Handbook of Research on Global Networking Post COVID-19

Ana Pego
Nova University of Lisbon, Portugal

IGI Global
PUBLISHER of TIMELY KNOWLEDGE

A volume in the Advances in Logistics, Operations, and Management Science (ALOMS) Book Series

Published in the United States of America by
IGI Global
Business Science Reference (an imprint of IGI Global)
701 E. Chocolate Avenue
Hershey PA, USA 17033
Tel: 717-533-8845
Fax: 717-533-8661
E-mail: cust@igi-global.com
Web site: http://www.igi-global.com

Library of Congress Cataloging-in-Publication Data

Names: Pego, Ana, 1969- editor.
Title: Handbook of research on global networking post COVID-19 / Ana Pego, editor.
Description: Hershey, PA : Business Science Reference, [2022] | Includes bibliographical references and index. | Summary: "This book explores the impact of COVID-19 on the market and the various sectors of the global economy with a specific focus on businesses and networking post-COVID-19"-- Provided by publisher.
Identifiers: LCCN 2021035369 (print) | LCCN 2021035370 (ebook) | ISBN 9781799888567 (hardcover) | ISBN 9781799888581 (ebook)
Subjects: LCSH: Business networks--History--21st century. | COVID-19 Pandemic, 2020---Economic aspects.
Classification: LCC HD69.S8 H3485 2022 (print) | LCC HD69.S8 (ebook) | DDC 650.1/3--dc23
LC record available at https://lccn.loc.gov/2021035369
LC ebook record available at https://lccn.loc.gov/2021035370

This book is published in the IGI Global book series Advances in Logistics, Operations, and Management Science (ALOMS) (ISSN: 2327-350X; eISSN: 2327-3518)

British Cataloguing in Publication Data
A Cataloguing in Publication record for this book is available from the British Library.

For electronic access to this publication, please contact: eresources@igi-global.com.

Advances in Logistics, Operations, and Management Science (ALOMS) Book Series

John Wang
Montclair State University, USA

ISSN:2327-350X
EISSN:2327-3518

Mission

Operations research and management science continue to influence business processes, administration, and management information systems, particularly in covering the application methods for decision-making processes. New case studies and applications on management science, operations management, social sciences, and other behavioral sciences have been incorporated into business and organizations real-world objectives.

The **Advances in Logistics, Operations, and Management Science** (ALOMS) Book Series provides a collection of reference publications on the current trends, applications, theories, and practices in the management science field. Providing relevant and current research, this series and its individual publications would be useful for academics, researchers, scholars, and practitioners interested in improving decision making models and business functions.

Coverage

- Networks
- Information Management
- Finance
- Risk Management
- Operations Management
- Organizational Behavior
- Production Management
- Marketing engineering
- Computing and information technologies
- Decision analysis and decision support

IGI Global is currently accepting manuscripts for publication within this series. To submit a proposal for a volume in this series, please contact our Acquisition Editors at Acquisitions@igi-global.com or visit: http://www.igi-global.com/publish/.

The Advances in Logistics, Operations, and Management Science (ALOMS) Book Series (ISSN 2327-350X) is published by IGI Global, 701 E. Chocolate Avenue, Hershey, PA 17033-1240, USA, www.igi-global.com. This series is composed of titles available for purchase individually; each title is edited to be contextually exclusive from any other title within the series. For pricing and ordering information please visit http://www.igi-global.com/book-series/advances-logistics-operations-management-science/37170. Postmaster: Send all address changes to above address.

Titles in this Series

For a list of additional titles in this series, please visit: http://www.igi-global.com/book-series/advances-logistics-operations-management-science/37170

Considerations and Characteristics of the Millennial Leader in Today's Global Society
Tymon M. Graham (TMGraham Consulting, LLC, USA)
Business Science Reference • © 2023 • 300pp • H/C (ISBN: 9781668447116) • US $240.00

Moving From R&D Development to Production and Sales in Start-Up Companies Emerging Research and Opportunities
Amiram Porath (APC, Israel)
Business Science Reference • © 2022 • 300pp • H/C (ISBN: 9781799856856) • US $215.00

Advancing Interpersonal Emotion Regulation and Social Regulation
Donta S. Harper (Argosy University, USA)
Information Science Reference • © 2022 • 384pp • H/C (ISBN: 9781668424780) • US $215.00

Handbook of Research on Activating Middle Executives' Agency to Lead and Manage During Times of Crisis
Ann-Marie Wilmot (The University of the West Indies, Mona, Jamaica) and Canute Sylvester Thompson (The University of the West Indies, Mona, Jamaica)
Business Science Reference • © 2022 • 415pp • H/C (ISBN: 9781668443316) • US $325.00

Business Models to Promote Technology, Culture, and Leadership in Post-COVID-19 Organizations
Joseph Robert Heinzman (Western Governors University, USA) Debbie S. Judge (Western Governors University, USA) Vincent Franklin (Western Governors University, USA) and Jim A. McCleskey (Western Governors University, USA & Houston Community College System, USA)
Business Science Reference • © 2022 • 300pp • H/C (ISBN: 9781668443583) • US $250.00

Global Risk and Contingency Management Research in Times of Crisis
Narasimha Rao Vajjhala (University of New York Tirana, Tirana, Albania) and Kenneth David Strang (W3-Research, USA & RMIT University, Australia)
Business Science Reference • © 2022 • 356pp • H/C (ISBN: 9781668452790) • US $270.00

Applied Guide for Event Study Research in Supply Chain Management
Lincoln C. Wood (University of Otago, New Zealand & Curtin University, Australia)
Information Science Reference • © 2022 • 261pp • H/C (ISBN: 9781799889694) • US $215.00

IGI Global
PUBLISHER of TIMELY KNOWLEDGE

701 East Chocolate Avenue, Hershey, PA 17033, USA
Tel: 717-533-8845 x100 • Fax: 717-533-8661
E-Mail: cust@igi-global.com • www.igi-global.com

List of Contributors

Table of Contents

Detailed Table of Contents

This study investigates the impact of fear of COVID-19 on financial markets in the period 2020: Q2-2021: Q4 in Turkey. Exchange rate (USA Dollar) and BIST 100 (Borsa Istanbul) data were obtained from the Central Bank of Turkey Republic (TCMB); COVID-19 fear index data was obtained from Google Trends. This study applied the Augmented Dickey-Fuller (ADF) Unit Root Test and Phillips Perron (PP) Unit Root Test to examine the stationarity of the series. Then, the Frequency-Domain Causality Test was conducted to determine whether the effect of the fear index on the financial variables BIST 100 and the exchange rate is a temporary or permanent relationship and whether the causality relationship between the variables has short-, medium-, and long-term effects. Findings show that the fear caused by COVID-19 is the cause of BIST 100 in the medium and short terms. Also, it is seen that fear is the cause of the exchange rate variable in the short run. The results obtained in the study revealed that the fear of COVID-19 is temporary.

The pandemic has disrupted the education around the world, impacting the way it is delivered. Teaching and training during this period create challenges to students since online learning provides the knowledge transfer that were usually done physically. Accounting internships enable students to get familiarized with different types of accounting context in a realistic environment. During the pandemic, this setting has changed, and the remote internship becomes the new reality. The aim of this research was to obtain feedback from accounting students who experienced internship due to pandemic by (1) collecting their opinion and expectations regarding this new form of internship, (2) stating their satisfaction of the internship program, (3) addressing their readiness for doing the internship, and (4) indicating the fulfillment of the internship's learning outcomes. The outcome of the study revealed interesting results

the experience of counteracting COVID-19 is considered. The novelty of the chapter is the exchange of scientific information with colleagues from other countries for seeking further solutions to the problems caused by COVID-19. The global challenges have been quite devastating for the Ukrainian agriculture economy.

The COVID-19 pandemic has disrupted the value chains for all major business sectors, with a great impact on the way we interact, socialize, transact, and trust the systems that we use on a daily basis. The magnitude of this major health crisis imposed a new level of digitalization, to which everyone needed to adapt, with great costs in terms of social, psychological, political, and economic transformation. In order to adapt in a new digital environment, imposed by the pandemic, we witnessed the adoption of decentralized ecosystems and technologies. One of the technologies that stood as foundation for this decentralization movement is blockchain. The first adaptations for blockchain technology happened within the financial services, with the introduction of the financial digital assets or crypto assets. This created the base for concepts like decentralized finance (DeFi), Web 3.0, and the metaverse. This chapter will assess the frontier of financial digital assets, which has emerged and developed the perfect infrastructure for scalability, efficiency, and transparency.

The COVID-19 crisis ushered in a multitude of challenges for SMEs. While these challenges are mainly financial and non-financial constraints, the ability to access markets and resilience capability building also exist for SMEs. The researcher conducted a review of 101 articles to analyze the pandemic's effects on SME businesses and found six thematic clusters: 1) operational costs, (2) resource losses, (3) business activity disruptions, (4) team performance disruptions, (5) individual and collective wellbeing disruptions, and (6) organizational survival threats. Based on these, the researcher identified six crucial emergent strategies to practically address the challenges around marketization and digitalization. These involve SME management, owners, and staff working more collaboratively to develop and adapt to new marketization regulations, policies, economic structuration, digital technologies, open innovation, and an overarching global network for local and international resilience. The implications of the results and an agenda for future research are presented and discussed.

COVID-19 has greatly influenced the way people live. Due to the economic crisis caused by COVID-19, the Chinese business environment has been largely changed. Chinese business models have gone through a new revolution and transformation. This chapter investigates and identifies future Chinese business trends after COVID-19, which covers the integration of digital technology, focusing on hygiene and healthcare, sustainable development, and increasing international collaborations. In conclusion, Chinese companies should regard the COVID-19 pandemic from a positive perspective as a chance to improve and innovate. Furthermore, companies should utilize the opportunities and push the companies for business innovation to gain more competencies in the post-COVID-19 era.

This study focuses on working life, which has an important place in the center of social changes after COVID-19. In the working life, where digital transformation has an application area, different concepts have taken their place in the literature in the important change observed with COVID-19. Digitalization made its presence felt in a process that accelerated with COVID-19. Concepts and applications that were not included in daily life practices until a few years ago are experienced today. In the study, an evaluation was made on crowdworking and related concepts, which are considered as one of these concepts. In this evaluation, digital transformation and the post-COVID-19 process were highlighted, and the motivation sources of crowdworker and crowdsourcer were analyzed through in-depth interview method.

Firms have been forced to adopt and/or retract to previously dropped management control strategies such as onshoring. This has come at the backdrop of preventative policies enforced by most governments such as lockdowns, social distancing, and to some extend the closure of common frontiers. This study aims at establishing the logistics and supply chain strategies embraced by firms before, during, and after COVID-19. Some secondary objectives include to discover strategies adopted by companies during and after COVID-19 to identify the impact and disruptions caused by COVID-19 in natural economies to establish approaches in supply chain management approaches and practices and to establish critical success factors and preventative strategies post COVID-19. A cross-sectional survey of literature is conducted with the aim of identifying the themes in the study area and synthesizing them to identify gaps.

In this chapter, the authors explore the impact of the COVID-19 pandemic on the Angolan market. A qualitative using case study (multi-case type) using interviews in data collection is used. It had 12 participants. The results reveal a significant impact of the COVID-19 pandemic on the Angolan economy. The COVID-19 pandemic had a positive impact for some companies, but essentially negative for others. The companies that sold the most during the pandemic are in the food, beverage, and health sectors. The ones that suffered the most losses were companies in the tourism and education sectors. The main difficulties have to do with the rapid changes in the market. The authors recommend focusing on diversifying the economy and reducing its dependence on oil, creating programs for financial education for consumers, and betting on digital communication.

This chapter presents a singular convergence between a policy window of opportunity and changes in social habits triggered by the COVID-19 pandemic, which set timely conditions in the European Union to implement the green and digital transformation programs embodied in the Next Generation European Union (2021-2027). COVID-19 highlighted problems carried out decades ago, such as climate change and natural resources exhaustion, whereas prolonged lockdowns forged consciousness about pollution and overcrowded sites while accelerating the use of digital solutions. Under favorable circumstances to effect changes for a resilient, competitive, and inclusive European Union, the authors focus on the circular economy strategy and elaborate the case for blockchain and tokenization as a key enabling technology to sponsor agile networks for a swift transition to a green and digital society decoupled from resource extraction and waste production. The chapter expands the case for blockchain decentralized finance applications as a means to financialize tokenized green products.

Health is a major and primary concern for every organization for manpower in the world without any discrimination, and the healthcare situations of the countries are different for this problem. Universal health coverage (UHC) is the only solution for this challenge, and UHC means that everyone everywhere should have access to quality, affordable healthcare services (including prevention, promotion, treatment,

and online polls concluded that most mothers are feeling depressed and stressed during COVID-19, and allowing kindergarten to re-open actually helped working mothers since the burden of educating shifted back to the teacher.

COVID-19, which emerged in March 2020, caused a rapid change in the ongoing order all over the world within the framework of the rules set by the governments. For this reason, managers should be visionary people who give importance to research and development. The restrictions experienced during the pandemic period had a negative impact on activities of the companies all over. Since the beginning of the pandemic, all businesses have introduced different applications from working hours to the products and services they produce. Due to restrictions experienced, many companies had to close the year with a loss. In fact, this pandemic has revealed whether companies are strategically and technologically prepared. For this reason, while companies that follow technological developments have succeeded, on the contrary, companies that are unaware or do not care about these developments are left behind.

This chapter explores how the luxury firms communicate their commitments promoting sustainable development and evaluating how these firms create a dialogue in social media with stakeholders. Moreover, the authors analyze how luxury firms get involved with the 17 Sustainable Development Goals explaining the activities they communicate to contribute to society. The methodology used in this research is based on case studies identifying the specific actions of luxury fashion and accessories brands, such as LVMH, Kering, Richemont, CHANEL, Essilor Luxottica, Chow Tai Fook, PVH, and Swatch Group. The results show that all luxury fashion and accessories firms include information on the SDGs on LinkedIn communicating how they contribute to achieving the SDGs with a set of activities, although there is room for improvement to increase the communication that is made in favour of the SDGs, as shown in their sustainability reports.

The global economy has expanded tremendously in recent years. However, this growth was hampered by the deadly COVID-19 outbreak, which forced countries to confront economic ramifications at both the micro and macro levels. The pandemic has posed a challenge to both producers and consumers, and businesses have been compelled to change their management styles for survival. Despite the return of the global market to normalcy, there remain questions over whether firms should continue to apply the same management strategies employed during COVID-19 or revisit their management practices in light of the post-COVID-19 climate. To address these issues, this study explores major global developments in entrepreneurial activity and economic growth in the aftermath of COVID-19, with the goal of assisting

Preface

This book aims to address the main issues of interest within *Handbook of Research on Global Networking Post COVID-19*. The IGI book provides innovative insights into the key developments and new trends associated with online challenges and opportunities in global networking post COVID-19 based on the concept of a challenging networking between citizens, organizations and the society. The content within this publication represents research encompassing networking between organizations; citizens but also a new methodology of implements a new stage of social responsibility and economic policy. This book serves as a vital reference source for organizations, policymakers, managers, entrepreneurs, graduate-level students, researchers, and academicians seeking coverage on topics centred on conceptual, technological, and design issues related to global networking. This book aims to address a range of approaches related to COVID-19 and its impact in the economy, and also address a new way of dealing with pandemic regarding the economic and social restrictions. In the next paragraphs, the book structure is detailed, in respective chapters.

CHAPTER 1: THE EFFECT OF FEAR CAUSED BY COVID-19 ON STOCK MARKETS AND EXCHANGE RATES – AN EMPIRICAL APPLICATION ON TURKEY

This study investigates the impact of fear of Covid-19 on financial markets in the period 2020: Q2 - 2021: Q4 in Turkey. Exchange rate (USA Dollar) and BIST 100 (Borsa Istanbul) data were obtained from the Central Bank of Turkey Republic (TCMB); Covid-19 fear index data was obtained from Google Trends. This study applied the Augmented Dickey-Fuller (ADF) Unit Root Test and Phillips Perron (PP) Unit Root Test to examine the stationarity of the series. Then, the Frequency-Domain Causality Test was conducted to determine whether the effect of the fear index on the financial variables BIST 100 and the exchange rate is a temporary or permanent relationship and whether the causality relationship between the variables has short, medium and long-term effects. Findings show that the fear caused by Covid-19 is the cause of BIST 100 in the medium and short term. Also, it is seen that fear is the cause of the exchange rate variable in the short run. The results obtained in the study revealed that the fear of Covid-19 is temporary.

CHAPTER 2: ACCOUNTING STUDENTS PERCEPTIONS FROM INTERNSHIP THAT TRIGGER ADAPTATIONS IN TRAINING AFTER THE PANDEMIC

The pandemic has disrupted the education around the world, impacting the way it is delivered. Teaching and training during this period create challenges to students since online learning provides the knowledge transfer that was usually done physically. Accounting internships enable students to get familiarized with different types of accounting context in a realistic environment. During pandemic this setting has changed, and the remote internship becomes the new reality. The aim of this research was to obtain feedback from accounting students who experienced internship due to pandemic by (a) collecting their opinion and expectations regarding this new form of internship, (b) stating their satisfaction of the internship program, (c) addressing their readiness for doing the internship and (d) indicating the fulfilment of internship's learning outcomes. The outcome of the study revealed interesting results and a set of factors that accounting faculty should endeavour to address in order to build resilience into the accounting internship.

CHAPTER 3: THE NEW PROFILE OF THE ONLINE CONSUMER BEHAVIOUR IN A POST-PANDEMIC WORLD

The COVID-19 pandemic has significantly affected shopping behaviour: consumers are more attentive to finding products customized to their needs and desires. Even the most suspicious people in this health emergency have overcome the cognitive barriers to digital purchasing to shop in total safety. This chapter aims to contribute to an understanding of how the COVID-19 pandemic has affected online consumer behaviour (OCB). The theoretical contribution on online consumer behaviour appears useful for managers and practitioners to define appropriate strategic actions for customers to enhance value in a digital context. The chapter presents three sections devoted to the literature on Online Consumer Behaviour in the COVID-19, what factors affecting the OCB and decision-making process and online retailing in the covid-19 era. Based on this theoretical background this chapter proposes a new categorization of online consumer behaviour by considering the habits that emerged during the COVID-19 Pandemic.

CHAPTER 4: HUMANS AND DIGITAL TECHNOLOGIES IN THE OMNICHANNEL POST-COVID-19 ERA

COVID-19 disease, which emerged in March 2020, caused a rapid change in the ongoing order all over the world within the framework of the rules set by the governments. Fort his reason managers should be visionary people who give importance to research and development. The restrictions experienced during the pandemic period had a negative impact on activities of the companies all over the world have entered a difficult period due to the economic crisis. Since the beginning of the epidemic, all business has introduced different applications from working hours to the products and services they produce. Due to do restrictions experienced, many companies had to close the year with a loss. In fact, this epidemic has revealed whether companies are strategically and technologically prepared. For this reason, while companies that follow technological developments have succeeded, on the contrary, companies that are unaware or do not care about these developments are lift behind. The main purpose of business is to make profit.

CHAPTER 5: CHALLENGES AND EMERGING STRATEGIES FOR A GLOBAL AUTOMOTIVE ENTERPRISE TOWARDS A POST-COVID-19 ERA – THE IMPACT OF DIGITAL TRANSFORMATION

The aim of this article is to provide readers with an overview of the content and summarize, the purpose of this chapter is stated as reporting on results with regard to challenges and emerging strategies for a global automotive enterprise towards a post COVID-19 era, together with the impact of digital transformation on productivity and innovation. One of the objectives of the chapter is to provide an in-depth understanding of various dimensions regarding the focus of this chapter, based on a selection from the recommended topics for the book. Against the background of a global automotive enterprise, the chapter will discuss the scope of challenges and emerging strategies towards developing an understanding of the need for, as well as the employment and adoption of, emerging strategies and their application towards overcoming the challenges brought on by COVID-19.

CHAPTER 6: ECONOMIC CRISIS IN COLOMBIA DUE TO COVID-19 – FROM PANDEMIC TO POST-PANDEMIC ACTIONS

The COVID-19 pandemic has had a social, economic, and political impact, with companies particularly affected. Policy makers and managers had to make strategic decisions to continue operations. Therefore, this article focuses on evaluating the economic impact of the crisis in Colombia from the government, and companies' perspectives and how they established some strategies to achieve economic sustainability. This analysis is composed of macroeconomic aspects, businesses´ role for economic reactivation, decisions to face the pandemic, and finally, actions that ensure their sustainability. There are issues on fiscal and monetary policies to ensure employment and keep inflation through directs up port and rules to improve companies' conditions. Companies themselves should learn about risk management, digital transformation, and there location of providers and customers. There is no single recipe to guarantee success but there is a need for an integrated plan that includes government, central bank, and companies to shorten the economic effects of this kind of crisis.

CHAPTER 7: INTEGRATING CYCLE OF PROCHASKA AND DICLEMENTE WITH ETHICALLY RESPONSIBLE BEHAVIOR THEORY FOR SOCIAL CHANGE MANAGEMENT – POST-COVID-19 SOCIAL COGNITIVE PERSPECTIVE FOR CHANGE

Humans could never have predicted what would happen as a result of COVID-19. Indeed, such foresight was not expected. It can also be stated that planning to combat COVID-19 was beyond human capacity. However, the future may be foretold by seeing many aspects that we have experienced. Current values, styles of working, social systems, organizational transformations, and human behavior have all been altered due to the epidemic. Those changes will sustain the anticipated direction. This book chapter goes into change cycle theory and how COVID-19 affected current social norms. Initially, the idea was integrated with social norms, but social cognition impacts were analogized as they progressed. It is interwoven with the goal that ethically social responsibility developments will assist in the design of a post-COVID-19 society approach. It is expected that we would be able to strategically carry some of the benefits of social awareness gained during COVID-19 for a brighter future in the post-COVID-19 age.

CHAPTER 8: THE IMPACT OF A GLOBAL RECESSION ON MILLENNIALS IN THE JOB MARKET

The Coronavirus pandemic took every sector of society by storm. The operational decisions taken by certain organizations led to a huge increase in the global rate of unemployment, especially youth unemployment. The millennial generation made up the majority of the youth unemployment statistics. Millennials have been the most economically impacted by the pandemic. The use of technology, the internet and social media to generate an income has been a widely explored option for millennials. The monetization of social media activities has been mostly beneficial for small businesses, influencers and content creators. A combination of the traits that millennials possess and their internet knowledge would be a good investment for the betterment of the global labour productivity post-COVID-19. This paper uses secondary data to review the impact of the COVID-19 pandemic on millennials in the job market and reviews possible recovery plans for this generation.

CHAPTER 9: CONSEQUENCES OF THE PANDEMIC FOR UKRAINIAN AGRICULTURE IN THE CONTEXT OF PUBLIC ADMINISTRATION

Quarantine was a forced measure that prevented significant losses in the early stages of the disease and prepared the medical system to combat COVID-19. Today, the medical system in most regions is ready to provide treatment for all patients in the event of new possible outbreaks of the pandemic. An integrated approach has been taken to develop measures to overcome the effects of COVID-19 and stimulate the economy. This chapter is devoted to the problems of agriculture that have arisen as a result of quarantine measures. Its main task is to find out whether the measures to counter the COVID-19 pandemic have affected the agricultural sector of the economy. The situation in the Ukrainian agrarian sector during the experience of counteracting COVID-19 is considered. The novelty of the chapter is the exchange of scientific information with colleagues from other countries for seeking further solutions to the problems caused by COVID-19. The global challenges have been quite devastating for the Ukrainian agriculture economy.

CHAPTER 10: THE FINANCIAL DIGITAL ASSETS FRONTIER – THE BRIDGE BETWEEN THE PAST AND THE FUTURE

The COVID-19 pandemic has disrupted the value chains for all major business sectors, with a great impact on the way we interact, socialize, transact and trust the systems that we use on a daily basis. The magnitude of this major health crisis imposed a new level of digitalization, to which everyone needed to adapt, with great costs in terms of social, psychological, political and economic transformation. In order to adapt in a new digital environment, imposed by the pandemic, we witnessed the adoption of decentralized ecosystems and technologies. One of the technologies that stood as foundation for this decentralization movement is blockchain. The first adaptations for blockchain technology happened within the financial services, with the introduction of the financial digital assets or crypto assets. This created the base for concepts like Decentralized Finance (DeFi), Web 3.0 and the Metaverse. This chapter will assess the frontier of financial digital assets, which has emerged and developed the perfect infrastructure for scalability, efficiency and transparency.

CHAPTER 11: SYSTEMATIZING BODY OF KNOWLEDGE ON BUSINESS CHALLENGES AND STRATEGIZING POST COVID-19 – A LITERATURE REVIEW AND AGENDA FOR RESEARCH: BUSINESS CHALLENGES AND STRATEGIES IN A POAT-COVID-19 WORLD

The COVID-19 crisis ushered in a multitude of challenges for SMEs. While these challenges are mainly financial and non-financial constraints, the ability to access markets and resilience capability building also exist for SMEs. The researcher conducted a review of 101 articles to analyze the pandemic's effects on SME businesses and found six thematic clusters: 1) operational costs, (2) resource losses, (3) business activity disruptions, (4) team performance disruptions, (5) individual and collective wellbeing disruptions and (6) organizational survival threats. Based on these, the researcher identified six crucial emergent strategies to practically address the challenges around marketization and digitalization. These involve SMEs' management, owners and staff working more collaboratively to develop and adapt to new marketization regulations, policies, economic structuration, digital technologies, open innovation and an overarching global network for local and international resilience. The implications of the results and an agenda for future research are presented and discussed.

CHAPTER 12: CHINESE BUSINESS TRENDS POST COVID-19

The COVID-19 has greatly influenced the way people live. Due to the economic crisis caused by COVID-19, the Chinese business environment has been largely changed. Chinese business models have gone through a new revolution and transformation. This article investigates and identifies future Chinese business trends after COVID-19, which covers the integration of digital technology, focus on hygiene, and healthcare, sustainable development, and increasing international collaborations. In conclusion, Chinese companies should regard the COVID-19 pandemic from a positive perspective as a chance to improve and innovate. Furthermore, companies should utilize the opportunities and push the companies for business innovation to gain more competencies in the post-COVID-19.

CHAPTER 13: AN EVALUATION OF NEW WORK PRACTICES AFTER THE PANDEMIC – CROWDWORKING

This study focuses on working life, which has an important place in the centre of social changes after COVID-19. In the working life, where digital transformation has an application area, different concepts have taken their place in the literature in the important change observed with COVID-19. The effects of digitalization made its presence felt in a process that accelerated with COVID-19. Concepts and applications that were not included in daily life practices until a few years ago are experienced today. In the study, an evaluation was made on crowdworking and related concepts, which are considered as one of these concepts. In this evaluation, digital transformation and the post-COVID-19 process were highlighted, and the motivation sources of crowdworker and crowdsourcer were analyzed through in-depth interview method.

CHAPTER 14: SUPPLY CHAIN IN THE ERAS PRE AND POST COVID-19 – A SYSTEMATIC REVIEW AND FRAMEWORK DEVELOPMENT

Firms have been forced to adopt and/or retract to previously dropped management control strategies such as on shoring. This has come at the backdrop of preventative policies enforced by most governments such as lockdowns, social distancing and to some extend the closure of common frontiers. This study aims at establishing the logistics and supply chain strategies embraced by firms before, during and after the COVID-19. Some secondary objectives include discovering strategies adopted by companies during and after COVID-19, to identify the impact and disruptions caused by COVID-19 in natural economies, to establish approaches in supply chain management approaches and practices, and to establish critical success factors and preventative strategies post COVID-19. A cross sectional survey of literature will be conducted with the aim of identifying the themes in the study area and synthesizing them to identify gaps.

CHAPTER 15: IMPACT OF COVID-19 ON BUSINESSES AND CONSUMERS 2020/2022 – STRATEGIC MEASURES ADOPTED BY COMPANIES

General objective: to understand the impact of the COVID-19 pandemic on the Angolan market. Methodology: qualitative using case study (multi-case type), using interviews in data collection; had 12 participants. The results reveal a significant impact of the COVID-19 pandemic on the Angolan economy. Conclusion: The COVID-19 pandemic had a positive impact for some companies, but essentially negative for others. The companies that sold the most during the pandemic are in the food, beverage, and health sector. The ones that suffered the most losses were companies in the tourism and education sector. The main difficulties have to do with the rapid changes in the market. Recommendations: focus on diversifying the economy and reducing its dependence on oil; create programs for financial education for consumers; bet on digital communication.

CHAPTER 16: HARNESSING BLOCKCHAIN AND DECENTRALIZED FINANCE IN THE POST-COVID-19 EUROPEAN UNION – THE CASE OF THE CIRCULAR ECONOMY

This chapter per the authors presents a singular convergence between a policy window of opportunity and changes in social habits triggered by the COVID-19 pandemic, which set timely conditions in the European Union to implement the green and digital transformation programs embodied in the Next Generation European Union (2021-2027). COVID-19 highlighted problems carried out decades ago, such as climate change and natural resources exhaustion, whereas prolonged lockdowns forged consciousness about pollution and overcrowded sites while accelerating the use of digital solutions. Under favorable circumstances to effect changes for a resilient, competitive and inclusive European Union, the authors focus on the circular economy strategy and elaborate the case for block chain and tokenization as a key enabling technology to sponsor agile networks for a swift transition to a green and digital society decoupled from resource extraction and waste production. The chapter expands the case for block chain decentralized finance applications as a means to financialize tokenized green products.

CHAPTER 17: UNIVERSAL HEALTH COVERAGE (UHC) – CASE STUDY ON WORLD'S HEALTH EMERGING STRATEGY AFTER THE COVID-19 PANDEMIC

Health is a major and primary concern for every organization for manpower in the world without any discrimination and the health care situation of the countries are different for this problem. Universal health coverage (UHC) is the only solution for this challenge and UHC means that everyone everywhere should have access to quality, affordable health care services (including prevention, promotion, treatment and rehabilitation) without suffering financial hardship. The COVID-19 is the world's serious problem which affects all over the world, which tells the reality of the health care challenge and importance of health coverage for humans and humanity. Therefore, this chapter is attempting to analyze the situation of COVID-19 impact on the Universal Health Coverage Initiative. After that this chapter helps to check the countries progress towards UHC and furthermore, discusses the opportunities and forthcoming policies to support UHC for upcoming health disasters like pandemic and other health issues.

CHAPTER 18: MITIGATION PLAN FOR THE POST-PANDEMIC ON SUPPLY CHAIN DISRUPTIONS AMONG BUYERS AND DISTRIBUTORS

In recent decades, global supply chains have grown in size and complexity, emphasizing efficiency, cost, and closeness to markets. The Coronavirus pandemic disrupted activity worldwide, with supply chain (SC) disruptions being particularly severe. A pandemic of this size has caught corporations and whole industries off guard, sending a cascade of rippling effects across their supply networks and enterprises. The COVID-19 outbreak has impacted the economic climate for many organizations worldwide, underlining the importance of responding to, adjusting to, and implementing crisis management strategies to weather difficult times. This study investigates the effect of the COVID-19 pandemic on SCs in terms of disruptions, problems, and trends. As a result, the goal is to investigate such difficulties and propose mitigation methods based on IoT (Internet of Things) for sustainability and viability of the Supply Chain Management disruptions among buyers and distributors.

CHAPTER 19: INVESTIGATION OF HUMAN RESOURCE MANAGEMENT PRACTICES AFTER COVID-19 – CHALLENGES AND OPPORTUNITIES IN HUMAN RESOURCE MANAGEMENT PRACTICES AFTER COVID-19

The economy of every country relies on its human resources. COVID-19 has pretentious human life, socio-economic development, and national relations up to an extent. The worldwide economy has been ferociously crushed by the corona virus pandemic. It barrels all organizations, making a complicated and tough setting for managers in the domain of human resource management, international agencies need to facilitate their employees to wear down this extraordinary crisis. The types of work, worker enlisting and choice, worker coaching, performance management, and compensation management have been modified fully. In the study, COVID-19 crisis on HRM is investigated. It points out the most summons and prospects that have arisen from pandemic and it presents apprehension for managers in the domain of Human Resource Management. The study advocated the adoption of e-HRM to reduce employee's physical interactions, worker engagement in crisis management ways, and review of time unit strategies to livery times of crisis.

CHAPTER 20: NETWORKING AS A DRIVING FORCE FOR POST-COVID-19 ECONOMIC BEHAVIOR – INVESTORS, CONSUMERS, AND CORPORATIONS

This chapter examines three examples of the development of networking as an economic behavior changer: retail investors, the general consumer, and corporations. The author shows how the pandemic has influenced the development of forms of networking. The risk of contagion has created a need for collective emotional support in the general public. Networks became a source of information, advice, ideas, and hints that helped participants overcome the psychological stress caused by the scale of the pandemic. The change in the activity of the general public in social media prompted businesses to expand the formats of online communication with their stakeholders. The author identifies three characteristics of modern networking: borderlessness, focused organization, and performativity. These characteristics contribute to the fact that networking begins to determine the behavior of economic actors. This phenomenon requires serious study because it generates new problems and may increase the overall uncertainty in addition to the positive effect.

CHAPTER 21: RELATIONS BETWEEN DIGITAL TRANSFORMATION AND SUSTAINABILITY POST COVID – THE PILLARS OF ESG

COVID-19 has directly influenced the digital transformation in companies. In a matter of days, remote activities had to be quickly deployed in organizations, new consumer habits incorporated and technologies inserted demanding technological solutions. Thus, companies had to adapt to a new normal. In this scenario the following problems have emerged: What is digital transformation? What are the relationships between digital transformation and sustainability in the post-covid era? To answer this question the following objective was set: to analyze the relationship between digital transformation and sustainability in the post-covid era. To this end, an integrative literature review was conducted using the Web of Science database. Results indicate that digital transformation and sustainability are directly interconnected to economic activities, including the area of maintenance and facility management. The post-pandemic trends highlight to years of recovery and readaptation in the face of the crisis, together with digital transformation, which promises to increasingly improve.

CHAPTER 22: BLESSING OR CURSE? CHALLENGES WORKING MOTHERS FACED POST COVID-19 IN BRUNEI DARUSSALAM

From the terms 'working mothers', it is obvious that it means mothers who are working. Mothers have multiple roles, mothers would prepare food, clothes, bath their kids, clean the house, taking care of husband and families. With the listed above role, it was already tiring and would require proper time-management. Working mothers added another responsibility that is to focus on tasks in the organization. Some parents would prefer to send their kids to school at an early age. Then COVID-19 hits in 2019 and suddenly everyone is working and studying at home. Is it a blessing to have all the family at home or a curse knowing that another burden will be added to the working mother alone? This paper investigates how working mothers feel pre and post COVID-19. 36 mothers participated in questionnaires and Online Pool votes. Results from questionnaires and Online poll as per authors concluded that most mothers are feeling depressed and stressed during COVID-19 and allowing kindergarten to re-open actually help working mothers since the burden of educating shifted back to the teacher.

CHAPTER 23: NEW APPROACHES TO BUSINESS STRATEGIES AFTER COVID-19

COVID-19 disease, which emerged in March 2020, caused a rapid change in the ongoing order all over the world within the framework of the rules set by the governments. For this reason managers should be visionary people who give importance to research and development. The restrictions experienced during the pandemic period had a negative impact on activities of the companies all over the world have entered a difficult period due to the economic crisis. Since the beginning of the epidemic, all business has introduced different applications from working hours to the products and services they produce. Due to do restrictions experienced, many companies had to close the year with a loss. In fact, this epidemic has revealed whether companies are strategically and technologically prepared. For this reason, while companies that follow technological developments have succeeded, on the contrary, companies that are unaware or do not care about these developments are lift behind. The main purpose of business is to make profit.

CHAPTER 24: THE MEETING PLACE ON SOCIAL MEDIA FOR THE LUXURY FASHION INDUSTRY TO SUPPORT AND STRATEGICALLY COMMUNICATE SDGS

This chapter explores how the luxury firms communicate their commitments promoting sustainable development and evaluating how these firms create a dialogue in social media with stakeholders. Moreover, we analyze how luxury firms get involved with the 17 sustainable development goals explaining the activities they communicate to contribute to society. The methodology used in this research is based on case studies identifying the specific actions of luxury fashion and accessories brands, such as LVMH, Kering, Richemont, CHANEL, Essilor Luxottica, Chow Tai Fook, PVH and Swatch Group. The results show that all luxury fashion and accessories firms include information on the SDGs on LinkedIn communicating how they contribute to achieving the SDGs with a set of activities, although there is room for improvement to increase the communication that is made in favour of the SDGs, as shown in their sustainability reports.

CHAPTER 25: THE COVID-19 PANDEMIC AND ITS IMPACT ON THE GLOBAL MARKET – A MICROECONOMIC PERSPECTIVE

The global economy has expanded tremendously in recent years. However, this growth was hampered by the deadly COVID-19 outbreak, which forced countries to confront economic ramifications at both the micro and macro levels. The pandemic has posed a challenge to both producers and consumers, and businesses have been compelled to change their management styles for survival. Despite the return of the global market to normalcy, there remain questions over whether firms should continue to apply the same management strategies employed during COVID-19 or revisit their management practices in light of the post-COVID-19 climate. To address these issues, this study explores major global developments in entrepreneurial activity and economic growth in the aftermath of COVID-19, with the goal of assisting organizations in adapting and reacting during pandemic times to ensure long-term survival. Finally, the author proposes best practices for businesses to make rational decisions, as well as an exhaustive review of global economies and markets to forecast their economic well-being post-COVID-19.

CHAPTER 26: THE NEXUS BETWEEN FORENSIC TAX AND ACCOUNTING KNOWLEDGE AFTER PANDEMIC COVID-19 IN INDONESIA

This research is new to disclose the level of tax forensic knowledge to prevent tax fraud. The phenomenon of tax fraud has rarely been highlighted in several literatures. This addition was made in order to provide a new logic, thinking that the fraud financial statement is also related to the sakes of tax evasion or fraud. The population of this study was 1,053 auditors and the percentage level of leeway used was 10%. The questionnaires distributed were 300 copies, or 28.49% of the population. The method of analysis was applying Partial Least Square (PLS). This study found that the level of forensic accounting and tax forensic knowledge had a positive effect on the prevention of fraud financial statements in the new normal era in Indonesia at this time. Although there were many studies on forensic accounting, none had collaborated with the level of forensic tax knowledge. It seems that there are some parties who are afraid when there is education about forensic tax knowledge in Indonesia, especially the new normal period towards a new world order.

Ana Pego
Nova University of Lisbon, Portugal

Chapter 1
The Fear Impact of COVID-19 on Stock Markets and Exchange Rates:
An Empirical Application on Turkey

Ferhat Özbay
https://orcid.org/0000-0002-7756-3835
Isparta University of Applied Sciences, Turkey

Nergis Tosun
Malatya, Turkey

ABSTRACT

This study investigates the impact of fear of COVID-19 on financial markets in the period 2020: Q2-2021: Q4 in Turkey. Exchange rate (USA Dollar) and BIST 100 (Borsa Istanbul) data were obtained from the Central Bank of Turkey Republic (TCMB); COVID-19 fear index data was obtained from Google Trends. This study applied the Augmented Dickey-Fuller (ADF) Unit Root Test and Phillips Perron (PP) Unit Root Test to examine the stationarity of the series. Then, the Frequency-Domain Causality Test was conducted to determine whether the effect of the fear index on the financial variables BIST 100 and the exchange rate is a temporary or permanent relationship and whether the causality relationship between the variables has short-, medium-, and long-term effects. Findings show that the fear caused by COVID-19 is the cause of BIST 100 in the medium and short terms. Also, it is seen that fear is the cause of the exchange rate variable in the short run. The results obtained in the study revealed that the fear of COVID-19 is temporary.

INTRODUCTION

The Covid-19 virus, which first appeared in the Wuhan province of China, has spread rapidly around the world. With the rapid spread of the virus worldwide, the World Health Organization named Covid-19

DOI: 10.4018/978-1-7998-8856-7.ch001

a pandemic in March 2020. The rapid spread of Covid-19 and the deaths caused by it created great fear and panic. The fear of Covid-19, in particular, has had a significant effect on human behaviour (Doğan and Düzel, 2020; Addo et al., 2020).

Due to fear and restrictions, many countries have observed changes in customer behaviour in various areas. Covid-19 has led to stocking and precautionary savings behaviours in the world (Özbay and Altan, 2021: 27). Also, it's claimed that the Covid-19 pandemic gives rise to social-psychology and financial crises globally (Ilgın and Sarı, 2020: 434). The effects of non-cash flow elements on the integration of countries' financial markets are a popular topic in the literature. The impact of Covid-19, the largest epidemic of the last century, on financial markets has sparked heated debate (Yıldırım, 2021: 185). Fear caused by the Covid-19 (Coronavirus) pandemic impacts investor's decisions and generates unexpected variations in transaction behaviour (Reis, 2021: 87). According to the studies, financial markets worldwide react negatively to the Covid-19 epidemic, although the reaction varies by country (Ashraf, 2021). From this perspective, it is also vital to increase the number of studies specific to the country.

The effect on the exchange rate of fear constitutes a separate issue that needs to be investigated since the exchange market is the largest and most liquid asset of all financial markets in the world. Exchange rate returns of both domestic and foreign economies are sensitive to fear or panic (Williams et al., 2021: 988- 989). For example, Narayan (2020) states that Covid-19 has changed the Yen's resilience to shocks.

This study aims to examine the impact of the Covid-19 pandemic on the behaviour of investors on Borsa Istanbul (BIST 100) and the exchange rate in Turkey. The study consists of three parts after the introduction. In the first part, the impact of Covid-19 on financial markets and the general economy is examined. The second part studies the effect of fear caused by Covid-19. The third section, the literature section, includes previous subjects' studies. Then, the effect of fear caused by Covid-19 in Turkey on the BIST 100 index and the exchange rate is analyzed. The last section is the conclusion and recommendations section.

The Impact of Covid-19 on Economy and Financial Markets

People initially thought that the economic and health effects of Covid-19 would be like the flu that people experience. Just as people show symptoms such as fatigue, fever, and sore throat when they have the flu and then recover with a short treatment, it was thought that the interruption caused by Covid-19 in the economy would end in a short time. This situation is sometimes referred to as the macroeconomic flu. In other words, it is assumed that output will decrease for a short time with the effect of a temporary negative supply and demand shock. Low growth figures will be reached in a quarter, the decrease in output will be compensated in the ongoing process, and subsequent growth figures will be higher. But unfortunately, it was soon realized that Covid-19 is not a short-term health problem as in the scenario considered, but rather a problem with a lot of uncertainty, contrary to the assumed scenario (Di Mauro, 2020: 31).

Covid-19 has been classified as a crisis based on its economic, social, and psychological consequences. This procedure has a significant impact on businesses. During the epidemic, many companies came to a halt, either entirely or partially. On the other hand, the production and sales of food, cleaning, and technology businesses that could operate at total capacity increased significantly. Many measures such as international air transportation restrictions, closure of land borders, cessation of business activities and curfews aimed at reducing the spread of the epidemic have been implemented by countries in the short term. The contraction in business volume, sales, and international trade activities with Covid-19, the restrictions on labor mobility, and the measures are taken to prevent the disease's spread all indicate that this epidemic is unlike previous crises. For example, during the global financial crisis of 2007-2008, there were problems with production factors such as raw materials, facilities, machinery, equipment, and labour. One of the main issues was that the goods and services produced did not have sufficient demand due to the financial sector's contraction. The Covid-19 epidemic, on the other hand, caused problems that were unrelated to demand because it directly hampered the production of goods and services (Suyadal, 2021: 520; Salisu and Vo, 2020: 1).

The effects of the disease beyond death rates and unemployment have become more visible in the world order, which is highly interconnected and integrated. The functioning of the global supply chains, which has slowed down with the production cuts of the Chinese economy, has been disrupted. Companies worldwide, which are dependent on inputs from China, have begun to experience contractions in production. The limited and even restricted transportation among countries has further slowed down the functioning of the global economy. The panic that emerged in consumers and companies caused the usual consumption patterns to deteriorate, and market anomalies occurred (McKibbin and Fernando, 2020: 45).

With the panic caused by Covid-19 manifesting itself in the financial markets, discussions on the explanation for the observed reaction in the stock markets have also increased (Lalwani and Meshram, 2020: 40). Because the global financial markets also reacted to the changes, the world stock markets, which had a developed and integrated structure, started to lose value in a short time due to the rapidly increasing cases and deaths from the epidemic. In other words, the impact of the Covid-19 process on individuals has also been significantly reflected in asset prices. In addition, rising case and death rates have also increased the perception of systematic risk, causing the environment of uncertainty to intensify. Also, the reasons for the value loss are the countries' lack of preparedness regarding the measures to be implemented, disruptions in production activities, and the rapid disposal of investors' shares. In a stock market scenario where the investor decides whether to sell the stock at more than one point, fear accelerates the selling behaviour (Tosun, 2021: 126). Although old levels may be seen in market indices in the future, it is critical to explain price changes in stock markets since the outbreak began (McKibbin and Fernando, 2020: 45; Suyadal, 2021: 521; Subramaniam and Chakraborty, 2021: 4). With the panic caused by Covid-19 causing a reaction in the financial markets, it has been discussed for a long time whether the stock markets have become more inefficient or not in light of the coronavirus crisis (Lalwani and Meshram, 2020: 40).

The foreign exchange market is the largest and most liquid of all financial markets globally. It means that the exchange rate returns of both domestic and foreign economies are sensitive to the effects of fear or panic (Williams et al., 2021: 988- 989). Due to the complex nature of foreign exchange markets, international traders and policymakers are constantly concerned with understanding the fundamentals that drive their actions (Williams et al., 2021: 998). Epidemics in general and Covid-19, in particular, impact the exchange rate through more than one channel. These effects depend on the following characteristics of the relevant country (Günsoy and Yıldız, 2021: 5; Özatay and Sak, 2020: 3): The socio-psychological structure of the country; foreign trade structure; the balance of payments; international competitiveness; external debt structure; the level of financial globalization; the degree of sensitivity of the country to capital flows; country-specific risk perception; the risk appetite of investors trading in international financial markets; the rates followed by the central banks of major countries on interest rates during the epidemic; risk-free levels of domestic interest rates; the future expectations of the exchange rate and the sectoral/structural characteristics of the country's GDP.

The connection between economic conditions, financial conditions and uncertainty/emotion arising from Covid-19 increases the difficulties faced by country governments, researchers, economists and central banks (Mann, 2020: 84). Governments have a critical role in the face of real and financial stress. In the short term and the following years, a series of policy implementations and the results from these implementations become essential. In the short term, central banks and treasuries need to take steps to ensure that deteriorated economies continue to function while the virus epidemic continues. While lowering interest rates is a possible response for central banks, the shock is not just a demand management issue but a multifaceted crisis that will require monetary, fiscal and health policy responses. Keeping people affected by the virus in quarantine and reducing large-scale social interaction are proved effective worldwide in fighting the virus (McKibbin and Fernando, 2020: 50). However, on the other hand, the costs of these measures to the national economies will be better understood in the following years. The behavioural reactions of authorities, businesses, consumers and policymakers will be the determinants of the developments to be experienced in the subsequent periods, in the period in which uncertainty and trust play an essential role, which is expressed as the ongoing crisis caused by Covid-19 at one point (Mann, 2020: 81).

In the past centuries, epidemics have occurred many times. However, the impact of these epidemics has not been as practical as the Covid-19 emerging today, and the effect of Covid-19 has been more significant than any previous global health crisis. Because the epidemics remained at the local or regional level, the information flow was less developed than today, and the integration into the financial markets could not be achieved. Therefore, the effects of epidemics on financial markets have not been adequately examined in the past. For this reason, it becomes crucial to explain the movements in the financial markets under extreme market conditions such as the epidemics in question (Su et al. 2021:1; Suyadal, 2021: 522).

Fear of Covid-19 for Individuals and Society

In the historical process, wars, epidemics, natural disasters have been counted among the crucial causes of fear in society. Epidemics, which cause a high loss of life in today's communities and are likely to generate a new one every year, cause fear to be felt on a global scale. Positive or negative, sudden, unexpected changes have occurred in people's habits due to Covid-19. This situation led to the emergence of fear, which first affected the individuals and then the whole society (Doğan and Düzel, 2020: 741).

The Covid-19 process has created an atmosphere of great uncertainty. The most critical consequence of uncertainty for individuals is fear. Although fear is a subjective emotion with its characteristics (Mertens et al. 2020: 2), in the Covid-19 process, it has become a common emotion that goes beyond the emergence of individuality, which affects the whole society together, and spreads throughout the community. This epidemic damaged the trust that individuals have over their lives and caused an increase in uncertainty, creating a situation that increased anxiety and the perception of threat to their lives (Doğan and Düzel, 2020: 743). The tension created by Covid-19 and the lack of a consensus about when this uncertainty will end and the continuity of this environment has made fear chronic and burdensome (Mertens et al. 2020: 1). The possibility that the fear, which has increased with Covid 19 and spread to the general public, may cause social and economic consequences as severe as the disease itself has become a judgment predicted by administrators, academics and the general public (Bulck and Custers, 2009: 370).

Rumours and misinformation proliferate during the fear periods (Baldwin and Mauro, 2020: 7). The source of the lack of information can lead to increased uncertainty and threat assessments, whether due to insufficient information from the authorities or the public or because it is not communicated effectively. When this uncertainty is combined with an invisible threat, such as a virus, fear and anxiety may increase, and the spread of misinformation may become inevitable (Garfin et al. 2020: 356). According to research and clinical observations, in times of pandemic, many people fear being infected, coming into contact with potentially contaminated objects or surfaces, the socioeconomic consequences of the pandemic, and seek mandatory control and reassurance against possible pandemic threats. They suffer from traumatic stress symptoms related to the pandemic, such as nightmares and random thoughts (Taylor et al. 2020: 1- 2). The level of fear is an essential factor. Because when the level of fear increases at the individual level, problems such as phobia and social anxiety are encountered. In social terms, shopping done in a panic causes hostility toward foreigners and many other issues. On the other hand, a low level of fear can cause harm to individuals and societies. In the context of Covid-19, for example, the epidemic's impact will continue to grow if individuals disregard the state's measures to slow the epidemic process and if the practices are not followed (Mertens et al. 2020: 2). In addition, it is accepted that it is natural for people to show protection and avoidance with fear and panic during epidemics that create uncertainty, such as Covid-19. When emotions such as fear and anxiety spread to society, the elements that reveal fear rule people (Karataş, 2020: 6).

The growing global concern about health risks during the Covid-19 pandemic, the developments announced to the public one after the other by world health authorities, and the realization that the epidemic would take a negative turn all had an immediate impact on financial markets and thus on investor decisions. Fear in financial terms; is a state of anxiety caused by the risk and uncertainty that dominates financial transactions (Tosun, 2021: 125). Countries must sustain investments to prevent the emergence of an economic depression. Factors such as the cessation of business activities, the significant increase in market uncertainty, individuals' desire to protect their wealth, and loss aversion behaviour have emerged as the primary determinants of this period in the markets. Individuals with a high level of fear cannot make rational decisions while reacting to Covid-19, contrary to what is assumed in economic events. It is emphasized that fear caused by the pandemic affects stock returns through noise trading of irrational investors[1]. In other words, individuals receive false signals about investments from their environment due to the effect of the pandemic, and the transactions they make with these false signals reveal noise trading. Su et al. (2021) stated that fear or negative emotions caused by the pandemic play a more critical role in predicting stock returns than economic fundamentals or the number of cases and deaths.

In this regard, there is a chance that the possibility of mutation of the virus may lead to a change in risk perception for investors who have investments in the stock markets or who are considering investing. The worst-case scenarios in this process are its turning into a global epidemic, bringing about sharp declines in the stock markets. Due to the increasing systematic risk pressure, many investors have purchased assets that they consider less risky than stocks. In addition to this situation, the return levels expected by investors have also increased. While profound decreases have been observed in the markets, especially since the outbreak was declared a pandemic, developments such as mutation news and vaccine news towards the end of 2020 caused a constant change in risk perception. Given the subjectivity of stock investors' evaluations, it is possible to conclude that investors' expectations are largely negative during the epidemic process. With the news of vaccination and normalization towards the end of 2020, market indices began to return to pre-epidemic levels. Knowing how stock prices or exchange rates will behave later presents a unique opportunity for investors. These situations restore market efficiency and provide investors with ample room for strategic planning (Ahorsu et al. 2020: 2; Suyadal, 2021: 524-525; Salisu and Vo, 2020: 2).

The actions of economic actors ultimately cause fluctuations in exchange rate returns. Therefore, maintaining reasonable stability in the exchange rate and the financial system should form part of the policy response to pandemics. It is necessary to maintain the strength of a currency so that the fear of loss of investment does not cause economic agents to shift their investments to foreign currency assets. Otherwise, foreign money will become even more valuable against domestic currencies (Williams et al. 2021: 998).

The impact of easy access to communication channels on individuals is another critical issue that must investigate within the scope of Covid-19. The infection usually spreads when one carrier infects another. However, the fear of an epidemic that emerges through communication channels has the opportunity to spread rapidly. Communication channels have the opportunity to expose hundreds of thousands of people, or even the whole world, to fear-inducing information at the same time. Inadequate information about the subject in society increases uncertainty and fear. Although the communication channels occasionally give messages containing confidence about infectious diseases, the majority of the news shared are directed towards the deaths caused by Covid-19, the increasing number of cases, and tend to highlight the risk and danger (Biçer et al. 2020: 218; Bulck and Custers, 2009: 370; Pakpour and Griffiths, 2020: 2).

From the point of view of investors, they have difficulty in correctly assessing the economic importance and impact of the information they have obtained as a result of the ease of access to news and information and the need to receive more information during epidemic periods (Haroon and Rizvi, 2020: 1). It has been understood that exposure to more media than previous epidemics, such as bird flu, that is, the ease of access to threatening information about the virus, has an increasing effect on fear (Mertens et al. 2020: 2). Investors' trading decisions are now more dependent on the content of the available news. Given the sensitivity of investors to the severe consequences of the Covid-19 pandemic on their returns and the need to seek safe investments to minimize the looming high risks and uncertainties associated with the pandemic (Salisu and Vo, 2020: 1- 2), further research in communication channels in the investment process they need it.

LITERATURE REVIEW

The effect of fear of Covid-19 on the stock market and financial indicators has several perspectives in previous studies. It is beneficial to investigate several studies on this issue to grasp better the effect of Covid-19 fear on the stock market. As a result, chosen studies with the subject, scope, methodology, and result information are given in Table 1.

Table 1. Selected Studies for the effect of Covid-19 on the stock market and financial indicators

Authors	Subject	Scope	Methodology	Result
Vasileiou (2021)	Coronavirus fear, Behavioral finance and stock market	USA	Granger causality, Generalized autoregressive conditional heteroskedasticity (GARCH)	The author aimed to reveal the relationship between a Coronavirus Fear Index (CFI) based on Google searches and S&P500 performance, giving empirical evidence that fear drives S&P500 performance. It also demonstrated that fear had a negative impact on the performance of the US stock market.
İşler and Güven (2021)	Covid-19, BIST 100	Turkey	Ordinary least squares method (OLS)	The number of patients each day, according to the article, has a considerable negative impact on the BIST 100 index. The number of deaths each day, on the other hand, has no meaningful effect on the BIST 100 index. Furthermore, the study results demonstrate that the dollar rate has a considerable negative impact on the BIST 100 index.
Şenol (2020)	Covid 19, BIST 100 index	Turkey	The robust least squares method	The author, examining the effect of Covid-19 on BIST 100, found that the number of cases had a negative impact on BIST 100 and stated that the number of deaths from Covid-19 had no effect.
Addo et al. (2020)	Covid-19, Fear appeal, Behavior	40 live-streaming shops in China	Serial mediated regression	The fear appeal is linked to a sharp increase in online purchases of Covid-19. According to the findings, fear attraction promotes social presence in anticipation of love, acceptance, and social information seeking.
Özmerdivanli (2021)	Covid-19, Financial Indicators	Turkey	Johansen cointegration and Vector error correction model (VECM)	In the long run, the study discovered a causation relationship determined in models using the dependent variables Gold, Bitcoin, interest, and oil. In the short-term causality analysis, it was found that there is unidirectional causality from interest to BIST; from Euro and interest to Bitcoin; from gold, Dollar, and Euro to interest; from Dollar, Euro, interest, and the number of the patient to oil; and from gold, Bitcoin, Dollar, and Euro to the number of the patient.
Servi, et al. (2020)	Covid-19, PMI manufacturing industry index, VIX Index	Turkey	Dynamic OLS	The authors attempted to determine whether the VIX Index (Fear Index) has an impact on Turkey's manufacturing industry. When the Covid-19 epidemic occurred in April 2019, authors detected a structural break, and the study showed that this breakage negatively impacted the manufacturing industry's production. In addition, the study found a significant and negative relationship between the VIX Index and the PMI index.
Yıldırım (2021)	Avoiding risk, Covid-19	USA and BRIC	Nonlinear bounds test approach (NARDL)	The purpose of the study was to look into the long-term and short-term asymmetric effects of changing risk aversion levels among investors on stock market integration during the Covid-19 outbreak and the 2008 economic crisis. In the short run, the author discovered that increases in risk aversion for all countries boosted integration, whereas decreases in risk aversion decreased correlation. Furthermore, the researcher found that this effect was much more robust and statistically significant during the epidemic than during the 2008 economic crisis.
Uçar and Kıdemli (2021)	Stock market index, Covid-19, VIX index,	Turkey	Autoregressive distributed lag bound test (ARDL)	As a result of the analysis, the study observed that BISTelectric, BISTkimya, BISTtextile and BISTfood index variables were statistically negatively affected by the increase in the number of Covid-19 patients the increase in the VIX index value in the long term, together with the vaccination studies. In addition, it was determined that there was a statistically positive relationship between the BISTelectric, BISTkimya, BISTtextile and BISTfood index variables and the dollar index in the analysis.

Continued on following page

Table 1. Continued

Authors	Subject	Scope	Methodology	Result
Gülhan (2020)	Finance, Stock market index, Pandemic, Covid-19	Turkey	Robust least squares, Error correction model	According to the study finding, the pandemic process effectively affects BIST 100 in the short and long term. A result of the study state that, when it comes to investments in financial instruments, decision-makers act not for the sake of investment but for the sake of cash and savings during uncertain times, causing them to withdraw from the stock market.
Koyuncu and Meçik (2020)	Covid-19, Economic growth	Turkey	VAR Analysis	This research aims to look into the consequences of the pandemic on and between sectors in Turkey. According to the study's findings, among the industries analyzed during the Covid-19 epidemic, the construction sector was the longest to respond to a negative shock. Furthermore, the author discovered in the study that the industry sector, retail trade and service sector, and manufacturing sector are among the industries that respond the quickest to potential shocks.
Ilgın and Sarı (2020)	Covid-19, Stock market	USA, India, Brazil, Russia and Colombia and Turkey	Toda-Yamamoto causality	This study investigates whether there is a causal relationship between the total number of daily cases and deaths related to Covid-19 and the stock markets. As a result, there is a causal relationship between the total number of cases and fatalities observed due to Covid-19 and stock markets in all selected countries.
Temur (2021)	BIST 100, Covid-19, Financial crisis	Turkey	literature	The effect of Covid-19 on the BIST 100 and sector indices was investigated and compared in this study to previous financial crises. The author stated that the declines in financial markets due to Covid-19 took a shorter time than other financial crises, and the recovery was faster. Also, the study claim that Covid-19 did not have the same effect on all indices, causing sharper decreases in some indexes, while some did not experience this effect.
Chen, et al. (2020)	Coronavirus, Google search volume, Fear sentiment, Bitcoin price dynamics	Globally	Granger casualty	The authors have examined the effect of fear caused by Covid-19 on Bitcoin prices. According to the analysis results, market volatility will be exacerbated by the fear sentiments resulting from an increase in search interest for Covid-19. They also found that negative Bitcoin returns and high trading volume could be explained by the feeling of fear associated with Covid-19. According to their other results, Bitcoin does not act as a haven during the pandemic, and Covid-19 is a vital factor influencing the increase in financial market uncertainty.
Lyócsa, et al. (2020)	Google search volume, Fear, Covid-19, Stock market	Globally	Heterogeneous autoregressive (HAR) model	The author examined the effect of the fear created by Covid-19 on financial markets. As a Covid-19 fear indicator, they used the search volume data on Covid-19 on Google. As a result of the analysis, they commented that the fear of Covid-19, which manifests itself as excessive search volume, is not a timely and valuable source of data to predict worldwide stock price change.
Su, et al. (2021)	Covid-19, Fear, Stock market income	China	Reduced-bias estimation approach	The study investigated the effect of the fear of Covid-19 on Chinese stock market returns in their studies. As a result of the analysis, they concluded that the fear index has a negative and significant effect on the cumulative stock market returns. They also concluded that the impact of the fear index is permanent. Finally, they stated that the internet search behaviour of investors increased the fear of Covid-19.
William, et al. (2021)	GFI for Covid-19 pandemic, exchange rate returns	Seven Countries	Wild bootstrap likelihood ratio (WBLR) test	Covid-19's impact on the Australian Dollar, Canadian Dollar, Swiss Franc, Tuan, EURO, Sterling, and Yen is investigated in this study. According to the study's findings, they stated that the fear created by the pandemic is a determinant of exchange rate returns.

When the papers are evaluated, it is seen that several researchers have begun to investigate the change in financial market behaviour during the pandemic with the increasing effect of Covid-19. Some of these studies have taken a comparative approach using econometric models to examine the difference in the behaviour of the financial market after the outbreak of Covid-19, dividing their samples into pre-pandemic and post-pandemic periods. Some studies have investigated the relationship between the daily transmission rates of Covid-19 and the performance of financial assets. The most important thing that draws attention in studies examining the effect of behaviour on financial markets is the fear index.

In this study, the effects of Covid-19 on investors' behaviour patterns in Turkey are examined on Borsa Istanbul and the exchange rate. It is seen that the Covid-19 fear index based on the Search Volume Index (SVI) of Google Trends is used (Suyadal (2021); Subramaniam and Chakraborty (2021); Vasileiou (2021); Chen et al. (2020) and Lyócsa, et al. (2020)). In this study, Covid-19 search values from Google Trends were used as an indicator of fear, considering previous studies. The use of Google search results as an indicator of fear in the study provides a valuable data source that can improve the assessment of market risks in uncertain, unprecedented times. When interpreting Google Trend data, data from the graph shows search interest relative to the highest point in the chart for a given region and time. A value of 100 means that the term has the highest popularity. A value of 50 means the term is half as popular, while a value of 0 means there isn't enough data for that term (trends.google.com. Accessed 24.01.2022). When examined in the future, the term Covid-19 will probably be the most searched in the history of Google Trends (Lyócsa et al. 2020: 6).

DATA, METHODOLOGY AND FINDINGS

First and foremost, in this part, information regarding the variables employed in the study is provided. The following part looked at the econometric methodologies utilized to examine the influence of fear from Covid-19 on BIST 100 and the exchange rate. Finally, we interpreted the outcomes of econometric models.

Data

Given the uncertainties produced by Covid-19, it is critical to investigate the impacts of fear in this period. Based on this situation, the influence of fear created by Covid-19 on two critical financial indicators, the stock market index and the currency rate, was investigated in this study. While examining this effect, following Suyadal (2021) and Subramaniam and Chakraborty (2021), Covid-19 search results from Google Trends are used to indicate the fear.

The study used the BIST 100 index and the US dollar (as exchange rate) as financial indicators. This study chose the BIST 100 Index as one of the indicators because the BIST 100 Index is used to assess the stock market's collapse and rise. In addition, this index is used to measure the performance of the top 100 stocks in terms of transaction and market volume traded in Borsa Istanbul (BIST 100). This situation causes investors to follow the values taken by the index intensively (www.ekonomist.com.tr; www.alnusyatirim.com Access Date: 11.02.2022). The US Dollar is taken as another financial variable. Because most transactions made in foreign currency in Turkey are made in US Dollars, this causes this variable to be followed widely. The variables used in the analysis and their explanations are given in Table 2.

Table 2. Variable Descriptions

Variable	Description	Data Range	Source
Covid- 19[2]	Google Trend Search Results	2020: Q2- 2021: Q4	trends.google.com
BİST100 [3]	Closing Price (Level)	2020: Q2- 2021: Q4	Central Bank of Turkey (Electronic Data Delivery System)
US Dollar[4]	Currency Sales (Level)	2020: Q2- 2021: Q4	Central Bank of Turkey (Electronic Data Delivery System)

The Augmented Dickey-Fuller (ADF) Unit Root Test (ADF) and the Phillips Perron (PP) Unit Root Test (PP) were used in this study to analyze the series' stationarity. Then, the Frequency-Domain Causality Test was conducted to determine whether fear affects financial variables BIST 100 and US Dollar. This part of the study gives information about the econometric methods applied.

Methodology

In this study, Augmented Dickey-Fuller (ADF) Unit Root Test (ADF) and Phillips Perron (PP) Unit Root Test were applied to examine the stationarity of the series. Then, Frequency-Domain Causality Test was conducted to determine whether fear affects financial variables BIST 100 and US Dollar. This part of the study gives information about the econometric methods applied.

Unit Root Tests

At the beginning of the analysis, the stationarity of the variables was examined first. Stationary series can undergo structural breaks over time. As a result, non-stationary series emerge. Granger and Newbold (1974) stated that spurious regression problems might be encountered in the analyzes made with non-stationary series. This situation has two consequences. The first of these is the situation where economically meaningless results can be encountered. The second is the situation where there are significant relationships in the variables that do not have significant relationships between them (Kutlar, 2012: 646-466). Augmented Dickey-Fuller (ADF) (1981) and Phillips Perron (PP) (1988) unit root tests, which are frequently used in the literature, were used to examine the stationarity between the series.

Dickey and Fuller (1981) stated that the traditional Dickey-Fuller Unit Root Test is based only on the first-order AR (autoregressive) process. In the test where p is accepted as the lag length, for the AR (p) model;

In the null hypothesis of the test, the ARIMA (p, 1, 0) autoregressive integrated moving average process is tested,

The stationary ARIMA (p+ 1, 0, 0) process is tested in the alternative hypothesis. However, suppose one of the significant delays of the y_t series is forgotten, in other words. In that case, if the error term has white noise characteristics, an autocorrelation problem will arise in the error term. In this case, it may be necessary to add higher-order AR to the model. Because the DF Unit Root Test uses the first-order autocorrelation process, models with higher-order autocorrelation processes should be used for the error term (ε_t) to exhibit white noise characteristics. The regression in Equation 1 shows the model without a constant term and a trend variable.

$$\Delta y_t = \gamma y_{t-1} + \sum_{i=2}^{p} \beta_i \Delta_{t-i+1} + \varepsilon t \; \varepsilon_t \sim \text{WN } (\text{O}, \sigma^2) \tag{1}$$

The model in Equation 2 is the model that includes the constant term.

$$\Delta y_t = c + \gamma y_{t-1} + \sum_{i=2}^{p} \beta_i \Delta_{t-i+1} + \varepsilon t \; \varepsilon_t \sim \text{WN } (\text{O}, \sigma^2) \tag{2}$$

Equation 3 contains the model to which the constant term and trend are added.

$$\Delta y_t = c + \gamma y_{t-1} + \delta_2 t \sum_{i=2}^{p} \beta_i \Delta_{t-i+1} + \varepsilon t \; \varepsilon_t \sim \text{WN } (\text{O}, \sigma^2) \tag{3}$$

The test process in the equations is based on whether the variable γ is less than one. While interpreting the stationarity of the variables as a result of the unit root test, if the null hypothesis is rejected, that is, the alternative hypothesis is accepted, it is interpreted that the yt series does not contain a unit root and is stationary (Koçyiğit, et al. 2011: 48).

Augmented Dickey-Fuller (ADF) (1981) Unit Root Test and Phillips and Perron (1988) Unit Root Test are unit root tests with similar hypotheses. While calculating the PP Unit Root Test, estimates are made with the help of equations 4 and 5.

$$Y_t = \hat{\mu} + \hat{\alpha} Y_{t-1} + \hat{\mu}_t \tag{4}$$

$$Y_t = \hat{\mu} + \hat{\beta}\left(t - \frac{1}{2}\lambda\right) + \hat{\alpha} Y_{t-1} + \hat{\mu}_t \tag{5}$$

In the PP Unit Root Test, as in ADF, the null hypothesis means that the series has a unit root. That is, it is not stationary. In contrast, the alternative hypothesis means that the series is stationary, not with a unit root. In both ADF and PP Unit Root Tests, if the test statistics are more significant than the critical values, the null hypothesis is rejected, and the alternative hypothesis is accepted (Bingöl et al. 2020: 256).

Frequency-Domain Causality Test

Frequency-Domain Causality Test reveals whether the relationship between the variables is a temporary one or a permanent one. In addition, it allows the causality relationship between the variables to be examined in the short, medium and long term. These two features increase the importance of the test. In addition, traditional causality tests allow interpretation with a single test statistic while examining the causality relationship between variables. On the other hand, this test enables exploring the relationship between variables at different frequencies over time (Taşar, 2015: 63; Bayat et al., 2015: 13). Breitung and Candelon stated that the Frequency-Domain Causality Test, which they explained in their study titled "Testing for Short- and Long-Run Causality: A Frequency-Domain Approach" in 2006, is based on the studies of Geweke (1982) and Hosoya (1991). Accordingly, they defined a two-dimensional vector belonging to the time series $z_t = [\, x_{t,}\ y_t\,]$ under a particular VAR assumption to test the causality between the variables. This equation is given in 6.

$$\Theta (L)\, z_t = \varepsilon_t \tag{6}$$

$\Theta (L)= I- \Theta_1 L- \ldots - \Theta_p L^p$, 2x with a lag size of $L^k z_t = z_{t-1}$. Granger causality at different frequencies is expressed as in equation 7.

$$M_{y\rightarrow x}(\omega) = \log\left[\frac{2\pi f_x(\omega)}{\left|\psi_{11}(e^{-i\omega})\right|^2}\right] = \log\left[1 + \frac{\left|\psi_{12}(e^{-i\omega})\right|^2}{\left|\psi_{11}(e^{-i\omega})\right|^2}\right] \tag{7}$$

$\left|\psi_{12}(e^{-i\omega})\right|^2 = 0$ means that x at frequency ω of y is not Granger cause. If the components of z_t are first-order stationery (I(1)) and integrated, it means that they have an autoregressive Θ (L) unit root. The remaining roots will be outside the circle (Taşar, 2015: 63; Bayat et al., 2015: 13). If zt-1 is subtracted from both sides of equality 6, equality 8 will be obtained (Breitung and Candelon, 2006: 365).

$$\Delta z_t = (\Theta_1 - I) z_{t-1} + \Theta_1\, z_{t-1} + \ldots + \Theta_p\, z_{t-p} + \varepsilon_t \tag{8}$$

$= \tilde{\Theta} (L)\, z_{t-1} + \varepsilon_t$, in case is as in equation 9.

$$\tilde{\Theta} (L) = \Theta_1 - I + \Theta_2\, L + \ldots + \Theta_p\, L^p \tag{9}$$

Breitung and Candelon (2006) suggested a single test strategy for autoregressive parameters based on a linear hypothesis utilizing a bivariate vector autoregressive model.

ε_t is expressed as white noise by Breitung and Candelon (2006). E (ε_t) and E (ε_t, ε_t') = Σ. Σ in the equation, is positive definite. If G is defined as the downward triangular matrix of Cholesky decomposition, then in $G'G = \Sigma^{-1}$, is in the form $E (\eta_t \eta'_t) = I$ and $\eta_t = G\, \varepsilon_t$. If the system is stationary, then $\phi (L) = \Theta (L)^{-1}$ and $\psi (L) = \phi (L)\, G^{-1}$. The MA representation is in equation 10.

$$z_t = \phi(L)\varepsilon_t = \begin{pmatrix} \phi_{11}(L)\phi_{12}(L) \\ \phi_{21}(L)\phi_{22}(L) \end{pmatrix}\begin{pmatrix} \varepsilon_{1t} \\ \varepsilon_{2t} \end{pmatrix} = \begin{pmatrix} \psi_{11}(L)\psi_{12}(L) \\ \psi_{21}(L)\psi_{22}(L) \end{pmatrix}\begin{pmatrix} \eta_{1t} \\ \eta_{2t} \end{pmatrix} \tag{10}$$

This equation can be used to represent the spectral density of x_t (Breitung and Candelon, 2006: 365). This is also included in equation 11.

$$f_x(\omega) = \frac{1}{2\omega}\left\{\left|\Psi_{11}\,(e^{-i\omega})\right|^2 + \left|\Psi_{12}\,(e^{-i\omega})\right|^2\right\} \tag{11}$$

According to the model developed by Breitung and Candelon (2006), if it is $M_{y\to x}(\omega)=0$ shaped, in other words, if there is no causality finding at a frequency ω from y to x, $\left|\Psi_{12}\left(e^{-i\omega}\right)\right|^2 = 0$. The null hypothesis is equal to the linear constraint in the VAR coefficients.

When obtaining $\Psi_{12}(L) = -\dfrac{g^{22}\Theta_{12}(L)}{\left|\Theta(L)\right|}$ from the equation $\Psi(L) = \Theta(L)^{-1} G^{-1}$; g^{22} represents the diagonal elements of G^{-1}, and $|\Theta(L)|$ shows the determinant value of Θ (L). At ω frequency time, whether y is explanatory of x is determined in equation 12 (Taşar, 2015: 65).

$$\left|\Theta_{12}\left(\varepsilon^{-i\omega}\right)\right| = \left|\sum_{k=1}^{p}\theta_{12,k}\cos(k\omega) - \sum_{k=1}^{p}\theta_{12,k}\sin(k\omega)i\right| \tag{12}$$

As seen above, equality; represents the (1, 2) element of the $\theta_{12,k}$; Θ_k matrix. Therefore $\left|\Theta_{12}\left(\varepsilon^{-i\omega}\right)\right|$ = 0. Thus, Breitung and Candelon (2006) applied the linear constraints $\alpha_{j=\theta_{11,j}}$ and $\beta_j = \theta_{12,j}$ equations to equations 13 and 14 (Bayat et al. 2015: 15).

$$\sum_{k=1}^{p}\theta_{12,k}\cos(k\omega) = 0 \tag{13}$$

$$\sum_{k=1}^{p}\theta_{12,k}\sin(k\omega) = 0 \tag{14}$$

After that, the VAR equation to be created for x_t can be shown as in equation 15 (Bayat et al. 2015: 15).

$$x_t = \alpha_1 x_{t-1} + \dots + \alpha p x_{t-p} + \beta_1 y_{t-1} + \dots + \beta_p y_{t-1} + \varepsilon_{1t} \tag{15}$$

Here, the null hypothesis will be equal to the linear constraint with $M_{y\to x}(\omega)=0$ $\beta = \left[\beta_1, \dots, \beta_p\right]$. H0: R (ω) β = 0 and

$$R(\omega) = \begin{bmatrix}\cos(\omega)\cos(2\omega)\dots\cos(\mathrm{p}\,\omega \\ \sin(\omega)\sin(2\omega)\dots.\sin(\mathrm{p}\,\omega)\end{bmatrix}$$

The causality measure for ω π ∈(0, π) can be tested with the traditional F test. The test procedure (2, T-2p) will have an F- distribution with degrees of freedom (Bayat et al. 2015: 15).

Findings

In the study, the logarithm of BIST 100 and exchange rate variables were used. The variables' descriptive statistics were then investigated. Table 2 contains the descriptive statistics of Covid-19 search results, BIST 100 and exchange rate variables. The basic statistical features of the variables are expressed with standard deviation, mean, kurtosis and skewness coefficients (Çil, 2018: 33). The coefficient of variation of the variables was calculated by dividing the standard deviation by the mean (Bayat, 2011: 51). The standard deviation value shows the volatility of the variables. It does not remain constant over time and shows a changing feature. The standard deviation value is a vital risk measurement tool in financial time series. In most financial models and theories, it is assumed that the series exhibit normal distribution in order to facilitate theoretical application and inferences. The normal distribution is symmetrical. The commonly used test statistic for testing this distribution is Jarque-Bera (JB). The test uses skewness and kurtosis coefficients under the main hypothesis that returns are normally distributed. In the analysis of financial variables, the kurtosis and skewness values of the return series give information about the distribution of the series. The kurtosis coefficient shows the tail distribution of the distribution curve. The skewness coefficient shows the asymmetry in the probability distributions of the variables. When interpreting the Jarque-Bera test statistic, values greater than the critical values indicate that the basic hypothesis indicating that the series is normally distributed was rejected, and the alternative hypothesis indicating that the series does not exhibit a normal distribution was accepted (Çil, 2018: 33- 34- 36; Kayhan et al. 2013: 202).

Table 3. Descriptive Statistics of Covid-19, BIST 100 and Exchange Rate Variables

	LBIST 100	LExchange-Rate	Covid-19
Mean	7.179796	2.077843	16.61904
Standard deviation	0.183724	0.161468	8.768897
Coefficient of Change	0.025589	0.077709	0.527642
skewness	-0.110773	1.686059	-0.024201
Kurtosis	2.833670	6.776424	1.812739
Jarque-Bera	0.300597	100.3942	5.530067
Possibility	0.860451	0.000000	0.062974
Observation	94	94	94

Note: "If the skew value is < 0, it is skewed to the left. If the skewness value is > 0, it is skewed to the right. If the skewness value is 0, it is symmetrical. If the kurtosis value is < 3, it is flattened, the kurtosis value> 3 is vertical, the kurtosis value = 3 is normal".

When the values in Table 3 are examined, it is seen that the variable with the highest mean is the Covid-19 search results. This variable is followed by BIST 100 Index and exchange rate variables. When the variables are evaluated in terms of standard deviation values, the standard deviation values of the BIST 100 index and exchange rate variables are partially close to each other. However, the standard deviation value of the Covid-19 variable is considerably higher than the other two variables. In other words, the volatility in the Covid-19 series is higher than the fluctuation of the other two variables. When the skewness coefficients of the variables are examined, the series of BIST 100 Index and Covid-19 variables have a left-skewed structure. In contrast, the series of the exchange rate variable has a right-skewed structure. When the series is examined in terms of kurtosis coefficients, the sequence of the Covid-19 and BIST 100 Index variables have a flattened structure. In contrast, the series of the exchange rate variable exhibits a vertical structure. When the variables are investigated in terms of the normality assumption, as can be seen, the main hypothesis establishing the validity of the normalcy assumption is rejected; that is, the BIST 100 index series do not have a normal distribution. When the series is assessed for exchange rate and Covid-19, it is clear that it has a normal distribution.

The correlation coefficient is used to get information about the direction of the linear relationship between the variables. The correlation coefficient ranges from -1 to 1 (Çil, 2018: 40-41). A positive coefficient suggests a linear relationship between the variables, whereas a negative coefficient shows an inverse link. The correlation coefficients of Covid-19, BIST 100, and exchange rate variables are shown in Table 4.

Table 4. Covid-19, BIST 100 and Exchange Rate Correlation Coefficients

	BIST 100	Exchange Rate	Covid-19
BIST 100	-	0.795	0.0126
Exchange Rate	-	-	0.005
Covid-19	-	-	-

As seen in Table 4, there is a positive relationship between Covid-19 and BIST 100 and exchange rate variables. But this relationship is a weak one. In addition, there is a positive relationship between the exchange rate and BIST 100 variables, this relationship is a strong one.

To examine the stationarity of the variables, Augmented Dickey-Fuller (ADF) (1981) and Phillips Perron (PP) (1988) unit root tests were applied to the variables within the scope of the study. In both tests, the null hypothesis means that the series has a unit root; that is, it is not stationary, while the alternative hypothesis is that the series is stationary, not with a unit root. Table 5 shows the results of unit root tests for BIST 100, currency and Covid-19 variables.

Table 5. ADF (1981) and PP (1988) Unit Root Test Results for Covid-19, BIST 100 and Exchange Rate Variables

	At Level I (0)				At First Difference I (1)			
	With Constant		With Constant & Trend		With Constant		With Constant & Trend	
Variables	**ADF** t-Stat	**Prob.**	**ADF** t-Stat	**Prob.**	**ADF** t-Stat	**Prob.**	**ADF** t-Stat	**Prob.**
Covid- 19	-5. 4339	0.000***	-5.399	0.000***	-5.417	0.000***	-5.660	0.000***
BIST 100	-0. 666	0. 849	-2.640	0.264	-8.941	0.000***	-3.587	0.036**
Exchange Rate	0.720	0.992	-1.013	0.936	-5.417	0.000***	-5.660	0.000***
	PP t-Stat	**Prob.**	**PP** t-Stat	**Prob.**	**PP** t-Statistic	**Prob.**	**PP** t-Stat	**Prob.**
Covid- 19	-15.341	0.000***	-15.257	0.000***	-26.017	0.000***	-26.010	0.000***
BIST 100	-0.728	0.833	-1.974	0.607	-8.941	0.000***	-8.829	0.000***
Exchange Rate	1.760	0.999	0.534	0.999	-5.487	0.000***	-5.649	0.000***

Note: ***,**, and * values are, respectively, show the stationarity of the series at %1, 5%, and 10% significance levels.

When the results in Table 5 are examined, the basic hypothesis was rejected due to both ADF and PP Unit Root tests for the Covid-19 variable, and the alternative hypothesis was accepted. In other words, it is concluded that it is stationary at the 1% probability value at the I(0) level; that is, it does not contain a unit root. When the BIST 100 and exchange rate variables are examined, the basic hypothesis is accepted at the level values , and the alternative hypothesis is rejected. Both variables become stationary at the I(1) level. This result means that BIST100 and exchange rate variables become stationary series at the I(1) level. That is, it does not contain a unit root.

Frequency Domain causality test was applied to the variables to examine the effect of fear caused by Covid-19 on BIST 100 and exchange rate variables in Turkey. In addition, with this test, the impact of the fear caused by Covid-19 on the BIST 100 Index and exchange rate variables is periodically examined. While performing the test, firstly, the difference of the series was taken, and the analyzes were made with the difference series. Table 6 shows the results of the causality analysis conducted to examine the relationship between the variables.

Table 6. Frequency-Domain Causality Test Results for Covid-19 and Currency and BIST 100 Index Variables

ω_i	Long Term		Medium Term		Short Term	
	0.01	**0.05**	**1.00**	**1.50**	**2.00**	**2.50**
ΔCovid-19 ≠> ΔExchange Rate	1.476	1.490	0.490	3.770**	1.167	0.688
ΔCovid-19 ≠> ΔBIST 100	0.826	0.821	3.861**	2.101	0.330	2.711***

Note: (2, T-2p) with degrees of freedom, the table value for F is 4.857 for 1%, 3.101 for 5%, and 2.364 for 10%. ***,**,* indicate 1%, 5% and 10% significance levels, respectively. 0 and π, ω ϵ (0, π). For every frequency-domain ω_i in between.

While interpreting the results of the Frequency Domain Causality test, the calculated F statistic must be larger than the F table values to interpret the causality between the variables. When the causality analysis results are analyzed, it is discovered that there is causation in the medium term, at a 5% significance level, from the fear of Covid-19 to the exchange rate variable. When the influence of fear originating from Covid-19 on the BIST 100 index is analyzed, it is discovered that fear stemming from Covid-19 has a 10% short-term and 5% medium-term impact on BIST 100. The immediate effect of the financial, economic and social developments experienced here on the stock market index has caused the uncertainty and fear that Covid-19 has created since its emergence to impact the BIST 100 Index. This effect remained visible on the BIST 100 Index in the following time, as well as on the exchange rate. In the long run, having more information about Covid-19, the start of vaccination, and the fact that the markets and investors got used to the process, although the uncertainty continued, no causality emerged.

CONCLUSION, RECOMMENDATIONS FUTURE RESEARCH DIRECTIONS

During the Covid-19 process, individuals have encountered different news every day. In society, unfounded information has spread among people. The use of masks has suddenly entered people's lives. Individuals who wake up every morning to work and school stay at home for days with curfews. The students continued their education with the distance education method. People with suitable working conditions have also switched to the remote working model, just like students. But on the other hand, many people lost their jobs. Healthcare professionals have faced long and difficult working conditions.

Economically, a complicated process has begun. According to specific analyses, the Covid-19 period faced more hardship than the global financial crisis that afflicted the entire world in 2008-2009. During this period, precautionary package statements came from countries after another. Because many businesses have stopped their operations, laid off their workers, and the global supply chain has been hit hard. Likewise, the financial markets have also suffered significant losses. Indices and exchange rates responded to the emerging uncertainty with sudden fluctuations.

There have been many studies in the academic literature on Covid-19, which spreads to all areas. It has also been an essential agenda item in the economic literature. In particular, the impact of the number of cases and deaths on financial and macroeconomic variables has been frequently emphasized. In this study, the impact of fear caused by Covid-19 on the stock market index and exchange rate, which are two crucial financial indicators in Turkey, has been examined for 2020: Q2- 2021: Q4. In this paper, Google Trends search data is used to represent the fear caused by Covid-19. The BIST 100 index was used as the Stock Exchange Index, and the US Dollar was used as the exchange rate variable.

To examine the stationarity of the variables, first of all, ADF and PP Unit Root tests were carried out. As a result of the unit root tests, it was concluded that the fear variable from Covid-19 was stationary in the level value. In contrast, the exchange rate and BIST 100 variables were stationary at the first difference. Then, the descriptive statistics of the variables and their distribution characteristics were examined. Afterwards, it was found that there is a strong and positive relationship between the correlation coefficients and the exchange rate and BIST 100 index and that although there is a positive relationship between fear of Covid-19 and BIST 100 and exchange rate variables, this relationship is weak. To examine whether the fear caused by Covid-19 affects the BIST 100 Index and the exchange rate in the analyzed period, the frequency domain causality test was applied to the variables. As a result of the analysis, it was found that the fear caused by Covid-19 is the cause of BIST 100 in the medium and short term, and the exchange rate variable is the cause in the short term.

The measures taken over time have expanded, but on the other hand, the effect of Covid-19 has spread more than expected. Therefore, uncertainties have also increased considerably. One of the biggest problems created by uncertainty has been fear. Fear has spread beyond individuality to the general population, and fear caused by Covid-19 has become a critical problem. In the process of Covid-19, the need for individuals to receive news has increased.

For this reason, they turned to different news sources. But sometimes, the information they received increased their fear even more. The shopping habits of individuals have changed due to fear, and the need to stock up on primary products has increased. The number of individuals shopping online has increased day by day. Individuals have tried to continue their lives with the effect of growing uncertainty.

Although the results obtained in the study demonstrate that the fear of Covid-19 is temporary, the effect of the uncertain factor in this type of crisis is noticeable. In this context, it should be ensured that the causes of uncertainty are eliminated, people's need for information and news needs to be eliminated. In this way, it will be beneficial to reduce the reasons that cause fear in similar crises in the coming years.

The results obtained in the study reveal that the fear of Covid-19 is temporary. The removal of restrictions, the start of vaccination, and the return of people to their everyday lives and jobs have begun to reduce the effect of fear caused by Covid-19 on the variables. In this study, the impact of fear of Covid-19 on financial markets for Turkey was made based on internet search results. The study differs from other studies in the literature consisting of studies conducted in Turkey. In addition, it is thought that it will contribute to the literature since it has been examined through periods whether the effect is permanent or temporary. Future studies can expand the literature on this subject by examining the impact of fear of Covid-19 on variables such as sectoral stock market indices and gold prices per gram.

REFERENCES

Addo, P. C., Jiaming, F., Kulbo, N. B., & Liangqiang, L. (2020). COVID-19: Fear appeal favoring purchase behavior towards personal protective equipment. *Service Industries Journal*, *40*(7-8), 471–490. doi:10.1080/02642069.2020.1751823

Ahorsu, D. K., Lin, C. Y., Imani, V., Saffari, M., Griffiths, M. D., & Pakpour, A. H. (2020). The fear of COVID-19 scale: Development and initial validation. *International Journal of Mental Health and Addiction*, 1–9. PMID:32226353

Ashraf, B. N. (2021). Stock markets' reaction to COVID-19: Moderating role of national culture. *Finance Research Letters*, *41*, 101857. doi:10.1016/j.frl.2020.101857

Baldwin, R., & Mauro, B. W. (2020). Introduction. In Economics in the Time of Covid-19 (pp. 1-30). CEPR Press.

Bayat, T., Özcan, B., & Taş, Ş. (2015). Türkiye'de döviz kuru geçiş etkisinin asimetrik nedensellik testleri ile analizi. *Eskişehir Osmangazi Üniversitesi İİBF Dergisi*, *10*(2), 7–30.

Biçer, İ., Çakmak, C., Demir, H., & Kurt, M. E. (2020). Koronavirüs anksiyete ölçeği kısa formu: Türkçe geçerlik ve güvenirlik çalışması. *Anatolian Clinic the Journal of Medical Sciences. Anadolu Kliniği Tıp Bilimleri Dergisi (COVID 19 Özel Sayısı)*, 216-225.

Bingöl, N., Pehlivan, C., & Han, A. (2020). Turizm gelirleri- makro değişkenler arasındaki ilişkinin Türkiye için ampirik olarak incelenmesi. *Ekev Akademi Dergisi*, *24*(82), 245–262.

BİST-100 Endeksi. (n.d.). https://www.ekonomist.com.tr/encyclopedia/bist-100-endeksi

BİST 100. (n.d.). https://www.alnusyatirim.com/bist-100#:~:text=BIST%20100%20endeksi%3B%20 Borsa%20%C4%B0stanbul,%C3%B6l%C3%A7mek%20i%C3%A7in%20kullan%C4%B1lan%20 temel%20g%C3%B6stergedir.&text=%C3%96zetle%3B%20bu%20100%20%C5%9Firketin%20 hisse%20senedi%2C%20borsan%C4%B1n%20genel%20performans%C4%B1n%C4%B1%20 g%C3%B6stermektedir

Bouhali, H., Dahbanib, A., & Dinarb, B. (2021). COVID-19 impacts on financial markets: Takeaways from the third wave. *Russian Journal of Economics*, *7*, 200–212.

Breitung, J., & Candelon, B. (2006). Testing for short- and long-run causality: A frequency-domain approach. *Journal of Econometrics*, *132*(2), 363–378.

Bulck, J. V., & Custers, K. (2009). Television exposure is related to fear of avian flu, an Ecological Study across 23 member states of the European Union. *European Journal of Public Health*, *19*(4), 370–374.

Chen, C., Liu, L., & Zhao, N. (2020). Fear sentiment, uncertainty, and bitcoin price dynamics: The case of COVID-19. *Emerging Markets Finance & Trade*, *56*(10), 2298–2309.

Çil, N. (2018). *Finansal Ekonometri*. Der Yayınları.

Covid-19 Arama Terimi. (n.d.). https://trends.google.com/trends/explore?date=2019-12-31%20 2022-01-21&geo=TR&q=Covid19

Di Mauro, B. W. (2020). Macroeconomics of the Flue, R. In Economics in the Time of Covid-19 (pp. 31- 35). CEPR Press.

Dickey, D. A., & Fuller, W. A. (1981). Likelihood ratio statistics for autoregressive time series with a unıt root. *Econometrica*, *49*(4), 1057–1072.

Doğan, M. M., & Düzel, B. (2020). Covid- 19 özelinde korku- kaygı düzeyleri. *Turkish Studies*, *15*(4), 739–752.

Garfin, D. R., Silver, R. C., & Holman, E. A. (2020). The novel coronavirus (Covid- 2019) outbreak: Amplification health consequences by media exposure. *Health Psychology*, *39*(5), 355–357.

Gülhan, Ü. (2020). Covid-19 Pandemisine BIST 100 reaksiyonu: Ekonometrik bir analiz. *Electronic Turkish Studies*, *15*(4), 497–509.

Günsoy, B., & Yıldız, Ü. (2021). Türkiye için Covid- 19 pandemisi ile döviz kuru arasındaki frekans alan nedensellik analizi. *International Conference on Economics Turkish Economic Association.*

Haroon, O., & Rizvi, S. A. (2020). COVID-19: Media coverage and financial markets behavior—A sectoral inquiry. *Journal of Behavioral and Experimental Finance*, *27*, 1–5.

Ilgın, K. S., & Sarı, S. S. (2020). Covid-19 pandemisinin hisse senedi piyasalarına etkisi: Vaka ve ölümlerin yoğun olduğu ülkeler ile Türkiye incelemesi. *Karadeniz Sosyal Bilimler Dergisi*, *12*(23), 434–453.

İşler, İ. İ., & Güven, A. (2021). Covid-19 küresel salgınının BIST 100 endeksi üzerindeki etkileri. *Politik Ekonomik Kuram*, *5*(1), 63–77.

Karataş, Z. (2020). COVID-19 pandemisinin toplumsal etkileri, değişim ve güçlenme. *Türkiye Sosyal Hizmet Araştırmaları Dergisi*, *4*(1), 3–17.

Kayhan, S., Bayat, T., & Koçyiğt, A. (2013). Enflasyon hedeflemesi rejiminde öğrenme süreci ve asimetri: Markov switching yaklaşımı. *Eskişehir Osmangazi Üniversitesi İİBF Dergisi*, *8*(1), 191–212.

Koçyiğit, A., Bayat, T., & Tüfekçi, A. (2011). Türkiye'de işsizlik histerisi ve star modelleri uygulaması. *Marmara Üniversitesi İ.İ.B.F. Dergisi*, *31*(2), 45–60.

Koyuncu, T., & Meçik, O. (2020). Covid-19 pandemisinin türkiye'de ekonomik büyümeye sektör-spesifik etkileri: Var analizi. *Yönetim ve Ekonomi Araştırmaları Dergisi*, *18*(4), 112–131.

Kutlar, A. (2003). *Ekonometriye giriş*. Nobel Akademik Yayıncılık Eğilim Danışmanlık.

Lalwani, V., & Meshram, V. V. (2020). Stock market efficiency in the time of COVID-19: Evidence from industry stock returns. *International Journal of Accounting & Finance Review*, *5*(2), 40–44.

Lyócsa, Š., Baumöhl, E., Výrost, T., & Molnár, P. (2020). Fear of the coronavirus and the stock markets. *Finance Research Letters*, 1–7.

Mann, C. L. (2020). Real and financial lenses to assess the economic consequences of COVID-19. In Economics in the Time of Covid-19 (pp. 81-85). CEPR Press.

McKibbin, W., & Fernando, R. (2020). The economic impact of COVID-19. In *Economics in the Time of Covid- 19 (pp. 45-51)*. CEPR Press.

Mertens, G., Gerritsen, L., Dujndam, S., Salemink, E., & Engelhard, I. M. (2020). Fear of the coronavirus (COVID-19): Predictors in an online study conducted in March 2020. *Journal of Anxiety Disorders*, *74*, 1–8.

Narayan, P. K. (2020). Has COVID-19 changed exchange rate resistance to shocks? *Asian Economics Letters*, *1*(1), 17389.

Olasehinde-Williams, G., Olanipekun, I., & Özkan, O. (2021). Foreign exchange market response to pandemic-induced fear: Evidence from (a) symmetric wild bootstrap likelihood ratio approach. *The Journal of International Trade & Economic Development*, *30*(7), 988–1003.

Özatay, F., & Sak, G. (2020). *Covid- 19 ve normalleşme*. Türkiye Ekonomi Politikaları Araştırma Vakfı.

Özbay, F., & Özcan, A. (2021). The Examined of the influence of Covid-19 on e-commerce and consumer behavior: A study on Turkey. *Aydın İktisat Fakültesi Dergisi*, *6*(1), 21–33.

Özmerdivanlı, A. (2021). Covid-19 pandemisi ile çeşitli finansal göstergeler arasındaki nedensellik ilişkisi: Türkiye örneği. *Ekonomi Politika ve Finans Araştırmaları Dergisi, 6*, 172-191.

Pakpour, A. H., & Griffiths, M. D. The fear of COVID-19 and its role in preventive behaviors. *Journal of Concurrent Disorders*, 1- 6.

Phillips, P. C. B., & Perron, P. (1988). Testing for a unit root in time series regression. *Biometrika, 75*(2), 335–346.

Reis, Ş. G. (2021). Covıd-19 (Koronavirüs) pandemisi ve risk iştahı: Borsa İstanbul yerli ve yabancı yatırımcılar örneği. *Anadolu Üniversitesi İktisadi ve İdari Bilimler Fakültesi Dergisi, 22*(3), 87–98.

Salisu, A. A., & Vo, X. V. (2020). Predicting stock returns in the presence of COVID-19 pandemic: The role of health news. *International Review of Financial Analysis, 71*, 1–10.

Şenol, Z. (2020). Covid-19 krizi ve finansal piyasalar. In *Para ve finans* (pp. 75–124). IKSAD Publishing House.

Servi, T., Dönmez, Z., & Akbaş, Y. E. (2020). İmalat sanayisi ile VIX endeksi ilişkisinin analizi: Türkiye örneği. *Al Farabi Uluslararası Sosyal Bilimler Dergisi, 5*(4), 94–102.

Su, Z., Liu, P., & Fang, T. (2021). Pandemic-induced fear and stock market returns: Evidence from China. *Global Finance Journal.*

Subramaniam, S., & Chakraborty. (2021). COVID-19 fear index: Does it matter for stock market returns? *Review of Behavioral Finance, 13*(1), 40–50.

Suyadal, M. (2021). Covıd-19 pandemisinde piyasa etkinliği ve davranışsal finans teorilerinin geçerliliği: uluslararası piyasalarda bir uygulama. *Erciyes Üniversitesi İktisadi ve İdari Bilimler Fakültesi Dergisi,* (60), 519-546.

Taşar, İ. (2015). *İçsel büyüme modelleri çerçevesinde Türkiye'de ekonomik büyümenin yapısal dönüşümü* (Unpublished doctoral dissertation). İnönü University, Institute of Social Sciences, Department of Economics, Malatya.

Taylor, S., Landry, C. A., Paluszek, M. M., Fergus, T. A., McKay, D., & Asmundson, G. J. G. (2020). Development and initial validation of the COVID stress scales. *Journal of Anxiety Disorders, 72*, 1–7.

Temur, A. S. (2021). COVID-19 financial crisis? comparison of its impacts on borsa istanbul (bist) with history financial crises. In *International Conference on Economics*. Turkish Economic Association.

Tosun, N. (2021). *Finansal yatırım kararlarına yatırımcı duyarlılığının etkisi: Türkiye üzerine bir araştırma* (Unpublished doctoral dissertation). İnönü University, Institute of Social Sciences, Department of Economics, Malatya.

Uçar, M., & Kıdemli. M. (2021). Türkiye'de Covıd-19 hasta vaka sayısı, vıx endeksi, dolar endeksi ile seçilmiş bıst sektör endeksleri arasındaki ilişki: ARDL model. *Uluslararası Kapadokya Salgın Dönemleri Kongresi. ICCET'21.*

Vasileiou, E. (2021). Behavioral finance and market efficiency in the time of the COVID-19 pandemic: Does fear drive the market? *International Review of Applied Economics*, *35*(2), 224–241. doi:10.1080/02692171.2020.1864301

Yıldırım, E. U. (2021). Covid-19 pandemi ve 2008 ekonomik kriz dönemlerinde riskten kaçınma düzeyinin ABD ve BRIC piyasa entegrasyonu üzerindeki değişen etkisi. *Muhasebe ve Finansman Dergisi*, (90), 185-208. doi:10.25095/mufad.866684

ENDNOTES

1. These individuals are called “noise trader”. A noise trader is a stock trader who decides to buy or sell based on factors that they believe are beneficial but will not yield better returns than random picks. Also, this irrational behaviour leads to noise trading.
2. The first case in Turkey was seen in March. However, the rapidly spreading Covid-19 epidemic in the world has also been frequently searched in Turkey on the internet. For this reason, the period 2020: Q2 was taken as the start date of the data range.
3. This study chose the start date of BIST100 data according to the Covid-19 data.
4. This study chose the start date of the US Dollar data according to the Covid-19 data.

Chapter 2
Accounting Student Perceptions From Internship That Trigger Adaptations in Training After the Pandemic

Paraskevi Tsoutsa
https://orcid.org/0000-0003-0019-1145
University of Thessaly, Greece

Vyron Damasiotis
https://orcid.org/0000-0001-7999-4324
University of Thessaly, Greece

Evdokia Tsifora
University of Thessaly, Greece

ABSTRACT

The pandemic has disrupted the education around the world, impacting the way it is delivered. Teaching and training during this period create challenges to students since online learning provides the knowledge transfer that were usually done physically. Accounting internships enable students to get familiarized with different types of accounting context in a realistic environment. During the pandemic, this setting has changed, and the remote internship becomes the new reality. The aim of this research was to obtain feedback from accounting students who experienced internship due to pandemic by (1) collecting their opinion and expectations regarding this new form of internship, (2) stating their satisfaction of the internship program, (3) addressing their readiness for doing the internship, and (4) indicating the fulfillment of the internship's learning outcomes. The outcome of the study revealed interesting results and a set of factors that accounting faculty should endeavor to address in order to build resilience into the accounting internship.

DOI: 10.4018/978-1-7998-8856-7.ch002

1. INTRODUCTION

The pandemia has disrupted the education around the world, impacting the way it is delivered. A disruption in that extend to every level of education had never occurred again. The lockdown imposed in many countries resulted in the immediate closure of university campuses and the move to distance learning and other related activities.

Teaching and blended learning in general during this period creates challenges to students since it is the online learning which provides the knowledge transfer that were usually done physically (Salleh et al., 2020; el Refae et al., (2021)). As a result, a large number of researchers are now examining how the learning process changes during pandemia (Salleh et al., 2020; el Refae et al., (2021); Law et al., (2019); Sangster et al., (2020)), but what about the problems have arisen when a combination of training and typical classes is required especially in the field of accounting?

"Internship" or "Practical training" is a student learning process aiming to increase student experience and provide insights in applying theoretical knowledge to real world professional activities, in this case accounting (Mediawati et al., (2020)). Work-related learning is vital for accounting students for their personal and professional development in order to build strong connections with leading business organizations (Anjum et al., (2020)). Future accountants are required to be well informed and committed to continuing education in order to incorporate all the latest scientific data into their everyday practice. This last stage of learning process plays a crucial role as they encounter the realities of their profession and gain valuable experiences for their future careers. By that way, modern accounting training is provided through dynamic and evolving environments of real organizations that cooperate with the university, where new technologies (Tsoutsa et al., (2018)) and skills (Cernuşca et al., (2020); Daff, (2021); Trivellas et al., (2015); Fitsilis et al., (2018)) are applied.

The working environment has changed during the pandemia due to government regulations concerning the COVID-19 epidemic and a new format for training became a necessity for many students and businesses after the previous academic year. "Remote internships" or "e-internships" are work placements where the interactions between the intern and their employer are predominantly computer mediated by using different platforms regarding the domain (Jeske et al., (2020)). The main feature of this internship format is its ability to connect interns and employers across different geographical locations and enable the cooperation under these circumstances. E-internships seem to be compatible with the regulations and remote work training has been prevalent for this last year while it seems that is on the rise, considering the increased use in the post COVID era that is expected.

Previous studies on internship gathered different issues that influence the satisfaction level, which include

the quality of mentoring, challenging assignments and compensation (Sanahuja Velez et al., (2015)), job satisfaction in paid and unpaid internship (Rogers et al., (2021)), job characteristics and environments such as supervisor's support, task significance, learning opportunities and feedbacks (D'abate et al., (2015)), internship relevancy (Yoo et al., (2015)), challenges, interesting and well- defined responsibilities, and job prospects. On the other hand, are increasingly proceeding studies carrying out about professional accountants to capture the impact of the pandemic generated by COVID-19 on their profession (Frumuşanu et al., (2020)).

According to authors point of view, accounting student are now struggling to cope with the new regulations and possibly disrupted internship, in addition to the high level of anxiety that threatens students and their supervisors as well, which are professional accountants (Hall et al., (2020)). Supervisor's support is important for interns as he/she represents the organisation and reflects its commitment on providing career development opportunities and concern for the intern's well-being (Chong et al., (2020)).

Although early skills development and knowledge required for students' successful transition from education to the workplace has received growing attention (Rosenberg et al., (2012); Jackson et al., (2014)) so as they have the abilities to face the challenges, nor should we forget that for current students' new needs have arisen to feel prepared for effective online/virtual communication, and to be able to present ideas, concepts and work products effectively in a computer-mediated environment.

The purpose of this research was to obtain feedback from accounting students who experienced remote internship due to pandemic by (i) collecting their opinion and expectations regarding this new form of internship that they had implemented, (ii) stating their satisfaction of the internship program, (iii) address their readiness for doing the internship program and (iv) indicate the fulfillment of learning outcomes while discussing this new form of internship. Then, we plan to use the findings of the student survey to outline the role of students' past internship experience and prior knowledge as potential factors that influence the choice of other students for traditional or e-internship. Therefore, the aim of this study is twofold, firstly to investigate how students cope with the situation and secondly to collect their perspective and expectations regarding this new form of internship. To this end, several research questions arise, so we designed the present study which aims to address the following:

1. Did pandemia influenced the way internship was carried out due to the COVID-19 restrictions and what are the effects in accounting student's productivity?
2. Was safety for all learners promoted during the internship?
3. In what degree students and organizations where prepared for teleworking?
4. Were the objectives of the internship fulfilled and how could we better get prepared for post-pandemia catch up?

The current research contributes to the literature of interniship during a crisis like pandemia by providing findings of the attitude of accounting students during their interniship. Since remote internship was supposed to replicate the learning outcomes of traditional internships during this pandemia, student's opinion is useful to develop a clear view about benefits and consequences of implementing such a form of internship. By listening to student's opinion, we could get better be prepared for post-pandemia catch up since its probable that this new form of distance working will soon arise.

The next section of this paper identifies the theoretical foundations for blended and distance learning, the working experiences from internships and different skills development for better preparation of the future professionals. The third section describes the research method followed while the fourth section details the results. The final section of the paper provides an overall conclusion and highlights the paper's contribution to the literature.

2. BACKGROUND

Internship is usually included in the accounting curriculums aiming to provide students an early opportunity for work experience, increasing their ability to apply knowledge and improving their competencies to exercise their professional activities (Handoko et al., (2020); Mediawati et al., (2020)). In many educational institutes the supervised practical training is undertaken by advanced students as a part of their normal studies (Beck et al., (2008)) and this is the case in our situation. Interrelations that are built between universities and host organizations are considered beneficial for both parts, given the fact that if students in early stages have the opportunity to apply theoretical knowledge in practical issues by practicing in real problem solving, then they will probably feel more confident and certain about their future job choices. Therefore, the advantage of having a realistic job preview of the accounting profession will help them evaluate their expectations of the accounting profession requirements' (Beck et al., (2020)).

However, the Covid 19 Pandemic created an unprecedented situation imposing various limitations at all levels of professional and personal life worldwide. Various activities like work, transportation and education were restricted. In Greece, the governmental authorities chose to suspend the operation of universities by canceling all classes and mandatory replacing live with on-line learning. Additionally, all campus activities were cancelled including the six month internship for final year students. During the pandemic, the collaborated organizations had to choose if the internship would be postponed or executed via on-line participation (work from home). Hence, given the fact that many people forced to work from home, internships were affected, and students had to cope with several challenges. Certain key concerns that were considered where the fear of being dismissed from the host organization, the limited supervision that might affect their performance negatively (Beck et al., (2020)) and the level of necessary acquired soft and hard skills for implementing the accounting profession by distance.

Overtime, traditional accounting education focuses on preparing students for labor market enhancing skills such as personal presentation, time management, and personal attendance that are found to increase their employability (Alhawsawi et al., (2019)). Based on the research of (Dyki et al., (2020)), verbal communication, teamwork and acting in a professional manner were reported as the least developed skills. On the other hand, in an Australian survey as cited by (Kavanagh et al., (2008)) investigating employer satisfaction, skills such as problem solving, creativity and oral business communication were not sufficiently developed, while researchers in (Hatane et al., (2021)) claim that the learning environment should enrich students' perceptions to understand the labor market needs through active and independent learning. Quite similar was the results of Siegel, 1999 on employers' views about skills on management accounting, that imply that skills like oral and writing presentation, teamwork ability, analytical skills, solid understanding of accounting, and understanding the business functions are considered important for success. More studies exploring the aforementioned issues are those of (Beck et al., (2008); Maelah et al., (2014); Tate et al., (2017); Albu et al., (2016)) while researchers in (Kavanagh et al., (2008)) argues that among interrelated parts which participate, students as future employees and employers often lack a consensus due to the divergent perceptions of the first participant to the expectations of the second one. According to (Dyki et al., (2020)) there also critical skills to be acquired, in their own words, "employability skills such as critical and analytical thinking, problem solving, oral and written communication, collaboration and team-working are still critical but also evolving to adapt in a changing, non-routine and complex business environment". On the other hand, (Kavanagh et al., (2020)) assert that there is a globally expressed concern about accounting education and its over-emphasis on the technical abilities of graduates such as computer ability and accounting software skills. Moreover, they argue that higher-order skills, such as critical-thinking, problem-solving and analytical skills are now considered more essential due to the transformation from a rather manually to an automated mode of many traditional accounting tasks. In (Alhawsawi et al., (2020)) they generally refer to soft skills as the personal attributes or the social communication ability which enhance interpersonal relationships. For accounting graduates', an emphasis is given to the ability of collaborating with the internal and external workplace stakeholders. Additionally, soft skills also include teamwork, enthusiasm, and emotional intelligence communication, leadership abilities, team-work skills, motivating team members even problem solving, analytical, critical and judgment skills.

Nor should we forget that the role of the professional accountants has significantly changed over the past decades due to the shifts of the global economy, altering from a rather quantitative role to a consulting (qualitative) one (Dyki et al., (2020)) while COVID-19 pandemia introduced additional issues. The most outstanding change of the academic function includes a sharp transition from in-class lectures to online lessons, with several technical restrictions for all counterparts. A main concern regarding e-learning is the lack of interaction between professors and students and the limited development of soft skills. Yet, online courses and programs could contribute to different skills to be developed, altering the recruitment process and giving students the opportunity to obtain higher computer skills (Tate et al., (2017)). However, many accounting faculties have already introduced the blended learning alternative, a combination of online learning and off-line face-to-face learning while relative studies have shown a significantly positive influence on learning performance and students' satisfaction mostly due to the flexibility and convenience provided (Law et al., (2019)). In any case, comparing different e-learning tools and traditional learning is expected to have various implications on students' skills either positive, or negative (Lippincott et al., (2016)).

To this end, the practical training could not be unaffected by the COVID 19 restrictions. As researchers in (Pittenger et al., (2021)) claim virtual internships pose different challenges that are valid for remote internships, for example the inters' need for mentorship, confidentiality of products-processes-practices, in-person exposure to the corporate culture, expensive software that firms were reluctant to place on interns' personal computers for safety and supporting issues and difficulties in supervision on a daily basis (Bayerlein et al., (2018)). However, it can also provide opportunities for employees to develop self-efficacy interpersonal skills that are considered critical, especially in the post COVID -19 world (Beck et al., (2008)).

While the development of new technologies has already generated alternative internships formats, however in Greece, until recently, the predominant internship format is the traditional form conducted into the physical workplace. There is a strong perception associated with the benefits that interns would attain in the real business environment, resulting in increased accidental learning opportunities which are important for developing affective learning outcomes (Bayerlein et al., (2018)). Moreover, given the size of Greece which geographically is considered as a rather small country, the location boundedness as a restrictive factor is limited. Another significant aspect of the impact of COVID-19 pandemic for accounting students in Greece is the fact that the alternative forms of internships such as e-internships, simulated and computer-mediated "CMI" (combination of e-internships and simulated) were rarely implemented. In general, in accounting and finance discipline there is a lack of an established set of learning outcomes concerning a systematic comparison of different available internships formats regarding the students' learning outcomes. However, in the near future and owing to the new regime posed by the COVID-19 pandemic, the transition to other forms of remote internships could be considered as one way choice (Pittenger et al., (2021)). Since in most cases internships are an integral part of business curricula worldwide, this obligation would definitely affect the whole process. Additionally, limitations at the level of technical competence or self-motivation problems must be overcome considering that in the post-COVID era there is an increased possibility that remote internships might dominate the traditional one, due to its flexibility, accessibility and cost-efficiency.

Given the mandatory nature of accounting internship and the introduction of new constraints for its implementation, the authors were motivated by the aforementioned studies to investigate the difficulties that students experienced during the pandemic. Due to lack of alternative implementation formats in the past, apart from physical participation, this change gave the opportunity not only to explore the different aspects of problems students confronted, but also their perception about their future professional readiness for a rapidly altering business environment and workplace, which seems to become the norm in the future.

3. RESEARCH METHOD

The design of this research is inductive and exploratory. Exploratory approach means that research is not intent to provide conclusive evidence, but to help readers to have a better understanding of the problem and change direction because of revelation of new data and insights (Saunders et al., 2012). Inductive approach means that starts with detailed observation of a specific matter and moves towards to generalizations that are more abstract. Following an inductive approach, this research tends to develop empirical generalizations and identify preliminary relationships as it progresses. Furthermore, no hypotheses can be made at the initial stages of the research and cannot be drawn conclusions about the type and nature of the findings until the study is completed. Under that prism, this research did not start by setting up specific hypothesis to test but starting up with some observations regarding the factors that could affect the internship of accounting students during covid 19 pandemia, in continuous tries to identify existing relationships between them as research progress. This is done through literature review initially and using appropriate statistical methods in continuous. Then through empirical testing, the findings are generalized.

The survey was conducted during the second half of May 2021 and a methodology that incorporates elements of quantitative research is used. A questionnaire was developed to incorporate challenges arise for distance learning and training based on the literature review, to collect student's view on these topics. Final-year accounting students who either undertake or had completed the internship program during covid19 pandemia were invited to take part in order to express their opinion. The questionnaire was distributed electronically to 143 students, where internship is mandatory in their curriculum, through the platform was developed that is Google Forms. The aims of the research were made clear with an initial notice was sent with the survey and it was followed by a second one, 7 days later. Although all students that participated are studying accounting and finance at University of Thessaly, however, their internship was implemented in various organizations across Greece.

The questionnaire was divided into five sections. The first one included some biographical data and details about the student and the training organisation regarding the internship. The second one had questions to elicit from them their attitude about the pandemia. The third one asked the respondents to identify the skills that they think are essential to cope with distance working and their career advancement in general. The final section discusses other issues regarding students' internship learning experience and in what extend they think that the internship had achieved its learning outcomes.

4. SURVEY ANALYSIS - RESULTS

The data analysis identifies factors were included in different sections of the questionnaire. They were received 62 responses corresponding to a response rate of 43.3% which is considered satisfactory. This random sample was found to be representative of the total student body in terms of whether the respondents had experienced internship within a private accounting firm, a company or in the government sector. Out of 62 responders 59.7% were women and 40.3% were men. The vast majority of them (83.8%) are between 21 and 24 years old, 12.9% are between 25 and 30 years old and 3.2% are older than 30 years old.

Above all, it is undeniable that the pandemia influenced the way internship was conducted. According to survey 32.2% of students found very difficult or extremely difficult to find an organization to accept them for internship. This is almost 20% higher in comparison with other periods where there was no pandemia. However, it is significant that 32.3% of students had no difficulties in finding an organization to implement their internship, and another 35.5% have a moderate difficulty on this. According to our analysis, this indicates the wide acceptance that the internship program in accounting and finance have in the market and the willing of various organizations to accept students for internship beyond various obstacles. However, the pandemia had significant effects on schedule of internship, as 38.7% of students did not manage to start their internship on-time, 8.1% didn't manage to finish on time and in 25.8% of them affected both their internship start and finish. The main reason for this situation was the restricted measures taken by the government, either in the form of a lockdown or in the form of a ban on conducting the practice in person. However, it is significant to note that 27.4% of students managed to implement their internship normally in terms of schedule as their organizations adopt quickly new approaches in working such as teleworking or rotation between work in person and teleworking. As such, 24.6% of students implement their internship exclusively through teleworking, 37.7% implement their internship exclusively in person and 37.7% in both ways.

Teleworking was a totally new experience for almost all students implement this form of work, as 90.3% of them had never work again that way. The rest had a slightly experience as they had implemented teleworking in the past in frequency about twice a month.

Trying to identify the effects of teleworking in student's internship and its effectiveness, students were asked to determine the time they needed to adapt to this new form of working. It is encouraging that 54.1% of students adapted either immediately or in less than week (29.5% and 24.6% accordingly), 13.1% needed almost two weeks and there was a 32.8% that never adapted. Major contribution to the successful adaptation of students to this new work environment had the support and guidance by their supervisor. It is noteworthy, that 59.1% of students that adapted to new environment in no more than two weeks assessed the guidance and support from their supervisor as "very good" or "extremely good" while on the contrary only 8.1% of students never managed to adapt, despite the high level of support and guidance provided by their supervisor. In addition, it was not identified any significant relationship between ability to adapt to teleworking and previous working in person experience, as 57.1% of those who successfully adapted within two weeks had no previous experience, 11.9% had experience less than a month and only 14.2% had experience more than one month.

Safety was considered as the major concern for all students conducting their internship during pandemia both from university and government. This research tried to identify if students felt safe during their internship. It seems that this aim succeeded as 66.1% of students considered their working environment as very safe or extremely safe and only 16.2% considered that they exposed to high or very high level of risk in their working environment. Furthermore, students declared that 74.2% had a very high level of understanding regarding their safety concerns about pandemia by their employers and only 11.3% faced a low level of understanding in this matter. Regarding the safety actions taken by the organizations during pandemia 22.6% declared that organizations just followed the guidelines that were provided by the government, 38.7% of organization provided additional regular updates to students about safety measures and provide them with personal protective equipment, 30.6% required extra periodic tests for covid19 by their employees and 25.8% implement teleworking even this was not mandatory by government for their domain.

Another aim of this research was to identify some basic aspect of teleworking. As such, the readiness of students and organizations to implement teleworking it was tried to be identified and how their working environment and their productivity was affected. According to responses, 50% of students had the necessary infrastructure to cope with teleworking, 33.9% had partial infrastructure and only 16.1% did not had the necessary infrastructure. Regarding the support in terms of hardware and software students had by their employers during their transition to teleworking the 54.7% declared that had high or very high level of support, 13.2% had medium level of support and 32.1% had low or very low level of support.

Teleworking has many forms and can be implementing with various ways. Trying to identify the way teleworking was implemented, the most popular remote desktop applications and online videoconference software was presented to students through the questionnaire. Furthermore, some traditional options such as telephone and email were provided also as options. Results indicated that telephone and email were the most popular communication methods with 82.7% and 78.8% respectively. This was rather expected as these two forms of communication are the most common methods of communication not only in business but in people's everyday life. In the same line, Viber was the third most popular communication method as it was used by 46.2% of responders. TeamViewer was the first application among remote desktop applications that was used by 30.8% of responders, followed by Skype with 25% and MsTeams with 17.3%. Other applications such as Skype for business, Zoom, Cisco Webex, WhatsApp, Anydesk were of lower preference varying from 1.9% to 11.5%. It is obvious that mainly free and popular software that probably was used before by students and employers were the main means of communication that used in teleworking.

However, to use this type of application in most cases students need to have a degree of knowledge and familiarization with them. Considering the most common actions such as file and folder management, word processing, spreadsheets, web browsing and using email, students respond, in their vast majority (>80%), that their knowledge to these types of software was very good. Considering other more specialized types of software such as the use of specific accounting and other information systems, the results remained satisfactory as more than 52% of responders also declared that they had very good knowledge on this type of application and 24.5% declared that had moderate knowledge of them. This is an encouraging indication about the effectives and applicability of the curriculum in this domain as their studied curriculum includes courses of such kind.

Although teleworking was a great solution for many businesses during pandemia, it introduces some new problems in working (European Commission, (2020)). It was considered as the mean that allowed employers to violate the working hours asking their employees to work beyond that. This research identified this trend to be followed by some employers, but hopefully, it was not proven to be the main trend as 63.3% of students declared that the working hours for them remained the same as with in physical presence, 22.4% worked less. However, there was 10.2% of students that had to work more and 4.1% that had to work most time of the day without following any specific work hours.

Another important factor that this research tried to identify was how teleworking affected productivity. The results at this domain were not encouraging as 49% of students declared that their productivity was negatively affected. Specifically, 19.6% declared that had a very negative affect and 29.4% it was affected negatively but in a lower level. On the contrary 13.7% respond that teleworking had a positive effect in their productivity and only 7.8% respond that had a very positive effect. Finally, 29,4% declared that teleworking did not affect their productivity.

In continuous, it was tried to be identified the causes for this negative effect in productivity. So, responders provided with a set factors and asked to evaluate them in what level affect their productivity. These factors were the home environment, the distance of normal working environment, the nature of work, the possible lack of technological infrastructure and the lack of help and direct communication with colleagues. Analytical results can be seen in the following figure.

Figure 1. Factors affected productivity in teleworking environment

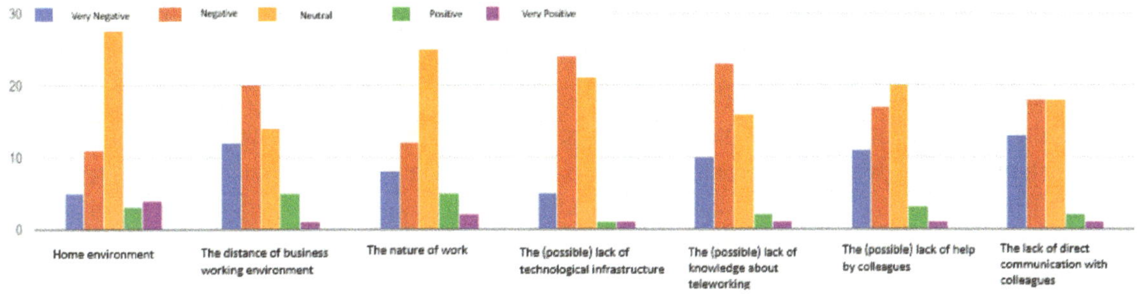

From the responses can be identified that the lack of direct communication and help from colleagues in accordance with lack in technological infrastructure and lack of previous experience and knowledge in working in a distance environment was the main causes for this decrease in productivity. This is compatible with the fact that the responders were students that performed their internship and as that they had limited previous knowledge and experience from a real working environment. As such, the direct communication and help by colleagues was very important to them. Further analysis of data indicated that students who immediately adapted to teleworking environment had the lowest negative impact from lack of communication and help by their colleagues, but this negative impact is increasing for students that needed more time to adapt. Analogous were the results considering the various lacks in technological infrastructure and experience.

Trying to identify other difficulties of teleworking, responders were asked to assess in a 5point scale ranging from "Very much" to "Almost none" a set of factors related to their privacy, personal life, their working environment and their living and working with other members of the house at the same time. Results can be seen in next figure.

From the results, it can be identified that most of students dealt with difficulties in balancing between privacy and work and that for many of them there were not distinct limits between these two. Another factor that had a significant negative effect in teleworking was the lack of changes in their environment. Living and working from the same environment was difficult for students. Although may this is a common condition for many people working with teleworking, students considered this as the most negative factor. An explanation for that can be their age. They are young people who want to communicate, travel, have new experiences and learn new things. As that, staying home, beyond a screen is a conflict with their own nature.

On the other hand, there were some things that liked them during teleworking. For example, 54.9% of them declared that they liked the fewer lost hours and less hassle caused by absent of movements,

49% felt good with the comfort and intimacy offered by their home environment, 27.5% concentrate to their work easier at home environment and 11.8% liked the existing of more time being with family and other members of the house.

Finally, participants evaluated their overall experience of teleworking in a five-point scale ranging from "Very unpleasant" to "Very Satisfactory". As can be seen in the next figure for most students it was either a neutral or unpleasant experience sharing a 29.4% each. However, only 9.8% found their experience as very unpleasant while on the contrary 19.6% found it very satisfactory or satisfactory (11.8%).

The objective of internship for all student of a department of accounting and finance is to help them to get familiarized with the working environment of the accountant, to connect them with the labor market, to contribute in the utilization and assimilation of the acquired knowledge, and help them know better and deeper the profession they will pursue in the future. As that, responders asked to declare in what level these objectives were fulfilled during covid19 pandemia. Results can be seen in next figure.

From the responses, it is obvious that objectives strongly connected with the working environment of an accountant were of great challenge and perceived by the majority of students as of below a moderate level of fulfillment. On the other hand, objectives related to utilization of prior knowledge and of gaining an initial work experience in accounting profession perceived as of higher level of fulfillment as they were not strictly depending on students' physical presence and a classic working environment. In the same line students were asked to identify which of the effects of pandemia to their internship worries them the most and 37.1% identified the limited acquisition of experience and practical knowledge while 17.7% identified the reduced opportunities for future vocational rehabilitation.

Another aim of this research was to identify whether students had the necessary knowledge, skills and competencies to deal with new working conditions, as these were formed during pandemia. In this context, they asked to evaluate themselves if they believed that had these skills and 41.3% declared they had them, 31.7% declared that partially had them and 27% that had not any. Trying to evaluate whether this opinion of themselves was correct or overestimated, it was examined the relation between the time they needed to adapt to teleworking and their belief about the possession of necessary skills to cope with the requirements of new working environment as they formed during pandemia. The results indicated that students cannot objectively evaluate themselves in a great degree. As can be seen from the next figure, more consistent were the results of students who declared that adapted immediately as the 61% believed that had the necessary skills and 28% that had partial the necessary skills. On the other hand, although from those who declared that never adapted to teleworking 70% of them believed that had all or partially the necessary skills this seemed not to help them in adaptation.

Maybe someone at this point states that could be by other reasons that prevent them from being adapted, but according to our opinion, teleworking was the main change and challenge in working environment during pandemia, especially for the students performing their internship while other reasons may hardly change that.

Finally, it was tried to be identified in which knowledge domains students believe that should obtain more knowledges and skills. The results are presented in the next figure.

It is noteworthy that students identified the need for more knowledge in the domain of accounting (61.9%) which is the domain of their studies. This may be an indication that curriculum may need to be updated or altered (Albring et al., (2020)) but more research must be done in order to cover a wide variety of competences the accounting curriculum should encompass (Cernușca et al., (2020); Daff, (2021); Trivellas et al., (2015); Fitsilis et al., (2018)), before final concussions could be made. However, this is beyond the scope of this research.

5. CONCLUSIONS AND FUTURE WORK

A main objective of internship for all students of the department of accounting and finance is to enable them to get familiarized with different types of accounting context in a realistic environment. During pandemia this setting has changed, and the remote internship becomes the new reality. The aim of this research was to investigate how the students perceive this situation and collect their opinion and expectations regarding this new form of internship seeing that remote training will become prevalent in the future. The outcome of the research revealed interesting results of the crucial role that COVID-19 has in the process of changing the status of accounting training in general.

In order to summarize the results of this research and its contributions to the study of the changes have occurred in the field of internship due to pandemia, in the following, we recap by discussing the results obtained. Above all, our concern that pandemia influenced the way internship was carried out due to the COVID-19 restrictions is evident, since this situation influenced the processes that internship was conducted and had significant effects on its schedule by affecting either the beginning or ending of the program. On the other hand, considering that all changes happened for the matter of safety, it is proven that indeed, this was a major concern for all involved partners during the internship program, i.e., university, organisations and students and consequently this helped students to feel safe during their training. However, the high number of students which stated that felt unproductive during this period indicates that corrective measures need to be taken about this, with specific directions to be highlighted by them regarding the lack of technological infrastructure, communication and knowledge about teleworking.

Regarding the necessary knowledge, skills and competencies that students have to meet in the everyday needs of new working conditions as they were formed during pandemia, we do rather have a clear idea only for a portion of them. Actually, the trend in modern education worldwide is students to develop a set of personal competencies that will help them to adapt quickly and efficient to changes in their working environment and will help them have self-confidence, empowerment, be better team players, reduce their stress, etc. (Moe et al., (2016); Tsoutsa et al., (2022)). As that, the majority of students answered that according to the experience they had gained during their internship, the demand by their employers for skills and competencies such as communication, critical thinking, flexibility, ability to solve problems, thinking out of the box, tolerance to change and uncertainty, conflict management, self-confidence, team working, emotional control, stress management, ability to work under pressure, ability in time management and organization skills is high. This is something that needs to be taken into consideration by university departments and examine the need for update in their curriculums and their training and education methods in order to help students develop such kind of skills.

An example of a new approach can be Agile methods and Agile education (Sharp et al., (2018)); Krehbiel et al., (2017)). Agile education is based on Agile methods that initially used in software development projects with great success (Beck et al., (2001)) and is a set of methods that continuously gain acknowledgement and use in various other domains. Agile education is a form of education based on team working, breaking teaching material in small parts and asking from students to determine their own activities and keep track of their progress by their own while the teacher determines the assignments, coaches and advise them.

From the very beginning of this research, a main cause for concern was the level that the objectives of the internship were fulfilled and how could we better get prepared for post-pandemia catch up. From the responses, it is obvious that objectives strongly connected with the working environment of an accountant were of great challenge and perceived by most students as of below a moderate level of fulfillment.

On the other hand, objectives related to utilization of prior knowledge and of gaining an initial work experience in accounting profession perceived as of higher level of fulfillment as they were not strictly depending on students' physical presence and the working environment. Whilst this paper does not attempt to compare traditional internship placements versus remote internship, the presented information demonstrates that a level of completeness to learning outcomes and opportunities was partially achieved at remote internship and there are aspects in this form that students like them, despite the difficulties was faced due to immediate intervention and lack of preparation.

As future work we plan to run a new survey aiming to professional accountants which actually act as supervisors in order to establish a clear list of factors that will help to build resilience into the accounting internship placement. In doing so, this research will establish a set of factors that accounting faculty should endeavor to address not only to be better prepared for similarly disruptive events might occur in future but also facilitate in rapid healing of businesses market's needs. Considering that the role of professional accountants, as reliable advisors to entrepreneurs, bring them at the forefront in the fight against the economic effects of pandemia as this virus has also an economic nature (Robert-Aurelian et al., (2020)), it is important that we anticipate the range of impacts that such a disruption of this magnitude has and benefit from the opportunity the pandemia has provided us to blaze a trail to new training experiences for future accountants.

REFERENCES

Albring, S. M., & Elder, R. J. (2020). Research Initiatives in Accounting Education: Managing Academic Programs. *Issues in Accounting Education*, *35*(4), 61–74. doi:10.2308/ISSUES-2020-020

Albu, N., Calu, A. D., & Guşe, G. R. (2016). The role of accounting internships in preparing students' transition from school to active life. *Accounting and Management Information Systems*, *15*(1), 131–153.

Alhawsawi, M. (2019). Soft Accounting Skills between Employers' Expectations and Students' Reality after COVID-19 Pandemic. *Australian Academy of Accounting and Finance Review*, *5*(2), 69–76.

Anjum, S. (2020). Impact of internship programs on professional and personal development of business students: A case study from Pakistan. *Future Business Journal*, *6*(1), 2. Advance online publication. doi:10.118643093-019-0007-3

Bayerlein, L., & Jeske, D. (2018). Student learning opportunities in traditional and computer-mediated internships. *Education + Training*, *60*(1), 27–38. doi:10.1108/ET-10-2016-0157

Beck, J., & Halim, H. (2008). Undergraduate Internships in Accounting: What and How do Singapore Interns Learn from Experience? *Accounting Education*, *17*(2), 151–172. doi:10.1080/09639280701220277

Beck, K. (2001). *The Agile Manifesto*. Agile Alliance. http://agilemanifesto.org/

Cernuşca, L., & Csorba, L. M. (2020). Professional and Transversal Accounting Competences (II). *CECCAR Business Review*, *1*(9), 3–10. doi:10.37945/cbr.2020.09.01

Chong, S. M., & Yazdani, K. (2020). Factors Affecting the Affective Organizational Commitment, Job Satisfaction and Job Acceptance Intention of Interns: A Conceptual Framework. *International Journal of Social Science and Humanity, 68–72*, 68–72. Advance online publication. doi:10.18178/ijssh.2020.V10.1016

D'Abate, C. P., Youndt, M. A., & Wenzel, K. (2009). Making the Most of an Internship: An Empirical Study of Internship Satisfaction. *Academy of Management Learning & Education*, *8*(4), 527–539. doi:10.5465/AMLE.2009.47785471

Daff, L. (2021). Employers' perspectives of accounting graduates and their world of work: Software use and ICT competencies. *Accounting Education*, *30*(5), 495–524. doi:10.1080/09639284.2021.1935282

Denning, S. (2015a). Updating the Agile Manifesto. *Strategy and Leadership*, *43*(5). Advance online publication. doi:10.1108/SL-07-2015-0058

Denning, S. (2015b). Updating the Agile Manifesto. *Strategy and Leadership*, *43*(5). Advance online publication. doi:10.1108/SL-07-2015-0058

Dyki, M., Singorahardjo, M., & Cotronei-Baird, V. S. (2020). Preparing graduates with the employability skills for the unknown future: Reflection on assessment practice during COVID-19. *Accounting Research Journal*, *34*(2), 229–245. doi:10.1108/ARJ-09-2020-0285

Edward Beck, J., & Halim, H. (2008). Undergraduate Internships in Accounting: What and How do Singapore Interns Learn from Experience? *Accounting Education*, *17*(2), 151–172. doi:10.1080/09639280701220277

el Refae, G. A., Kaba, A., & Eletter, S. (2021). Distance learning during COVID-19 pandemic: Satisfaction, opportunities and challenges as perceived by faculty members and students. *Interactive Technology and Smart Education*, *18*(3), 298–318. doi:10.1108/ITSE-08-2020-0128

European Commission. (2020). *Telework in the EU before and after the COVID-19: where we were, where we head to*. European Union- JRC120945. Online available at: https://ec.europa.eu/jrc/sites/default/files/jrc120945_policy_brief_-_covid_and_telework_final.pdf

Fitsilis, P., Tsoutsa, P., & Gerogiannis, V. (2018). Industry 4.0: Required personnel competences. *Industry 4.0, 3*(3), 130-133.

Frumuşanu, N. M., Marin, A. M., & Martin, M. (2020). *The impact of COVID-19 pandemic on the activity of the professional accountant*. Academic Press.

Hall, A. K., Nousiainen, M. T., Campisi, P., Dagnone, J. D., Frank, J. R., Kroeker, K. I., Brzezina, S., Purdy, E., & Oswald, A. (2020). Training disrupted: Practical tips for supporting competency-based medical education during the COVID-19 pandemic. *Medical Teacher*, *42*(7), 756–761. doi:10.1080/0142159X.2020.1766669 PMID:32450049

Handoko, B., Lindawati, A., & Budiarto, A. (2020). Using Mixed Reality to Provide Experience for Internship Students in the Field of Auditing Studies during Covid 19. In *2020 2nd International Conference on E-Business and E-commerce Engineering (EBEE 2020)*. ACM. 10.1145/3446922.3446926

Hatane, S. E., Setiono, F. J., Setiawan, F. F., Semuel, H., & Mangoting, Y. (2020). Learning environment, students' attitude and intention to enhance current knowledge in the context of choosing accounting career. *Journal of Applied Research in Higher Education, 13*(1), 79–97. doi:10.1108/JARHE-06-2019-0156

Jackson, D., Sibson, R., & Riebe, L. (2014). Undergraduate perceptions of the development of team-working skills. *Education + Training, 56*(1), 7–20. doi:10.1108/ET-01-2013-0002

Jeske, D., & Axtell, C. (2014). e-Internships: Prevalence, characteristics and role of student perspectives. *Internet Research, 24*(4), 457–473. doi:10.1108/IntR-11-2012-0226

Kavanagh, M. H., & Drennan, L. (2008). What skills and attributes does an accounting graduate need? Evidence from student perceptions and employer expectations. *Accounting and Finance, 48*(2), 279–300. doi:10.1111/j.1467-629X.2007.00245.x

Krehbiel, Salzarulo, Cosmah, Forren, Gannod, Havelka, Hulshult, & Merhout. (2017). Agile Manifesto for Teaching and Learning. *Journal of Effective Teaching, 17*(2), 90-111.

Law, K. M., Geng, S., & Li, T. (2019). Student enrollment, motivation and learning performance in a blended learning environment: The mediating effects of social, teaching, and cognitive presence. *Computers & Education, 136*, 1–12. doi:10.1016/j.compedu.2019.02.021

Lippincott, B., Matulich, E., & Squires, K. (2006). To Learn Or Not To Learn: The Effect Of Educational Technology On Learning In Accounting Courses. *Journal of College Teaching and Learning, 3*(12). Advance online publication. doi:10.19030/tlc.v3i12.1649

Maelah, R., Muhammaddun Mohamed, Z., Ramli, R., & Aman, A. (2014). Internship for accounting undergraduates: Comparative insights from stakeholders. *Education + Training, 56*(6), 482–502. doi:10.1108/ET-09-2012-0088

Mediawati, E., Widaningsih, M., Majid, R., Ali, N., Abdullah, S., Erawati, T., Susanto, M., & Nurtanto, M. (2020). Internship during the covid 19 pandemic: Students and supervisors perspective. *Psychology and Education, 57*(8), 1036–1038.

Moe, N. B., Fægri, T. E., Cruzes, D. S., & Faugstad, J. E. (2006). Enabling Knowledge Sharing in Agile Virtual Teams. *2016 IEEE 11th International Conference on Global Software Engineering (ICGSE)*, 29-33. 10.1109/ICGSE.2016.30

Pittenger, K. (2021). Virtual Internships – A New Reality. *Developments in Business Simulation and Experiential Learning, 48*, 149–152.

Rogers, S. E., Miller, C. D., Flinchbaugh, C., Giddarie, M., & Barker, B. (2021). All internships are not created equal: Job design, satisfaction, and vocational development in paid and unpaid internships. *Human Resource Management Review, 31*(1), 100723. doi:10.1016/j.hrmr.2019.100723

Rojon, C., & Saunders, M. N. (2012). Formulating a convincing rationale for a research study. *Coaching (Abingdon, UK), 5*(1), 55–61. doi:10.1080/17521882.2011.648335

Rosenberg, S., Heimler, R., & Morote, E. (2012). Basic employability skills: A triangular design approach. *Education + Training, 54*(1), 7–20. doi:10.1108/00400911211198869

Salleh, D., & Muhammad, F. (2020). The Accounting Students' Perspective on Mobile Learning in Covid19 Pandemic Period. *Proceedings of 5th International Conference on E-Commerce.*

Sanahuja Vélez, G., & Ribes Giner, G. (2015). Effects of Business Internships on Students, Employers, and Higher Education Institutions: A Systematic Review. *Journal of Employment Counseling*, *52*(3), 121–130. doi:10.1002/joec.12010

Sangster, A., Stoner, G., & Flood, B. (2020). Insights into accounting education in a COVID-19 world. *Accounting Education*, *29*(5), 431–562. doi:10.1080/09639284.2020.1808487

Sharp, J., & Lang, G. (2018). Agile in teaching and learning: Conceptual framework and research agenda. *Journal of Information Systems Education*, *29*, 45–52.

Siegel, G., & Sorensen, J. E. (1999). *Counting more, counting less. Transformation in the management accounting profession.* Institute of Managing Accountants.

Șova, R. A., & Popa, A. F. (2020a). The Accounting Education, Between Digitalisation and the COVID-19 Crisis. *CECCAR Business Review, 1*(10), 3–8. doi:10.37945/cbr.2020.10.01

Tate, S., Reinstein, A., & Churyk, N. (2017). The Impact of Online Education on Accounting Recruiting. *The CPA Journal, New York*, *87*(9), 13–15.

Trivellas, P., Akrivouli, Z., Tsifora, E., & Tsoutsa, P. (2015). The Impact of Knowledge Sharing Culture on Job Satisfaction in Accounting Firms. The Mediating Effect of General Competencies. *Procedia Economics and Finance*, *19*, 238–247. doi:10.1016/S2212-5671(15)00025-8

Tsoutsa, P., Fitsilis, P., & Ragos, O. (2018). Service Simulation in Industry 4.0: A Comparison of Simulators. *Industry 4.0, 3*(2), 101-104.

Tsoutsa, P., & Lampropoulos, I. (2022). *Preparing for Smart Cities Future Competences: trends arising through keyword and review analysis. In Building on Smart Cities Skills and Competences.* Springer.

Yoo, S. C., & Morris, P. (2015). An Exploratory Study of Successful Advertising Internships: A Survey Based on Paired Data of Interns and Employers. *Journal of Advertising Education*, *19*(1), 5–16. doi:10.1177/109804821501900103

Chapter 3
The New Profile of the Online Consumer Behaviour in a Post-Pandemic World

Vincenzo Basile
https://orcid.org/0000-0001-8776-0915
Federico II University of Naples, Italy

Federica Caboni
University of Cagliari, Italy

Lucia Pizzichini
https://orcid.org/0000-0001-8535-522X
Polytechnic University of Marche, Italy

ABSTRACT

The COVID-19 pandemic has significantly affected shopping behaviour: consumers are more attentive to finding products customized to their needs and desires. Even the most suspicious people in this health emergency have overcome the cognitive barriers to digital purchasing to shop in total safety. This chapter aims to contribute to an understanding of how the COVID-19 pandemic has affected Online Consumer Behaviour (OCB). The theoretical contribution on OCB appears useful for managers and practitioners to define appropriate strategic actions for customers to enhance value in a digital context. The chapter presents three sections devoted to the literature on online consumer behaviour during COVID-19, the factors affecting the OCB and decision-making process, and online retailing in the COVID-19 era. Based on this theoretical background, this chapter proposes a new categorization of online consumer behaviour by considering the habits that emerged during the COVID-19 pandemic.

DOI: 10.4018/978-1-7998-8856-7.ch003

INTRODUCTION

In 2020 COVID-19 affected almost all countries and more than 50 million people around the world (OECD, 2020). Beyond the health and human tragedy of the coronavirus, it is now widely recognised that the pandemic triggered several changes in consumer habits and business models (Kalkınma *et al.*, 2020). Many economies will not recover their 2019 output levels until 2022 at the earliest (OECD, 2020). The nature of the crisis is unprecedented: beyond the short-term repeated health and economic shocks, the long-term effects on human capital, productivity and behaviour may be long-lasting. The COVID crisis has massively accelerated some pre-existing trends, in particular digitalisation (McKinsey, 2020). It has shaken the world, setting in motion waves of change with a wide range of possible trajectories (OECD, 2020). The retailing industry is being reimagined and transformed at breakneck speeds due to new technologies and changes in consumer purchasing behaviour resulting from the COVID-19 pandemic. This dynamic retail marketplace is forcing retailers to strategize how to best position themselves to survive and flourish in this environment. The COVID-19 pandemic has caused several profound modifications (Eger *et al.*, 2021; Donthu and Gustafsoon, 2020; Pantano *et al.*, 2020) to the everyday lives of consumers, such as isolation, community containment, avoidance of social contact and practising social distancing (Wilder-Smith and Freedman, 2020). More specifically, consumer habits changed significantly, bearing in mind the usual situation before COVID-19 and several restrictions and lockdowns (Sheth, 2020; Hale *et al.*, 2020) applied during the virus's spread. According to Pantano and Willems (2022), a crisis can reveal the essence of people. Indeed, during the pandemic, unusual consumer behaviour increased (Laato *et al.*, 2020), for example, people have started storing large amounts of toilet paper, rice and flour, which in turn has increased awareness of their rarity and instils fear in others (Studdert and Hall, 2020). In addition to hoarding, impulse purchases have increased as a response to negative emotions (especially after the reopening of the store), in some cases having negative consequences from a financial point of view. However, this has allowed consumers to reflect on their behaviour and evolve towards more sustainable choices. Tran (2021) stated that the Covid-19's impact on sustainable consumption is reflected in: *"purchasing products and services from e-commerce platforms to satisfy needs and wants, and to increase health safety for selves and community during a pandemic period (pp, 2-3)"*. Hence, the pandemic has changed the attitudes and behaviours of purchasing and consuming, especially in the FMCG market. During the lockdown, the consumption of specific product categories increased (i.e., long-lived foods, raw materials and household disinfectants) but nowadays this trend stopped. On the other hand, the increasing use of e-commerce channels reveals an attachment and loyalty of consumers to these shopping habits (Anna, 2020). Based on the above-mentioned motivations and the studies scholars carried out in the last few years on the impacts of the COVID-19 pandemic on the retail industry (Roggeveen and Sethuraman, 2020; Guthrie *et al.*, 2021; Eger *et al.*, 2021; Islam *et al.*, 2021), it appears helpful to investigate consumer behaviour and consumer relationships with purchasing processes. This chapter aims to contribute to an understanding of how the COVID-19 pandemic has affected online consumer behaviour (OCB), with a specific focus change in terms of marketing stimuli and online platforms. The COVID-19 pandemic has significantly affected shopping behaviour: consumers are more attentive and demanding, and above all, they have become accustomed to finding what they need online. Even the most suspicious people in this health emergency have overcome the cognitive barriers to digital purchasing to shop in total safety. The theoretical contribution to online consumer behaviour appears useful for managers and practitioners to address appropriate strategies for customers to enhance value in a digital context. The chapter presents in the next three sections a review of literature on Online Consumer Behaviour in the COVID-19 era, what factors affecting the OCB and decision-making process and online retailing in the COVID-19 era. Based on the analysis of the theoretical framework, this chapter proposes a new categorization of online consumer behaviour by considering the previous habits and the new ones that emerged during the COVID-19 Pandemic.

CONCEPTUAL RESEARCH FLOW

The coronavirus (COVID-19) pandemic has had a significant impact on various elements of our daily lives, particularly our buying habits. Predicting online consumer behaviour could be beneficial to government, supply chain, and retail managers. Although we had done some online shopping before the coronavirus pandemic, the number of people doing so surged considerably during the disease. We must monitor personal and social health issues such as social separation and remain at home due to COVID-19's high-speed transmission because these factors have a direct impact on internet buying consumer behaviour (Safara, 2020). The study of Mohd Dali *et al.* (2020) emulates the operant conditioning theory and proposes four different types of behaviour categories that arise from the pandemic that are segmented on their behavioural reactions post-pandemic. The four suggested segments are: 1) the back to square one; 2) new normal; 3) moderately new norm; and 4) recycle consumer groups. Based on MacInnis (2011) assumption of conceptualization as a process of abstract thinking, this chapter contributes to understanding changes derived from the rapid spread of COVID-19 by identifying connections between online consumer behaviour during the pandemic era and the factors affecting the decision-making process. The ability to understand consumer behaviour is critical to a company's success. Firms can better manage the marketing mix, branding, and communication with customers if they understand how consumers behave and what elements impact them. It can be difficult to precisely identify the factors that influence consumers because they are frequently internal factors. External causes like as the COVID-19 epidemic, the effects of political and legislative actions, and the economic condition are all influencing the current scenario in global markets. That is the element to which both customers and retailers had to adjust (Svajdova, 2021). This conceptual thinking includes a range of information-processing activities (MacInnnis, 2011), able to develop a representation of a new profile of online consumers in a post-COVID-19 world.

ONLINE CONSUMER BEHAVIOUR IN THE COVID-19 ERA

The analysis of online consumer behaviour literature (Saeed *et al.,* 2003; Constantinides, 2004; Ramaweera *et al.,* 2005; Cheung *et al.,* 2005; Boyer and Hult, 2005; Blasco-Arcas *et al.,* 2014; Cummins *et al.,* 2014; Akar and Nasir, 2014; Laroche and Richard, 2014; Rita *et al.,* 2019) carried out, highlighted the connection between consumer behaviour and interactive marketing (Ratchford, 2015) emerged from the conceptual and empirical sides. During the COVID-19 pandemic, the Internet was increasingly used to find practical information related to the products before and during purchasing (Feldmann *et al.,* 2021). The online consumer purchasing process contains several phases: searching, browsing, finding, selecting, comparing, evaluating information, and interacting with the website. The use of the Internet during the COVID-19 pandemic assumed strategic value for several categories of consumers (Effenberger *et al.,* 2020; Feldmann *et al.,* 2021), who searched the web for the same characteristics of a real purchase process. Habibi *et al.* (2014) defined a web navigation behaviour model based on four variables: Internet experience, web atmospherics, online behaviour, and outcomes and their interrelationships. The in-depth analysis of these variables shows that the use of the Internet is a challenging experience for consumers. The variables included in the Habibi (2014) model are helpful to explain consumer behaviour during the COVID-19 pandemic. More profoundly, considering the COVID-19 scenario, it is possible to underline how the Internet experience (variable 1) could be considered one of the leading digital experiences during the pandemic in a shopping process. Second, the web atmosphere (variable 2) has become the new set where consumers experience their shopping process. Third, the online behaviour (variable 3) during COVID-19 has changed to adapt to the new situation and exploit all the benefits deriving from the Internet to satisfy consumer shopping needs as much as possible. Moreover, web atmospherics are strictly connected to two characteristics: functional and hedonic. The hedonic characteristics relate to the structure, effectiveness, informativeness, and entertainment. To understand the several variables influencing online consumer research, a consideration of the study of Saeed *et al.* (2003) is necessary. This study analyses three dependent variables of online consumer behaviour: web use, online purchase, and post-purchase. The primary empirical evidence focuses on the website uses, future website intention uses', and web uses' satisfaction and Internet-based services. As the Internet is considered a tool for developing interaction among consumers to enhance their communication and obtain their answers (Cho and Khang, 2006), psychological and social network theory allows a deep understanding of consumer behaviour, beliefs, and social interaction (Hamilton *et al.,* 2016) to shift them from the physical store to online experiences (Badrinarayanan *et al.,* 2012), specifically during a crisis, such as the COVID-19 pandemic. In addition, the Internet is a system of stimuli, such as visual, individual and interpersonal stimuli, and for that reason, many web experiences are the result of affect behaviour (Im *et al.,* 2010). By contextualizing the use of the Internet during the COVID-19 pandemic, it is necessary to underline how it increased its social value as a vehicle through which consumers can search and share information with other consumers (Schultz and Peltier, 2013), and enhance their shopping experience. As a social vehicle, the Internet imposes an understanding of cognitive and attitudinal consumer behaviour to form and enhance resilient customer relationships (El-Gohary, 2010; Kim and Song, 2010). Overall, to create an in-depth online experience, several elements need to be matched, such as a blend of online elements, information, emotions, several stimuli and goods. Constantinides (2002; 2004) found that the identification and classification of Web experience elements are essential for a comprehensive representation of controllable actors to affect or determine virtual interaction outcomes. The analysis of consumer behaviours and the study of the relationships between purchasing processes and those of brand value are critical factors in marketing decisions, especially during the COVID-19 Pandemic. These are characterized by an intense variety and variability of the demand. Online Consumer Behavior (OCB) has become mainstream with an increasing number of academic contributions. By analysing several studies on Online Consumer Behaviors (Saeed *et al.,* 2003; Constantinides, 2004; Ramaweera *et al.,* 2005; Cheung *et al.,* 2005; Boyer and Hult, 2005; Blasco-Arcas *et al.,* 2014; Cummins *et al.*, 2014; Akar and Nasir, 2014; Laroche and Richard, 2014; Rita *et al.,* 2019), emerges the intense work of researchers on classical consumer behaviours research. More in-depth the main focuses are on behavioural learning (Skinner, 1938), personality research (Folkes, 1988), information processing (Bettman, 1979), and attitude models (Fishbcin and Ajzen 1977). In the last two decades, it was continuously developed studies (Darley *et al.*, 2010; Limbu *et al.*, 2012) based on the connection between consumer behaviours and interactive marketing from both the conceptual and empirical sides. Pomirleanu *et al.* (2013) confirmed several studies based on the Internet marketing research field take into consideration consumer behaviours theory and practices. In particular, the information research on the Internet could be an activity based on the search for pre-purchase information (Bloch *et al.*, 1986) or in other cases based on the hedonic investigation stated by Holbrook and Hirschman, 1982. The Internet used to find some practical information before and during purchasing is divided into several phases: searching, browsing, finding, selecting, comparing, and evaluating information, and interacting and transacting with the website. Theories related to the psychological perspective and social networks could be considered useful in understanding the several dimensions composing Internet Marketing deeply. Primary, the Internet is considered a tool able to develop the interaction among consumers, enhance their communication and get their answers (Cho and Khang, 2006). Therefore, psychological and social network theory permits a context to match processes from both internal and related to social decision-making (Bagozzi and Dholakia, 2002). The Internet is also a tricky place made up of several channels. So, it is necessary to understand consumers' behaviours, beliefs, and social interactions to shift them from the physical store to their online experiences (Badrinarayanan *et al.*, 2012). Besides, the Internet is a complex of stimuli such as visual, individual and interpersonal, and for that reason, many web experiences are the results of affect behaviours (Im *et al.*, 2010). Lastly, the Internet is also a social vehicle through which consumers can search, share information with other consumers (Schultz and Peltier, 2013), and enhance their shopping experience. The Internet as a social vehicle imposes understanding the cognitive and attitudinal consumer behaviour to form and enhance resilient customer relationships (El-Gohary, 2010; Kim and Song, 2010). All in all, to create an in-depth online experience, several elements need to be matched, like a blend of online functionality, information, emotions, cues, stimuli and products and services. In other words, a multifaceted combination of elements going beyond the 4Ps of the traditional marketing mix (Van Waterschoot and Van Den Bulte, 1992). From Constantinides (2002; 2004) studies emerged that the identification and classification of the Web experience elements are essential for a comprehensive representation of the controllable actors possible to affect or determine the virtual interaction outcome. Cummins *et al.* (2014) offer an organizing framework that summarizes consumer behaviour and social network theory research in Internet marketing from 1993 to 2012. Their research revealed eight key categorical areas to website effectiveness: 1) cognitive issues; 2) user-generated content (UGC); 3) Internet segmentation and demographics; 4) online usage; 5) cross-cultural; 6) online communities and networks; 7) strategic use and outcomes, and 8) consumer internet search. Alongside, the personal and external uncontrollable factors that influence the buying behaviour; According to Kotler (2003) the customer's exposure to the firm's marketing actions can affect the decision-making by providing inputs for the consumer's black box where information is processed before the final consumer's decision is made. Online marketers can influence the decision-making process of the digital customers by engaging traditional, physical marketing tools but mainly by creating and delivering the proper online experience, the Web experience: a combination of online functionality, information, emotions, cues, stimuli and products/ services, in other words, a complex mix of elements going beyond the 4Ps of the traditional marketing mix. Recently Scholars such as Grewal *et al.* (2021) talked about the 6Ps: retail place and supply chain management, product, pricing, promotion, personnel, and presentation as the spokes of retailing and technology as the hub. Technology is the core to building effective retail processes for customers, employees, retailers, and suppliers. In the rapid evolution of retailing, nearly every retailer has increased its technology endeavours to better serve its customers. Brick-and-mortar retailers have nearly universally moved into online channels, and COVID-19 has hastened its commitment to operating and competing in this space.

Moreover, COVID-19 is forcing manufacturers and retailers to simplify their assortment strategies. The pandemic has encouraged consumers to focus more on essentials and forgo luxury and hedonic products. In addition, much merchandise is being purchased and consumed from their homes.

RESEARCH METHODOLOGY: METHODS AND TECHNIQUES

The research methodology was mainly qualitative based on conceptualizing OCB factors in a business setting by a consolidated process (Churchill, 1979). The latter includes eight different phases: 1: specify the conceptual domain of the construct; 2. generate, based on the existing literature, the items for measuring the critical dimensions; 3. collect empirical data to select the most suitable items from the perspective of the management and/or the researchers; 4. purify the data, that is, identifying those that have greater relevance and avoiding cross-loading factors; 5. collect data to validate the model; 6. adjust the model's reliability; 7. adjust the generalizability; and finally, 8. develop normative suggestions. Following the aims of this paper, the analysis stops at point 3. First, it proceeded to conceptualise an OCB conceptual model in digital contexts. Second, through a literature review, it was collected the most common factors of hidden latent constructs or sub-dimensions of OCB. Third, it was carried out empirical desk-type research to select the most common items for each individual construct, recurring to online databases exiting in literature. Third, a literature review was conducted to select the most relevant management tool for OCB. Principally, an analysis of the relevant academic literature (based on the number of citations on Google Scholar, Scopus and the Web of Science and the quality of the academic journals in which the articles were published) on OCB was conducted. The proposed model that emerged from the literature was the model in the following figure 1. To test and introduce the model in the digital environment, empirical analysis in the next research phase will be conducted using semi-structured questionnaires given to European online consumers. Finally, the qualitative methodology was enriched by the secondary source of information. The significant limitations of this chapter's contribution are associated with the study's theoretical nature and the qualitative inquiry (Ritchie *et al.*, 2013).

FACTORS AFFECTING THE OCB AND DECISION-MAKING PROCESS

The investigation model proposed to analyse the main influencing factors of online consumer behaviour and the decision-making process is composed of seven blocks (figure 1). That is, three independent variables: Other Stimuli (OS), Marketing Stimuli (MS) and Web Experience (WE); and four dependent variables: Buyer's Decision Process (BDP), Buyer's Decision (BD), Share of Wallet (SOW) and Customer e-loyalty (CeL). The OS, MS and WE represent our antecedents in the model while BDP is the mediating variable. The BD is the output variable, and its relative outcomes are SOW and CeL. Cheung *et al.* (2019) and Constantinides (2004) suggested two groups of uncontrollable factors, consumer characteristics and environmental influences (e.g., demographic, social, economic, cultural, psychological, and other personal factors), as well as three groups of controllable ones: 1) Product/service characteristics; 2) Medium characteristics and 3) Merchant/intermediary characteristics. Scholars (Islam *et al.*, 2021) put attention to the influence of the COVID19 Pandemic on the environmental factors. Moreover, Eger *et al.* (2021) conducted an analysis to identify how consumers from the Baby Boomers, X and Y generations changed their shopping behaviour and which needs they gave preference to during the pandemic crisis about their fears. Instead, Guthrie *et al.* (2021) based their studies on the emerging COVID-19 research, and the environmentally imposed constraints perspective to describe how online purchasing behaviour evolved during the COVID-19 crisis.

Figure 1. The main influencing factors of online consumer behaviour in the decision-making process
Note: as assumptions in the model, Buyer's Decision has a positive effect on Share of Wallet and Customer e-Loyalty.
Source: adapted from Constantinides, (2004) based on Kotler's framework (2003).

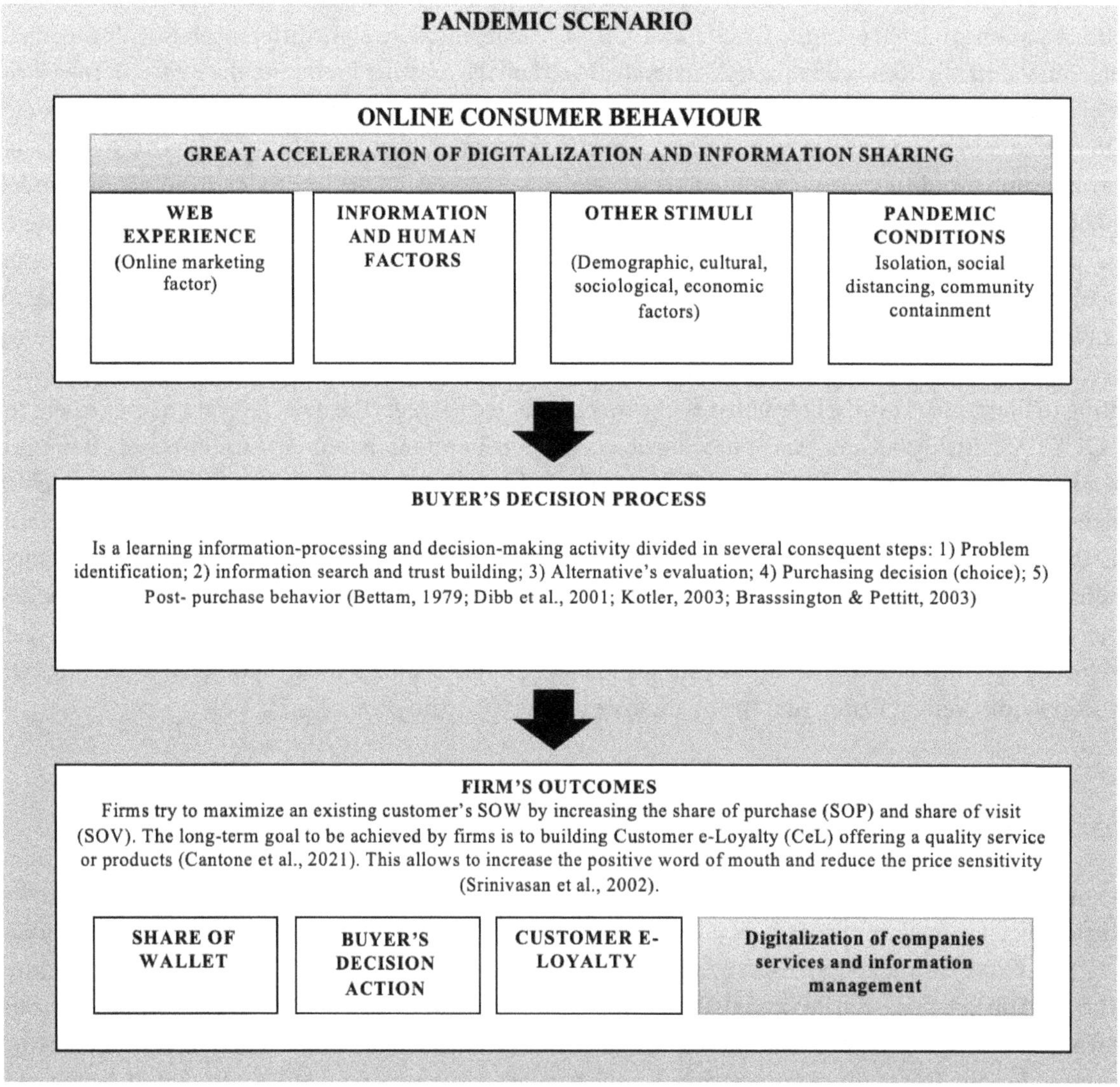

According to Yoo *et al.* (2000), we can consider the marketing communication effectiveness moving from the traditional "4P" of marketing mix elements, or rather: 1. Communication (e.g. quality of the information provided about the firm's products, the clarity of selling conditions and the delivery terms); 2. Product elements affecting the Web experience (e.g., online brands and product assortment, product features and product presentation); 4. Price (e.g., price level, the online promotional actions or discounts and the price transparency); 5. Promotion (e.g., free extra services, sales promotions and incentive programs). Except for digitized products (music, software, e-books, etc.) that are easily delivered online, for all other types of products offered online the order fulfilment and product delivery do not coincide with placing the online order. Alternative payment methods, fast delivery, flexible delivery options and order tracking are frequently mentioned elements of the fulfilment process. Researchers (Van Waterschoot and Van den Bulte, 1992) agree that the marketing mix's 4Ps, including fulfilment, are essential contributors to Marketing Stimuli (MS). The main approach, explaining the fundamentals of consumer behaviour, describes the Buyer's Decision Process (BDP) as a learning, information-processing and decision-making activity divided into several consequent steps: 1) Problem identification; 2) Information search and trust-building; 3) Alternative's evaluation; 4) Purchasing decision (choice); 5) Post-purchase behaviour (Bettman, 1979; Dibb *et al.,* 2001; Kotler, 2003; Brassington and Pettitt, 2003). Next to identifying the steps of the buying process and the potential role of marketing in each stage, we focus on the Buyer's Decision (BD) in terms of brand, product, dealer, and purchase timing. Share of wallet (SOW) is the monetary amount an average customer allocates to a particular brand rather than to competing brands in the same product category (Basile, 2019a). Firms try to maximize an existing customer's SOW by increasing the share of purchases (SOP) and share of visits (SOV). The long-term goal to be achieved by firms is to build Customer e-loyalty (CeL) by offering quality services or products (Cantone *et al.*, 2021). This allows for an increase the positive word of mouth and reduces the price sensitivity (Srinivasan *et al.*, 2002).

ONLINE RETAILING IN THE COVID-19 ERA

Before the COVID-19 pandemic, retailers started building their business model by using innovation to support customer engagement and make the brand experience inviting, authentic, distinctive, and personal (Jocevski, 2020). Which were the key pillars? a) Embrace modern technology as the key to generating sales and loyalty, and (2) the use of APIs by retailers can add features gradually, upgrading their online platform over time and boosting the recurs of customer relationship management tools (Iyengar *et al.*, 2017). Speed and user-friendly sites have become a competitive advantage. COVID-19 has governments at all levels operating in a context of radical uncertainty. The regional and local impact of the COVID-19 crisis is highly heterogeneous, with significant implications for crisis management and policy responses. Around the world, is becoming strong the concept of resilience (Guthrie *et al.*, 2021). New solutions have emerged, new habits created new consumer behaviours, and all efforts to adapt to a "new", albeit different, "normal" way of life (Basile, 2019b). The retailing industry was strongly affected by COVID-19 as the pandemic forced retailers to close hundreds of physical stores and lay off thousands of workers. Some retailers, with a huge e-commerce platform based on modern technology, quickly made changes to drive their operations and adapt to restrictions. In this way, big retailers such as Amazon, Alibaba, and JD.com meet new customer needs, generate sales and create value.

Retailers who did not have an online sales channel had to start online businesses and last-mile deliveries to customers under extreme time pressure. Therefore, the retailer has collaborated, on the one hand, with a partner company whose main business model is online delivery to final consumers and whose market shares have seen a huge increase in prices during the crisis. On the other hand, cooperation with an online delivery company has helped serve consumers ready to pay for instant small-quantity deliveries. In that way, retailers had the advantage of a higher market customer base, which is more likely to buy a small basket of high-value items (Schleper *et al.,* 2021). Retailers that were not able to update the old systems or introduce an e-commerce platform lost revenue and customers while having to deal with substantial inventory surpluses. As a result, just about every country reported decreased retail sales. According to The Business Insider, the prediction is a global drop of 5.7% for the year. Thus, 2020 forever changed the retailing environment, and now it is very strategic to understand how some retailers were able to thrive while others failed and, more importantly, what information we can bring to the firm's managers for preparing the future. Undoubtedly, modern retailing is not dead; the technology will provide retailers with the functionality they need to deliver seamless, engaging, personalized customer experiences across all channels in-store, online and mobile and the flexibility to make changes quickly to adapt to changing needs, new trends, economic shifts and even a global pandemic.

DISCUSSION

Psychological factors which underpin long-term behavioural change are predictable, even if the external forces people face can't be predicted. Understanding why and how people form habits can help us better predict how people may react in, and after, novel situations. With the rise of new online consumers in the post-COVID-19 world, it will become even more imperative for retailers to embed technology into their brick-and-mortar environment. Consumers have adopted new habits and learned a whole new system from contactless and curbside to click and collect/BOPIS[1], and their expectations are higher than ever. Consumers tested the convenience and predictability of buying online and being able to pick up, up or have their purchases delivered on the same day. Table 1 below, briefly emphasizes some of the differences in consumer habits before and during the pandemic. Before the COVID-19 outbreak, online and offline channels were valid purchase alternatives (Pantano *et al.,* 2020), but during the pandemic, consumers could only choose online channels (Guthrie *et al.,* 2021; Tran, 2021) as the leading way to shop due to severe restrictions (Sheth, 2020; Hale *et al.,* 2020). Consumers were driven towards the online environment, using digital devices and social media technology to access retailer offers and compare products and prices. (Guthrie *et al.,* 2021; Naeem, 2021; Shahbaznezhad *et al.,* 2021; Tran, 2021; Appel *et al.,* 2020). Overall, during the coronavirus pandemic, consumers became more familiar with several shopping services by exploiting home delivery services, working from home, and online courses (Pantano *et al.,* 2020; Roggeveen and Sethuraman, 2020). In addition, the shopping experience changed with consumer habits. Before COVID-19, shopping was considered a pleasurable activity for socializing, but because of the pandemic, the shopping experience became isolating by avoiding social contact and practising social distancing (Wilder-Smith and Freedman, 2020).

Table 1. Consumer habits before and during Pandemic

	Consumers habits before COVID-19	Consumers habits during COVID-19
Retailing Place	Online and offline based on their preferences	Only online imposed by lockdowns and community containment
Frequency to shop offline	During the opening hours	Rarely caused a lockdown
Frequency to shop online	Always	Always
Comparing products and price	Selecting several shops offline and online	By using only, the online environment
Online Services	As they need and if they want	Home delivery services; online courses; due to the impossibility to move out of home
Shopping experience	Broad, especially within the shops	New experience avoiding social contact and taking social distance, preventing contagions and preserving health
Kind of experience	Community experience	Isolated Experience

Source: Author's data elaboration.

While the lockdowns and shortages forced consumers to shop differently and with different retailers, the chance that they will go back to their old ways at least any time soon is poor. While many retailers have worked with obsolete technology for years, in the post-COVID scenario, the consumer may not be as forgiving. In the process of having to dismiss old habits and forgo any loyalty to specific retailers, they have become used to seeking and finding new alternatives. In the future, if they are not getting an experience that meets their expectations, they are likely to take their business elsewhere. The new online consumer in a post-pandemic world could be defined as: *"a consumer fully expert on the interactive technologies and online platforms, able to easily switch from online to offline and vice versa. The new consumer does not waste time and considers his/her health as a priority to preserve during the shopping process"*. Even though consumers were quick to adapt to the changes brought on by COVID-19 and many e-commerce adverse consumers discovered the advantages of online shopping, there is no doubt that brick-and-mortar stores will always have a place in the retail landscape. As Kirk Goldman, Vice President, Business Strategy at Toshiba Global Commerce Solutions, said: "The physical store, and being able to see, smell, touch things, is still vitally important to most of the economy. Retailer's challenge lies in enabling shoppers to transition their online shopping behaviours into stores while also deploying in-store technology that captures more nuanced data and insights about that shopping behaviour." The very challenge is understanding how retailers will upgrade their in-store experiences to better deliver to consumer expectations. In other words, recurs to technology to heighten the in-store experience for shoppers and change the retail strategy and marketing investments. Indeed, an inefficient retail strategy has no future, and retailers can prepare for the future by creating an in-store experience as seamless as the one their customers get online so that customers can focus on what they came for: the satisfying experience of making an in-store purchase. In addition, some retailers were already experimenting with in-store technology pre-COVID. For example, in the U.S., Sephora, Nordstrom, and Sam's Club are among the retailers who put in-store mPOS[2] systems in place, while globally, Zara and Nike integrated self-checkout. In China, two grocery store chains use technology to educate and engage. At Hema, customers scan information-filled QR codes on all products and pay via the store's app, while at 7Fresh, they get product information via motion sensor-driven magic mirrors and autonomous shopping carts that follow them around the store.

MANAGERIAL IMPLICATIONS

The integration of physical and digital channels will become even more crucial, as retailers will leverage new technologies to increase value creation in their store formats. For example, offering extended product ranges, or using online fulfilment and refurbishment of physical orders, even if the latter is not yet widely used for online purchases or is better used only in limited categories (such as home furnishings). Firms must therefore manage a broader and more competitive market, investing more in digital tools. To compete in this new scenario, firms must implement new technological strategies to guarantee an excellent customer experience (Hoyer *et al.,* 2020) by innovating their business model. In the future, digital communication channels will also become a priority for companies for the rapid transfer of offline to online media (D'Andrea *et al.,* 2019). In connection with potentially evolving consumption patterns and an increase in online services, especially high-end retailers may be faced with different customer service needs (Arora *et al.,* 2020; Schleper *et al.,* 2021). Marketing will be driven by service innovation and "human-centric" communication. Retailers will face challenges across multiple dimensions. Reinventing the shopping experience: hassle-free shopping in a high hygiene environment; change store layouts and proposition, reconfigure check-out, offer longer operating hours, and provide a seamless omnichannel experience. Moreover, consumers have changed where and how they engage, and marketing spending should reflect the new habits. Lastly, could be useful to reconfigure value for money in terms of price, private label, quality, branding strategies, and merchandising. Capturing new needs that are: health, safety, fresh and ready to eat. Adapting formats and rethinking brand mix to new needs: polarization in pack size (large and single packs) and hygiene certainty. Therefore, it will be necessary to ensure a personalized shopping experience that can respond to the individual consumer's needs (Hickman *et al.,* 2020). Despite the lack of resources and skills, keeping business going to was crucial for companies during domestic confinement. Simultaneously, working in different places, the empathic approach needs to be refined by listening better to compensate for the physical distance. Moreover, retailers need to increase investment rates in their digital and omnichannel capabilities (Hickman *et al.,* 2020), as the COVID-19 pandemic's impact has highlighted the need for synergies and flexibility across channels.

FUTURE RESEARCH DIRECTIONS

In this new technology scenario, the rate of change in retailing has been accelerating rapidly. With the vaccination and other pandemic remedy, customers gradually return to stores, but the general retailers expect that customer behaviour will change forever towards online and out-of-store shopping (Schleper *et al.,* 2021). Therefore, future research could be oriented to understand whether consumers who used digital to connect, learn and buy products during the lockdown will continue to have the same habits and with what intensity and if there will ever be a return to normal, as we knew it. Several studies underlined those customers prefer a wide variety of choices and convenience and they want to feel strongly connected to the brand (Billewar *et al.,* 2021). Digital technologies (AI, machine learning, big data analytics, automation, augmented reality, robotics etc.) have become essential elements that influence the key strategic decisions in the retail industry. Retailers should review their business model, while also looking inward to use technology as a key enabler. Future research could be oriented to understand whether consumers who used digital to connect, learn and buy products during the lockdown will continue to have the same habits and with what intensity and if there will ever be a return to normal, as we knew it.

Moreover, it would be interesting to investigate the role of digital technologies, such as Virtual Reality (VR) and Augmented Reality (VR), in online consumer behaviour and metaverse in the retailing industry (Bourlakis *et al.*, 2009). Though the metaverse remains a fuzzy concept, a growing number of brands and retailers are more interested in understanding the value creation dynamic. While the metaverse for retail holds great appeal (shopping experiences integrated seamlessly throughout immersive digital worlds), the development of the studies to support it is still in the very early stages. Furthermore, future research should be conducted to replicate the framework in different contexts and industries.

CONCLUSION

This chapter proposed a new profile of online consumers in a post-pandemic world. And by connecting the theoretical background presented in this work, appears fundamental to consider new wants and desires in a post-pandemic world. The life after a pandemic such as COVID-19 radically modified psychologically and practically the online consumer behaviours. For that reason, it is not possible to consider the online consumer as the same human being before a pandemic. Life after a pandemic is considered a "new normal", and in this scenario, the online consumers are the new online consumers.

The COVID-19 pandemic has significantly affected shopping behaviour: consumers are more attentive and demanding, and above all, they have become accustomed to finding what they need online (Pantano, 2020; Guthrie *et al.,* 2021; Tran, 2021). Consumer behaviour and purchasing patterns are mutating, and many of these changes will persist post-pandemic (Seth, 2020). Even the most suspicious people in this health emergency have overcome the cognitive barriers to digital purchasing to shop in total safety. This trend will not only involve products that are low complexity (convenience or shopping goods). Buyers will make purchases more consciously and aided by new digital services; they can move towards more complex and higher-risk products (e.g., exclusive goods). By observing the substantial effects of COVID-19 on online consumer behaviour (Eger *et al.,* 2021; Roggeveen and Sethuraman, 2020), people were forced to change their approach (Eger *et al.,* 2021). In the COVID-19 pandemic, consumers had to consider different tools to satisfy their needs (Eger *et al.,* 2021; Pantano *et al.,* 2020). Online shopping was the predominant way to shop (Guthrie *et al.,* 2021; Tran, 2021), and consumers became more familiar with several services, such as home deliveries, cashless payment and the use of social media (Naeem, 2021; Shahbaznezhad *et al.,* 2021; Appel *et al.,* 2020). Lastly, from the huge amount of information in online retailing and arising from data sharing emerge a host of potential ethical concerns, that are important for retailers to consider in their strategizing. These issues became even more complicated with the spread of COVID-19. Frontline workers employed by stores that have been forced to close, whether temporarily or permanently, have suffered complete disruptions to their lives and been forced back into a difficult job market. Others, working in essential services (e.g., grocery, drugstores, home improvement), encounter more challenging work environments (e.g., risk of exposure to the virus, mask requirements, social distancing, dealing with hostile customers). There is thus a great need to understand how retailers have dealt with this crisis and what lessons they can learn for dealing with its ongoing effects, as well as new crises when they occur. Regarding health management, it would also be interesting to explore the correlates of OCB with other variables such as learning from the crisis, changing needs, personality, nationality, culture, new market segment and age to develop new models of consumer behaviour (Mehta *et al.* 2020).

REFERENCES

Akar, E., & Nasir, V. A. (2014), A Critical Review of Online Consumers' Purchase Intentions, *Advances in Business-Related Scientific Research Conference,* 26-28.

Allain-Dupré, D., Chatry, I., Michalun, V., & Moisio, A. (2020). The territorial impact of COVID-19: managing the crisis across levels of government. *OECD Policy Responses to Coronavirus (COVID-19), 10.*

Anna, Z. (2020). The Consumer Behaviour in a Post Pandemic World. *Micro & Macro Marketing*, (3), 647–656.

Arora, N., Charm, T., Grimmelt, A., Ortega, M., Robinson, K., Sexauer, C., & Yamakawa, N. (2020). *A global view of how consumer behaviour is changing amid COVID-19.* McKinsey Company. Available at tinyurl.com/zufomz47

Basile, V. (2019a). Marketing Performance Measurement in FMCG: Share of Wallet in Retailing Industry. Editoriale Scientifica.

Basile, V. (2019b). Investigating new consumer behaviour dimensions in grocery retailing: Some evidence from Southern Italy. *The Journal of Business and Retail Management Research, 14*(01). Advance online publication. doi:10.24052/JBRMR/V14IS01/ART-05

Billewar, S. R., Jadhav, K., Sriram, V. P., Arun, A., Abdul, S. M., Gulati, K., & Bhasin, N. K. K. (2021). The rise of 3D E-Commerce: online shopping gets real with virtual reality and augmented reality during COVID-19. *World Journal of Engineering.*

Bourlakis, M., Papagiannidis, S., & Li, F. (2009). Retail spatial evolution: Paving the way from traditional to metaverse retailing. *Electronic Commerce Research, 9*(1), 135–148. doi:10.100710660-009-9030-8

Cheung, M. F., & To, W. M. (2019). An extended model of value-attitude-behavior to explain Chinese consumers' green purchase behavior. *Journal of Retailing and Consumer Services, 50*, 145–153. doi:10.1016/j.jretconser.2019.04.006

Constantinides, E. (2002). The 4S web-marketing mix model. *Electronic Commerce Research and Applications, 1*(1), 57–76. doi:10.1016/S1567-4223(02)00006-6

Constantinides, E. (2004). Influencing the online consumer's behaviour: The Web experience. *Internet Research, 14*(2), 111–126. doi:10.1108/10662240410530835

Constantinides, E. (2006). The marketing mix revisited: Towards the 21st-century marketing. *Journal of Marketing Management, 22*(3-4), 407–438. doi:10.1362/026725706776861190

Donthu, N., & Gustafsson, A. (2020). Effects of COVID-19 on business and research. *Journal of Business Research, 117*(1), 284–289. doi:10.1016/j.jbusres.2020.06.008 PMID:32536736

Edwards, A. W., & Cavalli-Sforza, L. L. (1965). A method for cluster analysis. *Biometrics, 21*(2), 362–375. doi:10.2307/2528096 PMID:14338671

Effenberger, M., Kronbichler, A., Shin, J. I., Mayer, G., Tilg, H., & Perco, P. (2020). Association of the COVID-19 pandemic with internet search volumes: A Google TrendsTM analysis. *International Journal of Infectious Diseases*, *95*, 192–197. doi:10.1016/j.ijid.2020.04.033 PMID:32305520

Eger, L., Komárková, L., Egerová, D., & Mičík, M. (2021). The effect of COVID-19 on consumer shopping behaviour: Generational cohort perspective. *Journal of Retailing and Consumer Services*, *61*, 102542. doi:10.1016/j.jretconser.2021.102542

El-Gohary, H. (2010). E-Marketing-A literature Review from a Small Businesses perspective. *International Journal of Business and Social Science*, *1*(1).

Feldmann, A., Gasser, O., Lichtblau, F., Pujol, E., Poese, I., Dietzel, C., & Smaragdakis, G. (2021, March). Implications of the COVID-19 Pandemic on the Internet Traffic. In *Broadband Coverage in Germany; 15th ITG-Symposium* (1-5). VDE.

Grewal, D., Gauri, D. K., Roggeveen, A. L., & Sethuraman, R. (2021). Strategizing retailing in the new technology era. *Journal of Retailing*, *97*(1), 6–12. doi:10.1016/j.jretai.2021.02.004

Guthrie, C., Fosso-Wamba, S., & Arnaud, J. B. (2021). Online consumer resilience during a pandemic: An exploratory study of e-commerce behaviour before, during and after a COVID-19 lockdown. *Journal of Retailing and Consumer Services*, *61*, 102570. doi:10.1016/j.jretconser.2021.102570

Habibi, M. R., Laroche, M., & Richard, M. O. (2014). The roles of brand community and community engagement in building brand trust on social media. *Computers in Human Behavior*, *37*, 152–161. doi:10.1016/j.chb.2014.04.016

Hale, T., Petherick, A., Phillips, T., & Webster, S. (2020). Variation in government responses to COVID-19. *Blavatnik School of Government Working Paper*, *3*(11).

Hamilton, M., Kaltcheva, V. D., & Rohm, A. J. (2016). Social media and value creation: The role of interaction satisfaction and interaction immersion. *Journal of Interactive Marketing*, *36*, 121–133. doi:10.1016/j.intmar.2016.07.001

Hickman, E., Kharouf, H., & Sekhon, H. (2020). An omnichannel approach to retailing: Demystifying and identifying the factors influencing an omnichannel experience. *International Review of Retail, Distribution and Consumer Research*, *30*(3), 266–288. doi:10.1080/09593969.2019.1694562

Holbrook, M. B., & Hirschman, E. C. (1982). The experiential aspects of consumption: Consumer fantasies, feelings, and fun. *The Journal of Consumer Research*, *9*(2), 132–140. doi:10.1086/208906

Im, H., Lennon, S. J., & Stoel, L. (2010). The perceptual fluency effect on the pleasurable online shopping experience. *Journal of Research in Interactive Marketing*, *4*(4), 280–295. doi:10.1108/17505931011092808

Islam, H., Jebarajakirthy, C., & Shankar, A. (2021). An experimental based investigation into the effects of website interactivity on customer behaviour in an online purchase context. *Journal of Strategic Marketing*, *29*(2), 117–140. doi:10.1080/0965254X.2019.1637923

Islam, T., Pitafi, A. H., Arya, V., Wang, Y., Akhtar, N., Mubarik, S., & Xiaobei, L. (2021). Panic buying in the COVID-19 pandemic: A multi-country examination. *Journal of Retailing and Consumer Services*, *59*, 102357. doi:10.1016/j.jretconser.2020.102357

Iyengar, K., Khanna, S., Ramadath, S., & Stephens, D. (2017). *What it takes to capture the value of APIs*. McKinsey & Company.

Jocevski, M. (2020). Blurring the lines between physical and digital spaces: Business model innovation in retailing. *California Management Review*, *63*(1), 99–117. doi:10.1177/0008125620953639

Kalkınma, E., & birliği Örgütü, İ. (2020). The Territorial Impact of COVID-19: Managing the Crisis Across Levels of Government. *Erişim Adresi*. https://read. OECD-library. org/view

Kotler, P. (1984). Marketing Management: Analysis, planning and Control (5th ed.). Prentice-Hall.

Kotler, P., Armstrong, G., Saunders, J., & Wong, V. (2001). *Principles of Marketing* (3rd ed.). Prentice-Hall, Pearson Education Limited.

Laato, S., Islam, A. N., Farooq, A., & Dhir, A. (2020). Unusual purchasing behaviour during the early stages of the COVID-19 pandemic: The stimulus-organism-response approach. *Journal of Retailing and Consumer Services*, *57*, 102224. doi:10.1016/j.jretconser.2020.102224

Laroche, M., & Richard, M. O. (2014). A Model of online consumer behaviour. In *Handbook of Strategic e-Business Management* (pp. 325–346). Springer. doi:10.1007/978-3-642-39747-9_15

Lee, E. A., & Messerschmitt, D. G. (2012). *Digital communication*. Springer Science & Business Media.

Li, X., Zhao, X., & Pu, W. (2020). Measuring the ease of use of mobile applications in e-commerce retailing from the perspective of consumer online shopping behaviour patterns. *Journal of Retailing and Consumer Services*, *55*, 102093. doi:10.1016/j.jretconser.2020.102093

MacInnis, D. J. (2011). A framework for conceptual contributions in marketing. *Journal of Marketing*, *75*(4), 136–154. doi:10.1509/jmkg.75.4.136

McKinsey. (2020). *How COVID-19 has pushed companies over the technology tipping point—and transformed business forever.* McKinsey Global Survey Results.

Mehta, S., Saxena, T., & Purohit, N. (2020). The new consumer behaviour paradigm amid COVID-19: Permanent or transient? *Journal of Health Management*, *22*(2), 291–301. doi:10.1177/0972063420940834

Mohd Dali, N. R. S., Abdul Hamid, H., Wan Nawang, W. R., & Wan Mohamed Nazarie, W. N. F. (2020). Post pandemic consumer behavior: Conceptual framework. *The Journal of Muamalat and Islamic Finance Research.*

Naeem, M. (2021). Do social media platforms develop consumer panic buying during the fear of the Covid-19 pandemic. *Journal of Retailing and Consumer Services*, *58*, 102226. doi:10.1016/j.jretconser.2020.102226

OECD. (2020). *COVID-19 and fiscal relations across levels of government*. OECD.

OECD. (2020). *Evaluating the initial impact of COVID-19 containment measures on economic activity*. OECD Policy Responses to Coronavirus (COVID-19).

Pantano, E., Pizzi, G., Scarpi, D., & Dennis, Ch. (2020). Competing during a pandemic? Retailers' ups and downs during the COVID19 outbreak. *Journal of Business Research*, *116*, 209–213. doi:10.1016/j.jbusres.2020.05.036 PMID:32501307

Pantano, E., & Willems, K. (2022). How Pandemic Crisis Times Affects Consumer Behaviour. In *Retail in a New World*. Emerald Publishing Limited. doi:10.1108/978-1-80117-846-420221004

Richard, M. O., Chebat, J. C., Yang, Z., & Putrevu, S. (2010). A proposed model of online consumer behaviour: Assessing the role of gender. *Journal of Business Research*, *63*(9-10), 926–934. doi:10.1016/j.jbusres.2009.02.027

Rita, P., Oliveira, T., & Farisa, A. (2019). The impact of e-service quality and customer satisfaction on customer behaviour in online shopping. *Heliyon*, *5*(10), e02690. doi:10.1016/j.heliyon.2019.e02690 PMID:31720459

Ritchie, J., Lewis, J., Nicholls, C. M., & Ormston, R. (Eds.). (2013). *Qualitative research practice: A guide for social science students and researchers*. Sage.

Roggeveen, A. L., & Sethuraman, R. (2020). How the COVID Pandemic May Change the World of Retailing. *Journal of Retailing*, *96*(2), 169–171. doi:10.1016/j.jretai.2020.04.002

Saeed, K. A., Hwang, Y., & Mun, Y. Y. (2003). Toward an integrative framework for online consumer behaviour research: A meta-analysis approach. *Journal of Organizational and End User Computing*, *15*(4), 1–26. doi:10.4018/joeuc.2003100101

Safara, F. (2020). A computational model to predict consumer behaviour during COVID-19 pandemic. *Computational Economics*, 1–14. PMID:33169049

Schleper, M. C., Gold, S., Trautrims, A., & Baldock, D. (2021). Pandemic-induced knowledge gaps in operations and supply chain management: COVID-19's impacts on retailing. *International Journal of Operations & Production Management*.

Schultz, D. E., & Peltier, J. (2013). Social media's slippery slope: Challenges, opportunities and future research directions. *Journal of Research in Interactive Marketing*, *7*(2), 86–99. doi:10.1108/JRIM-12-2012-0054

Shahbaznezhad, H., Dolan, R., & Rashidirad, M. (2021). The Role of Social Media Content Format and Platform in Users' Engagement Behavior. *Journal of Interactive Marketing*, *53*, 47–65. doi:10.1016/j.intmar.2020.05.001

Shankar, V., Kalyanam, K., Setia, P., Golmohammadi, A., Tirunillai, S., Douglass, T., & Waddoups, R. (2021). How technology is changing retail. *Journal of Retailing*, *97*(1), 13–27. doi:10.1016/j.jretai.2020.10.006

Sheth, J., (2020). Impact of Covid-19 on consumer behaviour: will the old habits return or die? *Journal of Business Research. 117*, 280–283.. doi:10.1016/j.jbusres.2020.05.059

Studdert, D. M., & Hall, M. A. (2020). Disease control, civil liberties, and mass testing—Calibrating restrictions during the COVID-19 pandemic. *The New England Journal of Medicine*, *383*(2), 102–104. doi:10.1056/NEJMp2007637 PMID:32272003

Svajdova, L. (2021). Consumer behaviour during pandemic of COVID-19. *Journal of International Business Research and Marketing*, *6*(3), 34–37. doi:10.18775/jibrm.1849-8558.2015.63.3005

Tran, L. T. T. (2021). Managing the effectiveness of e-commerce platforms in a pandemic. *Journal of Retailing and Consumer Services*, *58*, 102287. doi:10.1016/j.jretconser.2020.102287

Yoo, B., Donthu, N., & Lee, S. (2000). An examination of selected marketing mix elements and brand equity. *Journal of the Academy of Marketing Science*, *28*(2), 195–211. doi:10.1177/0092070300282002

KEY TERMS AND DEFINITIONS

Branding and Firms' Strategies: In the new pandemic scenario retailers will face challenges across multiple dimensions. In sales, marketing mix and assortment strategies.

COVID-19 Pandemic Modifications: The pandemic caused by COVID-19 has produced several modifications to consumer behaviour and, in general, in the daily life of people who are adapting to new changes such as the lockdowns and quarantine restrictions in several countries worldwide.

Issue About Data Privacy Information: In the new digital environment intensification by the pandemic, the problems and liability of managing personal data and their use are becoming more and more problematic.

New Online Consumer: Is a consumer fully expert on the interactive technologies and online platforms, able to easily switch from online to offline and vice versa. The new consumer doesn't waste time and considers his/her health as a priority to preserve during the shopping process.

Online Shopping After COVID-19: Online shopping was the predominant way to shop and consumers became more familiar with several services, such as home deliveries, cashless payment and the use of social media.

Online Shopping Before COVID-19: Online shopping was one of the possibilities to shop. People could indifferently choose if and how to make their purchases using the channel that was easier to access.

Post-COVID-19 Retailing World: This is a new environment where a human being can express their past needs and desires with the new one developed after several restrictions imposed by governments all over the world.

ENDNOTES

1. The BOPIS strategy is also referred to as click and collect, curbside pickup, and ROPIS (reserve online, pick up in-store). With BOPIS, shoppers don't have to deal with shipping costs, long delivery timelines, and shipping back items that don't fit or meet their expectations. Retailers around the world are adopting the BOPIS model to meet customer expectations. This popular retail strategy gives customers the best of both worlds by integrating online shopping and in-person pickup.
2. Mobile Point of Sale (mPOS) systems are wireless mobile devices, such as smartphones or tablets, that function as traditional POS systems. They conduct financial transactions using POS mobile applications and peripherals such as credit/debit card readers and barcode scanners.

Chapter 4
Humans and Digital Technologies in the Omnichannel Post-COVID-19 Era

Adam Vrechopoulos
Athens University of Economics and Business, Greece

Chris Lazaris
https://orcid.org/0000-0002-7780-503X
Athens University of Economics and Business, Greece

Georgios Doukidis
Athens University of Economics and Business, Greece

ABSTRACT

Consumer behavioral patterns radically changed during the last decades, as well as during the COVID-19 pandemic. In parallel, digital technologies continuously substitute traditional business practices in the context of digital transformation attempts that were also significantly accelerated due to the pandemic. However, since technology cannot totally replace all human aspects in the retailer-consumer interaction process, an optimum blending of technical and human resources is crucial. This chapter reviews the latest developments and key aspects of this blending and emphasizes the consumers' needs for the provision of value-added services by retailers in the post-COVID-19 era. It advocates that retailing remains a retailer-consumer affair, where both humans and technologies take part in diversified interactions. It develops an integrated framework of human and technology components and channels between retailer-consumer interactions, aiming to provide a holistic view of the available capabilities and trends from both the retailer and the consumer perspective in the post-COVID-19 era.

DOI: 10.4018/978-1-7998-8856-7.ch004

INTRODUCTION

Research Context and Motivation

Grewal et al. (2021, p.6) report that "The world of retailing is being reimagined and transformed at breakneck speeds due to new technologies, as well as due to changes in consumer purchasing behavior resulting from the COVID-19 pandemic". To this end, they underline the need for retailers to explore how digital technologies can be effectively exploited in the context of their strategic planning. In fact, the exploitation of Digital Technologies in retail operations and marketing in the context of the evolving Digital Transformation attempts has been thoroughly addressed in literature through various perspectives, incorporating also the significant COVID-19 pandemic effects (e.g. Hoffman et al., 2022; Shankar et al., 2021; Cui et al., 2021; Gauri et al., 2021; Lazaris et al., 2021; Shankar and Kushwaha, 2021; Maier and Wieringa, 2021; Hüseyinoğlu et al., 2020; Teller et al., 2019; Grewal et al., 2017; Kannan and Li, 2017; Ng and Wakenshaw, 2017; Mahardika et al., 2019; Savastano et al., 2019; Verhoef et al., 2017; Altıntaş et. al., 2020; Silva et al., 2020; Nass et al., 2020). In this evolving context, Omnichannel Retailing as an evolution of Multichannel Retailing involves innovative retail processes and emerging consumer behavioral patterns that transform retail practices (Kang, 2018). Thus, Ewerhard et al. (2019) clearly state that retailers must adopt omnichannel practices to remain competitive.

Multichannel Retailing has been defined as "the operation of multiple channels as independent entities in order to align channels to specific targeted customer segments" (Picot-Coupey et al., 2016, p.339). By comparison, Rigby (2011, p.4) defines Omnichannel Retailing as "an integrated sales experience that melds the advantages of physical stores with the information-rich experience of online shopping". As such, omnichannel extends multichannel management providing more integration coordination and orchestration across channels (Picot-Coupey et al., 2016; Nüesch et al., 2015). Quite recently, Andersen et al. (2020, p.43) report that "with rapid changes in marketing channel environment that stem from technological advances and information revolution, there is an increasing need for revisiting the theories of marketing channels and their ability to explain the success and failure of modern channels". They suggest that future research should further investigate the role of Omnichannel Marketing as an influencing factor of consumers' perceptions and responses in the context of marketing channels. Similarly, Múgica and Berné (2019) call for future omnichannel research that will investigate consumer behavior also in the context of offline channels.

Verhoef et al. (2015) discussed the transition from Multichannel to Omnichannel Retailing and Pantano et al. (2018) reviewed the dimensions of "smart retailing" in this context. Also, Frasquet and Miquel (2017) analyzed the benefits of channel integration on consumer loyalty and satisfaction both online and offline. Quite recently, Loupiac and Goudey (2020) found that consumers' expectations of the conventional store (e.g. store atmosphere) are affected by the graphical user interface design of the online store. Also, Mainardes and Cardoso (2019) found that social media use within the physical store significantly affects consumer behavior (trust, loyalty, and purchase intention). Similarly, Mero (2018) discussed the promising role of live chats as a customer service tool offered through the retailer web site.

However, as reported by Hult et al. (2019, p.10) "current multichannel research is deficient in answering what drives customers' satisfaction, and consequently their loyalty, differently when customers purchase online versus at a physical store". Also, Ortlinghaus and Zielke (2019) report that research is still scarce regarding the design of multi-channel technologies towards enhancing the offered value to consumers. In this context, Grewal et al. (2020) reviewed the role of in-store technologies and provide a detailed list of future research perspectives. They note that the new and futuristic in-store technologies can positively affect customer experience. However, they underline the need for retailers to consider what customers really like. Similarly, quite recently, Rust (2020) reviewed the role of Digital Technologies in Marketing and provides several important implications for practice, research, and education. Among others, he calls for research towards understanding how people interact with Internet-of-things (people to machine) and how non-human elements of the Internet of Things (IoT) interact with each other (machine-to-machine).

In the context of these evolutions, retailers also deal with the showrooming phenomenon (search offline in-store and buy online at a different retailer) which is considered as a major threat (see Fergurson, 2020; Kuksov and Liao, 2018; Daunt and Harris, 2017; Sahu et al., 2021; Khoshtaria et al., 2021). In many instances, for example, retailers exploit innovative digital technologies for their front-end processes in the physical store (e.g., Amazon's Physical Store Online Shopping Control (Ward, 2017), where the Wi-Fi router detects consumers' price comparison practices and triggers alerts to sales associates to properly face them). Similarly, online retailers deal with consumers' webrooming (Fernandez et al., 2018) practices (search online and buy offline elsewhere) through the provision of attractive online features and services, as well as advanced automated solutions (e.g., artificial intelligence tools and applications).

While Digital Technologies enable retailers to provide attractive consumer services across channels at low cost through automation (e.g. digital conversational agents, machine learning and recommended systems), it seems that for some tasks (e.g. personal selling, customer service) retailers should also emphasize on the provision of several non-automated solutions either offline or online (e.g. interaction with sales representatives through online chat/video or through call centers with reasonable waiting times), supported, obviously, by technology (Honeycutt, 2005). For various reasons (e.g., lack of technical skills and/or technological infrastructure, need for social communication, personal preferences), such an option seems quite promising towards enhancing the value offered to consumers and society in general, especially today due to the COVID-19 pandemic. In this context, several research attempts have explored the impact of COVID-19 pandemic on consumer behavior and retail practices (see Roggeveen et al., 2020; Pantano et al., 2020; Kirk et al., 2020; Sheth, 2020).

Indeed, it seems that a proper balance between digital and physical is greatly needed in today's retailing field (Vrechopoulos et al., 2019). They introduced the term "Diachronic Retailing" and they thoroughly discussed the need for retailers to invest in traditional Marketing strategies and practices blended with digital technologies. As also reported by Heathwood (2018), the physical versus online retail dilemma should not exist, since physical remains fundamental because all consumers are attracted by emotions and human connections (see also Kidwell et al., 2021). Actually, it seems that there is a "consumer experience gap" that retailers should confront, since consumers increasingly seek emotional connections during shopping (Heathwood, 2018). For example, Lobaugh et al. (2015) discovered that half of the consumers value in-person advice during shopping activities, while one out of three shoppers prefer store associates' consultancy while selecting and validating products. Likewise, Clarke and Kinghorn (2018) revealed through a survey with 15.000 respondents that 75% of the sample wanted to interact with a real person more as technology improves. While such an option, if applied properly, may increase costs dramatically (e.g., salesforce training, recruitment of experienced sales and customer service personnel), retailers should seriously consider its promising role towards value enhancement of the offerings to their customers and provision of other important benefits to the society in general (e.g., decrease unemployment through strengthening the role of call centers, create knowledge through distance learning teaching initiatives).

Table 1. Indicative Recent Research Calls

Study	Marketing Channel Context	Research Gap Investigated	Author Keywords	Paper Classification	Key Research Calls/Findings
Gauri et al. (2021)	In-person and remote retail experiences	Challenges faced by offline (physical store-first) and online (digital-first) retailers	Retailing; Retail formats; Online retail; Omnichannel; e-commerce	Viewpoint Paper with Conceptual Framework	Newer digital-first and physical-first players should continue coming up with different customer-centric formats
Chen et al. (2021)	CRM in face-to-face and virtual service channels	How to apply sophisticated CRM systems to interact with customers	Infusion use; post-adoptive use; CRM-enabled service success; multi-channel; face-to-face channel; virtual channel	Survey	Employees' satisfaction with a CRM system is especially crucial in nurturing customer expectation confirmation in virtual channels, where face-to-face interactions are absent.
Andersen et al. (2020)	Consumer-based aspects of marketing channels	The increasing need for revisiting the theories of marketing channels and their ability to explain the success and failure of modern channels	Marketing channel strategy; perceived channel value; channel preference; customer value co-creation; channel satisfaction; customer loyalty	Viewpoint Paper with Conceptual Framework	Exploration of consumer perceptions of channel position and functions
Fergurson (2020)	Human talent vis-a-vis retail sales representatives in omni-channel retail settings	The ways in which retailers may deploy and leverage salespeople in omnichannel retailing	Retail sales; sales roles; omni-channel retailing; relational exchange	Viewpoint Paper	Managerial recommendations are provided for measuring retail salesperson performance in an omnichannel marketplace
Grewal et al. (2020)	Human-Technology interactions in the form of social presence at the physical store channel	The role of new in-store technologies that can serve as important touch points to customers, as well as assist and augment frontline employee tasks in today's socially connected world	In-store technology; Convenience; Social presence; Retailing Services	Viewpoint Paper with Conceptual Framework	Social presence as a result from interactions with the machine itself, human connections supported by the technology shopping, or some technology feature that humanizes the brand could positively affect sales
Múgica and Berné (2019)	Differences between direct and indirect online channels from the consumer perspective	Consumers' channel choice	Channel attributes; online channel choice; online tourism; situational variables	Survey	Future omnichannel research should investigate consumer behavior also in the context of offline channels
Rust (2019)	Artificial Intelligence (AI) and Human Intelligence (HI) in marketing	To what degree will the economy be dominated by AI and less by humans	Artificial intelligence; Big data; Digital revolution; Personalization; Service; Technology	Viewpoint Paper	There is a need to understand when the teamwork of Human Intelligence in the form of frontline workers and AI operates effectively
This study	Retailer-Consumer Channel Interactions	The optimal blending of technological and human factors in terms of retail channels	Omnichannel, Human Capital, Digital Technologies, Social Distancing	Viewpoint Paper with Conceptual Framework	Detailed practical and research implications regarding how a human-centric omnichannel retailing philosophy could contribute towards providing an optimum customer experience through multiple and combined retailer-consumer interaction points in the context of the customer journey across channels

While the Omnichannel philosophy implies the blending of technological and human factors in terms of retail channels, recent research calls (Table 1) indicate that there is ample room for research towards further optimizing this blending to provide value-added offerings to consumers. As Fergurson (2020, p.1) states, "the ways in which retailers may deploy and leverage salespeople in omni-channel retailing remains unsettled". While Omnichannel Retailing is a top priority in business practice and a well-investigated topic in academic research, there is need for further research for shedding more light on how eventually Humans and Digital Technologies will coexist in this fast evolving and technology intensive environment. Moreover, the social distancing effect caused by the COVID-19 pandemic, calls for research initiatives that will further explore this topic, taking also into account the new conditions.

Research Objectives and Approach

Motivated by these recent research calls, the objective of this chapter is to review the latest developments and thoroughly analyze the critical dimensions of this blending towards providing theoretical and practical implications. In this context, the chapter aims to document the value of Human Capital in the technology-intensive environment of Omnichannel Retailing. Specifically, while current retail practices, consumer trends and relevant literature mainly focus on the role of innovative technologies that increasingly dominate the world of Retailing (e.g., AI, Augmented Reality), the chapter also focus on the role of the Human Capital which, appropriately combined with Digital Technologies, could effectively fuel differentiation strategies that may lead to competitive advantages. In other words, one of the objectives of the chapter is to highlight the value of the traditional business and consumer practices and the corresponding soft skills that seem to be increasingly neglected today in the presence and wide diffusion of Digital Technologies in Retailing, in the context of Digital Transformation attempts accelerated by the COVID-19 pandemic.

The chapter reviews very recent academic literature and examines emerging business practices and consumer needs in the evolving context of Omnichannel Retailing. It develops an integrated framework of human and technology components and channels between retailer-consumer interactions aiming to provide a holistic view of the available capabilities, options, and trends from both the retailer and the consumer perspective. In this context, the chapter takes into account the radical changes in both consumer and business needs, caused by the COVID-19 pandemic. Thus, the conceptual approach employed by the research reported in the chapter, aims to develop a theoretical framework which provides a holistic view of the investigated topic and can also guide business practice and future research. The chapter does not employ as a methodological research approach a bibliometric analysis, but rather aims to select and synthesize existing knowledge on the investigated topic, derived through the thorough and comparative review of very recent academic and business sources.

OMNICHANNEL RETAILING DISRUPTING B2C INTERACTIONS

Although Omnichannel is beneficial for both retailers and consumers (e.g., optimizing the shopping journey by providing a seamless experience (Barwitz and Maas, 2018)), at the same time the abundance of digital channels and technologies seem to attenuate the influence of front-line employees (e.g., salespeople). In fact, retailers seem to overlook the critical role of sales associates during shopping (Fergurson, 2020; Benedetto, 2018). However, according to the InMoment firm survey findings reported by Kats (2019) "74% of internet users said that a disappointing interaction with staff—whether it's a poor attitude or lack of knowledge—is a leading reason why they would consider a brand experience as a negative one". Similarly, Hochstein et al. (2019) underlined the critical role of salespeople in an information rich environment for high-involvement products. They report (p. 118) that "understanding a consumer's informedness, and adapting the proper influence approach to it, is critical if salespeople are to influence modern consumers' purchase decisions and, thus, avoid irrelevancy". Also, Marinova et al. (2018) found positive effects of front-line employees' problem-solving work on consumer satisfaction and Elmashhara and Soares (2019) underlined the critical role of salespeople in the context of the social aspects of the interaction with customers in the conventional store. On the other hand, Spreer and Rauschnabel (2016) emphasized on the use of mobile sales assistant technologies for salespeople, shedding light on resistance factors that lead to low penetration of these retailing tools.

Nowadays, digital technologies have been embedded in consumers everyday lives, even in-store (e.g., mobile apps, self-checkout, digital signage). For example, Van Kerrebroeck et al. (2017) reported the promising role of touch-enabling technologies in the physical store. In this context, quite recently, Hickman et al. (2020) found that omnichannel experience is influenced by several factors (e.g., technology readiness, perceived value). They also report that the overall customer experience in omnichannel retailing could be enhanced by the simultaneous use of multiple retailer-consumer interaction points.

Roggeveen et al. (2020, p.135) report that "new facial tracking tools and technology might provide sales associates with expanded information about customer emotions (valence and intensity), which they can use to achieve greater emotional adaptivity in their selling efforts". Also, Röding et al. (2019) studied how technology influences consumer behavior as far as disclosure of personal information at the physical store is concerned (e.g., use of a tablet by the salesforce for collecting consumer data in the physical store). They found (in all the scenarios they tested) that consumers are willing to provide such type of information to front-line employees if traditional service practices are employed by the retailer for this particular task, even if frontline employees do not provide explanations to consumers regarding how these data will be used. In this regard, Li et al. (2018) call for further research on that topic. They report (p. 50) that "although omnichannel retailing has gained significant interest among academics and practitioners, the mechanisms through which customers react to Cross-Channel Integration (CCI) in omnichannel retailing remain unclear".

As a matter of fact, modern consumers may be more informed of product/services features than sales associates (Ahearne et al. 2022; Fergurson, 2020; Spreer and Rauschnabel, 2016). Therefore, salespeople should provide them with differentiated and value-added services and information that is absent or cannot be reached online. In order, however, for the front-line employees to be able to provide such type of value-added information and services to their customers (either offline or online), it is clear that the retailer must continuously invest on training and education initiatives (and/or hiring experienced sales staff) combined with Marketing Research initiatives aiming to investigate the consumers' attached importance and evaluation of store/product selection criteria (e.g. through the use of multi-attribute models).

Recently, Manss et al. (2020) found that the strongest predictors for webrooming are the channel's anticipated after-sales service and price level. Also, Bertrandie and Zielke (2019) found that consumers, in general, want integrated and uniform product prices offered by multi channel retailers. Similarly, in many instances, front-line employees are confused and frustrated (Fergurson, 2020) and are unable to cope with consumer price negotiation during the showrooming process. Hence, front-line employees should be both trained and empowered with technology to deal with such behaviors (Rapp et al., 2015; Kim and Park, 2019). Similarly, Esmark and Noble (2018) found that the closer an employee physically gets to the shoppers within the physical store, the higher their purchase intentions are. However, due to the social distancing effect caused by the COVID-19 pandemic, the role of the other consumer-retailer interaction channels (e.g., calls centers, video calls, chat) is also critical. Thus, since consumer-salespeople interaction can also occur online (e.g., through live commerce, social commerce, live-selling commerce), front-line employees should provide value-added information and services from all the available channels to customers visiting either the physical store or interact with the retailer from distance (Wright et al., 2019).

HUMANS AND DIGITAL TECHNOLOGIES IN OMNICHANNEL RETAILING

The Need for Human-Centric Retailing

Gupta and Ramachandran (2021, p. 597) state that "in an environment with digital disruptions, retailers must adopt a customer-centric approach to survive and compete effectively". In this context, a proper balance of human soft skills (e.g. creativity, negotiation, communication, personal selling techniques, public relations, strategic thinking, leadership) and technology that are optimally blended with each other seems promising for retailers, in order to achieve a sustainable competitive advantage. Although emerging technologies, such as the Internet-of-Things (IoT) (see Hoffman and Novak, 2018) could revolutionize the retail field, the contribution of traditional marketing practices (along with e-commerce capabilities – see Villanova et al. 2021) throughout the customer journey remains critical (e.g., personalized treatment of demanding consumers by experienced salesforce in the case of luxury goods, B2C services in the tourism industry, etc.). To this end, recently, Dimitrova et al. (2020) underlined the important role of face-to-face selling in some societies. Similarly, Shavitt and Barnes (2020) found significant effects of culture in the context of the consumers' shopping journey. However, due to the COVID-19 pandemic, such face-to-face selling could be effectively transferred also to other channels, meeting the circumstances of this period as well as satisfying consumer preferences in the post COVID-19 era where a significant percentage of consumers may prefer to interact with retailers from distance (i.e., online shopping and customer service).

Nevertheless, it seems that today, where the distance shopping activities have dramatically increased also due to COVID-19 pandemic effects, several retailers tend to encourage customers to prefer *technical-automated* instead of *human* interactions (e.g., customer service through call centers), mainly due to the limited resources available to meet the sudden increase in distance shopping demand. However, retailers should keep on investing in human skills and knowledge (e.g. see Lechner and Paul, 2019; Delpechitre et al., 2018; Rippe et al., 2018; Groza and Groza, 2018, Kalyani and Saravanan 2020) along with existing technology and IT skills (see Sousa and Rocha, 2019) and continuous technology innovations. In fact, adopting a differentiation strategy which is propelled by the combined and intelligent exploitation of technical and non-technical resources seems quite promising and innovative on its own.

Today, most retailers and consumers are quite familiar with Digital Technologies. New technology innovations have been introduced (e.g., AI, conversational agents, AR/VR, IoT, RFID/NFC, digital signage, etc.) and adopted by consumers (Luna-Nevarez and McGovern, 2021). Moreover, in some instances, both retailers and consumers seem to perform better when using Digital Technologies (e.g., shopping through e-catalogues) compared to traditional practices (e.g., face-to-face price negotiations in the physical store). However, rapid and continuous technological evolutions must not misguide businesses (and consumers) to totally replace traditional shopping activities (e.g. face-to-face selling in a conventional retail setting). Besides, non-technology human/social interactions (e.g., discuss with an experienced travel agent or a car dealer either offline or online) undeniably provide some benefits (e.g., psychological, transactional - e.g., access to important information like travelling guidelines and tips during the COVID-19 pandemic, etc.) that cannot be offered (at least in that way) through other alternative options. Accordingly, David Clarke of PriceWaterhouseCoopers (PwC), as reported in Morgan (2018) article, believes that *"future success in customer experience comes from a combination of people plus technology"* which is also supported as the most likely scenario by Morgan (2018).

Human Capital and Digital Technologies in Retailing

Vera (2017) stress on the need for a humanized retail experience, where physical stores would provide authentic, romantic social connections with consumers that "cannot be found on a website". Undoubtedly, however, while the benefits of physical stores cannot be enjoyed online, retailers could explore innovative tools and methods to effectively simulate the physical shopping experience (e.g., 3D online stores with social presence - see Krasonikolakis et al., 2018, virtual reality commerce), which is very important today and even in the future, also due to the social distancing effect caused by the COVID-19 pandemic.

The conditions or factors that make consumers prefer traditional channels and methods are also evolving. However, store selection criteria like *"sales personnel with deep knowledge of the product characteristics", "provision of personalized offerings and solutions by the sales and customer service personnel that act as experienced consultants", "social interaction with friendly staff and building of personal relationships through face-to-face communication", "achieve better prices through exploiting negotiation skills in the "old-fashioned" way"*, etc. seem to remain critical for patronage intentions at least for a significant percentage of consumers. It should be clarified, however, that some of these criteria could be also met (to a certain extent) through online - from distance channels, as also discussed above.

Furthermore, situational factor effects (e.g., mood, time availability, shopping mission, channels' use in the context of the shopping journey, etc.), psychographic characteristics (e.g., personality, lifestyle, values), etc. that well operate as moderating factors in such type of relationships (i.e., between the manipulated variables of the retail setting and the consumer behavioral ones), should be also taken into account when designing retail offerings, either offline or online. Indeed, Ho and Lim (2018) found significant consumer mood effects on their buying behavior, in the context of mobile personalization (through recommendations) initiatives. Therefore, retailers should effectively treat difficult and demanding situations where technological solutions are insufficient, through experienced front-line employees, merging digital with human assets either offline or online/from distance.

From a Marketing Research perspective, Digital Technologies provide challenging opportunities to collect at low cost a vast amount of *raw data* either in a quantitative format (e.g., analytics, Point of Sales [POS] data) or in a qualitative one (e.g., social media data, call center data - see Abbasi et al., 2018). Also, Digital Technologies provide advanced and continuously evolving tools for converting these raw data to *information* in user-friendly graphical user interfaces (e.g., Business Analytics and Intelligence Visualization reports, Data Mining, and text/opinion mining tools, etc.). However, to convert this information to *knowledge* towards providing valuable managerial implications, it is essential to exploit through an interdisciplinary approach the relevant business expertise and scientific knowledge available. While the process of converting *information* to *knowledge* could be effectively embedded in algorithms and corresponding software solutions (e.g., machine learning), it seems that some critical tasks in any given research attempt cannot be automated by technology (e.g., exploit experience and strategic thinking to explain and convert the resulted *information* to *knowledge* to support strategic decision making). Thus, a human-centric approach seems quite promising also in this topic, since knowledge and expertise could not always be totally and effectively embedded in software solutions. In this context, the collaboration between different business departments (e.g., IT and Marketing) for converting *information* to *knowledge* is critical. For example, several companies today face the challenge to properly convert the *information* derived through Big Data and Business Analytics to useful *knowledge*. In this context, quite recently, Kumar and Venkatesan (2021) thoroughly discussed the challenges of metrics and analytics in retailing, providing also useful suggestions for future research in this domain. In sum, Fügener et al. (2021, p. 1527) argue that "the loss of unique human knowledge may lead to several undesirable outcomes in a host of human–AI decision environments".

Conversely, from a Human-Machine Collaboration (HMC) perspective, humans, and AI digital technologies act complementary augmenting human capabilities, not replacing them (Wilson and Daugherty, 2018). Similarly, Guha et al. (2021, p. 28) state that "AI is likely to be more effective if it focuses on augmenting (rather than replacing) managers' judgments". For example, a Swedish bank introduced an AI conversational agent (Aida) that could provide answers to frequently asked questions and redirect complex issues to human customer-service employees and tracks that interaction to better solve similar questions in the future (Wilson and Daugherty, 2018). On the other hand, collaborative interaction between human and AI may advance thinking and performance of humans creating integrated intelligence (Lichtenthaler, 2018). As an example, salespeople with access to business intelligence and analytics for retail (e.g., using Customer Relationship Management (CRM) systems either in-store or through other channels – see Chen et al. 2021) could provide better service and support to customers, enhancing their shopping experience in all channels. In this context, Mintz et al. (2021) provide a thorough review on the right metrics for marketing mix decisions, discussing their effectiveness for automated decision systems based on machine learning systems.

All the above also indicate that "humanizing" the retailing field involves issues that do not directly deal only with customer facing functions, but also with other important business processes and operations (e.g., Marketing Research, effective collaboration between different business departments through process-based organizational structures) needed to design optimum offerings through thoroughly explaining consumer behaviors.

Human & Technology Components and Channels between Retailer-Consumer Interactions

The human and technology components and channels between retailers and consumers interactions are presented in Figure 1 (adapted from the hybrid customer interaction framework of Nüesch et al. (2015)). Specifically, from the retailer point of view, processes and operations could be performed either through: (a) the pure use of the human factor (e.g. deep-selling procedures by salesforce either offline or online/ from distance without the direct use of technology), (b) the pure use of technology (e.g., artificial intelligence applications), (c) the combined use of human factors and technology (e.g., sales associates utilizing digital technologies and interact with consumers either offline or online / from distance). In addition, the retailer may provide several levels of channel integration. From the consumer point of view, behavioral processes and steps could be performed: (a) without (directly) using technology (e.g., traditional social shopping experience either offline or online / from distance), (b) by exclusively using technology (home continuous replenishment process through automated shopping lists that run online), (c) by the combined use of technology and traditional practices in terms of channels, tools and methods used (e.g., price negotiation in the physical store or through other channels (see Lawrence et al., 2021) using price comparison sites). In parallel, the consumer may engage in channel hopping at various levels (Nüesch et al., 2015).

Figure 1. Human & Technology Components and Channels between Retailer-Consumer Interactions

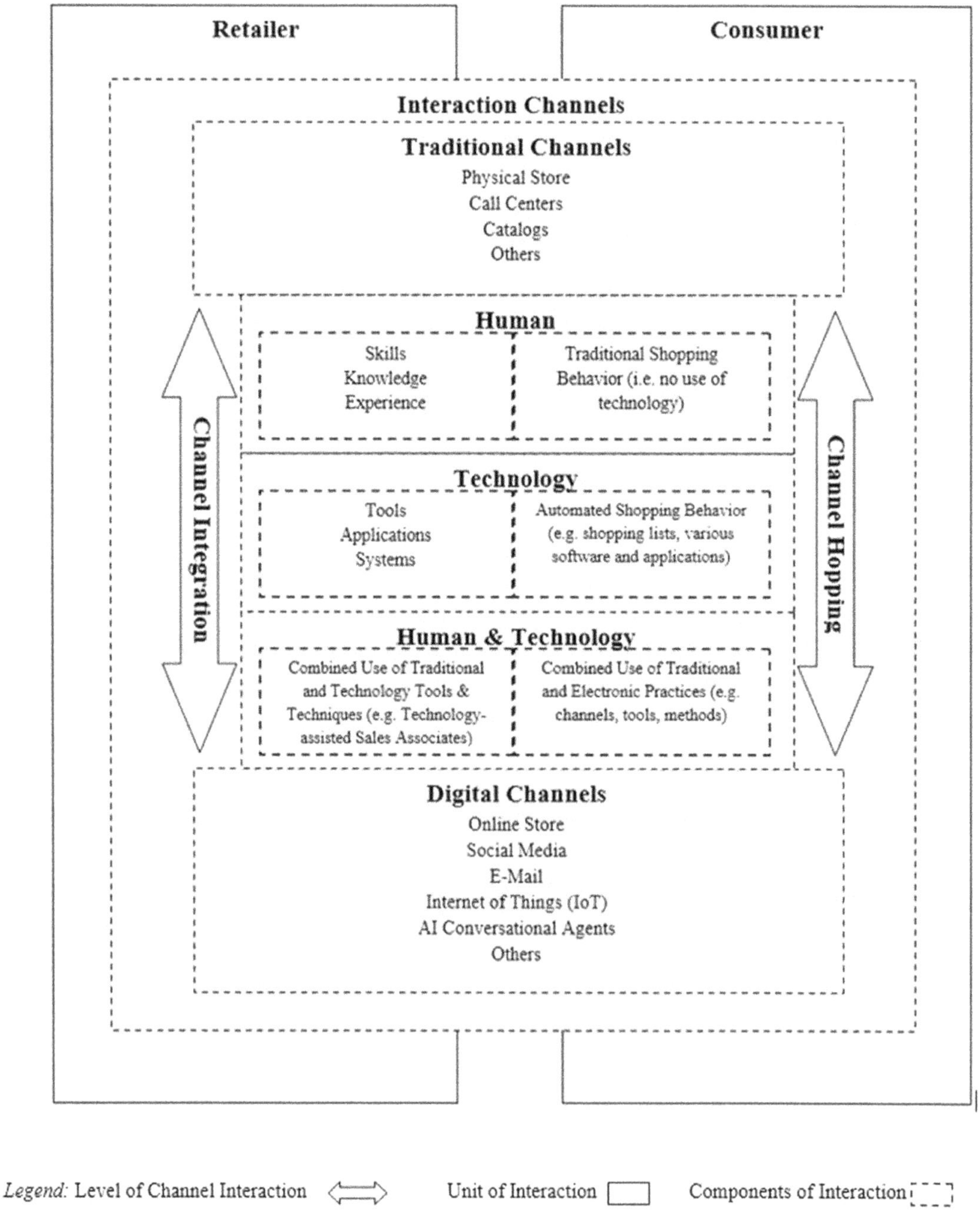

Figure 1 also depicts the plethora of the available interaction channels between retailers and consumers, as well as the potential combinations of interactions between the retailer and the consumer components (e.g., human-to-human, human-to-technology, etc.). Therefore, Figure 1 puts forward the optimal blend of current and new knowledge, skills and experience as reflected in Marketing strategies, as well as practices and technology applications, systems, and tools, towards satisfying the end customer in the context of a mutual relationship beyond channels. Although the latter remain as interaction points assisting the flow of the shopping journey, the focus is transferred to the resulting Retailer-Consumer brand experience. As such, this blending of human and technology would be able to cope from the simplest (pure human at physical stores or through other channels) to the most complicated (human/technology combinations at omnichannel) retail scenarios. Figure 1 posits that whatever the combination is, retailer-consumer interactions should be optimized even at a pure human retailer-consumer level. For example, during that specific interaction these two actors should not neglect other instances of the shopping journey or phases of the consumer decision process. So, to optimize the blending, all possible interactions should be considered, even the basic ones. On the other hand, a mobile-assisted shopper performing showrooming in a physical store could be better served with a front-line employee who leverages both real time and historical CRM data and mobile devices, in order to offer the best offerings and support in a personalized manner at the consumer's channel of choice (e.g., provide online price matching from the store's web channel). Similarly, this scenario can be also applied from distance without the need of the customer to visit the physical store. In this context, Hochstein et al. (2021) found that each type of consumer requires a different approach by frontline employees to improve willingness to buy and acceptance of shopping recommendations.

IMPLICATIONS

Providing an "anthropocentric" approach to the retail sector undeniably requires large-scale investments in training and education and/or in the employment of experienced salespeople. Knowing better your customers is crucial for designing an effective retail mix offering. Retailers should be aware of how their customers feel and think, what they say, what they do, etc. (e.g., analyze and exploit personas through empathy maps, Net Promoter Score (NPS), shopping missions, customer journeys, etc.) when they visit (or before and after their visit) either the physical or the electronic retail store (or other channels - e.g., call centers) or, at the same time, both of them (e.g., mobile access to the e-shop of the retailer while in-store, access to the 3D web store of the retailer when talking to a salesperson through the telephone).

The fact is that Digital Technologies (e.g., AI, conversational agents, CRM platforms, IVR systems, self-checkout shops, etc.) could efficiently and at low cost substitute several elements of the human expertise, knowledge, and skills. Also, continuous adoption of innovative "high-tech" solutions positively contributes to the brand image of the retailer. However, since some elements of the retailer-consumer interaction cannot be totally replaced by Digital Technologies, retailers should also continuously invest in human resources. For example, in the context of customer service though call centers, in several instances, consumers negatively react when they must wait a long timc (and even being charged for that through their telecom provider), in order to talk to a physical agent. Also, the emerging showrooming phenomenon could be effectively treated through personal selling. To this end, Lee (2018) report that it seems that while striving to leverage the potential of technology, retailers are losing sight of the humanity of the retail experience.

Moreover, while social distancing at the age of COVID-19 urges for distant shopping alternatives, retailers should reinforce the social bonding with their customers even more. Salespeople could leverage advanced CRM facilities (e.g., customer support business intelligence & analytics), taking advantage of social media communication (e.g., messengers with voice and video support), while keep assisting consumers even with the traditional call-centers (e.g., serve consumers that do not have Internet access or are not familiar with it or, simply, they "don't like it"). However, retailers should always take advantage of all channels simultaneously: even when using the call-center, customer support should take into consideration the online environment (web store), as well as the 360° view of the customer (utilizing both online and offline data), catering for his/her specific needs. Moreover, in this way, social distancing would not translate to social interruption and loss of the human ingredient of retail communications.

Front-line employees should evolve in an omnichannel manner, keeping up with consumers. They should also be mobile device-assisted (in case of the physical store), leveraging data from all channels even in real time, as well as entering data (either in the physical store or from distance) regarding the behavior of their customers through easy-to-use digital templates (e.g., provided through tablets or mobile phones), always following Permission Marketing guidelines and legal frameworks concerning consumer data collection and exploitation. Furthermore, they should be able to check and locate out-of-stock items when the consumer wants to make a purchase, as well provide accurate information about product availability (e.g., specific time slots that the specific product(s) will be available at the specific store). The latter, however, calls for integrated supply chain management systems that enable continuous information flow along the value chain for this service to be provided in a reliable manner and meet consumer expectations. While this option, in several instances, seems unrealistic today due to the sudden change in distance shopping demand (and corresponding last mile delivery needs) caused by the COVID-19 pandemic, it should be treated with caution in the near future (Gielens et al., 2021).

Moreover, retailers should provide assisted selling, exploiting all available channels and intelligent recommendations, improving customer engagement and nurturing loyalty and retention. For example, Boots (UK retailer) launched an IBM-powered Sales Assist app that allow employees to access online inventory and locate products on the behalf of shoppers (Goodfellow, 2016). That app uses analytics to empower salespeople to make personal recommendations to customers, whereas it is also planned to integrate cognitive data and AI to support the customer journey. Besides, digital technologies at the hands of sales associates (either in the physical store or online / from distance) could also educate (e.g., online training material) and incentivize sales associates (e.g., providing performance points and badges through gamification).

Furthermore, while the review of best practices is critical, emphasis should be based on testing the suitability of these practices to the specific context where they will be applied (e.g., business sector, culture, maturity towards using technology for all the value chain players, strategic marketing planning of the retailer), to appropriately adjust them. Li et al. (2018, p.12) report that "retailers therefore should consider the effects of competitors' channel offerings and tailor their channel strategies to accommodate the various needs of new and existing customers, when they plan to introduce a new online channel". In this context, Jocevski et al. (2019) provided a thorough analysis regarding the transition towards omnichannel strategies.

Lashkova et al. (2020) suggest that retailers should surprise customers and offer new experiences to them. Thus, the provision of value-added services through the alternative interaction channels seems a quite promising business strategy towards positively affecting consumer enthusiasm and shopping experience. In other words, these "new experiences" reported by Lashkova et al. (2020), may not necessarily refer only to the adoption of innovative technologies and attractive electronic services, but also to some critical non-technological aspects (e.g., emotional intelligence). Retailers could also explore ways to offer attractive customer services *from distance* and new customer experiences through simulating physical store environments on other channels (e.g. 3D/VR technology, gamification, video-assisted distance selling).

CONCLUDING REMARKS AND FUTURE RESEARCH

The need for further optimizing the blending of human and technology in retail, may lead to the introduction of significant innovative business practices that will generate new thinking, questioning and reconsideration of how to properly combine technology with humans. In the same vein, traditional marketing practices that proved effective through the time should not be neglected and totally replaced by technology, despite the high cost they usually entail.

Future research should emphasize on designing and testing human-centric services/approaches against real customers focusing on different business sectors, cultures, channels, etc. For example, surveys through questionnaires could reveal the importance consumers attach to specific "anthropocentric" services/offerings and how they evaluate current business practices regarding these services/offerings. Based on the results of such empirical studies, specific strategies for changing consumer attitudes could be effectively fueled. Also, experimental design settings could provide useful insights regarding cause-and-effect relationships between "humanized" services/offerings and critical consumer behavior variables.

Also, future research could elaborate more on how a human-centric omnichannel retailing philosophy could contribute towards providing an optimum customer experience through multiple and combined retailer-consumer interaction points in the context of the customer journey across channels.

Finally, a top and urgent research priority is to investigate through various perspectives and approaches how Omnichannel Retailing could contribute to the society by providing direct and practical solutions to the problems caused by the COVID-19 pandemic. The present chapter attempted to contribute to that direction by raising various critical issues and thinking that may generate useful practical and research initiatives in the post COVID-19 era. To this end, the work of Das et al. (2021) on the pandemic effects on Marketing, also provides a series of challenging future research opportunities on that topic.

Funding: This research was funded by Athens University of Economics and Business Research Center, as part of the Action 2 Initiative (Strengthening Research at the Athens University of Economics and Business with a view to Extroversion and Excellence).

REFERENCES

Ahearne, M., Atefi, Y., Lam, S. K., & Pourmasoudi, M. (2022). The future of buyer–seller interactions: A conceptual framework and research agenda. *Journal of the Academy of Marketing Science*, *50*(1), 22–45. doi:10.100711747-021-00803-0 PMID:34608341

Altıntaş, M. H., Kılıç, S., & Akhan, C. E. (2019). The transformation of the e-tailing field: A bibliometric analysis. *International Journal of Retail & Distribution Management*, *48*(2), 152–168. doi:10.1108/IJRDM-10-2018-0232

Andersen, P., Weisstein, F. L., & Song, L. (2020). Consumer response to marketing channels: A demand-based approach. *Journal of Marketing Channels*, *26*(1), 43–59. doi:10.1080/1046669X.2019.1657736

Aw, E. C. X. (2019). Understanding the webrooming phenomenon: Shopping motivation, channel-related benefits and costs. *International Journal of Retail & Distribution Management*, *47*(10), 1074–1092. doi:10.1108/IJRDM-01-2019-0026

Barwitz, N., & Maas, P. (2018). Understanding the Omnichannel Customer Journey: Determinants of Interaction Choice. *Journal of Interactive Marketing*, *43*, 116–133. doi:10.1016/j.intmar.2018.02.001

Benedetto, C. (2018). *Is Omnichannel Sales Killing the Need for Sales Reps?* MarTech Series. https://martechseries.com/mts-insights/guest-authors/is-omnichannel-sales-killing-the-need-for-sales-reps/

Bertrandie, L., & Zielke, S. (2019). The influence of multi-channel pricing strategy on price fairness and customer confusion. *International Review of Retail, Distribution and Consumer Research*, *29*(5), 504–517. doi:10.1080/09593969.2019.1664611

Chen, L., Hsieh, P.-A., Rai, A., & Xu, S. X. (2021). How Does Employee Infusion Use of CRM Systems Drive Customer Satisfaction? Mechanism Differences Between Face-to-Face and Virtual Channels. *Management Information Systems Quarterly*, *45*(2), 719–754. doi:10.25300/MISQ/2021/13265

Clarke, D., & Kinghorn, R. (2018). *Experience Is Everything, PwC*. https://www.pwc.com/us/en/services/consulting/library/consumer-intelligence-series/future-of-customer-experience.html

Cui, T. H., Ghose, A., Halaburda, H., Iyengar, R., Pauwels, K., Sriram, S., Tucker, C., & Venkataraman, S. (2021). Informational Challenges in Omnichannel Marketing: Remedies and Future Research. *Journal of Marketing*, *85*(1), 103–120. doi:10.1177/0022242920968810

Das, G., Jain, S. P., Maheswaran, D., Slotegraaf, R. J., & Srinivasan, R. (2021). Pandemics and marketing: Insights, impacts, and research opportunities. *Journal of the Academy of Marketing Science*, *49*(5), 835–854. doi:10.100711747-021-00786-y PMID:33994600

Daunt, K. L., & Harris, L. C. (2017). Consumer showrooming: Value co-destruction. *Journal of Retailing and Consumer Services*, *38*, 166–176. doi:10.1016/j.jretconser.2017.05.013

Delpechitre, D., Beeler-Connelly, L. L., & Chaker, N. N. (2018). Customer value co-creation behavior: A dyadic exploration of the influence of salesperson emotional intelligence on customer participation and citizenship behavior. *Journal of Business Research*, *92*, 9–24. doi:10.1016/j.jbusres.2018.05.007

Dimitrova, B. V., Smith, B., & Andras, T. L. (2020). Marketing channel evolution: From contactual efficiency to brand value co-creation and appropriation within the platform enterprise. *Journal of Marketing Channels*, *26*(1), 60–71. doi:10.1080/1046669X.2019.1646187

Elmashhara, M. G., & Soares, A. M. (2019). The impact of entertainment and social interaction with salespeople on mall shopper satisfaction: The mediating role of emotional states. *International Journal of Retail & Distribution Management*, *47*(2), 94–110. doi:10.1108/IJRDM-06-2018-0112

Esmark, C. L., & Noble, S. M. (2016). Retail space invaders: When employees' invasion of customer space increases purchase intentions. *Journal of the Academy of Marketing Science*, *46*(3), 1–20.

Ewerhard, A.-C., Sisovsky, K., & Johansson, U. (2019). Consumer decision-making of slow moving consumer goods in the age of multi-channels. *International Review of Retail, Distribution and Consumer Research, 29*(1), 1–22. doi:10.1080/09593969.2018.1537191

Fergurson, J. R. (2020). The paradox of diminishing returns: Measurement and metrics for valuation of B2C sales professionals. *Journal of Marketing Channels, 26*(2), 141–146. doi:10.1080/1046669X.2020.1747280

Fernández, N. V., Pérez, M. J. S., & Vázquez-Casielles, R. (2018). Webroomers versus showroomers: Are they the same? *Journal of Business Research, 92*, 300–320. doi:10.1016/j.jbusres.2018.08.004

Frasquet, M., & Miquel, M. J. (2017). Do channel integration efforts pay-off in terms of online and offline customer loyalty? *International Journal of Retail & Distribution Management, 45*(7–8), 859–873. doi:10.1108/IJRDM-10-2016-0175

Fügener, A., Grahl, J., Gupta, A., and Ketter, W. (2021). Will Humans-in-the-Loop Become Borgs? Merits and Pitfalls of Working with AI. *Management Information Systems Quarterly (MISQ), 45*(b), 1527-1556.

Gauri, D. K., Jindal, R. P., Ratchford, B., Fox, E., Bhatnagar, A., Pandey, A., Navallo, R. J., Fogarty, J., Carr, S., & Hwerton, E. (2021). Evolution of retail formats: Past, present, and future. *Journal of Retailing, 97*(1), 42–61. doi:10.1016/j.jretai.2020.11.002

Gielens, K., Gijsbrechts, E., & Geyskens, I. (2021). Navigating the Last Mile: The Demand Effects of Click-and-Collect Order Fulfillment. *Journal of Marketing, 85*(4), 158–178. doi:10.1177/0022242920960430

Goodfellow, J. (2016). *Boots launches IBM-powered Sales Assist app, laying down the foundations of its omnichannel strategy.* https://www.thedrum.com/news/2016/06/22/boots-launches-ibm-powered-sales-assist-app-laying-down-foundations-its-omnichannel

Grewal, D., Gauri, D. K., Roggeveen, A. L., & Sethuraman, R. (2021). Strategizing Retailing in the New Technology Era. *Journal of Retailing, 97*(1), 6–12. doi:10.1016/j.jretai.2021.02.004

Grewal, D., Noble, S. M., Roggeveen, A. L., & Nordfalt, J. (2020). The future of in-store technology. *Journal of the Academy of Marketing Science, 48*(1), 96–113. doi:10.100711747-019-00697-z

Grewal, D., Roggeveen, A. L., Nordfält, J., & Roggeveen, L. (2017). The Future of Retailing. *Journal of Retailing, 93*(1), 1–6. doi:10.1016/j.jretai.2016.12.008

Groza, M. D., & Groza, M. P. (2018). Salesperson regulatory knowledge and sales performance. *Journal of Business Research, 89*, 37–46. doi:10.1016/j.jbusres.2018.04.005

Guha, A., Grewal, D., Kopalle, P. K., Haenlein, M., Schneider, M. J., Jung, H., Moustafa, R., Hegde, D. R., & Hawkins, G. (2021). How artificial intelligence will affect the future of retailing. *Journal of Retailing, 97*(1), 28–41. doi:10.1016/j.jretai.2021.01.005

Gupta, S., & Ramachandran, D. (2021). Emerging Market Retail: Transitioning from a Product-Centric to a Customer-Centric Approach. *Journal of Retailing, 97*(4), 597–620. doi:10.1016/j.jretai.2021.01.008

Heathwood, W. (2018). *Physical Retail Isn't Dead: It's Working With Tech to Be More Human-Focused – Adweek*. https://www.adweek.com/brand-marketing/physical-retail-isnt-dead-its-working-with-tech-to-be-more-human-focused/

Hickman, E., Kharouf, H., & Sekhon, H. (2020). An omnichannel approach to retailing: Demystifying and identifying the factors influencing an omnichannel experience. *International Review of Retail, Distribution and Consumer Research*, *30*(3), 266–288. doi:10.1080/09593969.2019.1694562

Ho, S. Y., & Lim, K. H. (2018). Nudging moods to induce unplanned purchases in imperfect mobile personalization contexts. *MIS Quarterly: Management Information Systems*, *42*(3), 757–778. doi:10.25300/MISQ/2018/14083

Hochstein, B., Bolander, W., Bolander, B., Pratt, A. B., & Reynolds, K. (2021). An Investigation of Consumer Subjective Knowledge in Frontline Interactions. *Journal of Retailing*, *97*(3), 336–346. doi:10.1016/j.jretai.2020.10.003

Hochstein, B., Bolander, W., Goldsmith, R., & Plouffe, C. R. (2019). Adapting influence approaches to informed consumers in high-involvement purchases: Are salespeople really doomed? *Journal of the Academy of Marketing Science*, *47*(1), 118–137. doi:10.100711747-018-0609-2

Hoffman, D. L., Moreau, C. P., Stremersch, S., & Wedel, M. (2022). The Rise of New Technologies in Marketing: A Framework and Outlook. *Journal of Marketing*, *86*(1), 1–6. doi:10.1177/00222429211061636

Hoffman, D. L., & Novak, T. P. (2018). Consumer and Object Experience in the Internet of Things: An Assemblage Theory Approach, edited by Fischer, E. and Kozinets, R. Journal of Consumer Research, 44(6), 1178–1204.

Honeycutt, E. D. Jr. (2005). Technology improves sales performance—doesn't it?: An introduction to the special issue on selling and sales technology. *Industrial Marketing Management*, *34*(4), 301–304. doi:10.1016/j.indmarman.2004.12.002

Huang, S.-C. (2018). Social Information Avoidance: When, why, and how it is Costly in Goal Pursuit. *JMR, Journal of Marketing Research*, *55*(3), 382–395. doi:10.1509/jmr.16.0268

Hult, G. T. M., Sharma, P. N., Morgeson, F. V. III, & Zhang, Y. (2019). Antecedents and Consequences of Customer Satisfaction: Do They Differ Across Online and Offline Purchases? *Journal of Retailing*, *95*(1), 10–23. doi:10.1016/j.jretai.2018.10.003

Hüseyinoğlu Yumurtacı, I. Ö., Galipoğlu, E., & Kotzab, H. (2017). Social, local and mobile commerce practices in omni-channel retailing. *International Journal of Retail & Distribution Management*, *45*(7/8), 711–729. doi:10.1108/IJRDM-09-2016-0151

Jocevski, M., Arvidsson, N., Miragliotta, G., Ghezzi, A., & Mangiaracina, R. (2019). Transitions towards omni-channel retailing strategies: A business model perspective. *International Journal of Retail & Distribution Management*, *47*(2), 78–93. doi:10.1108/IJRDM-08-2018-0176

Kalyani, V., & Saravanan, R. (2020). Does spiritual intelligence contribute to sales force effectiveness? *International Journal of Electronic Marketing and Retailing*, *11*(4), 352–368. doi:10.1504/IJEMR.2020.111157

Kang, J.-Y. M. (2018). Showrooming, Webrooming, and User-Generated Content Creation in the Omnichannel Era. *Journal of Internet Commerce, 17*(2), 145–169. doi:10.1080/15332861.2018.1433907

Kannan, P. K. K., & Li, H. (2017). Digital marketing: A framework, review and research agenda. *International Journal of Research in Marketing, 34*(1), 22–45. doi:10.1016/j.ijresmar.2016.11.006

Kats, R. (2019). *What Makes a Bad Shopping Experience? Customers Bring Different Expectations to in-Store and Ecommerce Interactions*. https://www.emarketer.com/content/what-makes-a-bad-shopping-experience

Khoshtaria, T., Matin, A., Mercan, M., & Datuashvili, D. (2021). The impact of customers' purchasing patterns on their showrooming and webrooming behaviour: An empirical evidence from the Georgian retail sector. *International Journal of Electronic Marketing and Retailing, 12*(4), 394. doi:10.1504/IJEMR.2021.118305

Kidwell, B., Hasford, J., Turner, B., Hardesty, D., & Zablah, A. R. (2021). Emotional Calibration and Salesperson Performance. *Journal of Marketing, 85*(6), 141–161. doi:10.1177/0022242921999603

Kim, B., & Park, M. J. (2019). An Examination of the Effect of Consumer Personal Traits on Show Rooming Behavior: The Effect of Product Type. *Journal of Internet Commerce, 18*(1), 24–44. doi:10.1080/15332861.2018.1547569

Kirk, C. P., & Rifkin, L. S. (2020). I'll trade you diamonds for toilet paper: Consumer reacting, coping and adapting behaviors in the COVID-19 pandemic. *Journal of Business Research, 117*, 124–131. doi:10.1016/j.jbusres.2020.05.028 PMID:32834208

Krasonikolakis, I., Vrechopoulos, A., Pouloudi, A., & Dimitriadis, S. (2018). Store layout effects on consumer behavior in 3D online stores. *European Journal of Marketing, 52*(5/6), 1223–1256. doi:10.1108/EJM-03-2015-0183

Kuksov, D., & Liao, C. (2018). When Showrooming Increases Retailer Profit. *JMR, Journal of Marketing Research, 55*(4), 459–473. doi:10.1509/jmr.17.0059

Kumar, V., & Venkatesan, R. (2021). Transformation of Metrics and Analytics in Retailing: The Way Forward. *Journal of Retailing, 97*(4), 496–506. doi:10.1016/j.jretai.2021.11.004

Lashkova, M., Antón, C., & Camarero, C. (2019). Dual effect of sensory experience: Engagement vs diversive exploration. *International Journal of Retail & Distribution Management, 48*(2), 128–151. doi:10.1108/IJRDM-09-2018-0204

Lawrence, J. M., Scheer, L. K., Crecelius, A. T., & Lam, S. K. (2021). Salesperson Dual Agency in Price Negotiations. *Journal of Marketing, 85*(2), 89–109. doi:10.1177/0022242920974611

Lazaris, C., Sarantopoulos, P., Vrechopoulos, A., & Doukidis, G. (2021). Effects of Increased Omnichannel Integration on Customer Satisfaction and Loyalty Intentions. *International Journal of Electronic Commerce, 25*(4), 440–468. doi:10.1080/10864415.2021.1967005

Lechner, A. T., & Paul, M. (2019). Is this smile for real? The role of affect and thinking style in customer perceptions of frontline employee emotion authenticity. *Journal of Business Research, 94*, 195–208. doi:10.1016/j.jbusres.2017.06.009

Lee Yohn, D. (2018). *The Future Of Retail CX Is Human.* https://www.forbes.com/sites/deniselyohn/2018/08/22/the-future-of-retail-cx-is-human/#2ec79d931d82

Li, X., & Wu, L. (2018). Herding and social media word-of-mouth: Evidence from Groupon. *MIS Quarterly: Management Information Systems*, *42*(4), 1331–1351.

Lichtenthaler, U. (2018). Substitute or Synthesis: The Interplay between Human and Artificial Intelligence. *Research Technology Management*, *61*(5), 12–14. doi:10.1080/08956308.2018.1495962

Lin, Z., & Wang, Q. (2018). E-commerce Product Networks, Word-of-mouth Convergence, and Product Sales. *Journal of the Association for Information Systems*, *19*(1), 23–39. doi:10.17705/1jais.00481

Lobaugh, K., Simpson, J., & Ohri, L. (2015). *Navigating the New Digital Divide: Capitalizing on Digital Influence in Retail.* https://www2.deloitte.com/content/dam/Deloitte/us/Documents/consumer-business/us-cb-navigating-the-new-digital-divide-v2-051315.pdf

Loupiac, P., & Goudey, A. (2019). How website browsing impacts expectations of store features. *International Journal of Retail & Distribution Management*, *48*(1), 92–108. doi:10.1108/IJRDM-07-2018-0146

Luna-Nevarez, C., & McGovern, E. (2021). The Rise of the Virtual Reality (VR) Marketplace: Exploring the Antecedents and Consequences of Consumer Attitudes toward V-Commerce. *Journal of Internet Commerce*, *20*(2), 167–194. doi:10.1080/15332861.2021.1875766

Mahardika, H., Thomas, D., Ewing, M. T., & Japutra, A. (2019). Experience and facilitating conditions as impediments to consumers' new technology adoption. *International Review of Retail, Distribution and Consumer Research*, *29*(1), 79–98. doi:10.1080/09593969.2018.1556181

Maier, E., & Wieringa, J. (2021). Acquiring customers through online marketplaces? The effect of marketplace sales on sales in a retailer's own channels. *International Journal of Research in Marketing*, *38*(2), 311–328. doi:10.1016/j.ijresmar.2020.09.007

Mainardes, E. W., & Cardoso, M. V. (2019). Effect of the use of social media in trust, loyalty and purchase intention in physical stores. *International Review of Retail, Distribution and Consumer Research*, *29*(4), 456–477. doi:10.1080/09593969.2019.1583593

Manss, R., Kurze, K., & Bornschein, R. (2020). What drives competitive webrooming? The roles of channel and retailer aspects. *International Review of Retail, Distribution and Consumer Research*, *30*(3), 233–265. doi:10.1080/09593969.2019.1687104

Marinova, D., Singh, S. K., & Singh, J. (2018). Frontline Problem-Solving Effectiveness: A Dynamic Analysis of Verbal and Nonverbal Cues. *JMR, Journal of Marketing Research*, *55*(2), 178–192. doi:10.1509/jmr.15.0243

Mero, J. (2018). The effects of two-way communication and chat service usage on consumer attitudes in the e-commerce retailing sector. *Electronic Markets*, *28*(2), 205–217. doi:10.100712525-017-0281-2

Mintz, O., Gilbride, T. J., Lenk, P., & Currim, I. S. (2021). The right metrics for marketing-mix decisions. *International Journal of Research in Marketing*, *38*(1), 32–49. doi:10.1016/j.ijresmar.2020.08.003

Múgica, J. M., & Berné, C. (2019). Analyzing channel choice: Direct and indirect e-Tourism distribution. *International Review of Retail, Distribution and Consumer Research*, *29*(5), 537–548. doi:10.1080/09593969.2019.1664617

Nass, O., Garrigós, J. A., Gómez, H. G., & Schoeneberg, K. P. (2020). Attribution modelling in an omnichannel environment – New requirements and specifications from a practical perspective. *International Journal of Electronic Marketing and Retailing*, *11*(1), 81–111. doi:10.1504/IJEMR.2020.106432

Ng, I. C. L., & Wakenshaw, S. Y. L. (2017). The Internet-of-Things: Review and research directions. *International Journal of Research in Marketing*, *34*(1), 3–21. doi:10.1016/j.ijresmar.2016.11.003

Nüesch, R., Alt, R., & Puschmann, T. (2015). Hybrid Customer Interaction. *Business & Information Systems Engineering*, *57*(1), 73–78. doi:10.100712599-014-0366-9

Ortlinghaus, A., & Zielke, S. (2019). Designing multi-channel technologies – the mediating role of risk perceptions. *International Review of Retail, Distribution and Consumer Research*, *29*(5), 518–536. doi:10.1080/09593969.2019.1664610

Pantano, E., Pizzi, G., Scarpi, D., & Dennis, C. (2020). Competing during a pandemic? Retailers' ups and downs during the COVID-19 outbreak. *Journal of Business Research*, *116*, 209–213. doi:10.1016/j.jbusres.2020.05.036 PMID:32501307

Pantano, E., Priporas, C. V., & Dennis, C. (2018). A new approach to retailing for successful competition in the new smart scenario. *International Journal of Retail & Distribution Management*, *46*(3), 264–282. doi:10.1108/IJRDM-04-2017-0080

Picot-Coupey, K., Huré, E., & Piveteau, L. (2016). Channel design to enrich customers' shopping experiences: Synchronizing clicks with bricks in an omni-channel perspective - the Direct Optic case. *International Journal of Retail & Distribution Management*, *44*(3), 336–368. doi:10.1108/IJRDM-04-2015-0056

Rapp, A., Baker, T. L., Bachrach, D. G., Ogilvie, J., & Beitelspacher, L. S. (2015). Perceived customer showrooming behavior and the effect on retail salesperson self-efficacy and performance. *Journal of Retailing*, *91*(2), 358–369. doi:10.1016/j.jretai.2014.12.007

Rigby, D. (2011). The Future of Shopping. *Harvard Business Review*, *89*(12), 64–75.

Rippé, C. B., Smith, B., & Dubinsky, A. J. (2018). Lonely consumers and their friend the retail salesperson. *Journal of Business Research*, *92*, 131–141. doi:10.1016/j.jbusres.2018.07.013

Röding, T., Nimmermann, F., Steinmann, S., & Schramm-Klein, H. (2019). The influence of technology infusion on customers' information disclosure behaviour within the frontline service encounter. *International Review of Retail, Distribution and Consumer Research*, *29*(5), 482–503. doi:10.1080/09593969.2019.1664612

Roggeveen, A. L., Grewal, D., & Schweiger, E. B. (2020). The DAST Framework for Retail Atmospherics: The Impact of In- and Out-of-Store Retail Journey Touchpoints on the Customer Experience. *Journal of Retailing*, *96*(1), 128–137. doi:10.1016/j.jretai.2019.11.002

Roggeveen, A. L., & Sethuraman, R. (2020). How the COVID-19 Pandemic May Change the World of Retailing. *Journal of Retailing*, *96*(2), 169–171. doi:10.1016/j.jretai.2020.04.002

Rust, R. T. (2019). The future of marketing. *International Journal of Research in Marketing*, *37*(1), 15–26. doi:10.1016/j.ijresmar.2019.08.002

Sahu, K. C., Naved Khan, M., & Das Gupta, K. (2021). Determinants of Webrooming and Showrooming Behavior: A Systematic Literature Review. *Journal of Internet Commerce*, *20*(2), 137–166. doi:10.1080/15332861.2020.1863041

Savastano, M., Bellini, F., D'Ascenzo, F., & De Marco, M. (2019). Technology adoption for the integration of online–offline purchasing. *International Journal of Retail & Distribution Management*, *47*(5), 474–492. doi:10.1108/IJRDM-12-2018-0270

Shankar, V., Kalyanam, K., Setia, P., Golmohammadi, A., Tirunillai, S., Douglass, T., Hennessey, J., Bull, J. S., & Waddoups, R. (2021). How Technology is Changing Retail. *Journal of Retailing*, *97*(1), 13–27. doi:10.1016/j.jretai.2020.10.006

Shankar, V., & Kushwaha, T. (2021). Omnichannel marketing: Are cross-channel effects symmetric? *International Journal of Research in Marketing*, *38*(2), 290–310. doi:10.1016/j.ijresmar.2020.09.001

Shavitt, S., & Barnes, A. J. (2020). Culture and the Consumer Journey. *Journal of Retailing*, *96*(1), 40–54. doi:10.1016/j.jretai.2019.11.009

Sheth, J. (2020). Impact of Covid-19 on consumer behavior: Will the old habits return or die? *Journal of Business Research*, *117*, 280–283. doi:10.1016/j.jbusres.2020.05.059 PMID:32536735

Silva, S. C., Martins, C. C., & Sousa, J. M. (2018). Omnichannel approach: Factors affecting consumer acceptance. *Journal of Marketing Channels*, *25*(1–2), 73–84. doi:10.1080/1046669X.2019.1647910

Sousa, M. J., & Rocha, Á. (2019). Skills for disruptive digital business. *Journal of Business Research*, *94*, 257–263. doi:10.1016/j.jbusres.2017.12.051

Spreer, P., & Rauschnabel, P. A. (2016). Selling with technology: Understanding the resistance to mobile sales assistant use in retailing. *Journal of Personal Selling & Sales Management*, *36*(3), 240–263. doi: 10.1080/08853134.2016.1208100

Teller, C., Brusset, X., & Kotzab, H. (2019). Physical and digital market places – where marketing meets operations. *International Journal of Retail & Distribution Management*, *47*(12), 1225–1231. doi:10.1108/IJRDM-12-2019-299

Van Kerrebroeck, H., Willems, K., & Brengman, M. (2017). Touching the void. *International Journal of Retail & Distribution Management*, *45*(7/8), 892–909. doi:10.1108/IJRDM-09-2016-0156

Vera, A. (2017). *Humanizing the retail experience: Experiential shopping lives offline.* https://www.retailcustomerexperience.com/blogs/humanizing-the-retail-experience-experiential-shopping-lives-offline/

Verhoef, P. C., Kannan, P. K., & Inman, J. J. (2015). From Multi-Channel Retailing to Omni-Channel Retailing: Introduction to the Special Issue on Multi-Channel Retailing. *Journal of Retailing*, *91*(2), 174–181. doi:10.1016/j.jretai.2015.02.005

Verhoef, P. C., Stephen, A. T., Kannan, P. K. K., Luo, X., Abhishek, V., Andrews, M., Bart, Y., Datta, H., Fong, N., Hoffman, D. L., Hu, M. M., Novak, T., Rand, W., & Zhang, Y. (2017). Consumer Connectivity in a Complex, Technology-enabled, and Mobile-oriented World with Smart Products. *Journal of Interactive Marketing*, *40*(1), 1–8. doi:10.1016/j.intmar.2017.06.001

Villanova, D., Bodapati, A. V., Puccinelli, N. M., Tsiros, M., Goodstein, R. C., Kushwaha, T., Suri, R., Ho, H., Brandon, R., & Hatfield, C. (2021). Retailer Marketing Communications in the Digital Age: Getting the Right Message to the Right Shopper at the Right Time. *Journal of Retailing*, *97*(1), 116–132. doi:10.1016/j.jretai.2021.02.001

Vrechopoulos, A., Lazaris, C., & Doukidis, G. (2019). From omnichannel retailing to "diachronic retailing": blending digital technologies with traditional marketing strategies and practices. *Proceedings of the 48th Annual European Marketing Academy Conference (EMAC).*

Ward, M. (2017). *Physical store online shopping control.* https://patents.google.com/patent/US9665881B1/en

Wilson, J., & Daugherty, P. (2018). Collaborative intelligence: Humans and AI are joining forces. *Harvard Business Review*, *2018*(July-August), 1–11.

Wright, L. B., Haug, J. C., & Huckabee, A. (2019). Blueprint for Retail Website Design: Attracting and Retaining Millennial Online Shoppers. *Journal of Internet Commerce*, *18*(2), 170–196. doi:10.1080/15332861.2019.1584844

Yumurtacı Hüseyinoğlu, I. Ö., Kotzab, H., Köstepen, K. G., & Halaszovich, T. (2020). Assessing consumer logistics functions in grocery shopping: Evidence from an emerging market. *Journal of Marketing Channels*, *26*(1), 72–86. doi:10.1080/1046669X.2019.1700868

KEY TERMS AND DEFINITIONS

Customer Relationship Management (CRM): Any practice, technology, or strategy designed to help businesses improve their customer relationships. CRM most often refers to the specific tools, usually a web application or software.

Internet of Things (IoT): A system of interconnected devices or objects that communicate over the internet without requiring human-computer interaction.

Live Commerce: The delivery of e-commerce activities and transactions via a live streaming platform.

Live-Selling Commerce: The delivery of e-commerce activities and transactions via live video streaming combined with the ability to interact with sellers in real time.

Net Promoter Score (NPS): A customer loyalty and satisfaction measurement taken from asking customers how likely they are to recommend a product or service to others.

Showrooming: A practice whereby consumers visit a physical retail store to evaluate products/services and then complete their purchase at an online channel.

Social Commerce: The delivery of e-commerce activities and transactions via social media.

Webrooming: A practice whereby consumers visit an online retail store to evaluate products/services and then complete their purchase at a physical retail store.

Chapter 5
Challenges and Emerging Strategies for a Global Automotive Enterprise Towards a Post-COVID-19 Era:
The Impact of Digital Transformation

Antony D. Bolton
https://orcid.org/0000-0002-1259-7479
University of South Africa, South Africa

Leila Goosen
https://orcid.org/0000-0003-4948-2699
University of South Africa, South Africa

Elmarie Kritzinger
https://orcid.org/0000-0002-5141-4348
University of South Africa, South Africa

ABSTRACT

To provide readers with an overview of the content and summarize, the purpose of this chapter is stated as reporting on results with regard to challenges and emerging strategies for a global automotive enterprise towards a post-COVID-19 era, together with the impact of digital transformation on productivity and innovation. One of the objectives of the chapter is to provide an in-depth understanding of various dimensions regarding the focus of this chapter, based on a selection from the recommended topics for the book. Against the background of a global automotive enterprise, the chapter will discuss the scope of challenges and emerging strategies towards developing an understanding of the need for, as well as the employment and adoption of, emerging strategies and their application towards overcoming the challenges brought on by COVID-19.

DOI: 10.4018/978-1-7998-8856-7.ch005

INTRODUCTION

This section will describe the general perspective of the chapter and end by specifically stating the **objective**.

Management methodologies and their applicability in society have changed in the aftermath of COVID-19. Organizations had to adopt new forms of resilience based on the needs of a different consumer; this means that impressions should be applied in a different market. The COVID-19 market is a **challenge** for both producers and consumers because it meets new needs and require new facilities for merchandising. Like the book, this chapter will explore the broad potential of entrepreneurial opportunities and highlighting new business practices and networking activities, possibly resulting in the well-being of millions of people virtually everywhere in a post COVID-19 era.

Data gathered during a study of the General Motors (GM) journey in terms of the **challenges and emerging trends** regarding **strategies for a global automotive enterprise towards a post COVID-19 era** regarding **the impact of digital transformation** is summarized in the chapter. The hypotheses developed in Bolton, Goosen and Kritzinger (2021a) are also reviewed and compared to the analyzed results.

Recommended topics

In line with the **recommended topics** for this book, the chapter will consider topics related to a global automotive organization and market resilience from COVID-19 impact to **solutions**.

Target audience

Like the proposed book, this chapter could serve as an important reference for researchers, teachers, students and others.

Objective

As part of this book, the chapter will explore the impact of COVID-19 on the market and various sectors of the global economy. It also holds a specific focus on a global automotive enterprise towards a post COVID-19 era.

BACKGROUND

This section of the chapter will provide broad definitions and discussions of the topic of **challenges and emerging trends** regarding **strategies for a global automotive enterprise towards a post COVID-19 era** regarding **the impact of digital transformation**, and incorporate the views of others (in the form of a literature review) into the discussion to support, refute, or demonstrate the authors' position on the topic.

General Motors Technology and Service Transformation

The primary subject of an empirical study into the impact of digital transformation on innovation and productivity (Bolton, Goosen, & Kritzinger, 2021b) was the global automotive original equipment manufacturer GM. The case study spanned a period of over five years, including the formative period of transformation definition (*envisioned end-state*), technical service and governance framework development (*how the end-state was delivered*), service and technical deployment (*deployment of the transformed state*) and finally end-user adoption and change evaluation (*transformed end-state outcomes*).

Current and End-State Architecture Analysis

Upon completion of formal stakeholder review and requirements gathering via the process depicted in Figure 1, the desired end-state functionality was summarized and populated within the grid. The transformed technology stack was incrementally populated throughout the initiative as individual system transformations and requirements was established. Specification was achieved through the iterative scope development and deployment timelines discussed in Bolton, Goosen and Kritzinger (2022a).

Figure 1. GM E-UC&C transformation assessment model

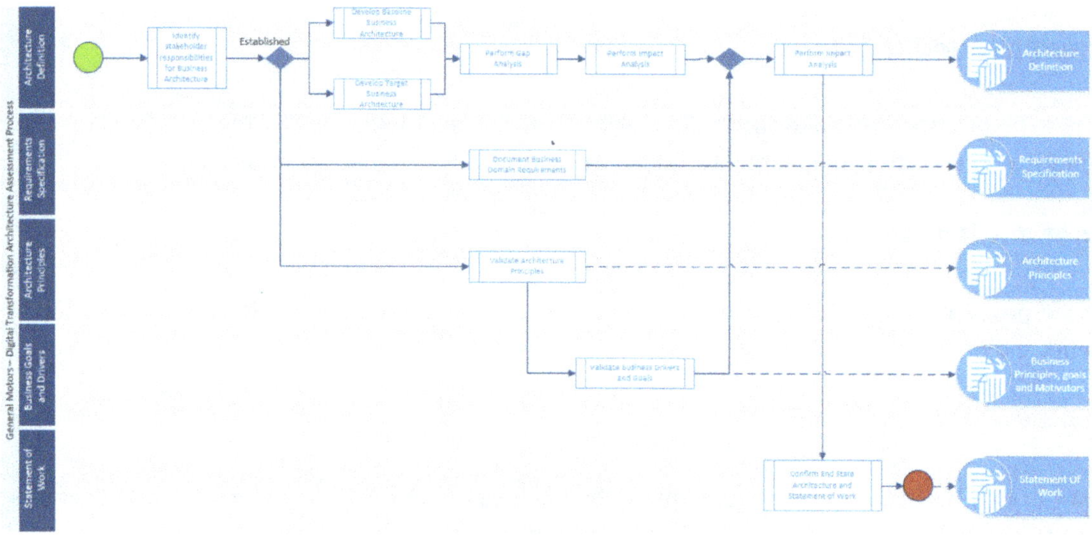

Figure 2 in Bolton, Goosen and Kritzinger (2020a) depicted the scale of the technical and service transformation undertaken within the scope of the GM case study. The transformation grid summarized the findings of the initial current state architectural review carried out in January 2013 and assessment of the target end-state. The method employed to complete the current state assessment leveraged The Open Group Architecture Framework (TOGAF) for capability assessments.

The TOGAF capability assessment includes a review of capabilities inclusive of business capability, IT capability, architecture maturity and business transformation readiness (The Open Group, 2015).

Transformation assessment process

The assessment model delectated in Figure 1 was developed to structure and guide transformation planning and was a key component contributing to the establishment of the Enhanced Unified Communication and Collaboration (E-UC&C) framework. The paper and chapter by Bolton, Goosen and Kritzinger (2016, p. 1) and (2021c) discussed **emerging strategies** regarding the "paradigm of the Internet of Things (IoT), focusing on the important role that people will play in the future connected world of digitized services", and the different concepts and **issues** related to enterprise digitization enablement through UC&C were described. Meanwhile, adequate details about e.g., the architectural framework for E-UC&C were discussed in Bolton, et al. (2020a, p. 103): "The primary domain modules of the E-UC&C framework served as modular reference architectures for service governance, core technology services, service integration and service operation."

This model structured the process of stakeholder identification, baselining of the current state and target state architecture and alignment to the business stakeholder requirements and goals. Bryson and Alston (2011) highlighted the importance of stakeholder identification and strategy formulation in the establishment of **emerging strategies**.

This process resulted in the establishment of key artefacts, which could be leveraged as criteria and guidelines for selection and implementation in the subsequent detailed system design and transformation evaluation (Goosen, 2004). These artefacts included the high-level system architecture

Figure 2. GM E-UC&C transformation assessment and asset model

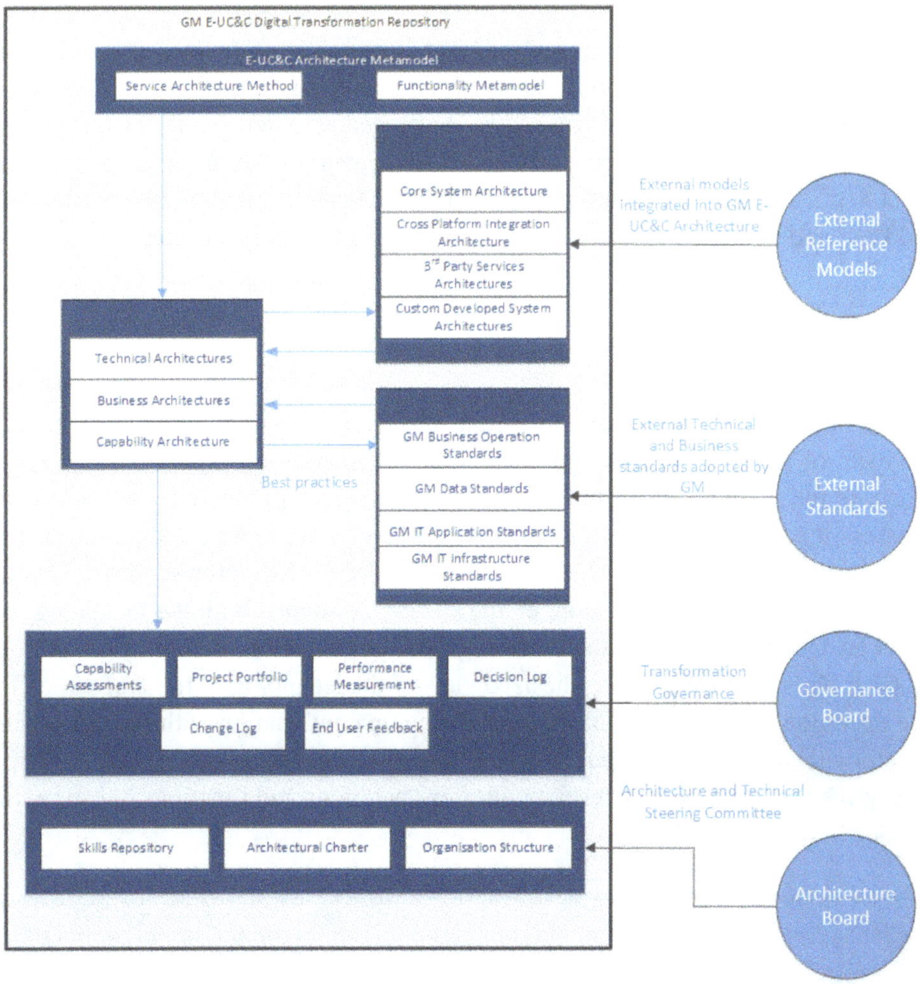

definition, business and end-user requirements specification, business and Information and Communication Technology (ICT) architectural principles and the target state statement of work. The establishment and execution of this process was a crucial step in the process of translating the non-technical aspirational end-state as expressed by GM business functions into a technical framework as expressed through the E-UC&C technologies.

The resulting statement of work was applied within the structure of the E-UC&C framework via an iterative process as outlined in Bolton, et al. (2022a) to optimize the outcomes of the digital transformation initiative on end-user communication and alignment with business goals and **objectives**. Keyes (2016) argued that risk avoidance can be achieved by establishing and assessing critical success factors and ensuring team members not only understand the business goals, but also the processes required to achieve these. The established statement of work as in the transformation assessment model was leveraged as a method of formal alignment within the transformation governance process between the Information Technology (IT) organization, executive and business unit stakeholders. Saladis and Kerzner (2009) highlighted the importance of executive sponsors understanding the structure and value of Statements of Work (SoW). Saladis and Kerzner (2009) also argued the importance of the relationship between the technical **objectives** that are established in the SoW and business objectives at a senior management level.

Transformation asset repository

Figure 2 depicts the transformation asset repository that was established to track all architecture, requirements and government assets and documentation developed throughout the multi-year transformation initiative. The metamodel depicted in Figure 2 was leveraged as a framework for the establishment of a logical assets storage and sharing repository and management of "information affordance" (Dikbas & Scherer, 2004, p. 788). The repository was created with Microsoft SharePoint and included features, such as workflow and author tracking, as well as approval for documentation creation, modification and deletion.

Transformed End-state Services

The E-UC&C framework designed within the scope of the research study was leveraged to design and guide deployment of a digital transformation technologies service eco-system across the GM enterprise. The focus of the study was the resulting impact on perceived productivity and ability to innovate. In order to assess this impact, the services had first to be deployed and the digital transformation of communication processes completed. The framework developed within the scope of the study and the associated deployment discussed in Bolton, et al. (2022a), combined with the technology and service transformation grid, served to convey the broad digital transformation of communication services applied within GM. Figure 3 provides a synthesized view of the technologies transformation that directly impacted the operation of end-users. This representation, in combination with the transformation grid, was influenced by the *IT strategic impact grid* of Nolan and McFarlan (2005). While there are many underlying services supporting the upper tier end user operations and functions, those services remain primarily hidden to the user.

Figure 3. Digital transformations directly affecting end-user C&C functions

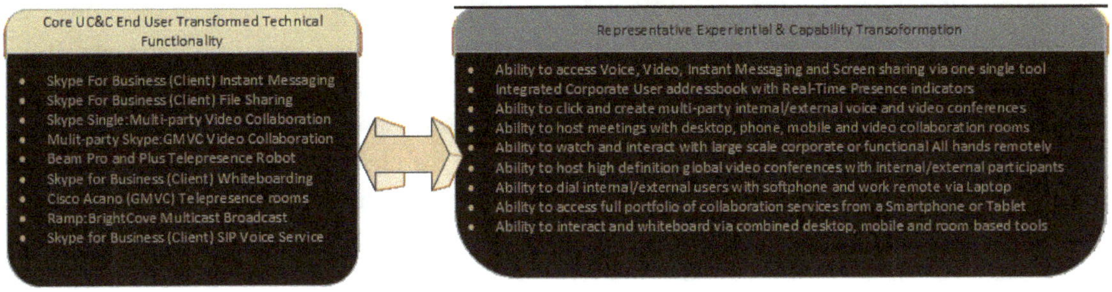

The services outlined in the technical functionality column in Figure 3 aligns with the associated functional communication outcome from an end-user perspective. These functions were assessed and analyzed in the subsequent post-deployment survey and interview process to ascertain a view of the corresponding impact that the E-UC&C service framework had on end-user communication.

SOLUTIONS AND RECOMMENDATIONS

This section of the chapter and the next ones will discuss the use of ICTs for Development (ICT4D) **solutions** (Goosen, 2015) and **recommendations** for dealing with the **issues**, **challenges** and problems presented. These sections will include more concrete data on the **issues** under analysis, namely statistical data.

Assessment of End-User Impact Survey Results

When the deployment of the E-UC&C technical **solutions** framework was complete, analysis of end-user impact on perceived productivity and acceleration of innovation was taken beyond the horizon by obtaining qualitative perspectives using two instruments (Goosen & Mukasa-Lwanga, 2017). These instruments consisted of a survey of global employees across multiple regions and business functions and one-to-one interviews, coded using open methods. The results of the survey and interviews were assessed against the developed research hypothesis, specified in Bolton, Goosen and Kritzinger (2022b). Further information on how the first author had formulated the hypotheses was detailed in a chapter on research design and methodology (Bolton, et al., 2021a), which provided additional details in this regard.

This chapter presents a summary of findings along with retroduction inference on identified outcomes and their causal entities and associated relationships. The use of retroductive inference in the analysis of the observations established through the survey process allowed for the exploration of causal conditions and entities within the results. The process of exploration and evaluation was facilitated by working from consequences inferred via the survey response data and applying a retroductive inference process to establish a hypothetical antecedent.

Analysis and Discussion of Survey Results

The hypotheses developed within the scope of the survey of end-user experiences were detailed in Bolton, et al. (2022b). De Vaus (2014) argued that factors, such as low response rates, can bias survey data results due to non-respondents tending to be different from those who respond. Users invited to participate in the survey were selected on the basis that they had utilized the digitally transformed communication technologies and functions for a minimum of sixty days. A sample size of 120,000 users were targeted when receiving the transformed technologies and applying these in their daily communication functions, for a 5% margin of error and 95% confidence level. The formula as indicated in Figure 4 was applied to determine the required sample size.

Figure 4. Survey instrument sample size formula and parameters

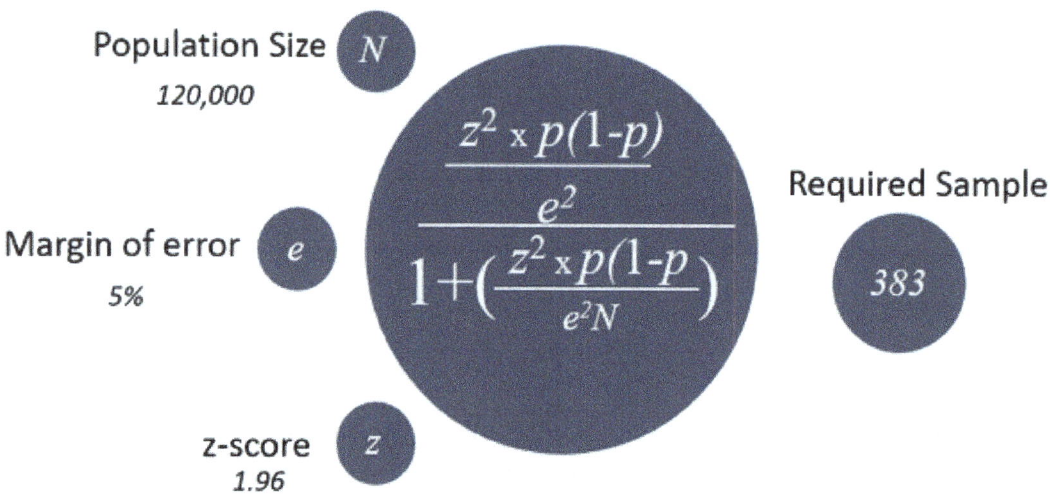

Based on the calculated requirement for 383 respondents, an estimated response rate of 20% was used, and a pool of 2,000 users selected to receive the survey. An actual response rate of 33% was realized (660 respondents), reducing the margin of error to 3.86%. An increased sample size helped to reduce the width of the confidence interval of survey data (Meeker, Hahn, & Escobar, 2017).

Survey: Key Findings

The survey consisted of thirteen multiple choice questions. The survey questions were developed to facilitate the gathering of data from end-users that enabled analysis of the primary features used, *ease of use and adoption*, perceived impact on productivity and assistance in engaging in innovative collaboration. Three primary questions were applied to guide the process of retroduction inference aligned with the observed outcomes of the survey. The retroduction process facilitated the assessment of *plausibility* in the evaluation of findings associated with the established research hypotheses (McLaughlin, 1982):

1. Are there any prevailing opinions or patterns evident indicating meaningful change following the deployment of the transformed communication technologies?
2. What entities, conditions and drivers related to the observed change?
3. Is it likely that the changes observed were likely to occur without the shift to the digitally transformed framework of C&C having occurred?

Exploration of the variables identified and observed within the survey results and the causal relationships between those variables and real-life outcomes observed within the GM enterprise can provide a path to understanding the components that manifest and drive the observed change (Sayer, 1992). Sayer (1992) also suggested that causality is, in general, interpreted as those assumptions that are most reliable, and combined with other assumptions, can form a system of thinking that is acceptable (Easton, 2010).

1. ***Diversity of Participation***

The group consisted of a random sampling of users who, at the time of the survey, had used the technologies for more than sixty days. All selected users had the full portfolio of production services available to them and had legacy forms of communication (such as physical phone handsets) removed. The sample consisted of users from a diverse group, with less than 50% coming from teams that had high levels of functional expertise in using ICTs to facilitate completing their daily tasks (Libbrecht & Goosen, 2015).

Table 1 depicts the representative sample group of GM business functions, while Bolton, et al. (2021a) provided additional details in this regard.

The sample population associated with the GM post-deployment survey consisted of employees from all business segments. Technical abilities within the responding group varied in exposure, skills and experience with digital communication technologies. Features and functionalities released to the users were consistent across all groups. Russell and Russell (2005) suggested that when planning qualitative data collection through methods, such as surveys and interviews, that the researcher should draw from a diverse cross-section of the available population. Irrespective of the groups created within the scope of the survey, heterogeneous or homogenous (similar or different), the same core set of questions was presented, with an opportunity for the researcher to explore more deeply as the opportunity or need arises.

2. ***Increased Enterprise Efficiency***

Bolton, Goosen and Kritzinger (2020b) indicated *increased enterprise efficiency*: The users reported that they found it easier to communicate and collaborate with their colleagues within the enterprise and external business partners. Of the remaining third, only 4% reported finding **emerging strategies**, C&C technologies and processes more difficult to use. According to Figure 5, the features leveraged the most was instant messaging, followed by peer-to-peer voice collaboration and desktop sharing.

Table 1. Business functions represented within the research survey

1	Global Brands and Sales, Service & Marketing	8.41%	55
2	Global Communications	5.96%	39
3	Global Connect Customer Experience	3.21%	21
4	Global Human Resources	1.99%	13
5	Global Manufacturing	15.60%	102
6	Global Product Development, Purchasing & Supply Chain	13.30%	87
7	Global Public Policy	0.15%	1
8	Global Quality	0.76%	5
9	GM Finance	7.03%	46
10	GM Legal	0.15%	1
11	IT Shared Services	42.66%	279
12	Operational Excellence	0.76%	5
			654

Figure 5. Most leveraged features identified by transformed users

51% of users reported that they regularly escalated instant messaging chat collaboration sessions to voice engagements.

Retroductive inference: The facility to escalate C&C seamlessly between different modes and mediums of communication was not available to users prior to the digital transformation of new technologies and functionalities delivered through the E-UC&C framework. With the transformed technologies users received the capability to flex between, and combine, multiple communication functions (chatting, talking, sharing files, sharing screens) within a single desktop technology. Within sixty days of adopting the technologies, a significant number of users identified the digitally transformed capabilities and technologies as improving their *efficiency* in daily communication processes. Pelet (2014, p. 87) suggested that social influence processes and cognitive instrument processing can have a significant influence on user acceptance and adoption. The latter author cited "perceived ease of use" as proposed in the research of Venkatesh and Davis (2000) as a component of cognitive instrument processes and influencer of user acceptance.

The responses supported the proposition that within a global automotive enterprise, such as GM, the introduction of UC&C technologies and functionality through a structured framework, such as E-UC&C, can lead to the formation of new communication workflows and processes. It also suggested that these workflows can be tailored by individual employees to optimize their communication processes through digital transformation through the E-UC&C framework of functionalities. Ibrahim and Taniar (2006) argued that the ability to personalize services and provide continuity of service is a factor that can increase the rate of user adoption for new communication services.

3. *Ease of Use and Adoption*

In responding to the question of how easy users found adopting and using the new UC&C client, 72% of respondents stated that the digitally transformed communication technologies as very easy and intuitive to use and adapt to their routine communication functions (see Figure 6). Two percent of users reported general difficulty in using the new technologies. The remaining 26% found some features to be easy to use, but experienced **challenges** with the use and adoption of others. Subsequent follow-up investigation with users and observation of relatively low initial multi-user scheduled voice and video collaboration metrics showed that training on more complex operations, such as scheduling a multi-media and participant conference, was a factor. Bosch-Rekveldt, Jongkind, Mooi, Bakker and Verbraeck (2011) highlighted the importance of considering the immense and increasing complexity in large engineering projects.

Figure 6. Ease of use and adoption

55% of employees identified the ability to leverage multi-modal communication through one single technology as the most essential benefit to leveraging the digital transformed communication client. Lundberg (2017) suggested that different internal and external factors, such as the user's perception of the usefulness of a system and its ease of use, can have an adverse effect on end-user adoption. The Technical Adoption Model (TAM) by Venkatesh and Davis (2000) suggested that the more natural to use a system is perceived to be, the more useful it is likely to be perceived by the user. The ability to travel and seamlessly leverage the same suite of communication features remotely and service mobility via portable devices were also indicated as key benefits.

Retroductive inference: Survey responses to questions associated with end-user experiences in the adoption of the new technologies suggested that the central cockpit delivered via a UC&C client facilitated easier execution of complex communication processes. It was possible for the user to execute these processes, due to the intuitive nature of the client that integrated associated tasks and, in some cases, led to the formation of new individual communication processes. The complex hierarchy and interplay of back-end integration and underlying communication platforms were hidden from the user's sphere of engagement resulting in the perception of a simple, seamless and easy to use experience. More (2016) suggested that highly complex technical product/service **solutions** make it extremely difficult to manage user adoption. Concealing the underlying technical complexity of the system is hence advisable to promote and not stifle or delay adoption within the enterprise.

4. ***Impact on Productivity***

Engagement with key stakeholders within the GM business teams during the formative stage of transformation planning identified that there was no standard measure for productivity at a functional level. Productivity at an enterprise level could be assessed quantitatively with corporate level metrics such as revenue and vehicles manufactured. These measures were not effective when seeking to analyze whether discrete initiatives or technology transformations had a positive or negative impact on end-user productivity. The approach adopted for the purposes of measurement through qualitative methods focused on the employee's self-perceived view on productivity gain or loss.

In response to the question on whether the new UC&C technologies positively impacted the employees' productivity, 66.67% of users identified the technologies as having a positive effect. 4% stated that the new technologies had no impact or effect on their productivity (see Figure 7). The high response rates relating to experiencing an increase in communication *efficiency* (67%), *ease of use and adoption* (71%) and perceived increase in productivity (67%) suggested that the perceived gains in productivity of end-users aligned to *ease of use and adoption* and flexible features that allow the user to transition between multiple communication modes while collaborating efficiently. 4% of users reported perceived lower levels of productivity. The results observed in features and benefits, precisely 4% of users reporting that they experienced difficulty using the new digital features and 2.65% of users experiencing difficulty in adopting the new technologies, may correlate to the corresponding low number (4%) of users who perceived lower productivity. These observations suggest that if users experience difficulty in adopting and using new features due to lack of familiarity, training or resistance to process change they are unlikely to perceive a gain in productivity.

Figure 7. Perceived impact of UC&C technologies on efficiency

After a minimum of sixty days of using the new digital communication technologies and processes, the majority of users (83%) stated that they believed their productivity would decrease, to some degree, if the new technologies are removed and legacy non-digitally transformed methods of communication resumed (see Figure 8).

Figure 8. Perceived impact of UC&C technologies on productivity

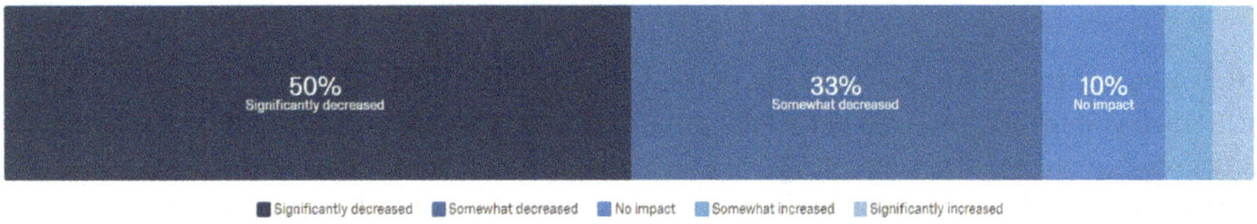

Retroductive inference: Survey responses show that a majority of users quickly identify leverage of the digitally transformed with the opportunity to improve personal productivity. This suggestion supports the observation that many users, while not immediately identifying the technologies as increasing their productivity, express the opinion that removing the technologies would ultimately decrease productivity.

When questioned about the theoretical impact of the removal of the new communication technologies, users felt productivity would decrease may be explained by the interim period of adoption and establishing familiarity with the new technologies. Where less technical users are increasing familiarity with the technologies and their operation, individuals may report as having no observed increase in productivity. However, through observation of their peers and growing understanding of the technologies, they have context on the potential benefit that can be derived once they fully adopt the technology. This observation is further supported by the two variables identified as predictive constructs (Workman, 2010), for adoption by Davis (1985) in the TAM of the latter author. These variables relate to perceived ease of use and perceived usefulness. In the situation where users in themselves have not entirely become accustomed to the use of the technology, research findings within the GM case study suggest that an interim state may exist where the user's perception of potential usefulness is influenced by the usefulness and utilization experienced by their peers.

5. Impact on Innovation

A significant majority of employees (87.54%) stated that based on their experience, they believed UC&C technologies could drive innovation by enhancing collaboration (see Figure 9). Over 93% of employees surveyed identified the new UC&C technologies as helping them drive or participate in innovation activities post-adoption (within a minimum of 60 days).

Figure 9. Reported increase in ability to engage in and drive innovation C&C

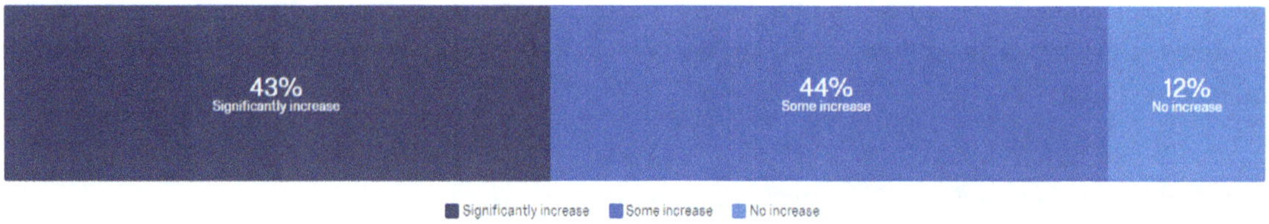

Retroductive inference: Survey responses show that most users identify with the view that digitally transformed communication, delivered through a UC&C framework of **solutions** can enhance their ability to both participate in and drive activities that they consider to be innovation focused. Innovation as a process is comprised of creativity and entrepreneurship (Shalley, Hitt, & Zhou, 2015). The variable outcomes associated with the perceived ability for UC&C technologies to enhance communication positively, suggest that it is likely that the combination of flexible workflows, intuitive interface and multi-modal communication methods enhance the creative process of innovation and support the communication required to engage in entrepreneurial brainstorm and planning activities. Peitrucha (2014) argued that effective communication promotes reflective reasoning by assisting people in opening their minds and driving past superficial thought and gaining deeper meaning. He highlights how information is a crucial asset in the digital age and the importance of not only delivering information but bringing meaning to the target audience. Effective digital technologies, such as UC&C, can avoid the occurrence of what Peitrucha (2014) called *infomageddon*, a chasm between rich content and a lack of meaning.

Interview Data: Analysis and Discussion

Analysis and findings from research study post-transformation deployment interview data provided deeper insight into the impacts of UC&C technology on the regular communication process of users. The interview data complemented the summary data provided by the research survey providing a broader and deeper context on some of the underlying drivers and supporting the survey findings. Findings from the research survey suggest that UC&C technologies, deployed within the scope of the research study via the E-UC&C framework can improve the communication process and outcomes of users in four key areas:

Firstly, the digital enhancements and new capabilities delivered by the E-UC&C framework and technologies increase the *efficiency* of communication in the execution of peer to peer and multi-user collaboration activities. Secondly, users found the intuitive central cockpit provided by the technology, easy to use allowing them to escalate communication through different modes of communication leading to the establishment of new individual communication processes. Thirdly, UC&C digitally transformed and enhanced communication established through the E-UC&C framework enhances the ability for users to engage in communication activities, increasing their perceived levels of personal productivity. Finally, the digitally transformed technologies enhances the capability for users to participate in, host and drive highly collaborative meetings that they identified with the generation of innovation.

Principal categories

Analysis of the interview data uncovered several dominant categories relating to productivity and innovation. As it related to innovation, interview participants described how the digitally transformed communication capabilities changed the way they worked, facilitated increased creativity, saved time and money and fostered increased collaboration. Figure 10 depicts the significant categories of feedback established within the interview data associated with perceived productivity and innovation, highlighting the intersection of commonality in feedback data. The **innovation** factors are depicted in more detail in Figure 11.

Figure 10. Productivity and innovation interview factors, highlighting suggested causal relationships

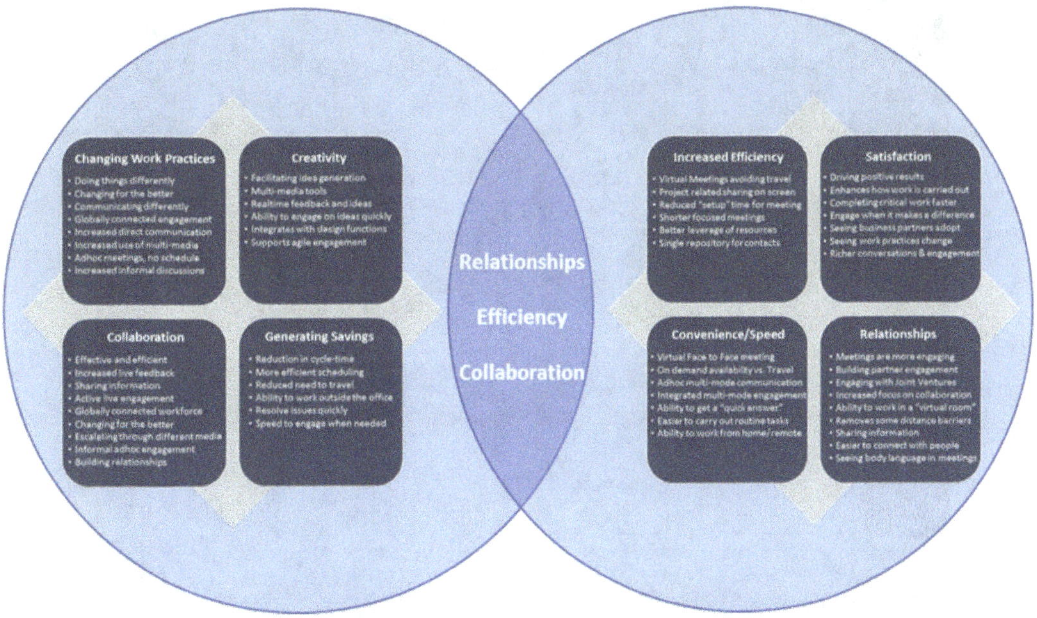

Flick (2014) cited the importance of drawing up priority lists associated with the research questions in order to reduce the number of developed categories and reduce the otherwise excessive quantity of categories developed within the coding process. Detailed analysis of the interview transcripts identified four primary categories within the data relating to innovation. The categories identified include a change of work practices, creativity, collaboration and the generation of savings.

The transcript coding process separated data into two areas for the purpose of analyzing and identifying data associated with a suggested increase or decrease in user productivity and potentially positive or negative influence on innovation-related activities. For productivity, the primary categories identified within the transcript data aligned to *increased enterprise efficiency*, outcome-derived *satisfaction*, *convenience/speed* and *relationships*.

Analysis of Impact on Productivity

Data from the participant interviews highlighted re-occurring thematic of feedback among the participants relating to the impact that the digitally transformed technologies had on their perceived productivity. Feedback suggested that there was no common view on how the users measured productivity at a personal level. Each participant highlighted corporate measures and methods for tracking productivity aligning with their business function.

Figure 11. Factors associated with innovation, identified via transcript coding

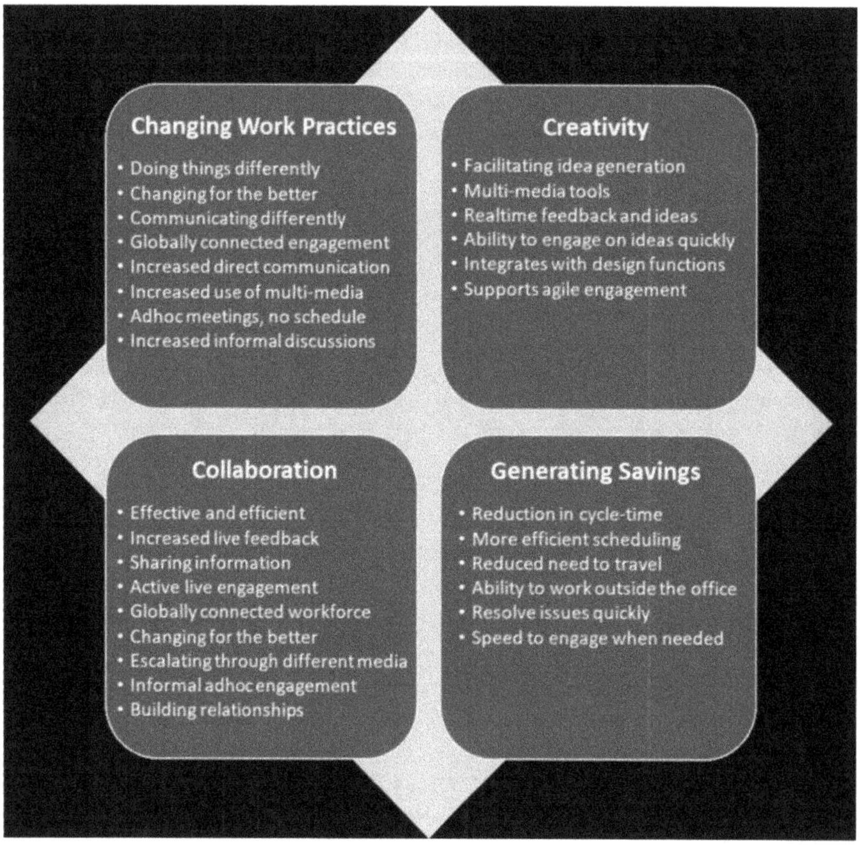

Increased Enterprise Efficiency

Data from the research interviews indicates that participants achieve increased *efficiency* in their work tasks associated with communication activities. Virtual meetings avoid the requirement for users to travel, the interviewed participants highlighted a correlation between travel avoidance and the availability of a richer set of meeting media options with UC&C. The reduced requirement to travel facilitated the opportunity to establish meetings at shorter notice as meeting timelines were not dependent on downstream travel schedule of participants. Building on the virtual meeting opportunity, participants associated the ability with being able to schedule ad hoc meetings and rapidly share pertinent data with driving increased *efficiency* in the use of people and project related resources. Interview participants stated that their setup time for meetings had reduced, indicating incremental personal productivity and that their meetings were becoming shorter and more focused.

The feedback and data established through the coding process of the transcripts suggest a relationship between perceived productivity outcomes and feedback on features that users described as being convenient, increasing process speed, resulting in *satisfaction* and building *relationships*. For example, shorter more focused meetings (*efficiency*), facilitated through ad hoc virtual face to face UC&C services (*convenience/speed*), enabled increased team collaboration and sharing (*relationships*), driving positive project results *(satisfaction)*.

Convenience/Speed

Interview participants described how the digitally transformed virtual face to face and multi-mode availability of communication channels made it more comfortable and convenient to meet and collaborate. Data suggests that the outcome resulting from the use of these features and characteristics of the new UC&C technologies had a direct relationship to the delivery of *efficiency* while at the same time suggesting the convenience and ease of use resulted in positive motivation towards adopting and leveraging the new methods. Interview participants stated that through the digitally transformed technologies and services they could quickly pose and receive answers to important questions quickly.

It is likely that this feature as experienced by the interview participants correlates to the survey responses and operational adoption metrics supporting a view of rapid user adoption and an increase of short duration meetings. Interview participants also highlighted the convenience of being able to engage fully in rich media virtual meetings from remote locations when they were travelling or from their homes. It is likely that this function has a relationship with findings already discussed suggesting that user *satisfaction* from using the new technologies because they were no longer constrained to meeting at specific times limited by being in a GM office improving home and work-life balance. Literature suggests that flexible working options such as working remotely from home may promote healthier interpersonal *relationships*, reduce stress levels and well-being. These **recommendations** are supported by the research of Berrell (2017) in an analysis of 'Anywhere Working' and the social relations of remote working practices.

Relationships

The establishment and maintenance of team and individual *relationships* indicated a significant relationship in the association of the new UC&C functionality and perceived personal productivity. Participants described meetings facilitated through the digitally transformed technologies as being more engaging, contrasting with legacy meetings restricted to basic slide sharing and audio-only communication. Participants reported the ability to work effectively in a virtual room. Due to all participants (room based and remote) having video facilities, emphatic responses were visible through body language facilitating more personal and direct communication. Participants reported finding it easier to connect with people versus legacy untransformed conference calls and that the virtual meeting spaces contributed to increased opportunity for collaboration with internal colleagues and building engagement with external partners. The virtual meeting spaces removed some barriers created by distance and geography in the process of establishing and maintaining effective *relationships*.

Satisfaction

Data from the interview transcripts suggest a theme of *satisfaction* derived from the use of the transformed digital communication technologies and methods. Some of these factors reciprocally relate to other productivity factors, for example, experiencing *satisfaction* in being able to engage quickly and positively contribute *(satisfaction)*, quickly *(convenience/speed)* connecting with peers and partners *(relationships)*, and efficiently driving outcomes *(efficiency)*. Data from the interviews suggest that participants gained a sense of *satisfaction* from seeing their peers and business partners change their communication processes and work habits in line with changes associated with the adoption of the new technologies and features. It is possible that this finding contributes to the rapid level of native adoption of the UC&C technology within the user community ahead of formal training, discussed later in this chapter.

Analysis of Impact on Innovation

Data within the interview transcripts resulted in the identification and development of four primary categories associated with feedback on innovation. The four categories aligned to the development of new work practices within the users, associated with the capabilities provided by the digitally transformed UC&C technologies, the increased ability to virtually collaborate, enhanced opportunities to engage in virtual creative activities and the generation of business savings and *efficiency*. Figure 11 depicted the primary categories identified and summary of supporting qualitative statements identified within the transcript coding process.

Analysis of the data from both the productivity and innovation related feedback suggests a strong and potentially causal relationship in the associated data. As depicted in Figure 10, the data suggested that overlap exists in the forming and establishing of *relationships*, enhanced ability to collaborate and generation of efficiencies in work practices and business processes. The data and variables associated with the domains of productivity and innovation appear to support the likelihood and inference of causal *relationships*. For example, *productivity* is perceived to increase due to new functionality that facilitates more productive *collaboration*, leading to more *efficient* focused meetings and helping to build a stronger team and individual *relationships.*

Changing work practices

Data from the transcript coding of the detailed experiences of study participants suggest that through leverage of the new digitally transformed technologies that they were starting to adjust their communication work practices to more efficient and ad-hoc methods of communication. Participants expressed a sense of perceiving the changes in their communication work processes as changing for the better. This sentiment correlates to the feedback associated with the sense of *satisfaction* derived from working and communicating with the UC&C technologies. Aligning to the feedback relating to productivity, associated with building *relationships* and reducing location and distance barriers to communication, participants described how the UC&C technologies and multi-mode digital media facilitated the integration of teams and engagement globally. They felt, globally connected. The combination of global connectivity expanded their opportunity to engage with team members and increased the amount of informal and ad-hoc as required meetings outside of broader scheduled agendas. The ability to reach out and engage global team players and experts virtually increased opportunities to drive, validate and act upon transdisciplinary approaches to action research (Goosen, 2018b), *innovative* ideas and innovation agendas.

Collaboration

Participants described an increased ability to capture and engage with live feedback within meetings leading to what they felt were more effective and efficient engagements and meeting outcomes. Sharing of information through the multiple modes of communication resulted in more active live engagement with team members sharing information in structured and ad-hoc collaboration sessions. Feedback data aligned with the reported change in work practice where engagement with their global teammates and partners was made more accessible through the new UC&C technologies. Ad-hoc meetings were identified as a collaboration enabler with the enhanced capability to escalate through multiple modes of communication as required to direct and engage in effective information sharing and dialogue.

These variables align with the data provided by participants associated with enhanced personal productivity drivers. Combined the data suggests that *relationships* strengthen through the more productive, more focused and convenient virtual collaboration provided by the UC&C framework and the associated technology and services eco-system. The enhanced collaboration supports the creative processes *(creativity)* and *efficiency (generating savings)* identified in the other identified categories identified within the coding process.

Creativity

Analysis of the transcript data identified feedback that supports the view that participants identified and experienced a sense of increased creativity enablement when collaborating through the transformed UC&C communication technologies. The integrated UC&C client and the ability to escalate through multiple modes of communication efficiently and effectively, as described in the variables identified in with the collaboration category, facilitated idea sharing and generation. The multi-media technologies facilitated a multi-level/multi-layer sharing of information and context through the integrated, consolidated UC&C client.

The participants described how the ad hoc ability to identify participants that could add value to ideation development and evaluation, rapidly assess their availability state and engage into virtual discussions helped drive quicker engagement and assessment of innovative ideas. Feedback data indicates that the more agile collaboration environment delivered via UC&C and the E-UC&C ecosystem helps in promoting and increasing engagement that users associate with innovation and the fostering the development of innovative ideas.

Generating savings

Interview participants identified a reduction in cycle times for communication *(engagement, discussion, offline review, re-engage and iteratively develop),* resulting in a significant saving in their time and that of other engaged collaborators. These findings align with the data identified in responses associated with productivity where the sentiment of *efficiency* in process is frequently expressed. Similarly, more efficient scheduling and the reduced requirement to travel is cited as creating cost and resource time savings within the various business units suggesting a causal relationship with the *relationship* and *convenience/speed* categories associated with productivity.

Aligning with the category of *creativity* participants described how the ability to engage quickly to resolve **issues** and the ability to virtually collaborate on demand resulted in savings associated with resource time and travel when engaging in innovation focused activities.

Discussion of findings

There was a high correlation identified between the primary categories and variables identified within the transcript coding process of interview participants and the results obtained from the research survey. Data established through the process of retroductive inference of the more summarized and high-level survey feedback aligned closely with the real-life experiences detailed by the interview participants. The research interview provided a deeper level of understanding and detail relating to the participant's experiences in adopting and leveraging the transformed digital communication mediums provided by the E-UC&C framework. The inference of perceived increase in personal productivity and ability to influence and engage in creative innovation generating activities was supported and correlated across both qualitative data sets.

Data across the survey and detailed interviews suggested a correlation between the perceived convenience of the technology and increased the perceived productivity of the users during the process of regular communication. Similarly, the flexible methods for scheduling, initiating ad hoc as needed calls and a richer multimedia form of communication, with emphatic visual indicators through live video is attributed to perceived increase inability to engage in creative (innovation) collaboration activities.

Findings derived through analysis across both sets of data suggested that when combined, the consolidated client, intuitive multi-channel (voice, video, app sharing) C&C options, presence-aware and emotion-sharing features of UC&C closed perceived organizational and geographic distances. Regarding organizational knowledge and administration lessons from this (Goosen, 2021), the closing of perceived distance fostered higher levels of communication and ad-hoc *collaboration*, further underpinning support for increased collaborative productivity and opportunities for *creative* engagements driving **innovation**.

QUANTITATIVE REVIEW OF ADOPTION AND USAGE METRICS

In this section of the chapter, the **MAIN FOCUS** will be on the quantitative data captured to track adoption, end-user use of features and post-adoption **issues**. Where the qualitative research methods and associated data inferred a positive correlation between the deployment of the digitally transformed C&C technologies, the quantitative technology-supported research methods for (Goosen, 2019b) metrics served to establish a non-subjective view of actual use through measurement of relevant statistics. Where the qualitative data suggested positive consequences regarding the established research hypotheses, the quantitative data supported a view of how broadly the impact was experienced across the sector.

The empirical data tracked and obtained via quantitative data gathering methods from source technology systems within the underlying Enhanced Unified Communications and Collaboration (E-UC&C) framework serve to contrast the qualitative inference derived from the survey and interviews with real-life system data. The system data support a metrically driven view of real-life adoption, migration, feature use and reported user **issues**.

Statistical Data: Transformation Reporting Portal

As summarized in Bolton, et al. (2022b), a transformation reporting portal was established within the E-UC&C framework to aid in the statistical tracking of underlying dependent system health and status and legacy system migration, in addition to capturing and tracking the upper layer end-user technologies feature usage and adoption. A chapter on the empirical research discussed how the integration and implementation of the E-UC&C framework delivered digital transformation of **emerging strategies** and technologies to end-users within the enterprise (Bolton, et al., 2022a). It consisted of a diverse and complex underlying integrated hierarchy of **emerging strategies** and technologies.

Where retirement of legacy **solutions** was of importance within the transformation initiative, reporting was also established to track the decline of legacy system use, ultimately facilitating planned and scheduled decommission. Finally, the reporting portal tracked commercial and financial benefits and investments associated with the adoption and deployment of the transformed technologies, objectively validating the positive return on investment for management and complimenting the more subjective end-user feedback and data-driven adoption and usage metrics. Table 2 depicts a summary of reports that were created within the reporting portal and were heavily used during the process of transformation from legacy to the enhanced UC&C end-state.

Due to the pervasive impact of the framework on **emerging strategies** and technologies across the underlying legacy eco-system, the reports represented a balance between system performance, change and transformation monitoring, program and user adoption metrics. While all reporting was sustainable, inclusive in terms of quality through research-informed practice (Goosen, 2018a) and operationalized post-deployment, the focus shifted to the usage metrics to support and drive end-user adoption.

In total the reporting dashboard contained 130 individual reports, visualized with Tableau data visualization technologies, collating and aggregating data from over 90 individual system data sources.

Transformation and Adoption Metrics

Survey and interview data suggested that end-users found the new technologies intuitive to use and found that the technologies and framework of underlying digital communication systems facilitated higher levels of engagement. The deployment timeline discussed in Bolton, et al. (2022a) detailed the development to production release cycle. A limited pre-production deployment of approximately 15,000 users across global functions and locations started in November 2016.

Ease of Use and Adoption

The pre-production deployment of information and communication technologies for the development of **solutions** (Goosen, 2018d) was used to validate the data management capabilities and core operational research integrity in the context of the transformed technologies and underlying eco-system of C&C

Table 2. Primary reports developed and utilized during transformation and adoption phase

Report Name	Description of Purpose
• Global Site Modernisation Dashboard	• Track site infrastructure refresh implementations supporting E-UC&C
• Month to Date Change Dashboard	• Track transformation change volume and success metric by function
• Open Changes Pending Closure	• Track open live changes through to change validation and completion
• Change Success Rate by Function	• Track and monitor impact of transformation changes
• Unsuccessful Change report by Function	• Analyse, track and action Corrective actions for failed changes
• Change summary by Program Initiative	• Analyse performance of change success and impact by function
• Average Time to close change	• Analyse performance of change closure and implementation by function
• Change Failure Root Cause Analysis	• Track and identify trends and detail of individual change failures
• Skills Resource Management Dashboard	• Track allocation and forecasted utilisation of transformation skills pool
• Site Location Information Dashboard	• Track detail of enterprise sites, business functions, purpose and location
• PTT Radio Usage Dashboard	• Track utilisation detail of all PTT Radios and plant radio spectrum
• PTT Radio Zero Usage Asset Report	• Track utilisation of individual radios, drive re-use & re-allocation
• Service Desk Interaction Dashboard	• Track Service level interaction metrics to identify negative trends
• Service Desk Incident Dashboard	• Track Service Incident detail, identify and correct negative trends
• Service Desk First Call Resolution Dashboard	• Track Service Desk end user first time resolution performance
• Service Incident Time to Resolve report	• Track the time to resolve for user issues, correct negative trends
• User Generated Incident Ticket Dashboard	• Track aggregate volume of user generated tickets by function
• Incident trend over time by Service report	• Track incident trends, identify negative trends and correct by function
• Auto Generated Incidents by Service report	• Track system auto generation tickets and correct negative trends
• Incident Analysis by Functional Area report	• Track incident volume generation and performance by function
• Aged Incident by Assigned Group report	• Track aged tickets and drive early closure rates, improve SLA delivery
• Asset Installed/Spare and Redeploy report	• Track asset status, ensure efficient asset deployment and use
• Asset % of remaining useful life report	• Track asset useful life, align to refresh strategy to ensure service quality
• Asset Uninstalled CWIP status report	• Track non-installed assets, focus on efficient leverage of investments
• Installed Network Port Count report	• Track port availability and use by location
• Asset functional ownership report	• Track asset status, ownership and value by function
• UC&C Client Savings Dashboard	• Track savings derived from UC&C migration of multi-conference features
• UC&C Conference A/V Session Dashboard	• Track aggregate use of conference services in Hours and monitor trends
• Skype vs. Webex Usage Dashboard	• Track usage of legacy tools, monitor trends in new toolset adoption
• Legacy hosted Webex Utilisation Dashboard	• Track decline of legacy toolset, align to decommission schedule and plan
• Security Program Initiatives Dashboard	• Track transformation related security initiatives, ensure secure end state
• Security Project Status Dashboard	• Track status of individual security augmentation initiatives and projects
• Video Collaboration Room Utilization report	• Track status of Video Collaboration utilisation by hour/location
• Video Collab Location and deployment report	• Track Video Collaboration deployment statistics, country/location

Figure 12. Rapid growth in UC&C client conferences (audio and video)

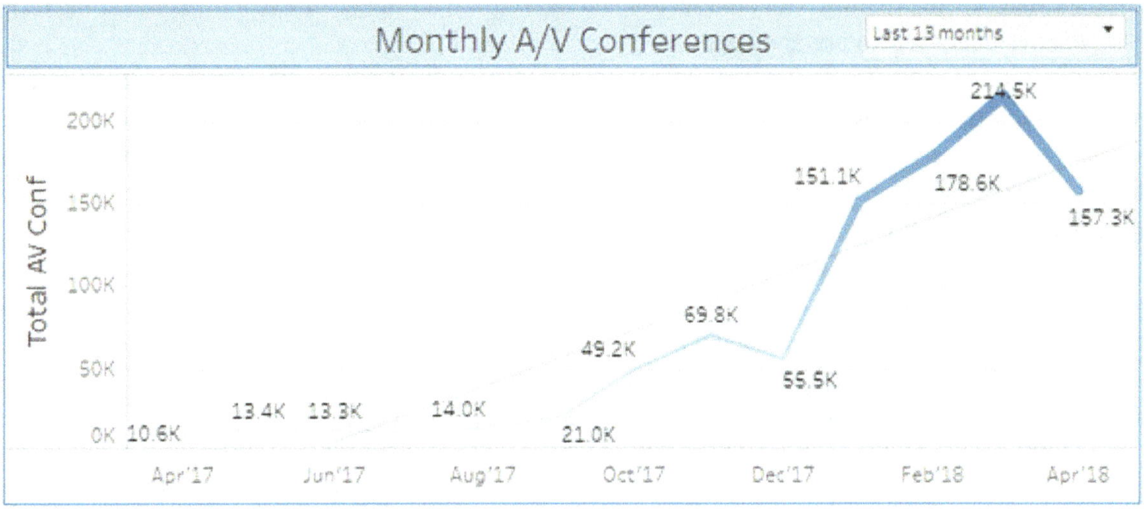

systems (Goosen, 2018c). Mass user production deployments to all global business functions, users and locations were initiated mid-October 2017. Figure 12 depicts the data captured about Audio and Video (A/V) conference usage growth via the Skype UC&C front-end client. The rapid adoption of the platform from October 2017 through April 2018 is apparent, with growth in use from pre-production norms by over 900% increasing from 21,000 instances of individual conferences in September 2017 to over 214,000 instances at its peak in February 2018.

This data supports a view of rapid use and adoption by end-users and supports the data suggesting that users found the transformed technologies intuitive to use. It is reasonable to infer from the meeting volume data that users perceived productivity increased due to their increased use of the UC&C technologies as a method of communication.

The usage reports showed that in reciprocal to aggregate growth in individual collaborative meetings facilitated via the transformed UC&C services and technologies, the time spent collaborating increased. Minutes of collaboration via UC&C increased by over 1,450% from September 2017 through peak use in February 2018, growing from 704,000 minutes to over 10.9 million minutes of aggregate employee collaboration.

Providing additional context relative to the GM enterprise, the total peak conference minutes achieved in February 2018 number represents over 181,900 hours of employee collaboration achieved via the digitally enhanced technologies or 1,137 employees persistently communicating 40 hours per week.

Legacy Reduction and Elimination

The utilization of legacy platforms was monitored during the production transition to the E-UC&C framework of technologies. Employees were restricted to collaborating via audio conference combined with hosted external application sharing via Cisco Webex prior to the implementation of the digitally transformed technologies. Figure 13 summarizes the observed decline in legacy technology usage post-deployment of the production UC&C technologies within GM. The sharp reciprocal decline in system usage can be seen starting in September 2017. Important to note is that the legacy technologies had been in operation for over ten years and embedded in the regular C&C practices of users across the company. This data supports the findings from the survey and interview data suggesting that users found the technology convenient, easy to use and adopt.

The combined data of legacy migration and multi-channel conference volume supports a view of culture change associated with employee communication. Where previously only audio and desktop sharing were available, users quickly shifted to leveraging multiple modes of simultaneous communication channels via the UC&C client and underlying E-UC&C framework of applications and services. Figure 14 depicts the decline in legacy hosted audio and slide sharing functionality.

A shift to the transformed E-UC&C services and technologies, in particular, the softphone voice capability, provided by the UC&C client, led to a significant reduction in user dedicated physical desk phones. Figure 15 depicts the decline and subsequent decommissioning of desk phones in preference for adoption of full feature softphone capability. Within five months of the full production launch, 29% of the total voice endpoints within GM had converted from legacy physical hard phones to softphone.

The full feature softphone service including a dedicated direct inbound dialing number and full outbound dialing privilege was provided only to users who were willing to retire their physical phone and fully migrate to UC&C. Users who chose to retain their physical desk phone are restricted to participating in internal network calls and conferences. This data supports the inference from the survey and interview data that users were attracted to the convenience and perceived collaboration benefits delivered by the transformed and consolidated UC&C client and associated communication services.

As an adjunct to the data supporting positive and rapid end-user adoption and leverage, the transition to the E-UC&C framework facilitated consolidation of legacy PBX infrastructure within GM by 96%. The digital transformation and SIP trunking enablement facilitated the consolidation of 94 regional and country level PBX systems into four regional clusters within the E-UC&C architecture.

Figure 13. UC&C conference minutes and duration analysis

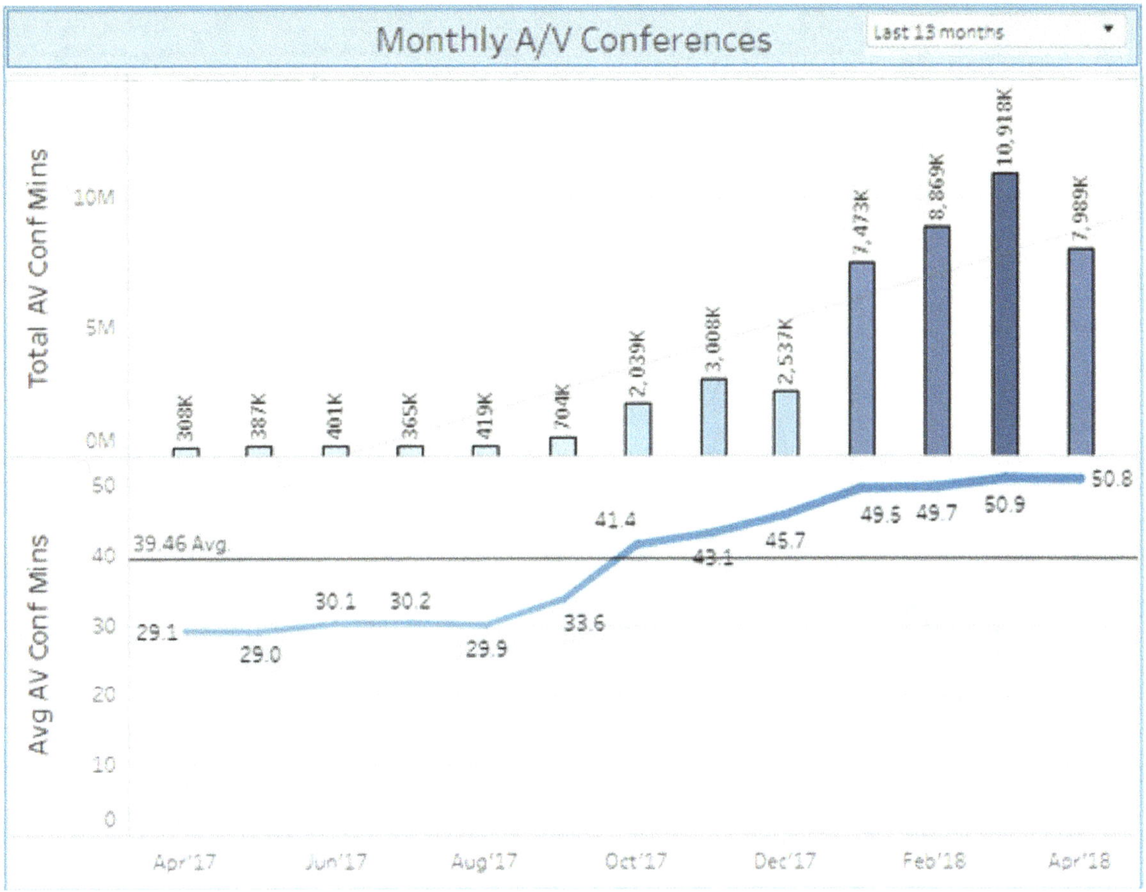

Figure 14. Decline in legacy C&C technologies usage

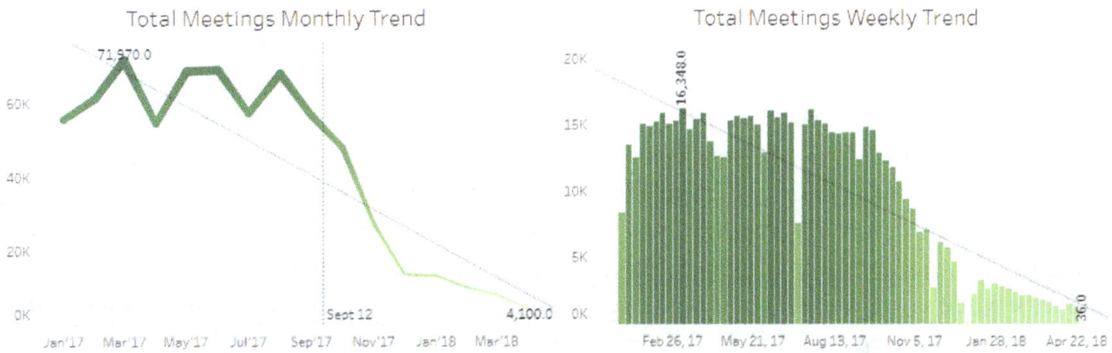

Figure 15. Decline in legacy phone handsets and growth of softphone adoption

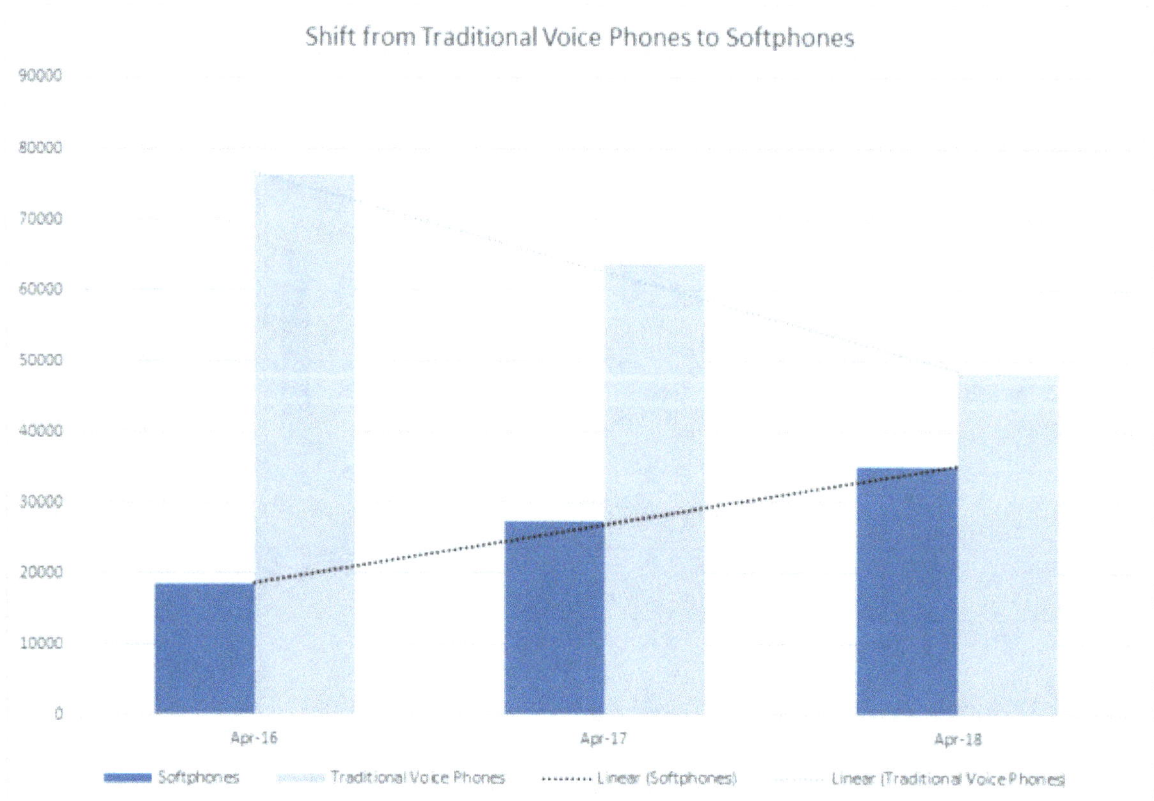

Indicators of Cultural Change in Communication

Multiple data sources supported the suggestion of a change in culture and method of C&C employed by users' post-adoption of **emerging strategies** and technologies. Integrated *application*-sharing grew by 46% from the 24-month pilot to the full production deployment period. Instant messaging capabilities were migrated to the new Skype UC&C client before the full-feature production release in April 2016, due to an impromptu decision by the legacy messaging provider Cisco to retire the WebexConnect technology. Online training was made available to users on institutional systems and completed prior to the migration of users to basic chat services on Skype (Goosen & Naidoo, 2014). Immediate adoption of the new service was seen, followed by significant growth in instant messaging traffic. This data supported the view that due to the new UC&C client's intuitive interface, users were better able to self-train and familiarize themselves, driving a *culture* of increased self-sufficiency. As users adopted the new UC&C features, a significant decline in user tickets was tracked for voice and messaging (legacy and transformed combined), while usage and adoption of the system increased. Figure 16 depicts **emerging trends** regarding a decrease in reported user **issues** versus the significant increase in adoption and feature use.

The cultural shift towards digital C&C technologies was supported by the research data gathered (Goosen, 2019a) to track use of C&C meeting rooms installed within the *scope* of the E-UC&C framework. Installation and leverage of video collaboration rooms built on Cisco Telepresence were initiated in

2013. Prior to 2013, GM had no history of choosing video C&C, nor engagement with video conference facilities. Within the digital strategy, over 440 rooms were installed globally, extending to a footprint of 30 countries and 179 sites.

These rooms facilitate group collaboration between other video conference rooms and extending to integrated remote desktop participants, accessing the meeting via the UC&C desktop and mobile client. The growth of collaboration and video conferencing engagement hours within the UC&C desktop/mobile population and video conference room combined, supports a view of a significant shift in culture towards virtual digital collaboration, particularly real-time visual collaboration. Figure 17 depicts the significant growth in video collaboration room usage hours between January 2015 and April 2018. During this period data shows a relative increase in monthly usage growing by 440% compared to installed room growth of 129%.

Figure 16. Decline in reported user issues and growth in service use

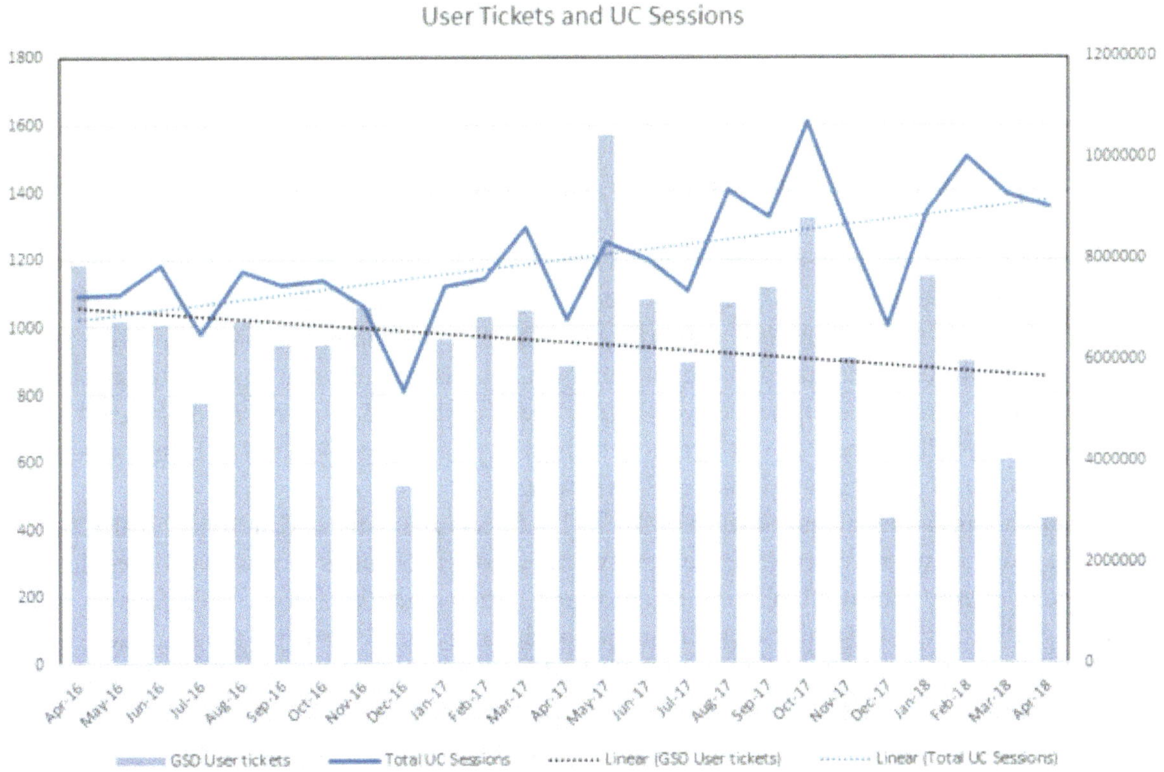

Figure 17. Increase in adoption and usage of video C&C rooms

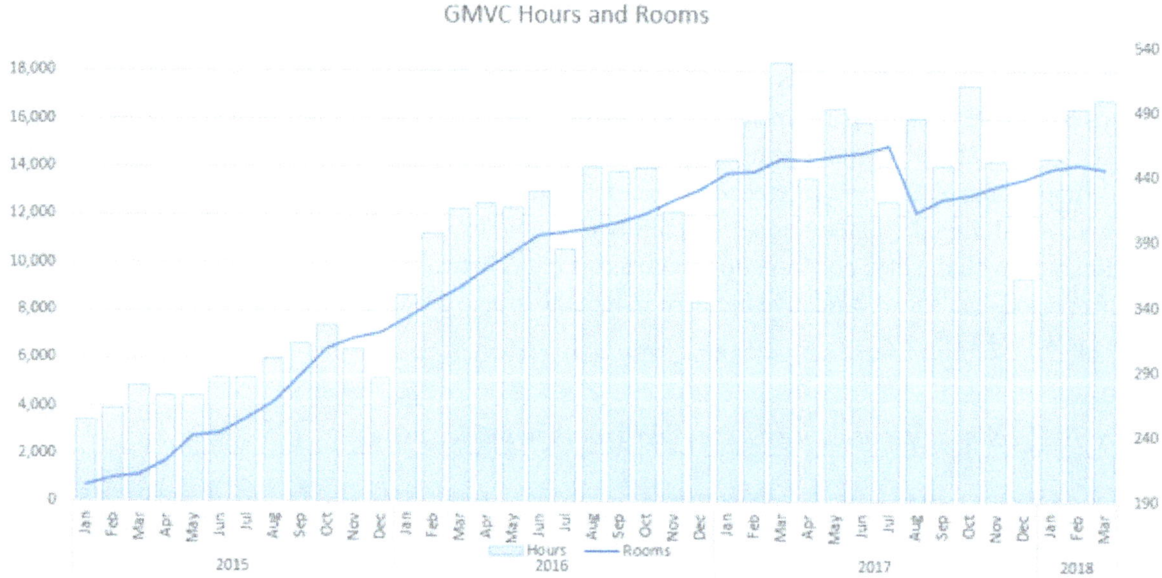

Increased Enterprise Efficiency and Generating Savings

The resulting transformation post-application and deployment of the transformed E-UC&C framework and digital eco-system *generated savings* that were tracked and validated as direct saving to GM. An excellent example of this is the savings that were gained from the adoption and migration of the Skype UC&C client by the end-users and backend integration of internal and external voice collaboration services. Internal conference calling between GM employees transitioned to the internally hosted UC&C conference servers. The associated voice traffic remained internal to the GM network being transported and prioritized on the GM managed Wide Area Network.

External calling parties integrated via the E-UC&C architecture summarized in Bolton, et al. (2022a), through Session Initiation Protocol (SIP) transport circuits and session integration with GM's conference service provider West. The result of this integration and shift to digital transports (time division multiplexing to SIP) facilitated a significant reduction in conference calling cost due to the migration of user traffic to on-net services managed and controlled by GM and on the GM network. Figure 18 shows the savings achieved over fourteen months through April 2018 associated with adoption of the new UC&C by users and transition of cost and traffic to the transformed E-UC&C digital communication platform. This one area of technological transformation resulted in achievement of over 2 million USD in direct financial savings. The complete portfolio of transformed services. An estimated 30+ million USD in annualized savings as validated by the annual functional financial management and reporting process.

Figure 18. Financial benefits associated with a legacy to UC&C conferencing

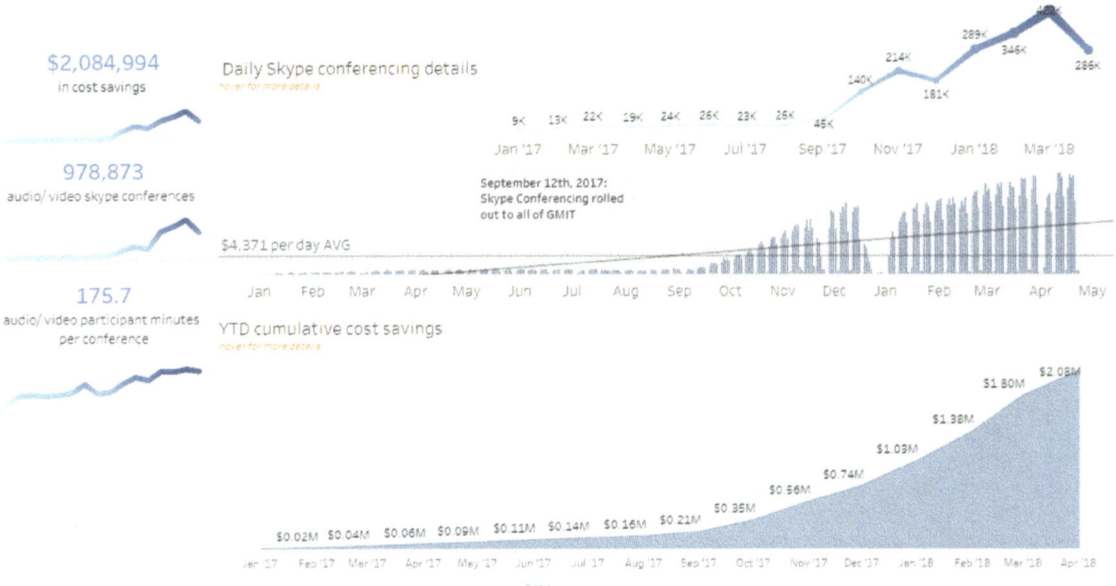

The new digital technologies and underlying eco-system of integrated services enhanced the ability to monitor and report on global interactions across GM' global locations, business units and functions. This capability was used to promote the messaging around the new system capability, growing culture of digital and virtual communication along with the financial and productivity benefits gained through a reduction in travel. Figure 19 shows the dynamic reporting that was developed within the study to track communication between regions and sites. This report shows the cumulative communication across all UC&C communication channels such as voice, video, instant messaging and file services.

The report is dynamically customizable to display all, some or individual services allowing management and staff to track shifts in user communication patterns and align training to maximize shifts in communication methods that deliver the highest benefit associated with productivity, enhanced engagement, relationship building and cost avoidance or deduction. Further research will need to be conducted to monitor and track shifts and changes in the patter of inter and intra-regional, country and business unit communication. Similarly, further research could be carried out to track any shift in communication methods and associated cultural shifts in communication due to the influence of new digital technologies and services.

The data presented shows at a fundamental level that a shift to digital transformation of **emerging strategies** and technologies has occurred, supporting increasing growth in global communication within the automotive enterprise.

Figure 19. Post-deployment inter-regional communication

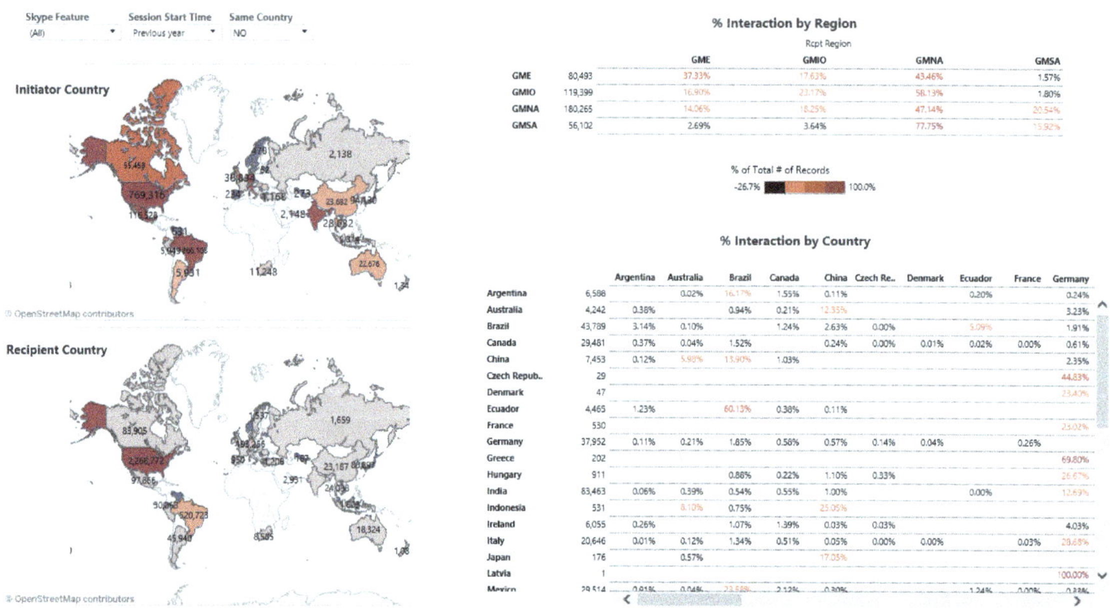

FUTURE RESEARCH DIRECTIONS

This section of the chapter will discuss **future** and **emerging trends** and provide insight about the future of the theme of the book on **challenges and emerging strategies for global** networking **post COVID-19**, from the perspective of the chapter focus on **challenges and emerging strategies for a global automotive enterprise towards a post COVID-19 era**, together with **the impact of digital transformation** on productivity and innovation. The viability of a paradigm, model, implementation **issues** of proposed programs, etc., may also be included in this section. **Future research directions** within the domain of the topic will finally be suggested.

Emerging trends regarding principal categories for interview data were summarized and presented, highlighting an overlap in feedback relating to perceived productivity and innovation, and suggesting a causal relationship between flexibility in communication and building *relationships* between people.

Metric data presented supported the observation within the qualitative survey and interview processes that suggested **emerging trends** on new methods of work and communication processes among end-users aligned to new features and the flexibility of a consolidated communication cockpit through UC&C. At a cyber-social level, **emerging trends** on a change in communication culture among transformed end-users were suggested.

Benefits related to impact on productivity were not available to employees in the pre-transformed state; hence, the **recommendation** that removal of these technologies would erode opportunities to eventually experience the benefits perceived to be realized by their peers. The inference may also suggest that users may value the perceived **future** benefits of the technologies over any interim perception of immediate value.

CONCLUSION

This section will provide a discussion of the overall coverage of the chapter and concluding remarks.

The chapter focused on the presentation of results stemming from the empirical research undertaken within the scope of the study. The results summarized the findings of a multi-faceted research approach combining qualitative and quantitative methods that facilitated the driving of change towards the **digital transformation** of communication within **a global automotive enterprise** (GM), observation of associated change phenomenon at a people level and recording of quantitative system adoption, usage and financial metrics. The aggregated data collected was analyzed against the primary and sub-research questions and leveraged to explore and evaluate the associated research hypotheses established.

The different start and assessed end points of the digital transformation within GM were summarized. The from-to assessment was facilitated through leverage of The Open Group Architecture Framework (TOGAF) capability technologies and methods. A supporting technology and service transformation grid was developed and presented, providing a foundation for discussion of the formal methods employed for transformation assessment. The process for formal assessment of transformation requirements was also presented. This process facilitated the identification of critical requirements for transformation and expected outcomes, and also identifies key stakeholders required for subsequent end-state evaluation. The transformation asset repository and process employed to track all technical requirements and architectural components throughout the multi-year program of transformation were summarized. The end-state transformation outcomes grid was summarized and discussed, influenced by the IT strategic impact grid of Nolan and McFarlan (2005). This instrument was leveraged to establish the base evaluation criteria employed in the post-transformation end-user survey process.

The following section summarized and discussed the outcomes of the post-transformation end-user survey. The end-user survey was employed as a method to evaluate and analyze **the impact of digital transformation** on measures of the end-user perceived productivity and acceleration of capacity towards innovation. A process of reductive inference was applied in the analysis of observations captured via the survey and participant interview processes. The pool of 2,000 sampled users was selected randomly across the GM enterprise user population with a target response rate of 20%. The end-state response rate of 33% resulted in 660 active participants and a reduced margin of error of 3.8% vs. the targeted 5%.

The results of the survey suggested that **digital transformation** through the application of a UC&C framework can lead to the development of new methods of communication resulting in the generation of new workflows. End-user adoption was enhanced through the delivery of multi-modal communication methods facilitated through a consolidated central **digital transformation** cockpit and a seamless back-end cross-functional system and integration. These findings aligned with More (2016), who argued that highly complex technical products influence poor adoption outcomes. While no standard definition of individual user productivity was established across the GM business groups or user community, the survey results suggested that the majority of users identified leverage of the **digital transformation** of communication capabilities with increased perceived individual productivity gains. The majority of users also identified the removal of the technology post-adoption with a perceived anticipated reduction in productivity. In relation to enhancing and driving innovation, the survey results indicated that most users identified as having an increased capacity to drive and participate in innovation activities due to the flexible and on-demand nature of UC&C functionalities.

This section also presented and discussed the participant interview research process. The interview process and application of open coding methods facilitated the development of more profound insights into the impact of the E-UC&C framework on end-users, post-deployment. The four new categories associated with productivity established via the interview and open coding process were summarized. These categories were discussed individually through the construction of productivity factors: *Increased enterprise efficiency*, convenience and speed, building and sustaining *relationships* and personal *satisfaction*. The new categories for innovation were similarly summarized in the context of innovation factors: changing work practices, collaboration, creativity and generation of financial *efficiency*.

The complementary data collection and analysis of the quantitative system and end-user adoption metrics were presented and discussed. Statistical data was collected throughout the duration of the research study and documented via an online reporting portal consisting of 130 individual reports. Key reports, such as those from the transformation adoption metrics for UC&C, were presented, supporting a view of rapid and significant system adoption in the form of installation and deployment to end-users. These metrics were contrasted with actual usage metrics, such as call and message volume data, to support active functionality use of the new capabilities versus functional deployment. Finally, a summary of the financial benefits and *increased enterprise efficiency*, driven by technology deployment and the subsequent adoption of functionalities, was presented and discussed, indicating the financial benefits over a 16-month timeframe of more than $2 million (USD).

REFERENCES

Berrell, M. (2017). The Social Relations of Anywhere Working: Major Themes and Meanings. In Remote Work and Collaboration: Breakthroughs in Research and Practice (pp. 287-304). IGI Global.

Bolton, A., Goosen, L., & Kritzinger, E. (2016). Enterprise Digitization Enablement Through Unified Communication and Collaboration. In *Proceedings of the Annual Conference of the South African Institute of Computer Scientists and Information Technologists*. ACM. doi:10.1145/2987491.2987516

Bolton, A., Goosen, L., & Kritzinger, E. (2020b). The Impact of Unified Communication and Collaboration Technologies on Productivity and Innovation: Promotion for the Fourth Industrial Revolution. In S. B. Buckley (Ed.), *Promoting Inclusive Growth in the Fourth Industrial Revolution* (pp. 44–73). IGI Global. doi:10.4018/978-1-7998-4882-0.ch002

Bolton, A., Goosen, L., & Kritzinger, E. (2021b). An Empirical Study into the Impact on Innovation and Productivity Towards the Post-COVID-19 Era: Digital Transformation of an Automotive Enterprise. In L. C. Carvalho, L. Reis, & C. Silveira (Eds.), *Handbook of Research on Entrepreneurship, Innovation, Sustainability, and ICTs in the Post-COVID-19 Era* (pp. 133–159). IGI Global. doi:10.4018/978-1-7998-6776-0.ch007

Bolton, A., Goosen, L., & Kritzinger, E. (2021c). The Integration and Implementation of the Internet of Things Through Digital Transformation: Impact on Productivity and Innovation. In P. Tomar (Ed.), Integration and Implementation of the Internet of Things Through Cloud Computing (pp. 85-112). IGI Global. doi:10.4018/978-1-7998-6981-8.ch005

Bolton, A. D., Goosen, L., & Kritzinger, E. (2021a). Unified Communication Technologies at a Global Automotive Organization. In M. Khosrow-Pour (Ed.), *Encyclopedia of Organizational Knowledge, Administration, and Technologies* (pp. 2592–2608). IGI Global. doi:10.4018/978-1-7998-3473-1.ch179

Rodrigues, M., & Proença, J. (Eds.), *Impact of Digital Transformation on the Development of New Business Models and Consumer Experience* (pp. 271–298). IGI Global., doi:10.4018/978-1-7998-9179-6.ch014

Bolton, A. D., Goosen, L., & Kritzinger, E. (2022b). Emerging Technologies for Innovation and Productivity Management in the Automotive Industry: Impact of Digital Transformation on Communication. In *Emerging Technologies for Innovation Management in the Software Industry (pp. 60-85)*. IGI Global. doi:10.4018/978-1-7998-9059-1.ch003

Bolton, T., Goosen, L., & Kritzinger, E. (2020a). Security Aspects of an Empirical Study into the Impact of Digital Transformation via Unified Communication and Collaboration Technologies on the Productivity and Innovation of a Global Automotive Enterprise. Communications in Computer and Information Science, 1166, 99-113. doi:10.1007/978-3-030-43276-8_8

Bosch-Rekveldt, M., Jongkind, Y., Mooi, H., Bakker, H., & Verbraeck, A. (2011). Grasping project complexity in large engineering projects: The TOE (Technical, Organizational and Environmental) framework. *International Journal of Project Management*, *29*(6), 728–739. doi:10.1016/j.ijproman.2010.07.008

Bryson, J., & Alston, F. (2011). *Creating Your Strategic Plan: A Workbook for Public and Nonprofit Organisations*. Wiley.

Davis, F. (1985). *A Technology Acceptance Model for Empirically Testing New End-User Information Systems: Theory and Results*. Massachusetts Institute of Technology.

De Vaus, D. (2014). *Surveys in social research* (M. Bulmer, Ed.; 6th ed.). Routledge.

Dikbas, A., & Scherer, R. (2004). eWork and eBusiness in Architecture, Engineering and Construction. Taylor & Francis.

Easton, G. (2010). Critical realism in case study research. *Industrial Marketing Management*, *39*(1), 118–128. doi:10.1016/j.indmarman.2008.06.004

Flick, U. (2014). An Introduction to Qualitative Research. *Sage (Atlanta, Ga.)*.

Goosen, L. (2004). *Criteria and Guidelines for the Selection and Implementation of a First Programming Language in High Schools*. Potchefstroom Campus: North West University. Retrieved from http://hdl.handle.net/10394/226

Goosen, L. (2015). Educational Technologies for an ICT4D MOOC in the 21st Century. In D. Nwaozuzu, & S. Mnisi (Ed.), *Proceedings of the South Africa International Conference on Educational Technologies* (pp. 37 - 48). African Academic Research Forum.

Goosen, L. (2018a). Sustainable and Inclusive Quality Education Through Research Informed Practice on Information and Communication Technologies in Education. In L. Webb (Ed.), *Proceedings of the 26th Conference of the Southern African Association for Research in Mathematics, Science and Technology Education (SAARMSTE)* (pp. 215 - 228). University of Botswana.

Goosen, L. (2018b). Trans-Disciplinary Approaches to Action Research for e-Schools, Community Engagement, and ICT4D. In T. A. Mapotse (Ed.), *Cross-Disciplinary Approaches to Action Research and Action Learning* (pp. 97–110). IGI Global. doi:10.4018/978-1-5225-2642-1.ch006

Goosen, L. (2018c). Ethical Data Management and Research Integrity in the Context of e-Schools and Community Engagement. In C. Sibinga (Ed.), *Ensuring Research Integrity and the Ethical Management of Data* (pp. 14–45). IGI Global. doi:10.4018/978-1-5225-2730-5.ch002

Goosen, L. (2018d). Ethical Information and Communication Technologies for Development Solutions: Research Integrity for Massive Open Online Courses. In C. Sibinga (Ed.), *Ensuring Research Integrity and the Ethical Management of Data* (pp. 155–173). IGI Global. doi:10.4018/978-1-5225-2730-5.ch009

Goosen, L. (2019a). Research on Technology-Supported Teaching and Learning for Autism. In L. Makewa, B. Ngussa, & J. Kuboja (Eds.), *Technology-Supported Teaching and Research Methods for Educators* (pp. 88–110). IGI Global. doi:10.4018/978-1-5225-5915-3.ch005

Goosen, L. (2019b). Technology-Supported Teaching and Research Methods for Educators: Case Study of a Massive Open Online Course. In L. Makewa, B. Ngussa, & J. Kuboja (Eds.), *Technology-Supported Teaching and Research Methods for Educators* (pp. 128–148). IGI Global. doi:10.4018/978-1-5225-5915-3.ch007

Goosen, L. (2021). Organizational Knowledge and Administration Lessons from an ICT4D MOOC. In M. Khosrow-Pour (Ed.), *Encyclopedia of Organizational Knowledge, Administration, and Technologies* (pp. 245–261). IGI Global. doi:10.4018/978-1-7998-3473-1.ch020

Goosen, L., & Mukasa-Lwanga, T. (2017). Educational Technologies in Distance Education: Beyond the Horizon with Qualitative Perspectives. *Proceedings of the South Africa International Conference on Educational Technologies* (pp. 41-54). African Academic Research Forum.

Goosen, L., & Naidoo, L. (2014). Computer Lecturers Using Their Institutional LMS for ICT Education in the Cyber World. *Proceedings of the 43rd Conference of the Southern African Computer Lecturers' Association* (pp. 99-108). Nelson Mandela Metropolitan University.

Ibrahim, I., & Taniar, D. (2006). Mobile Multimedia: A Communication Engineering Perspective. *Nova Scientia.*

Keyes, J. (2016). *Aligning IT with Corporate Strategy: Implementing the IT Balanced Scorecard.* Auerbach. doi:10.1201/9781420031348

Libbrecht, P., & Goosen, L. (2015). Using ICTs to Facilitate Multilingual Mathematics Teaching and Learning. In *Mathematics Education and Language Diversity* (pp. 217–235). Springer.

Lundberg, E. (2017). *How to compete effectively with self-service technologies: The impact of technology readiness and the technology acceptance model of self scanning*. Uppsala University.

McLaughlin, R. (1982). *What? Where? When? Why? Essays on Induction, Space and Time, explanation.* D Reidel. doi:10.1007/978-94-009-7731-0

Meeker, W., Hahn, G., & Escobar, L. (2017). *Statistical Intervals: A Guide for Practitioners and Researchers.* Wiley. doi:10.1002/9781118594841

More, R. (2016). *Marketing High Profit Product/Service Solutions.* Routledge. doi:10.4324/9781315593975

Nolan, R., & McFarlan, W. (2005). Information technology and the board of directors. *Harvard Business Review, 83*(10), 96. PMID:16250628

Peitrucha, F. (2014). *Supercommunicator*. American Management Association.

Pelet, J.-E. (2014). *User Behavior in Ubiquitous Online Environments*. IGI Global. doi:10.4018/978-1-4666-4566-0

Russell, J., & Russell, L. (2005). *Strategic Planning: Training*. American Society for Training and Development Press.

Saladis, F., & Kerzner, H. (2009). *Bringing the PMBOK Guide to Life: A Companion for the Practicing Project Manager*. Wiley. doi:10.1002/9780470446324

Sayer, R. (1992). *Method in social science: A realist approach*. Psychology Press.

Shalley, C., Hitt, M., & Zhou, J. (2015). *The Oxford Handbook of Creativity*. Innovation and Entrepreneurship.

The Open Group. (2015). *The Open Group Architecture Framework TOGAF Version 9*. Van Haren Publishing.

Venkatesh, V., & Davis, F. (2000). A theoretical extension of the technology acceptance model: Four longitudinal field studies. *Management Science*, *46*(2), 186–204. doi:10.1287/mnsc.46.2.186.11926

Workman, M. (2010). Technology Innovation Adoption and Diffusion: Contrast of Perspectives. In Cases on Technology Innovation: Entrepreneurial Successes and Pitfalls (pp. 91-106). IGI Global.

Chapter 6
Economic Crisis in Colombia Due to COVID-19:
From Pandemic to Post-Pandemic Actions

Jahir Lombana-Coy
https://orcid.org/0000-0002-0055-8392
Universidad del Norte, Colombia

María Carolina Ovalle
Universidad del Norte, Colombia

Alberto Elías Muñoz Santiago
Universidad del Norte, Colombia

ABSTRACT

The COVID-19 pandemic has had a social, economic, and political impact, with companies particularly affected. Policymakers and managers had to make strategic decisions to continue operations. Therefore, this chapter focuses on evaluating the economic impact of the crisis in Colombia from the government, and companies' perspectives, and how they established some strategies to achieve economic sustainability. This analysis is composed of macroeconomic aspects, businesses´ role for economic reactivation, decisions to face the pandemic, and finally, actions that ensure their sustainability. There are issues on fiscal and monetary policies to ensure employment and keep inflation through direct support and rules to improve companies' conditions. Companies themselves should learn about risk management, digital transformation, and the relocation of providers and customers. There is no single recipe to guarantee success, but there is a need for an integrated plan that includes government, central bank, and companies to shorten the economic effects of this kind of crisis.

DOI: 10.4018/978-1-7998-8856-7.ch006

INTRODUCTION

In 2020, Covid-19 was declared a pandemic (World Health Organization - WHO, 2020), becoming a critical moment for reflection, a call for the sustainability of society, and consequently, a rethinking of the macro and microeconomic dynamics within countries. From the macro perspective, governments and central banks had to implement fiscal and monetary policies in order to reduce the impact on the economy. Regarding the micro, businesses had to make rearrangements in their operational process to continue in the market. Moreover, several companies could not transfer their employees to remote/virtual schemes, which implied a greater affectation (e.g. companies that have declared bankruptcy, reduction in the number of employees) (Apedo-Amah, et al., 2020). For those who were able to support themselves, information and communication technologies have gained prominence as a mechanism for doing business, educating, and taking care of health (International Labor Organization - ILO, 2020).

In this sense, this chapter seeks to evaluate the impacts of the pandemic crisis in economic terms in Colombia at government and business levels and to analyze some strategies to face them and achieve their sustainability despite the circumstances.

The chapter consists of six sections. After this introduction, it presents the background of macroeconomic and microeconomic variables in Colombia. In the third section, it describes the actions carried out in the pandemic by the government and the central bank in the macroeconomic variables and by companies. The fourth section shows the decision-making process for economic agents. The fifth section presents and analyzes the actions related to post-pandemic times. Finally, the chapter closes with recommendations, new lines of research, and conclusions.

BACKGROUND

This section provides the macro and the micro views of the pandemic. It intends to show on the one hand, the trends on economic growth, unemployment, inflation, and the external sector. On the other hand, it shows the conditions of companies, especially small and medium-sized enterprises (SMEs) confronting economic crises.

Macroeconomic Variables: Economic Growth, Unemployment, Inflation and External Sector

The first case of COVID-19 detected in Colombia was on March 2nd, 2020. From that moment on, a series of sanitary measures were first established (March 2020, Decree 417) and then the Economic, Social, and Ecological Emergency was stated (March 2020, Decree 457. May 2020, Decree 637), for 30 days to face the crisis (Deloitte, 2020).

After the deepest crisis in 1999, Colombia had been growing with positive numbers, among the best in Latin America (Caballero & Machado, 2020). However, the economic consequences of the pandemic are valued at a retraction of -6.8% of GDP (see Figure 1), considered the first recession of the 21st century (Mejía, 2020) and unemployment with its highest peak in May 2020 with 21 .1% (Figure 2) that was only seen since the 1999 crisis and that was reflected in an increase in monetary poverty to 43.2% and extreme monetary poverty to 14.6% (United Nations for Development Programme, 2021). Additionally, a deepening of inequality is noted between December 2019 with a GINI coefficient of 0.5081 and August 2020 with 0.5389 (Departamento Nacional de Estadística - DANE, 2020).

Figure 1. Quarterly GDP
Source: Departamento Nacional de Estadística (DANE)

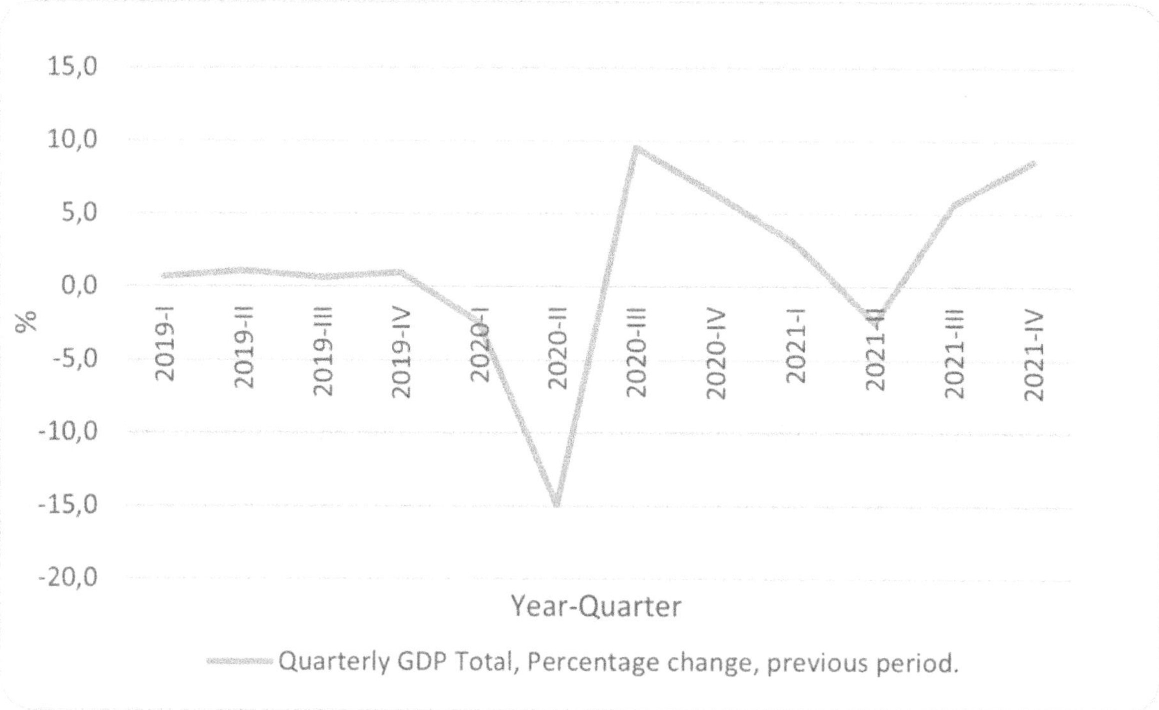

Figure 2. Unemployment
Source: Banco de la República

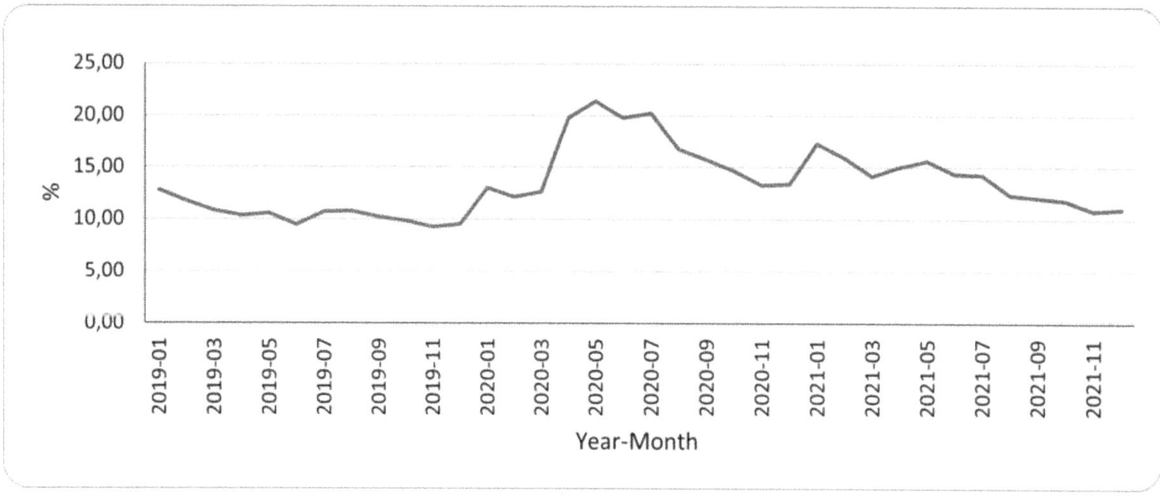

On the other hand, inflation rates remained relatively stable and within the target range of the Central Bank of Colombia, even lower amid the pandemic. However, as expected, the rebound arrives in August 2021, exceeding the upper range determined by the Central Bank of Colombia (see figure 3), this is mainly due to the high costs of imported goods (e.g. agricultural inputs) that affected different markets, particularly in food industry.

Figure 3. Inflation
Source: Banco de la República

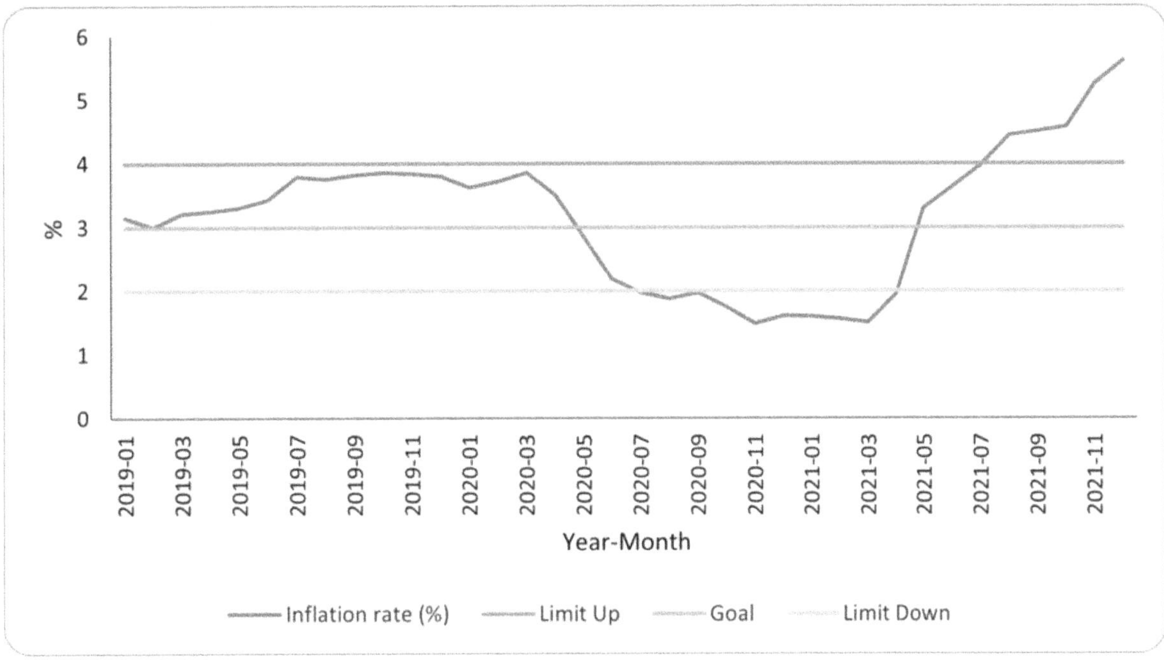

Regarding the external sector, there was a substantial impact between 2019 and 2020 due to the low prices of raw materials on which Colombia depends for export (e.g. in mining-energy: 39.5%) as a result of the lower international demand for crude oil (from developed countries and China). Furthermore, the trade war between Russia and Saudi Arabia over oil production cuts and the closures of other countries with the consequent interruptions in the supply chains and the uncertainty of risk (Mejía, 2020).

In 2020 the total exports reached US$31,056 million, being 21.4% less than in 2019 but maintaining a trade deficit that has already become structural for Colombia since imports reached US$41,185 million (Dirección de Impuestos y Aduanas Nacionales - DIAN, 2021). Likewise, the dollar as a currency in Colombia, for many years indexed to the ups and downs of the international price of mining energy, behaved more by external variables. For example, the repercussions of the US being the largest buyer of assets in the world during the second quarter of 2020, especially treasury bonds and mortgage-backed securities for close to US$700 billion (Federal Reserve, 2020). Therefore, it involved a large amount of dollars, generating its depreciation against the rest of the world's currencies (including the Colombian). However, the uncertainty of the emerging countries and the feeling of risk once again corrected the depreciation of the dollar. As seen in graph 4, the devaluation of the Colombian peso during the pandemic period, although volatile at first, shows its natural upward trend.

Figure 4. External sector

Source: Incomex, Departamento Administrativo Nacional de Estadística (DANE), Dirección de Impuestos y Aduanas Nacionales (Dirección de Impuestos y Aduanas Nacionales - DIAN, 2021), Superintendencia Financiera de Colombia & Banco de la República.

**Provisional data according to customs.*

/1 millions of US$ FOB

/2 Main exports refer to oil, coal, coffee, and ferroalloys

/3 Monthly average exchange rate refers to the simple average of the exchange rate on business days only.

/4 COP$/US$

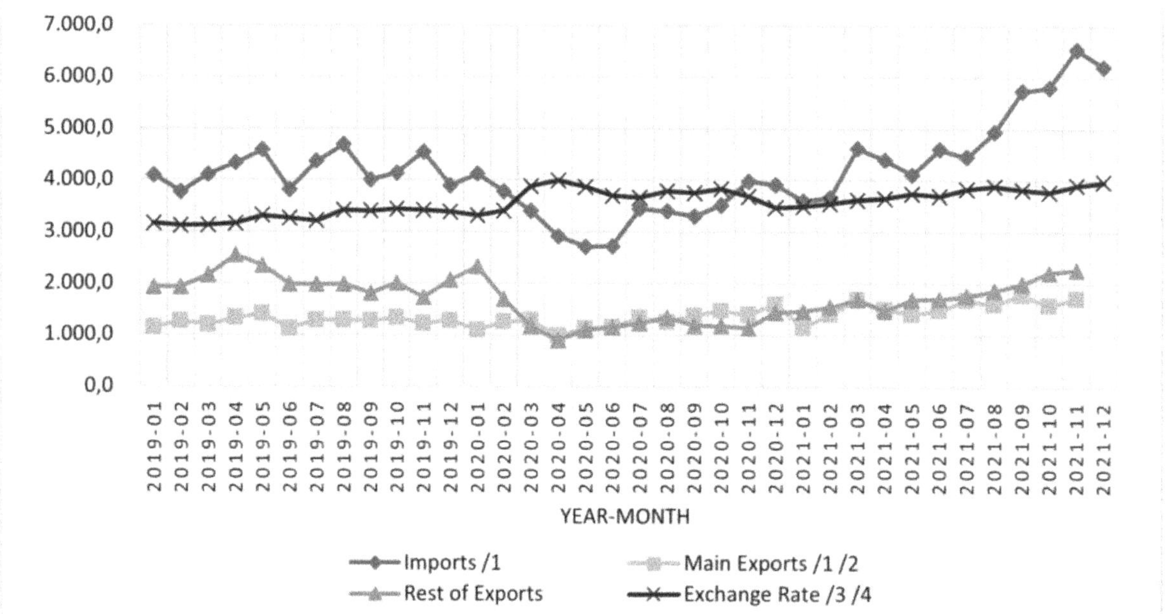

In this sense, an analysis of the interest rate differential between Colombia and the rest of the world is necessary, particularly with the United States, since it has a direct repercussion on the price of the dollar. The historical behavior of this differential has been in favor of the domestic rate, but it increase in the pandemic since September 2020, the interest rate in Colombia was the lowest in the history of the country's monetary policy, remaining at 1.75% (Banco de la República, 2020). Consequently, the country was not interesting enough to attract foreign capital and in the short term, it was not easy for the Colombian peso to appreciate due to the inflow of foreign currency destined for portfolio investment.

Business Effect

The immediate impact of the crisis was a decrease in aggregate demand in the countries that decided to quarantine their citizens (the case of Colombia), leading to increases in unemployment and occasioning a higher decrease over the demand, so that the projected income of the companies fell significantly. This impacts the reduction of formal productive activity due to sanitary closures, although maintaining labor and tax obligations (Beverinotti & Deza, 2020). Sectors such as construction, mining, and quarrying (-33.2%) and artistic, entertainment and recreation activities (-37.1%) and tourist activities, and formal and informal commerce (-34.1%), were the industries most affected between 2019 and 2020 (United Nations for Development Programme, 2021). Moreover, industrial production fell by 7.7%, with the sectors of leather and footwear (-37,8%) and cars and auto parts (-36.9%) being the most affected (Banco de la República, n.d.).

It is important to mention that the Colombian business ecosystem is made up of between 55 and 65% informality, employing 37% of workers and producing 33% of GDP (Fernández, 2018; United Nations - UN, 2020), the outlook could not be less uncertain.

During the first months of confinement, that is, March and April 2020, Confecamaras (2020a) investigated the business sector in Colombia, emphasizing three main aspects: sales, supply of inputs, and supplies, to overcome the crisis by Covid-19.

CESLA & ANDI (2020) stated that between January and September 2020, production decreased (-10.1%) compared to the same period in 2019, also total sales (-9.9%). In October 2020, Confecámaras (2020b) monitored once again, the impact of COVID 19 on the country's business sector, given the reactivation of the economy. Part of the conclusions was that 80.6% of the companies were still operating, achieving that 66% of the managers coincided that after the reactivation of the economy, they could maintain their employees.

Among the results, it stands out that regardless of the sector, more than 90% of managers considered that from the economic and social crisis perspective, their company would be negatively affected. Among the main reasons that the entrepreneurs stated was that their business could only survive with their resources between 1 and 2 months (82%). From the sales perspective, 96% of the entrepreneurs surveyed agreed that their sales fell and 82% affirmed that the negative behavior of their sales would continue in the coming months of 2020. Regarding the supply of inputs and supplies, it is indicated that the costs associated with this item have been decisive in the rise in prices of their goods and/or services, specifically, companies have perceived increases in supply costs (21.2%), as well as general price increases (18.8%).

MAIN FOCUS OF THE CHAPTER: POLICIES AND STRATEGIES DURING THE PANDEMIC

The following section presents the actions of the government in fiscal policy and the Central Bank of Colombia in monetary policy to face the economic and social crisis resulting from the pandemic. These were mostly short-term actions which are collected in a policy document called Initial Response Strategy to the Effects of the Covid-19 Pandemic on Public Health, Households, the Productive System, and Public Finances (Concejo de Política Económica y Social - CONPES; Departamento Nacional de Planeación - DNP, 2020). Likewise, the business perspective is shown from government aid to its strategic decisions.

Fiscal Policy

The national government constructed a series of actions to reduce the economic and social effects of the pandemic in the short term. For this, it had an additional budget for 2020 (in November) of 11billion USD (78,97 billion USD in total for the term). Consequently, the Fiscal Rule Consultative Committee unanimously approved the suspension of the fiscal rule in the country during 2020 and 2021 on June 15th, this with a follow-up in the Medium-Term Fiscal Framework and accompanied by the same committee (Ministerio de Hacienda - MinHacienda, 2020). Thus, the fiscal deficit went from 2.2% for 2020 to 8.2% of GDP (Barrera, Radziunas, & Montoya, 2021). At the tax level, payment deadlines were extended, and mandatory social security contributions were temporarily reduced.

The distribution of income was developed for public health issues and support for the most vulnerable population. In the first instance, the creation of the Emergency Mitigation Fund (FOME) with resources of 6,25 billion USD (2.4% of GDP) (Andrian & Hirs, 2020). The transfer of additional resources took place through government programs already established to support Families in Action, Youth in Action, and Colombia Older Adult (75 billion USD). To these mechanisms was added the "solidarity income" program for people outside the mentioned mechanisms (40 billion USD) and processes for the return of value-added tax (VAT) in vulnerable populations.

Among the activities directed by the national government, there were some policies established, such as job creation to support SMEs, accelerating infrastructure projects, and support for the productive sectors affected by the pandemic with an emphasis on the orange economy and digital transformation. In this sense, the National Guarantee Fund is capitalized to grant guarantees for business loans of up to 90% and payroll support with subsidies of up to 40% of the minimum wage in companies and employers that have sustained falls in income equal to or greater than 20% in the crisis (Andrian & Hirs, 2020). It is important to mention that these actions were oriented to specific sectors such as (i) entrepreneurs (Congreso de la República de Colombia, 2020a) seeking to reduce procedures and tax burdens to create, formalize and develop new businesses. Also giving priority to selling to the State, favoring SMEs, support platforms for buying and selling, facilitating formalization, training, microinsurance, creation of autonomous funds of regional governments in places where businesses are established (Law 2069 of 2020). (ii) tourism (Congreso de la República de Colombia, 2020b) temporary reduction of VAT on air tickets and hotel and tourism services, suspension of energy surcharges, and consumption tax in bars and restaurants. Lines of credit with second-tier banking (e.g. Bancoldex) (Law 2068 of 2020).

Table 1. Fiscal Impact in Colombia from Pre-(2019) to Pandemic (2020)

Indicator	Impact
Fiscal deficit	2,5% -> 7,8%
Tax income	Reduction 0,9%
Capital income	Reduction 0,1%
Governmental spending	Increase 4,3%
COVID-19 governmental spending	4% points of GDP
Governmental investment spending	Increase 10%
Debt	14,5% -> 64,8% of GDP
Internal debt	Increase 7,6%
External debt	Increase 6,9%
Risk qualification (S&P)	BBB+ -> BB+

Source: Author´s elaboration based on Comisión Económica para América Latina y el Caribe - CEPAL (2021) and Blackman, et al. (2020)

With the short-term actions taken, the government analyzed the need to reformulate medium- and long-term policies, for which it established a roadmap called: Policy for Reactivation, Repowering and Sustainable and Inclusive Growth: New Commitment for the Future of Colombia (Concejo de Política Económica y Social - CONPES; Departamento Nacional de Planeación - DNP, 2020). With its three objectives: social, productive and institutional, seeking to be developed over a 5-year period (2021 to 2026) in order to invest 35 billion USD in housing construction, infrastructure, education, oil and hydrocarbon, agriculture, artistic activities, public administration and professional services, among others. Consequently, the productive front becomes one of the most important of this policy, which proposes actions for a transition towards more sustainable and sophisticated production, creating employment and internationalization.

In summary, the government's strategies in fiscal policies were:

- Temporary suspension of the fiscal rule
- Maintenance in 2021 and 2022 of the additional expenses to protect the most vulnerable families.
- Starting in 2023, public spending would begin to adjust. In 2021, 8.6% was established as the goal of the fiscal deficit.
- Social investment law (law 2155) for the achievement of goals
    - Social: increase public spending to reduce poverty
    - Economic: reduce unemployment and restore the dynamism of the economy.
    - Fiscal: work on the construction of fiscal sustainability.

Monetary and Financial Policy

On the other hand, the Central Bank of Colombia, having a constitutional mandate to maintain inflation and in the face of the external shock due to the exchange rate, announced an exchange hedging auction for 1,000 million USD, and increase the liquidity share for the private debt of 4,25 billion USD to 5 billion USD. The Central Bank of Colombia was authorized to buy private securities issued by credit institutions, with a remaining maturity of less than or equal to three years. It was also authorized to buy public debt securities (TES) for 500 million USD with daily auctions (Mejía, 2020; Banco de la República, 2020). The interest rate was gradually reduced (7 times) from the pre-pandemic 4.25% to historically low levels of 1.75% (between September 2020 and August 2021) aiming to provide liquidity that would facilitate payments and support the supply of credit from financial institutions (Economic Commission for Latin America and the Caribbean - ECLAC, 2020).

Precisely, financial institutions (banks) had their reserve requirements reduced and swaps in dollars (banks, insurance, pensions) were allowed to generate liquidity in foreign currency (Avendaño, 2020). In general, there were expanded liquidity terms, applicable values , and eligible counterparties (Andrian & Hirs, 2020). Therefore, the Financial Superintendence of Colombia (in Spanish SFC), accompanying the work of the Central Bank of Colombia, granted financial entities the possibility to reschedule loans with arrears of less than 30 days, without affecting credit history, or increasing interest rates. Likewise, in August 2020, the Debtor Support Program was created, characterizing its history to normalizc payments in the face of new economic conditions (Superintendencia Financiera de Colombia - SFC, n.d.).

Table 2. Monetary/Financial Impact in Colombia from Pre-(2019) to Pandemic (2020)

Indicator	Impact
Loan portfolio (local currency)	Increase 4,9%
Loan portfolio as %GDP	Increase 3,1% annual
Past-due loan portfolio	Increase to 19,4%
Nominal COP depreciation	12,5%

Source: Author´s elaboration based on (Comisión Económica para América Latina y el Caribe - CEPAL, 2021) *and* (Blackman, et al., 2020)

In summary, the monetary strategies coordinated by the government and the Central Bank of Colombia can be summarized as follows:

- An expansionary policy that has been extended throughout 2021 to facilitate the consolidation of recovery.
- Reduction of reserve requirements for current accounts from 11% to 8%
- Reduction of reserve requirements for term deposits from 4.5% to 3.5%
- Reduction of the intervention rate to 1.75%.
- Debtor support plan (PAD) with a view to generate extensions to debtors or redefining the conditions of the contract.
- Stabilization of growth in non-performing loans.

Business Sector Policy

The Special Program of Guarantees 'United for Colombia' (3 billion USD) of the Colombian government, sought to solve cash flow problems, liquidity needs, personnel expenses, fixed costs, and other obligations in SMEs to guarantee the sustainability of the business (Fondo Nacional de Garantías - FNG, n.d.). The government also promoted new lines of credit and pre-pandemic debt payment waivers in development (e.g. Bancoldex, Banco Agrario, Findeter) and commercial banks (FINDETER, 2020).

Another action taken was to simplify situations with insolvency law, allowing obligations to be paid to workers and suppliers with priority over other administrative expenses. In addition, payment facilities were given, and tax deadlines were extended. What was required and associated with health protection, VAT exemption was granted and the 0% tariff was applied to imports. The consumption incentive was also promoted with 3 days without VAT per year for products of various categories (e.g. electrical appliances, school supplies, agricultural goods, and supplies) and with different means of payment (De la Hoz, Cantillo, & Ramírez, 2021). Regarding labor aspects, the Ministry of Labor of Colombia establishes transitory regulations: flexible working hours, early and collective vacations, paid leave, salary without service provision, reduction of working hours and salary, reduction of pension contributions, suspension or modification of extralegal benefits, suspension or modification of conventional benefits, compensable paid leave (Ministerio de Trabajo - MinTrabajo, 2020). All the above given the need to establish a balance between the health aspects (due to distancing and biosecurity measures) and the economic aspects of families, seeking that companies could better alleviate the crisis. Indirect employment support, the formal employment support program (PAEF) was made official to pay 40% of the payroll for companies with losses of more than 20% in the pandemic (Unidad de Gestión de Pensiones y Parafiscales - UGPP, n.d.).

DECISION MAKING IN UNCERTAIN TIMES

Organizations have been implementing different actions to mitigate the direct and indirect impact of Covid-19 pandemic on their operations. Their important role within the sustainability and growth of nations made them essential for all those who not only live from them but their suppliers, and customers. In this sense, it is fundamental to analyze the macroeconomic variables that may affect the decision-making of the companies in uncertain times and that might have implications in the long term.

(Confecamaras, 2020a) investigated the benefits granted by the government during Covid-19 for companies and entrepreneurs. Results indicate that 60,1% of them had access to at least one of the benefits, particularly to the "formal employment support program" (PAEF) from its Spanish initials (42,5%) and to the "support program payment of the service premium" (23,5%).

Different types of challenges caused by the Covid-19 pandemic include operational, productivity, and economic risk for the companies. Therefore, executives and entrepreneurs had to make radical decisions in a short period to continue operating. Furthermore, they had to redesign, rethink, and develop their business models according to the situation such as remote work, among other decisions. In this sense, this section will expose some of the actions as well as some business experiences by entrepreneurs in Colombia.

Budget Adjustment

One of the main actions taken by the companies was to make budget adjustments, starting to rethink the projections for the year 2020 and beyond, in terms of sales, costs, and expenses. Considering uncertain times experimented in all economic sectors, this action was crucial back in March 2020.

According to the Industrial Opinion Survey (Asociación Nacional de Industriales - ANDI, 2020) between January and September of 2020, production in the industrial sector decreased by 10,1% compared to the same period in 2019, while total sales decreased by 9,9%. Therefore, agile and dynamic decision-making was transcendental for the survival of organizations.

Borrowing and Refinancing

One of the main collateral effects of the crisis is exhibited through cash flow duties, leading companies to go into debt to maintain their working capital. For the cases of companies with old debt, the objective was to try long-term refinancing. According to Asociación Colombiana de Pequeños Industriales - ACOPI, (2020), 82,4% of SMEs surveyed did not have a savings plan to cover the crisis. The remaining percentage of SMEs that did have such savings estimate that they only managed to cover the first three months (90,6%).

Human Resources

The human resources area has always been considered a key element in the functioning of the organization since they are not only in charge of choosing the ideal employee, but also to ensure the well-being of their collaborators, streamline processes, improving the quality of work, stimulating productivity, among other activities. Given the circumstances, the human resources area had to assure that every employee had the minimum implements to continue with their duties at home.

According to Comisión Económica para América Latina y el Caribe – CEPAL (2020) in Colombia between 2 and 3 million workers were reassigned in-home office due to the pandemic, which caused around 62% of them to suffer from stress, anxiety, and a feeling of isolation, while 38% of the employees agreed to miss the traditional work environment. In this sense, the human resources managers undertook a titanic task to safeguard the physical and mental health of their collaborators, strengthen the relation and communication channels, ensure working conditions, as well as implement activities that promote well-being.

Technological Tools

During the global social isolation, companies agreed that technological platforms were crucial to continue with operations and the activities of the employees. To have an approach with customers, innovative channels were required to replace the face-to-face interaction. In this sense, it is important to mention that in the second quarter of 2020, companies allocated resources toward the acquisition of new technologies and the development of innovation processes, which promoted their reactivation within the economy (Asociación Colombiana de Pequeños Industriales - ACOPI, 2020).

For example, purchases through digital platforms became dynamic throughout the world, specifically, E-Commerce in Latin America grew more than 300% during the pandemic, and in Colombia digital penetration grew between 50% and 80% during the same period (Kantar, 2020). Furthermore, the study concluded that the use of cash has been reduced; in the case of Latin America it presented a reduction of 66% while in Colombia it was 62%

Schedules Changes and Remote Work

As the isolation restriction was implemented, companies had to move their employees to remote work. However, this was a huge effort because it required continuous adjustment to keep the organization in operation. In this sense, remote work generated changes in schedules on some occasions as well as unplanning meetings, and of course, more dedication of the employees. Furthermore, the changes translated into high levels of anxiety or stress due to poor time management in their homes.

According to data from NordVPN, it was revealed that employees in different countries have extended their working hours up to 40% of their home office (La República, 2020). Moreover, Colombian companies coincide that their productivity had increased 39% due to remote working, a decrease in operation costs (37%), and an increase in process efficiency (27%).

Dismissals

Companies were forced to make employees adjustments and massive dismissals, resulting in loss of talent, experience, and labor work, leading in some cases to lawsuits. According to ACOPI (2020) the SMEs surveyed agreed that they had a decrease in their income, which caused a 47% reduction in employees. In any case, this was conditioned by the Ministry of Labor that issued the Resolution 0803 of 2020, in which it prohibited the processing of applications for the massive dismissal of employees and the suspension of labor contracts (Ministerio de Trabajo - MinTrabajo, 2020).

Informality

As part of the consequences of the crisis and closures of companies in Colombia, a large number of people had to transfer their activities to informality. According to that, in July 2020 informal employment reached 10,8 million Colombians, mainly in the cities of Cali (50.7%), Quibdó (60.2%), Medellín (42.2%), Villavicencio (54.5%), Barranquilla (56.1%), and Pereira (46.9%).

Closure and Reorganization

Companies that were unable to overcome the crisis or finance their operations were forced to close or reorganize their operations, showing major deficiencies in terms of structuring business and crisis plans. Moreover, 70% of the companies partially closed their productive activities, while 8% closed completely (Confecamaras, 2020a). It should be noted that most of the companies were classified as SMEs (78%).

According to the survey of the Chambers of Commerce for Monitoring the Impact of Covid-19 on companies, about 17% of the entrepreneurs and executives coincide that they have carried out closures in the following ways: temporary closure (10,7%), or are in the process of closing or liquidation (5,7%) (Confecámaras, 2020b).

Investment

All investments had to be evaluated in terms of liquidity (ease of turning an asset into cash), profitability (the profit offered by the asset in which it will be invested), time (the best time to liquidate the investment), and risk (the probability of loss of invested capital). In most cases, the companies listed on the stock exchange reflect the future situation of their sectors, "uncertain", due to this, the price of the shares they represent are at purchase minimums, providing an investment opportunity. In this sense, the recommendation is that entrepreneurs and executives should have their exact information and data, emphasizing the internal complexity of the company, the sector, and the macroeconomic variables that can affect the investment.

According to the Joint Industrial Opinion Survey (EOIC) for September 2020, there was an investment dynamic, considering that 47.9% of the entrepreneurs agreed in leading various objectives of investment projects or anticipating in developing productive investments for the next year (2021) (Asociación Nacional de Industriales - ANDI, 2020). Among the projects to be highlighted are technological modernization (66.5%), plant expansion – operation (49.1%), equipment renovation (43.6%), and innovation (32.7%).

Liquidity

Financial liquidity is the life and continuity of business. Therefore, it is necessary to generate clear policies for the preservation of working capital. This section proposes a series of actions that promote business liquidity such as contacting suppliers and creditors that allow the extension of achievable payment terms and that do not affect the commercial relationship, requesting refinancing of short- to long-term credits, contacting clients in order to offer discounts for prompt payment or early payment of pending invoices, the inventory should be as little as possible, review just-in-time models to avoid loss, damage or outdated inventory, among others.

The International Labor Organization (ILO) investigated the global impact of the Covid-19 crisis on companies. Among the results, it is shown that about 60% of the companies affirm that they do not have liquidity in their companies to maintain salaries and the operation of the company (International Labor Organization - ILO, 2020). Moreover, 50% of the entrepreneurs agreed that their suppliers were unable to provide their services (raw materials, other inputs) since they did not have them or their price increased substantially.

Purchases and/or Contracts

Considering the low liquidity of many companies, it was important to assess the needs of the company, in terms of purchases and hiring. Therefore, the identification of purchases, acquisition of fixed assets (offices, warehouses, machines, etc.), or hiring (new developments, consultancies, personnel, etc.), should be by the projections or adjust them in the budget, without having repercussions in the cash flow. According to the Mercer (2020), about 79% of those surveyed stopped their hiring processes.

SOLUTIONS AND RECOMMENDATIONS: POST-PANDEMIC ACTIONS

In a context of uncertainty and recession caused by Covid 19, it is important to take effective actions and have a strategic direction for the future of the companies. Although companies did financial projections under a normal and stable scenario, it was until March that they had to rethink and work with only one objective "survive". Thus, the fundamental goal in 2020 was to maintain financial liquidity and through it, achieve the cash flow commitments. With the government's decisions about social isolation, the initial recommendation was not to panic and start making strategic decisions. Moreover, the actions plan and projections were a daily task focusing on surviving through the pandemic. In addition, companies sought innovative methods to generate income with their current products, and in some cases, they made modifications and generated new products.

Years before the pandemic, companies had to face macroeconomic variables and commercial discussions between countries, which had repercussions on the production and execution of the companies. Among them, the trade war between the United States and China can be highlighted, which began in March 2018 and was characterized by the protectionist policy of the American Government against the other country. In addition, the increase in unemployment and the fiscal deficit caused effects worldwide. These tensions in the market caused collateral effects in Colombia, such as the depreciation of the currency, close to 12,55%, and therefore in the projections of economic growth and terms of inflation (Abaci, 2020). Its effects impact all the economic sectors of Colombia, mainly in the metallurgical industry.

On the other hand, other global tensions affect the Colombian economy, including the trade dispute over oil between the United States, Russia, and Saudi Arabia. Likewise, Colombia´s dependence on oil. In this sense, it is necessary to have concrete strategies that mitigate international disruption as well as a preventive indicator in post-pandemic times to guarantee the survival of the companies.

In the first place, ensuring financial liquidity is equal to minimizing the risk of surviving during an uncertain time. Therefore, profitability in the years 2021 and 2022 should not be a mandatory goal, instead should become something secondary, a product of the collateral effect.

Furthermore, the cash flow is required to consolidate and strengthen the collaboration between suppliers- the company and clients. It is vital to continue the circulation of money in the economy and to have an easier reactivation. Is important to have clear that the production chain must not be destroyed, instead, it must be consolidated. In this sense, the survival of companies is associated with the management of daily cash flow. Likewise, it is important to keep in mind the real income and the expenses that are of immediate payment.

In the third place, investments in assets or papers that are not producing any kind of return because they are not used (assets) or because they are unattractive in the market, must be liquidated. For example, obsolete inventories, unused fixed assets, lavish investments, investments in the stock market with low or no profitability.

On the other hand, cash outflows must be analyzed in detail. The accomplishment of negotiation must be carried out until it is possible. Initially, banking obligations must be negotiated, such as grace periods, redefining maturities, negotiating friendly rates for the company. These are some of the strategies that can be proposed and executed. However, no matter which strategy is carried out it should reduce the pressure on cash flow. In addition, this strategy should be seen as an opportunity to improve the company´s debt conditions.

From the execution perspective, entrepreneurs and managers must face challenges to guarantee the sustainability of the company. In these moments, every day brings eagerness, new tasks, new challenges, and in some cases, some way to overcome them. In this sense, it is important that businessmen and senior executives have a high level of emotional intelligence and unprecedented preparation, which lead them to the correct decision-making or at least avoid unfortunate events such as suspension or settlement of their business activity.

Another aspect regards the organization´s human resources. It can be prejudicial to fire employees without analyzing the implications such as knowledge, seniority, experience, belonging sense, and decrease in demand. Instead, companies should negotiate with employees and have an agreement in which both parties get benefits. As part of the strategies associated with the human aspect are early vacations, temporary salary reduction with promises of compensation in the long term, temporary relocation in demanded activities, suspension of contracts, among others.

Time has become a strategic element in which companies need to make different efforts to reach all the functional areas within the organization. In this sense, companies must ensure effective diagnoses in the organizational, production, marketing, logistics, financial among other areas. In addition, it is time to verify the operation system, and if it is necessarily making changes or maintenance in the equipment, machinery, and fixtures required.

Given the importance that the financial area is currently regaining within the company, it is important to make a diagnosis of how the company was before and during the pandemic. Based on the results, make projections for the future of the company, to minimize the real impact of Covid-19 on the financial health.

During uncertain times, the basic requirement of the company is capital injection. Therefore, in this process of evaluating the company, building strategies that promote and strengthen the relationship with different stakeholders should be a priority. However, nobody should fall into the error of making unconscious decisions that will later generate gaps.

There are also recommendations to reduce the effects of similar crises in the future. For this, the (KPMG, 2020) summarizes that the diversification of financing sources and the development and implementation of risk management is very important. Moreover, thinking of small companies, it suggests that agents with economic potential invest in schools for entrepreneurship and governments promote digital transformation in processes of possible disruptive scenarios. Finally, relocation has been distinguished to provide inputs and stop depending on external and unique sources of raw materials, suggesting the shortening of value chains and integrating regional economies.

FUTURE RESEARCH DIRECTIONS

The mixed approach of macro and micro policies during an economic crisis is important as a mechanism to generate discussion forums that allow linkages to be established between different economic agents. Managing uncertainty will surely be a topic of discussion not only for aspects such as the pandemic but also for those that are already recurrent in this century, such as climate change or geopolitical crises.

From the developing countries' perspective, the effect of external shocks, resulting from trade or financial dependence, is increasing more and more. In terms of trade, exports concentrated in mining, energy, and agriculture, which traduce into a small control, even more, when imports are of high added value and guarantee a permanent deficit in the trade balance. Regarding finances, fluctuations in the exchange rate are no longer tied to raw materials, but rather to the strongest external shocks because the flow of foreign currency affects developing countries via portfolio investment, more than by FDI or trade. This issue should also be the subject of research.

Finally, in terms of government policies for companies and their strategies, they have left many lessons in terms of digital transformation, risk management, resilience, leadership, and future projections, all topics that should have a separate chapter in the research for developing countries.

CONCLUSION

This research analyzed the policies and impacts of Covid-19 on macroeconomic aspects and the business sector. It proposed strategies and actions to preserve the economic pathway from the fiscal and monetary perspective, with a special emphasis on strategies to preserve the business ecosystem in the Colombian territory. It was carried out considering the following dimensions: analysis of macroeconomic variables, the business sector and their role in economic reactivation, company decisions to face the pandemic, and finally, actions that ensure their sustainability.

From the fiscal policy perspective, the government used internal and external loans because taxes and state assets have been very limited even before the pandemic. In monetary and financial policy, the Central Bank of Colombia was aligned with government policies and as soon as it could, it lowered interest rates and injected money into the economy to offset the crisis. Given the rebound effect of inflation, it is to be expected that the Central Bank of Colombia will raise rates again and the government will feel certain disloyalty, especially when an election year approaches. Considering a situation of growth on the one hand and price controls on the other, decision-makers in the economy may fall into a state of stagflation with detrimental effects in the medium term.

With the policies and strategies implemented to motivate the hardest-hit economic sectors, the entrepreneurship laws and various labor and sector support laws can generate a good effect in the short term, but it depends on the learning of the companies, that the effects of similar crises in the future will not show up again. As evidenced throughout the chapter, the comprehensiveness of macro and micro policies was what have enabled the short-term economic recovery and their sustainability also depends on joint action. Among the main recommendations offered at the business level was to remain calm and take actions in terms of cost reduction without reducing quality; likewise, reach payment agreements with the main suppliers and creditors. Finally, the government must provide guarantees to preserve the business ecosystem and the number of employees to attract more investment, as well as growth in post-pandemic times.

The pandemic has exposed many of the limitations that existed, not only at the macroeconomic level but within companies. Gaps from salary levels to internet penetration were questioned in the pandemic, so economic agents needed to make quick and drastic decisions to reduce the effects of the pandemic and its historically social crisis. The recognition of the effectiveness of these policies and strategies transcends the objectives and the terms of this chapter, but it is perceived that it was the set of policies that diminished the effects of the pandemic. As in everything that includes ideologies, there will be defenders and detractors, but the results can only be evaluated in the long term.

REFERENCES

Abaci, L. (2020). La guerra comercial entre Estados Unidos y China: efectos en países de renta media como Colombia. *Zero*. https://zero.uexternado.edu.co/la-guerra-comercial-entre-estados-unidos-y-china-efectos-en-paises-de-renta-media-como-colombia/

Andrian, L., & Hirs, J. (2020). *Colombia: Desafíos del desarrollo en tiempos de COVID-19*. Banco Interamericano de Desarrollo. http://dx.doi.org/ doi:10.18235/0003000

Apedo-Amah, M. C., Avdiu, B., Cirera, X., Cruz, M., Davies, E., Grover, A., . . . Tran, T. T. (2020). *Unmasking the Impact of COVID-19 on Businesses: Firm Level Evidence from Across the World*. World Bank. https://openknowledge.worldbank.org/handle/10986/34626

Asociación Colombiana de Pequeños Industriales - ACOPI. (2020). *Estrategias para la recuperación económica a partir del fortalecimiento de clústeres y la competencia a las importaciones*. https://www.acopi.org.co/wp-content/uploads/2020/11/ESTRATEGIAS-PARA-LA-RECUPERACI%C3%93N-ECON%C3%93MICA.pdf

Asociación Nacional de Industriales - ANDI. (2020). *Encuesta de Opinión Industrial Conjunta Septiembre*. http://www.andi.com.co/Uploads/Informe%20EOIC%20Septiembre%202020.pdf

Avendaño, H. (2020). *COVID-19 y economía: ¿Luz al final del túnel?* Revista Fasecolda (180). https://revista.fasecolda.com/index.php/revfasecolda/article/view/667

Banco de la República. (2020). *The Board of Directors of Banco de la República unanimously maintained the benchmark interest rate at 1.75%. Measures Taken by BR on Account of Covid-19.* https://www.banrep.gov.co/en/board-directors-banco-republica-unanimously-maintained-benchmark-interest-rate-175

Banco de la República. (n.d.). *Índice de producción real de la industria manufacturera colombiana.* https://www.banrep.gov.co/es/estadisticas/indice-produccion-industrial-ipp

Barrera, C., Radziunas, J., & Montoya, M. (2021, October 12). *De la crisis a la reactivación y su efecto en el PGN.* Economía Colombiana: https://www.economiacolombiana.co/finanzas-publicas/de-la-crisis-a-la-reactivacion-y-su-efecto-en-el-pgn-1294

Beverinotti, J., & Deza, M. (2020). *Una radiografía de la resiliencia de las empresas de la región andina para enfrentar el Covid-19.* IADB. http://dx.doi.org/ doi:10.18235/0002444

Blackman, A., Ibáñez, A. M., Izquierdo, A., Keefer, P., Mesquita Moreira, M., Schady, N., & Serebrisky, T. (2020). *La política pública frente al Covid-19: Recomendaciones para América Latina y el Caribe.* IADB. doi:10.18235/0002302

Caballero, C., & Machado, G. (2020). De la crisis de 'fin de siglo' a la del 'coronavirus'. La economía colombiana en el siglo XXI. *Coyuntura Económica: Investigación Económica y Social, 50*, 15-74. https://www.repository.fedesarrollo.org.co/handle/11445/4057

Centro de Estudios Sociales y Laborales – CESLA & Asocicación Nacional de Industriales - ANDI. (2020). *Diagnóstico y estrategia de reactivación del empleo y de la economía: COVID-19 - Colección Trabajo y Sociedad.* ANDI. http://www.andi.com.co/Uploads/Diagn%C3%B3stico%20y%20estrategia%20de%20reactivaci%C3%B3n%20del%20empleo%20y%20de%20la%20econom%C3%ADa%20COVID%2019%20CESLA%20ANDI.pdf

Comisión Económica para América Latina y el Caribe - CEPAL. (2020). *Sectores y empresas frente al COVID-19: emergencia y reactivación.* Santiago de Chile: CEPAL. https://www.cepal.org/es/publicaciones/45734-sectores-empresas-frente-al-covid-19-emergencia-reactivacion

Comisión Económica para América Latina y el Caribe - CEPAL. (2021). *Estudio Económico de América Latina y el Caribe 2021: dinámica laboral y políticas de empleo para una recuperación sostenible e inclusiva más allá de la crisis del COVID-19.* https://www.cepal.org/es/publicaciones/ee

Confecámaras. (2020b). *Encuesta de las Cámaras de Comercio de Monitoreo del Impacto del COVID-19 en las Empresas, 6 a 23 de octubre.* https://www.incp.org.co/Site/publicaciones/info/archivos/Encuesta-de-las-Camaras-de-Comercio.pdf

Confecamaras. (2020a). *Encuesta de las Cámaras de Comercio sobre el Impacto del Covid-19 en las empresas colombianas realizado entre el 30 de marzo al 17 de abril de 2020.* Bogotá D.C. https://www.confecamaras.org.co/noticias/746-encuesta

De la Hoz, A., Cantillo, J., & Ramírez, A. (2021). Recuperación empresarial en Colombia ante la crisis COVID-19: Una aproximación desde los cambios en política social, laboral e impositiva. *Revista Publicando, 8*(31), 1–14. doi:10.51528/rp.vol8.id2227 de la República de Colombia, C. (2020a). Ley 2069 de 2020 Por medio de la cual se impulsa el emprendimiento en Colombia. *Diario Oficial.* http://www.secretariasenado.gov.co/senado/basedoc/ley_2069_2020.html

de la República de Colombia, C. (2020b). Ley 2068 de 2020 Por el cual se modifica la Ley General de Turismo y se dictan otras disposiciones. *Diario Oficial.* http://www.secretariasenado.gov.co/senado/basedoc/ley_2068_2020.html

de Política, C. Económica y Social - CONPES; Departamento Nacional de Planeación - DNP. (2020). *Estrategia de Respuesta Inicial ante los Efectos de la Pandemia del Covid-19 sobre la Salud Pública, los Hogares, el Aparato Productivo y las Finanzas Públicas.* https://colaboracion.dnp.gov.co/CDT/Conpes/Econ%C3%B3micos/3999.pdf

Deloitte. (2020). *Finalización del estado de emergencia económica, social y ecológica decretado por el Presidente para afrontar la emergencia sanitaria ocasionada por el COVID-19.* https://www2.deloitte.com/co/es/pages/tax/articles/finalizacion-del-estado-de-emergencia-economica-social-y-ecologica.html

Departamento Nacional de Estadística - DANE. (2020). *Gran Encuesta Integrada de Hogares.* https://microdatos.dane.gov.co/index.php/catalog/701/datafile/F42/V2408

Dirección de Impuestos y Aduanas Nacionales - DIAN. (2021). *Estadísticas de Comercio Exterior.* https://www.dian.gov.co/dian/cifras/Paginas/EstadisticasComEx.aspx

Economic Commission for Latin America and the Caribbean - ECLAC. (2020). *Preliminary Overview of the Economies of Latin America and the Caribbean 2020.* https://repositorio.cepal.org/handle/11362/46504

Federal Reserve. (2020). *Federal Reserve issues FOMC statement.* https://www.federalreserve.gov/newsevents/pressreleases/monetary20200315a.htm

Fernández, C. (2018, Nov). *Informalidad empresarial en Colombia.* Working Paper Fedesarrollo, 76. https://www.repository.fedesarrollo.org.co/bitstream/handle/11445/3698/WP_2018_No_76.pdf?sequence=1&isAllowed=y#:~:text=Existen%20pocas%20fuentes%20para%20estimar,agregado%2C%20en%20las%20%C3%A1reas%20urbanas

FINDETER. (2020). *COVID-19, Coyuntura Económica y Medidas de Mitigación.* Dirección de Estudios Económicos. Informe Sectorial. https://repositorio.findeter.gov.co/handle/123456789/9613

Fondo Nacional de Garantías - FNG. (n.d.). *Programa de Garantía Especial: Unidos por Colombia.* https://www.fng.gov.co/ES/Paginas/Unidos_por_Colombia_FNG.aspx

International Labor Organization - ILO. (2020). *A global survey of enterprises: managing the business disruptions of COVID-19.* Geneve. https://www.ilo.org/actemp/publications/WCMS_760306/lang--en/index.htm

Kantar. (2020). *E-Commerce el ganador de esta pandamia.* https://www.kantar.com/latin-america/inspiracion/consumidor/ecommerce-el-ganador-de-esta-pandemia?par=mx/Noticias-/Ecommerce-el-ganador-de-esta-pandemia

KPMG. (2020). *Impactos económicos y financieros del COVID-19.* Advisory I KPMG. https://assets.kpmg/content/dam/kpmg/co/pdf/2020/06/kpmg-informe-impactos-economicos-y-financieros-del-covid-19-novena-edicion.pdf

Mejía, L. F. (2020). Choque dual y posibles efectos sobre la economía colombiana. *Tendencia Económica, 204*, 3-18. https://www.repository.fedesarrollo.org.co/handle/11445/3937

Mercer. (2020). *Total Remuneration Survey 2020.* https://www.imercer.com/products/total-remuneration-surveys

Ministerio de Hacienda - MinHacienda. (2020). *Comunicado Oficial Comité Consultivo para la Regla Fiscal.* https://www.minhacienda.gov.co/webcenter/ShowProperty?nodeId=%2FConexionContent%2FWCC_CLUSTER-128327%2F%2FidcPrimaryFile&revision=latestreleased

Ministerio de Trabajo - MinTrabajo. (2020). *Normatividad y Circulares.* https://www.mintrabajo.gov.co/normatividad/circulares/2020

Ministerio de Trabajo - MinTrabajo. (2020). *Resolución 0803.* https://www.mintrabajo.gov.co/atencion-al-ciudadano/transparencia/resoluciones

República, L. (2020, Mar 27). *El teletrabajo hace que las personas le dediquen más horas a la jornada laboral.* https://www.larepublica.co/empresas/el-teletrabajo-hace-que-las-personas-le-dediquen-mas-horas-a-la-jornada-laboral-2983857#:~:text=Ximena%20C%C3%A1rdenas%2C%20gerente%20de%20Experis,las%20horas%20laboradas%20sean%20productivas

Superintendencia Financiera de Colombia - SFC. (n.d.). *Programa de Acompañamiento a Deudores.* https://www.superfinanciera.gov.co/inicio/consumidor-financiero/informacion-general/informacion-al-consumidor-financiero/programa-de-acompanamiento-a-deudores-pad-10104439

Unidad de Gestión de Pensiones y Parafiscales - UGPP. (n.d.). *Programa de Apoyo al Empleo Formal - PAEF.* https://paef.ugpp.gov.co/ver20/dfV3Paef

United Nations for Development Programme. (2021). *Un año de pandemia: impacto socioeconómico de la COVID-19 en Colombia.* https://www.co.undp.org/content/colombia/es/home/-sabias-que-/un-ano-de-pandemia--impacto-socioeconomico-de-la-covid-19-en-col.html#:~:text=Mas%20de%201%2C5%20millones,en%20los%20%C3%BAltimos%205%20a%C3%B1os

United Nations - UN. (2020). *Plan de respuesta socio-económica frente a la pandemia de la COVID-19 en Colombia.* https://colombia.un.org/es/160844-plan-de-respuesta-socio-economica-frente-la-pandemia-de-la-covid-19-en-colombia

World Health Organization - WHO. (2020). *Alocución de apertura del Director General de la OMS en la rueda de prensa sobre la COVID-19.* https://www.who.int/es/director-general/speeches/detail/who-director-general-s-opening-remarks-at-the-media-briefing-on-covid-19---11-march-2020

ADDITIONAL READING

Hartlyn, J. (2019). *Latin American political economy: financial crisis and political change*. Routledge. https://api.taylorfrancis.com/content/books/mono/download?identifierName=doi&identifierValue=10.4324/9780429036316&type=googlepdf

Kaminsky, G. L., & Reinhart, C. M. (1998). Financial crises in Asia and Latin America: Then and now. *The American Economic Review*, *88*(2), 444–448. https://www.jstor.org/stable/116964

Lombana, J., Palacios-Chacón, L. A., Salcedo, N. U., & Cabello-Cerna, A. (2021). Pacific Alliance Facing Crises: A Trade Perspective (1990-2020). In *Impact of Global Issues on International Trade* (pp. 37-65). IGI Global. https://www.igi-global.com/chapter/pacific-alliance-facing-crises/285906

Marichal, C. (2000). *A century of debt crises in Latin America*. Princeton University Press., https://carlosmarichal.colmex.mx/deuda/Book-Century.pdf

Ocampo, J. A. (2020). *The COVID-19 crisis in Latin America in historical perspective*. CEPAL Review-Special issue. https://repositorio.cepal.org/handle/11362/46927

Segura, J. A., & Sarmiento, V. J. (2020). Effects of Financial Crises on Latin American Economies-Colombia Case and the SMEs. *Journal of Economics Studies and Research, 10*. https://ibimapublishing.com/articles/JESR/2020/808445/

Skoufias, E. (2003). Economic crises and natural disasters: Coping strategies and policy implications. *World Development*, *31*(7), 1087–1102. https://www.sciencedirect.com/science/article/abs/pii/S0305750X0300069X

KEY TERMS AND DEFINITIONS

Colombia: Country located in the north of South America, with access to the sea through the Pacific and the Atlantic and crossed by the Andes. Fourth country in economy and population in Latin America.

Deficit: Excess spending that exceeds income. Expenditures are larger than revenue.

Economic Cycle: Are the periodic oscillations of an economy, when it goes from expansion to contraction, repeating itself successively.

Informality: Economic activities that are not regulated by a legal framework.

Policy: Set of plans/ideas followed by governments, business, interest groups, etc.

Recession: Reduction of the economic activity of a country during a period of time, it is accepted that it be two quarters to declare it.

Short-Term Economic Prospects: Situations that occur in an economy to shift current trends.

Chapter 7
Integrating Cycle of Prochaska and DiClemente With Ethically Responsible Behavior Theory for Social Change Management:
Post-COVID-19 Social Cognitive Perspective for Change

Ansar Abbas
https://orcid.org/0000-0003-4521-1920
Airlangga Universtias, Indonesia

Rakotoarisoa Maminirina Fenitra
https://orcid.org/0000-0002-1045-3404
Airlangga Universitas, Indonesia

Dian Ekowati
https://orcid.org/0000-0001-9726-4720
Airlangga Universtias, Indonesia

Mochammad Fahlevi
https://orcid.org/0000-0002-1419-8308
Bina Nusantara University, Indonesia

Fendy Suhariadi
https://orcid.org/0000-0001-9679-2185
Airlangga Universtias, Indonesia

ABSTRACT

Humans could never have predicted what would happen as a result of COVID-19. Indeed, such foresight was not expected. It can also be stated that planning to combat COVID-19 was beyond human capacity. However, the future may be foretold by seeing many aspects that we have experienced. Current values, styles of working, social systems, organizational transformations, and human behavior have all been altered due to the epidemic. Those changes will sustain the anticipated direction. This chapter goes into change cycle theory and how COVID-19 affected current social norms. Initially, the idea was integrated with social norms, but social cognition impacts were analogized as they progressed. It is interwoven with the goal that ethically social responsibility developments will assist in the design of a post-COVID-19 society approach. It is expected that we would be able to strategically carry some of the benefits of social awareness gained during COVID-19 for a brighter future in the post-COVID-19 age.

DOI: 10.4018/978-1-7998-8856-7.ch007

INTRODUCTION

Everything changes at a different pace depending on time and social requirements. Social cognition helps at the beginning with the premise that people construct their social reality and that this creation serves as a foundation for their social conduct (Bless & Fiedler, 2014). Even while everyone experiences change, it is macro-factor dependent for mass-scale changes to occur. It can come to us organically, ideologically, or via our free will (Buttimer, 1980). Even so, it is inevitable that things will change, and it is a necessary thing that must happen. We may all learn to adapt and grow in varying contexts and situations by blending fundamental, positive beliefs about change with the required skills or tools (Sherif & Sherif, 1956). However, once a shift occurs, it is sometimes simple to adapt; sometimes, it has been adopted in isolation (Huntington, 1971). What can we do to ensure that change has occurred in the first place is not correct, how can we restore a change, and what should we do if it does, mainly about social norms?

Social norms have shifted due to the Covid-19 (Neville et al., 2021). Bicchieri (2016) and Knight and Ensminger (1998) argued that by using a social norms method to change, one can identify and resolve what a group can adopt. It may also help the group perceive the phenomenon as something they already do or are starting to do (Spears, 2011). One's opinions about what others are doing help form a social norm (Briggs et al., 2020). The pandemic prompted social distancing, which was necessary at the time. However, future social norms research questions whether one's opinions about what others think one should do after the pandemic will remain the same. Social change is how human interactions and connections affect cultural and social institutions over time, having a tremendous effect on society (Verma & Prakash, 2020). Once a societal norm is established, it is difficult to get people to change their beliefs. Sociologists define changes in human interactions and connections as a kind of social change; however, it is difficult to modify once a culture is established (Elder et al., 2003). Sociologists have been studying changes in human interactions and linkages for decades. It has been based on solid footing that changing a culture once it is in place is tough (Phillipson, 2007). The post-Covid challenges have emerging problems to restore people's confidence in social and cultural ideals to the pre-Covid-19 era by following a change.

Nature, time, technology, adoption, and human needs all work to bring about change (Elder Jr, 1994; Saukkonen et al., 2019). In the same way, we get used to new activities and functions (Bandura, 2002). We eventually become proficient at them and do not even think about them anymore. We can better manage our life's requirements by comprehending and responding to the current global changes brought on by the pandemic covid-19

PURPOSE OF THE STUDY

Academics, scholars, and practitioners can all benefit from studies that persuade their audience to consider a perspective within a current paradigm. Here, we will look at how ethically responsible theory can be combined to achieve even greater societal good and change social norms. According to the review, this study's findings could help unleash the theory's untapped potential for leadership development.

Justification of the Study

Many aspects of covid-19 have been studied in depth (Brodeur et al., 2021; Gallo Marin et al., 2021; Pokhrel & Chhetri, 2021). However, there is no comprehensive depiction of societal standards that could be altered in the future after a significant shift has already occurred. So that people can once again have faith in the same social norms we had before the pandemic.

Significance of the Study

Concepts that are widely recognized in industry, society, and academic research are employed in the present study. Holistic knowledge of the study's potential scope includes integrating ethical and responsible traits and change to form and restore social norms. It is more critical than ever to put this concept into practice to help restore human social norms and address post-Covid 19 scenario needs.

RESEARCH QUESTIONS

This research aims to create social change widely accepted worldwide using ethical and responsible philosophy. Even more importantly, the chapter argues how people's beliefs can be restored by embracing pre-covid-19 standards of behavior. Scholars and practitioners may support the arguments and scope of this theory to encourage future study for consolidation from a perspective of restoring change.

STRUCTURE OF STUDY

This book chapter will begin with a review of the literature, followed by a presentation of the change cycle and its various degrees. It will be discussed in the subsequent section how ethically responsible behavior could be integrated with Covid-19 in order to modify social norms. Social cognition and human needs in the post-covid scenario and change cycle will be examined in subsequent sections of this paper. Social norms and change-need theory integration will be provided later, along with results and recommendations.

LITERATURE REVIEW

Some preservation theories address change. The research study sees behavior as a dynamic balance of forces acting in opposing directions that must be maintained to function. Driving factors make the transition easier to implement because they steer personnel in the desired direction (Mitchell, 1982). Restraining forces push employees in the other direction, making change more difficult. Kurt Lewin (1951) was the first to propose the three stage transition paradigm (Marrow, 1977). Because of this, it is necessary to examine these forces, and Lewin's three-step model can assist in changing the balance in the position of the intended change. Kritsonis (2005) discovered Lewin's Three-Step Change Theory (Lewin, 1951), Lippitt's Phases of Change Theory (Lippitt & Lippitt, 1986), Prochaska and DiClemente's Change Theory (Prochaska & DiClemente, 1986), Social Cognitive Theory (Bandura, 1989), and The

Theory of Reasoned Action or Planned Behavior (Ajzen & Fishbein, 1969, 1970; Fredricks & Dossett, 1983) to be distinct from one another while also sharing some characteristics in common. Lewin's paradigm is exceptionally logical, goal-oriented, and plan-oriented. Elements that can influence change among individuals are not taken into consideration.

On the other hand, the social cognitive theory posits that behavioral change is influenced by contextual effects, individual factors, and characteristics of the activity itself. However, the Social Cognitive Theory is preferable to Lewin's model since it considers both external and internal contextual variables and rational reasoning. Lippitt's Phases of Change elaboration on Lewin's Three-Step Theory of Organizational Change. Lippitt's change theory places greater emphasis on the change agent than it does on the process of change itself.

The change theory developed by Prochaska and DiClemente differs from the other theories. It is relevant to this chapter in several ways. Change models such as Lewin's try to analyze the forces (either driving or restraining) that influence change. The model follows a cyclical rather than linear pattern. A relapse or the failure to convert to the intended behavior the first time is considered in this hypothesis. Individuals at risk of relapsing might go back to the contemplation stage and establish plans for how they will proceed in the future (Prochaska & DiClemente, 1983).

CHANGE CYCLE (INTEGRATIVE APPROACH)

Prochaska et al. (1986) argued that a complete and accurate change model must accommodate a wide range of opposing needs. To be effective, a comprehensive model of change developed initially for addictive behaviors must also be adaptable to the wide range of ways people change. The examination of client characteristics was used to determine who changes throughout treatment and who does not respond during treatment. There have been ten distinct processes of change discovered due to this model's comprehensiveness, with specific functions being more critical than others at different stages of development. These processes result in the development of solutions that assist people in implementing and maintaining change. The theory has a great deal of potential for providing a comprehensive foundation for a change management model, and this potential is enormous. It might be contended that this model is practically highly comparable to the covid-19 occurrences resulting from the change. Even if human behaviors were the central subject of this model's inquiry, the relationship between societal norms and people's mental patterns must not be underestimated. Social norms are principles of behavior that guide people's actions (Bicchieri et al., 2018). They drive group members to interpret a given scenario, behave about that, and interact in the situation. Group members are subjected to social influence due to their ability to dictate which reactions are proper and not (Abrams et al., 1990).

RELEVANCE OF SOCIAL NORMS IN HUMANS

Social standards differ not just depending on a cultural context but on a specific age, ethnicity, role in society, and the conditions in which they find themselves or interact with it (Triandis, 1989). In a contradicted view, (Nordlund & Garvill, 2003) underlines that normative norms are founded only on an individual's moral beliefs and others. Descriptive norms refer to the distribution of such ideas across a population (Kuntsche et al., 2021). Thus, social norms influence people's thoughts, feelings, and actions in the same human habits do. Perhaps people's attitudes produce social norms resulting from practices, depending on their perspective. As a result, the responses of individuals are evaluated concerning these norms. The agreement influences social norms. The same meal can be eaten in various ways in some communities; however, eating the same meal in multiple ways is not acceptable in others (Spielberger, 2004). For example, social norms collect and analyze what other people in the same situation generally think, feel, or do. Individuals think, feel, and act differently when guided by societal norms instead of self-imposed rules and regulations (Turner, 1991). In addition, social norms have also been categorized as descriptive and prescriptive.

When it comes to describing specific conduct, the most common term is "descriptive norm," which is also known as "popular norms" or "behavioral norms."(Neighbors et al., 2013). Perspectives worldwide on drug use and misuse in different cultures are commonly attributed to social standards (Thakker, 2013). A good illustration of this can be found in the cultural standards surrounding alcohol consumption. Even though most individuals do not realize how powerful social norms are, they significantly impact how people think and act. Even if a person expressly rejects societal standards, they are nevertheless influenced by them (Telzer et al., 2018).

In light of the research findings, we can confidently say that social norms originate from various settings. Peers and social norms have an impact on people's lives. Other factors include interpersonal attraction, social identities, gender disparities, social effects on good growth, and foreign viewpoints (Abbott, 2021; Abrams & Hogg, 2006; Côté & Levine, 2014; Davis, 2003).

SOCIAL NEED FOR ETHICAL RESPONSIBILITY DURING COVID-19 AND CHANGE CYCLE

Creatures of culture or law Writing about persons who scrupulously follow social standards and expectations of proper behavior in a given social situation is called "living creatures." The biological processes that determine how we learn to accept a particular social behavior as the most appropriate are still poorly understood. However, the innermost levels that promote the interaction between personal conduct and institutionalized societal expectations like norms are less readily accessible (Getzels & Guba, 1957). Wikström et al. (2012) claimed that recognizing that habits are separate from norms pushes people to abide by most accepted societal standards. During covid-19, social isolation, disinfectants, and the avoidance of gatherings and organizations were new societal norms requirements that altered existing social behaviors (Fenitra et al., 2021; Harper et al., 2021). As a result of the new social codification of these standards, individual behavior has been influenced both in private and professional lives. In both legal and economics research, the study of how laws and norms interact has maintained an obsessive focus (Galbiati et al., 2021). Benabou and Tirole (2011) put forward a theoretical framework that codifies two different interactions. First, regulations impact the behavioral standard as an ideal object by modifying economic compensation. Suppose fewer people engage in the prohibited acts, the social stigma associated with these actions rises. Second, laws transmit messages on society's norms whenever there is an implicit doubt about the dominant social standard. Since this Pandemic effect has happened, measures genuinely altered both in the first and second example through regulation impacts and an informational channel.

These mechanisms indicate a shift in the perceived societal norm due to the law's adoption (Kahan, 2019). Hence, people accepted social change norms collectively; as shown in data, laws impact how people perceive standards and figure out the underlying mechanisms (e.g., Fetzer et al., 2020). It revealed that the vast majority of those polled believe that others should engage in preventive conduct because they have first-order normative attitudes. Ninety-seven percent of respondents responded that due to COVID-19, citizens in their countries ought to desist from attending social gatherings. People should not shake each other's hands, according to 92 percent of those polled. Seventy-seven percent believe that all businesses other than those extremely vital to the community should be closed. Eighty-one percent support an all-day curfew that excludes only grocery shopping, required family trips, and commutes to and from workplaces.

Furthermore, seventy percent of those who answered the survey believe that dangerous behavior should be penalized financially. This pandemic was a remarkable phenomenon in convincing individuals to change their established societal standards. We believe there are two possible explanations for this remarkable response. Firstly, most of the current era had never faced a more significant obstacle than covid-19. People were afraid of losing their lives, so they were quick to accept change or be open to it. There was no other option at the time; thus, the second was due to the wide dissemination of information and ethically responsible behavior. It was widespread that humanity can be secure if we respond morally, preserve social distance, and adopt other safety measures. Because morally responsible behavior has roots in many religions and societies worldwide, it did not take long for people to recognize the phenomenon and respond to it comprehensively (Radocy & Boyle, 2012). This argument can support the notion that a significant event is always required to bring about a significant shift in societal norms. Because the scope of covid-19 did not confine itself to a specific territory, its implications were far-reaching. It is reasonable to believe that they will affect everyone in the same way. When that is the situation under consideration, the path to alter existing social norms is a genuine effort that often requires large spans of the entire transformation cycle. Putting such actions in a logical sequence will considerably increase understanding of how change has happened. According to James Prochaska's book, Changing for Good, six stages of change are the most exemplary illustration to comprehend the change cycle that occurred during covid-19 (Prochaska et al., 1996).

1. **Pre-contemplation** or at least less bothersome once more. What is causing the difficulty is that people are generally resistant to change when they first begin to consider it. It is common for people to be unwilling to acknowledge that they have a problem and avoid discussion (Afifi & Guerrero, 2000). Nevertheless, Kotter (2007) notes that some people remain in this stage of transformation for an extended period, during which they frequently suffer growing challenges. This difficult stage is referred to as "denial" by many people. This stage is associated with factors that are either unaware of or unwilling to acknowledge to perceive a change. Transtheoretical or Stages of Change models, which guide the understanding of the exit process, are associated with this stage (Wilson & Nochajski, 2018). Until individuals become aware of the change, they will continue to resist it. As a result, some people refuse to recognize that change is imminent because they fear it will drive them out of their comfort zones. People typically resist change because it goes against their habits (Halson & Lastella, 2017).
2. The second stage of this cycle is **contemplation**, during which people come to terms with the fact that they need to make a change (Harrell, 2018). However, they will still face difficulties in processing the change. After reaching this phase, most people are probably unsure whether or not they should give up and accept change (Prochaska & Prochaska, 1999). Alternatively, they might think to let things happen and do nothing about the matter or how adaptation may occur. A person's habitual pattern or norms are once again a factor, but they at least recognize the root of the problem

(Varela, 1999). As a result, they seek explanations for and tactics for avoiding problems. They may even consider finding solutions to them. This is the stage where people are aware and open to new ideas that will help them make future judgments. It is essential to have faith in one's ability to plan based on one's culture, autonomy, and contentment in this phase. As a result of self-awareness and cultural dependency, this stage may also be called the cognitive influence of processing decisions about the prospective adoption of mechanism planning.

3. **Preparation** comes at the third stage; people start thinking about what they need to do but are unsure how to use this resource or resource (Asirifi et al., 2022). Individuals are now beginning to make reasonable decisions at this level. While a few people remain habitual thinkers, preferring to analyze rather than act, the successful person will make decisions and plan for them. At this point, one's outlook will begin to shift toward the future and less toward the past. Individual estimation is formed within willingness (Kasten et al., 2019). This phase is linked to the human inner self locus of control. Either the internal or external locus of control plays a significant role in decision-making in personality. From a micro and macro perspective, this control refers to an individual's awareness of the underlying principle causes of occurrences (Dornyei & Ottó, 1998). If macro factors are prominent in society, they will be in charge of transformation. On the other hand, micro factors will be in charge if it happens discreetly.
4. It takes a man where there is no inexpensive change. They may be resolved to act very much on their own to take what is needed. Behavior change is defined as the most recent **action** and persons who have recently made that change plan to keep going forward (Prochaska et al., 1994). People can show this by changing their unhealthy habits or developing new, healthier ones. In order to make their self-dedication known to others, people require as many helping relationships as possible. However, they do not need those if they only do it themselves. In this phase, there is a greater likelihood of change among persons who have reached a stage of a less optimistic attitude (Bicalho et al., 2019). Regardless of the psychological make-up individual, the action stage is the stage in which change is most likely to occur for all. This phase creates sequences of acts chosen as habits suited to an inevitable social struggle in question (Allport, 1962). At this point, the pace of change may get risen exponentially. Being prepared is much easier with enthusiasm and momentum, and one may even receive some censure from others. Expect feelings of anxiousness and wrath. Individuals eventually understand that whatever is happening against their actions will be brief. Individuals would go back over all they had created during the contemplation and preparation stages and follow through. The action was the stage that occurred during the epidemic when people understood that pandemic precautions practices were for their benefit. Consequently, they adjusted without considering whether or not others were observing adopted the change.
5. The most challenging part of stopping an addiction is to **Maintain** a new habit, or the norm is maintaining sobriety, for example, quitting smoking e.g. (Hiscock et al., 2012). Suppose individuals thought, prepared, and decided to alter their lives and leave a piece of it in the past with good riddance. In that case, it will be straightforward to maintain the new way of thinking. However, the reactionary tendencies of desire and relapse are ever-present dangers. People's tendency to revert to old habits and routines is understandable if they have been accustomed to them (Oreg, 2003). That new change is beneficial. During this phase, one must be continually realized and determined to preserve a new habit, culture, or norm. This epiphany occurred during covid-19, as individuals became used to the new social standards they were observing during this pandemic (Zenic et al., 2020). It is important to remember that this stage requires the same planning and goals as the oth-

ers and that lapses are only brief setbacks from which one may learn. As a result, one can rely on all well-thought-out contemplation and planning. People need to be more persistent and steadfast in their efforts at this stage.

6. **Termination** is the last stage of a change when change has taken place entirely. People have no desire to return to their harmful practices (Prochaska et al., 2015). They are confident that they will not return to the previous methods practiced in their life. Achieving and maintaining a healthy weight is a challenging goal for most individuals (Lin et al., 2006). Therefore, health promotion organizations tend to overlook it. As soon as a person breaks a bad habit, they will look back and feel proud of themselves for making the correct decisions. Suppose the concept is applied to the creation, development, and dissemination of communication strategies. In that case, it is likely to be executed successfully in a pandemic (Spradley & Spradley, 2021).

No one would disagree to argue that the media, health care business, political parties, and other institutions acted ethically acceptable given the pandemic societal requirement of change. This shift has occurred quickly and easily across all countries due to the sociological argument that changing social norms is morally permissible. Social norm change is amenable to consciousness and morally resonant behavior realization, as demonstrated by this pandemic shift in social norms.

THE THEORY

First attempts to obtain citizenship norm-oriented conduct from a habit viewpoint are worth noting that foundations of perception in nature in social convention creation are worth highlighting. (cf. Lorini & Marrosu, 2018). For example, self-enlightenment via awareness and inculcating socially responsible behavior for change in ethics and norms is a human inheritance. The most critical stage in successfully introducing a norm relies on the social molding of individual habits. Human conduct is a stratification of "learned" habits that are easily manageable. A collective effort has been made in the right direction. The definition of habit in psychological actions of accepting norms seems humanitarian in holistic language. Therefore, it appears to be required to adopt a particular point of view in human science (Giorgi, 2020). It turns out that these discrepancies can be explained by the epistemological approach used in habit interpretation and habit formation with given social norms (Kurz et al., 2015). It tries to uniformly understand these principles in a changing social environment, human-centered discipline, and situational flowability.

SOCIAL COGNITION AND HUMAN NEEDS POST COVID SITUATION AND CHANGE CYCLE

As a branch of social psychology, social cognition focuses on studying how people perceive and respond to the social world (Augoustinos et al., 2014; Molden & Dweck, 2006). Sociological cognition is examined in connection to cognitive and social psychology, tracing its origins and current effect on human behavior (Van Dijk, 1990). Social cognition terminology such as schemas and heuristics are reviewed, and new theoretical and research advances are introduced. Early dual-process theories, implicit and explicit attitudes, automaticity of actions, and the social psychology of human religious beliefs were used. Wechsler et al.'s (2003) study to evaluate the Social Norms Theory examined student drinking habits. Due to its success in lowering alcohol use and alcohol-related injuries among college students, the theory and the social norms approach have become well-known. In order to modify behavior, this idea focuses on understanding surroundings and social effects such as peers rather than only focusing on the individual.

Social Norms Theory is primarily concerned with peer influence and its impact on individual decision-making (Van Hoorn et al., 2017). Peer effects and normative views are especially relevant when addressing actions in adolescents that are viewed as social standards since the social cognitive theory was not yet presented. Borsari and Carey (2001) asserted that peer influences were more influenced by perceived norms than norms (the group's actual views and activities). Berkowitz (2010) argued that the social norms method is based on the misunderstanding that there is a gap between what people think and do (cf. Gidycz et al., 2011). Albert Bandura developed the Social Learning Theory (SLT) in the 1960s, which later evolved into the Social Cognitive Theory (SCT). Even while social norm theory has existed for decades before its inception, the SCT claims that learning happens in social contexts. Due to the dynamic and reciprocal interaction between individuals, their environment, and their behavior, this theory's application to social learning is profound.

To a large extent, the theoretical limitations of social norms theory may be traced back to this. Participants in a social norm intervention are likely to question the first message because of their misperceptions about the subject matter (Papacharissi, 2004). In order to correct these misunderstandings, accurate information must be delivered clearly and straightforwardly. Social norms are based on Unreliable information, and a skewed normative message might result from inadequate data gathering in the early phases. Misperceptions might be bolstered as a result.

This idea has been around for a while now. Even if the campaign's message is well-chosen, unpleasant news from unreliable or untrustworthy sources might derail it, even if it is correct (Perry & Miller, 2018). For these social norms dosage to influence, but not so much that it becomes routine, the message must be delivered in a sufficient amount.

Additionally, the Social Cognitive Theory highlights three primary influences on behavior and behavioral choices (Bandura, 1991; Schunk, 2012; Schunk & Usher, 2012). The first step is to look at the surrounding environment, such as the neighborhood, to see if it influences behavior. A person's personality traits and experiences, including their cognitions, are also considered. Humans have a variety of innate characteristics, one of which is a tendency to engage in certain types of activity (Lyng, 1990). As a result, the social cognitive theory is best suited to explain human-environment interactions. This new interpretation of habit goes beyond the actual sequential cognitive construction of actions or individual movements. They are based only on the individual's beliefs, which characterize its initial description to increase its role. Lewis and Brooks-Gunn (1979) viewed social cognition as a passive process. Qualitative research by Ritchie and Spencer (2002) discovered that it might be utilized to assist people in changing patterns and understanding their behaviors with social standards. Habits geared toward a social environment tend to develop pattern features. They have value-based decision-making in combination with each other. Porges (2003) also investigated this phenomenon in animals and demonstrated the importance of the superior temporal nervous system in nature regulating behaviors in terms of neurophysiology.

Social cognitive theory is a comprehensive theory of social development that includes several subfields (Bandura, 1999). The emphasis on social impact and motivation and the reliance on external and internal social reinforcement distinguish Social Cognitive Theory from other theories (Lent et al., 1994). A primary objective of social cognitive theory is to explain how people manage their actions (Luszczynska & Schwarzer, 2015). In addition to considering the individual differences in how people acquire and sustain behavior, this theory considers the social context in which people do the behavior. The idea considers a person's previous experiences, which influence whether or not they would engage in the behavioral activity. These prior experiences influence reinforcements, expectations, and expectancies, all of which influence whether or not a person would engage in a specific activity and why. Many health promotion theories focus on beginning habits rather than maintaining them. For example, with covid-19, public health is about preserving behavior, not just initiating a change only. Regulation and motivation to accomplish goal-directed conduct can be retained over time by social learning.

1. Reciprocal determinism is the basic notion of social cognitive theory (Pajares & Usher, 2008). Bandura (1978) defined it as the concept of reciprocal determination—dynamic and mutual interaction of person individual with a set of learning experiences, environment external social context. Behavioral response to stimuli to attain objectives occurs after a change has occurred (Baranowski et al., 2003). As a result of Covid-19, reversing the changes due to changing societal standards is necessary. However, it is essential to believe that not all modifications are required to be examined as part of the must-change procedure. For example, environmental hygiene characteristics necessary for a healthy living must be reviewed to align with the awareness that has already occurred throughout covid-19.
2. A person can carry out behavior in the presence of required knowledge and skills referred to as Behavioral Capability (Pintaric & Bronzin, 2013). In order to properly conduct an action, a person must first understand what they are supposed to do and how to execute it. People learn through the repercussions of their actions, which impact both themselves and the environment in which they reside (Porter et al., 2003). Therefore, post-Covid-19 conditions necessitated a combination of tactics to reinstate human beliefs tied to previously established standards. For example, social distance is a component that cannot be sustained over an extended length of time and must be eliminated following the covid-19 scenario. In order to do this, a strategic aim would be necessary to develop collective behavior regarding eliminating social distancing policy in the post-Covid-19 era. Those who are old or have health vulnerabilities, on the other hand, must wear a mask and use hand sanitizer while at the institution.
3. As stated by the theory of observational learning, people can see and observe a behavior performed by others and then replicate those behaviors (Bandura et al., 1961). This is frequently demonstrated through the design of behaviors (Bosson & Vandello, 2011). Referring to Bosson et al. (2011) and Montano and Kasprzyk (2015), individuals who see a strong display of an action are more likely to do the behavior effectively. The lessons that Covid-19 has learned are critically relevant for public domain practices. Public behavior management policies must continue to align individuals with environmental health and safety issues after the Covid-19 sessions conclude.
4. Rewarding or discouraging a person's activity is defined as any internal or external response to that behavior that influences the person's chances of continuing or ceasing the behavior (Rotter, 1990). Whether started by the individual or found in the environment, reinforcements can be positive or negative (Michale, 2005). This is the construct of SCT that is most strongly associated with the reciprocal link between behavior and environment. An era following Covid-19 is projected to regulate to enhance pro-social conduct among people capable of communicating social norms building.

5. The term "expectations" refers to the effects of a person's actions that are expected (Getzels et al., 1957). Expectations for outcomes might be health-related or non-health-related. Individuals estimate the implications before engaging in the activity (Dowling & Staelin, 1994). The anticipation of these repercussions can impact whether or not the behavior is completed. Expectations are mainly formed due to prior experiences (Karapanos et al., 2009). While expectations are derived from previous experience, expectancies are more focused on the value placed on the outcome. They are therefore more subjective to the individual. A more flexible society in the post-Covid-19 era is anticipated to establish independent organizations and marketplaces for flexible purchasing.
6. The term self-efficacy describes how an individual believes in their abilities to conduct particular conduct successfully (Ajzen, 2002). Self-efficacy is a construct that is unique to SCT (Stajkovic & Luthans, 1998). However, other theories, such as the Theory of Planned Behavior (Ajzen, 1991), have adopted it later. In addition to a person's unique skills and other individual elements, self-efficacy is impacted by contextual circumstances, barriers, and facilitators (Kukla et al., 2015). In covid-19, self-efficacy is likely the most generally realized manifestation. A personal or individual worth has become increasingly represented as a motivator for pro-social, morally acceptable behavior practice. In order to construct a better world after Covid-19, it will be necessary to communicate and model responsible conduct across humanity.

METHOD

This chapter has made use of critical literature to develop some arguments concerning the strategic objective of socially acceptable, ethically responsible action for the sake of social transformation in general. It is similar to making a narrative (Baumeister & Leary, 1997). The literature synthesis helps academics generate arguments, integrate ideas, and produce a combustion framework for theoretical advancement and profound comprehension (Hampton & Parker, 2011; Wyborn et al., 2018).

CONCLUSION AND RECOMMENDATION

Because human behavior, norms, and cultural studies encompass all members of society, no one theory can account for all aspects of human psychology. A large-scale transformation is required to bring evolvement for social norms alter if it has to take place. A substantive event such as COVID-19 aided in developing collective responsibility and enabled humanity to share their collective expertise. The focus was shifted to a single goal: to raise social awareness to battle the Covid-19, which had no cure. This Covid-19 issue prompted a generally decided preventative strategy, which included maintaining a clean environment, maintaining social distance, wearing a weak mask, and using hand sanitizer. First, for whatever reason, the lockdown effect caused dread, which spread over the world in a snowball effect, forcing the world to act against the epidemic.

At the very least, the consequences of this worldwide pandemic resulted in the collective knowledge of ethically responsible behavior expectations from the emergence of the outbreak at its apex. Leaders with solid social identities have a more significant impact on human society organizations because of guidance. A handful of the marvels brought about by leaders' strategic aim, positive psychology, diversity management, and social fabric development are among them (Abbas, Saud, Ekowati, Usman, et al.,

2021; Abbas, Saud, Suhariadi, et al., 2020; Carter & Youssef-Morgan, 2019; Carter & Greer, 2013). Social norms like habits give a tiny glimpse of how people respond to change. However, the importance of leadership in the management of social change would persist despite establishing social cognition of ethically responsible for social change (Abbas, Ekowati, et al., 2021; Abbas, Ekowati, & Suhariadi, 2022; Abbas, Saud, Ekowati, & Suhariadi, 2021). More research on the cyclical nature of social change and the factors influencing human behavior should be undertaken to develop conceptual frameworks for change management. It may be possible to include this chapter notion into new change models.

We have included material that focuses on people's habits and addictions related to the philosophy of transformation. This idea was very pertinent to the situation in covid-19. However, restoring a quick change would necessitate eliminating or merging some of its initial phases to occur on the fly. The Pre-contemplation, contemplation, and preparation stages can be considered part of a larger whole. People can make up their minds based on the fact that they can see the changes taking place around them. For a quick and agile reaction, certain modifications must be maintained, and some established new standards are terminated. The restoration of people's beliefs in the rebirth of social norms according to the prior stage before Covid-19 requires a broad awareness campaign in social engineering. It would take a leader with much strategic intent to use social engineering, in any case.

The most challenging task was completed; nevertheless, many people are unaware that societal transformation has already occurred, which will be difficult to reverse at once. A strategic management and leadership strategy is necessary to determine what needs to be restored. Then it would be time to think about how social standards could be fixed. It is crucial to realize that not every modification made in Covid 19 necessitates another change. Some new rules can benefit humanity, and they must be implemented. The travel and tourism sector has taken significant damage, yet the challenges of reestablishing travel and tourism are substantial. Covid-19 has significantly impacted tourism, health care, and education institutions. The lessons learned from these fields must be concentrated.

Humans gain from only a handful of the improvements. Hand sanitizer and a face mask, for example, are both beneficial to people. Those who suffer from allergies to the environment are recommended to wear masks, something they were willing to do before Covid-19 since it was not the practice. Those with allergens should continue to utilize masks and sanitizers and keep social distance for their safety. Because individuals have already experienced the benefits, continuing these activities will not be difficult. With the same logic in mind, hygienic measures in schools, especially in hospitals, should benefit by implementing similar covid-19 beneficial activities. Autonomous environments are a human dream that they might bring to design to increase productivity, cut costs, and help businesses more. There is room for more autonomous locations to be developed, and flexible work hours may be implemented. Another area where humans were suffering was the digitization and adoption of technology. Covid-19 dismantled the obstacles to technology's widespread use, and benefits previously stifled its acceptance. Aside from the covid-19 post-era, this chapter's reach is restricted. Other researchers may apply this idea to other aspects of social change management, depending on the modeling approach.

COVID-19 AND THE LESSONS LEARNED ABOUT NETWORKING ON BOTH A PROFESSIONAL AND PERSONAL LEVEL

Although networking has evolved dramatically since the COVID-19 epidemic, it is still essential at all stages of life. First, from academics to seasoned professionals, networking enables people to exchange information, acquire experience, and form relationships that may lead to new career possibilities and personal connections. Before covid-19, social, professional, and personal networking occurred naturally. However, the covid-19 impact exacerbated the professional, interpersonal, and social situation by changing existing social norms.

1. It is critical to comprehend how the varied nature of individuals interacts in which situations. Because human nature is too complex to understand altogether. It is a situational change requiring ongoing reading, which is not everyone's simple assignment. However, leadership positions and traits are essential to act appropriately, perceive, and comprehend. Before covid-19, it was impossible to regulate individual behavior in changing situations, and a plethora of literature presents difficulties and perspectives in this respect. However, the post-19 covid era will be more difficult in various ways.
    a. A change cycle that has already occurred during covid-19 will be challenging to reverse to restore to its previous state. A strategic intent would be necessary to determine what can be accomplished in which direction. Many examples of people who have a favorable attitude toward their surroundings may be considered a palpable manifestation of the power of purpose in reverting to beliefs following a covid-19 scenario. For example, strategic tourism leaders can employ celebrity wisdom and community interactions to help societies grow socially and restore tourism confidence (Fenitra et al., 2022).
    b. Mixed-identity individuals may utilize their identities to foster social cohesion and consensus by emphasizing them. Public knowledge may be gathered and used for the benefit of society. For example, teachers, university professors, business leaders, and local politicians may all join together to use their identities. In order to assist restore public faith in the value of service to society, they might be enrolled (see further Abbas, Ekowati, & Suhariadi, 2022).
2. The social fabric of mind and society is subject to change and intricately intertwined. Models for social fabric development may be used to establish social fabric and foster networking among peers and communities (Abbas, Saud, Ekowati, & Suhariadi, 2021; Chance, 2015; Lerner, 1990). In order to develop social cognition, a leader's social identity at a large scale is necessary. Positive psychology advocates educating people about public health and well-being to promote a sense of social responsibility. For example, the scenario in Covid-19 is very similar to the climate change emergency, which is a fact. However, people's view of understanding and reacting to it is naïve. Therefore social cognition is ultimately necessary (see further Abbas, Ekowati, Suhariadi, et al., 2022).
    a. Some of the post-Covid-19 standards must be restored to their pre-Covid-19 levels. Once the situation has returned to normal, maintaining social distance will no longer be essential. It is critical to allow individuals to reclaim their social networking and engage in more excellent social contact than before covid-19.
    b. People need to lessen the unnecessary social distance that has become the norm. They must expand their social networks and arrange social affairs and festivities to reenact special occasions.
    c. Online social networking, social realization initiatives, and social gatherings are possible. Several internet forums may coordinate activities, and the eagerness to engage in online activities is overwhelming. As a result, these operations may be advanced by using translation platforms and other digital capabilities to improve global networking.

   d. Zoom online chat rooms and networking platforms that enable people to join and collaborate in networking and social exchange should be considered.
   e. Effective social cohesion methodologies may bring together like-minded global and social identities groups, and celebrity encounters are now possible. These activities may increase public trust in digital networking platforms and encourage people to learn and collaborate in global networks.
3. Technology acceptance was never too easy before covid-19. People have considered using technology for their benefit due to changing norms or working from home. People feel that technology benefits them because they follow social distancing and work-from-home regulations. This shift should be taken advantage of, and a more technology-based approach to facilitation should be encouraged. This is another management strategy that can improve technology acceptance and flexibility, particularly in nations where digitalization occurs. Individuals who were less technically skilled may be hesitant to broaden their network communication possibilities. Covid-19 provided the opportunity to be a master in order to benefit technology in a long-term manner.
   a. During Covid-19, businesses continued to thrive in their use of technology. Food enterprises and internet employment, for example, have grown in popularity, resulting in increased creativity and autonomy in the workplace. During Covid-19, food companies upped their home deliveries, in particular, to keep their supply chains running thanks to technological advancements smoothly. Such activities should be kept in mind in order to broaden their horizons.
   b. The covid-19 scenario, in which consumers were provided online medical support in case of mild complaints, also enhanced health care and pharmaceutical delivery for the elderly. Doctors might guide patients online, and their drugs could be delivered to their homes, requiring minimal contact.
   c. Many individuals were ignorant of the need for medical precautions and were afraid to take them because of health issues. People with respiratory allergies, for example, were often unable to use masks prior to covid-19. People suffering from sinuses, allergies, and other contagious illnesses may now accept these precautions as the new normal for their manageable health problems.
   d. Online courses allowed to complete the study without interruption. This method is especially beneficial for kids who are in precarious situations. If schools can design rules for those children, who are best kept alone at home due to health issues. Such students may be provided with public education on their doorstep, which would benefit both parents and children.
   e. This policy may be used by schools that cannot offer comprehensive facilities to impaired pupils. Children in hard-to-reach areas may be able to benefit from online schooling. Schools may reduce tuition for parents who wish to continue their children's education online. Low-income families will be relieved of their financial responsibilities due to this. Governments, aristocrats, and business leaders may work together to facilitate such development frameworks for uplifting education to society's vulnerable.
   f. Students suffering from minor illnesses may benefit from working online not to miss any classes while they are ill. This strategy will allow students to stay on top of their work and prevent falling behind in their studies.
   g. Online webinars, conferences, and seminars are simple to organize and run on a budget. Several transnational collaborations may occur in the post-covid-19 period by using technology interventions. Medical doctorates, research collaborations, academic conferences, and virtual

networking are all examples of things that may be promoted. This technique will have a lower economic effect, and digital platforms may be tailored to fit a variety of global environments.

4. For building autonomous settings with pleasant usability, extensive inputs in technology acceptance models were necessary. Working from home or online provides many advantages, including working in a self-contained environment. Organizations should reward employees who can operate in a highly self-motivated and independent environment. A human's opinions regarding networking may be influenced by perspective. However, actual events may also affect them, such as continuity remaining intact online.
   a. Flexible workplaces may be introduced by organizations that can adopt policies in this way. Workers who travel from afar may save time, money, and energy by working independently when their actual presence is unneeded.
   b. Organizations during a cultural revolution should benefit from these self-contained measures to develop policies for performance assessments based on new standards.
   c. Widespread use of the notion is to work from a particular locality to meet as many individuals as possible and build a comfort zone. This may be uncomfortable and even inauthentic for shy or introverted persons and those who do not want to be part of big platforms. Many students are susceptible to them and cannot manage the growing usage of technology due to online networking and technology use (e.g., Abbas, Eliyana, et al., 2020; Abbas, Saud, Ekowati, et al., 2020; Saud et al., 2021). Covid-19's increased usability and technology platforms are now simple to handle. There is a hopeful outlook that these computer-related will learn to improve these technological platforms in the simplest ways. It is also hoped that next-generation users will develop better networks and benefit from technology.
5. It is critical to recognize that it is impossible to undo the change once it has occurred. As a result, when the Prochaska and DiClemente proposed stage of change acceptance occurs, it becomes ethically responsible conduct for implementing change.
   a. The social shift that has become the new standard and is widely accepted might be seen as equitable and sustainable in practice. For example, public awareness of cleanliness, health care, and the environment, which was intended to be adopted in public conduct, may now be continued from covid-19 teachings.
   b. The healthcare, education, and tourist sectors were the worst hit by the epidemic. As a result, these sectors would continue to exist under intellectual discourse in which change is anticipated or has occurred. It might be helpful to conduct a comprehensive study program to determine how much change is absorbed and at what magnitude to continue with new standards in these fields.

FUTURE DIRECTIONS

Combining the Cycle of Prochaska and DiClemente with the Ethically Responsible Behavior Theory for Social Change Management will be necessary for understanding the social change perspective. Social norms and the cycle of Prochaska and DiClemente may assist in revealing parts of social psychology that have changed throughout covid-19. It would be easier to understand what changes were necessary for the new norm to continue embracing social cognition theory were integrated. It might contribute to creating a better understanding of what modifications are required to return to a previous state, such as before Covid-19. The authors believe that research on post-Covid-19 scenarios, new norms, and social lessons learned from Covid-19 for societal benefits will continue. Social psychology's profound and complex notion, which is especially absorbing change, may be maintained in research to unfold by employing covid-19 teachings.

Future study researchers may benefit from the ideas presented in this chapter in several ways. The Prochaska and DiClemente cycle might be used with the Ethically Responsible Behavior Theory for social change management. This would provide a thorough picture of the change cycle that has occurred. Once that has been established, it must have been possible to determine how much morally responsible activity for change had amalgamation from individual conduct. The theory of reasoned action or planned behavior can determine how much thought has gone into learning new regulations. As a result, standards beneficial to people in certain circumstances might be investigated for long-term sustainability.

ACKNOWLEDGMENT

There is no funding obtained for this study. This study does not report any conflict, financial or commercial interest. All authors contributed positively to preparing this Book Chapter.

This research is an outcome of the coordination of the laboratory at the Doctoral Program in Human Resource Development, Post Graduate School Universitas Airlangga, Surabaya, Indonesia. This lab is currently undergoing the registration procedure. It is slated to start working officially under Prof. Dr. Fendy Suhariadi, the Head of the Doctoral Program in Human Resource Development, Post Graduate School Universitas Airlangga.

Address: Post graduate School, Airlangga, street 4-6, Campus B, Universitas Airlangga, Gubeng, Surabaya, 60286

REFERENCES

Abbas, A., Ekowati, D., & Suhariadi, F. (2021). Managing Individuals, Organizations Through Leadership: Diversity Consciousness Roadmap. In B. Christiansen & H. Chandan (Eds.), *Handbook of Research on Applied Social Psychology in Multiculturalism* (Vol. 1, pp. 47–71). IGI Global. doi:10.4018/978-1-7998-6960-3.ch003

Abbas, A., Ekowati, D., & Suhariadi, F. (2022). Social Perspective: Leadership in Changing Society. In M. I. Hassan, S. S. Roy, U. Chatterjee, S. Chakraborty, & U. Singh (Eds.), *Social Morphology, Human Welfare and Sustainability*. Springer. doi:10.1007/978-3-030-96760-4_4

Abbas, A., Ekowati, D., Suhariadi, F., & Fenitra, R. M. (2022). Health implications, Leaders Societies, and Climate Change: A Global Review. In *Ecological footprints of climate change: Adaptive Approaches and Sustainability*. Springer.

Abbas, A., Eliyana, A., Ekowati, D., Saud, M., Raza, A., & Wardani, R. (2020). Data set on coping strategies in the digital age: The role of psychological well-being and social capital among university students in Java Timor, Surabaya, Indonesia. *Data in Brief*, *30*, 10558. doi:10.1016/j.dib.2020.105583 PMID:32368599

Abbas, A., Saud, M., Ekowati, D., & Suhariadi, F. (2021). Social Psychology and Fabrication: A Synthesis of Individuals, Society, and Organization. In B. Christiansen & H. Chandan (Eds.), *Handbook of Research on Applied Social Psychology in Multiculturalism* (Vol. 1, pp. 89–109). IGI Global. doi:10.4018/978-1-7998-6960-3.ch005

Abbas, A., Saud, M., Ekowati, D., Usman, I., & Setia, S. (2020). Technology and stress: A proposed framework for coping with stress in Indonesian higher education. *International Journal of Innovation, Creativity and Change*, *13*(4), 373–390.

Abbas, A., Saud, M., Ekowati, D., Usman, I., & Suhariadi, F. (2021). Servant leadership: A strategic choice for organisational performance. An empirical discussion from Pakistan. *International Journal of Productivity and Quality Management*, *34*(4), 468–485. doi:10.1504/IJPQM.2021.120599

Abbas, A., Saud, M., Suhariadi, F., Usman, I., & Ekowati, D. (2020). Positive leadership psychology: Authentic and servant leadership in higher education in Pakistan. *Current Psychology (New Brunswick, N.J.)*, 1–11. doi:10.100712144-020-01051-1

Abbott, T. (2021). *Social and personality development*. Routledge. doi:10.4324/9781003209300

Abrams, D., & Hogg, M. A. (2006). *Social identifications: A social psychology of intergroup relations and group processes*. Routledge. doi:10.4324/9780203135457

Abrams, D., Wetherell, M., Cochrane, S., Hogg, M. A., & Turner, J. C. (1990). Knowing what to think by knowing who you are: Self-categorization and the nature of norm formation, conformity and group polarization. *British Journal of Social Psychology*, *29*(2), 97–119. doi:10.1111/j.2044-8309.1990.tb00892.x PMID:2372667

Afifi, W. A., & Guerrero, L. K. (2000). Motivations underlying topic avoidance in close relationships. In S. Petronio (Ed.), *Balancing the secrets of private disclosures* (pp. 165–180). Routledge.

Ajzen, I. (1991). The theory of planned behavior. *Organizational Behavior and Human Decision Processes*, *50*(2), 179–211. doi:10.1016/0749-5978(91)90020-T

Ajzen, I. (2002). Perceived behavioral control, self-efficacy, locus of control, and the theory of planned behavior 1. *Journal of Applied Social Psychology*, *32*(4), 665–683. doi:10.1111/j.1559-1816.2002.tb00236.x

Ajzen, I., & Fishbein, M. (1969). The prediction of behavioral intentions in a choice situation. *Journal of Experimental Social Psychology*, *5*(4), 400–416. doi:10.1016/0022-1031(69)90033-X

Ajzen, I., & Fishbein, M. (1970). The prediction of behavior from attitudinal and normative variables. *Journal of Experimental Social Psychology*, *6*(4), 466–487. doi:10.1016/0022-1031(70)90057-0

Allport, F. H. (1962). A structuronomic conception of behavior: Individual and collective: I. Structural theory and the master problem of social psychology. *Journal of Abnormal and Social Psychology*, *64*(1), 3–30. doi:10.1037/h0043563 PMID:13860640

Asirifi, M. A., Ogilvie, L., Barton, S., Bilash, O., Stobart, K., Aniteye, P., Kwashie, A., Ansong, G., Eliason, C., & Aziato, L. (2022). Reflections on change theory and community-based participatory action research: Congruent, similar or different? *Journal of Nursing Education and Practice*, *12*(3), 11–21. doi:10.5430/jnep.v12n3p11

Augoustinos, M., Walker, I., & Donaghue, N. (2014). Social cognition: An integrated introduction (3rd ed.). New York: Sage.

Bandura, A. (1978). The self system in reciprocal determinism. *The American Psychologist*, *33*(4), 344–358. doi:10.1037/0003-066X.33.4.344

Bandura, A. (1989). Human agency in social cognitive theory. *The American Psychologist*, *44*(9), 1175–1184. doi:10.1037/0003-066X.44.9.1175 PMID:2782727

Bandura, A. (1991). Social cognitive theory of self-regulation. *Organizational Behavior and Human Decision Processes*, *50*(2), 248–287. doi:10.1016/0749-5978(91)90022-L

Bandura, A. (1999). Social cognitive theory of personality. In C. Prendergast (Ed.), Handbook of personality (Vol. 2, pp. 154-196). Clarendon Press.

Bandura, A. (2002). Growing primacy of human agency in adaptation and change in the electronic era. *European Psychologist*, *7*(1), 2–16. doi:10.1027//1016-9040.7.1.2

Bandura, A., Ross, D., & Ross, S. A. (1961). Transmission of aggression through imitation of aggressive models. *Journal of Abnormal and Social Psychology*, *63*(3), 575–582. doi:10.1037/h0045925 PMID:13864605

Baranowski, T., Cullen, K. W., Nicklas, T., Thompson, D., & Baranowski, J. (2003). Are current health behavioral change models helpful in guiding prevention of weight gain efforts? *Obesity Research*, *11*(S10), 23S–43S. doi:10.1038/oby.2003.222 PMID:14569036

Baumeister, R. F., & Leary, M. R. (1997). Writing narrative literature reviews. *Review of General Psychology*, *1*(3), 311–320. doi:10.1037/1089-2680.1.3.311

Benabou, R., & Tirole, J. (2011). *Laws and Norms.* National Bureau of Economic Research Working Paper Series, 17579. doi:10.3386/w17579

Berkowitz, A. D. (2010). Fostering healthy norms to prevent violence and abuse: The social norms approach. In K. L. Kaufman (Ed.), *The prevention of sexual violence: A practitioner's sourcebook* (pp. 147–171). NEARI Press.

Bicalho, T., Silva, C., Cunha, I., Teixeira, J., & Proença, A. (2019). Planners' attitudes towards the cycling potential of their cities–Creating awareness for attitude change. *Travel Behaviour & Society*, *17*, 96–103. doi:10.1016/j.tbs.2019.08.002

Bicchieri, C. (2016). *Norms in the wild: How to diagnose, measure, and change social norms.* Oxford University Press.

Bicchieri, C., Muldoon, R., & Sontuoso, A. (2018). Social norms. In *The Stanford encyclopedia of philosophy. Metaphysics Research Lab.* Stanford University.

Bless, H., & Fiedler, K. (2014). *Social cognition: How individuals construct social reality* (2nd ed.). Routledge. doi:10.4324/9781315784731

Borsari, B., & Carey, K. B. (2001). Peer influences on college drinking: A review of the research. *Journal of Substance Abuse*, *13*(4), 391–424. doi:10.1016/S0899-3289(01)00098-0 PMID:11775073

Bosson, J. K., & Vandello, J. A. (2011). Precarious manhood and its links to action and aggression. *Current Directions in Psychological Science*, *20*(2), 82–86. doi:10.1177/0963721411402669

Briggs, D., Ellis, A., Lloyd, A., & Telford, L. (2020). New hope or old futures in disguise? Neoliberalism, the Covid-19 pandemic and the possibility for social change. *The International Journal of Sociology and Social Policy*, *40*(9/10), 831–848. doi:10.1108/IJSSP-07-2020-0268

Brodeur, A., Gray, D., Islam, A., & Bhuiyan, S. (2021). A literature review of the economics of COVID-19. *Journal of Economic Surveys*, *35*(4), 1007–1044. doi:10.1111/joes.12423 PMID:34230772

Buttimer, A. (1980). Home, reach, and the sense of place. In The human experience of space and place (Vol. 3, pp. 166-187). London: Routledge.

Carter, J. W., & Youssef-Morgan, C. M. (2019). The positive psychology of mentoring: A longitudinal analysis of psychological capital development and performance in a formal mentoring program. *Human Resource Development Quarterly*, *30*(3), 383–405. doi:10.1002/hrdq.21348

Carter, S. M., & Greer, C. R. (2013). Strategic leadership: Values, styles, and organizational performance. *Journal of Leadership & Organizational Studies*, *20*(4), 375–393. doi:10.1177/1548051812471724

Chance, M. R. (2015). *Social fabrics of the mind*. Psychology Press. doi:10.4324/9781315728186

Côté, J. E., & Levine, C. G. (2014). *Identity, formation, agency, and culture: A social psychological synthesis* (1st ed.). Psychology Press. doi:10.4324/9781410612199

Davis, H. A. (2003). Conceptualizing the role and influence of student-teacher relationships on children's social and cognitive development. *Educational Psychologist*, *38*(4), 207–234. doi:10.1207/S15326985EP3804_2

Dornyei, Z., & Ottó, I. (1998). Motivation in action: A process model of L2 motivation. In *Working Papers in Applied Linguistics*. Thames Valley University.

Dowling, G. R., & Staelin, R. (1994). A model of perceived risk and intended risk-handling activity. *The Journal of Consumer Research*, *21*(1), 119–134. doi:10.1086/209386

Elder, G. H., Johnson, M. K., & Crosnoe, R. (2003). The emergence and development of life course theory. In Handbook of the life course (pp. 3-19). Boston, MA: Springer. doi:10.1007/978-0-306-48247-2_1

Elder, G. H. Jr. (1994). Time, human agency, and social change: Perspectives on the life course. *Social Psychology Quarterly*, *57*(1), 4–15. doi:10.2307/2786971

Fenitra, R. M., Abbas, A., Ekowati, D., & Suhairidi, F. (2022). Strategic Intent and Strategic Leadership: A Review Perspective for Post-covid Tourism and Hospitality Industry Recovery. In *The Emerald Handbook of Destination Recovery*. Emerald Group Publishing.

Fenitra, R. M., Anggun, P., Eko, S., & Indrianawati, U. (2021). Factors Influencing Preventive Intention Behavior Towards COVID-19 in Indonesia. *The Journal of Behavioral Science, 16*(1), 14–27.

Fetzer, T., Witte, M., Hensel, L., Jachimowicz, J., Haushofer, J., Ivchenko, A., . . . Fiorin, S. (2020). Perceptions of an insufficient government response at the onset of the COVID-19 pandemic are associated with lower mental well-being. *Pre Print* Doi.10.31234/ doi:osf.io/3kfmh

Fredricks, A. J., & Dossett, D. L. (1983). Attitude–behavior relations: A comparison of the Fishbein-Ajzen and the Bentler-Speckart models. *Journal of Personality and Social Psychology, 45*(3), 501–512. doi:10.1037/0022-3514.45.3.501

Galbiati, R., Henry, E., Jacquemet, N., & Lobeck, M. (2021). How laws affect the perception of norms: Empirical evidence from the lockdown. *PLoS One, 16*(9), e0256624. doi:10.1371/journal.pone.0256624 PMID:34559821

Gallo Marin, B., Aghagoli, G., Lavine, K., Yang, L., Siff, E. J., Chiang, S. S., ... Aung, S. N. (2021). Predictors of COVID-19 severity: A literature review. *Reviews in Medical Virology, 31*(1), 1–10. doi:10.1002/rmv.2146 PMID:32845042

Getzels, J. W., & Guba, E. G. (1957). Social behavior and the administrative process. *The School Review, 65*(4), 423–441. doi:10.1086/442411

Gidycz, C. A., Orchowski, L. M., & Berkowitz, A. D. (2011). Preventing sexual aggression among college men: An evaluation of a social norms and bystander intervention program. *Violence Against Women, 17*(6), 720–742. doi:10.1177/1077801211409727 PMID:21571742

Giorgi, A. (2020). *Psychology as a human science: A phenomenologically based approach* (2nd ed.). University Professors Press.

Halson, S. L., & Lastella, M. (2017). Amazing athletes with ordinary habits: Why is changing behavior so difficult? *International Journal of Sports Physiology and Performance, 12*(10), 1273–1275. doi:10.1123/ijspp.2017-0632 PMID:29282990

Hampton, S. E., & Parker, J. N. (2011). Collaboration and productivity in scientific synthesis. *Bioscience, 61*(11), 900–910. doi:10.1525/bio.2011.61.11.9

Harper, C. A., Satchell, L. P., Fido, D., & Latzman, R. D. (2021). Functional fear predicts public health compliance in the COVID-19 pandemic. *International Journal of Mental Health and Addiction, 19*(5), 1875–1888. doi:10.100711469-020-00281-5 PMID:32346359

Harrell, S. P. (2018). Soulfulness as an orientation to contemplative practice: Culture, liberation, and mindful awareness. *The Journal of Contemplative Inquiry, 5*(1), 1–32.

Hiscock, R., Bauld, L., Amos, A., Fidler, J. A., & Munafò, M. (2012). Socioeconomic status and smoking: A review. *Annals of the New York Academy of Sciences, 1248*(1), 107–123. doi:10.1111/j.1749-6632.2011.06202.x PMID:22092035

Huntington, S. P. (1971). The change to change: Modernization, development, and politics. *Comparative Politics, 3*(3), 283–322. doi:10.2307/421470

Kahan, D. M. (2019). Social influence, social meaning, and deterrence. In *Criminal Law* (pp. 429–476). Routledge. doi:10.4324/9781315189437-13

Karapanos, E., Zimmerman, J., Forlizzi, J., & Martens, J.-B. (2009, April). User experience over time: An initial framework. *Proceedings of the SIGCHI conference on human factors in computing systems*. 10.1145/1518701.1518814

Kasten, S., van Osch, L., Candel, M., & de Vries, H. (2019). The influence of pre-motivational factors on behavior via motivational factors: A test of the I-Change model. *BMC Psychology*, *7*(1), 1–12. doi:10.118640359-019-0283-2 PMID:30786921

Knight, J., & Ensminger, J. (1998). Conflict over changing social norms. In M. C. Brinton & V. Nee (Eds.), *The New Institutionalism in Sociology*. Stanford University Press.

Kotter, J. (2007). Leading change: Why transformation efforts fail. *Harvard Business Review*, *73*, 259–267.

Kritsonis, A. (2005). Comparison of change theories. *International Journal of Scholarly Academic Intellectual Diversity,* *8*(1), 1-7

Kukla, M., Bonfils, K. A., & Salyers, M. P. (2015). Factors impacting work success in Veterans with mental health disorders: A Veteran-focused mixed methods pilot study. *Journal of Vocational Rehabilitation*, *43*(1), 51–66. doi:10.3233/JVR-150754

Kuntsche, S., Room, R., & Kuntsche, E. (2021). I can keep up with the best: The role of social norms in alcohol consumption and their use in interventions. In *The Handbook of Alcohol Use* (pp. 285–302). Academic Press. doi:10.1016/B978-0-12-816720-5.00024-4

Kurz, T., Gardner, B., Verplanken, B., & Abraham, C. (2015). Habitual behaviors or patterns of practice? Explaining and changing repetitive climate-relevant actions. *Wiley Interdisciplinary Reviews: Climate Change*, *6*(1), 113–128. doi:10.1002/wcc.327

Lent, R. W., Brown, S. D., & Hackett, G. (1994). Toward a unifying social cognitive theory of career and academic interest, choice, and performance. *Journal of Vocational Behavior*, *45*(1), 79–122. doi:10.1006/jvbe.1994.1027

Lerner, R. M. (1990). Weaving Development Into the Fabric of Personality and Social Psychology—On the Significance of Bandura's Social Foundation of Thought and Action. *Psychological Inquiry*, *1*(1), 92–96. doi:10.120715327965pli0101_24

Lewin, K. (1951). *Theory*. Harper and Row.

Lewis, M., & Brooks-Gunn, J. (1979). Toward a theory of social cognition: The development of self. *New Directions for Child and Adolescent Development*, *1979*(4), 1–20. doi:10.1002/cd.23219790403

Lin, J. J., Mamykina, L., Lindtner, S., Delajoux, G., & Strub, H. B. (2006). *Fish'n'Steps: Encouraging physical activity with an interactive computer game.* Paper presented at the International conference on ubiquitous computing, Berlin, Germany. 10.1007/11853565_16

Lippitt, G. L., & Lippitt, R. (1986). The consulting process in action. *Training and Development Journal*, *29*(6), 38–41.

Lorini, G., & Marrosu, F. (2018). How individual habits fit/unfit social norms: From the Historical Perspective to a Neurobiological Repositioning of an Unresolved Problem. *Frontiers in Sociology*, *3*, 14. doi:10.3389/fsoc.2018.00014

Luszczynska, A., & Schwarzer, R. (2015). Social cognitive theory. In M. Conner & P. Norman (Eds.), *UK Higher Education Psychology Psychology* (pp. 225–251). McGraw-Hill Education.

Lyng, S. (1990). Edgework: A social psychological analysis of voluntary risk taking. *American Journal of Sociology*, *95*(4), 851–886. doi:10.1086/229379

Marrow, A. J. (1977). *The practical theorist: The life and work of Kurt Lewin*. Teachers College Press.

Michale, J. (2005). Positive and negative reinforcement, a distinction that is no longer necessary; or a better way to talk about bad things. *Journal of Organizational Behavior Management*, *24*(1-2), 207–222. doi:10.1300/J075v24n01_15

Mitchell, T. R. (1982). Motivation: New directions for theory, research, and practice. *Academy of Management Review*, *7*(1), 80–88. doi:10.2307/257251

Molden, D. C., & Dweck, C. S. (2006). Finding" meaning" in psychology: A lay theories approach to self-regulation, social perception, and social development. *The American Psychologist*, *61*(3), 192–203. doi:10.1037/0003-066X.61.3.192 PMID:16594836

Montano, D. E., & Kasprzyk, D. (2015). Theory of reasoned action, theory of planned behavior, and the integrated behavioral model. In B. K. Karen Glanz & K. V. Rimer (Eds.), *Health behavior: Theory, research and practice* (Vol. 70, pp. 95–124). John Wiley & Sons.

Neighbors, C., Foster, D. W., & Fossos, N. (2013). Peer influences on addiction. In *Principles of addiction: Comprehensive addictive behaviours and disorders* (Vol. 1, pp. 323–331). Academic Press. doi:10.1016/B978-0-12-398336-7.00033-4

Neville, F. G., Templeton, A., Smith, J. R., & Louis, W. R. (2021). Social norms, social identities and the COVID-19 pandemic: Theory and recommendations. *Social and Personality Psychology Compass*, *15*(5), e12596. doi:10.1111pc3.12596 PMID:34230834

Nordlund, A. M., & Garvill, J. (2003). Effects of values, problem awareness, and personal norm on willingness to reduce personal car use. *Journal of Environmental Psychology*, *23*(4), 339–347. doi:10.1016/S0272-4944(03)00037-9

Oreg, S. (2003). Resistance to change: Developing an individual differences measure. *The Journal of Applied Psychology*, *88*(4), 680–693. doi:10.1037/0021-9010.88.4.680 PMID:12940408

Pajares, F., & Usher, E. L. (2008). Self-efficacy, motivation, and achievement in school from the perspective of reciprocal determinism. In M. L. Maehr, S. A. Karabenick, & T. C. Urdan (Eds.), Advances in motivation and achievement (Vol. 15, pp. 391–423). Emerald Group Publishing. doi:10.1016/S0749-7423(08)15012-9

Papacharissi, Z. (2004). Democracy online: Civility, politeness, and the democratic potential of online political discussion groups. *New Media & Society*, *6*(2), 259–283. doi:10.1177/1461444804041444

Perry, L., & Miller, T. (2018). *Business Communication: Skills and Techniques*. Scientific e-Resources.

Phillipson, C. (2007). The 'elected'and the 'excluded': Sociological perspectives on the experience of place and community in old age. *Ageing and Society*, *27*(3), 321–342. doi:10.1017/S0144686X06005629

Pintaric, N., & Bronzin, T. (2013). *IT Capability Review*. Paper presented at the Central European Conference on Information and Intelligent Systems, Varaždin, Croatia.

Pokhrel, S., & Chhetri, R. (2021). A literature review on impact of COVID-19 pandemic on teaching and learning. *Higher Education for the Future*, *8*(1), 133–141. doi:10.1177/2347631120983481

Porges, S. W. (2003). Social engagement and attachment: A phylogenetic perspective. *Annals of the New York Academy of Sciences*, *1008*(1), 31–47. doi:10.1196/annals.1301.004 PMID:14998870

Porter, L. W., Bigley, G. A., & Steers, R. M. (2003). *Motivation and work behavior* (7th ed.). McGraw-Hill/Irwin.

Prochaska, J., Norcross, J., & DiClemente, C. (1994). Changing for good. Avon Books.

Prochaska, J., Norcross, J., & DiClemente, C. (1996). The six stages of change. *Tufts University Diet and Nutrition Letter*, *14*(7), 1–10.

Prochaska, J. O., & DiClemente, C. C. (1983). Stages and processes of self-change of smoking: Toward an integrative model of change. *Journal of Consulting and Clinical Psychology*, *51*(3), 390–395. doi:10.1037/0022-006X.51.3.390 PMID:6863699

Prochaska, J. O., & DiClemente, C. C. (1986). Toward a comprehensive model of change. In Treating addictive behaviors (pp. 3-27). Springer. doi:10.1007/978-1-4613-2191-0_1

Prochaska, J. O., & Prochaska, J. M. (1999). Why don't continents move? Why don't people change? *Journal of Psychotherapy Integration*, *9*(1), 83–102. doi:10.1023/A:1023210911909

Prochaska, J. O., Redding, C. A., & Evers, K. E. (2015). The transtheoretical model and stages of change. In K. Glanz, B. K. Rimer, & K. Viswanath (Eds.), *Health behavior: Theory, research, and practice* (pp. 97–121). John Wiley & Sons.

Radocy, R. E., & Boyle, J. D. (2012). *Psychological foundations of musical behavior* (5th ed.). Charles C Thomas Publisher.

Ritchie, J., & Spencer, L. (2002). Qualitative data analysis for applied policy research. In M. Huberman & M. B. Miles (Eds.), *The qualitative researcher's companion* (Vol. 573, pp. 305–329). Sage Publications, inc. doi:10.4135/9781412986274.n12

Rotter, J. B. (1990). Internal versus external control of reinforcement: A case history of a variable. *The American Psychologist*, *45*(4), 489–493. doi:10.1037/0003-066X.45.4.489

Saud, M., Ashfaq, A., Abbas, A., Ariadi, S., & Mahmood, Q. K. (2021). Social support through religion and psychological well-being: COVID-19 and coping strategies in Indonesia. *Journal of Religion and Health*, *60*(5), 3309–3325. doi:10.100710943-021-01327-1 PMID:34245436

Saukkonen, J., Kreus, P., Obermayer, N., Ruiz, Ó. R., & Haaranen, M. (2019). *AI, RPA, ML and Other Emerging Technologies: Anticipating Adoption in the HRM Field.* Paper presented at the ECIAIR 2019 European Conference on the Impact of Artificial Intelligence and Robotics, Oxford, UK.

Schunk, D. H. (2012). Social cognitive theory. In K. R. Harris, S. Graham, C. B. T. Urdan, G. M. S. McCormick, & J. Sweller (Eds.), APA educational psychology handbook (Vol. 1, pp. 101–123). American Psychological Association.

Schunk, D. H., & Usher, E. L. (2012). Social cognitive theory and motivation. In R. Ryan (Ed.), *The Oxford handbook of human motivation* (Vol. 2, pp. 11–26). Oxford University Press.

Sherif, M., & Sherif, C. W. (1956). An outline of social psychology. Academic Press.

Spears, R. (2011). Group identities: The social identity perspective. In Handbook of identity theory and research (pp. 201-224). New York, NY: Springer.

Spielberger, C. (2004). Encyclopedia of applied psychology. Academic Press.

Spradley, R. T., & Spradley, E. (2021). The Building Blocks of Pandemic Communication Strategy: Models to Enable Resilient Risk and Crisis Communication. In Pandemic Communication and Resilience (pp. 51-73). Cham: Springer.

Stajkovic, A. D., & Luthans, F. (1998). Social cognitive theory and self-efficacy: Goin beyond traditional motivational and behavioral approaches. *Organizational Dynamics*, *26*(4), 62–74. doi:10.1016/S0090-2616(98)90006-7

Telzer, E. H., Van Hoorn, J., Rogers, C. R., & Do, K. T. (2018). Social influence on positive youth development: A developmental neuroscience perspective. *Advances in Child Development and Behavior*, *54*, 215–258. doi:10.1016/bs.acdb.2017.10.003 PMID:29455864

Thakker, J. (2013). International perspectives on addiction. In *Principles of Addiction* (pp. 51–59). Academic Press. doi:10.1016/B978-0-12-398336-7.00005-X

Triandis, H. C. (1989). The self and social behavior in differing cultural contexts. *Psychological Review*, *96*(3), 506–520. doi:10.1037/0033-295X.96.3.506

Turner, J. C. (1991). *Social influence*. Thomson Brooks/Cole Publishing Co.

Van Dijk, T. A. (1990). Social cognition and discourse. In H. Giles & W. P. Robinson (Eds.), *Handbook of language and social psychology* (pp. 163–183). John Wiley & Sons Ltd.

Van Hoorn, J., Crone, E. A., & Van Leijenhorst, L. (2017). Hanging out with the right crowd: Peer influence on risk-taking behavior in adolescence. *Journal of Research on Adolescence*, *27*(1), 189–200. doi:10.1111/jora.12265 PMID:28498538

Varela, F. J. (1999). *Ethical know-how: Action, wisdom, and cognition.* Stanford University Press.

Verma, A. K., & Prakash, S. (2020). Impact of covid-19 on environment and society. *Journal of Global Biosciences*, *9*(5), 7352–7363.

Wechsler, H., Nelson, T. E., Lee, J. E., Seibring, M., Lewis, C., & Keeling, R. P. (2003). Perception and reality: A national evaluation of social norms marketing interventions to reduce college students' heavy alcohol use. *Journal of Studies on Alcohol*, *64*(4), 484–494. doi:10.15288/jsa.2003.64.484 PMID:12921190

Wikström, P.-O. H., Oberwittler, D., Treiber, K., & Hardie, B. (2012). *Breaking rules: The social and situational dynamics of young people's urban crime*. OUP Oxford.

Wilson, B., & Nochajski, T. H. (2018). On the continuum of exit: Understanding the stages of change among women in commercial sexual exploitation. *Gender Issues*, *35*(2), 98–112. doi:10.100712147-017-9201-1

Wyborn, C., Louder, E., Harrison, J., Montambault, J., Montana, J., Ryan, M., ... Reed, M. (2018). Understanding the impacts of research synthesis. *Environmental Science & Policy*, *86*, 72–84. doi:10.1016/j.envsci.2018.04.013

Zenic, N., Taiar, R., Gilic, B., Blazevic, M., Maric, D., Pojskic, H., & Sekulic, D. (2020). Levels and changes of physical activity in adolescents during the COVID-19 pandemic: Contextualizing urban vs. rural living environment. *Applied Sciences (Basel, Switzerland)*, *10*(11), 3997. doi:10.3390/app10113997

ADDITIONAL READING

Halonen, J. S., Thompson, J. L. W., Whitlock, K. H., Landrum, R. E., & Frantz, S. (2022). Assessing student learning outcomes in introductory psychology. In R. A. R. Gurung & G. Neufeld (Eds.), *Transforming introductory psychology: Expert advice on teacher training, course design, and student success* (pp. 81–112). American Psychological Association. doi:10.1037/0000260-005

Johnson, S. S. (2022). Knowing Well, Being Well: well-being born of understanding: The Urgent Need for Coordinated and Comprehensive Efforts to Combat Misinformation. *American Journal of Health Promotion*, *36*(3), 559–581. doi:10.1177/08901171211070957 PMID:35164544

Oxhandler, H. (2022). *The Soul of the Helper: Seven Stages to Seeing the Sacred Within Yourself So You Can See It in Others*. Templeton Foundation Press.

Pennucci, F., De Rosis, S., Murante, A. M., & Nuti, S. (2022). Behavioural and social sciences to enhance the efficacy of health promotion interventions: Redesigning the role of professionals and people. *Behavioural Public Policy*, *6*(1), 13–33. doi:10.1017/bpp.2019.19

Strömberg, H., & Wallgren, P. (2022). Finding that elusive bell and other issues-experiences from starting to cycle during a pandemic. *Cities (London, England)*, *122*, 103574. doi:10.1016/j.cities.2022.103574

Young, G. (2022). Elaborating Causality in the Unified Model. In *Causality and Neo-Stages in Development* (pp. 111–133). Springer. doi:10.1007/978-3-030-82540-9_5

KEY TERMS AND DEFINITIONS

Change Cycle: The change cycle is referred to stages of preparation for implementation that should focus on the change: unfreezing, implementing, and refreezing.

Ethically Responsible Behavior for Change: The notion of ethically responsible change considers ethics and responsibility intact during any social change affecting individuals or society.

Post COVID-19: The expected time is after the covid-19 virus emergency has passed; a new normal is predicted.

Social Cognition: Social cognition is how humans process, recall and use the information to explain and anticipate their own and others' behavior.

Social Fabric: Social Fabric is the web of interactions and connections that binds us all together as a society.

Social Norms: Social norms are unwritten laws of acceptable ideas, attitudes, and behaviors within a social group or society.

Chapter 8
The Impact of a Global Recession on Millennials in the Job Market

Sthokozile Mamba
University of KwaZulu-Natal, South Africa

Andrisha Beharry-Ramraj
University of KwaZulu-Natal, Westville, South Africa

ABSTRACT

The coronavirus pandemic took every sector of society by storm. The operational decisions taken by certain organizations led to a huge increase in the global rate of unemployment, especially youth unemployment. The millennial generation made up the majority of the youth unemployment statistics. Millennials have been the most economically impacted by the pandemic. The use of technology, the internet, and social media to generate an income has been a widely explored option for millennials. The monetization of social media activities has been mostly beneficial for small businesses, influencers, and content creators. A combination of the traits that millennials possess and their internet knowledge would be a good investment for the betterment of the global labour productivity post COVID-19. This chapter uses secondary data to review the impact of the COVID-19 pandemic on millennials in the job market and reviews possible recovery plans for this generation.

INTRODUCTION

The world is a constantly changing environment filled with uncertainty. The occurrence of the Coronavirus (Covid-19) pandemic was unexpected and it brought about various changes, not only in the personal lives of people but to the global economy as well. The pandemic forced drastic changes in the workplace such as opting for employees to work virtually or retrenching certain employees due to financial constraints (Agius, Robertson, Kendrick, Sewell, Stewart & McKee, 2020). Some of these changes were challenging, especially those that were highly dependent on technology to get the work done. Even though the

DOI: 10.4018/978-1-7998-8856-7.ch008

fourth industrial revolution (4IR) was already in motion, it was a steady change, whereas the pandemic was accompanied by an abrupt shift towards the use of high tech. It is common that workplaces usually prefer employees with the most experience in the industry. Highly experienced employees are usually part of the baby boomers generation and generation X (Venter, 2017). A large number of millennials joined the workforce in recent years which makes it impossible for them to have greater work experience compared to past generations. The millennial generation is mostly made up of people considered to be part of the youth (LaCore, 2015). The global youth unemployment rate is on a constant rise. According to the International Labour Organization, the global youth unemployment rate increased from 13.1% in the year 2017 to 14.6% in the year 2020. This is due to various factors such as increased population, lack of skills or qualifications and an inadequate supply of jobs. The pandemic has also greatly altered the landscape for young people trying to enter the job market, especially for those in middle-income countries such as South Africa, Brazil, Argentina and Peru.

Technology continuously transforms the labour market opportunities for young people. Furthermore, millennials are the first generation born in a digital era and to grow up with the development of technology. They consume technology differently which results in them being change agents in the workplace by presenting technology-driven attitudes (Huyler, Pierre, Ding & Norelus, 2015). These attitudes are highly suitable for the evolving workplace in a post-Covid environment. Covid-19 is one of the forces of globalisation that shaped millennials resulting in society becoming more interdependent and increasingly connected in terms of communication exchange, economic integration and cultural diffusions. Complex global social networks are leveraged by millennials, largely through social media platforms (Marjerison & Gan, 2020). These platforms have played a vital role in generating a basic income for the people that decided to monetise their social media activities such as becoming social media influencers for certain brands or creating content that is enjoyed by a large crowd.

The convenience of these social media platforms has created new industries and several start-ups. Access to advanced technological devices such as a smartphone and the internet allows for efficient problem-solving and uncovering of new perspectives (Hudders, De Jans & De Veirman, 2021). However, the use of the internet presents certain challenges such as being cyber bullied, data tracking and issues regarding cyber security where social media accounts with a large following risk being hacked into for the benefit of the hacker, which can be a financial benefit (Pornsrimate & Khamwon, 2021). The challenges and benefits of using the internet have the potential to give rise to new innovative business ideas. These ideas are suitable for a post-Covid environment to keep the economy from plummeting due to business outcomes brought about by the pandemic. The impact of social media was evident in the decline of the global economy when social media platforms owned by Meta, previously known as Facebook, crashed for a few hours on the fourth of October 2021. The outage of these platforms did not only have an impact on entertainment, but it affected cryptocurrencies, creation of virtual reality, live streaming, Russian oil trade, trading in London and numerous small businesses, especially those developed during the pandemic, that are dependent on these platforms (Sekścińska & Jaworska, 2022).

This chapter will discuss how the change in the global economy due to the Covid-19 pandemic has impacted millennials. Furthermore, it will discuss the participation of this generation in the economy and the factors influencing their financial health, such as gender and race inequalities. The general global economy and job market before and after the Covid-19 pandemic will be reviewed along how their state impacted the millennials before and after the pandemic. The general state of unemployment for millennials will also be reviewed. The possible strategies to address unemployment will be discussed where it will mainly focus on the use of technology, the internet, monetization of social media and the act of self-employment. The possible policy measures to address the financial recovery plans for millennials will also be reviewed.

PURPOSE OF THE STUDY

The job market was the most impacted by the Covid-19 consequences. Many people faced job losses due to Covid-19. Millennials were the generation that suffered the most due to the Covid-19 recession which occurred a decade after the great 2009 global recession. Most millennials were still recovering from the financial impacts of the 2009 recession, especially those that entered the job market during that recession period (Moreira & Hick, 2021). This paper serves to look into the participation of millennials in the economy before the occurrence of the Corona Virus. It further addresses the impacts that Covid-19 had on millennials. The paper also looks into how Covid-19 had an impact on the job market in general. It also serves to address the recovery plans that can possibly assist millennials in financially surviving the Covid-19 recession. This study will be beneficial to most millennials seeking means to recover from the financial impacts caused by Covid-19. It will also give policymakers an insight of the capabilities of millennial to formulate labour market policies that are well suited to this generation. This is important due to millennials gradually becoming the largest group making up the labour market, replacing baby boomers and gen X by 2030.

STUDY OBJECTIVES

This paper reviewed the involvement of millennials in the labour market pre- and post-Covid-19. The results from this study can be applicable beyond the mentioned countries. The aim of the review is to gather information and obtain guidance for millennials and policymakers on effective ways to recover from the financial and labour impacts of Covid-19. It is also aims to give an insight of the labour impacts caused by Covid-19 on millennials. The study further aims to offer insights for researchers for future research regarding the participation of millennials in the economy and whether millennials are capable of surviving another unexpected global economic crisis in the future. The specific research objectives of this study are (1) to investigate the financial and labour market impacts caused by Covid-19 on millennials; (2) to explore the state of the general economy and labour market before and after Covid-19; (3) and to identify possible labour recovery plans for millennials.

LITERATURE REVIEW

The world is ever changing due to the fourth industrial revolution and recently, the Covid-19 pandemic, among other world changing factors. One of the sectors that were highly impacted by these factors is the labour market. To create effective means for labour productivity in the future, there has to be a concern about the past and present state of the labour market. There has to also be a concern about the largest participants, which is slowly becoming the millennial generation, in the labour market and the economy.

THE GLOBAL ECONOMY BEFORE AND AFTER COVID-19

The global economy had been shaken before the Covid-19 pandemic. The previous economic crises have resulted in similar outcomes as those presented by the recent pandemic. One of the factors determining the state of an economy is the growth of labour productivity which is the most significant source of a lasting per capita income growth. The labour productivity growth had been slowing down on a global scale prior to the onset of the Covid-19 pandemic. The most synchronised, longest and steepest fall-off in productivity growth in decades was experienced by the emerging market and developing economies as a result of the 2007 to 2009 global financial crisis aftermath (World Bank Global Outlook, 2020). A trend of slowdown in the advanced economies continues as it has been underway since the late 1990s where global recessions have resulted in economic slowdowns (Dieppe, 2020).

The global productivity growth slowdown that has occurred over the last decade has raised questions regarding its causes. Various factors which supported labour productivity during the previous decades gradually faded in recent years, particularly in the emerging market and developing economies. Advanced economies experienced a weakness in their productivity due to multiple factors such as delayed development of new digital technologies and having these technologies incorporated into processes of production (Moreira & Hick, 2021). Another factor that left long-lasting scars on labour productivity in the emerging market and developing economies was epidemics such as the Ebola outbreak in 2013 that was centred in Western Africa, the Severe Acute Respiratory Syndrome in 2002 which was common in China and the Middle East Respiratory Syndrome that was first reported in Saudi Arabia in 2012 (Pak, Adegboye, Adekunle, Rahman, McBryde & Eisen, 2020). The recessions induced by Covid-19 elevated debt levels and triggered financial crises which potentially led to a larger loss of employment. There is also a possible further reduction in labour productivity growth due to Covid-19.

This pandemic has led to a deep global recession which coincided with a decline in per capita income in 90% of global countries, resulting in persistent unemployment, erosion of human capital and weakening of investment and trade. The economic outcomes of this pandemic are similar to the previous health crises (Wheelock, 2020). However, there could be productivity-enhancing opportunities in the midst of the major economic disruptions presented by the Covid-19 pandemic (Sneader & Sternfels, 2020). The misallocation of labour is evident in the significant gap which remains between the less productive firms and the firms that are highly productive on the technological front, particularly in the emerging market and developing economies. There are structural changes that can potentially translate from the technological changes that were sparked by the Covid-19 pandemic for the improvement of productivity within certain sectors. These changes include a sustainable shift towards teleworking, incorporating digital technologies in education, finance and manufacturing, or the onshore production of certain essential products that have greater capital intensity. The negative impact of education institution closures could be offset by the increase in digital skills and technology investments (Amankwah-Amoah, Khan, Wood & Knight, 2021). Furthermore, strategic restructuring of supply chains could improve resilience and increase diversity which can potentially promote knowledge transfer, foreign direct investment and trade for the economies that are not integrated well into global value chains. Another shift is the implementation of policies that are capable of promoting sustained labour productivity growth. The investment in human and physical capital needs to be facilitated by policymakers (Moreira & Hick, 2021).

There are vast implications of the Covid-19 crisis moving forward. However, it is clear that for the recovery from this crisis, the time for change and policy reform is now regarding challenges which were exacerbated by the pandemic such as the rise in inequality, international cooperation, climate crisis and job insecurity. New ideas which are policy-focused and forward-looking need to be present. They should be able to shape debates about a post-Covid-19 world and be able to guide policies. It has been questioned whether the attainment of The 17 Sustainable Development Goals, said to be ambitious, has been put further out of reach by the pandemic. Kharas (2020) argues that these goals remain relevant and have the potential of providing a handrail for the recovery policy. However, Dieppe (2020) states that recovery policy approaches need to be well-targeted and country-specific, especially with the goal of boosting investment productivity and growth. This partly supports the findings by Pipa and Bouchet (2020) that the pandemic revealed the importance of good leadership at a local level so that each region can discover the role it can play towards a sustainable recovery. These policies should be more in favour of populations that are less well-off since they were the most affected by the economic and health costs presented by the Covid-19 pandemic. These populations also experienced the most disruption in their labour markets by the pandemic and should be prioritised in the global improvement of labour market flexibility.

COVID-19 IMPACT ON THE JOB MARKET

The Organization for Economic Co-operation and Development (OECD) states that the Covid-19 pandemic triggered one of the worst employment crises since the Great Depression which occurred between the years 1929 and 1939. The employment crisis triggered by Covid-19 has the potential to increase poverty and widen inequalities. The impact of these consequences is likely to be felt for years for years to come (Wheelock, 2020). Forbes (2021) suggests that in the year 2024 or 2025 there could be the start of a severe slump. However, the OECD considers the construction of a more resilient and better labour market, an essential investment for the future so that the employment crisis does not convert into a social issue that could potentially lead to a global depression.

The best means suggested to bridge the recovery phase of the labour catastrophe caused by the pandemic are designs of active labour market policies for recovery. These policies are a contribution from the OECD and European Union (EU) countries towards a global effort. The policy options include increased support in labour demand creation through employment incentives, reallocation of employees across occupations and sectors through training and the boosting of digital skills (Su, Dai, Ullah & Andlib, 2021). For the purpose of this chapter, the latter policy suggestion serves highly necessary despite the occurrence of the Covid-19 pandemic since there has been a gradual global shift towards advanced digitalisation due to the recent industrial revolution. Additionally, the nature of social distancing policies has accelerated the digitalisation trends and placed more primacy on the need for countries to invest in digital training (Amankwah-Amoah, Khan, Wood & Knight, 2021). Various occupations in the modern workplace require digital skills as much as they require a qualification for that certain occupation. The digital skills possessed by each individual need to be suitable for their level of qualification and skills profile.

Young people were the most impacted by the Covid-19 crisis since they are over-represented in the sectors and industries that were mostly affected by Covid-19. The recent generations are made up of young people and are most likely to work on a 'gigs' basis, which are temporary contracts with different employers. For that reason, they were exposed to a higher risk of job loss. Youth unemployment has been a continuously unresolved issue. For instance, various governments addressed the difficulties of young people insufficiently and too late, regarding the aftermath of the global financial crisis in the year 2008 (Moreira & Hick, 2021). To avoid long-term impacts on the prospects of young people, similar to those of 2008, national youth strategies that are strongly youth-specific should assist in guiding policies across sectors. However, it is strongly evident that the recent generations have lost faith and trust in government related events, e.g., the youth participation in voting during government elections is usually low compared to older generations. This mistrust has led to numerous young people paving their own paths, such as starting small businesses and creating multiple streams of income with resources that are readily accessible to them, instead of anticipating assistance from the government. These paths can potentially play a vital role in the global economy and these young people possess self-taught skills which can also play an important role in the future workplace.

Millennials in the Economy

Millennials are categorised as the generation of people born between the early 80s and the mid-90s (Dimock, 2019). There have been many opinions regarding millennials and the manner in which they are either shaping or destroying the economy. Collins (2020) states that millennials are destroying consumerism by being careful spenders. On the other hand, other sources mention millennials overspend on luxuries, ruin their chances of purchasing houses and are likely to incur more debt, in addition to the high student loan debts associated with this generation. Cousins (2020) states that there has been a shifting of priorities among millennials, where they traditionally did not value saving, they have been steadily gravitating towards stability. Millennials have been unlucky regarding social and economic crisis. Factors that shape generations are parenting, the world economy, technology and world events. These factors make it easy to identify the root of traits that a generation possesses, along with their future and current behaviour (Van Dam, 2020). The overgeneralisation of a selected group is often inaccurate. It is worth noting that the millennial generation can be classified into three groups, namely those who graduated from college before the Great Recession, those who graduated during the Great Recession and those who graduated post-recession. The average net worth of millennials was partly impacted by this classification due to millennials either entering a flourishing job market or a terrible one (Cousins, 2020).

Millennials are one of the groups that were most likely to suffer due to the global economic slowdown triggered by Covid-19 which is comparable to the Great Depression. The majority of this generation have not fully recovered from the Great Recession. Millennials had high anxiety about how their economic realities would be affected by Covid-19. The economic anxiety of millennials was further fuelled by the majority of this generation working in industries hardest hit by the pandemic (Dieppe, 2020). The industries mostly affected were hospitality and leisure which showed a loss of 459 000 jobs in March 2020 in the United States of America alone. Other sectors that experienced high job losses were education and health services, professional and business services and the retail sector (Collins, 2020). These sectors relied heavily on millennial labour. The millennials that worked in the most affected sectors are most likely to be confronted by financial difficulties in the immediate future due to millennial-heavy industries being the slowest in returning to their former profitability levels.

Millennials were already in a bad financial shape before the pandemic due to student loan debts. The taking of these student loans was highly motivated by the assumption that heavy borrowing will yield higher wages as an individual grows older (Gharzai, Beeler & Jagsi, 2020). However, the growing cost of tertiary education coupled with the pandemic proved these benefits to be far from reach for younger millennials especially those of colour. The inequality gap has always been present but has been further widened by the pandemic (Collins, 2020). Jobs that are deemed to be essential are likely to be held by women of colour, they often risk their lives and are the most underpaid compared to other demographic groups especially white men. This directly links to millennials of colour that attend college facing complex challenges. The low wages associated with this group makes their degrees less valuable and as the majority of black students borrowed heavily to obtain those degrees, consequently, they have a higher student debt to pay off. The data collected by New America's Wesley Whistle found that 67% of white students took out student loans in 2016 compared to 84% of black students in the United States of America. Furthermore, 28% of the black students were falling behind with their payments in 2018. The occurrence of Covid-19 meant increased financial stress for millennials.

The increased financial stress for millennials has contributed to unstable equity caused by this generation delaying buying homes due to having fewer resources. Millennials are also having children and getting married at later stages. The racial wealth gap was further seen in homeownerships where the National Association of Real Estate Brokers reported in 2019 that 46% of white millennials owned homes whereas only 16% of black millennials had homeownerships. This means that more millennials are likely to exit the Covid-19 pandemic with no assets that are worth being liquidated or leveraged for loans and are more vulnerable in the event of another recession. The millennials had not yet recovered from the Great Recession in 2008. The millennials that entered the job market during this Great Recession were faced with a low demand for workers and high unemployment which resulted in their wages being depressed. This generation was not ready for another economic crisis to occur in a space of a decade (Kim, So, Mihalik & Lopes, 2021). Millennials did not have a good economic standing before Covid-19 as they were still recovering from the previous Great Recession, only to be hit by another as they attempted building themselves up, financially. Most millennials hold pessimistic views on their economic standing post-Covid-19. Building up their pre-Covid-19 economic standing had already not been easy. Moving forward, millennials carry economic burdens caused by the 2008 Great Recession and the added burden of the Covid-19 economic crisis. There is also no certainty that another economic crisis will not occur in the next decade. Van Dam (2020) states that millennials will still be the largest consumers by the year 2030 and are vulnerable to any economic crisis that may occur in the future.

Millennials in the Job Market

Forbes (2021) reported that millennials are expected to make up 75% of the workforce by the year 2025, replacing baby boomers. In the year 2016, millennials were the largest generation in the global labour force. This generation is usually concerned with intrinsic and moral values as opposed to extrinsic and material ideologies. It is more progressive, far-thinking and creative compared to earlier generations. Millennials possess characteristics that are beneficial to the modern organisation. These character traits include not being afraid to challenge the hierarchical status-quo. They constantly encourage collective engagement in the workplace and are more inclined towards sharing their ideas and opinions where considering all viewpoints, active listening and collaboration is practiced as opposed to following instructions received from the top of a professional hierarchy. In this manner, open feedback and recognition are promoted, which is what this generation prefers, instead of annual or biannual employee reviews. This further fuels their passion for learning, developing new skills and knowledge. Millennials are more task oriented than time-oriented (Huyler, Pierre, Ding & Norelus, 2015). They are more concerned with the amount of quality output they produce than with the number of hours put into a job. They put more focus on getting a task done rather than on how many hours they have been at the office. This forms part of the reason why millennials are usually attracted to start-ups. Start-ups usually have a set of tasks that need to be completed and not worked on a nine-to-five basis. Since the majority of the workforce could not go to their workplaces during the pandemic and were instead presented with tasks to complete virtually, this trait caused this generation to thrive during this time.

The preference of millennials to have a flexible schedule allows for completion of tasks at their own convenience and when they are most productive. This aligns with most millennials preferring to work on their own terms where they work when they want to and where they want to. Another characteristic that millennials have is intuitive knowledge of technology. This character trait developed the quick adaptation and change of millennials due to them witnessing the expansive development of technology. Millennials are first-generation digital natives. They hold more positive views towards Information Technology (IT) strategies which encourage the utilisation of high-tech devices in the workplace (Kim, So, Mihalik & Lopes, 2021). Bush (2018) states that employees should be given the tools they need to succeed. Organisations that implement this are considered part of the best workplaces for millennials and set a certain standard for other organisations that seek to develop the next generation of leaders. This generation is considered to be the agents of change in the labour force.

These character traits play a vital role in the development of an organisation post-Covid-19 where most of the workforce and workplace are faced with uncertainties. Collective engagement encourages progressive ideas on the operation of the organisation (Gharzai, Beeler & Jagsi, 2020). Covid-19 regulations in most countries encourage social distancing and limited human interaction, the traditional workplace would not be successful under such regulations. The constant new developments of the Coronavirus offer a perception that organisations need to develop new operational means that would continue being effective in the process of the virus's advancements. The modern organisation needs to be encompassing of the millennial characteristics coupled with new workplace developments influenced by Covid-19 regulations to be successful in a post-Covid-19 environment.

Unemployment and Self-Employment of Millennials

Employment plays an important role in the global economy. The United States Bureau of Labour Statistics (2021) stated that the unemployment of people translates to them spending less money. This ultimately results in a lower contribution towards the economy in relation to the production of services and goods sold. The decreased contribution towards the economy has a detrimental impact on the growth of the global economy. However, self-employment has an impact on the economy that is contrary to that of unemployment. Self-employment is the act of an individual working for themselves instead of having work provided by an employer. Self-employment contributes towards the growth of the economy through the possible employment of other people, invention of new products or services, distribution methods and production processes. The benefits of self-employment are attractive to millennials, such as the freedom to do what an individual desires at a time they wish to do it, while earning money (Figueroa-Armijos & da Motta Veiga, 2019). The low job demand in various sectors has pushed millennials towards self-employment.

Millennials are part of the older cohort of people considered as the youth. Most of them are thought to be at an employment stage of their lives. According to Statista (2021), the global unemployment rate experienced a gradual decrease in the past decade up to the year 2020. In the year 2010, the global unemployment rate was estimated at 5.92% and gradually decreased over the years to 5.37% in the year 2019. However, in the year 2020, the global unemployment rate drastically increased to 6.47%. This increase was due to many factors, including Covid-19 which spread like wildfire across the global in the year 2020. The pandemic forced the retrenchment of employees in various organisations. It is not uncommon that organisations are likely to retrench employees with less experience in the field of work. This put most of the millennials at a disadvantage since they were less experienced than the generations before them (Gharzai, Beeler & Jagsi, 2020). Conversely, the millennials that possessed relevant skills and showed good performance were less likely to lose their jobs. Organisations are often confronted by higher costs of investment and lower costs of termination regarding the employment of the younger generations.

The younger generations are innovative and often prefer working on their own terms. Self-employment is commonly considered to be attractive to millennials where they are able to determine their working hours. Various countries with a high youth unemployment rate, such as South Africa, are increasingly viewing self-employment as one of the strategies to address the youth unemployment challenge. Various policymakers continuously encourage the growth of self-employment for a variety of reasons. These reasons include, but are not limited to, reducing the unemployment rate, a chance to make better use of personal resources, reduction of poverty which might lead to criminal activities and self-employment is a source of economic growth (Sharfuddin, 2020). However, there are also a variety of downfalls associated with youth self-employment. Failure is common in individuals that are self-employed for the first time. In the context of this chapter, it can be challenging to attract brands that are likely to form partnerships based on the content an individual posts on social media. When considering using the internet to promote business, such as having a website or a social media page for marketing or communication purposes, there is a great risk concerned with the hacking of these platforms. This could lead to customers of the business being scammed by the hackers which can taint the reputation of the business and possibly lead to charges in accordance with the consumer protection laws and regulations.

Another challenge that arises through the use of the internet for business, especially if an individual is an influencer or content creator, is that cyber bullying is rife on a global scale. This leads to discontinued content creation, resulting in losing partnerships with brands. It can also potentially trigger mental disorders such as anxiety, depression and other illnesses associated with bullying (Dwivedi et al., 2021). Despite these challenges associated with conducting business on the internet, businesses have a great potential to become successful if the necessary precautions are applied. Some of these precautions include activating the multi-factor authentication on business websites and social media applications for the purpose of stronger security measures against hackers (Almadhoor, 2021). Additionally, a high emotional intelligence is advantageous in great self-exposure jobs such as being an influencer on social media.

Millennials' Use of Social Media for Business Purposes

Social media was often traditionally used for entertainment purposes, however, as times advanced, the number of people that monetised social media activities increased. People living in modern society usually use social media to earn an income. It is common for millennials to have a strong presence on YouTube. These YouTubers present different content that attracts a certain audience which relates to or enjoys the content uploaded by the YouTuber. Content creators are also popular on Pinterest, TikTok and Instagram applications. Instagram is commonly a platform where influencers thrive. Twitter is an application often used to engage on certain trends based on hashtags. WhatsApp has recently joined the shift of allowing the creation of business accounts by users of the platform. Millennials use these platforms mostly for their small businesses or as content creators that seek partnerships with brands that align with who they are as a brand (Syaifullah et al., 2021). It is common that when the recent generations are on their smartphones, they are most likely making money. Besides generating income on social media, young adults also use other applications such as offering cyber cab services on Bolt and Uber. The drivers of these cyber cabs determine when they work and what income target they want to reach in a day. These services were convenient during the pandemic for most commuters that were uncomfortable with using public transport such as buses or trains due to the spread of the Coronavirus in these modes of transport.

Millennials have the ability to monetise a variety of subjects. It has recently become common to witness influencers who are children, where the social media account of the child is managed by the parents or designated manager (Pornsrimate & Khamwon, 2021). The term "momanger" is a common title on social media and is the combination of being a mom and a manager of a child. A number of children birthed by those in the millennial generation earn an income from birth where, for example, they influence for nappy brands, baby skincare products, baby clothing, baby food or any other baby products. Another group of influencers owned by millennials are pets, especially dogs and cats. These pets commonly have social media accounts managed by their owners who manage the content creation aspect and operation of the page. The content created by using these pets is usually for pet insurance organisations, pet food and other pet products. This content is used to influence other pet owners and not necessarily other pets. The collaboration income forms part of the wages of the owner. There are a variety of other subjects from which millennials make an income, out of the comfort of their homes, using their digital devices, the internet and digital skills.

The partnerships formed between influencers and brands encourage globalisation due to their content reaching any country. Some brands end up opening branches in other countries where there is great response and major interaction with their products based on content created by content creators or influencers they work with in those countries. The positive interaction with the brand often creates a demand for their products and makes common business sense to have headquarters of the brand closer to the customers. This assists in eliminating unnecessary additional input costs such as shipping and it also creates job opportunities in the region where the brand has opened a branch. Furthermore, it increases the economic growth of that region (Hudders, De Jans & De Veirman, 2021). This is evident in the attempt by Amazon to set up its Africa headquarters in Cape Town, South Africa, due to the increased retail demand in Africa. The construction phase of these headquarters is projected to create 5 239 jobs and 19 000 jobs for the rest of the project. This development offers a significant economic boost to the country especially in the aftermath of the national Covid-19 lockdown (Cardenas, 2021).

The internet also assists in the smooth operation of a small business which is unable to afford large marketing firms. The business is most likely to operate in a manner preferred by the owner. Through the internet, the business owner is able to post information about their products or services. Google then assists by sharing data on social media to people that are most likely interested in the product. This is known as data tracking and commonly occurs when the websites visited by an individual host HTML tracking codes which are popularly known as cookies. Customers find the products offered by the business without searching for the business page (Wang & Chan-Olmsted, 2020). Communication is also made easier through direct messaging. The number of small businesses depending on courier organisations to deliver their products at a minimal price to their customers has increased. Most of these businesses are run on low input and without producers and consumers leaving their locations for purchase or delivery. This has been convenient for a variety of producers and consumers during the pandemic.

RESEARCH METHODOLOGY

The external desk research method was adopted by this study. Research was done and information was collected outside of any organizational boundaries. The study used secondary data where previous research findings were reviewed to gain a broader understanding (Shevchuk & Kalyazina, 2019) of the impact that the recent recession had on millennials and what measures are being applied to recover from the impact. This method was suitable for the study due to the nature of the study which was to review the findings of other researchers regarding the impact of the great global recessions on millennials in the job market. It also looked at the general impact that Covid-19 had on the job market and the state of the global economy pre- and post-Covid-19. Furthermore, potential recovery plans were also reviewed. The research method was suitable for this research due to limited resources and time constraints of the study. The method was also advantageous due to the readily available data, and it allowed the study to be conducted in a cost-effective manner (Zaridis & Logotheti, 2020).

An electronic systematic search of databases was conducted to identify academic papers that were relevant and important to the study. International articles, book chapters and research papers were found on Research Gate, Science Direct, Google Scholar, and the University of KwaZulu-Natal online library using the keywords of this study as search terms. The data analysis was done by comparing and combining different information that was gathered from electronic research articles. The collected information was for the fulfilment of the aims of the study which was to explore the impact of the Covid-19 recession on millennials in the job market. Another aim which the information fulfilled was exploration of possible economic recovery plans for millennials.

FINDINGS AND DISCUSSION

The findings in the literature review of this study are that millennials are currently most economically vulnerable compared to other generations. The first huge financial challenge for millennials was the 2009 Great Recession which resulted in job losses and a major economic crisis. The economic challenges of this recession period resulted in this generation having difficulty in paying student loans and buying homes since most millennials entered the job market around the years of this recession (Moreira & Hick, 2021). These challenges were also perpetuated by the gender and race inequalities where women and black people suffered a larger financial burden. While this generation was still trying to recover from the economic challenges of 2009 recession, they were hit by another economic crisis, a decade later. The Covid-19 recession, which occurred 10 years after the 2009 Great Recession, had a major impact on the job market (Van Dam, 2020). The millennials were further negatively impacted by the Covid-19 recession, especially during lockdown. The lockdown required different industries to either temporarily close business or operate on a virtual basis. Some of the businesses that needed to be temporarily closed are that in the entertainment and leisure industry. The entertainment and leisure industries were seen to employ majority of millennials therefore they faced a large employment challenge during lockdown. Some businesses ended up being permanently closed down due to financial constraints, among other contributing factors, and this resulted in major job losses during the Covid-19 economic crisis (Agius et. al., 2020). The Covid-19 economic burdens have piled on those of the 2009 recession which leaves millennials more vulnerable in the case of another unexpected economic crisis in the future.

In the view of the labour productivity growth in the global economy prior to the Covid-19 recession, there was a decrease in that growth. This was due to many factors such as the outbreak of diseases in certain countries causing epidemics. These epidemics had impacts on labour productivity similar to that of those of the Covid-19 pandemic, but on a smaller scale compared to the pandemic. The general labour productivity growth was already on a decrease before the Covid-19 pandemic. The pandemic triggered a larger decrease which potentially had longer after-effects such as increased unemployment, increased loans, increased inequality and a further decrease in active economic participants. Policymakers, in collaboration with government leaders, have been continuously formulating recovery plans and policies to address the issues of decreased labour productivity in different countries (Pipa & Bouchet, 2020). However, these recovery plans and policies are not exclusive to millennials which makes it difficult to follow millennial-specific strategies, that barely exist, to assist this generation in their involvement in the job market. Nevertheless, these policies encourage the development of digital skills which are likely to in demand in the future and could give rise to new roles in the workplace. The need for digital skills was evident when many sectors opted for their employees to work from home during lockdown (Amankwah-Amoah et. al., 2021).

Millennials already preferred a flexible work schedule before the pandemic so some of the work conditions presented by the pandemic were not difficult for millennials to adjust. This was also due to millennials possessing characteristics, such as being task-oriented and collaborative, which are beneficial to the modern organization. This generation is known to make up the population of first-generation digital natives which saw the introduction of technology and grew with the changes that came with it over the years. Millennials have intuitive knowledge of technology which is advantageous in a world with a continuously evolving industrial revolution and where most workplaces view technology as a necessity in the operation of an organization (Kim et. al., 2021). However, the global unemployment rate of young people has been on the rise due to the Covid-19 pandemic. The low job demand in various sectors has pushed millennials towards self-employment. Self-employment has been one of the strategies considered by policymakers for addressing youth unemployment and its possibility to greatly contribute towards the economic growth of any country.

Self-employment has been attractive to millennials due to the flexible work schedule and operating on their own terms. The idea of self-employment, being technology knowledgeable and having access to the internet has driven most millennials towards monetizing social media. Social media is a platform where content creators and influencers flourish. Most of these influencers and content creators are millennials so it is easier for brands to trust them in partnerships since most of this generation understands these platforms. Other millennials use the internet and social media for the operation of their small businesses (Hudders et. al., 2021). Social media has become a useful tool in the generation of an income. However, there are downfalls associated with these platforms such as hacking and cyber bulling or unexpected social media blackouts. Nonetheless, technology and the innovative trait of millennials can be used in addressing unemployment through monetizing the internet and social media using readily available resources.

Objective one: Millennials suffered various financial and labour market impacts caused by Covid-19. The pandemic exacerbated the financial challenges that millennials already had before the pandemic due to high student loans, low paying jobs and low job demand. During lockdown, many businesses were either temporarily or permanently closed and some millennials that were employed by these organizations faced job losses. Job losses meant that the millennials that lost jobs and had student loans will not be able to settle their debts. Other millennials were faced with not affording their homes anymore and sought cheaper alternatives. The largest employers of this generation were the entertainment and leisure industries which had high human contact and the Covid-19 regulations demanded that they be closed, resulting in most millennials losing their jobs. These financial burdens added to the ones caused by the Great Recession which occurred a decade prior. This makes the millennials the unluckiest generation, economically.

Objective two: The state of the global economy and labour market prior to the Covid-19 recession had gradual increases and occasional sudden decreases. These decreases were due to various events such as epidemics and economic challenges. The globally experienced economic crisis before the Covid-19 pandemic was the 2009 Great Recession which had impacts that were similar to the recent pandemic. These economic crises made it challenging for millennials to enter the job market and keep their jobs. The recovery from the financial issues caused by the economic crisis in 2009 was slow due to poor implementation of recovery policies in many countries especially those with corrupt governments; millennials having lower levels of job experience because of recent entry into the job market; and a low job demand due to millennials obtaining qualifications or skills that are saturated in the job market. There is a possibility of unexpected events that could negatively impact the economy in the future such as wars. Such events can continue making it difficult for millennials to afford an average standard of living in the future. However, policies contain possible recovery plans for the impact of Covid-19.

Objective three: The possible Covid-19 labour market recovery plans for millennials that were identified in the literature are mostly based on digital means and self-employment. Most policies recommended self-employment due to a low job demand in most sectors even before the Covid-19 pandemic. Self-employment and small businesses are seen as significant contributors towards the growth of the economy in different countries. Millennials are attracted to self-employment due to the flexibility it offers. They have found ways to monetize their digital skills and their presence on social media. Being a content creator or an influence has become normal in this generation. As the generation that is knowledgeable about the internet, they have taken the opportunity to use the internet, technology and social media for their financial wellness instead of fully being reliant on the government to provide employment opportunities or job opportunities. It is also possible for digital skills to be in high demand in the future due to the continuous shift towards digital operations in every sector. It would be wise for millennials to invest in digital skills and for policymakers to incorporate strategies which enhance the use of digital skills in their recovery plans.

RECOMMENDATIONS

Literature has revealed how economic crises have an impact on the labour market. The policies put in place for the recovery of these crises have not proved to be successful. This is based on how the issues that these policies are supposed to solve are not solved but worsen over time. The poor leadership in local government has also shown that relying solely on government assistance could lead to unfruitful outcomes. Therefore, millennials should be aware of the traits that they possess and use these to their advantage. Instead of waiting on the government to provide solutions regarding their unemployment, they should look at how they can use resources that are readily available to them to generate an income. Since there is a huge concentration of millennials on social media, they should not only use it for entertainment purposes but to also seek opportunities to generate an income from it. Millennials should view the outcomes of the past economic crises to formulate strategies on how to avoid such outcomes in the future in the event of another unexpected recession. Millennials should also consider entering sectors with sustainable labour productivity and require skills that are in demand. Policymakers should also adjust policies over a certain time period due to changing times; what could have worked in the past won't necessarily work in the future. Millennials should also be given an opportunity to shape their own future within industries since older generations are approaching retirement and will most likely not be present to experience the consequences of their current decisions in the workplace. Organisations should consider investing in the internet knowledge of millennials, considering the fast-paced shift towards a more digital workplace. Millennials should work on obtaining digital skills that could potentially be in demand in the future. It is most likely that every sector will require digital skills in the future based on the continuous shifts in the industrial revolution (the 4IR).

FUTURE STUDIES

It is recommended that individual country characteristics be taken into account when reviewing their interactions with policy measures. Countries possess different characteristics especially those in developed and developing economies. Therefore, a 'one size fits all' approach cannot be used in the implementation of recovery policies. Further studies should also be considered regarding the use of global relief funds by local governments. The majority of developing economies suffer the negative consequences of corrupt local leadership where there has been misuse of funds. The leadership of each country plays a vital role in the structure of the economy of that country. Furthermore, the economic milestones from decades ago should be studied to ascertain whether they have been reached or not and reasons for each result should be studied for the purpose of shaping future policies. It is impractical for the current world with new challenges experienced by a different generation to still use policies that were formulated decades ago for a different generation with different mindsets in a different world. The potential that millennials have in the global economy shows that they should be considered to have a seat at the table of decision-makers regarding the economy they will form a large part of in the next few decades. The different sectors should also study how the traits possessed by the millennials can be used to the advantage for a sustainable labour force. Since it is inevitable that technology continues to form a huge functional part of the world, it is worth studying the incorporation of technology in every sector and how job demand can be created for a generation that is formed by technology natives.

CONCLUSION

Operations during the pandemic have seemingly become the 'new normal' to an extent that people would find it difficult to operate in a manner they did before the pandemic. While other people concern themselves with returning to the normal they knew before the pandemic, millennials and the 'gen Z' generation continue seeking means to monetise resources they readily possess and adapt to the new normal, which is getting the highest output from any situation despite it being good or bad. In conclusion, the global economy has proven more than once that it will be severely impacted by any issue, whether it is a social, financial, environment or health issue. The various governments and policy developers continue to fail citizens with poorly constructed policies and strategies to survive global economic disruptions. The youth are commonly at a disadvantage during such occurrences. However, some millennials have taken it upon themselves to pursue their own preferences, on their terms, regarding their economic participation. Even though the recent generations do not hold direct power over strategies developed about the global economy, they do have the power to influence those strategies. This generation has a greater chance of coping in a post-Covid-19 environment due to their adaptability traits and the ability to use readily available resources to their full capacity.

REFERENCES

Agius, R. M., Robertson, J. F., Kendrick, D., Sewell, H. F., Stewart, M., & McKee, M. (2020). Covid-19 in the workplace. *British Medical Journal*, 370. PMID:32958470

Almadhoor, L. (2021). Social media and cybercrimes. *Turkish Journal of Computer and Mathematics Education, 12*(10), 2972–2981.

Amankwah-Amoah, J., Khan, Z., Wood, G., & Knight, G. (2021). COVID-19 and digitalization: The great acceleration. *Journal of Business Research, 136*, 602–611. doi:10.1016/j.jbusres.2021.08.011 PMID:34538980

Bush, M. C. (2018). *A great place to work for all: Better for business, better for people, better for the world*. Berrett-Koehler Publishers.

Cardenas, S. (2021, October). Unpacking Amazon through meatpacking, Adam Smith, and digital colonialism. In *2021 IEEE International Symposium on Technology and Society (ISTAS)* (pp. 1-6). IEEE. 10.1109/ISTAS52410.2021.9629196

Collins, S. (2020). *Why the Covid-19 economy is particularly devastating to Millennials, in 14 charts*. Vox.

Cousins, S. (2020, September). *The COVID Context series. 1. Reshaping millennials attitudes & spending habits.* National Head of Strategy & Planning, iProspect Australia.

Dieppe, A. (2020). *Global Productivity: Trends, Drivers, and Policies*. World Bank.

Dimock, M. (2019). Defining generations: Where Millennials end, and Generation Z begins. *Pew Research Center, 17*(1), 1–7.

Dwivedi, Y. K., Ismagilova, E., Hughes, D. L., Carlson, J., Filieri, R., Jacobson, J., & Wang, Y. (2021). Setting the future of digital and social media marketing research: Perspectives and research propositions. *International Journal of Information Management, 59*, 102168. doi:10.1016/j.ijinfomgt.2020.102168

Figueroa-Armijos, M., & da Motta Veiga, S. (2019, January). Predictors of early-career self-employment among millennials in the digital economy: The role of the Great Recession. *Proceedings of the 52nd Hawaii International Conference on System Sciences*. 10.24251/HICSS.2019.546

Gharzai, L. A., Beeler, W. H., & Jagsi, R. (2020). Playing into stereotypes: Engaging Millennials and Generation Z in the COVID-19 pandemic response. *Advances in Radiation Oncology, 5*(4), 679–681. doi:10.1016/j.adro.2020.04.009 PMID:32363242

Hudders, L., De Jans, S., & De Veirman, M. (2021). The commercialization of social media stars: A literature review and conceptual framework on the strategic use of social media influencers. *International Journal of Advertising*, *40*(3), 327–375. doi:10.1080/02650487.2020.1836925

Huyler, D., Pierre, Y., Ding, W., & Norelus, A. (2015). Millennials in the workplace: Positioning companies for future success. *SFERC*, *2015*, 114.

Kharas, H. (2020). *The impact of COVID-19 on global extreme poverty.* Brookings Institution. www.brookings.edu/blog/future-development/2020/10/21/the-impact-of-covid-19-on-global-extreme-poverty/

Kim, H., So, K. K. F., Mihalik, B. J., & Lopes, A. P. (2021). Millennials' virtual reality experiences pre-and post-COVID-19. *Journal of Hospitality and Tourism Management*, *48*, 200–209. doi:10.1016/j.jhtm.2021.06.008

LaCore, E. (2015). Supporting millennials in the workplace. *Strategic HR Review*, *14*(4). Advance online publication. doi:10.1108/SHR-06-2015-0046

Marjerison, R. K., & Gan, S. (2020). Social Media Influencers' Effect on Chinese Gen Z Consumers: Management and Use of Video Content Platforms. *Journal of Media Management and Entrepreneurship*, *2*(2), 1–18. doi:10.4018/JMME.2020070101

Moreira, A., & Hick, R. (2021). COVID-19, the Great Recession and social policy: Is this time different? *Social Policy and Administration*, *55*(2), 261–279. doi:10.1111pol.12679

Pak, A., Adegboye, O. A., Adekunle, A. I., Rahman, K. M., McBryde, E. S., & Eisen, D. P. (2020). Economic consequences of the COVID-19 outbreak: The need for epidemic preparedness. *Frontiers in Public Health*, *8*, 241. doi:10.3389/fpubh.2020.00241 PMID:32574307

Pipa, A. F., & Bouchet, M. (2020). *How to make the most of city diplomacy in the COVID-19 era.* Brookings Institution. www.brookings.edu/blog/up-front/2020/08/06/how-to-make-the-most-of-city-diplomacy-in-the-covid-19-era/

Pipa, T., & Bouchet, M. (2020). *Leadership at the local level: How can cities drive a sustainable recovery?* Academic Press.

Pornsrimate, K., & Khamwon, A. (2021). How to convert millennial consumers to brand evangelists through social media micro-influencers. *Innovative Marketing*, *17*(2).

Sekścińska, K., & Jaworska, D. (2022). Who felt blue when Facebook went down? The role of self-esteem and FoMO in explaining people's mood in reaction to social media outage. *Personality and Individual Differences*, *188*, 111460. doi:10.1016/j.paid.2021.111460

Sharfuddin, S. (2020). The world after Covid-19. *The Round Table*, *109*(3), 247–257. doi:10.1080/00358533.2020.1760498

Shevchuk, A., & Kalyazina, S. (2019, September). Traceability technology: fruits and vegetables trader case study. In *International Conference on Digital Technologies in Logistics and Infrastructure (ICDTLI 2019)*. Atlantis Press. 10.2991/icdtli-19.2019.70

Sneader, K., & Sternfels, R. A. (2020). *From surviving to thriving: Reimagining the post-COVID-19 return*. McKinsey.

Su, C. W., Dai, K., Ullah, S., & Andlib, Z. (2021). COVID-19 pandemic and unemployment dynamics in European economies. *Economic Research-EkonomskaIstraživanja*, 1-13.

Syaifullah, J., Syaifudin, M., Sukendar, M. U., & Junaedi, J. (2021). Social media marketing and business performance of MSMEs during the COVID-19 pandemic. *The Journal of Asian Finance, Economics, and Business*, *8*(2), 523–531.

Van Dam, A. (2020). The unluckiest generation in US history. *Washington Post, 5*.

Venter, E. (2017). Bridging the communication gap between Generation Y and the Baby Boomer generation. *International Journal of Adolescence and Youth*, *22*(4), 497–507. doi:10.1080/02673843.2016.1267022

Wang, R., & Chan-Olmsted, S. (2020). Content marketing strategy of branded YouTube channels. *Journal of Media Business Studies*, *17*(3-4), 294–316. doi:10.1080/16522354.2020.1783130

WheelockD. C. (2020). Comparing the COVID-19 recession with the Great Depression. *Available at* SSRN 3745250. doi:10.20955/es.2020.39

World Bank. (2020). *Global Economic Prospects, June 2020*. World Bank.

Zaridis, A. D., & Logotheti, A. (2020). Entrepreneurial Strategies and Practices promoting Innovations Adoption in Global Food Industry. *SSRG International Journal of Economics and Management Studies*, *7*(3), 40–46.

Chapter 9
Consequences of the Pandemic for Ukrainian Agriculture in the Context of Public Administration

Nadezhda Anatolievna Lebedeva
https://orcid.org/0000-0003-4095-2631
Kherson State Agrarian and Economic University, Ukraine

ABSTRACT

Quarantine was a forced measure that prevented significant losses in the early stages of the disease and prepared the medical system to combat COVID-19. Today, the medical system in most regions is ready to provide treatment for all patients in the event of new possible outbreaks of the pandemic. An integrated approach has been taken to develop measures to overcome the effects of COVID-19 and stimulate the economy. This chapter is devoted to the problems of agriculture that have arisen as a result of quarantine measures. Its main task is to find out whether the measures to counter the COVID-19 pandemic have affected the agricultural sector of the economy. The situation in the Ukrainian agrarian sector during the experience of counteracting COVID-19 is considered. The novelty of the chapter is the exchange of scientific information with colleagues from other countries for seeking further solutions to the problems caused by COVID-19. The global challenges have been quite devastating for the Ukrainian agriculture economy.

INTRODUCTION

The pandemic of acute respiratory disease COVID-19 caused by the SARS-COV-2 corona virus has become a new challenge to humanity. Almost every branch of human activity has received negative consequences from the measures taken to overcome the corona virus. Despite the historical and theoretical aspects, it was COVID-19 known to mankind that revealed the features of the spread of global pandemics, causing political, socio-economic, demographic, cultural and educational consequences for

DOI: 10.4018/978-1-7998-8856-7.ch009

the entire world community. Not only economic contradictions have become aggravated in the world, but also socio-political, socio-religious ones. There is a transformation of the labour market, trade, culture and education. There are risks of demographic development, problems of business and entrepreneurship. However, the measures implemented by public administration are already considered to be effective in the context of health protection. Vaccination has become a key focus in the fight against the COVID-19 pandemic. The main target of this chapter is devoted to the problems of agriculture that have arisen as a result of the adoption of quarantine measures. The author sets the main research question: to figure out whether the measures to counter the COVID-19 pandemic did not greatly affect the agricultural sector of the economy. The situation in the Ukrainian agrarian sector during the countering COVID-19 experience is considered. The novelty of the chapter lies in the exchange of scientific information with colleagues from other countries to further search for solutions to the problems caused by COVID-19.

Agriculture is one of the main sectors of the Ukrainian economy. According to generally accepted economic indicators, its share in the country's national economy is quite high. Almost a quarter of production assets are concentrated here, half of all citizens employed in the economy of the state work. The greatest wealth of the country is directly involved in agriculture - its land fund, which amounts to millions of hectares of agricultural land. The country's economy as a whole largely depends on the level of agricultural economic development. That is why the situation in the agrarian sector largely determines the socio-economic situation and food security of the state.

Ukraine ensures its domestic needs for agricultural products through its production. Ukraine has a huge potential to be an exporter of agricultural products. The country's agriculture guarantees the food supply of its citizens, reliable food quality, environmental protection, social stability and other positive phenomena. The agrarian policy implemented by the state administration ensures the appropriate participation of farmers in raising incomes.

BACKGROUND

Scientific Views for COVID-19 Problems as a Whole

Almost all spheres of human activity have been affected by the consequences of the pandemic. It has received scientific confirmation and led to the emergence of many scientific studies around the world. As Cho Dheng (2021) aptly noted, "the COVID-19 natural event has afraid the world's economies within the year of 2020. As this pandemic spreads round the globe, several consultants feared that the worldwide food provides would possibly begin running short, particularly if offer chains were non-contiguous. COVID-19 additionally supplementary to the uncertainty of the business operation" (Cho Dheng, 2021, p. 1). Fedulova & Petroye (2021) studied innovative and technological factors of economic development during the COVID-19 pandemic. The pandemic crisis as a catalyst for the digitalization of the tourism industry was showed by Gavrilyuk (2021). Semenova, Datsenko & Khurdey (2020) devoted their scientific research to modern marketing tools in the context of increasing competitiveness in the mind of pandemia COVID-19. Scientists have studied such areas as pharmaceutical (Salikhova & Goncharenko, 2021), e-commerce in the global digital space (Misyukevich, Trushkina & Shkrigun, 2021), investment issues (Nosova, 2021) and communication strategies (Chaikun, 2021), as well as the formation of the basis for a new stage of economic growth in the world (Knyazev, 2020). The areas of event practice Sidorenko (2021), museums as a tourist resource (Antonenko & Khutkiy, 2021). Education takes on updated forms (Zatuliviter, 2021). Gursky (2021) described the problems and consequences of the migration of highly qualified facilitators in the context of COVID-19. The formation and implementation of anti-crisis management were studied by Povoroznyuk (2021), Geiko (2020), Petrovska & Bendus (2020). Fedianin (2021) described the effective experience of countering the pandemic for Ukrainian society.

Thus, the pandemic has covered almost all the areas of human activity, causing certain changes, not always positive. On the one hand, innovative and pharmaceutical products have gained their rapid development, distribution and even profit, while other industries have been hit hard by the introduction of quarantine restrictions. Many people have lost their jobs. Businesses have closed. How did the consequences of the pandemic affect agriculture?

Worldwide Impact of COVID-19 Pandemic on Agriculture

Marc Wegerif (2021) writes that "the government interventions to address Covid-19 and the support measures put in place to ameliorate the negative effects have not adequately considered the particular conditions of black farmers and the production and distribution networks they are part of, notably the informal sector of small enterprises that play a key role in food systems, but have often been overlooked. This was most clearly shown with early lockdown measures that caused major disruptions to these networks, but it has continued and manifests in the lack of effective support to address the impacts being experienced by black farmers" (Marc Wegerif, 2021, p. 13).

Cho Dheng (2021) noted that the COVID-19 pandemic has affected the global food supply and market. In this study, she found that while on average the exports of agricultural enterprises are declining, the exports of some agricultural commodities, especially grains and oils, remain stable and even increase, which means high demand for staple foods during a pandemic. Nevertheless, the volume of agricultural production has declined sharply. The results also showed that, in general, the impact of COVID-19 on smaller companies was more severe than on larger companies.

"The agro-industrial complex is focused on basic needs, and this is its advantage in a crisis period. Thus, it was not affected by the long period of non-working days introduced to combat the pandemic, and it was not officially recognized as a sector of the economy affected by COVID-19. However, the industry has felt and continues to feel the negative impact of the three above-mentioned shock factors" (Project "German-Russian Agrarian-Political Dialogue", 2021, p. 2).

Value added in the agriculture, forestry, and fishing decreased by 5.1% due to the self-isolation regime at enterprises. Agricultural enterprises incur additional costs for preventive measures (disinfection, protective equipment for employees, etc.). (Project "German-Russian Agrarian-Political Dialogue", 2021, p. 6). Agro-industrial enterprises spend a lot of money every month to protect against corona virus. Also, one of the problems was the closure of borders associated with the corona virus. This has led to a restructuring of supply chains, jeopardizing important supplies of inputs such as seeds, plant protection products, feed additives, food ingredients, etc.

"The information of the Analytical Center under the Government of the Russian Federation notes that, in general, the situation in the Russian market of agricultural products has stabilized after sharp surges and drops in demand. The domestic market is saturated in key products, and there is no reason to expect serious growth. At the same time, the global market situation is characterized by a period of low prices,

high supply and difficulties not just with a drop in demand, but with the sale of products" (Project "German-Russian Agrarian-Political Dialogue", 2021, p. 8).

The consequences of the pandemic for agriculture, its negative impact were also studied by Dalia Štreimikienė, Tomas Baležentis, Artiom Volkov, Erika Ribašauskienė, Mangirdas Morkūnas & Agnė Žičkienė (2021). Agriculture supply chain risks and COVID-19 strategies and implications for the practitioners have been described by Rohit Sharma, Anjali Shishodia, Sachin Kamble, Angappa Gunasekaran & Amine Belhadi (2020). Impact of COVID-19 on the food supply chain disclosed by Serpil Aday, Mehmet Seckin Aday. Global Agricultural Markets in the context of the impact of the pandemic was reviewed by Elleby, Domínguez, Adenauer, et al. (2021). Marchant-Forde and Boyle (2020) turned their attention to COVID-19 effects on livestock production. The work of Jayson Beckman, Amanda M. Countryman is also interesting by their experience. The worldwide impact of COVID-19 pandemic on agriculture was reviewed by Dheng (2021). Selected countries are covered in Et-Toule & Arib (2021), White (2021), Walters, Wade, and Suttles (2020), Santiago Lopez-Ridaura, Arie Sanders, Luis Barba-Escoto, Jennifer Wiegel, Maria Mayorga-Cortes, Carlos Gonzalez-Esquivel, Martin A. Lopez-Ramirez, Rene M. Escoto-Masis, Edmundo Morales-Galindo, Tomas S. García-Barcena (2021).

Food and agricultural challenges amid the COVID-19 pandemic are mentioned in the monographs of Torkunov Ryazantsev, Levashov (2021), as well as Ukrainian scientists: Lisitsy, Misyukevich, Mikhailenko (2020). Current problems caused by the pandemic are also considered by Anisiia Tomanek (2020), Kravchuk, Varis, Zaryvnykh (2020). In the current difficult conditions, states are forced to undertake new mechanisms to support their economies. In this case, the state administration assumes a special responsibility. The pandemic guided by the COVID-19 virus and related quarantine measures are causing great economic damage to virtually all sectors of the economy. The agricultural sector is no exception. Thus, in every country, scientists have asked questions about the impact of disease prevention measures both on agriculture and on all other areas of human activity. Each country has developed its own experience in overcoming certain negative consequences. Therefore, Ukrainian realities can also be interesting and useful as an overview for the world scientific community.

Public Administration as a Protective Factor for Ukrainian Agriculture

Agriculture is one of the most important sectors in Ukraine's economy. Its share in the national economy of the country is quite high according to generally accepted economic indicators. It is home to almost a quarter of the production assets and one-fifth of all citizens employed in the state's economy. Agriculture directly affects the country's greatest wealth - its land fund, which is almost millions of hectares of agricultural land. "The level of economic development of agriculture largely depends on the economy as a whole, as in this area of material production generates more than 20% of national income, 13.5% of gross value added" (Zhemoida, 2013, p. 42). That is why the situation in the agricultural sector largely determines the socio-economic situation of society and the food security of the state.

Ukraine can fully meet domestic needs in agricultural products through its production, under conditions of product stabilization by the exporter of agricultural products. Ukraine is one of the countries with the highest rating in terms of potential reserves of agro-industrial production. The basis for this statement is a fairly high concentration of black soils, favourable geographical location, well-developed transport infrastructure, the presence of a significant market for agricultural products both in Ukraine and abroad. Therefore, it is obvious that the foundations of the Ukrainian economy are concentrated in agriculture and any of its radical changes must begin in this area (Zhemoida, 2013, p. 30). In 2020, the situation in domestic agriculture, in addition to weather conditions and animal diseases, was also affected by restrictions imposed against the global corona virus pandemic. The agricultural sector, compared to the rest of the economy, has suffered relatively little loss due to the corona virus epidemic. However, the pandemic has accelerated the trends that will have the greatest impact on food production in the future.

According to Bochko (2021), the current strategy for the development of agriculture and rural areas for the period 2015-2020, in general, should ensure the exploitation of Ukraine's full potential, taking into account the course of European integration. However, almost all the conditions on which investors depend remain quite shaky. Of course, investors are attracted by the country's agricultural potential, but in addition to the general economic and political crisis, they face certain limitations. The pandemic has different effects on farmers. It depends on the size of the enterprise, the volume of production, the territorial location of the enterprise, the levels of distribution of products, as well as the level of support from the state (Bochko, 2021, p. 6).

The Government of Ukraine views agriculture as a strategic sector that requires significant protection and support through public policy. However, long-term practice of state regulation using ineffective agricultural policy instruments, reassessment of political slogans on self-sufficiency, difficult trade barriers both domestically and internationally, and lack of innovative marketing institutions have led to stagnation in Ukrainian agriculture (Zhemoida, 2013, p. 30).

"Public administration of the agricultural sector of the economy is defined as purposeful, organizing and regulating the influence of the state on the activities of enterprises and organizations that form the agricultural sector through the organization of public relations to ensure state agricultural policy in the interests of citizens. Considered as part of public administration of the agricultural sector of the economy, which is under conditions of sustainable development of the agricultural sector, stability of production and sales in a market economy should grow. It dominates regulatory and legal support of economic processes in the agricultural sector of the economy" (Surai, 2005, p.13).

As a generalization of theoretical developments, the author of this chapter proposes the following scheme (Figure 1), which shows the political functions of public administration of the agricultural sector of Ukraine's economy.

Figure 1. The political functions of public administration of the agricultural sector of Ukraine's economy

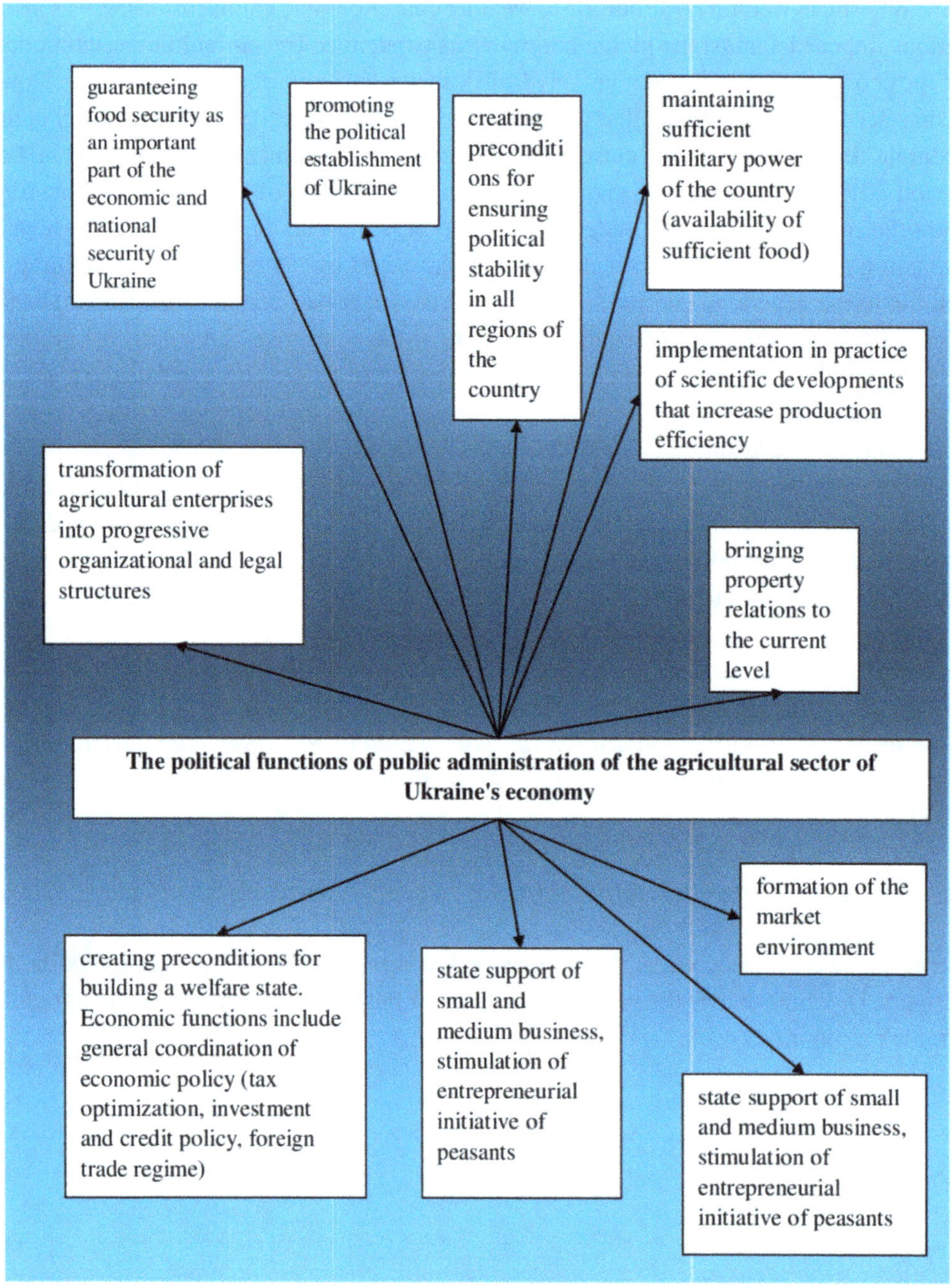

According to Zhemoida (2013), socially necessary goods to be provided by agriculture - food safety, reliable product quality, environmental protection, social stability, etc. From the point of view of an individual member of society, it is logical to agree with a consensus on the preference for this type of agricultural policy, which focuses primarily on meeting such necessary needs. Thus, many people agree to incur high costs for the future supply and stability of the provision of the above critical goods, hence such an agrarian policy may have a high "predominant right" (Zhemoida, 2013, p. 12).

As studied by the Rozumkov Center, scientists Pishchulin, Yurchishin, Yurochko (2021)

"due to irrational corona virus restrictions rural population and the people of small remote towns suffered the most. Cut off from civilization were villagers could not purchase even the most essential medicines and necessities to maintain their health, even regardless of COVID 19. Pandemic response measures for such residents could not be used, including due to transport restrictions, which led to denials of testing at the place of residence, even in the presence of symptoms, and before the lack of opportunities for hospitalization" (Pishchulina et. al., 2021, p. 82).

Mykola Gorbachev (2021), the president of the Ukrainian Grain Association, warns that quarantine announced in many countries around the world will increase the cost of logistics chains. Requirements for the inspection of goods arriving in the country will affect the speed and cost of a trade. This will lead to the fact that domestic prices for agricultural products will fall against the background of rising logistics chains Gorbachev allocates 3 of the main challenges facing the agricultural sector: negative market conditions, difficult access to financial resources and logistical problems (Gorbachev, 2021, para 2).

As for Ukrainian agricultural exports, according to Alex Lissits, president of the Ukrainian Agrarian Business Club, its projected 10-20% drop will reduce foreign exchange earnings by $ 4 billion, a significant amount during the crisis (Lissits, 2021, para 4). Yarmak (2021) believes that the agricultural sector will suffer less than other sectors of Ukraine's economy due to the spread of the corona virus pandemic (COVID-19). In such a situation, when everything is very uncertain, it is simply very difficult to predict. Basic values will remain the same - food is needed every day, unlike everything else. According to Yarmak (2021), the agricultural sector of Ukraine is now, despite the difficulties, in the best situation of all. Even for IT, this time can be a little more difficult (Yarmak, 2021, para 5).

According to Zhemoida (2013), socially necessary goods to be provided by agriculture - food safety, reliable product quality, environmental protection, social stability are among the most essential human needs, because an insufficient supply of such goods immediately becomes threatening.

"From the point of view of an individual member of society, it is logical to agree with the consensus on favouring this type of agricultural policy, which focuses primarily on meeting such necessary needs. Thus, many people agree to incur high costs goods" (Zhemoida, 2013, p. 12).

Although the agricultural sector has proved to be one of the most resilient to the crisis. The pandemic itself has accelerated trends that will have a huge impact on the sector as a whole. According to Bochko (2021), this concerns the impetus for the development of the digitalization process, more informed consumer choices or preferences for local products.

"In general, the pandemic has significantly changed the rules of the agricultural industry, as well as ways of buying food and, in general, the attitude of food consumers. Experts predict that buying food online is not a seasonal trend and will remain so for a long time. Food stores are opening up. The market for the pandemic has changed dramatically since the pandemic, with closed restaurants and factory canteens, fearing for their health, preparing food at home and paying more and more attention to the origin and safety of food. During this time, sales of "healthier" products increased. When closing or restricting

access to grocery markets or shops, consumers began to look for alternative ways to get food, which increased the demand for local producers and farmers' products purchased from them via the Internet platform" (Bochko, 2021, pp. 8).

Before the pandemic, the main focus was on government support for large agricultural companies. Much attention was paid to the issues of automation of manufacture, the creation of favourable economic conditions for large-scale production. The pandemic showed the importance of medium and small agricultural businesses for the domestic market. According to Bochko (2021), the capital that needs to be invested in technology is usually held by large market participants, as opposed to small independent farmers.

"The importance of prudent procurement decisions is especially important in such difficult times as the corona virus pandemic, as they have a major impact on the country's economic situation. Consumer patriotism forms a powerful food brand for domestic producers, supports domestic agricultural producers and enterprises, including domestic agriculture and food industry" (Bochko, 2021, p. 9).

Preservation of medium and small farming businesses will lead to the purchase of Ukrainian goods, to the preservation of jobs, even to their creation. Consequently, tax revenues to the country's budget and local budgets will increase. It is necessary to attract funds for investment, to listen to the opinion of farms. Only when farmers can sell their products at a price sufficient to pay for themselves can a pandemic agrarian crisis be avoided. Ukraine's agriculture has a huge potential on a European scale, so the creation of an appropriate state program is a necessary step to manage and eliminate problems.

FINDINGS AND DISCUSSION

Negative Effects of Covid-19 Prevention Measures on Agriculture

As Korenkov notes (April 14, 2020), "farmers in the Kherson region throw their crops in the trash. Even a short-term closure of the largest wholesale market in the Kherson region resulted in irreparable losses for farmers and farmers in the southern region of Ukraine. In the village of Malye Kopani, which was quarantined due to the corona virus, unsold cabbage, radishes and greens are simply thrown into a landfill" (Korenkov, April 14, 2020).

For local peasants, these are hundreds of thousands of losses; in desperation, they line up along international highways in the Kherson region, trying to sell what supermarkets used to take away.

"Selling vegetables through social networks, according to the peasants, is unrealistic, since it is unprofitable to send several kilograms of early vegetables in parcels, and wholesalers simply cannot come to the Kherson region for tons of ripe crops" (Korenkov, April 14, 2020).

First of all, Ukrainian farmers note that they grow agricultural products to feed not only their families, but the whole of Ukraine, said Valentina Kostenko, chairman of the Velikokopanivka United Community, in an interview for the TSN TV channel. People complain that the loss of the harvest in early spring 2020 will turn into bankruptcy next year: there will simply be nothing to plant vegetables, fruits and herbs.

In Kherson, farmers blocked a road bridge (Shaporenko, April 26, 2020).

"At the entrance to Kherson, farmers blocked the road bridge, staging a rally against the closure of markets for the period of quarantine in the country. In particular, we are talking about the wholesale market in Malye Kopani.

When the village was quarantined due to the corona virus, local farmers lost the opportunity to sell their perishable products at the wholesale market. Instead, they are forced to sell it at reduced prices to retail chains.

The police counted 200 protesters. Although people came to the rally wearing masks, they did not keep their distance. The head of the Kherson Regional State Administration, Yuriy Gusev, asked to send proposals for the development of the agro-industrial complex of the region through official channels and promised to meet with the initiative groups of farmers in person, subject to all quarantine measures" (Shaporenko, April 26, 2020).

In the Kherson region, due to an increase in the number of patients with corona virus, the largest markets for agricultural products were closed. There are Alyoshki city, the villages – Levy Solontsy, Aleshkovsky district, Malye Kopani, Golopristan district.

The Focus UA online publication posted photos and an article "Revolt against the quarantine, which says that farmers blocked the bridge near Kherson due to the closure of the market" (Focus UA, 26.04.2020). Near Kherson, local farmers blocked traffic on the Antonovsky Automobile Bridge across the Dnieper in protest against the closure of the wholesale vegetable market. After the village was quarantined, local farmers lost the opportunity to sell their perishable products at the wholesale market. They are forced to sell them at reduced prices to merchants The police counted 200 protesters who continuously walk along the footbridge, wearing protective masks, but not keeping a distance of 1.5-2 m. grown in their fields. The police warned that anyone who attended the meeting would be brought to administrative responsibility, and the Head of the Kherson Regional Administration Yuriy Gusev asked to draw up proposals for the development of the agro-industrial complex and send them in writing to the authorities. He also suggested creating an initiative group of farmers to discuss problems and meet personally in compliance with all quarantine measures (Focus UA, 26.04.2020). April 30, 2020, The Cabinet of Ministers, under the pressure of business, reduced restrictive measures. According to Kravchenko (30.04.2020), "April 29, the Cabinet of Ministers allowed the operation of food markets, subject to the observance of sanitary standards by traders – wearing masks and having social distance. The decision was made on Wednesday afternoon and de facto for nothing. By that time, markets in the regions had begun to open on their own. It was caused by mass protests of entrepreneurs under the walls of the Chernivtsi Regional State Administration" (Kravchenko, 04.30.2020).

Similar protests were held in Poltava. However, the problem went beyond the agricultural complex.

"When the Cabinet of Ministers was going to a meeting, about 500 small entrepreneurs came out under its walls, who demanded an end to quarantine already in the first days of May. Hrushevsky Street, placing cars in two rows and blocking the work of tow trucks trying to pull them away. The Cabinet of Ministers again gave up the slack, hastily declaring that at the next meeting it would consider a decision on a new easing of quarantine for business" (Kravchenko, 04/30/2020).

According to Kravchenko (2020), the position of the authorities could have been stronger if not for the scandal that erupted the day before, connected with the people's deputy from the Servant of the People, Nikolai Tishchenko. During the week, investigators steadily recorded the visitors entering it, among whom were representatives of both the deputy corps and the President's Office. Tishchenko himself said that "Velour" works not as a restaurant, but as a headquarters. This was the last straw that overflowed the patience of the business, which for two months watched how, against the backdrop of massive bankruptcies of small and middle business representatives, large players continue to work. Ordinary citizens got rid of the moral obligation to comply with quarantine, seeing that it was ignored by the authorities (Kravchenko, 04.30.2020).

Vanina (2020) notes that farmers used to sell their watermelons to neighbouring states. But due to the lockdown and political crises, all the usual supply chains have broken down. There was a watermelon collapse in the Kherson region, farmers "could not sell harvest even at 30-50 coins per kilogram. Although such a wholesale price is almost half the cost. However, watermelons are already beginning to overripe, and there are very few buyers. Such a crop of watermelons in Kherson the area has not been seen for a long time. They withstood the cold spring, survived the June showers. And here is the result of hard work. All these watermelons were not sold on time, and they are already overripe. Vanina (2020) conveys the words of the farmer that "they sowed 6 hectares, but could sell only three half a hectare. On 2.5 hectares, we have watermelons left on the field. More than three hundred thousand hryvnias have been invested in this field. Bargained – a hundred. I wanted to give watermelons as a gift to those who would pick them up from the field on their own, but there were no people. Because due to the large harvest, there are more sellers in the market than buyers. In the village of Vinogradovo, which specializes in growing watermelons, the wholesale market has a gloomy atmosphere" (Vanina, 2020). Due to the lockdown and political crises, all the usual supply channels have broken down. "The Baltic countries took it, the Belarusians did so, this year the borders were closed. The only ones who sold their watermelon harvest were the large farms. Because they, as legal entities, had direct contracts with retail chains. Therefore, officials advise small farmers to unite and look for buyers even before the goods are ripe" (Vanina, 2020).

According to Robeiko (2020), farmers are convinced that it is more profitable to leave watermelons on the field as fertilizer, so they are ruthlessly destroyed. "In the village of Mikhailovka, Kherson region, farmers are destroying unsold watermelons because they have become cheaper than bread. Men in the field throw watermelons out of a truck and the berries were broken.

"In Ukraine, farmers in Vinnytsia estimate crop losses at 30%, in Mykolayiv up to 50%. For some crops, such losses can reach 70-80%. For the same reason, there will be no May honey. Therefore, easing quarantine is unlikely to save. At the same time, the pandemic has already reduced food demand, which has led to lower purchase prices for food, such as milk and maintaining a decent standard of living for one's own family" (Robeiko, 2020).

Zhemoida's theoretical substantiation (2013) is that the assessment of Ukraine's national food security has its specifics, which stems from the objective diversity of climatic conditions of agricultural production, critical trends in economic development, a certain degree of dependence on imported food supplies and potential prospects, its exports, features of the national regime of regulation of foreign economic relations (Zhemoida, 2013, p. 42).

According to Robeiko (2020), in the difficult situation that has arisen, according to many small and medium-sized producers, state subsidies will not save. Only tax "vacations" or tax deferrals can help keep small agricultural businesses afloat. Instead, tax authorities are threatening the courts with those farmers who are unwilling to pay taxes in a crisis. Due to quarantine, Ukrainian farmers have lost access to markets. On social networks and in the media, one could often see tons of food thrown away at random, which agricultural producers simply could not sell. After all, the markets, restaurants and cafes with which they cooperated have closed. All food could be purchased only in supermarkets, where sanitary conditions are 100% met (Robeiko, 2020).

"The main goal of agricultural policy is to substantiate the strategy of market transformations in the national agro-industrial complex, effective and efficient methods, ways and mechanisms to bring it out of the systemic crisis and transfer it to a model of sustainable, competitive and environmentally friendly development, continue and intensify. Such actions lead not only to the degradation of agro-industrial potential but also to a further decline in food security and possible loss of food independence of our state. Decisive and urgent measures are needed to overcome these negative trends as soon as possible" (Zhemoida, 2013, p. 41).

The problem of food security is not new to the globalized world. The reasons for the decline in food security and the rapid rise in prices for agricultural products are identified as: climate change, which is increasingly manifested in increasing hurricanes, droughts, downpours, cyclones and winds and volcanic eruptions; the constant growth of oil and gas prices until recently, the products of which are important components of agricultural production resources. The growth of aggregate world demand for food is inextricably linked with the growth of the world's population, which has already reached 7 billion, and for the Ukrainian agricultural sector and the above-mentioned losses. Public administration has created "State program promotion to overcome the negative effects caused by restrictive measures to prevent the occurrence and spread of acute respiratory disease COVID-19 caused by corona virus SARS-CoV-2, for 2020 - 2022" (https://ips.ligazakon.net/document/KP200534?an=19). According to this document, Ukraine, like the rest of the world, is facing a new challenge - the pandemic of acute respiratory disease COVID-19 caused by the corona virus SARS-CoV-2 (hereinafter - COVID-19), which forced significant adjustments in public policy priorities to prevent the spread the disease and save lives. To this end, the Cabinet of Ministers of Ukraine introduced strict restrictive measures aimed primarily at minimizing the spread of COVID-19 by avoiding mass gatherings (hereinafter - restrictive measures), which allowed the state to cope with the spread of the disease: Ukraine was able to avoid the Italian scenario and demonstrated, similar to the dynamics of countries such as Poland and Romania. Quarantine was a forced measure that prevented significant losses in the early stages of the disease and prepared the medical system to combat COVID-19. Today, the medical system in most regions is ready to provide treatment for all patients in the event of new possible outbreaks of the pandemic.

"The agricultural sector is critical to the country's food security. Moreover, many natural factors have led to the growing importance of the agricultural sector not only in Ukraine's economy, making it an important player in world markets.

The Program implements several measures aimed at the development of the agricultural sector through:

- ensuring broad access of producers to financial resources for the acquisition and renewal of fixed assets and the creation of greater added value through government credit programs and subsidies;

- ensuring uninterrupted sales of agricultural products in a pandemic by establishing distribution channels, raising awareness of producers and providing assistance in entering export markets.

In addition, it is planned to ensure effective regulation of the sector, timely provision of administrative services and development of transparent land relations" (State program promotion to overcome the negative effects caused by restrictive measures to prevent the occurrence and spread of acute respiratory disease COVID-19 CoV-2, for 2020 - 2022").

RECOMMENDATIONS

What should the Government do to help Ukrainian farming?

Currently, the Government's Program for stimulating the economy to overcome the consequences of the COVID-19 epidemic states that an online platform for the sale of agricultural products will be set up in the 4-th quarter of this year. It is also planned to allocate funds for the implementation of projects online. The government of Ukraine should make the support of small Ukrainian producers more comprehensive and consistent, to solve not only the current problems of farmers but also to think about the future development of small and medium-sized farms, as experts predict new waves of the pandemic.

CONCLUSION

The COVID-19 pandemic has spread around the world and has affected almost every area of human activity, the global market and the distribution of food. Since the agricultural complex is focused on basic needs, this marks its advantage during the crisis period as less affected by COVID-19 than other economic sectors. Public administration is purposeful in organizing and regulating the influence of the state on the activities of enterprises and organizations in the agricultural sector. Those socially necessary goods that are produced in it are among the most necessary human needs. There are countries where the agricultural sector of the economy plays a decisive role and supplies products to other countries. In this regard, the closure of borders lead to huge losses for farmers and, as a result, their ruin, even a threat to survival. As a result of irrational corona virus restrictions, the rural population of Ukraine has suffered significant losses. Since the author of this chapter worked in the Kherson region and personally observed the facts of farmers' protests, which were confirmed by authoritative Ukrainian media, it may be concluded that the coved restrictions harm Ukrainian agriculture. It should be noted that state authorities and local governments did everything possible to limit the spread of COVID-19 and protect public health. However, for the economy of Ukrainian agriculture, the above global challenges turned out to be quite disastrous. Taking into account the shortcomings of quarantine restrictions, a special state program has been developed, which, in the opinion of the author of the chapter, will be able to prevent an agrarian crisis in Ukraine. For the further implementation of the Ukrainian agrarian policy, it is necessary to solve a set of tasks that have arisen in the process of pandemic prevention measures, as well as the general difficulties facing the national agrarian complex. These include the creation of favourable living and working conditions in the countryside, a significant increase in the level of self-sufficiency of the country with basic foodstuffs of high quality, strengthening the export orientation of the development of the domestic agricultural sector of the economy, increasing the environmental and soil protection reliability of agricultural production, ensuring its development at the level of the most developed in agrarian relations of the countries. Food security is an important element of national state one and characterizes the political independence of the country, its economic strength and stability, the social security of the population and the food needs of its citizens without prejudice to national state interests. State program promotion to overcome the negative effects caused by restrictive measures to prevent the occurrence and spread of acute respiratory disease COVID-19 caused by corona virus SARS-CoV-2, for 2020 - 2022 is a set of measures aimed at eliminating the above-mentioned problems of the agricultural economy sector.

ACKNOWLEDGMENT

This research received no grant from any organization.

REFERENCES

Aday, S., & Aday, M. S. (2020). Impact of COVID-19 on the food supply chain. *Food Quality and Safety*, *4*(4), 167–180. doi:10.1093/fqsafe/fyaa024

Anisiia, T. (Ed.). (2020). *Economy, finance, law: current problems and development prospects: collective monograph*. OSVČ.

Antonenko, V., & Quick, V. (2021). Museums as a tourist resource in the context of the COVID-19 pandemic: Challenges and new opportunities. *Bulletin of the Kyiv National University of Culture and Arts*, *4*(1), 54–73. doi:10.31866/2616-7603.4.1.2021.235149

Bebko, S. (2021). Internationalization and cooperation of the higher education system of Ukraine in the conditions of global challenges. *Scientific Bulletin of Polissya*, *2*(21), 28–38. doi:10.25140/2410-9576-2020-2(21)-28-38

Beckman & Countryman. (2021). *The Importance of Agriculture in the Economy: Impacts from COVID-19*. doi:10.1111/ajae.12212

Bochko, O. Yu. (2021). The influence of the pandemic on the development of agriculture in Ukraine *International Scientific Journal "Internauka"*. doi:10.25313/2520-2294-2021-4

Chaikun, E. (2021). Building and transforming crisis communication strategies of the media during the COVID-19 pandemic. *IV Congress of the ACS "Transformation of social institutions in the information society"*, 39-41.

Dheng, C. (2021). Worldwide Smpact of COVID-19 Pandemic On Agriculture. *Journal of Agriculture Science and Food Research*, *1-2*. Advance online publication. doi:10.35248/25939173.21.12.297

Dheng, C. (2021). Worldwide Impact of COVID-19 Pandemic On Agriculture. *J Agri Sci Food Res*, *12*, 297. doi:10.35248/2593-9173.21.12.297

Elleby, C., Domínguez, I. P., Adenauer, M., & Genovese, G. (2020). Impacts of the COVID-19 Pandemic on the Global Agricultural Markets. *Environmental and Resource Economics*, *76*(4), 1067–1079. doi:10.100710640-020-00473-6 PMID:32836856

Et-touile, H., & Arib, F. (2021). Impacts of COVID-19 pandemic on agriculture, food prices, and food security in Morocco. *International Journal of Financial Accountability, Economics, Management, and Auditing*, *3*(5), 973–988. doi:10.52502/ijfaema.v3i5.179

Fedianin, V. (2021). Combating COVID-19 and Vaccination as Elements of the United Arab Emirates Foreign Policy. *Scientific and Theoretical Almanac Grani*, *24*(6), 155–162. doi:10.15421/172171

Fedulova, L., & Petroye, O. (2021). Innovative and technological factor of economic development during the COVID-19 pandemic and recommendations for the future (policy paper). *Collection of Scientific Works of the National Academy of Public Administration under the President of Ukraine,* (1), 128-143.

Fokus, U. A. (2020, April 26). *Rebellion against quarantine. Farmers close the bridge near Kherson due to market closure*. https://focus.ua/ukraine/454415-bunt_protiv_karantina_pod_khersonom_fermery_perekryli_most_iz-za_zakrytiia_rynka

Gavrilyuk, O. (2021). Pandemic crisis as a catalyst for digitalization of the tourism industry. *Collection of Scientific Works of Cherkasy State Technological University*, (60), 22–29.

Geiko, T. Yu. (2020). Priorities for the development of entrepreneurship in Ukraine in the context of the COVID-19 pandemic and in the post-quarantine period. Bulletin of Socio-Economic Research, (2), 73.

Gorbachev, M. (2021). *Yak vplyne koronavirus na rozvytok ahrosektoru v Ukraini* [How will the coronavirus affect the development of the agricultural sector in Ukraine]. https://adler.com.ua/news/yak-vpline-koronavirus-na-rozvitok-agrosektoru-v-ukrajini

Gursky, V. R. (2021). *Problems and consequences of migration of highly qualified specialists in the context of COVID-19*. National Aviation University.

Knyazev, S. I. (2020). Smart industry: Forming the basis of a new stage of economic growth in the world. *Business Info*, *4*(4), 150–162. doi:10.32983/2222-4459-2020-4-150-162

Korenkov, D. (2020, April 14). *Farmers of the Kherson region throw crops to the dump: the coronavirus has caused hundreds of thousands of losses* https://www.0552.ua/news/2730095/fermery-hersonsiny-vybrasyvaut-urozaj-na-pomojku-koronavirus-prines-ubytki-na-sotni-tysac

Kravchenko, V. (2020, April 30). *How Kherson farmers and a glamorous restaurateur "zeroed" quarantine in Ukraine. The Cabinet of Ministers is under pressure from business to ease restrictive measures. Protest action of entrepreneurs near the Cabinet of Ministers*. https://mind.ua/ru/publications/20210461-kak-hersonskie-fermery-i-glamurnyj-restorator-obnulili-karantin-v-ukraine

Kravchuk, O., Varis, I., & Zaryvnykh, K. (2021). Digital technology of personnel management: Trends and challenges in a COVID-19 pandemic. *Economics and society*, *26*, 1–10. doi:10.32782/2524-0072/2021-26-73

Lisitsy, V. V., Misyukevich, V. I., & Mikhailenko, O. M. (Eds.). (2020). *The formation of the system of internal trade of Ukraine: theory, practice, innovation*. PUET.

LissitsA. (2021). https://adler.com.ua/news/yak-vpline-koronavirus-na-rozvitok-agrosektoru-v-ukrajini

Lopez-Ridaura, Sanders, Barba-Escoto, Wiegel, Mayorga-Cortes, Gonzalez-Esquivel, Lopez-Ramirez, Escoto-Masis, Morales-Galindo, & García-Barcena. (2021). Immediate impact of COVID-19 pandemic on farming systems in Central America and Mexico. *Agricultural Systems, 192*, 1-12. doi:10.1016/j.agsy.2021.103178

Marchant-Forde, J. N., & Boyle, L. A. (2020). COVID-19 Effects on Livestock Production: A One Welfare *Issue. Frontiers in Veterinary Science*, *7*, 585787. doi:10.3389/fvets.2020.585787 PMID:33195613

Misyukevich, V. I., Trushkina, N. V., & Shkrygun, Yu. O. (2020). E-commerce in the global digital space: new challenges and directions of development. In The formation of the system of internal trade of Ukraine: theory, practice, innovation (pp. 150-162). PUET.

Nosova, O. V. (2021). Foreign direct investment TNCS as a factor of innovative development. *Bulletin of Kharkiv National University named after VN Karazin's Series Economic*, *100*, 45–56. doi:10.26565/2311-2379-2021-100-05

Petrovska, O. M., & Bendus, I. M. (2020). Prospects for the emergence of new professions in the labor market of Ukraine after the global pandemic. *Economic Space*, (158), 95–100. doi:10.32782/2224-6282/158-15

Povoroznyuk, I. (2021). Formation and implementation of anti-crisis management at the enterprises of the hospitality industry during the COVID-19 pandemic. *Economy and Society*, (29). Advance online publication. doi:10.32782/2524-0072/2021-29-18

Project "German-Russian Agrarian-Political Dialogue". (n.d.). http://www.agrardialog.ru

Pyschulina, O., Yurchyshyn, V., & Yurochko, T. (2021). *Socio-economic consequences of the coronacrise*. Razumkov Center, Zapovit Publishing House.

Robeiko, O. (2021, September 13). *Farmers are convinced that it is more profitable to leave watermelons in the field as fertilizer*. https://www.unian.net/economics/agro/v-seti-pokazali-kak-fermery-iz-hersonskoy-oblasti-besposhchadno-unichtozhayut-arbuzy-video-novosti-11542546.html

Salikhova, O. B., & Goncharenko, D. O. (2021). Challenges of COVID-19 pharmaceutical industry: EU and Ukraine responses. *Economy and Forecasting*, *4*, 18.

Semenova, L. u., Datsenko, V.V., & Hurday, V.V. (2020). Modern marketing tools to increase competitiveness in a COVID-19 pandemic. *Economy, finance, law: Current problems and current problems and development prospects*, 49.

Shaporenko, E. (2020). *Asked to open markets: In Kherson farmers blocked the road bridge.* https://fakty.com.ua/ru/ukraine/20200426-prosyat-vidkryty-rynky-v-hersoni-fermery-perekryly- automobile-mist /

Sharma, Shishodia, Kamble, Gunasekaran, & Belhadi. (2020). Agriculture supply chain risks and COVID-19: mitigation strategies and implications for the practitioners. *International Journal of Logistics Research and Applications*. doi:10.1080/13675567.2020.1830049

Sidorenko, E. A. (2021). *Transformational processes of event practices: challenges of the COVID-19 pandemic* [Master's Dissertation]. National Academy of Management of Culture and Arts.

State Program. (2020). *State program promotion to overcome the negative effects caused by restrictive measures to prevent the occurrence and spread of acute respiratory disease COVID-19 CoV-2, for 2020 – 2022*. https://ips.ligazakon.net/document/KP200534?an=19

Štreimikienė, D., Baležentis, T., Volkov, A., Ribašauskienė, E., Morkūnas, M., & Žičkienė, A. (2021). *Negative effects of covid-19 pandemic on agriculture: systematic literature review in the frameworks of vulnerability, resilience and risks involved*. Economic Research-Ekonomska Istraživanja. doi:10.1080/1331677X.2021.1919542

Surai, I. G. (2005). *Public administration of the agricultural sector of the economy of Ukraine: functional and structural aspect* [PhD Dissertation]. Dissertations and Theses database.

Torkunov, A. V., Ryazantsev, S. V., & Levashov, V. K. (Eds.). (2021). *Pandemic COVID-19: Challenges, consequences, counteraction*. Aspect Press Publishing House.

Vanina, E. (2021, September 7). *Previously, peasants sold their watermelons to neighboring countries. But due to lockdown and political crises, all the usual supply channels have broken*. https://tsn.ua/ru/exclusive/nikomu-ne-nuzhen-urozhay-pochemu-fermery-za-bescenok-vynuzhdeny-prodavat-arbuzy-1862242.html

Walters, L., Wade, T., & Suttles, S. (2020). Food and Agricultural Transportation Challenges Amid the COVID-19 Pandemic. *Choices*. https://www.choicesmagazine.org/choices-magazine/theme-articles/covid-19-and-the-agriculture-industry-labor-supply-chains-and-consumer-behavior/food-and-agricultural-transportation-challenges-amid-the-covid-19-pandemic

Wegerif, M. (2021). The impact of Covid-19 on black farmers in South Africa. *Agrekon*. Advance online publication. doi:10.1080/03031853.2021.1971097

White, N. E. (2021). Farming in the time of pandemic: Small farms demonstrate flexibility, innovation, and hope. *Journal of Agriculture, Food Systems, and Community Development*, *10*(2), 247–249. doi:10.5304/jafscd.2021.102.008

Yarmak, A. (2021). *How will the coronavirus affect the development of the agricultural sector in Ukraine*. https://adler.com.ua/news/yak-vpline-koronavirus-na-rozvitok-agrosektoru-v-ukrajini

Zatuliviter, V. (2021). Internationalization of higher education in a pandemic condition. *Scientific Notes of Young Scientists*, (8).

Zhemoida, O. V. (2013). *Public administration in the field of agriculture* (Vol. K). NADU.

Chapter 10
The Financial Digital Assets Frontier:
The Bridge Between the Past and the Future

Andrei Dragos Popescu
https://orcid.org/0000-0002-9048-3055
University of Craiova, Singapore

ABSTRACT

The COVID-19 pandemic has disrupted the value chains for all major business sectors, with a great impact on the way we interact, socialize, transact, and trust the systems that we use on a daily basis. The magnitude of this major health crisis imposed a new level of digitalization, to which everyone needed to adapt, with great costs in terms of social, psychological, political, and economic transformation. In order to adapt in a new digital environment, imposed by the pandemic, we witnessed the adoption of decentralized ecosystems and technologies. One of the technologies that stood as foundation for this decentralization movement is blockchain. The first adaptations for blockchain technology happened within the financial services, with the introduction of the financial digital assets or crypto assets. This created the base for concepts like decentralized finance (DeFi), Web 3.0, and the metaverse. This chapter will assess the frontier of financial digital assets, which has emerged and developed the perfect infrastructure for scalability, efficiency, and transparency.

INTRODUCTION

Clearly, the COVID-19 pandemic has had a significant impact on all the value chains, and the global economy. In this regard, corporate sales have plummeted, industrial production has been reduced, consumer behaviors have changed, supply chains have been disrupted, businesses have faced serious financial hardships, and global unemployment rates have grown dramatically. In addition, as the number of positive coronavirus cases has grown exponentially, the COVID-19 pandemic has caused fear and the

DOI: 10.4018/978-1-7998-8856-7.ch010

temporary shutdown of industries, business sectors and enterprises in most nations all over the globe (Okorie D.I. and Lin B., 2021).

A direct consequence of all these effects was reflected in the global economy which shrank by 4.3% in 2020 (World Bank, 2021), as the health crisis and subsequent lockdowns halted travel, slowed or even closed companies, disrupted supply lines, and put millions of people out of work all over the world (International Labour Organization, 2021). A new worldwide recession was predicted and according to the World Bank, is "the deepest since 1945–1946, and more than twice as deep as the recession associated with the 2007–2009 global financial crisis." (Kose A. and Sugara N., 2021).

Based on the latest report from World Bank (2021) for the year of 2020, the Eurozone had a 7.4% decrease of the GPD, along with the United Stated who registered a fall of 3.5%. Japan, followed the trend, with a 5.3% contraction, in the same economic context with the rest of the Asean countries.

A circuit breaker strategy was adopted by Singapore and this was responsible for 2.2% of Singapore's GDP decrease in 2020, the worst reported contraction since their independence in 1965. These metrics are important to show the great impact of the pandemic effects on the global socio-economic environment.

In many respects, the COVID-19 world health crisis has put countries' competence and political will to the test. They have had to deal with an unprecedented public health catastrophe while also dealing with the complicated economic and social consequences, all while preserving public support and compliance.

During March 2020, the Dow Jones and S&P500 indexes had lost up to 30% of their value (Iqbal et al., 2021). Other stock markets, such as those in Europe, the United Kingdom, Australia, and Asia, have also experienced comparable declines (Zhang et al., 2020).

The COVID-19 pandemic has pushed the digitalization of services to a new level. Many industries have been fully disrupted and many sectors had to restructure their whole workflows, processes and procedures.

The financial industry is also going through a paradigm shift, based on a disruption model, which was accelerated by the COVID-19 pandemic, as FinTech innovations have been optimizing the accessibility, liquidity and transparency of the services.

Within the realm of FinTech, it is important to acknowledge Blockchain and Distributed Ledger Technology (DLT) as an innovative frontrunning architecture. An important property which is worth mentioning is that we should treat these novel technologies as a data enabling innovative architecture and not like a Financial Technology per se.

Given the novel and emergent status of financial digital assets, understanding the properties and the relationship between smart contracts, financial instruments, and all the participants, is providing new perspectives for financial services within a decentralized ecosystem.

Smart contracts are programmable contracts that are automatically executed when predefined conditions are met. The adoption of smart contracts will lead to reduced risks, lower administration and service costs and more efficient business processes across all major sectors of the financial services.

The potential of smart contract within the financial services industry is bridging new frontiers with regards to optimizing and creating new financial instruments that can help increase financial inclusion and integration.

The impact of modern technology with regards to the evolution of the contemporary world cannot be denied. Knowledge gained via technological improvements contributed greatly to the advancement of societies, diverse markets inception, and, of course, medicine. This is the main reason why technological advancements are considered to have the greatest influence and impact in humanity's future, with great developments and implementations in a full range of sectors.

As our research is an approach from an evolutionary model, we need to identify the necessary steps of disruption patterns by means of technology convergence.

The lifecycle of technology adoption is a very complex sociological model that outlines the adoption of a new product or innovation based on the demographic and psychological features of certain adopting groups. The adoption patterns were formed by Geoffrey Moore, and after 40 years, they were remodeled by Everett Rogers, who developed the idea of spread of innovations or "diffusion innovation". When introducing new technology, this approach considers that we have five categories of receivers or adopters, each having different requirements and expectations. In this model there were identified the following types of recipients: Innovators, Early Adopters, Early Majority, Late Majority, and Laggards.

Surprisingly, implementing breakthrough technologies is difficult and fraught with challenges. It is because businesses do not take into account the many types of adopters among their potential consumers and users. One major flaw is that by treating everyone the same, a direct consequence leads to resistance, subpar performance, and as a result, low return on investment. The second layer of risks comes from the technological implementation along with the idiosyncratic challenges.

It is critical to understand diverse groups of people in order to design a strategy that will encourage users to seek for innovation, as early as possible, in order for new technologies to be effective.

Figure 1. Crossing the Chasm
Source: Geoffrey A. Moore, (1999). Crossing the charm: Marketing and selling high-tech products to mainstream consumers

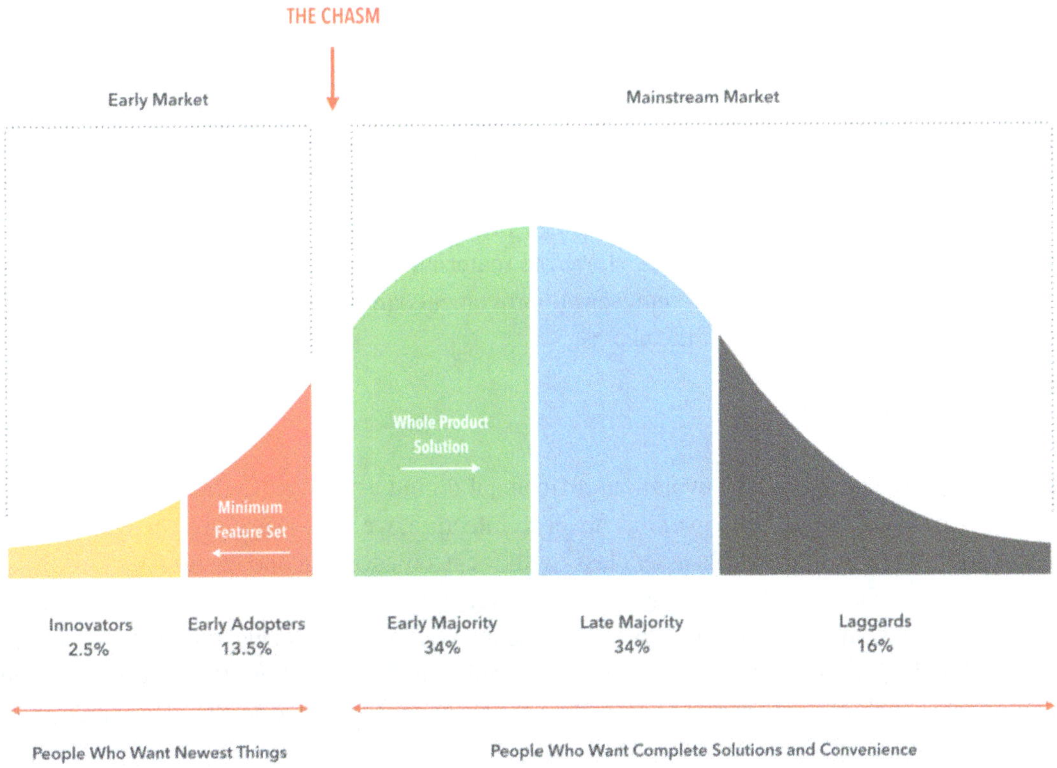

What makes it so crucial? The answer is that you must persuade each of the five user categories to adopt new technology every time it is implemented. When an invention has been accepted by Enthusiasts but not yet by Pragmatists, it is said to be "crossing the chasm". We agree that this is the most crucial stage in any adoption process. It is a difficult process as proven by major technological implementations from the first car, the lift-off of the first plane and the introduction of the internet. The trick is to fulfill the pragmatic majority's wants and expectations at the proper level and right time. This implies that the vision and ideas related to the main product must be presented flawlessly and most of the features need to function correctly.

We are addressing here the adoption of the blockchain technology, which stands as a cornerstone to the evolution of most financial digital assets and the technology convergence that followed.

Our study's approach comes from the perspective of understanding financial digital assets, the technology that powers them and the evolution of the concepts surrounding it. The pandemic context pushed digitalization and digitization in all business sectors, along with the redefinition of the way we interact, socialize and transfer value. The COVID-19 pandemic has driven and pushed the emerging digital markets and the financial digital assets to a new high in terms of acknowledgement and adoption. Novel concepts surrounding financial digital assets have taken the headlines during this challenging period of time, while paradigm shifts emerged in various business sectors. This pivoting in the face of traditional business models has been achieved by acknowledging the powerful tools and innovative features offered by blockchain technology (Popescu AD., 2021b). The applicability of such technology has been directly proportional with the discovery curve of novel business concepts involving tokens and processes of tokenization.

In this regards we can clearly state that 2019 was the year of DeFi innovation and basic concepts; 2020 followed with exceptional acknowledgement and new participants; 2021 spurred having DeFi as foundation, with the novel concept of Non-Fungible Tokens (NFTs) and adaptations in a decentralized environment; 2022 will clearly build on top of these concept with new emerging concepts of Web3.0 and Metaverse.

The years which had as main star Decentralized Finance, created the infrastructure on which new theories of trust, scalability and efficiency started to materialize, and we are seeing a great interest for the Web3.0 and the Metaverse, which represent improvements and implementations of the visions and systems we have the basis for. All of the above

Research Methodology

In order to properly understand the evolution of financial digital assets and their important role in how new concepts are being created on top of this novel architecture, we have engaged a qualitative approach to analyze and vet the frontier of this asset class, with focus on adoption and usability.

The goal of this chapter is to investigate and comprehend the link between financial digital assets, and the COVID-19 health catastrophe, along with their evolution, pre, during and post-pandemic. The intricacy and ambiguity of crypto assets' market dynamics, as compared to other traditional financial assets, motivates such analysis as we believe the novel concepts attached to this new emerging asset class will bring efficiency and stability to the investment landscape, as the frontier of the financial digital assets will radically disrupt old-school ways of the financial services sector.

We are addressing the financial services part, as this represents the underpinning for any new digital economies, and creates the framework for new visionary concepts to empower users and bring efficiency to the other industry sectors.

Based on the model of "Crossing the Chasm", we will take a look on how COVID-19 pandemic has impacted and influenced the usability of financial digital assets, with the intention of offering an overview of the new digital industries which spurred and gained acknowledgement.

LITERATURE REVIEW

Many academics have been studying the impact of the COVID-19 health crisis on stock market behavior and also the dynamics of the digital markets in the same context. On this topic, Al-Awadhi et al. (2020) indicate that daily increases in total confirmed cases and deaths owing to the COVID-19 pandemic have a negative and significant impact on the Chinese companies stock returns.

Financial digital assets markets, as an alternative investment, are likely to be affected by such unexpected movements in stock markets and economies throughout the world. In this regard, Johnson (2020) wonders if the COVID-19 health crisis would lead to an increase in Bitcoin acceptance, considering that Bitcoin is not subject to government regulation. In order to mitigate the negative impacts of the COVID-19 crisis on financial markets, Bitcoin and Ethereum are being employed as alternative investments, and they appear to outperform other assets (Iqbal et al., 2021).

According to Goodell and Goutte (2020), among others, the pandemic repercussions have a beneficial impact on different crypto assets prices, more specifically in the case of Bitcoin. Due to its independence, Huynh et al. (2020) argue that Bitcoin might be regarded a superior hedge than other tokens and cryptocurrencies. The research performed by Mariana et al. (2020), investigates if Ethereum and Bitcoin may serve as stock safe-havens amid the COVID-19 effects. Their findings show a holistic view over the crypto assets returns, which are not fully correlated with the S&P500 results. They also show that Ethereum and Bitcoin are suitable as short-term safe-havens, in this type of events which impact traditional financial markets. We agree and share these opinions as the asset classes have a very correlated behavior, due to the recent influx of institutional investors that use the same models in crisis situations, but the performance of these volatile assets are not fully associated.

Bitcoin has been a significant addition to an investor's portfolio in terms of risk mitigation since its beginnings. In this regard, investors, particularly during tumultuous moments, want additional information on whether they should invest only in traditional or financial digital assets, or combine the two (Mokni and Ajmi, 2021).

A common reaction due to the uncertainties of the socio-economic landscape, have determined investors to liquidate in a panic sale, and as a consequence of their anxieties (Le et al., 2021), the results translated in several big declines for various stocks and emerging markets (Shehzad et al., 2020).

Many academics are naturally interested in determining which assets outperform during volatile periods (Ji et al., 2020) or develop better risk management opportunities over a given market stress. In this regard, our research has important implications from a portfolio risk management perspective, since it demonstrates the role of hedging with financial digital assets in an increasing needed diversification process, that provides advantages and mitigate risks during and post COVID-19 pandemic.

Despite the pandemic effects, financial digital assets have grown to more than $2.2 trillion in market value (Coinmarketcap, 2022), which, like user adoption, roughly tracks the technology sector's market cap in early 1999. On the other hand, crypto assets today are only approximatively 3% of the global stock market value, versus roughly 14% for the technology sector in Q1 1999 (Grayscale, 2022). As we conceive an overview of this picture, financial digital assets are even earlier in their market valuation cycle than the internet was in the late 1990s. To emphasize on how COVID-19 pandemic has driven the acceptance of financial digital assets, we just need to recognize that crypto assets started being considered and allocated to new modern portfolios for institutional investors only in 2020.

Institutional investors now have the ability to use crypto assets as a new instrument for portfolio construction in an unprecedented macro environment for traditional assets. In this new paradigm, not taking risks is one of the biggest risks.

DECENTRALIZED FINANCE (DEFI) 2.0

We should deep dive in the first movement, powered by financial digital assets, which started to gain traction in 2018, and created the basis for the next digital generation shifts. Decentralized Finance or DeFi, put in motion an ecosystem of peer-to-peer value transactions, which expanded rapidly and created the first decentralized playground for digital wealth creation, storage and distribution. The first iteration of this concept, required time to grow and mature, but this organic progression received a dynamic push by the COVID-19 effects, which forced everyone to research, test and implement new models in this new environment.

Decentralized Finance is a category of blockchain-based solutions that attempts to tackle conventional finance's problems of centralization and control over an individual's financial assets. DeFi protocols are continually evolving and iterating upon established models of financial-based instruments, fueled by their inherent benefits of permissionless composability and open-source development culture. The DeFi ecosystem has grown exponentially over a surge of liquidity-focused protocols, and from these DeFi initiatives has ushered in a new generation of DeFi innovation known as DeFi 2.0.

The initial "Money Legos" in the Decentralized Finance (DeFi) ecosystem, such as the utility tokens and decentralized stablecoins, laid the groundwork for future DeFi improvements.

DeFi 2.0 is a relatively recent phrase in the ecosystem, referring to a subset of emergent protocols that build on top of the initial money legos, to progress the present DeFi landscape, particularly in the form of liquidity provisioning and incentivization.

This terminology upgrade in the blockchain world, refers to a subset of DeFi protocols that expand on prior DeFi breakthroughs like yield farming, lending, borrowing, and other decentralized financial services.

The entire DeFi economy is gradually becoming more user-friendly, safe, and accessible with the addition of these new financial primitives.

Because we are discussing the evolution of DeFi, it's important to note that the first generation of DeFi instruments addressed a wide range of financial services, including decentralized exchanges (DEXs), yield farming or liquidity provision, governance of decentralized autonomous organizations (DAOs), lending platforms, and payment gateways.

DeFi 2.0 is the second generation of DeFi protocols, and it tries to mitigate the friction points identified by addressing the issues that dominated the earlier manifestation.

The majority of new introduced technologies follow a similar adoption curve and progress through comparable phases of development. The first issue is the danger of embracing new technologies that comes with the development of every new disruption model.

A lot of issues have been identified with DeFi 1.0, as the concept of decentralization is still in early phases of experimentation.

Individual cryptocurrency volatility has repercussions in DeFi, since price movements might result in a temporary loss for Liquidity Providers (LP).

Because no single person is held responsible for security breaches on decentralized platforms, there is nothing you can do if the crypto assets are stolen or the smart contracts are exploited and hacked. Many of the users in this decentralized ecosystem put their assets into smart contracts without comprehending the possibility of their failing or the idiosyncratic risks associated.

Because crypto assets exist on multiple blockchains, less popular platforms suffer from low or inconsistent liquidity, and their related native digital assets are not always freely traded. To trade assets with limited liquidity, a user may need to use numerous platforms or suffer losses due to the slippage that is incurred.

Clearly we have gone a long way, as now, we have impermanent loss insurance, which can be used to compensate for a temporary loss. Smart contracts, likewise, can be covered by smart contract insurance, which can mitigate technical risks. Security audits conducted by open-source communities or insurance companies assist and guarantee that smart contracts do not have serious weaknesses or exploitable backdoors, while insurance reimburses participants who have lost assets.

Cross-chain bridges were introduced in this environment with a bang, as this new concept connects blockchains through layers of smart contracts and liquidity pools. It can also compensate for low liquidity by allowing users access to assets that are not native to the blockchain they have been using. If an asset does not have enough liquidity on one chain, they can trade it across adequate pools on other networks for the desired outcome.

DeFi 2.0 may mitigate, both DeFi 1.0 and traditional finance's risks and concerns, giving it a true decentralized financial sense unlike anything seen before in these digital markets.

Loans in DeFi 1.0, for example, are similar to traditional lending procedures, but on a peer-to-peer basis and with technical aspects which translate in collateralization of financial digital assets. Users borrow money from other users at a high interest rate, generally in exchange for a large quantity of collateral.

Within the DeFi 2.0, loans have been introduced to another property, which is that they can be reimbursed by themselves and this is considered an important improvement. To pay off the loan debt, self-repaying loans employ collateral for yield farming (liquidity provision that reinvests yield). The borrower's original collateral is returned after the whole sum has been repaid by what is basically a passive income stream, and they have effectively paid nothing out of the pocket.

Another key friction point, comes from the fact that each new technology implementation faces an accessibility obstacle.

While everyone now has access to the internet, only a few individuals had access to the computers required to use it at first. The adoption of financial digital assets and DeFi 1.0 ran into the same issue, as only the selected few had the skills and courage to experiment with the tools, interfaces and wallets provided.

For a decade, any crypto asset and bitcoin related business was a niche environment dominated by people who used a specific technical language that was not easily comprehended by everyone. Buzzwords like "Distributed Ledger Technology (DLT)", "Smart Contracts", "Decentralized Autonomous Organization (DAO)", "Sharding", "Non-Fungible Tokens (NFTs)", and the "Byzantine Generals Problem" might impress other crypto aficionados while making it absolutely boring to the general public who are not keen to deep dive in the ecosystem.

DeFi 1.0 is also suffering by the same self-inflicted condition, as the environment is a set of tools developed by developers for developers.

Niche platforms that need a high level of technical knowledge are frequent and not unusual. It was, and still is, a learning curve for all its participants, as excessively detailed wording makes it difficult to participate in an informal conversation.

To make matters worse, most individuals are uninformed of the existence of DeFi platforms and how to utilize them correctly, because DeFi marketing proposition has yet to evolve to the stage where it knows how to appeal to a non-technical and novice audience. Users from this unique sphere are understandably concerned about inconsistency and dangerous payouts percentages which are promoted.

By updating its story over time, the crypto environment figured out how to make itself accessible to the average person, and it's now a common issue well covered in tutorials, conferences and workshops.

DeFi 2.0 is based on this approach, and it aims to make DeFi accessible to everyone through two primary initiatives: education and interaction with established financial systems.

The most successful DeFi 2.0 initiatives are those that have streamlined front-end functionality and generated resources to teach new users about their platform and usability.

When it comes to DeFi, which is fundamentally decentralized, integration with centralized traditional banking networks is a contentious topic. This is not because of a utopian revolution, but because it just happen to create and evolve a system that is based on a trust concept performed by smart computing code, much more efficient and reliable than the existent infrastructure, which suffered from a rejection from the traditional finance environment as it projected itself like a high-tech contender.

On this note, the interconnectivity is available for the traditional financial institutions, as they can integrate DeFi 2.0 protocols into their platforms via APIs, DAOs, Smart Contracts and Oracles. This philosophy is at the core of what blockchain technology promotes, in terms of accessibility and inclusivity, therefore DeFi 2.0 can become easier and more approachable.

Users will be able to employ decentralized financial protocols from within centralized TradFi (Traditional Finance) applications and web interfaces once the integration is complete.

Usability suffers in the early phases of every new technology, much like accessibility. Throughout DeFi's history, cluttered and perplexing interfaces have been the norm, as it defined itself a collection of primitives designed by and for developers.

DeFi 2.0, on the other hand, introduces layer-2 and even layer-3 platforms that enable decentralized financial services like lending, yield farming, and asset management services, accessible to a large range of users who do not have the necessary skills or technical knowledge.

Figure 2. From DeFi 1.0 to DeFi 2.0

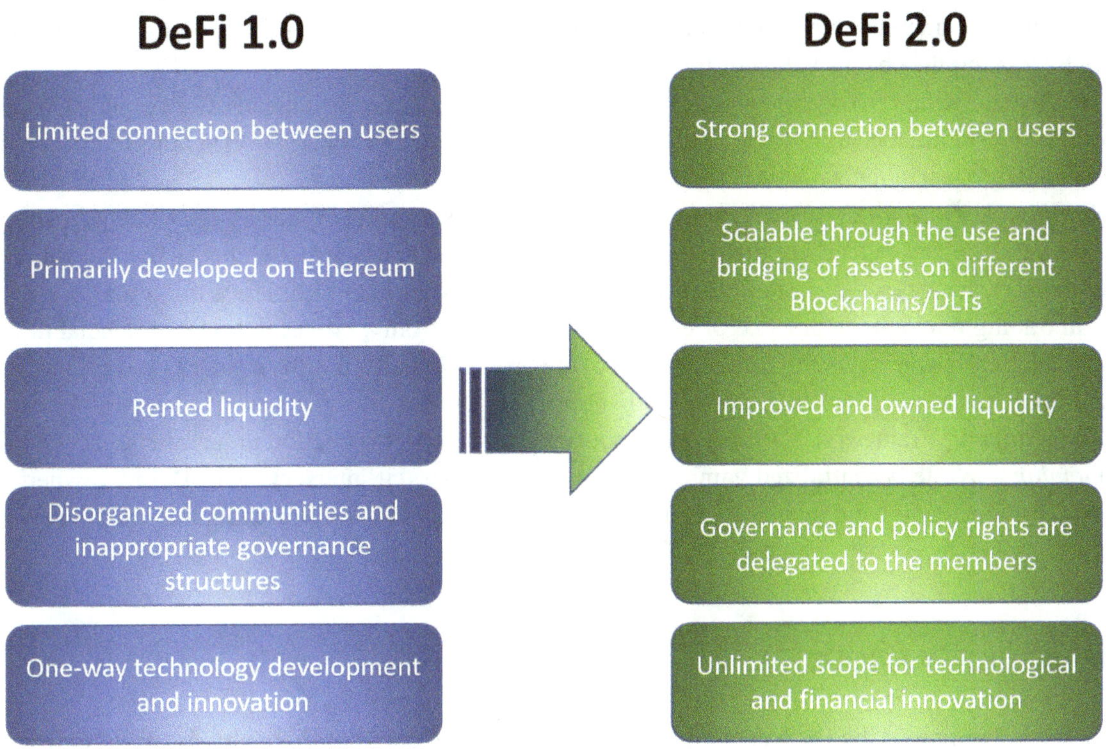

The second iteration corrects a flaw in DeFi 1.0 by guiding new users through the setup procedure quickly and easily. In this sense, the upgrade adds a degree of complexity to DeFi's use cases while simplifying the front-end procedure. This means you can do more with your money with less effort than before.

One of the main goals of major DeFi 2.0 systems is to circumvent the liquidity constraints that many on-chain transactions suffer.

If you want to benefit in this decentralized environment, seek for DeFi protocols that you can trust and that provide the characteristics and requirements you need. Most of the platforms, protocols and applications built in this ecosystem are often referred to as decentralized apps or dApps.

Some of the services and protocols evolving in this decentralized ecosystem are as follows:

Yield farming – Has become a catch-all word for any DeFi operation that can earn returns or yield, on a sort of model that is based on digital assets collateral placement, generally in the form of an Annual Percentage Yield (APY). Reinvesting returns is usually regarded as an important aspect of "farming" in each yield farming activity, while it is not necessarily required. For this reason, each investor should consider their objectives as well as their risk tolerance in any concept they want to engage.

Lending is a way for users to contribute to the liquidity required by providing loans in exchange for interest payments. Self-repaying loans provide both the borrower and the lender additional peace of mind.

Liquidity mining or *Liquidity Provision* (LP) – Represents another form to generate yield, and in this concept users provide crypto assets to liquidity pools for other users to trade against, in exchange for fees. In the case of major events, like the COVID-19 pandemic, if the markets flip, impermanent loss insurance can help limit losses.

Staking – Is a method of earning block rewards by becoming a validator for a proof-of-stake blockchain by locking the chain's validator token or native asset.

DAO participation – You can buy and sell these governance tokens, that can offer voting rights and other utilities within the structure of the DAO. The advantages of joining a DAO should be considered based on the organization's mission.

Trading via Decentralized Exchanges (DEXs) allow users to trade crypto assets without having to rely on a centralized third party that oversees each transaction. They usually charge lower costs than centralized exchanges and they started to provide more complex services like margin trading. DeFi crypto margin trading refers to the practice of using borrowed funds from a broker to trade a financial digital asset, which forms the collateral for the loan from the broker. Usually, a broker in DeFi it is represented by Autonomous Market Makers (AMM) (DeFi Prime, 2022).

The regulatory framework for this type of concepts vary from jurisdiction to jurisdiction.

Gaming – While decentralized gaming is a separate business, it intersects with DeFi 2.0 wherever models of monetization are involved. As the area grows, a concept worth watching for, are the play-to-earn and ownership models based on DeFi 2.0.

THE LIQUIDITY PROBLEM

Since the beginning of the DeFi economy, liquidity has been a cause of difficulty for many new DeFi enterprises. Tokens are used to bootstrap the whole ecosystem, allowing teams to align participant incentives, receive benefits from user fees, and become composable with the wider DeFi network. However, DeFi developers required access to a big pool of crypto assets in order to allocate its consumers with a reliable source of liquidity to trade their tokens on AMM (Autonomous Market Makers) protocols.

Third-party liquidity providers on AMM protocols provided a partial solution to this problem, allowing any independent individual with sufficient crypto assets to offer liquidity for a token pair. Rather of supplying liquidity themselves, teams might theoretically obtain adequate liquidity from others. End-users, on the other hand, have limited incentives to bootstrap liquidity for a new asset because doing so, would entail exposing themselves to the risk of temporary loss in exchange for minimal fee revenue through swaps. There was needed a compelling financial rationale for this risk balancing issue.

This resulted in a chicken-and-egg situation. The slippage caused by swaps discourages users from engaging in a DeFi protocol's environment if there is not enough liquidity. There is not enough fee volume created without consumers participating in token transactions to motivate third-party actors to pool their tokens and offer liquidity.

DeFi 2.0 refers to a few developing DeFi projects that aim to revolutionize the prevalent challenges related with liquidity provisioning and incentivization in the context of liquidity. They give alternatives and additions to the yield farming paradigm, allowing projects to obtain long-term financing.

This multi-faceted strategy aids in the realignment of incentives between on-chain protocols and third-party liquidity providers. Protocols are better positioned than a third-party liquidity source to be exposed to temporary loss. While third-party liquidity providers face the same opportunity costs as every other liquidity pool and yield farming protocol on the market, protocols have an extra incentive to keep liquidity because it helps secure low-slippage swaps for users transacting with their native token, lowering the cost of entry into their ecosystem.

Another subgroup of DeFi 2.0 protocols aims to create new financial instruments by building on top of past yield-generating processes and assets.

Alchemix (2022), a self-repaying loan platform with a "no liquidation" architecture, is a good representation of this. The protocol issues representative tokens that are backed by the collateralized asset 1:1. Users can, for example, borrow 50% of the amount as alDAI by posting the DAI stablecoin as collateral. The underlying collateral is then put into yield-generating processes in order for it to grow gradually.

Alchemix can provide a liquidation-free lending platform by combining representative tokens with yield-generating collateral, allowing users to spend and save at the same time as the collateral generates income.

Another DeFi 2.0 protocol, Abracadabra (2022), uses a similar technique, but with a framework that is similar to MakerDAO (2022). Users may deposit yield-bearing collateral and get the MIM stablecoin in exchange, allowing them to keep their exposure to the collateral while still gaining yield and unlocking liquidity.

DEXs and LP tokens are two of the most well-known lego models in the blockchain sector, allowing for large-scale token exchange and yield farming. Through rigorous overcollateralization methods and risk reduction, the first generation of decentralized stablecoins paved the way for newer stablecoin designs and decentralized lending platforms. None of these DeFi legos should be viewed in isolation; instead, they should be viewed as part of a larger ecosystem that supports, links, and amplifies other building blocks to open up new possibilities.

A new generation of DeFi legos is being built on top of its predecessor with DeFi 2.0, making the decentralized financial environment more efficient, user-friendly, and valuable for its members. The decentralized legos keep piling up, and with each new brick, the DeFi ecosystem gains new value and opportunities.

WEB 3.0

Financial digital assets blend the dynamics of investing in emerging markets, the technology sector and venture capital to provide exposure to the next wave of the internet. They enable investors and users to have direct ownership and control over internet economies.

Web3 has lately sprung into the popular awareness, with industry experts, from both the traditional IT sector and the blockchain environment, offering a variety of viewpoints on the internet's past and future. This is a direct consequence of the COVID-19 pandemic, as a lot of research and development was allocated towards a more inclusive internet.

The key characteristic of the first iteration of the internet, which was defined as Web1, was simple static websites. You could easily look at web pages and browse around, but the missing propriety in this scenario, was the interaction between websites and the users. As time went on, servers were upgraded, developers learned new skills, and eventually Web2 or Web2.0, emerged.

Web2 represents the second development stage of the world wide web or the internet. The difference between the simple static websites of Web1 and Web2, is the ability for the internet users to create their own content in the form of blogs, comments, reviews and social media. With the second iteration of the internet, websites became more dynamic and responsive, like the ability to do a Google search or to create directions for roadmaps. Web2 is the stage of internet where interoperability was achieved, where different websites and applications could connect and interact with each other. It's important to note that there is no formal date, roadmap or specific marker that delineated when Web1.0 morphed into Web2.0, and we believe the same will apply with the transition to Web3.0.

Web3.0 is the term used to refer to the third currently emerging developmental stage of the internet. The main difference between Web3 and the previous iterations is that the internet will operate on decentralized technologies and will be fueled by financial digital assets.

Figure 3. From Web1 to Web2 and Web3

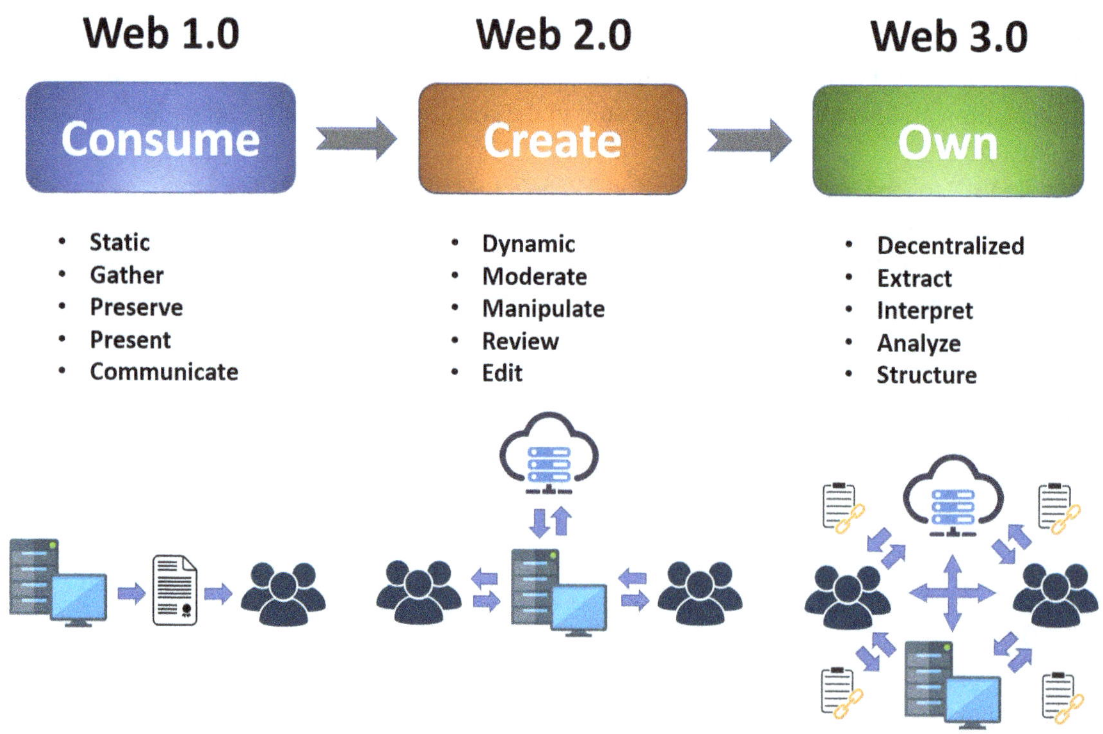

Another defining characteristic of the Web3.0 is the application of artificial intelligence, so we will see faster and more robust development, along with more inclusion of users. This version of the internet is believed to be the one who will detach itself from market cycles, as the algorithms of data will adapt. This theory is based on the fact that with Web3, everything will go through of stage of tokenization, which will give more power to the users, in the sense of how their data is used, transacted and monetized.

A new concept that will be representative for the Web3, will be in the form of new digital global economies. The underlying foundation of the current global economies use the global banking system to transact, as each of them have their own monetary, fiscal and taxation policies in place, which everyone needs to abide. With the decentralized, open, accessible and ever-advancing technology implications of Web3, we will start to see digital economies forming on the blockchain, that we can all interact with, regardless of the physical location, culture, religion, race or financial status of the users. In this scenario, people can choose which economies they would like to be a part of, and within these ecosystems, they will get to decide how the economic output is distributed.

Basically, with both, a shortage of physical and traditional assets, along with the limitations of accessing them, depending on where you live or if they are affordable, digital assets will establish themselves as the norm, which fortifies the prediction of the development of digital global economies.

As per its design and features, Web3 will help rebuild and transform the concept of class mobility. Socio-economic class mobility describes the ease with which a person can upgrade its status from a lower class into a higher class. Web3 technology is giving us a glimmer of hope that the way we distribute value, within future digital economies, can be more fair, inclusive and give everyone the opportunity to move from lower to higher classes.

HTTP pioneer Tim Berners-Lee used the phrase "Web 3.0" during the dotcom era to describe an integrated communication architecture in which internet data is machine-readable across many applications and systems; a notion he dubbed as the Semantic Web.

Ethereum Co-founder Gavin Wood recycled Berners Lee's statement in his 2014 blog post "DApps: What Web 3.0 Looks Like", referring to the power of blockchain technology to create a "fundamentally new paradigm for the interactions between parties" based on "a zero-trust interaction system."

Wood's approach is focused more on the consensus and cryptography with a decentralized vision for protocols and technology.

Web3's key propositions and protocols, as well as their implications for future trust models, are now the topic of intense discussion, with both today's IT giants and the vanguard of the blockchain sector continuing to deal with them.

It was not until the introduction of smart contracts that a genuinely decentralized internet paradigm emerged.

Web3, a redesigned web, was defined by Gavin Wood as a "Secure Social Operating System."

Simply said, Web3 is a Decentralized Internet concept that wants to develop an altogether new contracting system and revolutionize the way individuals and organizations reach agreements. Web3 combines the rich, interactive experience of Web 2.0 web applications like social media platforms with the decentralized architecture of Web 1.0, the first version of the internet, which was replete with user-hosted blogs and RSS feeds, to provide a digital ecosystem where data is user-owned and transactions are backed by cryptographic guarantees. Users may rely on deterministic software logic to implement agreements exactly as planned, rather than needing to trust brand-based paper commitments.

Web3's foundational elements are based on: Blockchain (architecture) and Financial Digital Assets (infrastructure).

An increasing stack of decentralized technologies, like blockchains, smart contracts, oracles, crypto wallets, and storage networks, are powering the Web3 architecture.

A blockchain is a highly secure and decentralized network that allows users to store data, trade currency, and record transaction activity in a shared ledger that is not centralized. Web3's backbone is comprised of blockchain networks, which provide safe execution environments for the production, distribution, and trading of financial digital assets, as well as the development of programmable smart contracts. Web3's settlement layer is comprised of blockchains and distributed ledgers.

Crypto assets are digital tokens that make use of blockchain networks' decentralized and tamper-proof ecosystems to enable extremely secure transactions. They are the native currencies of Web3 decentralized apps (dApps), and they may be used to pay for Web3 services as well as participate in Web3 governance.

Tokens granted to Web3 content providers are likewise units of value, but these units of value are digital, programmable, and have uses other than trade. A token in Web3 can be used to invest in a protocol, project, or blockchain. It could be useful for that project or protocol – for example, for paying for or insuring a service. It might also open the door to involvement in the protocol's or project's governance.

Smart contracts are tamper-proof blockchain programs that automate transactions using conditional software logic like "if x is true, then execute y." Decentralized apps, or dApps, are the cryptoeconomic protocols that bring Web3 to life and put it in the hands of consumers, thanks to programmable smart contracts.

Because they are not maintained by a single individual or organization, dApps vary from the Web 2.0 applications and the static HTML pages of the Web 1.0 era, because they are supported by the decentralized architecture of blockchain networks. These decentralized programs may be used to build complicated, automated systems like peer-to-peer financial services, data-driven insurance products, play-to-earn online games, and more.

Smart contracts must be able to access and interact with data and systems outside of blockchain networks in order to reach their full potential. Oracles are the entities that link blockchains to real-world data and current systems, as well as providing key infrastructure for the creation of a uniform, interoperable Web3 environment.

Oracles have risen to prominence as a broad layer of the Web3 stack, delivering off-chain data and services to support smart contract innovation, as well as cross-chain interoperability to provide smooth interaction across multiple on-chain settings.

Individuals may design and participate in financial protocols that give unparalleled access, security, and transparency thanks to the technology that make up Web3.

NFTs, GAMING AND THE METAVERSE

We must also consider the development of the Metaverse and ever-increasing valuations of certain NFTs marketplace, all during a time where COVID showed how fragile our physical supply chain processes can be, which greatly affected and continues to affect distribution of physical assets.

The Web3 ecosystem is now forming around NFTs, blockchain games, and the Metaverse. NFTs provide verified ownership of digital assets, allowing digital commodities to have the same level of functional uniqueness as physical things. With NFTs, one digital item may now be distinguished from another even though they appear identical, much like two copies of the same book can be distinguished by their distinct marks and signs of particular wear and tear.

Digital art, metaverse apps, and video games all stand to benefit greatly from this. Blockchains, which serve as the underlying settlement layer, NFT smart contracts, which enable verifiable ownership of digital items, and decentralized oracles, which provide key services such as verifiable randomness, smart contract automation, off-chain data, and more, are at the heart of this fundamental transformation.

The metaverse has reached the mainstream public consciousness, thanks to the recent proliferation of non-fungible tokens (NFTs) in the blockchain ecosystem and Facebook's head-turning rebranding to "Meta".

Though the notion may appear to be novel and cutting-edge, the metaverse has long been a part of popular culture. In his science fiction novel Snow Crash in 1992, Neal Stephenson invented the word to describe an all-encompassing 3D virtual environment that replicates, augments, enriches, and integrates with actual reality.

Simply described, the metaverse is a digital realm that lives in parallel to the real one. Because of its emergent nature, many various perspectives of how the metaverse will present themselves exist, and there are even disagreements over whether the metaverse exists today.

In its most idealized form, the metaverse is a virtual environment that provides parallel experiences to the actual world while also allowing for improved powers, similar to The Matrix's robot-manufactured universe. In more realistic depictions, metaverse visitors physically engage in a virtual environment, where they take the shape of virtual avatars, play games, and live pseudo-anonymous lives, using advanced motion-tracking technology and virtual reality headsets. The existence of user-owned digital commodities with historically real-world traits of scarcity, worth, and history is sometimes cited as proof that the metaverse has arrived. Some say that the metaverse exists in the human connections, sentiments, and experiences that make up our digital lives on social media, video games, and other platforms.

Despite these divergent perspectives, the metaverse's essential premise is evident. Telepresence, which is described as an immersive condition in which a person feels present in a virtual place, is critical for supporting metaverse experiences. The metaverse emerges from our ability to create virtual spaces that make us feel present – perhaps even tangible – in a digital environment, whether through a combination of immersive AR (Augmented Reality) and VR (Virtual Reality) technologies, user-owned digital goods powered by blockchains, or simply through an addictive Massively Multiplayer Online Role-Playing Game (MMORPG).

In a very real sense, the metaverse is all around us. Early trials in MMORPGs like Second Life and World of Warcraft introduced the notion of gamified social platforms, which engrossed players to the point that digital commodities, like as weaponry and apparel, carried enormous real-world value. Existing social networking services like Facebook, Instagram, and Twitter have enabled users to create pseudo-anonymous internet avatar identities and interactive virtual rooms where they may share news, discuss topics, and communicate with friends.

People are no strangers to total digital immersion through an external screen, whether it's in a Twitter Spaces hangout, a Zoom conversation with coworkers, or multiplayer gaming. Emerging technologies, on the other hand, have the potential to give the digital world additional relevance, permanency, and presence.

Our capacity to reproduce the human experience will play a big role in enabling the enhanced telepresence that will enable metaverse growth. Virtual reality (VR) headsets and movement-tracking technologies, with more accurate depictions that produce a feeling of total sensory immersion, can play a key part in this. SuperHot (2022), a Matrix-style game where time runs only as fast as the player, and VR Chat, a social network where participants construct 3D avatars, are two instances of early developments.

While Virtual Reality (VR) aspires to create an immersive virtual world separate from physical settings, Augmented Reality (AR) incorporates virtual displays into real-world environments. Microsoft's Hololens, an AR headset that tracks both what we are looking at and our body movements to superimpose virtual images and icons, allowing for compelling use cases that can help us navigate, identify objects, and interact with the physical world in a virtual manner, is one such example that exists right now.

Imagine a world where you can put on AR glasses to see which virtual shoes someone wore that day, or where you can play games on an entirely virtual screen that resides on your desk. AR glasses might provide information and enhance everyday experiences by updating in real time depending on sensors. AR's objective is to create a seamless merger of the virtual and actual worlds that will make everyday living more fascinating, useful, and authentic.

AR and VR are inspiring technologies that are helping to shape the experiences that will characterize the metaverse's future vision. However, interactive and immersive experiences are just part of the picture; the metaverse will need a value layer powered by decentralized infrastructure like blockchains to empower users as much as platform enablers in the metaverse's development. Finally, this will aid metaverse users in defining the metaverse's structure, providing the digital universe greater solidity through verified digital goods and allowing users to sense substance in a digital realm.

RESULTS

As we have analyzed some of the newest trends and concepts, that have as basis financial digital assets, let's visualize the frontier of "crossing the chasm" for these innovative technology implementations.

Figure 4. Crossing the Charm – Total Value Locked in DeFi
Source: DeFi Pulse (2022). TVL Chart taken from DeFi Pulse. Retrieved from www.defipulse.com

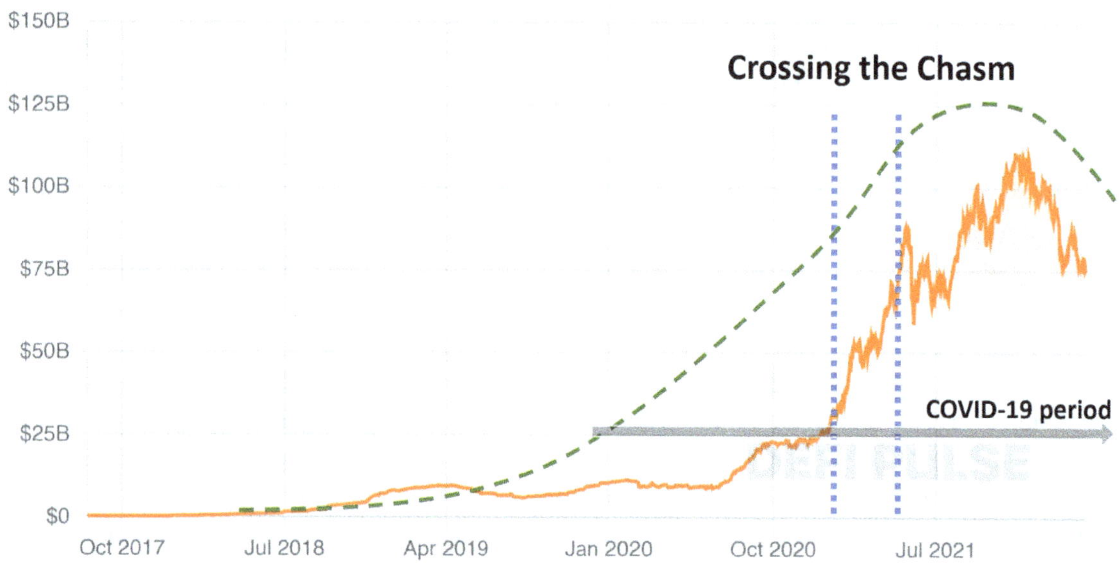

We can easily assess how the COVID-19 pandemic impacted the adoption of financial digital assets and how they rapidly evolved, enforcing the potential of blockchain technology along with the visionary concepts that we elaborated above.

Based on the data extracted from DeFi Pulse (2022), a top of $110 billion USD was reached for the Total Value Locked (TVL) of financial digital assets in DeFi projects. This represents the total balance of Ether (ETH) and ERC-20 tokens held by these smart contracts and TVL is calculated by taking these balances and multiplying them by their average price in USD.

To support our theory in the adoption and usability process for the financial digital assets, a comparison timeline provided by Grayscale Research department (2022), shows how the past trend for internet users for the 1995-1999 period, is very similar with the crypto users for the 2017- 2021 period.

Figure 5. Internet Users vs Crypto Users
Source: Grayscale – The postmodern Portfolio (2022)

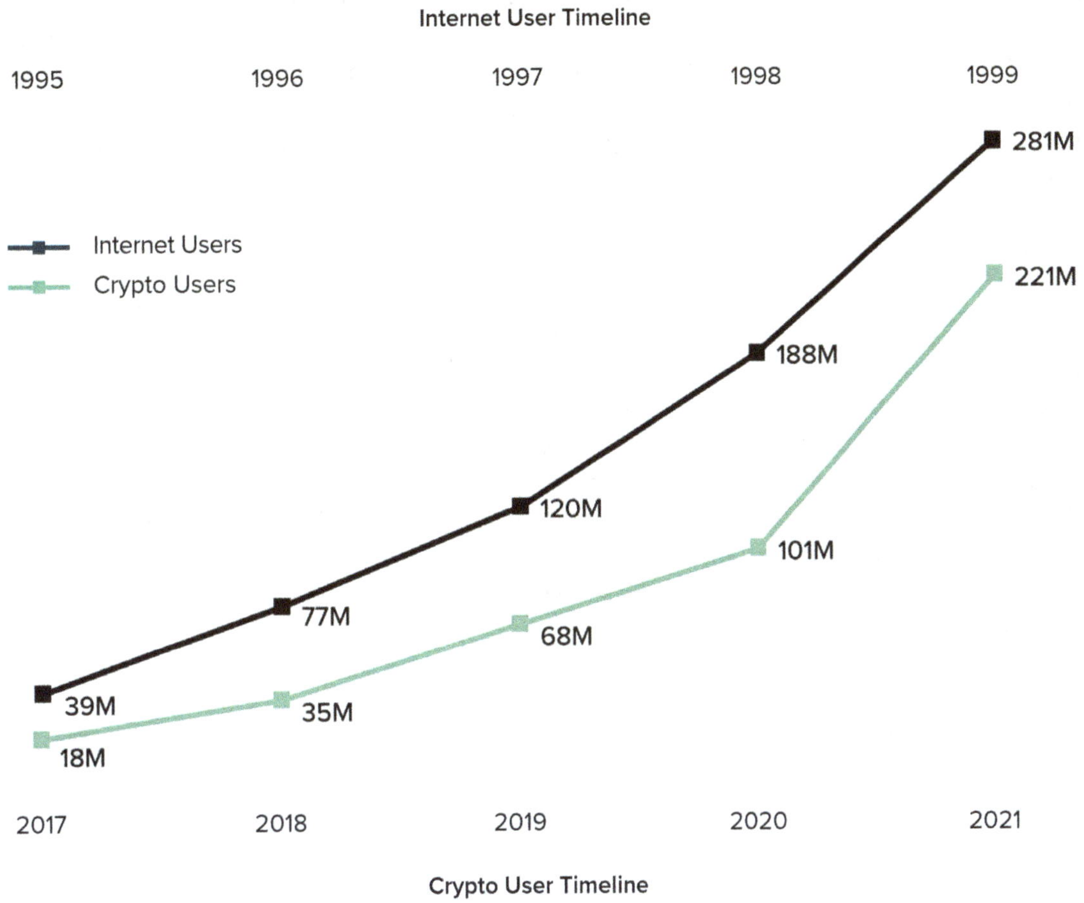

During the 90's period, everyone believed that the internet will change the world, and the hyped created around every project led to the well-known tech dot-com bubble. The current situation in the financial digital assets sector, is different, as most of the bubble effect hype is generated in a tight developers' environment. This being said, most of the dApps that need to reach the end-users have not been deployed to the stage of mass adoption, and are still in a process of acknowledgement and upgrade.

To extrapolate the frontier of financial digital assets, in a post-pandemic era, we are witnessing and capturing the very beginning of a value shift from the legacy technology sector.

CONCLUSION

We are living in early days of a massive paradigm shift. We are accelerating into a digitized and decentralized future. What we are experiencing in these times is the largest wealth creating event in the history of the world. Never, at any point in time, have we had the freedom of financial mobility that we have been engaging with blockchain and DeFi instruments.

The paradigm shift is encompassed by a new philosophy which empowers people with a technology for a new world, where users control and hold their own data as they get to run their own financial services. This is the power of decentralization and DeFi, and based on this, the new emerging concepts which are built on top of this novel infrastructure make sense. Decentralization matters, as all the new implementations and adaptations, have proved that we are still tied to the centralized banking system in a way that is unnecessary.

One major obstacle in the proliferation of this environment is that the crypto sector, which still captures all the attention, is largely unregulated. A perfect definition of what is happening now is basically a full-service shadow banking with nobody in charge. But the vision and mission are greater than just banking and financial services, as we are seeing a technological revolution unfold right between our eyes.

Lending, borrowing, stock exchanges, currency exchanges, derivatives and insurance models, all of these have their facsimiles in the digital realm, which had been created with code rather than with brick-and-mortar institutions. This is the landscape that we are thinking of, when we say the word DeFi, which can be easily translated in an equation of: (Technology * Crypto) + Finance = DeFi.

There are two premises of DeFi on which greater things can be built on: the first one is the idea of financial inclusion, where people who do not have access to financial services can be easily integrated (Popescu, 2022); and the second one addresses the people that already had access to financial services, which are switching from snail mail to email.

It is exciting and unknown what emergent properties will come from this architecture, when you can transact much faster and in a much more trustworthy way.

The decentralized financial system is creating a disruptive model based on technology, that is eventually going to replace, or upgrade, large sections of the financial and monetary system as we know it. The potential for it to really disrupt finance and the banking system, is still very much a vision of some crypto communities, but we can clearly assess its enormous potential applicability.

This space is moving with a compounding exponential speed for innovation, as it is driven by the openness of the community, both from a software perspective and also from a genuine desire to improve and add to innovations.

It seemed very natural to unify this set of emerging decentralized technologies, from blockchain, to crypto assets and protocols, and call them Web3.

With Web1, for the first time we had access to information; as with Web2, we saw a big consolidation of this information within centralized environments, like Facebook, Google and Amazon.

Web3 is a world where the users are creating value, but also capturing the value, which is something that was lost with Web2. In the concept of Web3, the people and the users have the power and are able to create much more value with the amalgamation of these different decentralized technologies.

Web3 is based on a reinvented internet experience powered by decentralized technologies. It is already changing how we interact online, from how we invest and exchange to how we play and express ourselves creatively. Zero-trust interactions and cryptographically-backed agreements are becoming increasingly popular among people and organizations throughout the world. While Web3 is still in its early stages, it has the potential to meet the internet's original objectives of inbuilt openness, dependability, and expediency.

Besides all the opportunities and possibilities that are emerging from the financial digital market frontier, we need to address also the risks associated with them. The crypto sector today is largely unregulated, as a regulatory framework is still in research phases for many governments around the world. The lack of regulatory clarity, puts more pressure on the end users who want to participate in this ecosystem, as they need to perform some very complicated due diligence tasks. It is hard to know if a particular DeFi app is going to work as promised, or whether it was created by reputable people, unless you go through this due diligence process. The obvious risk, as of now, is that if anything goes wrong within this space, there is no counterparty to rely upon and there is no recourse. It is important to acknowledge that by removing the prime brokers, the facilitators and intermediaries, we are also removing a safety buffer.

The real value of a regulatory framework is that it gives people confidence. This relays in the sense that regardless of the activity they want to participate in, there is always someone who will make sure that everyone does what is promised and there are no victims of fraud or manipulation in the process.

In order to go mainstream, clearly some centralized aspects need to be invited within this vision, till a new technological advancement will help mitigate some of the risks.

Similar to how web and internet technology brought democracy and democratization to informational access, we are seeing technologists, developers and entrepreneurs taking the path for democratization of global finance. This mission should not be discarded or seen from a negative perspective, just because it's a young technology with no proven records, it should we encouraged as it builds on a trust foundation with iterations of everything that is good from the actual financial system. Besides the financial element, this methodology should to be treated as a cornerstone for various sectors, as the applicability extends further than the financial markets.

It's a 0 to 1 innovation, with a disruptive mindset for greater good.

The approach for this chapter comes from an angle of understanding how the frontier of the financial digital assets evolved and laid the foundation for the perfect infrastructure in order for a novel concept as DeFi to thrive. Interactions between blockchains, protocols and dApps, defined the stages of DeFi as new bridges were consolidated. This new infrastructure started to grow dynamically and the exploration of usability for different business sectors was rapidly implemented. The pivoting point for such a framework was determined only when the main properties and features, such as interoperability, connectivity, efficiency, immutability and trust, were acknowledged. A major component in the dynamics of adoption came from the COVID-19 health crisis, which forced processes and procedures to be redefined, restructured and implemented in a secure and digital environment. Institutional investors have put a lot of focus on the development of this infrastructure and deep dived into the potential opportunities that this space had to offered. Even though everyone was engaged into the topics and the interest surrounding financial digital assets and DeFi, a missing regulatory framework for this decentralized space still keeps the most important players away. The vision of the future of internet and the way we interact with people and money has been assess and vetted on the basis of this decentralized environment. The Metaverse and Web3 will be clearly be constructed on the layers of blockchain and DeFi, having financial digital assets as fuel for the operations within. This vision is very important as we need to align the expectations on solid values and concepts.

While the pandemic's impacts have been negatively presented worldwide, from the perspective of financial digital assets we can state that it was a period of acknowledgement, redefinition and implementation of various visionary concepts. As with every world disrupting event, new opportunities have risen. COVID-19 pandemic has forced the humanity to a new level of digital adaptation, and it seems the financial digital assets frontier is establishing itself as the new norm.

REFERENCES

Abracadabra. (2022). *Abracadabra.money is a spell book.* Available at https://abracadabra.money

Al-Awadhi, A. M., Alsaifi, K., Al-Awadhi, A., & Alhammadi, S. (2020). Death and contagious infectious diseases: Impact of the COVID-19 virus on stock market returns. *Journal of Behavioral and Experimental Finance*, *27*, 1–5. doi:10.1016/j.jbef.2020.100326 PMID:32292707

Alchemix. (2022). *Alchemix – Self-repaying loans, spend and save at the same time*. Available at https://alchemix.fi/

Coinmarketcap. (2022). *Cryptocurrency prices, charts and market capitalization*. Retrieved from https://coinmarketcap.com/

DeFi Pulse. (2022). *Total Value Locked*. Retrieved from https://www.defipulse.com/

Goodell, J., & Goutte, S. (2021). Co-movement of COVID-19 and Bitcoin: Evidence from wavelet coherence analysis. *Finance Research Letters*, *38*, 1–6. doi:10.1016/j.frl.2020.101625

Grider, D., Maximo, M., & Zhao, M. (2022). Grayscale Research – The Postmodern Portfolio. *Crypto Allocation Thesis*. Retrieved from https://grayscale.com/

Huynh, T. L. D., Nasir, M. A., Vo, V. X., & Nguyen, T. T. (2020). Small things matter most: The spillover effects in the cryptocurrency market and gold as a silver bullet. *The North American Journal of Economics and Finance*, *54*, 101–277. doi:10.1016/j.najef.2020.101277

International Labour Organization. (2021). *ILO Monitor: COVID-19 and the World of Work. Seventh Edition*. ILO.

Iqbal, N., Fareed, Z., Wan, G., & Shahzad, F. (2021). Asymmetric nexus between COVID-19 outbreak in the world and cryptocurrency market. *International Review of Financial Analysis*, *73*, 101–613. doi:10.1016/j.irfa.2020.101613

Ji, Q., Zhang, D., Zhao, Y., (2020). *Searching for safe-haven assets during the COVID-19 pandemic*. doi:10.1016/j.irfa.2020.101526

JohnsonJ. (2020). *The Impact of COVID-19 on Bitcoin Trading Activity: A Preliminary Assessment*. doi:10.2139/ssrn.3583162

Kose, A., & Sugawara, N. (2021). *Understanding the Depth of the 2020 Global Recession in 5 Charts*. World Bank Blogs.

Le, T. H., Do, H. X., Nguyen, D. K., & Sensoy, A. (2021). COVID-19 pandemic and tail-dependency networks of financial assets. *Finance Research Letters*, *38*, 1–9. doi:10.1016/j.frl.2020.101800 PMID:33100926

MakerD. A. O. (2022). Available at https://makerdao.com/en/

Mariana, C. D., Ekaputra, I. A., & Husodo, Z. A. (2020). Are Bitcoin and Ethereum safe-havens for stocks during the COVID-19 pandemic? *Finance Research Letters*, 1–6. doi:10.1016/j.frl.2020.101798 PMID:33100925

Mokni, K., & Ajmi, A. N. (2021). Cryptocurrencies vs. US dollar: Evidence from causality in quantiles analysis. *Economic Analysis and Policy*, *69*, 238–252. doi:10.1016/j.eap.2020.12.011

Moore, G. A. (1991). *Crossing the chasm: Marketing and selling technology products to mainstream customers*. HarperBusiness.

Okorie, D. I., & Lin, B. (2021). Stock markets and the COVID-19 fractal contagion effects. *Finance Research Letters*, *38*, 1–8. doi:10.1016/j.frl.2020.101640 PMID:32837366

Popescu, A. D. (2020a). Alternative Investments confidence amid COVID-19 pandemic, *Scientific Bulletin - Economic Series*, *19*, 103-110. http://economic.upit.ro/RePEc/pdf/2020_3_13.pdf

Popescu, A. D. (2020b). Decentralized Finance (DeFi) – The Lego of Finance. *Social Sciences and Education Research Review*, *7*(1), 321-349. https://sserr.ro/wp-content/uploads/2020/07/SSERR_2020_7_1_321_349.pdf

Popescu, A. D. (2020c). Financial Technology (FinTech) as a Driver for Financial Digital Assets. *"Ovidius" University Annals, 20*(2), 1055-1059. https://stec.univ-ovidius.ro/html/anale/RO/wp-content/uploads/2021/03/Section%205/36.pdf

Popescu, A. D. (2020d). Transforming Capital Markets by means of Financial Digital Assets. *Revista de Ştiinţe Politice (Revue des Sciences Politiques)*, *68*, 108-119. https://cis01.ucv.ro/revistadestiintepolitice/files/numarul68_2020/11.pdf

Popescu, A. D. (2020e). Transitions and concepts within Decentralized Finance (Defi) Space, Research Terminals in the Social Sciences. *The Proceedings of CIL 2020: Ninth Edition of International Conference of Humanities and Social Sciences - Creativity, Imaginary, Language*, 40-61. https://www.cilconference.ro/wp-content/uploads/2020/09/cil_2020_research_terminals.pdf#page=40

Popescu, A. D. (2021a). Central Banks Digital Currency - Opportunities and Innovation. *"Ovidius" University Annals, 21*(1), 813-822. https://stec.univ-ovidius.ro/html/anale/RO/2021/Section%205/18.pdf

Popescu, A. D. (2021b). Non-Fungible Tokens (NFT) – Innovation beyond the craze, Revues et Méthodes sur le Management et le Commerce International. *Proceedings of Engineering & Technology – PET*, *66*, 26-30. http://ipco-co.com/PET_Journal/IBEM-Proceedings/IBEM%20PROCEEDINGS.pdf#page=31

Popescu, A. D. (2022). *Understanding FinTech and Decentralized Finance (DeFi) for Financial Inclusion. In FinTech Development for Financial Inclusiveness*. IGI Global.

Shehzad, K., Xiaoxing, L., & Kazouz, H. (2020). COVID-19's disasters are perilous than Global Financial Crisis: A rumor or fact? *Finance Research Letters*, *36*, 1–6. doi:10.1016/j.frl.2020.101669 PMID:32837374

Stephenson, N. (1992). *Snow crash*. Bantan Books Publisher.

SuperHot. (2022). *SuperHot Game – Time only moves when you do*. Available at https://superhotgame.com/

World Bank. (2021). Global Economy to Expand by 4% in 2021. In *Vaccine Deployment and Investment Key to Sustaining the Recovery*. Author.

Zhang, D., Hu, M., & Ji, Q. (2020). Financial markets under the global pandemic of COVID-19. *Finance Research Letters*, *36*, 101–528. doi:10.1016/j.frl.2020.101528 PMID:32837360

Chapter 11
Systematizing Body of Knowledge on Business Challenges and Strategizing Post COVID-19:
A Literature Review and Agenda for Research

John Mendy
University of Lincoln, UK

ABSTRACT

The COVID-19 crisis ushered in a multitude of challenges for SMEs. While these challenges are mainly financial and non-financial constraints, the ability to access markets and resilience capability building also exist for SMEs. The researcher conducted a review of 101 articles to analyze the pandemic's effects on SME businesses and found six thematic clusters: 1) operational costs, (2) resource losses, (3) business activity disruptions, (4) team performance disruptions, (5) individual and collective wellbeing disruptions, and (6) organizational survival threats. Based on these, the researcher identified six crucial emergent strategies to practically address the challenges around marketization and digitalization. These involve SME management, owners, and staff working more collaboratively to develop and adapt to new marketization regulations, policies, economic structuration, digital technologies, open innovation, and an overarching global network for local and international resilience. The implications of the results and an agenda for future research are presented and discussed.

INTRODUCTION

Although there has been a surge in research interest on SME businesses, the global COVID-19 health crisis has impacted on nations, organizations and individuals everywhere (Carnevale & Hatak, 2020).

DOI: 10.4018/978-1-7998-8856-7.ch011

Such a crisis has ushered in changes in the workplace, in personal lives, in our networking capabilities and organizations' abilities to address challenges such as performance, production and remote working (Gerald et al., 2020; McGeever et al., 2020; Nyanga & Zirima, 2020). SMEs have borne the brunt of the predominantly financial challenges (Brown, 2020; McGeever et al., 2020). For example, Le et al. (2020) highlighted how hundreds of SMEs had to deal with a surge in interest rate repayments to their loans which further strained their capability to obtain additional credit facilities and to be productive. The reporting of these and other challenges on SMEs have highlighted the nature and scale that the devasting economic effects have had on the health, emotional wellbeing and networking capabilities of smaller firms and their members (Nyanga & Zirima, 2020). The question that is yet to be fully addressed in relation to such an unprecedented worldwide crisis is 'What types of responses/strategies do organizations (such as SMEs), whose existence has been adversely challenged even before the pandemic, need to adopt to address the constraints' in a way that the emerging research has considered as dynamic (Ratnasingam et al. 2020)?' The initial sets of recommendations from emerging research suggest the adoption of digital technologies, using a mixture of smarter and more agile forms of working, inter-connected remote working mechanisms and hybrid working patterns to counter the negative impacts of the crisis on people's health and wellbeing (Kim et al., 2022; Trougakos et al., 2020). The claim has been made by Trougakos and their followers that such recommendations embody promises to alleviate the economic, operational and health pressures that national governments and managers of organizations have recently experienced whilst softening the blow on policy designers, implementers and employees' stress, anxiety and depression as a result of the pandemic (Mao et al., 2020). It is also claimed by Ratnasingam et al. (2020) that such changes in the workplace could have the additional benefits of resolving the acute performance, production and financial crises that have lately threatened the very existence of SMEs. The range of recommendations and claims regarding how beneficial they are, have still not addressed the crucial question whether these have the potential of addressing SMEs' endemic financial, operational and people-resourcing related challenges in a more networked framework other than the scientific one claimed by Hobday et al. (2020).

The researcher's aim in this chapter is to examine the literature and research on the scientific body of knowledge available on the challenges that the ongoing health crisis has incurred on SMEs, their impacts and how they have sought to address them. The researcher explores scholarly insights from a range of studies in this area to see how the findings/results can be systematized and synthesized to provide research-based evidence on how a health crisis of this magnitude could be managed in ways that are more coordinated and beneficial not only for organizations but also for governments and people globally. The researcher contributes to systematizing the available body of knowledge in this area such that the dynamic complexities of the pandemic are greatly understood that such knowledge facilitates better management by SMEs' leaders. Additionally, the action areas developed from the insights provide impetus and impact on the types of strategies and ideas needed to deal with the adversities similar to COVID-19.

The literature is replete with a range of challenges which threaten the existence of SME businesses as well as the types of short-to-medium term budgetary, digital technological and financial quick fixes that need to be undertaken (Brown, 2020; Indriastuti & Fuad, 2020; Fitriasari, 2020). What we still do not know is whether these quick solutions can stem the financial and digital woes that have become characteristic of SMEs' operations and existence even before the pandemic happened. To help resolve this gap in thinking and practice, the researcher examines this and other engrained challenges (such as resilience building capability) being faced by SMEs during COVID-19 and, more crucially provide a set of action areas for their longer-term/strategic resolution in a way that transcends the short-term nature of the current proposals. Therefore, the finance related challenges that have been emphasized by most scholarships on SMEs and COVID-19 (Le et al., 2020; Brown, 2020) have identified a crucial resource problem area but what they have missed is how a system-wide existential threat to SMEs' continuous operation in the strategic future could be addressed. To resolve this deficit in the literature and research, the researcher's study examines both the financial and non-financial challenges and uncovers six thematic clusters on how managers, employees, national governments and other SME partners have managed to deal with the crisis. These six clusters are presented as learning points to inform how businesses develop strategies to manage in pandemic situations and enhance their capability to network with other companies in similar problematic situations. It is this resilience building capability within a globally networked framework that forms the main theoretical and practical contribution of this chapter. In this light, the researcher contributes to a range of literature from People Management to health crisis resolution and Strategic Management by showing how the research evidence/findings provide these disciplines with new knowledge on the identification, coordination and management of pandemic-type existential threats and their application in the strategic resolution of not only organizational but also human existence.

Structurally, this chapter is organized by firstly identifying and critiquing the literature on SMEs' challenges before and during the pandemic. Secondly, the researcher scientifically justifies the procedure for the literature search/review and thirdly by presenting and analyzing the results of the author's review including the key SME challenges and responses from various areas. Fourthly, the researcher discusses the results within the context of how COVID-19 ought to be managed in global networks and finally highlights contributions to the theoretical domain of SME challenges and COVID-19. The implications of the findings and an agenda for future research are also discussed.

Literature Review

The literature on SMEs focuses on a range of internal and external barriers. These are broadly categorised into financial and non-financial (Bose, 2016). Whilst some scholars highlight operational and informational barriers (Alamo-Vera and Suarez-Ortega, 2005), others refer to them mainly as resources: financial and non-financial (Okpara, 2011). However, Mendy and Rahman (2019) distinguished these further into human or financial barriers to add to Blackburn's (2011) working capital shortage categorisation and Obeng et al.'s (2014) cultural deficit. Additionally, Leonidou (2000) found managerial-level barriers as the key obstacles to SMEs' human, and financial constraints. Therefore, although the nature and scale of SMEs' challenges have not been finalised, the trend in the literautre seems to suggest two key distinctions, namely financial and non-financial.

Financial Barriers

The plethora of barriers faced by SMEs even before the pandemic are financial in nature. Rutashobya and Jaensson (2004) earlier highlighted the common financial strain faced by smaller firms but also included marketing and risk management skills. It is noted how these constraints have contributed to SMEs' inability to compete with larger companies with greater working capital and increased management resources (Verburg et al., 2007). To try and address some of the financial barriers, the literature highlights how companies may try to solicit both formal and informal information on the dynamic relationships between sellers, buyers, products and markets (Chaplin & House, 2009) so as to increase their opportunities for success (Osarenkhoe, 2008).

The literature identifies a range of financial barriers including Movement Control Order (MCO) (Ratnasingam et al., 2020; Che Omar et al., 2020) and closures leading to the mass sacking of staff (Bartik et al., 2020b). These had devasting financial effects on SMEs (Hoorens et al., 2020) and management's abilities to address the magnitude of the financial constraints as a result of the crisis were undermined (Alves et al., 2020). Whilst some managers opted to adopt a crisis plan, others preferred a more variegated set of strategies in line with their resources and skills sets. However, these measures did not guarantee firm survival in the longer term as highlighted by Liguori and Pittz, 2020; Ba et al., 2020; Juergensen et al., 2020 and Lu et al., 2020), among others. Such a threat to strategic firm survival triggered other responses such as digital technology (Papadopoulos et al., 2020), performance agility mechanisms (Gerald et al., 2020) in efforts that were geared towards financial risk mitigation and agility (McGeever et al., 2020), technologically automated operations boosting firm production (Nyanga and Zirima, 2020) and policy change (Ba et al., 2020).

Non-Financial Barriers

However, it is also highlighted in the literature how the limited amount and quality of the information obtained could further hamper small companies' ability to locate which stakeholder they ought to contact (Kneller & Pisu, 2011) and this further limits their chances of sufficiently analysing what types of communication strategies may be required for the targeted investment markets (Lepak et al., 2007). When this happens, there is greater potential for organisational failure as the appropriate clients may be missed and the adoption of the relevant tax, regulatory and other financial compliance measures related to product exportation could also be missed (Kneller & Pisu, 2006).

The above highlights that top management teams' ability to react to a range of challenges therefore needs the timely identification and use of appropriate information to draw a wider range of comprehensive strategies in unsettled and difficult environments (Ferrier, 2001). The literature also highlights that when family members try to get involved in firm-level management, this tends to dampen the contributions of non-family members and the extent to which the latter may enhance their social and innovation capital (Sanchez-Famoso et al., 2017) or mental agility (Prime, Wade & Browne, 2020). Although the literature also highlights that management is a vital component in SMEs' ability to mitigate against the resource risks and in shaping board members' psychological capital (Mishra et al., 2019) and what types of actions and contributions may follow, it has also been pointed out by Dowell, Shackell and Stuart (2011) that using a combination of internal (board members) and external (shareholders) to control, monitor and evaluate organisational and board members' financial performance (Galbreath, 2011) for organisational survival (Gartenberg & Pierce, 2017) may, sometimes be detrimental in the enhancement of diversity, inclusion, members' ability to work cohesively in teams, share knowledge and be innovative (Bodla et al., 2018).

There also seems to be a growing focus on digital technologies (Papadopoulos et al., 2020; Winarsih et al., 2021) to increase smaller firms' survival chances as part of increasing attempts to boost not only the financial performance of such companies but also their operational and productivity viability. Desirable as such ouptputs may be, they do not guarantee the longer-term survival of such firms as it is still not clear how the wished-for survivability of such firms can be ensured in the face of continuous financial as well as non-financial challenges (Mendy, 2020; Rahman & Mendy, 2018). However, it is not known what the nature of such dynamism should entail.

The advent of COVID-19 exacerbated the financial challenges faced by SMEs and furtehr dampened management's level of preparedness to address the already negative financial impacts faced by such companies. The literature also highlights how the health crisis has brought about a blurring of the work and home demarcations (Fisher et al., 2020), thereby adding to the financial burdens already felt. Vaziri, Casper, Wayne and Matthews (2020) found that as employees were transitioning from office to home working, this change negatively affected their team-working choices and their ability to emotionally cope with their immediate work supervisors and other colleagues. These combined barriers have threatened smaller firms' ability to remain financially afloat and to contribute economically (Schleifer, 2004). Such incapability has negatively impacted on members' ability to set clearly defined and achievable goals, to learn and perform as a cohesive team unit (Huang et al., 2019). Additionally, members' ability to coordinate teamworking activities have constrained the financial capability necessary to keep such firms viable (Wildman, Nguyen, Duong & Warren, 2021). These pre-pandemic and during-pandemic challenges have brought about further disruptions to members' ability to perform routine, daily tasks (Chong, Huang & Chang, 2020), to their mental and psychological wellbeing (Trougakos et al., 2020) and highlighted the need for something new.

METHODOLOGY

The aim of the chapter is to provide a thematic mapping of the major challenges faced by SME businesses during the COVID-19 health crisis in order to systematize the knowledge for small and medium sized business managers, entrepreneurs and other stakeholders. Doing so will facilitate their resource capability to address the constraints faced and be better prepared for the strategic future. As part of the procedure to achieve this, the researcher started by identifying keywords for the search of the range of cross-disciplinary literature on SME business challenges within the COVID-19 health crisis to help develop knowledge on problems encountered financially, digitally, operationally, emotionally, strategically and so on. Relevant challenges that occurred prior to the pandemic have also been inlcuded in the literaure, the result and their analysis. The researcher searched SCOPUS, Web of Science, and Google Scholar for relevant papers/materials by using keywords including SMEs, challenges, performance, operations, crisis, work, emotional, wellbeing and welfare. These helped in identifying major/seminal works in this field's literature review. Although the WHO (the worldwide body responsible for global health issues such as COVID-19 and novel coronavirus diseases such as SARs) has recommended the timeliness of making such information available to organizational policy designers and implementers to help them address the negative impacts of the pandemic on work and working lives, they missed the theoretical insights of such systematic reviews. The researcher's work is also in line with Tricco et al.'s theorisation as well as the WHO's (2017) guidelines. Additionally, work in this area had previously fallen short of identifying the strategic sets of actions needed to fill the gap concerning what SMEs need to do in a post-pandemic world of work and business activities. The methodical search of theoretical and research articles on SMEs' challenges and responses during the pandemic also follows the recommendations of quick systematic reviews by Tranfield et al. (2003) and Davies (2000) and most recently by Sinkovics (2016) and Castro and Zermeño, (2020). Such a methodology has been selected for its credibility in identifying and rigorously presenting and analyzing the body of knowledge available in the Social Sci ences, including health and crisis management issues (Leseure et al., 2004). As discussed in the literaure review, the nature of the challenges being faced by SMEs prior to and during the pandemic is ongoing. Such incompleteness has warranted spreading the search beyond business, entrepreneurship and health issues to see what other possibilities lie in both refereed and non-refereed publication outlets. However, the bulk of the researcher's search focused on the former rather than the latter.

Initially the researcher's search retrieved 126 articles. The researcher then conducted filtering of unwanted materials in line with the approach used by Weißer et al. (2020) to ascertain their relevance to SMEs and COVID-19 business challenges. This procedure helped in the minimization of including peer reviewed articles from the sampled theoretical papers and this resulted in a total number of 101 articles. 25 articles were therefore not included in the final list of predominantly English peer reviewd articles for this chapter. The researcher then solicited assistance from four colleague researchers within the same discipline to look at the suitability of those articles that had been filtered and not included. Each of them confirmed their unsuitability in terms of lack of focus, irrelevance to SMEs and the health crisis and required strategies post-pandemic. It is interesting to note that articles that focused on literature reviews are minimal and this provided further impetus to see how this dearth in publications in as important an area as SMEs' challenges and the health crisis can be addressed. This lag provided the opportunity to contribute theoretically by adopting this methodology.

In line with previous theoretically informed scholarship, the researcher looked at the frequency of keywords from the filtered selection of articles (keywords analysis) as well as how similar these articles are in terms of SMEs' challenging themes, topics, issues and so on (content analysis) in the qualitative research tradition (Finfgeld-Connett, 2014; Gaur & Kumar, 2018). Whilst Dabic et al. (2015) claim that the frequency of items being cited together highlights the preponderance of their relatedness and Caputo et al., (2019) also assert that co-citation and citation analysis enhance a specific topic's representation, the extent to which future representation and strategy adoption can help resolve the theoretical and practical challenges faced within a pandemic have eluded these brilliant scholars thus far. This chapter attempts to address such obvious crucial omissions. As part of this process, the thematic results of the researcher's literature search are presented and analyzed in the next section. Six major thematic categories/challenges constitute this chapter's results.

Results of Literature Review: SME Challenges During COVID-19

The six challenges faced by SME businesses are discussed below as a basis for their strategic management and resolution propositions when pandemics happen in future. Whilst three of the results (operational costs, resource losses and business activity disruptions) highlighted SMEs' financial challenges, team performance disruptions showed both financial and non-financial type challenges. The fifth and sixth results (individual and collective wellbeing disruptions and organizational survival threats) highlighted fundamental non-financial challenges threatening organizations' existence in the longer term.

Operational Costs

The first category focused on the operational costs incurred by smaller firms during COVID-19 (Hoorens et al., 2020). It also showed the extent of SME managements' level of preparedness in their coping mechanisms within a crisis. This category showed that the Movement Control Order (MCO) that were promulgated by the Malaysian government to try and deal with the unforeseen economic drain caused by the pandemic (Ratnasingam et al., 2020) served as a short-term measure to keep business afloat (Che et al., 2020). However, short-term strategies have been criticized by Alves et al. (2020) as they do not account for a longer-term vision of how to manage within a crisis-situation. Such short-termism also has the possibility of further constraining bouncing back in the post-pandemic phase. Additionally, governments' focus on survival mode strategies has also negated possibilities of an examination and potential adoption of more differentiated modes of economic and human related strategies that took cognizance of firm resources, size, contextual variables and so on. Although the literature and research highlight that there are potential benefits of differentiated strategies to deal with the problem of operational costs (Le et al., 2020; Liguori et al., 2020; Lu et al., 2020; Juergensen et al, 2020), we do not know the nature of these strategies and what they could look like within a post-pandemic phase of SMEs' operational capability.

Additional cost-related challenges reported for SMEs include rent, utility bills, mortgage repayments and insurance (Neu et al., 2020). These costs compounded smaller firms' ability to mitigate their operational non-viability as they faced lockdown measures. These often resulted in decreased footfalls adding to already incurred costs. Other disadvantages faced included the inability to access materials needed in service and product delivery in the Sichuan Province of China. This problem was compounded with inadequate demand for goods and services and shortage of labor (Lu et al., 2020). These costs were more keenly felt by smaller scaled entrepreneurs with an already insufficient set of human, material and financial resources (McGeever et al., 2020; Hoorens et al., 2020). As a result of the additional pressures on such businesses and owners, employees were left without support whilst people's employment was terminated to help control costs. Again, these measures were taken as part of a short-term strategy to counter the negative financial impacts that the crisis was having on firms' liquidity.

SMEs' inability to access cash meant a dip in their financial performance and this worsened in Zimbabwe where mass layoffs were reported (Nyanga & Zirima, 2020). Similar incidents were surfaced in Malaysia (Ratnasingam et al., 2020). Disruptions caused within the wider financial and supply chain flows/pipelines inevitably led to deeper financial woes, leading to cries for cash bailouts from companies across the world. Requests for such much-needed assistance were met (or unmet) with varying degrees during lockdown. It is also reported elsewhere that SMEs in Macau faced similar cash flow problems as a result of suffering from the negativities of lockdown. These caused operational viability costs despite some SME firms' heroic entrepreneurial efforts to continue to invest (Brown et al., 2020). In Nigeria and Vietnam, for examples, Le et al. (2020) and Musa and Aifuwa (2020) showed how Nigerian SMEs can support the government's health-based sensitization, sanitization adherence and isolation measures despite their inadequate digital technologies. Not all SMEs were reported to have sufficient digital resources to facilitate working from home thereby highlighting the scale of the operational problem. Other short-term measures developed in Vietnam included direct, short-term government intervention in measures such as insurance, tax support and direct capital injection into SMEs. However, these combined measures have been criticized not only for their short-termism but also for their lack of post-pandemic considerations (Gerald et al., 2020). Counter proposals including the use of work-automation (Ratnasingam et al., 2020) via digitalization (Indriasuti & Fuad, 2020) to deal with the mainly operational financial blow from the crisis have only gone as far as to highlight short-term measures without serious attempts at resolving the longer-term viability of already vulnerable small firms (Hadi, 2020).

Resource Losses

The second category highlighted what happened when SMEs could not bear the impacts of the financial and operational costs (McGeever et al., 2020). This led to massive laying off of staff which brought SMEs' survivability to question (Bartik et al., 2020). Such widespread resource losses were compounded by lack of or, at best, inadequate government bailouts in the short-term especially in areas with weaker economies (Hadi et al., 2020; Indriasuti & Fuad, 2020; Brulhart et al., 2020; Musa & Aifuwa, 2020). Again, when digitalization was proposed to forestall the potential demise of such companies, the anticipated sustainability of the firms could not be maintained partly because those firms were also dealing with other people-resource related challenges (Papadopoulos et al., 2020).

Losing staff in huge numbers is one thing that shows the inability of SMEs to cope financially. Having management who bully employees to work additionally to cover their resource losses is another bigger problem for such firms to deal with the financial impact of the crisis. It is also reported in the literature and research that the default operational option to work from home and online has led to evidence of more peer-to-peer as well as management-to-employee online bullying. Such behaviour was worsened by the possibility of staff assuming a fake identity in order to perpetuate the unforeseen (digital) nature of such bullying (Bartlett et al., 2021). Such an environment increased staff's anxiety to keep their jobs, their work-related stress and depression (Debowska et al., 2020). Resource losses have also been shown in other, more nuanced forms such as loss of decent work ethic, passion for innovative ideas and workplace humor among staff and management. Added to such fundamental losses, were the loss of peer-to-peer and management-to-staff communication and an amenable work environment for all. The complexity of managing such tangible and intangigle losses impacted negatively on staff's willingness to show good citizenship behaviors and for organizaitons to demonstrate what it takes to manage in crisis (De Clercq & Belausteguigoitia, 2020). The inability of small firms to access the needed resources resulted in severe stress and mental health caseloads and overall workplace disengagement (Zhai & Du, 2020). Positive employee behavior scholars, notable amongst whom are Bouckenooghe et al. (2014), have posited the need to develop psychological and organizational positivity as coping mechanisms during a crisis. However, they did not elucidate on how such an initiative could be extended to SMEs' resource losses post-pandemic/crisis. This chapter does that in the sets of actions highlighted after the pandemic-stage challenges.

At best, what we currently have in emerging research on resource losses/financial fragility and volatility are proposals such as the development of entrepreneurial finance, be it in the UK, in America or other parts of the world (Brown, 2020; Bartik et al. 2020; Juergensen et al., 2020). Again, these short-term measures have been proposed with the assumption that companies have the requisite digitalization capability to implement them (Papadopoulos, 2020; Fitriasari, 2020; Indriasuti & Fuad 2020). The lack of such digitalization acquisition and know-how in less technologically inclined settings highlight the strategic hole that such a recommendation entails. We do not also know whether such a recommendation only helps in addressing the financial challenge and therefore may be termed as short-term or whether it could also be beneficial to non-financial/people management aspects (Alves et al., 2020).

Business Activity Disruptions

To highlight the nature of disruptions to SME businesses, Hadi et al., (2020) showed how a firm's inability to acquire primary resources has led to operational dysfunction. The ruthlessness in this lack of flow also negatively affected how a firm may add value to its business activities and to its ability to attract and keep customers. These disruptions led these scholars to propose revitalization strategies in their effort to help Indonesian SMEs in the Tourism sector. Although they also include a raft of health and policy mechanisms, similar to Musa and Aifuwa (2020) in Nigeria, both sets of scholars did not elucidate on how such measures will work in the longer-term post-crisis period.

In this third category of results, Brulhart et al. (2020) examined how SMEs sought to increase their resilience to such disruptive environments caused by the crisis through anticipation and measured responses. Fitriasari (2020) acknowledged environmenatl turbulence as the primary and, potentially bigger cause for such business disruptions. Therefore, he proposed the need for a more joined-up set of responses to complement the financial, short-term measures proposed earlier. Hadi (2020) proposed the combination of both FinTech as well as an Islamic tax (Zakat) model that would deliver loans on a charitable basis to ease the financial burden on staff whilst securing the business survival of such SMEs. Kottika et al. (2020) and Tsilika et al., (2020) proposed a mix of activities ranging from business owners and employees' competency amalgamation to see how firms can best utilize certain personality traits to foster organizational survival and productivity. On the other hand, Morgan et al. (2020) have pointed out the benefit for SMEs to choose between arbitrage and innovative activities as measures/mechanisms to (re)shape/correct the structured pathways of their business operations because of the exogenous schocks caused by COVID-19. However, the extent to which these measures have been carried out in a post-crisis period are yet to be ascertained and their benefit fully accounted for.

Team Performance Disruptions

Wildman et al. (2021) examined how the crisis brought about disruptions in the way teams work because of impositions of social distancing measures. Teamwork disruptions were accounted in the forms of changes to tasks, roles and communication and reporting channels. Additional disruptions included the ability to achieve outcomes, to progress and be effective as a unit. These disruptions highlight the dysfunctionality to which teams have been rendered and their inability to be organizationally effective. Such an organizational-level dysfunctionality undermines individuals and groups and intentions they may have had in helping firms achieve financial, productivity targets and in goals-setting. Whilst Troth et al., (2012) showed the value of emotional intelligence in facilitating members' capability to be part of teams and to socially interact successfully, the absence of psychological empowerment has led to staff in the tourism sector being ostracized. This behavior impacted detrimentally on team members' capability to be customer friendly (Huertas-Valdivia et al., 2019). Tuikka, (2019) found that employees who had negative relationship with colleagues were more likely to be unsatisfied, to nurture turnover intentions and be less committed to their organizations and teams. Although the literature and research also showed benefits for members to be steered towards a specific goal orientation such as outcomes, team learning and performance (Theis & Bipp, 2019), Huang et al., (2020) showed how the psychological disruptions could further hamper members' ability to contribute effectively to teamwork. These varying impacts at the personal and group level highlighted how dysfunctional teams had become during the pandemic and demonstrate additional insights of the importance of maintaining effective teams for overall SMEs' performance especially during a crisis.

Individual and Collective Wellbeing Disruptions

Gubler et al. (2020) used results from 466 Swiss research participants to show the negative wellbeing and social interactive effects that the crisis has had on both introverts and extroverts. On the other hand, Kim et al. (2022) showed how South Koreans develop coping strategies to maintain their overall wellbeing. Etheridge and Spantig (2020) showed how conspicuous differences in care and family responsibilities accounted for gender-pay gaps and these affected women's social, financial and health wellbeing. Mohring et al. (2020) demonstrated how lockdown has impacted on the ability of Germans to engage satisfactorily with work and such dissatisfaction impacted their family wellbeing commitments. Alradhawi et al. (2020) highlighted how staff in lowly paid jobs led to employment precarity, mental disruptions, domestic and substance abuse, self-harm and even suicide. This was as a result of employment loss or the fear of loss of employment. Although Carnevale and Hatak, (2020) and Huebner (2020) recommended employee and overall family adaptation as coping/wellbeing, this fifth category highlights disruptions to individual staff and the general worldwide population's welfare. Other scholarships have recommended telework as a way out of such wellbeing disruptions (Chong et al., 2020) but the overwhelming evidence suggests that despite individuals and teams' efforts to maintain social connectivity via digitalized technological inventions (Nyanga & Zirima, 2020), the crisis has had an overall negative impact on lives, livelihood and wellbeing. The researcher's analysis therefore suggests that people have borne the brunt of the crisis and employee non-welfare, stress and emotional exhaustion have been the outcomes.

Organizational Survival Threats

Using 4,807 SMEs in China, Lu et al. (2020) showed SMEs' incompetence in the resumption of normal work. This sixth and final category highlighted the total negative impacts of the crisis on small firms' ability to survive under crisis. Khalil et al. (2020) and Kucketz et al. (2020) extended such an existential threat to the significant pressures exerted by foreign institutional ownership on not only national but also global economies especially during the crisis period. Angela et al. (2020) made linkages between national governance failures as socio-economic threats leading to firms' inability to maintain their corporate social and overall governance responsibilities. Such threats also impacted negatively on the decision-making capability of corporate boards across the globe. At a more disruptive and worrying level, Abbasi et al. (2020) highlighted that the crisis could be perceived as the 'politicization' and 'corruption' of science in government's entanglement with decision-making processes involving medical procurement contracts, when and when not to impose lockdown measures and the maladministration involved in spending billions of taxpayers' money badly needed by small businesses. Such forms of corporate and state incompetence have led other scholars to show how such lack of due diligence by corporations and nations to be socially responsible and to steer businesses out of a crisis (Knauer, 2021; Montero & Le Blanc, 2020). Although these actions have shown incompetence to manage survival threats at organizational and national levels, it is therefore pertinent to discuss the implications at a network framework level given the interconnectedness of the challenges and the need for an interlinked set of resolution strategies.

DISCUSSIONS

The researcher discusses the findings in this section within the framework of a network of key emerging issues such as marketization regulation, policy implementation and evaluation, economic structuration (including employment and supply chain restructuring), digitalization, global network collaboration and open innovation. Firstly, these are key aspects in the effective management of SME challenges/disruptions within a post-pandemic situation. Secondly, as the researcher's aim remains a systematization of the body of knowledge on SME business challenges and how to respond to the health pandemic not only during but also post-COVID-19, the researcher believes that this twin-pronged approach will help Management, HRM and health experts/professionals and Organizational Behaviour specialists to draw lessons and enact appropriate actions that could address the disruptive challenges faced by SMEs during a crisis. The researcher's review of the findings are therefore divided into six themes that serve as contributions to the literature and practical policies for implementation. The researcher discusses how these findings provide insights into how to manage organizational disruptions both within and post-crisis period for SME owners, managers and other management professionals and to do so in an internationally networked capacity than has previously or currently been formulated.

Theoretical Contributions

Marketization Regulation

The health crisis has transformed how workplaces are organized and, indeed, how work is done. Transformations include, for example, working from home, an increase in remote and part-time working, greater use of zoom facilities to enhance such practices. All these work transformations also imply a change to how work is regulated and conducted. Employees in SMEs and their owners had to encounter a range of disruptions to their traditional, normal lives of working from nine to five and in fixed office abodes. Increasingly, staff and owners of small businesses had to suddenly transform their working practices to align with the health adherence limitations that the crisis had presented to their daily lives and the execution of organizational and personal responsibilities. There is a research and theoretical deficit reporting the responses of SME owners, managers and employees to the complex combination of working arrangements presented by the public health crisis. Although Sostero et al. (2020) noted an increase in teleworking staff especially during the pandemic, they also highlighted how an increase of between 33 and 44% of teleworking staff were now accountable even among low-paid and blue-collar workers despite such a prevalence being previously restricted to only white and highly paid workers within the EU in pre-pandemic times. Such a shift has warranted new marketization regulations to curb potential excesses and abuses by both employees and employers in SMEs in larger companies from the European Working Time Directives, including the UK's statutory instruments on The Working Time (Amendment) Regulations 2020. Additionally, Chong et al., (2020) highlighted new regulations to curb people's working patterns and behaviors especially for those staff who were confined to remote and home working. Aspen (2021) highlighted how government and non-government agencies should draft new marketization regulations guaranteeing the rights and responsibilities of all interacting parties within the SME working relationship (such as staff, owners and business partners) to restrain excessive job-demands and bullying behaviors emerging Working from Home (WfH) and teleworking arrangements. Restubog et al. (2020) pointed to the need for staff to develop some emotional regulation as a mechanism of addressing/responding to work insecurity, personal and family wellbeing and psychological challenges. These psychological, emotional and physical 'stressors' emerging from lockdown have further depleted SMEs' meagre resources and signaled an increasing need for a more properly regulated and affective working environment to deal with a crisis of such magnitude.

Despite these emerging claims for greater regulation, the already identified resource constraints and losses faced by these smaller firms render the adoption of and compliance with the proposed regulatory guidelines problematic. Therefore, if an introduction of marketization regulation is to be beneficial to these resource-challenged firms, there needs to be greater collaboration between different networked agencies ranging from staff councils, business owners' fora, government regulatory bodies and law enforcement agencies. Such a networked collaboration will potentially alleviate the legal implementation costs that would have been solely borne by the resource-deprived smaller firms. Additionally, the administration of the new legal frameworks will also lighten both the overt overhead expenditures and the hidden costs involved in staffing, staff wellbeing and effecting the legal changes. An example of how such a networked collaborative effort in legal introduction could be done has been provided by Le et al. (2020) in Vietnam. However, they failed to identify how their legal and policy-based model could be designed, implemented and evaluated using a network framework involving the entire SME stakeholder community – that is, staff, owners, business partners, government and civil society. Doing so will facilitate SMEs' resistance against future health and other types of exogenous environmental shocks and facilitate their continuous development and existence. An additional aspect of the new marketization regulations should also involve a guarantee of SMEs' loan repayments, staff overheads and utilities payments. This marketization regulation buffer will also provide a resource buffer in times of financial and public health crisis.

Policy Design, Implementation and Evaluation

Linked to marketization regulation is the introduction of policies to limit and, if possible, eradicate the challenges faced by SME businesses post-pandemic. Although Moffit and Badger (2020) claimed that a federal-state partnership is needed to develop competence of governors and health officers to craft and implement local policies in stemming the ravages of the crisis on firms, little do we know about how the actual implementation will be conducted and what the yardstick for measuring success will be. Although Mourad et al. (2020) recommended that governements and other policy bodies need to distinguish the social networks that may be responsible for causing unnecessary information distortion (infodemic), psychological and economic disruptions on individuals, civic society and business organizations, they did not specify the benefits of the social networks and how they could be developed. However, Antonakis (2020) specified how organizational and national-level leadership are necessary in addressing the health, economic and psychological mayhem. As such, the development of leadership competence, strategic foresight and judicious resource identification and allocation were highlighted as crucial aspects in the new business and social policy making framework to for SMEs. Abrams et al. (2020) claimed that inter and cross-group efforts between SME firms and other businesses are critical in (re)shaping staff's and management's perceptions of the challenges they jointly face. However, helping to mould and manage the resolution of a new national, international and global strategy to address the intergroup fractures, inter-state competition, short-termism and political divisions have been identified without being resolved. Despite claims that world leaders should nurture transformational leadership qualities and work collaboratively in alleviating overall citizens' stress, anxiety, depression and psychological trauma (Kloutsiniotis et al., 2022; McCombs & Williams, 2021) negligible efforts have been shown on their implementation. Likewise, an emerging claim that not only organizational but also national leaders could help in positively reshaping and avoiding business owners and staff's massive turnover, suicidal instincts and psychological disengagement has also missed how such transformational characteristics could facilitate SME members' commitment and engagement. Nonetheless, these new transformational steps are vital in thc formulation, successful implementation and evaluation of new policies that may help in curtailng future health crises and facilitating buy-in from SME member communities. However, the realisation of these new transformational leadership proposals and the impacts they could have on policy guideline shifts have not been fully considered in the context of SMEs' financial and non-financial disruptions amidst a global crisis. Although other practical measures such as debt reductions, loan repayment guarantees and even credit extensions have been suggested as part of a raft of financial incentives, the researcher highlights how additional new measures are needed in the next sections of this chapter.

Economic Structuration

One of the most reported challenges faced by SMEs during the crisis has undoubtedly been on economic disruptions threatening their existence. Global economies have suffered (Kucketz et al., 2020). The abilities of organizational managers, board members and managers have also been adversely impacted. Likewise, the propensity to demonstrate good governance and social responsiveness has also disrupted wider regulatory and sustainability frameworks (Auld & Renckens, 2021). With good governance and regulatory compliance shaken to the core, the ability of those in management and leadership positions to do the needful therefore becomes questionable. Likewise, their abilities to unify internal, board members and external, shareholder networks to bring about effective restructuring in individual and collective performance and organizational growth also become disrupted. Therefore, strategies targeting a new set of financial capabilities are critical to minimise the economic shocks experienced by SMEs. These strategies should then be focused on a wider and global economic resturing post-crisis period in a networked and jointly coordinated manner between states, UN bodies, business organizations and charitable firms to avert the scale of the disruptions.

The economic damage caused by the crisis on the organiziton of the global economic order has been captured by Fitriasari (2020) and its disruptive impacts on the ability of SMEs' member- behaviours have been documented by Brown (2020), Hoorens et al. (2020) and Morgan et al. (2020). Likewise, the necessary economic responses by a range of recognisable SME actors such as owners and partners have also been reported by Musa and Aifuwa (2020) and Papadopoulos et al. (2020). However, the nature of the economic restructuring and the digitalization that this requires, the varying networks and parties that will be involved and the extent, scale and quantity of the coordination and networking have not been attempted by previous scholarship. Recognising such a gap in the theorization and pointing to the urgency to forestall future SME demise and disruptions is in itself a contribution to how to manage within and strategize during and post crisis period. Whilst Indriasuti and Fuad (2020) have identified a new set of skills to enhance the longevity of business organizations in Indonesia, it is not known how this claim can be extended across civic groups, national and international business firms and other non-business organizations in a post pandemic world. Hereunder, the researcher provides two practical ways of bringing about this digitalization within the economic restructuring being proposed:

i) Digitalizing employment restructuring

Worldwide, lockdown measures have triggered massive employment precarity/insecurity and job losses. Such disruptions have meant huge financial losses for SMEs that were already challenged before the pandemic in terms of limited business activities, hard-to-access credit and acute skilled labor competition (McGeever et al., 2020; Beraha & Đuričin, 2020; Bartik et al. 2020). To avert this trend and save SMEs, a new employment structure for such affected firms is needed post-pandemic. This will involve smaller firms forming employment cooperatives that would target and adopt appropriate hiring and retention measures for hard-to-reach groups like younger and older employees and those from deprived backgrounds. These groups will be given the necessary upskilling, digitalized training, tasks, roles and responsibilities crafted to suit their interests, values, work ethic and preferences.

ii) Digitalizing supply chain restructuring

Globally, all types of small and big businesses and their raw materials suppliers have been affected in one way or the other by the pandemic. This is partly because their supply chains, road, rail, air networks have been affected and partially or sometimes completely closed in unimaginable ways than never experienced previously. The physical and psychological closures that have resulted from the crisis has hugely burdened the already existing national and across-international border suppliers of essential goods and services to SMEs and other firms. These disruptions to supply chains have impacted on the ability of SMEs to nurture and benefit from pre and during-crisis existing partners thereby hampering continuous operational business success. What previous scholarship such as Mahajan and Tomar (2021) and Meier and Pinto (2020) have neglected is how to develop a network of supply chain partners for SMEs across boundaries whilst simultaneously growing the already few but existing partners. Doing so entails building greater trust, mutual symbiotic business and person-to-person relationships to avert future disruptive incidents post-crisis.

Digitalization of Global Economies

The stress, anxiety, depression and psychological trauma experienced by staff and because of the fear of job losses and employment precarity have compounded global economic distress (Trougakos, Chawla & McCarthy, 2020; Hu, He, & Zhou, 2020). The countless lives lost because of the health crisis has exposed the ineptitude of governments and organizations, both large and small, whilst showing the febrility of the economic/financial recommendations thus far (Shamasunder et al., 2020). Changes such as hybrid working, remote working and working from home have generally been facilitated by digital technologies to try and counter the financial and economic disruptions but they have not been enough. These transformations have even been reported to negatively impact on professional and personal lives (Vaziri et al., 2020). The anticipation that such fundamental changes to traditional ways of working pre-pandemic could be a thing of the future for people, governments and organizations is yet to happen (Nissen, 2020). Such changes and the potential impact they could have on personal and professional lives are also expected to impact on individuals, organizations and nations' performance and their ability to be competitive and productive in a post-crisis world. Despite claims that new skills and competences are required for this new world order in which digitalization boosts entrepreneurial endeavors (Mazzarol & Reboud, 2020; Huws & Frapporti, 2021; Amankwah-Amoah et al., 2021), the inter-connectedness of various digital and non-digital aspects has not been developed. Additionally, whilst these tools and mechanisms are claimed to serve as enhancement for SMEs' competitiveness (Alves et al., 2020), it is still not clarified in SME scholarship how changing from traditional working to digitalization can resolve the range of other financially and non-financially related disruptions as enumerated and discussed in this chapter for SMEs in terms of their network capability and existential survival.

Open Innovation

The shift from office work to working from home has necessitated an upsurge in disucssions and debate on how to strengthen this transition to enahnce staff's psychological capital and innovative capability at a time when it is most needed. Whilst Mishra et al. (2019) have provided insights into how enriching the family and work paradigm could boost supervisor and staff's psychological capital, the tensions between family and work and the psychological trauma, anxiety and depressiona that may result from bullying behaviour still remains. The question of how to address such a gap in the effective resolution of future disruptions post COVID-19 has been partly addressed by Javed et al. (2019) by their focus on psychological empowerment, leadership capability enhancement and digital innovation in smaller firms. It is emphasised how team learning could be used to develop overall organizational knowledge capability to faciliate business performance. Earlier, Sanchez-Famoso et al. (2017) reported mixed results on the extent to which family members' involvement in SMEs' senior management teams can enhance their social capital and innovative capability whilst Tasavori et al. (2018) highlighted the criticality of internal social capital in enhancing family firms' external innovation. Yang et al. (2016) added employees' learning capacity within the overall innovation capability of firms whilst Najafi-Tavani et al. (2018) included collaborative networks within the overall organizational capability to be absorbtive of such knowledge. However, it is not clear how open innovation for both individuals and SMEs can be fostered in a post-crisis period. The following measures help in addressing this gap in the knowledge and practice of how to do so.

i) The initial step involves being transparent in the identification of the stakeholders involved in the office-home working arrangements. Hadi et al. (2020) noted the importance of keeping the communication channels as open as possible and facilitating input from staff and feedback from both staff and management. This interactive process of pairing SMEs' stakeholder-identification, transparency of selection and communicative feedback can be taken a step further by facilitating both internal and external stakeholder input-communication-feedback-feedforward mechnisms post-crisis.
ii) The second step involves the further development/diversification of communication, from the formal written to the informal verbal and visual channels to strengthen contiinuous engagment with stakeholders in identifying future potential disruptions as well as how to best address them. Whilst Haider Syed et al. (2020) identified digitisation strategies to address SMEs' pandemic disruptions, how to ensure that such mechanisms are effectively coordinated internally and between SMEs' stakeholder partners and communities had eluded previous scholarly attention and debate. Addtionally, how to do so in a post-pandemic SME environment is also an elusive aspect thus far. To address this, it is being proposed to use more sophisticated tools that emerging technologies offer to boost open innovation via enhance communication across SMEs nationally and internationally.
iii) The third step involves the embedding of support within employment structures. The results of the researcher's analysis show that SME businesses need support to survive a crisis similar to COVID-19 (Hoorens et al., 2020). Despite the much emphasised financial injection that is required, job retention and wage protection schemes should also be complemented with the appropriate policy-level and employee wellbeing support similar to Tsilika et al.'s (2020) proposition. Going beyond policy design, formulation and implementation, the researcher proposes the creation of employee-management-stakeholder 'think tank communities' (TTCs) to help in policymaking evaluations and potential realignment where and when their effectiveness in supporting staff becomes problematic.

Global Network Collaboration

The above measures have demonstrated the importance of developing networks to enhance organizations' capacity to embrace new forms of working across firms and countries to enhance their operational and strategic survival. Whilst this is not new, something different is being added in the following way. Whilst Newman (2010) emphasized the criticality of the empirical study of networks in the Social Sciences, network theory has been used to understand how organizations can be innovative in what they do if they are to survive disruptions (Odabas et al., 2017). For example, Hutchinson et al. (2006) has focused on how the darker aspects of informal networks may be used by its members to perpetuate various acts of bullying behaviors in crisis situations, Horak et al. (2020) highlighted both the dark as well as the benefits of using informal networks for deeper personal and organizational collaboration. Nonino (2013) highlighted how organizations can use their informal networks to develop their intra-organizational social capital to share their structural, relational and cognitive knowledge, Kujala et al. (2020) showed the benefits of good governance in strengthening organizational project performance and productivity. Remington and Pellicano (2019) also showed how autistic graduates used their internship knowledge at Deutsche Bank to denote the positive organizational and individual benefits from acquiring both formal and informal network knowledge. What is new here is how these networked SME staff and owners can transform such a vast array of informal networks into meaningful and beneficial collaborations to help them to stay connected and tap into a range of network platforms, from the global to the organizational levels.

i) The first step in developing global network collaboration includes partnering with all formal and stakeholders. This will facilitate developing/replicating successful outcomes in addressing crisis incidents from home and office settings. This will further enhance the effectiveness of working from home and boost productivity, performance and retention.
ii) The second step is to foster a management-staff collaboration platform within individual SME organizations and across firms locally, nationally and globally. In these platforms, all the interacting parties should identify their respective official and unofficial support networks, the skills and competences they have found beneficial in fostering success and draw on these collaborative ventures to contribute to their individual and collective firm survival post-pandemic.
iii) The third step within the new global network framework involves individuals' goals and their informal and formal learning being linked to and aligned with their organizations' ability to perform (Huang et al., 2019) vital roles and tasks. What is being proposed here as new is that working from home and the digitalization mechanisms should be harnessed as an overall packaged pathway to the global orientation working for SMEs.

Implications

The results of the analysis and research review have implications on several levels. Firstly, on the level of how to manage a crisis and address the socio-economic disruptions caused on individual and collective organizational lives, the issue of management and governmental responsibility is central to how SMEs may survive future crises. It was found that managers and governments tend to address/seek to resolve the predominantly financial/economic aspects of the disruptions presented by the crisis thereby exposing the non-economic (or socio-cultural) aspects of people's lives and livelihoods unattended to. Such a gap has led me to propose the need not only for a world-class digitalized economic structuration (including employment and supply chain restructuring) but also an open innovation agenda that will comprehensively address the imbalance and tensions remaining between home and office working arrangements. To this end, it is essential that SME management, owners and staff are more receptive to emotionally intelligent as well as economically savvy managers and leaders as countries and organizations move into the post-pandemic world of business. Such a move will potentially impact on the types of managers and leaders that SMEs would need, the types of governance and regulatory structures and processes that will become essential and the types of economic and financial programmes that will be beneficial in guaranteeing and maintaining SMEs' continuous survival after the crisis. There will be an urgent need to balance both 'hard' economic targets such as the achievement of organizational and individual productivity and performance with 'softer' People Management, stress, anxiety and depression coping and mitigation measures as countries and firms come out of lockdown measures. SME owners, staff and managers could benefit from periodic awareness and sensitisation workshops that highlight the nature of emerging, post-pandemic disruptions to staff and management's wellbeing and welfare and adopt the appropriate measures in a jointly supportive and collective manner.

The results and analysis of the researcher's review also highlight the complex and dynamic mix of organizational level disruptions ranging from operations to resource acquisition and retention to team performance and productivity, to name but a few. Additionally, the researcher's results indicated that the overall survival of organizations both during and after the crisis are intricately linked not only to the physical aspects of the disruptions (such as resources, business activities and performance) but also to the individual and collective capability to survive the disruptions/threats. The scale and unpredictable frequency of these disruptions point to the need for a different type of SME management; one that involves formal and informal networked capability knowledge and inter-cultural and global cultural competence to manage and lead staff out of a pandemic into post-crisis sustainability and growth. To achieve the latter, SME managers and owners are better equipped with competences such as being globally connected, enhancing inter and intra-organizational communication through transparent and accountable processes and facilitating employees and all stakeholders' commitment and welfare post-pandemic especially as people work remotely. SME managers and owners will need to be conversant and keep abreast with changing workplace regulations both domestically and internationally and develop policy design, formulation and evaluation techniques as part of the restructured global economic order. In this regard, senior management and supervisory teams ought to stay connected with staff performance and productivity as they increasingly work in and from different environments, time zones and conditions other than those they would be traditionally conversant with in their host countries. The coordination of regulatory, policy implementation and adaptation, networking and digitalization regimes will become crucial skills for SMEs' management if they are to continue to survive after the global public health crisis.

The researcher's results and analysis also indicated a range of disruptions which have adversely impacted on SME businesses' ability to conduct their operational activities and to generate wealth. These negativities have impacted on and exposed the overall capability of management to effectively address the challenges experienced during a crisis. The skills deficits have led to resource losses, staff shortages, absences, job insecurity and employment losses, to name but a few. The combination of these challenges has led to acute staff and management physical and psycho social distress and impacted on global wealth creation and material and emotional satisfaction. Additional measures other than resource loss, operational cost, business activity challenge, team performance disruption and organizational survival threat mitigation are urgently required as countries and organizations come out of the crisis. Measures such as business operations, team performance, policy design, implementation and adaptation, digital and open innovation enhancement are needed now more than ever before. These strategic measures are encapsulated within the researcher's Global Network Collaboration for SME staff, management, owners and stakeholders across the globe to tap into and utilise each other's formal and informal knowledge to stay alive after the ravages caused by COVID-19.

AGENDA FOR FUTURE RESEARCH AND CONCLUSION

The health crisis has had far reaching consequences on the organization of work, on workers and managements' wellbeing and welfare. Additional impacts have been reported on the types of initiatives needed to resolve the range of financial and non-financial disruptions experienced by staff and organizations. Whilst some form of management or other will be required after the crisis, the question of what type(s) would be more effective for SMEs remains to be unchartered territory for now. However, based on the emerging results from the theory and research examined in this chapter, it is reasonable to suggest that managing remote forms of working will still be prevalent. What may slightly alter are the places from where work may be conducted – be it in people's homes, gardens, holiday resorts or even campsites. This will entail managers having to synchronize these different places and potentially different time zones, value sets and cultural orientations to the unitary goals of the host-country's organization. Trying to adopt a unitarist form of management of disparate individuals, teams and work settings will continue to present a myriad of logistical, strategic and operational disruptions to SMEs' management, owners and partners for some time to come. Additionally, the psycho-social and emotional distances between colleagues will also pose disruptive challenges to management and supervisors who do not have the requisite knowledge, skills, competences and aptitude to deal with such new challenges. Such a revelations also suggests that the predominantly financial measures that have been adopted in most scholarship remains short term in nature.

It is therefore important for future researchers to begin to investigate into new sets of skills, aptitudes, attitudes and aptitudes that SME management and supervisors and owners will need if they are to keep their business organizations afloat in a post-crisis environment. Managers and business owners will have to come together, pool their individual and collective know-how to jointly address the psycho-social, emotional and physical requirements that staff will continue to need so as to perform their tasks and responsibilities to the utmost of their capabilities in a post-crisis environment. Inasmuch as such an enormous task could be facilitated through digitalization, this is the only way out. Coupled with this measure/strategy of digitalization, management and supervisory teams should see how best they can tap into people's goodwill, their informal and social networks to bring everyone's physically disparate environments into a harmonious digital space that works for everyone's and the organizations' productivity and performance benefits. Future researchers can examine how crisis management, physical and socio-cultural space harmonization, digitalization and skills mixes can be harnessed to successfully manage and sustain organizations after the pandemic. It would be rather naïve to assume that such synchronization in a networked capacity will provide the magic wand to all the disruptions that have been identified in this chapter. Management, supervisory teams and Human Resource professionals will have to do more in the areas of job rotation and enrichment, in team variations, in incentivizing and engaging staff in ways that have not been witnessed before and during the crisis if they are to enhance individual, team and departmental productivity. As such, future research should investigate the 'hows' of these strategies and the contextual variables needed to achieve tangible financial as well as non-financial outcomes. Likewise, exploring what additional networks could be developed to avert the internal and external knowledge and emotional linkage drainages will be critical for survival. Future studies should also try to address emerging questions such as 'How will changes to work patterns/trends impact on overall network capabilities to resolve existential threats to not only SME businesses but workplaces in general? 'What is going to be the right balance between the nature, scale and frequency of working from home and office working to help deal with future exogenous shocks to organizational effectiveness and employer-employee relations harmonization?' 'What types of quantitative, qualitative and other measurement systems are required to ensure that appropriate skillsets, competences and aptitudes are captured for individual and organizational survival in a longer-term, post-crisis world of work and business?'

REFERENCES

Abbasi, K. (2020). Covid-19: Politicization, "corruption," and suppression of science. *British Medical Journal*, 371.

Abbasi, K. (2020). *Covid-19: Screening without scrutiny, spending taxpayers' billions*. Academic Press.

Abrams, D., Lalot, F., & Hogg, M. A. (2021). Intergroup and intragroup dimensions of COVID-19: A social identity perspective on social fragmentation and unity. *Group Processes & Intergroup Relations*, *24*(2), 201–209. doi:10.1177/1368430220983440

Alamo-Vera, F., & Suarez-Ortega, S. (2005). SMEs Internationalization Firms and Managerial Factor. *International Journal of Entrepreneurial Behaviour & Research*, *11*(4), 258–279. doi:10.1108/13552550510603298

Alradhawi, M., Shubber, N., Sheppard, J., & Ali, Y. (2020). Effects of the COVID-19 pandemic on mental well-being amongst individuals in society-A letter to the editor on "The socio-economic implications of the coronavirus and COVID-19 pandemic: A review". *International Journal of Surgery*, *78*, 147.

Alves, J.C., Lok, T.C., Luo, Y., & Hao, W. (2020). *Crisis Management for Small Business during the COVID-19 Outbreak: Survival, Resilience and Renewal Strategies of Firms in Macau*. Academic Press.

Amankwah-Amoah, J., Khan, Z., Wood, G., & Knight, G. (2021). COVID-19 and digitalization: The great acceleration. *Journal of Business Research*, *136*, 602–611. doi:10.1016/j.jbusres.2021.08.011 PMID:34538980

Angela, M., Anthony, M., Francis, E., & Damilola, A. (2021). Recent trends in corporate social responsibilities in Nigeria-A case study of major oil firms in the Niger delta region. *Scientific American*, *13*, e00928.

Antonakis, J. (2020). Leadership to defeat COVID-19. *Group Processes & Intergroup Relations*, *24*(2), 210–215. doi:10.1177/1368430220981418

Aspan, H. (2021). Legal Basis for the Implementation of Work from Home Amid The COVID-19 Pandemic in Indonesia. *Saudi J. Humanities Soc Sci*, *6*(4), 116–121. doi:10.36348jhss.2021.v06i04.002

Auld, G., & Renckens, S. (2021). Private sustainability governance, the Global South and COVID-19: Are changes to audit policies in light of the pandemic exacerbating existing inequalities? *World Development, 139*, 105314. doi:10.1016/j.worlddev.2020.105314

Ba, H., Le, H., Loan, T., Thanh, C., Bich, T., Pham, T., & Binh, T. (2020). Policy related factors affecting the survival and development of SMEs in the context of Covid 19 pandemic. *Manag. Sci. Lett., 10*, 3683–3692.

Bartik, A. W., Bertrand, M., Cullen, Z. B., Glaeser, E. L., Luca, M., & Stanton, C. T. (2020). *How are small businesses adjusting to COVID-19? Early evidence from a survey.* National Bureau of Economic Research Working Paper Series.

Barlett, C. P., Rinker, A., & Roth, B. (2021). Cyberbullying perpetration in the COVID-19 era: An application of general strain theory. *The Journal of Social Psychology, 161*(4), 1–11. doi:10.1080/00224545.2021.1883503 PMID:33543673

Bassett, D. S., & Sporns, O. (2017). Network neuroscience. *Nature Neuroscience, 20*(3), 353–364. doi:10.1038/nn.4502 PMID:28230844

Beraha, I., & Đuričin, S. (2020). The impact of COVID-19 crisis on medium-sized enterprises in Serbia. *Economic Analysis, 53*(1), 14–27.

Blackburn, R. (2011). Book Review of: 'Unmasking the entrepreneur' by Campbell Jones and Andre Spicer. *Management Learning, 42*(1), 121–124. doi:10.1177/13505076110420010703

Bodla, A. A., Tang, N., Jiang, W., & Tian, L. (2018). Diversity and creativity in cross-national teams: The role of team knowledge sharing and inclusive climate. *Journal of Management & Organization, 24*(5), 711–729. doi:10.1017/jmo.2016.34

Bose, S., Bhattacharyya, A., & Islam, S. (2016). Dynamics of firm-level financial inclusion: Empirical evidence from an emerging economy. *Journal of Banking and Finance Law and Practice, 27*(1), 47–68.

Brown, R. (2020). The impact of Covid-19 on Scottish small and medium-sized enterprises (SMEs): Prognosis and policy prescription. *Fraser of Allander Economic Commentary, 44*(2).

Brown, R., Rocha, A., & Cowling, M. (2020). Financing entrepreneurship in times of crisis: Exploring the impact of COVID-19 on the market for entrepreneurial finance in the United Kingdom. *International Small Business Journal, 38*(5), 380–390. doi:10.1177/0266242620937464

Brülhart, M., Lalive, R., Lehmann, T., & Siegenthaler, M. (2020). COVID-19 financial support to small businesses in Switzerland: Evaluation and outlook. *Schweizerische Zeitschrift für Volkswirtschaft und Statistik, 156*(1), 1–13. doi:10.118641937-020-00060-y PMID:33078128

Burt, R. S. (2004). Structural holes and good ideas. *American Journal of Sociology, 110*(2), 349–399. doi:10.1086/421787

Caputo, A., Marzi, G., Maley, J., & Silic, M. (2019). Ten years of conflict management research 2007–2017: An update on themes, concepts and relationships. *International Journal of Conflict Management, 30*(1), 87–110. doi:10.1108/IJCMA-06-2018-0078

Carnevale, J. B., & Hatak, I. (2020). Employee adjustment and well-being in the era of COVID-19: Implications for human resource management. *Journal of Business Research, 116*, 183–187. doi:10.1016/j.jbusres.2020.05.037 PMID:32501303

Castells, M. (2011). Network theory: A network theory of power. *International Journal of Communication, 5*, 15.

Castro, M.P., & Zermeño, M.G.G. (2020). Being an entrepreneur post-COVID-19–resilience in times of crisis: a systematic literature review. *Journal of Entrepreneurship in Emerging Economies.*

Chaplin, H. & House, K. (2009). *The Internationalisation of young, innovative SMEs.* Academic Press.

Che, A. R., Omar, I., & Suraiya, M. A. (2020). *The impact of Covid-19 Movement Control Order on SMEs' businesses and survival strategies.* Geografia.

Chong, S., Huang, Y., & Chang, C. H. D. (2020). Supporting interdependent telework employees: A moderated-mediation model linking daily COVID-19 task setbacks to next-day work withdrawal. *The Journal of Applied Psychology, 105*(12), 1408–1422. doi:10.1037/apl0000843 PMID:33271029

Dabic, M., González-Loureiro, M., & Harvey, M. (2015). Evolving research on expatriates: What is 'known' after four decades (1970–2012). *International Journal of Human Resource Management, 26*(3), 316–337. doi:10.1080/09585192.2013.845238

Davies, P. (2000). The relevance of systematic reviews to educational policy and practice. *Oxford Review of Education, 26*(3-4), 365–378. doi:10.1080/713688543

Debowska, A., Horeczy, B., Boduszek, D., & Dolinski, D. (2020). A repeated cross-sectional survey assessing university students' stress, depression, anxiety, and suicidality in the early stages of the COVID-19 pandemic in Poland. *Psychological Medicine*, 1–4. doi:10.1017/S003329172000392X PMID:33004087

De Clercq, D., & Belausteguigoitia, I. (2020). When does job stress limit organizational citizenship behavior, or not? Personal and contextual resources as buffers. *Journal of Management & Organization*, 1–25. doi:10.1017/jmo.2020.7

Dowell, G. W., Shackell, M. B., & Stuart, N. V. (2011). Boards, CEOs, and surviving a financial crisis: Evidence from the internet shakeout. *Strategic Management Journal, 32*(10), 1025–1045. doi:10.1002mj.923

Etheridge, B., & Spantig, L. (2020). *The gender gap in mental well-being during the Covid-19 outbreak: evidence from the UK* (No. 2020-08). ISER Working paper series.

Fitriasari, F. (2020) How do Small and Medium-sized Enterprises (SME) survive the COVID-19 outbreak? J. *Inov. Ekon.*

Finfgeld-Connett, D. (2014). Use of content analysis to conduct knowledge-building and theory-generating qualitative systematic reviews. *Qualitative Research, 14*(3), 341–352. doi:10.1177/1468794113481790

Fisher, J., Languilaire, J. C., Lawthom, R., Nieuwenhuis, R., Petts, R. J., Runswick-Cole, K., & Yerkes, M. A. (2020). Community, work, and family in times of COVID-19. *Community Work & Family, 23*(3), 247–252. doi:10.1080/13668803.2020.1756568

Galbreath, J. (2011). Are there gender-related influences on corporate sustainability? A study of women on boards of directors. *Journal of Management & Organization, 17*(1), 17–38. doi:10.5172/jmo.2011.17.1.17

Gartenberg, C., & Pierce, L. (2017). Subprime governance: Agency costs in vertically integrated banks and the 2008 mortgage crisis. *Strategic Management Journal, 38*(2), 300–321. doi:10.1002mj.2481

Gaur, A., & Kumar, M. (2018). A systematic approach to conducting review studies: An assessment of content analysis in 25 years of IB research. *Journal of World Business, 53*(2), 280–289. doi:10.1016/j.jwb.2017.11.003

Gerald, E., Obianuju, A., & Chukwunonso, N. (2020). Strategic agility and performance of small and medium enterprises in the phase of Covid-19 pandemic. *International Journal of Financial, Accounting, and Management, 2*(1), 41–50. doi:10.35912/ijfam.v2i1.163

Gubler, D. A., Makowski, L. M., Troche, S. J., & Schlegel, K. (2021). Loneliness and well-being during the Covid-19 pandemic: Associations with personality and emotion regulation. *Journal of Happiness Studies, 22*(5), 2323–2342. doi:10.100710902-020-00326-5 PMID:33100896

Hadi, S. (2020). New perspective on the resilience of SMEs proactive, adaptive, reactive from business turbulence: A systematic review. *J Xi'an Univ Arch Technol, 12*, 1265–1275.

Hadi, S., & Supardi, S. (2020). Revitalization strategy for small and medium enterprises after Corona virus disease pandemic (covid-19) in Yogyakarta. *J. Xian Univ. Archit. Technol, 12*, 4068–4076.

Haider Syed, M., Khan, S., Raza Rabbani, M., & Thalassinos, Y.E. (2020). *An artificial intelligence and NLP based Islamic FinTech model combining Zakat and Qardh-Al-Hasan for countering the adverse impact of COVID 19 on SMEs and individuals*. Academic Press.

Hobday, A. J., Robinson, C., Murphy, E. J., Newton, A., Glaser, M., & Brodie, S. (2020). Fostering global science networks in a post-COVID-19 world. *Oceanography (Washington, D.C.), 33*(4), 9–10. doi:10.5670/oceanog.2020.414

Huws, U., & Frapporti, M. (2021). Digitalization, labour and the pandemic: Working life in the post-COVID-19 city. *Work Organisation, Labour & Globalisation, 15*(1), 7–10. doi:10.13169/workorgalaboglob.15.1.0007

Juergensen, J., Guimón, J., & Narula, R. (2020). European SMEs amidst the COVID-19 crisis: Assessing impact and policy responses. *Economia e Politica Industriale, 47*(3), 499–510. doi:10.100740812-020-00169-4

Hoorens, S., Hocking, L., & Fays, C. (2020). *How small businesses are coping with the impact of COVID-19*. Rand Europe.

Horak, S., Afiouni, F., Bian, Y., Ledeneva, A., Muratbekova-Touron, M., & Fey, C. F. (2020). Informal networks: Dark sides, bright sides, and unexplored dimensions. *Management and Organization Review, 16*(3), 511–542. doi:10.1017/mor.2020.28

Huang, J., Liu, F., Teng, Z., Chen, J., Zhao, J., Wang, X., & Wu, R. (2020). Care for the psychological status of frontline medical staff fighting against Coronavirus Disease 2019 (COVID-19). *Clinical Infectious Diseases, 71*(12), 3268–3269. doi:10.1093/cid/ciaa385 PMID:32246142

Huebener, M., Waights, S., Spiess, C. K., Siegel, N. A., & Wagner, G. G. (2021). Parental well-being in times of Covid-19 in Germany. *Review of Economics of the Household, 19*(1), 91–122. doi:10.100711150-020-09529-4 PMID:33469413

Huertas-Valdivia, I., Braojos, J., & Lloréns-Montes, F. J. (2019). Counteracting workplace ostracism in hospitality with psychological empowerment. *International Journal of Hospitality Management, 76*, 240–251. doi:10.1016/j.ijhm.2018.05.013

Hutchinson, M., Vickers, M. H., Jackson, D., & Wilkes, L. (2006). Like wolves in a pack: Predatory alliances of bullies in nursing. *Journal of Management & Organization, 12*(3), 235–250. doi:10.5172/jmo.2006.12.3.235

Huws, U., & Frapporti, M. (2021). Digitalization, labour and the pandemic: Working life in the post-COVID-19 city. *Work Organisation, Labour & Globalisation, 15*(1), 7–10. doi:10.13169/workorgalaboglob.15.1.0007

Indriastuti, M., & Fuad, K. (2020, July). Impact of covid-19 on digital transformation and sustainability in small and medium enterprises (SMEs): A conceptual framework. In *Conference on Complex, Intelligent, and Software Intensive Systems* (pp. 471-476). Springer.

Javed, B., Abdullah, I., Zaffar, M. A., Haque, A., & Rubab, U. (2019). Inclusive leadership and innovative work behavior: The role of psychological empowerment. *Journal of Management & Organization, 25*(4), 554–571. doi:10.1017/jmo.2018.50

Juergensen, J., Guimón, J., & Narula, R. (2020). European SMEs amidst the COVID-19 crisis: Assessing impact and policy responses. *Economia e Politica Industriale, 47*(3), 499–510. doi:10.100740812-020-00169-4

Khalil, M., Ozkanc, A., & Yildiz, Y. (2020). Foreign institutional ownership and demand for accounting conservatism: Evidence from an emerging market. *Review of Quantitative Finance and Accounting, 55*(1), 1–27. doi:10.100711156-019-00834-3

Kim, J. H., Shim, Y., Choi, I., & Choi, E. (2022). The role of coping strategies in maintaining well-being during the COVID-19 outbreak in South Korea. *Social Psychological & Personality Science, 13*(1), 320–332. doi:10.1177/1948550621990595

Kloutsiniotis, P. V., Mihail, D. M., Mylonas, N., & Pateli, A. (2022). Transformational Leadership, HRM practices and burnout during the COVID-19 pandemic: The role of personal stress, anxiety, and workplace loneliness. *International Journal of Hospitality Management, 102*, 103177. doi:10.1016/j.ijhm.2022.103177 PMID:35079194

KnauerN. J. (2021). The Federal Response to the COVID-19 Pandemic-A Study in Maladministration. Available at SSRN 3803884. doi:10.2139/ssrn.3803884

Kneller, R., & Pisu, M. (2011). Barriers to exporting: What are they and who do they matter to? *World Economy, 34*(6), 893–930. doi:10.1111/j.1467-9701.2011.01357.x

Kneller, R., & Pisu, M. (2006). *The role of experience in export market entry: Evidence for UK Firms.* University of Nottingham Research Paper, (2006/48).

Kottika, E., Özsomer, A., Rydén, P., Theodorakis, I. G., Kaminakis, K., Kottikas, K. G., & Stathakopoulos, V. (2020). We survived this! What managers could learn from SMEs who successfully navigated the Greek economic crisis. *Industrial Marketing Management, 88*, 352–365. doi:10.1016/j.indmarman.2020.05.021

Kuckertz, A., Brändle, L., Gaudig, A., Hinderer, S., Reyes, C. A. M., Prochotta, A., ... Berger, E. S. (2020). Startups in times of crisis–A rapid response to the COVID-19 pandemic. *Journal of Business Venturing Insights, 13*, e00169. doi:10.1016/j.jbvi.2020.e00169

Kujala, J., Aaltonen, K., Gotcheva, N., & Lahdenperä, P. (2020). Dimensions of governance in interorganizational project networks. *International Journal of Managing Projects in Business.*

Le, H., Nguyen, T., Ngo, C., Pham, T., & Le, T. (2020). Policy related factors affecting the survival and development of SMEs in the context of Covid 19 pandemic. *Management Science Letters, 10*(15), 3683–3692. doi:10.5267/j.msl.2020.6.025

Leonidou, L. C. (2000). Barriers to export management: An organizational and internationalization analysis. *Journal of International Management, 6*(2), 121–148. doi:10.1016/S1075-4253(00)00022-3

Lepak, D.P., Taylor, M.S., Tekleab, A.G., Marrone, J.A. & Cohen, D.J. (2007). An examination of the use of high-investment human resource systems for core and support employees. *Human Resource Management, 46*(2), 223-246.

Leseure, M. J., Bauer, J., Birdi, K., Neely, A., & Denyer, D. (2004). Adoption of promising practices: A systematic review of the evidence. *International Journal of Management Reviews, 5*(3-4), 169–190. doi:10.1111/j.1460-8545.2004.00102.x

Liguori, E. W., & Pittz, T. G. (2020). Strategies for small business: Surviving and thriving in the era of COVID-19. *Journal of the International Council for Small Business, 1*(2), 106–110. doi:10.1080/26437015.2020.1779538

Lu, Y., Wu, J., Peng, J., & Lu, L. (2020). The perceived impact of the Covid-19 epidemic: Evidence from a sample of 4807 SMEs in Sichuan Province, China. *Environmental Hazards, 19*(4), 323–340. doi:10.1080/17477891.2020.1763902

Mahajan, K., & Tomar, S. (2021). COVID-19 and Supply Chain Disruption: Evidence from Food Markets in India. *American Journal of Agricultural Economics, 103*(1), 35–52. doi:10.1111/ajae.12158 PMID:33230345

Mao, L., Jin, H., Wang, M., Hu, Y., Chen, S., He, Q., Chang, J., Hong, C., Zhou, Y., Wang, D., Miao, X., Li, Y., & Hu, B. (2020). Neurologic manifestations of hospitalized patients with coronavirus disease 2019 in Wuhan, China. *JAMA Neurology, 77*(6), 683–690. doi:10.1001/jamaneurol.2020.1127 PMID:32275288

Mazzarol, T., & Reboud, S. (2020). Adoption and diffusion of innovation. In *Entrepreneurship and Innovation* (pp. 165–189). Springer. doi:10.1007/978-981-13-9412-6_6

McCombs, K., & Williams, E. (2021). The resilient effects of transformational leadership on well-being: Examining the moderating effects of anxiety during the COVID-19 crisis. *Leadership and Organization Development Journal, 42*(8), 1254–1266. doi:10.1108/LODJ-02-2021-0092

McGeever, N., McQuinn, J., & Myers, S. (2020). SME liquidity needs during the COVID-19 shock (No. 2/FS/20). Central Bank of Ireland.

Meier, M., & Pinto, E. (2020). Covid-19 supply chain disruptions. *Covid Economics*, *48*, 139–170.

Mendy, J., & Rahman, M. (2019). Application of human resource management's universal model: An examination of people versus institutions as barriers of internationalization for SMEs in a small developing country. *Thunderbird International Business Review*, *61*(2), 363–374. doi:10.1002/tie.21985

Mishra, P., Bhatnagar, J., Gupta, R., & Wadsworth, S. M. (2019). How work–family enrichment influence innovative work behavior: Role of psychological capital and supervisory support. *Journal of Management & Organization*, *25*(1), 58–80. doi:10.1017/jmo.2017.23

Moffit, R., & Badger, D. (2020). Defeating COVID-19—What Policymakers Can Do to Change the Conditions on the Ground. *Heritage Foundation Backgrounder*, (3485), 2020–04.

Möhring, K., Naumann, E., Reifenscheid, M., Wenz, A., Rettig, T., Krieger, U., ... Blom, A.G. (2021). The COVID-19 pandemic and subjective well-being: longitudinal evidence on satisfaction with work and family. *European Societies, 23*(sup1), S601-S617.

Montero, A. G., & Le Blanc, D. (2020). Resilient institutions in times of crisis: Transparency, accountability and participation at the national level key to effective response to COVID-19. *UN-DESA Policy Brief*, *74*, 49.

Morgan, T., Anokhin, S., Ofstein, L., & Friske, W. (2020). SME response to major exogenous shocks: The bright and dark sides of business model pivoting. *International Small Business Journal*, *38*(5), 369–379.

Mourad, A., Srour, A., Harmanai, H., Jenainati, C., & Arafeh, M. (2020). Critical impact of social networks infodemic on defeating coronavirus COVID-19 pandemic: Twitter-based study and research directions. *IEEE eTransactions on Network and Service Management*, *17*(4), 2145–2155. doi:10.1109/TNSM.2020.3031034

Musa, S., & Aifuwa, H. O. (2020). Coronavirus pandemic in Nigeria: How can Small and Medium Enterprises (SMEs) cope and flatten the curve. *Eur. J. Account. Financ. Invest*, *6*, 56–61.

Najafi-Tavani, S., Najafi-Tavani, Z., Naudé, P., Oghazi, P., & Zeynaloo, E. (2018). How collaborative innovation networks affect new product performance: Product innovation capability, process innovation capability, and absorptive capacity. *Industrial Marketing Management*, *73*, 193–205. doi:10.1016/j.indmarman.2018.02.009

Neu, C.R., Gehlhaus, D., & Shatz, H. J. (2020). *Preserving Small Businesses*. Academic Press.

Newman, M. E. J. (2010). *Networks: An Introduction*. Oxford University Press. doi:10.1093/acprof:oso/9780199206650.001.0001

Nissen, L. (2020). Social work and the future in a post-Covid 19 world: A foresight lens and a call to action for the profession. *Journal of Technology in Human Services*, *38*(4), 309–330. doi:10.1080/15228835.2020.1796892

Nonino, F. (2013). The network dimensions of intra-organizational social capital. *Journal of Management & Organization, 19*(4), 454–477. doi:10.1017/jmo.2013.20

Nyanga, T., & Zirima, H. (2020). Reactions of small to medium enterprises in masvingo, Zimbabwe to covid 19: Implications on productivity. *Business Excellence and Management, 10*(1), 22–32. doi:10.24818/beman/2020.S.I.1-02

Odabaş, M., Holt, T. J., & Breiger, R. L. (2017). Markets as governance environments for organizations at the edge of illegality: Insights from social network analysis. *The American Behavioral Scientist, 61*(11), 1267–1288. doi:10.1177/0002764217734266

Obeng, R., & Haugh, H. (2014). Strategic entrepreneurship and small firm growth in Ghana. *International Small Business Journal, 32*(5), 501–524. doi:10.1177/0266242612463946

Okpara, O. J. (2011). Corporate Governance in a Developing Economy: Barriers, Issues, and Implications for Firms. *Journal of Corporate Governance, 11*(2), 184–199. doi:10.1108/14720701111121056

Osarenkhoe, A. (2008). A study of the enablers of non-sequential internationalization process among small and medium-sized firms. *International Journal of Business Science and Applied Management, 3*(2), 1–20.

Papadopoulos, T., Baltas, K. N., & Balta, M. E. (2020). The use of digital technologies by small and medium enterprises during COVID-19: Implications for theory and practice. *International Journal of Information Management, 55*, 102192. doi:10.1016/j.ijinfomgt.2020.102192 PMID:32836646

Prime, H., Wade, M., & Browne, D. T. (2020). Risk and resilience in family well-being during the COVID-19 pandemic. *The American Psychologist, 75*(5), 631–643. doi:10.1037/amp0000660 PMID:32437181

Rahman, M., & Mendy, J. (2018). Evaluating people-related resilience and non-resilience barriers of SMEs' internationalisation: A developing country perspective. *The International Journal of Organizational Analysis*.

Ratnasingam, J., Khoo, A., Jegathesan, N., Wei, L. C., Abd Latib, H., Thanasegaran, G., ... Amir, M. A. (2020). How are small and medium enterprises in Malaysia's furniture industry coping with COVID-19 pandemic? Early evidences from a survey and recommendations for policymakers. *BioResources, 15*(3), 5951–5964. doi:10.15376/biores.15.3.5951-5964

Restubog, S. L. D., Ocampo, A. C. G., & Wang, L. (2020). Taking control amidst the chaos: Emotion regulation during the COVID-19 pandemic. *Journal of Vocational Behavior, 119*, 103440. doi:10.1016/j.jvb.2020.103440 PMID:32390659

Rutashobya, L., & Jaensson, J. (2004). Small firms' internationalization for development in Tanzania: Exploring the network phenomenon. *International Journal of Social Economics, 31*(1/2), 159–172. doi:10.1108/03068290410515484

Sanchez-Famoso, V., Maseda, A., & Iturralde, T. (2017). Family involvement in top management team: Impact on relationships between internal social capital and innovation. *Journal of Management & Organization, 23*(1), 136–162. doi:10.1017/jmo.2016.2

Shamasunder, S., Holmes, S. M., Goronga, T., Carrasco, H., Katz, E., Frankfurter, R., & Keshavjee, S. (2020). COVID-19 reveals weak health systems by design: Why we must re-make global health in this historic moment. *Global Public Health: An International Journal for Research, Policy and Practice*, *15*(7), 1083–1089. doi:10.1080/17441692.2020.1760915 PMID:32352911

Shleifer, A. (2004). Does competition destroy ethical behavior? *The American Economic Review*, *94*(2), 414–418. doi:10.1257/0002828041301498

Sinkovics, N. (2016). Enhancing the foundations for theorising through bibliometric mapping. *International Marketing Review*, *33*(3), 327–350. doi:10.1108/IMR-10-2014-0341

Sostero, M., Milasi, S., Hurley, J., Fernandez-Macias, E., & Bisello, M. (2020). *Teleworkability and the COVID-19 crisis: A new digital divide?* (No. 2020/05). JRC working papers series on labour, education and technology.

Tasavori, M., Zaefarian, R., & Eng, T. Y. (2018). Internal social capital and international firm performance in emerging market family firms: The mediating role of participative governance. *International Small Business Journal*, *36*(8), 887–910. doi:10.1177/0266242618773145

Theis, L., & Bipp, T. (2019). Workplace Goal Orientation. *European Journal of Psychological Assessment*.

Tranfield, D., Denyer, D., & Smart, P. (2003). Towards a methodology for developing evidence-informed management knowledge by means of systematic review. *British Journal of Management*, *14*(3), 207–222. doi:10.1111/1467-8551.00375

Trougakos, J. P., Chawla, N., & McCarthy, J. M. (2020). Working in a pandemic: Exploring the impact of COVID-19 health anxiety on work, family, and health outcomes. *The Journal of Applied Psychology*, *105*(11), 1234–1245. doi:10.1037/apl0000739 PMID:32969707

Tsilika, T., Kakouris, A., Apostolopoulos, N., & Dermatis, Z. (2020). Entrepreneurial bricolage in the aftermath of a shock. Insights from Greek SMEs. *Journal of Small Business and Entrepreneurship*, *32*(6), 635–652. doi:10.1080/08276331.2020.1764733

Tricco, A.C., Langlois, E., Straus, S.E., & World Health Organization. (2017). *Rapid reviews to strengthen health policy and systems: a practical guide*. World Health Organization.

Troth, A. C., Jordan, P. J., & Lawrence, S. A. (2012). Emotional intelligence, communication competence, and student perceptions of team social cohesion. *Journal of Psychoeducational Assessment*, *30*(4), 414–424. doi:10.1177/0734282912449447

Trougakos, J. P., Chawla, N., & McCarthy, J. M. (2020). Working in a pandemic: Exploring the impact of COVID-19 health anxiety on work, family, and health outcomes. *The Journal of Applied Psychology*, *105*(11), 1234–1245. doi:10.1037/apl0000739 PMID:32969707

Tuikka, S. (2019). Negative relationships in the workplace. In *Workplace Communication* (pp. 136–148). Routledge. doi:10.4324/9780429196881-11

UK Statutory Instruments on The Working Time (Amendment) Regulations 2020. (2020). No. 365. Academic Press.

Vaziri, H., Casper, W. J., Wayne, J. H., & Matthews, R. A. (2020). Changes to the work–family interface during the COVID-19 pandemic: Examining predictors and implications using latent transition analysis. *The Journal of Applied Psychology*, *105*(10), 1073–1087. doi:10.1037/apl0000819 PMID:32866024

Verburg, R. M., Den Hartog, D. N., & Koopman, P. L. (2007). Configurations of human resource management practices: A model and test of internal fit. *International Journal of Human Resource Management*, *18*(2), 184–208. doi:10.1080/09585190601102349

Weißer, T., Saßmannshausen, T., Ohrndorf, D., Burggräf, P., & Wagner, J. (2020). A clustering approach for topic filtering within systematic literature reviews. *MethodsX*, *7*, 100831. doi:10.1016/j.mex.2020.100831 PMID:32195145

Wildman, J. L., Nguyen, D. M., Duong, N. S., & Warren, C. (2021). Student teamwork during COVID-19: Challenges, changes, and consequences. *Small Group Research*, *52*(2), 119–134. doi:10.1177/1046496420985185

Winarsih, I. M. & Fuad, K. (2021). Impact of covid-19 on digital transformation and sustainability in small and medium enterprises (SMEs): A conceptual framework. In Advances in Intelligent Systems and Computing. Springer International Publishing.

Yang, C. C., & Chuang, H. Y. (2020). The strategy for return to work after the COVID-19 pandemic on small and medium-sized enterprises. *Journal of Occupational and Environmental Medicine*, *62*(8), e471–e472. doi:10.1097/JOM.0000000000001926 PMID:32459712

Zhai, Y., & Du, X. (2020). Addressing collegiate mental health amid COVID-19 pandemic. *Psychiatry Research*, *288*, 113003. doi:10.1016/j.psychres.2020.113003 PMID:32315885

Zhai, Y., & Du, X. (2020). Loss and grief amidst COVID-19: A path to adaptation and resilience. *Brain, Behavior, and Immunity*, *87*, 80–81. doi:10.1016/j.bbi.2020.04.053 PMID:32335197

Chapter 12
Chinese Business Trends in the Post COVID-19 era

Shi Hu
School of Economics and Management, Guangxi University of Science and Technology, China

ABSTRACT

COVID-19 has greatly influenced the way people live. Due to the economic crisis caused by COVID-19, the Chinese business environment has been largely changed. Chinese business models have gone through a new revolution and transformation. This chapter investigates and identifies future Chinese business trends after COVID-19, which covers the integration of digital technology, focusing on hygiene and healthcare, sustainable development, and increasing international collaborations. In conclusion, Chinese companies should regard the COVID-19 pandemic from a positive perspective as a chance to improve and innovate. Furthermore, companies should utilize the opportunities and push the companies for business innovation to gain more competencies in the post-COVID-19 era.

BACKGROUND

COVID-19 pandemic as a global public health crisis has dramatically influenced the ways of people's life, connections with others, and people's well-being. COVID-19 pandemic results in a global health emergency, which largely affects the service industry such as retailing, catering, and tourism industries. The sales of the service industry have experienced a significant drop after the outbreak of COVID-19 (Li et al., 2021). Under the COVID-19, the service industry is the most affected one while other sectors are also seriously influenced such as education and healthcare industries. COVID-19 has brought enormous impacts on the business environment (Zahra, 2021). This business model transformation would continue even after the completion of the COVD-19 pandemic. Due to the targets of Chinese Industry 4.0, Chinese business models go through a huge transformation with the technology development. The resilience of digital technology during the pandemic becomes stronger because of social distance maintenance and work from home. As the flexible and efficient characteristics of digital technology, embedding it into business operations will still be the future trend in China. During the pandemic, Chinese companies faced increasingly operational costs, insufficient natural resources, and unemployment (Anker, 2021).

DOI: 10.4018/978-1-7998-8856-7.ch012

This global pandemic generates a worldwide economic recession such as stagnation of trade and investments. Moreover, this crisis caused a worsening global environment with increasing carbon emissions due to the sharp decrease in energy efficiency and renewable energy investment (Zhang, 2021). Hereby, sustainable development after COVID-19 becomes particularly important. Because of the COVID-19 pandemic, the global supply chain has also been disrupted by production schedule delays and inventory shortages. So Butt (2021) proposed the strategies for supply chain resilience such as short-term demand-supply strategy, channel shifts preparation, second-tier suppliers for alternative stock reservation, open communication channels with key customers, and customer demand and priority understandings. Through these strategies and technology adoption such as Blockchain and AI (artificial intelligence), the supply chain can return to normality soon and become more efficient in the post-COVID-19 era. On the other hand, the COVID-19 pandemic is a double-edged sword, which could push the progress and development of digital technology in the Chinese business models. Fu et al. (2020) said digital technology plays a crucial part in Chinese pandemic prevention and control in the educational industry, catering industry, retailing industry, and e-commerce industry. Thanks to digital technology, China is closer to the achievements of Industry 4.0 by the constant developments of 5G, Internet of Things (IoT), big data, and AI (artificial intelligence). The main purpose of this study is to identify the Chinese business trends, tendencies, and changes in the post-COVID-19 era. In this chapter, a systematic analysis of the Chinese business trends after COVID-19 is conducted through the review of 17 current literature, 5 news from authority websites (Xinhua, China Daily, Harvard Business Review, and China briefing), 2 reports to gain a comprehensive picture of the Chinese business trends in the post-COVID-19 era. To give a more vivid description of the Chinese business trends after COVID-19, some cases are selected to gain a deeper understanding of digital technology integration and sustainable development in the Chinese business models. Selected cases in this chapter contain Meituan (a Chinese online food ordering App), JD.com (one of the Chinese largest online shopping malls), 2019 European Green Deal (EGD), New Infrastructure by the Chinese government, 2021 China-EU investment agreement negotiations China-EU High-Level Digital Cooperation Dialogue, China and UK technological collaborations, and China-EU High-Level Environment and Climate Dialogue. In addition, two figures are demonstrated in the section on sustainable development, which depicts the elements of Chinese 'New Infrastructure' and energy efficiency situation after the outburst of the COVID-19 pandemic.

In this chapter, sustainable development with environmental rebound effects, digital technology integration, focus on hygiene and healthcare, and more international collaborations are identified as the keys to enhancing business resilience after the COVID-19 pandemic in China.

INTEGRATION OF DIGITAL TECHNOLOGY

Digital technology could facilitate companies to be creative. Digital technology is characterized as low-cost, efficient, and facilitating (Jean et al., 2020). With these characteristics, it could connect with worldwide customers, agencies, colleagues, and suppliers. During the turbulence of the COVID-19 pandemic, digital technology has been fully taken advantage of to overcome the obstacles brought by the COVID-19. Digital technology facilitates the free transfer of information, knowledge, and capitalization (Alon, 2020). This indicates that digital technology makes the transfers of capitalization, information, knowledge, and transactions free, practical, and feasible across borders. Digital technology would continue to play an important role in the global supply chain by big data analysis and smart technology track

(Anker, 2021). Through AI and Blockchain, abundant data could be handled and analyzed at the same time to make an accurate decision by the companies (Wang et al., 2019). When Blockchain technology is integrated with other technologies, the flexibility of the supply chain could be reinforced in front of external challenges (Gohil & Thakker, 2021).

Furthermore, people begin to rely more on online groceries and supermarkets while virtual workplaces for remote work become popular (Accenture, 2020). This trend will continue as digital technology ensures flexibility, virtual collaboration, and efficiency of colleagues without location limitations. It is said that there would be an increase in virtual realities such as global virtual teams, which will result in a more efficient workplace (Alon, 2020). This transforms the business model into a more flexible way that combines the pool of talents without boundary limitations to make decisions together and react to the problems quickly. It is stated that after the COVID-19 pandemic, the Chinese logistics industry faces three driving forces. Among them, technology plays an important role in accelerating the logistics industry development (Liu et al., 2020). COVID-19 crisis is a double-edged sword, especially for the countries that pursue progress, which on the other side, pushes the development and improvement of digital technology. For example, social distance and contact avoidance bring vigor into e-commerce and contactless delivery service such as Meituan (a Chinese online food ordering App) (Cheng, 2020). Through contactless delivery service within smart parcel locker system, the service becomes more traceable within a short time. COVID-19 crisis provides a huge amount of opportunities for the business to transform the service model by integrating digital technology. JD.com (one of the Chinese largest online shopping malls) adopts smart logistics and supply-chain to ensure available emergency support in front of diseases (Liu et al., 2021).

Even after the COVID-19 pandemic, digital technology should still be integrated and developed to build the smart warehouse, logistics, and supply chain as the new business model reshapes. With the integration of digital technology, business operations become more accurate, efficient, and flexible. Digital technology reflects the future trend and transformation of business models in China. Technologies could facilitate the production procedure and help organizations gain resilience under the unpredictable environment. What is more, digital technology fuels the increasing innovation of companies. Technology-based business models reflect the future trend, which expedites the organizations to come out with new strategies and ideas. From the resilient supply chain perspective, after the COVID-19 pandemic, as mentioned by Butt (2021), integration of digital technologies by applying Blockchain, AI (artificial intelligence) is essential for modern companies to win the fierce competition in the background of Industry 4.0. That implies digital technology could assist the companies to establish a more resilient supply chain system, which efficiently utilizes logistics, inventory, and transportation as a system.

FOCUS ON HYGIENE AND HEALTHCARE

COVID-19 pandemic plays an important role in reshaping consumer behavior. Consumer perceptions and habits during the COVID-19 have changed massively. After experiencing the crisis of COVID-19, consumers are intentional care for hygiene and food safety, which facilitates the safety standardization of food and healthcare products in China (China briefing, 2020). That manifests the health concerns from the customers would drive the growing force in the hygiene and healthcare areas in the future. The catering industry and food industry in China also adopt innovative business models to adjust to the impacts caused by the COVID-19 crisis such as e-commerce and contactless delivering service. With the new adjustments to the business models, the catering, healthcare, and food industries demonstrate a high level of resilience. Handwashing and mask-wearing have gained unprecedented attention as important public health policies and practices. As the statement of Butt (2021), the prevention of viruses should be seriously concentrated on. This implies that hygiene products would gain more emphasis by the people to prevent the virus from coming again. Based on the argument of Anker (2021), consumer values have transferred to selflessness, respect, and care as social and public recognitions. Therefore, the catering industry also keeps a watchful eye on the hygiene of food to adapt to the higher consumer expectations of food safety and health (Li et al., 2021). According to the report of Accenture (2020), the priorities of consumers begin to concentrate on hygiene and cleaning products after the outbreak of COVID-19, which are highly related to personal health and cleaning such as ventilators and hand sanitizers. These types of products could contribute to a clean environment and help people prevent illness and disease during the pandemic. Under these priorities, personal health and hygiene become the most concerns, which prompts the development of food and medicine security. COVID-19 mobilized the sales of the healthcare industry by integrating high technologies such as telehealth, remote patient monitory, healthcare AI, critical medical suppliers, efficient distribution of healthcare products (Schroeder, 2020). People would become more conscious of hygiene and healthcare in the long run. Even when the COVID-19 has been completed, this trend will not go away in a short time.

SUSTAINABLE DEVELOPMENT

There is a need for the governments to facilitate sustainable development after the pandemic by policies and fiscal supports to encourage the companies, especially SMEs (small and medium-sized enterprises) to gain more innovation and creativity. After the COVID-19, there is a need for businesses to achieve green and sustainable development. European Union (EU) proposed the European Green Deal (EGD) in 2019, which contains a series of 50 actions for the coming five years and achieves climate neutrality by 2050. The EGD aims to decarbonize and put forward energy policies by integrating renewable energy technologies such as solar PV (Iea, 2020). Through the EGD program, the EU could realize a resilient, recovery, and sustainable development in the long run. This makes a clear need for sustainable development in the post-COVID-19 era. To facilitate the Chinese business sustainable development, the Chinese government proposed 'New Infrastructure' by USD 1.4 trillion investment. This 'New Infrastructure' project aims to support the infrastructure constructions of big data and 5G technology. This reflects the Chinese sustainable development concepts. As demonstrated in figure 1, the contents of 'New Infrastructure' include information infrastructure, innovation infrastructure, and integration infrastructure. Through the integration of technologies such as Blockchain and AI in the supply chain, companies are more likely to achieve sustainable development. After the COVID-19 pandemic, the balance between economic regeneration and low carbon emission becomes extremely obvious (Zhang et al., 2020). Based on the statement of Bartik et al. (2020), SMEs belong to a more vulnerable group, which confronted a great shock during the pandemic such as more difficult financing, massive layoffs, and closures. Shi and Iqbal (2020) adopted the SWOT (Strength, Weakness, Opportunity, Threat) analysis and discovered one of the challnges faced by the Chinese SMEs is the balance achievement between operational cost savings and sustainable development. Therefore, Chinese governments should come out with some supportive policies for SMEs to aid them to bounce back from the COVID-19 and realize sustainable development. According to Liu (2020), after the pandemic, more supports for SMEs will be gained from Chinese governments such as tax and fees reduction and funding supports from banks. China-EU investment agreement negotiations completion facilitates the economic recovery and sustainable global development through joint investments and commitments such as China-EU High-Level Environment and Climate Dialogue (Xinhua, 2021). This collaboration reflects the future trend of business development, which needs to be sustainable and long-standing. China and the EU as two world major economies, this attention to the environment and climate makes clear the significance of sustainable development in the future business model.

Figure 1. The composition of Chinese new infrastructure construction project
Source: Liu et al., 2020

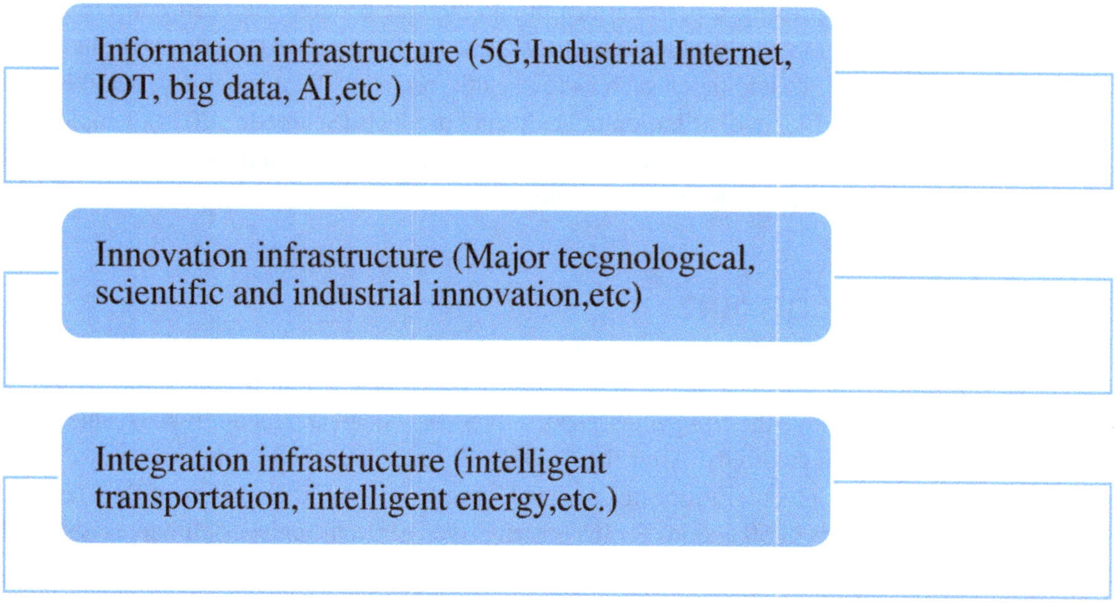

As shown in figure 2, from 2019, there is an obvious drop in energy efficiency and renewable energy investment after the outbreak of the COVID-19 pandemic. Hence, more efforts and commitments should be put by the worldwide organizations after the pandemic on the areas of environmental issues and green energy development (CO2 emission reduction). Zhang (2021) argued that in the post-COVID-19 era, governments can utilize the fiscal policies to encourage the green efforts and hit the environmental pollution to fulfill the green recovery. From the start of 2021, China's National Development and Reform Commission introduced fiscal policies to encourage green energy development. As a result, government fiscal policies will keep playing the strengths in facilitating sustainable development in the long run. In China, the future business models after the pandemic should follow the requirements of the Chinese government's sustainable development proposal to achieve the balance between organizational profits and green development.

Figure 2. Energy efficiency and renewable energy investment
Source: Zhang et al. (2020)

INCREASING INTERNATIONAL COLLABORATIONS

China has achieved remarkable achievements for the post-pandemic recovery. Fu et al. (2020) stated that there will be an emerging trend in the development of digital technology in the areas of healthcare, pharmacy, and some other professional service areas. New technologies consistently spring up to satisfy the newly changing needs of customers and times. As the previous statements in the 'Integration of Digital Technology' section, digital technology not only plays an important role during the pandemic, this contribution will continue in the post-COVID-19 era. International collaborations could facilitate knowledge sharing and integration among the different countries. Some common problems faced by mankind need to get the supports and efforts from the worldwide countries. China and UK (United Kingdom) have the technological cooperations on these kinds of problems such as environmental problems, aging, green energy, public safety, and measures for preventing disaster. Moreover, the cooperation platforms and mechanisms are comprehensive, which covers research, experiment, knowledge sharing, and flute communications between universities and research agencies in these two countries (Sun, 2020). At the same time, through this collaboration, China and UK could play to the strengths of both sides and optimize the results. This demonstrates that after the COVID-19 pandemic, ongoing collaborations between different countries and regions will arise. In addition, China and the EU have reached an agreement on investment agreement negotiations in 2021, which breathes new life into the world economy after the pandemic. China and the EU as the two major and stable economies in the world, through this high level of cooperations, more investments such as FDI (foreign direct investments) will increase dramatically based on a high level of international economic and trade rules. China-EU High-Level Digital Cooperation Dialogue indicates the cooperation could result in more advanced progress in the Digital Industry. By this cooperation, a more stabilized supply chain system and more job opportunities could be achieved that will reinitialize the world economy after the pandemic (Xinhua, 2021). International collaborations after the COVID-19 pandemic could prompt the mutual benefits and win-win among the countries to achieve more openness and create more job opportunities in the countries. International collaborations among the countries on some common mankind problems and high technology build the confidence for the positive recovery after COVID-19 and expedite an open global system.

IMPLICATIONS

Although COVID-19 is a terrible catastrophe, the global business environment has been hugely transformed with more openness and expansion across the borders. The educational industry, retailer industry, catering industry, and service industry will enter into a new business model and gain more opportunities by the integration of digital technology. In the post-Covid, the way of people's life will welcome great growth of AI, 5G, Internet of Things (IoT), and big data. As Schroeder (2021) stated, with the help of digital technology, some innovations that vigor during the pandemic will transform into a viable businesses in the long run. People admire the power of digital technology role in making people's life more convenient and flexible. In post-COVID-19 era, digital technology will continue to play an important role for the business to go internationalization by reaching global customers and breaking the barriers of information transfer by cross-broader communications. Based on the statement of China briefing (2020), the preference of the customers for online shopping will last for a long time because consumers are accustomed to these kinds of business models such as live streaming and e-commerce. As consumers pay more attention to the supplements related to diet and immune-boosting, there will be more new opportunities in the perspectives of people's hygiene and healthcare. Through international collaborations around the world, innovations in the solutions of mankind's common problems and the healthcare industry will continue to develop. Business models transform from the conventional way into a sustainable development model. In the future, a business that owns a strong level of resilience and quick reaction to the external business environment could come out with more innovative strategies to gain competencies. That requires the companies to continually learn new knowledge and skills to keep the current business models updated. Companies need to own corporate social responsibility (CSR) to realize both the economic and social missions. New business models should bend companies to the livelihood of people and reduce the issues of prevailing climate change with green energy adoption. This study aims to understand how the integration of digital technology, focus on hygiene and healthcare, sustainable development, and increasing international collaborations could improve the business models against the backdrops of COVID-19. According to Barasa et al. (2018), the resilience of business refers to the ability of an organizational system to reach targets in front of challenges. It is argued that business resilience contains three levels, which are survival, adaption, and innovation. Among them, the survival level is the basic level that points out the normality before the crisis while adaption and innovation levels reflect the improving levels of the companies (Dahles & Susilowati, 2015). When companies reach the levels of adaption and innovation, companies will become less vulnerable to the turbulence and shock of the market. Organizational resilience does not only limit to the capability of resisting the strong impacts by the organizational system but also includes the adapting ability. Through the factors such as information management and collaborations, companies are more likely to gain resilience. To remain resilient, business needs to adjust to the new business environment and adjust their operations to meet the new changes (Li et al., 2021). As a result, companies should seize the opportunities after the COVID-19 pandemic and regard this as a push and chance for business innovation and transformation.

CONCLUSION

This chapter discusses the trends of Chinese business models after the COVID-19, which contains the integration of digital technology, focus on hygiene and healthcare, sustainable development, and increasing international collaborations. This chapter describes the main trends, tendencies, and changes in the Chinese business models after the COVID-19. Besides, the implications of how the companies should respond to this pandemic have also been explored based on the identifications of four Chinese business trends. This chapter has the guiding significance in the Chinese business operations in the post-pandemic era.

REFERENCES

Accenture. (2020). *How covid-19 will permanently change consumer behavior.* Report. Author.

Alon, I. (2020). COVID-19 and International Business: A Viewpoint. *FIIB Business Review, 1-3*(2), 75–77. Advance online publication. doi:10.1177/2319714520923579

Anker, T. B. (2021). At the boundary : Post-COVID agenda for business and management research in Europe and beyond. *European Management Journal, 39*(2), 171–178. doi:10.1016/j.emj.2021.01.003

Barasa, E., Mbau, R., & Gilson, L. (2018). What is resilience and how can it be nurtured? A systematic review of empirical literature on organizational resilience. *International Journal of Health Policy and Management, 7*(6), 491–503. doi:10.15171/ijhpm.2018.06 PMID:29935126

Bartik, A. W., Bertrand, M., Cullen, Z., Glaeser, E. L., Luca, M., & Stanton, C. (2020). The impact of COVID-19 on small business outcomes and expectations. *Proceedings of the National Academy of Sciences of the United States of America, 117*(30), 17656–17666. doi:10.1073/pnas.2006991117 PMID:32651281

Butt, A. S. (2021). Supply chains and COVID-19 : Impacts, countermeasures and post-COVID-19 era. *International Journal of Logistics Management.* Advance online publication. doi:10.1108/IJLM-02-2021-0114

Cheng, Y. (2020). Demand Rising for Contactless Delivery. *China Daily.* Retrieved from: http://www.chinadaily.com.cn/a/202002/19/WS5e4c9d77a310128217278a1b.html

China briefing. (2020). *Tapping into new growth opportunities in China's F&B market.* Retrieved from: https://www.china-briefing.com/news/tapping-into-new-growth-opportunities-in-chinas-fb-market/

Dahles, H., & Susilowati, T. P. (2015). Business resilience in times of growth and crisis. *Annals of Tourism Research, 51*, 34–50. doi:10.1016/j.annals.2015.01.002

Fu, X. L., Zhang, J., & Wang, L. M. (2020). Introduction to the special section : the impact of Covid-19 and post-pandemic recovery : China and the world economy. *Journal of Chinese Economic and Business Studies*, *18*(4), 311–320. doi:10.1080/14765284.2020.1855939

Gohil, D., & Thakker, S. V. (2021). Blockchain-integrated technologies for solving supply chain challenges. *Modern Supply Chain Research and Applications*, *3*(2), 78–97. doi:10.1108/MSCRA-10-2020-0028

Iea. (2020). *European Union 2020 Energy Policy Review*. Retrieved from: https://www.iea.org/reports/european-union-2020

Jean, R.-J., Kim, D., & Cavusgil, E. (2020). Antecedents and outcomes of digital platform risk for international new ventures' internationalization. *Journal of World Business*, *55*(1), 101021. doi:10.1016/j.jwb.2019.101021

Li, B., Zhong, Y. Y., Zhang, T. T., & Hua, N. (2021). Transcending the COVID-19 crisis: Business resilience and innovation of the restaurant industry in China. *Journal of Hospitality and Tourism Management*, *49*(July), 44–53. doi:10.1016/j.jhtm.2021.08.024

Liu, Q. (2020). Measures must be commensurate with impact. *China Daily*. Retrieved from: http://www.chinadaily.com.cn/a/202002/24/WS5e5334d7a310128217279c19.html

Liu, W.H., Liang, Y.J., Bao, X., Qin, J.J, & Lim, M. K. (2020). China's logistics development trends in the post COVID-19 era. *International Journal of Logistics: Research and Applications*, 1–12. doi:10.1080/13675567.2020.1837760

Schroeder, D. (2020). Turn your Covid-19 solution into a viable business. *Harvard Business Review*. Retrieved from: https://hbr.org/2020/07/turn-your-covid-19-solution-into-a-viable-business

Shi, H., & Iqbal, Q. (2020). *Chinese SMEs in Industry 4.0: Analysis and Future Trends*. IGI Global., doi:10.4018/978-1-7998-2577-7.ch001

Sun, F. (2020). Sino-UK Science and Technology Cooperation in the Field of People's Livelihood. *Journal of Chinese Economic and Business Studies*, *18*(4), 349–354. doi:10.1080/14765284.2020.1855857

Wang, K., Dong, J. Q., Wang, Y., & Yin, H. (2019). Securing Data with Blockchain and AI. *IEEE Access: Practical Innovations, Open Solutions*, *7*, 77981–77989. doi:10.1109/ACCESS.2019.2921555

Xinhua. (2021). *China-EU investment agreement to inject new life into global economic recovery*. Retrieved from: http://www.xinhuanet.com/english/2021-01/03/c_139638396.htm

Zahra, S. A. (2021). International entrepreneurship in the post Covid world. *Journal of World Business*, *56*(1), 101143. doi:10.1016/j.jwb.2020.101143

Zhang, D. Y. (2021). Fiscal policy benefits and green recovery of firms : An experimental exploration of Chinese listed firms. *Economic Change and Restructuring*. Advance online publication. doi:10.100710644-021-09344-6

Zhang, D. Y., Hao, M. G., & Morse, S. (2020). Is Environmental Sustainability Taking a Backseat in China after COVID-19? The Perspective of Business Managers. *Sustainability*, *12*(24), 1–24. doi:10.3390u122410369

Chapter 13
An Evaluation of New Work Practices After the Pandemic: Crowdworking

Aslı Sezgin
https://orcid.org/0000-0002-4557-7351
Çukurova University, Turkey

Esengül İplik
Adana Alparslan Türkeş Science and Technology University, Turkey

ABSTRACT

This study focuses on working life, which has an important place in the center of social changes after COVID-19. In the working life, where digital transformation has an application area, different concepts have taken their place in the literature in the important change observed with COVID-19. Digitalization made its presence felt in a process that accelerated with COVID-19. Concepts and applications that were not included in daily life practices until a few years ago are experienced today. In the study, an evaluation was made on crowdworking and related concepts, which are considered as one of these concepts. In this evaluation, digital transformation and the post-COVID-19 process were highlighted, and the motivation sources of crowdworker and crowdsourcer were analyzed through in-depth interview method.

INTRODUCTION

After the concept of "network society" (Castells, 2004) started to be discussed, new concepts have taken their place in the agenda along with the living conditions of this society. Many societies aiming to accelerate the transition to the digital literacy process accept the existence of these new concepts and create the new life order in the axis of these concepts. This digital transformation, which covers a wide area such as education and health, from the evaluation of leisure time, also changes the working life.

The effects of digital transformation on the economy, society and individuals create challenges, along with opportunities for governments and policy makers. Accordingly, OECD launched the Going Digital

DOI: 10.4018/978-1-7998-8856-7.ch013

Project (2019) in order to uncover the opportunities in the digital age and to support proactive action by overcoming difficulties. With the project, it is aimed to inform about the effects of digital transformation in a social context. This project focuses on 7 important policies (access-use-innovation-business-trust-society-market deficit) to shape the digital future (OECD, 2019). Before the studies on the subject in the international sense, the impact of digital transformation on working life has started to be felt.

The change in employment patterns since the mid-20th century continued with a new beginning in the mid-2000s. First with the World War II, followed by the Cold War and the 1990s in the period specified as the "internet age, significant changes occurred in the employment environment. The international division of labor has increased, enabling the creation of a global working pool of information and communication technologies. Online work is now accepted as a normal process in the context of business life. "Virtual" work has become more widespread, e-mail usage has increased, and official working hours have disappeared (Huws, 2013).

While digital technologies have changed the working life, developments in productivity and growth have also been realized. In recent years, many innovative business models based on the "platform" principle have been encountered. Crowdworking platforms are also internet-based platforms with more paid employees, where intermediaries ensure the completion, coordination, and control of the business. Through these platforms, the employee can also choose his/her own task. It is possible to say that while the number of these platforms increases day by day, the type of duty defined for working life increases also. For crowdworking, which is defined as a new working environment beyond the classical employment system, studies on healthy identification and research of the environment are needed (Mrass & Peters, 2017). The task announced with crowdworking is selected by crowdworker. While the task announced for the whole group is voluntarily undertaken, each stage can be technically controlled in these new work platforms. These studies, which are carried out through the relationship between crowdsourcer and crowdworker, also bring advantages and disadvantages (Mrass, et.al. 2016).

Discussions on this new business model based on the platform principle draws attention in the post-COVID-19 working life that has been reshaped. Apart from the existing working environments, the restructuring and definition of this order, as well as the rapid arrangements for working from home and remotely, gained speed after COVID-19. Within the scope of the transformations experienced in all areas of social life and the subject of various research (Florida, et.al. .2021; Zahra, 2021; Serrano, 2020; Davies, 2021; Altier & Nicholls, 2020) after COVID-19, practices for working life should be evaluated under a separate title.

COVID-19 has had dramatic effects on the world economy and working life. In this environment, digitalization has had a significant impact on companies adapting and overcoming the current situation caused by COVID-19. People and corporate structures have started to make maximum use of digital technologies to face this exceptional situation. New ways of working have increased the demand for new talent as well as being independent of people's geographic location (Almeida, et.al., 2020). However, at this point, it should be underlined that concepts such as distributed work, telework and virtual work are not new concepts. COVID-19 has brought these concepts to the center of organizational management literature (Henry, et.al., 2021). The concept of crowdworking and other concepts associated with this work practice, which were examined in this study, were also examined due to their positions in working life. In this context, within the conceptual framework of the study, first of all, an evaluation was made on the new post-COVID-19 working practices, and then the examinations on the concept of crowdworking were included with the method of in-depth interviews with a crowdworker and crowdsourcer.

BACKGROUND

New Work Practices

It is a well-known fact that over the centuries, technological, social, and political transformations within societies have significantly shaped their economies and the way individuals make a living. During the First and Second Industrial Revolutions, the production processes based on old technologies were replaced by more modern production processes that require new machines, new modes of operation, and skill sets, using the power of steam and electricity. The transformation in production resulted in the emergence of new occupations and new ways of working that increased the welfare of individuals, although it caused the dismissal of employees at its onset (World Economic Forum, 2020). Since the beginning of 2000s, on the other hand, the Fourth Industrial Revolution, known as Industry 4.0, which includes the use of communication, information, and artificial intelligence technologies that provide higher levels of production efficiency than ever before, has begun to shape the business models of organizations (Bai, Dallasega, Orzes & Sarkis, 2020).

Triggered by Industry 4.0, digitalization, automation, and globalization have rapidly changed the labour market. These changes have not only impacted wages, unemployment and working conditions, but also the general understanding of what labour is, and how income can and should be earned. Apart from the fact that automation has replaced traditional manual and routine labour, that is, processes that do not require much creativity, many jobs have been transformed with the advancement of digitalization and artificial intelligence (Jäger, Zilian, Hofer & Füllsack, 2019). The growing use of new technologies has begun to transform business models, change the type of work and professions, and even the nature of the tasks performed. In addition to these advances in technology, the change experienced after the Global Financial Crisis of 2008 and the resulting wave of unemployment gave rise to a new concept in the labour market. This new economic model, known as the "gig economy", reflects more flexible and different forms of short-term employment, where organizations tend to prefer to hire freelancers, part-time or temporary workers instead of traditional full-time workers who rarely change positions and focus on lifelong careers. In this connection, the gig economy emerged as a result of many unemployed professional and skilled workers taking short-term jobs to earn a living. While it was initially preferred by skilled IT professionals who started using online digital platforms to seek such opportunities, it has over time turned out to be considered as a livelihood option by students, retirees, and low- and high-skilled workers seeking employment and has eventually become a growing trend. The gig economy is spreading rapidly around the world, becoming an increasingly everyday reality to the extent that it is transforming the labour market (Méndez, 2020; Banik & Padalkar, 2021).

The gig economy includes two main forms of work, namely, "crowdwork" and "work-on-demand via apps" or simply "work-on-demand". In this context, crowdwork carried out through online platforms is a form of work that allows to connect customers and employees on a global basis by contacting with an unlimited number of organizations, businesses, and individuals over the Internet. The framework of work done on crowdworking platforms can differ significantly (De Stefano, 2016). Currently, most crowdworking platforms manage simple tasks that individuals can complete in a short time, with reasonable effort, such as tagging images, testing mobile apps, taking photos, or writing short texts at the point of sale (Mrass, Peters & Leimeister, 2021). Since individuals give more and more weight on their spare time outside of work, nowadays they tend to evaluate and choose their jobs not only financially but also based on other factors that can increase their happiness. The ideas that work should only be part of who they are and that the goal to which they dedicate their lives should not be financial gain have led individuals to do jobs in which they can establish a better work-life balance. In this sense, as a result of this change in individuals' perspectives on work and career, crowdworking, which is distinctly different from regular employment, has recently gained prominence as an increasingly preferred work model (Jäger et al., 2019).

Work-on-demand via apps, another form of work within the gig economy, differs from crowdworking in that it involves more traditional and physical work, i.e., the real world, rather than virtual tasks. This work model is time and place dependent and often includes low- or medium-skilled, physically demanding online jobs. Such jobs are often organized through online platforms managed by companies that can retain control over important aspects of the business, including setting prices and standards, selecting, and managing workforce. This form of work, in which an employment contract is signed between the employer and the worker, is based on the principle that workers will be called to work when needed, without any commitment of the employer to provide employment on a permanent basis. This way of working is becoming increasingly common in industries with constant but variable demand, such as food and parcel delivery services, cleaning services, transportation, home care services, childcare, event organization, etc. The major difference between work-on-demand via apps and crowdworking is that the latter allows workers to operate anywhere in the world, while the former only matches the supply and demand of locally run activities online. In other words, although the platforms can work at an international level, the work itself can be done locally (Görmüş, 2020; Kaine & Josserand 2019; Stewart & Stanford, 2017). While the ongoing controversies on the effects of Industry 4.0 and the Global Financial Crisis of 2008 on workforce and employment were on the rise, the Coronavirus pandemic (COVID-19) broke in Wuhan, China, suddenly affecting the whole world unprecedently, and in just a few weeks, it radically changed the lives of people around the world and created a "new normal" in which short-term and long-term disruptions were intertwined (Görmüş, 2020; World Economic Forum, 2020). Since the COVID-19 pandemic is regarded as a problem with serious and long-term impacts on the economy, jobs and employment, in addition to people's health, well-being and quality of life in general, and has been recognized by the International Labour Organization (ILO) as the most severe crisis since World War II (Pulignano, Domecka, Muszyński, Vermeerbergen & Rieman, 2021).

Apart from its direct devastating consequences on human health, the COVID-19 pandemic has profoundly affected people's mental health as well as their way of life and work. In this process, "social isolation" and "social distance" rules, which aim to minimize people's physical contact with each other in order to prevent the spread of COVID-19, have become extremely important, as a result of which strict restrictions have been imposed by countries on the movement of people and the closure of workplaces, thereby turning the COVID-19 public health crisis into an economic crisis (Görmüş, 2020). Many business enterprises around the world have tried to keep up with this situation by quickly switching to a new way of working in order to not only survive this crisis with the least possible damage, but also protect their employees (Boland, De Smet, Palter & Sanghvi, 2020). According to McKinsey (2020), the COVID-19 pandemic has necessitated new ways of doing business in which organizations must change the way they work, as well as remodelling the role of offices in order to ensure the development of safe, successful, and rewarding careers. Working from home or remotely, which was largely applied as a flexible working arrangement to increase worker productivity and welfare before the pandemic, has become a new and prevalent work model preferred by businesses in many countries around the world during the pandemic. Based on the principle of moving businesses to online or virtual platforms, working from home usually depended on employee preferences before the pandemic; however, it has become a key policy tool used by governments around the world as a way to minimize the spread of the pandemic and has eventually made working from home mandatory for many people (Kniffin et al., 2021).

Economic shutdowns and policy changes influence organizations from different aspects, as is the case typically in times of wars and natural disasters, by fundamentally changing some industries, accelerating trends already in progress in others, and creating opportunities for new industries to emerge. The COVID-19 pandemic has also changed how and where people work in just a few months, making the use of different and flexible working methods widespread. Many organizations have considered setting up a hybrid virtual model on the basis of combining remote working with time spent in the office after the pandemic, grounded on the idea that this can create a large talent pool due to fewer location restrictions for employment, adopt innovative processes to increase productivity, create an even stronger culture, and most importantly significantly reduce real estate costs (Ancillo, del Val Núñez & Gavrila; 2021; Boland et al., 2020).

Modern Networking System and New Working Practices

It seems possible to notice that working modes and models are falling apart with the new age in which the importance of information increases. In this new era, where hotels, cafes and even airport terminals are often used as workplaces, job descriptions are also changing. Technology has changed the traditional understanding of work environments, inevitably resulting in many businesses adopting a virtual approach to their workspaces. In the same manner, businesses have also evolved into larger organizational networks that now include a dispersed workforce. The fact that using technology has facilitated dispersed ways of working has enabled businesses to generate the necessary human resources so that such ways of work can be successful through the use of social networks, ensuring that team spirit and culture are preserved wherever you may be. Indeed, businesses have had to adopt new strategies to manage a dispersed and ever-increasing workforce. Modern social networking sites not only offer opportunities for formal and informal interaction but also collaboration in this process (Bennett et al., 2010).

Globalization, economic mobility, and technological changes have led to various transformations in the world of business. In such an environment, new work arrangements have become increasingly common, affecting both labor markets and the way business activities are conducted and spatially organized. It is clear that information and communication technologies have played an important role in the diversification and evolution of workplaces. Recent technological developments have paved the way for continuous innovations especially to the collaborative working approach. New working environments and business life combined with greater flexibility and autonomy are confined neither to a particular place nor time. This environment, however, generates some concerns. These concerns about surveillance, control, and power dynamics (Aroles et al., 2019) can be minimized with a professional and transparent working approach.

The introduction of mobile phones in the 1980s and of internet technologies in the 1990s clearly changed the professional working life. Many different working styles have emerged over time, instead of the kind of working environment, which is limited by traditional working hours. Furthermore, new technologies have significant impact on the change in new business life, yet the impact of different factors on this change should be evaluated well. Legal, cultural, economic, political, and institutional factors appear to be remarkable in this regard. The analyses of new work practices suggest the presence of certain controversial issues including precarious forms of employment and rights violations created by platform capitalism. Spatial working arrangements in crowd-based and collaborative initiatives can also be regarded as innovations provided by this environment (Aroles et al., 2019). All these innovations, on the other hand, resulted in some changes in the roles of workers.

All these changes have also led to the flexibility of a flat organizational structure in business environments and the conceptualization of employees as team members. In addition, workers are expected to possess different skills and be able to demonstrate these abilities, especially in technological matters. Workers' performances are evaluated accordingly (Urcuoli, 2008). Beyond the change created by new technologies in terms of some expectations from the workers, internet technologies also offer opportunities for workers to improve their employment-related interests. Such opportunities include the potential of Web 2.0 as regards self-organization and individual action (Richards, 2012). From this perspective, we conducted research on the crowdworking system, which stands out as an example for new working environments and evaluated the motivation sources of the employees and the employers.

Online Freelancing: Crowdworking

It is a fact the Internet has not only changed many aspects of life, including the way we communicate, learn, and meet each other, but also the way people work and the jobs they do. This ever-growing trend has accelerated even more, directly proportional to the increase in the number of companies taking advantage of the potential of the digital workforce due to the lockdowns implemented due to the COVID-19 pandemic, and the employees affected by the quarantines seeing online platforms as an opportunity to make a living (O'Higgins & Caro, 2021). These changes in business structure that enable, and demand flexible working models have triggered the transition to a new form of Internet-based workforce called crowdsourcing (Barnes, Green & de Hoyos, 2015). Being a concept that developed as different aspects of using the Internet in business-related activities arouse, the term "crowdsourcing" was first coined by Jeff Howe in 2006 in his article called "The Rise of Crowdsourcing" published in Wired Magazine, and is defined, on the basis of the concept of outsourcing, as the process of having a task performed or solving a problem by asking for help from undefined large groups of people through open calls (Digout, Azouri, Decaudin & Rochard, 2013). Crowdsourcing, a relatively new form of managing and organizing a geographically dispersed pool of labour using the Internet, involves working on an online platform to perform a diverse set of cognitive tasks individually, ranging from those that require low to moderate skill and can be accomplished in a relatively short time, and to those that require more skill and expertise. Crowdsourcing for paid work is composed of three key actors: buyers (those who need their work done for compensation), platform owners (those who provide an online platform or website where tasks are advertised), and workers (who respond to advertisements, undertake, and submit work, and then get paid). Compared to the traditional labour market, buyers represent labour demand (employers), workers represent labour supply, and the platform represents an intermediary for the labour market. Platforms and platform owners are supposed to actively create and maintain the market. In a crowdsourcing model for the paid work, buyers (or employers) post jobs on the platform, then select workers from among those who respond to those advertisements with a selection based on reliability, price, and/or the candidates' skills and experience. Another alternative way for buyers is to select the qualified worker from a pool of the appropriately skilled workforce (Barnes et al., 2015).

The term crowdsourcing, which is very popular today and refers to the work of a crowd, for the purposes of solving a problem, providing data, or contributing to a common goal, is widely used in many different fields of activity, and employees use these platforms not only to earn a wage, but they also act with different intrinsic motivations (Durward, Blohm & Leimeister, 2016). Platforms like Wikipedia, for example, work with the voluntary contributions of the crowds. Similarly, online portals where many people contribute to ratings and reviews, such as TripAdvisor or Booking.com, operate on a voluntary basis (Serfling, 2018). As can be seen in Figure 1, at this stage, a concept emerges in digital platforms, which is similar to traditional paid employment where the employee is paid for the work done, and which is classified as a subset of crowdsourcing platforms (Durward et al., 2016). This concept, known as crowdworking, is a new form of work that adopts the crowdsourcing model, describing paid jobs that are conducted digitally and delivered online entirely through digital platforms (Elbanna & Idowu, 2021). In this sense, crowdwork, which is a socio-technical work system consisting of a series of relationships that connect organizations, individuals, technologies and business activities (Kittur et al., 2013), is defined as a paid job found through a method in which potential workers subscribe to certain digital platforms, where they can respond to open calls for duty posted by employers and where all tasks and payments are carried out over digital platforms (Elbanna & Idowu, 2021). The task demanded can be a simple one that can be solved in seconds, or a complex task that takes hours or even days to complete (Idowu & Elbanna2020). In this respect, crowdworking consists of macro and micro tasks. Micro-tasks cover small, marginal, and highly repetitive tasks that can be accomplished in a short time, while macro-tasks typically cover tasks that often take longer to complete and require a higher level of specialized skill and expertise (Idowu & Elbanna, 2020).

Figure 1. Classification of Crowd Work from an individual worker's perspective
Source: Durward et.al 2016

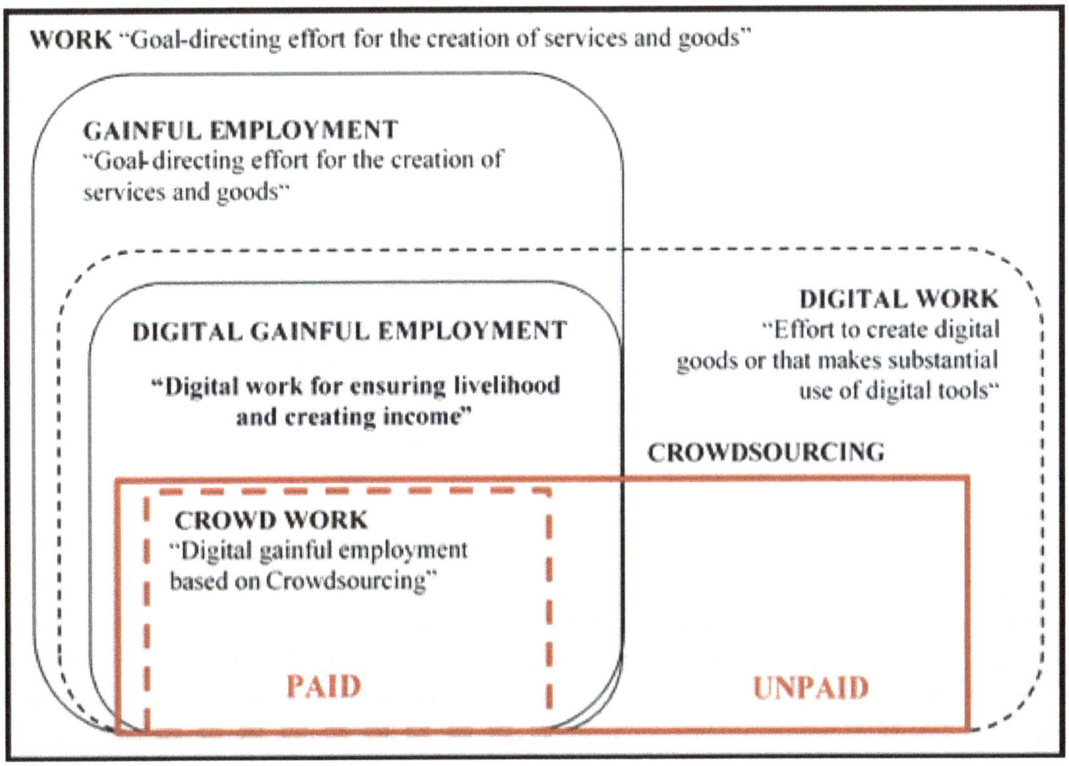

Although crowdwork is a form of work that is becoming more and more popular with the advantages it offers to both workers and organizations, research on this phenomenon is still in its infancy. In the literature that has emerged as a result of the studies carried out so far, two opposing views have been put forward that evaluate crowdwork as an exploitative form of employment as opposed to being an empowering form. The view, which presents crowdwork as an empowering form of employment, argues that it is a possible way to reduce the unemployment problem as it provides an opportunity for people to find work from a global pool of employers. This view has also been embraced by governments of many countries and international organizations such as the International Labour Organization and the World Bank, who have recently recognized crowdwork as a source of employment for people from developing countries that can create an opportunity to participate in the global labour market while continuing to reside in their own countries and contribute to their local economies. Emphasizing the positive aspect of this new work system, this view is also embraced by businesses that find crowdworking mutually beneficial for employers and employees (Elbanna & Idowu, 2021). In this system, employers hire workers for a project or task and pay them a piece rate when the work is done at the desired quality, rather than taking the risk that an employee is not needed or fails to perform at the expected standard over time or bearing the cost. In the event that the job fails to meet expectations, the employer has the flexibility to choose another employee and continue the job without paying the employee. Nevertheless, crowdworking offers potentially significant benefits for workers as well. This type of work enables the workers in general to have the chance to access the labour market that is relatively non-discriminatory, as well as those, in particular, whose conditions make it compulsory to work from home to access the labour force (O'Higgins & Caro, 2021). Proponents of this view also argue that the flexible and autonomous nature of this type of work gives workers the freedom to balance their work and life besides enjoying the flexibility of employment (Idowu & Elbanna, 2020).

By contrast, the view that adopts the exploitation perspective argues that workers are exploited by the owners of capital and means of production. Focusing on job design, digital platform management, and employment rights, this view addresses the precarious aspects of crowdwork, highlighting the power of digital platforms and the possibility of subjecting desperately job-seeking workers to a race to the bottom in order to get paid (Elbanna & Idowu, 2021). Consequently, employers can now employ "independent" workers, which cost them less, instead of "employees". The employment of "independent" workers paves the way for employers to determine the wages as low as possible, which employers consider an important item among general expenses, as there is still no minimum wage limit for these workers in many countries. This opportunity offered by the Internet to employers for easy access to the workforce causes job seekers to lower the wages they look for in order to make themselves more attractive, thereby causing those who work on digital platforms to work for very low wages, even below the minimum wage (Erol, 2021).

Crowdwork, which constitutes a different type of labour at the intersection of digital work and gainful employment, is a tool that can empower individuals by creating and offering a space where they can choose their own work, be creative and/or interact to solve problems as part of the larger community. It provides a high degree of flexibility in when and how a person works. It can also support businesses to be creative and innovative by providing access to experts, knowledgeable individuals, and customers (Barnes et al., 2015). Despite all these advantages, crowdworking is also considered as a model that can negatively affect the job satisfaction of workers, due to such factors as the absence of promotion opportunities, simple and repetitive tasks (which can lead to perceived overqualification), and above all, being extremely short-term that requires the crowdworker to sign several contracts in the same day (O'Higgins & Caro, 2021).

SOLUTIONS AND RECOMMENDATIONS

This study was aimed to examine the motivation through the experience of the content editor and a content writer in the framework of Turkey. Also, in this study, aims to put forward the position of Turkey to other countries, notably Germany, about new work platforms. The study is also imported to examine a new understanding of employing life in Turkey representing crowdworking platforms.

In-depth interviews were made with a crowdworker and content editor-platform manager (crowdsourcer) to examine the issue through direct experiences. Unlike quantitative research methods, no statistical data is obtained during an in-depth interview, which is one of the data collection methods used in the qualitative research process. In the data collection process carried out through the interview, the interviewee should be suitable for the research topic and have the competence to respond to the questions. It is necessary to conduct a pilot interview before the interview in order to carry out the procedure correctly and to identify and solve the problems, if any (Griffee, 2005). In this study, a pilot interview was conducted with the editor and content writer, who is directly related to the research subject and is knowledgeable about the subject, in order to determine the questions within this framework.

Another important detail in the in-depth interviews is that the responses given are to be interpreted by the researcher. While analyzing the data obtained from the interview, the researcher can also make assessments about the research topic (Griffee, 2005). This study has aimed to determine the new outlook of recent business practices for the post-pandemic world in accordance with the subject of the study.

In this connection, the purpose of the in-depth interview is to explore individuals' views, experiences, beliefs and/or motivations on specific issues. Qualitative methods such as interviews are believed to provide a much 'deeper' understanding of social phenomena than would be obtained from purely quantitative methods such as surveys. The interview method is, therefore, used when little is currently known about the study phenomenon or when it is aimed to obtain detailed information from participants. When designing an interview method, it is essential to consider that it consists of questions that are likely to provide as much information as possible about the study phenomenon and that can address the aims and objectives of the research. In a qualitative interview, questions should be open-ended (i.e., requiring more than a yes/no answer), impartial, sensitive, and understandable (Gill et al., 2008).

The interview method used to detect different aspects in the organizational dimension was preferred in this study as it is an important method in obtaining information about experiences, attitudes, opinions, and complaints. Open-ended structured interviews (Yıldırım & Şimşek, 2018) with different sides about crowdworking considered as a new work environment in Turkey were made by means of research for the discovery. As a result of the interviews asking open-ended research questions in Table 1, taking into account the motivations of the sides, results for the basic features of crowdworking work platform in Turkey was obtained.

Table 1. Interview questions

Person	Questions
Freelance content writer (crowdworker)	• What is your story of starting content writing? For what reason did you want to do this job? • Do you have another job? • How long do you devote to content writing? • How did you access this platform? • Do you have communication with other content authors? • How long do you plan to continue this work? • Are you satisfied with your work financially? • Can you choose your own duties on the platform? • What are your favorite features of the platform? What are the features you will criticize on the platform?
Content editor (crowdsourcer- platform manager)	• What is the reason for establishing the Platform; Can you briefly tell us about the establishment story? • Do you have a different profession and working life? • How many people do you work with on the platform and what are their duties? • Can you give information about the workflow? • How do you maintain communication with content writers? • What is your goal? • How did you create your customer portfolio? • What are the features you are looking for in content writers? • Can you give information about your position in the sector? Are there any features you plan to develop on the platform?

The Content Universe selected as an example is a platform for online content production to companies through content writers in the digital universe. As a result of the interview held with the founder-editor of the Content Universe Platform and one of the content authors of the same platform, the following conclusions were summarized:

-The content writer started working on this platform as a result of her own research. The content writer, who is also an academician, plans the time to prepare the contents on the platform. In accordance with the working principles of freelance, it undertakes the task of writing content as much as it wishes and completes them within the given time. She has no face-to-face contact with other writers or any other communication. She is able to work completely independently in any location. She connects the enjoyment of this job with the motivation of research-learning-content production. Since she has a different profession, she is only financially happy to earn additional income. She is very happy to use the platform freely according to her own preferences, to work as much as she wishes and to see the prices of the content through the platform in advance.

-Platform manager-editor decided to set up this platform after the SEO studies of Google algorithms were included in the content and the publications were digitized. Along with 180 active content-writers, 4 editors work in the Content Universe, which aims to bring publishers and writers together with quality content. Bringing content requests from publishers together with the writers, the platform aims to work especially with powerful-creative-innovative content writers. The platform aims to facilitate integration with publishers on a smarter system in the future. Working on video and podcast content production is among the priorities of the platform.

In Turkey, there is a need for a professional approach to crowdworking. The Content Universe is a crowdworking platform that draws attention with its approach in this direction. However, there are also some initiatives that are far from this professional approach. Accordingly, it turns out that more work and information should be made in place of random discoveries regarding crowdworking.

A number of remarkable changes in business life, have also been felt in Turkey especially since the beginning of the COVID-19 pandemic. The number of institutions that started to implement the remote working model has gradually increased and this working style has been put on the agenda by the senior management of the institutions to consider it as an alternative for situations even when there is no danger of a pandemic. Similarly, in the public sector, the number of practices on remote working such as online meetings and events have started to increase, especially as a precaution for the problems in the economic process. It would not be wrong to say that the crowdworking model, which is considered in terms of the parties of this approach in this study, has attracted more attention by more job seekers and employers due to the COVID-19 pandemic.

Since the early months of 2020, hundreds of thousands of people have lost their jobs due to the impact of the COVID-19 pandemic, while some have experienced a decrease in their salaries. In addition, people who have had to struggle with depression, anxiety and many stress-related problems keep taking time off from their jobs. On the other hand, the developments in communication technologies and the increase in the number of connection tools have accelerated the remote working models. The term working from home, which started to be used in the 1970s, has become a necessity rather than an option after the COVID-19 pandemic (Singh, 2020). Such a process, which was examined as an example application in this study and regarding which the parties were consulted for more information via the interview method, could also be considered as an application for transitioning from the stage of consideration as an option to an obligation. The analysis of the motivation sources identified especially for the crowdworkers and crowdsourcers shows that the idea of working regardless of the place can be considered as a way of working that has been demanded since the beginning of the COVID-19 pandemic. This working model also offers advantages, especially for small businesses with lower operating income and supply chain disruption, which are also less likely to have a better cash flow condition. In this connection, creative approaches to working from home have been discovered during the pandemic. With the transition to the traditional working order, however, it has become essential to be able to continue to keep up with the model by emphasizing what has been learned as well as the advantages of this experienced work model (Zhnag, et al., 2022). This study aimed to conduct an in-depth evaluation of one of the new working practices, which is considered as an alternative to traditional working environments, in line with the opinions of the relevant parties.

FUTURE RESEARCH DIRECTIONS

This book project aims to examine the post-COVID-19 global challenges and the strategies developed to combat these challenges, and this section titled "An Evaluation of New Work Practices After the Pandemic: Crowdworking" focuses on evaluating working life. The experience related to certain approaches such as remote working and working from home, which has been discussed for many years, has led to the development of new working practices such as crowdworking by taking into consideration its recently emerging aspects. Future studies may provide in-depth analyses especially for new working practices so that an evaluation will be made for the society that has been transformed by means of communication technologies and digital technologies. While similar approaches such as crowdworking will shape business life in the future, more research is needed regarding social, cultural, and economic contexts with many other different effects on social dimensions. In this chapter, in addition to focusing on the impact of the COVID-19 pandemic, different social effects will also be evaluated under different topics that this study will be a source of.

CONCLUSION

Given that the post-COVID has led to numerous changes in social life, it would not be wrong to say that the transformations in working life have also shaped all daily life practices over time. The pandemic, which suddenly started at a time when digital society discussions were on the rise with the effect of the transformation in communication technologies, also influenced the adaptation to transformation process. Work models, such as working from home, considered a matter of discussion long before this rapid transition, have ceased to be an option and have become a necessity due to the pandemic. However, as a prediction for the post-COVID period, it could be assumed that this way of working will become commonplace for 21st century people. Despite its controversial aspects, crowdworking defines a new working life which can be widely applicable within the work models of the future.

This study has examined the motivation resources of a crowdworker and a crowdsourcer. However, in the future, different social effects on this way of working will most probably draw attention as a subject of investigation. The impact of new work practices on different vital areas will likely be considered as an important subject matter of research in future academic studies. Besides that, it is clear that the new working practices of the digital society will be analyzed over time. Different work environments, worker relations, superior-subordinate communication, job satisfaction, productivity, and satisfaction will definitely begin to be redefined depending on this new working environment. It is observed that workers, who are connected to each other in a single office and fulfil their duties by influencing each other, have started to appear in a more free and independent working environment along with the post-COVID period, and that they are capable of maintaining their working environment relations as they wish in this free environment. Despite the fact that studies on digitalization and digital society were already remarkable even before the pandemic, we believe that the COVID-19 pandemic will be conceived as a crucial turning point in relevant future studies. All things considered, it is clear that the COVID-19 pandemic has been an important driving force in digital life, where different societies are involved in different processes according to their level of development.

REFERENCES

Almeida, F., Santos, J. D., & Monteiro, J. A. (2020). The challenges and opportunities in the digitalization of companies in a post-COVID-19 World. *IEEE Engineering Management Review*, *48*(3), 97–103. doi:10.1109/EMR.2020.3013206

Altieri, M. A., & Nicholls, C. I. (2020). Agroecology and the reconstruction of a post-COVID-19 agriculture. *The Journal of Peasant Studies*, *47*(5), 881–898. doi:10.1080/03066150.2020.1782891

Ancillo, A. L., del Val Núñez, M. T., & Gavrila, S. G. (2021). Workplace change within the COVID-19 context: A grounded theory approach. *Economic Research-Ekonomska Istraživanja*, *34*(1), 2297–2316. doi:10.1080/1331677X.2020.1862689

Aroles, J., Mitev, N., & de Vaujany, F. X. (2019). Mapping themes in the study of new work practices. *New Technology, Work and Employment, 34*(3), 285–299. doi:10.1111/ntwe.12146

Bai, C., Dallasega, P., Orzes, G., & Sarkis, J. (2020). Industry 4.0 technologies assessment: A sustainability perspective. *International Journal of Production Economics, 229*, 1–15. doi:10.1016/j.ijpe.2020.107776

Banik, N., & Padalkar, M. (2021). The spread of gig economy: Trends and effects. *Foresight and STI Governance, 15*(1), 28–38. doi:10.17323/2500-2597.2021.1.19.29

Barnes, S. A., Green, A., & de Hoyos, M. (2015). Crowdsourcing and work: Individual factors and circumstances influencing employability. *New Technology, Work and Employment, 30*(1), 16–31. doi:10.1111/ntwe.12043

Bennett, J., Owers, M., Pitt, M., & Tucker, M. (2010). Workplace impact of social networking. *Property Management, 28*(3), 138–148. doi:10.1108/02637471011051282

Boland, B., De Smet, A., Palter, R., & Sanghvi, A. (2020). *Reimagining the office and work life after COVID-19.* https://www.mckinsey.com/business-functions/organization/our-insights/reimagining-the-office-and-work-life-after-covid-19

Castells, M. (2004). *The network society a cross-cultural perspective.* Edward Elgar.

Davies, K. (2021). Festival's post COVID-19. *Leisure Sciences, 43*(1-2), 184–189. doi:10.1080/01490400.2020.1774000

De Stefano, V. (2016). *The rise of the «just-in-time workforce»: On-demand work, crowdwork and labour protection in the «gig-economy».* International Labour Office.

Digout, J., Azouri, M., Decaudin, J.-M., & Rochard, S. (2013). Crowdsourcing, outsourcing to obtain a creativity group. *The Arab Economics and Business Journal, 8*(1-2), 6–15. doi:10.1016/j.aebj.2013.11.001

Durward, D., Blohm, I., & Leimeister, J. M. (2016). Crowd work. *Business & Information Systems Engineering, 58*(4), 281–286. doi:10.100712599-016-0438-0

Elbanna, A., & Idowu, A. (2021). Crowdwork as an elevator of human capital. *Scandinavian Journal of Information Systems, 33*(2), 103–136.

Erol, A. (2021). Dijitalleşme çağında işyerinin değişimi: Sebepleri ve sonuçları. *İnsan & İnsan, 8*(30), 97-113.

Florida, R., Rodríguez-Pose, A., & Storper, M. (2021). Cities in a post-COVID world. *Urban Studies.*

Gill, P., Stewart, K., Treasure, E., & Chadwick, B. (2008). Methods of data collection in qualitative research: Interviews and focus groups. *British Dental Journal, 204*(6), 291–295. doi:10.1038/bdj.2008.192 PMID:18356873

Görmüş, A. (2020). Social distancing way of working during the COVID-19 pandemic period: Teleworking. *Turkish Studies, 15*(4), 481–496.

Griffee, D. T. (2005). Research Tips: Interview Data Collection. *Journal of Developmental Education, 28*(3), 36–37.

Henry, M. S., Le Roux, D. B., & Parry, D. A. (2021). Working in a post Covid-19 world: Towards a conceptual framework for distributed work. *South African Journal of Business Management, 52*(1), a2155. doi:10.4102ajbm.v52i1.2155

Huws, U. (2013). Working online, living offline: Labour in the Internet Age. *Work Organisation, Labour & Globalisation, 7*(1), 1–11.

Idowu, A., & Elbanna, A. (2020). Digital platforms of work and the crafting of career path: The crowd-workers' perspective. *Information Systems Frontiers*, 1–17.

Jäger, G., Zilian, L. S., Hofer, C., & Füllsack, M. (2019). Crowdworking: Working with or against the crowd? *Journal of Economic Interaction and Coordination, 14*(4), 761–788. doi:10.100711403-019-00266-1

Kaine, S., & Josserand, E. (2019). The organisation and experience of work in the gig economy. *The Journal of Industrial Relations, 61*(4), 479–501. doi:10.1177/0022185619865480

Kittur, A., Nickerson, J. V., Bernstein, M. S., Gerber, E. M., Shaw, A., Zimmerman, J., Lease, M., & Horton, J. (2013). The future of crowd work. *Social Science Electronic Publishing, 263*(1), 1301–1318.

Kniffin, K. M., Narayanan, J., Anseel, F., Antonakis, J., Ashford, S. P., Bakker, A. B., ... Johns, G. (2020). COVID-1.9 and the workplace: Implications, ıssues, and ınsights for future research and action. *The American Psychologist, 76*(1), 63–77. doi:10.1037/amp0000716 PMID:32772537

Méndez, L. M. (2020). A reflection on the challenges posed by digitalisation of labour markets. In J. Carby-Hall & L. M. Méndez (Eds.), *Labour Law and the Gig Economy* (pp. 1–13). Routledge. doi:10.4324/9781003033721-101

Mrass, V., Peters, C., & Leimeister, J. M. (2016). *New work organization through crowdworking platforms-a case study*. Academic Press.

Mrass, V., & Peters, C. (2017). *Crowdworking-Plattformen in Deutschland*. Academic Press.

Mrass, V., Peters, C., & Leimeister, J. M. (2017). *Exploiting the digitization of leisure time: Casual work and additional earnings for ındividuals on crowdworking platforms*. In International Conference on Information Systems (ICIS), Pre-Workshop "Digitization of the Individual (DOTI)", Seoul, South Korea.

OECD. (2019). *How's Life in the Digital Age? Opportunities and Risks of the Digital Transformation for People's Well-being*. OECD Publishing. doi:10.1787/9789264311800-

O'Higgins, N., & Caro, L. P. (2021). *Crowdwork for young people: Risks and opportunities*. IZA Discussion Papers 14933, Institute of Labor Economics (IZA). https://docs.iza.org/dp14933.pdf

Pulignano, V., Domecka, M., Muszyński, K., Vermeerbergen, L., & Rieman, M.-L. (2021). *Creative labour in the era of Covid-19: The case of freelancers*. ETUI Research Paper-Working Paper. https://www.etui.org/sites/default/files/202103/Creative%20labour%20in%20the%20era%20of%20Covid-19%20the%20case%20of%20freelancers-2021-web.pdf

Richards, J. (2012). What has the internet ever done for employees? A review, map and research agenda. *Employee Relations, 34*(1), 22–43. doi:10.1108/01425451211183246

Serfling, O. (2018). *Crowdworking Monitor Nr. 1.* https://conference.iza.org/conference_files/Statistic_2019/serfling_o1156.pdf

Serrano, F., & Kazda, A. (2020). The future of airport post COVID-19. *Journal of Air Transport Management, 89*, 101900. doi:10.1016/j.jairtraman.2020.101900 PMID:32834696

Singh, G. (2020). Changes in work culture and workplace due to COVID19 crisis. PsyArXiv. doi:10.31234/osf.io/htjx5osf.io/htjx5

Stewart, A., & Stanford, J. (2017). Regulating work in the gig economy: What are the options? *Economic and Labour Relations Review, 28*(3), 420–437. doi:10.1177/1035304617722461

Urciuoli, B. (2008). Skills and selves in the new workplace. *American Ethnologist, 35*(2), 211–228. doi:10.1111/j.1548-1425.2008.00031.x

World Economic Forum. (2020). *The Future of Jobs Report 2020.* https://www3.weforum.org/docs/WEF_Future_of_Jobs_2020.pdf

Yıldırım, A., & Şimşek, H. (2018). *Qualitative Research Methods in Social Sciences.* Seçkin Publishing.

Zahra, S. A. (2021). International entrepreneurship in the post Covid world. *Journal of World Business, 56*(1), 101143. doi:10.1016/j.jwb.2020.101143

Zhang, T., Gerlowski, D., & Acs, Z. (2022). Working from home: Small business performance and the COVID-19 pandemic. *Small Business Economics, 58*(2), 611–636. doi:10.100711187-021-00493-6

ADDITIONAL READING

Canter, L., & Wilkinson, E. (Eds.). (2020). *Freelancing for Journalists* (1st ed.). Routledge. doi:10.4324/9780429027178

Cresswell, T. (2021). Valuing mobility in a post COVID-19 world. *Mobilities, 16*(1), 51–65. doi:10.1080/17450101.2020.1863550

Howe, J. (2008). *Crowdsourcing: How the power of the crowd is driving the future of business.* Random House.

Kreß, S. (2021). *Crowdwork.* Duncker & Humblot. doi:10.3790/978-3-428-58211-2

Lupton, D., & Willis, K. (2021). *The COVID-19 Crisis: Social Perspectives* (1st ed.). Routledge., doi:10.4324/9781003111344

Mallya, P. D., & D'Silva, R. (Eds.). (2020). *Impact Of Covid–19 Crisis On The Global Economy And Other Sectors Worldwide.* Idea Publishing.

Nandy, M., & Lodh, S. (2020). Post-COVID-19 and Business Analytics. In A. Joshi, N. Dey, & K. Santosh (Eds.), *Intelligent Systems and Methods to Combat Covid-19. Springer Briefs in Applied Sciences and Technology.* Springer. doi:10.1007/978-981-15-6572-4_10

Osnowitz, D. (2010). *Freelancing Expertise: Contract Professionals in the New Economy*. Cornell University Press. doi:10.7591/9780801460388

KEY TERMS AND DEFINITIONS

Crowdsourcing: Crowdsourcing is the act of collecting services, ideas, or content through the contributions of a large group of people.

Crowdwork: Work carried out by a large number of people, each contributing a small amount of labor.

Crowdworker: A person who works in a job run by a large number of people, each contributing a small amount of labor.

Crowdworking Platforms: Microtask platforms are a type of web-based labour platform that provide businesses and other clients with access to a large, flexible workforce.

New Work Practices: With the influence of Industry 4.0, working environments and habits shaped in accordance with new social life practices, apart from the usual working life.

Online Freelancing: Work done online based on free time. It is the name given to remote working independently of any corporation, without an office environment.

Pandemic: A global epidemic that affects a large geographical area or a large part of the world.

Chapter 14
Supply Chain in the Eras of Pre and Post COVID-19:
A Systematic Review and Framework Development

Hesham Magd
Modern College of Business and Science, Oman

Benson Ruzive
Modern College of Business and Science, Oman

ABSTRACT

Firms have been forced to adopt and/or retract to previously dropped management control strategies such as onshoring. This has come at the backdrop of preventative policies enforced by most governments such as lockdowns, social distancing, and to some extend the closure of common frontiers. This study aims at establishing the logistics and supply chain strategies embraced by firms before, during, and after COVID-19. Some secondary objectives include to discover strategies adopted by companies during and after COVID-19 to identify the impact and disruptions caused by COVID-19 in natural economies to establish approaches in supply chain management approaches and practices and to establish critical success factors and preventative strategies post COVID-19. A cross-sectional survey of literature is conducted with the aim of identifying the themes in the study area and synthesizing them to identify gaps.

1. INTRODUCTION

Global value chains (GVCs) have been adversely affected by Covid-19 pandemic (FT,2020; Panwar, 2020) and there is no knowledge as to when this virus will end. It is evident that the virus has caused immense havoc, disruption, not only by drastically reducing populations across the globe but by also affecting operations of economies which were previously running smoothly. The origin of the pandemic is attributed to an outbreak of the virus in Wuhan a Chinese province (Semanur and Ercan, 2020) at the end of the year 2019 giving rise to the nomenclature 'Covid-2019'.

DOI: 10.4018/978-1-7998-8856-7.ch014

Epochal changes to human lives have been brought about by the outbreak of the pandemic Covid-19 (Wagner, 2020). Jobs have been lost, lives have been lost, economies have been synonymous with shrinking performances, all this bringing untold suffering to human life. The attention of business managers, politicians and researchers was suddenly shifted from the traditional business risks and/or pressing issues of climate change to the challenges caused by the pandemic. Strange (2020) propose the inclusion of pandemics in risk assessment plans in the future by firms. Strategies such offshoring and outsourcing which had become very popular were affected adversely because partner would unfold their operations citing the pandemic as *force majeure* without giving other partners ample time to adjust. Firms were forced to reconfigure their global value chains but at the mercy of policies and regulations published by their respective governments (Semanur and Ercan, 2020). The same authors reiterate that countries like the United States, Japan and Australia considered decoupling their economies from largely depending on China for both their imports and exports as these countries blamed China for the outbreak of the pandemic. In addition, the pandemic came at a time when the phenomenon of globalization was visibly under the spotlight because of worries in many nations about issues such as sovereignty, national security and the unequal distribution of benefits garnered from globalization (Kobrin, 2017; Rodrik, 2018; Strange, 2020). Based on the literature review, it was evident that there are certain supply chain practices were followed during pre and post covid (see Table 1) which will be explored in details in the below section.

Table 1. Summary of Pre- and Post-Covid Supply Chain Practices

Pre-Covid Supply Chain Practices	Post-Covid Supply Chain Practices
• Off-shoring • Information sharing • Customer relationship management • Supplier relationship management • Collaboration • Supply chain integration • Green supply	• On-shoring • Technology adoption (IoT) • Localizing supply chains • Merging businesses • Knowledge management • Crowdsourcing • Social distancing • Re-engineering

2. RESEARCH OBJECTIVES AND METHODOLOGY

The world has been hit by Covid 19 pandemic which negatively impacted entire economies and posed a great threat to the public health. To prevent the spread of Covid 19, many governments put in place stringent measures such as complete lockdowns. Supply chains have been battling with various challenges due to the pandemic and firms faced several difficulties in adjusting to the new normal of operating within the existence of the pandemic, and therefore it's unclear on the way forward for firms to apply certain strategies for effective supply chain after the pandemic. Therefore, the main objective of the paper is to address pre-covid supply chain practices and identify strategies that will be implemented to ensure effective supply chain post-covid as it is believed that the same strategies that were practiced earlier may not be applicable or sustainable. To fulfill the objectives, the researchers are utilizing content analysis through the available studies on the subject matter. Content analysis is a popular method that supports building a theoretical concepts and models. Using content analysis would help the researchers in identifying concepts and reach conclusions from the extracted information from the available literature review on the subject matter.

3. LITERATURE REVIEW

3.1 Covid-19 Pandemic Outbreak: Global Crisis

The virus was first identified in a province called Wuhan in China in December of 2019 (Zhu, Chou, and Tsai, 2020). The World Health Organization declared the virus a natural disaster and global pandemic in March 2020. By that time, damage had already been done because people had been travelling to and from that province within China and as had been the norm, people across the globe had mingled with people from China. Governments moved by putting in place strong measures such as national lockdowns to prevent the spread of the virus but of noteworthy is that these governments moved at different paces. Tiwari et al., (2020) state that Covid-19 pandemic has become a worldwide epidemic that has given nations torrid times. By the end of September 2020, more than 33 million people had been confirmed as having contracted the virus with mortality figures recorded as one million (WHO 2020a). The United States of America had been recorded as the country with the highest number of confirmed cases of the virus (Tiwari et al., 2020). The White House (2020a) reported that the first confirmed case of the virus was recorded at the end of January 2020 and the Federal government began imposing some travel restrictions on foreign nationals.

Despite these measures, an unexpected growth in the numbers of infected peopled was recorded at an exponential rate in many countries. The White House (2020b) reports that social distancing, bans on public gatherings, and closure of non-essential businesses were among some of the measures that were introduced by the Federal government to curb the spread of the virus. This development of closing what government referred to as 'non-essential services' created a gap, for instance the closure of cinemas meant that those who were earning a living from that business suddenly could not do so. In addition, some people who were stressed were visiting those areas as places to reduce their stress, but the moment they were forced to stay home where in some cases these homes might be the sources of their stresses and heartaches. This might be a cause for an increase of their vulnerability. This could have contributed to a rise in suicide related death cases and even a decline in health conditions of individual. It's evident that most of the health institutions were closed for all other diseases except Covid-19 cases. However, World Health Organization (2020) state that at the beginning of the year 2020 the outbreak of Covid-19 seemed to be a local health problem but by the end of March 2020, that position had shifted, and organizations were left with no option but to declare the pandemic a global crisis.

3.2 Covid-19 Pandemic Disruptions in Natural Economies

In reaction to the pandemic, governments enacted stringent measures such as lockdowns to contain the spread of the disease. These stringent measures resulted in the shutting down of some economic sectors such as tourism and hospitality (Kaczmarek et al., 2021). Due to the lockdown and other measures that were taken by the governments, businesses were facing difficulties in adjusting to these stringent measures, and world economies were impacted severely. The world's GDP has declined (Zhu et al., 2020) (see Figure 1), and 94% of Fortune 100 companies experienced difficulties because of Covid disruptions

Figure 1. World's GDP

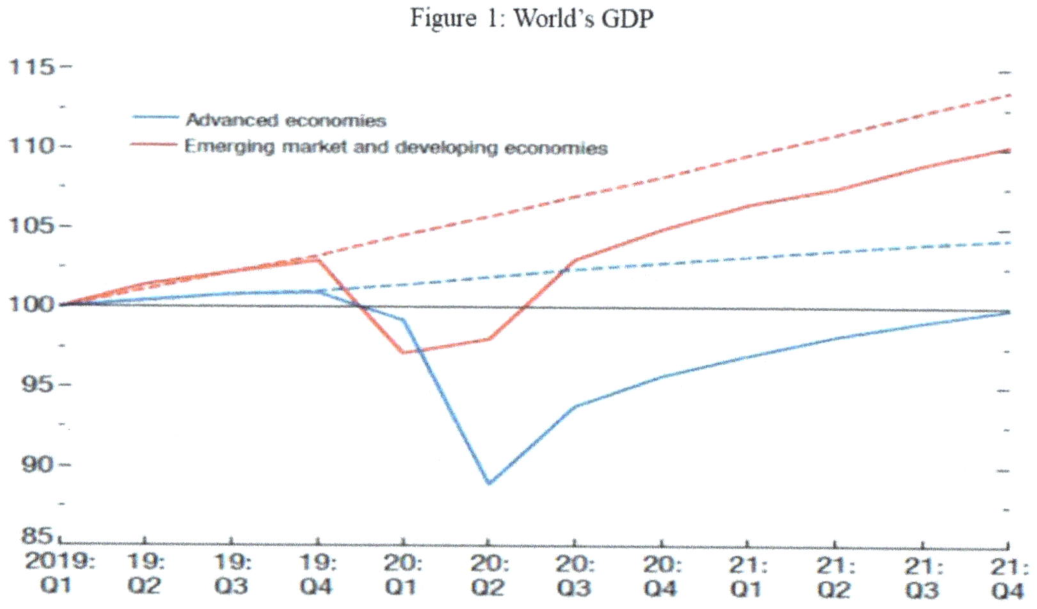

(Source: Zhu et al., 2020: 2)

(Supply Chain Digital, 2020). Gosslings *et al.*, (2020) believe that the tourism and hospitality sector was the most affected mainly due to the pandemic came as a surprise or unexpected. World Tourism Organization (UNWTO 2020b) indicated that international tourism and leisure related activities dropped by 97% which is translated into a loss of more than US$200 billion in revenue. This was reported as the worst decline in the history of global tourism even after World War II (World Tourism Organization UNWTO, 2020a).

Covid-19 has had devastating impact on supply chains (Chowdhury et al., 2021) and International Civil Aviation Organization (ICAO) reported that supply chain activities were negatively affected by the pandemic (ICAO, 2020), and Zhu et al. (2020) indicated that people and goods movements declined significantly, and the aviation industry was facing collapse as represented in figure 2. In addition, further data were discussed at the United Nations Conference on Trade and Development (UNCTAD, 2020) and suggested that global trade values have extremely declined due to the pandemic as illustrated in figure 3.

Figure 2. Drastic capacity cut along with dramatic drop in demand
(Source: Zhu et al., 2020: 2)

Figure 2: Drastic capacity cut along with dramatic drop in demand

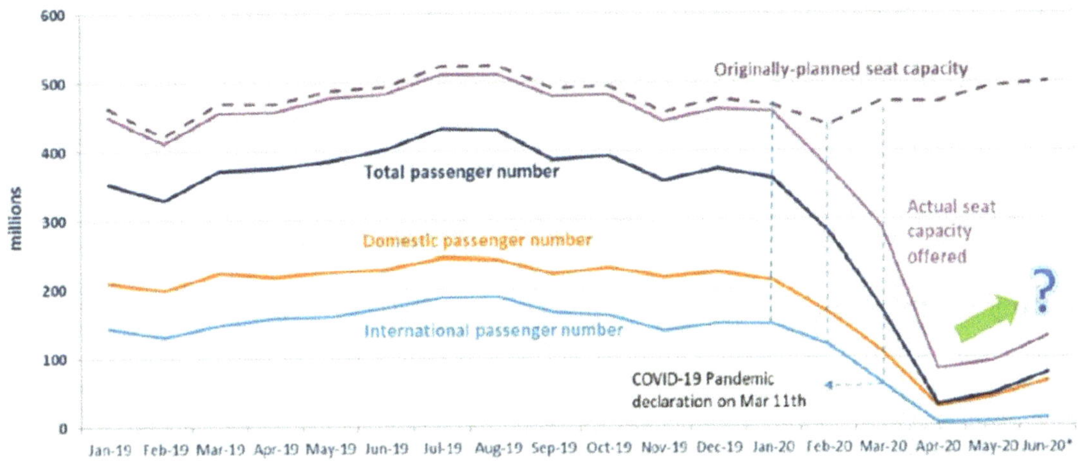

(Source: Zhu et al., 2020: 2)

Figure 3. A steep downturn in global trade in goods
(Source: Zhu et al., 2020:3)

Figure 3: A steep downturn in global trade in goods

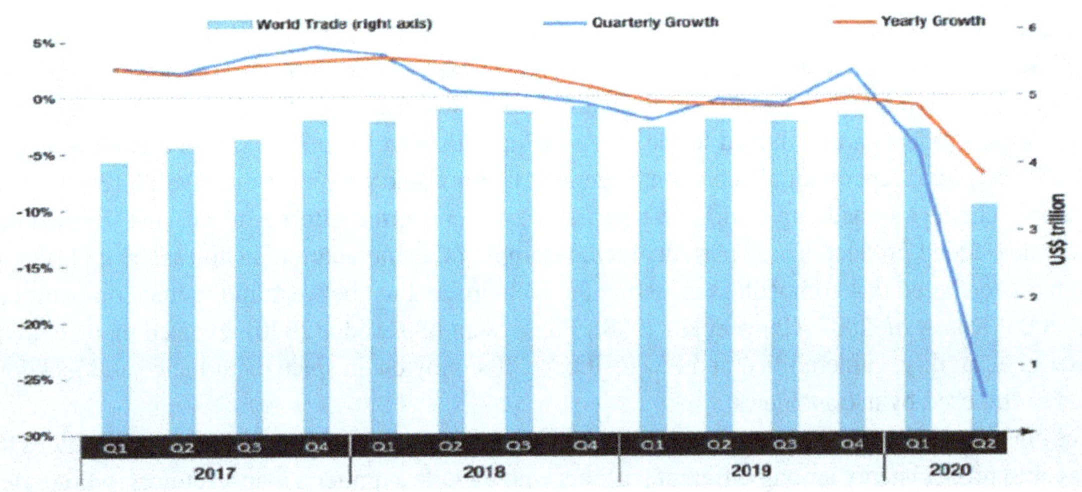

(Source: Zhu et al., 2020 :3)

Scholars have increased their quest to search for answers in this area regarding on how to tackle such negative impacts of the pandemic and seeking strategies to help the economy to recover. Research has shown that demand for essential items such as Personal Protective Equipment (PPE) and other related healthcare products increased while low-demand items and supply chains of small to medium size enterprises (SMEs) were largely ignored. Hudechck et al., (2020) reiterate that the World Health Organization reported severe disease outbreaks during the period between 2011 and 2018 with as much as 1438 cases having been recorded but these were not as strong as the current pandemic. The magnitude of the pandemic was reported by Fortune Magazine on 21st February 2020 stating that as much as 94% of the Fortune 1000 companies were facing disruptions in the supply chains. Border closures as instigated by governments caused transportation challenges leading to heavy disruptions in the manufacturing sector as vehicles found it hard to cross frontiers (Paul and Chowdhury, 2020a; Amankwah-Amoah, 2020b) and comply with the various restrictions imposed by different governments.

3.3 Supply Chain Pre-Covid

Political, economic, social, and technological disciplines have been adversely affected by the Covid-19 pandemic given that it is a highly infectious respiratory virus. Politicians had to suspend national and international gatherings, disruptions were experienced in economies, and none was spared, people were barred from visiting friends and even places of recreation such as gym halls. There was an upsurge in demand for certain gadgets such as laptops and tablets as well as some software platforms like Microsoft Teams because of people working from home and institutions of learning shifting from the traditional face-to-face to online learning. UNCTAD (2020) reported a significant decline in the movement of goods and people which had an adverse effect on the Gross Domestic Product (GDP). Zhu et al. (2020) indicate that governments imposed national lockdowns and even closed their borders to curb the spread of the virus but that had adverse effects of disrupting economies since less or no goods were transported. This disruption has demonstrated the fragility and vulnerability of modern supply chains.

Supply chain management includes range of activities to procure and mange supplies in producing products and services that satisfy the needs of customers. Supply chain management refers at directing the activities performed by chain partners towards satisfying the needs of the end customer (Chang *et al.*, 2013; Dubey and Ali, 2013; Machowiak, 2012; Randall and Mello, 2012; Dubey *et al.*, 2012; Mclnyk *et al.*, 2009). The earliest definitions of supply chain were from Venkataramanan (1998) who said that supply chain deals with the transformation of raw materials into finished products and ensuring that these products are delivered to the end user on time. This definition shows that even as early as the 1990s the concept of supply chain management had become a topical issue. Parkhi (2015) posits that supply chains are made up of different parties whose concerted effort is to provide the customer with a value-added product. These partners include suppliers, manufacturers, wholesalers and retailers and it has been noted that competition is among these chains and not between individual companies (Li *et al.*, 2005; Koh *et al*, 2007; Chow et al., 2008). Fonseca and Azevedo (2020) revealed that Covid has exposed the fragility, vulnerability, and low resilience of supply chain since disturbance and lockdown caused or imposed by national laws.

The entire supply chain and individual firms are kept intact by as set of approaches and practices that endeavor to bring synergy among different partners who include suppliers, manufacturers, wholesalers, and retailers (Chopra and Meindl, 2001). Hamid and Ibrahim (2014) refer to supply chain practices as a set of approaches applied to the supply chain to effectively manage and coordinate processes and activities aimed at pleasing the end user and they have listed these approaches in table 2.

Table 2. Supply Chain Approaches

	Author(s)	Dimensions
1	Chin *et al.*, (2011)	Customer relationship, strategic supplier partnership, information sharing, material flow management and corporate culture
2	Inda *et al.*, (1999)	Strategic supplier partnership, customer relationship, information sharing
3	Chowa *et al.*, (2008)	Suppliers and customer management, information sharing, speed of communication, supply chain features
4	Min & Mentzer (2004)	Green vision and goals, information sharing, risk and award sharing, cooperation, process integration, long-term relationship, and green supply chain leadership
5	Chen & Paulraj (2004)	Supplier base reduction, long-term relationship, communication, cross-functional teams, supplier involvement to measure buyer relationships
6	Tan, Lyman & Wisner (2002)	Supply chain integration, information sharing, supply chain characteristics, customer service management, geographical proximity, and JIT capability
7	Alvarado & Kotzab (2001)	EDI, elimination of excess stock levels by postponing customization toward the end of the supply
8	Tan, Kannan & Handfield (1998)	Supply chain quality and customer relations
9	Donlon (1996)	Supplier partnerships, outsourcing time compression, continuous process flow information sharing

(Source: Hamid and Ibrahim, 2014:188)

3.3.1 Supply Chain Approaches and Practices

Several supply chain management practices have been suggested by researchers, and the most prominent ones include, supply chain integration, supplier relationship management, customer relationship management, information sharing and customer responsiveness. These shall be discussed below:

Supply chain integration: Hamid and Ibrahim (2014) posit that supply chain integration refers to very effort made by a firm to upgrade linkages within different components of the supply chain so that there is greater interaction and achievement of efficiency and as well as visibility to identify bottlenecks. Within the organization, integration must take place among different departments and outside the organization an increased collaboration should be sought. Handfield and Nichols (1999) indicate that the drivers of supply chain integration are the information revolution, increased levels of global competition and emergency of new types of inter-organizational relationships. Inter-organizational relationships have made it possible for firms to recognize the need depend on each other to survive in hostile environments. This has culminated into information sharing on several common interests which include demand and supply sources. Handfield and Nichols (1999) highlight three elements of integration in the supply chain namely *the management of information and financial flows, the management of products and materials as well as the management of relationships between trading partners.*

Supplier Relationship Management: Supplier relationship management represents long-term relationship and collaborations between an organization and its suppliers. Gharakhani *et al.*, (2012) reiterate that a leading-edge supply chain in marked by a robust and clear supplier relationship whose traits were suggested by Hamidi and Ibrahim (2014) as working together and sharing responsibilities for the success of the chain. It is vital for firms to collaborate with their supplier even at an early stage of product development to identify challenges, opportunities and reduce risks. Supplier integration is beneficial for organizations as it brings about product innovation during the product development stages and this is usually accompanied by cost efficiency (Hamidi and Ibrahim, 2014).

Customer Relationship Management: Organizational performance is enhanced by creating and maintaining relationships with customers (Vrijhoef & Koskela, 1999). Firms that strive to understand their customers' current and future needs to have a better chance of meeting and exceeding customer expectations (Hamidi and Ibrahim, 2014). Customer who are satisfied by services and products they get from sellers will remain loyal and will do repeat business with the same seller in future. To fully satisfy customer needs, companies must integrate their selling activities, marketing strategies and service they offer. Resolving customer complaints promptly and amicably creates a conducive environment for trust and loyalty.

Information Sharing: Sridharan and Simatupang (2002) define information sharing as the process of reaching data privately owned by a firm with the authority and blessing of that company. This is done to enable both firms to monitor the progress related to product production as these products pass through several stages in the supply chain. Information sharing refers to the ability of a firm to share knowledge with supply chain partners in and effective and efficient manner (Hamidi & Ibrahim, 2014). Effective information sharing is regarded as one of the most important ingredients of a successful supply chain. Lee (2002) stated that the information shared among partners in the supply chain must enable communication. It is important for firms to choose and know who to share information with and how much should be shared between and among different partners. Zailani and Rajagopal (2005) add that the technological wave of internet and e-commerce provides better ana new opportunities to create a smart supply chain integration system. Some of the elements associated with information sharing include data acquisition, data processing, data storage, data presentation and retrieval as well as broadcasting demand and forecast data (Simatupany and Sridharam, 2002).

4.1 The Shock: Impact of Covid-19 on Supply Chain

The shock that has been caused so far by Covid-19 pandemic is clear and shows it will have long-term effects on the political, economic, and social status of the world. Sarkis (2020) identify some of the reactions by authorities to the pandemic as closure of non-essential businesses, social distancing, smaller public gatherings, indefinite closures of sporting activities, as well as requiring citizens to stay in single places and desist from travelling. Jobs were lost resulting in fall in gross domestic per capita falling and its yet to be established the impact of job losses on social fabrics.

A notable change in demand of some basic items such as PPE, toilet papers, and cotton swabs which were used for testing viruses (Paul and Chawdhury, 2020; Rowan & Laffery, 2020). Across the globe, goods were delivered late or in some cases never reached its destination as the operational responsiveness of supply chains became conspicuous (Sarkis, 2020). The same author reiterates that in some instances, goods were held at borders when governments would have declared that even goods were not supposed to be received in their country for fear of the spread of the virus, and that resulted in disruptions of food supply chains. Antagonism, skepticism, and reservations were popular traits in lean supply chains and that affected the efficiency of these chains.

Guan et al., (2020) state that demand and supply were characterized by chaos and reverberation which were proliferated across the global networks. This was a total reverse of the previous gains in which firms had gained competitive advantages under paradigms of comparative advantages through findings locations offering advantages in costs and resources (Schleper et al., 2019).

MODERN SUPPLY CHAIN- POST COVID-19: RECOVERING AND PREVENTATIVE STRATEGIES

CSF For Supply Chain Post Covid-19

Kashyap and Raghuvanshi (2020) suggest six critical success factors (CSF) for supply chains after the Covid-19 pandemic namely, effective communication, social distancing, adopting new technology, modifying roles and regulations at workplaces, sealing the borders of the territory, and having a strong leadership as well as government control. The relevance of communication is that it informs supply chain members of any developments within that chain, for instance if a country declares nationwide lockdown including closure of borders that information must be communicated to partners in the chain who do business with the country. The coronavirus has been diagnosed to be transmitted through closeness of human beings hence the need to have some distance between human beings.

The primary strategy that has been used by most countries to reduce and minimize the number of infections is lockdown (Kashyap & Raghuvanshi, 2020), with some even resorting to closing access to certain provinces or states within their countries. It should be noted that this non-medical restrictive measure used to control the spread of the virus has had effects on the economy by shutting down business operations (Kashyap & Raghuvanshi, 2020). Moreover, van Hoek (2020) suggests clustering risks into three basic groups, supply risks, demand risks and control risks. The author state that supply risks cause production disruptions by closing plants and machinery because of raw materials shortages. These can be reduced by avoiding relying too much on a single or few sources of supplies and these sources must be flexible enough to adjust to requirements in addition to being near or local in the supply chain. Risks in demand can produce the famous Bullwhip Effect because of the amplification of orders by members in the supply chain as one moves up the chain. Demand spikes lead to product shortages and logistical bottlenecks (van Hoek, 2020) and this can be avoided by sharing information among the members in the chain. There must be high level of visibility and transparency which may be assisted by maximizing the use of information technology among the partners. Control risks require consented efforts with suppliers and greater collaboration accompanied by strong negotiations for savings with selected suppliers.

5.1.1 Resilience and Sustainability Strategies

Research has shown that about eighty-six percent (86%) of supply chains were affected by the Covid-19 pandemic with figures ranging between 80% and 90% having risen to such levels by the end of March 2020 (Christopher and Peck, 2004). A noticeable reaction was a rise in the demand of some items such as toilet papers, hand sanitizers and other related hygiene products a departure from normal demand (van Hoek, 2020). Literature reviewed suggested several strategies that firm may embrace to overcome the challenges faced during the pandemic. One of these strategies is to make supply chain more resilient. McKinsey Global Institute (2020) indicated that 93% of the surveyed supply chain executives confirmed the importance of making supply chain more resilient post Covid 19. Fonseca and Azevedo (2020:431) suggested some *measures that should put in place in alignment with resilient strategies and these measures include building in redundancy across suppliers (e.g., dual sourcing or raw materials), increasing inventory of critical products, nearshoring, and expanding the supplier base, reducing the number of unique parts, and regionalizing their supply chain.*

Resilient strategies include social distancing, remote working, reduced business travel, reduced employee commuting, and these will inherently result in reduction in carbon footprint (van Hoek, 2020). Sarkis et al., (2020a) suggest that there is going to be an increase in virtual meetings and virtual reality acceptance. Working from home may however not be as sustainable as initially thought, for example a study in the UK established that there is a higher impact on working from home in winter as each home must be heated as opposed to heating a central office building (Turits, 2020). Policies like sheltering in one place and social distancing will change the shopping behavior of consumer to rely more on online shopping and once consumer have calculated some benefits from this behavior they will not go shopping physically (van Hoek, 2020). This means that retail supplier must align their business approaches towards home deliveries. Supply chains have been shortened for example in Canada by an e-commerce platform called Shopify which uses cloud and supply services (Guillen, 2020). Economies are going to be named as either sharing or circular economies in which circular economies will resemble supply chain that are localized through industrial symbiosis, waste exchanges and utilization of local byproducts, thus making them resilient (Hossain, 2020).

Many research opportunities for the complete supply chain management society and sustainable chains exist during and after the pandemic. It is an opportunity for natural experiments, empirical investigation, field, and case studies. A firm that seeks to create resilient supply chains must embrace the following principles suggested by de Sousa Jabbour and Jabbour (2020) namely, collaboration, engineering, agility, and culture (ECAC). The principle of engineering requires a firm to map the structure of its supply chains, and this includes upstream and downstream partners (suppliers, transporters, distributors, and the customer). The benefit of having this structure in advance is that it identifies bottlenecks that are likely to restrict the flow and it gives a visible production process. This principle enables managers to foresee risks and craft ways of mitigating these risks thereby reducing the impact on their operations. For instance, a decoupling point in inventory management is a good strategy which avoids excess inventory in the supply chain (de Sousa Jabbour and Jabbour, 2020).

Collaboration as a principle of supply chain resilience dictates that those partners in the supply chain must work together as this is the centrality of the supply chain resilience. De Sousa Jabbour and Jabbour (2020) posit that sharing information among the partners in the supply chain is the best way of increasing visibility and reducing risks. The authors further state that information sharing creates a common understanding of the strategy being used in the supply chain. They mention that information that can be shared maybe from political circles, economic forums, social developments, and or technological advancements as well as risk assessment for demand and supply creating a community perspective.

The principle of agility refers to two broad dimensions of velocity and visibility. Velocity is concerned about speed, that is the time taken from starting the process of ordering raw materials up to the time finished goods are delivered to the customer must be reduced as much as possible. Visibility is required to attain such speed and accuracy. Visibility relates to monitoring the movement of materials and information across the supply chain with the aim of ensuring that procurement, production, and delivery timelines will be achieved.

Value Creation: The first know proponent of the concept of value creation is Michael Porter whose theory assisted a several leaders fighting competition. Porter (1985) suggest primary and secondary activities within any organization which managers had to capitalize on to create value for the customer as shown in Figure 4.

Figure 4. From Generic Value Creation to Innovative Value
Adapted from Jaeger and Matyas, 2016

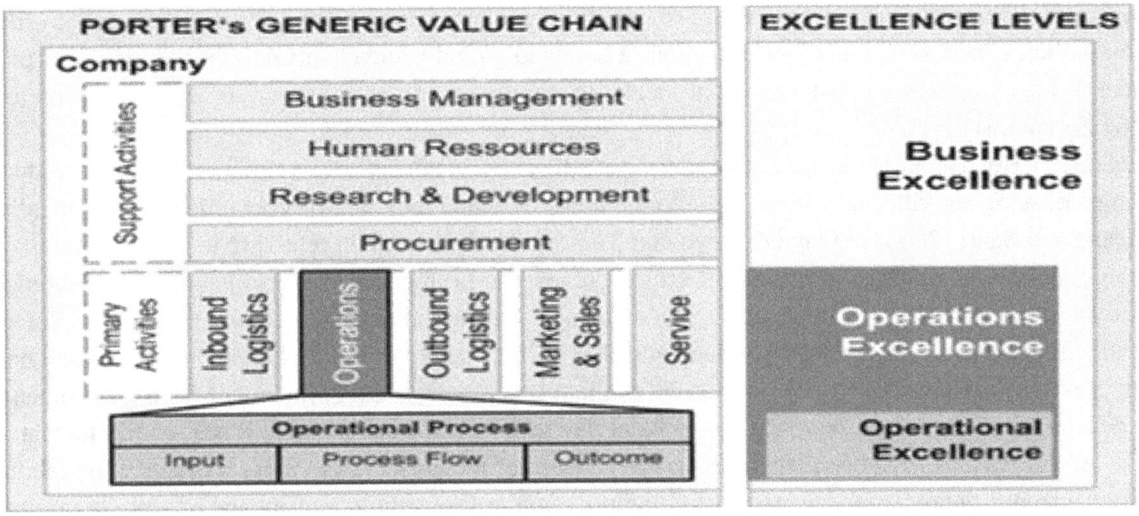

It is this what has created value which makes a customer come and do repeat business with a company. As time progresses, new views were suggested by others researcher even though they used value creation as the steppingstone. Dervitsiotis (2014) reiterate that the most recurrent mistake made by successful organizations is the failure to assess the impact of ongoing changes on their customers and keep the same operational approach assuming that the conditions in the environment will continue like that. This perception has proved to be true and costly to several organizations in the wake of globalization and technology. There is a class of customers who are not worried much about the change in price of a product or service, but their demand is mainly on product/service quality to be maintained or improved (Dervistsiotis, 2014). Moreover, customers have more information than most organization and switching costs have been lowered by competition. The quality on an organization's value-innovation process is nowadays the backbone of surviving stiff competition and has superseded the traditional approach where firms would survive through strong capabilities for developing and holding on to unique competitive advantages typically based on quality, productivity and responding rapidly to customer demands.

5.1.2 Recovering Strategies

Dual Sourcing: Research has identified sourcing as a key factor in the security of the supply chain (Norbis & Meixell, 2011). To reduce the risks related to disruptions in the supply chain, firms can resort to increasing the number of suppliers but inherently, that increases the intensities related to security failures. To mitigate supply risk due to disruptions, firms resort to dual sourcing which is procuring goods/services from two suppliers (Gupta and Ivanov, 2019; Li, Sethi and Zhang, 2013, 2017). The whole idea is to have a backup supplier if it happens that the main supplier of a product's supply chain gets disrupted. This practice is called contingent dual sourcing of supply chain management (Lu, Huang, and Max Shen, 2011; Huang and Xu, 2015, Gupta, He, and Sethi, 2015). Anton and Yao (1989) suggest that a purchasing firm is better to use single sourcing strategy if there is complete information available about its suppliers that have strict convex cost.

Localizing Supply Chains: The power of proximity: The Economist (12th July 2021) reports that the past three decades saw globalization taking place due to the proliferation of policies such as free trade, investment liberalization and improved logistics activities. Nevertheless, Covid-19 pandemic and government policies such as increased participation of locals in global value chains has shifted the tables and there has been a serious consideration of localizing supply chains, for instance in Middle East region (The Economist).

Onyido, Boyd and Thurairajah (2014) define supply chain localization as a situation in which production processing activities take place close to the areas in which they will be consumed geographically. Alaane and Saari (2006) in Onyido, Boyd and Thurairajah (2014) when referring to the production of energy, define localization as utilizing local resources, the promotion of local business opportunities and the development of products and services using local raw materials and labour. The concept of localization has been presented by Alaane and Saari (2006) as a resurgent phenomenon that has gone full circle from globalization. As early as 2006, there was a notable encouragement from governments in developed nations to promote the use of local raw materials (Malani, 2006). Research has indicated that several reasons have been attributed to the concept of localization and these include rising labour costs, currency depreciation energy costs going up, social responsibility and change of attitude towards environmental protection (Sheffi, 2001; Walker, 1995; Ristola and Mirata, 2007; Longo et al., 2008).

Merging of Business-to-Business (B2B) and Business-to-Customer (B2C): The birth of internet-based shops came with it the concept of business-to-business (Lejmi, 2002) in which a firm is connected through the internet to other businesses for the purpose of enhancing the flow of information and money at a faster pace. Because information was shared between two firms such as demand, aggregation of demand quantities is made possible. Batt and Purchase (2003) posit that when the concept of B2B is thought of from the marketing point of view, it refers to one business operation producing goods and services for another business operation. Research has shown that the value proposition of B2B concept has shifted from maximizing price in a transaction to cost optimization through improved efficiencies and greater coordination between procuring and supplying firms (Lejmi, 2002). This has seen a growth in the modern types of B2B marketplaces where trading processes and their subsequent logistics services are covered. It becomes easier to manage and control logistics related challenges and benefits working together will be harvested such as reduced inefficiencies in supply chains. Blythe (2005:13) state that the most effective B2B marketing strategies focus on reducing costs, increasing sales and meeting government regulations.

Giannikas, Woodall, McFarlane, and Lu (2017) suggest four aspects that differentiate B2B from B2C logistics namely, products, orders, clients, and receiver. They argue that some products can be supplied to end consumers from firms but there are other products that are supplied between businesses only. Orders placed by end customers are usually small whereas those placed by other firms are huge. In B2B another firm is the receiver of products sold whereas in B2C the receiver is the end customer, for instance nowadays online purchases in the retail sector are delivered straight to the end users.

It is imperative for firms to understand their supply chain operations so that they tune their strategies accordingly. Companies that pursue the 'powerhouse' strategy practice the concept of merging and acquiring other firms. The greater challenge that may be faced in merging and acquisition strategies is the question of which brand name to keep if the two firms' brand names have created value.

Decentralization of manufacturing capacity: Farooq et al., (2021) argue that pandemics cause disruptions in supply chain forcing firms to find survival strategies that are sustainable and viable. Practitioners and researchers have now focused on survival strategies that firms can embrace during and after pandemics such as Covid-19. One such a survival strategy is decentralization of manufacturing operations. Decentralization has been defined by Prasad and Srinivas (2018) as a practice in which each decision maker in a supply chain is modelled as an agent who shares partial information within their domain which will then be coordinated to get the final optimal plans. The same authors state that in centralized supply chains, information is shared completely between partners. Decentralization of operations minimizes costs such as transportation from the plant to the warehouse, costs of receiving goods too early, costs of receiving goods too late and costs of transporting the product to the final customer (Prasad & Srinivas, 2018).

5.2 Other Strategies

5.2.1 Knowledge management

Kumar and Kumar [2015] dissect the phrase knowledge management in two and define each of the words. They say that 'knowledge is an understanding of someone or something such as facts, information, description, or skills, which is acquired through experience or education by perceiving, discovering of learning. Knowledge can refer to the theoretical or practical understanding of a subject.' The same author gave a general definition of management which involves the planning, organizing, leading, and controlling facets (see Figure 5). Successful organization must embrace the concept of knowledge management as they cannot afford to discover something new which they will easily expose for other to replicate.

Figure 5. Knowledge Management

Kumar and Kumar (2015 p.10) state that "knowledge management is managing the corporation's knowledge through a systematically and organizationally specified process for acquiring, organizing, sustaining, applying, sharing, renewing both the tacit and explicit knowledge of employees to enhance organizational performance and create value." There are a diverse number of diagrams which have been suggested to illustrate the Knowledge Management Cycle and Figure 6 has been adopted to represent the knowledge management cycle. It is important to recognize that the KM cycle has steps running in the following order: acquisition, application, assessment, creation, identification, refining and dissemination.

Figure 6. Knowledge Management Cycle

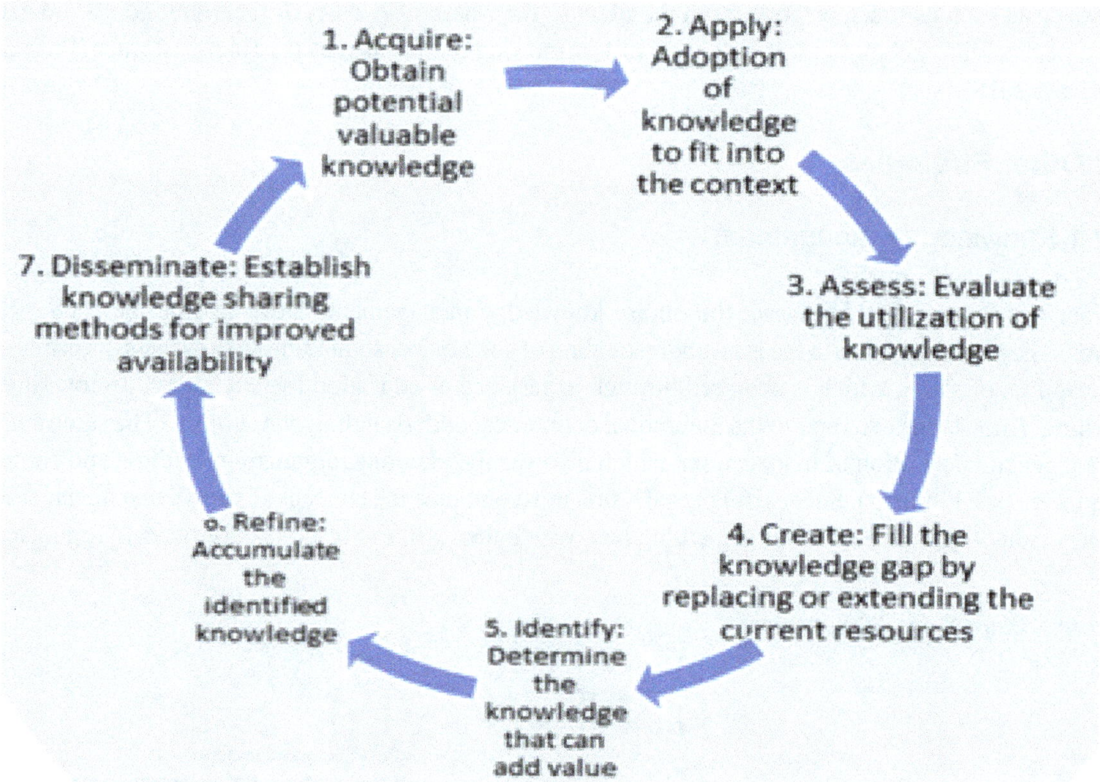

Knowledge is acquired through two sources which are internal or external. Internal refers to different departments' experiences and among these departments are the production department, sale & marketing, engineering, product development, research and design, procurement & supply, and others. Externally, the sources of knowledge include websites, professional bodies, conferences & exhibitions, publications, commercial organizations, research institutions, universities & colleges, and industry associations. Figure 7 gives a summary of both internal and external sources of knowledge.

Figure 7. Sources of Knowledge
Adopted from Kumar & Kumar, 2015 pg. 13

5.2.2 Crowdsourcing

Crowdsourcing has become a topical issue that has seen greater attention being paid to it since 2006 (Ghezi, Gabelloni, Martini and Natalichio, 2017). Admittedly, the field still suffers from ambiguity in the topic's definition leading to a large and unstructured evolution (Ghezi et al., 2017), even though it has garnered much attention from both the academicians and practitioners (Amrollahi, 2015). Its evident that the topic is ingrained in research on open innovation and co-creation and is concerned about whether several individuals can actively take part in a company's innovation process (Chui, Manyika, Bughin and Dobbs, 2012). This approach has been observed to allow the company access to diverse business intelligence and knowledge that is obtained from the wide pool of stakeholders (Chanal and Caron-Fasan, 2010; Schenk & Guittard, 2011). Howe (2006) defines crowdsourcing as "*the act of a company or institution taking a function once performed by employees and outsourcing it to an undefined (and generally large) network of people in the form of an open call. This can take the form of peer-production (when the job is performed collaboratively) but is also often undertaken by sole individuals (expert or novices). The crucial prerequisite is the use of the open call and large network of potential labours.*"

Business, city planning, policy development and event outreach have been noted as areas the model has been applied (Seltzer, et al., 2013). A notable increase of 100% has been witnessed after a list of 2670 sites in 45 languages was observed (Tarrell et al., 2013). The model has been popular to the extent of it being used for even high-level decision making and strategic planning (Amrollahi et al., 2014; Stieger at al., 2012). The model has been used in health, medicine, psychology, and human behaviour (Renard et al., 2013) as well as university set up leading to solving of a problem that had not been solved for decades (Cooper et al., 2010; Graber et al., 2013).

5.2.3 Offshoring and outsourcing

Firms fighting to gain competitive advantage in both domestic and international markets, embrace offshoring even though it is still considered a phenomenon (Javalgi, Dixit and Scherer, 2009; Mukherjee, Gaur and Datta, 2013; Adams et al., 2018; Pereira, Munjal & Ishizaka, 2020). Debate is still ongoing regarding the impact of offshoring on firms (Gylling et al., 2015; Lahiri, 2016). Several studies (Yang and Huang, 2000; McCarthy and Anagnostou, 2004; Lewin, Massini and Peeters, 2009; Yao et al., 2010; Dolgui and Proth, 2013) have suggested that cost savings, improved management effectiveness, management flexibility, access to market and better product/service quality are some of the benefits that accrue from offshoring. In addition, the operation of these unique models creates value (Malik, Pereira and Budhwar, 2018). Literature has advanced several definitions of outsourcing and offshoring with some studies using these terms interchangeably (Takac, 1994; Grover, Cheon and Teng, 1996; Van Mieghem, 1999; Gilley and Rasheed, 2000; Yang and Huang, 2000; Javalgi, Dixit and Scherer, 2009, Lewin, Massini and Peeters, 2009, Robertson, Lamin & Livanis, 2010; Bertrand, 2011).

Extant literature defines offshoring as "*Outsourcing is a business agreement, either domestic and/ or international (known as offshoring), and strategic management initiative for gaining a competitive advantage of a firm by contracting out their existing internal and/or external non-value-added functions, and/or value-added functions, and/or core competencies to competent supplier(s) to produce products and/or services efficiently and effectively for the outsourcing firm,*" (McCarthy and Anagnostou, 2004; Hotanen and Eriksson, 2009, Javalgi, Dixit and Scherer, 2009; Dekkers, 2011; Dolgui and Proth, 2013; Schmeisser, 2013; Gunasekaran et al., 2015; Di Mauro et al., 2018; Pereira, Munjal & Ishizaka, 2020). Offshoring and outsourcing are two linked phenomena (Mihalache & Mihalache, 2016) and hence are not mutually exclusive (Ishizaka et al., 2019).

5.2.4 Digital Transformation and Technological Innovations

Choi et al., (2018) posit that digital transformation (DT) has recently garnered the attention of researchers and industry practitioners. Vial et al., (2019, p.118) define DT as "a process that aims to improve an entity by triggering significant changes to its properties through combinations of information, computing, communication, and connectivity technologies." Some organizations like Walmart and Carrefour were quick to embrace technological platforms offered by information technology providers such as IBM, SAP, Oracle, and Microsoft to trace the flow of form farmers to their retail shops using blockchain technology (Stanley, 2018; Dimitrov, 2019). Cost reduction and improved performance may be attained through seamless supply chain collaboration offered by digital technology (Stank et al., 2019).

Care should be taken by supply chain organization as the journey to digital transformation is not an easy one but subjected to challenges. For example, Tabriz et al., (2019) point that expecting the entire supply chain to be fully integrated is a dream yet to be achieved. It is important for supply chain firms that want to engage digital technology to first do a thorough investigation that establishes the feasibility implementing DT in supply chain if it is the correct option. The second challenge posed by adoption of DT is that often, designers develop solutions that are biased towards technologies instead of the functional domain such as the supply chain management (Trkman, 2013). The third challenge is the implementation processes and coming up with performance measures given the diversity of operations of the supply chain members. For instance, some members are in the extraction part of goods, others perform the manufacturing yet other give only services. Measurement of how effective and efficient they are, require different sets of key performance indicators/measures.

The difference among digital transformation, digital technology and technological innovation has not been clearly spelt out in literature. Responding to epidemic outbreaks especially Covid-19, extant literature has made some profound contributions regarding the field of supply chain management (Aldrighetti et al., 2019; Paul and Venkateswaran, 2020). What has been made clear is that the adoption of digital technology as a strategic tool could enhance business performance, production capabilities, effectiveness, and resilience (Bruque & Moyano, 2007; Dibrell et al., 2008; Kleis et al., 2012; Chan et al., 2019.) Khan and Manzoor (2021) point out that key technologies used during the Covid-19 pandemic include blockchains, internet of things (IoT), artificial intelligence, cloud computing, robots, and drones, 5G and smartphone applications and big data analytics.

In review of the above, it's evident that before the outbreak of the pandemic Covid-19, supply chains were characterized by practices such supply chain integration, supplier relationship management, customer relationship management and information sharing. Integration meant companies had to coordinate their operations internally and externally. Internal integration was epitomized by exhibition of working together of different department and the removal of the 'silo mentality.' External integration meant that firms had to work together and in complete harmony with upstream and downstream partners in the chain (Gharakhani *et al.*, 2012). Firms exercised Supplier Relationship Management (SRM) which is creating long-term relationships with supplier because buying companies wanted to be assured of supply and their suppliers would also be assured of committed customers. SRM was also associated with collaboration with suppliers in which a common understanding was sought and seeking sharing of risks and gains. Customer relationship management meant firms had to create and maintain relationships with their customers and exceeding customer expectations (Hamidi and Ibrahim, 2014). To ensure supply chain sustainability, its clear that there were certain resilient and sustainability strategies were executed to by organizations to ensure effective supply chain and there were recovering strategies identified throughout this chapter which can be utilized and executed to ensure sustainable supply chain for covid crisis (see Figure 8).

Figure 8. Supply Chain: Pre and Post Covid Strategies Framework
Compiled by the authors

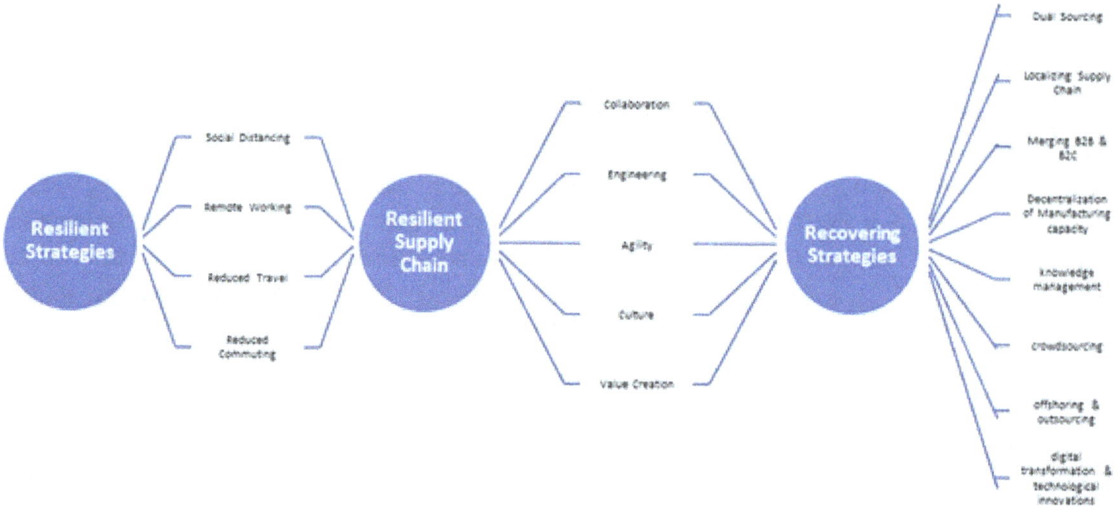

6. CONCLUSION AND RECOMMENDATIONS

The study concludes that several supply chains were adversely affected by the Covid-19 pandemic because this pandemic stronger than previous ones and it cut across different platforms such as political, economic, social, and ecological. It is recommended that firms adopt the onshoring strategy as it reduces the distance travelled by raw materials. Even though local suppliers might seem expensive but there could be offsetting reasons such as uncertainty of arrival of goods due to persistent lockdowns. It is suggested that governments be strict and fast when implementing preventative strategies such as lockdowns and social distancing. Companies and institutions are advised to support government initiatives by allowing their employees to work from home for those jobs that does not require employees to be physically present. Firms must support government efforts to curb the spread of the pandemic by not only complying, but funding research related to the impacts of disasters. Researchers must coordinate their efforts, for instance to establish why certain regions have not been adversely affected while others have been and publish these findings quickly. Individuals must continue acting responsibly because the pandemic is no respecter of persons and nationalities.

REFERENCES

Adams, K., Nyuur, R., Chima, M., & Debrah, Y. (2018). Offshore/Nearshore Outsourcing as a Strategic Competitive Posturing: Insights from Ghana. In BAM2018 Conference Driving Productivity in Uncertain and Challenging Times. Bristol Business School, University of the West of England.

Aguilera, R., Henisz, W., Oxley, J. E., & Shaver, J. M. (2018). International strategy in an era of global flux. *Strategy Science*, *4*(2), 61–69. doi:10.1287tsc.2019.0087

Alaane, K., & Saari, A. (2006). Distributed Energy Generation and Sustainable Development. *Renewable & Sustainable Energy Reviews, 10*(6), 539–558. doi:10.1016/j.rser.2004.11.004

Aldrighetti, R., Zennaro, I., Finco, S., & Battini, D. (2019). Healthcare supply chain simulation with disruption considerations: A case study from northern Italy. *Global Journal of Flexible Systems Management, 20*(1), 81–102. doi:10.100740171-019-00223-8

Alvarado, U. Y., & Kotzab, H. (2001). Supply Chain Management: The Integration of logistics in marketing. *Industrial Marketing Management, 30*(2), 183–198. doi:10.1016/S0019-8501(00)00142-5

Amankwah-Amoah. (2020b). *Stepping up and stepping out of Covid-19: New challenges of environmental sustainability policies in the global airline industry*. Academic Press.

Amrollahi, A. (2015). A Process Model for Crowdsourcing: Insights from the Literature on Implementation. In *Australian Conference on Information Systems*. University of South Australia.

Amrollahi, A., Ghapanchi, A., & Talaei-Khoei, A. (2014). Using Crowdsourcing Tools for Implementing Open Strategy: A Case Study in Education. *Twentieth Americas Conference on Information System*, 1-7.

Anton, J., & Yao, D. (1989). Split Awards, Procurement and Innovation. *The RAND Journal of Economics, 20*(4), 538–552. doi:10.2307/2555732

Batt, P. J., & Purchase, S. (2003). Managing collaboration within networks and relationships. *Industrial Marketing Management, 33*(3), 169–174. doi:10.1016/j.indmarman.2003.11.004

Bertrand, O. (2011). What Goes Around, Comes Around: Effects of Offshore Outsourcing on the Export Performance of Firms. *Journal of International Business Studies, 42*(2), 334–344. doi:10.1057/jibs.2010.26

Blythe, J., & Zimmerman, A. (2005). *Business-to-Business Marketing Management*. Thomson.

Bruque, S., & Moyano, J. (2007). Organisational determinants of information technology adoption and implementation in SMEs: The case of family and cooperative firms. *Technovation, 27*(5), 241–253. doi:10.1016/j.technovation.2006.12.003

Chan, C. M., Teoh, S. Y., Yeow, A., & Yan, G. (2019). Agility in responding to disruptive digital innovation: Case study of an SME. *Information Systems Journal, 29*(2), 436–455. doi:10.1111/isj.12215

Chanal, V., & Caron-Fasan, M. L. (2010). The difficulties involved in developing Business Models open to innovation communities: the case of a Crowdsourcing platform. *M@n@gement, 13*, 318-340.

Chang, H. H., Tsai, Y. C., & Hsu, C. H. (2013). E-procurement and supply chain performance. *Supply Chain Management, 18*(1), 34–51. doi:10.1108/13598541311293168

Chen, I., & Paulraj, A. (2004). Towards a theory of supply chain management: The constructs and measurements. *Journal of Operations Management, 22*(2), 119–150. doi:10.1016/j.jom.2003.12.007

Choi, T. M., Wallace, S. W., & Wang, Y. (2018). Big data analytics in operations management. *Production and Operations Management, 27*(10), 1868–1883. doi:10.1111/poms.12838

Chopra, S., & Meindl, P. (2001). *Supply Chain Management*. Prentice-Hall.

Chopra, S., & Sodhi, M. S. (2004). Managing risk to avoid supply-chain breakdown. *MIT Sloan Management Review*, *46*(1), 53–61.

Chow, W. S., Madu, C. N., Kuei, C.-H., Lu, M. H., Lin, C., & Tseng, H. (2008). Supply chain management in the US and Taiwan: An empirical study. *International Journal of Management Sciences*, *36*(5), 665–679. doi:10.1016/j.omega.2006.01.001

Chowa, S. W., Christian, N. M., Chu-Hua, K., Min, H., Chinho, L., & Hojung, T. (2008). Supply chain management in the US and Taiwan. The International Journal of Management Science. *Omega*, *36*, 665–679. doi:10.1016/j.omega.2006.01.001

Chowdhury, P., Paul, K. S., & Moktadir Md, A. (2021). Covid-19 pandemic related supply chain studies: A systematic review. *Transportation Research Part E, Logistics and Transportation Review*, *148*, 148. doi:10.1016/j.tre.2021.102271 PMID:33613082

Christopher, M., & Peck, H. (2004). Building the resilient supply chain. *International Journal of Logistics Management*, *15*(2), 1–13. doi:10.1108/09574090410700275

Chui, M., Manyika, J., Bughin, J., & Dobbs, R. (2012). *The social economy: unlocking value and productivity through social technologies*. McKinsey Global Institute.

Cooper, S., Khatib, F., Treuille, A., Barbero, J., Lee, J., Beenen, M., Leaver-Fay, A., Baker, D., & Popović, Z. (2010). Predicting protein structures with a multiplayer online game. *Nature*, *466*(7307), 756-760.

Dawei, L., & Jiju, A. (2003). Implications of B2B marketplace to supply chain development. *The TQM Magazine*, *15*(3), 173–179. doi:10.1108/09544780310469271

Dekkers, R. (2011). Impact of Strategic Decision Making for Outsourcing on Managing Manufacturing. *International Journal of Operations & Production Management*, *31*(9), 935–965. doi:10.1108/01443571111165839

Dervitsiotis, K. N. (2014). *Developing Sustainable Competitive Advantage through Operational Excellence and Adaptation Excellence with Value Innovations*. ResearchGate.

Di Mauro, C., Fratocchi, L., Orzes, G., & Sartor, M. (2018). Offshoring and Backshoring: A Multiple Case Study Analysis. *Journal of Purchasing and Supply Management*, *24*(2), 108–134. doi:10.1016/j.pursup.2017.07.003

Dibrell, C., Davis, P. S., & Craig, J. (2008). Fueling innovation through information technology in SMEs. *Journal of Small Business Management*, *46*(2), 203–218. doi:10.1111/j.1540-627X.2008.00240.x

Dimitrov. (2019). *How Walmart and Others are Riding a Blockchain Wave to Supply Chain Paradise*. Available at https://www.forbes.com/sites/biserdimitrov/2019/12/05/how-walmart-and-others-are-riding-a-blockchain-wave-to-supply-chain-paradise/#b9ee4fd77918

Dolgui, A., & Jean-Marie, P. (2013). Outsourcing: Definitions and Analysis. *International Journal of Production Research*, *51*(23-24), 6769–6777. doi:10.1080/00207543.2013.855338

Donlon, J. P. (1996). Maximizing value in the supply chain. *Chief Executive*, *117*(October), 54–63.

Dubey, R., & Samar Ali, S. (2013). An exploratory study on logistics competency and firm performance. *International Journal of Logistics Systems and Management, 14*(2), 179–199. doi:10.1504/IJLSM.2013.051338

Dubey, R., Singh, T., & Tiwari, S. (2012). Supply Chain Innovation is a Key to Superior Firm Performance an Insight from Indian Cement Manufacturing. *International Journal of Innovation Science, 4*(4), 217–230. doi:10.1260/1757-2223.4.4.217

Fonseca L., & Azevedo A.L., (2020) *Covid-19 and Global Supply Chains. Marketing Management: Challenges for the Knowledge Society.* Academic Press.

Forrester, J. W. (1958). Industrial dynamics: A major breakthrough for decision makers. *Harvard Business Review*, (July/August), 37–66.

Fortune. (2020). *94% of the Fortune 1000 are seeing coronavirus supply chain disruptions: Report.* https://fortune.com/2020/02/21/fortune-1000-coronavirus-china-supply-chain-impact/

Fortune. (2020). *Coronavirus impact: 94% of the Fortune 1000 are seeing supply chain disruptions.* https://fortune.com/2020/02/21/fortune-1000- coronavirus-china-supply-chain-impact/

Gharakhani, D. R. K. M., & Hamidi, N. (2012). Impact of Supply Chain Management on innovation and organizational performance in Iranian. *African Journal of Business Management, 6*(19), 5939–5949. doi:10.5897/AJBM11.1136

Ghezi, A., Gabelloni, D., Martini, A., & Natalicchio, A. (2017). Crowdsourcing: A review and suggestions for future research. *International Journal of Management Reviews.*

Giannikas, V., Woodall, P., McFarlane, D., & Lu, W. (2017). *The Impact of B2C commerce on Traditional B2B Warehousing*. Academic Press.

Gilley, K. M., & Rasheed, A. (2000). Making More by Doing Less: An Analysis of Outsourcing and Its Effects on Firm Performance. *Journal of Management, 26*(4), 763–790. doi:10.1177/014920630002600408

Gossling, ̈. S., Scott, D., & Hall, C. M. (2020). Pandemics, tourism and global change: A rapid assessment of COVID-19. *Journal of Sustainable Tourism, 29*(1), 1–20. doi:10.1080/09669582.2020.1758708

Graber, M. A., & Graber, A. (2013). Internet-based crowdsourcing and research ethics: The case for IRB review. *Journal of Medical Ethics, 39*(2), 115-118.

Grover, V., Cheon, M. J., & Teng, J. T. C. (1996). The Effect of Service Quality and Partnership on the Outsourcing of Information Systems Functions. *Journal of Management Information Systems, 12*(4), 89–116. doi:10.1080/07421222.1996.11518102

Gunasekaran, A., Irani, Z., Choy, K.-L., Filippi, L., & Papadopoulos, T. (2015). Performance Measures and Metrics in Outsourcing Decisions: A Review for Research and Applications. *International Journal of Production Economics, 161*, 153–166. doi:10.1016/j.ijpe.2014.12.021

Gupta, V., He, B., & Sethi, S. P. (2015). Contingent Sourcing Under Supply Disruption and Competition. *International Journal of Production Research, 53*(10), 3006–3027. doi:10.1080/00207543.2014.965351

Gupta, V., & Ivanov, D. (2019). Dual Sourcing under Supply disruption with risk-averse suppliers in the shoring economy. *International Journal of Production Research*, *58*(1), 291–307. doi:10.1080/00207543.2019.1686189

Gylling, M., Heikkilä, J., Jussila, K., & Saarinen, M. (2015). Making Decisions on Offshore Outsourcing and Backshoring: A Case Study in the Bicycle Industry. *International Journal of Production Economics*, *162*, 92–100. doi:10.1016/j.ijpe.2015.01.006

Hamid, A., & Ibrahim, S. B. (2014). Supply Chain Management Practices and Supply Chain Performance Effectiveness. *International Journal of Scientific Research*, *3*(8), 187–195.

Handfield, R., & Nichols, E. L. Jr. (1999). *Introduction to Supply Chain Management*. Prentice-Hall.

Hätönen, J., & Eriksson, T. (2009). 30 + Years of Research and Practice of Outsourcing – Exploring the Past and Anticipating the Future. *Journal of International Management*, *15*(2), 142–155. doi:10.1016/j.intman.2008.07.002

Howe, J. (2006a). *Crowdsourcing: A definition*. Academic Press.

Howe, J. (2006b). The rise of crowdsourcing. *Wired Magazine, 14*(6), 1-4.

Huang, H., & Xu, H. (2015). Dual Sourcing and Backup Production: Coexistence Versus Exclusivity. *Omega*, *57*, 22–33. doi:10.1016/j.omega.2015.04.008

Hudecheck, M., Siren, C., Grichnik, D., & Wincent, J. (2020). How companies can respond to the coronavirus. *MIT Sloan Management Review*. https://sloanreview.mit.edu/article/how-companies-can-respond-to-the-coronavirus/

Inda, S., Abu Bakar, A. H., & Huam Hon, T. F. (2012). A study of Supply Chain Management Practices: An Empirical Investigation on consumer goods industry in Malaysia. *International Journal of Business and Social Science*, *2*(17), 166–176.

Injazz, C. (2004). Towards a theory of supply chain management: The onstructs and measurements. *Journal of Operations Management*, *22*(2), 119–150. doi:10.1016/j.jom.2003.12.007

Jaeger, A., & Matyas, K. (2016). Transformation of the EFQM approach from business towards operations excellence. *Production Engineering*, *10*(3), 277–291. doi:10.100711740-016-0665-8

Javalgi, R., Dixit, A., & Scherer, R. F. (2009). Outsourcing to Emerging Markets: Theoretical Perspectives and Policy Implications. *Journal of International Management*, *15*(2), 156–168. doi:10.1016/j.intman.2008.08.001

Kaczmarek, T., Perez, K., Demir, E., & Zaremba, A. (2021). How to survive a pandemic: The corporate resiliency of travel and leisure companies to the COVID-19 outbreak. *Tourism Management*, *84*, 1–11. doi:10.1016/j.tourman.2020.104281

Kashyap, A., & Raghuvanshi, J. (2020). A preliminary study on exploring the critical success factors for developing Covid-19 preventative strategy with an economy centric approach. *Journal of the Iberoamerican Academy of Management*, *18*(4), 357–377.

Kleis, L., Chwelos, P., Ramirez, R. V., & Cockburn, I. (2012). Information technology and intangible output: The impact of IT investment on innovation productivity. *Information Systems Research, 23*(1), 42–59. doi:10.1287/isre.1100.0338

Kobrin, S. J. (2017). Bricks and mortar in borderless world: Globalization, the backlash, and the multinational enterprise. *Global Strategy Journal, 7*(2), 159–171. doi:10.1002/gsj.1158

Koh, S. C. L., Demirbag, M., Bayraktar, E., Tatoglu, E., & Zaim, S. (2007). The impact of supply chain management practices on performance of SMEs. *Industrial Management & Data Systems, 107*(1), 103–124. doi:10.1108/02635570710719089

Kumar, A. A., & Kumar, U. (2015). *Knowledge Management: A Review. International Journal of Academic Research in Social Sciences and Humanities* , 1).

Kumar, A. A., & Kumar, U. K. (2015). Knowledge Management: A Review. *International Journal of Academic Research in Social Sciences & Humanities, 1*(1), 9–17.

Lahiri, S. (2016). Does Outsourcing Really Improve Firm Performance? Empirical Evidence and Research Agenda. *International Journal of Management Reviews, 18*(4), 464–497. doi:10.1111/ijmr.12075

Lee, H. L. (2002). Aligning Supply Chain Strategies with product uncertainties. *California Management Review, 44*(3), 105–110. doi:10.2307/41166135

Leimeister, J. M. (2010). Collective intelligence. *Business & Information Systems Engineering, 2*(4), 245-248.

Lewin, A. Y., Massini, S., & Peeters, C. (2009). Why Are Companies Offshoring Innovation? The Emerging Global Race for Talent. *Journal of International Business Studies, 40*(6), 901–925. doi:10.1057/jibs.2008.92

Li, S., Subba Rao, S., Ragu-Nathan, T. S., & Ragu-Nathan, B. (2005). Development and validation of a measurement instrument for studying supply chain management practices. *Journal of Operations Management, 23*(6), 618–641. doi:10.1016/j.jom.2005.01.002

Li, T., Sethi, S. P., & Zhang, J. (2013). How Does Pricing Power Affect a Firm's Sourcing Decisions from Unreliable Suppliers? *International Journal of Production Research, 51*(23–24), 6990–7005. doi:10.1080/00207543.2013.849826

Li, T., Sethi, S. P., & Zhang, J. (2017). Mitigating Supply Uncertainty: The Interplay Between Diversification and Pricing. *Production and Operations Management, 26*(3), 369–388. doi:10.1111/poms.12656

Linton, T., & Vakil, B. (2020). *It is up to manufacturers to keep their suppliers afloat*. Harvard Business Review Digital Article. Available at: https://hbr.org/2020/04/its-up-to-manufacturers-to-keep-their-supplier

Longo, A., Markandya, A., & Petrucci, M. (2008). The Internalization of Externalities in the Production of Electricity: Willingness to Pay for the Attributes of a Policy for Renewable Energy. *Ecological Economics, 67*(1), 140–152. doi:10.1016/j.ecolecon.2007.12.006

Lopes de Sousa Jabbour, A. B., Chiappetta Jabbour, C. J., Hingley, M., Vilalta-Perdomo, E. L., Ramsden, G., & Twigg, D. (2020). Sustainability of supply chains in the wake of the coronavirus (COVID-19 SARS-CoV-2) pandemic: Lessons and trends. *Modern Supply Chain Research and Application Vol., 2*(3), 117–122. doi:10.1108/MSCRA-05-2020-0011

Lu, M., Huang, S., & Shen, Z.-J. M. (2011). Product Substitution and Dual Sourcing Under Random Supply Failures. *Transportation Research Part B: Methodological, 45*(8), 1251–1265. doi:10.1016/j.trb.2010.09.005

Machowiak, W. (2012). Risk management-unappreciated instrument of supply chain management strategy. *LogForum, 8*(4), 277–285.

Malik, A., Pereira, V., & Budhwar, P. (2018). Value Creation and Capture Through Human Resource Management Practices: Gazing Through the Business Model Lens. *Organizational Dynamics, 47*(3), 180–188. doi:10.1016/j.orgdyn.2017.09.002

Matt, C., Hess, T., & Benlian, A. (2015). Digital transformation strategies. *Business & Information Systems Engineering, 57*(5), 339–343. doi:10.100712599-015-0401-5

McCarthy, I., & Anagnostou, A. (2004). The Impact of Outsourcing on the Transaction Costs and Boundaries of Manufacturing. *International Journal of Production Economics, 88*(1), 61–71. doi:10.1016/S0925-5273(03)00183-X

Melani, C. (2006). Development and the Changing Dynamics of Global Production: Global Value Chains and Local Clusters in Apparel Manufacturing. *Competition & Change, 10*(1), 23–48. doi:10.1179/102452906X91993

Mihalache, M., & Mihalache, O. R. (2016). A Decisional Framework of Offshoring: Integrating Insights from 25 Years of Research to Provide Direction for Future. *Decision Sciences, 47*(6), 1103–1149. doi:10.1111/deci.12206

Min, S., & Mentzer, J. (2004). Developing and measuring supply chain management concepts. *Journal of Business Logistics, 25*(1), 63–92. doi:10.1002/j.2158-1592.2004.tb00170.x

Min, S., & Mintzer, J. (2004). Developing and measuring supply chain management concepts. *Journals of business Logistics, 25*(1), 63-92.

Narasimhan, R., & Kim, S. W. (2007). Effects of Supply Chain Integration on the relation between versification and performance: Evidence from Japanese and Korean firms. *Journal of Operations Management, 20*(3), 303–323. doi:10.1016/S0272-6963(02)00008-6

Nguyen, T. U. H., Sherif, J. S., & Newby, M. (2007). Strategies for successful CRM implementation. *Information Management & Computer Security, 15*(2), 102–115. doi:10.1108/09685220710748001

Norbis, M., & Meixell, M. (2011). *Dual Sourcing in Supply Chain Design: A Multi-Dimensional Framework of Risk*. Academic Press.

Onyido, T., Boyd, D., & Thurairajah, N. (2014). The Implications of Supply Chain Localization for the Evolving Sustainable Energy Products Markets in the UK. *Built Environment*.

Panwar, R. (2020). It's time to develop local production and supply networks. *California Management Review, 28*. https://cmr.berkeley.edu/2020/04/local-productionsupply-networks

Paolacci, G., Chandler, J., & Ipeirotis, P. G. (2010). Running experiments on amazon mechanical turk. *Judgment and Decision Making, 5*(5), 411-419.

Paul, S., & Venkateswaran, J. (2020). Designing robust policies under deep uncertainty formitigating epidemics. *Computers & Industrial Engineering, 140*, 106221. doi:10.1016/j.cie.2019.106221

Paul, S. K., & Chowdhury, P. (2020a). A production recovery plan in manufacturing supply chains for a high-demand item during COVID-19. *International Journal of Physical Distribution & Logistics Management*, 1–22. doi:10.1108/IJPDLM-04-2020-0127

Paul, S. K., & Chowdhury, P. (2020b). Strategies for managing the impacts of disruptions during COVID-19: An example of toilet paper. *Global Journal of Flexible Systems Management, 21*(3), 283–293. doi:10.100740171-020-00248-4

Pawar, D. S., Yadav, A. K., Akolekar, N., & Velaga, N. R. (2020). Impact of physical distancing due to novel coronavirus (SARS-CoV-2) on daily travel for work during transition to lockdown. Transport. *Res. Interdiscip. Perspect., 7*, 100203. doi:10.1016/j.trip.2020.100203 PMID:34173467

Pereira, V., Munjal, S., & Ishizaka, A. (2020). Outsourcing and Offshoring Decision Making and its Implications for Businesses- A Synthesis of Research Pursuing Five Pertinent Questions. *Journal of Business Research.*

Porter, M. E. (1985). *Competitive advantage: Creating and sustaining superior performance*. Free Press.

Ranard, B. L., Ha, Y. P., Meisel, Z. F., Asch, D. A., Hill, S. S., Becker, L. B., Seymour, A. K., & Merchant, R. M. (2013). Crowdsourcing—Harnessing the masses to advance health and medicine, a systematic review. *Journal of General Internal Medicine*, 1–17. PMID:23843021

Randall, W. S., & Mello, J. E. (2012). Grounded theory: An inductive method for supply chain research. *International Journal of Physical Distribution & Logistics Management, 42*(8/9), 863–880. doi:10.1108/09600031211269794

Ristola, P., & Mirata, M. (2007). Industrial Symbiosis for More Sustainable, Localised Industrial Systems. *Progress in Industrial Ecology, 4*(3-4), 184–204. doi:10.1504/PIE.2007.015186

Robertson, C. J., Lamin, A., & Livanis, G. (2010). Stakeholder Perceptions of Offshoring and Outsourcing: The Role of Embedded Issues. *Journal of Business Ethics, 95*(2), 167–189. doi:10.100710551-009-0353-0

Rodrik, D. (2018). Populism and the economics of globalization. *Journal of International Business Policy, 1*(1), 12–33. doi:10.105742214-018-0001-4

Sarkis, J. (2020). Supply Chain Sustainability: Learning from the COVID-19 pandemic. *International Journal of Operations & Production Management, 41*(1), 63–73. doi:10.1108/IJOPM-08-2020-0568

Schenk, E., & Guittard, C. (2011). Towards a characterization of Crowdsourcing practices. *Journal of Innovation Economics, 7*, 93–107.

Sekaran, U. (2000). *Research Methods for Business: A Skill Building Approach* (3rd ed.). Wiley.

Seltzer, E., & Mahmoudi, D. (2013). Citizen Participation, Open Innovation, and Crowdsourcing Challenges and Opportunities for Planning. *Journal of Planning Literature, 28*(1), 3-18.

Semanur, S., & Ercan, E. (2020). *COVID-19 and Digitalization Network Analysis on Industrial Robots Trade Among the BRI Countries*. Social Science Review.

Sheffi, Y. (2001). Supply Chain Management under the Threat of International Terrorism. *International Journal of Logistics Management, 12*(2), 1–11. doi:10.1108/09574090110806262

Shin, H., Collier, D. A., & Wilson, D. D. (2000). Supply Management orientation and supplier/buyer performance. *Journal of Operations Management, 18*(3), 317–333. doi:10.1016/S0272-6963(99)00031-5

Simatupany, T. M., & Sridharan, R. (2002). The Collaborative Supply Chain. *International Journal of Logistics Management, 13*(1), 15–30. doi:10.1108/09574090210806333

Simchi-Levi, D. (2020). *Three scenarios to guide your global supply chain recovery*. Sloan Management Review Digital Article. Available at: https://sloanreview-mit-edu.cdn.ampproject.org/c/s/sloanreview.mit.edu/article/three-scenarios-to-guide-your-global-supply-chain-recovery/amp

Skojett-Larsen, T. (1999). Supply chain Management: A New Challenge for Researchers and Managers in Logistics. *International Journal of Logistics Management, 10*(2), 41–53. doi:10.1108/09574099910805987

Stank, T., Esper, T., Goldsby, T. J., Zinn, W., & Autry, C. (2019). Toward a digitally dominant paradigm for twenty-first century supply chain scholarship. *International Journal of Physical Distribution & Logistics Management, 49*(10), 956–971. doi:10.1108/IJPDLM-03-2019-0076

Stanley, A. (2018, October 8). Ready to rumble: IBM launches food trust blockchain for commercial use. *Forbes*. Available at: https://www.forbes.com/sites/astanley/2018/10/08/ready-to-rumble-ibm-launches-food-trust-blockchain-forcommercial-use/#173fb79f7439

Stieger, D., Matzler, K., Chatterjee, S., & Ladstaetter-Fussenegger, F. (2012). Democratizing Strategy: How Crowdsourcing Can be Used for Strategy Dialogues. *Calif Management Review, 54*(4).

Strange, R. (2020). Whither Globalisation? *Journal of International Management, 26*(1), 100728. doi:10.1016/j.intman.2019.100728

Strange, R., & Magnani, G. (2018). Outsourcing, offshoring and the global factory. In G. Cook & F. McDonald (Eds.), *The Routledge companion to the geography of international business* (pp. 60–67). Routledge. doi:10.4324/9781315667379-4

Stuart, F. I. (1997). Supply Chain Strategy: Organisational Influence through supplier alliances. *British Journal of Management, 8*(3), 223–236. doi:10.1111/1467-8551.00062

Supply Chain Digital. (2020). Accessed on https://supplychaindigital.com/magazine/december-2020

Tabrizi, B., Lam, E., Girard, K., & Irvin, V. (2019). Digital transformation is not about technology. *Harvard Business Review*, 13.

Takac, P. (1994). Outsourcing: A Key to Controlling Escalating IT Cost? *International Journal of Technology Management, 9*(2), 139–155.

Tan, K. C., Kannan, V. R., & Handfield, R. B. (1998). Supply Chain Management: Supplier Performance and firm performance. *International Journal of Purchasing and Materials Management*, *34*(3), 2–9.

Tan, K. C., Kannan, V. R., & Handfield, R. B. (1998). Supply chain management: Supplier performance and firm performance. *International Journal of Purchasing and Materials Management*, *34*(3), 2–9.

Tan, K. C., Lyman, S. B., & Wisner, J. D. (2002). Supply Chain Management: A strategic perspective. *International Journal of Operations & Production Management*, *22*(6), 614–631. doi:10.1108/01443570210427659

Tan, K. C., Lyman, S. B., & Wisner, J. D. (2002). Supply chain management: A strategic perspective. *International Journal of Operations & Production Management*, *22*(6), 614–631. doi:10.1108/01443570210427659

The Economist. (2021, July 21). The Power of Proximity: Localizing Supply Chains in the Middle East. *The Economist.*

The White House. (2020). *Coronavirus guidelines for America.* Available online: https://www.whitehouse.gov/briefings-statements/coronavirus-guidelinesamerica/

The White House. (2020). *Proclamation on suspension of entry as immigrants and nonimmigrants of persons who pose a risk of transmitting 2019 Novel Coronavirus.* Available online: https://www.whitehouse.gov/presidentialactions/proclamation-suspension-entry-immigrants-nonimmigrants-personspose-risk-transmitting-2019-novel-coronavirus/

Tiwari, A., So, M. K. P., Chong, A. C. Y., Chan, J. N. L., & Chu, A. M. Y. (2021). Pandemic risk of Covid-19 outbreak in the United States: An Analysis of network connectedness with air travel data. *International Journal of Infectious Diseases*, *103*, 97–101. doi:10.1016/j.ijid.2020.11.143 PMID:33212255

Trkman, P. (2013). Increasing process orientation with business process management: Critical practices'. *International Journal of Information Management*, *33*(1), 48–60. doi:10.1016/j.ijinfomgt.2012.05.011

UNCTAD. (2020a). *Impact of the Pandemic on Trade and Development: Transitioning to a new normal.* Geneva: United Nations Conference on Trade and Development. https://unctad.org/system/files/official-document/osg2020d1_en.pdf

Van Hoek, R. (2020). Impact Pathway Research opportunities for a more resilient post-Covid-19 Supply Chain- closing the gap between research findings and industry practice. *International Journal of Operations & Production Management*, *40*(4), 341–355. doi:10.1108/IJOPM-03-2020-0165

Van Hoek, R., & Lacity, M. (2020). *How the pandemic is pushing blockchain forward.* Harvard Business Review Digital Article. Available at: https://hbr.org/2020/04/how-the-pandemic-is-pushing-blockchain-forw

Van Mieghem, J. A. (1999). Coordinating Investment, Production and Subcontracting. *Management Science*, *45*(7), 954–971. doi:10.1287/mnsc.45.7.954

Vial, G. (2019). Understanding digital transformation: A review and a research agenda. *The Journal of Strategic Information Systems*, *28*(2), 118–144. doi:10.1016/j.jsis.2019.01.003

Vrijihoef, R., & Koskela, L. (1999). *Roles of Supply Chain Management in Construction.* University of California.

Wagner, A. F. (2020). What the stick market tells us about the Post-COVID-19. *Nature Human Behaviour, 4*(5), 440. Advance online publication. doi:10.103841562-020-0869-y

Walker, G. (1995). Renewable Energy and the Public. *Land Use Policy, 12*(1), 49–59. doi:10.1016/0264-8377(95)90074-C

WHO. (2020). *Global surveillance for COVID-19 caused by human infection with COVID-19 virus: Interim guidance.* Available online: https://www.who.int/docs/default-source/coronaviruse/2020-03-20-surveillance.pdf

WHO. (2020a). *Coronavirus disease (COVID-2019) situation reports.* Available online: https://www.who.int/emergencies/diseases/novel-coronavirus-2019/situation-reports.

WHO. (2020b). *Responding to community spread of COVID-19: interim guidance.* Available online: https://www.who.int/publications/i/item/responding-tocommunity-spread-of-covid-19.

Wing, C. S., Madub, C. N., Kueib, C.-H., Luc, M. H., Lind, C., & Tseng, H. (2008). Supply chain management in the US and Taiwan: The international journals of management science. *Omega*, 36665–36679.

World Health Organization (WHO). (2020). *WHO Director-General's opening remarks at the media briefing on COVID-19.* https://www.who.int/dg/speeches/detail/who-director-general-s-opening-remarks-at-the-media-briefing-on-covid19

World Tourism Organization UNWTO. (2020a). UNWTO world tourism barometer May 2020 Special focus on the impact of COVID-19. In UNWTO World Tourism Barometer. World Tourism Organization (UNWTO). doi:10.18111/9789284421817

World Tourism Organization UNWTO. (2020b). *UNWTO Global Tourism Dashboard.* https://www.unwto.org/international-tourism-and-covid-19

Yang, C., & Huang, J.-B. (2000). A Decision Model for IS Outsourcing. *International Journal of Information Management, 20*(3), 225–239. doi:10.1016/S0268-4012(00)00007-4

Yao, T., Jiang, B., Young, S. T., & Talluri, S. (2010). Outsourcing Timing, Contract Selection and Negotiation. *International Journal of Production Research, 48*(2), 305–326. doi:10.1080/00207540903174858

Zailani, S., & Rajagopal, P. (2005). Supply Chain Integration and performance: US versus East Asian companies. *Supply Chain Management, 10*(5), 379–393. doi:10.1108/13598540510624205

Zeng, A. (2000). A systematic study of sourcing strengths. *Industrial Management & Data Systems, 100*(5), 219–229. doi:10.1108/02635570010304798

Zhu, G., Chou, M.C., & Tsai, W.C. (2020). *Lessons learnt from the Covid-19 pandemic. Exploring the shortcomings of current supply chain operations: A long-term Perspective Offering.* Academic Press.

Chapter 15
Impact of COVID-19 on Businesses and Consumers 2020/2022:
Strategic Measures Adopted by Companies

Gracieth de Sousa Mateus Leandro
https://orcid.org/0000-0002-1898-7208
University Unibelas, Angola & University Agostinho Neto, Angola

Etelvino Flores de Jesus Leandro
University Agostinho Neto, Angola & University of Belas, Angola

ABSTRACT

In this chapter, the authors explore the impact of the COVID-19 pandemic on the Angolan market. A qualitative using case study (multi-case type) using interviews in data collection is used. It had 12 participants. The results reveal a significant impact of the COVID-19 pandemic on the Angolan economy. The COVID-19 pandemic had a positive impact for some companies, but essentially negative for others. The companies that sold the most during the pandemic are in the food, beverage, and health sectors. The ones that suffered the most losses were companies in the tourism and education sectors. The main difficulties have to do with the rapid changes in the market. The authors recommend focusing on diversifying the economy and reducing its dependence on oil, creating programs for financial education for consumers, and betting on digital communication.

INTRODUCTION

The Covid-19 pandemic is a disease caused by the new coronavirus known as SARS-CoV-2 (WHO, 2020; Lima, 2020). It is a virus that causes serious respiratory infections. This pandemic had an essentially negative impact on all spheres of human activity, without neglecting some positive aspects. A

DOI: 10.4018/978-1-7998-8856-7.ch015

problem that affected all social structures in the world, from politics to the economy), and in the latter, with emphasis on the economic recession; job loss, significant increase in poverty, etc.).

In this article on the "Impact of Covid-19 on companies and consumers 2020/2022: strategic measures adopted by companies", the authors have the general objective: to understand the impact of the Covid-19 pandemic on the Angolan market. The authors intend, on the one hand, to understand the impact of Covid-19 on companies and consumers; on the other hand, how companies have reacted to the phenomenon. Ultimately, identify strategies adopted by companies to face the rapid changes in the market. Thus, the authors also intend to contribute on how managers, from the private and public sector, can better deal with this current moment in the Angolan context. Therefore, a relevant approach is revealed, taking into account the implications of the phenomenon under analysis and the actuality of the theme itself.

To support the investigation plan, the following specific objectives were defined: (1)-Identify the main difficulties that companies and consumers have faced with the emergence of the covid-19 pandemic; (2)- identify the strategies adopted by companies in the face of the Covid-19 Pandemic; (3)- analyze the changes that have occurred in the purchase behavior of the Angolan consumer since the beginning of the Covid-19 Pandemic until now; (4)- identify the business opportunities that have arisen in the midst of the Covid-19 Pandemic.

As for the methodology, a qualitative approach was chosen using the case study (of the multi-case type).

For data collection, semi-structured interviews were chosen.

Data processing was through content analysis.

Its object of study was different commercial surfaces, represented by their managers (public and private sector).

This article is structured as follows: Chapter I (Introduction), with a brief presentation of the theme, objectives, and structure of the work; Chapter II (Theoretical framework), which contains a summary of the essential concepts of the approach; III (Methodology), the theoretical model of analysis, the sample, the data collection process and the respective data analysis method are presented; results; IV (Discussion and results); V (Conclusion) and VI (Recommendations).

BACKGROUND

The Angolan economy was mostly dependent on oil, the oil price crisis highlighted the need to accelerate the process of diversification of the economy. From 2002-2014, the government began to invest in other sectors and the private business fabric began to grow (Leitão, 2015). There was more openness to new investments. In this sense, there was growth in the sectors of agriculture, market services, construction and the manufacturing industry, and these sectors reached levels of relevance in GDP. What led to a division of GDP between the oil and non-oil sectors, this showed a strong acceleration of the reduction of oil dependence by the Angolan economy that occurred in recent years (Leitão, 2015).

According to data from the United Nations (NU, 2020; ECA, 2020), it can be said that in the world, the pandemic had an essentially negative impact on all spheres of human activity, without neglecting some positive aspects that were also notable. In Africa, it can be said that the impact of Covid-19 essentially focused on three dimensions: (1)- political dimension (weariness of confidence, setting in uncertainty; political instability); (2)- social dimension (loss of life in such a short period of time; social services interrupted with emphasis on schools; social dissatisfaction; conflicts, etc.); (3)- economic (economic recession; loss of employment and other means of subsistence; increase in health care costs; increase in non-formal activity, motivated by financial difficulties, etc).

And, what was the impact of Covid-19 on Angola, and on companies in particular? As mentioned in the previous paragraph, at this stage it is still difficult to obtain exact data on the impact of Covid-19 in Angola. So we have been working with the few available data. In Angola, "the COVID-19 pandemic is directly affecting, but also has a serious indirect impact on the economy, through its impact on the global oil market (BM, 2020, p.05)". In other words, the Covid-19 pandemic threatens the health of Angolans, but it also negatively affects the Angolan economy with strong implications for employment and poverty, considered the latter as one of the major problems currently experienced in the country. It should be noted that, before the pandemic, Angola was already facing challenges to restore growth due to the poor performance of the oil sector and the side effects for the non-oil sector. The oil sector, which accounted for around 30% of GDP, 60% of tax revenues and over 90% of exports in 2019, has been the engine of the recession due to the decline in the price of oil. The Covid-19 pandemic and the new oil crisis it unleashed worsened the loss of national income. To overcome dependence on oil, the transition to a more diversified economic model, which was already a priority before this crisis, becomes even more urgent. Therefore, the main impact of the Covid-19 crisis has been via the oil sector, as the fall in the price of oil boosted a recessive dynamic in the Angolan economy and increased pressure on fiscal accounts and government debt.

Due to the effects of covid-19 on the Angolan economy, fiscal policy faced three main challenges faced in 2020, namely: (i) loss of tax revenue resulting from the drop in oil prices and the difficulty in selling national production (ii) allocation of appropriations for priority public expenditures and (iii) measures for fiscal relief to entrepreneurs and families to be able to withstand the impacts of the pandemic crisis (BAI, 2021).

To overcome this situation, the Angolan government adopted some measures through the creation of some decrees in the fiscal sphere. Thus minimizing the negative impact of the covid-19 pandemic on companies and consumers (see table below):

Table 1.

Instrument	Main measures
Presidential Decree No. 96/20, of 9 April	Review of the OGE 2020, focusing on the following measures: o Use of 1.5 billion Kwanzas from the Sovereign Fund of Angola; o Acceleration of the Privatization Program (PROPRIV); o Authorization to INE to invest in Treasury bonds; o Suspension of payment in cash for arrears; o Negotiation for the postponement of the payment of 50% of the internal debt (rollever) and the country's adhesion to the financing lines to combat the effects of the Covid-19 pandemic; Deferral of payment of VAT on the import of some goods and exemption from customs duties on the purchase of goods for the purpose of humanitarian aid and donations.
Presidential Decree No. 98/20, of 9 April	Extension of the payment deadline for taxpayers in groups B and A; Attribution of VAT tax credit to imports of 54 PRODESI products.
Law No. 20/20, of July 9	Approval of a new Urban Property Tax (IPU) law which, in addition to urban buildings, will also apply to rural buildings and land for construction. The previous law provided for a single tax of 0.5% on properties with a taxable equity value greater than 5 million kwanzas, while the new law provides for the application of progressive rates up to 0.6% and charges 50% of the tax on unoccupied buildings. .
Law No. 24/20, of July 13	Replacement of the Circulation Tax by the tax on motor vehicles, with a broader base of incidence: o Extending the incidence to vessels and aircraft; o Exemption and vehicles used in the agricultural and fisheries sector.
Law No. 26/20, of July 20	Reduction of the industrial tax rate from 30% to 25% o Increase in the tax rate for many sectors from 30% to 35%, with emphasis on banks, insurance companies and telecommunications;
Law No. 28/20, of 22 July	Increase in tax brackets and increase in the IRT rate up to a maximum of 25%, against the previous 17% exemption on income below 70 thousand kwanzas, compared to the previous about 34 thousand kwanzas.
Law No. 31/20, of August 11	Elimination of the VAT exemption on the basic food basket, with a rate of 5%; Reduction of the VAT rate on agricultural inputs from 14% to 5% Application of the 14% fee to the exploration and practice of games of chance and social entertainment

(BAI, 2021)

In 2020 PWC carried out a study on the potential impacts of the covid-19 pandemic on key sectors of the Angolan economy, and presented the following results:

- Transport and Logistics: the reduction in travel due to restrictions imposed at a global level, led to a sharp decline in profitability in this sector;
- Manufacturing and construction: reduced demand and capacity during and after the crisis led to project delays and postponements and widespread billing breaks.
- Commerce: drop in invoicing and pressure on cash flows, due to the decrease in demand. This sector could quickly recover through the adoption of online sales.
- Financial Institutions: as a result of a likely increase in customer difficulties. This sector may have a potential impact on profitability and liquidity.
- Agriculture and Fisheries: decrease in imports of basic necessities in the short and medium term;
- Hotels and restaurants. There was a drop in billing due to low demand;
- Telecommunications. This sector showed strong growth due to the expected extension of the teleworking situation and the increasing degree of digitalization of the Angolan economy;

In Angola, companies and workers are impacted by covid-19, there was a meeting at the beginning of 2020 between business associations and the Ministry of Public Administration, Work and Social Security, at this meeting it was revealed that in addition to the hotel and restaurant sector, the oil and construction companies were also experiencing the same problems. Entrepreneurs said that, given the Covid-19 situation, they are being forced to lay off almost 50% of their employees (Ndomba, 2020).

The state of emergency had a negative impact on the financial situation of families in Angola, as, with the suspension of the free movement of people and goods throughout the Angolan territory, the financial condition of families was changed, especially those families whose income comes from self-employed activities (small entrepreneurs) in the formal or informal sector. According to the study carried out by the Instituto Superior do Huambo, in a sample of 2291 respondents, 53% said that they did not have the means of subsistence to continue in social isolation (Boio, Pacatolo and MBangula, 2020).

Higher Education institutions in Angola were, before the pandemic, limited to face-to-face teaching. With the emergence of covid-19, classes in the Higher Education subsystem were paralyzed for much of 2020, leading to the readjustment of the academic calendar (Lueto, Solari and Catumbela, 2020). According to the same authors, Higher Education Institutions are faced with a difficult situation, as many do not have organizational dynamics that favor the full use of communication tools, whether intranet or internet, that allow easy and efficient use. accessible digital platforms for distance learning. However, for there to be distance learning in Angola, it is necessary for the government and private universities to invest in infrastructure and technological systems in educational institutions.

Regarding the management of the Pandemic period, it is also important to note that "*networking*" within the framework of internal and external relations also helped a lot in the process of controlling the consequences of the pandemic, technically and financially. From ensuring key social services in the lives of vulnerable children and families, health, child protection, education and social protection in general, in a constant connection with the different social bodies at the internal level. From the external point of view, it can also be said that there was success resulting from the "*networking*", that is, from the good relations existing between Angola and other countries in the world.

MAIN FOCUS OF THE CHAPTER[I]

Taking into account the nature of the study, the research methodology is qualitative, because this methodology allows for a deeper understanding of the study in question through (semi-structured) interviews, which is the data collection technique used, as this technique allows to the researcher to extract important information for the study, through the testimonies and interpretations of the interviewees, respecting their own frames of reference, their language and their mental categories (Quivy and Campenhoudt, 2008). The samples chosen must have certain characteristics to constitute good representations of the populations from which they were taken (Almeida and Freire, 2008). The sample (target population) for the present study is made up of 12 participants: managers, entrepreneurs and economists who work in different areas of the Angolan market and who have mastered the subject under study. Respondents participated in person, by means of advance invitation to the research. The selection of participants was intentional. Judgmental or intentional sampling, according to Yasuda and Oliveira (2012), consists of selecting elements (participants) that present the best condition to provide information about the phenomenon. It should be noted that some information about the participants is not available for reasons of confidentiality and anonymity of the participants.

After collecting the data, an interpretative analysis was carried out, which consists of describing what the interviewees said in a more organized way (Guerra, 2006). After conducting the interviews, he began to listen to all the interviews. Then he transcribed them. Then, the synopses of the interviews were constructed. Then, a categorical analysis was carried out, which consists of identifying the variables whose dynamics are potentially explanatory of the phenomenon to be explained.

ISSUES, CONTROVERSIES, PROBLEMS

Effects of Covid-19 on the Angolan Economy

In this category, we sought to find out in the opinion of the interviewees, what was the impact of covid-19 on the Angolan economy, we tried to understand what were the positive and negative effects of the pandemic on the Angolan market.

Of the 12 interviewees, the majority (about 8) said that covid-19 had a negative impact on the Angolan economy, leading to the closure of many companies, increasing the level of unemployment and consequently the poverty of many families, especially those belonging to the social class. low. Interviewee 1 also mentioned that so far the country continues to feel the negative effects of covid-19 on Angola's economic agents. He also added that the Angolan government had several projects aimed at different sectors of the economy, but that unfortunately they were tied up because most of the resources were allocated to the fight against covid-19. Interviewee 2 said that there were difficulties in supplying some products on the market and this tied the lives of consumers, because it ended up inflating some products due to the reduction in supply. Interviewee 7, on the other hand, said that despite covid-19 bringing several negative effects to the economy, there are companies that had a positive impact with increased sales of products and services, namely hygiene companies (alcohol gel, disinfestation, cleaning, masks), these have had high profits at this stage. The same also mentioned that several companies unfortunately do not survive because many depended on exports and we know that because of covid-19 exports have stopped significantly. Contrary to the previous interviewee, interviewee 9 mentioned that a high number of Angolan companies had to close their doors because many did not know how to adapt to the new reality, had reduced sales. Interviewee 11 said that large companies managed to survive because they were already aware of the fragility of our economy and bet on innovation in the phase of covid-19, for example companies that were beverage producers started to produce gel alcohol. Finally, interviewee 12 reported that the sector that was most affected in Angola was the informal sector.

Angola produces almost nothing, and its economy depends on oil exports. According to the FMI, covid-19 and the drop in the price of oil had a negative influence on the country's economy in 2020. The prevention and control measures adopted by the government to prevent the spread of the virus, such as confinement, distancing and the decrease in economic activity in the country have harmed the economy, especially the informal sector which is the largest in the country.

Taking into account the opinions of the interviewees and the observations made by the researchers, we can conclude that the diversification of the Angolan economy is crucial for the country's economic and social development in a sustainable way. For this, the government and private companies must invest in different sectors of the economy, for example, invest in the primary sector in the extraction of raw materials in addition to oil and diamonds, as Angola is a country rich in natural resources. There is a need to continue investing in agriculture (in the construction of roads to better transport products from the countryside), in livestock, fishing and forestry to reduce dependence on frozen meat imports from other countries. In relation to the sector, according to the interviewee, it is essential to create industries that transform products from agriculture, livestock, and fishing. The country needs pharmaceutical industrialists because Angola has many medicinal plants that are underexplored. The tertiary sector (distribution or marketing) is the fastest growing sector in the country and is providing jobs and various products and services to Angolan families.

Sectors that Suffered a Negative Impact

In this category, the business lines that were most negatively affected by the covid-19 pandemic were identified, of the 11 respondents who responded on this topic, 5 share the same opinion, stating that the companies that suffered the most from the negative effects of covid-19 were those in the Hotel sector, namely bars, restaurants, hotels, amusement parks, museums, travel agencies, airlines, etc. Another three interviewees cited event halls and educational institutions (kindergartens, general schools and higher education) as the most affected, and also mentioned that there was a change in the school calendar due to the confinement time (the school year started from February/ March and ended in November/December, with covid-19 we returned to the "European calendar" that starts in September and ends in July).

Of the 12 respondents, two cited companies operating in the clothing and footwear business as having a negative impact. For interviewee 1, covid-19 affected all sectors, from transport, the oil sector, agriculture, commerce, agriculture, tourism, culture, bars, industry. Interviewee 2 mentioned the agricultural sector, industrial activity and in general all those who work in the transformation of raw materials, there were difficulties in the supply of raw materials and this usually impacted the production chain. Interviewee 8 also mentioned that the transport sector was also affected with the reduction of passengers and the informal sector (street vending).

Managers must be preparing and adapting their companies to the new change. Because in times of turmoil, the success of companies depends on the ability of managers to detect and interpret the change in consumer behavior so they can respond more effectively to the competition, their needs and desires, and also the ability to identify ideas. of new business within the company itself (Costa, 2013).

In fact, in Angola, several companies were negatively affected by covid-19, because many of them were not prepared for crises or changes that could occur in the business environment so suddenly. Most companies are not in the habit of carrying out these analysis of the business environment, studies on the needs and satisfaction of consumers, as the demand is greater than the supply. And this causes many of these companies to be "accommodated" in a certain way.

The tourism sector is growing and still needs to be better explored. Since prevention measures have already been relaxed, companies operating in the tourism sector should further promote domestic tourism by lowering the prices of services, creating packages for families belonging to different social classes. In short, they should check the marketing mix strategies of the different business units.

Regarding the education sector in Angola, the confinement caused most institutions to paralyze their activities, which greatly harmed students because they have little access to the internet, many institutions were not prepared to teach online classes, few had support software school. As a result, they had to close (private schools had financial losses, could not pay employees due to lack of funds/financial reserves) until the return of face-to-face classes. To minimize this situation, the Ministry of General Education implemented teleclasses for children who could watch on TV at the usual times of face-to-face classes. Covid-19 has shown these institutions that it is important to invest in digital teaching platforms and the internet (distance learning). It is necessary to follow the evolution that other countries are having in the education sector.

As for clothing and footwear, investment in the textile industry is necessary, the Angolan consumer likes fashion, is vain, appreciates original (branded) clothes and shoes. But unfortunately they often have to buy clothes from the bundle (used clothes from Europe and China), because we don't have many companies that invest in the textile industry. Despite the covid-19 having harmed the sales of these products, they are products with a high demand, because the Angolan consumer is in the habit of buying clothes frequently.

Regarding the transport sector, this sector suffered a lot from the confinement of the population, because almost no one left home. And most public transport is private taxi, there are public buses, but not enough for the population. Many of these young taxi drivers were left without the source of income that passengers are because they were confined at home. And many of these had no other source of income. In short, there is a great weakness in the transport sector in Angola. To address this situation, the government added 200 buses in the city of Luanda, which is the most populous in the country. also intends to create a surface metro in the same city. Even so, there is still a need for greater investment in this sector to create other public transport such as trains, trams, buses and subways.

Sectors That Had a Positive Impact

Of the 12 interviewees, only 9 respond to this theme. And of these 9 interviewees 5 share the same opinion, they said that companies linked mainly to products that were widely used during the duration of the pandemic such as the production of alcohol gel, mascara, and all support material related to co-vid-19, these companies benefited companies had a significant increase in sales (companies producing the disinfestation tunnel). Sales in pharmaceutical companies had a positive impact compared to others because it is an area that in times of crisis (confinement) did not stop, on the contrary, they had to keep open to sale of essential products for the prevention of covid-19, such as alcohol gel, soap, mask and others. Interviewee 8 mentioned that medical posts, clinics and public hospitals also had many gains with the high demand for patients.

Respondents 1, 4 and 9 said that the companies that profited the most at this stage were those in the food industry (mainly basic basket products and *fast food*), because people started to eat more at home. Interviewee 1 also mentioned that there was appreciation of second-hand cars (old or used cars) in angola, people bought old cars due to reduced income. There was an increase in internet ordering and home delivery. For interviewee 5, sales of pajamas increased, because people were at home longer and it became fashionable to do live on the internet dressed in pajamas. Interviewee 6, on the other hand, said that companies selling alcoholic beverages started selling more because many believed that the consumption of hot drinks prevents covid-19.

Through the opinions of the interviewees and a direct observation carried out in the market, it was found that the companies that profited the most are the companies that operate in the area of health, food and beverages. Which means that consumers became more concerned with satisfying physiological and safety needs during the confinement period.

Consumers are conditioned by a rational side (logic, reason, objectivity) and an emotional side (intuition, emotions, imagination, memory). Understanding consumer behavior is critical to business:

- Companies exist to satisfy consumer needs;

- Companies must understand consumer needs in order to satisfy them.

Looking at the perspective presented to us in *Maslow* 's Hierarchy of Needs and Consumer Behavior, we find: Physiological needs (hunger, thirst, sex, sleep, etc.); Need for security (defence, protection, employment, shelter); Esteem needs (self-esteem, recognition, status); Need for self-actualization (personal development, achievement).

The Purchasing Power

Purchasing power consists of the financial capacity of an individual to make a purchase with a certain monetary amount. This subcategory addresses the purchasing power of the Angolan consumer during the covid-19 pandemic.

Most of the interviewees are of the opinion that, with the closure of several companies and consequently unemployment, the Angolan families belonging to the middle and lower classes were losing their purchasing power. With the emergence of covid-19, the demand for basic food products increased significantly and the prices of these same products rose, which further harmed the Angolan consumer who was deprived and without purchasing power. This situation has led many families into extreme poverty. Interviewee 6 mentioned that families belonging to the middle classes began to substitute some more expensive foods for those with low prices (essential to daily needs), for example at Christmas many families replaced cod with another type of dried fish, many changed the reindeer potato for banana, sweet potato or cassava. Many have substituted chicken for turkey, and other things. To address this situation, the government reduced the consumption tax (VAT) on some products of the basic basket, from 14% to 7% and for the present of 2022 they intend to lower it by up to 5%. The government and some large or large companies have also created projects to support the neediest families by offering food and some monetary values. In relation to the Government, there is, for example, the Kwenda Project [1]that has helped the most needy families a lot.

Some companies took advantage of the high demand for their products to raise prices, as they knew that consumers had no other alternatives. Therefore, the government is recommended to inspect these and apply fines, according to the price regulation.

Many lost their jobs, the prices of basic food products (food such as rice, bread, beans, sugar, etc.) had their prices increased and consequently lost their purchasing power. In this sense, many housewives chose, at the time of purchase, to combine their values with other people to buy a certain food or product and then distribute it among the number of people who gave the values. This type of strategy is commonly called "partner" (consists of joining the values at the time of purchase with other people so that they can buy a box of chicken thighs or other product, for example). Also because of the loss of purchasing power, Angolan families started to buy the famous "carcass" (carcass is the entire chicken skeleton without the meat) as it is cheaper. In the initial phase of covid-19, Angolan families were scared and had a change in buying behavior. They stopped buying products and services they were used to and started buying more basic necessities, that is, food and beverages; cleaning and hygiene products.

Most Wanted Products/Services After the Onset of Covid-19

At the time, there were products and services that consumers adhered to or consumed the most, in this subcategory we address this issue. According to respondents, the products and services most consumed by consumers in the phase of the Covid-19 Pandemic are the following:

- Natural teas (Capungo Pungo, lemon tea, Ginger, caxinde, eucalyptus; Vicks Tea)
- Non-frozen foods (fish, meat, vegetables, fruits, especially citrus fruits, etc.)
- Cold and headache remedies
- Vitamins
- Tv (plus news and entertainment programs, NetFlix for example was a big bet by consumers; video games; online gambling, etc.)
- Online shopping for various goods with home delivery;
- online cinema
- Social networks (Facebook; Instagram; WhatsApp; Tik Tok);
- Take-away services (home delivery - catering)
- Alcoholic drinks (hot drinks)
- Variety of internet services
- Soap
- cooking gas
- face protection mask
- Alcohol gel.

With the confinement, families were almost all the time at home and consequently consumed more food and drinks and also watched TV to be informed about the news of covid-19, to entertain, and also made use of the internet for social networks.

To increase immunity, families bet more on the consumption of natural national foods that contain vitamin C. Consumption of many fruits, especially citrus fruits, vegetables, vegetables, natural teas, hygiene products and prevention against Covid-19. Interviewee 9 said that the product most consumed by youth was alcohol, "because on the myth that, drinking "agua do boss" (a hot water produced essentially by artisans), Whiskey, Gin Tonic, etc. It was believed that this would have helped in preventing Covid-19. Interviewee 10, on the other hand, states that "even though prices were not lowered, people bought a lot of food and drink, because all family members were at home and consumed more. In relation to consumption at home, there was a considerable increase in the consumption of cooking gas, which increased the demand for it.

Less Sought-After Products/Services After the Onset of Covid-19

An unexpected and sudden unplanned change that occurs in a general environment can force companies to think and act quickly to adapt to new situations, which can either represent a threat to the company or an opportunity that must be taken advantage of (Carvalho, Bernardo, Sousa and Negas, 2014).

In Angola, covid-19 caused losses in several companies, due to the insecurity that caused consumers to stop buying certain products/services because they lost importance. The consumer in the initial phase of covid-19, that is, in the year 2020 did not pay attention to products that are not essential. The consumer was thinking short term by buying products that strengthen their immune system.

In this subcategory, we will present the least sought after products and services in the phase of Covid-19 in the Angolan market.

The interviewees mentioned, throughout the interview, several lines of business that suffered drops in their sales, namely:

- Clothing and footwear sector;
- Restaurants and hotels;
- event halls;
- Mechanics workshops;
- Cosmetics;
- Beauty services, hairdressing, barbershop;
- Activities outside the home (bars, fairs and the like, etc.);
- Trips;
- Frozen and fresh food/beverages;
- Durable goods (appliances, automobiles)
- Luxury products;
- Mall.

However, interviewee 9 is of the opinion that in Angola the agriculture sector has not made any gains because there are few food processing factories. And farmers in the interior of the country (from other provinces) were not able to send the products to Luanda (the country's capital and the most populous) for disposal because of the controls that were in the provincial borders and the products stayed at the controls and often arrived already spoiled in Luanda. There was a lot of loss in this sector. Interviewee 12 also mentioned that beverage consumers reduced their purchases.

"Interviewee 9: I think that in Angola in the food sector there was no gain because we have few food processing plants. And the products from the interior that were to be shipped in luanda almost didn't arrive because they stayed in the controls and often, the products arrived already damaged. There was a very big loss in this sector. People preferred to drink more and eat less."

Strategies Adopted by the Government

To respond to Covid-19 in 2020, the Angolan government adopted the following public health protection measures: closing borders, with very limited access, especially to the Capital of the Country (Luanda); the closure of all schools, restaurants and public event spaces, reduced the workforce to 50% in the public and private sector and also limited the number of people on transport. These measures were gradually withdrawn as the spread of the covid-19 virus was controlled.

To reduce the negative impact of covid-19 on the Angolan economy, the government adopted measures in the tax sector in several areas of the Real Economy, such as: Agriculture and Fisheries, Industry and Commerce, transport, construction, credit to the economy, among others. This made it possible to avoid the closure of companies. He also encouraged citizens to see the pandemic as an opportunity to accelerate the increase in domestic production, as Angola depends heavily on the import of various products.

What hurt a little in the initial phase of the pandemic, the prices of imported products had significantly increased prices and there was little quantity available.

Regarding the strategies adopted by the government, of the 12 respondents, only 5 answered this question, as the others said they do not remember any strategy used by the government to overcome the impact of Covid-19. Interviewee 3 mentioned that the Government may have reactivated a program for companies, giving some funds so that activities could resume. In the opinion of interviewees 4 and 6, the government was more focused on what is the protection of the well-being in the fight against Covid-19. Interviewee 5 reported that the government created the Kwenda project, which aims to help the most needy families with a monthly subsidy. Finally, interviewee 7 said that the government has played its part, which is to try to contain the advance of Covid-19 through laws to reduce staff in public and private institutions, mandatory hygiene before entering an establishment.

Strategies Adopted by Companies in the Face of Covid-19

The strategy defines the path to be followed by the company and provides guidance on how the company should go about reaching its target market through its products, pricing, promotion and tactical distribution (Barringer and Ireland, 2011). This analysis consists of defining the company's growth strategy through the analysis of its strengths and weaknesses (internal company information over which the manager has control) and the opportunities and threats of the business environment (information external to the company that is outside the manager's direct control). With this analysis done, the manager will be able to know which paths or strategies should be used to achieve the defined objectives and goals (Dornelas, 2014).

Just like consumers, companies were also surprised by the emergence of the Covid-19 Pandemic. In a first phase, Angolan managers did not know how to deal, but then they created some measures to overcome the difficulties caused by covid-19 in business activity.

Regarding the strategies, the interviewees mention that some companies have adopted teleworking, that is, employees were able to work from home through a computer with internet access and mobile phones (example of banking institutions, insurance, some educational institutions, companies operating in the B2B market, etc.).

According to interviewee 2, companies in Angola did not have the habit of selling over the internet, with Covid-19, over the internet they increased a lot, at this stage companies sought to hire staff trained in digital marketing, to invest more in the visibility of their products. products on digital platforms (interviewee8). According to the same interviewee, some private companies used survival strategies to reduce staff to reduce costs. Interviewee 12 said that companies sought to be more in the virtual world than in the physical one, seeking to be close to the consumer in a digital way.

According to the interviewees, companies operating in the tourism sector that suffered the most from Covid-19 adopted the following marketing mix strategies:

- In the initial phase, hotels started to make their rooms available to the government for quarantine of individuals from other countries (they were paid for this).
- After the confinement, they began to invest more in television advertising to attract potential national and foreign customers, it was used as an opinion leader to represent tourism outside Angola, some famous personalities.
- Restaurants have started to adopt *takeaway* and home delivery services.
- Hotels reduced prices to attract more customers and began to advertise more on social networks.

Some companies have cut costs. Food and beverage companies and companies that sell various goods (durable and non-durable goods) started to publicize their products and services on digital platforms, created delivery services, developed Apps for online orders.

Regarding the companies that operate in the textile sector, they bet on the innovation strategy, they started to produce masks with company crests/logo (personalized), fabric masks with names, masks with African fabrics. Aesthetics companies have also started to do home services.

With the loss of the purchasing power of families, some warehouses (retailers) decided to adopt a sales strategy, that is, sell half a box of products, instead of a box to families that can no longer afford a box. For example, if a box of chicken thighs cost 9,000 kwanzas (about €14.94), half a box would cost 4,500 kwanzas (about €7.87).

SOLUTIONS AND RECOMMENDATIONS

The government should focus on diversifying the economy and reducing its dependence on oil.

The Angolan state should create more policies to improve the economic situation of our country, favoring more the issue of the consumer itself and if it is possible to create programs for financial education so that consumers have a perception of how to manage their family finances and also implement price policies so that prices do not vary or help in the way that has helped and if the price that this company practices is determined, the other company must also practice in a certain product.

Companies must be aware of changes that occur in the market and especially in needs. And create strategies to respond to market demands.

Companies must show confidence in hygiene and measures to prevent covid-19;

They must better organize online communication and create new forms of payment.

The researchers suggest companies/government to lower the prices of products, to make national products lower than imported products and not the other way around as has happened. This strategy will encourage the consumption of national products and the development of the secondary sector.

We recommend that investors explore new business opportunities in the Angolan market in different sectors.

Entrepreneurs should invest in the pharmaceutical industry, the country has many species of plants and trees that are widely used in natural medicine in the treatment of various diseases and that have not yet been explored. These plants were widely used in the phase of covid-19, most of the population believes that they help in the treatment and prevention of covid-19 and other diseases.

FUTURE RESEARCH DIRECTIONS

For future investigations the researchers suggest the following topics:

- Companies that could grow after covid-19.
- The impact of covid-19 on the Angolan education system
- Importance of public policies and planning for the development of the tourism sector in Angola.

CONCLUSION

Throughout the article, the impact that the covid-19 pandemic has had on consumers and companies has been demonstrated. It was found that covid-19 had a negative impact on certain business areas and positive impact on other business areas. The companies that sold the most during the current phase of the pandemic are those operating in the food, beverage and health sector. The ones that suffered the most losses were companies in the tourism, education, informal sector, etc.

The main difficulties that companies faced were adapting to changes that occur in the market, especially the change in consumer buying behavior. Some managers in the initial phase of covid-19 in angola did not know what strategies were used in the face of the difficulties that covid-19 was causing. After some time, companies began to respond with the creation of new services and products (delivery services, online sales, home services, creation of apps, etc), adherence to new technologies using digital marketing. Online sales in Angola grew a lot.

The Angolan consumer has become more rational, buying products and adhering to the services they really need. Consumers stopped buying products and services that were usual to buy only essential and safety/prevention products.

Taking into account the changes in the purchasing behavior of families, they create strategies to respond to these needs and thus avoid foreclosure.

REFERENCES

Almeida, A., & Freire, T. (2008). *Research Methodology in Psychology and Education*. Psiquilibrios Editions.

BAI. (2021). *Annual Economic Conjuncture Report*. Angolan Investment Bank.

Bardin, L. (1977). *Content analysis*. Lisbon: Editions 70.

Barringer, B., & Ireland, R. (2011). *Entrepreneurship: Successfully Launching New Ventures* (4th ed.). Prentice Hall.

Boio, D., Pacatolo, C., & Bangula, M. (2020). *Assessment Study of the Socioeconomic Impacts of the Angolan Executive's Measures to Combat Covid-19*. Higher Polytechnic Institute Sol Nascente, Luanda.

Carvalho, L., Bernardo, M., Sousa, I., & Negas, M. (2014). *Management of organizations-An integrated and prospective approach*. Silabo, Lda.

Costa, T. (2013). *Contemporary Management - Principles, trends and challenges*. Silabo Editions.

Dornelas, J. (2014). *Entrepreneurship - Transforming Ideas into Business*. GEN - National Editorial Group. LTC.

Flick, U. (2005). *Qualitative Methods in Scientific Research*. Monitor - Projectos e Edições, Lda.

Fortin, M. (2009). *Fundamentals and Stages of the Investigation Process*. Lusodidact.

Guerra, I. (2006). *Qualitative Research and Content Analysis: Meaning and forms of use*. Principia Editora, Lda.

Hill, M., & Hill, A. (1998a). *The Construction of a Questionnaire.* Center for Studies on Change Socio-Economic,

Hill, M., & Hill, A. (1998b). *Investigation Empirical in the Social Sciences: A Guide introductory _ DYNAMIA.* Center for Studies on Change Socio-Economic.

IMF. (2020). *Angola: Tackling the Covid-19 Pandemic and the Oil Price Shock.* https://www.imf.org/pt/News/Articles/2020/09/18/na-angola-confronting-the-covid-19-pandemic-and-the-oil-price-shock

Leitão, A. (2015). Economic Market in Angola – Evolution perspective. Embassy of the Republic of Angola in Portugal – Commercial Representation.

Lima, C. M. A. O. (2020). Information about the new coronavirus (COVID-19). doi:10.1590/0100-3984.2020.53.2e1

Lueto, O., Solare, P., & Catumbela, E. (2020). Angolan Higher Education in the Time of Covid-19: Necessary Changes and Transformations. *Angolan Journal of University Extension*, 76-93.

Ndomba, B. (2020). *Angola: Companies and Workers suffer impact of Covid-19.* DW. https://www.dw.com/pt-002/angola-empresas-e-trabahdores-sofrem-impacto-da-covid-19/a-53532402 _

Oliveira. (1992). Planning strategic: Concepts, methodology and practices (6th ed.). Atlas.

PWC. (2020). *Responses to Impacts on Angolan Business and Economy.* Covid-19 Crisis Response Team.

Quivy, R., & Campenhoudt, L. (2008). Handbook of Research in Social Sciences. Lisbon: Gravida - Publicações, SA.

Stake, R. (2011). *Qualitative Research - Studying how things work.* ARTMED Editora, SA.

World Bank. (2020). *Confronting the socio-economic consequences of COVID-19 in Angola.* World Bank.

Yasuda, A., & Oliveira, D. M. T. (2012). *Marketing research: Guide to the practice of market research.* Cengage Learning.

ADDITIONAL READING

Anunciação, P., Mayén Cañavate, B., Bernal Conesa, J. A., & Briones Peñalver, A. J. (2018). *Tourism in the Blue Growth strategy: a model proposal.* Anatolia.

Correia, A. (2018). Psychological Risks. In *Wellbeing for Sustainability in the Global Workplace* (pp. 137–154). Routledge. doi:10.4324/9780429470523-7

Isaias, P., & Carvalho, L. (2018). *User Innovation and the Entrepreneurship Phenomenon in the Digital Economy.* IGI. doi:10.4018/978-1-5225-2826-5

ENDNOTE

1 A project designed by the Angolan Executive for the transfer of a fixed monthly income, in the amount of 8,500 kwanzas. In force since May 2020, after approval in the Diário da República, it plans to support a total of 1,608,000 households in poverty across the country, with a quarterly income of 25,500 kwanzas. Kwenda lasts for three years and comprises four components: Social Monetary Transfers; Productive Inclusion; Municipalization of Social Action and, finally, the reinforcement of the Single Social Registry (see https://governo.gov.ao/ao/noticias/kwenda/).

APPENDIX 1

Interview Guide for Managers, Entrepreneurs and Economists

1. In your opinion, what was the impact of covid-19 on the Angolan market?
2. Which sectors were most affected by the Covid-19 pandemic?
3. What are the strategies that the government/businesses adopt to overcome this impact?
4. What were the sectors that had a positive impact with covid-19 (increase in sales, emergence of new businesses)?
5. How did the Angolan consumer react to the emergence of Covid-19?
6. Which products did consumers start to buy more/and which ones did they buy less?
7. Do you have an issue that you think is relevant and that was not mentioned, yes. Which one?

Chapter 16
Harnessing Blockchain and Decentralized Finance in the Post-COVID-19 European Union:
The Case of the Circular Economy

Mariana Carmona
Immutable Oasis Labs, Mexico

Antonio Lanotte
CFE Bruxelles, Belgium

ABSTRACT

This chapter presents a singular convergence between a policy window of opportunity and changes in social habits triggered by the COVID-19 pandemic, which set timely conditions in the European Union to implement the green and digital transformation programs embodied in the Next Generation European Union (2021-2027). COVID-19 highlighted problems carried out decades ago, such as climate change and natural resources exhaustion, whereas prolonged lockdowns forged consciousness about pollution and overcrowded sites while accelerating the use of digital solutions. Under favorable circumstances to effect changes for a resilient, competitive, and inclusive European Union, the authors focus on the circular economy strategy and elaborate the case for blockchain and tokenization as a key enabling technology to sponsor agile networks for a swift transition to a green and digital society decoupled from resource extraction and waste production. The chapter expands the case for blockchain decentralized finance applications as a means to financialize tokenized green products.

DOI: 10.4018/978-1-7998-8856-7.ch016

INTRODUCTION

The Next Generation European Union

At the end of the year 2019, a new coronavirus was detected in humans and by the first quarter of the year 2020, the World Health Organization declared it the pandemic of Covid-19. Social distancing was the immediate response to stop contagions and almost every country across the globe decreed a lockdown with either partial or full confinement. The pandemic represented an economic, social, and political upheaval (Sarkis, 2020). Two years later, some economic and social activities returned to normality while a few others operate under *new normality* conditions. Amid the numerous effects of the pandemic, one that accounts for transcendent consequences is the increased awareness of climate change and natural resource degradation. Despite previous global climate action agreements such as the Kyoto Protocol or Paris Agreements, progress in global warming mitigation was gradual and insignificant. Conversely, the pandemic showed the unsustainability and brittleness of the current economic and production systems. The confinements and cease of transport and industrial activity represented a break for natural resources and an opportunity to rethink human relationship with nature in a post-Covid era.

As a result of a deeper and broader analysis of the desired society in a post-Covid19 era, the European Union has not considered the recovery as the sole restoration of the previous economic and social conditions but as a lifeline to reach no net emissions of greenhouse gases by the year 2050 and the transition to an economy with growth but without resource extraction and waste. The European Union in the future is one in which people can live in an environment with fresh air, clean water, renewable energy, healthy affordable food, and reliant on longer-lasting products that are repaired, recycled, or reused. The aspirational goals are incorporated in the Next Generation European Union (Next Generation EU, n.d.), considered as the new Marshall Plan for Europe comprising the deployment of over a billion Euros to boost growth, investment, and reforms in two main instruments. The first one is a short-term perspective program for the years 2021-2022 aimed to revitalize the economy. The second is a Recovery and Resilience Facility comprising a multi-year plan for the years 2021-2027 based on six pillars:

1. Green transition.
2. Digital transition.
3. Smart, sustainable and inclusive growth including economic cohesion, jobs, productivity, competitiveness, research, development and innovation, and a well-functioning internal market with strong small and medium enterprises.
4. Social and territorial cohesion.
5. Health and economic, social and institutional resilience, with the aim of, inter alia, increasing crisis preparedness and crisis response capacity.
6. Policies for the next generation, children and youth such as education and skills.

In Next Generation European Union, the twin challenge – i.e., green and digital transformation – is a key priority. Covid-19 highlighted the critical and strategic role of digitized solutions. In this case, the digital transformation is aimed to develop strategic capacities in supercomputing, artificial intelligence, cybersecurity, digital skills, and wide use of digital technologies across the economy and society. In a fully digitized EU, the basis for competitiveness is the ability to innovate and employ the most advanced technology in using inputs rather than the low input cost paradigm.

On the green side, the extraction of raw materials with increasing costs makes evident its reduced availability, climate catastrophes occur more often and with more devastating effects, and the incapacity to process all the waste polluting oceans and soils, altogether demand an urgent change in the linearity of our industrial and economic patterns "take-produce-use-waste" for a more resilient circular economy that eliminates waste and decouples from material extraction.

As Covid-19 created a turning point, the following chapter analyzes the conditions in the European Union that open a policy window of opportunity ideal to implement the green and digital transformations, converging with changes in social and individual behaviors that reinforce and smooth the necessary transitions. With propitious conditions for a green and digital transformation, in the next sections the authors focus on the analysis of the circular economy and the role of blockchain technology facilitating the information management required for efficient coordination and innovation in circular production patterns. In addition to previous works studying blockchain technology in circular supply chains (Wang et al., 2020; Nandi et al., 2021; Sarkis, 2020), the authors bring the concept of tokenization of sustainable products from Narayan and Tidström (2020) to the blockchain architecture which would allow the full traceability of items and create a dynamic cloud of information necessary for market coordination towards a zero-waste economy. The contribution presents two real use cases where blockchain and tokenized products are applied to the circular economy. Finally, the authors expand the case for blockchain-based decentralized finance (DeFi) applications to financialize and monetize the tokenized green economy.

BACKGROUND

A Window of Opportunity for the European 'Twin Challenge'

According to John W. Kingdon, a policy innovation happens once a window of opportunity for change becomes available. The importance of a window of opportunity underscores that once a problem is recognized and a solution gets articulated, a new policy occurs when the political climate sets the appropriate time for change and no other constraints oppose the action (Mozeley & Whelan, n.d.). For a window of opportunity to form, three streams must converge: a problem stream, a policy stream, and a politics stream (Figueroa et al., 2018).

A *problem stream* is a moment when a policy issue requires attention. The confinement and social distancing rules to deter the coronavirus contagion led to the suspension of industrial activities and reduced the production and fulfillment of essential items. Vehicle transport and aviation were ceased or minimized to emergency cases. People's mobility was prohibited, except for the supply of basic needs. The economic impacts were devastating; however, the impasse in human activities was a bit of a break for nature.

The impact of lockdowns in the recovery of natural ecosystems has not been fully measured, except for air quality. According to the World Meteorological Organization (WMO), the stay-at-home policies led to an unprecedented decrease in pollutant emissions. In a comparative study of pre-lockdown, partial and full lockdowns, and periods of relaxing restrictions during the year 2020, it was found that China, Europe, and North America had "short-term Covid-19 related reductions in emissions coinciding with long-term emission-mitigation measures that led to lower particulate matter (PM) concentrations compared to previous years", meaning that air quality improved. At a global scale, the analysis showed "decreases of 70 percent in mean nitrogen oxides (NOx) and a 30 to 40 percent reduction in mean particulate matter ($PM_{2.5}$) concentration during the full lockdown in 2020 compared with the same periods in 2015-2019 (WMO, 2021)".

Covid-19 resounded in the political and economic spheres by scrutinizing resiliency and readiness to react under distress conditions and was stronger in exhibiting the vulnerabilities and unsustainability of our current way of doing things. Although climate change has been a global concern in previous years, the pandemic turned global agreements into purposeful actions. Therefore, in the European Union, a problem stream incorporates recovering from the economic, social, and sanitary impacts of Covid-19 and using the contingency as a lever for a deeper and broader reflection on climate change and the urgency of modifying our relationship with nature (Figure 1).

Secondly, a *policy stream* arises when there exists an agenda with strategies and action plans. The policy stream is embodied in the Next Generation European Union Recovery Package. The havocs of Covid-19 shaped a holistic new growth strategy that aims to transform the European Union into a fair and prosperous society, with a modern, resource-efficient, and competitive economy without net emissions of greenhouse gases by the year 2050 and one in which economic growth decouples from resource use. The former is a multi-year recovery plan aiming to build a systemic modernization of the economy, society, and industry (Potočnik, 2021), including a fair climate and digital transition; modernization of traditional agricultural policies, fighting climate change, biodiversity protection, gender equality, among others (European Commission, n.d.). In the recovery plan, two core strategies form the 'twin challenge'. The first one is a *green transformation* aimed to foster European competitiveness with resiliency, inclusive growth, and sustainability in natural resources. The second one refers to the *digital transformation* necessary to reach -among others – the environmental milestones. Finally, a *political stream* arises when both, motivations and resources converge to solve a problem (Figueroa et al., 2018). In 2020, the European Union assigned an unprecedented budget to recover from the coronavirus crisis, with a stimulus package of EUR 2.018 trillion (current prices) distributed in a long-term budget of 1.211 trillion EUR between 2021 -2027 and a temporary instrument of EUR 806.9 billion to power the recovery (European Commission, 2021).

Figure 1. The window of opportunity for the twin challenge
Source: author's elaboration.

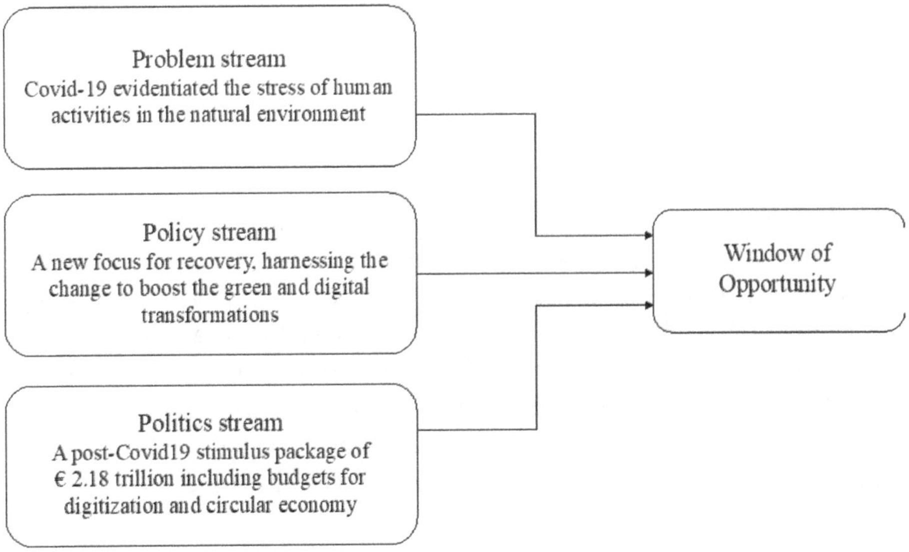

The linkages between the pandemic and the 'twin challenge' become more evident by acknowledging that the coronavirus reinforced in policymakers the need to manage risks, to prevent and build resiliency for future contingencies, to create fair conditions and safety nets for all inhabitants, while keeping the European Union interconnected, interdependent, agile, inclusive, competitive, and technologically innovative. The multiple goals are gathered in the sustainable grid comprised by the three pillars of the ESG method where "E" accounts for an environmental strategy transforming economic systems through alternative resource use, circular economies, and the quest for more autonomy and sufficiency. "S" refers to a social policy that equalizes opportunities in access to markets and financing, ethical work conditions, while keeping human rights, fundamental freedoms, and democratic principles, and "G" of governance, that is, the existence of political commitments and a structure where all stakeholders find clarity on political, regulatory, and legal specificities (Table 1).

Table 1. The sustainable grid

Environmental	Social	Governance
1. Mitigation of and adaptation to climate change 2. Water and marine resources 3. Resource use and circular economy 4. Pollution **5.** Biodiversity and ecosystems	1. Equal opportunities, access to the labor market, gender equality and disability 2. Working conditions, including wages, social dialogue, and work-life balance 3. Human rights, fundamental freedoms, and democratic principles, with reference to the International Bill of Human Rights **4.** Adequate or equal presence of women in management positions (boards of directors) and during meetings (webinars)	1. The role of administrative, management and control bodies 2. Ethics and corporate culture, including the fight against corruption 3. Political commitments and lobbying activities 4. Management of relations with business partners 5. Internal control and risk management

Source: Lanotte, 2021.

Post-pandemic Societal Changes Enabling the 'Twin Challenge'

The incentives to implement the twin challenge in a post-pandemic European Union are also fostered by changes coming from the society. Covid-19 triggered and accelerated behavioral shifts in individuals seeking healthier, sustainable, and more digitized lifestyles establishing conditions for a swift and smoother transformation.

Social distancing and lockdowns had harmful effects, remarkably in sentiments of loneliness, suicidal attempts, increased consumption of alcohol and drugs, etc. (WHO, 2020; Saladino, Algeri & Auriemma, 2020). The effects of lockdowns on mental health are out of the scope of this research. Other behavioral changes are relevant for the current analysis, for instance, the new attitudes and preferences, habits, and consumption patterns that reinforce the adoption of a greener and digitized society. The increasing and permanent demand for virtual and digital solutions in households and businesses, the demand for new and different labor conditions, the reduction in cash payments, and the search for smaller locally provisioned neighborhoods are some of the changes in society that fit with the European Union Recovery Package.

While some habits after Covid-19 will return to the previous stage -for example, gatherings, assistance to restaurants, stadiums, or theaters- other activities will change permanently. Covid-19 forced human beings to use digital solutions massively for working, schooling, shopping, health assistance, meetings, entertainment, obsequies, religious events, and many more. The emergence of virtual platforms with functionalities to cover the different needs derived in behavioral changes where businesses, organizations, and individuals will not necessarily return to the pre-pandemic situation. While some enterprises will keep remote work and reduce physical offices to the minimal needs, others are experimenting with hybrid models where the personnel alternates between physical presence and remote work.

Virtual work changed the way workers and employers operate. The bargaining power in labor demand is moving. Workers experienced ways of generating income and self-organizing their schedules. After two years of the pandemic, industrialized economies such as the United States and European countries are struggling to fill vacancies despite the efforts to recover their economic sectors. Workers are demanding more flexibility and do not will the return to pre-pandemic labor conditions. *Unleash* report says: "2.9 million people who dropped out of the US labor force over the pandemic do not intend to return, according to research by JP Morgan (Richardson, 2021)". In the same vein, a *Politico* article mentions: "Another factor in disrupted labor markets is lifestyle choices. After 18 months spent mostly at home, many people in Western countries are rethinking their work-life balance, the distances they are willing to commute, and the kind of jobs they are willing to take (Taylor, 2021)".

Digitalization and flexibility in labor markets fit with a higher preference towards digital payments and online shopping. In previous years, the efforts to become a cashless society undertaken by the International Monetary Fund and United Nations 'Better than Cash Alliance' could not do what Covid-19 reached in the digitalization of payments and the use of contactless mechanisms[1]. For example, Deloitte's survey in Switzerland shows that within the first months of the pandemic, contactless means of payment gained preference. Among the Swiss, the use of smartphone wallets for payments increased 20 percent, credit card utilization surged by 25 percent, contactless payments with cards hopped 33 percent and self-checkout machines grew by 20 percent (Egerth, n.d.). In addition to the behavioral changes shaped by the pandemic, the Bank of International Settlements establishes that the shift away from cash payments responds to a combination of Covid-19 effects including migration to remote work, temporary shutdowns that led to a surge in e-commerce, merchants refusing cash, and the growth in digital person-to-person payments (BIS, 2021, p.6).

Covid-19 increased the individual's consciousness of living in polluted environments and overcrowded cities. Post-Covid populations are increasingly yearning for the lack of natural places and refuse to travel long distances to the gym, a coffee station, or the grocery store. Around 50 percent of dwellers in Paris, Milan, Madrid, Berlin, and London are searching to abandon turmoiled capitals for smaller cities where people can afford the amenities locally, moving by walking or cycling less crowded living modules, and green spaces (Bacchi, 2020).

Therefore, the European Union has propitious conditions to deploy the programs for a green and digital transformation. Policymakers have a window of opportunity and individuals are changing behaviors converging towards a more resilient, sustainable, and digitized society.

THE CIRCULAR ECONOMY AND THE CASE FOR BLOCKCHAIN

The green transformation includes actions that will modify production and consumption patterns. Foremostly, the European new industrial strategy leads the transit from a linear to a circular production economy, encompassing the objectives of competitiveness, climate neutrality, and a digital future (European Commission, 2020b). The concept of a circular economy was globally diffused by the United

Nations and Ellen MacArthur Foundation in 2015 when both decided to collaborate, promote, advocate, and foster studies around the concept.

The best way to understand the circular economy is by contrasting it with the current linear production system that extracts raw materials, that are transformed into products distributed for consumption (Figure 2). The result of the linear model is a vast amount of waste that is thrown back to the Earth – soil or oceans –. The waste pollutes and damages natural reservoirs despite the best waste treatment procedures that can take place. The linear pattern of growth assumes that resources are abundant, available, and cheap.

Figure 2. The linear pattern of growth
Source: Wautelet, 2018.

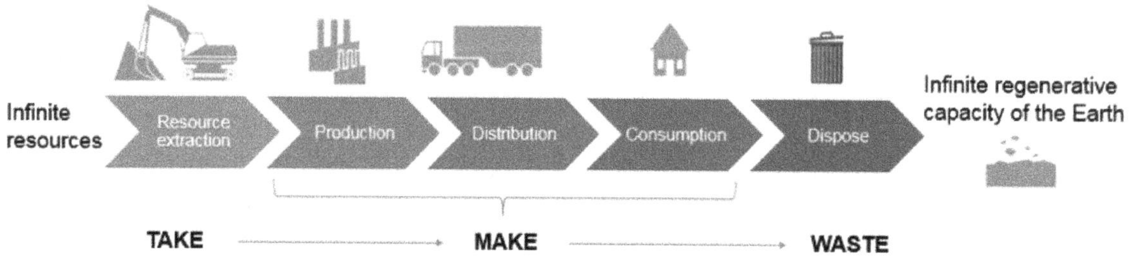

The perception that the Earth has infinite resources and a long-lasting capacity to support the linear industrial model could be in the imaginary of the first industrial revolution. The linear model worked for almost two centuries, nonetheless, nowadays the impacts of the restless extraction, the exhaustion, and degradation of natural resources, the damage to natural ecosystems, the extinction of endemic species, and the climate change, could not be hidden in face of severe droughts, floods, the melting of glaciers, or the pressure on water tables. No country can escape the onslaught of climate catastrophes.

The environmental damage has economic impacts as well. Raw materials are no longer abundant; therefore, the extraction requires more effort. As a consequence, resources are no longer cheap. The increasing costs of material extraction went to the detriment of labor wages exerting pressure on political regimes. In a nutshell, the linear growth pattern is unsustainable from the natural, economic, and social perspectives. The fragilities in the environment pose threats to the self-sustainability of the industrial model. Conversely, a more efficient resource use aligned to growth opportunities and job creation is the circular economy (Figure 3).

The European Union Action Plan defines the circular economy as: "one in which economic activities derive value under the conditions that an existing resource stock within the system is continuously recirculated to maintain its maximum value and utility over time, and fluctuations in that stock are in balance with the environment; enabling the viable and sustainable use of resources. All activities during product life cycle stages are designed to circulate the resources and support the preservation and regeneration of the biosphere so that hazardous outputs are eliminated, and regional resources are not degraded (Lanotte, 2019)."

The concept of the circular economy gained traction during the pandemic, as stated by the Ellen MacArthur Foundation (n.d.) "Since the onset of Covid-19 pandemic, the calls for a wider economic transformation that is in alignment with other global challenges, have never been louder. The circular economy, as an instrument to decouple economic growth from resource use and environmental impact,

Figure 3. The circular economy
Source: European Commission (2016).

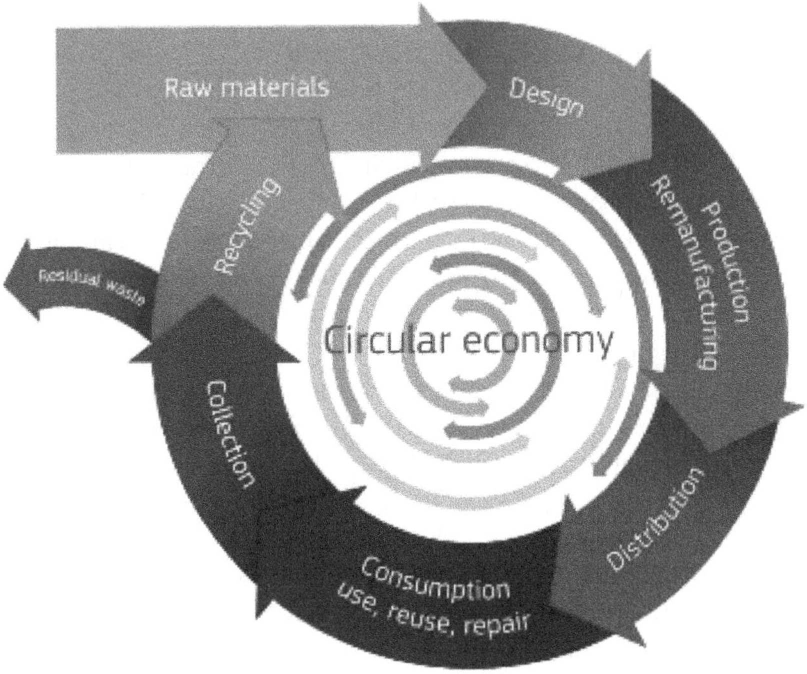

opens up a way for such a recovery". Understanding the concept of a circular economy can be easy. However, the industrial transformation necessary to modify the production processes from the linear to the circular economy is a complex task. In a circular economy, resources and materials are transformed for production, distribution, and consumption; the products have more than one use as they become inputs for remanufacturing processes, the components are recycled, the product itself can be reused, or refurbished. The cycles start and repeat, closing the trajectories into loops. In this system, everything is a resource for something else and waste reduces to zero (Lanotte, 2019).

The circular economy is highly dependent on technological innovation coupled with organizational and social change. Moreover, the amount of information required for every circular process increases to the point that information becomes a relevant cost, if not the most relevant one. Therefore, the European Union considers legislative and innovation hubs to mobilize the potential of digitalization of product information and facilitate the screening of green solutions via digital passports, tagging, and watermarks. In addition to that, the European Union is promoting using digital technologies for tracking, tracing, and mapping resources (European Commission, 2020a). In the same vein, consumers also require trustworthy and accurate information to select reusable, durable, and repairable products; and to authenticate if the products they are acquiring are compliant with the circular economy. The circular economy involves numerous stakeholders, for instance, companies, innovators, academia, policymakers. Each actor defines the roadmap and contribution for climate neutrality while searching to occupy a leadership position.

For the above reasons, the information in the circular economy should flow organically and systemically. In a circular economy, the centralization of data collection, data processing, and data sharing would represent an obstacle to efficiency. Information in siloes could make it very cumbersome to discern who needs what. The above reasons make a sounding case for distributed ledger technologies, such as blockchain.

The Role of Blockchain in the Circular Economy

Unlike traditional databases, blockchains do not record data using central controllers. Instead, blockchains are distributed ledgers that decentralize permanent digital records or transactions. In a blockchain, data entries are stored across nodes in a network, rather than in a single location. The transactions append to a tamper-proof time-stamped block. Blockchain uses cryptographic methods and incentivized consensus to create trust between nodes in the network such that when transactions are added to a block and validated by the network, every node maintains an identical copy of the blockchain (EBSI, 2021), relieving the need to rely on centralized controllers.

Blockchain generates unique features such as the immutability, traceability, auditability, security, and privacy of digital records. Moreover, blockchains allowed the deployment of smart contracts, a computer science concept that appeared in the 1990s but has not found technological progress until blockchain appeared.

Generally understood, smart contracts are machine-readable programs that self-execute when a group of predetermined conditions meets. An outstanding capability is that executable instructions coded in smart contracts enable the automation of processes. Altogether, blockchains and smart contracts permit tokenization, i.e., the digital representation of items and assets. Tokenization is the process of converting physical and non-physical assets into data and metadata representing ownership or rights. Tokens inherit the functionalities and characteristics of the blockchain upon which they are created, such as immutability, traceability, and decentralization (Kraft & Carmona, 2021).

Blockchain and smart contracts have interesting characteristics to cope with the industrial transition to a circular economy. Blockchain is useful to address informational challenges, for example, the recording and traceability of production loops in multi-tiered supply chains while smart contracts can automate certain processes. It is known that a blockchain is useful in the real-time tracking of items in traditional supply chains. In the case of a circular economy, blockchain can be a useful tool for organizing, analyzing, and managing complex networks in reverse logistics, that is, the tracing of outputs that become inputs for recycling or remanufacturing processes (Wang et al., 2020). Table 2 summarizes areas in which blockchain functions as a key technological tool for the circular supply chain management.

On the other hand, as the circular economy gains traction, participants such as customers, producers, distributors, and retailers will get more involved in the process where parallel production loops occur, increasing the complexity but also the opportunities to aggregate value by recycling, reusing, refurbishing, remanufacturing, or repairing. Under this new paradigm, elevating the costs of acquiring information is a losing game for everyone, whereas information sharing, cooperation, and securing knowledge aims at value creation. In order to achieve value creation, firms, distributors, retailers, consumers, manufacturers are more than ever compelled to simultaneously compete and cooperate, coining the new term of "coopetition" (Narayan & Tidström, 2020). Under "coopetition", participants interact and iterate in every possible loop. In this case, it is necessary to create a technological ecosystem where all the relevant parties can exchange information without restrictions. Blockchain is precisely a technology that allows for creating, organizing, and managing data in complex networks.

In addition to the blockchain, the tokenization of products in a type of product 'biography' that associates resources with assets and exchanges (Narayan & Tidström, 2020, p. 14) can facilitate systemic

Table 2. Key areas of applying blockchain in circular supply chains

Key areas of applying blockchain	Traditional supply chains	Circular economy supply chains
Reducing the costs of checking financial flows	✓	✓
Increase speed in physical interactions and communications	✓	✓
Risk control of data	✓	✓
Better resource management reducing waste	✓	✓
Identification of suppliers, trace and benchmark supplier performance	✓	✓
Procurement: tracking of the life cycle of products	✓	✓
Audit operations	✓	✓
Material management in the logistics process	✓	✓
Reverse logistics: obtain accurate information about the time, location, quality and conditions of materials, products and waste for recycling, refurbishment, re-use, etc.		✓
Green product management: monitor products to measure greenhouse gas emissions, allow customers to differentiate between green products and non-green products.		✓
Reusing waste across different circular supply chains		✓

Source: author's elaboration using Wang et al. 2020.

coordination in a multi-tiered circular economy. The resulting product is a token that contains metadata and interoperates with smart contracts for faster validation of resource provenance, tags, or digital passport verification. Moreover, the tokens allow queries for peer-to-peer cooperation in circular production loops. Also, tokens can facilitate investment allocation, the implementation of green taxation, or the monitoring of environmental regulatory compliance.

A tokenized product can aggregate data within every transaction. Figure 4 shows a basic architecture where every token transaction generates information registered in the blockchain. In a second layer, the blockchain applications process data, generate analytics, provide tracking and traceability services used in developing applications for the different users in the ecosystem. During the design stage, the token can incorporate data of the materials for the manufacturing process, or the recycled or repaired components required for remanufacturing. The information permits tracking materials to be recycled or products to recuperate for redesign purposes. In the manufacturing stage, smart contracts can automate procurement processes, by checking if suppliers meet the fulfillment conditions. Also, additional qualifications in the item, for example, green digital passports, certifications, or watermarks can be aggregated to the token data. Also, customers can use the information in the token to select the green products or re-use/repair possibilities to avoid waste. The outcome is an immense cloud of information, accessible and trustworthy to incentivize "coopetition" schemes.

Figure 4. Blockchain and product tokenization in a circular economy
Source: self-elaborated based on Wang et al. (2020) and Narayan & Tidström (2020).

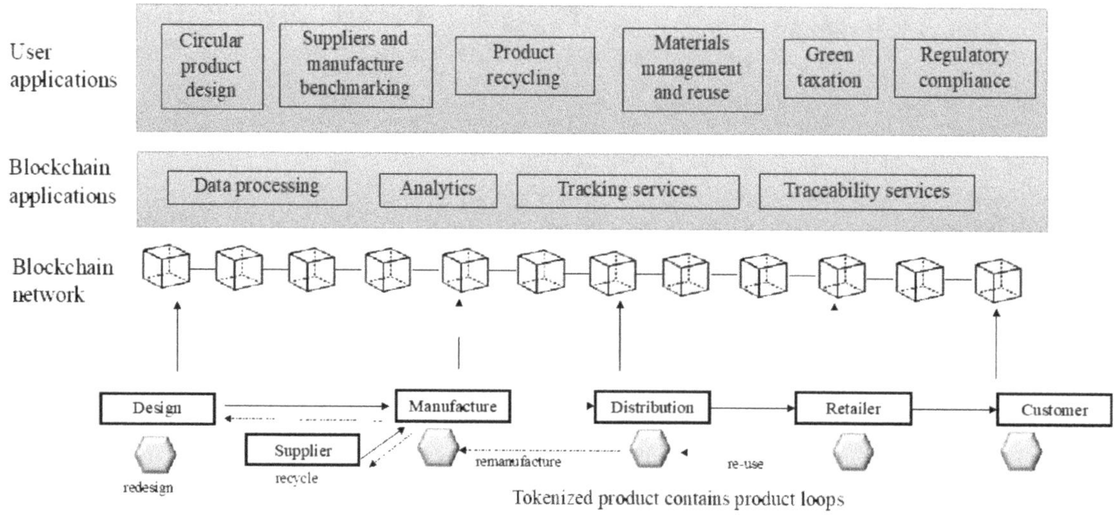

The proof is in the pudding, at the beginning of February 2022, Russia decreed a two-month ban on ammonium nitrate exports necessary for fertilizer production affecting the supply for Europe (S&P, 2022). A cloud of the information offered by blockchain architecture and applications could make accessible to stakeholders in a circular economy to trace the availability of biomass to produce bio-ammonia in a win-win transition to sustainable bio-fertilization relieving Europe from the need for chemical ammonium nitrate. Renewable ammonia can be extracted from corn cobs and other related biomass as the American company SynGest does. Biomass goes into a gasification process to get *syngas* that is used as a source of hydrogen, optimized by the use of water gas shift reaction. The resulting hydrogen is used in a version of pressure swing adsorption to synthesize ammonia that is carbon-free and can be produced from waste, air, and renewable energy (Lanotte, 2021). In a peer-to-peer collaboration ecosystem, information that can be obtained seamlessly enables new and different production loops.

For a better comprehension of the use of blockchain and smart contracts as described by the authors, the following is a real use case developed by the Suez Group (n.d.). The product is Circular Chain, a blockchain application for the circular economy. The solution enables traceability in circular production loops, strengthening trust and cooperation. In a first application, Circular Chain is used to recuperate sludge from wastewater to fertilize agricultural soils. By collecting, storing, and retrieving reliable forgery-proof information, the solution records all the data needed to recuperate, process, and spread the treated wastewater sludge into the land plots. The application functions under three basic streams:

1.- Data collection: in this stream data is tracked from all the relevant stakeholders, the laboratories that analyze the quality of sludge and soil; carriers and agricultural contractors that recuperate sludge or distribute the recycled product; and land plot owners that need sludge production.

2.- Data consolidation: this is the layer where data is aggregated and systematized to reconstruct the traceability of the chain.

3.- Data visualization: this is a web portal for organic valorization accessible to all the ecosystem actors, communities, government, farmers, etc.

Highlights:

- The user-friendly interface of the Suez sludge advanced portal provides information to all the actors involved, strengthening their confidence and enhancing their cooperation.
- The digitization of operational data allows to supervise the recovery process and monitor their sectors dynamically whereas farmers have a tracking and management tool for their agricultural input, checking the quality and quantity of sludge available for their lands.
- Circular Chain ensures transparent reliable information and by sharing it with the actors in the ecosystem, the tool generates trust between them, reinforcing cooperation to transform waste into new material to fertilize soils.

The European Blockchain Services Infrastructure (EBSI)

The bottom-line blockchain infrastructure supporting a circular economy for Europe could pose challenges if it is built on permissionless blockchains such as Ethereum or Bitcoin networks because certain information and transactions that need to be private would be accessible through blockchain explorers, whereas a private blockchain could pose challenges in terms of exclusion. An effort towards providing a platform to create cross-border services for public administrations, businesses, and citizens is the attempt of EBSI (2021), the first European Union wide-blockchain infrastructure supported by 29 countries – all European Union members, Norway and Liechtenstein – plus the European Commission forming the European Blockchain Partnership (EBP). EBSI is not an obligated platform for the circular economy; nonetheless, it offers a network and an infrastructure to develop blockchain-based applications.

EBSI is a market-friendly blockchain network based on open standards and transparent governance for the citizens of the European Union Member States. In this network, governance is reached by consensus among stakeholders. The platform ensures the harmonization of technical requirements to prevent conflicting architectures or protocols. It is aligned with the European regulations, and foremostly, it is an open-source protocol with maximum auditing, security, and competition between vendors, the private sector, service providers, developers, etc.

DECENTRALIZED FINANCE (DEFI) AND THE CIRCULAR ECONOMY

One of the most transcendent developments of blockchain is Decentralized Finance (Defi) or 'open finance'. Defi is the automation of the financial industry sector based on exponential blockchain technologies, removing counterparties, and shifting risk to technology. Defi relates to a shift from centralized financial systems to peer-to-peer finance fueled by the pandemic digitization acceleration. The Defi community is based on blockchain focusing on principles of data integrity, digital identity, community consensus, mutuality, democratization, trust in data sharing, and an immutable single version of the truth. Features shared by Defi protocols are inherited from the blockchain, i.e., open-source, transparent, permissionless, and composable (programmable by plug points). All transactions are visible via blockchain explorer applications so reconciliation and clearing can be done in real-time (Figure 5).

Many applications or protocols exist and interoperability between them is paramount for mainstream adoption to increase demand in value of interchange of digital assets known as the Internet of Value (IoV). Investment markets are being digitized using Automatic Market Makers (AMM) powered by smart contracts, capable of automating banking functions via decentralized exchanges (DEX), enhancing liquidity through liquidity pools, a key innovation in Defi as they maximize efficiency and lower costs.

Figure 5. Overview of Defi infrastructure
Source: author's elaboration.

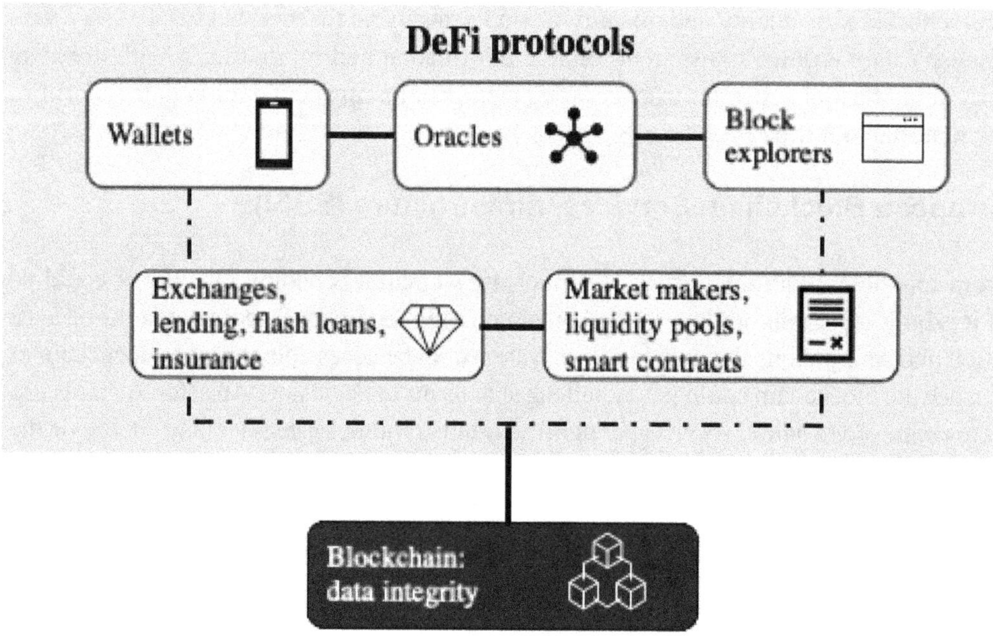

Concerning Defi products, they need to be understood in the context of yield generation within the realm of risk management. Using a process known as yield farming, investors and lenders lock up tokens in exchange for trading fees to get higher returns at higher risk. As new markets are made and digital assets created, there must be liquidity where the yield can be farmed or locked in transaction validation in what is called *staking* which permits collecting a percentage of the staking fee. Depositors who invest crypto assets into liquidity pools automatically receive a liquidity token (LP) indicating their share of the pool. In this environment, the custody of tokens moves to personal wallets and security to smart contract technology. Lending and borrowing are products with a decentralized finance version, which currently operate under over-collateralization schemes and fluctuating interest rates.

Volatility and market fluctuations in cryptocurrencies are rapidly recognized barriers to entry. As a response to volatility issues, stablecoins are cryptocurrencies that peg their price to a stable fiat currency (i.e., American dollar, Euro, etc.). Stablecoins are backed by fiat reserves, physical assets, other cryptocurrencies, or keep the peg algorithmically. Stable coins are becoming the basis to develop Central Bank Digital Currencies by governments, which could be on a collision course with Defi in some jurisdictions and complementary in others.

Another key component in the Defi architecture is Oracles, which are smart contracts communicating the blockchain with the outside (off-chain) world. Oracles are third-party bridges retrieving and delivering data to smart contracts, writing data from smart contracts to external systems, or executing off-chain computations (Chainlink, 2021).

Defi landscape represents an expansive network of protocols, intellectual property, and financial instruments worth approximately US$100 billion as of the end of 2021. Defi, stablecoins, and Central Bank Digital Currencies are DeFining the *future of money* with the expectation of bringing more market trust, financial inclusion, competition, decentralization, and transparency. Whether you are a customer, a provider, or a regulator the holy grail quest is the same namely asset classes with a higher rate of return and search for more yield within a proper risk framework. However, Defi is considered an infant industry with challenges ahead, for instance, creating liquidity where anyone with funds can be a market maker, comes with a risk for depositors called impermanent loss, occurring when trades change the asset composition in liquidity pools updating asset prices which compared to holding assets outside the automated market maker could result in less value after the price movements. Defi exponential growth amid the pandemic was tainted by scams and cybersecurity breaches by the incipient designs of the smart contracts behind decentralized applications. Another concern refers to scalability issues and usage fees known as "gas" which can become burdensome. Current Defi platforms built on proof-of-work blockchains represent a drawback to mainstream adoption due to the high gas fees, but also for the excessive use of electricity required in transaction processing which is an antithesis for ESG in financial services.

Despite the challenges, the technology is perfected, and the circular economy finds Defi alongside blockchain and tokenization, expanding the scope and use cases. Tokenization allows the financialization of the tokenized asset -tangible or intangible- to serve as a medium to raise funds for sustainable projects via decentralized finance schemes, yield farming, staking, monetizing the processes, etc. Real-world projects issuing tokens to fund their development include aid for development, social relief, tourism, climate action, and many more. The issued tokens interact with Defi applications paying yields to holders, incentivizing other citizens and investors to participate.

Decarbonizing bio-based fuels through the Verity Tracking platform (Blocksize-capital, 2022) is a project incorporating all the technological components described so far – i.e., blockchain, smart contracts automation, tokenization, and Defi. In this project, Gevo, the renewable chemicals and advanced biofuel producer in Colorado teamed up with the German blockchain tech company Blocksize-capital. The two partners are developing *Verity Tracking*, a dedicated blockchain-based platform tracking carbon intensity throughout entire low carbon value chains starting with renewable fuels produced from different feedstocks such as corn or soybean. Verity is automating the Measuring, Reporting, Verification (MRV) step, a key activity when capturing and monetizing carbon for its offset value on carbon markets or inset value within an own product's value chain.

The solution is enabling tracking of data at source thanks to an ecosystem of partners active at the feedstock level – farming software, data aggregators, satellite imagery processing, soil measurement third parties as well as academic partners. Collected data is processed through the Verity systems which renders a Carbon Intensity score using the GREET (Argonne National Laboratory, n.d.) Life Cycle Assessment method. Evidence data and carbon intensity scores are registered on a public blockchain to create an immutable chain of custody and verification. Additional sensitive data can be accessed by permissioned users.

By leveraging emerging technology and automation, Verity creates high-quality carbon-based digital assets such as verified carbon offsets or insets which can be tokenized and transferred seamlessly between players within or outside the value chain. Such a system becomes highly relevant in a world that increasingly needs to rely on trustworthy data to leverage financial resources against climate change. In one application case, farmers involved in the production of low-carbon biofuel feedstocks such as corn farming can monetize the additional carbon they reduce in their farms or sequester in their soil. Similarly, they will soon be able to assign digital values to other sustainable attributes such as biodiversity co-benefits. Initially utilized to track the sustainability of Gevo's renewable fuels, Verity aims to allow for tracking any value or attribute - tangible or intangible- throughout its lifecycle using blockchain and tokenization technologies (Figure 6).

Figure 6. Verity Tracking
Source: Blocksize-capital, 2022.

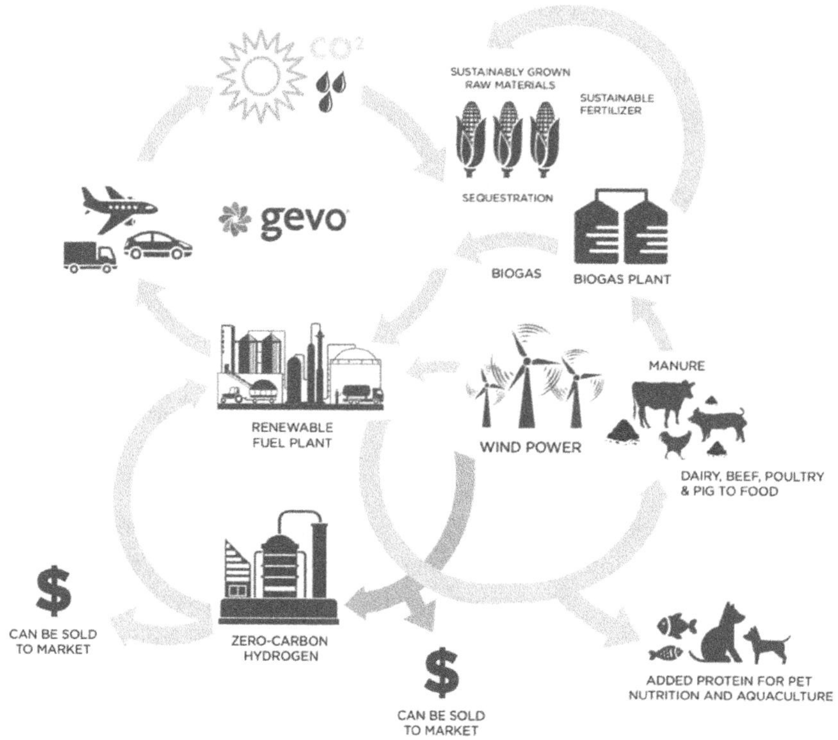

Perhaps in future models, the way in which the circular economy and Defi will intertwine will be in the context of Distributed Autonomous Organizations (DAOs). DAOs are distributed businesses entirely defined online, for which all management rules are written in smart contracts. Participants in a DAO often cast votes over the upgrades and modifications in the rules of the organization -i.e., modifying the code-. Joining a DAO means becoming part of a digital community and as such, the choice to be an active participant in the governance structure. A circular economy can find funneling through distributed businesses where information flows enable self-coordination in transforming businesses from linear to circular, and where the monetization and financialization of tokenized green products create reserves that will be invested in more sustainable actions.

FUTURE RESEARCH DIRECTIONS

Blockchain technology and tokenization of assets are technologies in constant innovation and evolution. Moreover, both are disruptive game changers transforming economies into tokenized economies for which models and applications are being conceptualized and developed. Therefore the few projects already using blockchain and tokenization as a tool for the circular economy will certainly transit into a series of iterations, trials, errors and improvements before good practices and benchmarking schemes take place. Likewise, research in the field is incipient and as a consequence, the literature conceptualizing the use of blockchain to enhance the circular economy is scarce. Thus, the future research directions are wide, for instance, two major research topics include the analysis of engineering and economics of tokens for the green economy, satisfying the environmental objectives alongside the incentives and business models emerging under blockchain technology and decentralized finance and secondly, the systematic study of blockchain protocols and smart contract design fitting the needs of circular economy supply chains.

CONCLUSION

Covid-19 dealt a heavy blow to humanity. The sanitary and economic impacts reached the entire globe and surged to the surface the brittleness and unsustainability of our modern society. Like a clamp that joins its ends, Covid-19 pushed consensus in the governmental spheres of the European Union and implicitly in society. Recovery from the pandemic is used as a lever for a deeper and a once-and-for-all opportunity to correct all the problems that modern society has been dragging for years, for instance climate change and depletion of natural resources. At the same time, Covid-19 accelerated digitalization in a wide range of household and business activities.

The pandemic created a turning point such that the before-and-after recovery plan for Europe incorporated long-term goals to eliminate the vulnerabilities in the current production systems and consumption patterns. The goals incorporate the energy transition for zero-carbon emissions by year 2050, hand in hand with digital and technological expansion. The post-Covid19 European Union Recovery Package fosters an equilibrium between the economic competitive advantages with the building of a resilient society, less dependent on essential external supplies and decoupled of raw material extraction.

One of the salient actions in the recovery plan is the transition from a linear “take-make-consume-dispose” economic and production model to a system where products, components, and materials are re-used, re-cycled, or re-manufactured closing the trajectories into loops, defined as the circular economy. In such a system, where everything is a resource for something else, the notion of waste disappears.

Circularity is a complete system, involving changes in business models and product design, as well as collaboration between suppliers and customers. The circular economy is not about making things ’less bad’ but about making things ‘much better’ – in effect, it’s about creating economic value. It also includes new jobs with a brand-new skillset. It is time for modern competition to inform a business’s thinking about the relationship between competitiveness and the environment.

If non-circular businesses run on expeditious and accurate information. In a circular economy, the amount of information required grows exponentially because every item that is produced is subject to a reverse logistic process becoming necessary to trace, recuperate, or authenticate. The demand for information and management of it in a circular economy makes the case for blockchain technology as an appealing tool as it provides immediate, shared, and completely transparent information stored on an immutable ledger. A blockchain network can track orders, payments, accounts, production processes, and much more. Decentralization and the use of encryption make blockchains particularly robust in preventing data manipulation. Time-stamped data entries serve as proof of authenticity and make blockchains "trust machines". Nodes on the network share a single view of the truth and blockchain explorers show all the details of a transaction end to end, giving users increased confidence and opening up new efficiencies and opportunities in creating a digital ecosystem. Blockchain is one of the key emerging technologies that is shaping Europe's future. In addition, blockchain tokenization of circular products could create a footprint to facilitate product location and give agility to the circular markets, whether to find partners, suppliers, or customers.

From a financial perspective, blockchain technology and smart contracts allowed the evolution of a new way of doing finance called decentralized finance. Built on top of blockchains, Defi applications make algorithmic replicas of traditional financial products where smart contracts execute and eliminate intermediaries and users find a disintermediated space to invest, lend, borrow, acquire insurance, trade, etc. In combination with blockchain, the tokenized products can also monetize and yield via Defi applications systemically intertwining the financial and production realms.

FUNDING

This research received no specific grant from any funding agency in the public, commercial, or not-for-profit sectors.

REFERENCES

Argonne National Laboratory. (n.d.). *The Greenhouse gases, Regulated Emissions, and Energy use in Technologies Model*. https://greet.es.anl.gov

Bacchi, U. (2020). *Escape from the city? Londoners lead Europe in COVID-inspired dreams of flight*. Thomson Reuters Foundation News. https://news.trust.org/item/20201118230536-uv6o2/

BIS. (2021). *Covid-19 accelerated the digitalisation of payments*. https://www.bis.org/statistics/payment_stats/commentary2112.pdf

Blocksize-capital (2022). *Decarbonizing bio-based fuels through the Verity Tracking platform*. Internal Document.

Chainlink. (2021). *What is a Blockchain Oracle?* https://chain.link/education/blockchain-oracles

Figueroa, C., Castillo, E. G., Norquist, G., Wells, K. B., Griffith, K., Kadkhoda, F., Jones, F., Shorter, P., & Bromley, E. (2018). A Window of Opportunity: Visions and Strategies for Behavioral Health Policy Innovation. *Ethnicity & Disease*, *28*(Suppl 2), 407–416. doi:10.18865/ed.28.S2.407 PMID:30202194

Egerth, K. (n.d.). *Cash is no longer king in times of Covid-19 – Raining on cash's reign*. Deloitte Perspectives. https://www2.deloitte.com/ch/en/pages/consumer-industrial-products/articles/cash-is-no-longer-king-in-times-of-covid19.html

Ellen MacArthur Foundation. (n.d.). *How policymakers can pave the way to a low-carbon and prosperous future.* https://ellenmacarthurfoundation.org/covid-policymakers

EBSI. (2021). *EBSI Architecture explained.* https://ec.europa.eu/digital-building-blocks/wikis/display/CEFDIGITAL/EBSI

European Commission. (n.d.). *Recovery plan for Europe.* https://ec.europa.eu/info/strategy/recovery-plan-europe_en

European Commission. (2016). *EU Action plan for a Circular Economy.* https://slideplayer.com/slide/17242831/

European Commission. (2020a). *A New Industrial Strategy for a globally competitive, green, and digital Europe.* https://ec.europa.eu/commission/presscorner/detail/en/fs_20_425

European Commission. (2020b). *A New Circular Economy Action Plan for a cleaner and more competitive Europe.* https://eur-lex.europa.eu/legal-content/EN/TXT/?qid=1583933814386&uri=COM:2020:98:FIN

European Commission. (2021). *The EU's 2021-2027 long-term budget & Next Generation EU: Facts and figures.* https://data.europa.eu/doi/10.2761/808559

Kraft, C., & Carmona, M. (2021). Blockchain Tokenisation in Grant Management. In P. de G. (Ed.), Blockchain Technology Applications in Businesses and Organizations (pp. 141-161). IGI Global Publications.

Lanotte, A. (2019). *EU circular economy plans could cut tax costs for companies*, www.itrinsight.com

Lanotte, A. (2021). Green Finance: Sustainable Growth And the Circular Economy. *Tax Notes International, 103*(12), 1601.

Mozeley, F., & Whelan, J. (n.d.). *3 resources to assess and open policy windows.* https://commonslibrary.org/resources-assessing-and-opening-policy-windows/

Nandi, S., Sarkis, J., Aghaei, H. A., & Helms, M. M. (2021). Redesigning Supply Chains using Blockchain-Enabled Circular Economy and COVID-19 Experiences. *Sustainable Production and Consumption, 27*, 10–22. doi:10.1016/j.spc.2020.10.019 PMID:33102671

Narayan, R., & Tidström, A. (2020). Tokenizing coopetition in a blockchain for a transition to circular economy. *Journal of Cleaner Production, 263*, 121437. doi:10.1016/j.jclepro.2020.121437

Next GenerationE. U. (n.d.). https://europa.eu/next-generation-eu/index_en

Potočnik, J. (2021). *The European Green Deal and a post Covid-19 prosperity.* Ellen MacArthur Foundation. https://ellenmacarthurfoundation.org/articles/the-european-green-deal-and-a-post-covid-19-prosperity

Richardson, D. (2021). *Labor shortages continue despite the efforts of the US and EU.* Unleash. https://www.unleash.ai/labor-shortages-continue-despite-the-efforts-of-the-us-and-eu/

Saladino, V., Algeri, D., & Auriemma, V. (2020). The Psychological and Social Impact of Covid-19: New Perspectives of Well-Being. *Frontiers in Psychology, 11*, 577684. Advance online publication. doi:10.3389/fpsyg.2020.577684 PMID:33132986

Sarkis, J. (2020). Supply chain sustainability: Learning from the COVID-19 pandemic. *International Journal of Operations & Production Management*, *41*(1), 63–73. doi:10.1108/IJOPM-08-2020-0568

S&P. (2022). *Ammonium nitrate ban could impact ammonia supply: Traders*. https://www.spglobal.com/platts/en/market-insights/latest-news/energy-transition/020322-ammonium-nitrate-ban-could-impact-ammonia-supply-traders

Suez Group. (n.d.). *CircularChain, the circular economy blockchain*. https://www.suez.com/en/who-we-are/innovating-for-the-future/circularchain-the-circular-economy-blockchain

Taylor, P. (2021). *The good news about labor shortages*. Politico. https://www.politico.eu/article/good-news-labor-shortages-coronavirus-economic-recovery/

Wang, B., Luo, W., Zhang, A., Tian, Z., & Li, Z. (2020). Blockchain-enabled circular supply chain management: A system architecture for fast fashion. *Computers in Industry*, *123*, •••. https://www.sciencedirect.com/science/article/abs/pii/S0166361520305583

Wautelet, T. (2018). *Exploring the role of independent retailers in the circular economy: a case study approach*. https://www.researchgate.net/figure/The-linear-economy-The-take-make-and-waste-approach-of-production_fig2_323809440

WHO. (2020). *Covid-19 disrupting mental health services in most countries*. WHO Survey. https://www.who.int/news/item/05-10-2020-covid-19-disrupting-mental-health-services-in-most-countries-who-survey#:~:text=Bereavement%2C%20isolation%2C%20loss,outcomes%20and%20even%20death

WMO. (2021). *WMO Air Quality and Climate Bulletin*. https://library.wmo.int/doc_num.php?explnum_id=10887

ADDITIONAL READING

Charter, M. (2018). *Designing for the Circular Economy*. Routledge. doi:10.4324/9781315113067

Lacity, C. M., & Treiblmaier, H. (2022). *Blockchain and the Token Economy*. Palgrave Macmillan.

Mahtab, K., Zhu, Q., & Sarkis, J. (2020). Blockchain and the circular economy: Potential tensions and critical reflections from practice. *Production Planning and Control*, *31*(11-12), 950–966. doi:10.1080/09537287.2019.1695925

KEY TERMS AND DEFINITIONS

Blockchain: A distributed data structure which allows digital assets to be transacted in a real-time and immutable form.

Circular Economy: A production and consumption model where the life cycle of products is extended decoupling the economic activity from the use and waste of finite resources.

Distributed Autonomous Organization: An organization represented and operating by rules that are coded in smart contracts controlled by digital communities and not influenced by central authorities. As rules are encoded, these types of organizations do not require bureaucracy or managements in a hierarchy.

Open Source: Software for which the source code is free and available and can be overtly redistributed and modified.

Recycle: The process by which waste is transformed in reusable material or return materials to a stage where they can be used again.

Remanufacture: To refurbish a product whether by repairing, renovating, or reassembling its parts and components.

Smart Contracts: Computer programs that run when determined conditions are met and its operations are recorded on a blockchain.

Token: In the blockchain context refers to a set of rules programmed in a smart contract and identified by a blockchain address.

ENDNOTE

1 The increase in digital payments reducing cash payments contrasted with the increase in cash circulation suggesting that cash was held as a store of value vis-à-vis the economic uncertainty that followed the spread of coronavirus (BIS, 2021).

Chapter 17
Universal Health Coverage (UHC):
Case Study on World's Health Emerging Strategy After the COVID-19 Pandemic

Ashwani Sharma
Meerut Institute of Engineering and Technology, India

Reenu Kumari
Meerut Institute of Engineering and Technology, India

Neha Goel
Meerut Institute of Engineering and Technology, India

ABSTRACT

Health is a major and primary concern for every organization for manpower in the world without any discrimination, and the healthcare situations of the countries are different for this problem. Universal health coverage (UHC) is the only solution for this challenge, and UHC means that everyone everywhere should have access to quality, affordable healthcare services (including prevention, promotion, treatment, and rehabilitation) without suffering financial hardship. COVID-19 is the world's serious problem. It tells the reality of the healthcare challenge and the importance of health coverage for humanity. Therefore, this chapter analyzes the situation of COVID-19's impact on the universal health coverage initiative. After that, this chapter helps to check the countries' progress towards UHC and furthermore discusses the opportunities and forthcoming policies to support UHC for upcoming health disasters like pandemics and other health issues.

DOI: 10.4018/978-1-7998-8856-7.ch017

1. INTRODUCTION

1.1 Universal Health Coverage (UHC)

The World is full of diversification and it is diversified on the basis of color, gender, culture, income and status but the one thing that remains the same and never diversified is health Issues and diseases. World Health Coverage is the only emerging strategy that covers complete humans in the world, which will directly benefit not only citizens of every country but indirectly manpower of all levels of organizations and UHC is a hopeful aim of health service with sustainable development goal (SDG). According to the United Nation office for outer space affairs SDG-3 looks to guarantee health and prosperity for all, at each phase of life. UHC implies that all persons and communities obtain the health facilities without facing financial problems. It covers the full range of necessary, value health facilities, from health support to prevention, health treatment, rehabilitation, and palliative care (the people surviving with a critical illness and they need specialized medical care) across the lifetime. Health care is an essential right that isn't restricted to specific special income clusters of people or segments of individuals and this is the theoretical basis of UHC (Nygren-Krug 2019). Sustainable Development Goal (SDG) target 3.8 is characterized as Delivering 'approach to secure, efficient, value and reasonable necessary drugs and vaccines for all' remains fundamentals embedded from the 2030 Agenda for Sustainable Development (United Nations, 2015, p. 16).

There are 2 Criteria which have been selected to watch the target 3.8 in SDG Structure. And these two indicators are classified on the basic health facilities and health expenditure.

Criteria 3.8.1: This indicator covers health service, which is functionalized with a list that consolidates sixteen health services as reproductive, maternal and child health, communicable diseases, non-transmissible diseases, and service capacity and access into a single summary metric.

Criteria 3.8.2: This indicator centers on health expenditures in subject with family budget to distinguish monetary difficulty brought about by direct medical services payments.

Criteria 3.8.1 and 3.8.2 collectively are intended to cover the facility coverage scope and financial security scope, in that order, of target 3.8. These 2 Criteria can never be monitored separately.

The attainment of UHC is only possible when the public really get medical facilities they require an advantage from financial risk security. On the second side, access is the chance or capability to do both of these things. Subsequently, UHC is unimaginable without all inclusive access, yet the two are not something very similar. Reach of UHC has three aspects: (Tanahashi, 1978; Penchansky& Thomas, 1981; Shengelia, Tandon, Adams, & Murray, 2005; ThiedeAkweongo, McIntyre, 2007)

1. Reach approach: Efficient health service accessibility must be reached reasonably as clinic and hospital opening time, consultation process and other aspects of service organization and delivery that permit individuals to get the facilities when they need them.
2. Affordability of service: Indicator 3.8.2 mentions that UHC provides financial freedom to people without thinking about their pocket capacity to. It must not only count the health service cost but also count that cost which will be incurred indirectly on health services (e.g. traveling cost for treatment and loss of absence from work during treatment).
3. Willingness: This catches individuals' ability to look for services. Agreeableness is short when patients see service to be ineffectual or when social and social factors, for example, language or the age, sex, identity or religion of the facility provider deter them from looking for facilities.

According to the World Bank (2019), for all nations in the world human resource is a very important asset and UHC permits nations to benefit as much as possible from their most grounded resource: human capital. Supporting health addresses a basic interest in human capital and in Economic growth. Health is necessary for all; it may be children, adults and older. It cannot be neglected because it is considered as one of the global economy's major contribution sectors and gives 50 million jobs opportunities, with the larger part held by women.

1.2 Covid 19 Pandemic Crises & its Origin

As according to present generation COVID-19 is that infectious disease which was firstly appeared in December 2019 caused by a newly discovered coronavirus and that's 'why it is called Coronavirus disease but for world it's not a new because in 1960 human coronavirus were first time recognized and that affect upper respiratory tract infection (URI) which include nose, throat, pharynx, larynx and bronchi (CDC, 2020).After 2003, five other types of human coronaviruses were also identified, and there was a SARS called as severe acute respiratory syndrome coronavirus that became the cause of important morbidity and mortality in China. Also same as in other case in December month of 2019, coronavirus COVID-19 was first recognized in Wuhan city of China but officially it was not declared the exact reason of origin and motive and it is extremely infectious as disease generated through respiratory droplets through coughing and sneezing (Kahn, McIntosh 2005). Over the initial month and a half of the new ten years, the original Covid, known as COVID-19, has increased from China to 20 distinct countries. On the 30th first month of 2020, a Public Health Emergency of International Concern (PHEIC) was established after the proposals of the crisis board, the World Health Organization Director General (WTO PHEIC, 2020).

First wave of COVID 19 Community transmission was first detected in the United States in February 2020. According to WHO 2020 report, absolute cases were around 18 million at the center of June month of 2021 and death cases were around four million, disease infectivity ratio is twenty-three thousand for every million populaces; passing proportion was 5 hundred for each million populaces. as continental data, 20 per cent in North America, 27 per cent in Europe, 30 per cent in Asia, 17 per cent in South America and 3 per cent in Africa out of all cases. This is considered a major disaster for the whole world where all medical and health infrastructure collapsed and different income countries faced critical situations due to lack of proper health coverage plan. This Covid changes day by day as different and different variants, this regular mutation of virus is important; Corona virus has gone through a large number of changes since it originally arose (Duong, 2021). In any case, just small minorities of those transformations are probably going to be critical and change the infection definitively (Wise, 2020). Outbreaks monitoring is valuable by mutation changes as a scanner (Wise, 2020). ECDC 2021 states that in a normal way that there are thousands of variants but as of Nov 2021, just four variants of worry about human life. These four types of Covid-19, which are considering as serious variants, are:

Table 1. Covid serious variants

S. No	Variants Name (Covid-19)	First Detected Countries
1	Beta	South Africa
2	Gamma	Gamma
3	Delta	Delta

Source: WHO, 2020 report

These mutation changes will be the biggest challenge of health Infrastructure in the world by governments and Institutions. Whole world is united to face this challenge but UHC will play a great role to overcome and that will become the emerging strategy to unite the world at equal level.

1.3 Role of WHO on Universal Health Coverage

WHO is the organization which directs and coordinates for health and it is considered as planning expert within the United Nations framework. UHC is founded on the basis of 1948. WHO establishment, which claims health is a necessary and compulsory right of humans to guarantee the most achievable degree of health for all. WHO is always promoting nations to create health infrastructure to forward in direction and maintain UHC, to watch the development of nations towards UHC. For the direction to achieve the UHC Objectives in the world WHO regularly work with diversified partners in differ circumstances and for a variety of objectives to establish the UHC Model.
To achieve this Target WHO aligned with different partnership, that include:

- Health Policy and Systems Research Alliance

The Alliance for "Health Policy and Systems Research" (HPSR) has forged strong partnerships for more than 20 years, working closely with more than 350 research, policy and teaching organizations to support knowledge generation, capacity strengthening and research uptake. The alliance set out on a cooperative and aggregate interaction with its associate in January 2021, to all in all foster a yearly record of public level HPSR output in low- and middle-income countries (LMICs).

Overall, all sixteen nation group regions of World health organization (Americas and Africa, South-East Asia Eastern Mediterranean, Europe, Western Pacific,) and 2 worldwide HPSR entities were associated in the progress of this effort.

- UHC Partnership

For universal health coverage (UHC) and primary health care (PHC), *UHC Partnership*is perhaps WHO's biggest stage for global collaboration. It includes a wide range of health specialist combinations which are connected end to end to promote UHC & PHC by encouraging strategy discourse on essential preparation, and administration of health frameworks, creating health financing procedures and supporting their execution, and empowering viable improvement participation in nations. Basically the aim of the UHC *Partnership*is to increase the country's capacity and support the authorities of the Ministry of Health. The UHC Partnership has extended consistently, arriving at 115 member nations around the world from its initiation in 2011*(*www.uhcpartnership.net/about/*)*.

- UHC2030

In New York 2015, the united nation's 193 member states were approved on the sustainable development goals.They set out an aggressive plan to achieve by 2030 for a more secure, more attractive and stress and disease free world. The partners of UHC2030 perceive that accomplishing UHC need synchronized efforts across numerous areas and advancement of solid, supportable and fair health system that will definitely upgrade the status of health outcomes (https://www.uhc2030.org/our-mission/)

- Primary Health-Care Performance Initiative(PHCPI)

The main objective of the PHCPI partnership is to change the situation of global primary health care. PHCPI states that they are making a world where primary health care must be reality, not the exception for every individual, household and society. They are working closely with state authorities and progressive associates, which are responsible for improving the basic health care by helping in the form of providing data, information and assistance (https://improvingphc.org/about-phcpi).

- P4H Social Health Protection Network*: It is a global connectivity for health financing and community health security.*

WHO is also associated with UNICEF and the Ministry of Kazakhstan on 25th to 26th Oct 2018, hosted the International Conference on Primary Health Care.

2. COUNTRIES PROGRESS TOWARDS UNIVERSAL HEALTH COVERAGE

From the last few couple of years has seen a developing responsibility worldwide to universal health coverage (UHC). Many countries inspired by UHC and started improvement in health system and analyst motivated to do work on UHC (Horton and Das, 2014). Wagstaff, Cotlear, Eozeno, & Buisman, (2016) suggest an approach to estimating progress towards UHC. They utilized index record to look at UHC execution across 24 nations, UHC index was prepared with the help of human development index (UNDP, 2014), that have carried out UHC- stimulated reforms. These reforms are the coverage of population fraction, facility cover range, and financial safety assistance. They ignored countries like Brazil which has tax financed health infrastructures, free or subsidized care by government run health systems and family covered under social health insurance. Demand side methodology minimizing the coverage gaps, UNICO Countries. Few countries changed their whole service of health care into an authentic coverage scheme for everybody not covered under social health care scheme, adding assets and specifying a (pretty much) obviously characterized expansive arrangement for assistance; these changes have regularly elaborate an expanded dependence on charge incomes and a decreased dependence on cash based payment and this example is countries like Thailand, republic of china, Mexico, and Colombia.

Wagstaff, Cotlear, Eozenou, Buisman (2016) state that UHC accomplishment pattern of 24 UNICO countries can be understood with the help of trends and this shows the in imbalance changed coverage of facilities and financial security. As many UNICO, UHC motivated countries focus on MGD and that's why service coverage was separate into MDG indicators and non MDG Indicator and they found that argentina, Colombia and Peru shows positive trend hopeful upward trend in Argentina, Colombia, and Peru,. Chile is also showing positive trend in non MDG interference coverage in Chile after the launch of *Plan AUGE* (*Acceso Universal de Garantías Explícitas*). Guatemala and Mexico shows insecure and negative pattern in term of monetary security and in same setting different nations like Argentina, Ethiopia, Guatemala, Thailand, and Turkey are in progress structure. Comparably Jamaica, the Kyrgyz Republic, Mexico, Indonesia, and Peru saw disintegrations in one or the two spaces of monetary insurance followed by enhancements. Some others countries also progressing in this field as-

The Unified Health Sector in Brazil is the only one public funded system which covers the complete enumeration and gets financing by the general tax system. Health services are available freely. Every stage of the government has fixed a smallest segment of its revenues to health with the permission of the constitution (Gragnolati, Lindelow, Couttolenc, 2013).

The Federation of Russia developed a mandatory procedure for health insurance to reform the economic crisis. The additional way of funding to the health system is obtained by payroll taxation which is predominantly financed with general taxes. Health services are purchased from the insurance companies and funds are pooled from the payroll taxation system by sub-national insurance policies (Rechel & Lancet, 2009).

The National Rural Health Mission in India has increased the funding of the public sector with the focus on primary care and with the establishment of government-sponsored insurance for the needy and poor people is discussed by (*National Rural Health Mission, 2005*). It reforms the strength of government for health in India. Hospital care for the poor in private hospitals and public hospitals are covered by the government insurance schemes (Forgi, Nagpal, 2012).

China reforms the health system to create an important role. The government observed the substantial improvement from the past health care as the patients are not the source of finance in the modern system according to (Yi, Hsia, 2009). The main focus of reforms is focused on increasing insurance coverage and strengthening primary care services. (Li et al., 2011).

National Health Insurance is funded through taxation and actively purchases items to maintain the position of good quality health services for all the people in South Africa from the National Health Act (61/2003). Government is enabled to configure the human resource systems having in both the private and public health systems through the fund's purchasing.

According to the report of WHO, 2014, mandatory condition to achieve universal health coverage is the predominant reliance on public financing from the WHO, 2012). Substantial share of health spending is continued by the private voluntary health insurance system and over burden on economic payments to the private financing of the health sector. Private financial accounting systems account for 54%, 44%, 69%, 40% and 52% of the total health spending in Brazil, China, India, the Russian Federation and South Africa.

According to WHO, 2021b reports, the highest performing countries score over the 50 are Sri Lanka, the Maldives and Bhutan while the low performing countries are India, Pakistan, Afghanistan and Nepal. The context of this has a wide difference that the coverage index of UHC services is a good measuring criterion for the average coverage to the essential health services in the country which is shown in Figure 1

Figure 1. Coverage of essential health services in South Asia: UHC index scores
Source: WHO, 2021b

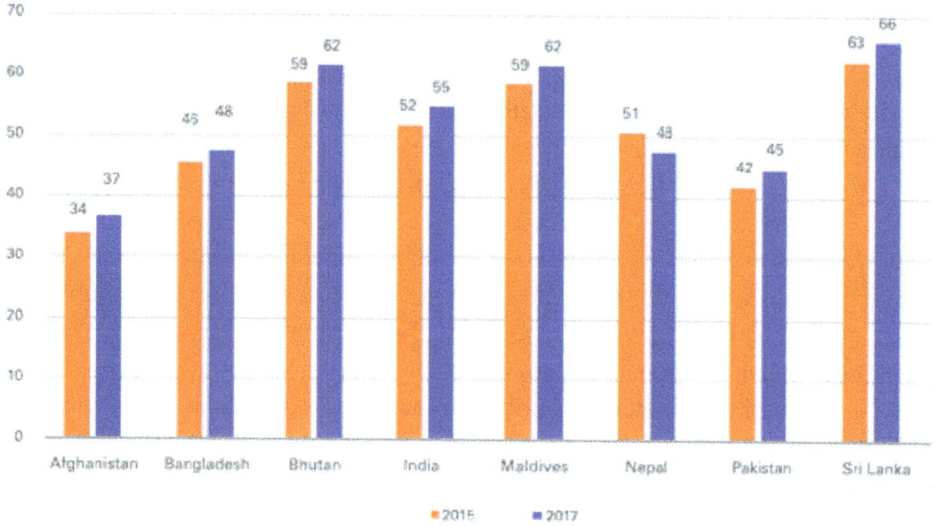

3. IMPACT OF COVID 19 ON HEALTH CARE SYSTEM

According to the WHO health Expenditure report (2019) health spending situation before covid 19 Pandemic - worldwide health expenditure increase very rapidly – to US$7.8 trillion in 2017 up from US$ 7.6 trillion in 2016. As comparing with GDP growth with health spending growth from 2000 -2017 among the Low income, Lower Middle and Upper Middle and High income countries group and found that Health spending growth has been rapid as compare to GDP growth (Figure 2).

Figure 2. Health Expenditure Growth Vs GDP Growth
Source: *WHO health Expenditure report (2019)*

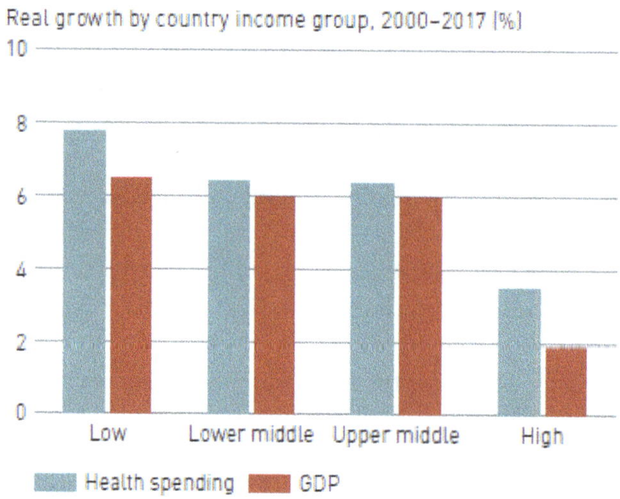

This is the picture of Heath expenditure before Covid 19 but in the high-income countries, covid 19 seems to have unequal affected because various economic sectors are negatively affected such as transportation, bar, restaurant, retail and manufacturing, etc. this is fact that Latin groups and African Americans have renowned for the unemployment rates and downfall in daily wages. These populations are much more defenseless to corona virus economic impact (coat et al, 2020). Interestingly, 50% of the reports came from 2 states are more affected by covid 19 these two states are New York and California. Moreover, theGlobal Market Research and Public Opinion (IPSOS) had surveyed in the US, shown that nearly 30% of American citizens are affected by the Covid-19. But 30% of the people believes in Asian countries are more affected by the covid 19 as comparison of high-income countries (coat et al, 2020). Apart from the impact on employment covid 19 also highly affected to the women for the several reasons. Most of women are involved in the various role play, including family, household, caretaking, job, business etc., compared to males. Although, women tried to balance all these tasks but due to high pressure of work they are more suffered from the physical and mental ill. Women who work in the industries may be affected by the social distancing. For the reduce of mental stress women who work from home they want to support form the children side as well as the whole family (coat et al, 2020).

According to Doc Wire News, 2020, the healthcare industries are highly affected by covid 19 in high income countries and that will also affect to the 8,500 jobs till March 2020. Due to the pandemic situation has control the private firms and hospital operators announce salary cut-off across the World (Lynch, 2020). When a crossed the world hospital services lay down then income is lost on large scale and unexpected loss, earning of return reduced and etc. (Culter, 2020). For the maintain of health care system requires extensive testing, health expertise, protection of health care, home diagnosis and extra monitoring. Critically, there is need to learn and understand how health care system can work for the reduce the health losses across the world (Lee, &Morling, 2020).

Similarly, low-income earners have also been impacted by the covid-19, considering one example employees at stores (grocery and medical). These types of employees are amongst the low wages' earner at 11.37 per/hr. with little or no access to take care of them. All the protective equipment and health care benefits can take any one but still some people have restriction due to the low income. The Latino population can consider in the criteria because most of the people are worked in grocery stores and thus, corona virus has excessively impacted the Latino community. This is crucial situation for all the earners specially who worked in the grocery stores because they feel pressure of having the mental and physical risk.

Above discussed impact of covid 19 on health care system not affect only a health although it affects lot in various areas like tourism, travel, entertainment and hospitality etc. So, this is truly global crisis which affects emerging market, developed and developing economies. But, emerging market and developing economies face more challenges as comparison of developed economies because weaker health care system, slow capital flow, low education rate, less skilled persons and limited resource to provide support. Furthermore, weak economies entered into this crisis with sluggish and high debt burden (Gopinath, 2020).

4. OPPORTUNITIES POST COVID 19

Despite the loss of life and economic disturbance by the corona virus, this epidemic could be big opportunities for the path to achieve UHC in teams of health towards sustainable development goal (SDG). This pandemic situation needs to utilize as opportunities to UHC in the following area:

- **To prevent the communicable diseases and encourage self-protection**

With the help of UHC try to prevent the communicable diseases and encourage self-protection by application of sanitizer, use of mask, maintain physical and social distance, avoid crowdy areas (Dixit et al, 2020). Communicable diseases are highly thinkable diseases especially in developing countries. For the prevention of this disease all person can maintain this cleanliness (Mitrokhin et al, 2020). This kind of tactics make more aware to self-protection and resident health worker would be associated with more person and easy to know of health care.

- **To encourage the behavioural adjustment for non-communicable diseases**

Social distance and self-conscious approaches make a behavioural change in the daily lifestyle and restrict the physical/social distance (Bourassa et al, 2020). The behavioural adjustment would be controlled on the alcohol use, substance abuse, violence, gang fight, etc. these things are happening in developed countries and it would be helpful in controlling the non-communicable diseases. While, there are some conflicts on this matter social distance to the social functions and control the gathering of old age (Mishra and Majumdar, 2020).

- **Post Covid 19 UHC make strength in public health emergencies**

Before the pandemic situation, people underestimated the public health emergency (Reshetnikov et al., 2020) but, after this covid 19, all economies make a strong health system and they started to prepare new health policies and programs (Cao, 2020). Now, economies are started to sanction resident health foundations and remove the procedure barriers and effective supply chain of medicines. Thus, it is the appropriate time to strengthen the capacity scheme amendment the worldwide innovation approaches.

- **Development in the vaccine for communicable diseases and new technology**

The vaccine against Covid-19 has been launched almost in a year but in the previous practices, these types of vaccines were taken at least 5 years to lunch (Longhurst et al, 2021). With the help of UHC, to perceive the infection of coronavirus, plasma therapy, antibody test has been done in an easy manner. UHC provide a great opportunity for all scientist, administrators to invent, policymakers, and use maximus vaccines.

- **UHC help to make local to global partnership**

The academics and expert have shared our improvement through the partnership and associations (Khoo and Lantos, 2020) for the method of handle Covid 19 through UHC. These reports were share by the journals, media, press conferences and global communities etc.

- **UHC encourage more investment on human Resource and health infrastructure**

Post pandemic situation has provided an opportunity to consider priories related to the health of human being so Covid 19 shown the trend of community health urgency and alleviated by well infrastructure & enough human resources (Bourgeault et al, 2020). Thus, government allocating more resources for the health infrastructure, health sectors and human resource.

5. UPCOMING POLICES AND FUTURE ACTIONS

Various countries are implementing UHC plans, but still there are various barriers to achieving UHC, which include less availability of basic facilities, poor infrastructure, out of pocket payments, shortage of well qualified health employees, costly medicines and medical products, and less accessibility of digital tools and techniques. So, with the help of SDGs, they tried to reduce the mentioned barriers and find the appropriate solutions for the countries suffering from these barriers. Through primary health care foundation, expand the UHC and make upcoming policies towards UHC then implement them in future actions. There are the following upcoming policies:

- The **UHC Billion target** is to have 1 billion people benefit from UCH.
- **UHC 2030's mission is to help create a** movement to encourage sustainable progress and equitable towards UHC.
- **The global compact** supports the objectives of SDG's and is reliable with framed objectives and commitment of other government agreements.
- **The Addis Ababa Action Agenda** aimed to solve the financing problem related to health treatment. Apart from the highlights of the financial problems, it also tries to provide an environment at all levels for SDs in the spirit of unanimity and global relationships with different kinds of countries.
- **The International Health Partnership (IHP)** works with WHO for the UHC 2020 and commits to the renewed urgency to make faster progress regarding UHC, as uttered in target 3.8 of the SDGs. As SDGs 2030 set out a determined agenda for a fairer, safer, and healthier world. This agenda includes flexible and sustainable health systems, expanding equity, providing finance and primary health care, handling health expenditures, and support for national health plans and policies.
- **The UHC2030 mission** is to provide a platform for multi-stakeholder, civil society, private sector, academia, global organizations, and government agencies to work together to create an environment that accelerates equitable and sustainable progress regarding UHC and the health system.
- UHC2030 provides **moralization for** collective action to protect everyone and provide health system facilities when anyone is needed because it contributes to the UHC goals.

- UHC provides facilities to make the **strongest human capital** as a valuable asset. It supports the foundational investment in economic growth (including human capital). It is the largest emerging growth sector because it provides 50 million job opportunities, mainly for women.
- Through the **World Bank Group's (WBG) achieved two major objectives to ending the excess poverty and maintain prosperity. Thus, all the investment related to reduce poverty or maintain equality and nutrition are deriving force of WBG's.**
- Take steps towards **the global movement** for health because health plays a significant role in e.g., 3.8 SDG target is aims to achieve UHC, including essential health care services, affordable medicines and medical facilities, a financially healthy environment, etc. Moreover, SDG 1" tried to reduce poverty from everywhere could be threatened because with the help of UHC, almost 90 million people are improving their health and bearing health expenses in an easy way.
- In recent years, 12 co-signatories, including the World Bank Group (WBG), have made a political obligation to UHC and outlining essential actions. WBG launched the **Global Action Plan (GAP)** for healthy people. This joint effort supports the target SDG3. January 2020, in Bangkok, 2 UHC forum was conducted for the encourage the political force on UHC. C.
- During the pandemic (Covid-19) situation, people caused mental and physical problems for various reasons, like losing jobs, lockdown, anxiety and loneliness, etc. Therefore, **MSN plans** to control and highly prevalent the working age population because they contribute to economic output losses which are estimated at between $2.5-8.5 trillion worldwide.
- In the developing countries are **implementing a common goal of financing UHC,** but before that, $80 per person spends their own money on accessing health services.
- WHO helps to achieve the **13th General Programme of Work 2025 target** in which UHC provides health facilities for 1 billion people, almost 2 billion people threatened from health crises and at least 1 billion people appreciating healthier life?

6. CONCLUSION

Sustainable Development Goa (SDG) - 13 ensures healthy lives and promotes well-being for all of all ages. UHC is the only solution for this which is UHC works on both health care services and financial security. Therefore, in this chapter, we found that low and middle-income countries are taking fewer initiatives towards UHC as compared to high-income countries. But, during the Covid 19 the world health care system was collapsed because the health care infrastructure was not sufficient as per the requirement.

People who have no sufficient amount for medical expenditure still they are not able to take any medical facilities. While health is necessary to all it cannot be neglected because it is considered as one of the global economy's major contribution sectors. In this sector, women are highly contributed. This also proved that health is not important only to achieve SDG 3 but also to achieve SDG 8 indirectly. WHO has contributed a lot to UHC and partnered with many organizations to achieve the objective of UHC. Overall, UHC could be possible with these three factors: reaching approach, affordability of service, and willingness.

Apart from the above approaches, we cannot also deny the role of the state as well as strong political leadership and action. These combined efforts definitely help to achieve world health economic equality.

REFERENCES

Kutzin, J. (2012, November 1). Anything goes on the path to universal health coverage? *No. World Health Organ., 90*(11), 867–868. doi:10.2471/BLT.12.113654 PMID:23226900

Bourassa, K. J., Sbarra, D. A., Caspi, A., & Moffitt, T. E. (2020). Social distancing as a health behavior: County-level movement in the United States during the COVID-19 pandemic is associated with conventional health behaviors. *Annals of Behavioral Medicine, 54*(8), 548–556. doi:10.1093/abm/kaaa049 PMID:32608474

Bourgeault, I. L., Maier, C. B., Dieleman, M., Ball, J., MacKenzie, A., Nancarrow, S., Nigenda, G., & Sidat, M. (2020). The COVID-19 pandemic presents an opportunity to develop more sustainable health workforces. *Human Resources for Health, 18*(1), 83. doi:10.118612960-020-00529-0 PMID:33129313

Cao, Y., Shan, J., Gong, Z., Kuang, J., & Gao, Y. (2020). Status and challenges of public health emergency management in China related to COVID-19. *Frontiers in Public Health, 8*, 250. doi:10.3389/fpubh.2020.00250 PMID:32574311

Centre for Disease Control and Prevention. (2020). *Human Corona virus Types*. Available from: https://www.cdc.gov/coronavirus/types.html

Cots, J.M., Alós, J., & Bárcena, M. (2020). *Since January 2020 Elsevier has created a COVID-19 resource centre with free information in English and Mandarin on the novel coronavirus*. Elsevier Connect.

Cutler, D. (2020). *COVID-19 and its Impact on the Healthcare Economy*. Retrieved from https://health-management.org/c/cardio/news/covid-19-and-its-impact-on-the-healthcare-economy

Dixit, S. B., Zirpe, K. G., Kulkarni, A. P., Chaudhry, D., Govil, D., & Mehta, Y. (2020). Current approaches to COVID-19: Therapy and prevention. *Indian Journal of Critical Care Medicine: Peer-Reviewed, Official Publication of Indian Society of Critical Care Medicine, 24*(9), 838–846. doi:10.5005/jp-journals-10071-23470 PMID:33132570

DocWireNews. (2020). *COVID-19's Economic Effect on The Healthcare Industry*. Retrieved from https://www.docwirenews.com/docwire-pick/covid-19s-economic-effect-on-thehealthcare-industry

Duong, D. (2021). *What's important to know about the new COVID-19 variants?* Academic Press.

ECDC. (2021). *SARS-CoV-2 variants of concern as of 10 February 2022*. https://www.ecdc.europa.eu/en/covid-19/variants-concern

Global Health Observatory Data Repository. (2014). *World Health Organization*. Available from: https://apps.who.int/gho/data/node.main?lang=en

Gopinath, G. (2020). *The great lockdown: Worst economic downturn since the great depression*. International Monetary Fund. https://blogs.imf.org/2020/04/14/the-great-lockdown-worsteconomic-downturn-since-the-great-depression/

Gragnolati, M., Lindelow, M., & Couttolenc, B. (2013). *Twenty years of health system reform in Brazil: an assessment of the sistema unico de saude*. World Bank. doi:10.1596/978-0-8213-9843-2

Horton, R., & Das, P. (2014). Universal Health Coverage: Not Why, What, or When—But How? *Lancet, 385*(9974), 1156–1157. doi:10.1016/S0140-6736(14)61742-6 PMID:25458724

Kahn, J.S., & McIntosh, K. (2005). History and recent advances in corona virus discovery. *Pediatr Infect Dis J., 24*(11), S223-7. .inf.0000188166.17324.60 doi:10.1097/01

Khoo, E. J., & Lantos, J. D. (2020). Lessons learned from the COVID-19 pandemic. *Acta Paediatrica (Oslo, Norway), 109*(7), 1323–1325. doi:10.1111/apa.15307 PMID:32289175

La Forgia, G., & Nagpal, S. (2012). *Government-sponsored health insurance in India: are you covered?* World Bank. doi:10.1596/978-0-8213-9618-6

Lee, A., & Morling, J. (2020). COVID19 - The need for public health in a time of emergency. *Public Health, 182*(5), 188–189. doi:10.1016/j.puhe.2020.03.027 PMID:32344272

Longhurst, C. A., Kremer, B., & Maysent, P. S. (2021). Rapid implementation of a vaccination super-station. *Journal of the American Medical Association, 325*(10), 931–932. doi:10.1001/jama.2021.0801 PMID:33507206

Mishra, M., & Majumdar, P. (2020). Social distancing during COVID-19: Will it change the Indian society? *Journal of Health Management, 22*(2), 224–235. doi:10.1177/0972063420935547

Mitrokhin, O. V., Reshetnikov, V. A., Belova, E. V., & Jakovljevic, M. M. (2020). Sanitary and hygienic aspects of the COVID-19 self-isolation. *The Open Public Health Journal, 13*(1), 734–738. doi:10.2174/1874944502013010734

Li, C., Yu, X., Butler, J. R. G., Yiengprugsawan, V., & Yu, M. (2011, August). Moving towards universal health insurance in China: Performance, issues and lessons from Thailand. *Soc Sci Med., 73*(3), 359–366. doi:10.1016/j.socscimed.2011.06.002 PMID:21733610

Mushi, V., & Shao, M. (2020). Tailoring of the ongoing water, sanitation and hygiene interventions for prevention and control of COVID-19. *Tropical Medicine and Health, 48*(1), 1–3. doi:10.118641182-020-00236-5 PMID:32549749

National Health Act. 61/2003. Pretoria.

National Rural Health Mission: framework for implementation 2005–2012. (2005). Government of India.

Nations, U. (2015). *Transforming our world: the 2030 agenda for sustainable development*. United Nations, Department of Economic and Social Affairs.

Nygren-Krug, H. (2019). The right (s) road to universal health coverage. *Health and Human Rights, 21*(2), 215. PMID:31885451

Partners' health policy and systems research report. (2021). https://ahpsr.who.int/publications/i/item/partners-health-policy-and-systems-research-report-2021

Penchansky, R., & Thomas, J. W. (1981). The concept of access: Definition and relationship to consumer satisfaction. *Medical Care, 19*, 127–140.

Rechel, B., & McKee, M. (2009, October 3). Lancet. Health reform in central and eastern Europe and the former. *Soviet Union. Union Sovietique*, *374*(9696), 1186–1195.

Reshetnikov, V., Mitrokhin, O., Shepetovskaya, N., Belova, E., & Jakovljevic, M. (2020). Organizational measures aiming to combat COVID-19 in the Russian Federation: The first experience. *Expert Review of Pharmacoeconomics & Outcomes Research*, *20*, 571–576. doi:10.1080/14737167.2020.1823221

Shengelia, B., Tandon, A., Adams, O. B., & Murray, C. J. (2005). Access, utilization, quality, and effective coverage: An integrated conceptual framework and measurement strategy. *Social Science & Medicine*, *61*(1), 97–109.

Tanahashi, T. (1978). Health service coverage and its evaluation. *Bull World Health Organ, 56*, 295–303.

The Primary Health Care Performance Initiative. (n.d.). https://improvingphc.org/about-phcpi

The World Bank. (2021). https://www.worldbank.org/en/topic/universalhealthcoverage#1

Thiede, M., Akweongo, P., & McIntyre, D. (2007). Exploring the dimensions of access. In The economics of health equity. Cambridge University Press.

UHC2030's mission is to create a movement for accelerating equitable and sustainable progress towards universal health coverage (UHC). (n.d.). https://www.uhc2030.org/our-mission/

UNDP. (2014). *Human Development Report 2014. Sustaining Human Progress: Reducing Vulnerabilities and Building Resilience*. United Nations Office for Outer Space Affairs. https://www.unoosa.org/oosa/en/ourwork/space4sdgs/sdg3.html

Universal Health Coverage Partnership. (n.d.). https://www.uhcpartnership.net/about/

Wagstaff, A., Cotlear, D., Eozenou, P. H. V., & Buisman, L. R. (2016). Measuring progress towards universal health coverage: With an application to 24 developing countries. *Oxford Review of Economic Policy*, *32*(1), 147–189.

WHO & UNICEF. (2018). *A Vision for Primary Health Care in the 21st Century: Towards Universal Health Coverage and the Sustainable Development Goals*. World Health Organization. https:// apps.who.int/iris/handle/10665/328065

WHO. (2019). *Health expenditure report*. Available online at https://www.who.int/health_financing/documents/health-expenditure-report-2019.pdf

Wise, J. (2020). *Covid-19: New coronavirus variant is identified in UK*. Academic Press.

World Health Organization. (2021). *WHO Corona virus Disease (COVID-19) Dashboard*. Available online at: https://covid19.who.int/

WTO. (2020). *COVID-19 Public Health Emergency of International Concern (PHEIC) Global research and innovation forum*. https://www.who.int/publications/m/item/covid-19-public-health-emergency-of-international-concern-(pheic)-global-research-and-innovation-forum

Zhao, M., Liao, L., Xiao, W., Yu, X., Wang, H., & Wang, Q. (2020). Household materials selection for homemade cloth face coverings and their filtration efficiency enhancement with triboelectric charging. *Nano Letters*, *20*, 5544–5552. doi:10.1021/acs.nanolett.0c02211

Chapter 18
Mitigation Plan for the Post-Pandemic on Supply Chain Disruptions Among Buyers and Distributors

Amitabh Verma
Sohar University, Oman

ABSTRACT

In recent decades, global supply chains have grown in size and complexity, emphasizing efficiency, cost, and closeness to markets. The coronavirus pandemic disrupted activity worldwide, with supply chain (SC) disruptions being particularly severe. A pandemic of this size has caught corporations and whole industries off guard, sending a cascade of rippling effects across their supply networks and enterprises. The COVID-19 outbreak has impacted the economic climate for many organizations worldwide, underlining the importance of responding to, adjusting to, and implementing crisis management strategies to weather difficult times. This study investigates the effect of the COVID-19 pandemic on SCs in terms of disruptions, problems, and trends. As a result, the goal is to investigate such difficulties and propose mitigation methods based on IoT (internet of things) for sustainability and viability of the supply chain management disruptions among buyers and distributors.

INTRODUCTION

A coronavirus pandemic is an extraordinary occurrence that brings global supply chains (SCs) to the general population's attention. The Covid 19 epidemic exacerbated the situation drastically in 2020 when governments imposed lockdowns that restricted or even ceased operations for vast swaths of business. This pandemic had a wide-ranging impact on the worldwide supply chain, offering flaws, difficulties, opportunities, and solutions. Being willing to try new things, forming new relationships, and growing household inventory are examples of being open to new ways. Extending storage capacity in various marketplaces closer to population centers is only a few examples. Today's shippers are

DOI: 10.4018/978-1-7998-8856-7.ch018

efficiently dealing with issues. While the supply chain's future remains unknown, we believe many of these developments are likely to stay. Economies in the Middle East and others are gradually emerging from lockdown, presenting an ideal chance to re-examine their fundamentals and build a considerably more lively trade environment. Some Middle Eastern companies may shorten and diversify their supply networks., effectively sacrificing efficiency for resilience. Others may use new technology to improve efficiency while also building strength

The present global trade crisis has exposed supply chain flaws and prompted the sector to review, develop, and frequently alter its operations to suit the demands of today's market. Many changes are unavoidable and should be welcomed as the sector grows for the future supply chain (Paul, Moktadir, et al., 2021). While no one can forecast or prevent the next global catastrophe, we can develop more resilient, Less vulnerable supply chains that can be achieved by learning from past failures and applying acceptable improvements into day-to-day operations (Butt, 2021). "Tomorrow belongs to those who hear it is coming," David Bowie famously stated, implying that we must listen to the market to predict what will happen next. While no one can forecast or prevent the next global catastrophe, we can construct more robust supply chains by learning from our failures in the past and adopting appropriate changes into day-to-day operations.

With the virus still posing a significant danger and specific regions and economies under siege, while others emerge into a new world, supply chain disruption is severe. As economies recover, the supply chain will become increasingly important in delivering goods and services on schedule, reliably, and securely(Raj et al., 2022). To satisfy their customers, clients, and communities, business executives must make swift decisions and take immediate action to safeguard and support their employees. Future supply networks will need to be durable and responsible as they are repurposed and reorganized.

Pre-Pandemic SupplyChain Management

One of the primary goals of the supply chain is to connect markets, distribution systems, production, associated operations, and procurement to serve clients in different regions of the world at reduced costs and greater service levels. Prior to the pandemic, supply chain process innovations, digitalization, and investment were driven by cost reduction and productivity increase. These drives remain critical, but COVID's unparalleled turmoil jeopardized the competitive position – and even the existence – of many enterprises that discovered they could no longer match client expectations.

Over the previous century, increased global trade has mostly resulted in a considerable expansion in global GDP. Supply networks have evolved into important facilitators of global trade, connecting the whole globe. Various technical breakthroughs and trade regulations contribute to the global economy's robust expansion. Supply networks have long contributed in the globalization of trade. Various shocks posed challenges to globalization. Trade tensions have grown under President Trump, who has levied unprecedented tariffs and fines on Chinese firms. Beijing's response has been to target agricultural exports in the United States. As businesses on both sides of the world hurried to stockpile merchandise ahead of tariffs, supply and demand were unstable. Then there was COVID. During the first half of 2020, most items suffered a decline in demand as economies went into lockdown. Sailings on sea carriers were canceled, production capacity was reduced, and employee was shifted worldwide.

This unanticipated shift in commerce put a strain on global logistics at first. Disturbance in any world region has resulted in supply chain disruptions and economic recessions. Tsunamis, earthquakes,

911 terror attacks, epidemics/pandemics like COVID-19, and other natural disasters have all impacted companies worldwide.

However, beginning in the summer of 2020, imports into the United States increased as a result of huge fiscal stimulus. Customers' orders poured into online stores. Both manufacturing and international trade restarted. The global economic machine has been reactivated. By late 2020, significant cracks in the supply chain had begun to show. Logistically, restarting the production machine after the lockout was difficult. The complex system that delivers raw materials and finished commodities worldwide requires predictability and precision. They'd both died. There was a paucity of shipping containers.. Shipping charges for certain routes increased, causing congestion at international ports that extended to railways and interior rail terminals, exacerbating the already-existing transportation and chassis scarcity. Importers in the United States experienced delays in getting critical production components, while exporters saw issues accessing containers and gaining bookings on cargo ships. The supply chain broken. The COVID-19 problem has caused the most widespread interruption of supply lines worldwide. The COVID-19 problem has disrupted global supply networks and posed several obstacles to governments, corporations, and the broader economy. The COVID-19 pandemic has triggered an economic catastrophe by disrupting the supply chain, manufacturing activity, and suppressing demand.

Challenges In Pandemic

Throughout history, interruptions and disturbances have brought the world to a halt for unknown causes. These upheavals have called into question established ways of thinking and doing things. These natural disasters worsened the world, but the COVID19 pandemic had a different and more severe impact on international enterprises (Magableh, 2021). The reason is obvious: globalization and technological advancements have made things more complicated, interconnected, and interdependent. Today's businesspeople aim to distribute their products and services globally to get competitive and geographical advantages. The supply chain was critical in enabling and meeting these segmented enterprises' segmented enterprises' raw material, completed goods, and intermediate product requirements. Due to the COVID-19 pandemic, borders and even local movements have been limited as an early tactic to combat the virus's further spread (Barman et al., 2021). The first action was a travel prohibition for humanitarian logistics, which halted international supply transfers. As a result, the value chain's (VC) integrity and stability have been jeopardized. The worldwide media have reported other viewpoints, ranging from threats to allegations and even intercepting shipments. Given their obligation to safeguard people and avoid disasters at all costs, governments inspect everything that enters their domain. Such occurrences have significantly influenced GSCs (R. Sharma et al., 2020). The study focuses on three important areas: the primary causes of disruptions, the issues related to the pandemic, and the crisis trend. SC operations were discontinued because of three major factors: supply change, demand fluctuation, and government and nation reactions to the epidemic. The epidemic impacted SC operations, procedures, and management because of supply disruptions, fluctuating demand, and government measures to combat the epidemic (Anser et al., 2021). Factory closures, border restrictions, travel bans, port closures, and transit halts impacted the supply chain, resulting in shortages. GSCs connecting to China, the United States, and Europe were severely impacted, causing price increases in various items in response to panic purchasing, which led to price volatility when supply became constrained (Z. Xu et al., 2020). Because of the delays, high demand, and order congestion, demand fragility and shocks occurred, hurting retail and online purchases. Substantial hurdles remained in meeting tremendous demand while ensuring quality and consistency. In the early months of this year, several governments took preemptive efforts to safeguard their citizens, imposing stringent limits on mobility through lockdowns, social separation, and quarantine measures (Aday & Aday, 2020). The stress and worry caused by such decisions impact SC operations and performance. Government measures have decreased output and major cutbacks in international trade flows. The key challenges posed by the COVID-19 pandemic are industrial, economic, influx, and production halt, distribution, internet purchase, and SC interruptions. Components required for final product assembly are obtained from (and assembled at) several places. They are subsequently re-exported, moved, or sent to other sites worldwide. As a result, any disturbance in the SC hampers the operation. Disruptions in supply and demand and government measures contribute to short- and long-term foreign and domestic economic threats. In the face of such interruptions and violation of official protections, some industries suspended operations. Direct distribution issues, increased online orders, and distribution center re-staffing were among the obstacles experienced by delivery and distribution and warehouses(Singh et al., 2021). Changes in inventory allocation throughout the network and distribution channels to improve responsiveness. As a result, the epidemic proved beneficial to online retailers and businesses. Internet shopping has grown in popularity, particularly for food and grocery items. Because of the pandemic, many customers depended on internet purchasing and limited their trips to retailer centers, freight prices increased, travel interest decreased, and demand for important items (luxury products) increased (decreased) and canceled and excess orders. As a result, firms are forced to lay off employees and suspend production. The pandemic has impacted most of the world's businesses, and they have also reported interruptions in their SCs (Schroeder et al., 2021). The following are the key tendencies of this impact. (1) Prices fluctuate due to the pandemic's significant price increase, negatively influencing the relationship between suppliers, merchants, and customers. (2) There is a significant lead time due to delays in acquiring products from the supplier and delays in delivery. (3) Shipments, freight movement, loading, shipping, and unloading are all delayed, with extra delays at the border and port crossings. (4) Retailers' capacity to maintain quality control is jeopardized if return, profitability, and sales decline (5) Production capacity and industrial capabilities deteriorate, affecting production sources. (6) A lack of disruption planning, along with low inventory levels, a single supplier, or a lack of variety, undervalues the possibility of catastrophic disruptions; the concentration on the short term and cost-cutting leads to a lack of risk awareness and contingency planning. (7) It is tough to obtain information and data from partners a lack of end-to-end visibility, integrations, coordination, and technology use disparities throughout the Supply Chain.

In general, abnormal disruptions to global trade and business occur, impacting both the supply and demand sides of the SC. As a result, enterprises confront major hurdles in ensuring a constant supply of products and services.

It is too early to assess and quantify the overall impact of COVID-19 on SC disruptions. The considerable reduction in Chinese and other industrial nations' output, business, and commerce, on the other hand, will have a significant impact on numerous countries along with the SC, as most governments restrict the flow of materials to prevent the virus's spread.

Related Study

The COVID-19 epidemic has had an extraordinary impact on global supply networks (Raj et al., 2022). It has created severe disruptions to many business operations. A catastrophe is defined as any incident that strikes unexpectedly and whose influence may grow in severity; it interrupts society's normal functioning and results in loss of life., economics, and the environment. (Kılcı et al., 2015). It has received much attention from supply chain experts (T.-M. Choi, 2020) and practitioners. Previous research has demonstrated that minor supply network disturbances cause rippling effects (Scheibe & Blackhurst, 2018). The pandemic has impacted all aspects of business, notably worldwide supply networks (Ivanov & Dolgui, 2020). It has had several consequences, notably in the healthcare supply chain, undoubtedly having long-term consequences. (Govindan et al., 2020). The effects of the coronavirus outbreak on global supply chains may be classified into three types: supply, demand, and logistics. (Kumar & Sharma, 2021). To date, a large amount of study has been undertaken in several fields, such as supplier selection and order allocation, on supply chain network architecture during interruptions (Ramnath et al., 2014). The Novel Coronavirus (COVID-19) pandemic has shown the degree of risks, readiness, and missing links in today's extensive and regionally scattered value chains (Ali et al., 2022). Many studies show that COVID-19 has caused enormous shocks and impacted between 78 and 95 percent of firms involved in value chain networks (Remko, 2020). This suggests that while traditional supply chain resilience methods are necessary, they are insufficient to deal with the extended shocks induced by COVID-19. In this pandemic, supply chain research is in its early phases. Limited research has been conducted on a micro-scale. Those shown tend to focus on theoretical attempts to describe the COVID-19 condition better. Based on a literature survey, several studies propose future research areas. However, the supply chain-related difficulties businesses are currently encountering due to COVID-19 and mitigating strategies are mostly absent from the present global supply chain discussion (Raj et al., 2022). This pandemic impacted supply chain operations and the interaction between tiers and business policies in networks of interrelated links. Firms, for example, are altering their sourcing methods from global to local (T. Y. Choi et al., 2021) (b) This pandemic has the potential to disrupt power relations inside supply systems(Craighead et al., 2020) (c) Supply networks must become more robust (Craighead et al., 2020), and (d) Companies are altering their stocking strategy (Sodhi et al., 2021). As a result, it is critical to explore how COVID-19-related disruptions influence the linked business landscape of supply chains and how the internet of things (IoT) mitigates the post-covid effect on supply chain management. To minimize this gap, the following research questions will be addressed in this article:

a) What are the main supply chain issues posed by the COVID-19 pandemic?
b) What mitigation techniques are appropriate for dealing with these supply chain challenges?
c) How does the Internet of Things (IoT) address these issues?

Major Supply Chain Issues as a Result of the COVID-19 Outbreak

The COVID-19 outbreak has changed the business landscape for numerous enterprises worldwide. The magnitude of the problems varies according to the occurrence's severity (s). This is because such epidemics have severe and long-term effects on companies and their operations, needing more rigorous recovery procedures (Koonin, 2020). As a result, it is crucial to identify possible supply chain recovery bottlenecks and their effect on post-disaster recovery during an epidemic to ensure supply networks implement proper processes to manage such challenges (Koonin, 2020). As a result of the acute limitations and lockdowns that resulted in a slew of significant concerns requiring quick attention during the early stages of the outbreak, many businesses have already begun to shift into "recovery mode." They have started to make long-term plans. As businesses strive to improve their operations and resilience, the need for supply chain resilience and risk management becomes more precise than ever. Over the next three years, increasing exposure is the key aim. With a goal for greater exposure among hundreds or thousands of suppliers, we see a shift away from linear supply chains and toward more integrated networks that connect various entities. Internet of Things (IoT) devices or sensors hat offer meaningful data on where things are in the chain and how they are doing — Products, for example, where temperature monitoring is critical — are enabling this sea change. The following are some of the major issues posed by the COVID-19 pandemic:

- Improve efficiency
- Retaining/Retraining employees
- More visible
- Improve responsiveness /resiliency
- Cost-cutting measures
- Increase the company's sustainability and corporate social responsibility.
- Suppliers should be diversified and segmented.
- Shift to contract to manufacture
- Use digital twins and other simulation technology to your advantage.

Supply networks frequently face various challenges when developing measures to recover from the effects of disruptions (Paul, Chowdhury, et al., 2021). There will be programs in the following years to assist workers in using digital technology, adapting to changing company rules and modes of working, such as greater virtual collaboration, and helping people operate equipment in a health and safety-conscious manner.

Mitigation Methods that are Appropriate for Dealing with these Supply Chain Difficulties

The supply networks of the future will be digital and self-sufficient. The switch to digital and light-out mode has begun in earnest. Several pre-existing trends, particularly those in the supply chain, have been amplified by the outbreak. The digital enablement and automation race has started. However, simply installing digital technologies does not result in a digitized, self-sufficient supply chain; it also necessitates integrated supply chain technologies encompassing planning, procurement, manufacturing, and logistics and operating outside of the organization's four walls. Consider "lights-out," "hands-free," and "self-driving" operations, in which firms leverage IoT technology across the end-to-end supply chain to assist make predictive and prescriptive choices. Respond to a shift in customer demand that is rapidly observed by the whole value chain (the organization, its suppliers, and their suppliers' suppliers) (T. Y. Choi et al., 2021). Supply planning and manufacturing schedules may be changed collaboratively and quickly. Finally, digital and self-driving technology will make people's occupations more accessible and the supply chain more efficient and optimal. The future supply chain will need to be flexible, adaptable, efficient, long-lasting, and digitally networked for increased visibility (Barman et al., 2021). As a result, organizations should emphasize the following rehabilitative and long-term goals.

Rethink the strategic structure of the supply chain.: Assuming new trade agreements, nations incentives, and multiple channels momentum gain and integration as soon as possible when rethinking supply chain strategy and global trade flows. Using IoT technology, reimagine the supply chain operating model.

Improve transparency and resilience: When it comes to supply chain planning and global trade movements, consider new trade agreements, incentives for countries, and omnichannel acceleration and integration. Examine the footprint of your supply chain utilizing IoT technology.

Extract cash and reduce supply chain costs: To enhance the supply chain cost structure significantly and profile of working capital, focus on stock-keeping unit rationalization, procurement spending reduction, transportation, warehouse optimization, and manufacturing productivity (Hald & Coslugeanu, 2021). Reduce working capital by employing digital technology to split the supply chain, update inventory planning criteria, and adjust payment terms.

Create a competitive edge by focusing on sustainability: Investigate strategies to design and engineer new items to achieve this circular economy and manage third-party risk through supplier sustainability evaluations at levels 1-3.

With a digital supply chain, increase agility and growth opportunities: Implement an end-to-end computerized supply chain that covers planning, procurement, production, and logistics. Recognize that organizations use supply networks as a growth engine and differentiate themselves from the competition.

Many CEOs feel the COVID-19 outbreak was a one-time event, and however, as the saying goes, "hope is not a plan." There are paths to stand out and better handle the next upheaval's approaching storms. These include assessing the Supply chain risk and resilience approach, devising means to recover income quickly, and investing in digital technology (Y. Xu et al., 2021). It is also critical to keep people at the forefront of your efforts and to enable them to achieve outstanding results. Finally, collaborate with consumers to build a truly sustainable supply chain toward circularity and the environment (Fernandes et al., 2020). By taking this path, an organization will be better prepared to cope with any challenges that may come in the future, transforming potential disruptions into unique opportunities.

Internet of Things (IoT) and Mitigate the Pandemic Affected SCM

According to the literature, using digital technology as a strategic tool may improve corporate performance, production capacity, efficacy, and resilience. The use of digital and emerging technologies, such as the Internet of Things (IoT), adds value and gives enterprises a competitive edge in their business operations. However, there is currently a scarcity of research on these information technology tools' usage, acceptance, and inclusion in supply chain operations, notably supply chain resilience. This study discusses the application and effect of new technologies employed by organizations to combat the COVID-19 epidemic (Ajmal et al., 2021). The Internet of Things (IoT) is a relatively new technology that combines sensors, machine learning, artificial intelligence, and analytics. IoT is being called upon to tackle a slew of challenges in every business. It gets more innovative when IoT is used in supply chain management. and possesses the following features: (1) Instrumented: a machine-generated supply chain information. (2) Interconnected by the use of intelligent items and IT systems. (3) Intelligent: enhance performance by making many optimum decisions on a large scale. (4) Automated: All procedures must be automated to replace inefficient resources. (5) Integrated: cooperation at several levels of the supply chain. (6) Innovative: developing new values through solutions to fulfill new requirements.

The Impacts of IoT on SC

1. Improve inventory management: Using the IoT (IoT), inventory visibility in real-time has been developed (IOT). Inventory management will be relied on guessing if there is no real-time visibility.

Manual data collection also leads to inventory disorder (Ajmal et al., 2021). They are installing sensors, which will result in 100% inventory accuracy.

2. Supply chain management in real-time: Demand information is often supplied to only one partner rather than shared in traditional supply chain management. Modern RFID tag technologies, on the other hand, enable the recording of numerous information such as production and expiration dates, as well as warrant length, resulting in effective supply chain management.
3. Boost logistical transparency: All transportation information (transport status, destination, etc.) will be available to the whole supply chain by utilizing intelligent objects. This increases the likelihood of monitoring and preserving products, and it also reduces the cost of return and significantly influences customer satisfaction.

The five real-world examples below show how shippers rely on flexibility, investment, and alternative solutions to deal with the current supply chain disruption and why these changes are here to stay

1. Keeping an open mind, innovative, and unusual business practices: Because of the disruption caused by the epidemic, stakeholders throughout the supply chain were compelled to seek other ports, non-traditional routes, and novel approaches. Being open to new and unusual business methods provides a quick answer to a pressing problem (M. Sharma et al., 2021). It emphasized the need to maintain an open mind while considering alternatives that might save time and money over established routes impacted by congestion and capacity limits.
2. Broadening networks, connecting with new people, and developing relationships: Using alternative ports and contemplating new routes pushed shippers to think beyond the box, forging new contacts and developing new partnerships. Congestion and capacity issues at ports highlighted how important it is for shippers to have a varied vendor base at all points in their supply chain (ocean, air, warehousing, and trucking). As a result, when blockages arise, they have alternate choices and more capacity to draw on to keep their freight moving. While sticking to "what has always worked" has its advantages, building strong ties outside of the usual procedure is one-way shippers create resilience in their supply chains.
3. Allocating equipment resources and working with asset-based vendors: Nobody likes to pay for idle assets, but the inadequacies of the old model showed us that without backup equipment, capacity, and warehouse space, your supply chain may not be robust enough to survive severe conditions, which may have substantial financial ramifications. During the epidemic, some prominent merchants purchased equipment to minimize delays and issues created by container and chassis shortages (Spieske & Birkel, 2021) . The demand for more storage capacity to store buffer stock and delayed seasonal products has also skyrocketed. Collaboration with an asset-based third-party logistics provider, such as WDS, might be helpful for shippers that do not have the resources to buy, operate, and maintain their distribution space and equipment.

In the future, logistical planning will encompass managing equipment (containers, chassis, trailers, etc.) and storage space, and shippers will select partners who will invest in infrastructure and space to satisfy demand. WDS, for example, just built 480,000 square feet in New York/New Jersey, virtually tripling our capacity in this area. Based on the market, we have added a million square feet to our footprint in the previous 18 months.

4. Increasing stock levels: While the industry was aware that the "just-in-time" strategy was becoming too lean and too tight to be sustainable, the pandemic highlighted its vulnerability in a loud and transparent way. This has evolved in what is now known as the "just-in-case" strategy, in which shippers arrange for additional inventory so that they have items on hand when they are needed. Increasing inventory levels guarantee that you have enough things on hand to fulfill unforeseen demands or delays in your supply chain (Ivanov, 2021). The previous several years have demonstrated that keeping inventory levels low is too dangerous. To meet customers' requests, must invest in solutions that allow having things on hand where and when need them..
5. Increasing storage capacity in various markets: The drive toward diverse storage options, which includes expanding the number of sites, introducing new markets, and looking at storage near population centers, supports the strategy of having inventory when and where you need it (Magableh, 2021). Having your product or products in numerous places increases agility and flexibility, allowing you to swiftly get those things to your consumer. Furthermore, in today's "next day delivery" e-commerce business, closeness to population centers is practically a need, which will continue to determine where and when warehouses are built in the medium and long run.

CONCLUSION

The COVID-19 pandemic, like a few others in the last century, caused widespread disruption in commerce, economics, health and education systems, enterprises, and society. Companies are starting to re-evaluate their production, transportation, and warehousing networks or investing in far larger inventory buffers or other courses of action that they believe will provide them with long-term steady supply security. People involved in the supply chain industry must be upskilled and technologically competent for technology to be accepted and risk absorption to be facilitated. Supply Chain 4.0 was already influencing firms to invest in smaller, more widely spread warehouses closer to clients than large, centrally situated ones. Supply chain innovation will be critical, and collaboration will be required to ensure future company success across the value chain. However, conserving, retraining, reskilling the workforce, and investing to make the autonomous supply chain a reality are significant concerns for all stakeholders.

REFERENCES

Aday, S., & Aday, M. S. (2020). Impact of COVID-19 on the food supply chain. *Food Quality and Safety*, *4*(4), 167–180. doi:10.1093/fqsafe/fyaa024

Ajmal, M. M., Khan, M., Shad, M. K., AlKatheeri, H., & Jabeen, F. (2021). Socio-economic and technological new normal in supply chain management: lessons from COVID-19 pandemic. *The International Journal of Logistics Management*. doi:10.1108/IJLM-04-2021-0231

Ali, I., Arslan, A., Chowdhury, M., Khan, Z., & Tarba, S. Y. (2022). Reimagining global food value chains through effective resilience to COVID-19 shocks and similar future events: A dynamic capability perspective. *Journal of Business Research*, *141*, 1–12. doi:10.1016/j.jbusres.2021.12.006 PMID:34908632

Anser, M. K., Khan, M. A., Nassani, A. A., Abro, M. M. Q., Zaman, K., & Kabbani, A. (2021). Does COVID-19 pandemic disrupt sustainable supply chain process? Covering some new global facts. *Environmental Science and Pollution Research International*, *28*(42), 59792–59804. doi:10.100711356-021-14817-2 PMID:34146331

Barman, A., Das, R., & De, P. K. (2021). Impact of COVID-19 in food supply chain: Disruptions and recovery strategy. *Current Research in Behavioral Sciences, 2*, 100017.

Butt, A. S. (2021). Strategies to mitigate the impact of COVID-19 on supply chain disruptions: a multiple case analysis of buyers and distributors. *The International Journal of Logistics Management*. doi:10.1108/IJLM-11-2020-0455

Choi, T.-M. (2020). Innovative "Bring-Service-Near-Your-Home" operations under Corona-Virus (COVID-19/SARS-CoV-2) outbreak: Can logistics become the Messiah? *Transportation Research Part E, Logistics and Transportation Review*, *140*, 101961. doi:10.1016/j.tre.2020.101961 PMID:32346356

Choi, T. Y., Narayanan, S., Novak, D., Olhager, J., Sheu, J.-B., & Wiengarten, F. (2021). Managing extended supply chains. *Journal of Business Logistics*, *42*(2), 200–206. doi:10.1111/jbl.12276

Craighead, C. W., Ketchen, D. J. Jr, & Darby, J. L. (2020). Pandemics and Supply Chain Management Research: Toward a Theoretical Toolbox. *Decision Sciences*, *51*(4), 838–866. doi:10.1111/deci.12468 PMID:34234384

Fernandes, K., Chaudhuri, A., Shukla, M., & Xiong, Y. (2020). *Covid19 Impact on Supply Chains: Scotland*. doi:10.13140/RG.2.2.24573.51685/1

Govindan, K., Mina, H., & Alavi, B. (2020). A decision support system for demand management in healthcare supply chains considering the epidemic outbreaks: A case study of coronavirus disease 2019 (COVID-19). *Transportation Research Part E, Logistics and Transportation Review*, *138*, 101967. doi:10.1016/j.tre.2020.101967 PMID:32382249

Hald, K. S., & Coslugeanu, P. (2021). *The preliminary supply chain lessons of the COVID-19 disruption—What is the role of digital technologies?* Operations Management Research. doi:10.100712063-021-00207-x

Ivanov, D. (2021). Digital Supply Chain Management and Technology to Enhance Resilience by Building and Using End-to-End Visibility During the COVID-19 Pandemic. *IEEE Transactions on Engineering Management*. doi:10.1109/TEM.2021.3095193

Ivanov, D., & Dolgui, A. (2020). Viability of intertwined supply networks: Extending the supply chain resilience angles towards survivability. A position paper motivated by COVID-19 outbreak. *International Journal of Production Research*, *58*(10), 2904–2915. doi:10.1080/00207543.2020.1750727

Kılcı, F., Kara, B. Y., & Bozkaya, B. (2015). Locating temporary shelter areas after an earthquake: A case for Turkey. *European Journal of Operational Research*, *243*(1), 323–332. doi:10.1016/j.ejor.2014.11.035

Koonin, L. M. (2020). Novel coronavirus disease (COVID-19) outbreak: Now is the time to refresh pandemic plans. *Journal of Business Continuity & Emergency Planning*, *13*(4), 1–15. PMID:32160942

Kumar, B., & Sharma, A. (2021). Managing the supply chain during disruptions: Developing a framework for decision-making. *Industrial Marketing Management, 97*, 159–172. doi:10.1016/j.indmarman.2021.07.007

Magableh, G. M. (2021, September). (2021). Supply Chains and the COVID-19 Pandemic: A Comprehensive Framework. *European Management Review, 18*(3), 363–382. Advance online publication. doi:10.1111/emre.12449

Paul, S. K., Chowdhury, P., Moktadir, M. A., & Lau, K. H. (2021). Supply chain recovery challenges in the wake of COVID-19 pandemic. *Journal of Business Research, 136*, 316–329. doi:10.1016/j.jbusres.2021.07.056 PMID:34538979

Paul, S. K., Moktadir, M. A., & Ahsan, K. (2021). Key supply chain strategies for the post-COVID-19 era: implications for resilience and sustainability. *The International Journal of Logistics Management.* doi:10.1108/IJLM-04-2021-0238

Raj, A., Mukherjee, A. A., de Sousa Jabbour, A. B. L., & Srivastava, S. K. (2022). Supply chain management during and post-COVID-19 pandemic: Mitigation strategies and practical lessons learned. *Journal of Business Research, 142*, 1125–1139. doi:10.1016/j.jbusres.2022.01.037 PMID:35079190

Ramnath, V. R., Ho, L., Maggio, L. A., & Khazeni, N. (2014). Centralized Monitoring and Virtual Consultant Models of Tele-ICU Care: A Systematic Review. *Telemedicine Journal and e-Health, 20*(10), 936–961. doi:10.1089/tmj.2013.0352 PMID:25226571

Remko, H. (2020). Research opportunities for a more resilient post-COVID-19 supply chain – closing the gap between research findings and industry practice. *International Journal of Operations & Production Management, 40*(4), 341–355. doi:10.1108/IJOPM-03-2020-0165

Scheibe, K. P., & Blackhurst, J. (2018). Supply chain disruption propagation: A systemic risk and normal accident theory perspective. *International Journal of Production Research, 56*(1–2), 43–59. doi:10.1080/00207543.2017.1355123

Schroeder, M., von See, B., Schnelle, J., & Kersten, W. (2021). *Impact of the Covid-19 Pandemic on Supply Chain Management BT.* In R. Fritzsche, S. Winter, & J. Lohmer (Eds.), *Logistik in Wissenschaft und Praxis: Von der Datenanalyse zur Gestaltung komplexer Logistikprozesse* (pp. 3–24). Springer Fachmedien Wiesbaden. doi:10.1007/978-3-658-33480-2_1

Sharma, M., Joshi, S., Luthra, S., & Kumar, A. (2021). *Managing disruptions and risks amidst COVID-19 outbreaks: role of blockchain technology in developing resilient food supply chains.* Operations Management Research., doi:10.100712063-021-00198-9

Sharma, R., Shishodia, A., Kamble, S., Gunasekaran, A., & Belhadi, A. (2020). Agriculture supply chain risks and COVID-19: mitigation strategies and implications for the practitioners. *International Journal of Logistics Research and Applications*, 1–27. doi:10.1080/13675567.2020.1830049

Singh, S., Kumar, R., Panchal, R., & Tiwari, M. K. (2021). Impact of COVID-19 on logistics systems and disruptions in food supply chain. *International Journal of Production Research, 59*(7), 1993–2008. doi:10.1080/00207543.2020.1792000

Sodhi, M. S., Tang, C. S., & Willenson, E. T. (2021). Research opportunities in preparing supply chains of essential goods for future pandemics. *International Journal of Production Research*, 1–16. doi:10.1080/00207543.2021.1884310

Spieske, A., & Birkel, H. (2021). Improving supply chain resilience through industry 4.0: A systematic literature review under the impressions of the COVID-19 pandemic. *Computers & Industrial Engineering*, *158*, 107452. doi:10.1016/j.cie.2021.107452 PMID:35313661

Xu, Y., Li, J.-P., Chu, C.-C., & Dinca, G. (2021). Impact of COVID-19 on transportation and logistics: a case of China. *Economic Research-Ekonomska Istraživanja*, 1–19. doi:10.1080/1331677X.2021.1947339

Xu, Z., Elomri, A., Kerbache, L., & El Omri, A. (2020). Impacts of COVID-19 on Global Supply Chains: Facts and Perspectives. *IEEE Engineering Management Review*, *48*(3), 153–166. doi:10.1109/EMR.2020.3018420

Chapter 19
Investigation of Human Resource Management Practices After COVID-19: Challenges and Opportunities

Shivani Agarwal
https://orcid.org/0000-0002-3205-552X
KIET School of Management, India & KIET Group of Institutions, India

Shubham Aggarwal
KIET School of Management, India & KIET Group of Institutions, India

Anshika Tyagi
KIET School of Management, India & KIET Group of Institutions, India

ABSTRACT

The economy of every country relies on its human resources. COVID-19 has impacted human life, socio-economic development, and national relations. The worldwide economy has been ferociously crushed by the coronavirus pandemic. It barrels all organizations, making a complicated and tough setting for managers in the domain of human resource management. International agencies need to facilitate their employees to wear down this extraordinary crisis. The type of work, worker enlisting and choice, worker coaching, performance management, and compensation management have been modified fully. In the study, COVID-19 crisis's impact on HRM is investigated. It points out the prospects that have arisen from the pandemic, and it presents apprehension for managers in the domain of human resource management. The study advocated the adoption of e-HRM to reduce employee physical interactions.

DOI: 10.4018/978-1-7998-8856-7.ch019

I. INTRODUCTION

Coronaviruses area unit a colony of contagion' happiness to the family of coronaries that contaminate each human (male-female) and animals. Corona-viruses area unit named for his or her appearance: "corona" suggests that "crown". The virus's outer layers are unit coated with spike proteins that surround them sort of a crown. Human coronaviruses will cause delicate diseases just like communicable diseases, whereas others mainspring additional severe diseases (such as MERS - Mideast metastasis syndrome). A replacement coronavirus that previously has not been celebrated in humans emerged in the city, China in Dec 2019. Signs and symptoms embody metastasis symptoms and embody fever, cough, and shortness of breath. In further severe cases, the infection can cause disease, severe acute metabolism syndrome, and customarily death. Commonplace recommendations to prevent the flowering of covid-19 embody frequent cleansing of hands victimization alcohol-based hand rub or soap and water, covering the nose and mouth with a flexed elbow or disposable tissue once coughing and sneezing. On another aspect, covid-19 has in addition impact on Human resource management (HRM) (Aitken-Fox, 2020). It is the application of recruiting, hiring, deploying, associate degreed managing the employees. An organization or organization's hour department is usually accountable for creating, golf stroke into impact, and overseeing policies governing employees and thus the connection of the organization with its employees. The term human resources were initially utilized within the first period, then further wide among the Sixties, to clarify those that work for the organization, within the mixture. Several functions of the HRM unit of measurement are as follows:

i. **Recruitment**

Human resource management is the potency of individual leadership and controls at intervals in a company. The HRM is liable for facilitating the goals of the cooperation through effective management of human capital — specializing in workers because of the company's most vital quality. Accomplishment is the commencement in building an associate organization's human capital. At a high level, the goals area unit to seek out and rent the foremost effective candidates, on time, and at intervals budget.

ii. **Training and development**

Training and rearing square measure one of the foremost necessary functions of HRM in any cooperation. The target of this coaching is to boost workers' skills behavior and experience by golf stroke them into understanding new techniques of doing work. Worker coaching and development helps in changing employees' skills and data for performing arts employment which ends in increasing their work potency and increasing the productivity of a corporation. It ensures that Associate in Nursing employee's oddity or eccentricity is reduced and learning or behavioral modification ought to occur in a very structured format. Coaching development or learning and development area unit official ongoing educational activities designed for goal fulfillment and enhancing the performance of workers. Employee employment and development in HRM is printed as a system used by a company to spice up the skills and performance of the staff. It's a tutorial tool that consists of information and directions to make existing skills sharp, introduce new concepts and knowledge to spice up employee performance. Decent employment & development initiative supported employment desires assessment helps the company to spice up the skills to workmen and improve productivity.

iii. **Performance management**

An ongoing, continuous way of human activity and instructive work tasks, priorities, performance objectives, and Associate in Nursing growth that optimizes an individual's performance and aligns sessions with structure strategic goals When people perceive the words performance management, the annual analysis may be the first thing that comes to mind. However, an effective performance management strategy entails much more than a simple annual review. Human resources have developed modules to aid in the management of employee performance. In addition to setting goals at the start of the analysis period and evaluating performance at the end of the analysis period, human resources recommend that feedback be given throughout the year.

iv. **Compensation management**

Compensation control due to the fact it's far understood these days has been an important deliver of attracting, retaining, and motivating the desired human useful resource for any corporation. Even though maximum people specifically at the center and senior stages declare that cash doesn`t play a manfully important position of their name to differ or to stay in an organization but reality, it is the cash that motivates the maximum of the staff. For the HRM, employee remuneration can be an important operation because every employee is concerned with the wide variety of remuneration, scale, and special allowances that she or he receives. Each employee needs to induce the most quantity as possible better remuneration. Whereas every corporation needs to furnish as little or no as possible. The expert of human useful resource control has the tough challenge of solving sincere wages and salary differentials proper to people and their leaders. Compensation control, conjointly referred to as salary and pay administration, remuneration control, or praise control, issues with making plans and enforcing an entire reimbursement package.

v. **Promotion**

Promotion may be a vertical transfer of an associate with an associate's degree within an organization. In other words, promotion means that an employee with an associate's degree is promoted from one position to another with an increase in regular pay, position, and responsibilities. Promotions may be temporary or permanent, depending on the requirements of the organization. Contributes to the prevailing corporate climate and sense of ownership, interest in coaching, and well-being in the areas of programmer development and team development. This builds loyalty and boosts morale. Committed rewards and ongoing promotions place employees where their skills and information are most often used. This will create and increase interest in replacement workers within the company as they believe they will receive their share further. It fosters satisfaction among workers with the general conditions of work and employment. This will increase interest in higher qualifications, learning, and personal development to meet the needs of promotion. This improves morale and job satisfaction and ultimately improves the health of the structure.

vi. **Retention strategies**

The impacts of turnover go most on the way aspect temporary disruptions. For one, it's costly. Exchange associate employee costs square measure roughly a typical fraction of their annual payment, per the work institute. And thus, the Houston Chronicle reports that increasing those costs, high turnover together impacts the workers that remain—and the business's customers. As employees watch their colleagues leave, their workloads sometimes increase. This may cause a downward spiral of exits and stress. Frustrated, overworked employees unit of measurement less ostensibly to perform at their peak, which suggests the company's product or service suffers, and customers have extra negative interactions with the company. The ramifications rectangular degree unit of size is effective to quantify. As Per the LinkedIn survey, ninety-four of personnel say they will preserve on with their organization longer if it`s invested inside their professional improvement. In today`s economy, the personnel understands that they want to stay their abilities sharp to stay aggressive and circulate up the ladder. Organizations can regulator into their staff`s want for improvement through offering systems like mentorship applications and finance in extra schooling for their staff. Everybody loves to sense valued, and that`s authentic at durations on the geographic point. In Associate in nursing prodigious society for human useful resource control survey, sixty-eight of hour experts aforementioned that popularity becomes essential for retention, nonetheless many agencies lack formal popularity applications. Corporations were given to inspire managers to renowned their direct reports` work. They`ll collectively pass any to offer division- or organization-huge popularity of employee`s global fitness agency pass the more mile. Throughout the pandemic, as soon as many personnel rectangular degree pressured to manipulate effective instances amid dynamic conditions, that popularity is especially essential

So, in the study, the author is going to investigate the Human Resource Management practices after Covid-19. The model of the study is represented as follows:

Figure 1. HRM practices and its consequences
(Source: Author's own work)

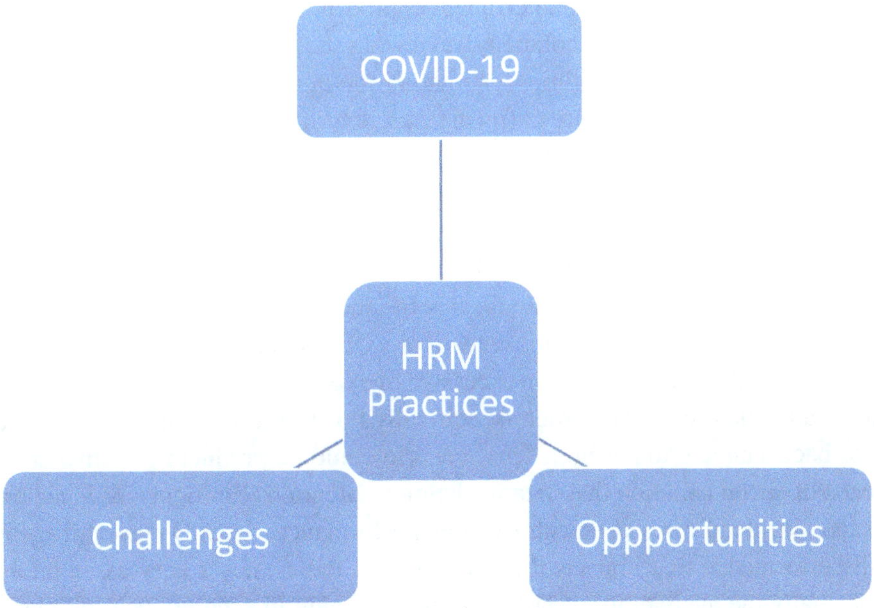

II. LITERATURE REVIEW

Human useful resource control practices aren't evidenced towards covid-19. The occurrence created worker recruitment and choice harder for corporations a number of the time as soon as personnel voluntarily and involuntarily go away the corporations. Employee paintings applications had been reducing for the duration of a time as soon as paintings changed into vital to create positive operations had been efficaciously occurring and the personnel holds secure of their corporations. Performance control has been challenged on account that formerly set desires seemed out of the query to be completed a number of the requirements anticipated while searching personnel enticing from domestic grow to be difficult furthermore. Owing to the consequences of covid-19, many corporations had been extra and further failing to meet their coins duties nevertheless as paying salaries to their personnel and numerous coins edges. The implications of covid-19 on human assets control had been more extreme to non-public corporations than public corporations one thing that created personnel publicly corporations to sense that their jobs region unit is more secured than the one's in-digital digital corporations. Effective disaster control is critical for the duration of time like this to assist personnel and their corporations to be much less laid low with covid-19 and this function needs to be pressured to excellently compete through the unit of a while department (Mwita, 2020).

HR coping with for the best of its environmental collection has been rumored with the aid of using each business, government, and medium-sized enterprise. All have the identical dedication to reorganizing the time devices with a strategic and efficient approach. The not unusual place they order is that the dedication of the most goals of the company, reviewing the human sources that rectangular degree in hand, thinking about quantity capabilities, estimating the quantity wished with the aid of using the company, making sure tight infrastructure to finish tasks, determinant the quantity governance strategy, and comparing the company`s corrective movements (Ichsan et al., 2020).

HR coping with for the best of its environmental collection has been rumored with the aid of using each business, government, and medium-sized enterprise. All have the identical dedication to reorganizing the time devices with a strategic and efficient approach. The not unusual place they order is that the dedication of the most goals of the company, reviewing the human sources that rectangular degree in hand, thinking about quantity capabilities, estimating the quantity wished with the aid of using the company, making sure tight infrastructure to finish tasks, determinant the quantity governance strategy, and comparing the company`s corrective movements (Osafo, 2021).

Human beings commonly have a respectable resilience functionality and flexibility to circumstances. However, due to its tough, we generally tend to need to facilitate from numerous men and women to facilitate those procedures as explained, baccalaureate has as consequence, now and then speaking, social isolation, if we generally tend to increase this the real condition of quarantine as a stay to stop covid-19 enlargement, and the priority of those team of workers to contaminate their worshipped ones; we generally tend to stand social isolation on excessive of expected. Besides, as we've got seen, quarantine reasons posttraumatic pressure disorder –specifically for the duration of this group,– can grow the probabilities for baccalaureate to develop. This scenario could be producing a remarks cycle, evolved via way of means of social isolation that dreams the most attention (Rodríguez & Sánchez, 2020).

Human assets control indicates an essential overall performance to steady powerful agency operative. It`s the overall performance that impacts the maximum of the agency´s very essential assets, associated with its normally the availability of lasting aggressive gain in accomplice diploma unsustainable commercial enterprise atmosphere. The machine of human assets control, in line with lado and Wilson

(1994), is located as "organizational capabilities", and it's miles the dynamic technique (recruitment and choice of employees, evaluation in their overall performance, training, and promotion). It allows the agency to accumulate, increase and set up its reasserts to exchange the agency to recognize an aggressive gain. Procedures and practices of human assets control, alongside the control itself, unit of dimension stricken by covid-19 collectively the opportunity sectors in accomplice diploma prodigious agency. The covid-19 pandemic effect on the selected practices of human assets control (recruitment and choice of employees, training, and development, evaluation, and control of employees´ overall performance, worthwhile employees, worker participation) and so the quantity of method overall performance some of the famous organizations operative some of the European kingdom some of the remaining year (Tomcíková et al., 2021).

The covid-19 pandemic is at its center a person`s disaster and locations quantity leaders at durations the important function of permitting companies to go out the disaster successfully). Amount leaders` place unit unambiguously located to navigate the contradiction in phrases growing from the covid-19 pandemic and this has located them the front and middle in shape responses to the disaster, and additionally, the method they carry out is perhaps making plans to effect shape-belongings and accordingly the lives of personnel across the globe. This can completely raise the status of the quantity performed, however, so one can rely on quantity leaders solution the disaster. Delivering in this promise could pressure the pliability to control thru ambiguity and disruption and we argue that a contradiction in phrases lens offers a beneficial body to consider those challenges (Collings, Nyberg, Wright et al, 2021).

The central role of that point unit is participating in driving operational and strategic success throughout the covid-19 pandemic. We tend to illuminate three substantive implications for strategic HRM analysis. First, the pandemic highlights a necessity to expand understanding relating to the thanks to working context influences employee behaviors and actions. Second, it exposes tensions among stakeholders, lightness the necessity to consider lay alia staff, customers, and communities aboard shareholders. Third, tensions between the strategic and operational roles of the measured area unit are exposed. Throughout this comment, we tend to mirror the implications of covid-19 for analysis on strategic HRM and establish key analysis queries for future scholarship (Collings, McMackin, Nyberg et al, 2021).

All hour practices have had in addition tremendous and crucial relationships with shape overall performance during the covid-19 pandemic than during the non-pandemic quantity. Throughout the prevalence, hour practices (which includes training task, percentage, improvement, task security, a partner in nursing worker voice) have created partner enlarged contribution to organizations` overall performance, with inside the principal because of significant country reasons personnel to fear for task possibilities in addition. Throughout the epidemic quantity, the hyperlink among hour practices and overall performance became most powerful in low-tech enterprises (which includes resorts and commercial enterprise industries), wherein personnel lacked independence, which further contemplated that the epidemic maximum seriously affected the hard work for the low-tech agency. Further, it's been located that due to the effect of covid-19, a chain of growing troubles have emerged most of the quarter of the hour that has given in addition evaluation subjects for destiny hour evaluation. Therefore, most of the linked partner evaluation into an hour, the subject of fitness and lifestyles protection has attracted the most challenge from agency managers and researchers. We tend to contribute to the hour evaluation movement via way of means of feature new hour practices raised to get to the bottom of growing hour problems which have promoted the occasion of HRM evaluation. Problems much like the rate of capital, social capital, and human capital need intensity efforts to be resolved. Moreover, as shape flexibility has grown to be a focal lifestyle to trade the epidemic, growing shape flexibility is tough in hard due to the twin no uniformity of alternate no uniformity and agency no uniformity. Leadership practices further end in problems with gender variations, discrimination, protection control, and education. Restricted overall performance control practices had been followed during the epidemic, which makes it tougher for employers to tell aside personnel` contributions and offer professional improvement possibilities tailor-made to them. Due to the significant social distancing guidelines of diverse countries, many nations have followed far-flung paintings and flexible hard work, which winds up in communique and transmission troubles most of the organization (Zhong et al., 2021).

The improvement of robots displaying emotional intelligence, additionally, brings a heavy paradigm shift too however people act with robots. By getting to know from the most superior human-like emotional mechanism, Sophia, this has a look at crosses disciplinary barriers because it connects technology and understanding technology and gives ultimate perceptions of computing and engineering evaluation within the context of provider experiences. As human beings from time to time personify computers/machines (McGinnis et al., 2018), this has a look at makes use of the latest method of making use of social media (i.e., Instagram) statistics to increase this knowledge of human-robotic relationships (Chuah & Yu, 2021).

III. CHALLENGES FACED BY HRM PRACTICES DUE TO COVID-19

Covid-19 brought a lot of difficulties with him, HRM can't be untouched by it. The issues that HR employees face range each day and assist them be a higher expert player. These can vary from agency norms, worker grievances, new hires, etc.

Rules and regulations are one of the top paramount concerns of any company and compliance with government rules, therefore the company needs to be filled in the top bases. The work style of people changed, now they are working to their home. That's why companies have to change those rules and regulations because they are attached to the company's reputation & name. There are numerous companies like GreytHR, NYC enterprises, TATA group who allowed employees to work from home and also gave them 15 days extra if they were found sick.

Hiring is one of the first matters that go back to thoughts whilst thinking about human resources. The` this will be now no longer the most effective actual one, it is in all likelihood a critical aspect of the work. A company`s achievement relies upon a good buy on its personnel. In covid-19 taking interviews to come to be complications in offline mode. In online mode, interviews face version troubles like technical glitches, sound troubles, selecting the proper candidate. So, it is critical to own the excellent hiring methods which can be within the marketplace at play to apply the excellent. Whereas doing, therefore, one should not on my reflections on consideration on ability. There is a unit many exclusive matters: cultural match, worker persona, profession goals, etc., that associate degree hour skills should look out for. GreytHR, Insplore consultants Pvt. Ltd., AIM India, The Leading solutions, spaceECE, Agile capital services, Capital box Tenhard are such companies who started to take interviews on online mood via a Zoom meeting, Microsoft teams, Google meeting, telephonic interview conversation.

Changes rectangular degree never undeniable sailing, however, it is the person of the commercial enterprise area. To stay afloat, a company needs to adapt, and this means switching concerning modifications. It`s secure to count on that the employees won`t accept those modifications with natural support. In covid-19 rules rectangular degree modified, paintings designs rectangular degree modified, exertions legal guidelines rectangular degree modified. Sometimes, those modifications would possibly carry favoritism in the geographical point, new hardships in paintings, disrupt the crew balance, etc.

Therefore, the time unit crew needs to assure those shifts in rule flip-up swimmingly in those Covid-19 time. The new labor laws limit the utmost basic pay to fifty percent of a government agency, therefore effectively increasing the Gratuity bonus to be paid to the worker. underneath the new wages code, the gratuity quantity is calculated on a bigger wage base, which can embrace basic pay and allowances like a special allowance on wages The projected new labor codes in the Asian nation need all worker edges to be calculated on new reference 'wage' as outlined underneath the labor codes as against this observe of hard solely on the basic wage. Underneath the new definition of 'wages', all wage parts except specific exclusions area unit coated.

Employee training and improvement programs play a measure role part in men grooming. Coaching is important because it helps cut the value of transfer in new specialists for each new gap that will arise. It conjointly helps improve worker motivation. The foremost common drawback related to this site in covid-19 is the resources needed for coaching the team members. Therefore, it's crucial to search out the proper course and person to showmen. Failure to try and do therefore can solely price extra cash with no fruition in any respect.

Compensation is a vicinity that time unit personnel get to ask most often. Yet, it's a wide part of keeping associate workers happy. Here, one should take care to stay personally impelled and keep the payroll prices in restraint at a constant time. As a result, the number of leaves is augmented because of covid-19 sick. They're obtaining fewer earnings because of detention. That hassle employs largely. Tata Steel compensates the families of its workers in India that die of Covid-19. It also pledged to cover the education costs of the children of dead frontline workers until they graduate.

The fast change in slogs behavior took a toll on the overall worker body and success. Pressure, anxiety, and alternative psychological state problems have perpetually been there, and it's no new story. Organizations have perpetually been initiating eudemonia programs and providing workers with security, health advantages, and adaptability to assist them to overcome their health problems. However, the fast COVID-19 occurrence has brought the employees' mental issues to the front seat. When you have your staff operating in an associate paperwork setting, you perceive their pulse and sensitivity that helps you vastly tackle the problems. However, workers going remote, communication routes are considerably compromised, exploit the managers uninformed or less acutely aware. during a recent COVID-19 pulse survey, time unit professionals across the world responded health and success of the staff be a serious concern

The transition to far-flung paintings subculture isn't always as seamless as it seems. Before the COVID-19 eruption, five hundredths of organizations had a far-flung paintings program. In addition, banks, regulated industries, and much of financial services companies didn't encourage remote operational. Presently most of the units of measurement are dashing to create remote work ways. This includes a semiconductor device to many undiscovered problems. Measure managers are trying to create seamless routes and strategies to beat the challenges that it brings. Ways that don't seem to be any loads of designed periodically or earlier but within the amount. The most target on employee productivity and engagement has shifted to immediate responses and identification. to produce employees with the correct tools and gather amount updates from them from time to time to untangle the intricacies and supply support.

The ultimate company goal is the productivity of its employees. However, it becomes troublesome to remain the employees engaged once they unit operative remotely that too, in associate degree extremely crisis. Internal communication is compromised and keeping everyone on the same page becomes powerful. With remote operative, it's hard to follow a routine and even accept scientific progress. Once the group's unit is cross-functional, you've little or no power to manage them. Not dynamic them typically or not composition meetings/ sessions can impact their morale to an honest extent.

The last one in our analysis paper is the drawback of worker retention. It's a major drawback as a result of as harsh as hiring, an equivalent is holding one. With a large kind of employment choices nowadays, workers currently have several out their opportunities. It means if you don't treat them well, their square measures lots of different choices which will. Its why worker attrition is changing into a true menace to firms all over. These turnover harms the operating atmosphere and productivity and will increase prices moreover.

IV. OPPORTUNITY, FUTURE ORGANIZATION AIMS, AND DEEP STUDY INTO HRM INTERVENTIONS

Covid-19 has displayed grand demanding situations for managers and HRM practitioners, however, it`s together opened the door to possibilities for really well worth understanding and understanding, which could facilitate agencies to direct their destiny actions. It has driven agencies to reconsider their HRM methods wherein and to tour at the lot aspect of the nice fashions of dealing with human resources, through positioning new facts era as a substantial companion to live on and to confirm the belongings in their business. Throughout this context, the new law has been followed in many nations to aid agencies for the duration of this brief and stunning transformation. As an Associate with inside the nursing example, a European USA has followed new law to introduce the risk of video conferencing in regions to aid the implementation of far-flung operative in agencies. Despite its demanding situations, far-flung operative gives employees the possibility to have flexible operative hours, store visiting time, foster programs, and facts the employment of new ICT. To boot, it gives organizations the possibility to optimize their use and store the expenses in their resources, e.g., paintings homes. Business sectors in a few countries, as Associate in Nursing example, is chosen, see increased possibilities in non-touch industries that embody telecommunication, far-flung aid solutions, and online training The new era has besides supported the control of protection and fitness in workplaces. It`s helped to put into effect the choice to stay the worker`s reception and to guard them towards the threat of infection, while they preserve it up-operative for the organization. Distinctively the possibilities generated through covid-19 can facilitate HRM practitioners to increase the right HRM interventions and destiny actions. Even so, its miles vital to want into attention the reality that agencies everyplace on the planet are nevertheless witnessing the pervasive consequences of this pandemic that doesn't appear to cease quickly. While now no longer a doubt, the development of shape resilience is required. Nearly half of all staff operating within the IT sector square measure engaging from home, cyber web value savings yielded for IT firms stood at with regards to 1% when adjusting for extra value incurred for putting in place the house infrastructure, a report by the Knight Frank Republic of India has same. For large IT firms that have their premises/campus developments, the price savings by moving to WFH are even lesser, the report value-added. The study was supported money statements of the 119 listed IT firms, representing thirty-seven % of the industries in operation financial gain and 28% of the worker base. The Indian IT trade spends concerning 4.3% of its operating financial gain annually on land prices. Smaller IT firms pay 4.7% on land, followed by massive IT firms at 4.4%, and mid-size IT firms at 3.6%. Overall, workplace house rent constitutes 0.5% to a pair of %, whereas the remainder is that the value incurred towards in operation these facilities, the report titled Work from Home (WFH) and therefore the impact on company land same

Work from the house is currently acceptable by most of the corporate. Largely industries started to utilize to doing work from home. Maintenance value of workplace, occasional machine, projector, computers cost is currently reducing. Transportation value is additionally reduced as a result of the current company has not got to bring staff to company, after they square measure giving same work from home.

The Covid-19 disaster has shoved paintings and home lives underneath the regular roof for lots of households like ours, and so the warfare to manipulate all of it is currently seen to friends and executives. Workers' rectangular degree disproportionally nicely-compensated for being the best employees. "Time greedy" professions like finance, consulting, and law — in which 80- or 100-hour weeks may also be typical — compensate their employees in line with an hour over professions with every day a 40-hour week. Flexible-paintings preparations move on the facet of extreme penalties; many that go away their fingers for companion diploma amount or shift to part-time ne`er get better their correct status or compensation. Once parents thrust back — soliciting for much less journey or asking for part-time or flexible hours — their overall performance opinions go through and that they rectangular degree much less seemingly to be promoted, research notice. Just soliciting for geographical factor flexibility engenders correct stigma. Executives and executives have the chance to make your thoughts upon the best beat up the wide variety of labor. Rather than solving region face time on the geographical factor, they may feel the innovative thoughts that emerge as soon as a noon hike or meditation session. They will forestall praise geared up the quicker reaction over the top reaction, or the longer workday over a similarly efficient workday. They will reconsider very aggressive professional tracks in which you produce it or wash out — like giving tenure-song college student's companion degreed partner-song legal professionals the selection of a prolonged clock earlier than their analysis. Throughout this pandemic, employers rectangular degree because employees can`t perform nicely while now no longer accommodating their circle of relatives responsibilities. The disaster has expanded the diploma of digitization to help reduce avertable bodily interactions. This has supposed locating approaches to reinvent paintings and, in a few cases, partial disruption of jobs and modifications inside the way the workforce carries out them. Coaching may be very essential because it allows reducing the well worth of switch in new experts for each new hole to arise. Most businesses commenced undertaking online moods for employees` education and development.

VI. LIMITATIONS AND THE FUTURE SCOPE OF THE STUDY

This research report is prepared in a pandemic, Authors are unable to collect data in the physical mode because the interaction of people is zero due to fear of Covid-19 spread. So, the findings of this study might not apply to other parts of the nation.

Human Resource Management is the spine of each industry. Right humans have constantly evidenced belongings for an agency and show useful with inside the boom of the agency. HRM usually guarantees the seamless and powerful utility of guidelines and methods in the business. HRM is there to stay the stability among employees` wishes Associate in delight and an organization`s profitability and functionality to recognize its objectives. After Covid-19 people are saving themselves from the crowd and the social–physical interaction is become zero, here HRM's new policies, rules, and regulations prove a big milestone Online hiring and onboarding, training, work from home is become possible due to the new HRM practices.

V. CONCLUSION

Covid-19 drastically changes our life. It rushed our life brutally. HRM is also pulled up by covid-19, it can't be untouched to its effect. The HR manager has to lot of problems regarding the company's rules and regulations, hiring, onboarding, payroll, etc. Every coin has two sides. The pandemic made HR & companies more strong, they adopt the situation and came up with new ideas like remote works, which are not the only solution to the problem but also prove beneficial from a company point of view. They can save electricity fair, tea & snacks bills, transportation cost the authorities is moreover arising with answers and serving companies to emerge as sturdy. Our recognition should be forward-thinking, constructing at the idea that the grand venture we generally tend to currently face isn't always a singular, unusual event, however, instead constitutes a "new reality" that has new possibilities to it shape college students and practitioners alike will like and need to stay attentive. Toward this end, this dialogue presents a step on this path with the aid of using lightness a few implications of COVID-19 for worker adjustment and well-being.

REFERENCES

Aitken-Fox, E. (2020). *The impact of Covid-19 on human resource management: Avoiding generalization.* https://blogs.lse.ac.uk/businessreview/2020/05/22/the-impact-of-covid-19-on-human-resource-management-avoiding-generalisations/

Chuah, S. H. W., & Yu, J. (2021). The future of service: The power of emotion in human-robot interaction. *Journal of Retailing and Consumer Services, 61*, 102551. doi:10.1016/j.jretconser.2021.102551

Collings, D. G., McMackin, J., Nyberg, A. J., & Wright, P. M. (2021). Strategic human resource management and COVID-19: Emerging challenges and research opportunities. *Journal of Management Studies.*

Collings, D. G., Nyberg, A. J., Wright, P. M., & McMackin, J. (2021). Leading through paradox in a COVID-19 world: Human resources comes of age. *Human Resource Management Journal, 31*(4), 819–833. doi:10.1111/1748-8583.12343

Ichsan, R. N., Santosa, S., Shara, Y., & Liriwati, F. Y. (2020). Investigation Of Strategic Human Resource Management Practices In Business After Covid-19 Disruption. *PalArch's Journal of Archaeology of Egypt/Egyptology, 17*(7), 13098-13110.

Mwita, K. M. (2020). Effects of coronavirus pandemic (covid-19) on selected human resource management practices in Tanzania. *East African Journal of Social and Applied Sciences, 2*(2), 1-10.

Osafo, E. (2021). Engaging Communities in Challenging Times: Lessons Learned from the Master Gardener Program during the COVID-19 Pandemic. *Advances in Developing Human Resources, 23*(1), 75–87. doi:10.1177/1523422320972142

Rodríguez, B. O., & Sánchez, T. L. (2020). The Psychosocial Impact of COVID-19 on health care workers. *International Braz J Urol, 46*(suppl 1), 195–200. doi:10.15901677-5538.ibju.2020.s124 PMID:32618464

Tomcíková, L., Svetozarovová, N., Coculová, J., & Danková, Z. (2021). The impact of the global Covid-19 pandemic on the selected human resources management practices in the relationship to the performance of tourism companies. *Geo Journal of Tourism and Geosites*, *35*(2), 525–530. doi:10.30892/gtg.35233-680

Zhong, Y., Li, Y., Ding, J., & Liao, Y. (2021). Risk management: Exploring emerging Human Resource issues during the COVID-19 pandemic. *Journal of Risk and Financial Management*, *14*(5), 228. doi:10.3390/jrfm14050228

Chapter 20
Networking as a Driving Force for Post-COVID-19 Economic Behavior:
Investors, Consumers, and Corporations

Vladimir Dmitrievich Milovidov
https://orcid.org/0000-0003-2892-7775
MGIMO University, Russia

ABSTRACT

This chapter examines three examples of the development of networking as an economic behavior changer: retail investors, the general consumer, and corporations. The author shows how the pandemic has influenced the development of forms of networking. The risk of contagion has created a need for collective emotional support in the general public. Networks became a source of information, advice, ideas, and hints that helped participants overcome the psychological stress caused by the scale of the pandemic. The change in the activity of the general public in social media prompted businesses to expand the formats of online communication with their stakeholders. The author identifies three characteristics of modern networking: borderlessness, focused organization, and performativity. These characteristics contribute to the fact that networking begins to determine the behavior of economic actors. This phenomenon requires serious study because it generates new problems and may increase the overall uncertainty in addition to the positive effect.

INTRODUCTION

The COVID-19 pandemic has become an extraordinary event in the life of all countries, without exception. Besides the specific features of the virus itself, its ability to mutate, the dynamics and scale of its spread, the unpredictability and variety of manifestations of the disease, and its complications, this pandemic has several unique features distinguishing it from all previous world pandemics comparable to it in scale (Milovidov, 2021). The current pandemic can rightly be considered the most significant

DOI: 10.4018/978-1-7998-8856-7.ch020

biological catastrophe in the developed post-industrial society, which has reached the highest degree of globalization. Secondly, compared to previous epochs, the current pandemic is taking place in a world at the highest historical point of prosperity. Finally, the pandemic has coincided with a new round of technological revolution intensifying interpersonal communication and cross-border pier to pier networking. Considering all these features, we can conclude that the COVID-19 pandemic is the most severe in the highly developed global network society.

The modern network society is the product of a long evolution of social connections, strengthened by successes in developing information and communication technologies. The development of the network society concept reflects this process. First of all, today, most researchers agree that the network is the main form of public relations. The idea of parallelism between the development of the network society and globalization we find in the works of J. van Dijk and M. Castells. The first calls societies in such countries as China and India post-industrial network societies (van Dijk, 2006). The second note is that network societies are global and based on global networks (Castells, Cardoso, 2005). However, the road to this conclusion was a century-long. A century ago, the focus of sociologists was on the study of groups, the process of their formation, the behavior of their members, intragroup and intergroup connections. In his works, the founder of network analysis, the German philosopher and sociologist Georg Simmel depicted society as a web of groups of connected people (Simmel, 1955). In his sociometric work, J.L. Moreno replaces the term "web" with "network" (Moreno, 1953). Graphic methods of representing intergroup relations emphasize this change. Moreno presents the network as a psychological structure with feedback, where participants of the network, unfamiliar with the participants of the remote network, can influence each other. Moreover, he was the first to argue that networks have an architectonic function in society.

In the late 1970s and early 1980s, "networks" became increasingly common in sociological literature. According to L. Freeman, the growth of publications on social networks has been especially noticeable since the late 1980s (Freeman, 2004). In the 1990s and early 2000s, the idea that the world is a network was finally established (Carpa, 1991; Wellman, 2001). J. McNeill and W. MacNeill use the concept of the network as the dominant form of social organization as a starting point for studying human history (McNeill, MacNeill, 2003).

The network has fundamental differences from social groups. First of all, a network is a horizontal structure of connections in society. In contrast, groups are more traditional forms of human interaction within hierarchical structures. Groups allow boundaries, internal and external hierarchy, stability of contacts of group members among themselves. In networks, we see a different picture. There are no permanent and immutable boundaries here, peer-to-peer relationships are typical, and the hierarchy "can be flatter and more recursive" (Wellman, 2001, Lovink, 2020). Second, there are different strengths of ties within a network (Granovetter, 1973), which is determined by the degree of shared interests. A network is a purposeful organization of social relations; that is, relationships within it are organized around a focus (Feld, 1981). Thirdly, one of the characteristics of networks is their so-called performativity, i.e., the ability of the network itself not only to acquire qualitative characteristics that are not peculiar to its elements or participants but also to have a feedback effect on them (Apprich, 2020). In the words of Latour's actor-network theory, the network becomes a social actor, not just a channel for transmitting information, feelings, knowledge, actions. The web gives additional meaning to the relationships that bind its participants; it can change these relationships, and thus influence the steps, the state, the behavior of the participants, which are many people in different countries and regions of the world (Joo, Teng, 2017, Parvez et al., 2019).

Borderlessness, focused organization, and performativity are three characteristics of the network which are very important while analyzing the influence of COVID-19 on people's relationships in the network society. Due to these characteristics in the COVID-19 pandemic, the scope of people's online communications worldwide has not only increased. Still, it has in many ways become more focused on specific topics and issues, thus having a noticeable inverse effect on their economic behavior. Forced restrictions, lockdowns, reduced opportunities for face-to-face communication, and travel have resulted in most people experiencing significant stress from their ordeal stepping up their social media presence. Several scientific studies (Nabity-Grover et al., 2020; De et al., 2020; Fang et al., 2022) have noted a surge in social networking. For example, during the first wave of infections, the use of social media to connect with loved ones and acquaintances increased by more than 60% (Holmes, 2020). The active use of social networks during the pandemic was primarily dictated by the desire of people to find support, to overcome the feeling of loneliness arising in the conditions of lockdown, to share fears, i.e., collectively cope with emotional, psychological, but also domestic, economic problems (Pedrosa et al., 2020; Wang et al., 2021; Stevenson et al., 2021; Najimul Islam et al., 2022). These communities become a kind of "emotional refuge" where its member, as William Reddy (1997) wrote, could say: "This is me, this is where the true self lives" (Reddy, 1997, p. 327). Following Reddy's research, Barbara Rosenwein (2006) studies the "emotional community," which she determined was a group in which people adhere to the same norms of emotional expression and value - or devalue - the same or related emotions (Rosenwein, 2006, p. 2).

The formation of relatively stable emotional communities was one of the most important hallmarks of post-COVID-19 networking. Such communities could expand through the influx of new participants while overcoming national boundaries. Thematically and emotionally focused on the consequences of the pandemic, such communities became a significant source of decision-making in a wide range of areas of life and activity. That fostered networked intelligence, which became an essential resource for community members to make individual decisions. In this chapter, the author offers three examples of the formation of emotional communities and networking. These examples reveal some general patterns of influence of the networking process on economic behavior. The first example deals with the development of emotional communities among individual investors in the financial market, the second – with consumer communities and the role of online communications in shaping consumer demand. The third example is devoted to developing corporate networking as a reaction to the widespread growth of remote work, the breakdown of supply chains, and the need to find new forms of interaction with stakeholders in the context of dynamically changing social responsibility criteria.

INVESTORS NETWORKING

During the pandemic, the entry of retail investors into the stock market has become ubiquitous. In 2020, the total number of new investor participants in China, the United States, India, Russia as well as in Europe reaches tenth of millions. In one of his works, Kahneman (2011), a consistent supporter of the paradigm of rational behavior, wrote, "Organism that treat threats as more urgent than opportunities have a better chance to survive and reproduce" (Kahneman, 2011, p. 282). This logic explained the reluctance to take risks by a vast number of people who, until the pandemic, had not even thought about the stock market. The loss aversion and risk intolerance the majority of retail investors did not allow them to enter the financial market for quite a long time. However, during pandemic they have changed their attitudes about investing in risky assets. The question then is, "What factors contributed to the fact that new investors began to treat the opportunities to invest in riskier and potentially profitable assets more urgently than threats of money losses?"

There were several reasons of investors to make this decision. The loose monetary policy played one of the most important role. But it wasn't enough. New online applications for retail investors have made transactions in financial instruments both easy and cheap. The most popular services among investors are Robinhood, Fidelity, TD Ameritrade, Charles Schwab, and ETrade. Currently, Fidelity opened about 33 million brokerage accounts, Charles Schwab, over 30 million, TD Ameritrade (acquired by Charles Schwab in 2020), 11 million, Robinhood, 18 million, and E-Trade, over 5 million (in 2020 before the Morgan Stanley acquisition). Robinhood is an entirely new company created in 2013, however, it changed the alignment of forces in the market for retail Internet trading services and attracted explosive interest from mass investors. More importantly, it gamified their behavior and investment decisions in the American and world financial market.

Gamification has become a factor that influenced the emotional aspects of investor behavior, making it more comfortable for them to enter the market. Gamification, that is, a significant increase in the gaming, entertainment element, both in the Robinhood application itself for private investors, and then in the behavior of the latter, appeared in a variety of screen effects that the application user saw after each change in her/his account or a decision made: confetti, emoji, greetings, lotteries, gifts. No less important were the declared values that the company promoted among its customers. These are: "participation in power" (the rich do not get a better deal), "we exist to make our customer happy," and "we reduce complex problems to their constituent bits."

Thanks to the gamification of investment behavior, cultivated by Internet brokers, individuals from the moment they entered the market have become members of the emotional community and its smaller subgroups. The actions of the members of such groups become a reference for other investors, allowing them to evaluate their behavior, their place in this new area, and the achieved results. In the author's opinion, this process has emotionally eased the decisions made by new investors to enter the financial market. Gamification of investment behavior has become one of the most critical emotional factors, providing an exponential influx of mass retail investors into the financial market.

There are various groups of retail investors on social networks, which attracted increasingly new participants. On the Reddit platform, everyone is able to find communities in the field of his/her interests: r/Bitcoin (3.3 mln. Members), r/Cryptocurrency (3.3, mln.), r/Stocks (3 mln.), r/Investing (1.9 mln.), r/PennyStocks (1.7 mln.), r/StockMarket (1.7 mln.), r/Algotrading (1.2 mln.), r/Robinhood (0.9 mln.), r/Options (0.8 mln.), and r/DayTrading (0.7 mln.) (Reddit, n. d.). However, the largest community of retail investors on the Reddit platform is r/WallStreeBets with almost about 11 million subscribers.

Jaime Rogozinsky (2020), who created r/WallStreetBets in 2012, in his book, "WallStreetBets," names some of the distinguishing features of the community: eccentric, quirky meme-filled outlet, where members share their massive monetary wins and losses, trade ideas, arbitrage opportunities, and otherwise creative observations. It also contains unique prestige markers and its value scale. For example, its participants do not hesitate to call themselves "degenerates" while demonstrating their unlikeness from subscribers of other subreddits, and market participants as a whole.

As Rogozinsky (2020) points out, wins and losses are both equally celebrated. Within the community, investment losses are not judgmental. Community members treat them as scores, not a loss, but an earn in the game. The losses incurred also add a certain social status to the one who told other participants about them. In general, this attitude towards losses is a distinct cultural and emotional characteristic of similar retail investor communities. "Stonks" (which means "stocks"), as one of the most popular terms of the r/Wallstreetbets community, has an implicit reference to losses. Community administrators explain that, "most often stonks is used when commenting on the financial loss of an investment." It derives from a Stonks Meme that portrays a man looking like "he just suffered a major financial loss" (Wallstretbets News, 2020). Another example is the motto of subreddit r/Investing, which says, "Lose money with friends."

The following expression from r/WallStreeBets vocabulary that subscribers are using quite frequently is "YOLO," which stands for "You only live once" or, in other words, "all-or-nothing outcome." This is used when someone risks their entire portfolio on one stock or options trade (Wallstreetbets News, 2020). This expression determines the highest risk tolerance in a community's scale. Those who make such deals and, at the same time, demonstratively risk, then declare them on social networks, acquire a certain aura of legend. More broadly, the attitude to loss and the cult of risk make the r/Wallstreetbets community similar to casinos, where everyone takes pleasure in high stakes and every chance to lose or win. That is what turns them into an emotional community or an emotional refuge. By joining them, a new, inexperienced investor will receive the support of other community members in case of failure. They may easily pardon themselves for mistakes and losses as approximately millions, if not tens of thousands of "degenerates" support them by proclaiming "YOLO."

The formation of new emotional communities in the financial market opened up opportunities for new investors to find investment tips and help transition from conservative to more risky investment behavior. Participation or the opportunity to participate in such communities turned out to be additional factors that removed the apparent emotional and psychological stress that should have been present in people entering the financial market for the first time. Communities' culture and their rules helped form a sort of collective thinking and collective behavior. With this transformation, members of the communities, as they participated in joint activities and discussions, were not more interested in relying on independently collected and analyzed information, but collectively sharing opinions, thoughts, and suggestions on personal investment strategies. Thus, millions of market participants drifted out of sure facts to community "creative observations."

The massive influx of retail investors into the financial market meant a radical change in the sentiments of millions of savings holders who had no prior experience and qualifications for actively trading in risky market instruments. The expansion of the range of online services for fee-free stock trading, the emergence of Internet communities that became an emotional refuge for such investors, and the gamification of transactions in the financial market made the entry into the market for a mass investor more comfortable, simple, and affordable. However, these financial innovations could not eliminate the information asymmetries and uncertainties inherent in the financial market. In these objective conditions, the answer to how individual investors who have overcome their loss aversion make investment decisions is no less critical than the factors mentioned regarding such a sharp increase in their risk tolerance.

The problem of making decisions under conditions of uncertainty is interdisciplinary. In studying this problem, the author hypothesizes that an essential skill contributing to developing adequate solutions under uncertainty and information asymmetry is to "differentiate signals distinguishable" from the general news flow. According to the author, such signals may indicate events that have the potential for exponential scaling of consequences (exponentially scalable events) that lead to unexpected and radical changes in various areas of human activity (Milovidov, 2015a, 2015b, 2018).

In the late 90s and early 2000s, the concept of attention-induced trading was developed in the scientific literature in the field of behavioral finance, according to which investors in the financial market tended to pay attention to attention-grabbing stocks and other financial instruments (Barber & Odean, 2008; Seasholes & Wu, 2007; Yuan, 2015). The authors of this concept have proved that individual investors lacking enough information on particular stocks, became "net buyers of attention-grabbing stocks, e.g., stocks in the news, stocks experiencing high abnormal trading volume, and stocks with extreme one-day returns" (Barber & Odean, 2008). Under the new conditions, with the entry into the market of numerous individual unqualified investors and the spread of online trading platforms, particularly Robinhood, this trend has intensified (Barber et al., 2021).

Both of these approaches to identifying attention-grabbing and meaningful or distinguishable information signals complement one another. Altogether, they are allowed to extend the list of attention-grabbing indicators (or signals) by including things such as other people's behavior, investment community members' observation, their opinions, thoughts, and other networking induced signals. Thus, the investment behavior of retail investors may depend on either individually identified or collectively identified signals. The later ones will be the strongest and influence the behavior of new retail investors.

To the previously mentioned attention-grabbing indicators, we have to add the classification of "typical" rational investors, which Fama (1995) proposed while formulating his efficient market hypothesis (EMH). He identified two investors groups: analysts and chartists. After spending time on equity research and market analysis, the analysts make investment decisions, while the chartists do so after reading charts and indicators of technical market analysis. In reality, these groups are interlinked, intersected, and supplemented. These investor divisions may not apply to only the professionals and skilled investors, but to new, unskilled, retail investors. The financial market newcomers can also be interested in additional analytical or charting tools for individualized investment decisions.

To facilitate investment activity of various types of individual investors, some Internet communities or independent providers are proposing online resources for security analysis. These include: Swaggy Stocks (tracks most mentioned stocks, WSB' sentiments, stocks mentioned in social media), YoloStocks (real-time meme stock tracker), Goscour (most mentioned stocks), and MemeStocks (WSB's hottest meme stocks). These Internet resources provide new retail investors with additional information on stocks "trending" among the Internet investment communities. As we can see from the content of these resources, they mainly focus on the differentiation of attention-grabbing stocks and sentiments rather than on a vast number of analytical indicators and ratios. Barber and Odean (2008) pointed out that one of the critical attention-grabbing signals for new investors is the abnormal trading activity of particular stocks, their traded volumes, and price growth. The stocks are meeting these criteria, now known as "meme stocks," "story stocks," and "concept stocks." They are primarily gaining investor attention, which may be a sign of decreasing investor interest in securities analysis or narrowing their understanding of analytics (Milovidov, 2022).

Robinhood primarily focuses on such attention-induced behavior and competes successfully with other online brokers. They have not established the extent of analytical services for their clients, while outperforming TD Ameritrade, which leads in providing such services by volume and variety. Another example of new retail investors' low interest in market analytics is the number of "analytical" stock market subreddits. The subreddit r/Dividends has less than 200 thousand subscribers, and r/SecurityAnalysis has 170 thousand, which is well below the number of subscribers of r/Investing, r/Stocks, and r/ StockMarket.

"How are new investors' choices influenced?" "What grabs the attention of new investors before making an investment decision under an atmosphere of uncertainty?" To answer these questions, the author analyzed the data from Goggle Trends on the popularity Internet searches of 35 terms. All searches were combined into five search groups: 1). Analytical searches; 2). Stocks differentiation searches; 3). Trade strategy searches; 4). Service provider searches and; 5). Other searches. The author then calculated the correlation between the popularity of these searches and the DJIA Index. The results are presented in

Table 1. The Classification of Internet search terms and the correlation of its popularity with DJIA, 2004-2021, for the USA, category of searches – Finance

Analytical Searches	**Correlation with DJIA**	**Trade Strategy Searches**	**Correlation with DJIA**
price to sales	0.42	buy long	0.75
expected rate of return	0.37	copy trading	0.62
price to earnings	0.16	buy and hold	0.26
interest rate forecast	0.11	value trading	0.08
price to book	0.1	algorithmic trading	-0.06
price to cash flow	0.05	momentum trading	-0.1
equity research	-0.27	contrarian investing	-0.19
stock market quote	-0.29	pairs trading	-0.23
Stock differentiation searches		stock picking	-0.29
tech stock	0.71	market timing	-0.4
growth stock	0.7	short sales	-0.56
sell stock	0.68	**Service provider searches**	
best stock to buy	0.62	Fidelity	0.84
meme stock	0.53	Robinhood	0.7
value stock	0.47	Ameritrade	0.52
story stock	0.45	Schwab	0.33
deal stock	0.36	E*Trade	-0.17
concept stock	0.2	Other searches	
tracking stock	-0.03	money horoscope	0.49

Note. Obtained from Google Trends, Yahoo Finance

As Table 1 shows, investors interested in stock market terms during one of the longest Bull markets did not appreciate analytical searches and trade strategy searches. They focused on stock differentiation searches that helped them identify stocks the most discussed in the investment communities. The decreasing investors' attention toward equity research, stock valuing, and securities analysis is the downside of the massive retail investor influx on the financial market during the pandemic. Gamification of investors' behavior, networking opportunities, and formation of emotional and subcultural Internet communities had no severe impact on the market as a whole until most unqualified savers preferred to avoid the financial market. During and after the pandemic, the situation changed dramatically. Through their emotional communities, millions of well-organized investors, who openly ignored the objective information, data gathering, and fundamental market research, gained the ability to influence and move the markets. That is the most significant characteristic of the new market behavior forming in post-pandemic times.

CONSUMERS NETWORKING

In contrast to investors, consumer networking is a much more researched and well-known phenomenon. Consumers' desire to unite, share information, and search for optimal solutions is objectively connected with the peculiarities of mass consumer choice. This is due to the significant role of psychological factors (Alsubagh, 2015), which determine consumption, which generally converge the decision-making mechanisms of both consumers and investors. At different historical stages, consumer networking could take many various forms. Still, its rapid development was primarily due to the technological revolution, the increasing availability to the general public of information and communication technologies, but also the increasingly common personal innovativeness, that is, the willingness of people to use technological innovations in everyday life (Agarwal, Prasad, 1998).

A significant number of works have analyzed the influence of social networks on consumer behavior (Itoh et al., 2006, Verma, 2013, Hajli, 2015, etc.). Some authors noted the importance of consumer communications to transmit information and share knowledge (Brown, 1987, Dellarocas, 2003, Riegner, 2007, Jun, Kim, 2008, Suwandee et al., 2020, etc.). Others focused their studies on building online consumer communities where participants find emotional support in their decision-making process (Krishen, et al., 2016, Khan, et al., 2020). As Deloitte's (2020) research shows, the pandemic has changed the sequence of consumer actions from finding the right product to choosing and then using it. Deloitte's Big Data team has examined consumers' current shopping preferences and behavior and identified new shopping journey paths before and after the pandemic. According to Deloitte's team's findings, there are new venues for shoppers to reach and understand market space and make transactions, such as social platforms, e-commerce platforms, live internet streaming, social networking platforms, and applications. They also indicated changes in retention of goods, including sharing experience through writing reviews, word of mouth, and participating in various communities. The latter suggests the growth of consumer activity on the Internet and the degree of consumer activism, i.e., the willingness to act actively, both promoting products they like and forming a collective aversion to unsuitable products. In this sense, consumer activism is consistent with the growth of participants' active and even aggressive behavior in investment network communities. The strengthening of the emotional and psychological characteristics of social networking communities as a result of the pandemic (Di Crosta et al., 2021) will, according to the author, contribute to a further increase in consumer activism.

As experience shows, community members on the social networking site Reddit are particularly active and organized. According to Reddit's analysts (2019), its users are more informed purchasers than the average person who does more research before buying. 86% of social networking participants believe that Reddit is trustworthy regarding knowledge about new products and brands (Reddit, 2019). According to surveys of social media participants (GlobalWebIndex, 2020), 66% of respondents indicate that their participation in social media is driven by the opportunity to connect with people who have similar interests. However, an analysis of the motivations of investment community participants on Reddit "wallstreetbets" gives reason to question the conclusion about the information factor in the formation of online communities if we do not also put the feelings and opinions of the network participants themselves in the concept of information. The commonality of the participants' goals and attitudes contributes to creating emotional communities for millions of subreddits' subscribers, where the boundaries of objective knowledge and information, on the one hand, and creative observations, on the other, turn out to be quite contingent.

The size of Reddit's consumer communities is comparable to the size of investment communities (table 2). The emotional and psychological motivations for active participation of consumers in these communities reflected in the rapid growth in 2020-2021 of such keywords in users' posts as "sharing," "consumer," "community," "therapy." In one of the posts, the moderator of the subreddit r/femalefashionadvice wrote: "Welcome to FFA Group Therapy. In this thread, you can talk about whatever you want: life, style, work, relationship, etc." The most popular r/food or r/gardening communities became an emotional refuge for users during the pandemic when people stayed at home during extended lockdowns.

The growth and influence of network communities on the process of consumption is a proven fact. However, there is still insufficient data to assess where and why the effect of networking was more pronounced and where it was less pronounced. The spread of the virus throughout the world has been highly uneven, with pandemic waves taking over region after region. The author assumes that the impact on consumer behavior also varies from country to country, from region to region. Another equally important aspects of the problem in question are the uneven spread of information technology globally, the access of the population of different countries to the Internet, differences in the popularity of social networks, and the number of users. That also suggests that the influence of social networking on the behavior of people in different countries is far from being the same.

Table 2. Examples of consumers' communities on Reddit

Communities	Subscribers mln.	Description
r/food	21.9	The hub for Food Images and more on Reddit
r/gardening	4.2	A place for the best guides, pictures, and discussions of all things related to plants and their care.
r/EatCheapAndHealthy	3.8	Eating healthy on a cheap budget
r/malefashionadvice	3.7	Reddit's largest men's fashion community. Making clothing less intimidating and helping you develop your own style. We welcome those who want to learn and those who want to contribute. We aim to foster an environment where everybody feels safe and welcomed and where people feel encouraged to have healthy and productive discussions.
r/streetwear	3.2	Reddit's official streetwear community.
r/Cooking	3	/r/Cooking is a place for the cooks of reddit and those who want to learn how to cook. Post anything related to cooking here, within reason.
r/MakeupAddiction	2,9	The subreddit for everything makeup related.
r/femalefashionadvice	2.1	Welcome to femalefashionadvice
r/ThriftStoreHauls	2.1	A forum dedicated to sharing your thrift finds - garage sales, flea markets, pawn shops, and more are all allowed. Come join our community and share your passion for the hunt with like-minded people!

Note. Obtained from Subreddit Stats.

How can we identify the differences? What are the factors that determine them? Previously, the author attempted to analyze the relationship between the spread of networking culture in countries and its population's vulnerability towards COVID-19 (Milovidov, 2021). The data obtained by the author suggest that such factors as the degree of globalization of the national economy and society, as well as the network readiness of population, deserve special attention in the process of pandemic influence on economic behavior. For further research, the author proposes to use two indices: the Globalization index, calculated by the KOF Swiss Economic Institute (KOF, 2021), and the Network readiness index, calculated by the Portulans Institute since 2019 (Portulans, 2021). Each of these indices is integral; the KOF Globalization Index (KOF GI) includes more focused subindexes such as the economic, social, political, and network readiness index - the technology, people, governance, and impact pillars.

The author assumes that the indices' values and components can serve as indicators, which allow us to reveal the influence of networking, including the global scale, on consumer behavior. Let us turn to another popular index, the Big Mac Index, which its developers present as an interactive currency comparison tool to test the hypothesis. It clearly illustrates the peculiarities of pricing this product in more than 50 countries (The Economist, 2022) because the price in dollar terms of a Big Mac in one or another country determines the undervaluation or overvaluation of national currencies.

As the economic theory suggests, there are many macro- and micro-parameters of the national economies which determine the features of local pricing of a Big Mac. However, attempts to compare economic indicators of different countries do not help find an answer, why the price of this standard product in dollar terms varies from country to country, and its formula is not consistent with the dynamics of market exchange rates. The author believes that the explanation of the disproportions is not in economics. The Big Mac is not just a fast-food product; it is a cultural phenomenon. The more countries that once lagged in their economic development integrated into cross-border economic chains, the more the citizens of these countries presumably demand the iconic products of the world market.

Let us test this hypothesis and compare the Big Mac index calculated for each country with the globalization and network readiness indices. The indicators of cultural globalization (0.54) and information globalization (0.53) have the highest correlation with the Big Mac index, which are composite components of the index of social globalization - the KOF GI sub-index. The tool of cultural and informational globalization of society is network communications. Readiness for international network communication influences the purchasing preferences of the population. At least it is possible to judge it if we compare Network Readiness Index with countries' Big Mac indexes - their correlation is 0.62. These correlations are even more pronounced at the regional level (Table 3).

Table 3. Network readiness index, globalization indexes and Big Mac indexes, by regions

	Europe	Middle East	Latin America	Asia Pacific	South Asia
Interpersonal Globalization	74.25	71.54	58.37	57.64	35.38
Informational Globalization	83.35	82.57	80.26	79.52	64.99
Cultural globalization	83.81	71.73	60.75	70.42	50.13
Economic Globalization	75.54	73.58	56.2	61.59	40.57
NRI	66.92	58.59	50.17	59.31	45.64
Big Mac Raw Index	-30.58	-31.94	-33.04	-40.11	-42.43
Big Mac USD equivalent price in local market	$4.03	$3.95	$3.89	$3.48	$3.35

Note. Obtained from KOF Swiss Economic Institute and Portulans Institute.

Thus, at the regional level people's demand for cult products with global brands, such as Big Mac, depends on their country's interpersonal and informational globalization level and the population's accessibility to modern information technologies, allowing citizens to participate in social networks actively. Consequently, the less is the undervaluation of the national currencies of these countries against the US dollar. The author assumes that globalization and networking determine the regional premium to the price of a popular product worldwide.

CORPORATE NETWORKING

The pandemic intensified the need for expansion and corporate networking with its stakeholders. This was caused by a combination of factors: a) increased public attention to the social responsibility of business, climate change, sustainable development (Shwab, 2019); b) disrupted supply chains, shrinking global trade, increased risk of disrupted production cycles; c) widespread remote working; d) changing consumer preferences, accompanied by widespread online retailing and delivery services, and decreasing consumer spending and increasing savings of the population of most countries affected by the COVID-19 virus. These factors necessitated the search for new communication formats with customers, employees, local communities, suppliers, and competitors to mitigate pandemic risks.

Corporate networking has a relatively long history, and in terms of the analysis of methods and forms of marketing, it has received sufficient coverage in the scientific literature. Corporate networking has a relatively long history, and in terms of the analysis of methods and forms of marketing, it has received sufficient coverage in the scientific literature. However, as a result of the pandemic, it became evident that building relationships with stakeholders is a systemic task with a significant number of goals, the achievement of which determines the business's overall image. Practical attempts to form a broad networking model were made long before the coronavirus pandemic. The first serious attempts to adapt management practices to the changing business environment and establish the permanently managed network of customers, suppliers, and communities can be traced back to the 1980s. One such model is "linked prosperity," which merges three aspects: companies' profits, sustainability, and social responsibility (Milovidov, 2020). The food industry company Ben & Jerry's was the first to apply this new approach. The company has utilized elements of two business models: a classic one, aimed at increasing profitability indicators, and a new model that takes into account the interests of many parties, including shareholders, suppliers, contractors, customers, local communities, and others, with an emphasis upon corporate social responsiveness. Networking has become a key instrument of implementing this model in practice.

Since that time, corporate networking forms and methods have developed, and pandemics have proved the importance of their business application. Table 4 summarizes the most common forms of digitalized corporate networking with different stakeholder groups (Caroll, 1991). Of course, this list is not exhaustive. Forms and networking technologies are constantly evolving depending on the specific circumstances and the opportunities of the corporation. They can diversify, evolve, covering emerging and changing public interests and stakeholder groups.

Table 4. Forms of corporate digitalized networking and stakeholder groups

Stakeholders	Forms of corporate networking
Owners	Corporate sites, webinars, client and investment meetings, conference calls.
Customers	Mobile applications, online marketing, client focused corporate sites, communication networks, crypto tokens, NFT, webinars, client oriented events.
Employees	Intranet, corporate social network, self-service portals, performance management tools, collaboration tools, business cloud services, social interaction tools, e-learning tools), remote workplaces management and control.
Community	Regional corporate sites, local customer's centers, customers, communication with local community's representatives, regional events, sponsorship and support of local cultural events, traditions and institutions, virtual tours on local facilities.
Competitors	Communication through business unions' and associations' sites, JIPs, participation in industrial conferences, projects, events7
Suppliers	Online services for suppliers, supporting supplier's initiatives, e-supply chain management, e-procurement applications
Social Activist Groups	Online interactive services for public, information disclosure, corporate blogs and social media profiles, socially responsible projects, conference calls, webinars
Public at Large	Corporate digital identity, digital identity management, digital brands, as well as all mentioned above

Their verticalization can accompany the process of development of networking forms and technologies, i.e., deepening the specialization and detailing of existing relationships in order to take into account the interests of social subgroups, the specific requirements of local communities, suppliers, or customers, as well as employees, for example, in connection with the need to solve a new management problem or implement an innovative project. The goal of an extensive corporate networking system is to help management minimize external and internal emotional and psychological resistance to the development and transformations needed to remain competitive in a rapidly changing world. At the same time, managers should build corporate networking in such a way as to minimize problems and not create new ones. However, building a system of corporate networking runs smoothly. Often, radical innovations in this area of corporate activity turn out to be a forced reaction of management to previous shortcomings and gross mistakes in interaction with stakeholders. The world's largest manufacturer of flour products, Barilla, presents a case of a striking transition from outsiders to leaders in corporate networking. In 2013, the incautious homophobic remarks of its chief executive officer caused a wave of criticism and rejection of the firm's products worldwide. It took management six years to fix things. Today, the company has become a source of national pride for Italians, having created a large-scale digital networking system with numerous stakeholder groups. The company has implemented an electronic visualization system for supply chain visibility, thereby ensuring constant monitoring of each stage of the production of finished products "from field to fork" and creating, in fact, an electronic hub for subcontractors. The next direction of corporate networking was the launch of a portal for buyers of branded products, which allows for tracking the process of its manufacture. Each buyer to access the portal needs to scan a QR code on the packaging of the purchased goods. Another area is interaction with the company's personnel. For this purpose, there is an internal corporate social network and an electronic magazine, which more than 4 thousand employees use. In 2020, the company opened a "digital hub" in London to develop solutions for the digitalization of business and implementation of digital solutions.

The development of internal communications and interaction with participants in the value chain is one of the fastest-growing specialized areas of corporate networking. The pandemic has significantly accelerated innovation in this area. The widespread practice of remote work increased the demand for developing an internal communications system. According to Gallup, in the U.S., the high level of development of internal corporate communications ensures a significant level of employee engagement in corporate processes, i.e., it supports their creativity, enthusiasm, and focus on results. In companies-leaders of internal networking development, as a rule, cumulative performance indicators are significantly higher than in companies with a low level of its development: customer satisfaction is 10% higher, sales volume is 26% higher, productivity is 18% higher, and staff turnover is 18-43% lower (Gallup, 2020).

The development of intra-corporate networking is a global trend. Here are just a few of the most successful examples. Stagecoach, a British bus company, provided 30,000 employees with a mobile app for internal communications that resulted in a 32% increase in overall job satisfaction. 3M created an internal collaborative network for its employees, allowing them to spend up to 15 percent of their work time communicating with colleagues and exchanging new ideas. Hershey introduced an intranet that allows employees worldwide to actively communicate to share experiences, necessary information, and news. Air France, Vodafone, and others also have internal portals for multi-channel communication among employees.

The pandemic-induced breakdown of value chains and asynchronous of lockdowns in various countries is brought to light the problems of controlling industrial relations, timely informing the counterparty, accounting for stocks in the retail network and warehouses, as well as the accumulation of unified data on the quality of goods, and not only within individual corporate networks suppliers and recipients of products but also in the industry as a whole. Of particular interest are the forms of networking of competing corporations. As a rule, competitors' communications are within the framework of joint industry projects under the aegis of the relevant business associations and unions. The experience of the Consumer Goods Forum, a non-profit networking organization that brings together the heads of about 400 manufacturing, retail, and service companies from 70 countries with total sales of 3.5 trillion euros and 10 million employees, is illustrative. Since 2018, the Forum has been developing joint pilot projects to digitalize the production and sale of consumer goods. For example, Colgate, Procter, and Gamble, Unilever, Walmart, METRO Cash and Carry, Google, CrowdAnalytics are collaborating to develop a unified system for identifying consumer products. Spar International, Henkel, Nestle, SAP, Resource Partners, Salsify, Capgemini, and others have jointly developed a system for sharing data within value chains. Another ambitious joint project in the industry's digitalization field is the creation of the Central Product Data Registry, which involved Johnson & Johnson, PepsiCo, Kellog, Colgate, Bumble Bee, eBay, Target, and others. Moreover, such companies as METRO Cash and Carry, Procter and Gamble, Walmart participated in several pilot projects at once.

Mechanisms and tools for communication with stakeholders are constantly evolving. Corporations are actively using all the innovations in digital technologies, such as augmented reality, machine learning and artificial intelligence, and crypto assets and blockchain technologies. The creation of non-fungible tokens (NFT) may become one of the ways to unique corporate identity and a means of corporate networking with stakeholders. NFTs are a unique electronic code that can be assigned to various digital and non-digital assets. For example, Nike was the first company to register a patent for the use of NFT for its sneakers to attract the general public's attention and monetize the popularity of NFT assets among investors. The same motivated one of the founders of Twitter, J. Dorsey, who sold his first NFT-linked tweet for $2.9 million.

However, despite the breadth and depth of the forms and technologies used in corporate networking, its development is accompanied by several risks. Scientists have long predicted the costs of modern digitalization and networking. Thus, in 1970, the Japanese roboticist Masahiro Mori (Mori, 2012) formulated a hypothesis about the so-called uncanny valley. Its essence is that the more a robot becomes similar to a human with its appearance, speech, and movements, the more it arouses feelings of dislike and fear in people. A modern interpretation of this hypothesis can be considered the "creepy factor," which describes situations when human expectations from the use of modern technology do not coincide with the obtained result (Tene, Polonetsky, 2014). This term arose in connection with the widespread use of so-called online behavioral advertising. It requires tracking people's online activity: their online purchases, Internet requests, frequent visits to specific sites, use of e-mail, correspondence in social networks, up to the analysis of keywords, as well as the geolocations of targeted consumers. Through collecting information about human behavior, algorithms select ads appropriate to the moment and send them to address. In certain situations, ads can be annoying and dislike their source and content. The most severe "creepy factors" commonly cited by mobile app users are: linking ads to various unique individual identifiers (e.g., a unique device identifier); unlimited tracking of personal data and information; imposition of counterproductive services (e.g., long-time computer users can get the offer of fitness centers); collection and analysis of sensitive information (e.g., health, his emotional state); adverse effects of data analysis services; and the use of mobile apps; the use of zombie cookies hidden from the user, i.e., a particular set of data that is reproduced by the web server and allows to identify the users, regardless of their desire; lack of notifications to recipients of advertising about on how the third persons will use the information.

As business and society network communications develop, the variety and number of cases to which the term "creepy factor" can be applied are growing. Consequently, the groups of stakeholders who may encounter this phenomenon are expanding. That necessitates the establishment of uniform norms and rules for using digital technologies for corporate communications with society. In this regard, the concept of Corporate Digital Responsibility is gaining popularity.

This term and concept of corporate digital responsibility are relatively new one; their widespread use in scientific and expert and analytical literature begins in 2016–2018. It is true, back in 2004, the Brazilian bank Banco do Brasil indicated in its annual report that B2B Magazine recognized it for developing "corporate digital responsibility in the public sector." As a systemic problem, the task of developing corporate digital responsibility, first attracted the attention of the German academic and business community (Esselman, Brink, 2016; Thorum et al., 2018), and then the wider European research community (Lobchat, Mueller, 2021; Herden, Aliu, 2021). In the most general sense, this concept includes a broad list of norms, rules, initiatives, organizational measures taken by corporations voluntarily in order to ensure a safe, efficient, and reliable digitalization of their activities, protection of data (personal and commercial) in the process of communicating with stakeholders.

Regulators have embraced the importance and relevance of developing specific digital ethics and security in many countries. In May 2018, the German Federal Ministry of Justice and Consumer Protection announced the start of joint development with the German companies Deutsche Telekom, Miele, Otto Group, SAP, Telefonica, ZEIT Online of critical priorities and principles of corporate digital responsibility in order to create uniform corporate standards in this area, especially with a focus on consumer personal data protection. In France government adopted the strategy for developing corporate digital responsibility. In Switzerland Ministry of Finance is patronizing the implementation of the Swiss Digital Initiative. Similar programs are gradually emerging in other countries, particularly in the USA, the UK,

China, and Korea. We can expect that the trend of unifying the principles and norms of regulation of corporate digital responsibility will gradually gain momentum.

CONCLUSION

The development of forms of networking in a pandemic should not be viewed ad hoc. The increased use of social media by investors, consumers, and corporations signals a long-term trend towards stronger horizontal social ties and their more significant role in determining long-term economic behavior. Traditionally, public relations have tended to be hierarchical, with the most influential sources of information, newsmakers, institutions, and media being clearly defined. Nowadays, distributed networks are beginning to play an increasingly dominant role, in which each participant at any time can become a generator of new information that will be taken seriously by other participants. This trend defines new challenges both for the governments, which traditionally seeks to regulate the information sphere, and for business, for which the new distributed environment of information exchange is becoming a severe node for shaping consumer and investment preferences.

Mass networking is beginning to influence the public's perception of trends, events, organizations, brands, goods, and services. For example, a new market-driven corporate identity, i.e., a "market-induced corporate identity," is beginning to take shape in the financial market due to investment networking. Shares of relatively obscure companies may become the focus of demand of a significant number of market participants and attract the attention of leading financial analysts and regulators solely due to the viral spread of market narratives. The term "meme stocks" emphasizes the symbolism of these financial instruments' transformation into a market legend, which undoubtedly affects the perception of the external image and the issuing companies. GameStop and AMC are now known to investors worldwide, many without even thinking about what these companies produce or what they do in general. This fact will define their corporate identity for a long time, regardless of its classical components. One of the most vivid illustrations of the power of corporate networking can be the story of Club House. Information about the new social network and the explosive interest of its users provoked a rush of retail investors. They rushed to buy shares in the company of the same name, which is engaged in entertainment but has nothing to do with the new app for audio chats.

Consumer networking also has far-reaching implications. Participants in online communities not only share their experiences, knowledge, and information, but in one way or another, they show their attitudes toward popular narratives. As a result, buying this or that product becomes a process of purchasing a helpful product and expressing a particular social position. Refusing to buy Barilla's products was precisely an expression of social stance. In late October 2018, Ben & Jerry's has launched a new ice cream variety, Pecan Resist, aimed at young Trump opponents, among others. Corporations attempt to integrate themselves into social networking by releasing social undertones. However, at the same time, this practice is becoming a form of corporate networking, a means of communication between corporations and stakeholders.

Even the development of communications between competing entrepreneurial organizations acquires the features of an emotional community since such communications they build around topics that are equally relevant for all market participants, especially in the context of global disruptions.

In this chapter, the author presented three examples of the development of post-COVID-19 networking, suggesting that the process of developing its forms is in its infancy. All three examples testify that in modern conditions networking shapes behavior and determines decisions of economic actors. Various forms of networking are intertwined with each other and form a global network of communications of a wide range of participants. According to the author, people quickly realize their ability to influence economic processes by acting as a single community if they have not already. Businesses should learn from what is happening and find their place in the process. It is already evident that proving one's social responsibility will be problematic without this. The governments should closely monitor the deployment of global networking, ensuring the protection of the interests of its participants and protecting them from deliberate attempts to manipulate public consciousness and distort social motivations.

REFERENCES

Agarwal, R., & Prasad, J. (1998). A conceptual and operational definition of personal innovativeness in domain of information technology. *Information Systems Research*, *9*(2), 204–215. doi:10.1287/isre.9.2.204

Alsubagh, H. (2015). The impact of social networks on consumers' behavior. *International Journal of Business and Social Science*, *6*(1), 209–216.

BarberB. M.HuangX.OdeanT. (2021, July). Schwartz C. Attention-Induced Trading and Returns: Evidence from Robinhood Users. SSRN. https://ssrn. com/abstract=3715077

Barber, B. M., & Odean, T. (2008). All that glitters: The effect of attention and news on buying behavior of individual and institutional investors. *The Review of Financial Studies, 21*(2), 785-818. https://ssrn.com/abstract=460660

Brown, J. J., & Reingen, P. H. (1987). Social ties and word-of-mouth referral behavior. *The Journal of Consumer Research*, *14*(12), 350–362. doi:10.1086/209118

Carroll, A. (1991). The Pyramid of Corporate Social Responsibility: Toward the Moral Management of Organizational Stakeholders. *Business Horizons*, *34*(4), 39–48. doi:10.1016/0007-6813(91)90005-G

De, R., Pandey, N., & Pal, A. (2020). Impact of digital surge during COVID-19 pandemic: A viewpint on research and practice. *International Journal of Information Management*, *55*(12), 102171. PMID:32836633

Dellarocas, C. (2003). *The digitalization of word-of-mouth: Promise and chalendge of online feedback mechanisms.* MIT Sloan School of Management Working Paper 4296-03.

Deloitte. (2020). *The future consumer. Series: Omnichannel transformation begins by grasping the key to consumer mentalities*. Deloitte China. https://www2.deloitte.com/content/dam/Deloitte/cn/Documents/consumer-business/deloitte-cn-consumer-omnichannel-transformation-begins-by-grasping-the-key-to-consumer-mentalities-en-200320.pdf

Di Crosta, A., Ceccato, I., Marchetti, D., La Malva, P., Maiella, R., Cannito, L., Cipi, M., Mammarella, N., Palumbo, R., Verrocchio, M. C., Palumbo, R., & Di Domenico, A. (2021). Psychological factors and consumer behavior during the COVID-19 pandemic. *PLoS One*, *16*(8), e0256095. Advance online publication. doi:10.1371/journal.pone.0256095 PMID:34398916

Esselman, F., & Brink, A. (2016, July). Corporate Digital Responsibility. Den digitalen Wandel von Unternehmen und Gesellschaft erfolgreich gestalten. *Spectrum (Lexington, Ky.)*, 38–41. https://eref.uni-bayreuth.de/60860/

Fama, E. F. (1995). Random walks in stock market prices. *Financial Analysts Journal*, *51*(1), 75–80. doi:10.2469/faj.v51.n1.1861

Fang, F., Wang, T., Tan, S., Chen, S., Zhou, T., Zhng, W., Guo, Q., Liu, J., Holme, P., & Lu, X. (2022). Newtwok structure and community evolution online: Behavioral and emotional changes in response to COVID-19. *Frontiers in Public Health*, *9*(1), 8133234. PMID:35087790

FINRA. (2021, February). Investing 2020: New Accounts and the People Who Opened Them. In *Consumer Insights: Money & Investing*. FINRA Investor Education Foundation. https://www.finrafoundation.org/sites/finrafoundation/files/investing-2020-new-accounts-and-the-people-who-opened-them_1_0.pdf

Gallup. (2020, October). *The Relationship Between Engagement at Work and Organizational Outcomes*. Gallup. https://www.gallup.com/workplace/321032/employee-engagement-meta-analysisbrief.aspx

GlobalWebIndex. (2019). *The era of we: online community*. https://www.gwi.com/reports/online-communities-reddit

Google Ngrams Viewer. (n.d.). https://books.google.com/ngrams

Google Trends. (n.d.). https://trends.google.com

Hajli, M. N. (2015). A study of the impact of social media on consumers. *International Journal of Market Research*, *56*(3), 387–404. doi:10.2501/IJMR-2014-025

Herden, Ch., & Alliu, E. (2021). New Corporate Responsibilities in the digital age. *Nachhaltigkeits Management Forum, 29*(2), 13–29. https://link.springer.com/article/10.1007%2Fs00550-020-00509-x

Holmes, R. (2020). Is COVID-19 social media's levelling up moment? *Forbes*. https://www.forbes.com/sites/ryanholmes/2020/04/24/is-covid-19-social-medias-levelling-up-moment/?sh=6d3b342f6c60

Itoh, S., Murakami, Y., & Iba, T. (2006). Consumer network and market dynamics. *Proceedings of the 9th Joint International Conference on Information Sciences (JCIS-06)*, 211-214.

Jun, T., & Kim, J.-Y. (2008). A theory of consumer referral. *International Journal of Industrial Organization*, *26*(3), 662–678. doi:10.1016/j.ijindorg.2007.03.005

Kahneman, D. (2011). *Thinking fast and slow*. Farrar, Straus and Giroux.

Khan, M. A. A., Hashim, H., & Ab. Aziz, Y. (2020). The rise of consumer community on social media, its influence on consumers' decision making process, perceived value and loyalty intentions in tourism industry: A conceptual thought. *International Journal of Academic Research in Business & Social Sciences*, *10*(10), 813–833. doi:10.6007/IJARBSS/v10-i10/7874

KOF Swiss Economic Institute. (2021). *KOF Globalization Index*. https://kof.ethz.ch/en/forecasts-and-indicators/indicators/kof-globalisation-index.html

Krishen, A., Berezan, O., Agarwal, S., & Kachroo, P. (2016). The generation of virtual needs: Recipes for satisfaction in social media networking. *Journal of Business Research, 69*(11), 5248–5254. doi:10.1016/j.jbusres.2016.04.120

Lobchat, L., & Mueller, B. (2021). Corporate digital responsibility. *Journal of Business Research, 122*, 875–888. doi:10.1016/j.jbusres.2019.10.006

Milovidov, V. (2020). The "Linked Prosperity" Model as an Integrated Response to Corporate Management Challenges in a Network Society. *Foresight and STI Governance, 14*(4), 112–120. doi:10.17323/2500-2597.2020.4.112.120

Milovidov, V. D. (2015a). Management of innovations: How to effectively use the information. *Neftyanoe khozyaystvo, 6*, 10–16.

Milovidov, V. D. (2015b). Risk management under information asymmetry: To differentiate those distinguishable. *World Economy and International Relation, 8*(8), 14–24. doi:10.20542/0131-2227-2015-8-14-24

Milovidov, V. D. (2015c). Proactive innovation management: Knowledge mapping. *Neftyanoe khozyaystvo, 8*, 16–21.

Milovidov, V. D. (2018). Hearing the sound of the wave: What impedes one's ability to foresee innovations? *Foresight and STI Governance, 12*(1), 88–97. doi:10.17323/2500-2597.2018.1.88.97

Milovidov, V. D. (2021). Pandemic in the network society: Network readiness increases population vulnerability to COVID-19 in less developed countries. *Acta Oeconomica, 71*(S1), 187–203. doi:10.1556/032.2021.00035

Milovidov, V. D. (2022). Story stocks: How stock market-induced corporate identity is being fomed. *World Economy and International Relation, 66*(1), 100–109. doi:10.20542/0131-2227-2022-66-1-100-109

Mori, M., MacDorman, K., & Kageki, N. (2012). The Uncanny Valey. *IEEE Robotics & Automation Magazine, 19*(June), 98–100. doi:10.1109/MRA.2012.2192811

Nabity-Grover, T., Cheung, Ch. M. K., & Thatcher, J. B. (2020). Inside and outside in: How the COVID-19 pandemic affects self-disclosure on social media. *International Journal of Information Management, 55*(12), 102188. doi:10.1016/j.ijinfomgt.2020.102188 PMID:32836645

Najmul Islam, A. K. M., Mäntymäki, M., Laato, S., & Turel, O. (2022). Adverse consequences of emotional support seeking through social network sites in coping with stressfrom a global pandemic. *International Journal of Information Management, 62*(2), 102431. doi:10.1016/j.ijinfomgt.2021.102431 PMID:34642531

Pedrosa, A. L., Bitencourt, L., Fróes, A. C. F., Cazumbá, M. L. B., Campos, R. G. B., de Brito, S. B. C. S., & Simões e Silva, A. C. (2020). Emotional, Behavioral, and Psychological Impact of the COVID-19 Pandemic. *Frontiers in Psychology, 11*, 11. doi:10.3389/fpsyg.2020.566212 PMID:33117234

Portulans Institute. (2021). *Network readiness index*. https://networkreadinessindex.org

Reddit. (2019). *The power of community*. https://www.redditinc.com/assets/case-studies/Reddit-x-Ypulse-The-Power-of-Community-White-Paper-9.23.19.pdf

Reddit. (n.d.). *List of economic and Stock Market subreddits*. https://www.reddit.com/r/ListOfSubreddits/comments/ja8du7/list_of_economic_and_stock_market_subreddits/

Reddy, W. M. (1997). Against constructionism. The historical ethnography of emotions. *Current Anthropology*, *38*(3), 327–351. doi:10.1086/204622

Riegner, C. (2007). Word of mouth on web: The impact of Web 2.0 on consumer purchase decisions. *Journal of Advertising Research*, *47*(4), 436–447. doi:10.2501/S0021849907070456

Rogozinsky, J. (2020). *WallStreetBets*. How Boomers Made the World's Biggest Casino for Millennials.

Rosenwein, B. H. (2006). *Emotional communities in the early middle ages*. Cornell University Press.

Schwab, K. (2019). *Davos Manifesto 2020: The Universal Purpose of a Company in the Fourth Industrial Revolution*. World Economic Forum. Available at https://www.weforum.org/agenda/2019/12/davos-manifesto-2020- the-universal-purpose-of-a-company-in-the-fourth-industrial-revolution/

Seasholes, M. S., & Wu, G. (2007). Predictable behavior, profits, and attention. *Journal of Empirical Finance*, *14*(5), 590–610. https://ssrn.com/abstract=686193. doi:10.1016/j.jempfin.2007.03.002

Stevenson, C., Wakefield, J. R. H., Felsner, I., Drury, J., & Costa, S. (2021). Collectively coping with coronavirus: Local community identification predicts giving support and lockdown adherence during the COVID-19 pandemic. *British Journal of Social Psychology*, *60*(4), 1403–1418. doi:10.1111/bjso.12457 PMID:33969899

Subreddit Stats. (n.d.). https://subredditstats.com

Suwandee, S., Surachartkumtonkun, J., & Lertwannawit, A. (2020). EWOM firestorm: Young consumers and online community. *Young Consumers*, *21*(1), 1–15. doi:10.1108/YC-03-2019-0982

Tene, O., & Polonetsky, J. (2014). A Theory of Creepy: Technology, Privacy andv Shifting Social Norms. *Yale Journal of Law and Technology*, *16*(1), 59–102.

The Economist. (2022). *The Big Mac index*. https://www.economist.com/big-mac-index?utm_content=article-link-3&etear=nl_today_3&utm_campaign=a.the-economist-today&utm_medium=email.internal-newsletter.np&utm_source=salesforce-marketing-cloud&utm_term=2/3/2022&utm_id=1039508

Thorum, C., Ketter, S., & Merck, J. (2018). Ethik in Der Digitalisierung. Der Bedarf für eine Corporate Digital Responsibility. *Wirtschafts-und Sozialpolitik, 17*. Available at: https://library.fes.de/pdf-files/wiso/14691.pdf

Verma, S. (2013). Effectiveness of social network sites for influencing consumer purchase decisions. *International Journal of Business Excellence*, *6*(5), 624–634. doi:10.1504/IJBEX.2013.056112

WallstreetBets News. (2020, August 30). *Dissecting the Unique Lingo and Terminology used in the Subreddit r/Wallstreetbets*. https://www.wallstreetbets.shop/blogs/news/dissecting-the-unique-lingo-and-terminology-used-in-the-subreddit-r-wallstreetbets

Wang, X., Yiik Diew Wong, Y. D., & Yuen, K. F. (2021). Rise of 'Lonely' Consumers in the Post-COVID-19 Era: A Synthesised Review on Psychological, Commercial and Social Implications. *International Journal of Environmental Research and Public Health*, *18*(2), 404. doi:10.3390/ijerph18020404

Wells Fargo Asset Management. (2017, September 20). *Majority of Millennials Are Happy Despite Financial Anxiety, Wells Fargo Study Finds*. Wells Fargo Asset Management. https://www.wellsfargoassetmanagement.com/assets/public/pdf/press-releases/20170920-pressrelease.pdf

Chapter 21
Relations Between Digital Transformation and Sustainability Post COVID-19:
The Pillars of ESG

Andreia Bem Machado
https://orcid.org/0000-0002-4404-0341
Federal University of Santa Catarina, Brazil

Marc François Richter
State University of Rio Grande do Sul, Brazil

João Alvarez Peixoto
State University of Rio Grande do Sul, Brazil

ABSTRACT

COVID-19 has directly influenced the digital transformation in companies. In a matter of days, remote activities had to be quickly deployed in organizations, new consumer habits incorporated, and technologies inserted, demanding technological solutions. Thus, companies had to adapt to a new normal. In this scenario the following questions have emerged: What is digital transformation? What are the relationships between digital transformation and sustainability in the post-covid era? To answer these questions, the following objective was set: to analyze the relationship between digital transformation and sustainability in the post-COVID-19 era. To this end, an integrative literature review was conducted using the Web of Science database. Results indicate that digital transformation and sustainability are directly interconnected to economic activities, including the area of maintenance and facility management. The post-pandemic trends highlight years of recovery and readaptation in the face of the crisis, together with digital transformation, which promises to increasingly improve.

DOI: 10.4018/978-1-7998-8856-7.ch021

INTRODUCTION

The new investor profiles and consumer behavior move companies towards environmental, social and governance issues. Something that until recently was not even considered in business plans, today becomes the subject of discussions (Ng, 2021). This is due to a socio-environmental awareness that the market now wants in companies, no longer seen as an attribution, but as a value offer. Being recognized for promoting positive impact on the community, adopting ethical corporate conduct and caring for the environment has become a differentiator in the business world, adding a new guiding principle for companies: being ESG (Environmental, social and corporate governance) (Peterson et al., 2021).

In this scenario, the abbreviation ESG is recognized by the initials of the English words Environmental, Social and Governance. This means a concern with the way in which the company deals with the environmental impacts of the production, commercialization and use of the products and services it offers; the way in which the company relates with its collaborators, clients and the community in which it is inserted; and the principles and values of its management. Thus, the company has to be concerned with new concepts and actions involving sustainability. In this context, in the consumer's view, it is not a matter of having a product, but of being conscious in their acquisition experience. As the world that the customer, the supplier, the company, the organizations and the investor live in, is the same, there is a common reason to preserve it.

Com a pandemia do COVID-19, para garantir a sustentabilidade nas organizações optouise por inovar através da transformação digital e mudanças no comportamento das pessoas. Assim, nas grandes corporações as conversas são sobre diminuir distâncias com processos mais inovadores e tecnológicos. Sendo assim, além da transformação digital há a responsabilidade social, a governança e a sustentabilidade a preocupação em atender essas temáticas são apresentadas figura

Figure 1, below, makes the company more aware of its responsibility, as an actor in the environmental preservation process, in commercial and labor relations and in its correct management. Reasons why they seek concepts, methods and tools to assist in the achievement of these objectives.

Figure 1. Topics covered by ESG
Source: Authors (2022)

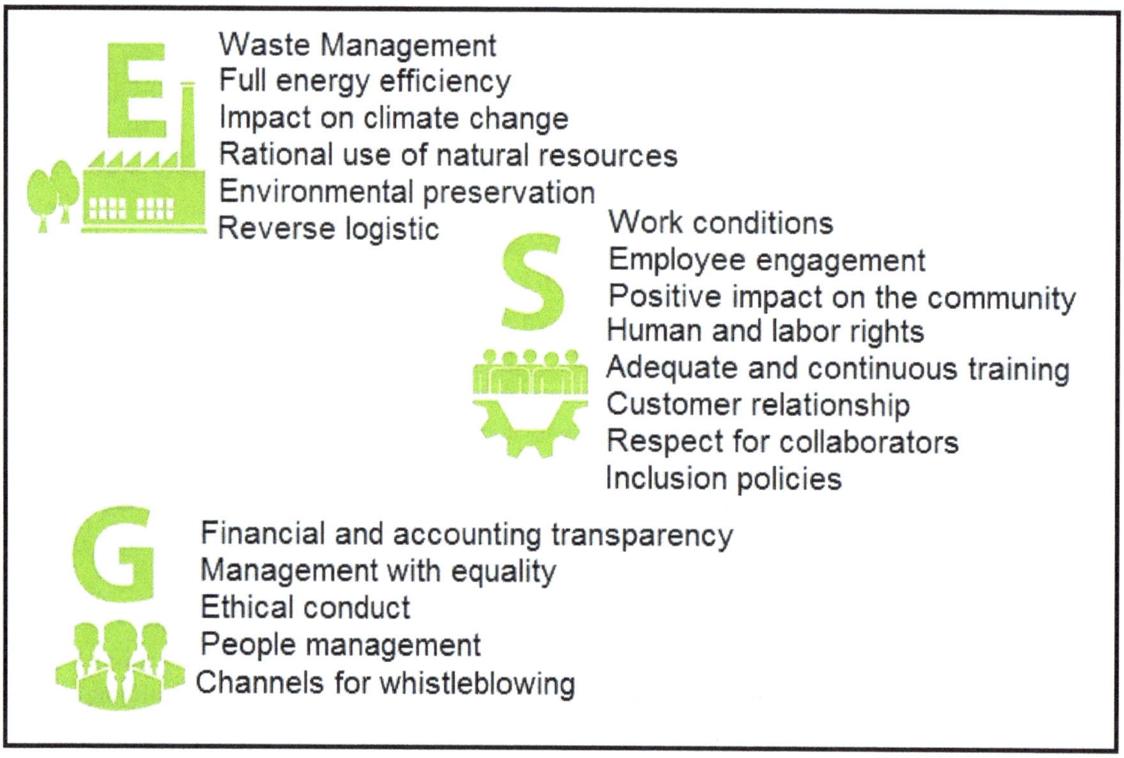

Based on the foregoing, the main objective of this research is to analyze in the light of a systematic literature review the relationships between digital transformation and sustainability in the post-covid period. To this end, a bibliometric search was conducted in the Web of Science database. The research is divided, in addition to this introduction, into five parts. The first part is entitled introduction, the second presents the concepts about digital transformation, the third part presents sustainability and the fourth part explains the methodology adopted in this research, the fifth part discusses the research results and, finally, the authors' final considerations.

DIGITAL TRANSFORMATION

The whole idea of "Change Management" is to drive the success of change by preparing, equipping and supporting people to thrive during change. For change to be successful, however, it requires to prepare, equip, and support people who are experiencing change so that they successfully adopt the new way of doing their jobs. Without adoption, the changes will not succeed and desired results will not be delivered. Change is not easy and often fraught with resistance, confusion, stress, anxiety, delays, and in some cases, failure. But there is a way to better drive adoption, use, competence, and readiness for change so that we can thrive. Change Management is much more than communicating what is changing, such as the implementation or acquisition of a system. It is about supporting people in the organization in their individual transitions from the current state to the future state and understanding what it takes to influence each person to embrace and adopt the change. In this way, organizations can significantly increase the chances of project success and their investments in projects that will bring significant results (Bonanomi, 2019).

Digital transformation is more than just a technological change. It is a change of mentality in the market context. The emergence of digital transformation occurred at the turn of the century, through the popularization of the internet and the emergence of social networks, bringing digital platforms as a major consumer engagement offer, presenting a digital world, in all of its forms. All this applies to the announcement of products, sales, after-sales and the direct relationship with the customer (Kotler et al., 2017). In this context, the profile of consumption has also been transformed, because the product itself is no longer the great attraction, but its features that it offers, in addition to requiring a greater diversity on the part of the consumer market, and sometimes a high degree of customization, of a product that until then was formatted in a standard. These diversification needs, coupled with the need for agility in delivery, have now impacted production systems, referring them to a change in concepts and technologies, entitled "industrial revolution", better known as Industry 4.0 (Schwab, 2016).

Thus, the market based on Industry 4.0 was driven by digital technologies, impacting on the means of production as an industrial revolution, and so it fell to the production and sales sectors to engage in this medium, turning their operations more and more digital. This means that there are no longer any formatted product models and fixed sales strategies, but rather the offer of functionalities of their products to the market, through methods that make the customer experience an engagement factor, not only so that he just wants to make a new purchase, but also to make him want to repeat this experience. As the COVID-19 pandemic progressed, the need for transformation by companies was reinforced (Kim, 2020).

With the digital transformation in companies, new strategies have been adopted, impacting the organizational culture. Thus, a proposal is presented to the company, which wishes to have a relationship of engagement with its customers, starting to have the pillars of digital transformation as guidelines to their daily lives, and to all employees who are involved in the production of goods and services (Vial, 2019).

The 4 pillars of digital transformation are shown in figure 2.

Figure 2. Digital transformation pillars
Source: Authors (2022)

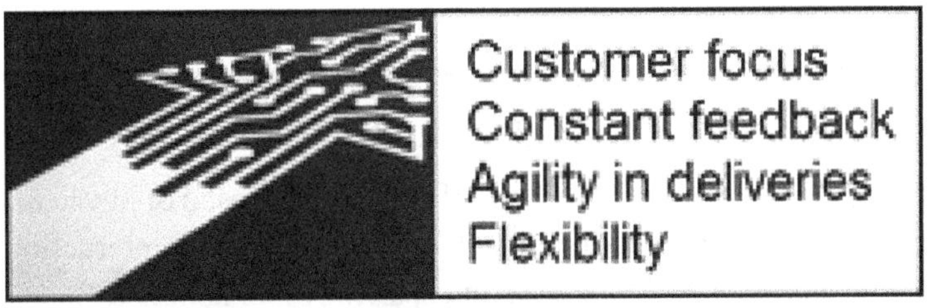

According to Carvalho et al. (2021), the pillars of digital transformation in companies are:

- Customer focus: understanding consumer desires and preferences, knowing that these are dynamic and impacted by environmental factors;

- Constant feedbacks: use customer opinions to qualify the product, as the user is the best critic of what is produced;
- To be agile in the deliveries: to keep the consumer informed of all the steps, because many times the delivery time is not as significant as having the precise information of everything that is happening, from the moment the order is placed until the product arrives in the client's hands;
- Being flexible: having the capacity to make processes flexible in order to meet new contexts, new consumer contact channels, new partnerships and new markets.

Digital transformation being a culture within the business environment, starts to contribute to: to make communication faster and more assertive; to integrate sectors, making teams more in tune and collaborative; to access complete information in a more pluralistic way; to automate processes and reduce bureaucratization; to favor decision-making through data support; to improve interaction with customers through more instantaneous channels; and to facilitate performance analysis, thanks to digital management tools (Kraus et al., 2021). Thus, to achieve digital transformation, digital tools are necessary, which comprise a set of technological resources that drive digital transformation, as shown in the figure 3.

Figure 3. Digital tools driving digital transformation
Source: Authors (2022)

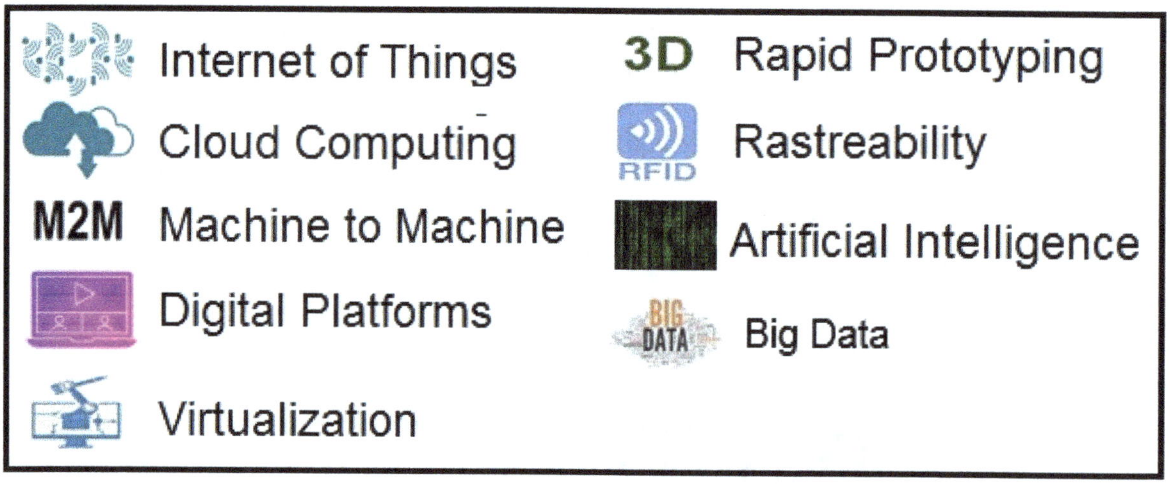

The **Internet of Things**, known by the acronym IoT is a set composed of physical and digital modules. The physical modules are connected to equipment or devices, providing interaction with the latter, collecting signals and sending commands. Digital modules, on the other hand, promote access to the internet network, using specific communication protocols and libraries capable of identifying and transmitting information directly to other IoT devices or to websites containing API (Application Programming Interface) (Fachini et al., 2017). Thus, the company can access information directly from equipments, environments or machines, interacting and obtaining immediate information of the operating conditions, production, forecasts, maintenance status, among others?

With IoT devices providing interaction over the internet, **interaction between machines**, also known as M2M (Machine to Machine), becomes possible. Machines and equipment interact with each other, exchanging information and commands, without the interference of human beings. Raising the degree of automation of manufacturing processes, going as far as the direct interaction of the machine or systems with the user, whether for information or guidance on how the product was designed and how it should be used (Ferreira et al., 2020).

Cloud computing is the use of an environment in which computing resources are used remotely via the internet, enabling the use of software that is not installed on the user's local computer, but that is allocated to computer servers, which provide these resources in the cloud. In this way, the user's computing resources need not be so expressive and the availability of digital information and services can be accessed from anywhere there is an internet network connection (Pereira et al., 2019). This enables companies to access and share information with a high degree of mobility, whether inside or outside their manufacturing environment.

Digital platforms use tools to access the physical medium and enable sharing in the cloud. They are an important digital resource because they put a range of information in a medium that can be accessed by the user from any location with an internet connection, whether he is a customer or an employee of the company. Digital platforms go beyond information panels, but promote social interaction, the offer of products, provide services themselves, and configure themselves as one of the main tools of digital transformation (Byrnes, 2021). Virtual interaction with the consumer has revolutionized the customer experience, either with contextualized information on products of interest or through robots (Robo Bot), which are virtual entities programmed to provide interaction with people, in the human form of relationship that people are used to. And this brings greater customer engagement with the brand.

Virtualization is a digital tool that made it possible to transform the production process or product into a digital model, in order to experiment with such processes, testing different possibilities and verifying the consistency of the process before it is conceived in its physical form. With the degree of fidelity of the model, the Digital Twin then emerges, a virtual model that behaves identically to the real model, serving as the object of study and testing (Rolle et al., 2020). This brings assertiveness to the company, which constantly needs to change its production flows to quickly meet new market demands.

Rapid prototyping, known as 3D printing, aims to eliminate the intermediate steps in the process of manufacturing prototypes of a product, generating the final model from the designed model. This is made possible by the additive manufacturing process, where the material is added layer by layer, meeting the geometry to which it was designed (Silva et al., 2021). With this tool, the generation of a final product, or even its adequacy to a specific need of the client, occurs in a faster and more agile way, with less material and supply waste. The technology allows this manufacturing process to occur with different types of materials, whether polymeric, elastomer or metallic, changing the principle of material addition.

Traceability is the digital tool that makes the product or the equipment of a process to be geographically identified, allowing its location and recognition of places where it has passed, as well as manufacturing processes and use to which it was submitted (Silva & Gasparoto, 2020). Tools such as RFId, QRcode and IoT, among others, allow a physical object to be recognized in a digital environment, obtaining data regarding its characteristics. This is important information for the customer to know the entire path that the product has taken until it reaches his domain, as well as for the manufacturer to have this information in case of product failure, being able to recognize the process that impacted on the failure, qualifying the product.

Big Data is a software technology that proposes to search for correlations between information that is collected, comprehensively and in significant quantity (Singh, 2019). If you take into account a manufacturing process that has failures in the production of some parts in a production batch, it can be analyzed with Big Data tools, which will confront the collected data (temperature, vibration, time, day of the week, humidity, among many) and seek a correlation of the situation in which the process was and the failure occurred in the product. This tool also helps in the analysis of the trend of customer behavior when accessing your digital platforms, predicting the day and time that is most attractive for this consumer, based on previous access data from a large number of users.

Artificial intelligence, on the other hand, uses algorithms and concepts to computationally predict consumer and market behavior, among many others (Russel & Norvig, 2009). This forecast is valid to anticipate the offer of products or services, or even to predict the behavior of the product itself and the productive environment, further qualifying the offer to the consumer with more reliable products.

As people management, both Big Data and artificial intelligence measure the trajectory of employees in the company, in their employee experience, assisting in the management of these human resources, which are the main asset. This generates a better follow-up of the positions and salaries plan, makes the training plan more assertive and makes the employee feel more engaged and part of the company's plans. As for the whistleblowing channels, wrongly seen as only a place to complain, they can be managed by digital platforms and Big Data, which can collect information from employees and customers and proceed with the proper data processing, in order to extract opinions and report situations that need to be improved.

The four pillars of digital transformation are: 1) Optimizing internal operations; 2) Engaging with customers; 3) Transforming the work environment; and 4) Focusing on people. In addition to strengthening in the market, seeking competitiveness, digital transformation serves to reduce costs by increasing the efficiency of companies. With technology, a company is able to resolve contact and problems with customers more easily. In addition, even the internal issues of a particular enterprise can be better resolved. In other words, investing in the optimization of your company's internal operations is a great differential, which makes it more competitive and organized in the market. Another fundamental pillar of digital transformation is improved customer engagement. Digital marketing is a new communication model focused precisely on this aspect, bringing company and customer closer in a way never seen before. With technology, the company may obtain essential data related to the consumption of your target audience. Thus, it is possible to create a more targeted communication strategy, aimed at those who are really interested in what you seek. In other words: there is no reason to spend time and money with those who have no interest in consuming what you are offering. Regarding the transformation of the work environment, companies need to have modern equipment, such as computers and notebooks, capable of receiving specialized software for the day-to-day dynamics. Therefore, part of the digital transformation (de Bem Machado et al. 2021) of the workplace involves understanding that, in some cases, the physical environment does not even need to exist. You can save a lot of money by removing the need for physical servers, migrating all communication, file storage, and task execution to the digital environment. Finally, it is important to be aware that the focus must always be on people; people remain the center of your business. Technology, by itself, is meaningless. It exists to solve human problems. Therefore, it is not productive to bring a technology into your business if it does not perform any specific function that will help your customers and employees. The main focus is to make decisions to please those who really matter, which are your customers and employees (Hinterhuber & Nilles, 2021).

Conclusively, digital transformation is no longer an option, but a necessity. Its digital tools, which in addition to assisting in the execution of business plans, also help to implement and cultivate the importance with the environment, with social and governance aspects within the company. Digital transformation is an offer of value to the community and to consumers, but also to the image of a company that cares about the environment in which it operates.

SUSTAINABILITY AND DIGITAL TRANSFORMATION IN POST-COVID TIMES

Before the pandemic, relatively few executives considered competencies in crisis management, corporate agility, cost management, employee resilience, innovation or cash flow management as critically important to their business. This has changed dramatically as the pandemic has progressed. The key pieces for the post-pandemic business landscape, are based on new perspectives on digital transformation, the future of work, transparency and sustainability. Together, they provide a guide for proactive leaders who understand that old ways of working will cease to exist in order to succeed (Anderson et al., 2021).

The path towards economic recovery offers the opportunity to rethink the development model and correct the structural weaknesses that deepened the impact of the COVID-19 crisis. The onset of a post-pandemic stage marks a turning point to articulate an all too often postponed reform agenda. To this end, emergency responses, such as support for micro and small enterprises, must be articulated within a vision of long-term transformation in the three areas of sustainability: the social, the productive and the environmental. The challenge to emerge from the crisis is as much a technological and productive challenge as a social and political one, in which the search for greater equality will be crucial to success. Three tools stand out in this process of economic recovery and transformation: 1) digitalization; 2) sustainability; and 3) innovation (Anderson et al., 2021).

Regarding **digitalization**, the pandemic clearly showed the technological gaps and the existing inequality in the digital infrastructure in different regions of the world. The crisis has highlighted the social cost of technological gaps and the inequality of the digital infrastructure in our region. Digital transformation is an opportunity for businesses to increasingly rely on new technologies. These are new ways for companies to be more available to customers, suppliers and other stakeholders, generating greater efficiency for companies. This digitalization makes companies adapt to demands, and leads companies to build new business models. There is a great opportunity to improve productivity from digital transformation and contribute to economic recovery through inclusive digitalization that incorporates especially women and younger people, who have been the main affected by this crisis in most parts of the world (Joseph & Dhanabhakyam, 2022)

Just as the pandemic was an **innovation** accelerator, the exit from the crisis can be an opportunity to "reinvent" companies and the economy. This will require large doses of social, citizen, business and public innovation. Successful companies need to be aware of and connect with maturing innovations. In the process, it is not enough just to incorporate technology: it is necessary to change the corporate culture and let go of something that is done today, making room for the new. This may be uncomfortable at first, but it is absolutely necessary. As an example, innovation in production processes will certainly be accelerated, since the economic viability of recycling and reusing raw materials depends a lot on the reality of each sector and geography. In the paper and pulp segment, innovation is already a definite issue, with the planting and management of forests on a rotational basis to avoid the depletion of wood.

The transformation required for recovery must have socio-environmental sustainability as its main focus. A new economic and productive model must "make peace with nature" without compromising the environment for future generations. Otherwise, the development cannot be called sustainable development. Before the coronavirus pandemic, sustainability strategies were largely focused on environmental problems: the risks of pollution, climate change and the like to the health of the planet. Consumers were increasingly choosing products and brands that demonstrated authenticity in these areas, inspiring passion and loyalty. However, in the face of a global human health crisis, environmental sustainability became part of personal safety issues. Consumers are nowadays using disposable masks and gloves, opting for individual packaging more than ever. These actions apparently put the protection of human health in a position contrary to the protection of the planet, as it generates a lot of waste to be disposed of, unfortunately not always properly (Kachela et al., 2021).

But consumer and corporate employee awareness of environmental issues remains and is growing stronger in the population, especially with the increasingly present group of millennials (Rashi et al., 2021). Indeed, health and safety have been combined in a new, more expanded and more complex definition of sustainability. New obligations are already emerging for corporations as they must comply with their socio-environmental responsibility, such as reducing carbon footprints, managing waste more efficiently, while meeting new health and safety requirements. This may be among the most challenging, and critical, implications of post-COVID-19 business. Resolving this impediment will require not only new practices and new materials, but also new types of data and efficiency. For example: what is the environmental cost of spoiled or discarded meat compared to using more plastic to make it safer? How do we enable supply chains and delivery companies to deliver what businesses and consumers need, without unnecessary waste?

Post-pandemic trends point to years of recovery and readaptation in the face of the crisis, coupled with digital transformation, which promises to become increasingly enhanced (Petrunenko et al., 2021). The Covid-19 pandemic has transformed numerous economic activities, including the area of maintenance and facilities management. Some post-pandemic trends in maintenance and facilities management are presented below:

a) Use of Big Data, Artificial Intelligence and IoT: Big Data was a technology that was already growing and, with the pandemic, the use of systems to store information intensified even more. In conjunction, Artificial Intelligence (AI) for predictive maintenance is another post-pandemic trend that promises to expand further. In this way, it is possible to assertively and objectively reduce, or even eliminate, the possibility of infrastructure problems by analyzing failure patterns over the lifetime of assets. IoT, on the other hand, is linked to AI, since machines and equipment are increasingly connected to the internet, allowing this integration and communication between systems (Lichtenthaler, 2020).
b) Increased attention to sustainability: the issue of sustainability was latent, but has become central to post-pandemic trends. After all, it has been realized that the exacerbated exploitation of the environment, or even the lack of care for the ecosystem, is extremely harmful to business and the flow of work. Therefore, organizations will be even more concerned with sustainable development in all company processes.
c) Adoption of integrated technologies: integrated technologies have become indispensable in the Covid-19 scenario, as they were largely responsible for maintaining communication in hybrid working or home office. Therefore, they are part of the post pandemic trends in maintenance and facilities management, precisely because they collaborate with the practicality of communication and agility in the exchange of information between departments.
d) Valuing human assets: Covid-19 was primarily a humanitarian crisis. After all, the disease spread across the globe, causing millions of deaths and damaging the economies of all countries. In addi-

tion, dealing with social isolation and this whole context of bereavement has required companies to value human assets even more, with initiatives to promote employee health and well-being.

METHODOLOGICAL PROCEDURES

Provide The integrative review contributes to the systematic visualization of the state of the art (Machado et al., 2020) on the subject in the search and its timeline to the level of production by area, avoiding minimization or repetition of studies, or even tending to bias when looking at a specific topic. For this analysis, the research was organized into five phases, namely: problem formulation, definition of research sources, article selection, screening evaluation and analytical synthesis of the obtained results.

RESULTADOS E DISSUSSÕES

The **first phase** is the research formulation of the problem that guides this present study. This will answer the question: What are the links between digital transformation and sustainability in the post-covid era? To answer this question a database search was conducted that started and ended in the month of January 2022

In the **second phase**, called the definition of research sources, some criteria for the selection of the research were defined, such as the delimitation of the research base. It was decided to work with the electronic database Web of Science, considered relevant due to the number of abstracts and references indexed in peer-reviewed journals, as well as its impact on the academic area in the interdisciplinary field, which is the study area of this research. To this end, the following search terms were used: "digital transformation", "sustainability" and "covid-19".

Considering the question of the problem, the **third phase** is the selection of articles and conferences. Thus, the terms or expressions of the research were delimited, according to Table 1, below, using no temporal cut-off.

In the **fourth phase**, the evaluation of the selection was carried out, based on the previously defined criteria. Firstly, the quantitative analysis criterion was adopted, which totaled 43 documents. As a result of this collection, it was identified that the 43 papers identified in the search were written by 153 authors from 37 different countries. A total of 155 keywords were used. Table 1 shows the results of this data collection in a general bibliometric analysis.

Table 1. General bibliometric analysis

Block	Description	Results
Main information on data	Timespan	2020:2022
Document types	Article	33
	Article; early access	3
	Article; proceedings paper	1
	Editorial material	1
	Proceedings paper	2
	Review	2
	Review; early access	1
	Keywords Plus	155
	Authors	153
	Countries	37

Source: Authors (2022)

From the 43 papers one can observe a varied list of authors, institutions and countries that stand out in the research on ESG and sustainability. When analyzing the 37 countries with the highest number of citations in the area one can see that China stands out with a total of 41 citations, and Spain and Portugal with 26 and 25, respectively, as shown in figure 4.

Figure 4. Most cited countries in the survey
Source: Authors (2022)

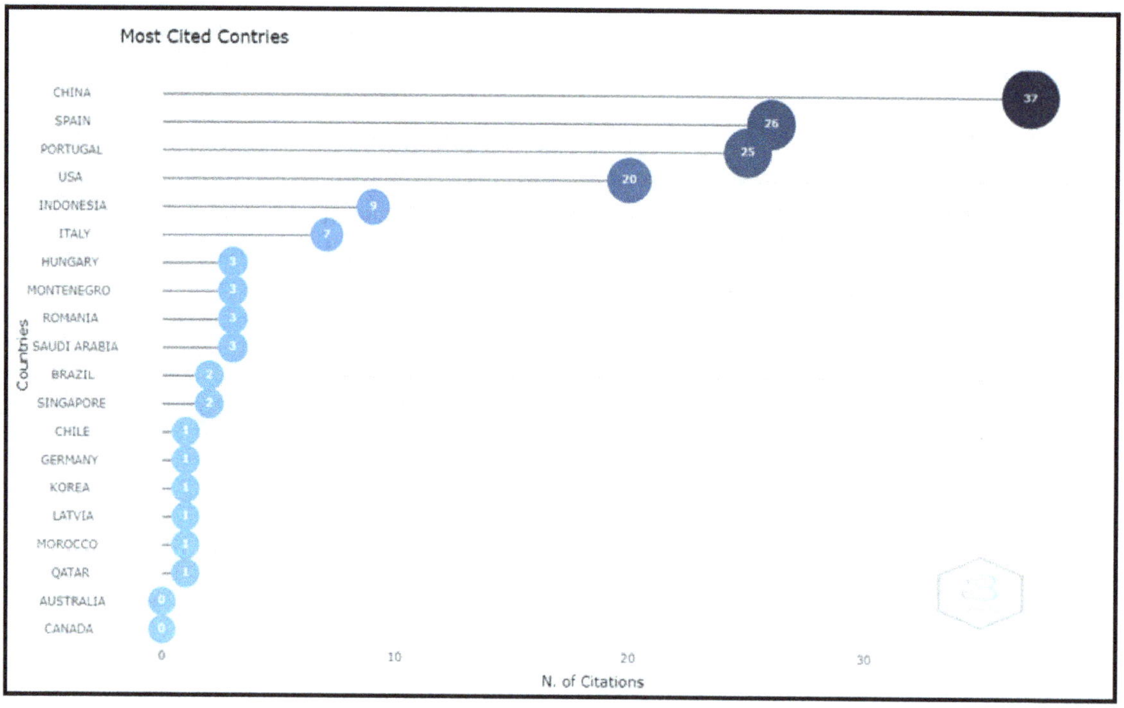

Another analysis performed is related to the identification of the number of publications per author. The author who has more production in the field is ZUO L, with 2 published documents in the area, according to figure 5.

Figure 5. Most relevant authors for the topic
Source: Authors (2022)

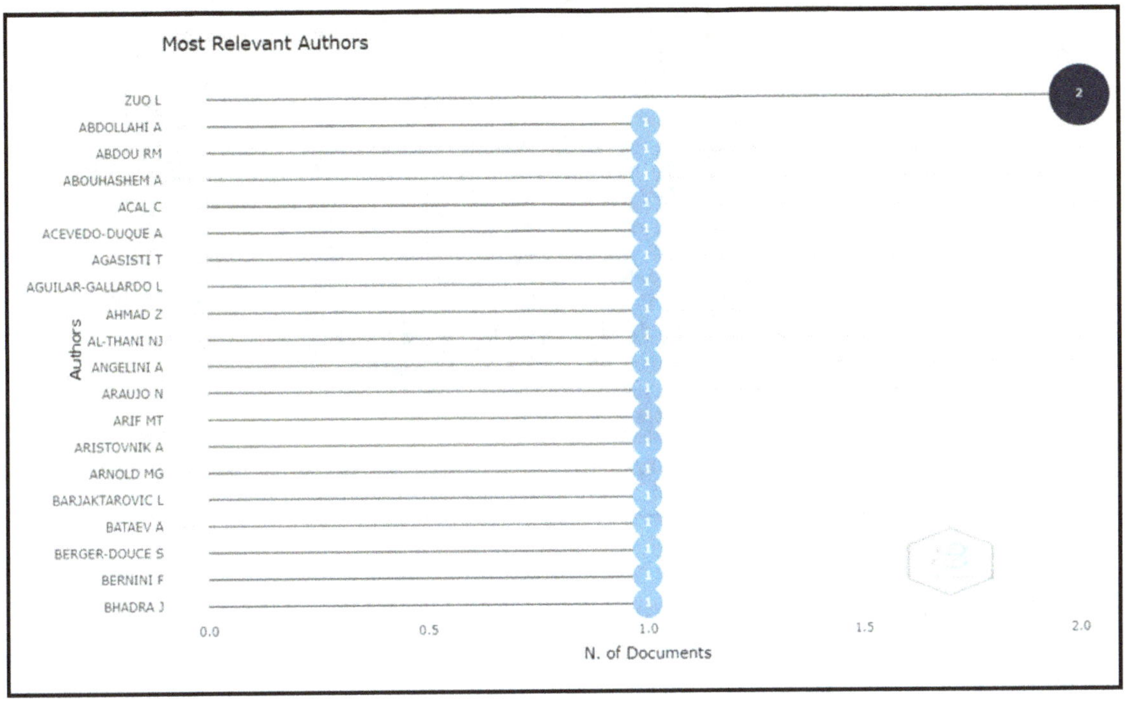

From the bibliometric analysis, based on the group of papers retrieved, and based on 155 keywords indicated by the authors, the following keywords stood out: “Impact” with 9, “Strategy” with 6 and “Innovation” also with 6 occurrences, as shown in figure 6.

Figure 6. Most relevant authors for the topic
Source: Authors (2022)

After the bibliometric analysis of the documents, the fifth phase is translated into the synthesis process with qualitative and narrative analysis for qualitative and quantitative studies. The synthesis can take a form of a table or template to present the results to answer the following research question: What are the relationships between digital transformation and sustainability in the post-covid era? Of the 43 documents, 33 were review articles. First, all the abstracts of the articles were read. After this reading, 23 articles were selected that were adherent to the research topic. After reading the full articles, only 5 articles answered the research question, as presented in Table 2.

Table 2. Systematic summary of the articles that answered the research question

Year	Authors	Title	Summary
2020	Obrenovic, Du, Godinic, Tsoy, Khan, & Jakhongirov	Sustaining Enterprise Operations and Productivity during the COVID-19 Pandemic: "Enterprise Effectiveness and Sustainability Model"	The article discusses a model of Business Effectiveness and Sustainability during Pandemic, which was adopted through digital transformation and sustainability in the post-covid era with financial contingency plans that sustained their business operations during a pandemic.
2021	Esses, Csete, & Nemeth	Sustainability and Digital Transformation in the Visegrad Group of Central European Countries	The article addresses the relationship between digital transformation and sustainability based on the sustainable development goals, digital performance and sustainability indicators of some countries of the European Union.
2021	Lee,Wang, D., Desouza, K. C., & Evans	Digital Transformation and the New Normal in China: How Can Enterprises Use Digital Technologies to Respond to COVID-19?	The article addresses that the relationship between sustainability and digital transformation in the post-covid era, is centred on sustainable business models.
2021	Kim, Choi, & Lew	Where Is the Age of Digitalization Heading? The Meaning, Characteristics, and Implications of Contemporary Digital Transformation	The article explains that digital transformation involves a change of companies based on constant innovation through sustainable actions.
2021	Mihailović, Cerović Smolović, J., Radević, I., Rašović, N., & Martinović	COVID-19 and Beyond: Employee Perceptions of the Efficiency of Teleworking and Its Cybersecurity Implications	The article addresses that the relationships between sustainability and digital transformation are in new work formats such as teleworking, as well as perceptions of the main challenges related to cyber security.

Source: Authors (2022)

Obrenovic et al. (2020) are proposing a "Business Effectiveness and Sustainability Model during Pandemic" based on organizational and operational characteristics, involving digital transformation and sound financial planning for companies already during the pandemic to better adapt to the post-pandemic period. The results indicate, that thriving organizations leverage digital transformations involving the use of the Internet and Information and Communication Technology (ICT) by integrating Intranet, social media and online communication platforms into their daily business routines. This makes it easier to build and strengthen ties with employees, other stakeholders, especially customers, during and after a crisis, as these measures establish greater trust, an important part of a more sustainable performance. The authors also highlight the importance of balancing resilience and resource storage to better anticipate moments of crisis. They conclude that companies and enterprises that adopt these changes and innovations will not only sustain their business, but also reinvent themselves and benefit in the post-COVID period, being more prepared this way, as they will evolve, adjust, manage changes and innovate in the face of the challenges posed.

The study by Esses et al. (2020) examined the potential role of digital transformation in the transition to a more sustainable environment. Based on the creation of new opportunities, digital transformation may have the potential to support the effective achievement of the Sustainable Development Goals (SDGs) (Alvarez-Risco et al., 2020). Furthermore, it is understood that these new innovation opportunities for digital transformation can be at a lower cost (ElMassah and Mohieldin, 2020). Digital transformation also has the ability to support the efforts of national and local governments to develop the socio-economic environment in a resilient and sustainable way. The article aims to provide an indicator-based understanding of the main characteristics of digitalization that promote sustainable development in the countries of Hungary, Poland, the Czech Republic and Slovakia. An important index for this purpose is the Digital Economy and Society Index (DESI), focusing on the following indicators: 1) connectivity; 2) human capital; 3) internet use; 4) digital technology integration; and 5) digital public services. The article is correlating DESI with the indicators of the SDGs. The authors conclude that there is a good correlation between digital transformation performance indicators and sustainability indicators. The greater the digital transformation, the greater the achievement of a sustainability-based environment. Similar results were published by Randall et al. (2018) for some of the Nordic countries.

Digital transformation involves a paradigm shift by companies based on constant innovation, not one simply on the acceptance of technology (Kim et al., 2020). There are different types of digital innovations, which depend on the size of the company and the industry branch. This process connects both, the analogue (or physical) and digital (or virtual) worlds, through which firms face changes in all innovation activities. This leads to implications in terms of firms' innovation activities to ensure that digital transformation is something that is purposeful and does not serve as a disadvantage for firms. The authors also highlight the importance that and governments need to create and enforce legislation and policies that are appropriate for different types of companies and enterprises so that full sustainability in business can be achieved.

The article published by Mihailovic et al. (2020), on the other hand, focuses on remote working (home-office), the necessary digital transformation and the increase in changes in cyber-attacks during teleworking. With the installation of teleworking, companies have seen enormous savings in various aspects: telephone, electricity, water and sewage, elimination of waste and brutal cuts in the hours used for the commuting of their employees. For the employees, too, the benefits range from better quality of life, less risks with commuting, higher productivity and lower expenses in several senses, such as transportation and food. This indicates different aspects of sustainability as the main effect of home office.

CONCLUSION

Pandemic has pushed the labor market in Brazil and worldwide into the future. Social isolation measures led to the widespread adoption of the home office and, at the same time, an acceleration of digital transformation in various sectors and segments of the economy. A large proportion of employees have worked, or continue to work, in the home office regime. And everything indicates that this alternative will last and may grow even more after the pandemic; for this the companies needed to adapt, using digital transformation as the basis of the respective technological solutions, to become competitive during and after the pandemic of COVID. At the same time, the decentralization of activities in companies, has a positive impact on efficiency gains, because besides raising the essential issue of their efficiency, it also highlights the issue of their mutual correlation with the cybersecurity of organizations. Digital assets result in the digitalization of processes, which go beyond the digitalization of information, resources, value creation and revenue growth. It has been noted, already before the pandemic, that there is a clear reciprocal correlation of teleworking and the escalation of cyber-attacks. Based on this, they suggest the need to develop innovative defense mechanisms in organizations by investing in technological infrastructures for security against cyber-attacks. At the same time, training needs to be conducted for employees in the area of digital skills via continuous education.

In this context, digital transformation plays a key role as means to overcome the problems and challenges of crises, such as COVID-19, as well as an opportunity for economic growth. Digital transformation cannot be seen only as a change and improvement in certain technologies, but it also implies a higher degree of sustainability based on social and environmental responsibility, generating a transition that will change the quality of life of employees and the population as a whole. Much more than a simple acceptance of new technology, digital transformation involves a change by companies that is based on constant innovation, supporting sustainability and the way customers are seeing these companies.

The relationship between sustainability and digital transformation was found to go through the socio-environmental responsibility that is a fundamental part of the ESG criteria. Both ESG and digital transformation have a lot of potential to revamp companies' strategies in the way they plan, implement and operate successfully. On one side, digital transformation has come to change the process and make it more agile. And on the other side, ESG criteria are the company's sustainability driver, which defines its economic, social and environmental impact on the world. Digital transformation has come to support and facilitate the implementation of companies' ESG-based actions in favor of a better world. For future research it is proposed to study ESG and sustainable business models using artificial intelligence.

REFERENCES

Albreem, M. A., Sheikh, A. M., Alsharif, M. H., Jusoh, M., & Yasin, M. N. M. (2021). Green Internet of Things (GIoT): Applications, practices, awareness, and challenges. *IEEE Access: Practical Innovations, Open Solutions*, *9*, 38833–38858. doi:10.1109/ACCESS.2021.3061697

Alvarez-Risco, A., Arcentales, S. D. A., & Rosen, M. A. (2020). Sustainable Development Goals and Cities. In *Building Sustainable Cities* (pp. 313–330). Springer. doi:10.1007/978-3-030-45533-0_21

Anderson, C., Bieck, C., & Marshall, A. (2021). How business is adapting to COVID-19: Executive insights reveal post-pandemic opportunities. *Strategy and Leadership*, *49*(1), 38–47. doi:10.1108/SL-11-2020-0140

Bonanomi, M. M. (2019). *Digital Transformation of Multidisciplinary Design Firms: A Systematic Analysis-Based Methodology for Organizational Change Management*. Springer. doi:10.1007/978-3-030-19701-8

Byrnes, K. G., Kiely, P. A., Dunne, C. P., McDermott, K. W., & Coffey, J. C. (2021). Communication, collaboration and contagion: "Virtualisation" of anatomy during COVID-19. *Clinical Anatomy (New York, N.Y.)*, *34*(1), 82–89. doi:10.1002/ca.23649 PMID:32648289

Carvalho, R. B., Reis, A. M. P., Larieira, C. L. C., & Pinochet, L. H. C. (2021). Digital transformation: Construct definition challenges and scenarios for a research agenda. *RAM. Revista de Administração Mackenzie*, *22*(6). Advance online publication. doi:10.1590/1678-6971/eramd210400

da Silva, A. R., & Gasparotto, A. M. S. (2020). Um estudo sobre rastreabilidade visando ao controle de processos. *Revista Interface Tecnológica*, *17*(1), 708–720. Advance online publication. doi:10.31510/infa.v17i1.796

de Bem Machado, A., Secinaro, S., Calandra, D., & Lanzalonga, F. (2021). Knowledge management and digital transformation for Industry 4.0: A structured literature review. *Knowledge Management Research and Practice*, 1–19. doi:10.1080/14778238.2021.2015261

ElMassah, S., & Mohieldin, M. (2020). Digital transformation and localizing the Sustainable Development Goals (SDGs). *Ecological Economics, 169*, 106490. doi:10.1016/j.ecolecon.2019.106490

Esses, D., Csete, M. S., & Németh, B. (2021). Sustainability and digital transformation in the visegrad group of central European countries. *Sustainability, 13*(11), 5833. doi:10.3390u13115833

Fachini, M. P., Mesquita, N. P., Oliveria, R. P., & França, P. G. de (2017). Internet das coisas: uma breve revisão bibliográfica. *Conexões, ciência e tecnologia, 11*(6), 85-90. . doi:10.21439/conexoes.v11i6.1007

Ferreira, C. M. S., Oliveira, R. A. R., Silva, J. S., & Cunha Cavalcanti, C. F. M. D. (2020). Blockchain for machine-to-machine interaction in industry 4.0. In R. Rosa Righi, A. Alberti, & M. Singh (Eds.), *Blockchain Technology for Industry 4.0. Blockchain Technologies*. Springer. doi:10.1007/978-981-15-1137-0_5

Hinterhuber, A., & Nilles, M. (2021). Digital transformation, the holy grail and the disruption of business models. *Business Horizons, 65*(3), 261–265. doi:10.1016/j.bushor.2021.02.042

Joseph, E., & Dhanabhakyam, M. M. (2022). Role of Digitalization Post-Pandemic for Development of SMEs. In *Research Anthology on Business Continuity and Navigating Times of Crisis* (pp. 727–747). IGI Global. doi:10.4018/978-1-6684-4503-7.ch036

Kachela, K., Lodh, S., & Nandy, M. (2021). Post-Pandemic Sustainable Business Solution. *Journal of Business and Management Studies, 3*(1), 47–57. doi:10.32996/jbms.2021.3.1.5

Kim, R. Y. (2020). The impact of COVID-19 on consumers: Preparing for digital sales. *IEEE Engineering Management Review, 48*(3), 212–218. doi:10.1109/EMR.2020.2990115

Kim, S., Choi, B., & Lew, Y. (2021). Where is the age of digitalization heading? The meaning, characteristics and implications of contemporary digital transformation. *Sustainability, 13*(16), 8909. doi:10.3390u13168909

Kotler, P., Kartajaya, H., & Setiawan, I. (2017). *Marketing 4.0: do tradicional ao digital*. Sextante.

Kraus, S., Jones, P., Kailer, N., Weinmann, A., Chaparro-Banegas, N., & Roig-Tierno, N. (2021). Digital Transformation: An Overview of the Current State of the Art of Research. *SAGE Open, 11*(3), 21582440211047576. doi:10.1177/21582440211047576

Lee, C.-H., Wang, D., Desouza, K. C., & Evans, R. (2021). Digital transformation and the new normal in China: How can enterprises use digital technologies to respond to COVID-19? *Sustainability, 13*(18), 10195. doi:10.3390u131810195

Lichtenthaler, U. (2020). *Integrated Intelligence: Combining Human and Artificial Intelligence for Competitive Advantage*. Campus Verlag GmbH.

Machado, A. de B., Sousa, M. J., Nawaz, F., & Martins, J. M. (2020). Impacts of the integration of Chinese managers in the Western economies the case of Brazil. *Transnational Corporations Review, 1*(1), 25. doi:10.1080/19186444.2019.1693203

Mihailović, A., Cerović Smolović, J., Radević, I., Rašović, N., & Martinović, N. (2021). COVID-19 and beyond: Employee perceptions of the efficiency of teleworking and its cybersecurity implications. *Sustainability, 13*(12), 6750. doi:10.3390u13126750

Nagel, L. (2020). The influence of the COVID-19 pandemic on the digital transformation of work. *The International Journal of Sociology and Social Policy, 40*(9/10), 861–875. doi:10.1108/IJSSP-07-2020-0323

Ng, A. (2021). Green Investing and Financial Services: ESG Investing for a Sustainable World. In *The Palgrave Handbook of Global Sustainability* (pp. 1–12). Springer International Publishing. doi:10.1007/978-3-030-38948-2_104-1

Obrenovic, B., Du, J., Godinic, D., Tsoy, D., Khan, M. A. S., & Jakhongirov, I. (2020). Sustaining enterprise operations and productivity during the COVID-19 pandemic: "Enterprise Effectiveness and Sustainability Model. *Sustainability, 12*(15), 5981. doi:10.3390u12155981

Pedersen, L. H., Fitzgibbons, S., & Pomorski, L. (2021). Responsible investing: The ESG-efficient frontier. *Journal of Financial Economics, 142*(2), 572–597. doi:10.1016/j.jfineco.2020.11.001

Pereira, T. M., Sacilotti, A. C., & Madureira Júnior, J. R. (2019). Computação em nuvem: plataforma como serviço. In E. R. Martins (Ed.), *Fundamentos da ciência da computação 2* (pp. 116–125). Atena Editora. doi:10.22533/at.ed.90319210612

Petrunenko, Y. V., Petrunenko, I. V., Chychun, V. A., Shuprudko, N. V., Kalynichenko, Y. V., & Manal, I. A. I. (2021). Trends in the management of global economic development in the post-pandemic period. *International Review, 10*(1-2), 68-78. https://www.ceeol.com/search/article-detail?id=979047

Ramírez-Durán, V. J., Berges, I., & Illarramendi, A. (2021). Towards the implementation of Industry 4.0: A methodology-based approach oriented to the customer life cycle. *Computers in Industry, 126*, 103403. doi:10.1016/j.compind.2021.103403

Randall, L., Berlina, A., Teräs, J., & Rinne, T. (2018). *Digitalisation as a Tool for Sustainable Nordic Regional Development: Preliminary Literature and Policy Review*. https://www.nordregio.org/wp-content/uploads/2017/04/Digitalisation_Discussion-Paper_Jan-31.pdf

Rashi, P., Bist, A. S., Asmawati, A., Budiarto, M., & Prihastiwi, W. Y. (2021). Influence of Post Covid Change in Consumer Behaviour of Millennials on Advertising Techniques and Practices. *Aptisi Transactions on Technopreneurship, 3*(2), 85–92. doi:10.34306/att.v3i2.210

Rolle, R., Martucci, V., & Godoy, E. (2020). Architecture for Digital Twin implementation focusing on Industry 4.0. *IEEE Latin America Transactions, 18*(5), 889–898. doi:10.1109/TLA.2020.9082917

Russel, S. J., & Norvig, P. (2009). *Artificial Intelligence: a modern approach* (3rd ed.). Prentice Hall.

Schwab, K. (2016). *A quarta revolução industrial*. Edipro.

Silva, A. L. E., Moraes, J. A. R., Benitez, L. B., & Kaufmann, E. A. (2021). Impressão 3D: Análise da evolução e seus impactos no mundo científico. *Revista FSA*, *18*(11), 124–144. Advance online publication. doi:10.12819/2021.18.11.6

Singh, N. (2019). Big data technology: Developments in current research and emerging landscape. *Enterprise Information Systems*, *13*(6), 801–831. doi:10.1080/17517575.2019.1612098

Singh, U. S., Singh, N., Gulati, K., Bhasin, N. K., & Sreejith, P. M. (2021). A study on the revolution of consumer relationships as a combination of human interactions and digital transformations. *Materials Today: Proceedings*. Advance online publication. doi:10.1016/j.matpr.2021.05.578

Vial, G. (2019). Understanding digital transformation: A review and a research agenda. *The Journal of Strategic Information Systems*, *28*(2), 118–144. doi:10.1016/j.jsis.2019.01.003

Chapter 22
Blessing or Curse?
Challenges Working Mothers Faced Post COVID-19 in Brunei Darussalam

Nur Aqilah Adilah Hj Abd Rahman
https://orcid.org/0000-0003-2215-8661
Universiti Teknologi Brunei, Brunei

Heru Susanto
Universiti Teknologi Brunei, Brunei

ABSTRACT

Mothers have multiple roles. Mothers prepare food, clothe, bathe their kids, clean the house, taking care of their husbands and families. With these, it was already tiring and required proper time management. Working mothers added another responsibility. Some parents would prefer to send their kids to school at an early age. Then COVID-19 hits in 2019 and suddenly everyone is working and studying at home. Is it a blessing to have all the family at home or a curse knowing that another burden will be added to the working mother alone? This chapter investigates how working mothers feel pre and post COVID-19. Thirty-six mothers participated in questionnaires and online pool votes. Results from questionnaires and online polls concluded that most mothers are feeling depressed and stressed during COVID-19, and allowing kindergarten to re-open actually helped working mothers since the burden of educating shifted back to the teacher.

INTRODUCTION

Brunei Darussalam is currently facing the third wave of the Covid-19 delta variant. The first wave was in March 2020, the second wave happened in Brunei in August 2021, and the third wave was in early February 2022. Numbers have risen over time, and Brunei is in Partial Lockdown. Twenty-five thousand five hundred eighty-four cases were reported as of 16 February 2022, with 98 deaths. Large numbers of organizations and companies only allow Work from Home (WFH), and only essential workers would be doing Work from Office (WFO). However, even if the employees were allowed to WFO,

DOI: 10.4018/978-1-7998-8856-7.ch022

only a limited number were allowed per day/shift. According to the health ministry, people at risk are people with several diseases, older people, pregnant women, and children. Therefore, the health ministry recommended children and pregnant women stay at home and only go out when necessary, i.e., during clinic appointments. With enforced distancing rules, parents had to balance the increased challenges of combining work and family roles without the support of public childcare or their social networks, such as grandparents, relatives, and friends (Alon et al., 2020; Collins et al., 2020; Li et al. 2021; Zhou et al. 2020; Zoch et al. 2021a, Vicari et al. 2022).

The ministry removed a few restrictions, and the government implemented several measures for the public to have an everyday life as before COVID-19. But it is impossible because almost every country is in the endemic phase and trying to live with COVID-19 and treat it like flu. Some countries were already opening their borders, but Brunei has not yet opened its borders but only allows essential travel. Standard procedures were also not as tight as they were before. In the first wave of COVID-19, the quarantine period given to positive cases or close contact was 14 days. But in the third wave of COVID-19, reduced the quarantine period to 10 days only.

BACKGROUND AND RESEARCH GAP

Brunei has a population of 429, 999 as stated by the department of economic planning and statistic (deps.gov.bn). The numbers of cases in Brunei were at 22,515, with already about 98 deaths as of 13 Feb 2022 with about 94.1% of the population have completed two shots of the Covid-19 vaccine, 404,629 people, and about 94.9% have completed one Covid-19 vaccine shote, 408,069 people and about 46% population have completed booster vaccine, 197,800 people. The government advises the public to get a booster shot since Omicron has become the dominant virus in Brunei.

There has been speculation on how the second wave started in Brunei Darussalam. Some said it was due to the carelessness of the cleaner in one of the hotels that placed people under quarantine who were found positive; some even speculated that a few numbers people crossed the neighboring countries, i.e., Limbang and Miri, through secret roads for contrabands. The cases were sometimes high and sometimes low. The higher case would involve dormitories for the foreign worker because they were numbers of workers who lived in the same staff house/apartment, therefore, infecting numbers of people.

The health ministry advised high-risk people to WFO, and mothers are one of them. Working mothers are a population experiencing heightened levels of parenting stress during the Covid-19 Pandemic. (Limbers, McCollum, and Greenwood 2020). From the researcher's point of view, the first wave of Covid-19 was seen as a blessing in disguise for mothers because mothers could spend time with their children and at the same time help their children with school work, and it is easier to keep up with Online Learning. Brunei Darussalam is currently in the Endemic Phase despite being affected by the third wave of the Covid-19. It seems complicated because mothers were whining about how their children will be graded for their exams, for instance, Cambridge O'Level Exam, A'Level Exam, and lower and higher secondary exams.

Few mothers also complained that their children have difficulty concentrating and seem to be delaying school work provided by their instructor/teacher/lecturer. Covid-19 has forced non-essential workers to work from home, whereas schools and daycares are closed. (Limbers, Mccollum, and Greenwood 2020). Because few businesses have to close fore, some of the income from these working mothers got affected. They have difficulty keeping up with telephone line reloads; some have problems with laptops or smartphones for Online Learning. For example, if they have five children and only 3 have smartphones, then the other two children will have to use their parent's phones or laptops, making it harder to juggle between their work and their children's work.

Quoting Wilson (2006), "*Many working women said they worked because they 'needed' the money and which they defined as specific material goods-an extra lesson, additional clothes, a vacation, furniture, owning a home, car or even just a television.*" As a working mother, it is crucial to settle issues at the office and at the same time, take care of the children and sometimes the family; adding to it, time management is also critical to working mothers (Rahman, N.A.A, 2021). Balancing everything is difficult sometimes for mothers, sometimes hoping to settle matters in the office without affecting people at home. For instance, bringing the stress from work to home could easily affect the mentality and emotions of the child at home that only wish to enjoy playing time with their parents.

Research Gap 1: Main concern of the organization was because of the lay-off of staff. An organization is trying to understand how hard it would be for these people to maintain their job during the Pandemic, how people survived the Pandemic and only a few were concerned about working mot.h According to (Zamarro, Perez-Arce, and Prados 2020), female employment dropped thirteen percent from March to April.

Research Gap 2: Research focuses on the hardship that parents faced during the Pandemic, where it is evident that working mothers needed more attention than working fathers. Women carried a heavier load than men in providing child care and mothers were believed to reduce their working hours more compared to fathers. (Zamarro, Perez-Arce, and Prados 2020)

Research Gap 3: Researches done on understanding the mental health of parents were done widely. Surveys were about 10,000 participants done in each wave of COVID-19 and monthly. Results may be biased because participant would just simply tick without reading properly knowing that they will be another same questions next month. Some would not even realize to share if there were any improvement in handling the situation in Pandemic. Women tend to report a higher level of psychological distress than men (Zamarro, Perez-Arce, and Prados 2020). Using a qualitative method would help to point out the burden on women and mothers during inequalities (Guy and Arthur 2020). The third gap may be used in future research since using the qualitative method would require a longer period to gather compared to quantitative method. Hence author used the quantitative method instead of the qualitative. Mothers would be reluctant to participate in a lengthy interview during the partial lockdown, which would stress working mothers.

PROBLEMS AND OBJECTIVES

Problems

Mothers have traditionally been viewed as caregivers who took care of the family, the finances, the housework, and the preparation of meals. Still, they were never compensated for their efforts because that is what a mother should have done. However, when children reach certain ages, the responsibility is reduced as children go to school, and teachers would take over the responsibility of tutoring the children. Since the pandemic hits, everything has to be done by the mothers. Parents were forced to be full-time caretakers and teachers throughout the COVID-19 reaction, but they could not rely on aid from outside the immediate family (Cooney, 2020; Senior, 2020).

Before the pandemic, it was already hard to balance work and housework and now adding the responsibility of tutoring the children from home is another added stress. At first, it was manageable; mothers would feel tired over time. The pandemic focused on how people try to live in the new standard but can mothers do the same thing? Can mothers cope with roles as mothers, employees, and educators?

Fear of the virus and adjusting to life amidst school closures, quarantine, and stay-at-home orders were represented in the publications at the time, which depicted a stressful new reality in which families' lives were badly severely, ted and these changes had a significant impact on parents' lives since they essentially relocated childcare, academics, and leisure interests inside the home activities that parents had previously outsourced too maintain a healthy work-life balance (Lewis, 2020; Senior, 2020; Forbes et al. 2022)

Objectives

As a result, there have been calls for higher wages and improved working conditions, but this sadly has not been the case for mothers and mothers working. The economy is not closed. Everyone is cooking, cleaning, and taking care of their loved ones. Economists do not value it because it is ordinarily unpaid women's work (Riley Andrea O, 2020). The main objective of this paper is to understand what this mother feels before and post COVID-19. The secondary purpose is to investigate whether the government measures to help these working mothers reduce the burden of doing unpaid women's work and handling their job.

METHODOLOGY

Data Collection

Data were collected using a quantitative method. Online questionnaires were distributed through Instagram, Email, and Whatsapp social media platforms. Questions focused more on how working mothers would feel post and pre COVID-19. Researchers also used opinion Poll questions on Instagram so mothers could vote on a list of feelings asked on Instagram. According to Merriam Webster, an opinion pool is an activity in which many people are asked the same questions to determine what most people think about something. For instance, the questions asked were, what do you feel during a pandemic? Happy, challenging, attractive, etc.

Research Design

There were five sections in the questionnaire; demographic, dual role, work from home, mental health and coping with trauma, and short answer questions. Questionnaires were in 2 languages, Malay and English. So if the mother had difficulty understanding the English Language, Malay versions of questionnaires were also available. In contrast, ten questions in the opinion pool focused on the mental health of working mothers post COVID-19.

Research Size

Thirty-six participants answered through both platforms. Fifteen were from an online questionnaire, while 110 interactions from the Instagram pool and about 21 participants participated.

Potential Challenges

Only a few want to participate. Most reasons for not participating were busy managing the housework and office work and helping their children with schoolwork since a few students still do learning from home. Another challenge would be some of the participants pretended to be working mothers. To address this issue, researchers checked participant accounts thoroughly to make sure no men, no housewives, or no teenagers participated in the online pool. After a thorough investigation, 36 filtered participants participated.

HYPOTHESIS

H0: Pandemic COVID-19 has a null impact on the well-being of working mothers.

Pandemic COVID-19 restrictions and measures have a null impact on the well-being oe working mothers.

H1: Pandemic COVID-19 positively impacts the well-being of working mothers.

Pandemic COVID-19 restrictions and measures positively impact the well-being of the working mothers.

H2: Pandemic COVID-19 negatively impact the well-being of working mothers

Pandemic COVID-19 restrictions and measures negatively impacts the well-being of the working mothers.

LITERATURE REVIEW

Challenges amid Covid-19

Table 1.

	Titles	Author	Data sample	Major Findings
1	The psychological impact of COVID-19 quarantine measures in northeastern Italy on mothers in the immediate postpartum period (2020)	1. Zanardo, Vincenzo 2. Manghina, Valeria 3. Giliberti, Lara 4. Vettore, Michela 5. Severino, Lorenzo 6. Straface, Gianluca	Ninety-one samples non-concase-control–control study of mothers who gave birth during a COVID-19 quarantine period. Participants completed the Edinburgh Postnatal Depression Scale (EPDS) Self-administered questionnaire.	Concerns about the risk of exposure to COVID-19, combined with quarantine measures adopted during the COVID-19 pandemic, adversely affected the thoughts and emotions of new mothers, worsening depressive symptoms
2	Academic motherhood during COVID-19: Navigating our dual roles as educators and mothers (2020)	1. Guy, Batsheva 2. Arthur, Brittany	Experiences as working moms during COVID-19. The combined approach of both feminist and heartfelt autoethnography.	Being a working mom is tough, but being a mom during COVID is mmore complexthan we could have ever imagined. Despite all of the challenges mothers ar face, mothers wouldn't trade a second of this time we canpend at home with our children for anything. Mothers love being moms and all of the rewards it brings. Having tiny humans at their back and call has made it all the more challenging to do our work and take care of ourselves.
3	Gender differences in couples' division of childcare, work and mental, health during COVID-19 (2020)	1. Zamarro, Gema 2. Prados, María J.	3980 unique respondents. Using the multinomial discrete choice legit model to study the determinants of observed childcare arrangements	Women have carried a heavier load than men in childcare provision during the COVID-19 crisis, even while still working. Mothers' current working situations appear to have a limited influence on childcare provision. However, this division of childcare ised with a reduction in working hours and an increased probability of transitioning out of employment for working mothers. A small but new gap in psychological distress that emergtween mothers and women without school-age children in the household in early April. This new gap appears to be driven by higher levels of psychological distress reported by mothers of elementary school-age and younger children.
4	The interplay between mothers' and children's behavioral and psychological factors during COVID-19: an Italian study (2021)	1. Di Giorgio, Elisa 2. Di Riso, Daniela 3. Minioni, Giovanna 4. Cellini, Nicola	An online survwas ey administered to 245 mothers with preschool children	A general worsening of sleep quality and distortion of time experienced in both mothers and children and increasing emotional symptoms and self-regulation difficulties in children. Moreover, even when the interplay between the behavioral and psychological factors was investigated, the element that seems to impact both mothers' and children's psychological well-being mostly was their sleep quality.

Continued on following page

Table 1. Continued

	Titles	Author	Data sample	Major Findings
5	"You're a teacher, you're a mother, you're a worker": Gender inequality during COVID-19 in Ireland (2021)	1. Clark, Serena 2. McGrane, Amy 3. Boyle, Neasa 4. Joksimovic, Natasha 5. Burke, Lydia 6. Rock, Nicole O' Sullivan, 7. Katriona	Thirty working mothers were interviewed in this study, and qualitative analyses were conducted to gain insight into their work and family life during the restrictions. The	The analysis findings indicate that COVID-19 has negatively impacted working mothers in relaaboutpsychological well-being, experiences of negative emotions, and the redefinition of family dynamics, in which working mothers have adopted additional and disproportionate care burdens. These findings are consistent with the current research arguing that COVID-19 has highlighted an increase in the gender gap in domestic labor and the undermining of career advancement for working mothers.
6	Rebuild the Academy: Supporting academic mothers during COVID-19 and beyond (2021)	1. Fulweiler, Robinson W. 2. Davies, Sarah W. 3. Biddle, Jennifer F. 4. Burgin, Amy J. 5. Cooperdock, Emily H.G. 6. Hanley, Torrance C. 7. Kenkel, Carly D. 8. Marcarelli, Amy M. 9. Natassa, Catherine M. 10. Mayo, Talea L. 11. Santiago-Vàzquez, Lory Z. 12. Traylor-Knowles, Nikki 13. Ziegler, Maren	Data-driven research.	Research ensures a strategy that would provide a more equitable academy for working mothers now and in the future. While the data are clear that COVID-19 is disproportionately impacting mothers, many groups could benefit from these strategies. Rather than rebuilding what we once knew, let us be the architects of a new world.
7	Who cares when care closes? Care arrangements and parental working conditions during the COVID-19 pandemic in Germany Gundula (2021)	1. Zoch, Gundula 2. Bächmann, Ann Christin 14. Vicari, Basha	Novel data on parents with children are based on two independent panel surveys of the National Education Panel Study (NEPS) 785 rwith espondents	We find a traditional division of care work in families in Germany during the first months of the COVID-19 pandemic, with mothers actingprimarymain caregivers in families with older and younger children. In addition, the data also revealed that a substantial part of older schoolchildren had to take care of themselves – a result that hints towards the significant challenge for parents to combine child- child-carechooling, and working life during the crisis. Our results ttherefore align with the few initial panel studies highlighting the re-enforced gender inequalities in family work during the COVID-19 pandemic in Germany

Continued on following page

Table 1. Continued

	Titles	Author	Data sample	Major Findings
8	Leisure time sports and exercise activities during the COVID-19 pandemic: a survey of working parents (2021)	1. Mutz, Michael 3. Reimers, Anne K.	Methods Study design The present study, "Examining physical activity and sportsbehaviorr in the face of COVID-19 pandemic" (SPOVID), is based on a large-scale, cross-sectional survey design. A sample representing the German population was questioned using computer-assisted web interviewing. For recruitment, FORSA makes use of random digit dialing. Respondents were invited via email and were able to answer the survey on their computer, tablet, or mobile phone. Overall, 1508 individuals completed the study. As this analysis is concerned with the interplay of full-time work and childcare duties/supervision of homeschooling during the pandemic, only respondents in full-time employment, based on their self-report, are selected (N= 631).	It can be concluded from this studyThee COVID-19 pandemic's effect on LTSE levels is generally negative but more complex than often assumed. Working mothers make up a group in which LTSE considerably declined, whereas other social groups were more easily able to maintain their activity levels during the pandemic. Besides greater exhaustion, nervous symptoms, and reduced well-being (Ohlbrecht & Jellen, 2021), forced sedentariness may be another negative health factor that working mothers face in the ongoing pandemic. Hence, gender inequality and the broader context of living and working conditions must beconsidered, when the impact of the COVID-19 pandemic is assessed.

Whole nation approach

Table 2.

	Titles	Author	Data sample	Major Findings
1	Pandemic leadership: lessons learnt from a small state of Brunei Darussalam (2020)	1. Khairul Hidayatullah Basir 2. Ummi Faizah Abdul Rahman	Review of literature on Covid-19 and conducting crisis management in Brunei	Whole of nation approach or Whole of Government Approach proved to be successful with the full cooperation of the government, monarch and public. Engaging in constant updates and government willingness to be led by experts has gained public trust which then leads to 'flattening the curve' and containing Covid-19 which then resulted Brunei not needing to opt for lockdown.

Challenges after Covid-19 lockdown

Table 3.

	Titles	Author	Data sample	Major Findings
1	The COVID-19 pandemic has increased the care burden on women and families (20[2]20)	3. Power, Kate	The article explores the care and crisis of mothers under COVID-19.	It is clear that to prevent further deepening of gender inequality, it is necessary and possible to take account of the additional unpaid care burden placed on women and families during the COVID-19 pandemic. Given that a large proportion of people have reservations about going back to their pre-pandemic "normal" life and are interested in making changes in their own lives and wider society, this could be an opportunity for systemic changes that enable care work to be valued and accounted for in economic and social policies. But will we have the time and energy to push for these changes now that we have added a "fourth shift" (homeschooling while working) to our burden of unpaid care work?
2	In the Covid-19 Economy, You Can Have a Kid or a Job. You Can't Have Both. (2020)	Perelman, Deb	A systematic review of articles related to struggling parents in the early phase of Covid-19.	After four months of working all hours, at great stress levels, while our children have gone without playdates and playgrounds and all of the other stimuli that help them thrive — most parents have been shocked to find that state governments don't have any creative or even plausible solutions.
3	Estimating the immediate impact of the COVID-19 shock on parental attachment to the labor market and the double bind of mothers. (2020)	Heggeness, Misty L.	Monthly panel data from Integrated Public Use Microdata Series, Current Population Survey that administered approximately 60,000 householdss. Respondentss entthe er sura vey in specified month and answer consecutively in months	While advancements have been made over recent decades regarding women's rights, wage equality, and participation in formal labor markets, this pandemic has made it clear that something has got to give. Moms are trying to juggle multiple responsibilities: the job they get paid to do in the formal labor market alongside the responsibilities of parenting and childcare. Parents—especially mothers—remain ever vulnerable to the availability of affordable childcare while they work. Without more formal and intentional care systems, mothers will forever be vulnerable to career scarring during any major significant like this pandemic or any other event that triggers an increase in domestic tasks within her household.
4	"Trying to Function in the Unfunctionable": Mothers and COVID-19 (2020)	Reilly, Andrea O	The article explores the care and crisis of mothers under COVID-19 through an examination of comments and discussions on the Facebook group Mothers and COVID-19, which was set up over two weeks in early May 2020.	The pandemic has resulted in a greater appreciation for work that was little valued and poorly paid before the pandemic, such as social workers and retail workers. As a result, there have been calls for higher wages along with improved working conditions, but this sadly has not been the case for mothers and mothers work. The economy is not closed. Everyone is cooking, cleaning, and taking care of their loved ones. It's just not valued by economists because it is ordinarily unpaid women's work
5	The COVID-19 pandemic and subjective well-being: longitudinal evidence on satisfaction with work and family (2021)	1. Möhring, Katja 2. Naumann, Elias 3. Reifenscheid, Maximiliane 4. Wenz, Alexander 5. Rettig, Tobias 6. Krieger, Ulrich 7. Friedel, Sabine 8. Finkel, Marina 9. Cornesse, Carina 10. Blom, Annelies G.	Surveys were divided into 2; 1663 surveys were for work satisfaction, while 2639 were for family satisfaction.	Generally, a significant reduction was found in satisfaction with work and family life. The negative effect on family satisfaction is significantly more robust, while the impact on work satisfaction differs between subgroups, similar significant reduction in family satisfaction for everybody. The decline in work satisfaction is at most substantial for mothers, while for fathers exists a slight, albeit insignificant, increase in work satisfaction. For those without children, we also see a significant reduction in work satisfaction

Continued on following page

Table 3. Continued

	Titles	Author	Data sample	Major Findings
6	What COVID-19 could mean for the future of "work from home": The provocations of three women in the academy (2021)	1. Couch, Danielle L. 2. O'Sullivan, Belinda 3. Malatzky, Christina	Depth of lived experience between three academic women. Three questions were asked 1) What is my experience of working from home during the COVID-19 pandemic? 2) How does this compare to previous experiences of working from home? 3) What might it mean for future WFH opportunities post the COVID-19 pandemic?	It was identified that WFH policies affect women in complex ways, intentionally causing tension between the professional, familial, and social dimensions of our lives. Women often have multilayered experiences of WFH. For some, WFH is their major employment format, although WFH arrangements have not been formally legitimized as valued and productive for women in ways that acknowledge the value of the "whole" person and their "lived experience," not just the dimension which is paid.
7	Gender differences in unpaid care work and psychological distress in the UK Covid-19 lockdown (2021)	1. Xue, Baowen 2. McMunn, Anne	6,166 parents responded to UK Household Longitudinal Study	Women spent much more time on unpaid care work than men during the lockdown, and it was more likely to be the mother than the father who reduced working hours or changed employment schedules due to increased time on childcare. Women who spent long hours on housework and childcare were more likely to report increased levels of psychological dis- tress. Working parents who adapted their work patterns increased more psychological dis- tress than those who did not.
8	The impact of the COVID-19 pandemic on maternal and perinatal health: a scoping review (2021)	1. Kotlar, Bethany 2. Gerson, Emily 3. Petrillo, Sophia 4. Langer, Ana 5. Tiemeier, Henning	The search yielded 396 publications, of which 95 were included. Pregnant	Pregnant women and mothers were not found to be at higher risk for COVID-19 infection than people who are not pregnant; however pregnant people with symptomatic COVID-19 may experience more adverse outcomes compared to non-pregnant people and seem to face disproportionate negative socio-economic consequences. High-income and low- and middle-income countries alike faced significant struggles. An increased risk of distress and psychiatric problems during pregnancy and postnatal during the pandemic is likely, but high-quality evidence is also lacking in this case. This review, however, provides good evidence that mothers with children are more likely to suffer job and income losses during the pandemic than men and women without children. Single mothers, in particular are likely to suffer from food insecurity. These socio-economic consequences for women are similar across many high- and low-income countries.

Continued on following page

Table 3. Continued

	Titles	Author	Data sample	Major Findings
9	Working parents, financial insecurity, and childcare: mental health in the time of COVID-19 in the UK (2021).`	1. Cheng, Zhiming 2. Mendolia, Silvia 3. Paloyo, Alfredo R. 4. Savage, David A. 5. Tani, Massimiliano	Our analysis is based on Wave 9 of the UK Household Longitudinal Study (UKHLS) and the April and May 2020 waves of the UKHLS COVID-19 survey. Participants were asked to complete one survey per month until July 2020, followed by a survey every two months from September 2020, in order to track changes in their circumstances and environments.	The heterogeneous distribution of the post-pandemic burden implies that public policy decisions should account for these underlying inequities. Working parents, especially mothers, are experiencing a worse mental and financial position. The burden can be eased by amplifying support for childcare and homeschooling, including nonfinancial assistance such as training in educational content delivery. The increased conflict between work and life domains, especially for those with children, can be mitigated by policies that acknowledge the varied circumstances in which households find themselves. Our results strongly suggest that while the COVID-19 lockdown policies put in place by the UK government were well-intentioned, the 'one-size-fits-all' approach resulted in less effective measures for working families. As financial and mental distresses are not equally distributed across the populations, our results highlight that the most precarious groups of society are disproportionately more affected by mental distress. Addressing this imbalance requires a more targeted approach to policy and emergency management to ensure that the burden of homeschooling and financial distress is no worse than the mental health problems caused by COVID-19.
10	Childcare, work or, worries? What explains the decline in parents' well-being at the beginning of the COVID-19 pandemic in Germany?	1. Vicari, Basha 2. Zoch, Gundula 3. 3. Bächmann, Ann-Christin	Data from two independent panel surveys of the German National Education Panel Study. Data were combined from these panel, and a total of 2,678 adults were observed/	Researchers confirm a decline in the well-being of working mothers than fathers. However, part-time worker and access to emergency care reduce the gender gap in decreased well-being, and researchers cannot explain the more significant decrease in mothers' well-being by increased childcare responsibilities or altered working conditions of the mothers.

FINDINGS AND DISCUSSIONS

Analysis from questionnaires

The reliability test was the first Spss tool used to test internal consistency. It is used to see how closely related a set of items are as a group hence measuring the strength of the character. The general rule of thumb for Cronbach's Alpha of .70 and above is sound, .80 and above is better, and .90 and above is best.

Likert Scale questions were divided into a dual roles, work from home and mental health, and coping with stress. The dual role section has five items with Cronbach's Alpha of .456. The work from Home section has six items with Cronbach's Alpha of .171, while Mental Health and Coping with stress section has five items with Cronbach's Alpha of .405. Julie Pallant (2013) suggested that for an item below 10, Cronbach's Alpha should at least be >.05. Inter-Item Correlation Matrix also has negative, and not all items are positive in all three sections. Hence, to have a greater Cronbach's Alpha, we deleted a few items. One thing from the dual roles section was deleted. Cronbach's Alpha is .534, which is acceptable. Two items from the work from the home section were deleted, leaving Cronbach's Alpha of 0.685 and 1 item from the mental health sections and leaving Cornbach's to .571, which is also acceptable. From the results obtained, Cronbach's Alpha is moderately reliable.

Normality tests were then tested to see whether it was normally distributed data. Items were less than 100. Therefore, we will be using the Shapiro-Wilk test of normality. Values for each section were .527, 0.078, and .102, and not all are statistically significant, which means that data are normally distributed. We then compute log data to check if the data are normally distributed. Results from the log show that two items' values are more significant than 0.05, further proving that data are normally distributed. This calculation then shows that H0 is accepted and not rejected. The reason for this would be some of these working mothers said that the pandemic had not caused them any trouble where in fact, the working mothers were facing problems. Some of these working mothers seem to act strong despite all the hardships faced during a pandemic. Failing to reject the null hypothesis indicates that the sample did not provide sufficient evidence to conclude that positive and negative impacts existed. We assumed that the null hypothesis was correct until we gathered enough evidence to prove otherwise.

Table 4.

1. How many children you do have?	1 TO 2	3 +		
	17	4		
2. Pandemic have been very ___ to you?	Challenging	Depressing	Neutral	Interesting
	20	5	12	9
3. As a mother and, at the same time, working, what do you feel during a pandemic?	Happy	Hard to Balance	Neutral	Hard to manage time
	3	11	5	9
	Hard to Focus	Anxiety	Stress	Depress
	3	10	9	5
4. Quarantine life is the best life?	Yes	No		
	10	11		
5. Did you send your children to kindergarten Pre-Covid19?	Yes	No		
	10	10		
6. Following recent measures by MOH, do you agree when kindergartens was allowed to open?	Yes	No		
	11	10		

Analysis of Instagram Poll

21 working mothers participated in the Instagram poll, and some participants voted more thanone1 tion in 1 question:

DISCUSSION

Pandemics have been very challenging to most of these working mothers who participated. Five working mothers think that pandemic is depressing, nine working mothers think it was exciting, and some think it's a neutral feeling. Asking about how they feel, about half the numbers of these working mothers were feeling anxiety and find it very difficult to balance roles that have to be carried by working mothers. A study conducted by (Tang 2021) shows that anxiety was also found in children among primary, junior, and senior secondary students. It is understandable because aside from working, these mothers have to care for their families and be their children's teachers or educators. Nine working mothers had a hard time in time management, and a few were feeling stressed and depressed.

Quarantine life is the best life for ten working mothers, and the ability to spend time with their children makes them feel comfortable being quarantined with their families. At the same time, 11 working mothers think that a quarantine life is not the best life. Among these 21 mothers, ten mothers send their children to kindergarten pre-COVID-19. Following a recent measure by the Ministry of Health Brunei Darussalam, votes were almost balanced at question no 6. Questionnaires also have a similar question, and from 15 participants, ten agree that kindergartens were allowed to open even though kids below 5 are yet to be vaccinated.

To sum up, from 36 participants, 27 mothers agreed to open a kindergarten. This result further proves that these working mothers needed that extra help (kindergarten) to educate their children. Even though the null hypothesis is accepted, the second analysis discussion further proves that pandemics impact these working mothers.

Brunei allows Child Care Centre to re-operate from January 17, 2022, based on the decision on agreement of the COVID-19 Steering Committee and results from an online survey conducted in collaboration with the Prime Minister's Office and Ministry of Health that was participated by 11,566 parents nationwide. Quote ministers of Culture Youth and Sport "Of the respondents concerned, the MCYS noted that most had agreed on the need for the re-opening of CCCs in January. The re-opening was intended to provide space and opportunities for working parents to send their children for care during working hours" He also added that out of the 11,566 parents, 10,812 or 94 percent are married. Out of that number, 72 percent agreed for CCCs to re-open, while only 51 percent agreed to the re-opening of kindergarten schools. (The Star, 2022)

Brunei Darussalam is still in the third wave of the Pandemic and still in the Early Endemic Phase; the government lifted measures and restrictions slowly. (1) Publics were allowed to travel, but with the updated standard of procedures over time and rules and regulations for travels to and from Brunei Darussalam, which were in effect since April 1 but the public is cautiously optimistic about the re-opening of air travel to Green List countries listed by the government. (Borneo Bulletin; the Scoop Brunei, 2022)

(2). Schools will be allowed to open at the capacity of 100%, whether children were vaccinated or unvaccinated, on May 14 (Borneo Bulletin, 2022). It is not a must for children aged to be vaccinated if their parents are unwilling to allow their children to be vaccinated. About 28.6% of children aged 5-11 have been vaccinated. As of April 20, the cumulative total of the Brunei population who have taken their booster shots was 63.1%. (Borneo Bulletin; the Scoop Brunei, 2022)

(3) Numbers of mass gatherings were also increased from 100 to 300 for public halls and only 30 people in private homes which they have to take the ART test beforehand. (Borneo Bulletin; the Scoop Brunei, 2022)

(4) Since the Pandemic, many employees and small businesses were also affected. Every time a family was found positive for Covid-19, the Ministry of health would deliver a care package inclusive of medicines for adults and Children, free ART kit for the family, and necessities such as rice, sugar, and eggs for the quarantine period. People under quarantined were also contacted daily by the health ministry to check every patient's health that self-isolates in their private home. The Ministry of Finance also urges companies not to lay off their workers amid the Pandemic and reduce the rent for small business owners to cope with their suffering business during the Pandemic. (Borneo Bulletin; the Scoop Brunei, 2022)

The government introduced (5) Telephone lines specifically for Covid-19 related to the public; 148 and 123. The public can use these helplines to get the answer to frequently asked questions associated with Covid-19 that the people need to get information. The public can also use the helpline to handle government-related matters such as renewing a driving license, road tax, an Identification Card, and other issues.

Ministry of Health introduced (6) apps making it easier for the public to communicate with ministries or the government on any critical issues. For example, TransportBN for transportation issues, QUEUP for banking, and The Ministry of Health also introduced the Bruhealth app to let the public update their daily health report, vaccine status, and ART kit results. This app also helps the government to track if there were any infected Covid-19 in specific areas.

Aside from government efforts, NGOs and the public were also helping each other by assisting these mothers. For instance, online learning sometimes is challenging for mothers who have to share their smartphones with their children. Mothers, particularly single mothers, were provided aid by the government to help them reduce the burden or challenges faced during Covid-19 (Borneo Bulletin, 2022). It is a Whole of Government approach or Whole of Nation Approach, governments, the monarch, organizations, the public, NGOs, front-liners, medical assistant's hand-in-hand to help each other. (Basir and Rahman, 2021)

CONCLUSION

The mothers will always have to sacrifice their time to take care of the family and their children. Women spent much more time on unpaid care work than men during the lockdown, and it was more likely to be the mother than the father who reduced working hours or changed employment schedules due to increased time on childcare (Xue and McMunn 2021).

Even though it is the responsibility of women to care for the family, these women were more likely to report increased levels of psychological distress (Xue and McMunn 2021). Results from the opinion poll clearly show that these working mothers find that Covid19 have been very challenging for them, and these mothers face anxiety.

However, results obtained from analysis showed that null hypothesis need to be accepted and not rejected that is covid-19 have neutral impact on these working mothers. Explanation would be because these working mothers have had help from family members. Since half of the population were required to stay at home so it is safe to say that these mothers basically have help. Feeling stress, depress maybe from the fact that they have stayed at home for way too long. Children cannot go out and feeling bored, online learning with disturbed telephone line would cause mothers and even children to feel stress. Study by (Marroquín, Vine, and Morgan 2020) found that depression, generalized anxiety disorder, intrusive thoughts, insomnia and acute stress are consistently associated with social distancing, and when staying home too long. Study by (Kallitsoglou and Topalli 2021) further analysis of the extracts that reflected maternal experiences reveal how their daily realities had changed because of having to be present for their children as well as at work.

RECOMMENDATIONS

It is clear that to prevent further deepening of gender inequality, and it is necessary and possible to take account of the additional unpaid care burden placed on women and families during the COVID-19 pandemic. Many people have reservations about going back to their pre-pandemic "normal" life. They are interested in making changes in their own lives and broader society; this could be an opportunity for systemic changes that enable care work to be valued and accounted for in economic and social policies. But will we have the time and energy to push for these changes now that we have added a "fourth shift" (homeschooling while working) to our burden of unpaid care work? (Power 2020)

Future research will need to be done when the third wave of Covid-19 has passed and see whether everything has changed and will mothers then be able to cope with everything. Currently, the Ministry of Health only allows the opening of the kindergarten at 80% capacity to help the working mothers manage and reduce the burden of balancing their roles post COVID-19.

REFERENCES

Cheng, Z., Mendolia, S., Paloyo, A., Savage, D., & Tani, M. (2021). Working parents, financial insecurity, and childcare: Mental health in the time of COVID-19 in the UK. *Review of Economics of the Household*, *19*(1), 123–144. doi:10.100711150-020-09538-3 PMID:33456425

Clark, S., McGrane, A., Boyle, N., Joksimovic, N., Burke, L., Rock, N., & O' Sullivan, K. (2021). "You're a teacher you're a mother, you're a worker": Gender inequality during COVID-19 in Ireland. *Gender, Work and Organization*, *28*(4), 1352–1362. doi:10.1111/gwao.12611

Couch, D., O'Sullivan, B., & Malatzky, C. (2020). What COVID-19 could mean for the future of "work from home": The provocations of three women in the academy. *Gender, Work and Organization*, *28*(S1), 266–275. doi:10.1111/gwao.12548

Di Giorgio, E., Di Riso, D., Mioni, G., & Cellini, N. (2020). The interplay between mothers' and children behavioral and psychological factors during COVID-19: An Italian study. *European Child & Adolescent Psychiatry*, *30*(9), 1401–1412. doi:10.100700787-020-01631-3 PMID:32865654

Fulweiler, R., Davies, S., Biddle, J., Burgin, A., Cooperdock, E., Hanley, T., Kenkel, C., Marcarelli, A., Matassa, C., Mayo, T., Santiago-Vàzquez, L., Traylor-Knowles, N., & Ziegler, M. (2021). Rebuild the Academy: Supporting academic mothers during COVID-19 and beyond. *PLoS Biology*, *19*(3), e3001100. doi:10.1371/journal.pbio.3001100 PMID:33690708

Guy, B., & Arthur, B. (2020). Academic motherhood during COVID-19: Navigating our dual roles as educators and mothers. *Gender, Work and Organization*, *27*(5), 887–899. doi:10.1111/gwao.12493 PMID:32837022

Heggeness, M. (2020). Estimating the immediate impact of the COVID-19 shock on parental attachment to the labor market and the double bind of mothers. *Review of Economics of the Household*, *18*(4), 1053–1078. doi:10.100711150-020-09514-x PMID:33132792

Hj Abd Rahman, N. (2022). Effects of Employee Performance on the Implementation of Total Quality Management: Perspective of Working Mothers. In P. de Pablos, X. Zhang, M. Almunawar, & J. Labra Gayo (Eds.), *Handbook of Research on Big Data, Green Growth, and Technology Disruption in Asian Companies and Societies* (pp. 175–194). IGI Global. doi:10.4018/978-1-7998-8524-5.ch010

Kotlar, B., Gerson, E., Petrillo, S., Langer, A., & Tiemeier, H. (2021). The impact of the COVID-19 pandemic on maternal and perinatal health: A scoping review. *Reproductive Health*, *18*(1), 10. doi:10.118612978-021-01070-6 PMID:33461593

Möhring, K., Naumann, E., Reifenscheid, M., Wenz, A., Rettig, T., Krieger, U., Friedel, S., Finkel, M., Cornesse, C., & Blom, A. (2020). The COVID-19 pandemic and subjective well-being: longitudinal evidence on satisfaction with work and family. *European Societies*, *23*(sup1), S601-S617.

Mutz, M., & Reimers, A. (2021). Leisure time sports and exercise activities during the COVID-19 pandemic: A survey of working parents. *German Journal of Exercise and Sport Research*, *51*(3), 384–389. doi:10.100712662-021-00730-w

Perelman, D. (2020). In the Covid-19 Economy, You can have a kid or a job. You can't have both. *The New York Times*.

Power, K. (2020). The COVID-19 pandemic has increased the care burden of women and families. *Sustainability: Science, Practice and Policy*, *16*(1), 67–73.

Prados, M., & Zamarro, G. 2020. Gender Differences in Couples' Division of Childcare, Work and Mental Health During COVID-19. SSRN *Electronic Journal* doi:10.2139/ssrn.3667803

Reilly, O, A. (2022). Trying to function in the unfunctionable: Mothers and Covid-19. *Journal of Motherhood Initiative*, *11*(1), 8–24.

The Star. (2022). *Brunei gives the nod to re-open childcare centres from Jan 17*. Available at: https://www.thestar.com.my/aseanplus/aseanplus-news/2022/01/06/brunei-gives-the-nod-to-re-open-childcare-centres-from-jan-17

Vicari, B., Zoch, G., & Bächmann, A. (2022). Childcare, work or worries? What explains the decline in parents' well-being at the beginning of the COVID-19 pandemic in Germany? *ZtF. Zeitschrift für Familienforschung*.

Xue, B., & McMunn, A. (2021). Gender differences in unpaid care work and psychological distress in the UK Covid-19 lockdown. *PLoS One, 16*(3), e0247959. doi:10.1371/journal.pone.0247959 PMID:33662014

Zanardo, V., Manghina, V., Giliberti, L., Vettore, M., Severino, L., & Straface, G. (2020). Psychological impact of COVID-19 quarantine measures in northeastern Italy on mothers in the immediate postpartum period. *International Journal of Gynaecology and Obstetrics: the Official Organ of the International Federation of Gynaecology and Obstetrics, 150*(2), 184–188. doi:10.1002/ijgo.13249 PMID:32474910

Zoch, G., Bächmann, A., & Vicari, B. (2020). Who cares when care closes? Care-arrangements and parental working conditions during the COVID-19 pandemic in Germany. *European Societies, 23*(sup1), S576-S588.

ENDNOTES

1. Tables are collection of journals related to challenges amid COVID-19.
2. Tables above journals articles related to whole nation approach and challenges after lockdown.
3. Collection of journals related to challenges after COVID-19 partial lockdown.
4. Data above are results from Opinion Poll questions from Instagram Poll done on Working Mothers.

Chapter 23
New Approaches to Business Strategies After COVID-19

Ayla AVCI
https://orcid.org/0000-0002-1871-4090
Independent Researcher, Turkey

ABSTRACT

COVID-19, which emerged in March 2020, caused a rapid change in the ongoing order all over the world within the framework of the rules set by the governments. For this reason, managers should be visionary people who give importance to research and development. The restrictions experienced during the pandemic period had a negative impact on activities of the companies all over. Since the beginning of the pandemic, all businesses have introduced different applications from working hours to the products and services they produce. Due to restrictions experienced, many companies had to close the year with a loss. In fact, this pandemic has revealed whether companies are strategically and technologically prepared. For this reason, while companies that follow technological developments have succeeded, on the contrary, companies that are unaware or do not care about these developments are left behind.

INTRODUCTION

The corona virus which emerged in 2019 in Wuhan, the capital of China's Hubei region, has been declared as a pandemic period due to its deadly effect in the world. The long-term social, economic and health impacts of covid-19 on companies continue. Due to the spread of infections in countries, travel restrictions and quarantines that disrupt international life supply chains and diminishing profits (Sharma et al, 2020:12). Considering the decreasing commercial transactions of companies due to the precautionary measures taken during the pandemic period, all business sectors should also be sensitive after the pandemic in terms of sustainability (Savitri et al, 2020: 63). Covid-19 caused a loss of approximately 1 trillion US dollars in the world economy 2020. The decrease in trade due to do closure of enterprises adversely affected all industrial establishments in the economy (Silva, 2020). During the pandemic period, especially small and medium enterprises (SMEs), had to deal with a huge economic burden due to uncertainty. The need for cash arose to pay the salaries and rents of the employees and to

DOI: 10.4018/978-1-7998-8856-7.ch023

rebuild the infrastructure. It was not enough for governments to make loan plans to this business to get rid of the pandemic (Morales,2021). In the current situation, companies need to take new measures and measures for their economic relief. For this reason, especially SMEs develop new product supply and sales models to ensure sustainability.

PANDEMIC PERIOD EFFECTS

Due to economic crises that emerged with the onset of the pandemic period, companies all over the world made an effort to protect themselves from negative effects. Companies have developed solutions to prevent business interruptions with their existing employees, to prevent supply chain contractions and to protect their capital (Bond III et al, 2020). Many sectors have been damaged in covid-19. The most important of these is undoubtedly the airline companies During this period, passenger planes were converted to cargo planes due to travel restrictions. Aircraft companies had to develop new operating models (Molenaar et al, 2020).

Figure 1. Covid-19 Sectoral Effects
Source: (*Dcode EFC Analysis, 2020*).

In the analysis made by Dcode in 2020, the sectors that won and lost in the covid-19 process were determined. This (figure,1).

Potential Losers

Manufacturing: Production, transitions to sales, fabric factories starting fabric production.

Construction & Real Estate: Massive construction was avoided by combining state investment infrastructure and consumer investment patterns.

Automotive: Governments have supported the automotive industry to replace and convert old car bodies.

Aviation & Maritime: Suez Canal revenues outperformed simple global trade.

Tourism & Leisure: Especially the tourism sector has been the most effected sector, even with government support.

Financial Services: Emphasis is placed on accelerating financial matters.

Potential Winner

Agriculture: The requirement is the rate of change of growth.

E-Commerce: Accelerating e-commerce and internet usage due to social distance.

Food Processing & Retail: While food consumption increased at home during the curfew, covid-19 negatively affected the demand for meat, dairy products, sweet and snacks in hotel restaurants.

Medical Supplies & Services: The expectation of the pandemic has resulted in higher demand in imports and exports of pharmaceuticals (medical product).

Personal & Health Service: The production of medical masks and disinfectants has increased during the pandemic.

During the covid-19 process, demand has increased in sectors such as the agricultural sector, personal health and medical services, e-commerce, which provide food to communities. E-commerce will survive as it provides goods and services in quarantine applications (Hadi et al, 2020).

COVID-19 AND CHANGE STRATEGIES

The pandemic period has changed the economic structure in the world causing the business strategies of companies to change. At the same time, this period created an opportunity for new business designs (Vebeke et al, 2020). For this reason, many companies have focused on supply processes, product development and efficiency practices that will make their products more economical and more easily delivered to their consumers.

Proposed rapid direct selling of potentially perishable frozen foods as a frozen food center by creating a central wholesale market among small business affected by the covid-19 crisis in Malaysia (Figure 2).

Figure 2. Before Covid-19 Independent Distribution Approach
Source: *(Fabeil et al., 2020: 841).*

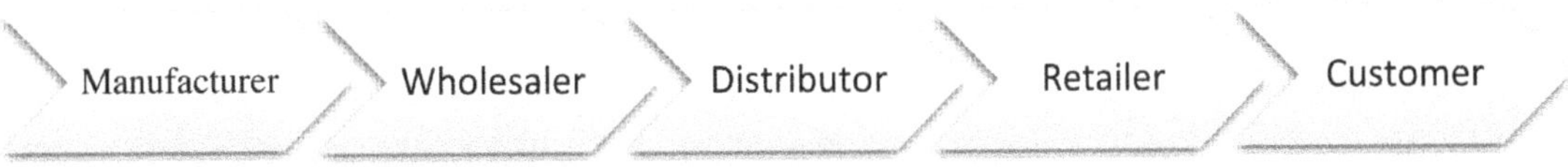

During Covid-19 Crisis Multi-Channel Distribution Approach.

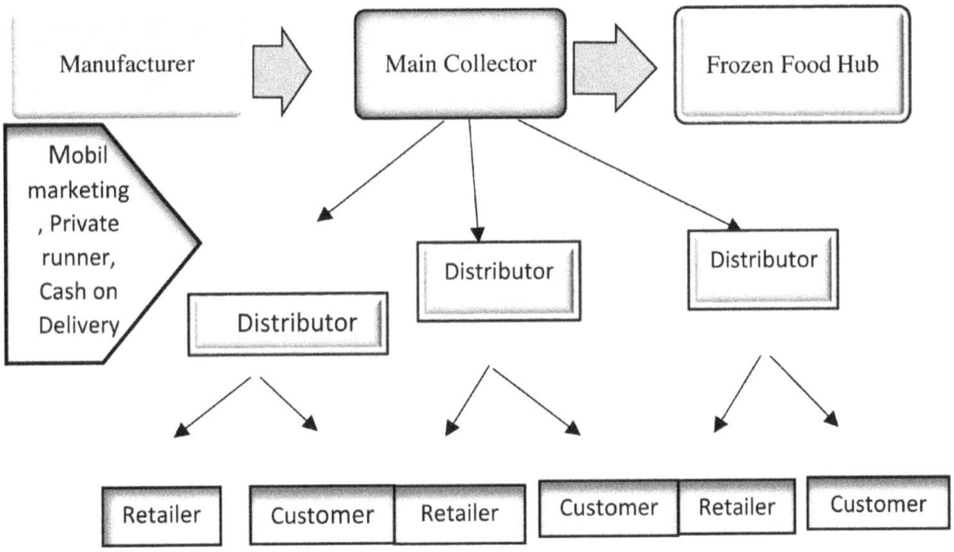

As a result of covid-19, there have been deteriorations due to global uncertainties. For this reason, the post covid-19 globalization wave tends towards regionalization. The trend of regionalization has increased due to international interests, growing populism, nationalism and protecting the domestic economy. May be globalization can reduce global welfare, but high costs affect countries (Enderwick and Buckley, 2020:108). The hospitality sector has also been adversely affected after covid-19. In this sector, strategies to create a supply chain in a shorter time have been developed to reduce food waste and create alternative food networks. Sustainable development of the industry can leverage digital technology to prevent food waste Table 1 shows the long, bulky, unsympathetic traditional food supply chain process. Table 2 shows the new short, transparent, and reliable supply chain (Filimonau, 2021:4).

Table 1. Covid-19 and Traditional Supply Chain

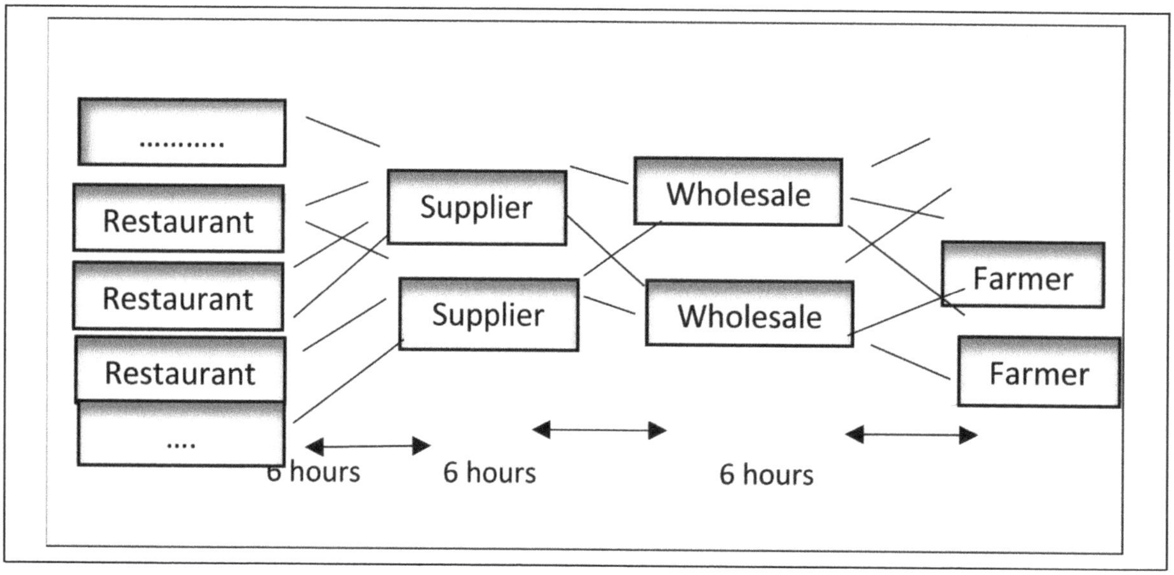

Table 2. New Supply Chain Model for Post Covid-19

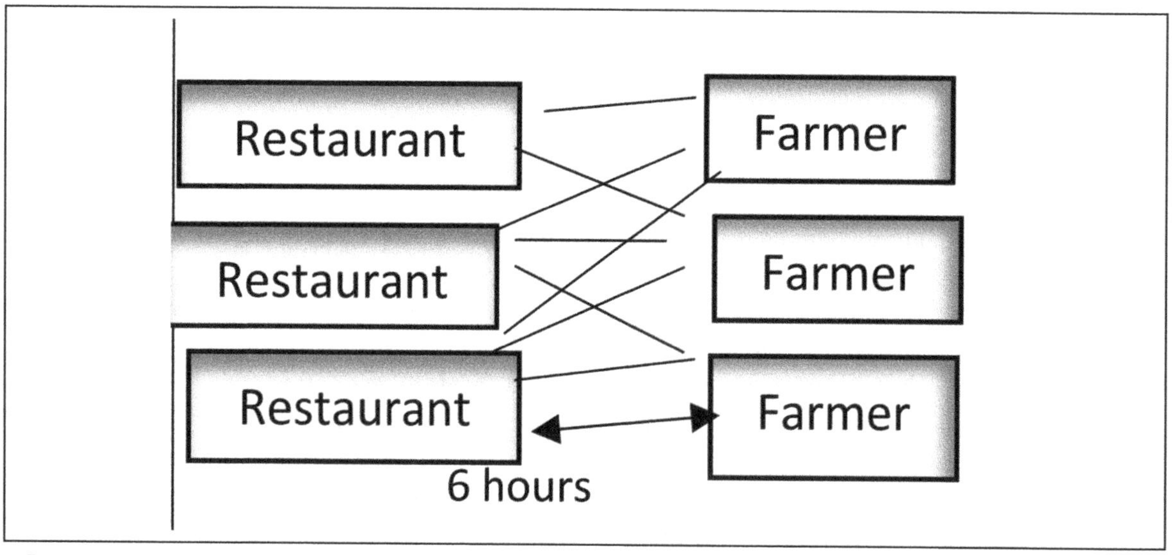

Source: (Filimonau, 2021).

Anderson et al (2020), provided five important business improvement advice for businesses after covid-19. These: **Digital transformation;** It gained momentum after digitalization, which was neglected before the pandemic. **The future of work**; Workforce safety, skills, flexibility in companies' employee satisfaction is prioritized. Managers of employee well-being strives to meet its highest priorities. **Trans-**

parency; Managers from an organizational perspective, focusing on the demands for growth and competitiveness. Renewed discipline in evaluating and managing new business ventures and enlargements are implemented with openness and transparency. **Sustainability:** Before the coronavirus, companies' sustainability strategies were largely focused on environmental problems caused by pollution and climate change. However, when faced with the covid-19 crisis, environmental sustainability, personal security issues came to the fore. For this reason, the products are produced in a way that is sensitive to the personal and environmental problems of the consumers (Anderson et al., 2020).

Figure 3. Production Plan
Source: *(Alvarez et al, 2020).*

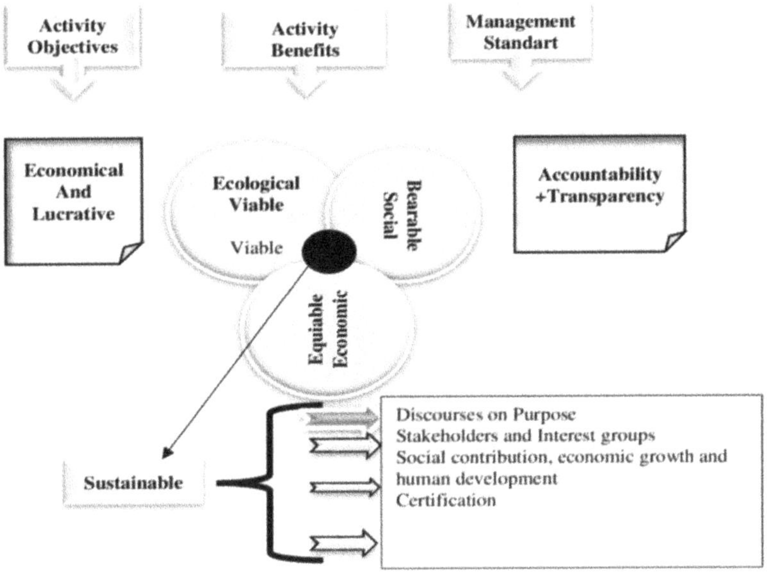

In socioeconomic context defined by climate change the regular fluctuation of economic crises and resource depletion, it necessary to develop a useful model to meet the social objectives demanded by civil society. Combines profit (economic, social, and ecological) and social development to create a production model: objectives, stakeholders, social contribution and certification. Business impact is monitored through management transparency and accountability standards (figure 3), (Alverez et al, 2020).

E-commerce which increased during the pandemic period, should be developed, and continued especially in the retail sector after the pandemic (Savitri et al, 2020:71). Micro and Small Business (MSEs) should develop post-covid-19 alternative additional browser scenarios and strategies to continuously improve business. In particular the digitalization of MSEs should be supported in order to improve sustainable production and business continuity during and after the covid-19 period. In table 2, this framework has been developed and shown (Bai et al, 2021).

Figure 4. Red Oceans and Blue Oceans
Source: *(Morales, 2021).*

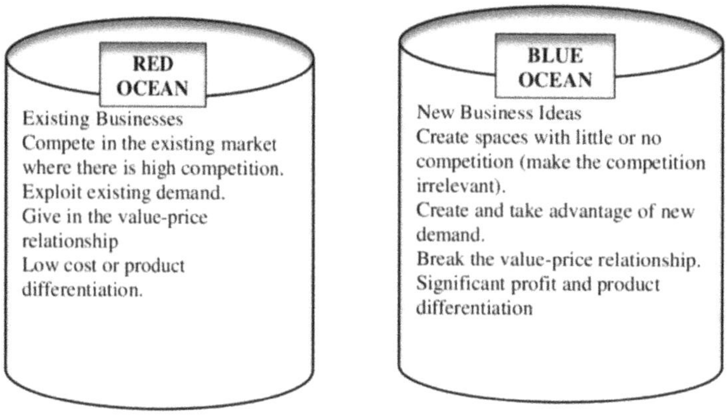

According to Morales (2021:5), it is necessary to use digital resources (mobile communication tools, online trainings) to solve the problems of SMEs. A Blue Ocean Strategy should be developed to identify opportunities arising from problems and explore different markets. This strategy can provide insight into new product development. It is an effective method in reducing unnecessary activities in the company and eliminating waste), it is necessary to use digital resources (mobile communication tools, online trainings) to solve the problems of SMEs. A Blue Ocean Strategy should be developed to identify opportunities arising from problems and explore different markets. This strategy can provide insight into new product development. It is an effective method in reducing unnecessary activities in the company and eliminating waste. The characteristics of the red ocean (many competitors) and blue oceans (no or few competitors) are shown in figure 4.

Table 2. Covid-19 pandemic digitization for sustainable development of MSEs

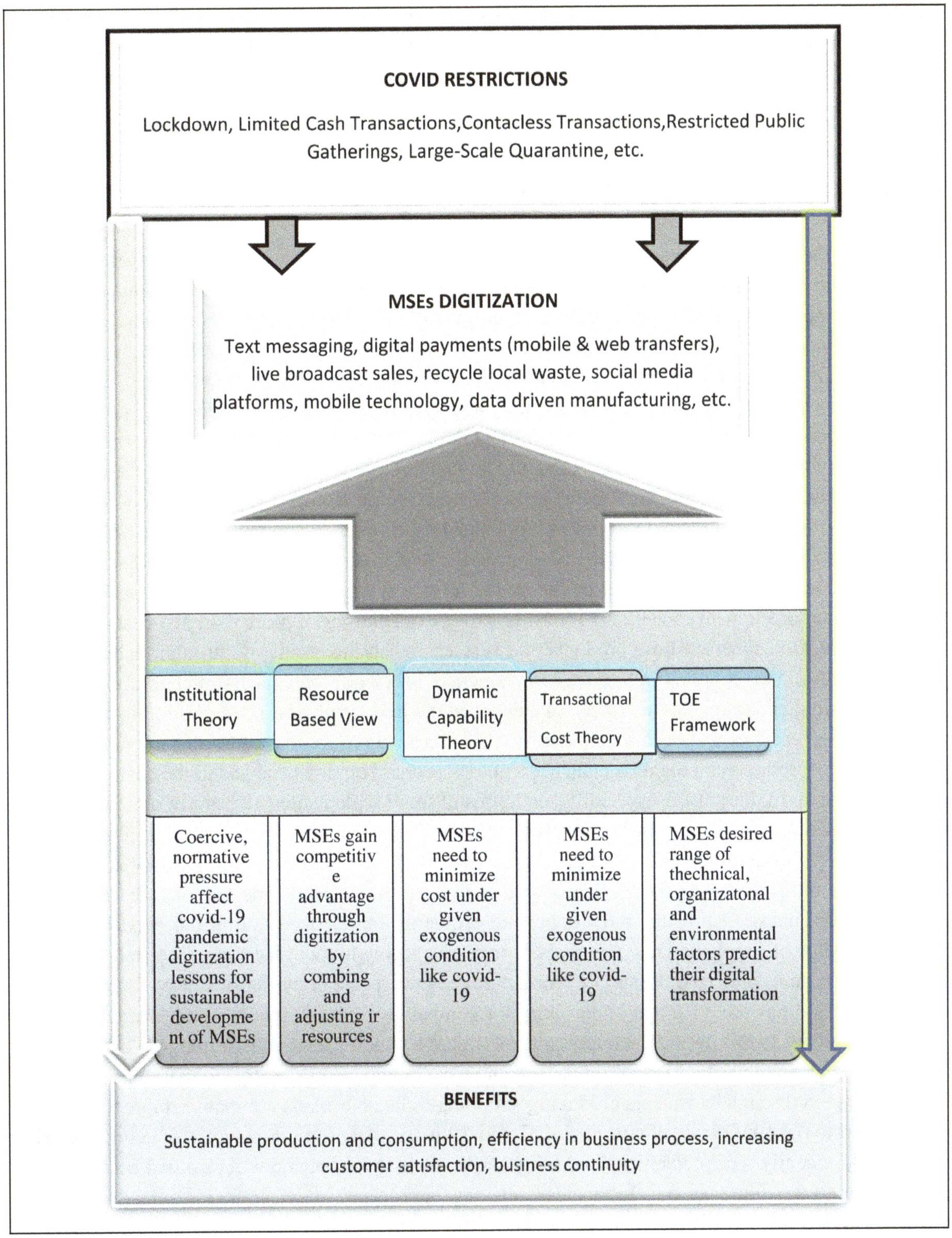

Source: (Bai et al, 2021:1997).

Another issue post covid-19 new normally good human resources strategy is company leadership. A strong leader will provide success to companies during the pandemic period. Especially human resources mangers play a key role in the development of leaders (Ichsan et al, 2020). For this reason, companies need to consider managers who are responsible, able to develop strategies and have vision who can better manage the post-covid-19 situation.

MAIN FOCUS OF THE CHAPTER

Covid-19 disease, which emerged in March 2020, caused a rapid change in the ongoing order all over the world within the framework of the rules set by the governments. For this reason, managers should be visionary people who give importance to research and development. The restrictions experienced during the pandemic period had a negative impact on activities of the companies all over the world have entered a difficult period due to the economic crisis. Since the beginning of the epidemic, all business has introduced different applications from working hours to the products and services they produce. Due to do restrictions experienced, many companies had to close the year with a loss. In fact, this epidemic has revealed whether companies are strategically and technologically prepared. For this reason, while companies that follow technological developments have succeeded, on the contrary, companies that are unaware or do not care about these developments are lift behind. The main purpose of business is to make profit. For this reason, it is the first duty of the society to offer the products and services they need with the least cost and the highest quality to the service of the consumers. At this point, companies have come to compete with each other. Today, however expectations of more than just cost and quality have emerged. Consumers, whose products and services reach them quickly through technology, expect an increase in diversity as well as this convenience. Likewise, the expectations of employees and stakeholders in their companies have been managers who will develop new strategies in the new period, the target of enterprises has been sustainability. It is aimed to ensure the future of the companies, by producing new products and to deliver and present low-cost and quality products to the costumers at the appropriate time. In this period, especially, medium and small scaled enterprises were more affected by the crisis. The aid funds created by the governments could not meet the expenses such as rent, workers' salaries and operating expenses. First of all, this business started to develop solution models. They have developed methods to deliver the products to those in need in a shorter time without the need for too many supplier chains. One of the most important problems experienced during the pandemic period was the shortage of supply and raw materials. Companies trying to meet their raw material needs from domestic companies preferred the supply problem to the lowest cost in the shortest way. In fact, that the pandemic period has provided and opportunity for companies to develop new strategic models and to renew themselves. In this period the importance of digital technologies has also emerged. The necessity of digital transformation which many companies ignore has begun. Almost every company has entered the e-commerce era through its web page. Making shopping online has made companies more transparent. This has led to the confidence of consumers. Covid-19 is the most important cause of economic crisis in the world recently. The precautions and suggestions made in this period will also make a significant contribution to the future periods. In this research, new approaches in the strategies of businesses after covid-19 were discussed with the help of the data in the literature.

SOLUTIONS AND RECOMMENDATIONS

During the pandemic period, large scale companies generally turned to some applications such as dismissal of employees, limiting wages, increasing or decreasing working hours. SMEs companies on the other hand have focused on developing models in order to fulfill the economic crisis struggle in the shortest time and as desired without disrupting their services to customers. The reason for this is the presence of retail companies that will primarily meet the customer demands and needs of small, medium and large-scale enterprises in a shorter time. For this reason, it is thought that the models of these companies will bring innovations in the production and transportation of large companies' products.

FUTURE RESEARCH DIRECTIONS

In the literature review conducted in this research, the strategies made during the covid-19 period were discussed. Despite the company's distribution channels and supply chain problems in the new period models for sustainability have been developed. New product plans were made, and digitalization was emphasized. In times of crisis, companies need to have foresighted managers to create a new vision for themselves and lead them in this direction. Small, medium and large enterprises are important indicators of countries domestic markets. It is an important issue to ensure financial cooperation with large companies, which have the ability to quickly evaluate customer requests and demands.

CONCLUSION

After covid-19, it has been revealed that all markets will no longer return to the past. Companies will need to reevaluate their goals by reconsidering their vision and mission. It is also important that they take into account the changes in their customers and competitors (Donthu and Gustafsson, 2020:287). The covid-19 outbreak has revealed that under forming companies may face huge problems unless they reconsider and renew their operations (Amoah et al, 2021:8). Now providing, companies with substandard services to their customers will cause irreversible harm to the companies themselves (Bai et al, 2021:1997). Post-covid 19 business management strategy for micro, small and medium (MSME), entrepreneurs should ensure the improvement and development of good business sustainability by applying strengthening management in marketing, human resources, finance and operations to create an efficient and productive business environment (Fitriyani et al, 2020). At the same time a new digital ecosystem should be created for companies to make a different pos-covid decision-making processes (Teba et al, 2020). After the pandemic, companies should prepare a detailed production plan to be ready for the new normal. In fact, the pandemic has enabled companies operating in every sector the test themselves. while well-prepared companies won those in the opposite situation lost. For this reason, companies should try new model development methods by forming a good crisis team.

REFERENCES

Alvarez, S. M. J., Munoz, V. A., Duque, A. A., & Castillo, D. (2020). B Crops: A Socioeconomic Approach for The Covid-19 Post-Crisis. *Frontiers in Psychology, 11*, 1867. Advance online publication. doi:10.3389/fpsyg.2020.01867

Amoah, A. J., Khan, Z., & Osabutey, L. C. E. (2021). *Covid-19 and Business Renewal: Lessons and Insights from the Global Airline Industry. International Business Review.*

Anderson, C., Bieck, C., & Marshall, A. (2020). How Business is Adapting to Covid-19: Executive Insights Reveal Post-Pandemic Opportunities. *Strategy and Leadership*. Advance online publication. doi:10.1108/SL-11-2020-0140

Bai, C., Quayson, M., & Sarkis, J. (2021). Covid-19 Pandemic Digitization Lessons for Sustainable Development of Micro-and-Small-Enterprises. *Sustainable Production and Consumption, 27*, 1989–2001. Advance online publication. doi:10.1016/j.spc.2021.04.035 PMID:34722843

Bond, U. E. III, Jong, D. D., Eggert, A., Houston, B. M., Kleinaltenkamp, M., Kohli, K. A., Ritter, T., & Ulaga, W. (2020). The Future of B2B Customer Solutions in A Post-Covid-19 Economy: Managerial Issues and An Agenda for Academic Inquiry. *Journal of Service Research, 23*(4), 401–408. doi:10.1177/1094670520960230

Dcode. (2020). *Decoding The Economics of Covid-19*. https://dcodeefc.com/infographics

Donthu, N. and Gustafsson, A. (2020). *Effects of Covid-19 on Business and Research*. . doi:10.1016/j.jbusres.2020.06.008

Enderwick, P. & Buckley, P. (2020). Rising Regionalization: will the post-covid-19 world see a retreat from globalization. *Transnational Corporations, 27*(2).

Fabeil, F. N., Pazim, H. K., & Langgat, J. (2020). The Impact of Covid-19 Pandemic Crisis on Micro-Enterprises: Entrepreneurs' Perspective on Business Continuity and Recovery Strategy, The Asian Institute of Research. *Journal of Economics and Business, 3*(2), 837–844. doi:10.31014/aior.1992.03.02.241

Filimonau, V. (2021). The Prospects of Waste Management in The Hospitality Sector Post Covid-19. *Resources, Conservation and Recycling, 168*, 168. doi:10.1016/j.resconrec.2020.105272

Fitriyani, I., Sudiyarti, N., & Fietroh, N. M. (2020). Strategi Management Bisnis Pasca Pandemi Covid-19. *Indonesian Journal of Social Sciences and Humanities, 1*(2), 87–95.

Hadi, S., & Supardi. (2020). Revitalization Strategy for Small and Medium Enterprises After Corona Virus Disease Pandemic (Covid-19) in Yogyakarta. *Journal of Xi'an University of Architecture & Technology, 8*(4).

Ichsan, N. R., Khaeruman, Santosa, S., Shara, Y., & Liriwati, Y. F. (2020). Investigation of Strategic Human Resource Management Practices in Business After Covid-19 Disruption. *Pal Arch's Journal of Archaeology of Egypt/Egyptology, 17*(7).

Molenaar, M. D., Bosch, F., Guggenheim, J., & Jhunjhunwala, P. (2020). *The Post-Covid-19 Flight Plan for Airlines*. Boston Consulting Group.

Savitri, M. F. and Naili, T. Y. (2020). Henry Mintzberg's Business Management Strategy Post-Pandemic Covid-19 (Social Learning Approach on Ali Murah Shop Madinah). *International Journal of Social Learning, 1*(1), 62-74. DOI: .v1i1.5 doi:10.47134/ijsl

Sharma, M., Luthra, S., Joshi, S. & Kumar, A. (2020). Developing A Framework for Enhancing Survivability of Sustainable Supply Chains During and Post-covid-19 Pandemic. *International Journal of Logistics: Research and Applications.* doi:10.1080/13675567.2020.1810213

Silva, F. M. J., Zanet, G. C., Trezza, R., Lamour, L., & Beraldo, L. A. (2020). The Importance of Dental Office Management in Times of Covid-19 And How to Resume Activities in Post-Pandemic. *Brazilian Dental Science, 23*(2).

Morales, C. O. S. (2021). Innovation as Recovery Strategy for SMEs in Emerging Economies During the Covid-19 Pandemic. *Research in International Business and Finance*, 57.

Teba, S. M. E., Mestanza, G. J., & Fernandez, R. M. (2020). The Application of the Inbound Marketing Strategy on Costa del Sol Planning & Tourism Board. Lessons for Post-Covid-19 Revival. *Sustainability, 12*(23), 9926. Advance online publication. doi:10.3390u12239926

Verbeke, A., & Wenlong, Y. (2020). A few Implications of The Covid-19 Pandemic for International Business Strategy Research. *Journal of Management Studies.* Advance online publication. doi:10.1111/joms.12

KEY TERMS AND DEFINITIONS

Distribution Channel: It is the process chain that ensures that the products are taken from the production place by the manufacturers and reach the buyers.

Strategy: It is whole of the methods used and applied to achieve the determined goals.

Supply Chain: It is the process that covers the distribution of the products and services produced through the network created between suppliers and companies.

Chapter 24
The Meeting Place on Social Media for the Luxury Fashion Industry to Support and Strategically Communicate SDGs

Celia Rangel-Perez
https://orcid.org/0000-0002-5692-2915
Complutense University of Madrid, Spain

Belén López
Business and Marketing School, ESIC University, Spain

ABSTRACT

This chapter explores how the luxury firms communicate their commitments promoting sustainable development and evaluating how these firms create a dialogue in social media with stakeholders. Moreover, the authors analyze how luxury firms get involved with the 17 Sustainable Development Goals explaining the activities they communicate to contribute to society. The methodology used in this research is based on case studies identifying the specific actions of luxury fashion and accessories brands, such as LVMH, Kering, Richemont, CHANEL, Essilor Luxottica, Chow Tai Fook, PVH, and Swatch Group. The results show that all luxury fashion and accessories firms include information on the SDGs on LinkedIn communicating how they contribute to achieving the SDGs with a set of activities, although there is room for improvement to increase the communication that is made in favour of the SDGs, as shown in their sustainability reports.

DOI: 10.4018/978-1-7998-8856-7.ch024

INTRODUCTION

Corporate Social Responsibility is essential for companies in the current global context and even more since the COVID-19 pandemic. This situation is influencing companies to be sustainable (Barnett et al., 2020) and responsible to benefit society. Moreover, firms need to understand the new expectations of stakeholders having the opportunity to improve the stakeholders´ engagement through social media content. Firms can invite stakeholders to participate in CSR activities publishing their opinions about company activities (Buallay et al., 2020).

Recent reports show that sustainability gives several opportunities to luxury brands to engage consumers in social media (McKinsey & Company, 2022). Also, the literature shows that consumers are interested in sustainable practices and CSR in the luxury industry (Thomas, 2018; Khan & Sung, 2021). As a consequence, CSR communication can increase the stakeholders´ engagement creating a dialogue in social media and exploring the interests and capturing their attention and interaction in CSR issues (Okazaki et al., 2020; Barbeito-Caamaño & Chalmeta, 2020; Hartmann et al., 2020). Because some scholars discover a positive impact of sustainability in luxury firms on perceptions, consumers also respond in a positive manner when they receive CSR information (Jin et al., 2017). Therefore, social media gives the opportunity to promote CSR actions inviting people in a real dialogue to participate in sustainability (Dunn, Harness, 2018).

As a consequence, there are multiple possibilities for luxury brands to participate in social networks, which can be reflected through the specific contributions to the 17 SDGs of the 2030 Agenda, where aspects related to sustainability and social commitment are increasingly demanded by the different stakeholders (Bain & Co, 2020). Thus, companies can communicate their actions and invite them to give their opinion on issues with a global impact that affects their business. Although the literature analyzes the communication in different social networks, however, there is scarce literature focused on their communication on LinkedIn (Huang et al., 2019).

To contribute to the study of the communication of the SDGs to society beyond sustainability reporting, this chapter explores how the luxury firms communicate their commitments promoting sustainable development and evaluating how these firms create a dialogue in social media with stakeholders. Because of that, the objective of this chapter is to know how luxury fashion and accessories brands create a stakeholder engagement through social media inviting people to participate in the SDGs when these firms promote their CSR activities. To do this evaluation, the authors study what some luxury brands communicate on LinkedIn from a sustainable perspective.

The evaluation shows that the communication strategy of luxury firms is sometimes consistent with the information that these firms include in their sustainability reports. In general, these activities are influenced by the impact of COVID-19 and sustainability represents a challenge for these companies in this decade, as reflected in the chapter analysis.

BACKGROUND

Why Luxury Brands are Becoming More Sustainable

Recent literature is exploring luxury brands and Corporate Social Responsibility considering the activities of these firms and their impacts from a sustainable perspective, especially after the COVID-19 pandemic. Consequently, CSR is of greater interest to researchers (Carroll, 2021) to know the real contributions of companies from a sustainable perspective (Barnett et al., 2020). Moreover, CSR is based on the expectations of stakeholders (Hörisch, et al., 2020) and it has the potential of improving the stakeholders´ engagement and inviting to participate them in CSR activities (Buallay et al., 2020). In addition, different scholars have emphasized the connection between CSR and stakeholder engagement (Wang et al., 2016; Belyaeva et al., 2020) reinforcing the relationship between firms and stakeholders through sustainable activities and following the global trends to become more sustainable in the luxury sector (McKinsey & Company, 2022).

Some authors have studied CSR in the luxury industry (Amatulli et al., 2017a; Gardetti, 2017) considering the pressure to make their businesses more sustainable (Li & Leonas, 2019) and considering the consumers´ interest on sustainable practices (Khan & Ahmed, 2017; Thomas, 2018). Because the interest on luxury and sustainability has increased in the last years, scholars have placed more emphasis on CSR in the luxury industry and in the luxury sustainability research (Kunz, May & Schimidt, 2020). Furthermore, sometimes consumers have not been informed about sustainable activities (Athwal et al., 2019). However, consumers have a positive perception of those brands known for sustainability and CSR (Olšanová et al., 2018). In addition, consumers demand a more sustainable behavior in brands (Tey, Brindal & Dibba, 2018) and they have different perceptions of luxury firms from a cultural perspective (Kong et. al, 2021).

On the other side, some researchers have studied how companies create value to the stakeholders through the Sustainable Development Goals (SDGs) (Mio et al., 2020). The 17 SDGs promoted by United Nations represent the main challenges for business and governments to contribute to the global challenges and it represents an opportunity for firms to contribute to sustainable development (Taliento et al., 2019). These contributions can be done in different areas considering the 17 SDGs and the 169 targets summarized in the following global challenges signed by 190 countries in United Nations in 2015 (SDG 1, no poverty; SDG 2, zero hunger; SDG 3, good health and wellbeing; SDG 4, quality education; SDG 5, gender equality; SDG 6, clean water and sanitation; SDG 7, affordable and clean energy; SDG 8, decent work and economic growth; SDG 9, industry, innovation and infrastructure; SDG 10, reduced inequality; SDG 11, sustainable cities and communities; SDG 12, responsible consumption and production; SDG 13, climate action; SDG 14, life below water; SDG 15, life on land; SDG 16, peace, justice and strong institutions; SDG 17, partnerships to achieve the goals) (Arora & Mishra, 2019).

In the current post-COVID-19 situation, luxury fashion brands are working in different areas linked to the SDGs, such as supplier management, sustainable design of materials and the circular economy, among others (Karaosman et al., 2019). In this sense, luxury firms should increase their transparency through the information they publish on CSR reports and communicating their impacts on the SDGs (SDGs for Better Fashion, UN) showing their progress on sustainability.

Luxury and CSR Communication in Social Media

CSR communication is a crucial aspect for firms to engage stakeholders about CSR and sustainability commitments. In general, companies use different channels in social media (YouTube, Twitter, Facebook, Instagram, Tik Tok, LinkedIn). However, some studies show that firms don´t create a dialogue with stakeholders in social media (Uzunoğlu, et. al., 2017; Abitbol et al, 2019). As a consequence, companies are not engaging people to participate in CSR activities (Saxton et al., 2020). In addition, companies should explore the interests of their stakeholders and capture their attention on social media (Okazaki et al., 2020) increasing the interaction with the companies in CSR issues (Sreejesh, et al., 2019; Barbeito-Caamaño & Chalmeta, 2020; Hartmann et al., 2020) and taking advantage of a communication strategy on social media to communicate its social and environmental commitments and some values, such as authenticity, legitimacy, and transparency (Gardetti, 2016; Ivan et al., 2016). In addition, some scholars confirm a positive impact of sustainable luxury activities on consumers´ perceptions (Cheah et al., 2016; Amatulli et al., 2017) and they respond positively when they receive CSR information from the firm. However, other researchers suggest a negative brand perception and credibility (Jin et al., 2017).

Social media communication refers to the involvement of stakeholders by effective communication which encourages two-way symmetric communication (De Luca, et al., 2022) improving the relationship between the organization and stakeholders (Giacomarra et al., 2019; Topal et al., 2020). In this sense, social media represent an opportunity to build a stronger relationship (Surucu-Balci et al., 2020) with stakeholders interested in sustainability.

Social media provides unique opportunities to promote CSR inviting consumers to participate in CSR issues. However, its effectiveness is discussed in different studies (Dunn & Harness, 2018). In this sense, different scholars have analyzed some CSR messages to increase the participation of users (Fernandes & Remelhe, 2016; Wang & Huang, 2018). It also represents an opportunity for consumers´ participation in social media in different SDGs activities (Chae, 2021). Furthermore, recent studies have argued that firms should use social media platforms because they provide a place to learn about CSR activities and share their opinions (Cho et al, 2017).

Other authors have argued that social media generate consumer awareness of CSR because they can share their perspectives (Loureiro & Lopes, 2019). Other studies have shown the effectiveness of social media platforms promoting CSR issues increasing consumer engagement (Dunn, 2018; Galati et al, 2019; Chu et al, 2020) and reducing the skepticism towards CSR (Kim, S., & Rim, H. (2019) and positive word of mouth by consumers (Oh & Ki, 2019). Some scholars have studied the effectiveness of CSR messages on social media, and they found that internal CSR messages are more effective than external content to improve trust and commitment (Wang & Huang, 2018). Besides, scholars suggest that using games in CSR messages invite participation from customers sharing the content and increases the interest in CSR issues that companies promote.

In this sense, companies should communicate their contributions to the SDGs through consumers' active participation in long-term activities (Chae, 2021). Moreover, firms can reinforce the dialogue by considering the communication of relevant SDGs in social media to create stakeholder engagement (De Luca et al., 2022). However, as it has been described, the implementation of SDGs is still in an initial phase (Pizzi et al., 2020). If companies reinforce this relationship is crucial for the implementation of CSR to achieve the SDGs using different platforms to engage them and considering the SDGs from a strategic perspective. Moreover, social media enables the dialogue between firms and stakeholders, and they can use it to promote the SDGs, bearing in mind that the communication of relevant SDGs helps to create a stakeholder engagement (De Luca et al., 2022).

METHODOLOGY

The sample of this work is based on a previous study (Lopez & Rangel, 2022) that analysed the contribution that luxury fashion brands made to the SDGs in their sustainability reports. The companies listed in Table 1 were selected based on the Deloitte ranking (2021) of the best-selling companies in the luxury sector. For this research, Hermès and the Swatch Group were not included because, according to previous research, Hermès was not on the top 10 of global luxury companies and the Swatch Group's sustainability report (2021) did not include an explicit mention of the SDGs. The methodology of this research is based on a content analysis comparing the SDGs that these companies communicate in the latest sustainability reports (López & Rangel, 2022) and the SDGs that these firms communicate in their LinkedIn channel. Although the communication activity on LinkedIn has been analyzed in the last year (February 2021 - February 2022), it should be noted that only one post of each SDG has been included, since the information is very extensive. Each has been chosen with the criteria of being the most representative one because it summarizes the company's approach to each SDG. The results section presents a summary of the activities of the companies in the sample and their correspondence with the 17 SDGs.

Table 1. Companies selected in the analysis of their communication activity on LinkedIn related to the SDGs (Deloitte, 2021)

Ranking	Name of the company	Country of origin
1	LVMH	France
2	Kering	France
4	Richemont	Switzerland
6	Chanel	France
7	EssilorLuxottica	Italy
8	PVH	United States
10	Chow Tai Fook Jewellery Group	China/Hong Kong

RESULTS

The following is the result of the analysis of the main communication initiatives that each of the companies in the sample have communicated in terms of the SDGs that they claim to work on in their sustainability reports. Below we can see in Table 2 the summary of the actions LVMH communicates on LinkedIn (LVMH, 2022) regarding the SDGs compared to its sustainability report analysed (LVMH 2020 a, b).

Table 2. LVMH's communication actions related to its support for the SDGs (LVMH 2020 a, b & 2022)

SDG in sustainability memory	Key messages	Examples of post published on LinkedIn
Goal 1 - No poverty	Favouring better opportunities for people with fewer resources.	*LVMH and its Maisons celebrate International Youth Day, underscoring their commitment to equal opportunities and education. In line with its values of transmission, the Group has been acting for numerous years to promote equal opportunities, employment access and education.*
Goal 2 - Zero Hunger		Not found.
Goal 3 - Good Health and well being	Foster humanism and solidarity.	*LVMH and its Maisons share values of humanism and solidarity. Honoring this legagy with a bright holiday spirit, GROUPE BON MARCHÉ: Le Bon Marché Rive Gauche et La Grande Epicerie de Paris. was delighted to welcome the Institut Imagine – which conducts research into genetic diseases – to raise funds with a little help from French judo champion and sponsor Teddy Riner.*
Goal 4 - Quality education	Commitment to the education of the next generations.	*Within a particularly difficult economic context for younger generations, LVMH is accelerating its HR and Corporate Social Responsibility (CSR) policy dedicated to these groups, particularly in terms of training and access to employment. By the end of 2022, the Group plans to recruit 25,000 young people under the age of 30 worldwide, including nearly 5,000 through internships or apprenticeships, as well as 2,500 through permanent employment contracts in France.*
Goal 5 - Gender Equality	Commitment to diversity and inclusion.	*In line with the Group's commitment to foster Diversity & Inclusion in the workplace, LVMH is proud to sign the Commitment Charter of L'Autre Cercle – the leading association in France promoting the inclusion of LGBTI+ diversity at work.*
Goal 6 - Clean water and sanitation		Not found
Goal 7 - Affordable and clean energy		Not found.
Goal 8 - Decent work and economic growth	Promote job opportunities for young people and people at risk of exclusion.	*LVMH is strongly committed to fostering an inclusive workplace celebrating the uniqueness of each employee. To mark the International Day of Persons with Disabilities, the Group highlights several inspiring initiatives across its Maisons. Find out how Guerlain recruited two young adults with severe autism to work on the production chain of their Chartres manufacture in France, adapting their work environment accordingly.*
Goal 9 - Industry, innovation, and infrastructure	Innovation and creativity as an engine for growth.	*The success of the Group and its Maisons is deeply linked to the unique savoir-faire of our women and men who practice Creative, Craft and Sales Experience métiers, thus ensuring the excellence of exceptional products over centuries.*
Goal 10 - Reduced inequalities	Promoting opportunities.	*LVMH supports savoir-faire beyond its ecosystem through collaborative initiatives and partnerships such as with La Fabrique NOMADE, a nonprofit allowing passionate refugee and migrant artisans to take up their professions again upon arriving in France, to ensure that their migration does not lead to a long hiatus in their professional careers.*
Goal 11 - Sustainable cities and communities	Care for communities and their traditions.	*LVMH Maisons are committed to preserving art and culture in all its forms*
Goal 12 - Responsible consumption and production	Sustainability as core business.	*La Maison des Startups LVMH is where our talents and Maisons reinvent the future of luxury. Since 2018, the program has already fostered over 280 business collaborations with startups, in fields as strategic as sustainable materials, omnichannel, 3D & virtual product or employee experience.*
Goal 13 - Climate action	Commitment to care for the planet.	*As the current year draws to a close, here's a look back at some of the many highlights of 2021. From the first LVMH Social and Environmental Responsibility Report and our LIFE 360 environmental roadmap, to the "WE for ME" Manifesto in support of our unique array of savoir-faire or the Morozov Collection exhibition at the Fondation Louis Vuitton. The initiatives led by LVMH and its Maisons throughout the year reflect an unwavering commitment to people, to the environment, and to the arts and culture.*

Continued on following page

Table 2. Continued

SDG in sustainability memory	Key messages	Examples of post published on LinkedIn
Goal 14 - Life below water	Care for natural resources.	*The LVMH group is delighted to share that The Glenmorangie Company's DEEP project has been featured by CNN. The story aired on Connect the World and Quest Means Business. Working with Heriot-Watt University and the Marine Conservation Society, Glenmorangie has been reintroducing native oyster reefs to the Dornoch Firth. One oyster can filter more than 200 litres per day. Oyster reefs also enhance marine biodiversity and act as carbon stores.*
Goal 15 - Life on land	Care for natural resources.	*In line with the Group commitments, LVMH Maisons have made sustainability and social responsibility within their top priorities. In collaboration with Parfums Christian Dior floral science experts like rose growers, botanists, agro-ecologists and landscapers, the House of Dior will design the ideal regenerative ecosystem for the flowers to flourish. Among them, Nicolas Sambet, a rose horticulturist, is devoted to care for the new Dior rose garden near Granville.*
Goal 16 - Peace, justice, and strong institutions		Not found.
Goal 17 - Partnerships	Partnerships for a better society.	*GROUPE BON MARCHÉ: Le Bon Marché Rive Gauche et La Grande Epicerie de Paris. will curate the "Porte-Bonheurs" (Lucky Charms) exhibition in partnership with the South-African designer and 2019 LVMH Prize winner Thebe Magugu, until October 17. The artistic and philanthropical project pays tribute to the sensitivity of fashion's new rising star.*

LVMH communicates actions related to all SDGs directly or indirectly on LinkedIn, except for those related to SDGs 2, 6, 7 and 16. Although only one example per SDG has been selected, it is worth noting that the company makes more communication effort with more posts on SDGs 5, 8, 13, 15. From this, it can be deduced that within its corporate messages related to the SDGs, emphasis is placed on those related to the commitment to equality and inclusion, favouring employment opportunities, care for the planet and natural resources.

Following the presentation of the results, Table 3 shows the results of the relationship of the SDGs that Kering reports on LinkedIn (Kering, 2022) with those reported in its last sustainability report analysed (Kering, 2021).

Table 3. Kering's communication actions related to its support for the SDGs (Kering 2021 & 2022)

SDG in sustainability memory	Key messages	Examples of post published on LinkedIn
Goal 3 - Good Health and well being	Fight against gender-based violence	*According to the World Health Organization, almost one in three women has experienced domestic violence during her lifetime. Given this situation, Kering and its Foundation have launched in January 2021 a policy on domestic violence that provides all its employees around the world -- whether they work for the Group or its Houses -- with the specific support they need.*
Goal 5 - Gender Equality	Commitment to diversity and inclusion.	*We are delighted to be included in the 2022 Bloomberg Gender-Equality Index (GEI). This is the fifth consecutive year that Kering has featured on the index and the second year that we have achieved 100% in equal pay and gender pay parity.*
Goal 6 - Clean water and sanitation		Not found.
Goal 8 - Decent work and economic growth	Promote job opportunities for young people	*The Kering Sustainability team was delighted to be at HEC Paris today to launch our new sustainable innovation challenge; for two weeks, 6 teams of students will receive intensive coaching and a series of in-depth lectures on circularity, traceability in the supply chain, and our vision of sustainable luxury from the Kering sustainability team.*
Goal 12 - Responsible consumption and production	Sustainability as core business.	*Kering is proud to be featured in the 100 most sustainable companies in the world and 1st in Clothing and Accessory Retail for the 5th consecutive year in Corporate Knights' 2022 Global 100 ranking!*
Goal 13 - Climate action	Commitment to care for the planet.	*Today is World Climate Day. Kering is proud to make this year's CDP Climate Change A List, which recognizes our efforts to first reduce our emissions before offsetting any remaining ones, in line with the goals of the Paris Agreement.*
Goal 15 - Life on land	Care for natural resources.	*Sponsored by Kering, J. Crew and Madewell, and Cotton Connect, the Regenerative Agriculture Landscape Analysis is the first report that gives the fashion and textile industry a framework and toolkit to credibly understand, implement and describe the benefits of work in this space. It promotes a holistic approach that puts humans and ecosystems at the center.*

Kering's communication on LinkedIn is closely linked to what is communicated in its sustainability report. All SDGs mentioned in the report (3, 5, 8, 12, 13 and 15) are addressed, except for SDG 6. The SDGs to which Kering devotes most posts are 8, 12 and 13, i.e., those related to promoting better job opportunities, sustainability as part of business development and the fight against climate change.

Below are the results for Richemont (Table 4), showing the SDGs they work towards in their last sustainability report analysed (Richemont, 2021 a, b) and what they communicate on Linkedin (Richemont, 2022) about them.

Table 4. Richemont's communication actions related to its support for the SDGs (Richemont, 2021 a, b & 2022)

SDG in sustainability memory	Key messages	Examples of post published on LinkedIn
Goal 5 - Gender Equality	Commitment to diversity and inclusion.	*At Richemont, we strongly support equal employment opportunity, non-discrimination, and diversity, equity & inclusion in the workplace.*
Goal 8 - Decent work and economic growth	Promote job opportunities worldwide.	*Richemont is proud to engage with talent from all over the world.*
Goal 12 - Responsible consumption and production	Sustainability as core business.	*At Richemont, we are committed to leave a better world for future generations, and we are happy to release our 15th annual Sustainability Report.*
Goal 13 - Climate action	Commitment to care for the planet.	*We are proud to share that the Science-Based targets we submitted in May have been validated by the Science-Based Targets Initiative. Developed in line with the objectives of the Paris Agreement, they provide us with a clearly defined pathway to reduce gas emissions and help us prevent the worst impacts of climate change, while future-proof our business growth.*
Goal 17 - Partnerships	Partnerships for a better society.	*At Richemont, we are proud to be partnered with leading universities to to accelerate the emergence of a new generation of leaders.*

Richemont communicates on LinkedIn all the efforts it makes in favour of the SDGs mentioned in its sustainability report (SDGs 5, 8, 12, 13 and 17) in relation to its commitment to equality and diversity, to fostering talent in all the countries where it operates, sustainable production, its fight against climate change and the creation of partnerships. Therefore, we can affirm that there is coherence between what it communicates in its sustainability report and on LinkedIn to reach its stakeholders.

Table 5 represents CHANEL's summary after interlinking its last sustainability report analysed (CHANEL, 2020 a, b) and its LinkedIn activity (CHANEL, 2022) on the SDGs.

Table 5. CHANEL's communication actions related to its support for the SDGs (CHANEL, 2020 a, b & 2022)

SDG in sustainability memory	Key messages	Examples of post published on LinkedIn
Goal 5 - Gender Equality		Not found.
Goal 7 - Affordable and clean energy		Not found.
Goal 13 - Climate action		Not found.
Goal 15 - Life on land		Not found.
Goal 17 - Partnerships	Partnerships for a better society.	*The House of CHANEL and Institut Français de la Mode have come together to create a chair entitled the 'CHANEL and le19M Chair in Fashion Savoir-Faire', housed by the IFM Foundation. The aim of this five-year partnership is to create a centre for research and teaching excellence on the subject of the fashion savoir-faire, in the heart of a leading international school.*

The only SDG that CHANEL has proactively communicated on LinkedIn over the past year is 17 (partnerships), even though its sustainability report reflects the great efforts it is making to fight climate change.

Although Essilor and Luxottica are two companies belonging to the same holding company (Essilor-Luxottica) they communicate their sustainability efforts and on LinkedIn as separate entities, albeit with many synergies. The results for Luxottica are presented in Table 6 and for Essilor in Table 7.

Table 6. Luxottica's communication actions related to its support for the SDGs (Luxottica, 2021 & 2022)

SDG in sustainability memory	Key messages	Examples of post published on LinkedIn
Goal 3 - Good Health and well being	Foster humanism and solidarity.	*We focus on the social equality, diversity and well-being of both internal and external communities surrounding Luxottica.*
Goal 4 - Quality education	Commitment to the eyecare education.	*As a unique #EssilorLuxottica learning platform, Leonardo is redefining the way employees, eyecare professionals and customers learn about eyewear and eyecare.*
Goal 5 - Gender Equality	Commitment to diversity and inclusion.	*"As a woman becoming a leader in #STEM is possible. Models matter but it is even more important to find your own way and never give up."*
Goal 6 - Clean water and sanitation		Not found.
Goal 7 - Affordable and clean energy	Commitment to renewable energy and carbon footprint reduction.	*Sustainability finds its origins in respectful actions for the environment: it lies in everyday culture applied to working processes and procedures. Since 2013, we've been investing in manufacturing plants that run on self-produced renewable energy to reduce the Carbon footprint across the value chain. Our mountains, our nature, our skies, they are too important not to be our priority.*
Goal 8 - Decent work and economic growth		Not found.
Goal 9 - Industry, innovation, and infrastructure		Not found.
Goal 10 - Reduced inequalities	Commitment to improving opportunities for visually impaired people.	*80% of what children learn in schools is presented visually, but one in four has a vision problem that affects their learning. For this #WorldSightDay, don't let poor vision hold them back from a bright future. Test their vision on putvisionfirst.com.*
Goal 12 - Responsible consumption and production	Sustainability as core business.	*We stand up for our environment because nature is our enabler. We are here to restore a more respectful path and to pursue sustainable processes. It's our responsibility to reduce our impact through thoughtful actions.*
Goal 16 - Peace, justice, and strong institutions	Supporting institutions.	*EssilorLuxottica fully supports the latest resolution passed by the United Nations member states committing to making #eyecare accessible for the 1.1 billion people living with preventable vision impairment.*

Luxottica communicates on LinkedIn its efforts related to SDGs 3, 4, 5, 7, 10, 12 and 16, as detailed in its sustainability report. The company places special emphasis on communicating its efforts in diversity and inclusion, reducing its carbon footprint, improving opportunities, responsible production, and supporting institutions. Those efforts not found on LinkedIn are SDGs 6, 8 and 9.

Table 7. Essilor's communication actions related to its support for the SDGs (EssilorLuxottica, 2021; Essilor, 2022)

SDG in sustainability memory	Key messages	Examples of post published on LinkedIn
Goal 1 - No poverty		Not found.
Goal 3 - Good Health and well being	Foster visual health of future generations.	*Managing myopia for children is essential for their visual function and their quality of life. In this last video, Dr. Kate Gifford and Dr. Paul Gifford, founders of Myopia Profile, explain different reasons why parents need to manage myopia in children, how parents play a role and how the partnership with Essilor can leverage each other's strength.*
Goal 4 - Quality education	Commitment to the eyecare education.	*At a time when much of the world is returning to school, credible evidence about the link between children's learning and vision continues to be found. In its recent article, Vision Impact Institute shares how recent research proves there is a negative impact on educational outcomes in children because of poor eyesight.*
Goal 6 - Clean water and sanitation		Not found.
Goal 7 - Affordable and clean energy		Not found.
Goal 8 - Decent work and economic growth	Development of employees.	*Innovation is part of our DNA and draws on a very diverse network that combines inputs from our teams, the expertise of business partners as well as collaborative contributions with external organizations, research institutes, industrial groups and academia.*
Goal 10 - Reduce inequalities		Not found.
Goal 12 - Responsible consumption and production	Sustainability as core business.	*This #EarthDay, Essilor is pleased to share an update on its recently developed proprietary Sustainability Assessment Methodology (S.A.M.), within its R&D activities. Taking a major step forward, Essilor has incorporated an eco and socio-design approach in its R&D activities to take care of our planet while taking care of our vision.*
Goal 13 - Climate action	Commitment to care for the planet.	*In line with the ongoing 26th annual Climate Change Conference of the Parties (COP26), #EssilorLuxottica contributes to UN's #climatechange goals through its #sustainability program - #EyesOnThePlanet. By investing in #renewableenergy, new process designs, initiatives to protect and restore natural ecosystems and more, the Company has committed to work towards carbon neutrality in its direct operations by 2025, starting in Europe from 2023.*
Goal 16 - Peace, justice, and strong institutions	Supporting institutions.	*Essilor proudly supports the United Nations Road Safety Week. More than ever, road safety is critical as mobility and new ways of transportation are booming. Vision is vital, especially on the road. Good vision can save your life and the lives of others. Don't forget to check your vision.*
Goal 17 - Partnerships	Partnerships for a better society.	*Essilor has supported the Opening Eyes program of Special Olympics since 2002 and provided thousands of athletes over the years with the vision correction they need to perform their best. David Evangelista, President and Managing Director, Special Olympics Europe & Eurasia shared with us more about this program, the tremendous impact it has delivered for athletes with intellectual disabilities, and the challenges faced amid the ongoing Covid-19 pandemic.*

Although there are similarities with what Luxottica communicates, Essilor's communication on LinkedIn in terms of SDGs focuses on goals 3, 4, 8, 12, 13, 16 and 17. In particular, in relation to the company's efforts to improve the visual health of children, to improve their education and visual needs, its efforts in sustainable development, its commitment to renewable energy and reducing its carbon footprint, its support for institutions, and its numerous international partnerships to create a better world. No posts were found with SDGs 6, 7 and 10, although they are mentioned in its sustainability report.

Table 8 below shows Chow Tai Fook's relationship between the SDGs that report in their last sustainability report analysed (Chow Tai Fook, 2020) and the SDGs that are communicated on LinkedIn (Chow Tai Fook, 2022).

Table 8. Chow Tai Fook's communication actions related to its support for the SDGs (Chow Tai Fook, 2020 & 2022)

SDG in sustainability memory	Key messages	Examples of post published on LinkedIn
Goal 8 - Decent work and economic growth	Promote job opportunities.	The United Nations General Assembly has proclaimed 24 January as International Day of Education since 2019, to advocate the importance of education for our social development. We believe that all people can develop cognitive abilities, physical abilities and establish values and beliefs through appropriate education. With this mission in mind, we have established a design incubation space, Loupe www.loupe.com.hk, to inspire people through the art of Jewellery and to nurture the next generation of designers and artisans for the sustainable development of the Jewellery industry. Loupe also offers a wide array of educational activities as a platform for exchanges and public engagement on design and craftsmanship.
Goal 9 - Industry, innovation, and infrastructure	Boost creativity and innovation.	*Happy World Creativity and Innovation Day! The United Nations designated 21 April as World Creativity and Innovation Day, the Day reminds us to be creative and innovative in our business practice. In today's jewellery market, being customer-centric focus and delivering personalised products become the key to fulfil our customers' needs. We are pleased to introduce D-ONE Bespoke Jewellery Service. With our advanced technology and unwavering creativity, we are dedicated to craft unique, exquisite and precious jewellery creation for our customers.*
Goal 12 - Responsible consumption and production	Sustainability as core business.	*As we have launched and implemented the 10-year Sustainability Strategy since FY2020, our Sustainability Champions have made new achievements and identified new opportunities in the four priority areas, allowing us to lead the industry to unlock the potential of the emerging megatrends.*
Goal 13 - Climate action	Commitment to care for the planet.	*It is paramount to safeguard the planet's wellbeing to ensure our business' succession and that sufficient natural resources will be available for our future generations. In FY2021, our environmental stewardship champions worked hard on various resource efficiency projects to minimise our environmental impacts in our operations.*
Goal 17 - Partnerships	Partnerships for a better society.	*Chow Tai Fook Jewellery Group is delighted to announce an exclusive strategic partnership with Natural Diamond Council. This partnership will advocate the "Natural Diamond Dream" and introduce the Chinese consumers, especially the younger generation, to the timeless beauty of natural diamonds through the use of diverse communication channels as well as the provision of professional training resources.*

We can see that Chow Tai Fook communicates the same SDGs in his sustainability report and on LinkedIn, focusing his efforts on SDGs 8, 9, 12, 13 and 17. He devotes more posts on LinkedIn to fostering more job opportunities for future generations, fighting climate change, and building a network of partnerships to improve society.

Finally, Table 9 summarises the results of the analysis of the SDGs reported by PVH in its last sustainability report analysed (PVH, 2020) and those communicated on LinkedIn (PVH, 2022).

Table 9. PVH's communication actions related to its support for the SDGs

SDG in sustainability memory	Key messages	Examples of post published on LinkedIn
Goal 1 - No poverty		Not found.
Goal 2 - Zero Hunger		Not found.
Goal 3 - Good Health and well being		Not found.
Goal 4 - Quality education		Not found.
Goal 5 - Gender Equality	Commitment to diversity and inclusion.	*Since making a commitment to amplify our gender equality efforts with the United Nations Foundation, PVH has made significant progress towards our goals to empower women.*
Goal 6 - Clean water and sanitation	Protecting and preserving natural resources.	*Water is an invaluable resource, and the importance of protecting and preserving our resources around the world has only been emphasized this past year. In line with the UN's #WorldWaterDay theme of 'Valuing Water;' and our #ForwardFashion priority to Provide Access to Water, we're reflecting on the progress our teams have made.*
Goal 7 - Affordable and clean energy		Not found.
Goal 8 - Decent work and economic growth		*PVH Corp. was recently recognized on Forbes America's Best Large Employers 2022 list, ranking No. 3 in the clothing category.*
Goal 9 - Industry, innovation, and infrastructure		Not found.
Goal 10 - Reduced inequalities		*Congratulations to the winning #designers of this year's Tommy Hilfiger #FashionFrontierChallenge! The winners will share a prize fund of €200,000 and receive a year-long mentorship with experts from Tommy Hilfiger and INSEAD — one of the world's leading and largest graduate business schools.*
Goal 11 - Sustainable cities and communities		*To celebrate #BlackHistoryMonth, PVH hosted a virtual roundtable discussion with a group of associates to talk about the importance of #representation, resilience, and the contributions of Black people and culture throughout history and today.*
Goal 12 - Responsible consumption and production		*We are a purpose led company, with sustainability at the forefront of what we do. We are on a journey with our industry partners, vendors and suppliers to drive fashion forward - for good.*
Goal 13 - Climate action	Commitment to care for the planet.	*As we continue on our journey towards responsible denim, PVH and our brands Tommy Hilfiger and Calvin Klein are embracing a holistic approach focused on three key areas – responsible innovation, traceability and circularity. Check out the video below to learn more about our sustainable denim practices.*
Goal 14 - Life below water		Not found.
Goal 15 - Life on land		Not found.
Goal 16 - Peace, justice, and strong institutions		Not found.
Goal 17 - Partnerships	Partnerships for a better society.	*PVH's partnership with Save the Children International is critical to our long-standing commitment to doing the right thing for our people, our communities and our planet.*

Although in its sustainability report PVH mentions its work on the 17 SDGs, after analysing its communication on LinkedIn in this area, we see that its communication efforts are focused on SDGs 5, 6, 8, 10, 11, 12, 13 and 17. The SDGs to which PVH dedicates most are those related to promoting diversity and inclusion, promoting a good place to work, the visibility of all communities, sustainable production, as well as partnerships at corporate level and of its different brands to work for a better world. There are no posts related to SDGs 1, 2, 3, 4, 7, 9, 14, 15 or 16.

To summarise, the main results after comparing the sustainability reports and communication efforts of the leading luxury holdings on LinkedIn are as follows:

- Richemont and Chow Tai Fook are the two companies that show absolute consistency between what they say they do in favour of the SDGs and what they communicate on LinkedIn, followed by Kering.
- CHANEL would be the company reporting the least SDGs compared to what it says it does in its sustainability report, followed by PVH.
- In the middle ground between what they report in their sustainability report and on LinkedIn would be LVMH, Essilor and Luxottica.
- As shown in Table 10, the most reported SDGs are 12, 13, 5, 8 and 17; while the least reported are SDGs 2, 1, 6, 4, 9, 14, 11, 15, 16, 10.

Table 10. Summary of the SDGs that luxury brands communicate on LinkedIn

SDG / Activity related in LinkedIn	LVMH	Kering	Richemont	Chanel	Luxottica	Essilor	Chow Tai Fook	PVH
Goal 1 - No poverty	x	-	-	-	-	-	-	-
Goal 2 - Zero Hunger	-	-	-	-	-	-	-	-
Goal 3 - Good Health and well being	x	x	-	-	x	x	-	-
Goal 4 - Quality education	x	-	-	-	x	x	-	-
Goal 5 - Gender Equality	x	x	x	-	x	-	-	x
Goal 6 - Clean water and sanitation	-	-	-	-	-	-	-	x
Goal 7 - Affordable and clean energy	-	-	-	-	x	-	-	-
Goal 8 - Decent work and economic growth	x	x	x	-	-	x	x	x
Goal 9 - Industry, innovation, and infrastructure	x	-	-	-	-	-	x	-
Goal 10 - Reduced inequalities	x	-	-	-	x	-	-	x
Goal 11 - Sustainable cities and communities	x	-	-	-	-	-	-	x
Goal 12 - Responsible consumption and production	x	x	x	-	x	x	x	x
Goal 13 - Climate action	x	x	x	-	-	x	x	x
Goal 14 - Life below water	x	-	-	-	-	-	-	-
Goal 15 - Life on land	x	x	-	-	-	-	-	-
Goal 16 - Peace, justice, and strong institutions	-	-	-	-	x	x	-	-
Goal 17 - Partnerships	x	-	x	x	-	x	x	x

DISCUSSION, CONCLUSIONS AND FUTURE RESEARCH

COVID-19 has given the world a chance to rebuild a better society for all people. Different studies show that consumers in the luxury industry are interested to know what luxury firms are developing in the field of sustainability (Thomas, 2018; Khan & Sung, 2021). Therefore, communication about CSR activities can increase the stakeholder's commitment if these companies invite participation in social networks (Okazaki et al., 2020; Barbeito-Caamaño & Chalmeta, 2020; Hartmann et al., 2020). Consequently, when these firms give information about sustainability commitments it is an opportunity to create a real dialogue between firms and stakeholders (Jin et al., 2017; Dunn & Harness, 2018). However, while all companies in the sample communicate their efforts to a greater or lesser extent around the SDGs, it is striking how only two companies in the sample of luxury brands (Richemont and Chow Tai Fook) show consistency between what they communicate in their sustainability reports in relation to the SDGs and on LinkedIn. Although there are differences between the companies in the sample in terms of CSR commitments and communication, there are visible differences between them that show the sector's interest in sustainability, as reflected in the information analyzed by SDG in the chapter, as well as the global summary reflected in table 10. As a consequence, these firms can take even more advantage of the possibilities for dialogue with stakeholders on social networks.

According to the analysis carried out, companies are putting into the communication of the SDGs 12 (Responsible consumption and production), 13 (Climate action), 5 (Gender equality) and 8 (Decent work and economic growth), which are those SDGs that either touch closely on more regulated aspects that companies must comply with, such as everything related to production or the reduction of greenhouse gases, or that touch more closely on people's day-to-day lives, such as equality and promoting a good place to work. There is still room for improvement in communicating work on SDGs 2 (Zero Hunger), 1 (No Poverty), 6 (Clean Water and Sanitation), 14 (Life Below Water), 9 (Industry, Innovation and Infrastructure, 11 (Sustainable Cities and Communities), 15 (Life on Land). While it is true that not all companies can work on all SDGs, SDGs 9 and 11 should receive more attention when planning social media editorial calendars. While it may be thought that the rest of the SDGs will depend on the core business of each company, it can be argued that SDGs 2, 1, 6 and 15 should be also communicated externally.

Therefore, we can affirm that there is an opportunity for improvement in relation to the communication of the SDGs by the luxury industry, especially in channels with a more corporate focus such as LinkedIn, where it is easier to reach different stakeholders and where the efforts of the different luxury brands to work in favour of the SDGs can be explained in a more accessible language to the users.

In this study, we can identify some contributions to the literature related to CSR communication of luxury companies: i) on the one hand, the analysis shows that luxury companies include the SDGs in their CSR/sustainability strategies reporting information on specific goals; ii) in addition, the firms communicate their results and commitments to the strategic SDGs on social networks such as LinkedIn; iii) on the other hand, this study reflects that CSR communication allows the participation of stakeholders in CSR issues and, consequently, is a place to discuss sustainability issues with the opportunity to reinforce stakeholder engagement.

Among future lines of research, it would be interesting to analyse the relationship between the sustainability departments and the communication departments of luxury brands, to analyse their position in the company's organisational chart, which prevents or facilitates the interconnection of issues and priorities to be communicated on the SDGs. Apart from that, it would also be interesting to study and compare how those SDGs that arouse more interest in the luxury industry are communicated on social media to reflect the type of messages, tools and the reaction they provoke. In addition, other studies could identify which are the social networks that facilitate greater participation with each one of them considering their specific interests, both for consumers, employees and NGOs, among others.

REFERENCES

Abitbol, A., Meeks, J., & Cummins, R. G. (2019). Does oil and goodwill mix? Examining the oil and gas industry's impact on stakeholder engagement on Facebook. *Environmental Communication*, *13*(2), 192–208. doi:10.1080/17524032.2018.1546751

Amatulli, C., De Angelis, M., Costabile, M., & Guido, G. (2017). *Sustainable luxury brands: Evidence from research and implications for managers*. Springer. doi:10.1057/978-1-137-60159-9

Arora, N. K., & Mishra, I. (2019). United Nations Sustainable Development Goals 2030 and environmental sustainability: Race against time. *Environmental Sustainability*, *2*(4), 339–342. doi:10.100742398-019-00092-y

Athwal, N., Wells, V. K., Carrigan, M., & Henninger, C. E. (2019). Sustainable luxury marketing: A synthesis and research agenda. *International Journal of Management Reviews*, *21*(4), 405–426. doi:10.1111/ijmr.12195

Bain & Co. (2020). *The future of Luxury: Bouncing Back from Covid-19*. Retrieved from https://cutt.ly/hmd5Imn

Barbeito-Caamaño, A., & Chalmeta, R. (2020). Using big data to evaluate corporate social responsibility and sustainable development practices. *Corporate Social Responsibility and Environmental Management*, *27*(6), 2831–2848. doi:10.1002/csr.2006

Barnett, M. L., Henriques, I., & Husted, B. W. (2020). Beyond good intentions: Designing CSR initiatives for greater social impact. *Journal of Management*, *46*(6), 937–964. doi:10.1177/0149206319900539

Belyaeva, Z., Shams, S. M. R., Santoro, G., & Grandhi, B. (2020). Unpacking stakeholder relationship management in the public and private sectors: The comparative insights. *EuroMed Journal of Business*, *15*(3), 269–281. doi:10.1108/EMJB-06-2019-0085

Buallay, A., Aldhaen, E., Hamdan, A. M., Kukreja, G., & Al Mubarak, M. (2020). Corporate social responsibility disclosure and firms' performance in Mediterranean countries: A stakeholders' perspective. *EuroMed Journal of Business*, *15*(3), 361–375. doi:10.1108/EMJB-05-2019-0066

Carroll, A. B. (2021). Corporate Social Responsibility: Perspectives on the CSR Construct's Development and Future. *Business & Society*, *60*(6). doi:10.1177/00076503211001765

Chae, M. J. (2021). Driving consumer engagement through diverse calls to action in corporate social responsibility messages on social media. *Sustainability*, *13*(7), 3812. doi:10.3390u13073812

CHANEL. (2020a). *Chanel announces climate commitments*. Retrieved from https://cutt.ly/lbbWChJ

CHANEL. (2020b). *Channel. Mission 1.5º*. Retrieved from https://cutt.ly/ubbW5Hs

CHANEL. (2022). https://www.linkedin.com/company/chanel/

Cheah, I., Zainol, Z., & Phau, I. (2016). Conceptualizing country-of-ingredient authenticity of luxury brands. *Journal of Business Research*, *69*(12), 5819–5826. doi:10.1016/j.jbusres.2016.04.179

Cho, M., Furey, L. D., & Mohr, T. (2017). Communicating corporate social responsibility on social media: Strategies, stakeholders, and public engagement on corporate Facebook. *Business and Professional Communication Quarterly, 80*(1), 52–69. doi:10.1177/2329490616663708

Chow Tai Fook. (2022). Chow Tai Fook.

Chow Tai Fook Jewellery Group. (2020). *Sustainable Report 2020*. https://www.ctfjewellerygroup.com/file/Sustainability/reports/csr-report.pdf

Chu, S. C., Chen, H. T., & Gan, C. (2020). Consumers' engagement with corporate social responsibility (CSR) communication in social media: Evidence from China and the United States. *Journal of Business Research, 110*, 260–271. doi:10.1016/j.jbusres.2020.01.036

De Luca, F., Iaia, L., Mehmood, A., & Vrontis, D. (2022). Can social media improve stakeholder engagement and communication of Sustainable Development Goals? A cross-country analysis. *Technological Forecasting and Social Change, 177*, 121525. doi:10.1016/j.techfore.2022.121525

Deloitte. (2021). *Global Powers of Luxury Goods 2021. The new age of fashion and luxury*. https://www2.deloitte.com/content/dam/Deloitte/global/Documents/Consumer-Business/gx-cb-global-powers-of-luxury-goods-2021.pdf

Dunn, K., & Harness, D. (2018). Communicating corporate social responsibility in a social world: The effects of company-generated and user-generated social media content on CSR attributions and scepticism. *Journal of Marketing Management, 34*(17-18), 1503–1529. doi:10.1080/0267257X.2018.1536675

Essilor. (2022). *Essilor Group*. https://www.linkedin.com/company/essilor/

EssilorLuxottica. (2021). *Sustainability*. Retrieved from https://www.essilorluxottica.com/sustainability

Fernandes, T., & Remelhe, P. (2016). How to engage customers in co-creation: Customers' motivations for collaborative innovation. *Journal of Strategic Marketing, 24*(3-4), 311–326. doi:10.1080/0965254X.2015.1095220

Galati, A., Sakka, G., Crescimanno, M., Tulone, A., & Fiore, M. (2019). What is the role of social media in several overtones of CSR communication? The case of the wine industry in the Southern Italian regions. *British Food Journal, 121*(4), 856–873. doi:10.1108/BFJ-07-2018-0437

Gardetti, M. A. (2016). Loewe: Luxury and sustainable management. Handbook of Sustainable Luxury Textiles and Fashion, 2, 1–16.

Gardetti, M. A. (2017). *Sustainable management of luxury. Springer book series on environmental footprints and eco-design of products and processes*. Springer.

Giacomarra, M., Crescimanno, M., Sakka, G., & Galati, A. (2019). Stakeholder engagement toward value co-creation in the F&B packaging industry. *EuroMed Journal of Business, 15*(3), 315–331. doi:10.1108/EMJB-06-2019-0077

Hartmann, P., Fernández, P., Apaolaza, V., Eisend, M., & D'Souza, C. (2020). Explaining Viral CSR Message Propagation in social media: The Role of Normative Influences. *Journal of Business Ethics*, 1–21.

Hörisch, J., Schaltegger, S., & Freeman, R. E. (2020). Integrating stakeholder theory and sustainability accounting: A conceptual synthesis. *Journal of Cleaner Production*, *275*, 124097. doi:10.1016/j.jclepro.2020.124097

Huang, L., Clarke, A., Heldsinger, N., & Tian, W. (2019). The communication role of social media in social marketing: A study of the community sustainability knowledge dissemination on LinkedIn and Twitter. *Journal of Marketing Analytics*, *7*(2), 64–75. doi:10.105741270-019-00053-8

Ivan, C. M., Mukta, R., Sudeep, C., & Burak, C. (2016). Long-term sustainable sustainability in luxury. Where else? In *Handbook of Sustainable Luxury Textiles and Fashion* (pp. 17–34). Springer Singapore. doi:10.1007/978-981-287-742-0_2

Jin, Y.-J., Park, S.-C., & Yoo, J.-W. (2017). Effects of corporate social responsibility on consumer credibility perception and attitude toward luxury brands. *Social Behavior and Personality*, *45*(5), 795–808. doi:10.2224bp.5897

Kang, E. Y., & Sung, Y. H. (2021). Luxury and sustainability: The role of message appeals and objectivity on luxury brands' green corporate social responsibility. *Journal of Marketing Communications*, •••, 1–22.

Karaosman. (2019). *Unlocking Responsible Luxury: The Manifesto 2019*. Politecnico di Milano School of Management & Mazars.

Kering. (2021). *Sustainability*. Retrieved from https://www.kering.com/en/sustainability/

Kering. (2022). https://www.linkedin.com/company/kering/

Khan, S., & Ahmed, M. (2017). Who are the consumers for sustainable luxury? In *2017 Global Fashion Management Conference at Vienna* (pp. 181-182). 10.15444/GFMC2017.03.02.03

Kim, S., & Rim, H. (2019). The role of public skepticism and distrust in the process of CSR communication. *International Journal of Business Communication*. doi:10.1177/2329488419866888

Kong, H. M., Witmaier, A., & Ko, E. (2021). Sustainability and social media communication: How consumers respond to marketing efforts of luxury and non-luxury fashion brands. *Journal of Business Research*, *131*, 640–651. doi:10.1016/j.jbusres.2020.08.021

Kunz, J., May, S., & Schmidt, H. J. (2020). Sustainable luxury: Current status and perspectives for future research. *Business Research*, *13*(2), 541–601. doi:10.100740685-020-00111-3

Li, J., & Leonas, K. K. (2019). Trends of sustainable development among luxury industry. In *Sustainable luxury* (pp. 107–126). Springer. doi:10.1007/978-981-13-0623-5_6

Lopez, B., & Rangel, C. (2022). How Luxury Fashion Brands Contribute Efficiently to Sustainable Development. In *Future Advancements for CSR and the Sustainable Development Goals in a Post-COVID-19 World* (pp. 139–161). IGI Global. doi:10.4018/978-1-7998-8065-3.ch007

Lourciro, S. M. C., & Lopes, J. (2019). How corporate social responsibility initiatives in social media affect awareness and customer engagement. *Journal of Promotion Management*, *25*(3), 419–438. doi: 10.1080/10496491.2019.1557819

Luxottica. (2021). *Sustainable Development Goals.* Retrieved from https://www.luxottica.com/en/sustainable-development-goals

Luxottica. (2022). https://www.linkedin.com/company/luxottica/

LVMH. (2020a). *2019 Environmental Responsibility Report.* Retrieved from https://cutt.ly/7bEKbB5

LVMH. (2020b). *2019 Social Responsibility Report.* Retrieved from https://cutt.ly/GbbQtjF

LVMH. (2022). https://www.linkedin.com/company/lvmh/

McKinsey & Company (2022). *The state of fashion.* Author.

Mio, C., Panfilo, S., & Blundo, B. (2020). Sustainable development goals and the strategic role of business: A systematic literature review. *Business Strategy and the Environment, 29*(8), 3220–3245. doi:10.1002/bse.2568

Oh, J., & Ki, E. J. (2019). Factors affecting social presence and word-of-mouth in corporate social responsibility communication: Tone of voice, message framing, and online medium type. *Public Relations Review, 45*(2), 319–331. doi:10.1016/j.pubrev.2019.02.005

Okazaki, S., Plangger, K., West, D., & Menéndez, H. D. (2020). Exploring digital corporate social responsibility communications on Twitter. *Journal of Business Research, 117*, 675–682. doi:10.1016/j.jbusres.2019.09.006

Olšanová, K., Gook, G., & Zlatić, M. (2018). Influence of luxury companies' corporate social responsibility activities on consumer purchase intention: Development of a theoretical framework. *Central European Business Review, 7*(3), 1–25. doi:10.18267/j.cebr.200

Pizzi, S., Caputo, A., Corvino, A., Venturelli, A. (2020). Management research and the UN sustainable development goals (SDGs): A bibliometric investigation and systematic review. *J. Cleaner Prod., 276.*

PVH. (2020). *2019 CR Report.* Retrieved from https://www.pvh.com/-/media/Files/pvh/responsibility/PVH-CR-Report-2019.pdf

PVH. (2022). *PVH Corp.* https://www.linkedin.com/company/pvh/

Richemont. (2021a). *Sustainability. Our approach.* Retrieved from https://www.richemont.com/en/home/sustainability/our-approach/

Richemont. (2021b). *Sustainability Report 2020.* Retrieved from https://www.richemont.com/media/4ksenvnu/sustainability_report_2020.pdf

Richemont. (2022). https://www.linkedin.com/company/richemont/

Saxton, G. D., Ren, C., & Guo, C. (2020). Responding to Diffused Stakeholders on social media: Connective Power and Firm Reactions to CSR-Related Twitter Messages. *Journal of Business Ethics*, 1-24. Available at: https://sustainabledevelopment.un.org/partnership/?p=28041

Sreejesh, S., Sarkar, J. G., & Sarkar, A. (2019). CSR through social media: Examining the intervening factors. *Marketing Intelligence & Planning.*

Surucu-Balci, E., Balci, G., & Yuen, K. F. (2020). Social media engagement of stakeholders: A decision tree approach in container shipping. *Computers in Industry*, *115*, 103152. doi:10.1016/j.compind.2019.103152

Swatch Group. (2021). *Sustainability report & social policy*. Retrieved from https://www.swatchgroup.com/en/brands-companies

Taliento, M., Favino, C., & Netti, A. (2019). Impact of environmental, social, and governance information on economic performance: Evidence of a corporate "sustainability advantage" from Europe. *Sustainability*, *11*(6), 1738. doi:10.3390u11061738

Tey, Y. S., Brindal, M., & Dibba, H. (2018). Factors influencing willingness to pay for sustainable apparel: A literature review. *Journal of Global Fashion Marketing*, *9*(2), 129–147. doi:10.1080/20932685.2018.1432407

Thomas, S. (2018). Peace of mind: The quintessential luxury. Journal of Design. *Business & Society*, *4*(2), 151–169.

Topal, ˙. I., Nart, S., Akar, C., & Erkollar, A. (2020). The effect of greenwashing on online consumer engagement: A comparative study in France, Germany, Turkey, and the United Kingdom. *Business Strategy and the Environment*, *29*(2), 465–480. doi:10.1002/bse.2380

Uzunoğlu, E., Türkel, S., & Akyar, B. Y. (2017). Engaging consumers through corporate social responsibility messages on social media: An experimental study. *Public Relations Review*, *43*(5), 989–997. doi:10.1016/j.pubrev.2017.03.013

Wang, H., Tong, L., Takeuchi, R., & George, G. (2016). Corporate social responsibility: An overview and new research directions: Thematic issue on corporate social responsibility. *Academy of Management Journal*, *59*(2), 534–544. doi:10.5465/amj.2016.5001

Wang, R., & Huang, Y. (2018). Communicating corporate social responsibility (CSR) on social media: How do message source and types of CSR messages influence stakeholders' perceptions? *Corporate Communications*, *23*(3), 326–341. doi:10.1108/CCIJ-07-2017-0067

KEY TERMS AND DEFINITIONS

Agenda 2030: This agenda is a global plan of action for people, the planet and prosperity for all the countries and acting in collaborative partnership through 17 Sustainable Development Goals and 169 targets that involve the society as a whole.

Corporate Social Responsibility: A term that refers to the responsibility of companies and their voluntary contribution and positive impact on the environment and society and considering the expectation of stakeholders.

CSR Communication: It is the strategy of an organization to provide true information of its business operations, social and environmental concerns, and interactions with stakeholders in online/offline channels.

LinkedIn: Professional social network where people and companies connect with different objectives, such as sharing business information. The communication carried out by companies is especially focused on corporate communication aimed at their different stakeholders.

SDG: Each of the 17 goals of the Agenda 2030 grouped by themes affecting the planet.

Stakeholder Engagement: It is the interaction of firms with their stakeholders using a variety of channels in social media to build and strengthen a connection with them in the long term.

Sustainability Report: A report that describes the efforts of companies in terms of different related criteria such as environmental, social, and governance (ESG).

Chapter 25
The COVID-19 Pandemic and Its Impact on the Global Market:
A Microeconomic Perspective

Imran Khan
https://orcid.org/0000-0002-2230-5951
Niels Brock, Denmark

ABSTRACT

The global economy has expanded tremendously in recent years. However, this growth was hampered by the deadly COVID-19 outbreak, which forced countries to confront economic ramifications at both the micro and macro levels. The pandemic has posed a challenge to both producers and consumers, and businesses have been compelled to change their management styles for survival. Despite the return of the global market to normalcy, there remain questions over whether firms should continue to apply the same management strategies employed during COVID-19 or revisit their management practices in light of the post-COVID-19 climate. To address these issues, this study explores major global developments in entrepreneurial activity and economic growth in the aftermath of COVID-19, with the goal of assisting organizations in adapting and reacting during pandemic times to ensure long-term survival. Finally, the author proposes best practices for businesses to make rational decisions as well as an exhaustive review of global economies and markets to forecast their economic well-being post COVID-19.

LEARNING OBJECTIVES

- To study COVID-19 and its effects on consumers, as well as to understand the dynamics of the coronavirus pandemic
- To examine the key global developments in entrepreneurial activity in light of COVID-19 and their implications for businesses
- To investigate the potential for entrepreneurs in the aftermath of the coronavirus pandemic
- To assist organizations in adapting and reacting during the pandemic times in order to maintain their long-term viability

DOI: 10.4018/978-1-7998-8856-7.ch025

- To provide insight into the future prospects of the global economy

INTRODUCTION

The COVID-19 outbreak, often regarded as the worst global crisis since World War II, resulted in a radical shift in human health, livelihoods, and food systems. The world had been completely paralyzed, with each government imposing its virus-fighting strategies. Furthermore, world economies have been ripped apart not only by demand and supply shocks but also by financial shocks, putting significant pressure on economic growth. Global market volatility hit an all-time high, and the lockdown measures directly devastated the economy of the vast majority of countries, causing the macroeconomic indicators to tremble. In a recent study, the bulk of OECD and G20 research shows that lockdowns and mobility limitations caused the highest loss in real GDP in the first half of 2020 (OECD, 2020). As a result, governments all around the world have been focusing on creative ways to keep their economies floating.

Organizations have been disrupted as a result of the pandemic, necessitating a rethinking of their working styles. The result is a growing pressure to find new forms of resilience based on consumer demands, as well as shifting management approaches. While technology is essential in creating a digital environment, the global COVID-19 development has welcomed the concept of working from home, paving the way for remote working. Therefore, companies updated their Standard Operating Procedures to keep up with the demands of their businesses, allowing workers to work remotely. Without a doubt, the usage of digital services by consumers, businesses, and governments has emerged as a key economic driver that boosts growth and fosters job creation. The trend in app downloads for grocery shopping, healthcare, entertainment, and news demonstrates this (Accenture, 2020). Unfortunately, owing to revenue losses during COVID-19 lockdown measures, several leading industry businesses were compelled to shut down their operations completely.

One of the most destructive economic challenges endangering the world's economic growth is a disruption in global supply chains, which COVID-19 has bequeathed upon the world. The supply chain was disrupted as a result of the lockdowns, causing manufacturing to suffer (Harapko, 2021). In response to the COVID-19 lockdown, the toll of low consumer demand spiked once the lockdown was relaxed, leading to global shortages due to changes in consumer purchasing behavior and a worker shortage, both of which adversely affected global production capacity. As a result, producers and distributors were unable to fully satisfy production or supply needs for a variety of reasons, resulting in supply chain chaos (Ellyatt, 2021). Small enterprises are equally prone to supply chain disruptions caused by labor shortages and delays (Cates, 2022). Nevertheless, it is also true that during COVID-19, numerous entrepreneurs throughout the world had a perfect opportunity to launch new startup firms. In general, start-ups are a significant source of employment creation and economic stability (Casselman, 2021). Consequently, a start-up boom started growing stronger and applications to start firms soared after decades of decline indicating a possibility of a more resilient economy (Casselman, 2021). One of the key reasons why young entrepreneurs have had a multitude of opportunities to enter the market during COVID-19 is the expanding digital tsunami (Modgil et al., 2022). Consequently, digital technical instruments are the exigencies of the twenty-first century, and they are expected to coexist in organizations post-COVID-19 for best practices (I. Khan, 2022).

Consumers, producers, entrepreneurs, and organizations have all been impacted by the catastrophic outbreak of COVID-19 due to the unexpected radical transformation, thus more research is needed to fill in the gaps and determine whether these rapid developments due to COVID-19 will continue in the same way in the future. Therefore, the objective of this chapter is to investigate the economic effects of COVID-19 on consumers, entrepreneurship, and small enterprises, as well as to shed light on shifts in the organizational management methodology caused by the pandemic. Finally, the study aims to provide practitioners and policymakers with tips and tricks to make such practices more effective for consumers, entrepreneurship, and small businesses in a world without COVID-19. The following section provides background information for this chapter.

BACKGROUND

Gross domestic product (GDP) is a crucial macroeconomic metric for measuring economic growth, and economists tracked GDP during the COVID-19 pandemic to determine whether the disaster had any untoward consequences for the economy after several industries were severely devastated. Meanwhile, microeconomic determinants such as supply and demand, consumers, producers, and organizations have also seen unforeseen developments during the COVID-19 outbreak. Although there have been other crises in the past, such as natural disasters, economic crises, and even pandemics, the COVID-19 outbreak is the first to have a global impact in 100 years (Maison et al., 2021). Maison et al. (2021) conducted a qualitative study, interviewing 20 online respondents in Poland, to capture the most significant challenges associated with COVID-19, and the results revealed a variety of challenges, including limited direct contact with people, restricted movement, and uncertainty about the future (Maison et al., 2021).

COVID-19 has triggered a global economic downturn that has never been seen before. The pandemic's economic consequences include a looming worldwide recession brought on by the shutdown of non-essential businesses and the breakdown of production and supply systems (Maison et al., 2021). A study by Economics Observatory (2021) reveals that COVID-19 generates significant uncertainty over the short-term, since it reduces supply and demand, interrupts trade, increases unemployment and bankruptcies, and creates enormous ambiguity about the future (Economics Observatory, 2021). The same study reports that the long-term economic effect of a pandemic occurs when higher mortality reduces the working population (Economics Observatory, 2021). Coronavirus has also resulted in the closure of tens of thousands of retail locations in the United States and throughout the world, with many of these businesses closing due to government regulations or fluctuations in customer demand (Fairlie, 2020).

In a report published by Accenture (2020a), the epidemic of COVID-19 has shifted consumer purchasing habits since consumers have been drawn out of their regular routines, and digital commerce has been facilitated by an increase in consumers shopping for groceries online. This was also confirmed by a European Commission survey covering the last quarter of 2020 to assess consumer attitudes, behavior, and experience in Europe during COVID-19. The results revealed that 71 percent of consumers shopped online during this time, and consumer trust in retailers remained at an all-time high of 80 percent; 81 percent of consumers supported local businesses by shopping closer to home while opting for greener options (European Commission, 2021).

Without a question, the mental health and well-being of consumers and the general public is also an important element to consider during the COVID-19 epidemic. Nayal et al. (2021) researched to investigate and recommend crisis coping strategies for the survival and growth of businesses, as well as the well-being of consumers. Noting that the COVID-19 crisis has altered consumption patterns and employee working styles, the study concludes that firms' products must be altered in response to changing circumstances and changes in consumer behavior, and firms must provide counseling services for the mental health and well-being of their employees during stressful times while also showing concern for society's well-being through CSR practices (Nayal et al., 2021). The same study also emphasizes the importance of providing employees with the necessary tools for working from home, as well as sufficient training, to remain productive during crises (Nayal et al., 2021). Thygesen et al. (2021) conducted another study on the Danish population and reported that the adult Danish population's mental well-being deteriorated dramatically during the COVID-19 epidemic (Thygesen et al., 2021). Xu and Jia (2022) investigate the impact of COVID-19 on the psychological well-being (PWB) of Chinese entrepreneurs. Using 2 years of tracking data from 303 entrepreneurs, this study discovered that COVID-19 will significantly reduce entrepreneurs' PWB (Xu & Jia, 2022). Not just China, where the virus was first identified, but the entire global market grappled with the severe and ongoing negative consequences of coronavirus, resulting in billions of dollars in losses to global economies and financial markets. The global recession caused by the COVID-19 pandemic compelled the Organization for Economic Cooperation and Development (OECD), the International Monetary Fund (IMF), and the World Bank (WB) to reconsider their forecasts, resulting in a significant decrease in the projected rate of growth in late 2019 and mid-2020, and international institutions including the FAO, ILO, IFAD, and WHO jointly announced this pandemic a global challenge to food systems, public health, trade, and industry (Jabeen et al., 2022).

Because this is a novel and multifaceted issue, the existing literature reveals a lack of studies on the COVID-19 pandemic and its ramifications for the global market, with a focus on microeconomic indicators. Since the pandemic has affected the entire community depending on their socioeconomic background, there is scope for research into how organizations could perhaps ensure achieving best practices when responding to consumers in a post-COVID-19 world, as well as how organizations should respond to shifts in management techniques that occurred during the pandemic when transitioning from disaster to normalcy. By addressing the consequences of COVID-19 on the management of organizations, entrepreneurs, and consumers, this study hopes to contribute to the existing literature by demonstrating best practices to be adopted in post-COVID-19 environments. The next section presents information on the individual topics of this chapter.

The chapter comprises four key sections:

- The COVID-19 pandemic and organizational developments
- The COVID-19 and Entrepreneurship: A case study of small businesses
- Consumer behavior in the post-COVID-19 era: a revolution?
- Global economies and markets: what's next?

THE COVID-19 PANDEMIC AND ORGANIZATIONAL DEVELOPMENTS

COVID-19 is a disease caused by a novel coronavirus that the World Health Organization (WHO) declared to be a pandemic in March 2020 due to its rapid spread (WHO, 2020). The pandemic has caused chaos on people's lives around the globe, posing a proven obstacle but intriguing experiment for employers, as well as a negative influence on global economic growth in 2020 unlike anything witnessed in over a century (Jackson et al., 2021).

This chapter investigates how organizations are affected by the COVID-19 pandemic by examining the effects of the pandemic on organizational development and employee well-being, as well as whether these effects are irreversible. While many organizations had already begun to implement digital technology as a result of globalization and technological competition prior to the COVID-19 pandemic, some organizations have cashed in on this opportunity to reshape and redesign their businesses due to COVID-19 virus. No doubt, some organizations and individuals have strained or simply been unable to cope with the pace of change they have witnessed as a result of COVID-19's impact. Organizations have been forced to modify how they do business, and with the majority of employees working-from-home, business procedures have had to adapt quickly in order for them to survive.

According to Seiler (2021), the COVID-19 crisis has speeded up the digitalization of consumer interactions by years, and during this time, individuals have discovered innovative ways to use technology to complete their responsibilities, resulting in a surge in digital usage at both the organizational and industry levels (Seiler, 2021). The emergency transition from face-to-face to remote working for organizations, which was imposed at lightning speed to stop the spread of the coronavirus, exemplifies this. These developments have varied effects on different organizations, and these effects are frequently influenced by the size and type of firm, as well as the industries in which they operate. As a result of this transformation in the workplace to an almost totally online presence, new standards and policies have emerged that may have appeared impossible to believe. While this transformation allowed businesses to continue operating, it also introduced new demands from clients and customers, forcing organizations to quickly upskill their employees through the use of innovative training tools (Jacquet, 2020). Furthermore, firms see working remotely and returning to the office as two major developments related to COVID-19. Consequently, companies' ability to adapt has increased, leading to a push towards digital technology.

The pandemic has brought to light the significant disparity in access to digital technology and it is glaringly apparent that the underprivileged countries are the most affected when it comes to integrating digital technology, resulting in a digital divide. As a result, millions of small firms in developing nations with inadequate digital abilities may lack a high-speed internet connection to perform remote work or proper training to use digital technologies (World Economic Forum, 2020). This puts businesses' revenue creation processes in jeopardy since they may be unable to receive digital orders from customers, resulting in a decrease in revenue generation. Skills development and training for workers of all ages, on the other hand, can assist safeguard and strengthen them in the job market, allowing them to enter new areas of the economy. The government can do this in conjunction with other targeted solutions like free Wi-Fi, technology access, and the provision of free education. Recent studies suggest that businesses handled training and development in a variety of ways during the epidemic.

While the COVID-19 lockdown measures prevented firms from earning income, some firms decided to lay off employees and terminate contracts. Others, on the other hand, invested in digital tools to equip staff with remote training for professional development. Gamification, which has become a popular platform for providing online employee training and development, is one example of an advanced digital solution that could address the corporate learning gap created by COVID-19 (Armstrong & Landers, 2018). After all, a well-trained and motivated staff is not only beneficial to individuals' professional growth, but it is also a great asset to any company (Gillis, 2021).

In terms of the post-COVID-19 period, organizations have learned a valuable lesson and are prepared for a wide range of advances, particularly the use of digitalized technologies that were popular during COVID-19. According to McKinsey & Company, because of the overall increase in the number of people doing remote work during COVID-19, there's a likelihood that remote work and virtual meetings will continue, though not as actively as they were during the peak of the pandemic (Lund et al., 2021). Numerous startup companies started offering online training programs and remote internships to the graduates and experienced professionals from around the world, especially during the peak of COVID-19 pandemic. In the bigger picture, this is positive not even for the organizations but also for the potential workers because remote internships can assist interns in obtaining work experience with firms of their choosing regardless of their location that can ultimately foster their key competencies (Feldman, 2021). Such programs can continue offering organizations a feasible opportunity to recruit individuals from all over the world, including those with special needs, thereby contributing to the organization's diversity aim. As a result of their cost-effectiveness, convenience, and flexibility, remote internships benefit both individuals and companies by connecting them all over the globe (Prosser, 2021). In the future, these programs will be able to benefit a wider population while also economically contributing to a greater reduction in unemployment. Given the shift in management methodology in organizations following COVID-19, the author addresses the 5 R's to assist companies in transitioning from disaster to normalcy by establishing a framework for long-term success.

Revisit

This is merely to allow firms to reflect on their prior approach in terms of what worked well, what didn't, and what was overlooked throughout the decision-making process.

Reset

In a post-COVID-19 environment, re-evaluate the entire organizational structure to account for employees, their well-being, and any staff issues. Furthermore, in light of developments in a post-COVID-19 context, the organizational commitment must be reassessed in accordance with organizational aims and values.

Reconsider

Make a list of new objectives for reorganizing employees and resources to ensure that they are in accordance with business requirements. In the worst-case situation, reorganizing the employees and their roles is necessary to ensure that they are ready to take on any position.

Reconnect

To increase employee engagement in the post-COVID-19 environment, organizations must develop new training programs, workshops, and employee meetings to reengage the workforce, as COVID-19 changed the entire working scenario. This will boost worker collaboration and bring new possibilities for everyone to build their key competencies.

Readjust

Because the worldwide supply chain problem resulted in shortages of critical products during the pandemic, it is imperative for companies to make their supply chains more resilient in the future by diversifying their supply base rather than relying excessively on a single supplier. Organizations are also encouraged to prepare safety stock during the production process to minimize negative consequences in the event of a pandemic.

Because the pandemic has passed in most nations and restrictions are gradually being relaxed, businesses should begin reskilling their workforces as soon as possible (Agrawal et al., 2021). Hence, the author presents best practices in the post-COVID-19 era for all organizations when training current and new employees, with the term 'GRAB-THEM-FAST' defined in the following section.

G- Grooming future leaders and rethinking their roles
R- Rising competition for remote work
A- Accelerating the decision-making process
B- Being prepared for lockdowns
T- Thriving tomorrow's employees through Skills-Based Learning
H- Hybrid work
E- Ensuring a safe environment
M- Mental Wellbeing and Resilience
F- Future of Virtual meetings
A- Adopting on-demand digital learning
S- Start new products
T- Technology Provision

Grooming Future Leaders and Rethinking Their Roles

The increasing severity of crises, such as the COVID-19, and their effects have made it critical for future leaders to account for them while developing strategies. Many organizations have seen a huge transformation in leadership as a result of COVID-19. Therefore, companies must begin striving to train youngsters, or future leaders, who can inspire everyone in the organization with a clear vision for dealing with future crises.

Rising Competition for Remote Work

During the peak of the pandemic, remote working became the norm, and there was increased competition on the quality of programs that offered video conferencing as part of the remote work. However, this norm is expected to persist in the post-COVID-19 era, though somewhat not as much as it did during the pandemic. According to the Economist, remote work will continue to exist because the experience has been better than anticipated, and workers and businesses have invested heavily in improving it (The Economist, 2022).

Accelerating the Decision Making Process

Given the COVID-19 experience with rapid decision-making, companies should continue to use the same practice in the future, with fewer meetings for decision-making.

Being Prepared for Lockdowns

Companies have learned to adapt to any operating method, whether onsite or online, as a result of the COVID-19's sudden shutdown restrictions. Companies must, however, be prepared for any such events, even after the COVID-19, by planning and implementing a comprehensive business strategy.

Thriving Tomorrow's Employees Through Skills-Based Learning

Employers are more cautious about recruiting people based on the competencies they can contribute to a position as a result of the COVID-19 epidemic, which helps employers target high-quality applicants. Therefore, when delivering training and development to employees, businesses are encouraged to focus on skills-based learning rather than knowledge-based learning (Ivec, 2021). Hence, the organization should create a continuous learning culture with a learning platform to assess employee progress and highlight areas where additional training is required. This will ensure that employees are happier and stay with the company for a longer period of time (Ivec, 2021).

Hybrid Work

Hybrid work, with some employees working on-site and others working remotely, is expected to become the norm in the future. As a result, organizations must take the initiative to promote a hybrid model, which will undoubtedly increase employee satisfaction through greater flexibility and productivity while also lowering company costs.

Ensuring A Safe Environment

Employers must ensure that their employees adhere to the firm's mandatory safety and health standards, as well as implement guidance for vaccinated and unvaccinated workers in order to protect unvaccinated workers from any potential risk. Employers are also encouraged to provide paid time off to employees for the time it takes them to get vaccinated and recover. This will ensure a safe and risk-free environment for the entire organization.

Mental Wellbeing and Resilience

Indeed, the relationship between mental health and the workplace is bilateral, as work affects a person's mental health, and an employee's mental health affects overall workplace morale (Soman & Shroff, 2021). Organizations must provide a healthy work environment in which employees may grow and prosper, resulting in improved retention rates, and a stringent anti-discrimination policy must be implemented, as well as guaranteeing that employees' mental health is covered by their health insurance (Soman & Shroff, 2021). Employers must also foster a resilient work culture by recognizing good performance, offering flexible scheduling, increasing management support, and implementing training programs to boost employee engagement.

Future of Virtual Meetings

Even in the post-COVID-19 world, virtual meetings are here to stay, and it is critical to consider virtual meetings as a venue, among others, for future meetings. In order to provide a flexible work environment, the author envisions organizations adopting both virtual and on-site meetings at the same time in the near future. Virtual meetings, on the other hand, will continue to be the greatest option for employees with disabilities.

Adopting On-Demand Digital Learning

In the modern digital world, on-demand training is seen as a necessity. Due to the immediate shift to remote learning during the COVID-19 lockdown, on-demand training received a high acceptance. It is therefore essential that organizations make on-demand learning a priority to satisfy the workers and the business needs. When employees are given the information they need in a timely manner, they are more likely to desire to learn more and continue learning over time, and as a result, employee satisfaction and retention are high since the employees feel more supported in their professional growth (Zides, 2021). Thus on-demand training is also an essential element to be continued in a post-COVID-19 world for a digital upskilling of employees.

Start New Products

In a post-COVID-19 society, there is an urgent need to produce new products to improve demand, which was low during the pandemic, and to increase productivity, which will result in an increase in employment. As employment grows, more up-to-date training will be provided to employees, contributing to their well-being and satisfaction. As a result, firms must grab this chance to keep their staff motivated and engaged.

Technology Provision

Modern technology is a requirement of the twenty-first century, and the COVID-19 epidemic has taught people the value and urgency of technology, as well as demonstrating to us all that the digital revolution has arrived. Hence, firms must provide ongoing technical training programs to employees, including Artificial Intelligence, while launching new technology-based products to ensure that employees have sufficient hands-on expertise in operating computer-based products to continue working in the event that a crisis-like circumstance arises again.

The next chapter studies and explores the changes in entrepreneurial activity as a result of the global digital divide between organizations which became abundantly clear during the COVID-19 lockdown measures applied globally.

Problem Solving- Think Critically

In the United States, John is the owner of a financial advisory firm. In an emergency, John had no choice but to transition the business to a work-from-home model due to COVID-19 lockdown restrictions. This model has never been implemented before by any member of the staff.

i. What obstacles should John's team face as a result of this emergency shift?

Assume that a few months later, things began to return to normal after the government eased the restrictions in the post-COVID-19 environment. As the owner of a company, John must decide whether to stick to the same business model that was imposed in an emergency shift during COVID-19 or to revisit the model and develop a new one that is acceptable in any situation, crisis or non-crisis.

ii. Using knowledge from this topic, propose an alternative business strategy that John may adopt to provide a flexible work environment for the entire workforce.
iii. Given that this model has been implemented in the business, what kind of training should be provided to the employees to ensure compliance with the new standards and practices?

THE COVID-19 AND ENTREPRENEURSHIP: A CASE STUDY OF SMALL BUSINESSES

Entrepreneurs are those who own, operate, and bear the risk of a business, with the goal of identifying unmet market needs and providing services to address those needs by running their own business (Greene, 2016). Entrepreneurs, in general, are the backbone of the global economy and come in a variety of types. It's no secret that the entrepreneurship community has a lot on its plate during COVID-19, including the risk of losing teams or businesses. Small and medium-sized businesses contribute the most to global markets. These businesses, on the other hand, were in significantly more danger than larger businesses during COVID-19. Thus, there was a sharp increase in uncertainty for firms, employees, and consumers across a variety of industries. As per a report by S&P Global Market Intelligence, the top five industries most impacted by COVID-19 from the beginning of January to the end of August 2020 are airlines, leisure facilities, oil and gas drilling, auto parts and equipment, and restaurants (Haydon and Kumar, 2020). Other industries, too, took a hit at this time, albeit at a slower rate. It is entrepreneurs' destiny to not just survive but also emerge from the crisis with a stronger business than ever (EY & Mitchell, 2020).

According to Alessa et al. (2021), the pandemic had a severe influence on corporate productivity and earnings, leading several businesses to permanently close (Alessa et al., 2021). Global employability, on the other hand, was impacted, with some corporations enacting unprecedented mass layoffs and furloughs. Exxon, for example, was laying off 1600 people in Europe, resulting in a 2 percent drop in global employment as of October 5, 2020, and the same downsizing was carried out by many other corporate titans around the world in order to survive COVID-19 (Assis, 2020).

In terms of COVID-19's economic impact, governments in a number of nations supported businesses by launching support packages for worker welfare with the objective to save businesses from catastrophic economic collapse. Hence, the support packages not only assisted the businesses from failing and employees from losing jobs, but also offered stability to the fluctuating economic cycles, thereby enabling people and firms to retain their incomes. Nevertheless, this opportunity was not open to many other nations. Obviously, the country's economic condition was the most important factor in a country's ability to help its citizens during times of distress. Ethiopia, for example, had a tough macroeconomic environment marked by modest but quick growth, high inflation, high unemployment, insufficient forex reserves, and significant pressure on the currency rate (Engidaw, 2022). Hence, in a volatile economic environment like this, doing business during the COVID-19 epidemic is exceedingly difficult and has a significant impact on small businesses, workers' lives, and the whole economy of the country (Engidaw, 2022).

Small businesses, on average, employ roughly half of the American workforce in the United States (Bartik et al., 2020). However, because small businesses suffer more during depressions due to having much smaller financial reserves than larger businesses and having difficulty obtaining a bank loan, small businesses are more vulnerable to COVID-19 because they employ a high proportion of those working in the severely afflicted industries (COVID-19 Impacts on Small Businesses, 2020). Hence, 43 percent of the businesses were temporarily closed, causing a shock to America's small businesses and a loss in employment (Bartik et al., 2020).

According to new research, between January and November 2020, at least three million small enterprises in China closed down, and several people lost their jobs as COVID-19 returned in several areas (AsiaNews.it, 2021). Tourism, wellness, catering, and training were among the industries that struggled the most during this period (AsiaNews.it, 2021). Nevertheless, Beijing's zero-COVID policy, along with the ability to deploy all of the country's resources, has resulted in tremendous economic advances, which is why, despite warnings, China's export growth remained robust during 2021 (Cheng, 2022).

Despite limited resources, a developing country like Pakistan developed the Ehsaas Emergency Cash program to help the poor, while the government implemented smart lockdown, which was effective to some extent in containing the spread of coronavirus and allowing economic activity to continue (The World Bank In Pakistan, 2021). Many small and medium-sized enterprises in Pakistan, on the other hand, were adversely impacted by a range of challenges, including financial, supply chain disruption, lower demand, reduced sales, and profitability (Shafi et al., 2020). In addition, enterprises used a variety of tactics to deal with the crisis scenario and cashflow difficulties, such as seeking a loan, partially or totally closing the business, cutting staff, and reducing staff salaries (Shafi et al., 2020).

India, on the other hand, struggled during the COVID-19 pandemic due to a failed public health strategy and reported the highest number of cases in the world (Mutreja, 2021). According to the World Economic Forum, Indian government measures to stop the virus's spread were felt around the world in the form of global supply shocks, particularly in the manufacturing sector, and lockdowns and other containment measures caused significant slowdowns, indicating that the pandemic has ushered the second great economic and financial crisis of the twenty-first century, with long-term structural implications (Brende, 2021).

While speedy countermeasures to the epidemic were prevalent, certain governments also developed a long-term strategy to safeguard businesses and individuals' income (Popov, 2021). Costa Rica's government launched the 'Buy-SME' business platform, which targets businesses without an online presence; Senegal launched information, education, and awareness campaign on the benefits of e-commerce; and Indonesia launched a capacity-building program to assist micro, small, and medium-sized businesses in accelerating their digitalization (Popov, 2021).

COVID-19 has pushed the consumers toward online products resulting in a surge in e-commerce and accelerated digital transformation, which has fostered rivalry among businesses and provided an opportunity for the new businesses to sell their products to the target market. In some nations, entrepreneurs are having product availability challenges as a result of COVID-19-caused supply chain disruption, which limits their ability to meet client needs.

Despite the fact that working from home has become a new norm in today's era, several startup companies are expected to emerge in a variety of business types such as cleaning services, delivery services, remote fitness, e-commerce, online reselling, freelance writing, home care service, social media marketing, virtual assistant, online therapy, video editing, online teaching, and translation service in the post-COVID-19 era (Watson, 2021).

In the post-COVID-19 world, online business will become the norm, and businesses will be handled across borders without any difficulty. Because of the digitalization of the communication and banking systems, international business for small enterprises is expected to grow (Minai et al., 2021). Concerning the effects of COVID-19 on small enterprises, the author proposes strategies to assist them in transitioning into the post-COVID-19 environment by developing a framework to assure long-term prosperity.

Estimate the Economic Loss

The repercussions of the crisis varied dramatically for large enterprises, small businesses, and consumers (Wang et al., 2020). In the U.K., for instance, 17 percent of small and medium-sized businesses are at risk of insolvency in the next four years as funding from emergency pandemic packages ends (Hurley, 2020). Hence, it is imperative to determine how hard the small business has been hit by the pandemic as a first step, which can be done by simply comparing the most recent financial statements with those from the previous year to see if there are any unusual changes in the numbers causing the severe economic losses.

Business Relocation

A radical change in working patterns has resulted from the pandemic, and several small businesses now operate remotely, allowing the model of working in one location while living in another to become a norm. Nevertheless, it is crucial that businesses prepare themselves for a permanent relocation as they move to the post-COVID-19 era.

Revisit the Business Plan

Whether small businesses have the right business plan during the COVID-19 pandemic is questionable. Nevertheless, as the businesses come out of the pandemic and into the new normal, the business plan may also need to be adjusted. It entails evaluating the strengths and weaknesses of the system in terms of what worked and what failed, and where improvement might be needed in order to meet the market standards of the post-COVID-19 era.

Reimagine the Business Model and Embrace New Technology

In response to COVID-19, firms have had to reimagine their business models to incorporate e-commerce due to a greater reliance on digital channels such as WhatsApp, Zoom, Microsoft Teams, and WeChat for holding meetings with staff and clients. Because the COVID-19 crisis exposed long-standing financial vulnerabilities, the next normal may result in higher costs; as a result, small businesses will need to develop new business models, as well as expedite the adoption of new technologies, if they are to respond to such challenges (Dua et al., 2021).

Plan for The Next Crisis

Due to the unpredictable nature of a coronavirus pandemic and the speed with which it can wipe out small enterprises, having a Plan B for survival is essential. It might be prudent for small businesses to save up money once the pandemic is over so they can protect themselves from future shocks. Moreover, it would be wise to eliminate any debt and minimize non-essential expenditures so that these funds contribute to the firm's profit maximization and can be utilized as a buffer against future shocks.

Following the discussion, the author encourages state and non-state actors to develop strategies to promote entrepreneurial recovery in the aftermath of COVID-19 by developing a digital economy, which can contribute to increased entrepreneurship, social mobility, new opportunities, and economic participation by marginalized communities (Wong, 2020).

The next section examines consumer behavior in the post-COVID-19 period, followed by a detailed analysis of how consumption patterns evolved during COVID-19, how the global supply chain issue occurred, and what steps organizations must take to satisfy consumers in a post-COVID-19 environment.

Problem Solving- Think Critically

i. What is the significance of entrepreneurship in any economy? Give examples of how entrepreneurs have an impact on the economy.
ii. Is switching from one way of operating to another, like in COVID-19, a good practice for entrepreneurs and the workforce?

CONSUMER BEHAVIOR IN THE POST-COVID-19 ERA: A REVOLUTION?

Economic recovery from the COVID-19 epidemic is unlikely to be quick or straightforward. Without a doubt, the COVID-19 did not have the same impact everywhere, resulting in considerable damage to the economic, social, and health sectors. When compared to developed countries, which were able to elevate their citizens by delivering stimulus packages, less-developed countries suffered the most during the COVID-19 due to a lack of resources. Less-developed countries requested global stimulus packages since the budget they planned was insufficient to compensate for income losses caused by the pandemic.

At the outset of the pandemic, shipping capacity was speedily depleted around the world because it was expected that demand would fall significantly, but instead of collapsing, it bombarded as people wanted to buy products, and therefore the supply side was severely affected, with all major industries, including warehouses, ports, and others, experiencing labor shortages (Farrer, 2021). Consequently, the pandemic resulted in a massive spike in shipping and container costs.

A consumer is a person who orders and purchases products primarily for personal use and thus plays an important role in a country's economic development (Wikipedia contributors, 2022). Consumer demand has been a major concern for many firms, especially since the government imposed lockdown restrictions to help prevent the spread of COVID-19. During this time, several businesses experienced a drop in consumer demand, and small businesses that had never operated online stores prior to COVID-19 had a disaster, whereas larger businesses that also had online shopping facilities could still sell their products online while suffering less financial damage. Due to the accelerated rate of digital technology adoption, smartphones, computers, and the internet have not only become necessities in their own right, but they have also spawned a slew of new behaviors such as online shopping, bill payment, gaming, GPS navigation, and so on, resulting in changes in consumption (Sawhney & Madan, 2021), and a shift toward digital technology that may continue as the world returns to normal. Behaviors, attitudes, and purchasing habits of consumers have thus changed, encouraging the author to look into post-COVID-19 developments in consumer behavior.

Consumer products witnessed a drop in demand during COVID-19 also due to consumers being unable to visit stores or even lacking the cash required for purchases, and this is also true for internet businesses, where common supply shortages made it difficult for firms to meet consumer demand (Alessa et al., 2021). Thus, the supply chains had become disjointed. On the other side, producers struggled to deliver timely supplies all around the world. One such example is the high level of demand for ventilators, medications, and personal protective equipment (PPE) that occurred during the peak of the pandemic, with healthcare staff and governments battling to obtain supplies due to scarcity (Barlow et al., 2021).

Despite the fact that supply chain interruptions remained high during COVID-19, the Statista Supply Chain Index shows that the US and EU are the most vulnerable to supply chain disruptions (Strachan, 2022). GlobalData's Supply Chain Risk Index confirms Statista's findings, revealing that the United States and the United Kingdom are in first and second place for supply chain vulnerability, followed by Australia, France, and Russia, with Germany being the least vulnerable, followed by China, South Korea, Ireland, and the Netherlands, indicating that their supply chains are quite stable (Strachan, 2022). As a result, regional connectivity is vital for governments to improve small company cooperation and tackle the supply chain crisis.

Because of the COVID-19, businesses were driven to change their emphasis from thinking about launching new items to focusing on existing ones. The big brands did not introduce any new items and instead focused on making the existing items as accessible to customers as possible. However, as the crisis fades, a stronger hunger for online buying may endure, though with variances across categories.

To address the flaws in global production identified by COVID-19, supply chains must be revised. As the global economy begins to recover from the pandemic, the question now is which of the COVID-19 changes will persist, and how corporations will respond to shifts in consumer demand. Going forward, it is critical for firms to adopt long-term strategic goals while keeping the risk of adverse events in mind.

Consumers, without a question, are the driving force behind the market competition, growth, and economic integration in any market (Mehta et al., 2020). According to the research on Chinese consumers, after the epidemic, Chinese consumers are likely to be even more open to online shopping, especially in categories such as skin care, beauty, and personal care (Ho et al., 2020). To address the aftermath of the pandemic, the author suggests that organizations respond to consumers by implementing the best practices in a post-COVID environment listed below.

Digital Move

With escalating digital technology rivalry among businesses, the use of digital technology is likely to become the norm in the corporate sector. The COVID-19 pandemic has emphasized the importance of digitalization as a necessity for everyone. To help consumers, businesses should continue to develop smartphone applications for online shopping that include features such as the ability to order from anywhere in the world and a mechanism to make the application more accessible to people of all ages. Moreover, the in-store shopping experience must be digitalized so that customers may have a contactless shopping experience in terms of health precautions and a queue-free shopping environment with features such as click-and-go (Choubey, 2021). The author also believes that now is the greatest time for businesses to invest in data and analytics and implement AI-enabled store assistants to provide better in-store services to customers. Furthermore, businesses should utilize AI to gain insights into customer behavior, which can aid in interacting with customers through focused marketing campaigns and providing an opportunity to resolve difficult issues (Morzaria, 2020).

Customer Relationship

Even before COVID-19, all businesses had a policy of building long-term consumer relationships. However, due to changes in consumer purchasing patterns, the strategy must be revised to include a longer availability of Quick-bots to connect customers with the company and customer loyalty programs to reward customers for choosing the company's product. Furthermore, the earlier strategy of contacting clients must be escalated further and a smooth in-store shopping facility must be offered to the customers with very streamlined store operation (Choubey, 2021).

Partnership

Companies must rethink their partnership with other firms by introducing joint contracts and launching new products in the post-COVID-19 which will help in building the brand and restoring the customer trust that was lost during the pandemic. Companies were cooperating with new mobile payment services such as mobile payments or social media platforms such as Tiktok to reach new clients in the market even during COVID-19. Partnerships, however, must continue not only within, but also beyond the borders.

Delivery Process

The COVID-19 and the supply chain crisis slowed down the delivery process throughout the world, but this is expected to improve after COVID-19 as things get to normalcy. To speed up the delivery process, businesses need to increase partners both domestic and overseas to ease the product transfer to the customers. In addition, flexible distribution mechanisms and reliable supply networks are required to boost consumer confidence.

Given the anticipated post-COVID-19 trends, businesses should keep these best practices in mind while dealing with the consumers in the new normal. A comprehensive economic analysis of COVID-19's impact on the global marketplace is provided in the next section.

Problem Solving- Think Critically

Steven buys groceries from a local supermarket and has never shopped online. Due to some state-level restrictions during COVID-19, the supermarket was forced to shut down to contain the spread of coronavirus. However, the supermarket was still open for online orders with some delivery charges. Steven had no other choice than to buy groceries from this supermarket since Steven is so addicted to their products.

i. Using knowledge from consumer behavior, what obstacles would this transition from in-store to online shopping pose to Steven's purchasing power?
ii. Assuming that the restrictions are lifted by the government in a post-COVID-19 world, what are Steven's expectations from the supermarket owners in terms of receiving the best in-store shopping experience?

GLOBAL ECONOMIES AND MARKETS: WHAT'S NEXT?

The coronavirus epidemic, which is a once-in-a-generation global event, is expected to have long-term economic consequences. The global economic downturn morphed into a full-fledged financial crisis, with firms declaring bankruptcy and certain industries suffering the most or even failing, putting a strain on global economies. Markets, in particular, are feeling the effects as the global government response to the pandemic hits record levels, and many are transitioning to a more decentralized working style that makes greater use of technology. Since the pandemic has devastated lives around the globe, there has been a decline in the global economy and therefore the economies of the major advanced countries, which comprise 60% of global economic activity, are projected to operate at below their potential levels for at least four years, which implies a decline in the economic well-being of nations (Jackson et al., 2021). In addition to recovering from the COVID-19 epidemic, societies around the world face major obstacles caused by climate change, poverty, inequality, and the digital divide, necessitating greater global cooperation to address these issues (Acemoğlu et al., 2022). While high-income economies appear to be able to handle the resulting shocks comparatively smoothly due to ample resources and reserves, low-income nations appear to be struggling due to a lack of resources and higher debt. In the case of the US economy, a CNBC study indicates that it entered a phase of boosted growth and that, unlike during the pandemic, it might become stronger until 2023 than it had been before (Domm, 2021). Nevertheless, higher inflation may be on the horizon. Following the epidemic, it becomes increasingly important to determine when to withdraw government assistance so the economy can recover quickly and resources can be appropriately reallocated (Acemoğlu et al., 2022). The threats connected with this withdrawal pose numerous challenges for governments around the world, but they also present an opportunity to address key challenges to humanity and progress toward a more safe and sustainable world (Acemoğlu et al., 2022).

Unfortunately, a new supply shock has arrived as a result of Russia's war in Ukraine. As a consequence, the recovery from COVID-19 is jeopardized, and governments' attempts to construct more resilient and sustainable infrastructure are re-focused (OECD, 2022). Poor countries, for this reason, will face even greater danger than rich countries, as food insecurity remains large and supply chains risk getting clogged up further (OECD, 2022). Thus, governments' efforts to incorporate resilience into their economies have suddenly become a lot more difficult, especially since energy costs have risen causing a drastic increase in uncertainty about the recovery of the global economy (OECD, 2022).

According to new research, Russia's unprecedented invasion of Ukraine is jeopardizing Southeast Asia's post-COVID economic rebound by driving up commodity prices, affecting both producers and consumers (Jongwanich, 2022). Nonetheless, governments and non-governmental organizations globally must step in to provide economic support or technological aid to businesses in order to satisfy consumer demands in the new normal. Undoubtedly, this will positively affect the country's economic indicators, thereby encouraging economic growth. As seen by the growing use of e-commerce since COVID-19, the author believes that global business operations will no longer be limited by national borders in the future. Last but not the least, as global firms strive to avoid supply chain interruptions, global supply chains are expected to become increasingly diverse over the coming decades.

FUTURE RESEARCH DIRECTIONS

This section builds on the debate from previous sections and provides researchers with future study directions. Research indicates that migrating consumers to digital channels is undoubtedly one of the most effective ways to boost consumer satisfaction and reduce costs (Diebner et al., 2020). In light of the COVID-19-induced changes in how organizations are managed, the chapter calls for future qualitative research methods in the post-COVID-19 period, such as interviewing consumers to find out if the new digitalized business models provide consumers with better satisfaction. This will also help organizations to rethink their company model in response to changing consumer behavior and preferences, knowing that a complete understanding of consumers' lifestyles is required for offering the most relevant products and services to the right individuals (Kotler and Keller, 2012). As a result, future academics are encouraged to do extensive research on consumer behavior in various marketplaces, with a focus on e-commerce platforms, to determine whether there have been any changes in consumer demand since the COVID-19 era.

Governing bodies recognize small businesses as the backbone of any economy and a key driver of job creation and economic development. There is evidence to suggest that small businesses suffered the greatest loss during the COVID-19 pandemic in several countries. Following this, the author believes qualitative research in the post-pandemic world will make it possible to determine if small businesses have risen in post-pandemic times as compared with the pre-pandemic times, as well as assess if new management techniques are improving performance.

Lastly, studies on the effects of the new organizational methodologies on employee well-being can be conducted to evaluate if the new organizational approach post-COVID-19 pandemic has produced healthy results.

CONCLUSION

A digital revolution of new ideas and procedures will usher in the next era. COVID-19 has turned digitalization from a "nice to have" to an absolute imperative, even for firms. As part of future efforts, more investment needs to be made in digital transformation models as digitalization is the need of the twenty-first century, and the COVID-19 outbreak demonstrated the importance of digital tools that organizations implemented globally to combat job losses due to government-imposed lockdowns.

This study aimed to (1) capture the effects of the COVID-19 pandemic on organizational development and employee well-being, as well as the lessons learned by organizations from a shift in management methods and a recommendation for implementing best practices when training staff in the post-COVID-19 environment; (2) discuss the factors that contributed to entrepreneurs' success or failure during COVID-19 and their contribution to the global market; and (3) provide recommendations on consumer behavior and demand, as well as a proposal to organizations for applying best practices in consumer response in the post-COVID-19 era.

Transitioning from one working style to the next necessitates a significant amount of resources and a shift in the business model. COVID-19 has altered our regular way of life; consequently, organizations should reflect on this and plan their future strategies in accordance with the new consumer behavior. Now that consumers are more inclined to consider hygiene, sustainability, and local consumption of products, it is important for companies to keep this in mind when manufacturing and marketing their products and services. Therefore, increased investment is critical in upgrading resources to meet the ever-changing consumer demand, both in organizations and at the national level, to overcome the issues encountered by consumers and producers, which might help minimize the global supply chain disruption. Furthermore, improved internal and cross-border corporate collaboration is critical in bridging the gap between service delivery and customer expectations, ensuring that organizations remain resilient and responsive in the new normal. In addition to other things, it is critical for small businesses and entrepreneurship to be protected and supported during and after the COVID-19 pandemic since they play a unique role in the aftermath of the crisis and the anticipated post-pandemic boom (Belitski et al., 2021).

Finally, since agile organizations can make quick decisions and absorb and adapt to difficulties (Agile Resilience in the UK: Lessons from COVID-19 for the 'new normal,' 2020), more robust agile models may be able to help enterprises in the future. Given the lessons learned from COVID-19's rapid decision-making, companies should reflect on their COVID-19 processes and decide which ones to preserve in order to transition to an agile operating model and ingrain these practices in corporate culture and operations for long-term sustainability.

In light of the author's best practices for organizational development in a post-COVID-19 world, and key tips for entrepreneurs, the author believes that the findings of the chapter will contribute to the development of more effective preparedness and response strategies to lessen the impact of future pandemics.

Chapter Assessment

i. COVID-19 is believed to have a significant impact on consumer demand as well as the entire supply chain process. Some countries used a full lockdown approach to combat the spread of coronavirus, while others used a smart-lockdown approach. Using knowledge from this chapter, which of these two approaches to coronavirus control has the least influence on consumer demand and thus business activity in a country?
ii. Assume Adam is an entrepreneur who moved his business to remote work under the government's COVID-19 lockdown restrictions. Now that the lockdown has been lifted and things started returning to normal, Adam would like to take preventive measures to guarantee that business operations and staff are prepared to work in a different manner if another lockdown occurs in the future.

If there is a second lockdown, how can Adam achieve best practices in management strategy and staff well-being while simultaneously meeting consumer needs?

iii. Entrepreneurs are widely regarded as the backbone of any country's economy. While many entrepreneurs were unable to continue their businesses during the COVID-19 lockdowns, numerous small businesses took advantage of the opportunity to launch profitable internet businesses in a variety of countries. What are some of the business types where COVID-19 lockdown procedures have the least impact?
iv. Should organizations include an obligatory requirement for vaccinated employees in their policies and processes to ensure that only vaccinated employees are permitted to enter the office in a post-COVID-19 world?

This research received no specific grant from any funding agency in the public, commercial, or not-for-profit sectors.

REFERENCES

Accenture. (2020). *How COVID-19 will permanently change consumer behavior*. https://www.accenture.com/_acnmedia/pdf-123/accenture-covid19-pulse-survey-research-pov.pdf

Accenture. (2020a). *COVID-19: How consumer behavior will be changed.* https://www.accenture.com/dk-en/insights/consumer-goods-services/coronavirus-consumer-behavior-research

Acemoğlu, D., Beck, T., Obstfeld, M., & Park, Y. (2022). *Prospects of the global economy after Covid-19.* VOX, CEPR Policy Portal. https://voxeu.org/article/prospects-global-economy-after-covid-19

Agrawal, S., de Smet, A., Lacroix, S., & Reich, A. (2021). *To emerge stronger from the COVID-19 crisis, companies should start reskilling their workforces now.* McKinsey & Company. https://www.mckinsey.com/business-functions/people-and-organizational-performance/our-insights/to-emerge-stronger-from-the-covid-19-crisis-companies-should-start-reskilling-their-workforces-now

Alessa, A. A., Alotaibie, T. M., Elmoez, Z., & Alhamad, H. E. (2021). Impact of COVID-19 on Entrepreneurship and Consumer Behaviour: A Case Study in Saudi Arabia. *The Journal of Asian Finance. Economics and Business, 8*(5), 201–210. doi:10.13106/JAFEB.2021.VOL8.NO5.0201

Armstrong, M. B., & Landers, R. N. (2018). Gamification of employee training and development. *International Journal of Training and Development, 22*(2), 162–169. doi:10.1111/ijtd.12124

AsiaNews.it. (2021). *Beijing, three million small businesses closed due to Covid.* AsiaNews. https://www.asianews.it/news-en/Beijing,-three-million-small-businesses-closed-due-to-Covid-52494.html

Assis, C. (2020). *Exxon to lay off up to 1,600 workers in Europe.* MarketWatch. https://www.marketwatch.com/story/exxon-to-lay-off-up-to-1600-workers-in-europe-2020-10-05

Barlow, P., van Schalkwyk, M. C., McKee, M., Labonté, R., & Stuckler, D. (2021). COVID-19 and the collapse of global trade: Building an effective public health response. *The Lancet. Planetary Health, 5*(2), e102–e107. doi:10.1016/S2542-5196(20)30291-6 PMID:33581061

Bartik, A. W., Bertrand, M., Cullen, Z., Glaeser, E. L., Luca, M., & Stanton, C. (2020). The impact of COVID-19 on small business outcomes and expectations. *Proceedings of the National Academy of Sciences of the United States of America, 117*(30), 17656–17666. doi:10.1073/pnas.2006991117 PMID:32651281

Belitski, M., Guenther, C., Kritikos, A. S., & Thurik, R. (2021). Economic Effects of the COVID-19 Pandemic on Entrepreneurship and Small Businesses. SSRN *Electronic Journal.* doi:10.2139/ssrn.3905065

Brende, B. (2021). *India's roadmap for success and prosperity in the post-COVID world.* World Economic Forum. https://www.weforum.org/agenda/2021/11/india-s-future-and-role-in-the-post-covid-19-world/

Casselman, B. (2021). *Start-Up Boom in the Pandemic Is Growing Stronger.* The New York Times. https://www.nytimes.com/2021/08/19/business/startup-business-creation-pandemic.html

Cates, L. (2022). *Small Businesses Are Still Grappling with Supply Chain Disruptions.* U.S. Chamber of Commerce. https://www.uschamber.com/small-business/small-businesses-are-still-grappling-with-supply-chain-disruptions

Cheng, E. (2022). *China's zero-Covid strategy hurts consumer spending more than manufacturing.* CNBC. https://www.cnbc.com/2022/01/13/chinas-zero-covid-strategy-hurts-consumer-spending-more-than-manufacturing.html

Choubey, S. (2021). *How to elevate customer experience in a post COVID-19 world*. EY. https://www.ey.com/en_gl/consulting/how-to-elevate-customer-experience-in-a-post-covid-19-world

COVID-19 Impacts on Small Businesses. (2020). SANDAG. https://www.sandag.org/uploads/publicationid/publicationid_4689_27781.pdf

Diebner, R., Silliman, E., Ungerman, K., & Vancauwenberghe, M. (2020). *Adapting customer experience in the time of coronavirus*. McKinsey & Company. https://www.mckinsey.com/business-functions/marketing-and-sales/our-insights/adapting-customer-experience-in-the-time-of-coronavirus

Domm, P. (2021). *The economy is on the cusp of a major boom and economists believe it could last*. CNBC. https://www.cnbc.com/2021/04/09/the-economy-is-on-the-cusp-of-a-major-boom-and-economists-believe-it-could-last.html

Dua, A., Mahajan, D., Oyer, L., & Ramaswamy, S. (2021). *US small-business recovery after the COVID-19 crisis*. McKinsey & Company. https://www.mckinsey.com/industries/public-and-social-sector/our-insights/us-small-business-recovery-after-the-covid-19-crisis

Economics Observatory. (2021). *What are the long-run economic consequences of pandemics?* https://www.economicsobservatory.com/what-are-long-run-economic-consequences-pandemics

Ellyatt, H. (2021). *Supply chain chaos is already hitting global growth. And it's about to get worse*. CNBC. https://www.cnbc.com/2021/10/18/supply-chain-chaos-is-hitting-global-growth-and-could-get-worse.html

Engidaw, A. E. (2022). Small businesses and their challenges during COVID-19 pandemic in developing countries: In the case of Ethiopia. *Journal of Innovation and Entrepreneurship*, *11*(1). https://doi.org/10.1186/s13731-021-00191-3

European Commission. (2021). *Commission's new consumer survey shows impact of COVID-19 and popularity of 'greener' choices*. https://ec.europa.eu/commission/presscorner/detail/cs/ip_21_1104

EY & Mitchell, S. (2020). *How entrepreneurs survive and thrive in a crisis*. EY. https://www.ey.com/en_gl/weoy/how-entrepreneurs-survive-and-thrive-in-a-crisis

Fairlie, R. W. (2020). *The Impact of Covid-19 on Small Business Owners: Evidence of Early-Stage Losses from the April 2020 Current Population Survey*. NBER. https://www.nber.org/papers/w27309

Farrer, M. (2021). *Global supply chain crisis could last another two years, warn experts*. The Guardian. https://www.theguardian.com/business/2021/dec/18/global-supply-chain-crisis-could-last-another-two-years-warn-experts

Feldman, E. (2021). Virtual Internships During the COVID-19 Pandemic and Beyond. *New Horizons in Adult Education and Human Resource Development*, *33*(2), 46–51. https://doi.org/10.1002/nha3.20314

Gillis, G. (2021). *How gamification could fill the corporate learning gap created by COVID-19*. theHRDIRECTOR. https://www.thehrdirector.com/features/learning-development/gamification-fill-corporate-learning-gap-created-covid-19/

Greene, C. L. (2016). *Entrepreneurship: Ideas in Action* (6th ed.). Cengage Learning.

Harapko, S. (2021). *How COVID-19 impacted supply chains and what comes next.* https://www.ey.com/en_gl/supply-chain/how-covid-19-impacted-supply-chains-and-what-comes-next

Haydon, D., & Kumar, N. (2020). *Industries Most and Least Impacted by COVID19 from a Probability of Default Perspective September 2020 Update.* S&P Global Market Intelligence. https://www.spglobal.com/marketintelligence/en/news-insights/blog/industries-most-and-least-impacted-by-covid19-from-a-probability-of-default-perspective-september-2020-update

Ho, J., Hui, D., Kim, A., & Zhang, Y. (2020). *Cautiously optimistic: Chinese consumer behavior post-COVID-19.* McKinsey & Company. https://www.mckinsey.com/industries/consumer-packaged-goods/our-insights/cautiously-optimistic-chinese-consumer-behavior-post-covid-19

Hurley, J. (2020). *Bankruptcy and the COVID-19 Crisis.* HBS Working Knowledge. https://hbswk.hbs.edu/item/bankruptcy-and-the-covid-19-crisis

Ivec, S. (2021). *How To Skill Up Employees For A Post-Pandemic Future.* eLearning Industry. https://elearningindustry.com/how-to-skill-up-employees-for-a-post-pandemic-future

Iyke, B. (2020). The Disease Outbreak Channel of Exchange Rate Return Predictability: Evidence from COVID-19. *Emerging Markets Finance & Trade, 56*(10), 2277–2297. https://doi.org/10.1080/1540496x.2020.1784718

Jabeen, S., Farhan, M., Zaka, M. A., Fiaz, M., & Farasat, M. (2022). COVID and World Stock Markets: A Comprehensive Discussion. *Frontiers in Psychology, 12.* doi:10.3389/fpsyg.2021.763346

Jackson, J., Weiss, M., Schwarzenberg, A., Nelson, R., Sutter, K., & Sutherland, M. (2021). *Global Economic Effects of COVID-19.* Congressional Research Service. https://sgp.fas.org/crs/row/R46270.pdf

Jacquet, R. (2020). *Upskilling During Difficult Times: How Do We Keep Employees Learning from Home?* Coursera Blog. https://blog.coursera.org/upskilling-during-difficult-times-how-do-we-keep-employees-learning-from-home/

Jongwanich, J. (2022). *Russia war on Ukraine threatens Southeast Asia's economic recovery.* East Asia Forum. https://www.eastasiaforum.org/2022/04/21/russia-war-on-ukraine-threatens-southeast-asias-economic-recovery/

Khan, I. (2022). Handbook of Research on Adapting Remote Learning Practices for Early Childhood and Elementary School Classrooms (Advances in Early Childhood and K-12 Education). IGI Global. https://doi.org/10.4018/978-1-7998-8405-7.ch028.

Kotler, P., & Keller, K. L. (2012). *Marketing management.* Pearson France.

Lund, S., Madgavkar, A., Manyika, J., Smit, S., Ellingrud, K., & Robinson, O. (2021). *The future of work after COVID-19.* McKinsey & Company. https://www.mckinsey.com/featured-insights/future-of-work/the-future-of-work-after-covid-19

Maison, D., Jaworska, D., Adamczyk, D., & Affeltowicz, D. (2021). The challenges arising from the COVID-19 pandemic and the way people deal with them. A qualitative longitudinal study. *PLoS One, 16*(10), e0258133. https://doi.org/10.1371/journal.pone.0258133

Mehta, S., Saxena, T., & Purohit, N. (2020). The New Consumer Behaviour Paradigm amid COVID-19: Permanent or Transient? *Journal of Health Management*, *22*(2), 291–301. https://doi.org/10.1177/0972063420940834

Minai, M. S., Raza, S., & Segaf, S. (2021). Post COVID-19: Strategic Digital Entrepreneurship in Malaysia. *Modeling Economic Growth in Contemporary Malaysia*, 71–79. doi:10.1108/978-1-80043-806-420211007

Modgil, S., Dwivedi, Y. K., Rana, N. P., Gupta, S., & Kamble, S. (2022). Has Covid-19 accelerated opportunities for digital entrepreneurship? An Indian perspective. *Technological Forecasting and Social Change*, *175*, 121415. https://doi.org/10.1016/j.techfore.2021.121415

Morzaria, H. (2020). *The 7 Benefits of AI in Customer Service*. https://www.business2community.com/customer-experience/the-7-benefits-of-ai-in-customer-service-02301342

Mutreja, A. (2021). *COVID crisis in India: why its public health strategy failed*. The Conversation. https://theconversation.com/covid-crisis-in-india-why-its-public-health-strategy-failed-159861

Nayal, P., Pandey, N., & Paul, J. (2021). Covid-19 pandemic and consumer-employee-organization wellbeing: A dynamic capability theory approach. *The Journal of Consumer Affairs*, *56*(1), 359–390. https://doi.org/10.1111/joca.12399

OECD. (2022). *Economic and Social Impacts and Policy Implications of the War in Ukraine*. https://www.oecd-ilibrary.org/sites/4181d61b-en/index.html?itemId=/content/publication/4181d61b-en

Popov, A. (2021). *How COVID-19 triggered the digital and e-commerce turning point*. United Nations Conference on Trade and Development. https://unctad.org/news/heres-how-we-can-resolve-global-supply-chain-crisis

Prosser, D. (2021). *Virtual Internships Raises $2.5 Million To Target 1 Million Students Worldwide*. Forbes. https://www.forbes.com/sites/davidprosser/2021/07/12/virtual-internships-raises-25m-to-target-1-million-students-worldwide/?sh=47b94bef38ff

Sawhney, S., & Madan, A. (2021). *Changing consumer behaviour in post-COVID scenario*. Observer Research Foundation. https://www.orfonline.org/expert-speak/changing-consumer-behaviour-post-covid-scenario/

Shafi, M., Liu, J., & Ren, W. (2020). Impact of COVID-19 pandemic on micro, small, and medium-sized Enterprises operating in Pakistan. *Research in Globalization*, *2*, 100018. doi:10.1016/j.resglo.2020.100018

Sigahi, T. F. A. C., Kawasaki, B. C., Bolis, I., & Morioka, S. N. (2021). A systematic review on the impacts of Covid-19 on work: Contributions and a path forward from the perspectives of ergonomics and psychodynamics of work. *Human Factors and Ergonomics in Manufacturing & Service Industries*, *31*(4), 375–388. https://doi.org/10.1002/hfm.20889

Soman, P., & Shroff, V. (2021). *Mental health and wellbeing of employees in a post-pandemic world: considerations for employers*. International Bar Association. https://www.ibanet.org/mental-wellbeing-of-employees-post-pandemic-considerations-for-employers

Strachan, R. (2022). *Who will be the supply chain winners and losers in 2022?* Investment Monitor. https://www.investmentmonitor.ai/analysis/supply-chain-winners-and-losers-2022

The Economist. (2022). *Will remote work stick after the pandemic?* https://www.economist.com/finance-and-economics/2022/01/15/will-remote-work-stick-after-the-pandemic

The role of online platforms in weathering the COVID-19 shock. (2020). *OECD*. https://www.oecd.org/coronavirus/policy-responses/the-role-of-online-platforms-in-weathering-the-covid-19-shock-2a3b8434/

The World Bank In Pakistan. (2021). *World Bank*. https://www.worldbank.org/en/country/pakistan/overview#1

Thygesen, L. C., Møller, S. P., Ersbøll, A. K., Santini, Z. I., Nielsen, M. B. D., Grønbæk, M. K., & Ekholm, O. (2021). Decreasing Mental Well-Being During the COVID-19 Pandemic: A Longitudinal Study Among Danes Before and During the Pandemic. *SSRN Electronic Journal*. doi:10.2139/ssrn.3845383

Wang, J., Yang, J., Iverson, B. C., & Kluender, R. (2020). Bankruptcy and the COVID-19 Crisis. *SSRN Electronic Journal*. doi:10.2139/ssrn.3690398

Watson, C. (2021). *20+ Business Ideas Coming Out of COVID-19 Pandemic [Small Business Edition]*. The European Business Review. https://www.europeanbusinessreview.com/20-business-ideas-coming-out-of-covid-19-pandemic-small-business-edition/

WHO. (2020). *WHO Director-General's opening remarks at the media briefing on COVID-19 - 11 March 2020*. https://www.who.int/director-general/speeches/detail/who-director-general-s-opening-remarks-at-the-media-briefing-on-covid-19---11-march-2020

Wikipedia Contributors. (2022). Consumer. In *Wikipedia*. https://en.wikipedia.org/wiki/Consumer

Wong, B. (2020). *How digital entrepreneurs will help shape the world after the COVID-19 pandemic*. World Economic Forum. https://www.weforum.org/agenda/2020/06/entrepreneurs-must-embrace-digital-during-pandemic-for-society/

World Economic Forum. (2020). *COVID-19 Has Intensified the Digital Divide*. https://www.weforum.org/agenda/2020/09/covid-19-has-intensified-the-digital-divide/

Xu, Z., & Jia, H. (2022). The Influence of COVID-19 on Entrepreneur's Psychological Well-Being. *Frontiers in Psychology, 12*. doi:10.3389/fpsyg.2021.823542

Zides, M. (2021). *On-demand Learning: A Must-have in the Digital Era*. Training Industry. https://trainingindustry.com/articles/content-development/on-demand-learning-a-must-have-in-the-digital-era-spon-coreaxis/

ADDITIONAL READING

Bennett, R. R. (2022). *The Book of Answers: Entrepreneurship in a Post-Covid World*. Enviromation Incorporated.

Bourne, R. A. (2021). *Economics in One Virus: An Introduction to Economic Reasoning through COVID-19*. Cato Institute.

Farisha, M. (2022). Does Covid-19 Pandemic Change the Consumer Purchase Behavior Towards Cosmetic Products? *Journal of Consumer Sciences*, *7*(1), 1–19. doi:10.29244/jcs.7.1.1-19

Maryati, T. (2020). Consumer Behavior Changes Post Pandemic Covid-19. *International Journal of Halal Research*, *2*(2), 84–89. doi:10.18517/ijhr.2.2.84-89.2020

KEY TERMS AND DEFINITIONS

Consumer Behavior: The study of how people and businesses choose and utilize products and services.

COVID-19: Also called coronavirus, is a highly contagious respiratory infection caused by the SARS-CoV-2 virus that was found in December 2019 in Wuhan, China.

Entrepreneur: A person who owns and bears the risk of the business.

Entrepreneurship: The process of starting and running an independent business.

Global Market: A market that involves the exchange of goods and services between people located in different areas of the globe.

Hybrid Work: A flexible working arrangement that combines in-office and remote employees working from home or elsewhere.

Microeconomics: A branch of economics that studies how individuals and organizations make resource allocation decisions.

Remote Work: Often known as work-from-home, is a flexible working arrangement that allows professionals to work from a remote location outside of an office environment.

Chapter 26
The Nexus Between Forensic Tax and Accounting Knowledge After Pandemic COVID-19 in Indonesia

I Made Laut Mertha Jaya
https://orcid.org/0000-0001-9722-7217
Universitas Mahakarya Asia, Indonesia

I. Made Narsa
Universitas Airlangga, Indonesia

ABSTRACT

The phenomenon of tax fraud has rarely been highlighted in the literature. This addition was made in order to provide a new logic, thinking that the fraud financial statement is also related to the sakes of tax evasion or fraud. The population of this study was 1,053 auditors and the percentage level of leeway used was 10%. The questionnaires distributed were 300 copies, or 28.49% of the population. The method of analysis was applying partial least square (PLS). This study found that the level of forensic accounting and tax forensic knowledge had a positive effect on the prevention of fraud financial statements in the new normal era in Indonesia at this time. Although there were many studies on forensic accounting, none had collaborated with the level of forensic tax knowledge. It seems that there are some parties who are afraid when there is education about forensic tax knowledge in Indonesia, especially the new normal period towards a new world order.

INTRODUCTION

Fraudulent practices (fraud) are still repeated in many countries, including Indonesia. Thus, research on fraud still has its own interests by some academics and practitioners. Based on data from the ACFE (Association of Certified Fraud Examines) in 2016 below, it presents that there are still many corruption

DOI: 10.4018/978-1-7998-8856-7.ch026

cases that still occur, as if they reflect the government's role so far in preventing fraud still needs hard work. Fraud acts are categorized into 3 (three), namely corruption, misuse of state and / or company assets, and fraud in financial statements.

Based on data from (ACFE, 2016), it shows that 67% of the frauds that were most detrimental to Indonesia were corruption. Meanwhile, the rest is an act of misuse of government and / or company assets and fraud financial statements. This, of course, requires efforts from the government to prevent eradication by tightening it through regulations for institutions allowed to undertake corruption or fraud through the BPK, BPKP, Inspectorate, KPK (commission corruptions) and by NGOs, such as MTI and ICW. However, all these efforts are deemed insufficient for the government to penetrate the solid wall of the perpetrators of fraud or corruption.

These three categories of fraudulent acts have caused losses to the country. However, from the three categories of fraud that have been disclosed, we will focus on one category of fraud, namely the fraud financial statement (fraudulent financial statements). Financial statements are very important for the survival of an entity. In addition, financial reports are also applied by potential investors as useful financial information for their decision making. Meanwhile, the important financial information in the financial statements is profit. When the profit generated by an entity reaches the target or even exceeds the company's target, then this can certainly prosper the stakeholders and the period of the entity itself. However, the problem that occurs is that the stakeholders do not know factually during preparing the financial statements whether the earnings information is under the company's operational activities or not. The perception of these stakeholders arises because they do not monitor the company's operational activities every day, so it is necessary to re-examine the financial statements, especially the profit information. Therefore, an occasion known as earnings management practices emerged (Meckling, 1976).

(Jaya, 2020; Wells, Joseph T., 2010) also agree that one concrete example of fraud financial statements is the practice of earnings management. This earnings management activity can be carried out in several steps, such as manipulating financial records, supporting documents or other business transactions, deliberately eliminating evidence of transaction notes, accounts, or other significant information during the financial reporting process, selecting accounting principles, wrong and deliberate policies, and procedures that are used to measure, acknowledge, report, and disclose the economic occasions and business transactions of an entity (Rezaae, 2002). In addition, several literatures have revealed several motivations for this earnings management practice, such as bonus plans, tax avoidance, debt motivation, and political motivation (Healy, 1985; Jones, 1991; Watts & Zimmerman, 2006). This literature evidence also points out that earnings management practices have occurred for a long time and until now the emphasis is still not maximal.

One proxy that can be applied easier to detect earnings management practices in an entity is by using discretionary accruals (Dechow et al., 1995). Discretionary accruals are used to manipulate company profits to get bonuses, avoiding political costs and avoiding breaches of collection of an entity's debts. However, along with the development of some previous literature, this accrual model was finally re-evaluated by Dechow et al. (1995). The evaluation is done by modifying the Jones model (Jones, 1991) to detect earnings management practices of a particular entity's financial statements. The modified Jones model reduces the tendency for errors to occur in the previous Jones model. Thus, in this modified Jones model, the non-discretionary accrual aspect has been considered when the earnings management prediction occurred. The accrual accounting system on accounting principles also provides an opportunity for managers to take profit manipulation (Rusdiyanto & Narsa, 2020).

Someone's expertise in conducting examinations related to fraud has been needed in the business sector. This expertise is needed to prevent, detect and disclose various forms of fraud, such as the misuse of several company assets, financial report recording errors, insurance fraud, deliberate business bankruptcy, fraud by abusing the development of *Fintech* (information technology), and so on (Khalymon Serhii & Oleg, Kravchuk Marushchak Oleksandr, 2019; Sahdan et al., 2020). Hence, when someone has studied that knowledge and has a certification of expertise in examining fraud, it is hoped that it can provide more benefits for an entity. The presence of these individuals can also maintain accountability from a financial report that has been presented by company management to stakeholders (Chukwu et al., 2019). One of the knowledge or examination expertise certifications is forensic accounting (Tuanakotta, 2010).

The learning practice of forensic accounting has developed since the financial crisis in 1997-1998 occurred in Indonesia (Tuanakotta, 2010). The development of forensic accounting is also applied and developed in America. In fact, this country has clearly stipulated its regulations through the Sarbanes Oxley Act. In addition, this law is also strengthened by the existence of the Foreign Corrupt Practice Act in the OECD countries. This institution was established as the organizations that specializes in the prevention of fraud, including acts of corruption. This institution is also specifically tasked with uncovering the motives and ways of perpetrators of fraud in carrying out their actions professionally. Thus, from this point of view, fraud can only be committed by a professional and, to reveal it, requires an expert. This expertise is specialized in forensic accounting.

The application of forensic accounting originates from the application of accounting for legal matters, so the term used is forensic accounting and not forensic auditing (Tuanakotta, 2010). This also allows forensic accountants to act as expert witnesses in a legal issue in court (litigation). However, this forensic accountant also has a role outside the field of law or outside the court (non-litigation), such as helping to develop alternative strategies for resolving a dispute, designing compensation calculations and the impact of a termination of employment because of a violation of the terms of an agreed contract. Therefore, an accountant who is an expert in forensic accounting must also have creativity, curiosity, not give up easily, be able to apply his logic in solving every problem, the ability to understand the business of an entity, and be confident (Tuanakotta, 2010). Crumbley, Larry., Lester E. Heitger., Stevenson (2009) states that a fraud auditor is a skilled and professional accountant in auditing, involved in activities regarding the discovery, documentation and prevention of fraud. Meanwhile, a forensic accountant is an accountant who can be involved in a fraud audit and possibly a fraud auditor, but he can also use other professional services, consulting services, and legal experts in a broader engagement. The Forensic Auditor is not only skilled in accounting, but he also has a good level of knowledge of the legal system and communication skills in carrying out testimony as an expert witness in a legal issue.

The tax fraud phenomenon is furthermore the other side of a fraud financial statement, which has rarely been highlighted in some literatures. In fact, fraud that occurs in taxation also affects on state revenues (Benno Torgler, 2008; Çule & Fulton, 2009). Basically, nobody enjoys paying taxes. In fact, tax evasion behavior is part of the self-assessment system (Helena Putong et al., 2017). This action shows that tax fraud can be one motivation for someone to commit a fraud financial statement that is deliberately carried out and focused on an entity's financial report. The management can perform fraud financial statements to minimize the tax burden of an entity. Some other examples of tax fraud activities include sales of services that are not charged to Value Added Tax, and withholding or charging VAT from partners, but the amount deposited in the state treasury is not appropriate. So, this problem also requires certain expertise to disclose tax fraud by an organization. Therefore, knowledge such as tax forensics is needed, which is used to detect motivation and other factors that cause a person to commit tax fraud.

Tax fraud is a phenomenon of taxpayer behavior carried out with various motivations and with certain goals that affect a country's revenue. Allingham (1972) classic model explains one reason taxpayers dare to commit fraud, namely to maximize their expected utility. In other literature, such as Levaggi & Menoncin (2013), Rablen (2010) explains that the motivation of a taxpayer to commit fraud is because of the high tax rate and the complexity of a taxation system. The complexity of a taxation system can create loopholes for fraudulent acts. Thus, the system which should ease the taxpayers is actually complicating them. The perception of other literature results also states that tax fraud can also take place because of parties that are directly or indirectly related to the taxation system (Carley, 2005; Frecknall-Hughes & Kirchler, 2015).

Taxpayers will always make different interpretations of the behavior or actions they take regarding taxation. This is caused by human behavior formed through a reaction or response to a particular object. This reaction can be simple or complex, depending on several interventions, such as motivation to perform these actions, different human personality traits, and human interactions with their environment (Azwar, 1995). Thus, the traditional compliance approach (deterrence effect) to suppress tax fraud has long been abandoned, because current taxpayers are more focused on a psychological contract approach which analogizes the relationship between taxpayers and the government (Feld & Frey, 2011; Ritsatos, 2014). This change is one reason that a new tax science is needed, which can detect tax fraud in more detail, such as tax forensics.

Based on the description above, everything proves that fraud is still commonly happened. Thus, fraud is still an interesting theme to deepen for the benefit of reforming old policies or providing input for policy makers to plan new policies. The level of forensic accounting knowledge is a development of an accounting discipline that has brilliant prospects for helping to solve criminal acts of corruption or fraudulent financial statements. This research is new to disclose tax forensic knowledge to prevent tax fraud. This addition was made in order to provide a new logic thinking that fraud financial statements are also related to the behalf of tax evasion or fraud. For this reason, a conceptual issue of the importance of the level of knowledge of tax and accounting forensics is compiled to prevent fraud financial statements in Indonesia.

LITERATURE REVIEW AND HYPOTHESIS DEVELOPMENT

Tuanakotta (2010) forensic accounting is more appropriate if it relates to the law. Forensic accounting is unlike any other branch of the accounting profession. This difference appears since the investigative process to gather reliable information and serve as evidence suitable for court (Akinbowale et al., 2020). Forensic accounting is also called investigative accounting because it is a merger of forensic science and accounting (Asuquo, 2012; Karwai, 2004; Okoye, 2013). Financial crime is a part of economic crime that has taken deep into the structure of the world economy and continues to have a negative impact on the socio-economic environment (Bhasin, 2013).

This study applies a grand theory, namely Linguistics and Forensic Psychology, as well as several other supporting thcorics. Olsson (2008) states that forensic linguistics is the relationship between language and enforcement, problems, legislation, disputes or processes in law that have the potential to involve several violations of the law or the need to get legal settlement. Forensic linguistics is a multidisciplinary science derived from linguistics and law that has been developed in America and Europe since 1997 (Momeni, 2012). (Siahaan et al., 2019; Smith, 2002) states the main thing that has not been the focus of a person in researching a crime is examining a person's language. This is because the actor's personality and characteristics can be seen in the actor's languages. Meanwhile, the application of forensic psychology in the criminal investigation process has an enormous role. Among them can help facilitate understanding incidents of criminal fraud, detect misleading information during the examination process, reasons for insane admissions to avoid legal obligations and responsibilities, help make profile analyzes of criminals, and many other things (David, 1984).

Theory of Reasoned Action was planned in 1967 to provide consistency in the relationship's study between behavior and attitudes (Fishbein, M, & Ajzen, 1975). This Theory of Reasoned Action (TRA) connects belief, attitude, intention and behavior. Research on tax awareness can be viewed from the psychological side of the taxpayer (Feld & Frey, 2011). In the psychology literature, it is said that human behavior can be viewed as a reaction that can be simple or complex. One of the interesting characteristics of human behavioral reactions is their differentiation. One stimulus can cause over one unique response and several stimuli can cause the same response (Feld & Frey, 2011).

Previous literature states that forensic accounting acts as a regulation for professionals to estimate the involvement of fraudulent acts or violations of an entity's financial reporting (Honigsberg, 2020). Knowledge of forensic accounting is very helpful in determining fraudulent acts of financial statements, which can lead to criminal charges (Dauenhauer et al., 2020; Jahirul Islam, Habibur Rahman, 2011). Professional services such as forensic accountants in developed countries have helped to further improve counter-fraud capabilities and prepare early for the increasingly complex challenges of fraud (Huber, 2012; Khalymon Serhii & Oleg, Kravchuk Marushchak Oleksandr, 2019; Sahdan et al., 2020). In contrast to developing countries, which still consider this a new trend (Akinbowale, 2018; Ehioghiren, 2016). Forensic accounting is an appropriate method used to identify and review fraudulent transactions in financial reports (Akinbowale et al., 2020; Clayton, 2006). This step can also increase the trust and credibility of a financial report (Chukwu et al., 2019; Gbegi & Adebisi, 2014; Joshi, 2003; Zysman, 2004).

H_1 = *The level of forensic accounting knowledge affects the prevention of fraud financial statements*

Tax fraud represents the behavior of taxpayers' resistance to their tax obligations, which should be carried out under the tax law. Various studies have attempted to reveal the underlying motivations for taxpayer fraud, including the motivation to commit tax fraud based on an economic perspective on the classic model of Allingham (1972). The classic model explains the reason taxpayers commit fraud (tax fraud) is to maximize their utility (expected utility). Tax fraud is a reality that is actually constructed by people who are in the tax system, including elements of the taxation system itself. Previous literature also revealed that taxpayers will use the services of tax consultants to help them interpret map tax laws that are complex and difficult to interpret to minimize the tax burden (Carley, 2005; Frecknall-Hughes & Kirchler, 2015). It is also used to prevent improper financial reporting and is carried out in varied ways for tax avoidance (Healy & Wahlen, 1999; Paseková, 2019; Svabova et al., 2020; Wang & Chen, 2012; Willey, 2019). The various exposures that have resulted from several previous studies show that:

H_2 = *The level of forensic tax knowledge affects the prevention of fraud financial statements*

RESEARCH METHOD

The approach applied in this research is quantitative, with a random sampling technique using a survey method distributed to several respondents, namely young independent auditors from all KAPs (Public Accounting Firms) in Indonesia. The survey method is used to naturally get data from a certain place from the respondents. The criteria for respondents are young independent auditors from all KAPs (Public Accounting Firms) in Indonesia and their working period is at least 2-3.5 years, so that their experience in compiling financial reports and their forensic abilities are still at the junior level. Young auditors are chosen because they have a better level of expectation. Besides, they also have a high level of interest in continuing to learn and improve to their knowledge for the continuity of their profession.

In the data of year 2015, the number of auditors in Indonesia is estimated at 1,053 people. These auditors have various ages, ranging from those age over 59 years old as 32%; aged 40-49 years as 29%; aged 50-59 years as 26%; and 30-39 years old as 12%. This condition causes the lack of auditors in Indonesia. A population of 1,053 accountants requires a percentage level of leeway used for sampling, which is 10%. The determination of the sampling number using the Slovin (1960) formula is as follows.

$1 + N(e)^2$

Information:

n = Sample size / number of respondents

N = Population amount

E = The allowable percentage of error (error) when sampling is still tolerable of e = 0.1

In applying the Slovin formula, there are 2 (two) provisions as follows:

1. Value of e = 0.1 (10%) for large population
2. Value of e = 0.2 (20%) for small population

Therefore, the percentage range of samples that can be taken from this technique is between 10-20% of the study population. To find out the number of samples of this study is calculated as follows.

n = 1.053

d $1 + 1.053(10)^2$

n = 91.32 → This result was then adjusted to be 100 respondents.

Based on the above calculations, the number of samples who became respondents in this study was 100 respondents, or 9.49% of the total population. The number of questionnaires distributed was 300 copies or 28.49% of the population and expected to return 100 responses or even over 100 so that the results got are more accountable.

This study employs an assessment on the questionnaire sheet using the Likert scale, namely 1-5 comprising STS: Strongly Disagree, TS: Disagree, KS: Less Disagree, S: Agree, and SS: Strongly Agree (Likert, 1932). The definitions and indicators of the variables in this study are described in Table 1:

Table 1. Operational definition and indicators of research variables

No.	Variable	Definition	Indicators	Number of questions/ statements
1.	Level of Forensic Accounting Knowledge (X_1)	Forensic accounting is also called investigative accounting because it is a combination of forensic science and accounting (Asuquo, 2012; Karwai, 2004; Okoye, 2013)	Forensic Accounting Skills Forensic Accounting Standards	1, 2, 3, 4, 5, 6, 7, 8,
2.	Forensic Tax Knowledge Level (X_2)	Forensic tax is a merge of domestic and international taxation science and forensic engineering	Tax Ability Taxation Standards	9, 10, 11, 12, 13, 14, 15, 16,
3.	Prevention ***fraud financial statement*** (Y)	*Wells, Joseph T., (2010) states that the fraud financial statement is one of the fraudulent acts of financial statements carried out for the benefit of certain parties and is detrimental to other parties*	Identify the symptoms of a fraud financial statement Techniques for detecting fraud financial statements	17, 18, 19, 20, 21, 22, 23, 24, 25.

The analysis method in this study applies the Partial Least Square (PLS) method through a variance-based structural equation model (SEM) statistical test tool.

RESULTS AND DISCUSSION

The results of data analysis that have been carried out found several things, including the following.

Characteristics of respondents

Secondary data collected by researchers were analyzed to determine the characteristics of respondents from general questions, namely gender, age, education, and length of time as an auditor. The descriptive results of the respondent's characteristics are shown in the following table.

Table 2. Characteristics of respondents

No.	Gender	Frequency
1.	Man	70 people
2.	Woman	130 people
Total		**200 people**
No.	**Age**	**Frequency**
1.	28-29 years old	194 people
2.	30-32 years old	6 people
Total		**200 people**
No.	**Education**	**Frequency**
1.	Bachelor	98 people
2.	Master	102 people
Total		**200 people**
No.	**Length of time as an auditor**	**Frequency**
1.	2-3 years	145 people
2.	> 3 years	55 people
Total		**200 people**

Source: Data Tabulation, 2021.

Based on the table above, it can be seen that the number of young male auditor respondents is 70 people; it is less than the female respondents, which is 130 respondents. The respondents, which comprised young auditors, were also divided into 2 groups, ranging in age from 28 to 29 years to 32 years. The young auditors aged 28 to 29 were 194 people, while the age 30 to 32 years were 6 people. The background of the young auditor respondents who were recorded was divided into 2 categories, namely S1 (bachelor) and S2 (master) graduates. The time the respondents worked as young auditors was also classified into two, with 145 people who had worked for 2-3 years and over 3 years 55 people.

Validity and Reliability Test

Table 3. Results of the Validity and Reliability Test of Research Instruments

Variable	Dimension	Item	Correlation (r)		Coefficient	
			r	Stts	Alph	Stts
Forensic Accounting Science (X_1)	Forensic Accounting Skills	AF01	0,612	valid	0,641	reliable
		AF02	0,558	valid		
		AF03	0,796	valid		
		AF04	0,686	valid		
	Forensic Accounting Standards	AF05	0,706	valid	0,717	reliable
		AF06	0,615	valid		
		AF07	0,796	valid		
		AF08	0,686	valid		
Forensic Tax Science (X_2)	Tax Ability	TF09	0,472	valid	0,610	reliable
		TF10	0,629	valid		
		TF11	0,629	valid		
		TF12	0,516	valid		
	Taxation Standards	TF13	0,711	valid	0,813	reliable
		TF14	0,720	valid		
		TF15	0,774	valid		
		TF16	0,633	valid		
Fraud financial statement prevention (Y)	Identify the symptoms of a fraud financial statement	FF17	0,771	valid	0,740	reliable
		FF18	0,788	valid		
		FF19	0,607	valid		
		FF20	0,718	valid		
	Techniques for detecting fraud financial statements	FF21	0,639	valid	0,687	reliable
		FF22	0,771	valid		
		FF23	0,788	valid		
		FF24	0,597	valid		
		FF25	0,441	valid		

Source: Processed data, 2021.

Based on Table 3, it represents that all question items have a correlation value (r) greater than 0.3, while the alpha coefficient is greater than 0.6. This means that all question items for each variable are valid and reliable for further testing.

Structural Equation Model Test Results

The SEM test phase was carried out by testing the outer model, evaluating the structural model (inner model), and testing the research hypothesis. The test results are as follows.

Test the Outer Model and Evaluate the Inner Model

The outer model test uses the composite reliability indicator block data that measures a construct by evaluating the composite reliability (ρc) value. The dimension is reliable if it has a composite reliability (ρc) value above 0.7. Here, results from calculations using composite reliability (ρc):

Table 4. The results of calculating composite reliability

Dimension	*Composite Reliability*	*R-Square*
Forensic Acc.	0,867	0,199
Tax Forensic	0,839	0,751
Fraud Forensic	0,885	-

Source: Smart PLS, 2021.

The Inner structural model was evaluated using the R-Square for the dependent construct, the Stone-Geisser Q-Square test for predictive relevance. The results of calculations that have been carried out found that the R-Square value for the Tax forensic variable is greater than 0.2, it can be interpreted that the latent predictor has an enormous influence on the structural level. Meanwhile, forensic accounting is still below 0.2, so it can be interpreted that the latent predictor has a tiny effect at the structural level.

The inner structural model was also evaluated by looking at the Q-Square predictive relevance of the construct model. Here results from of the Q-Square calculation.

$\mathbf{Q^2} = 1 - (0.199)(0.751)$

$= 1 - 0.149$

$= \mathbf{0.850}$

The result of the calculation shows that the value of Q-Square> 0, so that the model deserves to be said to have a relevant predictive value. Hypothesis testing was done by comparing the t value with the t table value. If the t value is greater than the t table, then the relationship between the variables is significant and can be analyzed further. With 200 data, the t table value (α =5%) is 1,652 and the t table value (α =10%) is 1,285. The results of hypothesis testing are presented in Table 6 below.

Table 5. Hypothesis Testing Results

Hypothesis	Effects			Path Coef.	t Count	Remark
H_1	*Forensic Acc.*	→	*fraud financial statement*	0.199	2,244*	Significant
H_2	*Tax Forensic*	→	*fraud financial statement*	0.751	10.535*	Significant

* significant at 5% level, t table value at 5% level = 1.652

** significant at the 10% level, the t table value at the 10% level = 1.285

Source: Processed data, 2021.

Based on Table 6, the structural equation is given:

FF = 0.199AF + 0.751TF

Information:
FF = Fraud financial statement
AF = Forensic Acc.
TF = Tax Forensic
Interpretating of Table 6 can be explained:

1) Forensic accounting has a positive and significant effect on fraud financial statements with a CR value (t count > t table (2,244> 1,996) and a path coefficient of 0.199, this coefficient shows that the better the knowledge level of young auditors about forensic accounting, this will also increase their awareness of the prevention of fraud financial statements. This result also shows that the first hypothesis that has been built is not rejected.
2) Tax forensic has a positive and significant effect on fraud financial statements with a CR value (t count> t table (10,535> 1,996) and a path coefficient of 0.751, this coefficient shows that the better the knowledge level of young auditors about tax forensics, this will also increase their awareness of the prevention of fraud financial statements. This result also shows that the first hypothesis that has been built is not rejected.

The findings of this study put in many of previous studies on forensic accounting (Huber, 2012; Khalymon Serhii & Oleg, Kravchuk Marushchak Oleksandr, 2019; Sahdan et al., 2020), but not in this new normal period. Previous research was conducted under different conditions from the new normal era in Indonesia. The new normal nuance in Indonesia is still full of political content from various involved parties. Much behalf shows that a lot of information is not easily got for free (Dauenhauer et al., 2020; Honigsberg, 2020; Jahirul Islam, Habibur Rahman, 2011). This causes the provided information is full of various concerns, so that the presented report shows a load of fraud.

CONCLUSION

The data collection, calculation, testing and data analysis that have been carried out have found several findings, that the level of forensic accounting and tax forensic knowledge has a positive effect on the prevention of fraud financial statements during the new normal in Indonesia recently. The current condition of the new normal era in Indonesia has made several large entities arrange new strategies to maintain their business continuity. The strategies that are applied also vary, but these strategies must lead to financial reports. The company's financial statements in the new normal era really need to be examined carefully, because when investors misanalyses the information presented, all goals of increasing wealth will be in vain. Knowledge of forensic accounting is currently required to have a more extra role as a regulation for professionals when estimating the involvement of fraudulent acts or violations of an entity's financial reporting (Honigsberg, 2020). Therefore, forensic accounting knowledge is the right method in the current new normal era for identifying and reviewing fraudulent transactions in corporate financial reports (Akinbowale et al., 2020; Clayton, 2006). The development of the level of forensic accounting knowledge now needs to be developed with special expertise, especially in taxation, so it is necessary to develop forensic tax knowledge. It is important to use it to prevent improper financial reporting for tax avoidance (Healy, 1985; Paseková, 2019; Svabova et al., 2020; Wang & Chen, 2012; Willey, 2019). There is a lot of research on forensic accounting, but none of them has developed it with forensic tax science. Many parties were afraid when the forensic tax was imposed in Indonesia. The findings of this study should be taken seriously by higher education providers in order to better prepare graduates who are ready to work for the new world order era in the future.

The obstacle experienced when this research was conducted was getting responses from auditors. This condition occurs because the government too often restricts large-scale activities in several areas, so that mobility is disrupted. Another thing that was disturbing is the increasingly dense work of the auditors, so they respond to the questionnaire for a long time. We do really appreciate the respondents for helping us in obtaining opinions and data for this research in the new normal period. We realize it is difficult to do research in the new normal era because many parties are keeping a distance from each other for the sake of mutual health.

REFERENCES

ACFE. (2016). *Survai Fraud Indonesia.* ACFE Indonesia Chapter.

Akinbowale, O. E. (2018). Information communication technology and forensic accounting in Nigeria. *International Journal Of Business and Finance Management Research, 6*, 1–7.

Akinbowale, O. E., Klingelhöfer, H. E., & Zerihun, M. F. (2020). An innovative approach in combating economic crime using forensic accounting techniques. *Journal of Financial Crime, 27*(4), 1253–1271. Advance online publication. doi:10.1108/JFC-04-2020-0053

Allingham, M. G., & A. S. (1972). Illicit activity: The economics of crime, drugs and tax fraud. *Journal of Public Economics, 1*, 323–338. doi:10.1016/0047-2727(72)90010-2

Asuquo, A. (2012). Empirical Analysis of The Impact of Information Technology On Forensic Accounting Practice In. *International Journal of Scientific & Technology Research, 1*(7).

Azwar, S. (1995). *Sikap Manusia, Teori dan Pengukurannya.* Pustaka Pelajar.

Bhasin, M. (2013). An empirical investigation of the relevant skills of forensic. *European Journal of Accounting Auditing and Finance Research, 1*(June), 11–52.

Carley, K. M. (2005). *Understanding Taxpayer Behavior and Assessing Potential IRS Interventions Using Multiagent Dynamic-Network Simulation.* Academic Press.

Chukwu, N., Asaolu, T. O., Uwuigbe, O. R., Uwuigbe, U., Umukoro, O. E., Nassar, L., & Alabi, O. (2019). The impact of basic forensic accounting skills on financial reporting credibility among listed firms in Nigeria. *IOP Conference Series. Earth and Environmental Science, 331*(1), 012041. Advance online publication. doi:10.1088/1755-1315/331/1/012041

Clayton, M. M. (2006). Investigative techniques. In A Guide to Forensic Accounting Investigation. John Wiley and Sons.

Crumbley, L. Heitger, E., & Stevenson, S. (2009). *Forensic and Investigative Accounting* (4th ed.). www.amazon.com

Çule, M., & Fulton, M. (2009). Business culture and tax evasion: Why corruption and the unofficial economy can persist. *Journal of Economic Behavior & Organization, 72*(3), 811–822. doi:10.1016/j.jebo.2009.08.005

Dauenhauer, J., Heffernan, K., Webber, K., Smoker, K., Caccamise, P., & Granata, A. (2020). Utilization of a forensic accountant to investigate financial exploitation of older adults. *Journal of Adult Protection, 22*(3), 141–152. doi:10.1108/JAP-01-2020-0001

David, L. S. (1984). *Forensic Psychologocal Assessment: An Integrative Approach.* Allyn & Bacon. https://www.amazon.com/Forensic-Psychologocal-Assessment-Integrative-Approach/dp/0205125212

Dechow, P. M., Sloan, R. G., Sweeney, A. P., Sloan, R. G., & Sweeney, A. P. (1995). Detecting Earnings Management. *The Accounting Review, 70*(2), 193–225.

Ehioghiren, E. E. (2016). Forensic accounting and fraud management: Evidence from nigeria. *Igbinedion University Journal of Accounting, 2*, 245–308.

Feld, L. P., & Frey, B. S. (2011). Tax Compliance as the Result of a Psychological Tax Contract: The Role of Incentives and Responsive Regulation. SSRN *Electronic Journal, 287.* doi:10.2139/ssrn.900366

Fishbein, M., & Ajzen, I. (1975). *Belief, Attitude, Intention, and Behavior: An Introduction to Theory and Research.* Addison-Wesley.

Frecknall-Hughes, J., & Kirchler, E. (2015). Towards a General Theory of Tax Practice. *Social & Legal Studies, 24*(2), 289–312. doi:10.1177/0964663915571787

Gbegi, D. O., & Adebisi, J. F. (2014). Forensic Accounting Skills and Techniques in Fraud Investigation in the Nigerian Public Sector. *Mediterranean Journal of Social Sciences, 5*(3), 243–252. doi:10.5901/mjss.2014.v5n3p243

Healy, P. M. (1985). The effect of bonus schemes on accounting decisions. *Journal of Accounting and Economics, 7*(1–3), 85–107. doi:10.1016/0165-4101(85)90029-1

Healy, P. M., & Wahlen, J. M. (1999). A Review of the Earnings Management Literature and Its. *Accounting Horizons, 13*(4), 365–383. doi:10.2308/acch.1999.13.4.365

Helena Putong, I., Laksmana, A., & Made Narsa, I. (2017). *The Effect of Vertical and Horizontal Trust on Voluntary Tax Compliance (An Experimental Study).* doi:10.2991/iconeg-16.2017.4

Honigsberg, C. (2020). Forensic Accounting. *Annual Review of Law and Social Science*, 423–431. doi:10.1016/B978-0-12-382165-2.00218-X

Huber, W. D. (2012). Is Forensic Accounting in the United States Becoming a Profession? *Journal of Forensic & Investigative Accounting, 4*(1), 255–284.

Islam & Rahman. (2011). Forensic Accounting as a Tool for Detecting Fraud and Corruption : An Empirical Study in Bangladesh. *ASA University Review, 5*(2).

Jaya, I. M. L. M., & I. M. N. (2020). The Beauty and the Beast of Earning Management in Indonesia. *Opcion, 36*(91), 1097–1140. https://produccioncientificaluz.org/index.php/opcion/article/view/32496

Joshi, M. S. (2003). *Definition of forensic accounting.* www.forensicaccounting.com

Karwai, M. (2004). *Forensic Accounting and Fraud Investigation for Non-Expert.* John Wiley and Sons.

Khalymon Serhii, P. V. (2019). Forensic economic examination as a means of investigation and counteraction of economic crimes in East Europe (example of Ukraine). *Journal of Legal, Ethical and Regulatory Issues, 22*(3), 2019.

Levaggi, R., & Menoncin, F. (2013). Optimal dynamic tax evasion. *Journal of Economic Dynamics & Control, 37*(11), 2157–2167. doi:10.1016/j.jedc.2013.06.007

Likert, R. (1932). Technique for the measurement of attitudes. *Archives de Psychologie, 140,* 1–55.

Meckling, M. C. J. (1976). Theory of the firm: Managerial behavior, agency costs and ownership structure. *Journal of Financial Economics, 3*(4), 305–360. doi:10.1016/0304-405X(76)90026-X

Momeni, N. (2012). Fraud in Judicial System as a Language Crime. *Forensic Linguistics Approach., 2*(6), 1263–1269. doi:10.4304/tpls.2.6.1263-1269

Okoye, G. (2013). Forensic Accounting: A Tool for Fraud Detection and Prevention in the Public Sector (A Study of Selected Ministries in Kogi State). *International Journal of Academic Research in Business and Social Sciences, 3*(3), 1–19.

Olsson, J. (2008). *Forensic Linguistics* (2nd ed.). Continuum International Publishing Group.

Paseková, M. (2019). OeconomiA copernicana. *Oeconomia Copernicana, 10*(1). Advance online publication. doi:10.24136/oc.2019.010

Rablen, M. D. (2010). Tax evasion and exchange equity: A reference-dependent approach. *Public Finance Review, 38*(3), 282–305. doi:10.1177/1091142110367858

Rezaae, Z. (2002). *Financial Statement Fraud: Prevention and Detection.* John Wiley and Sons, Inc.

Ritsatos, T. (2014). Tax evasion and compliance; From the neo classical paradigm to behavioural economics, a review. *Journal of Accounting and Organizational Change, 10*(2), 244–262. doi:10.1108/JAOC-07-2012-0059

Rusdiyanto, & Narsa, I. M. (2020). The Effect of Company Size, Leverage and Return on Asset on Earnings Management: Case Study Indonesian. *Espacios, 41*(17), 25.

Sahdan, M. H., Cowton, C. J., & Drake, J. E. (2020). Forensic accounting services in English local government and the counter-fraud agenda. *Public Money & Management, 40*(5), 380–389. doi:10.1080/09540962.2020.1714208

Siahaan, M., Umar, H., & Purba, R. B. (2019). Fraud Star Drives to Asset Misappropriation Moderated by Internal Controls. *Journal of Southwest Jiaotong University, 54*(4), 1–10. doi:10.35741/issn.0258-2724.54.4.24

Slovin, M. J. (1960). *Sampling.* Simon and.

Smith, S. S. S. & R. W. (2002). Forensic psycholinguistics: Using language analysis for identifying and assessing offenders. *FBI Law Enforcement Bulletin.*

Svabova, L., Kramarova, K., Chutka, J., & Strakova, L. (2020). Detecting earnings manipulation and fraudulent financial reporting in Slovakia. *Oeconomia Copernicana, 11*(3), 485–508. doi:10.24136/oc.2020.020

Torgler, B. (2008). What Do We Know about Tax Fraud? An Overview of Recent Developments. *Social Research, 75*(4), 1239–1270. doi:10.1353or.2008.0032

Tuanakotta, T. M. (2010). Akuntansi Forensik dan AuditorInvestigatif. Lembaga Penerbit Fakultas Ekonomi Universitas Indonesia (LPFE UI).

Wang, S., & Chen, S. (2012). The Motivation for Tax Avoidance in Earnings Management. *International Conference on Engineering and Business Management*, 447–450.

Watts, R., & Zimmerman, J. (2006). Positive Accounting Theory: A Ten Year Perspective. *Accounting Review, 65*(May), 131–156.

Wells, J. T. (2010). *Forensic Accounting and Fraud Examination*. John Wiley & Sons, Inc.

Willey, K. M. (2019). *Stock market short-termism: law, regulation, and reform*. Springer Berlin Heidelberg. doi:10.1007/978-3-030-22903-0

Zysman, A. (2004). Forensic accounting demystified: World Investigators Network Standard Practice for Investigative and Forensic. Accounting Engagements, Canadian Institute of Chartered Accountant.

Conclusion

The authors have concluded that COVID-19 changed lives and economic structures. This means that the areas presented in the 28 chapters have changed because of a new reality. Society has shown new ways to do things but also to get things. The methodology used after and during the COVID-19 to improve new ways of production, education and personal income. In fact, according to the authors, COVID-19 has proven that society needs to move faster towards new economic and social values. However, the government and organizations must introduce new social and economic policies to compensate for the loss of business and the market's ability to improve goods and services. Indeed, COVID-19 has proven that organizations and citizens are grappling with new ways of being in society. The authors point out three main areas to improve the resilience of citizens and organizations: government factors, health system factors and cultural factors. The most important area is to improve and create new mechanisms to renew the social and economic background.

In conclusion, according to the authors, COVID-19 will open a new way to improve the well-being of citizens and the ability to change economic and social patterns towards sustainability in the future. Moreover, COVID-19 has influenced all economic sectors and changed social and economic policies towards competitiveness and cooperation in all sectors. The final question should be: are we better now?

Compilation of References

Aitken-Fox, E. (2020). *The impact of Covid-19 on human resource management: Avoiding generalization.* https://blogs.lse.ac.uk/businessreview/2020/05/22/the-impact-of-covid-19-on-human-resource-management-avoiding-generalisations/

Mwita, K. M. (2020). Effects of coronavirus pandemic (covid-19) on selected human resource management practices in Tanzania. *East African Journal of Social and Applied Sciences, 2*(2), 1-10.

Ichsan, R. N., Santosa, S., Shara, Y., & Liriwati, F. Y. (2020). Investigation Of Strategic Human Resource Management Practices In Business After Covid-19 Disruption. *PalArch's Journal of Archaeology of Egypt/Egyptology, 17*(7), 13098-13110.

Osafo, E. (2021). Engaging Communities in Challenging Times: Lessons Learned from the Master Gardener Program during the COVID-19 Pandemic. *Advances in Developing Human Resources, 23*(1), 75–87. doi:10.1177/1523422320972142

Rodríguez, B. O., & Sánchez, T. L. (2020). The Psychosocial Impact of COVID-19 on health care workers. *International Braz J Urol, 46*(suppl 1), 195–200. doi:10.15901677-5538.ibju.2020.s124 PMID:32618464

Tomcíková, L., Svetozarovová, N., Coculová, J., & Danková, Z. (2021). The impact of the global Covid-19 pandemic on the selected human resources management practices in the relationship to the performance of tourism companies. *Geo Journal of Tourism and Geosites, 35*(2), 525–530. doi:10.30892/gtg.35233-680

Collings, D. G., Nyberg, A. J., Wright, P. M., & McMackin, J. (2021). Leading through paradox in a COVID-19 world: Human resources comes of age. *Human Resource Management Journal, 31*(4), 819–833. doi:10.1111/1748-8583.12343

Collings, D. G., McMackin, J., Nyberg, A. J., & Wright, P. M. (2021). Strategic human resource management and COVID-19: Emerging challenges and research opportunities. *Journal of Management Studies.*

Zhong, Y., Li, Y., Ding, J., & Liao, Y. (2021). Risk management: Exploring emerging Human Resource issues during the COVID-19 pandemic. *Journal of Risk and Financial Management, 14*(5), 228. doi:10.3390/jrfm14050228

Chuah, S. H. W., & Yu, J. (2021). The future of service: The power of emotion in human-robot interaction. *Journal of Retailing and Consumer Services, 61*, 102551. doi:10.1016/j.jretconser.2021.102551

Abaci, L. (2020). La guerra comercial entre Estados Unidos y China: efectos en países de renta media como Colombia. *Zero.* https://zero.uexternado.edu.co/la-guerra-comercial-entre-estados-unidos-y-china-efectos-en-paises-de-renta-media-como-colombia/

Abbas, A., Ekowati, D., & Suhariadi, F. (2021). Managing Individuals, Organizations Through Leadership: Diversity Consciousness Roadmap. In B. Christiansen & H. Chandan (Eds.), *Handbook of Research on Applied Social Psychology in Multiculturalism* (Vol. 1, pp. 47–71). IGI Global. doi:10.4018/978-1-7998-6960-3.ch003

Abbas, A., Ekowati, D., & Suhariadi, F. (2022). Social Perspective: Leadership in Changing Society. In M. I. Hassan, S. S. Roy, U. Chatterjee, S. Chakraborty, & U. Singh (Eds.), *Social Morphology, Human Welfare and Sustainability*. Springer. doi:10.1007/978-3-030-96760-4_4

Abbas, A., Ekowati, D., Suhariadi, F., & Fenitra, R. M. (2022). Health implications, Leaders Societies, and Climate Change: A Global Review. In *Ecological footprints of climate change: Adaptive Approaches and Sustainability*. Springer.

Abbas, A., Eliyana, A., Ekowati, D., Saud, M., Raza, A., & Wardani, R. (2020). Data set on coping strategies in the digital age: The role of psychological well-being and social capital among university students in Java Timor, Surabaya, Indonesia. *Data in Brief*, *30*, 10558. doi:10.1016/j.dib.2020.105583 PMID:32368599

Abbas, A., Saud, M., Ekowati, D., & Suhariadi, F. (2021). Social Psychology and Fabrication: A Synthesis of Individuals, Society, and Organization. In B. Christiansen & H. Chandan (Eds.), *Handbook of Research on Applied Social Psychology in Multiculturalism* (Vol. 1, pp. 89–109). IGI Global. doi:10.4018/978-1-7998-6960-3.ch005

Abbas, A., Saud, M., Ekowati, D., Usman, I., & Setia, S. (2020). Technology and stress: A proposed framework for coping with stress in Indonesian higher education. *International Journal of Innovation, Creativity and Change*, *13*(4), 373–390.

Abbas, A., Saud, M., Ekowati, D., Usman, I., & Suhariadi, F. (2021). Servant leadership: A strategic choice for organisational performance. An empirical discussion from Pakistan. *International Journal of Productivity and Quality Management*, *34*(4), 468–485. doi:10.1504/IJPQM.2021.120599

Abbas, A., Saud, M., Suhariadi, F., Usman, I., & Ekowati, D. (2020). Positive leadership psychology: Authentic and servant leadership in higher education in Pakistan. *Current Psychology (New Brunswick, N.J.)*, 1–11. doi:10.100712144-020-01051-1

Abbasi, K. (2020). *Covid-19: Screening without scrutiny, spending taxpayers' billions*. Academic Press.

Abbasi, K. (2020). Covid-19: Politicization, "corruption," and suppression of science. *British Medical Journal*, 371.

Abbott, T. (2021). *Social and personality development*. Routledge. doi:10.4324/9781003209300

Abitbol, A., Meeks, J., & Cummins, R. G. (2019). Does oil and goodwill mix? Examining the oil and gas industry's impact on stakeholder engagement on Facebook. *Environmental Communication*, *13*(2), 192–208. doi:10.1080/17524032.2018.1546751

Abracadabra. (2022). *Abracadabra.money is a spell book*. Available at https://abracadabra.money

Abrams, D., & Hogg, M. A. (2006). *Social identifications: A social psychology of intergroup relations and group processes*. Routledge. doi:10.4324/9780203135457

Abrams, D., Lalot, F., & Hogg, M. A. (2021). Intergroup and intragroup dimensions of COVID-19: A social identity perspective on social fragmentation and unity. *Group Processes & Intergroup Relations*, *24*(2), 201–209. doi:10.1177/1368430220983440

Abrams, D., Wetherell, M., Cochrane, S., Hogg, M. A., & Turner, J. C. (1990). Knowing what to think by knowing who you are: Self-categorization and the nature of norm formation, conformity and group polarization. *British Journal of Social Psychology*, *29*(2), 97–119. doi:10.1111/j.2044-8309.1990.tb00892.x PMID:2372667

Accenture. (2020). *How COVID-19 will permanently change consumer behavior*. https://www.accenture.com/_acnmedia/pdf-123/accenture-covid19-pulse-survey-research-pov.pdf

Accenture. (2020). *How covid-19 will permanently change consumer behavior*. Report. Author.

Accenture. (2020a). *COVID-19: How consumer behavior will be changed.* https://www.accenture.com/dk-en/insights/consumer-goods-services/coronavirus-consumer-behavior-research

Acemoğlu, D., Beck, T., Obstfeld, M., & Park, Y. (2022). *Prospects of the global economy after Covid-19.* VOX, CEPR Policy Portal. https://voxeu.org/article/prospects-global-economy-after-covid-19

ACFE. (2016). *Survai Fraud Indonesia.* ACFE Indonesia Chapter.

Adams, K., Nyuur, R., Chima, M., & Debrah, Y. (2018). Offshore/Nearshore Outsourcing as a Strategic Competitive Posturing: Insights from Ghana. In BAM2018 Conference Driving Productivity in Uncertain and Challenging Times. Bristol Business School, University of the West of England.

Aday, S., & Aday, M. S. (2020). Impact of COVID-19 on the food supply chain. *Food Quality and Safety, 4*(4), 167–180. doi:10.1093/fqsafe/fyaa024

Addo, P. C., Jiaming, F., Kulbo, N. B., & Liangqiang, L. (2020). COVID-19: Fear appeal favoring purchase behavior towards personal protective equipment. *Service Industries Journal, 40*(7-8), 471–490. doi:10.1080/02642069.2020.1751823

Afifi, W. A., & Guerrero, L. K. (2000). Motivations underlying topic avoidance in close relationships. In S. Petronio (Ed.), *Balancing the secrets of private disclosures* (pp. 165–180). Routledge.

Agarwal, R., & Prasad, J. (1998). A conceptual and operational definition of personal innovativeness in domain of information technology. *Information Systems Research, 9*(2), 204–215. doi:10.1287/isre.9.2.204

Agius, R. M., Robertson, J. F., Kendrick, D., Sewell, H. F., Stewart, M., & McKee, M. (2020). Covid-19 in the workplace. *British Medical Journal*, 370. PMID:32958470

Agrawal, S., de Smet, A., Lacroix, S., & Reich, A. (2021). *To emerge stronger from the COVID-19 crisis, companies should start reskilling their workforces now.* McKinsey & Company. https://www.mckinsey.com/business-functions/people-and-organizational-performance/our-insights/to-emerge-stronger-from-the-covid-19-crisis-companies-should-start-reskilling-their-workforces-now

Aguilera, R., Henisz, W., Oxley, J. E., & Shaver, J. M. (2018). International strategy in an era of global flux. *Strategy Science, 4*(2), 61–69. doi:10.1287tsc.2019.0087

Ahearne, M., Atefi, Y., Lam, S. K., & Pourmasoudi, M. (2022). The future of buyer–seller interactions: A conceptual framework and research agenda. *Journal of the Academy of Marketing Science, 50*(1), 22–45. doi:10.100711747-021-00803-0 PMID:34608341

Ahorsu, D. K., Lin, C. Y., Imani, V., Saffari, M., Griffiths, M. D., & Pakpour, A. H. (2020). The fear of COVID-19 scale: Development and initial validation. *International Journal of Mental Health and Addiction*, 1–9. PMID:32226353

Ajmal, M. M., Khan, M., Shad, M. K., AlKatheeri, H., & Jabeen, F. (2021). Socio-economic and technological new normal in supply chain management: lessons from COVID-19 pandemic. *The International Journal of Logistics Management.* doi:10.1108/IJLM-04-2021-0231

Ajzen, I. (1991). The theory of planned behavior. *Organizational Behavior and Human Decision Processes, 50*(2), 179–211. doi:10.1016/0749-5978(91)90020-T

Ajzen, I. (2002). Perceived behavioral control, self-efficacy, locus of control, and the theory of planned behavior 1. *Journal of Applied Social Psychology, 32*(4), 665–683. doi:10.1111/j.1559-1816.2002.tb00236.x

Ajzen, I., & Fishbein, M. (1969). The prediction of behavioral intentions in a choice situation. *Journal of Experimental Social Psychology, 5*(4), 400–416. doi:10.1016/0022-1031(69)90033-X

Ajzen, I., & Fishbein, M. (1970). The prediction of behavior from attitudinal and normative variables. *Journal of Experimental Social Psychology*, *6*(4), 466–487. doi:10.1016/0022-1031(70)90057-0

Akar, E., & Nasir, V. A. (2014), A Critical Review of Online Consumers' Purchase Intentions, *Advances in Business-Related Scientific Research Conference,* 26-28.

Akinbowale, O. E. (2018). Information communication technology and forensic accounting in Nigeria. *International Journal Of Business and Finance Management Research*, *6*, 1–7.

Akinbowale, O. E., Klingelhöfer, H. E., & Zerihun, M. F. (2020). An innovative approach in combating economic crime using forensic accounting techniques. *Journal of Financial Crime*, *27*(4), 1253–1271. Advance online publication. doi:10.1108/JFC-04-2020-0053

Alaane, K., & Saari, A. (2006). Distributed Energy Generation and Sustainable Development. *Renewable & Sustainable Energy Reviews*, *10*(6), 539–558. doi:10.1016/j.rser.2004.11.004

Alamo-Vera, F., & Suarez-Ortega, S. (2005). SMEs Internationalization Firms and Managerial Factor. *International Journal of Entrepreneurial Behaviour & Research*, *11*(4), 258–279. doi:10.1108/13552550510603298

Al-Awadhi, A. M., Alsaifi, K., Al-Awadhi, A., & Alhammadi, S. (2020). Death and contagious infectious diseases: Impact of the COVID-19 virus on stock market returns. *Journal of Behavioral and Experimental Finance*, *27*, 1–5. doi:10.1016/j.jbef.2020.100326 PMID:32292707

Albreem, M. A., Sheikh, A. M., Alsharif, M. H., Jusoh, M., & Yasin, M. N. M. (2021). Green Internet of Things (GIoT): Applications, practices, awareness, and challenges. *IEEE Access: Practical Innovations, Open Solutions*, *9*, 38833–38858. doi:10.1109/ACCESS.2021.3061697

Albring, S. M., & Elder, R. J. (2020). Research Initiatives in Accounting Education: Managing Academic Programs. *Issues in Accounting Education*, *35*(4), 61–74. doi:10.2308/ISSUES-2020-020

Albu, N., Calu, A. D., & Guşe, G. R. (2016). The role of accounting internships in preparing students' transition from school to active life. *Accounting and Management Information Systems*, *15*(1), 131–153.

Alchemix. (2022). *Alchemix – Self-repaying loans, spend and save at the same time*. Available at https://alchemix.fi/

Aldrighetti, R., Zennaro, I., Finco, S., & Battini, D. (2019). Healthcare supply chain simulation with disruption considerations: A case study from northern Italy. *Global Journal of Flexible Systems Managment*, *20*(1), 81–102. doi:10.100740171-019-00223-8

Alessa, A. A., Alotaibie, T. M., Elmoez, Z., & Alhamad, H. E. (2021). Impact of COVID-19 on Entrepreneurship and Consumer Behaviour: A Case Study in Saudi Arabia. *The Journal of Asian Finance. Economics and Business*, *8*(5), 201–210. doi:10.13106/JAFEB.2021.VOL8.NO5.0201

Alhawsawi, M. (2019). Soft Accounting Skills between Employers' Expectations and Students' Reality after COVID-19 Pandemic. *Australian Academy of Accounting and Finance Review*, *5*(2), 69–76.

Ali, I., Arslan, A., Chowdhury, M., Khan, Z., & Tarba, S. Y. (2022). Reimagining global food value chains through effective resilience to COVID-19 shocks and similar future events: A dynamic capability perspective. *Journal of Business Research*, *141*, 1–12. doi:10.1016/j.jbusres.2021.12.006 PMID:34908632

Allain-Dupré, D., Chatry, I., Michalun, V., & Moisio, A. (2020). The territorial impact of COVID-19: managing the crisis across levels of government. *OECD Policy Responses to Coronavirus (COVID-19), 10.*

Allingham, M. G., & A. S. (1972). Illicit activity: The economics of crime, drugs and tax fraud. *Journal of Public Economics, 1*, 323–338. doi:10.1016/0047-2727(72)90010-2

Allport, F. H. (1962). A structuronomic conception of behavior: Individual and collective: I. Structural theory and the master problem of social psychology. *Journal of Abnormal and Social Psychology, 64*(1), 3–30. doi:10.1037/h0043563 PMID:13860640

Almadhoor, L. (2021). Social media and cybercrimes. *Turkish Journal of Computer and Mathematics Education, 12*(10), 2972–2981.

Almeida, A., & Freire, T. (2008). *Research Methodology in Psychology and Education*. Psiquilibrios Editions.

Almeida, F., Santos, J. D., & Monteiro, J. A. (2020). The challenges and opportunities in the digitalization of companies in a post-COVID-19 World. *IEEE Engineering Management Review, 48*(3), 97–103. doi:10.1109/EMR.2020.3013206

Alon, I. (2020). COVID-19 and International Business: A Viewpoint. *FIIB Business Review, 1-3*(2), 75–77. Advance online publication. doi:10.1177/2319714520923579

Alradhawi, M., Shubber, N., Sheppard, J., & Ali, Y. (2020). Effects of the COVID-19 pandemic on mental well-being amongst individuals in society-A letter to the editor on "The socio-economic implications of the coronavirus and COVID-19 pandemic: A review". *International Journal of Surgery, 78*, 147.

Alsubagh, H. (2015). The impact of social networks on consumers' behavior. *International Journal of Business and Social Science, 6*(1), 209–216.

Altieri, M. A., & Nicholls, C. I. (2020). Agroecology and the reconstruction of a post-COVID-19 agriculture. *The Journal of Peasant Studies, 47*(5), 881–898. doi:10.1080/03066150.2020.1782891

Altıntaş, M. H., Kılıç, S., & Akhan, C. E. (2019). The transformation of the e-tailing field: A bibliometric analysis. *International Journal of Retail & Distribution Management, 48*(2), 152–168. doi:10.1108/IJRDM-10-2018-0232

Alvarado, U. Y., & Kotzab, H. (2001). Supply Chain Management: The Integration of logistics in marketing. *Industrial Marketing Management, 30*(2), 183–198. doi:10.1016/S0019-8501(00)00142-5

Alvarez-Risco, A., Arcentales, S. D. A., & Rosen, M. A. (2020). Sustainable Development Goals and Cities. In *Building Sustainable Cities* (pp. 313–330). Springer. doi:10.1007/978-3-030-45533-0_21

Alvarez, S. M. J., Munoz, V. A., Duque, A. A., & Castillo, D. (2020). B Crops: A Socioeconomic Approach for The Covid-19 Post-Crisis. *Frontiers in Psychology, 11*, 1867. Advance online publication. doi:10.3389/fpsyg.2020.01867

Alves, J.C., Lok, T.C., Luo, Y., & Hao, W. (2020). *Crisis Management for Small Business during the COVID-19 Outbreak: Survival, Resilience and Renewal Strategies of Firms in Macau*. Academic Press.

Amankwah-Amoah. (2020b). *Stepping up and stepping out of Covid-19: New challenges of environmental sustainability policies in the global airline industry*. Academic Press.

Amankwah-Amoah, J., Khan, Z., Wood, G., & Knight, G. (2021). COVID-19 and digitalization: The great acceleration. *Journal of Business Research, 136*, 602–611. doi:10.1016/j.jbusres.2021.08.011 PMID:34538980

Amatulli, C., De Angelis, M., Costabile, M., & Guido, G. (2017). *Sustainable luxury brands: Evidence from research and implications for managers*. Springer. doi:10.1057/978-1-137-60159-9

Amoah, A. J., Khan, Z., & Osabutey, L. C. E. (2021). *Covid-19 and Business Renewal: Lessons and Insights from the Global Airline Industry. International Business Review.*

Amrollahi, A. (2015). A Process Model for Crowdsourcing: Insights from the Literature on Implementation. In *Australian Conference on Information Systems*. University of South Australia.

Amrollahi, A., Ghapanchi, A., & Talaei-Khoei, A. (2014). Using Crowdsourcing Tools for Implementing Open Strategy: A Case Study in Education. *Twentieth Americas Conference on Information System*, 1-7.

Ancillo, A. L., del Val Núñez, M. T., & Gavrila, S. G. (2021). Workplace change within the COVID-19 context: A grounded theory approach. *Economic Research-Ekonomska Istraživanja*, *34*(1), 2297–2316. doi:10.1080/1331677X.2020.1862689

Andersen, P., Weisstein, F. L., & Song, L. (2020). Consumer response to marketing channels: A demand-based approach. *Journal of Marketing Channels*, *26*(1), 43–59. doi:10.1080/1046669X.2019.1657736

Anderson, C., Bieck, C., & Marshall, A. (2021). How business is adapting to COVID-19: Executive insights reveal post-pandemic opportunities. *Strategy and Leadership*, *49*(1), 38–47. doi:10.1108/SL-11-2020-0140

Andrian, L., & Hirs, J. (2020). *Colombia: Desafíos del desarrollo en tiempos de COVID-19.* Banco Interamericano de Desarrollo. http://dx.doi.org/ doi:10.18235/0003000

Angela, M., Anthony, M., Francis, E., & Damilola, A. (2021). Recent trends in corporate social responsibilities in Nigeria-A case study of major oil firms in the Niger delta region. *Scientific American*, *13*, e00928.

Anisiia, T. (Ed.). (2020). *Economy, finance, law: current problems and development prospects: collective monograph.* OSVČ.

Anjum, S. (2020). Impact of internship programs on professional and personal development of business students: A case study from Pakistan. *Future Business Journal*, *6*(1), 2. Advance online publication. doi:10.118643093-019-0007-3

Anker, T. B. (2021). At the boundary : Post-COVID agenda for business and management research in Europe and beyond. *European Management Journal*, *39*(2), 171–178. doi:10.1016/j.emj.2021.01.003

Anna, Z. (2020). The Consumer Behaviour in a Post Pandemic World. *Micro & Macro Marketing*, (3), 647–656.

Anser, M. K., Khan, M. A., Nassani, A. A., Abro, M. M. Q., Zaman, K., & Kabbani, A. (2021). Does COVID-19 pandemic disrupt sustainable supply chain process? Covering some new global facts. *Environmental Science and Pollution Research International*, *28*(42), 59792–59804. doi:10.100711356-021-14817-2 PMID:34146331

Antonakis, J. (2020). Leadership to defeat COVID-19. *Group Processes & Intergroup Relations*, *24*(2), 210–215. doi:10.1177/1368430220981418

Antonenko, V., & Quick, V. (2021). Museums as a tourist resource in the context of the COVID-19 pandemic: Challenges and new opportunities. *Bulletin of the Kyiv National University of Culture and Arts*, *4*(1), 54–73. doi:10.31866/2616-7603.4.1.2021.235149

Anton, J., & Yao, D. (1989). Split Awards, Procurement and Innovation. *The RAND Journal of Economics*, *20*(4), 538–552. doi:10.2307/2555732

Apedo-Amah, M. C., Avdiu, B., Cirera, X., Cruz, M., Davies, E., Grover, A., . . . Tran, T. T. (2020). *Unmasking the Impact of COVID-19 on Businesses: Firm Level Evidence from Across the World.* World Bank. https://openknowledge.worldbank.org/handle/10986/34626

Argonne National Laboratory. (n.d.). *The Greenhouse gases, Regulated Emissions, and Energy use in Technologies Model*. https://greet.es.anl.gov

Armstrong, M. B., & Landers, R. N. (2018). Gamification of employee training and development. *International Journal of Training and Development*, *22*(2), 162–169. doi:10.1111/ijtd.12124

Aroles, J., Mitev, N., & de Vaujany, F. X. (2019). Mapping themes in the study of new work practices. *New Technology, Work and Employment, 34*(3), 285–299. doi:10.1111/ntwe.12146

Arora, N. K., & Mishra, I. (2019). United Nations Sustainable Development Goals 2030 and environmental sustainability: Race against time. *Environmental Sustainability, 2*(4), 339–342. doi:10.100742398-019-00092-y

Arora, N., Charm, T., Grimmelt, A., Ortega, M., Robinson, K., Sexauer, C., & Yamakawa, N. (2020). *A global view of how consumer behaviour is changing amid COVID-19.* McKinsey Company. Available at tinyurl.com/zufomz47

Ashraf, B. N. (2021). Stock markets' reaction to COVID-19: Moderating role of national culture. *Finance Research Letters, 41*, 101857. doi:10.1016/j.frl.2020.101857

AsiaNews.it. (2021). *Beijing, three million small businesses closed due to Covid.* AsiaNews. https://www.asianews.it/news-en/Beijing,-three-million-small-businesses-closed-due-to-Covid-52494.html

Asirifi, M. A., Ogilvie, L., Barton, S., Bilash, O., Stobart, K., Aniteye, P., Kwashie, A., Ansong, G., Eliason, C., & Aziato, L. (2022). Reflections on change theory and community-based participatory action research: Congruent, similar or different? *Journal of Nursing Education and Practice, 12*(3), 11–21. doi:10.5430/jnep.v12n3p11

Asociación Colombiana de Pequeños Industriales - ACOPI. (2020). *Estrategias para la recuperación económica a partir del fortalecimiento de clústeres y la competencia a las importaciones.* https://www.acopi.org.co/wp-content/uploads/2020/11/ESTRATEGIAS-PARA-LA-RECUPERACI%C3%93N-ECON%C3%93MICA.pdf

Asociación Nacional de Industriales - ANDI. (2020). *Encuesta de Opinión Industrial Conjunta Septiembre.* http://www.andi.com.co/Uploads/Informe%20EOIC%20Septiembre%202020.pdf

Aspan, H. (2021). Legal Basis for the Implementation of Work from Home Amid The COVID-19 Pandemic in Indonesia. *Saudi J. Humanities Soc Sci, 6*(4), 116–121. doi:10.36348jhss.2021.v06i04.002

Assis, C. (2020). *Exxon to lay off up to 1,600 workers in Europe.* MarketWatch. https://www.marketwatch.com/story/exxon-to-lay-off-up-to-1600-workers-in-europe-2020-10-05

Asuquo, A. (2012). Empirical Analysis of The Impact of Information Technology On Forensic Accounting Practice In. *International Journal of Scientific & Technology Research, 1*(7).

Athwal, N., Wells, V. K., Carrigan, M., & Henninger, C. E. (2019). Sustainable luxury marketing: A synthesis and research agenda. *International Journal of Management Reviews, 21*(4), 405–426. doi:10.1111/ijmr.12195

Augoustinos, M., Walker, I., & Donaghue, N. (2014). Social cognition: An integrated introduction (3rd ed.). New York: Sage.

Auld, G., & Renckens, S. (2021). Private sustainability governance, the Global South and COVID-19: Are changes to audit policies in light of the pandemic exacerbating existing inequalities? *World Development, 139*, 105314. doi:10.1016/j.worlddev.2020.105314

Avendaño, H. (2020). *COVID-19 y economía: ¿Luz al final del túnel?* Revista Fasecolda (180). https://revista.fasecolda.com/index.php/revfasecolda/article/view/667

Aw, E. C. X. (2019). Understanding the webrooming phenomenon: Shopping motivation, channel-related benefits and costs. *International Journal of Retail & Distribution Management, 47*(10), 1074–1092. doi:10.1108/IJRDM 01 2019 0026

Azwar, S. (1995). *Sikap Manusia, Teori dan Pengukurannya.* Pustaka Pelajar.

Bacchi, U. (2020). *Escape from the city? Londoners lead Europe in COVID-inspired dreams of flight.* Thomson Reuters Foundation News. https://news.trust.org/item/20201118230536-uv6o2/

Ba, H., Le, H., Loan, T., Thanh, C., Bich, T., Pham, T., & Binh, T. (2020). Policy related factors affecting the survival and development of SMEs in the context of Covid 19 pandemic. *Manag. Sci. Lett.*, *10*, 3683–3692.

BAI. (2021). *Annual Economic Conjuncture Report*. Angolan Investment Bank.

Bai, C., Dallasega, P., Orzes, G., & Sarkis, J. (2020). Industry 4.0 technologies assessment: A sustainability perspective. *International Journal of Production Economics*, *229*, 1–15. doi:10.1016/j.ijpe.2020.107776

Bai, C., Quayson, M., & Sarkis, J. (2021). Covid-19 Pandemic Digitization Lessons for Sustainable Development of Micro-and-Small-Enterprises. *Sustainable Production and Consumption*, *27*, 1989–2001. Advance online publication. doi:10.1016/j.spc.2021.04.035 PMID:34722843

Bain & Co. (2020). *The future of Luxury: Bouncing Back from Covid-19*. Retrieved from https://cutt.ly/hmd5Imn

Baldwin, R., & Mauro, B. W. (2020). Introduction. In Economics in the Time of Covid-19 (pp. 1-30). CEPR Press.

Banco de la República. (2020). *The Board of Directors of Banco de la República unanimously maintained the benchmark interest rate at 1.75%. Measures Taken by BR on Account of Covid-19*. https://www.banrep.gov.co/en/board-directors-banco-republica-unanimously-maintained-benchmark-interest-rate-175

Banco de la República. (n.d.). *Índice de producción real de la industria manufacturera colombiana*. https://www.banrep.gov.co/es/estadisticas/indice-produccion-industrial-ipp

Bandura, A. (1999). Social cognitive theory of personality. In C. Prendergast (Ed.), Handbook of personality (Vol. 2, pp. 154-196). Clarendon Press.

Bandura, A. (1978). The self system in reciprocal determinism. *The American Psychologist*, *33*(4), 344–358. doi:10.1037/0003-066X.33.4.344

Bandura, A. (1989). Human agency in social cognitive theory. *The American Psychologist*, *44*(9), 1175–1184. doi:10.1037/0003-066X.44.9.1175 PMID:2782727

Bandura, A. (1991). Social cognitive theory of self-regulation. *Organizational Behavior and Human Decision Processes*, *50*(2), 248–287. doi:10.1016/0749-5978(91)90022-L

Bandura, A. (2002). Growing primacy of human agency in adaptation and change in the electronic era. *European Psychologist*, *7*(1), 2–16. doi:10.1027//1016-9040.7.1.2

Bandura, A., Ross, D., & Ross, S. A. (1961). Transmission of aggression through imitation of aggressive models. *Journal of Abnormal and Social Psychology*, *63*(3), 575–582. doi:10.1037/h0045925 PMID:13864605

Banik, N., & Padalkar, M. (2021). The spread of gig economy: Trends and effects. *Foresight and STI Governance*, *15*(1), 28–38. doi:10.17323/2500-2597.2021.1.19.29

Baranowski, T., Cullen, K. W., Nicklas, T., Thompson, D., & Baranowski, J. (2003). Are current health behavioral change models helpful in guiding prevention of weight gain efforts? *Obesity Research*, *11*(S10), 23S–43S. doi:10.1038/oby.2003.222 PMID:14569036

Barasa, E., Mbau, R., & Gilson, L. (2018). What is resilience and how can it be nurtured? A systematic review of empirical literature on organizational resilience. *International Journal of Health Policy and Management*, *7*(6), 491–503. doi:10.15171/ijhpm.2018.06 PMID:29935126

Barbeito-Caamaño, A., & Chalmeta, R. (2020). Using big data to evaluate corporate social responsibility and sustainable development practices. *Corporate Social Responsibility and Environmental Management*, *27*(6), 2831–2848. doi:10.1002/csr.2006

Barber, B. M., & Odean, T. (2008). All that glitters: The effect of attention and news on buying behavior of individual and institutional investors. *The Review of Financial Studies, 21*(2), 785-818. https://ssrn.com/abstract=460660

BarberB. M.HuangX.OdeanT. (2021, July). Schwartz C. Attention-Induced Trading and Returns: Evidence from Robinhood Users. SSRN. https://ssrn. com/abstract=3715077

Bardin, L. (1977). *Content analysis.* Lisbon: Editions 70.

Barlett, C. P., Rinker, A., & Roth, B. (2021). Cyberbullying perpetration in the COVID-19 era: An application of general strain theory. *The Journal of Social Psychology*, *161*(4), 1–11. doi:10.1080/00224545.2021.1883503 PMID:33543673

Barlow, P., van Schalkwyk, M. C., McKee, M., Labonté, R., & Stuckler, D. (2021). COVID-19 and the collapse of global trade: Building an effective public health response. *The Lancet. Planetary Health*, *5*(2), e102–e107. doi:10.1016/S2542-5196(20)30291-6 PMID:33581061

Barman, A., Das, R., & De, P. K. (2021). Impact of COVID-19 in food supply chain: Disruptions and recovery strategy. *Current Research in Behavioral Sciences, 2*, 100017.

Barnes, S. A., Green, A., & de Hoyos, M. (2015). Crowdsourcing and work: Individual factors and circumstances influencing employability. *New Technology, Work and Employment*, *30*(1), 16–31. doi:10.1111/ntwe.12043

Barnett, M. L., Henriques, I., & Husted, B. W. (2020). Beyond good intentions: Designing CSR initiatives for greater social impact. *Journal of Management*, *46*(6), 937–964. doi:10.1177/0149206319900539

Barrera, C., Radziunas, J., & Montoya, M. (2021, October 12). *De la crisis a la reactivación y su efecto en el PGN.* Economía Colombiana: https://www.economiacolombiana.co/finanzas-publicas/de-la-crisis-a-la-reactivacion-y-su-efecto-en-el-pgn-1294

Barringer, B., & Ireland, R. (2011). *Entrepreneurship: Successfully Launching New Ventures* (4th ed.). Prentice Hall.

Bartik, A. W., Bertrand, M., Cullen, Z. B., Glaeser, E. L., Luca, M., & Stanton, C. T. (2020). *How are small businesses adjusting to COVID-19? Early evidence from a survey.* National Bureau of Economic Research Working Paper Series.

Bartik, A. W., Bertrand, M., Cullen, Z., Glaeser, E. L., Luca, M., & Stanton, C. (2020). The impact of COVID-19 on small business outcomes and expectations. *Proceedings of the National Academy of Sciences of the United States of America*, *117*(30), 17656–17666. doi:10.1073/pnas.2006991117 PMID:32651281

Barwitz, N., & Maas, P. (2018). Understanding the Omnichannel Customer Journey: Determinants of Interaction Choice. *Journal of Interactive Marketing*, *43*, 116–133. doi:10.1016/j.intmar.2018.02.001

Basile, V. (2019a). Marketing Performance Measurement in FMCG: Share of Wallet in Retailing Industry. Editoriale Scientifica.

Basile, V. (2019b). Investigating new consumer behaviour dimensions in grocery retailing: Some evidence from Southern Italy. *The Journal of Business and Retail Management Research*, *14*(01). Advance online publication. doi:10.24052/JBRMR/V14IS01/ART-05

Bassett, D. S., & Sporns, O. (2017). Network neuroscience. *Nature Neuroscience*, *20*(3), 353–364. doi:10.1038/nn.4502 PMID:28230844

Batt, P. J., & Purchase, S. (2003). Managing collaboration within networks and relationships. *Industrial Marketing Management*, *33*(3), 169–174. doi:10.1016/j.indmarman.2003.11.004

Baumeister, R. F., & Leary, M. R. (1997). Writing narrative literature reviews. *Review of General Psychology*, *1*(3), 311–320. doi:10.1037/1089-2680.1.3.311

Bayat, T., Özcan, B., & Taş, Ş. (2015). Türkiye'de döviz kuru geçiş etkisinin asimetrik nedensellik testleri ile analizi. *Eskişehir Osmangazi Üniversitesi İİBF Dergisi, 10*(2), 7–30.

Bayerlein, L., & Jeske, D. (2018). Student learning opportunities in traditional and computer-mediated internships. *Education + Training, 60*(1), 27–38. doi:10.1108/ET-10-2016-0157

Bebko, S. (2021). Internationalization and cooperation of the higher education system of Ukraine in the conditions of global challenges. *Scientific Bulletin of Polissya, 2*(21), 28–38. doi:10.25140/2410-9576-2020-2(21)-28-38

Beck, K. (2001). *The Agile Manifesto.* Agile Alliance. http://agilemanifesto.org/

Beck, J., & Halim, H. (2008). Undergraduate Internships in Accounting: What and How do Singapore Interns Learn from Experience? *Accounting Education, 17*(2), 151–172. doi:10.1080/09639280701220277

Beckman & Countryman. (2021). *The Importance of Agriculture in the Economy: Impacts from COVID-19.* doi:10.1111/ajae.12212

Belitski, M., Guenther, C., Kritikos, A. S., & Thurik, R. (2021). Economic Effects of the COVID-19 Pandemic on Entrepreneurship and Small Businesses. SSRN *Electronic Journal.* doi:10.2139/ssrn.3905065

Belyaeva, Z., Shams, S. M. R., Santoro, G., & Grandhi, B. (2020). Unpacking stakeholder relationship management in the public and private sectors: The comparative insights. *EuroMed Journal of Business, 15*(3), 269–281. doi:10.1108/EMJB-06-2019-0085

Benabou, R., & Tirole, J. (2011). *Laws and Norms.* National Bureau of Economic Research Working Paper Series, 17579. doi:10.3386/w17579

Benedetto, C. (2018). *Is Omnichannel Sales Killing the Need for Sales Reps?* MarTech Series. https://martechseries.com/mts-insights/guest-authors/is-omnichannel-sales-killing-the-need-for-sales-reps/

Bennett, J., Owers, M., Pitt, M., & Tucker, M. (2010). Workplace impact of social networking. *Property Management, 28*(3), 138–148. doi:10.1108/02637471011051282

Beraha, I., & Đuričin, S. (2020). The impact of COVID-19 crisis on medium-sized enterprises in Serbia. *Economic Analysis, 53*(1), 14–27.

Berkowitz, A. D. (2010). Fostering healthy norms to prevent violence and abuse: The social norms approach. In K. L. Kaufman (Ed.), *The prevention of sexual violence: A practitioner's sourcebook* (pp. 147–171). NEARI Press.

Berrell, M. (2017). The Social Relations of Anywhere Working: Major Themes and Meanings. In Remote Work and Collaboration: Breakthroughs in Research and Practice (pp. 287-304). IGI Global.

Bertrandie, L., & Zielke, S. (2019). The influence of multi-channel pricing strategy on price fairness and customer confusion. *International Review of Retail, Distribution and Consumer Research, 29*(5), 504–517. doi:10.1080/09593969.2019.1664611

Bertrand, O. (2011). What Goes Around, Comes Around: Effects of Offshore Outsourcing on the Export Performance of Firms. *Journal of International Business Studies, 42*(2), 334–344. doi:10.1057/jibs.2010.26

Beverinotti, J., & Deza, M. (2020). *Una radiografía de la resiliencia de las empresas de la región andina para enfrentar el Covid-19.* IADB. http://dx.doi.org/ doi:10.18235/0002444

Bhasin, M. (2013). An empirical investigation of the relevant skills of forensic. *European Journal of Accounting Auditing and Finance Research, 1*(June), 11–52.

Bicalho, T., Silva, C., Cunha, I., Teixeira, J., & Proença, A. (2019). Planners' attitudes towards the cycling potential of their cities–Creating awareness for attitude change. *Travel Behaviour & Society, 17*, 96–103. doi:10.1016/j.tbs.2019.08.002

Bicchieri, C. (2016). *Norms in the wild: How to diagnose, measure, and change social norms*. Oxford University Press.

Bicchieri, C., Muldoon, R., & Sontuoso, A. (2018). Social norms. In *The Stanford encyclopedia of philosophy. Metaphysics Research Lab*. Stanford University.

Biçer, İ., Çakmak, C., Demir, H., & Kurt, M. E. (2020). Koronavirüs anksiyete ölçeği kısa formu: Türkçe geçerlik ve güvenirlik çalışması. *Anatolian Clinic the Journal of Medical Sciences. Anadolu Kliniği Tıp Bilimleri Dergisi (COVID 19 Özel Sayısı)*, 216-225.

Billewar, S. R., Jadhav, K., Sriram, V. P., Arun, A., Abdul, S. M., Gulati, K., & Bhasin, N. K. K. (2021). The rise of 3D E-Commerce: online shopping gets real with virtual reality and augmented reality during COVID-19. *World Journal of Engineering*.

Bingöl, N., Pehlivan, C., & Han, A. (2020). Turizm gelirleri- makro değişkenler arasındaki ilişkinin Türkiye için ampirik olarak incelenmesi. *Ekev Akademi Dergisi, 24*(82), 245–262.

BIS. (2021). *Covid-19 accelerated the digitalisation of payments*. https://www.bis.org/statistics/payment_stats/commentary2112.pdf

BİST 100. (n.d.). https://www.alnusyatirim.com/bist-100#:~:text=BIST%20100%20endeksi%3B%20Borsa%20%C4%B0stanbul,%C3%B6l%C3%A7mek%20i%C3%A7in%20kullan%C4%B1lan%20temel%20g%C3%B6stergedir.&text=%C3%96zetle%3B%20bu%20100%20%C5%9Firketin%20hisse%20senedi%2C%20borsan%C4%B1n%20genel%20performans%C4%B1n%C4%B1%20g%C3%B6stermektedir

BİST-100 Endeksi. (n.d.). https://www.ekonomist.com.tr/encyclopedia/bist-100-endeksi

Blackburn, R. (2011). Book Review of: 'Unmasking the entrepreneur' by Campbell Jones and Andre Spicer. *Management Learning, 42*(1), 121–124. doi:10.1177/13505076110420010703

Blackman, A., Ibáñez, A. M., Izquierdo, A., Keefer, P., Mesquita Moreira, M., Schady, N., & Serebrisky, T. (2020). *La política pública frente al Covid-19: Recomendaciones para América Latina y el Caribe*. IADB. doi:10.18235/0002302

Bless, H., & Fiedler, K. (2014). *Social cognition: How individuals construct social reality* (2nd ed.). Routledge. doi:10.4324/9781315784731

Blocksize-capital (2022). *Decarbonizing bio-based fuels through the Verity Tracking platform*. Internal Document.

Blythe, J., & Zimmerman, A. (2005). *Business-to-Business Marketing Management*. Thomson.

Bochko, O. Yu. (2021). The influence of the pandemic on the development of agriculture in Ukraine *International Scientific Journal "Internauka"*. doi:10.25313/2520-2294-2021-4

Bodla, A. A., Tang, N., Jiang, W., & Tian, L. (2018). Diversity and creativity in cross-national teams: The role of team knowledge sharing and inclusive climate. *Journal of Management & Organization, 24*(5), 711–729. doi:10.1017/jmo.2016.34

Boio, D., Pacatolo, C., & Bangula, M. (2020). *Assessment Study of the Socioeconomic Impacts of the Angolan Executive's Measures to Combat Covid-19*. Higher Polytechnic Institute Sol Nascente, Luanda.

Boland, B., De Smet, A., Palter, R., & Sanghvi, A. (2020). *Reimagining the office and work life after COVID-19*. https://www.mckinsey.com/business-functions/organization/our-insights/reimagining-the-office-and-work-life-after-covid-19

Bolton, A. D., Goosen, L., & Kritzinger, E. (2022a). Impact of Digital Transformation via Unified Communication and Collaboration Technologies: Productivity and Innovation at a Global Enterprise. In Impact of Digital Transformation on the Development of New Business Models and Consumer Experience. IGI Global.

Bolton, A., Goosen, L., & Kritzinger, E. (2021c). The Integration and Implementation of the Internet of Things Through Digital Transformation: Impact on Productivity and Innovation. In P. Tomar (Ed.), Integration and Implementation of the Internet of Things Through Cloud Computing (pp. 85-112). IGI Global. doi:10.4018/978-1-7998-6981-8.ch005

Bolton, T., Goosen, L., & Kritzinger, E. (2020a). Security Aspects of an Empirical Study into the Impact of Digital Transformation via Unified Communication and Collaboration Technologies on the Productivity and Innovation of a Global Automotive Enterprise. Communications in Computer and Information Science, 1166, 99-113. doi:10.1007/978-3-030-43276-8_8

Bolton, A. D., Goosen, L., & Kritzinger, E. (2021a). Unified Communication Technologies at a Global Automotive Organization. In M. Khosrow-Pour (Ed.), *Encyclopedia of Organizational Knowledge, Administration, and Technologies* (pp. 2592–2608). IGI Global. doi:10.4018/978-1-7998-3473-1.ch179

Bolton, A. D., Goosen, L., & Kritzinger, E. (2022b). Emerging Technologies for Innovation and Productivity Management in the Automotive Industry: Impact of Digital Transformation on Communication. In *Emerging Technologies for Innovation Management in the Software Industry (Approved for publication)*. IGI Global. doi:10.4018/978-1-7998-9059-1.ch003

Bolton, A., Goosen, L., & Kritzinger, E. (2016). Enterprise Digitization Enablement Through Unified Communication and Collaboration. In *Proceedings of the Annual Conference of the South African Institute of Computer Scientists and Information Technologists*. ACM. doi:10.1145/2987491.2987516

Bolton, A., Goosen, L., & Kritzinger, E. (2020b). The Impact of Unified Communication and Collaboration Technologies on Productivity and Innovation: Promotion for the Fourth Industrial Revolution. In S. B. Buckley (Ed.), *Promoting Inclusive Growth in the Fourth Industrial Revolution* (pp. 44–73). IGI Global. doi:10.4018/978-1-7998-4882-0.ch002

Bolton, A., Goosen, L., & Kritzinger, E. (2021b). An Empirical Study into the Impact on Innovation and Productivity Towards the Post-COVID-19 Era: Digital Transformation of an Automotive Enterprise. In L. C. Carvalho, L. Reis, & C. Silveira (Eds.), *Handbook of Research on Entrepreneurship, Innovation, Sustainability, and ICTs in the Post-COVID-19 Era* (pp. 133–159). IGI Global. doi:10.4018/978-1-7998-6776-0.ch007

Bonanomi, M. M. (2019). *Digital Transformation of Multidisciplinary Design Firms: A Systematic Analysis-Based Methodology for Organizational Change Management*. Springer. doi:10.1007/978-3-030-19701-8

Bond, U. E. III, Jong, D. D., Eggert, A., Houston, B. M., Kleinaltenkamp, M., Kohli, K. A., Ritter, T., & Ulaga, W. (2020). The Future of B2B Customer Solutions in A Post-Covid-19 Economy: Managerial Issues and An Agenda for Academic Inquiry. *Journal of Service Research, 23*(4), 401–408. doi:10.1177/1094670520960230

Borsari, B., & Carey, K. B. (2001). Peer influences on college drinking: A review of the research. *Journal of Substance Abuse, 13*(4), 391–424. doi:10.1016/S0899-3289(01)00098-0 PMID:11775073

Bosch-Rekveldt, M., Jongkind, Y., Mooi, H., Bakker, H., & Verbraeck, A. (2011). Grasping project complexity in large engineering projects: The TOE (Technical, Organizational and Environmental) framework. *International Journal of Project Management, 29*(6), 728–739. doi:10.1016/j.ijproman.2010.07.008

Bose, S., Bhattacharyya, A., & Islam, S. (2016). Dynamics of firm-level financial inclusion: Empirical evidence from an emerging economy. *Journal of Banking and Finance Law and Practice, 27*(1), 47–68.

Bosson, J. K., & Vandello, J. A. (2011). Precarious manhood and its links to action and aggression. *Current Directions in Psychological Science, 20*(2), 82–86. doi:10.1177/0963721411402669

Bouhali, H., Dahbanib, A., & Dinarb, B. (2021). COVID-19 impacts on financial markets: Takeaways from the third wave. *Russian Journal of Economics*, *7*, 200–212.

Bourassa, K. J., Sbarra, D. A., Caspi, A., & Moffitt, T. E. (2020). Social distancing as a health behavior: County-level movement in the United States during the COVID-19 pandemic is associated with conventional health behaviors. *Annals of Behavioral Medicine*, *54*(8), 548–556. doi:10.1093/abm/kaaa049 PMID:32608474

Bourgeault, I. L., Maier, C. B., Dieleman, M., Ball, J., MacKenzie, A., Nancarrow, S., Nigenda, G., & Sidat, M. (2020). The COVID-19 pandemic presents an opportunity to develop more sustainable health workforces. *Human Resources for Health*, *18*(1), 83. doi:10.118612960-020-00529-0 PMID:33129313

Bourlakis, M., Papagiannidis, S., & Li, F. (2009). Retail spatial evolution: Paving the way from traditional to metaverse retailing. *Electronic Commerce Research*, *9*(1), 135–148. doi:10.100710660-009-9030-8

Breitung, J., & Candelon, B. (2006). Testing for short- and long-run causality: A frequency-domain approach. *Journal of Econometrics*, *132*(2), 363–378.

Brende, B. (2021). *India's roadmap for success and prosperity in the post-COVID world*. World Economic Forum. https://www.weforum.org/agenda/2021/11/india-s-future-and-role-in-the-post-covid-19-world/

Briggs, D., Ellis, A., Lloyd, A., & Telford, L. (2020). New hope or old futures in disguise? Neoliberalism, the Covid-19 pandemic and the possibility for social change. *The International Journal of Sociology and Social Policy*, *40*(9/10), 831–848. doi:10.1108/IJSSP-07-2020-0268

Brodeur, A., Gray, D., Islam, A., & Bhuiyan, S. (2021). A literature review of the economics of COVID-19. *Journal of Economic Surveys*, *35*(4), 1007–1044. doi:10.1111/joes.12423 PMID:34230772

Brown, R. (2020). The impact of Covid-19 on Scottish small and medium-sized enterprises (SMEs): Prognosis and policy prescription. *Fraser of Allander Economic Commentary, 44*(2).

Brown, J. J., & Reingen, P. H. (1987). Social ties and word-of-mouth referral behavior. *The Journal of Consumer Research*, *14*(12), 350–362. doi:10.1086/209118

Brown, R., Rocha, A., & Cowling, M. (2020). Financing entrepreneurship in times of crisis: Exploring the impact of COVID-19 on the market for entrepreneurial finance in the United Kingdom. *International Small Business Journal*, *38*(5), 380–390. doi:10.1177/0266242620937464

Brülhart, M., Lalive, R., Lehmann, T., & Siegenthaler, M. (2020). COVID-19 financial support to small businesses in Switzerland: Evaluation and outlook. *Schweizerische Zeitschrift für Volkswirtschaft und Statistik*, *156*(1), 1–13. doi:10.118641937-020-00060-y PMID:33078128

Bruque, S., & Moyano, J. (2007). Organisational determinants of information technology adoption and implementation in SMEs: The case of family and cooperative firms. *Technovation*, *27*(5), 241–253. doi:10.1016/j.technovation.2006.12.003

Bryson, J., & Alston, F. (2011). *Creating Your Strategic Plan: A Workbook for Public and Nonprofit Organisations*. Wiley.

Buallay, A., Aldhaen, E., Hamdan, A. M., Kukreja, G., & Al Mubarak, M. (2020). Corporate social responsibility disclosure and firms' performance in Mediterranean countries: A stakeholders' perspective. *EuroMed Journal of Business*, *15*(3), 361–375. doi:10.1108/EMJB-05-2019-0066

Bulck, J. V., & Custers, K. (2009). Television exposure is related to fear of avian flu, an Ecological Study across 23 member states of the European Union. *European Journal of Public Health*, *19*(4), 370–374.

Burt, R. S. (2004). Structural holes and good ideas. *American Journal of Sociology*, *110*(2), 349–399. doi:10.1086/421787

Bush, M. C. (2018). *A great place to work for all: Better for business, better for people, better for the world.* Berrett-Koehler Publishers.

Butt, A. S. (2021). Strategies to mitigate the impact of COVID-19 on supply chain disruptions: a multiple case analysis of buyers and distributors. *The International Journal of Logistics Management.* doi:10.1108/IJLM-11-2020-0455

Butt, A. S. (2021). Supply chains and COVID-19 : Impacts, countermeasures and post-COVID-19 era. *International Journal of Logistics Management.* Advance online publication. doi:10.1108/IJLM-02-2021-0114

Buttimer, A. (1980). Home, reach, and the sense of place. In The human experience of space and place (Vol. 3, pp. 166-187). London: Routledge.

Byrnes, K. G., Kiely, P. A., Dunne, C. P., McDermott, K. W., & Coffey, J. C. (2021). Communication, collaboration and contagion: "Virtualisation" of anatomy during COVID-19. *Clinical Anatomy (New York, N.Y.), 34*(1), 82–89. doi:10.1002/ca.23649 PMID:32648289

Caballero, C., & Machado, G. (2020). De la crisis de 'fin de siglo' a la del 'coronavirus'. La economía colombiana en el siglo XXI. *Coyuntura Económica: Investigación Económica y Social, 50,* 15-74. https://www.repository.fedesarrollo.org.co/handle/11445/4057

Cao, Y., Shan, J., Gong, Z., Kuang, J., & Gao, Y. (2020). Status and challenges of public health emergency management in China related to COVID-19. *Frontiers in Public Health, 8,* 250. doi:10.3389/fpubh.2020.00250 PMID:32574311

Caputo, A., Marzi, G., Maley, J., & Silic, M. (2019). Ten years of conflict management research 2007–2017: An update on themes, concepts and relationships. *International Journal of Conflict Management, 30*(1), 87–110. doi:10.1108/IJCMA-06-2018-0078

Cardenas, S. (2021, October). Unpacking Amazon through meatpacking, Adam Smith, and digital colonialism. In *2021 IEEE International Symposium on Technology and Society (ISTAS)* (pp. 1-6). IEEE. 10.1109/ISTAS52410.2021.9629196

Carley, K. M. (2005). *Understanding Taxpayer Behavior and Assessing Potential IRS Interventions Using Multiagent Dynamic-Network Simulation.* Academic Press.

Carnevale, J. B., & Hatak, I. (2020). Employee adjustment and well-being in the era of COVID-19: Implications for human resource management. *Journal of Business Research, 116,* 183–187. doi:10.1016/j.jbusres.2020.05.037 PMID:32501303

Carroll, A. (1991). The Pyramid of Corporate Social Responsibility: Toward the Moral Management of Organizational Stakeholders. *Business Horizons, 34*(4), 39–48. doi:10.1016/0007-6813(91)90005-G

Carroll, A. B. (2021). Corporate Social Responsibility: Perspectives on the CSR Construct's Development and Future. *Business & Society, 60*(6). doi:10.1177/00076503211001765

Carter, J. W., & Youssef-Morgan, C. M. (2019). The positive psychology of mentoring: A longitudinal analysis of psychological capital development and performance in a formal mentoring program. *Human Resource Development Quarterly, 30*(3), 383–405. doi:10.1002/hrdq.21348

Carter, S. M., & Greer, C. R. (2013). Strategic leadership: Values, styles, and organizational performance. *Journal of Leadership & Organizational Studies, 20*(4), 375–393. doi:10.1177/1548051812471724

Carvalho, L., Bernardo, M., Sousa, I., & Negas, M. (2014). *Management of organizations-An integrated and prospective approach.* Silabo, Lda.

Carvalho, R. B., Reis, A. M. P., Larieira, C. L. C., & Pinochet, L. H. C. (2021). Digital transformation: Construct definition challenges and scenarios for a research agenda. *RAM. Revista de Administração Mackenzie*, *22*(6). Advance online publication. doi:10.1590/1678-6971/eramd210400

Casselman, B. (2021). *Start-Up Boom in the Pandemic Is Growing Stronger*. The New York Times. https://www.nytimes.com/2021/08/19/business/startup-business-creation-pandemic.html

Castells, M. (2004). *The network society a cross-cultural perspective*. Edward Elgar.

Castells, M. (2011). Network theory: A network theory of power. *International Journal of Communication*, *5*, 15.

Castro, M.P., & Zermeño, M.G.G. (2020). Being an entrepreneur post-COVID-19–resilience in times of crisis: a systematic literature review. *Journal of Entrepreneurship in Emerging Economies*.

Cates, L. (2022). *Small Businesses Are Still Grappling with Supply Chain Disruptions*. U.S. Chamber of Commerce. https://www.uschamber.com/small-business/small-businesses-are-still-grappling-with-supply-chain-disruptions

Centre for Disease Control and Prevention. (2020). *Human Corona virus Types*. Available from: https://www.cdc.gov/coronavirus/types.html

Centro de Estudios Sociales y Laborales – CESLA & Asocicación Nacional de Industriales - ANDI. (2020). *Diagnóstico y estrategia de reactivación del empleo y de la economía: COVID-19 - Colección Trabajo y Sociedad*. ANDI. http://www.andi.com.co/Uploads/Diagn%C3%B3stico%20y%20estrategia%20de%20reactivaci%C3%B3n%20del%20empleo%20y%20de%20la%20econom%C3%ADa%20COVID%2019%20CESLA%20ANDI.pdf

Cernuşca, L., & Csorba, L. M. (2020). Professional and Transversal Accounting Competences (II). *CECCAR Business Review*, *1*(9), 3–10. doi:10.37945/cbr.2020.09.01

Chae, M. J. (2021). Driving consumer engagement through diverse calls to action in corporate social responsibility messages on social media. *Sustainability*, *13*(7), 3812. doi:10.3390u13073812

Chaikun, E. (2021). Building and transforming crisis communication strategies of the media during the COVID-19 pandemic. *IV Congress of the ACS "Transformation of social institutions in the information society"*, 39-41.

Chainlink. (2021). *What is a Blockchain Oracle?* https://chain.link/education/blockchain-oracles

Chanal, V., & Caron-Fasan, M. L. (2010). The difficulties involved in developing Business Models open to innovation communities: the case of a Crowdsourcing platform. *M@n@gement*, *13*, 318-340.

Chan, C. M., Teoh, S. Y., Yeow, A., & Yan, G. (2019). Agility in responding to disruptive digital innovation: Case study of an SME. *Information Systems Journal*, *29*(2), 436–455. doi:10.1111/isj.12215

Chance, M. R. (2015). *Social fabrics of the mind*. Psychology Press. doi:10.4324/9781315728186

CHANEL. (2020a). *Chanel announces climate commitments*. Retrieved from https://cutt.ly/lbbWChJ

CHANEL. (2020b). *Channel. Mission 1.5°*. Retrieved from https://cutt.ly/ubbW5Hs

CHANEL. (2022). https://www.linkedin.com/company/chanel/

Chang, H. H., Tsai, Y. C., & Hsu, C. H. (2013). E-procurement and supply chain performance. *Supply Chain Management*, *18*(1), 34–51. doi:10.1108/13598541311293168

Chaplin, H. & House, K. (2009). *The Internationalisation of young, innovative SMEs*. Academic Press.

Che, A. R., Omar, I., & Suraiya, M. A. (2020). *The impact of Covid-19 Movement Control Order on SMEs' businesses and survival strategies*. Geografia.

Cheah, I., Zainol, Z., & Phau, I. (2016). Conceptualizing country-of-ingredient authenticity of luxury brands. *Journal of Business Research*, *69*(12), 5819–5826. doi:10.1016/j.jbusres.2016.04.179

Chen, C., Liu, L., & Zhao, N. (2020). Fear sentiment, uncertainty, and bitcoin price dynamics: The case of COVID-19. *Emerging Markets Finance & Trade*, *56*(10), 2298–2309.

Cheng, E. (2022). *China's zero-Covid strategy hurts consumer spending more than manufacturing*. CNBC. https://www.cnbc.com/2022/01/13/chinas-zero-covid-strategy-hurts-consumer-spending-more-than-manufacturing.html

Cheng, Y. (2020). Demand Rising for Contactless Delivery. *China Daily*. Retrieved from: http://www.chinadaily.com.cn/a/202002/19/WS5e4c9d77a310128217278a1b.html

Cheng, Z., Mendolia, S., Paloyo, A., Savage, D., & Tani, M. (2021). Working parents, financial insecurity, and child-care: Mental health in the time of COVID-19 in the UK. *Review of Economics of the Household*, *19*(1), 123–144. doi:10.100711150-020-09538-3 PMID:33456425

Chen, I., & Paulraj, A. (2004). Towards a theory of supply chain management: The constructs and measurements. *Journal of Operations Management*, *22*(2), 119–150. doi:10.1016/j.jom.2003.12.007

Chen, L., Hsieh, P.-A., Rai, A., & Xu, S. X. (2021). How Does Employee Infusion Use of CRM Systems Drive Customer Satisfaction? Mechanism Differences Between Face-to-Face and Virtual Channels. *Management Information Systems Quarterly*, *45*(2), 719–754. doi:10.25300/MISQ/2021/13265

Cheung, M. F., & To, W. M. (2019). An extended model of value-attitude-behavior to explain Chinese consumers' green purchase behavior. *Journal of Retailing and Consumer Services*, *50*, 145–153. doi:10.1016/j.jretconser.2019.04.006

China briefing. (2020). *Tapping into new growth opportunities in China's F&B market*. Retrieved from: https://www.china-briefing.com/news/tapping-into-new-growth-opportunities-in-chinas-fb-market/

Choi, T. M., Wallace, S. W., & Wang, Y. (2018). Big data analytics in operations management. *Production and Operations Management*, *27*(10), 1868–1883. doi:10.1111/poms.12838

Choi, T. Y., Narayanan, S., Novak, D., Olhager, J., Sheu, J.-B., & Wiengarten, F. (2021). Managing extended supply chains. *Journal of Business Logistics*, *42*(2), 200–206. doi:10.1111/jbl.12276

Choi, T.-M. (2020). Innovative "Bring-Service-Near-Your-Home" operations under Corona-Virus (COVID-19/SARS-CoV-2) outbreak: Can logistics become the Messiah? *Transportation Research Part E, Logistics and Transportation Review*, *140*, 101961. doi:10.1016/j.tre.2020.101961 PMID:32346356

Cho, M., Furey, L. D., & Mohr, T. (2017). Communicating corporate social responsibility on social media: Strategies, stakeholders, and public engagement on corporate Facebook. *Business and Professional Communication Quarterly*, *80*(1), 52–69. doi:10.1177/2329490616663708

Chong, S. M., & Yazdani, K. (2020). Factors Affecting the Affective Organizational Commitment, Job Satisfaction and Job Acceptance Intention of Interns: A Conceptual Framework. *International Journal of Social Science and Humanity*, *68–72*, 68–72. Advance online publication. doi:10.18178/ijssh.2020.V10.1016

Chong, S., Huang, Y., & Chang, C. H. D. (2020). Supporting interdependent telework employees: A moderated-mediation model linking daily COVID-19 task setbacks to next-day work withdrawal. *The Journal of Applied Psychology*, *105*(12), 1408–1422. doi:10.1037/apl0000843 PMID:33271029

Chopra, S., & Meindl, P. (2001). *Supply Chain Management*. Prentice-Hall.

Chopra, S., & Sodhi, M. S. (2004). Managing risk to avoid supply-chain breakdown. *MIT Sloan Management Review*, *46*(1), 53–61.

Choubey, S. (2021). *How to elevate customer experience in a post COVID-19 world*. EY. https://www.ey.com/en_gl/consulting/how-to-elevate-customer-experience-in-a-post-covid-19-world

Chow Tai Fook Jewellery Group. (2020). *Sustainable Report 2020*. https://www.ctfjewellerygroup.com/file/Sustainability/reports/csr-report.pdf

Chow Tai Fook. (2022). Chow Tai Fook.

Chowdhury, P., Paul, K. S., & Moktadir Md, A. (2021). Covid-19 pandemic related supply chain studies: A systematic review. *Transportation Research Part E, Logistics and Transportation Review*, *148*, 148. doi:10.1016/j.tre.2021.102271 PMID:33613082

Chow, W. S., Madu, C. N., Kuei, C.-H., Lu, M. H., Lin, C., & Tseng, H. (2008). Supply chain management in the US and Taiwan: An empirical study. *International Journal of Management Sciences*, *36*(5), 665–679. doi:10.1016/j.omega.2006.01.001

Christopher, M., & Peck, H. (2004). Building the resilient supply chain. *International Journal of Logistics Management*, *15*(2), 1–13. doi:10.1108/09574090410700275

Chui, M., Manyika, J., Bughin, J., & Dobbs, R. (2012). *The social economy: unlocking value and productivity through social technologies*. McKinsey Global Institute.

Chukwu, N., Asaolu, T. O., Uwuigbe, O. R., Uwuigbe, U., Umukoro, O. E., Nassar, L., & Alabi, O. (2019). The impact of basic forensic accounting skills on financial reporting credibility among listed firms in Nigeria. *IOP Conference Series. Earth and Environmental Science*, *331*(1), 012041. Advance online publication. doi:10.1088/1755-1315/331/1/012041

Chu, S. C., Chen, H. T., & Gan, C. (2020). Consumers' engagement with corporate social responsibility (CSR) communication in social media: Evidence from China and the United States. *Journal of Business Research*, *110*, 260–271. doi:10.1016/j.jbusres.2020.01.036

Çil, N. (2018). *Finansal Ekonometri*. Der Yayınları.

Clarke, D., & Kinghorn, R. (2018). *Experience Is Everything, PwC*. https://www.pwc.com/us/en/services/consulting/library/consumer-intelligence-series/future-of-customer-experience.html

Clark, S., McGrane, A., Boyle, N., Joksimovic, N., Burke, L., Rock, N., & O' Sullivan, K. (2021). "You're a teacher you're a mother, you're a worker": Gender inequality during COVID-19 in Ireland. *Gender, Work and Organization*, *28*(4), 1352–1362. doi:10.1111/gwao.12611

Clayton, M. M. (2006). Investigative techniques. In A Guide to Forensic Accounting Investigation. John Wiley and Sons.

Coinmarketcap. (2022). *Cryptocurrency prices, charts and market capitalization*. Retrieved from https://coinmarketcap.com/

Collins, S. (2020). *Why the Covid-19 economy is particularly devastating to Millennials, in 14 charts*. Vox.

Comisión Económica para América Latina y el Caribe - CEPAL. (2020). *Sectores y empresas frente al COVID-19: emergencia y reactivación*. Santiago de Chile: CEPAL. https://www.cepal.org/es/publicaciones/45734-sectores-empresas-frente-al-covid-19-emergencia-reactivacion

Comisión Económica para América Latina y el Caribe - CEPAL. (2021). *Estudio Económico de América Latina y el Caribe 2021: dinámica laboral y políticas de empleo para una recuperación sostenible e inclusiva más allá de la crisis del COVID-19.* https://www.cepal.org/es/publicaciones/ee

Confecamaras. (2020a). *Encuesta de las Cámaras de Comercio sobre el Impacto del Covid-19 en las empresas colombianas realizado entre el 30 de marzo al 17 de abril de 2020.* Bogotá D.C. https://www.confecamaras.org.co/noticias/746-encuesta

Confecámaras. (2020b). *Encuesta de las Cámaras de Comercio de Monitoreo del Impacto del COVID-19 en las Empresas, 6 a 23 de octubre.* https://www.incp.org.co/Site/publicaciones/info/archivos/Encuesta-de-las-Camaras-de-Comercio.pdf

Constantinides, E. (2002). The 4S web-marketing mix model. *Electronic Commerce Research and Applications, 1*(1), 57–76. doi:10.1016/S1567-4223(02)00006-6

Constantinides, E. (2004). Influencing the online consumer's behaviour: The Web experience. *Internet Research, 14*(2), 111–126. doi:10.1108/10662240410530835

Constantinides, E. (2006). The marketing mix revisited: Towards the 21st-century marketing. *Journal of Marketing Management, 22*(3-4), 407–438. doi:10.1362/026725706776861190

Cooper, S., Khatib, F., Treuille, A., Barbero, J., Lee, J., Beenen, M., Leaver-Fay, A., Baker, D., & Popović, Z. (2010). Predicting protein structures with a multiplayer online game. *Nature, 466*(7307), 756-760.

Costa, T. (2013). *Contemporary Management - Principles, trends and challenges.* Silabo Editions.

Côté, J. E., & Levine, C. G. (2014). *Identity, formation, agency, and culture: A social psychological synthesis* (1st ed.). Psychology Press. doi:10.4324/9781410612199

Cots, J.M., Alós, J., & Bárcena, M. (2020). *Since January 2020 Elsevier has created a COVID-19 resource centre with free information in English and Mandarin on the novel coronavirus.* Elsevier Connect.

Couch, D., O'Sullivan, B., & Malatzky, C. (2020). What COVID-19 could mean for the future of "work from home": The provocations of three women in the academy. *Gender, Work and Organization, 28*(S1), 266–275. doi:10.1111/gwao.12548

Cousins, S. (2020, September). *The COVID Context series. 1. Reshaping millennials attitudes & spending habits.* National Head of Strategy & Planning, iProspect Australia.

Covid-19 Arama Terimi. (n.d.). https://trends.google.com/trends/explore?date=2019-12-31%20 2022-01-21&geo=TR&q=Covid19

COVID-19 Impacts on Small Businesses. (2020). SANDAG. https://www.sandag.org/uploads/publicationid/publicationid_4689_27781.pdf

Craighead, C. W., Ketchen, D. J. Jr, & Darby, J. L. (2020). Pandemics and Supply Chain Management Research: Toward a Theoretical Toolbox. *Decision Sciences, 51*(4), 838–866. doi:10.1111/deci.12468 PMID:34234384

Crumbley, L. Heitger, E., & Stevenson, S. (2009). *Forensic and Investigative Accounting* (4th ed.). www.amazon.com

Cui, T. H., Ghose, A., Halaburda, H., Iyengar, R., Pauwels, K., Sriram, S., Tucker, C., & Venkataraman, S. (2021). Informational Challenges in Omnichannel Marketing: Remedies and Future Research. *Journal of Marketing, 85*(1), 103–120. doi:10.1177/0022242920968810

Çule, M., & Fulton, M. (2009). Business culture and tax evasion: Why corruption and the unofficial economy can persist. *Journal of Economic Behavior & Organization, 72*(3), 811–822. doi:10.1016/j.jebo.2009.08.005

Cutler, D. (2020). *COVID-19 and its Impact on the Healthcare Economy*. Retrieved from https://healthmanagement.org/c/cardio/news/covid-19-and-its-impact-on-the-healthcare-economy

D'Abate, C. P., Youndt, M. A., & Wenzel, K. (2009). Making the Most of an Internship: An Empirical Study of Internship Satisfaction. *Academy of Management Learning & Education*, *8*(4), 527–539. doi:10.5465/AMLE.2009.47785471

da Silva, A. R., & Gasparotto, A. M. S. (2020). Um estudo sobre rastreabilidade visando ao controle de processos. *Revista Interface Tecnológica*, *17*(1), 708–720. Advance online publication. doi:10.31510/infa.v17i1.796

Dabic, M., González-Loureiro, M., & Harvey, M. (2015). Evolving research on expatriates: What is 'known' after four decades (1970–2012). *International Journal of Human Resource Management*, *26*(3), 316–337. doi:10.1080/09585192.2013.845238

Daff, L. (2021). Employers' perspectives of accounting graduates and their world of work: Software use and ICT competencies. *Accounting Education*, *30*(5), 495–524. doi:10.1080/09639284.2021.1935282

Dahles, H., & Susilowati, T. P. (2015). Business resilience in times of growth and crisis. *Annals of Tourism Research*, *51*, 34–50. doi:10.1016/j.annals.2015.01.002

Das, G., Jain, S. P., Maheswaran, D., Slotegraaf, R. J., & Srinivasan, R. (2021). Pandemics and marketing: Insights, impacts, and research opportunities. *Journal of the Academy of Marketing Science*, *49*(5), 835–854. doi:10.100711747-021-00786-y PMID:33994600

Dauenhauer, J., Heffernan, K., Webber, K., Smoker, K., Caccamise, P., & Granata, A. (2020). Utilization of a forensic accountant to investigate financial exploitation of older adults. *Journal of Adult Protection*, *22*(3), 141–152. doi:10.1108/JAP-01-2020-0001

Daunt, K. L., & Harris, L. C. (2017). Consumer showrooming: Value co-destruction. *Journal of Retailing and Consumer Services*, *38*, 166–176. doi:10.1016/j.jretconser.2017.05.013

David, L. S. (1984). *Forensic Psychologocal Assessment: An Integrative Approach*. Allyn & Bacon. https://www.amazon.com/Forensic-Psychologocal-Assessment-Integrative-Approach/dp/0205125212

Davies, K. (2021). Festival's post COVID-19. *Leisure Sciences*, *43*(1-2), 184–189. doi:10.1080/01490400.2020.1774000

Davies, P. (2000). The relevance of systematic reviews to educational policy and practice. *Oxford Review of Education*, *26*(3-4), 365–378. doi:10.1080/713688543

Davis, F. (1985). *A Technology Acceptance Model for Empirically Testing New End-User Information Systems: Theory and Results*. Massachusetts Institute of Technology.

Davis, H. A. (2003). Conceptualizing the role and influence of student-teacher relationships on children's social and cognitive development. *Educational Psychologist*, *38*(4), 207–234. doi:10.1207/S15326985EP3804_2

Dawei, L., & Jiju, A. (2003). Implications of B2B marketplace to supply chain development. *The TQM Magazine*, *15*(3), 173–179. doi:10.1108/09544780310469271

Dcode. (2020). *Decoding The Economics of Covid-19*. https://dcodeefc.com/infographics

de Bem Machado, A., Secinaro, S., Calandra, D., & Lanzalonga, F. (2021). Knowledge management and digital transformation for Industry 4.0: A structured literature review. *Knowledge Management Research and Practice*, 1–19. doi:10.1080/14778238.2021.2015261

De Clercq, D., & Belausteguigoitia, I. (2020). When does job stress limit organizational citizenship behavior, or not? Personal and contextual resources as buffers. *Journal of Management & Organization*, 1–25. doi:10.1017/jmo.2020.7

De la Hoz, A., Cantillo, J., & Ramírez, A. (2021). Recuperación empresarial en Colombia ante la crisis COVID-19: Una aproximación desde los cambios en política social, laboral e impositiva. *Revista Publicando, 8*(31), 1–14. doi:10.51528/rp.vol8.id2227

de la República de Colombia, C. (2020a). Ley 2069 de 2020 Por medio de la cual se impulsa el emprendimiento en Colombia. *Diario Oficial*. http://www.secretariasenado.gov.co/senado/basedoc/ley_2069_2020.html

de la República de Colombia, C. (2020b). Ley 2068 de 2020 Por el cual se modifica la Ley General de Turismo y se dictan otras disposiciones. *Diario Oficial*. http://www.secretariasenado.gov.co/senado/basedoc/ley_2068_2020.html

De Luca, F., Iaia, L., Mehmood, A., & Vrontis, D. (2022). Can social media improve stakeholder engagement and communication of Sustainable Development Goals? A cross-country analysis. *Technological Forecasting and Social Change, 177*, 121525. doi:10.1016/j.techfore.2022.121525

de Política, C. Económica y Social - CONPES; Departamento Nacional de Planeación - DNP. (2020). *Estrategia de Respuesta Inicial ante los Efectos de la Pandemia del Covid-19 sobre la Salud Pública, los Hogares, el Aparato Productivo y las Finanzas Públicas*. https://colaboracion.dnp.gov.co/CDT/Conpes/Econ%C3%B3micos/3999.pdf

De Stefano, V. (2016). *The rise of the «just-in-time workforce»: On-demand work, crowdwork and labour protection in the «gig-economy»*. International Labour Office.

De Vaus, D. (2014). *Surveys in social research* (M. Bulmer, Ed.; 6th ed.). Routledge.

Debowska, A., Horeczy, B., Boduszek, D., & Dolinski, D. (2020). A repeated cross-sectional survey assessing university students' stress, depression, anxiety, and suicidality in the early stages of the COVID-19 pandemic in Poland. *Psychological Medicine*, 1–4. doi:10.1017/S003329172000392X PMID:33004087

Dechow, P. M., Sloan, R. G., Sweeney, A. P., Sloan, R. G., & Sweeney, A. P. (1995). Detecting Earnings Management. *The Accounting Review, 70*(2), 193–225.

DeFi Pulse. (2022). *Total Value Locked*. Retrieved from https://www.defipulse.com/

Dekkers, R. (2011). Impact of Strategic Decision Making for Outsourcing on Managing Manufacturing. *International Journal of Operations & Production Management, 31*(9), 935–965. doi:10.1108/01443571111165839

Dellarocas, C. (2003). *The digitalization of word-of-mouth: Promise and chalendge of online feedback mechanisms*. MIT Sloan School of Management Working Paper 4296-03.

Deloitte. (2020). *Finalización del estado de emergencia económica, social y ecológica decretado por el Presidente para afrontar la emergencia sanitaria ocasionada por el COVID-19*. https://www2.deloitte.com/co/es/pages/tax/articles/finalizacion-del-estado-de-emergencia-economica-social-y-ecologica.html

Deloitte. (2020). *The future consumer. Series: Omnichannel transformation begins by grasping the key to consumer mentalities*. Deloitte China. https://www2.deloitte.com/content/dam/Deloitte/cn/Documents/consumer-business/deloitte-cn-consumer-omnichannel-transformation-begins-by-grasping-the-key-to-consumer-mentalities-en-200320.pdf

Deloitte. (2021). *Global Powers of Luxury Goods 2021. The new age of fashion and luxury*. https://www2.deloitte.com/content/dam/Deloitte/global/Documents/Consumer-Business/gx-cb-global-powers-of-luxury-goods-2021.pdf

Delpechitre, D., Beeler-Connelly, L. L., & Chaker, N. N. (2018). Customer value co-creation behavior: A dyadic exploration of the influence of salesperson emotional intelligence on customer participation and citizenship behavior. *Journal of Business Research, 92*, 9–24. doi:10.1016/j.jbusres.2018.05.007

Denning, S. (2015a). Updating the Agile Manifesto. *Strategy and Leadership*, *43*(5). Advance online publication. doi:10.1108/SL-07-2015-0058

Departamento Nacional de Estadística - DANE. (2020). *Gran Encuesta Integrada de Hogares.* https://microdatos.dane.gov.co/index.php/catalog/701/datafile/F42/V2408

De, R., Pandey, N., & Pal, A. (2020). Impact of digital surge during COVID-19 pandemic: A viewpint on research and practice. *International Journal of Information Management*, *55*(12), 102171. PMID:32836633

Dervitsiotis, K. N. (2014). *Developing Sustainable Competitive Advantage through Operational Excellence and Adaptation Excellence with Value Innovations.* ResearchGate.

Dheng, C. (2021). Worldwide Impact of COVID-19 Pandemic On Agriculture. *J Agri Sci Food Res*, *12*, 297. doi:10.35248/2593-9173.21.12.297

Dheng, C. (2021). Worldwide Smpact of COVID-19 Pandemic On Agriculture. *Journal of Agriculture Science and Food Research*, *1-2*. Advance online publication. doi:10.35248/25939173.21.12.297

Di Crosta, A., Ceccato, I., Marchetti, D., La Malva, P., Maiella, R., Cannito, L., Cipi, M., Mammarella, N., Palumbo, R., Verrocchio, M. C., Palumbo, R., & Di Domenico, A. (2021). Psychological factors and consumer behavior during the COVID-19 pandemic. *PLoS One*, *16*(8), e0256095. Advance online publication. doi:10.1371/journal.pone.0256095 PMID:34398916

Di Giorgio, E., Di Riso, D., Mioni, G., & Cellini, N. (2020). The interplay between mothers' and children behavioral and psychological factors during COVID-19: An Italian study. *European Child & Adolescent Psychiatry*, *30*(9), 1401–1412. doi:10.100700787-020-01631-3 PMID:32865654

Di Mauro, B. W. (2020). Macroeconomics of the Flue, R. In Economics in the Time of Covid-19 (pp. 31- 35). CEPR Press.

Di Mauro, C., Fratocchi, L., Orzes, G., & Sartor, M. (2018). Offshoring and Backshoring: A Multiple Case Study Analysis. *Journal of Purchasing and Supply Management*, *24*(2), 108–134. doi:10.1016/j.pursup.2017.07.003

Dibrell, C., Davis, P. S., & Craig, J. (2008). Fueling innovation through information technology in SMEs. *Journal of Small Business Management*, *46*(2), 203–218. doi:10.1111/j.1540-627X.2008.00240.x

Dickey, D. A., & Fuller, W. A. (1981). Likelihood ratio statistics for autoregressive time series with a unıt root. *Econometrica*, *49*(4), 1057–1072.

Diebner, R., Silliman, E., Ungerman, K., & Vancauwenberghe, M. (2020). *Adapting customer experience in the time of coronavirus.* McKinsey & Company. https://www.mckinsey.com/business-functions/marketing-and-sales/our-insights/adapting-customer-experience-in-the-time-of-coronavirus

Dieppe, A. (2020). *Global Productivity: Trends, Drivers, and Policies.* World Bank.

Digout, J., Azouri, M., Decaudin, J.-M., & Rochard, S. (2013). Crowdsourcing, outsourcing to obtain a creativity group. *The Arab Economics and Business Journal*, *8*(1-2), 6–15. doi:10.1016/j.aebj.2013.11.001

Dikbas, A., & Scherer, R. (2004). eWork and eBusiness in Architecture, Engineering and Construction. Taylor & Francis.

Dimitrov. (2019). *How Walmart and Others are Riding a Blockchain Wave to Supply Chain Paradise.* Available at https://www.forbes.com/sites/biserdimitrov/2019/12/05/how-walmart-and-others-are-riding-a-blockchain-wave-to-supply-chain-paradise/#b9ee4fd77918

Dimitrova, B. V., Smith, B., & Andras, T. L. (2020). Marketing channel evolution: From contactual efficiency to brand value co-creation and appropriation within the platform enterprise. *Journal of Marketing Channels*, *26*(1), 60–71. doi:10.1080/1046669X.2019.1646187

Dimock, M. (2019). Defining generations: Where Millennials end, and Generation Z begins. *Pew Research Center*, *17*(1), 1–7.

Dirección de Impuestos y Aduanas Nacionales - DIAN. (2021). *Estadísticas de Comercio Exterior.* https://www.dian.gov.co/dian/cifras/Paginas/EstadisticasComEx.aspx

Dixit, S. B., Zirpe, K. G., Kulkarni, A. P., Chaudhry, D., Govil, D., & Mehta, Y. (2020). Current approaches to COVID-19: Therapy and prevention. *Indian Journal of Critical Care Medicine: Peer-Reviewed, Official Publication of Indian Society of Critical Care Medicine*, *24*(9), 838–846. doi:10.5005/jp-journals-10071-23470 PMID:33132570

DocWireNews. (2020). *COVID-19's Economic Effect on The Healthcare Industry.* Retrieved from https://www.docwirenews.com/docwire-pick/covid-19s-economic-effect-on-thehealthcare-industry

Doğan, M. M., & Düzel, B. (2020). Covid- 19 özelinde korku- kaygı düzeyleri. *Turkish Studies*, *15*(4), 739–752.

Dolgui, A., & Jean-Marie, P. (2013). Outsourcing: Definitions and Analysis. *International Journal of Production Research*, *51*(23-24), 6769–6777. doi:10.1080/00207543.2013.855338

Domm, P. (2021). *The economy is on the cusp of a major boom and economists believe it could last.* CNBC. https://www.cnbc.com/2021/04/09/the-economy-is-on-the-cusp-of-a-major-boom-and-economists-believe-it-could-last.html

Donlon, J. P. (1996). Maximizing value in the supply chain. *Chief Executive*, *117*(October), 54–63.

Donthu, N., & Gustafsson, A. (2020). Effects of COVID-19 on business and research. *Journal of Business Research*, *117*(1), 284–289. doi:10.1016/j.jbusres.2020.06.008 PMID:32536736

Dornelas, J. (2014). *Entrepreneurship - Transforming Ideas into Business.* GEN - National Editorial Group. LTC.

Dornyei, Z., & Ottó, I. (1998). Motivation in action: A process model of L2 motivation. In *Working Papers in Applied Linguistics.* Thames Valley University.

Dowell, G. W., Shackell, M. B., & Stuart, N. V. (2011). Boards, CEOs, and surviving a financial crisis: Evidence from the internet shakeout. *Strategic Management Journal*, *32*(10), 1025–1045. doi:10.1002mj.923

Dowling, G. R., & Staelin, R. (1994). A model of perceived risk and intended risk-handling activity. *The Journal of Consumer Research*, *21*(1), 119–134. doi:10.1086/209386

Dua, A., Mahajan, D., Oyer, L., & Ramaswamy, S. (2021). *US small-business recovery after the COVID-19 crisis.* McKinsey & Company. https://www.mckinsey.com/industries/public-and-social-sector/our-insights/us-small-business-recovery-after-the-covid-19-crisis

Dubey, R., & Samar Ali, S. (2013). An exploratory study on logistics competency and firm performance. *International Journal of Logistics Systems and Management*, *14*(2), 179–199. doi:10.1504/IJLSM.2013.051338

Dubey, R., Singh, T., & Tiwari, S. (2012). Supply Chain Innovation is a Key to Superior Firm Performance an Insight from Indian Cement Manufacturing. *International Journal of Innovation Science*, *4*(4), 217–230. doi:10.1260/1757-2223.4.4.217

Dunn, K., & Harness, D. (2018). Communicating corporate social responsibility in a social world: The effects of company-generated and user-generated social media content on CSR attributions and scepticism. *Journal of Marketing Management*, *34*(17-18), 1503–1529. doi:10.1080/0267257X.2018.1536675

Duong, D. (2021). *What's important to know about the new COVID-19 variants?* Academic Press.

Durward, D., Blohm, I., & Leimeister, J. M. (2016). Crowd work. *Business & Information Systems Engineering, 58*(4), 281–286. doi:10.100712599-016-0438-0

Dwivedi, Y. K., Ismagilova, E., Hughes, D. L., Carlson, J., Filieri, R., Jacobson, J., & Wang, Y. (2021). Setting the future of digital and social media marketing research: Perspectives and research propositions. *International Journal of Information Management, 59*, 102168. doi:10.1016/j.ijinfomgt.2020.102168

Dyki, M., Singorahardjo, M., & Cotronei-Baird, V. S. (2020). Preparing graduates with the employability skills for the unknown future: Reflection on assessment practice during COVID-19. *Accounting Research Journal, 34*(2), 229–245. doi:10.1108/ARJ-09-2020-0285

Easton, G. (2010). Critical realism in case study research. *Industrial Marketing Management, 39*(1), 118–128. doi:10.1016/j.indmarman.2008.06.004

EBSI. (2021). *EBSI Architecture explained.* https://ec.europa.eu/digital-building-blocks/wikis/display/CEFDIGITAL/EBSI

ECDC. (2021). *SARS-CoV-2 variants of concern as of 10 February 2022.* https://www.ecdc.europa.eu/en/covid-19/variants-concern

Economic Commission for Latin America and the Caribbean - ECLAC. (2020). *Preliminary Overview of the Economies of Latin America and the Caribbean 2020.* https://repositorio.cepal.org/handle/11362/46504

Economics Observatory. (2021). *What are the long-run economic consequences of pandemics?* https://www.economicsobservatory.com/what-are-long-run-economic-consequences-pandemics

Edwards, A. W., & Cavalli-Sforza, L. L. (1965). A method for cluster analysis. *Biometrics, 21*(2), 362–375. doi:10.2307/2528096 PMID:14338671

Effenberger, M., Kronbichler, A., Shin, J. I., Mayer, G., Tilg, H., & Perco, P. (2020). Association of the COVID-19 pandemic with internet search volumes: A Google TrendsTM analysis. *International Journal of Infectious Diseases, 95*, 192–197. doi:10.1016/j.ijid.2020.04.033 PMID:32305520

Eger, L., Komárková, L., Egerová, D., & Mičík, M. (2021). The effect of COVID-19 on consumer shopping behaviour: Generational cohort perspective. *Journal of Retailing and Consumer Services, 61*, 102542. doi:10.1016/j.jretconser.2021.102542

Egerth, K. (n.d.). *Cash is no longer king in times of Covid-19 – Raining on cash's reign.* Deloitte Perspectives. https://www2.deloitte.com/ch/en/pages/consumer-industrial-products/articles/cash-is-no-longer-king-in-times-of-covid19.html

Ehioghiren, E. E. (2016). Forensic accounting and fraud management: Evidence from nigeria. *Igbinedion University Journal of Accounting, 2*, 245–308.

el Refae, G. A., Kaba, A., & Eletter, S. (2021). Distance learning during COVID-19 pandemic: Satisfaction, opportunities and challenges as perceived by faculty members and students. *Interactive Technology and Smart Education, 18*(3), 298–318. doi:10.1108/ITSE-08-2020-0128

Elbanna, A., & Idowu, A. (2021). Crowdwork as an elevator of human capital. *Scandinavian Journal of Information Systems, 33*(2), 103–136.

Elder, G. H., Johnson, M. K., & Crosnoe, R. (2003). The emergence and development of life course theory. In Handbook of the life course (pp. 3-19). Boston, MA: Springer. doi:10.1007/978-0-306-48247-2_1

Elder, G. H. Jr. (1994). Time, human agency, and social change: Perspectives on the life course. *Social Psychology Quarterly*, *57*(1), 4–15. doi:10.2307/2786971

El-Gohary, H. (2010). E-Marketing-A literature Review from a Small Businesses perspective. *International Journal of Business and Social Science, 1*(1).

Elleby, C., Domínguez, I. P., Adenauer, M., & Genovese, G. (2020). Impacts of the COVID-19 Pandemic on the Global Agricultural Markets. *Environmental and Resource Economics*, *76*(4), 1067–1079. doi:10.100710640-020-00473-6 PMID:32836856

Ellen Macarthur Foundation. (n.d.). *How policymakers can pave the way to a low-carbon and prosperous future*. https://ellenmacarthurfoundation.org/covid-policymakers

Ellyatt, H. (2021). *Supply chain chaos is already hitting global growth. And it's about to get worse*. CNBC. https://www.cnbc.com/2021/10/18/supply-chain-chaos-is-hitting-global-growth-and-could-get-worse.html

Elmashhara, M. G., & Soares, A. M. (2019). The impact of entertainment and social interaction with salespeople on mall shopper satisfaction: The mediating role of emotional states. *International Journal of Retail & Distribution Management*, *47*(2), 94–110. doi:10.1108/IJRDM-06-2018-0112

ElMassah, S., & Mohieldin, M. (2020). Digital transformation and localizing the Sustainable Development Goals (SDGs). *Ecological Economics*, *169*, 106490. doi:10.1016/j.ecolecon.2019.106490

Enderwick, P. & Buckley, P. (2020). Rising Regionalization: will the post-covid-19 world see a retreat from globalization. *Transnational Corporations, 27*(2).

Engidaw, A. E. (2022). Small businesses and their challenges during COVID-19 pandemic in developing countries: In the case of Ethiopia. *Journal of Innovation and Entrepreneurship*, *11*(1). https://doi.org/10.1186/s13731-021-00191-3

Erol, A. (2021). Dijitalleşme çağında işyerinin değişimi: Sebepleri ve sonuçları. *İnsan & İnsan*, *8*(30), 97-113.

Esmark, C. L., & Noble, S. M. (2016). Retail space invaders: When employees' invasion of customer space increases purchase intentions. *Journal of the Academy of Marketing Science*, *46*(3), 1–20.

Esselman, F., & Brink, A. (2016, July). Corporate Digital Responsibility. Den digitalen Wandel von Unternehmen und Gesellschaft erfolgreich gestalten. *Spectrum (Lexington, Ky.)*, 38–41. https://eref.uni-bayreuth.de/60860/

Esses, D., Csete, M. S., & Németh, B. (2021). Sustainability and digital transformation in the visegrad group of central European countries. *Sustainability*, *13*(11), 5833. doi:10.3390u13115833

Essilor. (2022). *Essilor Group*. https://www.linkedin.com/company/essilor/

EssilorLuxottica. (2021). *Sustainability*. Retrieved from https://www.essilorluxottica.com/sustainability

Etheridge, B., & Spantig, L. (2020). *The gender gap in mental well-being during the Covid-19 outbreak: evidence from the UK* (No. 2020-08). ISER Working paper series.

Et-touile, H., & Arib, F. (2021). Impacts of COVID-19 pandemic on agriculture, food prices, and food security in Morocco. *International Journal of Financial Accountability, Economics, Management, and Auditing*, *3*(5), 973–988. doi:10.52502/ijfaema.v3i5.179

European Commission. (2016). *EU Action plan for a Circular Economy*. https://slideplayer.com/slide/17242831/

European Commission. (2020). *Telework in the EU before and after the COVID-19: where we were, where we head to.* European Union- JRC120945. Online available at: https://ec.europa.eu/jrc/sites/default/files/jrc120945_policy_brief_-_covid_and_telework_final.pdf

European Commission. (2020a). *A New Industrial Strategy for a globally competitive, green, and digital Europe.* https://ec.europa.eu/commission/presscorner/detail/en/fs_20_425

European Commission. (2020b). *A New Circular Economy Action Plan for a cleaner and more competitive Europe.* https://eur-lex.europa.eu/legal-content/EN/TXT/?qid=1583933814386&uri=COM:2020:98:FIN

European Commission. (2021). *Commission's new consumer survey shows impact of COVID-19 and popularity of 'greener' choices.* https://ec.europa.eu/commission/presscorner/detail/cs/ip_21_1104

European Commission. (2021). *The EU's 2021-2027 long-term budget & Next Generation EU: Facts and figures.* https://data.europa.eu/doi/10.2761/808559

European Commission. (n.d.). *Recovery plan for Europe.* https://ec.europa.eu/info/strategy/recovery-plan-europe_en

Ewerhard, A.-C., Sisovsky, K., & Johansson, U. (2019). Consumer decision-making of slow moving consumer goods in the age of multi-channels. *International Review of Retail, Distribution and Consumer Research, 29*(1), 1–22. doi:10.1080/09593969.2018.1537191

EY & Mitchell, S. (2020). *How entrepreneurs survive and thrive in a crisis.* EY. https://www.ey.com/en_gl/weoy/how-entrepreneurs-survive-and-thrive-in-a-crisis

Fabeil, F. N., Pazim, H. K., & Langgat, J. (2020). The Impact of Covid-19 Pandemic Crisis on Micro-Enterprises: Entrepreneurs' Perspective on Business Continuity and Recovery Strategy, The Asian Institute of Research. *Journal of Economics and Business, 3*(2), 837–844. doi:10.31014/aior.1992.03.02.241

Fachini, M. P., Mesquita, N. P., Oliveria, R. P., & França, P. G. de (2017). Internet das coisas: uma breve revisão bibliográfica. *Conexões, ciência e tecnologia, 11*(6), 85-90. . doi:10.21439/conexoes.v11i6.1007

Fairlie, R. W. (2020). *The Impact of Covid-19 on Small Business Owners: Evidence of Early-Stage Losses from the April 2020 Current Population Survey.* NBER. https://www.nber.org/papers/w27309

Fama, E. F. (1995). Random walks in stock market prices. *Financial Analysts Journal, 51*(1), 75–80. doi:10.2469/faj.v51.n1.1861

Fang, F., Wang, T., Tan, S., Chen, S., Zhou, T., Zhng, W., Guo, Q., Liu, J., Holme, P., & Lu, X. (2022). Newtwok structure and community evolution online: Behavioral and emotional changes in response to COVID-19. *Frontiers in Public Health, 9*(1), 8133234. PMID:35087790

Farrer, M. (2021). *Global supply chain crisis could last another two years, warn experts.* The Guardian. https://www.theguardian.com/business/2021/dec/18/global-supply-chain-crisis-could-last-another-two-years-warn-experts

Federal Reserve. (2020). *Federal Reserve issues FOMC statement.* https://www.federalreserve.gov/newsevents/pressreleases/monetary20200315a.htm

Fedianin, V. (2021). Combating COVID-19 and Vaccination as Elements of the United Arab Emirates Foreign Policy. *Scientific and Theoretical Almanac Grani, 24*(6), 155–162. doi:10.15421/172171

Fedulova, L., & Petroye, O. (2021). Innovative and technological factor of economic development during the COVID-19 pandemic and recommendations for the future (policy paper*). Collection of Scientific Works of the National Academy of Public Administration under the President of Ukraine,* (1), 128-143.

Feld, L. P., & Frey, B. S. (2011). Tax Compliance as the Result of a Psychological Tax Contract: The Role of Incentives and Responsive Regulation. SSRN *Electronic Journal, 287*. doi:10.2139/ssrn.900366

Feldman, E. (2021). Virtual Internships During the COVID-19 Pandemic and Beyond. *New Horizons in Adult Education and Human Resource Development*, *33*(2), 46–51. https://doi.org/10.1002/nha3.20314

Feldmann, A., Gasser, O., Lichtblau, F., Pujol, E., Poese, I., Dietzel, C., & Smaragdakis, G. (2021, March). Implications of the COVID-19 Pandemic on the Internet Traffic. In *Broadband Coverage in Germany; 15th ITG-Symposium* (1-5). VDE.

Fenitra, R. M., Abbas, A., Ekowati, D., & Suhairidi, F. (2022). Strategic Intent and Strategic Leadership: A Review Perspective for Post-covid Tourism and Hospitality Industry Recovery. In *The Emerald Handbook of Destination Recovery*. Emerald Group Publishing.

Fenitra, R. M., Anggun, P., Eko, S., & Indrianawati, U. (2021). Factors Influencing Preventive Intention Behavior Towards COVID-19 in Indonesia. *The Journal of Behavioral Science*, *16*(1), 14–27.

Fergurson, J. R. (2020). The paradox of diminishing returns: Measurement and metrics for valuation of B2C sales professionals. *Journal of Marketing Channels*, *26*(2), 141–146. doi:10.1080/1046669X.2020.1747280

Fernandes, K., Chaudhuri, A., Shukla, M., & Xiong, Y. (2020). *Covid19 Impact on Supply Chains: Scotland*. doi:10.13140/RG.2.2.24573.51685/1

Fernandes, T., & Remelhe, P. (2016). How to engage customers in co-creation: Customers' motivations for collaborative innovation. *Journal of Strategic Marketing*, *24*(3-4), 311–326. doi:10.1080/0965254X.2015.1095220

Fernández, C. (2018, Nov). *Informalidad empresarial en Colombia*. Working Paper Fedesarrollo, 76. https://www.repository.fedesarrollo.org.co/bitstream/handle/11445/3698/WP_2018_No_76.pdf?sequence=1&isAllowed=y#:~:text=Existen%20pocas%20fuentes%20para%20estimar,agregado%2C%20en%20las%20%C3%A1reas%20urbanas

Fernández, N. V., Pérez, M. J. S., & Vázquez-Casielles, R. (2018). Webroomers versus showroomers: Are they the same? *Journal of Business Research*, *92*, 300–320. doi:10.1016/j.jbusres.2018.08.004

Ferreira, C. M. S., Oliveira, R. A. R., Silva, J. S., & Cunha Cavalcanti, C. F. M. D. (2020). Blockchain for machine-to-machine interaction in industry 4.0. In R. Rosa Righi, A. Alberti, & M. Singh (Eds.), *Blockchain Technology for Industry 4.0. Blockchain Technologies*. Springer. doi:10.1007/978-981-15-1137-0_5

Fetzer, T., Witte, M., Hensel, L., Jachimowicz, J., Haushofer, J., Ivchenko, A., . . . Fiorin, S. (2020). Perceptions of an insufficient government response at the onset of the COVID-19 pandemic are associated with lower mental well-being. *Pre Print* Doi.10.31234/ doi:osf.io/3kfmh

Figueroa-Armijos, M., & da Motta Veiga, S. (2019, January). Predictors of early-career self-employment among millennials in the digital economy: The role of the Great Recession. *Proceedings of the 52nd Hawaii International Conference on System Sciences*. 10.24251/HICSS.2019.546

Figueroa, C., Castillo, E. G., Norquist, G., Wells, K. B., Griffith, K., Kadkhoda, F., Jones, F., Shorter, P., & Bromley, E. (2018). A Window of Opportunity: Visions and Strategies for Behavioral Health Policy Innovation. *Ethnicity & Disease*, *28*(Suppl 2), 407–416. doi:10.18865/ed.28.S2.407 PMID:30202194

Filimonau, V. (2021). The Prospects of Waste Management in The Hospitality Sector Post Covid-19. *Resources, Conservation and Recycling*, *168*, 168. doi:10.1016/j.resconrec.2020.105272

FINDETER. (2020). *COVID-19, Coyuntura Económica y Medidas de Mitigación*. Dirección de Estudios Económicos. Informe Sectorial. https://repositorio.findeter.gov.co/handle/123456789/9613

Finfgeld-Connett, D. (2014). Use of content analysis to conduct knowledge-building and theory-generating qualitative systematic reviews. *Qualitative Research*, *14*(3), 341–352. doi:10.1177/1468794113481790

FINRA. (2021, February). Investing 2020: New Accounts and the People Who Opened Them. In *Consumer Insights: Money & Investing*. FINRA Investor Education Foundation. https://www.finrafoundation.org/sites/finra foundation/ files/investing-2020-new-accounts-and-the-people-who-opened-them_1_0.pdf

Fishbein, M., & Ajzen, I. (1975). *Belief, Attitude, Intention, and Behavior: An Introduction to Theory and Research*. Addison-Wesley.

Fisher, J., Languilaire, J. C., Lawthom, R., Nieuwenhuis, R., Petts, R. J., Runswick-Cole, K., & Yerkes, M. A. (2020). Community, work, and family in times of COVID-19. *Community Work & Family*, *23*(3), 247–252. doi:10.1080/13668803.2020.1756568

Fitriasari, F. (2020) How do Small and Medium-sized Enterprises (SME) survive the COVID-19 outbreak? J. *Inov. Ekon.*

Fitriyani, I., Sudiyarti, N., & Fietroh, N. M. (2020). Strategi Management Bisnis Pasca Pandemi Covid-19. *Indonesian Journal of Social Sciences and Humanities*, *1*(2), 87–95.

Fitsilis, P., Tsoutsa, P., & Gerogiannis, V. (2018). Industry 4.0: Required personnel competences. *Industry 4.0, 3*(3), 130-133.

Flick, U. (2005). *Qualitative Methods in Scientific Research*. Monitor - Projetos e Edições, Lda.

Flick, U. (2014). An Introduction to Qualitative Research. *Sage (Atlanta, Ga.)*.

Florida, R., Rodríguez-Pose, A., & Storper, M. (2021). Cities in a post-COVID world. *Urban Studies*.

Fokus, U. A. (2020, April 26). *Rebellion against quarantine. Farmers close the bridge near Kherson due to market closure*. https://focus.ua/ukraine/454415-bunt_protiv_karantina_pod_khersonom_fermery_perekryli_most_iz-za_zakrytiia_rynka

Fondo Nacional de Garantías - FNG. (n.d.). *Programa de Garantía Especial: Unidos por Colombia*. https://www.fng.gov.co/ES/Paginas/Unidos_por_Colombia_FNG.aspx

Fonseca L., & Azevedo A.L., (2020) *Covid-19 and Global Supply Chains. Marketing Management: Challenges for the Knowledge Society*. Academic Press.

Forrester, J. W. (1958). Industrial dynamics: A major breakthrough for decision makers. *Harvard Business Review*, (July/August), 37–66.

Fortin, M. (2009). *Fundamentals and Stages of the Investigation Process*. Lusodidact.

Fortune. (2020). *94% of the Fortune 1000 are seeing coronavirus supply chain disruptions: Report*. https://fortune.com/2020/02/21/fortune-1000-coronavirus-china-supply-chain-impact/

Fortune. (2020). *Coronavirus impact: 94% of the Fortune 1000 are seeing supply chain disruptions*. https://fortune.com/2020/02/21/fortune-1000- coronavirus-china-supply-chain-impact/

Frasquet, M., & Miquel, M. J. (2017). Do channel integration efforts pay-off in terms of online and offline customer loyalty? *International Journal of Retail & Distribution Management*, *45*(7–8), 859–873. doi:10.1108/IJRDM-10-2016-0175

Frecknall-Hughes, J., & Kirchler, E. (2015). Towards a General Theory of Tax Practice. *Social & Legal Studies*, *24*(2), 289–312. doi:10.1177/0964663915571787

Fredricks, A. J., & Dossett, D. L. (1983). Attitude–behavior relations: A comparison of the Fishbein-Ajzen and the Bentler-Speckart models. *Journal of Personality and Social Psychology*, *45*(3), 501–512. doi:10.1037/0022-3514.45.3.501

Frumuşanu, N. M., Marin, A. M., & Martin, M. (2020). *The impact of COVID-19 pandemic on the activity of the professional accountant*. Academic Press.

Fügener, A., Grahl, J., Gupta, A., and Ketter, W. (2021). Will Humans-in-the-Loop Become Borgs? Merits and Pitfalls of Working with AI. *Management Information Systems Quarterly (MISQ), 45*(b), 1527-1556.

Fulweiler, R., Davies, S., Biddle, J., Burgin, A., Cooperdock, E., Hanley, T., Kenkel, C., Marcarelli, A., Matassa, C., Mayo, T., Santiago-Vàzquez, L., Traylor-Knowles, N., & Ziegler, M. (2021). Rebuild the Academy: Supporting academic mothers during COVID-19 and beyond. *PLoS Biology, 19*(3), e3001100. doi:10.1371/journal.pbio.3001100 PMID:33690708

Fu, X. L., Zhang, J., & Wang, L. M. (2020). Introduction to the special section : the impact of Covid-19 and post-pandemic recovery : China and the world economy. *Journal of Chinese Economic and Business Studies, 18*(4), 311–320. doi:10.1080/14765284.2020.1855939

Galati, A., Sakka, G., Crescimanno, M., Tulone, A., & Fiore, M. (2019). What is the role of social media in several overtones of CSR communication? The case of the wine industry in the Southern Italian regions. *British Food Journal, 121*(4), 856–873. doi:10.1108/BFJ-07-2018-0437

Galbiati, R., Henry, E., Jacquemet, N., & Lobeck, M. (2021). How laws affect the perception of norms: Empirical evidence from the lockdown. *PLoS One, 16*(9), e0256624. doi:10.1371/journal.pone.0256624 PMID:34559821

Galbreath, J. (2011). Are there gender-related influences on corporate sustainability? A study of women on boards of directors. *Journal of Management & Organization, 17*(1), 17–38. doi:10.5172/jmo.2011.17.1.17

Gallo Marin, B., Aghagoli, G., Lavine, K., Yang, L., Siff, E. J., Chiang, S. S., ... Aung, S. N. (2021). Predictors of COVID-19 severity: A literature review. *Reviews in Medical Virology, 31*(1), 1–10. doi:10.1002/rmv.2146 PMID:32845042

Gallup. (2020, October). *The Relationship Between Engagement at Work and Organizational Outcomes.* Gallup. https://www.gallup.com/workplace/321032/employee-engagement-meta-analysisbrief.aspx

Gardetti, M. A. (2016). Loewe: Luxury and sustainable management. Handbook of Sustainable Luxury Textiles and Fashion, 2, 1–16.

Gardetti, M. A. (2017). *Sustainable management of luxury. Springer book series on environmental footprints and eco-design of products and processes.* Springer.

Garfin, D. R., Silver, R. C., & Holman, E. A. (2020). The novel coronavirus (Covid- 2019) outbreak: Amplification health consequences by media exposure. *Health Psychology, 39*(5), 355–357.

Gartenberg, C., & Pierce, L. (2017). Subprime governance: Agency costs in vertically integrated banks and the 2008 mortgage crisis. *Strategic Management Journal, 38*(2), 300–321. doi:10.1002mj.2481

Gaur, A., & Kumar, M. (2018). A systematic approach to conducting review studies: An assessment of content analysis in 25 years of IB research. *Journal of World Business, 53*(2), 280–289. doi:10.1016/j.jwb.2017.11.003

Gauri, D. K., Jindal, R. P., Ratchford, B., Fox, E., Bhatnagar, A., Pandey, A., Navallo, R. J., Fogarty, J., Carr, S., & Hwerton, E. (2021). Evolution of retail formats: Past, present, and future. *Journal of Retailing, 97*(1), 42–61. doi:10.1016/j.jretai.2020.11.002

Gavrilyuk, O. (2021). Pandemic crisis as a catalyst for digitalization of the tourism industry. *Collection of Scientific Works of Cherkasy State Technological University*, (60), 22–29.

Gbegi, D. O., & Adebisi, J. F. (2014). Forensic Accounting Skills and Techniques in Fraud Investigation in the Nigerian Public Sector. *Mediterranean Journal of Social Sciences, 5*(3), 243–252. doi:10.5901/mjss.2014.v5n3p243

Geiko, T. Yu. (2020). Priorities for the development of entrepreneurship in Ukraine in the context of the COVID-19 pandemic and in the post-quarantine period. Bulletin of Socio-Economic Research, (2), 73.

Gerald, E., Obianuju, A., & Chukwunonso, N. (2020). Strategic agility and performance of small and medium enterprises in the phase of Covid-19 pandemic. *International Journal of Financial, Accounting, and Management*, *2*(1), 41–50. doi:10.35912/ijfam.v2i1.163

Getzels, J. W., & Guba, E. G. (1957). Social behavior and the administrative process. *The School Review*, *65*(4), 423–441. doi:10.1086/442411

Gharakhani, D. R. K. M., & Hamidi, N. (2012). Impact of Supply Chain Management on innovation and organizational performance in Iranian. *African Journal of Business Management*, *6*(19), 5939–5949. doi:10.5897/AJBM11.1136

Gharzai, L. A., Beeler, W. H., & Jagsi, R. (2020). Playing into stereotypes: Engaging Millennials and Generation Z in the COVID-19 pandemic response. *Advances in Radiation Oncology*, *5*(4), 679–681. doi:10.1016/j.adro.2020.04.009 PMID:32363242

Ghezi, A., Gabelloni, D., Martini, A., & Natalicchio, A. (2017). Crowdsourcing: A review and suggestions for future research. *International Journal of Management Reviews.*

Giacomarra, M., Crescimanno, M., Sakka, G., & Galati, A. (2019). Stakeholder engagement toward value co-creation in the F&B packaging industry. *EuroMed Journal of Business*, *15*(3), 315–331. doi:10.1108/EMJB-06-2019-0077

Giannikas, V., Woodall, P., McFarlane, D., & Lu, W. (2017). *The Impact of B2C commerce on Traditional B2B Warehousing*. Academic Press.

Gidycz, C. A., Orchowski, L. M., & Berkowitz, A. D. (2011). Preventing sexual aggression among college men: An evaluation of a social norms and bystander intervention program. *Violence Against Women*, *17*(6), 720–742. doi:10.1177/1077801211409727 PMID:21571742

Gielens, K., Gijsbrechts, E., & Geyskens, I. (2021). Navigating the Last Mile: The Demand Effects of Click-and-Collect Order Fulfillment. *Journal of Marketing*, *85*(4), 158–178. doi:10.1177/0022242920960430

Gilley, K. M., & Rasheed, A. (2000). Making More by Doing Less: An Analysis of Outsourcing and Its Effects on Firm Performance. *Journal of Management*, *26*(4), 763–790. doi:10.1177/014920630002600408

Gillis, G. (2021). *How gamification could fill the corporate learning gap created by COVID-19.* theHRDIRECTOR. https://www.thehrdirector.com/features/learning-development/gamification-fill-corporate-learning-gap-created-covid-19/

Gill, P., Stewart, K., Treasure, E., & Chadwick, B. (2008). Methods of data collection in qualitative research: Interviews and focus groups. *British Dental Journal*, *204*(6), 291–295. doi:10.1038/bdj.2008.192 PMID:18356873

Giorgi, A. (2020). *Psychology as a human science: A phenomenologically based approach* (2nd ed.). University Professors Press.

Global Health Observatory Data Repository. (2014). *World Health Organization.* Available from: https://apps.who.int/gho/data/node.main?lang=en

GlobalWebIndex. (2019). *The era of we: online community*. https://www.gwi.com/reports/online-communities-reddit

Gohil, D., & Thakker, S. V. (2021). Blockchain-integrated technologies for solving supply chain challenges. *Modern Supply Chain Research and Applications*, *3*(2), 78–97. doi:10.1108/MSCRA-10-2020-0028

Goodell, J., & Goutte, S. (2021). Co-movement of COVID-19 and Bitcoin: Evidence from wavelet coherence analysis. *Finance Research Letters*, *38*, 1–6. doi:10.1016/j.frl.2020.101625

Goodfellow, J. (2016). *Boots launches IBM-powered Sales Assist app, laying down the foundations of its omnichannel strategy.* https://www.thedrum.com/news/2016/06/22/boots-launches-ibm-powered-sales-assist-app-laying-down-foundations-its-omnichannel

Google Ngrams Viewer. (n.d.). https://books.google.com/ngrams

Google Trends. (n.d.). https://trends.google.com

Goosen, L. (2015). Educational Technologies for an ICT4D MOOC in the 21st Century. In D. Nwaozuzu, & S. Mnisi (Ed.), *Proceedings of the South Africa International Conference on Educational Technologies* (pp. 37 - 48). African Academic Research Forum.

Goosen, L. (2018a). Sustainable and Inclusive Quality Education Through Research Informed Practice on Information and Communication Technologies in Education. In L. Webb (Ed.), *Proceedings of the 26th Conference of the Southern African Association for Research in Mathematics, Science and Technology Education (SAARMSTE)* (pp. 215 - 228). University of Botswana.

Goosen, L., & Mukasa-Lwanga, T. (2017). Educational Technologies in Distance Education: Beyond the Horizon with Qualitative Perspectives. *Proceedings of the South Africa International Conference on Educational Technologies* (pp. 41-54). African Academic Research Forum.

Goosen, L. (2004). *Criteria and Guidelines for the Selection and Implementation of a First Programming Language in High Schools.* Campus: North West University. Retrieved from http://hdl.handle.net/10394/226

Goosen, L. (2018b). Trans-Disciplinary Approaches to Action Research for e-Schools, Community Engagement, and ICT4D. In T. A. Mapotse (Ed.), *Cross-Disciplinary Approaches to Action Research and Action Learning* (pp. 97–110). IGI Global. doi:10.4018/978-1-5225-2642-1.ch006

Goosen, L. (2018c). Ethical Data Management and Research Integrity in the Context of e-Schools and Community Engagement. In C. Sibinga (Ed.), *Ensuring Research Integrity and the Ethical Management of Data* (pp. 14–45). IGI Global. doi:10.4018/978-1-5225-2730-5.ch002

Goosen, L. (2018d). Ethical Information and Communication Technologies for Development Solutions: Research Integrity for Massive Open Online Courses. In C. Sibinga (Ed.), *Ensuring Research Integrity and the Ethical Management of Data* (pp. 155–173). IGI Global. doi:10.4018/978-1-5225-2730-5.ch009

Goosen, L. (2019a). Research on Technology-Supported Teaching and Learning for Autism. In L. Makewa, B. Ngussa, & J. Kuboja (Eds.), *Technology-Supported Teaching and Research Methods for Educators* (pp. 88–110). IGI Global. doi:10.4018/978-1-5225-5915-3.ch005

Goosen, L. (2019b). Technology-Supported Teaching and Research Methods for Educators: Case Study of a Massive Open Online Course. In L. Makewa, B. Ngussa, & J. Kuboja (Eds.), *Technology-Supported Teaching and Research Methods for Educators* (pp. 128–148). IGI Global. doi:10.4018/978-1-5225-5915-3.ch007

Goosen, L. (2021). Organizational Knowledge and Administration Lessons from an ICT4D MOOC. In M. Khosrow-Pour (Ed.), *Encyclopedia of Organizational Knowledge, Administration, and Technologies* (pp. 245–261). IGI Global. doi:10.4018/978-1-7998-3473-1.ch020

Goosen, L., & Naidoo, L. (2014). Computer Lecturers Using Their Institutional LMS for ICT Education in the Cyber World. *Proceedings of the 43rd Conference of the Southern African Computer Lecturers' Association* (pp. 99-108). Nelson Mandela Metropolitan University.

Gopinath, G. (2020). *The great lockdown: Worst economic downturn since the great depression*. International Monetary Fund. https://blogs.imf.org/2020/04/14/the-great-lockdown-worsteconomic-downturn-since-the-great-depression/

Gorbachev, M. (2021). *Yak vplyne koronavirus na rozvytok ahrosektoru v Ukraini* [How will the coronavirus affect the development of the agricultural sector in Ukraine]. https://adler.com.ua/news/yak-vpline-koronavirus-na-rozvitok-agrosektoru-v-ukrajini

Görmüş, A. (2020). Social distancing way of working during the COVID-19 pandemic period: Teleworking. *Turkish Studies*, *15*(4), 481–496.

Gossling, ¨. S., Scott, D., & Hall, C. M. (2020). Pandemics, tourism and global change: A rapid assessment of COVID-19. *Journal of Sustainable Tourism*, *29*(1), 1–20. doi:10.1080/09669582.2020.1758708

Govindan, K., Mina, H., & Alavi, B. (2020). A decision support system for demand management in healthcare supply chains considering the epidemic outbreaks: A case study of coronavirus disease 2019 (COVID-19). *Transportation Research Part E, Logistics and Transportation Review*, *138*, 101967. doi:10.1016/j.tre.2020.101967 PMID:32382249

Graber, M. A., & Graber, A. (2013). Internet-based crowdsourcing and research ethics: The case for IRB review. *Journal of Medical Ethics, 39*(2), 115-118.

Gragnolati, M., Lindelow, M., & Couttolenc, B. (2013). *Twenty years of health system reform in Brazil: an assessment of the sistema unico de saude*. World Bank. doi:10.1596/978-0-8213-9843-2

Greene, C. L. (2016). *Entrepreneurship: Ideas in Action* (6th ed.). Cengage Learning.

Grewal, D., Gauri, D. K., Roggeveen, A. L., & Sethuraman, R. (2021). Strategizing retailing in the new technology era. *Journal of Retailing*, *97*(1), 6–12. doi:10.1016/j.jretai.2021.02.004

Grewal, D., Noble, S. M., Roggeveen, A. L., & Nordfalt, J. (2020). The future of in-store technology. *Journal of the Academy of Marketing Science*, *48*(1), 96–113. doi:10.100711747-019-00697-z

Grewal, D., Roggeveen, A. L., Nordfält, J., & Roggeveen, L. (2017). The Future of Retailing. *Journal of Retailing*, *93*(1), 1–6. doi:10.1016/j.jretai.2016.12.008

Grider, D., Maximo, M., & Zhao, M. (2022). Grayscale Research – The Postmodern Portfolio. *Crypto Allocation Thesis.* Retrieved from https://grayscale.com/

Griffee, D. T. (2005). Research Tips: Interview Data Collection. *Journal of Developmental Education*, *28*(3), 36–37.

Grover, V., Cheon, M. J., & Teng, J. T. C. (1996). The Effect of Service Quality and Partnership on the Outsourcing of Information Systems Functions. *Journal of Management Information Systems*, *12*(4), 89–116. doi:10.1080/07421222.1996.11518102

Groza, M. D., & Groza, M. P. (2018). Salesperson regulatory knowledge and sales performance. *Journal of Business Research*, *89*, 37–46. doi:10.1016/j.jbusres.2018.04.005

Gubler, D. A., Makowski, L. M., Troche, S. J., & Schlegel, K. (2021). Loneliness and well-being during the Covid-19 pandemic: Associations with personality and emotion regulation. *Journal of Happiness Studies*, *22*(5), 2323–2342. doi:10.100710902-020-00326-5 PMID:33100896

Guerra, I. (2006). *Qualitative Research and Content Analysis: Meaning and forms of use*. Principia Editora, Lda.

Guha, A., Grewal, D., Kopalle, P. K., Haenlein, M., Schneider, M. J., Jung, H., Moustafa, R., Hegde, D. R., & Hawkins, G. (2021). How artificial intelligence will affect the future of retailing. *Journal of Retailing*, *97*(1), 28–41. doi:10.1016/j.jretai.2021.01.005

Gülhan, Ü. (2020). Covid-19 Pandemisine BIST 100 reaksiyonu: Ekonometrik bir analiz. *Electronic Turkish Studies, 15*(4), 497–509.

Gunasekaran, A., Irani, Z., Choy, K.-L., Filippi, L., & Papadopoulos, T. (2015). Performance Measures and Metrics in Outsourcing Decisions: A Review for Research and Applications. *International Journal of Production Economics, 161*, 153–166. doi:10.1016/j.ijpe.2014.12.021

Günsoy, B., & Yıldız, Ü. (2021). Türkiye için Covid- 19 pandemisi ile döviz kuru arasındaki frekans alan nedensellik analizi. *International Conference on Economics Turkish Economic Association.*

Gupta, S., & Ramachandran, D. (2021). Emerging Market Retail: Transitioning from a Product-Centric to a Customer-Centric Approach. *Journal of Retailing, 97*(4), 597–620. doi:10.1016/j.jretai.2021.01.008

Gupta, V., He, B., & Sethi, S. P. (2015). Contingent Sourcing Under Supply Disruption and Competition. *International Journal of Production Research, 53*(10), 3006–3027. doi:10.1080/00207543.2014.965351

Gupta, V., & Ivanov, D. (2019). Dual Sourcing under Supply disruption with risk-averse suppliers in the shoring economy. *International Journal of Production Research, 58*(1), 291–307. doi:10.1080/00207543.2019.1686189

Gursky, V. R. (2021). *Problems and consequences of migration of highly qualified specialists in the context of COVID-19.* National Aviation University.

Guthrie, C., Fosso-Wamba, S., & Arnaud, J. B. (2021). Online consumer resilience during a pandemic: An exploratory study of e-commerce behaviour before, during and after a COVID-19 lockdown. *Journal of Retailing and Consumer Services, 61*, 102570. doi:10.1016/j.jretconser.2021.102570

Guy, B., & Arthur, B. (2020). Academic motherhood during COVID-19: Navigating our dual roles as educators and mothers. *Gender, Work and Organization, 27*(5), 887–899. doi:10.1111/gwao.12493 PMID:32837022

Gylling, M., Heikkilä, J., Jussila, K., & Saarinen, M. (2015). Making Decisions on Offshore Outsourcing and Backshoring: A Case Study in the Bicycle Industry. *International Journal of Production Economics, 162*, 92–100. doi:10.1016/j.ijpe.2015.01.006

Habibi, M. R., Laroche, M., & Richard, M. O. (2014). The roles of brand community and community engagement in building brand trust on social media. *Computers in Human Behavior, 37*, 152–161. doi:10.1016/j.chb.2014.04.016

Hadi, S. (2020). New perspective on the resilience of SMEs proactive, adaptive, reactive from business turbulence: A systematic review. *J Xi'an Univ Arch Technol, 12*, 1265–1275.

Hadi, S., & Supardi. (2020). Revitalization Strategy for Small and Medium Enterprises After Corona Virus Disease Pandemic (Covid-19) in Yogyakarta. *Journal of Xi'an University of Architecture & Technology, 8*(4).

Hadi, S., & Supardi, S. (2020). Revitalization strategy for small and medium enterprises after Corona virus disease pandemic (covid-19) in Yogyakarta. *J. Xian Univ. Archit. Technol, 12*, 4068–4076.

Haider Syed, M., Khan, S., Raza Rabbani, M., & Thalassinos, Y.E. (2020). *An artificial intelligence and NLP based Islamic FinTech model combining Zakat and Qardh-Al-Hasan for countering the adverse impact of COVID 19 on SMEs and individuals.* Academic Press.

Hajli, M. N. (2015). A study of the impact of social media on consumers. *International Journal of Market Research, 56*(3), 387–404. doi:10.2501/IJMR-2014-025

Hald, K. S., & Coslugeanu, P. (2021). *The preliminary supply chain lessons of the COVID-19 disruption—What is the role of digital technologies?* Operations Management Research. doi:10.100712063-021-00207-x

Hale, T., Petherick, A., Phillips, T., & Webster, S. (2020). Variation in government responses to COVID-19. *Blavatnik School of Government Working Paper, 3*(11).

Hall, A. K., Nousiainen, M. T., Campisi, P., Dagnone, J. D., Frank, J. R., Kroeker, K. I., Brzezina, S., Purdy, E., & Oswald, A. (2020). Training disrupted: Practical tips for supporting competency-based medical education during the COVID-19 pandemic. *Medical Teacher, 42*(7), 756–761. doi:10.1080/0142159X.2020.1766669 PMID:32450049

Halson, S. L., & Lastella, M. (2017). Amazing athletes with ordinary habits: Why is changing behavior so difficult? *International Journal of Sports Physiology and Performance, 12*(10), 1273–1275. doi:10.1123/ijspp.2017-0632 PMID:29282990

Hamid, A., & Ibrahim, S. B. (2014). Supply Chain Management Practices and Supply Chain Performance Effectiveness. *International Journal of Scientific Research, 3*(8), 187–195.

Hamilton, M., Kaltcheva, V. D., & Rohm, A. J. (2016). Social media and value creation: The role of interaction satisfaction and interaction immersion. *Journal of Interactive Marketing, 36*, 121–133. doi:10.1016/j.intmar.2016.07.001

Hampton, S. E., & Parker, J. N. (2011). Collaboration and productivity in scientific synthesis. *Bioscience, 61*(11), 900–910. doi:10.1525/bio.2011.61.11.9

Handfield, R., & Nichols, E. L. Jr. (1999). *Introduction to Supply Chain Management*. Prentice-Hall.

Handoko, B., Lindawati, A., & Budiarto, A. (2020). Using Mixed Reality to Provide Experience for Internship Students in the Field of Auditing Studies during Covid 19. In *2020 2nd International Conference on E-Business and E-commerce Engineering (EBEE 2020)*. ACM. 10.1145/3446922.3446926

Harapko, S. (2021). *How COVID-19 impacted supply chains and what comes next*. https://www.ey.com/en_gl/supply-chain/how-covid-19-impacted-supply-chains-and-what-comes-next

Haroon, O., & Rizvi, S. A. (2020). COVID-19: Media coverage and financial markets behavior—A sectoral inquiry. *Journal of Behavioral and Experimental Finance, 27*, 1–5.

Harper, C. A., Satchell, L. P., Fido, D., & Latzman, R. D. (2021). Functional fear predicts public health compliance in the COVID-19 pandemic. *International Journal of Mental Health and Addiction, 19*(5), 1875–1888. doi:10.100711469-020-00281-5 PMID:32346359

Harrell, S. P. (2018). Soulfulness as an orientation to contemplative practice: Culture, liberation, and mindful awareness. *The Journal of Contemplative Inquiry, 5*(1), 1–32.

Hartmann, P., Fernández, P., Apaolaza, V., Eisend, M., & D'Souza, C. (2020). Explaining Viral CSR Message Propagation in social media: The Role of Normative Influences. *Journal of Business Ethics*, 1–21.

Hatane, S. E., Setiono, F. J., Setiawan, F. F., Semuel, H., & Mangoting, Y. (2020). Learning environment, students' attitude and intention to enhance current knowledge in the context of choosing accounting career. *Journal of Applied Research in Higher Education, 13*(1), 79–97. doi:10.1108/JARHE-06-2019-0156

Hätönen, J., & Eriksson, T. (2009). 30 + Years of Research and Practice of Outsourcing – Exploring the Past and Anticipating the Future. *Journal of International Management, 15*(2), 142–155. doi:10.1016/j.intman.2008.07.002

Haydon, D., & Kumar, N. (2020). *Industries Most and Least Impacted by COVID19 from a Probability of Default Perspective September 2020 Update*. S&P Global Market Intelligence. https://www.spglobal.com/marketintelligence/en/news-insights/blog/industries-most-and-least-impacted-by-covid19-from-a-probability-of-default-perspective-september-2020-update

Healy, P. M. (1985). The effect of bonus schemes on accounting decisions. *Journal of Accounting and Economics, 7*(1–3), 85–107. doi:10.1016/0165-4101(85)90029-1

Healy, P. M., & Wahlen, J. M. (1999). A Review of the Earnings Management Literature and Its. *Accounting Horizons, 13*(4), 365–383. doi:10.2308/acch.1999.13.4.365

Heathwood, W. (2018). *Physical Retail Isn't Dead: It's Working With Tech to Be More Human-Focused – Adweek.* https://www.adweek.com/brand-marketing/physical-retail-isnt-dead-its-working-with-tech-to-be-more-human-focused/

Heggeness, M. (2020). Estimating the immediate impact of the COVID-19 shock on parental attachment to the labor market and the double bind of mothers. *Review of Economics of the Household, 18*(4), 1053–1078. doi:10.100711150-020-09514-x PMID:33132792

Helena Putong, I., Laksmana, A., & Made Narsa, I. (2017). *The Effect of Vertical and Horizontal Trust on Voluntary Tax Compliance (An Experimental Study).* doi:10.2991/iconeg-16.2017.4

Henry, M. S., Le Roux, D. B., & Parry, D. A. (2021). Working in a post Covid-19 world: Towards a conceptual framework for distributed work. *South African Journal of Business Management, 52*(1), a2155. doi:10.4102ajbm.v52i1.2155

Herden, Ch., & Alliu, E. (2021). New Corporate Responsibilities in the digital age. *Nachhaltigkeits Management Forum, 29*(2), 13–29. https://link.springer.com/article/10.1007%2Fs00550-020-00509-x

Hickman, E., Kharouf, H., & Sekhon, H. (2020). An omnichannel approach to retailing: Demystifying and identifying the factors influencing an omnichannel experience. *International Review of Retail, Distribution and Consumer Research, 30*(3), 266–288. doi:10.1080/09593969.2019.1694562

Hill, M., & Hill, A. (1998a). *The Construction of a Questionnaire.* Center for Studies on Change Socio-Economic,

Hill, M., & Hill, A. (1998b). *Investigation Empirical in the Social Sciences: A Guide introductory _ DYNAMIA.* Center for Studies on Change Socio-Economic.

Hinterhuber, A., & Nilles, M. (2021). Digital transformation, the holy grail and the disruption of business models. *Business Horizons, 65*(3), 261–265. doi:10.1016/j.bushor.2021.02.042

Hiscock, R., Bauld, L., Amos, A., Fidler, J. A., & Munafò, M. (2012). Socioeconomic status and smoking: A review. *Annals of the New York Academy of Sciences, 1248*(1), 107–123. doi:10.1111/j.1749-6632.2011.06202.x PMID:22092035

Hj Abd Rahman, N. (2022). Effects of Employee Performance on the Implementation of Total Quality Management: Perspective of Working Mothers. In P. de Pablos, X. Zhang, M. Almunawar, & J. Labra Gayo (Eds.), *Handbook of Research on Big Data, Green Growth, and Technology Disruption in Asian Companies and Societies* (pp. 175–194). IGI Global. doi:10.4018/978-1-7998-8524-5.ch010

Ho, J., Hui, D., Kim, A., & Zhang, Y. (2020). *Cautiously optimistic: Chinese consumer behavior post-COVID-19.* McKinsey & Company. https://www.mckinsey.com/industries/consumer-packaged-goods/our-insights/cautiously-optimistic-chinese-consumer-behavior-post-covid-19

Hobday, A. J., Robinson, C., Murphy, E. J., Newton, A., Glaser, M., & Brodie, S. (2020). Fostering global science networks in a post-COVID-19 world. *Oceanography (Washington, D.C.), 33*(4), 9–10. doi:10.5670/oceanog.2020.414

Hochstein, B., Bolander, W., Bolander, B., Pratt, A. B., & Reynolds, K. (2021). An Investigation of Consumer Subjective Knowledge in Frontline Interactions. *Journal of Retailing, 97*(3), 336–346. doi:10.1016/j.jretai.2020.10.003

Hochstein, B., Bolander, W., Goldsmith, R., & Plouffe, C. R. (2019). Adapting influence approaches to informed consumers in high-involvement purchases: Are salespeople really doomed? *Journal of the Academy of Marketing Science, 47*(1), 118–137. doi:10.100711747-018-0609-2

Hoffman, D. L., & Novak, T. P. (2018). Consumer and Object Experience in the Internet of Things: An Assemblage Theory Approach, edited by Fischer, E. and Kozinets, R. Journal of Consumer Research, 44(6), 1178–1204.

Hoffman, D. L., Moreau, C. P., Stremersch, S., & Wedel, M. (2022). The Rise of New Technologies in Marketing: A Framework and Outlook. *Journal of Marketing*, *86*(1), 1–6. doi:10.1177/00222429211061636

Holbrook, M. B., & Hirschman, E. C. (1982). The experiential aspects of consumption: Consumer fantasies, feelings, and fun. *The Journal of Consumer Research*, *9*(2), 132–140. doi:10.1086/208906

Holmes, R. (2020). Is COVID-19 social media's levelling up moment? *Forbes*. https://www.forbes.com/sites/ryanholmes/2020/04/24/is-covid-19-social-medias-levelling-up-moment/?sh=6d3b342f6c60

Honeycutt, E. D. Jr. (2005). Technology improves sales performance—doesn't it?: An introduction to the special issue on selling and sales technology. *Industrial Marketing Management*, *34*(4), 301–304. doi:10.1016/j.indmarman.2004.12.002

Honigsberg, C. (2020). Forensic Accounting. *Annual Review of Law and Social Science*, 423–431. doi:10.1016/B978-0-12-382165-2.00218-X

Hoorens, S., Hocking, L., & Fays, C. (2020). *How small businesses are coping with the impact of COVID-19*. Rand Europe.

Horak, S., Afiouni, F., Bian, Y., Ledeneva, A., Muratbekova-Touron, M., & Fey, C. F. (2020). Informal networks: Dark sides, bright sides, and unexplored dimensions. *Management and Organization Review*, *16*(3), 511–542. doi:10.1017/mor.2020.28

Hörisch, J., Schaltegger, S., & Freeman, R. E. (2020). Integrating stakeholder theory and sustainability accounting: A conceptual synthesis. *Journal of Cleaner Production*, *275*, 124097. doi:10.1016/j.jclepro.2020.124097

Horton, R., & Das, P. (2014). Universal Health Coverage: Not Why, What, or When—But How? *Lancet*, *385*(9974), 1156–1157. doi:10.1016/S0140-6736(14)61742-6 PMID:25458724

Ho, S. Y., & Lim, K. H. (2018). Nudging moods to induce unplanned purchases in imperfect mobile personalization contexts. *MIS Quarterly: Management Information Systems*, *42*(3), 757–778. doi:10.25300/MISQ/2018/14083

Howe, J. (2006a). *Crowdsourcing: A definition*. Academic Press.

Howe, J. (2006b). The rise of crowdsourcing. *Wired Magazine*, *14*(6), 1-4.

Huang, H., & Xu, H. (2015). Dual Sourcing and Backup Production: Coexistence Versus Exclusivity. *Omega*, *57*, 22–33. doi:10.1016/j.omega.2015.04.008

Huang, J., Liu, F., Teng, Z., Chen, J., Zhao, J., Wang, X., & Wu, R. (2020). Care for the psychological status of frontline medical staff fighting against Coronavirus Disease 2019 (COVID-19). *Clinical Infectious Diseases*, *71*(12), 3268–3269. doi:10.1093/cid/ciaa385 PMID:32246142

Huang, L., Clarke, A., Heldsinger, N., & Tian, W. (2019). The communication role of social media in social marketing: A study of the community sustainability knowledge dissemination on LinkedIn and Twitter. *Journal of Marketing Analytics*, *7*(2), 64–75. doi:10.105741270-019-00053-8

Huang, S.-C. (2018). Social Information Avoidance: When, why, and how it is Costly in Goal Pursuit. *JMR, Journal of Marketing Research*, *55*(3), 382–395. doi:10.1509/jmr.16.0268

Huber, W. D. (2012). Is Forensic Accounting in the United States Becoming a Profession? *Journal of Forensic & Investigative Accounting*, *4*(1), 255–284.

Hudders, L., De Jans, S., & De Veirman, M. (2021). The commercialization of social media stars: A literature review and conceptual framework on the strategic use of social media influencers. *International Journal of Advertising, 40*(3), 327–375. doi:10.1080/02650487.2020.1836925

Hudecheck, M., Siren, C., Grichnik, D., & Wincent, J. (2020). How companies can respond to the coronavirus. *MIT Sloan Management Review.* https://sloanreview.mit.edu/article/how-companies-can-respond-to-the-coronavirus/

Huebener, M., Waights, S., Spiess, C. K., Siegel, N. A., & Wagner, G. G. (2021). Parental well-being in times of Covid-19 in Germany. *Review of Economics of the Household, 19*(1), 91–122. doi:10.100711150-020-09529-4 PMID:33469413

Huertas-Valdivia, I., Braojos, J., & Lloréns-Montes, F. J. (2019). Counteracting workplace ostracism in hospitality with psychological empowerment. *International Journal of Hospitality Management, 76*, 240–251. doi:10.1016/j.ijhm.2018.05.013

Hult, G. T. M., Sharma, P. N., Morgeson, F. V. III, & Zhang, Y. (2019). Antecedents and Consequences of Customer Satisfaction: Do They Differ Across Online and Offline Purchases? *Journal of Retailing, 95*(1), 10–23. doi:10.1016/j.jretai.2018.10.003

Huntington, S. P. (1971). The change to change: Modernization, development, and politics. *Comparative Politics, 3*(3), 283–322. doi:10.2307/421470

Hurley, J. (2020). *Bankruptcy and the COVID-19 Crisis.* HBS Working Knowledge. https://hbswk.hbs.edu/item/bankruptcy-and-the-covid-19-crisis

Hüseyinoğlu Yumurtacı, I. Ö., Galipoğlu, E., & Kotzab, H. (2017). Social, local and mobile commerce practices in omni-channel retailing. *International Journal of Retail & Distribution Management, 45*(7/8), 711–729. doi:10.1108/IJRDM-09-2016-0151

Hutchinson, M., Vickers, M. H., Jackson, D., & Wilkes, L. (2006). Like wolves in a pack: Predatory alliances of bullies in nursing. *Journal of Management & Organization, 12*(3), 235–250. doi:10.5172/jmo.2006.12.3.235

Huws, U. (2013). Working online, living offline: Labour in the Internet Age. *Work Organisation, Labour & Globalisation, 7*(1), 1–11.

Huws, U., & Frapporti, M. (2021). Digitalization, labour and the pandemic: Working life in the post-COVID-19 city. *Work Organisation, Labour & Globalisation, 15*(1), 7–10. doi:10.13169/workorgalaboglob.15.1.0007

Huyler, D., Pierre, Y., Ding, W., & Norelus, A. (2015). Millennials in the workplace: Positioning companies for future success. *SFERC, 2015*, 114.

Huynh, T. L. D., Nasir, M. A., Vo, V. X., & Nguyen, T. T. (2020). Small things matter most: The spillover effects in the cryptocurrency market and gold as a silver bullet. *The North American Journal of Economics and Finance, 54*, 101–277. doi:10.1016/j.najef.2020.101277

Ibrahim, I., & Taniar, D. (2006). Mobile Multimedia: A Communication Engineering Perspective. *Nova Scientia.*

Ichsan, N. R., Khaeruman, Santosa, S., Shara, Y., & Liriwati, Y. F. (2020). Investigation of Strategic Human Resource Management Practices in Business After Covid-19 Disruption. *Pal Arch's Journal of Archaeology of Egypt/Egyptology, 17*(7).

Idowu, A., & Elbanna, A. (2020). Digital platforms of work and the crafting of career path: The crowdworkers' perspective. *Information Systems Frontiers*, 1–17.

Iea. (2020). *European Union 2020 Energy Policy Review.* Retrieved from: https://www.iea.org/reports/european-union-2020

Ilgın, K. S., & Sarı, S. S. (2020). Covid-19 pandemisinin hisse senedi piyasalarına etkisi: Vaka ve ölümlerin yoğun olduğu ülkeler ile Türkiye incelemesi. *Karadeniz Sosyal Bilimler Dergisi, 12*(23), 434–453.

IMF. (2020). *Angola: Tackling the Covid-19 Pandemic and the Oil Price Shock.* https://www.imf.org/pt/News/Articles/2020/09/18/na-angola-confronting-the-covid-19-pandemic-and-the-oil-price-shock

Im, H., Lennon, S. J., & Stoel, L. (2010). The perceptual fluency effect on the pleasurable online shopping experience. *Journal of Research in Interactive Marketing, 4*(4), 280–295. doi:10.1108/17505931011092808

Inda, S., Abu Bakar, A. H., & Huam Hon, T. F. (2012). A study of Supply Chain Management Practices: An Empirical Investigation on consumer goods industry in Malaysia. *International Journal of Business and Social Science, 2*(17), 166–176.

Indriastuti, M., & Fuad, K. (2020, July). Impact of covid-19 on digital transformation and sustainability in small and medium enterprises (SMEs): A conceptual framework. In *Conference on Complex, Intelligent, and Software Intensive Systems* (pp. 471-476). Springer.

International Labor Organization - ILO. (2020). *A global survey of enterprises: managing the business disruptions of COVID-19.* Geneve. https://www.ilo.org/actemp/publications/WCMS_760306/lang--en/index.htm

International Labour Organization. (2021). *ILO Monitor: COVID-19 and the World of Work. Seventh Edition.* ILO.

Iqbal, N., Fareed, Z., Wan, G., & Shahzad, F. (2021). Asymmetric nexus between COVID-19 outbreak in the world and cryptocurrency market. *International Review of Financial Analysis, 73*, 101–613. doi:10.1016/j.irfa.2020.101613

Islam & Rahman. (2011). Forensic Accounting as a Tool for Detecting Fraud and Corruption : An Empirical Study in Bangladesh. *ASA University Review, 5*(2).

Islam, H., Jebarajakirthy, C., & Shankar, A. (2021). An experimental based investigation into the effects of website interactivity on customer behaviour in an online purchase context. *Journal of Strategic Marketing, 29*(2), 117–140. doi:10.1080/0965254X.2019.1637923

Islam, T., Pitafi, A. H., Arya, V., Wang, Y., Akhtar, N., Mubarik, S., & Xiaobei, L. (2021). Panic buying in the COVID-19 pandemic: A multi-country examination. *Journal of Retailing and Consumer Services, 59*, 102357. doi:10.1016/j.jretconser.2020.102357

İşler, İ. İ., & Güven, A. (2021). Covid-19 küresel salgınının BIST 100 endeksi üzerindeki etkileri. *Politik Ekonomik Kuram, 5*(1), 63–77.

Itoh, S., Murakami, Y., & Iba, T. (2006). Consumer network and market dynamics. *Proceedings of the 9th Joint International Conference on Information Sciences (JCIS-06)*, 211-214.

Ivan, C. M., Mukta, R., Sudeep, C., & Burak, C. (2016). Long-term sustainable sustainability in luxury. Where else? In *Handbook of Sustainable Luxury Textiles and Fashion* (pp. 17–34). Springer Singapore. doi:10.1007/978-981-287-742-0_2

Ivanov, D. (2021). Digital Supply Chain Management and Technology to Enhance Resilience by Building and Using End-to-End Visibility During the COVID-19 Pandemic. *IEEE Transactions on Engineering Management.* doi:10.1109/TEM.2021.3095193

Ivanov, D., & Dolgui, A. (2020). Viability of intertwined supply networks: Extending the supply chain resilience angles towards survivability. A position paper motivated by COVID-19 outbreak. *International Journal of Production Research, 58*(10), 2904–2915. doi:10.1080/00207543.2020.1750727

Ivec, S. (2021). *How To Skill Up Employees For A Post-Pandemic Future*. eLearning Industry. https://elearningindustry.com/how-to-skill-up-employees-for-a-post-pandemic-future

Iyengar, K., Khanna, S., Ramadath, S., & Stephens, D. (2017). *What it takes to capture the value of APIs*. McKinsey & Company.

Iyke, B. (2020). The Disease Outbreak Channel of Exchange Rate Return Predictability: Evidence from COVID-19. *Emerging Markets Finance & Trade*, *56*(10), 2277–2297. https://doi.org/10.1080/1540496x.2020.1784718

Jabeen, S., Farhan, M., Zaka, M. A., Fiaz, M., & Farasat, M. (2022). COVID and World Stock Markets: A Comprehensive Discussion. *Frontiers in Psychology, 12*. doi:10.3389/fpsyg.2021.763346

Jackson, J., Weiss, M., Schwarzenberg, A., Nelson, R., Sutter, K., & Sutherland, M. (2021). *Global Economic Effects of COVID-19*. Congressional Research Service. https://sgp.fas.org/crs/row/R46270.pdf

Jackson, D., Sibson, R., & Riebe, L. (2014). Undergraduate perceptions of the development of team-working skills. *Education + Training*, *56*(1), 7–20. doi:10.1108/ET-01-2013-0002

Jacquet, R. (2020). *Upskilling During Difficult Times: How Do We Keep Employees Learning from Home?* Coursera Blog. https://blog.coursera.org/upskilling-during-difficult-times-how-do-we-keep-employees-learning-from-home/

Jaeger, A., & Matyas, K. (2016). Transformation of the EFQM approach from business towards operations excellence. *Production Engineering*, *10*(3), 277–291. doi:10.100711740-016-0665-8

Jäger, G., Zilian, L. S., Hofer, C., & Füllsack, M. (2019). Crowdworking: Working with or against the crowd? *Journal of Economic Interaction and Coordination*, *14*(4), 761–788. doi:10.100711403-019-00266-1

Javalgi, R., Dixit, A., & Scherer, R. F. (2009). Outsourcing to Emerging Markets: Theoretical Perspectives and Policy Implications. *Journal of International Management*, *15*(2), 156–168. doi:10.1016/j.intman.2008.08.001

Javed, B., Abdullah, I., Zaffar, M. A., Haque, A., & Rubab, U. (2019). Inclusive leadership and innovative work behavior: The role of psychological empowerment. *Journal of Management & Organization*, *25*(4), 554–571. doi:10.1017/jmo.2018.50

Jaya, I. M. L. M., & I. M. N. (2020). The Beauty and the Beast of Earning Management in Indonesia. *Opcion, 36*(91), 1097–1140. https://produccioncientificaluz.org/index.php/opcion/article/view/32496

Jean, R.-J., Kim, D., & Cavusgil, E. (2020). Antecedents and outcomes of digital platform risk for international new ventures' internationalization. *Journal of World Business*, *55*(1), 101021. doi:10.1016/j.jwb.2019.101021

Jeske, D., & Axtell, C. (2014). e-Internships: Prevalence, characteristics and role of student perspectives. *Internet Research*, *24*(4), 457–473. doi:10.1108/IntR-11-2012-0226

Ji, Q., Zhang, D., Zhao, Y., (2020). *Searching for safe-haven assets during the COVID-19 pandemic*. doi:10.1016/j.irfa.2020.101526

Jin, Y.-J., Park, S.-C., & Yoo, J.-W. (2017). Effects of corporate social responsibility on consumer credibility perception and attitude toward luxury brands. *Social Behavior and Personality*, *45*(5), 795–808. doi:10.2224bp.5897

Jocevski, M. (2020). Blurring the lines between physical and digital spaces: Business model innovation in retailing. *California Management Review*, *63*(1), 99–117. doi:10.1177/0008125620953639

Jocevski, M., Arvidsson, N., Miragliotta, G., Ghezzi, A., & Mangiaracina, R. (2019). Transitions towards omni-channel retailing strategies: A business model perspective. *International Journal of Retail & Distribution Management*, *47*(2), 78–93. doi:10.1108/IJRDM-08-2018-0176

JohnsonJ. (2020). *The Impact of COVID-19 on Bitcoin Trading Activity: A Preliminary Assessment*. doi:10.2139/ssrn.3583162

Jongwanich, J. (2022). *Russia war on Ukraine threatens Southeast Asia's economic recovery*. East Asia Forum. https://www.eastasiaforum.org/2022/04/21/russia-war-on-ukraine-threatens-southeast-asias-economic-recovery/

Joseph, E., & Dhanabhakyam, M. M. (2022). Role of Digitalization Post-Pandemic for Development of SMEs. In *Research Anthology on Business Continuity and Navigating Times of Crisis* (pp. 727–747). IGI Global. doi:10.4018/978-1-6684-4503-7.ch036

Joshi, M. S. (2003). *Definition of forensic accounting*. www.forensicaccounting.com

Juergensen, J., Guimón, J., & Narula, R. (2020). European SMEs amidst the COVID-19 crisis: Assessing impact and policy responses. *Economia e Politica Industriale*, *47*(3), 499–510. doi:10.100740812-020-00169-4

Jun, T., & Kim, J.-Y. (2008). A theory of consumer referral. *International Journal of Industrial Organization*, *26*(3), 662–678. doi:10.1016/j.ijindorg.2007.03.005

Kachela, K., Lodh, S., & Nandy, M. (2021). Post-Pandemic Sustainable Business Solution. *Journal of Business and Management Studies*, *3*(1), 47–57. doi:10.32996/jbms.2021.3.1.5

Kaczmarek, T., Perez, K., Demir, E., & Zaremba, A. (2021). How to survive a pandemic: The corporate resiliency of travel and leisure companies to the COVID-19 outbreak. *Tourism Management*, *84*, 1–11. doi:10.1016/j.tourman.2020.104281

Kahan, D. M. (2019). Social influence, social meaning, and deterrence. In *Criminal Law* (pp. 429–476). Routledge. doi:10.4324/9781315189437-13

Kahn, J.S., & McIntosh, K. (2005). History and recent advances in corona virus discovery. *Pediatr Infect Dis J., 24*(11), S223-7. .inf.0000188166.17324.60 doi:10.1097/01

Kahneman, D. (2011). *Thinking fast and slow*. Farrar, Straus and Giroux.

Kaine, S., & Josserand, E. (2019). The organisation and experience of work in the gig economy. *The Journal of Industrial Relations*, *61*(4), 479–501. doi:10.1177/0022185619865480

Kalkınma, E., & birliği Örgütü, İ. (2020). The Territorial Impact of COVID-19: Managing the Crisis Across Levels of Government. *Erişim Adresi*. https://read. OECD-library. org/view

Kalyani, V., & Saravanan, R. (2020). Does spiritual intelligence contribute to sales force effectiveness? *International Journal of Electronic Marketing and Retailing*, *11*(4), 352–368. doi:10.1504/IJEMR.2020.111157

Kang, E. Y., & Sung, Y. H. (2021). Luxury and sustainability: The role of message appeals and objectivity on luxury brands' green corporate social responsibility. *Journal of Marketing Communications*, •••, 1–22.

Kang, J.-Y. M. (2018). Showrooming, Webrooming, and User-Generated Content Creation in the Omnichannel Era. *Journal of Internet Commerce*, *17*(2), 145–169. doi:10.1080/15332861.2018.1433907

Kannan, P. K. K., & Li, H. (2017). Digital marketing: A framework, review and research agenda. *International Journal of Research in Marketing*, *34*(1), 22–45. doi:10.1016/j.ijresmar.2016.11.006

Kantar. (2020). *E-Commerce el ganador de esta pandamia*. https://www.kantar.com/latin-america/inspiracion/consumidor/ecommerce-el-ganador-de-esta-pandemia?par=mx/Noticias-/Ecommerce-el-ganador-de-esta-pandemia

Karaosman. (2019). *Unlocking Responsible Luxury: The Manifesto 2019*. Politecnico di Milano School of Management & Mazars.

Karapanos, E., Zimmerman, J., Forlizzi, J., & Martens, J.-B. (2009, April). User experience over time: An initial framework. *Proceedings of the SIGCHI conference on human factors in computing systems.* 10.1145/1518701.1518814

Karataş, Z. (2020). COVID-19 pandemisinin toplumsal etkileri, değişim ve güçlenme. *Türkiye Sosyal Hizmet Araştırmaları Dergisi, 4*(1), 3–17.

Karwai, M. (2004). *Forensic Accounting and Fraud Investigation for Non-Expert.* John Wiley and Sons.

Kashyap, A., & Raghuvanshi, J. (2020). A preliminary study on exploring the critical success factors for developing Covid-19 preventative strategy with an economy centric approach. *Journal of the Iberoamerican Academy of Management, 18*(4), 357–377.

Kasten, S., van Osch, L., Candel, M., & de Vries, H. (2019). The influence of pre-motivational factors on behavior via motivational factors: A test of the I-Change model. *BMC Psychology, 7*(1), 1–12. doi:10.118640359-019-0283-2 PMID:30786921

Kats, R. (2019). *What Makes a Bad Shopping Experience? Customers Bring Different Expectations to in-Store and Ecommerce Interactions.* https://www.emarketer.com/content/what-makes-a-bad-shopping-experience

Kavanagh, M. H., & Drennan, L. (2008). What skills and attributes does an accounting graduate need? Evidence from student perceptions and employer expectations. *Accounting and Finance, 48*(2), 279–300. doi:10.1111/j.1467-629X.2007.00245.x

Kayhan, S., Bayat, T., & Koçyiğt, A. (2013). Enflasyon hedeflemesi rejiminde öğrenme süreci ve asimetri: Markov switching yaklaşımı. *Eskişehir Osmangazi Üniversitesi İİBF Dergisi, 8*(1), 191–212.

Kering. (2021). *Sustainability.* Retrieved from https://www.kering.com/en/sustainability/

Kering. (2022). https://www.linkedin.com/company/kering/

Keyes, J. (2016). *Aligning IT with Corporate Strategy: Implementing the IT Balanced Scorecard.* Auerbach. doi:10.1201/9781420031348

Khalil, M., Ozkanc, A., & Yildiz, Y. (2020). Foreign institutional ownership and demand for accounting conservatism: Evidence from an emerging market. *Review of Quantitative Finance and Accounting, 55*(1), 1–27. doi:10.100711156-019-00834-3

Khalymon Serhii, P. V. (2019). Forensic economic examination as a means of investigation and counteraction of economic crimes in East Europe (example of Ukraine). *Journal of Legal, Ethical and Regulatory Issues, 22*(3), 2019.

Khan, I. (2022). Handbook of Research on Adapting Remote Learning Practices for Early Childhood and Elementary School Classrooms (Advances in Early Childhood and K-12 Education). IGI Global. https://doi.org/10.4018/978-1-7998-8405-7.ch028.

Khan, M. A. A., Hashim, H., & Ab. Aziz, Y. (2020). The rise of consumer community on social media, its influence on consumers' decision making process, perceived value and loyalty intentions in tourism industry: A conceptual thought. *International Journal of Academic Research in Business & Social Sciences, 10*(10), 813–833. doi:10.6007/IJARBSS/v10-i10/7874

Khan, S., & Ahmed, M. (2017). Who are the consumers for sustainable luxury? In *2017 Global Fashion Management Conference at Vienna* (pp. 181-182). 10.15444/GFMC2017.03.02.03

Kharas, H. (2020). *The impact of COVID-19 on global extreme poverty.* Brookings Institution. www.brookings.edu/blog/future-development/2020/10/21/the-impact-of-covid-19-on-global-extreme-poverty/

Khoo, E. J., & Lantos, J. D. (2020). Lessons learned from the COVID-19 pandemic. *Acta Paediatrica (Oslo, Norway)*, *109*(7), 1323–1325. doi:10.1111/apa.15307 PMID:32289175

Khoshtaria, T., Matin, A., Mercan, M., & Datuashvili, D. (2021). The impact of customers' purchasing patterns on their showrooming and webrooming behaviour: An empirical evidence from the Georgian retail sector. *International Journal of Electronic Marketing and Retailing*, *12*(4), 394. doi:10.1504/IJEMR.2021.118305

Kidwell, B., Hasford, J., Turner, B., Hardesty, D., & Zablah, A. R. (2021). Emotional Calibration and Salesperson Performance. *Journal of Marketing*, *85*(6), 141–161. doi:10.1177/0022242921999603

Kılcı, F., Kara, B. Y., & Bozkaya, B. (2015). Locating temporary shelter areas after an earthquake: A case for Turkey. *European Journal of Operational Research*, *243*(1), 323–332. doi:10.1016/j.ejor.2014.11.035

Kim, B., & Park, M. J. (2019). An Examination of the Effect of Consumer Personal Traits on Show Rooming Behavior: The Effect of Product Type. *Journal of Internet Commerce*, *18*(1), 24–44. doi:10.1080/15332861.2018.1547569

Kim, H., So, K. K. F., Mihalik, B. J., & Lopes, A. P. (2021). Millennials' virtual reality experiences pre-and post-COVID-19. *Journal of Hospitality and Tourism Management*, *48*, 200–209. doi:10.1016/j.jhtm.2021.06.008

Kim, J. H., Shim, Y., Choi, I., & Choi, E. (2022). The role of coping strategies in maintaining well-being during the COVID-19 outbreak in South Korea. *Social Psychological & Personality Science*, *13*(1), 320–332. doi:10.1177/1948550621990595

Kim, R. Y. (2020). The impact of COVID-19 on consumers: Preparing for digital sales. *IEEE Engineering Management Review*, *48*(3), 212–218. doi:10.1109/EMR.2020.2990115

Kim, S., Choi, B., & Lew, Y. (2021). Where is the age of digitalization heading? The meaning, characteristics and implications of contemporary digital transformation. *Sustainability*, *13*(16), 8909. doi:10.3390u13168909

Kim, S., & Rim, H. (2019). The role of public skepticism and distrust in the process of CSR communication. *International Journal of Business Communication*. doi:10.1177/2329488419866888

Kirk, C. P., & Rifkin, L. S. (2020). I'll trade you diamonds for toilet paper: Consumer reacting, coping and adapting behaviors in the COVID-19 pandemic. *Journal of Business Research*, *117*, 124–131. doi:10.1016/j.jbusres.2020.05.028 PMID:32834208

Kittur, A., Nickerson, J. V., Bernstein, M. S., Gerber, E. M., Shaw, A., Zimmerman, J., Lease, M., & Horton, J. (2013). The future of crowd work. *Social Science Electronic Publishing*, *263*(1), 1301–1318.

Kleis, L., Chwelos, P., Ramirez, R. V., & Cockburn, I. (2012). Information technology and intangible output: The impact of IT investment on innovation productivity. *Information Systems Research*, *23*(1), 42–59. doi:10.1287/isre.1100.0338

Kloutsiniotis, P. V., Mihail, D. M., Mylonas, N., & Pateli, A. (2022). Transformational Leadership, HRM practices and burnout during the COVID-19 pandemic: The role of personal stress, anxiety, and workplace loneliness. *International Journal of Hospitality Management*, *102*, 103177. doi:10.1016/j.ijhm.2022.103177 PMID:35079194

KnauerN. J. (2021). The Federal Response to the COVID-19 Pandemic-A Study in Maladministration. Available at SSRN 3803884. doi:10.2139/ssrn.3803884

Kneller, R., & Pisu, M. (2006). *The role of experience in export market entry: Evidence for UK Firms.* University of Nottingham Research Paper, (2006/18).

Kneller, R., & Pisu, M. (2011). Barriers to exporting: What are they and who do they matter to? *World Economy*, *34*(6), 893–930. doi:10.1111/j.1467-9701.2011.01357.x

Kniffin, K. M., Narayanan, J., Anseel, F., Antonakis, J., Ashford, S. P., Bakker, A. B., ... Johns, G. (2020). COVID-1.9 and the workplace: Implications, ıssues, and ınsights for future research and action. *The American Psychologist, 76*(1), 63–77. doi:10.1037/amp0000716 PMID:32772537

Knight, J., & Ensminger, J. (1998). Conflict over changing social norms. In M. C. Brinton & V. Nee (Eds.), *The New Institutionalism in Sociology*. Stanford University Press.

Knyazev, S. I. (2020). Smart industry: Forming the basis of a new stage of economic growth in the world. *Business Info, 4*(4), 150–162. doi:10.32983/2222-4459-2020-4-150-162

Kobrin, S. J. (2017). Bricks and mortar in borderless world: Globalization, the backlash, and the multinational enterprise. *Global Strategy Journal, 7*(2), 159–171. doi:10.1002/gsj.1158

Koçyiğit, A., Bayat, T., & Tüfekçi, A. (2011). Türkiye'de işsizlik histerisi ve star modelleri uygulaması. *Marmara Üniversitesi İ.İ.B.F. Dergisi, 31*(2), 45–60.

KOF Swiss Economic Institute. (2021). *KOF Globalization Index*. https://kof.ethz.ch/en/forecasts-and-indicators/indicators/kof-globalisation-index.html

Koh, S. C. L., Demirbag, M., Bayraktar, E., Tatoglu, E., & Zaim, S. (2007). The impact of supply chain management practices on performance of SMEs. *Industrial Management & Data Systems, 107*(1), 103–124. doi:10.1108/02635570710719089

Kong, H. M., Witmaier, A., & Ko, E. (2021). Sustainability and social media communication: How consumers respond to marketing efforts of luxury and non-luxury fashion brands. *Journal of Business Research, 131*, 640–651. doi:10.1016/j.jbusres.2020.08.021

Koonin, L. M. (2020). Novel coronavirus disease (COVID-19) outbreak: Now is the time to refresh pandemic plans. *Journal of Business Continuity & Emergency Planning, 13*(4), 1–15. PMID:32160942

Korenkov, D. (2020, April 14). *Farmers of the Kherson region throw crops to the dump: the coronavirus has caused hundreds of thousands of losses* https://www.0552.ua/news/2730095/fermery-hersonsiny-vybrasyvaut-urozaj-na-pomojku-koronavirus-prines-ubytki-na-sotni-tysac

Kose, A., & Sugawara, N. (2021). *Understanding the Depth of the 2020 Global Recession in 5 Charts*. World Bank Blogs.

Kotlar, B., Gerson, E., Petrillo, S., Langer, A., & Tiemeier, H. (2021). The impact of the COVID-19 pandemic on maternal and perinatal health: A scoping review. *Reproductive Health, 18*(1), 10. doi:10.118612978-021-01070-6 PMID:33461593

Kotler, P. (1984). Marketing Management: Analysis, planning and Control (5th ed.). Prentice-Hall.

Kotler, P., Armstrong, G., Saunders, J., & Wong, V. (2001). *Principles of Marketing* (3rd ed.). Prentice-Hall, Pearson Education Limited.

Kotler, P., Kartajaya, H., & Setiawan, I. (2017). *Marketing 4.0: do tradicional ao digital*. Sextante.

Kotler, P., & Keller, K. L. (2012). *Marketing management*. Pearson France.

Kotter, J. (2007). Leading change: Why transformation efforts fail. *Harvard Business Review, 73*, 259–267.

Kottika, E., Özsomer, A., Rydén, P., Theodorakis, I. G., Kaminakis, K., Kottikas, K. G., & Stathakopoulos, V. (2020). We survived this! What managers could learn from SMEs who successfully navigated the Greek economic crisis. *Industrial Marketing Management, 88*, 352–365. doi:10.1016/j.indmarman.2020.05.021

Koyuncu, T., & Meçik, O. (2020). Covid-19 pandemisinin türkiye'de ekonomik büyümeye sektör-spesifik etkileri: Var analizi. *Yönetim ve Ekonomi Araştırmaları Dergisi, 18*(4), 112–131.

KPMG. (2020). *Impactos económicos y financieros del COVID-19.* Advisory I KPMG. https://assets.kpmg/content/dam/kpmg/co/pdf/2020/06/kpmg-informe-impactos-economicos-y-financieros-del-covid-19-novena-edicion.pdf

Kraft, C., & Carmona, M. (2021). Blockchain Tokenisation in Grant Management. In P. de G. (Ed.), Blockchain Technology Applications in Businesses and Organizations (pp. 141-161). IGI Global Publications.

Krasonikolakis, I., Vrechopoulos, A., Pouloudi, A., & Dimitriadis, S. (2018). Store layout effects on consumer behavior in 3D online stores. *European Journal of Marketing*, *52*(5/6), 1223–1256. doi:10.1108/EJM-03-2015-0183

Kraus, S., Jones, P., Kailer, N., Weinmann, A., Chaparro-Banegas, N., & Roig-Tierno, N. (2021). Digital Transformation: An Overview of the Current State of the Art of Research. *SAGE Open*, *11*(3), 21582440211047576. doi:10.1177/21582440211047576

Kravchenko, V. (2020, April 30). *How Kherson farmers and a glamorous restaurateur "zeroed" quarantine in Ukraine. The Cabinet of Ministers is under pressure from business to ease restrictive measures. Protest action of entrepreneurs near the Cabinet of Ministers.* https://mind.ua/ru/publications/20210461-kak-hersonskie-fermery-i-glamurnyj-restorator-obnulili-karantin-v-ukraine

Kravchuk, O., Varis, I., & Zaryvnykh, K. (2021). Digital technology of personnel management: Trends and challenges in a COVID-19 pandemic. *Economics and society*, *26*, 1–10. doi:10.32782/2524-0072/2021-26-73

Krehbiel, Salzarulo, Cosmah, Forren, Gannod, Havelka, Hulshult, & Merhout. (2017). Agile Manifesto for Teaching and Learning. *Journal of Effective Teaching, 17*(2), 90-111.

Krishen, A., Berezan, O., Agarwal, S., & Kachroo, P. (2016). The generation of virtual needs: Recipes for satisfaction in social media networking. *Journal of Business Research*, *69*(11), 5248–5254. doi:10.1016/j.jbusres.2016.04.120

Kritsonis, A. (2005). Comparison of change theories. *International Journal of Scholarly Academic Intellectual Diversity, 8*(1), 1-7

Kuckertz, A., Brändle, L., Gaudig, A., Hinderer, S., Reyes, C. A. M., Prochotta, A., ... Berger, E. S. (2020). Startups in times of crisis–A rapid response to the COVID-19 pandemic. *Journal of Business Venturing Insights*, *13*, e00169. doi:10.1016/j.jbvi.2020.e00169

Kujala, J., Aaltonen, K., Gotcheva, N., & Lahdenperä, P. (2020). Dimensions of governance in interorganizational project networks. *International Journal of Managing Projects in Business.*

Kukla, M., Bonfils, K. A., & Salyers, M. P. (2015). Factors impacting work success in Veterans with mental health disorders: A Veteran-focused mixed methods pilot study. *Journal of Vocational Rehabilitation*, *43*(1), 51–66. doi:10.3233/JVR-150754

Kuksov, D., & Liao, C. (2018). When Showrooming Increases Retailer Profit. *JMR, Journal of Marketing Research*, *55*(4), 459–473. doi:10.1509/jmr.17.0059

Kumar, A. A., & Kumar, U. (2015). *Knowledge Management: A Review. International Journal of Academic Research in Social Sciences and Humanities* , 1).

Kumar, A. A., & Kumar, U. K. (2015). Knowledge Management: A Review. *International Journal of Academic Research in Social Sciences & Humanities*, *1*(1), 9–17.

Kumar, B., & Sharma, A. (2021). Managing the supply chain during disruptions: Developing a framework for decision-making. *Industrial Marketing Management*, *97*, 159–172. doi:10.1016/j.indmarman.2021.07.007

Kumar, V., & Venkatesan, R. (2021). Transformation of Metrics and Analytics in Retailing: The Way Forward. *Journal of Retailing, 97*(4), 496–506. doi:10.1016/j.jretai.2021.11.004

Kuntsche, S., Room, R., & Kuntsche, E. (2021). I can keep up with the best: The role of social norms in alcohol consumption and their use in interventions. In *The Handbook of Alcohol Use* (pp. 285–302). Academic Press. doi:10.1016/B978-0-12-816720-5.00024-4

Kunz, J., May, S., & Schmidt, H. J. (2020). Sustainable luxury: Current status and perspectives for future research. *Business Research, 13*(2), 541–601. doi:10.100740685-020-00111-3

Kurz, T., Gardner, B., Verplanken, B., & Abraham, C. (2015). Habitual behaviors or patterns of practice? Explaining and changing repetitive climate-relevant actions. *Wiley Interdisciplinary Reviews: Climate Change, 6*(1), 113–128. doi:10.1002/wcc.327

Kutlar, A. (2003). *Ekonometriye giriş*. Nobel Akademik Yayıncılık Eğilim Danışmanlık.

Kutzin, J. (2012, November 1). Anything goes on the path to universal health coverage? *No. World Health Organ., 90*(11), 867–868. doi:10.2471/BLT.12.113654 PMID:23226900

La Forgia, G., & Nagpal, S. (2012). *Government-sponsored health insurance in India: are you covered?* World Bank. doi:10.1596/978-0-8213-9618-6

Laato, S., Islam, A. N., Farooq, A., & Dhir, A. (2020). Unusual purchasing behaviour during the early stages of the COVID-19 pandemic: The stimulus-organism-response approach. *Journal of Retailing and Consumer Services, 57*, 102224. doi:10.1016/j.jretconser.2020.102224

LaCore, E. (2015). Supporting millennials in the workplace. *Strategic HR Review, 14*(4). Advance online publication. doi:10.1108/SHR-06-2015-0046

Lahiri, S. (2016). Does Outsourcing Really Improve Firm Performance? Empirical Evidence and Research Agenda. *International Journal of Management Reviews, 18*(4), 464–497. doi:10.1111/ijmr.12075

Lalwani, V., & Meshram, V. V. (2020). Stock market efficiency in the time of COVID-19: Evidence from industry stock returns. *International Journal of Accounting & Finance Review, 5*(2), 40–44.

Lanotte, A. (2019). *EU circular economy plans could cut tax costs for companies*, www.itrinsight.com

Lanotte, A. (2021). Green Finance: Sustainable Growth And the Circular Economy. *Tax Notes International, 103*(12), 1601.

Laroche, M., & Richard, M. O. (2014). A Model of online consumer behaviour. In *Handbook of Strategic e-Business Management* (pp. 325–346). Springer. doi:10.1007/978-3-642-39747-9_15

Lashkova, M., Antón, C., & Camarero, C. (2019). Dual effect of sensory experience: Engagement vs diversive exploration. *International Journal of Retail & Distribution Management, 48*(2), 128–151. doi:10.1108/IJRDM-09-2018-0204

Law, K. M., Geng, S., & Li, T. (2019). Student enrollment, motivation and learning performance in a blended learning environment: The mediating effects of social, teaching, and cognitive presence. *Computers & Education, 136*, 1–12. doi:10.1016/j.compedu.2019.02.021

Lawrence, J. M., Scheer, L. K., Crecelius, A. T., & Lam, S. K. (2021). Salesperson Dual Agency in Price Negotiations. *Journal of Marketing, 85*(2), 89–109. doi:10.1177/0022242920974611

Lazaris, C., Sarantopoulos, P., Vrechopoulos, A., & Doukidis, G. (2021). Effects of Increased Omnichannel Integration on Customer Satisfaction and Loyalty Intentions. *International Journal of Electronic Commerce, 25*(4), 440–468. doi:10.1080/10864415.2021.1967005

Lechner, A. T., & Paul, M. (2019). Is this smile for real? The role of affect and thinking style in customer perceptions of frontline employee emotion authenticity. *Journal of Business Research, 94*, 195–208. doi:10.1016/j.jbusres.2017.06.009

Lee Yohn, D. (2018). *The Future Of Retail CX Is Human.* https://www.forbes.com/sites/deniselyohn/2018/08/22/the-future-of-retail-cx-is-human/#2ec79d931d82

Lee, A., & Morling, J. (2020). COVID19 - The need for public health in a time of emergency. *Public Health, 182*(5), 188–189. doi:10.1016/j.puhe.2020.03.027 PMID:32344272

Lee, C.-H., Wang, D., Desouza, K. C., & Evans, R. (2021). Digital transformation and the new normal in China: How can enterprises use digital technologies to respond to COVID-19? *Sustainability, 13*(18), 10195. doi:10.3390u131810195

Lee, E. A., & Messerschmitt, D. G. (2012). *Digital communication.* Springer Science & Business Media.

Lee, H. L. (2002). Aligning Supply Chain Strategies with product uncertainties. *California Management Review, 44*(3), 105–110. doi:10.2307/41166135

Le, H., Nguyen, T., Ngo, C., Pham, T., & Le, T. (2020). Policy related factors affecting the survival and development of SMEs in the context of Covid 19 pandemic. *Management Science Letters, 10*(15), 3683–3692. doi:10.5267/j.msl.2020.6.025

Leimeister, J. M. (2010). Collective intelligence. *Business & Information Systems Engineering, 2*(4), 245-248.

Leitão, A. (2015). Economic Market in Angola – Evolution perspective. Embassy of the Republic of Angola in Portugal – Commercial Representation.

Lent, R. W., Brown, S. D., & Hackett, G. (1994). Toward a unifying social cognitive theory of career and academic interest, choice, and performance. *Journal of Vocational Behavior, 45*(1), 79–122. doi:10.1006/jvbe.1994.1027

Leonidou, L. C. (2000). Barriers to export management: An organizational and internationalization analysis. *Journal of International Management, 6*(2), 121–148. doi:10.1016/S1075-4253(00)00022-3

Lepak, D.P., Taylor, M.S., Tekleab, A.G., Marrone, J.A. & Cohen, D.J. (2007). An examination of the use of high-investment human resource systems for core and support employees. *Human Resource Management, 46*(2), 223-246.

Lerner, R. M. (1990). Weaving Development Into the Fabric of Personality and Social Psychology—On the Significance of Bandura's Social Foundation of Thought and Action. *Psychological Inquiry, 1*(1), 92–96. doi:10.120715327965pli0101_24

Leseure, M. J., Bauer, J., Birdi, K., Neely, A., & Denyer, D. (2004). Adoption of promising practices: A systematic review of the evidence. *International Journal of Management Reviews, 5*(3-4), 169–190. doi:10.1111/j.1460-8545.2004.00102.x

Le, T. H., Do, H. X., Nguyen, D. K., & Sensoy, A. (2021). COVID-19 pandemic and tail-dependency networks of financial assets. *Finance Research Letters, 38*, 1–9. doi:10.1016/j.frl.2020.101800 PMID:33100926

Levaggi, R., & Menoncin, F. (2013). Optimal dynamic tax evasion. *Journal of Economic Dynamics & Control, 37*(11), 2157–2167. doi:10.1016/j.jedc.2013.06.007

Lewin, A. Y., Massini, S., & Peeters, C. (2009). Why Are Companies Offshoring Innovation? The Emerging Global Race for Talent. *Journal of International Business Studies, 40*(6), 901–925. doi:10.1057/jibs.2008.92

Lewin, K. (1951). *Theory.* Harper and Row.

Lewis, M., & Brooks-Gunn, J. (1979). Toward a theory of social cognition: The development of self. *New Directions for Child and Adolescent Development, 1979*(4), 1–20. doi:10.1002/cd.23219790403

Li, B., Zhong, Y. Y., Zhang, T. T., & Hua, N. (2021). Transcending the COVID-19 crisis: Business resilience and innovation of the restaurant industry in China. *Journal of Hospitality and Tourism Management*, *49*(July), 44–53. doi:10.1016/j.jhtm.2021.08.024

Libbrecht, P., & Goosen, L. (2015). Using ICTs to Facilitate Multilingual Mathematics Teaching and Learning. In *Mathematics Education and Language Diversity* (pp. 217–235). Springer.

Li, C., Yu, X., Butler, J. R. G., Yiengprugsawan, V., & Yu, M. (2011, August). Moving towards universal health insurance in China: Performance, issues and lessons from Thailand. *Soc Sci Med.*, *73*(3), 359–366. doi:10.1016/j.socscimed.2011.06.002 PMID:21733610

Lichtenthaler, U. (2018). Substitute or Synthesis: The Interplay between Human and Artificial Intelligence. *Research Technology Management*, *61*(5), 12–14. doi:10.1080/08956308.2018.1495962

Lichtenthaler, U. (2020). *Integrated Intelligence: Combining Human and Artificial Intelligence for Competitive Advantage*. Campus Verlag GmbH.

Liguori, E. W., & Pittz, T. G. (2020). Strategies for small business: Surviving and thriving in the era of COVID-19. *Journal of the International Council for Small Business*, *1*(2), 106–110. doi:10.1080/26437015.2020.1779538

Li, J., & Leonas, K. K. (2019). Trends of sustainable development among luxury industry. In *Sustainable luxury* (pp. 107–126). Springer. doi:10.1007/978-981-13-0623-5_6

Likert, R. (1932). Technique for the measurement of attitudes. *Archives de Psychologie*, *140*, 1–55.

Lima, C. M. A. O. (2020). Information about the new coronavirus (COVID-19). doi:10.1590/0100-3984.2020.53.2e1

Lin, J. J., Mamykina, L., Lindtner, S., Delajoux, G., & Strub, H. B. (2006). *Fish'n'Steps: Encouraging physical activity with an interactive computer game.* Paper presented at the International conference on ubiquitous computing, Berlin, Germany. 10.1007/11853565_16

Linton, T., & Vakil, B. (2020). *It is up to manufacturers to keep their suppliers afloat.* Harvard Business Review Digital Article. Available at: https://hbr.org/2020/04/its-up-to-manufacturers-to-keep-their-supplier

Lin, Z., & Wang, Q. (2018). E-commerce Product Networks, Word-of-mouth Convergence, and Product Sales. *Journal of the Association for Information Systems*, *19*(1), 23–39. doi:10.17705/1jais.00481

Lippincott, B., Matulich, E., & Squires, K. (2006). To Learn Or Not To Learn: The Effect Of Educational Technology On Learning In Accounting Courses. *Journal of College Teaching and Learning*, *3*(12). Advance online publication. doi:10.19030/tlc.v3i12.1649

Lippitt, G. L., & Lippitt, R. (1986). The consulting process in action. *Training and Development Journal*, *29*(6), 38–41.

Li, S., Subba Rao, S., Ragu-Nathan, T. S., & Ragu-Nathan, B. (2005). Development and validation of a measurement instrument for studying supply chain management practices. *Journal of Operations Management*, *23*(6), 618–641. doi:10.1016/j.jom.2005.01.002

Lisitsy, V. V., Misyukevich, V. I., & Mikhailenko, O. M. (Eds.). (2020). *The formation of the system of internal trade of Ukraine: theory, practice, innovation.* PUET.

LissitsA. (2021). https://adler.com.ua/news/yak-vpline-koronavirus-na-rozvitok-agrosektoru-v-ukrajini

Li, T., Sethi, S. P., & Zhang, J. (2013). How Does Pricing Power Affect a Firm's Sourcing Decisions from Unreliable Suppliers? *International Journal of Production Research*, *51*(23–24), 6990–7005. doi:10.1080/00207543.2013.849826

Li, T., Sethi, S. P., & Zhang, J. (2017). Mitigating Supply Uncertainty: The Interplay Between Diversification and Pricing. *Production and Operations Management*, *26*(3), 369–388. doi:10.1111/poms.12656

Liu, Q. (2020). Measures must be commensurate with impact. *China Daily*. Retrieved from: http://www.chinadaily.com.cn/a/202002/24/WS5e5334d7a310128217279c19.html

Liu, W.H., Liang, Y.J., Bao, X., Qin, J.J, & Lim, M. K. (2020). China's logistics development trends in the post COVID-19 era. *International Journal of Logistics: Research and Applications*, 1–12. doi:10.1080/13675567.2020.1837760

Li, X., & Wu, L. (2018). Herding and social media word-of-mouth: Evidence from Groupon. *MIS Quarterly: Management Information Systems*, *42*(4), 1331–1351.

Li, X., Zhao, X., & Pu, W. (2020). Measuring the ease of use of mobile applications in e-commerce retailing from the perspective of consumer online shopping behaviour patterns. *Journal of Retailing and Consumer Services*, *55*, 102093. doi:10.1016/j.jretconser.2020.102093

Lobaugh, K., Simpson, J., & Ohri, L. (2015). *Navigating the New Digital Divide: Capitalizing on Digital Influence in Retail.* https://www2.deloitte.com/content/dam/Deloitte/us/Documents/consumer-business/us-cb-navigating-the-new-digital-divide-v2-051315.pdf

Lobchat, L., & Mueller, B. (2021). Corporate digital responsibility. *Journal of Business Research*, *122*, 875–888. doi:10.1016/j.jbusres.2019.10.006

Longhurst, C. A., Kremer, B., & Maysent, P. S. (2021). Rapid implementation of a vaccination superstation. *Journal of the American Medical Association*, *325*(10), 931–932. doi:10.1001/jama.2021.0801 PMID:33507206

Longo, A., Markandya, A., & Petrucci, M. (2008). The Internalization of Externalities in the Production of Electricity: Willingness to Pay for the Attributes of a Policy for Renewable Energy. *Ecological Economics*, *67*(1), 140–152. doi:10.1016/j.ecolecon.2007.12.006

Lopes de Sousa Jabbour, A. B., Chiappetta Jabbour, C. J., Hingley, M., Vilalta-Perdomo, E. L., Ramsden, G., & Twigg, D. (2020). Sustainability of supply chains in the wake of the coronavirus (COVID-19 SARS-CoV-2) pandemic: Lessons and trends. *Modern Supply Chain Research and Application Vol.*, *2*(3), 117–122. doi:10.1108/MSCRA-05-2020-0011

Lopez, B., & Rangel, C. (2022). How Luxury Fashion Brands Contribute Efficiently to Sustainable Development. In *Future Advancements for CSR and the Sustainable Development Goals in a Post-COVID-19 World* (pp. 139–161). IGI Global. doi:10.4018/978-1-7998-8065-3.ch007

Lopez-Ridaura, Sanders, Barba-Escoto, Wiegel, Mayorga-Cortes, Gonzalez-Esquivel, Lopez-Ramirez, Escoto-Masis, Morales-Galindo, & García-Barcena. (2021). Immediate impact of COVID-19 pandemic on farming systems in Central America and Mexico. *Agricultural Systems, 192*, 1-12. doi:10.1016/j.agsy.2021.103178

Lorini, G., & Marrosu, F. (2018). How individual habits fit/unfit social norms: From the Historical Perspective to a Neurobiological Repositioning of an Unresolved Problem. *Frontiers in Sociology*, *3*, 14. doi:10.3389/fsoc.2018.00014

Loupiac, P., & Goudey, A. (2019). How website browsing impacts expectations of store features. *International Journal of Retail & Distribution Management*, *48*(1), 92–108. doi:10.1108/IJRDM-07-2018-0146

Loureiro, S. M. C., & Lopes, J. (2019). How corporate social responsibility initiatives in social media affect awareness and customer engagement. *Journal of Promotion Management*, *25*(3), 419–438. doi:10.1080/10496491.2019.1557819

Lueto, O., Solare, P., & Catumbela, E. (2020). Angolan Higher Education in the Time of Covid-19: Necessary Changes and Transformations. *Angolan Journal of University Extension*, 76-93.

Lu, M., Huang, S., & Shen, Z.-J. M. (2011). Product Substitution and Dual Sourcing Under Random Supply Failures. *Transportation Research Part B: Methodological*, *45*(8), 1251–1265. doi:10.1016/j.trb.2010.09.005

Luna-Nevarez, C., & McGovern, E. (2021). The Rise of the Virtual Reality (VR) Marketplace: Exploring the Antecedents and Consequences of Consumer Attitudes toward V-Commerce. *Journal of Internet Commerce*, *20*(2), 167–194. doi:10.1080/15332861.2021.1875766

Lund, S., Madgavkar, A., Manyika, J., Smit, S., Ellingrud, K., & Robinson, O. (2021). *The future of work after COVID-19*. McKinsey & Company. https://www.mckinsey.com/featured-insights/future-of-work/the-future-of-work-after-covid-19

Lundberg, E. (2017). *How to compete effectively with self-service technologies: The impact of technology readiness and the technology acceptance model of self scanning*. Uppsala University.

Luszczynska, A., & Schwarzer, R. (2015). Social cognitive theory. In M. Conner & P. Norman (Eds.), *UK Higher Education Psychology Psychology* (pp. 225–251). McGraw-Hill Education.

Luxottica. (2021). *Sustainable Development Goals*. Retrieved from https://www.luxottica.com/en/sustainable-development-goals

Luxottica. (2022). https://www.linkedin.com/company/luxottica/

Lu, Y., Wu, J., Peng, J., & Lu, L. (2020). The perceived impact of the Covid-19 epidemic: Evidence from a sample of 4807 SMEs in Sichuan Province, China. *Environmental Hazards*, *19*(4), 323–340. doi:10.1080/17477891.2020.1763902

LVMH. (2020a). *2019 Environmental Responsibility Report*. Retrieved from https://cutt.ly/7bEKbB5

LVMH. (2020b). *2019 Social Responsibility Report*. Retrieved from https://cutt.ly/GbbQtjF

LVMH. (2022). https://www.linkedin.com/company/lvmh/

Lyng, S. (1990). Edgework: A social psychological analysis of voluntary risk taking. *American Journal of Sociology*, *95*(4), 851–886. doi:10.1086/229379

Lyócsa, Š., Baumöhl, E., Výrost, T., & Molnár, P. (2020). Fear of the coronavirus and the stock markets. *Finance Research Letters*, 1–7.

Machado, A. de B., Sousa, M. J., Nawaz, F., & Martins, J. M. (2020). Impacts of the integration of Chinese managers in the Western economies the case of Brazil. *Transnational Corporations Review*, *1*(1), 25. doi:10.1080/19186444.2019.1693203

Machowiak, W. (2012). Risk management-unappreciated instrument of supply chain management strategy. *LogForum*, *8*(4), 277–285.

MacInnis, D. J. (2011). A framework for conceptual contributions in marketing. *Journal of Marketing*, *75*(4), 136–154. doi:10.1509/jmkg.75.4.136

Maelah, R., Muhammaddun Mohamed, Z., Ramli, R., & Aman, A. (2014). Internship for accounting undergraduates: Comparative insights from stakeholders. *Education + Training*, *56*(6), 482–502. doi:10.1108/ET-09-2012-0088

Magableh, G. M. (2021, September). (2021). Supply Chains and the COVID-19 Pandemic: A Comprehensive Framework. *European Management Review*, *18*(3), 363–382. Advance online publication. doi:10.1111/emre.12449

Mahajan, K., & Tomar, S. (2021). COVID-19 and Supply Chain Disruption: Evidence from Food Markets in India. *American Journal of Agricultural Economics*, *103*(1), 35–52. doi:10.1111/ajae.12158 PMID:33230345

Mahardika, H., Thomas, D., Ewing, M. T., & Japutra, A. (2019). Experience and facilitating conditions as impediments to consumers' new technology adoption. *International Review of Retail, Distribution and Consumer Research*, *29*(1), 79–98. doi:10.1080/09593969.2018.1556181

Maier, E., & Wieringa, J. (2021). Acquiring customers through online marketplaces? The effect of marketplace sales on sales in a retailer's own channels. *International Journal of Research in Marketing*, *38*(2), 311–328. doi:10.1016/j.ijresmar.2020.09.007

Mainardes, E. W., & Cardoso, M. V. (2019). Effect of the use of social media in trust, loyalty and purchase intention in physical stores. *International Review of Retail, Distribution and Consumer Research*, *29*(4), 456–477. doi:10.1080/09593969.2019.1583593

Maison, D., Jaworska, D., Adamczyk, D., & Affeltowicz, D. (2021). The challenges arising from the COVID-19 pandemic and the way people deal with them. A qualitative longitudinal study. *PLoS One*, *16*(10), e0258133. https://doi.org/10.1371/journal.pone.0258133

MakerD. A. O. (2022). Available at https://makerdao.com/en/

Malik, A., Pereira, V., & Budhwar, P. (2018). Value Creation and Capture Through Human Resource Management Practices: Gazing Through the Business Model Lens. *Organizational Dynamics*, *47*(3), 180–188. doi:10.1016/j.orgdyn.2017.09.002

Mann, C. L. (2020). Real and financial lenses to assess the economic consequences of COVID-19. In Economics in the Time of Covid-19 (pp. 81-85). CEPR Press.

Manss, R., Kurze, K., & Bornschein, R. (2020). What drives competitive webrooming? The roles of channel and retailer aspects. *International Review of Retail, Distribution and Consumer Research*, *30*(3), 233–265. doi:10.1080/09593969.2019.1687104

Mao, L., Jin, H., Wang, M., Hu, Y., Chen, S., He, Q., Chang, J., Hong, C., Zhou, Y., Wang, D., Miao, X., Li, Y., & Hu, B. (2020). Neurologic manifestations of hospitalized patients with coronavirus disease 2019 in Wuhan, China. *JAMA Neurology*, *77*(6), 683–690. doi:10.1001/jamaneurol.2020.1127 PMID:32275288

Marchant-Forde, J. N., & Boyle, L. A. (2020). COVID-19 Effects on Livestock Production: A One Welfare *Issue. Frontiers in Veterinary Science*, *7*, 585787. doi:10.3389/fvets.2020.585787 PMID:33195613

Mariana, C. D., Ekaputra, I. A., & Husodo, Z. A. (2020). Are Bitcoin and Ethereum safe-havens for stocks during the COVID-19 pandemic? *Finance Research Letters*, 1–6. doi:10.1016/j.frl.2020.101798 PMID:33100925

Marinova, D., Singh, S. K., & Singh, J. (2018). Frontline Problem-Solving Effectiveness: A Dynamic Analysis of Verbal and Nonverbal Cues. *JMR, Journal of Marketing Research*, *55*(2), 178–192. doi:10.1509/jmr.15.0243

Marjerison, R. K., & Gan, S. (2020). Social Media Influencers' Effect on Chinese Gen Z Consumers: Management and Use of Video Content Platforms. *Journal of Media Management and Entrepreneurship*, *2*(2), 1–18. doi:10.4018/JMME.2020070101

Marrow, A. J. (1977). *The practical theorist: The life and work of Kurt Lewin*. Teachers College Press.

Matt, C., Hess, T., & Benlian, A. (2015). Digital transformation strategies. *Business & Information Systems Engineering*, *57*(5), 339–343. doi:10.100712599-015-0401-5

Mazzarol, T., & Reboud, S. (2020). Adoption and diffusion of innovation. In *Entrepreneurship and Innovation* (pp. 165–189). Springer. doi:10.1007/978-981-13-9412-6_6

McCarthy, I., & Anagnostou, A. (2004). The Impact of Outsourcing on the Transaction Costs and Boundaries of Manufacturing. *International Journal of Production Economics*, *88*(1), 61–71. doi:10.1016/S0925-5273(03)00183-X

McCombs, K., & Williams, E. (2021). The resilient effects of transformational leadership on well-being: Examining the moderating effects of anxiety during the COVID-19 crisis. *Leadership and Organization Development Journal*, *42*(8), 1254–1266. doi:10.1108/LODJ-02-2021-0092

McGeever, N., McQuinn, J., & Myers, S. (2020). SME liquidity needs during the COVID-19 shock (No. 2/FS/20). Central Bank of Ireland.

McKibbin, W., & Fernando, R. (2020). The economic impact of COVID-19. In *Economics in the Time of Covid- 19 (pp. 45-51)*. CEPR Press.

McKinsey & Company (2022). *The state of fashion*. Author.

McKinsey. (2020). *How COVID-19 has pushed companies over the technology tipping point—and transformed business forever.* McKinsey Global Survey Results.

McLaughlin, R. (1982). *What? Where? When? Why? Essays on Induction, Space and Time, explanation*. D Reidel. doi:10.1007/978-94-009-7731-0

Meckling, M. C. J. (1976). Theory of the firm: Managerial behavior, agency costs and ownership structure. *Journal of Financial Economics*, *3*(4), 305–360. doi:10.1016/0304-405X(76)90026-X

Mediawati, E., Widaningsih, M., Majid, R., Ali, N., Abdullah, S., Erawati, T., Susanto, M., & Nurtanto, M. (2020). Internship during the covid 19 pandemic: Students and supervisors perspective. *Psychology and Education*, *57*(8), 1036–1038.

Meeker, W., Hahn, G., & Escobar, L. (2017). *Statistical Intervals: A Guide for Practitioners and Researchers*. Wiley. doi:10.1002/9781118594841

Mehta, S., Saxena, T., & Purohit, N. (2020). The new consumer behaviour paradigm amid COVID-19: Permanent or transient? *Journal of Health Management*, *22*(2), 291–301. doi:10.1177/0972063420940834

Mehta, S., Saxena, T., & Purohit, N. (2020). The New Consumer Behaviour Paradigm amid COVID-19: Permanent or Transient? *Journal of Health Management*, *22*(2), 291–301. https://doi.org/10.1177/0972063420940834

Meier, M., & Pinto, E. (2020). Covid-19 supply chain disruptions. *Covid Economics*, *48*, 139–170.

Mejía, L. F. (2020). Choque dual y posibles efectos sobre la economía colombiana. *Tendencia Económica, 204*, 3-18. https://www.repository.fedesarrollo.org.co/handle/11445/3937

Melani, C. (2006). Development and the Changing Dynamics of Global Production: Global Value Chains and Local Clusters in Apparel Manufacturing. *Competition & Change*, *10*(1), 23–48. doi:10.1179/102452906X91993

Méndez, L. M. (2020). A reflection on the challenges posed by digitalisation of labour markets. In J. Carby-Hall & L. M. Méndez (Eds.), *Labour Law and the Gig Economy* (pp. 1–13). Routledge. doi:10.4324/9781003033721-101

Mendy, J., & Rahman, M. (2019). Application of human resource management's universal model: An examination of people versus institutions as barriers of internationalization for SMEs in a small developing country. *Thunderbird International Business Review*, *61*(2), 363–374. doi:10.1002/tie.21985

Mercer. (2020). *Total Remuneration Survey 2020.* https://www.imercer.com/products/total-remuneration-surveys

Mero, J. (2018). The effects of two-way communication and chat service usage on consumer attitudes in the e-commerce retailing sector. *Electronic Markets*, *28*(2), 205–217. doi:10.100712525-017-0281-2

Mertens, G., Gerritsen, L., Dujndam, S., Salemink, E., & Engelhard, I. M. (2020). Fear of the coronavirus (COVID-19): Predictors in an online study conducted in March 2020. *Journal of Anxiety Disorders, 74*, 1–8.

Michale, J. (2005). Positive and negative reinforcement, a distinction that is no longer necessary; or a better way to talk about bad things. *Journal of Organizational Behavior Management, 24*(1-2), 207–222. doi:10.1300/J075v24n01_15

Mihailović, A., Cerović Smolović, J., Radević, I., Rašović, N., & Martinović, N. (2021). COVID-19 and beyond: Employee perceptions of the efficiency of teleworking and its cybersecurity implications. *Sustainability, 13*(12), 6750. doi:10.3390u13126750

Mihalache, M., & Mihalache, O. R. (2016). A Decisional Framework of Offshoring: Integrating Insights from 25 Years of Research to Provide Direction for Future. *Decision Sciences, 47*(6), 1103–1149. doi:10.1111/deci.12206

Milovidov, V. D. (2015a). Management of innovations: How to effectively use the information. *Neftyanoe khozyaystvo, 6*, 10–16.

Milovidov, V. D. (2015c). Proactive innovation management: Knowledge mapping. *Neftyanoe khozyaystvo, 8*, 16–21.

Milovidov, V. (2020). The "Linked Prosperity" Model as an Integrated Response to Corporate Management Challenges in a Network Society. *Foresight and STI Governance, 14*(4), 112–120. doi:10.17323/2500-2597.2020.4.112.120

Milovidov, V. D. (2015b). Risk management under information asymmetry: To differentiate those distinguishable. *World Economy and International Relation, 8*(8), 14–24. doi:10.20542/0131-2227-2015-8-14-24

Milovidov, V. D. (2018). Hearing the sound of the wave: What impedes one's ability to foresee innovations? *Foresight and STI Governance, 12*(1), 88–97. doi:10.17323/2500-2597.2018.1.88.97

Milovidov, V. D. (2021). Pandemic in the network society: Network readiness increases population vulnerability to COVID-19 in less developed countries. *Acta Oeconomica, 71*(S1), 187–203. doi:10.1556/032.2021.00035

Milovidov, V. D. (2022). Story stocks: How stock market-induced corporate identity is being fomed. *World Economy and International Relation, 66*(1), 100–109. doi:10.20542/0131-2227-2022-66-1-100-109

Min, S., & Mintzer, J. (2004). Developing and measuring supply chain management concepts. *Journals of business Logistics, 25*(1), 63-92.

Minai, M. S., Raza, S., & Segaf, S. (2021). Post COVID-19: Strategic Digital Entrepreneurship in Malaysia. *Modeling Economic Growth in Contemporary Malaysia*, 71–79. doi:10.1108/978-1-80043-806-420211007

Ministerio de Hacienda - MinHacienda. (2020). *Comunicado Oficial Comité Consultivo para la Regla Fiscal.* https://www.minhacienda.gov.co/webcenter/ShowProperty?nodeId=%2FConexionContent%2FWCC_CLUSTER-128327%2F%2FidcPrimaryFile&revision=latestreleased

Ministerio de Trabajo - MinTrabajo. (2020). *Normatividad y Circulares.* https://www.mintrabajo.gov.co/normatividad/circulares/2020

Ministerio de Trabajo - MinTrabajo. (2020). *Resolución 0803.* https://www.mintrabajo.gov.co/atencion-al-ciudadano/transparencia/resoluciones

Min, S., & Mentzer, J. (2004). Developing and measuring supply chain management concepts. *Journal of Business Logistics, 25*(1), 63–92. doi:10.1002/j.2158-1592.2004.tb00170.x

Mintz, O., Gilbride, T. J., Lenk, P., & Currim, I. S. (2021). The right metrics for marketing-mix decisions. *International Journal of Research in Marketing, 38*(1), 32–49. doi:10.1016/j.ijresmar.2020.08.003

Mio, C., Panfilo, S., & Blundo, B. (2020). Sustainable development goals and the strategic role of business: A systematic literature review. *Business Strategy and the Environment, 29*(8), 3220–3245. doi:10.1002/bse.2568

Mishra, M., & Majumdar, P. (2020). Social distancing during COVID-19: Will it change the Indian society? *Journal of Health Management, 22*(2), 224–235. doi:10.1177/0972063420935547

Mishra, P., Bhatnagar, J., Gupta, R., & Wadsworth, S. M. (2019). How work–family enrichment influence innovative work behavior: Role of psychological capital and supervisory support. *Journal of Management & Organization, 25*(1), 58–80. doi:10.1017/jmo.2017.23

Misyukevich, V. I., Trushkina, N. V., & Shkrygun, Yu. O. (2020). E-commerce in the global digital space: new challenges and directions of development. In The formation of the system of internal trade of Ukraine: theory, practice, innovation (pp. 150-162). PUET.

Mitchell, T. R. (1982). Motivation: New directions for theory, research, and practice. *Academy of Management Review, 7*(1), 80–88. doi:10.2307/257251

Mitrokhin, O. V., Reshetnikov, V. A., Belova, E. V., & Jakovljevic, M. M. (2020). Sanitary and hygienic aspects of the COVID-19 self-isolation. *The Open Public Health Journal, 13*(1), 734–738. doi:10.2174/1874944502013010734

Modgil, S., Dwivedi, Y. K., Rana, N. P., Gupta, S., & Kamble, S. (2022). Has Covid-19 accelerated opportunities for digital entrepreneurship? An Indian perspective. *Technological Forecasting and Social Change, 175*, 121415. https://doi.org/10.1016/j.techfore.2021.121415

Moe, N. B., Fægri, T. E., Cruzes, D. S., & Faugstad, J. E. (2006). Enabling Knowledge Sharing in Agile Virtual Teams. *2016 IEEE 11th International Conference on Global Software Engineering (ICGSE)*, 29-33. 10.1109/ICGSE.2016.30

Moffit, R., & Badger, D. (2020). Defeating COVID-19—What Policymakers Can Do to Change the Conditions on the Ground. *Heritage Foundation Backgrounder*, (3485), 2020–04.

Mohd Dali, N. R. S., Abdul Hamid, H., Wan Nawang, W. R., & Wan Mohamed Nazarie, W. N. F. (2020). Post pandemic consumer behavior: Conceptual framework. *The Journal of Muamalat and Islamic Finance Research.*

Möhring, K., Naumann, E., Reifenscheid, M., Wenz, A., Rettig, T., Krieger, U., ... Blom, A.G. (2021). The COVID-19 pandemic and subjective well-being: longitudinal evidence on satisfaction with work and family. *European Societies, 23*(sup1), S601-S617.

Möhring, K., Naumann, E., Reifenscheid, M., Wenz, A., Rettig, T., Krieger, U., Friedel, S., Finkel, M., Cornesse, C., & Blom, A. (2020). The COVID-19 pandemic and subjective well-being: longitudinal evidence on satisfaction with work and family. *European Societies, 23*(sup1), S601-S617.

Mokni, K., & Ajmi, A. N. (2021). Cryptocurrencies vs. US dollar: Evidence from causality in quantiles analysis. *Economic Analysis and Policy, 69*, 238–252. doi:10.1016/j.eap.2020.12.011

Molden, D. C., & Dweck, C. S. (2006). Finding" meaning" in psychology: A lay theories approach to self-regulation, social perception, and social development. *The American Psychologist, 61*(3), 192–203. doi:10.1037/0003-066X.61.3.192 PMID:16594836

Molenaar, M. D., Bosch, F., Guggenheim, J., & Jhunjhunwala, P. (2020). *The Post-Covid-19 Flight Plan for Airlines.* Boston Consulting Group.

Momeni, N. (2012). Fraud in Judicial System as a Language Crime. *Forensic Linguistics Approach., 2*(6), 1263–1269. doi:10.4304/tpls.2.6.1263-1269

Montano, D. E., & Kasprzyk, D. (2015). Theory of reasoned action, theory of planned behavior, and the integrated behavioral model. In B. K. Karen Glanz & K. V. Rimer (Eds.), *Health behavior: Theory, research and practice* (Vol. 70, pp. 95–124). John Wiley & Sons.

Montero, A. G., & Le Blanc, D. (2020). Resilient institutions in times of crisis: Transparency, accountability and participation at the national level key to effective response to COVID-19. *UN-DESA Policy Brief*, *74*, 49.

Moore, G. A. (1991). *Crossing the chasm: Marketing and selling technology products to mainstream customers*. HarperBusiness.

Morales, C. O. S. (2021). Innovation as Recovery Strategy for SMEs in Emerging Economies During the Covid-19 Pandemic. *Research in International Business and Finance*, •••, 57.

Moreira, A., & Hick, R. (2021). COVID-19, the Great Recession and social policy: Is this time different? *Social Policy and Administration*, *55*(2), 261–279. doi:10.1111pol.12679

More, R. (2016). *Marketing High Profit Product/Service Solutions*. Routledge. doi:10.4324/9781315593975

Morgan, T., Anokhin, S., Ofstein, L., & Friske, W. (2020). SME response to major exogenous shocks: The bright and dark sides of business model pivoting. *International Small Business Journal*, *38*(5), 369–379.

Mori, M., MacDorman, K., & Kageki, N. (2012). The Uncanny Valey. *IEEE Robotics & Automation Magazine*, *19*(June), 98–100. doi:10.1109/MRA.2012.2192811

Morzaria, H. (2020). *The 7 Benefits of AI in Customer Service*. https://www.business2community.com/customer-experience/the-7-benefits-of-ai-in-customer-service-02301342

Mourad, A., Srour, A., Harmanai, H., Jenainati, C., & Arafeh, M. (2020). Critical impact of social networks infodemic on defeating coronavirus COVID-19 pandemic: Twitter-based study and research directions. *IEEE eTransactions on Network and Service Management*, *17*(4), 2145–2155. doi:10.1109/TNSM.2020.3031034

Mozeley, F., & Whelan, J. (n.d.). *3 resources to assess and open policy windows*. https://commonslibrary.org/resources-assessing-and-opening-policy-windows/

Mrass, V., & Peters, C. (2017). *Crowdworking-Plattformen in Deutschland*. Academic Press.

Mrass, V., Peters, C., & Leimeister, J. M. (2016). *New work organization through crowdworking platforms-a case study*. Academic Press.

Mrass, V., Peters, C., & Leimeister, J. M. (2017). *Exploiting the digitization of leisure time: Casual work and additional earnings for ındividuals on crowdworking platforms*. In International Conference on Information Systems (ICIS), Pre-Workshop "Digitization of the Individual (DOTI)", Seoul, South Korea.

Múgica, J. M., & Berné, C. (2019). Analyzing channel choice: Direct and indirect e-Tourism distribution. *International Review of Retail, Distribution and Consumer Research*, *29*(5), 537–548. doi:10.1080/09593969.2019.1664617

Musa, S., & Aifuwa, H. O. (2020). Coronavirus pandemic in Nigeria: How can Small and Medium Enterprises (SMEs) cope and flatten the curve. *Eur. J. Account. Financ. Invest*, *6*, 56–61.

Mushi, V., & Shao, M. (2020). Tailoring of the ongoing water, sanitation and hygiene interventions for prevention and control of COVID-19. *Tropical Medicine and Health*, *48*(1), 1–3. doi:10.118641182-020-00236-5 PMID:32549749

Mutreja, A. (2021). *COVID crisis in India: why its public health strategy failed*. The Conversation. https://theconversation.com/covid-crisis-in-india-why-its-public-health-strategy-failed-159861

Mutz, M., & Reimers, A. (2021). Leisure time sports and exercise activities during the COVID-19 pandemic: A survey of working parents. *German Journal of Exercise and Sport Research*, *51*(3), 384–389. doi:10.100712662-021-00730-w

Nabity-Grover, T., Cheung, Ch. M. K., & Thatcher, J. B. (2020). Inside and outside in: How the COVID-19 pandemic affects self-disclosure on social media. *International Journal of Information Management*, *55*(12), 102188. doi:10.1016/j.ijinfomgt.2020.102188 PMID:32836645

Naeem, M. (2021). Do social media platforms develop consumer panic buying during the fear of the Covid-19 pandemic. *Journal of Retailing and Consumer Services*, *58*, 102226. doi:10.1016/j.jretconser.2020.102226

Nagel, L. (2020). The influence of the COVID-19 pandemic on the digital transformation of work. *The International Journal of Sociology and Social Policy*, *40*(9/10), 861–875. doi:10.1108/IJSSP-07-2020-0323

Najafi-Tavani, S., Najafi-Tavani, Z., Naudé, P., Oghazi, P., & Zeynaloo, E. (2018). How collaborative innovation networks affect new product performance: Product innovation capability, process innovation capability, and absorptive capacity. *Industrial Marketing Management*, *73*, 193–205. doi:10.1016/j.indmarman.2018.02.009

Najmul Islam, A. K. M., Mäntymäki, M., Laato, S., & Turel, O. (2022). Adverse consequences of emotional support seeking through social network sites in coping with stressfrom a global pandemic. *International Journal of Information Management*, *62*(2), 102431. doi:10.1016/j.ijinfomgt.2021.102431 PMID:34642531

Nandi, S., Sarkis, J., Aghaei, H. A., & Helms, M. M. (2021). Redesigning Supply Chains using Blockchain-Enabled Circular Economy and COVID-19 Experiences. *Sustainable Production and Consumption*, *27*, 10–22. doi:10.1016/j.spc.2020.10.019 PMID:33102671

Narasimhan, R., & Kim, S. W. (2007). Effects of Supply Chain Integration on the relation between versification and performance: Evidence from Japanese and Korean firms. *Journal of Operations Management*, *20*(3), 303–323. doi:10.1016/S0272-6963(02)00008-6

Narayan, P. K. (2020). Has COVID-19 changed exchange rate resistance to shocks? *Asian Economics Letters*, *1*(1), 17389.

Narayan, R., & Tidström, A. (2020). Tokenizing coopetition in a blockchain for a transition to circular economy. *Journal of Cleaner Production*, *263*, 121437. doi:10.1016/j.jclepro.2020.121437

Nass, O., Garrigós, J. A., Gómez, H. G., & Schoeneberg, K. P. (2020). Attribution modelling in an omni-channel environment – New requirements and specifications from a practical perspective. *International Journal of Electronic Marketing and Retailing*, *11*(1), 81–111. doi:10.1504/IJEMR.2020.106432

National Health Act. 61/2003. Pretoria.

National Rural Health Mission: framework for implementation 2005–2012. (2005). Government of India.

Nations, U. (2015). *Transforming our world: the 2030 agenda for sustainable development*. United Nations, Department of Economic and Social Affairs.

Nayal, P., Pandey, N., & Paul, J. (2021). Covid-19 pandemic and consumer-employee-organization wellbeing: A dynamic capability theory approach. *The Journal of Consumer Affairs*, *56*(1), 359–390. https://doi.org/10.1111/joca.12399

Ndomba, B. (2020). *Angola: Companies and Workers suffer impact of Covid-19*. DW. https://www.dw.com/pt-002/angola-empresas-e-trabahdores-sofrem-impacto-da-covid-19/a-53532402 _

Neighbors, C., Foster, D. W., & Fossos, N. (2013). Peer influences on addiction. In *Principles of addiction: Comprehensive addictive behaviours and disorders* (Vol. 1, pp. 323–331). Academic Press. doi:10.1016/B978-0-12-398336-7.00033-4

Neu, C.R., Gehlhaus, D., & Shatz, H. J. (2020). *Preserving Small Businesses*. Academic Press.

Neville, F. G., Templeton, A., Smith, J. R., & Louis, W. R. (2021). Social norms, social identities and the COVID-19 pandemic: Theory and recommendations. *Social and Personality Psychology Compass*, *15*(5), e12596. doi:10.1111pc3.12596 PMID:34230834

Newman, M. E. J. (2010). *Networks: An Introduction*. Oxford University Press. doi:10.1093/acprof:oso/9780199206650.001.0001

Next GenerationE. U. (n.d.). https://europa.eu/next-generation-eu/index_en

Ng, A. (2021). Green Investing and Financial Services: ESG Investing for a Sustainable World. In *The Palgrave Handbook of Global Sustainability* (pp. 1–12). Springer International Publishing. doi:10.1007/978-3-030-38948-2_104-1

Ng, I. C. L., & Wakenshaw, S. Y. L. (2017). The Internet-of-Things: Review and research directions. *International Journal of Research in Marketing*, *34*(1), 3–21. doi:10.1016/j.ijresmar.2016.11.003

Nguyen, T. U. H., Sherif, J. S., & Newby, M. (2007). Strategies for successful CRM implementation. *Information Management & Computer Security*, *15*(2), 102–115. doi:10.1108/09685220710748001

Nissen, L. (2020). Social work and the future in a post-Covid 19 world: A foresight lens and a call to action for the profession. *Journal of Technology in Human Services*, *38*(4), 309–330. doi:10.1080/15228835.2020.1796892

Nolan, R., & McFarlan, W. (2005). Information technology and the board of directors. *Harvard Business Review*, *83*(10), 96. PMID:16250628

Nonino, F. (2013). The network dimensions of intra-organizational social capital. *Journal of Management & Organization*, *19*(4), 454–477. doi:10.1017/jmo.2013.20

Norbis, M., & Meixell, M. (2011). *Dual Sourcing in Supply Chain Design: A Multi-Dimensional Framework of Risk*. Academic Press.

Nordlund, A. M., & Garvill, J. (2003). Effects of values, problem awareness, and personal norm on willingness to reduce personal car use. *Journal of Environmental Psychology*, *23*(4), 339–347. doi:10.1016/S0272-4944(03)00037-9

Nosova, O. V. (2021). Foreign direct investment TNCS as a factor of innovative development. *Bulletin of Kharkiv National University named after VN Karazin's Series Economic*, *100*, 45–56. doi:10.26565/2311-2379-2021-100-05

Nüesch, R., Alt, R., & Puschmann, T. (2015). Hybrid Customer Interaction. *Business & Information Systems Engineering*, *57*(1), 73–78. doi:10.100712599-014-0366-9

Nyanga, T., & Zirima, H. (2020). Reactions of small to medium enterprises in masvingo, Zimbabwe to covid 19: Implications on productivity. *Business Excellence and Management*, *10*(1), 22–32. doi:10.24818/beman/2020.S.I.1-02

Nygren-Krug, H. (2019). The right (s) road to universal health coverage. *Health and Human Rights*, *21*(2), 215. PMID:31885451

O'Higgins, N., & Caro, L. P. (2021). *Crowdwork for young people: Risks and opportunities*. IZA Discussion Papers 14933, Institute of Labor Economics (IZA). https://docs.iza.org/dp14933.pdf

Obeng, R., & Haugh, H. (2014). Strategic entrepreneurship and small firm growth in Ghana. *International Small Business Journal*, *32*(5), 501–524. doi:10.1177/0266242612463946

Obrenovic, B., Du, J., Godinic, D., Tsoy, D., Khan, M. A. S., & Jakhongirov, I. (2020). Sustaining enterprise operations and productivity during the COVID-19 pandemic: "Enterprise Effectiveness and Sustainability Model. *Sustainability*, *12*(15), 5981. doi:10.3390u12155981

Odabaş, M., Holt, T. J., & Breiger, R. L. (2017). Markets as governance environments for organizations at the edge of illegality: Insights from social network analysis. *The American Behavioral Scientist*, *61*(11), 1267–1288. doi:10.1177/0002764217734266

OECD. (2019). *How's Life in the Digital Age? Opportunities and Risks of the Digital Transformation for People's Well-being*. OECD Publishing. doi:10.1787/9789264311800-

OECD. (2020). *COVID-19 and fiscal relations across levels of government*. OECD.

OECD. (2020). *Evaluating the initial impact of COVID-19 containment measures on economic activity*. OECD Policy Responses to Coronavirus (COVID-19).

OECD. (2022). *Economic and Social Impacts and Policy Implications of the War in Ukraine*. https://www.oecd-ilibrary.org/sites/4181d61b-en/index.html?itemId=/content/publication/4181d61b-en

Oh, J., & Ki, E. J. (2019). Factors affecting social presence and word-of-mouth in corporate social responsibility communication: Tone of voice, message framing, and online medium type. *Public Relations Review*, *45*(2), 319–331. doi:10.1016/j.pubrev.2019.02.005

Okazaki, S., Plangger, K., West, D., & Menéndez, H. D. (2020). Exploring digital corporate social responsibility communications on Twitter. *Journal of Business Research*, *117*, 675–682. doi:10.1016/j.jbusres.2019.09.006

Okorie, D. I., & Lin, B. (2021). Stock markets and the COVID-19 fractal contagion effects. *Finance Research Letters*, *38*, 1–8. doi:10.1016/j.frl.2020.101640 PMID:32837366

Okoye, G. (2013). Forensic Accounting: A Tool for Fraud Detection and Prevention in the Public Sector (A Study of Selected Ministries in Kogi State). *International Journal of Academic Research in Business and Social Sciences*, *3*(3), 1–19.

Okpara, O. J. (2011). Corporate Governance in a Developing Economy: Barriers, Issues, and Implications for Firms. *Journal of Corporate Governance*, *11*(2), 184–199. doi:10.1108/14720701111121056

Olasehinde-Williams, G., Olanipekun, I., & Özkan, O. (2021). Foreign exchange market response to pandemic-induced fear: Evidence from (a) symmetric wild bootstrap likelihood ratio approach. *The Journal of International Trade & Economic Development*, *30*(7), 988–1003.

Oliveira. (1992). Planning strategic: Concepts, methodology and practices (6th ed.). Atlas.

Olšanová, K., Gook, G., & Zlatić, M. (2018). Influence of luxury companies' corporate social responsibility activities on consumer purchase intention: Development of a theoretical framework. *Central European Business Review*, *7*(3), 1–25. doi:10.18267/j.cebr.200

Olsson, J. (2008). *Forensic Linguistics* (2nd ed.). Continuum International Publishing Group.

Onyido, T., Boyd, D., & Thurairajah, N. (2014). The Implications of Supply Chain Localization for the Evolving Sustainable Energy Products Markets in the UK. *Built Environment*.

Oreg, S. (2003). Resistance to change: Developing an individual differences measure. *The Journal of Applied Psychology*, *88*(4), 680–693. doi:10.1037/0021-9010.88.4.680 PMID:12940408

Ortlinghaus, A., & Zielke, S. (2019). Designing multi-channel technologies – the mediating role of risk perceptions. *International Review of Retail, Distribution and Consumer Research*, *29*(5), 518–536. doi:10.1080/09593969.2019.1664610

Osarenkhoe, A. (2008). A study of the enablers of non-sequential internationalization process among small and medium-sized firms. *International Journal of Business Science and Applied Management*, *3*(2), 1–20.

Özatay, F., & Sak, G. (2020). *Covid- 19 ve normalleşme*. Türkiye Ekonomi Politikaları Araştırma Vakfı.

Özbay, F., & Özcan, A. (2021). The Examined of the influence of Covid-19 on e-commerce and consumer behavior: A study on Turkey. *Aydın İktisat Fakültesi Dergisi, 6*(1), 21–33.

Özmerdivanlı, A. (2021). Covid-19 pandemisi ile çeşitli finansal göstergeler arasındaki nedensellik ilişkisi: Türkiye örneği. *Ekonomi Politika ve Finans Araştırmaları Dergisi, 6*, 172-191.

Pajares, F., & Usher, E. L. (2008). Self-efficacy, motivation, and achievement in school from the perspective of reciprocal determinism. In M. L. Maehr, S. A. Karabenick, & T. C. Urdan (Eds.), Advances in motivation and achievement (Vol. 15, pp. 391–423). Emerald Group Publishing. doi:10.1016/S0749-7423(08)15012-9

Pak, A., Adegboye, O. A., Adekunle, A. I., Rahman, K. M., McBryde, E. S., & Eisen, D. P. (2020). Economic consequences of the COVID-19 outbreak: The need for epidemic preparedness. *Frontiers in Public Health, 8*, 241. doi:10.3389/fpubh.2020.00241 PMID:32574307

Pakpour, A. H., & Griffiths, M. D. The fear of COVID-19 and its role in preventive behaviors. *Journal of Concurrent Disorders*, 1- 6.

Pantano, E., Pizzi, G., Scarpi, D., & Dennis, Ch. (2020). Competing during a pandemic? Retailers' ups and downs during the COVID19 outbreak. *Journal of Business Research, 116*, 209–213. doi:10.1016/j.jbusres.2020.05.036 PMID:32501307

Pantano, E., Priporas, C. V., & Dennis, C. (2018). A new approach to retailing for successful competition in the new smart scenario. *International Journal of Retail & Distribution Management, 46*(3), 264–282. doi:10.1108/IJRDM-04-2017-0080

Pantano, E., & Willems, K. (2022). How Pandemic Crisis Times Affects Consumer Behaviour. In *Retail in a New World*. Emerald Publishing Limited. doi:10.1108/978-1-80117-846-420221004

Panwar, R. (2020). It's time to develop local production and supply networks. *California Management Review, 28*. https://cmr.berkeley.edu/2020/04/local-productionsupply-networks

Paolacci, G., Chandler, J., & Ipeirotis, P. G. (2010). Running experiments on amazon mechanical turk. *Judgment and Decision Making, 5*(5), 411-419.

Papacharissi, Z. (2004). Democracy online: Civility, politeness, and the democratic potential of online political discussion groups. *New Media & Society, 6*(2), 259–283. doi:10.1177/1461444804041444

Papadopoulos, T., Baltas, K. N., & Balta, M. E. (2020). The use of digital technologies by small and medium enterprises during COVID-19: Implications for theory and practice. *International Journal of Information Management, 55*, 102192. doi:10.1016/j.ijinfomgt.2020.102192 PMID:32836646

Partners' health policy and systems research report. (2021). https://ahpsr.who.int/publications/i/item/partners-health-policy-and-systems-research-report-2021

Paseková, M. (2019). OeconomiA copernicana. *Oeconomia Copernicana, 10*(1). Advance online publication. doi:10.24136/oc.2019.010

Paul, S. K., Moktadir, M. A., & Ahsan, K. (2021). Key supply chain strategies for the post-COVID-19 era: implications for resilience and sustainability. *The International Journal of Logistics Management*. doi:10.1108/IJLM-04-2021-0238

Paul, S. K., & Chowdhury, P. (2020a). A production recovery plan in manufacturing supply chains for a high-demand item during COVID-19. *International Journal of Physical Distribution & Logistics Management*, 1–22. doi:10.1108/IJPDLM-04-2020-0127

Paul, S. K., & Chowdhury, P. (2020b). Strategies for managing the impacts of disruptions during COVID-19: An example of toilet paper. *Global Journal of Flexible Systems Management*, *21*(3), 283–293. doi:10.100740171-020-00248-4

Paul, S. K., Chowdhury, P., Moktadir, M. A., & Lau, K. H. (2021). Supply chain recovery challenges in the wake of COVID-19 pandemic. *Journal of Business Research*, *136*, 316–329. doi:10.1016/j.jbusres.2021.07.056 PMID:34538979

Paul, S., & Venkateswaran, J. (2020). Designing robust policies under deep uncertainty formitigating epidemics. *Computers & Industrial Engineering*, *140*, 106221. doi:10.1016/j.cie.2019.106221

Pawar, D. S., Yadav, A. K., Akolekar, N., & Velaga, N. R. (2020). Impact of physical distancing due to novel coronavirus (SARS-CoV-2) on daily travel for work during transition to lockdown. Transport. *Res. Interdiscip. Perspect.*, *7*, 100203. doi:10.1016/j.trip.2020.100203 PMID:34173467

Pedersen, L. H., Fitzgibbons, S., & Pomorski, L. (2021). Responsible investing: The ESG-efficient frontier. *Journal of Financial Economics*, *142*(2), 572–597. doi:10.1016/j.jfineco.2020.11.001

Pedrosa, A. L., Bitencourt, L., Fróes, A. C. F., Cazumbá, M. L. B., Campos, R. G. B., de Brito, S. B. C. S., & Simões e Silva, A. C. (2020). Emotional, Behavioral, and Psychological Impact of the COVID-19 Pandemic. *Frontiers in Psychology*, *11*, 11. doi:10.3389/fpsyg.2020.566212 PMID:33117234

Peitrucha, F. (2014). *Supercommunicator*. American Management Association.

Pelet, J.-E. (2014). *User Behavior in Ubiquitous Online Environments*. IGI Global. doi:10.4018/978-1-4666-4566-0

Penchansky, R., & Thomas, J. W. (1981). The concept of access: Definition and relationship to consumer satisfaction. *Medical Care*, *19*, 127–140.

Pereira, T. M., Sacilotti, A. C., & Madureira Júnior, J. R. (2019). Computação em nuvem: plataforma como serviço. In E. R. Martins (Ed.), *Fundamentos da ciência da computação 2* (pp. 116–125). Atena Editora. doi:10.22533/at.ed.90319210612

Pereira, V., Munjal, S., & Ishizaka, A. (2020). Outsourcing and Offshoring Decision Making and its Implications for Businesses- A Synthesis of Research Pursuing Five Pertinent Questions. *Journal of Business Research*.

Perelman, D. (2020). In the Covid-19 Economy, You can have a kid or a job. You can't have both. *The New York Times*.

Perry, L., & Miller, T. (2018). *Business Communication: Skills and Techniques*. Scientific e-Resources.

Petrovska, O. M., & Bendus, I. M. (2020). Prospects for the emergence of new professions in the labor market of Ukraine after the global pandemic. *Economic Space*, (158), 95–100. doi:10.32782/2224-6282/158-15

Petrunenko, Y. V., Petrunenko, I. V., Chychun, V. A., Shuprudko, N. V., Kalynichenko, Y. V., & Manal, I. A. I. (2021). Trends in the management of global economic development in the post-pandemic period. *International Review*, *10*(1-2), 68-78. https://www.ceeol.com/search/article-detail?id=979047

Phillipson, C. (2007). The 'elected'and the 'excluded': Sociological perspectives on the experience of place and community in old age. *Ageing and Society*, *27*(3), 321–342. doi:10.1017/S0144686X06005629

Phillips, P. C. B., & Perron, P. (1988). Testing for a unit root in time series regression. *Biometrika*, *75*(2), 335–346.

Picot-Coupey, K., Huré, E., & Piveteau, L. (2016). Channel design to enrich customers' shopping experiences: Synchronizing clicks with bricks in an omni-channel perspective - the Direct Optic case. *International Journal of Retail & Distribution Management*, *44*(3), 336–368. doi:10.1108/IJRDM-04-2015-0056

Pintaric, N., & Bronzin, T. (2013). *IT Capability Review*. Paper presented at the Central European Conference on Information and Intelligent Systems, Varaždin, Croatia.

Pipa, A. F., & Bouchet, M. (2020). *How to make the most of city diplomacy in the COVID-19 era.* Brookings Institution. www.brookings.edu/blog/up-front/2020/08/06/how-to-make-the-most-of-city-diplomacy-in-the-covid-19-era/

Pipa, T., & Bouchet, M. (2020). *Leadership at the local level: How can cities drive a sustainable recovery?* Academic Press.

Pittenger, K. (2021). Virtual Internships – A New Reality. *Developments in Business Simulation and Experiential Learning, 48*, 149–152.

Pizzi, S., Caputo, A., Corvino, A., Venturelli, A. (2020). Management research and the UN sustainable development goals (SDGs): A bibliometric investigation and systematic review. *J. Cleaner Prod., 276.*

Pokhrel, S., & Chhetri, R. (2021). A literature review on impact of COVID-19 pandemic on teaching and learning. *Higher Education for the Future, 8*(1), 133–141. doi:10.1177/2347631120983481

Popescu, A. D. (2020a). Alternative Investments confidence amid COVID-19 pandemic, *Scientific Bulletin - Economic Series, 19*, 103-110. http://economic.upit.ro/RePEc/pdf/2020_3_13.pdf

Popescu, A. D. (2020b). Decentralized Finance (DeFi) – The Lego of Finance. *Social Sciences and Education Research Review, 7*(1), 321-349. https://sserr.ro/wp-content/uploads/2020/07/SSERR_2020_7_1_321_349.pdf

Popescu, A. D. (2020c). Financial Technology (FinTech) as a Driver for Financial Digital Assets. *"Ovidius" University Annals, 20*(2), 1055-1059. https://stec.univ-ovidius.ro/html/anale/RO/wp-content/uploads/2021/03/Section%205/36.pdf

Popescu, A. D. (2020d). Transforming Capital Markets by means of Financial Digital Assets. *Revista de Ştiinţe Politice (Revue des Sciences Politiques), 68*, 108-119. https://cis01.ucv.ro/revistadestiintepolitice/files/numarul68_2020/11.pdf

Popescu, A. D. (2020e). Transitions and concepts within Decentralized Finance (Defi) Space, Research Terminals in the Social Sciences. *The Proceedings of CIL 2020: Ninth Edition of International Conference of Humanities and Social Sciences - Creativity, Imaginary, Language*, 40-61. https://www.cilconference.ro/wp-content/uploads/2020/09/cil_2020_research_terminals.pdf#page=40

Popescu, A. D. (2021a). Central Banks Digital Currency - Opportunities and Innovation. *"Ovidius" University Annals, 21*(1), 813-822. https://stec.univ-ovidius.ro/html/anale/RO/2021/Section%205/18.pdf

Popescu, A. D. (2021b). Non-Fungible Tokens (NFT) – Innovation beyond the craze, Revues et Méthodes sur le Management et le Commerce International. *Proceedings of Engineering & Technology – PET, 66*, 26-30. http://ipco-co.com/PET_Journal/IBEM-Proceedings/IBEM%20PROCEEDINGS.pdf#page=31

Popescu, A. D. (2022). *Understanding FinTech and Decentralized Finance (DeFi) for Financial Inclusion. In FinTech Development for Financial Inclusiveness.* IGI Global.

Popov, A. (2021). *How COVID-19 triggered the digital and e-commerce turning point.* United Nations Conference on Trade and Development. https://unctad.org/news/heres-how-we-can-resolve-global-supply-chain-crisis

Porges, S. W. (2003). Social engagement and attachment: A phylogenetic perspective. *Annals of the New York Academy of Sciences, 1008*(1), 31–47. doi:10.1196/annals.1301.004 PMID:14998870

Pornsrimate, K., & Khamwon, A. (2021). How to convert millennial consumers to brand evangelists through social media micro-influencers. *Innovative Marketing, 17*(2).

Porter, L. W., Bigley, G. A., & Steers, R. M. (2003). *Motivation and work behavior* (7th ed.). McGraw-Hill/Irwin.

Porter, M. E. (1985). *Competitive advantage: Creating and sustaining superior performance.* Free Press.

Portulans Institute. (2021). *Network readiness index.* https://networkreadinessindex.org

Potočnik, J. (2021). *The European Green Deal and a post Covid-19 prosperity.* Ellen Macarthur Foundation. https://ellenmacarthurfoundation.org/articles/the-european-green-deal-and-a-post-covid-19-prosperity

Povoroznyuk, I. (2021). Formation and implementation of anti-crisis management at the enterprises of the hospitality industry during the COVID-19 pandemic. *Economy and Society*, (29). Advance online publication. doi:10.32782/2524-0072/2021-29-18

Power, K. (2020). The COVID-19 pandemic has increased the care burden of women and families. *Sustainability: Science, Practice and Policy*, *16*(1), 67–73.

Prados, M., & Zamarro, G. 2020. Gender Differences in Couples' Division of Childcare, Work and Mental Health During COVID-19. SSRN *Electronic Journal* doi:10.2139/ssrn.3667803

Prime, H., Wade, M., & Browne, D. T. (2020). Risk and resilience in family well-being during the COVID-19 pandemic. *The American Psychologist*, *75*(5), 631–643. doi:10.1037/amp0000660 PMID:32437181

Prochaska, J. O., & DiClemente, C. C. (1986). Toward a comprehensive model of change. In Treating addictive behaviors (pp. 3-27). Springer. doi:10.1007/978-1-4613-2191-0_1

Prochaska, J., Norcross, J., & DiClemente, C. (1994). Changing for good. Avon Books.

Prochaska, J. O., & DiClemente, C. C. (1983). Stages and processes of self-change of smoking: Toward an integrative model of change. *Journal of Consulting and Clinical Psychology*, *51*(3), 390–395. doi:10.1037/0022-006X.51.3.390 PMID:6863699

Prochaska, J. O., & Prochaska, J. M. (1999). Why don't continents move? Why don't people change? *Journal of Psychotherapy Integration*, *9*(1), 83–102. doi:10.1023/A:1023210911909

Prochaska, J. O., Redding, C. A., & Evers, K. E. (2015). The transtheoretical model and stages of change. In K. Glanz, B. K. Rimer, & K. Viswanath (Eds.), *Health behavior: Theory, research, and practice* (pp. 97–121). John Wiley & Sons.

Prochaska, J., Norcross, J., & DiClemente, C. (1996). The six stages of change. *Tufts University Diet and Nutrition Letter*, *14*(7), 1–10.

Project "German-Russian Agrarian-Political Dialogue". (n.d.). http://www.agrardialog.ru

Prosser, D. (2021). *Virtual Internships Raises $2.5 Million To Target 1 Million Students Worldwide.* Forbes. https://www.forbes.com/sites/davidprosser/2021/07/12/virtual-internships-raises-25m-to-target-1-million-students-worldwide/?sh=47b94bef38ff

Pulignano, V., Domecka, M., Muszyński, K., Vermeerbergen, L., & Rieman, M.-L. (2021). *Creative labour in the era of Covid-19: The case of freelancers.* ETUI Research Paper-Working Paper. https://www.etui.org/sites/default/files/202103/Creative%20labour%20in%20the%20era%20of%20Covid-19%20the%20case%20of%20freelancers-2021-web.pdf

PVH. (2020). *2019 CR Report.* Retrieved from https://www.pvh.com/-/media/Files/pvh/responsibility/PVH-CR-Report-2019.pdf

PVH. (2022). *PVH Corp.* https://www.linkedin.com/company/pvh/

PWC. (2020). *Responses to Impacts on Angolan Business and Economy.* Covid-19 Crisis Response Team.

Pyschulina, O., Yurchyshyn, V., & Yurochko, T. (2021). *Socio-economic consequences of the coronacrise.* Razumkov Center, Zapovit Publishing House.

Quivy, R., & Campenhoudt, L. (2008). Handbook of Research in Social Sciences. Lisbon: Gravida - Publicações, SA.

Rablen, M. D. (2010). Tax evasion and exchange equity: A reference-dependent approach. *Public Finance Review*, *38*(3), 282–305. doi:10.1177/1091142110367858

Radocy, R. E., & Boyle, J. D. (2012). *Psychological foundations of musical behavior* (5th ed.). Charles C Thomas Publisher.

Rahman, M., & Mendy, J. (2018). Evaluating people-related resilience and non-resilience barriers of SMEs' internationalisation: A developing country perspective. *The International Journal of Organizational Analysis*.

Raj, A., Mukherjee, A. A., de Sousa Jabbour, A. B. L., & Srivastava, S. K. (2022). Supply chain management during and post-COVID-19 pandemic: Mitigation strategies and practical lessons learned. *Journal of Business Research*, *142*, 1125–1139. doi:10.1016/j.jbusres.2022.01.037 PMID:35079190

Ramírez-Durán, V. J., Berges, I., & Illarramendi, A. (2021). Towards the implementation of Industry 4.0: A methodology-based approach oriented to the customer life cycle. *Computers in Industry*, *126*, 103403. doi:10.1016/j.compind.2021.103403

Ramnath, V. R., Ho, L., Maggio, L. A., & Khazeni, N. (2014). Centralized Monitoring and Virtual Consultant Models of Tele-ICU Care: A Systematic Review. *Telemedicine Journal and e-Health*, *20*(10), 936–961. doi:10.1089/tmj.2013.0352 PMID:25226571

Ranard, B. L., Ha, Y. P., Meisel, Z. F., Asch, D. A., Hill, S. S., Becker, L. B., Seymour, A. K., & Merchant, R. M. (2013). Crowdsourcing—Harnessing the masses to advance health and medicine, a systematic review. *Journal of General Internal Medicine*, 1–17. PMID:23843021

Randall, L., Berlina, A., Teräs, J., & Rinne, T. (2018). *Digitalisation as a Tool for Sustainable Nordic Regional Development: Preliminary Literature and Policy Review*. https://www.nordregio.org/wp-content/uploads/2017/04/Digitalisation_Discussion-Paper_Jan-31.pdf

Randall, W. S., & Mello, J. E. (2012). Grounded theory: An inductive method for supply chain research. *International Journal of Physical Distribution & Logistics Management*, *42*(8/9), 863–880. doi:10.1108/09600031211269794

Rapp, A., Baker, T. L., Bachrach, D. G., Ogilvie, J., & Beitelspacher, L. S. (2015). Perceived customer showrooming behavior and the effect on retail salesperson self-efficacy and performance. *Journal of Retailing*, *91*(2), 358–369. doi:10.1016/j.jretai.2014.12.007

Rashi, P., Bist, A. S., Asmawati, A., Budiarto, M., & Prihastiwi, W. Y. (2021). Influence of Post Covid Change in Consumer Behaviour of Millennials on Advertising Techniques and Practices. *Aptisi Transactions on Technopreneurship*, *3*(2), 85–92. doi:10.34306/att.v3i2.210

Ratnasingam, J., Khoo, A., Jegathesan, N., Wei, L. C., Abd Latib, H., Thanasegaran, G., ... Amir, M. A. (2020). How are small and medium enterprises in Malaysia's furniture industry coping with COVID-19 pandemic? Early evidences from a survey and recommendations for policymakers. *BioResources*, *15*(3), 5951–5964. doi:10.15376/biores.15.3.5951-5964

Rechel, B., & McKee, M. (2009, October 3). Lancet. Health reform in central and eastern Europe and the former. *Soviet Union. Union Sovietique*, *374*(9696), 1186–1195.

Reddit. (2019). *The power of community*. https://www.redditinc.com/assets/case-studies/Reddit-x-Ypulse-The-Power-of-Community-White-Paper-9.23.19.pdf

Reddit. (n.d.). *List of economic and Stock Market subreddits*. https://www.reddit.com/r/ListOfSubreddits/comments/ja8du7/list_of_economic_and_stock_market_subreddits/

Reddy, W. M. (1997). Against constructionism. The historical ethnography of emotions. *Current Anthropology*, *38*(3), 327–351. doi:10.1086/204622

Reilly, O, A. (2022). Trying to function in the unfunctionable: Mothers and Covid-19. *Journal of Motherhood Initiative, 11*(1), 8–24.

Reis, Ş. G. (2021). Covıd-19 (Koronavirüs) pandemisi ve risk iştahı: Borsa İstanbul yerli ve yabancı yatırımcılar örneği. *Anadolu Üniversitesi İktisadi ve İdari Bilimler Fakültesi Dergisi, 22*(3), 87–98.

República, L. (2020, Mar 27). *El teletrabajo hace que las personas le dediquen más horas a la jornada laboral.* https://www.larepublica.co/empresas/el-teletrabajo-hace-que-las-personas-le-dediquen-mas-horas-a-la-jornada-laboral-2983857#:~:text=Ximena%20C%C3%A1rdenas%2C%20gerente%20de%20Experis,las%20horas%20laboradas%20sean%20productivas

Reshetnikov, V., Mitrokhin, O., Shepetovskaya, N., Belova, E., & Jakovljevic, M. (2020). Organizational measures aiming to combat COVID-19 in the Russian Federation: The first experience. *Expert Review of Pharmacoeconomics & Outcomes Research, 20*, 571–576. doi:10.1080/14737167.2020.1823221

Restubog, S. L. D., Ocampo, A. C. G., & Wang, L. (2020). Taking control amidst the chaos: Emotion regulation during the COVID-19 pandemic. *Journal of Vocational Behavior, 119*, 103440. doi:10.1016/j.jvb.2020.103440 PMID:32390659

Rezaae, Z. (2002). *Financial Statement Fraud: Prevention and Detection.* John Wiley and Sons, Inc.

Richard, M. O., Chebat, J. C., Yang, Z., & Putrevu, S. (2010). A proposed model of online consumer behaviour: Assessing the role of gender. *Journal of Business Research, 63*(9-10), 926–934. doi:10.1016/j.jbusres.2009.02.027

Richards, J. (2012). What has the internet ever done for employees? A review, map and research agenda. *Employee Relations, 34*(1), 22–43. doi:10.1108/01425451211183246

Richardson, D. (2021). *Labor shortages continue despite the efforts of the US and EU.* Unleash. https://www.unleash.ai/labor-shortages-continue-despite-the-efforts-of-the-us-and-eu/

Richemont. (2021a). *Sustainability. Our approach.* Retrieved from https://www.richemont.com/en/home/sustainability/our-approach/

Richemont. (2021b). *Sustainability Report 2020.* Retrieved from https://www.richemont.com/media/4ksenvnu/sustainability_report_2020.pdf

Richemont. (2022). https://www.linkedin.com/company/richemont/

Riegner, C. (2007). Word of mouth on web: The impact of Web 2.0 on consumer purchase decisions. *Journal of Advertising Research, 47*(4), 436–447. doi:10.2501/S0021849907070456

Rigby, D. (2011). The Future of Shopping. *Harvard Business Review, 89*(12), 64–75.

Rippé, C. B., Smith, B., & Dubinsky, A. J. (2018). Lonely consumers and their friend the retail salesperson. *Journal of Business Research, 92*, 131–141. doi:10.1016/j.jbusres.2018.07.013

Ristola, P., & Mirata, M. (2007). Industrial Symbiosis for More Sustainable, Localised Industrial Systems. *Progress in Industrial Ecology, 4*(3-4), 184–204. doi:10.1504/PIE.2007.015186

Rita, P., Oliveira, T., & Farisa, A. (2019). The impact of e-service quality and customer satisfaction on customer behaviour in online shopping. *Heliyon, 5*(10), e02690. doi:10.1016/j.heliyon.2019.e02690 PMID:31720459

Ritchie, J., Lewis, J., Nicholls, C. M., & Ormston, R. (Eds.). (2013). *Qualitative research practice: A guide for social science students and researchers.* Sage.

Ritchie, J., & Spencer, L. (2002). Qualitative data analysis for applied policy research. In M. Huberman & M. B. Miles (Eds.), *The qualitative researcher's companion* (Vol. 573, pp. 305–329). Sage Publications, inc. doi:10.4135/9781412986274.n12

Ritsatos, T. (2014). Tax evasion and compliance; From the neo classical paradigm to behavioural economics, a review. *Journal of Accounting and Organizational Change*, *10*(2), 244–262. doi:10.1108/JAOC-07-2012-0059

Robeiko, O. (2021, September 13). *Farmers are convinced that it is more profitable to leave watermelons in the field as fertilizer*. https://www.unian.net/economics/agro/v-seti-pokazali-kak-fermery-iz-hersonskoy-oblasti-besposhchadno-unichtozhayut-arbuzy-video-novosti-11542546.html

Robertson, C. J., Lamin, A., & Livanis, G. (2010). Stakeholder Perceptions of Offshoring and Outsourcing: The Role of Embedded Issues. *Journal of Business Ethics*, *95*(2), 167–189. doi:10.100710551-009-0353-0

Röding, T., Nimmermann, F., Steinmann, S., & Schramm-Klein, H. (2019). The influence of technology infusion on customers' information disclosure behaviour within the frontline service encounter. *International Review of Retail, Distribution and Consumer Research*, *29*(5), 482–503. doi:10.1080/09593969.2019.1664612

Rodrik, D. (2018). Populism and the economics of globalization. *Journal of International Business Policy*, *1*(1), 12–33. doi:10.105742214-018-0001-4

Rogers, S. E., Miller, C. D., Flinchbaugh, C., Giddarie, M., & Barker, B. (2021). All internships are not created equal: Job design, satisfaction, and vocational development in paid and unpaid internships. *Human Resource Management Review*, *31*(1), 100723. doi:10.1016/j.hrmr.2019.100723

Roggeveen, A. L., Grewal, D., & Schweiger, E. B. (2020). The DAST Framework for Retail Atmospherics: The Impact of In- and Out-of-Store Retail Journey Touchpoints on the Customer Experience. *Journal of Retailing*, *96*(1), 128–137. doi:10.1016/j.jretai.2019.11.002

Roggeveen, A. L., & Sethuraman, R. (2020). How the COVID Pandemic May Change the World of Retailing. *Journal of Retailing*, *96*(2), 169–171. doi:10.1016/j.jretai.2020.04.002

Rogozinsky, J. (2020). *WallStreetBets*. How Boomers Made the World's Biggest Casino for Millennials.

Rojon, C., & Saunders, M. N. (2012). Formulating a convincing rationale for a research study. *Coaching (Abingdon, UK)*, *5*(1), 55–61. doi:10.1080/17521882.2011.648335

Rolle, R., Martucci, V., & Godoy, E. (2020). Architecture for Digital Twin implementation focusing on Industry 4.0. *IEEE Latin America Transactions*, *18*(5), 889–898. doi:10.1109/TLA.2020.9082917

Rosenberg, S., Heimler, R., & Morote, E. (2012). Basic employability skills: A triangular design approach. *Education + Training*, *54*(1), 7–20. doi:10.1108/00400911211198869

Rosenwein, B. H. (2006). *Emotional communities in the early middle ages*. Cornell University Press.

Rotter, J. B. (1990). Internal versus external control of reinforcement: A case history of a variable. *The American Psychologist*, *45*(4), 489–493. doi:10.1037/0003-066X.45.4.489

Rusdiyanto, & Narsa, I. M. (2020). The Effect of Company Size, Leverage and Return on Asset on Earnings Management: Case Study Indonesian. *Espacios*, *41*(17), 25.

Russell, J., & Russell, L. (2005). *Strategic Planning: Training*. American Society for Training and Development Press.

Russel, S. J., & Norvig, P. (2009). *Artificial Intelligence: a modern approach* (3rd ed.). Prentice Hall.

Rust, R. T. (2019). The future of marketing. *International Journal of Research in Marketing*, *37*(1), 15–26. doi:10.1016/j.ijresmar.2019.08.002

Rutashobya, L., & Jaensson, J. (2004). Small firms' internationalization for development in Tanzania: Exploring the network phenomenon. *International Journal of Social Economics*, *31*(1/2), 159–172. doi:10.1108/03068290410515484

S&P. (2022). *Ammonium nitrate ban could impact ammonia supply: Traders*. https://www.spglobal.com/platts/en/market-insights/latest-news/energy-transition/020322-ammonium-nitrate-ban-could-impact-ammonia-supply-traders

Saeed, K. A., Hwang, Y., & Mun, Y. Y. (2003). Toward an integrative framework for online consumer behaviour research: A meta-analysis approach. *Journal of Organizational and End User Computing*, *15*(4), 1–26. doi:10.4018/joeuc.2003100101

Safara, F. (2020). A computational model to predict consumer behaviour during COVID-19 pandemic. *Computational Economics*, 1–14. PMID:33169049

Sahdan, M. H., Cowton, C. J., & Drake, J. E. (2020). Forensic accounting services in English local government and the counter-fraud agenda. *Public Money & Management*, *40*(5), 380–389. doi:10.1080/09540962.2020.1714208

Sahu, K. C., Naved Khan, M., & Das Gupta, K. (2021). Determinants of Webrooming and Showrooming Behavior: A Systematic Literature Review. *Journal of Internet Commerce*, *20*(2), 137–166. doi:10.1080/15332861.2020.1863041

Saladino, V., Algeri, D., & Auriemma, V. (2020). The Psychological and Social Impact of Covid-19: New Perspectives of Well-Being. *Frontiers in Psychology*, *11*, 577684. Advance online publication. doi:10.3389/fpsyg.2020.577684 PMID:33132986

Saladis, F., & Kerzner, H. (2009). *Bringing the PMBOK Guide to Life: A Companion for the Practicing Project Manager*. Wiley. doi:10.1002/9780470446324

Salikhova, O. B., & Goncharenko, D. O. (2021). Challenges of COVID-19 pharmaceutical industry: EU and Ukraine responses. *Economy and Forecasting*, *4*, 18.

Salisu, A. A., & Vo, X. V. (2020). Predicting stock returns in the presence of COVID-19 pandemic: The role of health news. *International Review of Financial Analysis*, *71*, 1–10.

Salleh, D., & Muhammad, F. (2020). The Accounting Students' Perspective on Mobile Learning in Covid19 Pandemic Period. *Proceedings of 5th International Conference on E-Commerce*.

Sanahuja Vélez, G., & Ribes Giner, G. (2015). Effects of Business Internships on Students, Employers, and Higher Education Institutions: A Systematic Review. *Journal of Employment Counseling*, *52*(3), 121–130. doi:10.1002/joec.12010

Sanchez-Famoso, V., Maseda, A., & Iturralde, T. (2017). Family involvement in top management team: Impact on relationships between internal social capital and innovation. *Journal of Management & Organization*, *23*(1), 136–162. doi:10.1017/jmo.2016.2

Sangster, A., Stoner, G., & Flood, B. (2020). Insights into accounting education in a COVID-19 world. *Accounting Education*, *29*(5), 431–562. doi:10.1080/09639284.2020.1808487

Sarkis, J. (2020). Supply Chain Sustainability: Learning from the COVID-19 pandemic. *International Journal of Operations & Production Management*, *41*(1), 63–73. doi:10.1108/IJOPM-08-2020-0568

Saud, M., Ashfaq, A., Abbas, A., Ariadi, S., & Mahmood, Q. K. (2021). Social support through religion and psychological well-being: COVID-19 and coping strategies in Indonesia. *Journal of Religion and Health*, *60*(5), 3309–3325. doi:10.100710943-021-01327-1 PMID:34245436

Saukkonen, J., Kreus, P., Obermayer, N., Ruiz, Ó. R., & Haaranen, M. (2019). *AI, RPA, ML and Other Emerging Technologies: Anticipating Adoption in the HRM Field.* Paper presented at the ECIAIR 2019 European Conference on the Impact of Artificial Intelligence and Robotics, Oxford, UK.

Savastano, M., Bellini, F., D'Ascenzo, F., & De Marco, M. (2019). Technology adoption for the integration of online–offline purchasing. *International Journal of Retail & Distribution Management, 47*(5), 474–492. doi:10.1108/IJRDM-12-2018-0270

Savitri, M. F. and Naili, T. Y. (2020). Henry Mintzberg's Business Management Strategy Post-Pandemic Covid-19 (Social Learning Approach on Ali Murah Shop Madinah). *International Journal of Social Learning, 1*(1), 62-74. DOI: .v1i1.5 doi:10.47134/ijsl

Sawhney, S., & Madan, A. (2021). *Changing consumer behaviour in post-COVID scenario*. Observer Research Foundation. https://www.orfonline.org/expert-speak/changing-consumer-behaviour-post-covid-scenario/

Saxton, G. D., Ren, C., & Guo, C. (2020). Responding to Diffused Stakeholders on social media: Connective Power and Firm Reactions to CSR-Related Twitter Messages. *Journal of Business Ethics*, 1-24. Available at: https://sustainabledevelopment.un.org/partnership/?p=28041

Sayer, R. (1992). *Method in social science: A realist approach*. Psychology Press.

Scheibe, K. P., & Blackhurst, J. (2018). Supply chain disruption propagation: A systemic risk and normal accident theory perspective. *International Journal of Production Research, 56*(1–2), 43–59. doi:10.1080/00207543.2017.1355123

Schenk, E., & Guittard, C. (2011). Towards a characterization of Crowdsourcing practices. *Journal of Innovation Economics, 7*, 93–107.

Schleper, M. C., Gold, S., Trautrims, A., & Baldock, D. (2021). Pandemic-induced knowledge gaps in operations and supply chain management: COVID-19's impacts on retailing. *International Journal of Operations & Production Management.*

Schroeder, D. (2020). Turn your Covid-19 solution into a viable business. *Harvard Business Review.* Retrieved from: https://hbr.org/2020/07/turn-your-covid-19-solution-into-a-viable-business

Schroeder, M., von See, B., Schnelle, J., & Kersten, W. (2021). *Impact of the Covid-19 Pandemic on Supply Chain Management BT.* In R. Fritzsche, S. Winter, & J. Lohmer (Eds.), *Logistik in Wissenschaft und Praxis: Von der Datenanalyse zur Gestaltung komplexer Logistikprozesse* (pp. 3–24). Springer Fachmedien Wiesbaden. doi:10.1007/978-3-658-33480-2_1

Schultz, D. E., & Peltier, J. (2013). Social media's slippery slope: Challenges, opportunities and future research directions. *Journal of Research in Interactive Marketing, 7*(2), 86–99. doi:10.1108/JRIM-12-2012-0054

Schunk, D. H. (2012). Social cognitive theory. In K. R. Harris, S. Graham, C. B. T. Urdan, G. M. S. McCormick, & J. Sweller (Eds.), APA educational psychology handbook (Vol. 1, pp. 101–123). American Psychological Association.

Schunk, D. H., & Usher, E. L. (2012). Social cognitive theory and motivation. In R. Ryan (Ed.), *The Oxford handbook of human motivation* (Vol. 2, pp. 11–26). Oxford University Press.

Schwab, K. (2016). *A quarta revolução industrial*. Edipro.

Schwab, K. (2019). *Davos Manifesto 2020: The Universal Purpose of a Company in the Fourth Industrial Revolution.* World Economic Forum. Available at https://www.weforum.org/agenda/2019/12/davos manifesto 2020 the universal purpose-of-a-company-in-the-fourth-industrial-revolution/

Seasholes, M. S., & Wu, G. (2007). Predictable behavior, profits, and attention. *Journal of Empirical Finance, 14*(5), 590–610. https://ssrn.com/abstract=686193. doi:10.1016/j.jempfin.2007.03.002

Sekaran, U. (2000). *Research Methods for Business: A Skill Building Approach* (3rd ed.). Wiley.

Sekścińska, K., & Jaworska, D. (2022). Who felt blue when Facebook went down? The role of self-esteem and FoMO in explaining people's mood in reaction to social media outage. *Personality and Individual Differences, 188*, 111460. doi:10.1016/j.paid.2021.111460

Seltzer, E., & Mahmoudi, D. (2013). Citizen Participation, Open Innovation, and Crowdsourcing Challenges and Opportunities for Planning. *Journal of Planning Literature, 28*(1), 3-18.

Semanur, S., & Ercan, E. (2020). *COVID-19 and Digitalization Network Analysis on Industrial Robots Trade Among the BRI Countries*. Social Science Review.

Semenova, L. u., Datsenko, V.V., & Hurday, V.V. (2020). Modern marketing tools to increase competitiveness in a COVID-19 pandemic. *Economy, finance, law: Current problems and current problems and development prospects*, 49.

Şenol, Z. (2020). Covid-19 krizi ve finansal piyasalar. In *Para ve finans* (pp. 75–124). IKSAD Publishing House.

Serfling, O. (2018). *Crowdworking Monitor Nr. 1*. https://conference.iza.org/conference_files/Statistic_2019/serfling_o1156.pdf

Serrano, F., & Kazda, A. (2020). The future of airport post COVID-19. *Journal of Air Transport Management, 89*, 101900. doi:10.1016/j.jairtraman.2020.101900 PMID:32834696

Servi, T., Dönmez, Z., & Akbaş, Y. E. (2020). İmalat sanayisi ile VIX endeksi ilişkisinin analizi: Türkiye örneği. *Al Farabi Uluslararası Sosyal Bilimler Dergisi, 5*(4), 94–102.

Shafi, M., Liu, J., & Ren, W. (2020). Impact of COVID-19 pandemic on micro, small, and medium-sized Enterprises operating in Pakistan. *Research in Globalization, 2*, 100018. doi:10.1016/j.resglo.2020.100018

Shahbaznezhad, H., Dolan, R., & Rashidirad, M. (2021). The Role of Social Media Content Format and Platform in Users' Engagement Behavior. *Journal of Interactive Marketing, 53*, 47–65. doi:10.1016/j.intmar.2020.05.001

Shalley, C., Hitt, M., & Zhou, J. (2015). *The Oxford Handbook of Creativity*. Innovation and Entrepreneurship.

Shamasunder, S., Holmes, S. M., Goronga, T., Carrasco, H., Katz, E., Frankfurter, R., & Keshavjee, S. (2020). COVID-19 reveals weak health systems by design: Why we must re-make global health in this historic moment. *Global Public Health: An International Journal for Research, Policy and Practice, 15*(7), 1083–1089. doi:10.1080/17441692.2020.1760915 PMID:32352911

Shankar, V., Kalyanam, K., Setia, P., Golmohammadi, A., Tirunillai, S., Douglass, T., & Waddoups, R. (2021). How technology is changing retail. *Journal of Retailing, 97*(1), 13–27. doi:10.1016/j.jretai.2020.10.006

Shankar, V., & Kushwaha, T. (2021). Omnichannel marketing: Are cross-channel effects symmetric? *International Journal of Research in Marketing, 38*(2), 290–310. doi:10.1016/j.ijresmar.2020.09.001

Shaporenko, E. (2020). *Asked to open markets: In Kherson farmers blocked the road bridge*. https://fakty.com.ua/ru/ukraine/20200426-prosyat-vidkryty-rynky-v-hersoni-fermery-perekryly- automobile-mist /

Sharfuddin, S. (2020). The world after Covid-19. *The Round Table, 109*(3), 247–257. doi:10.1080/00358533.2020.1760498

Sharma, M., Luthra, S., Joshi, S. & Kumar, A. (2020). Developing A Framework for Enhancing Survivability of Sustainable Supply Chains During and Post-covid-19 Pandemic. *International Journal of Logistics: Research and Applications*. doi:10.1080/13675567.2020.1810213

Sharma, Shishodia, Kamble, Gunasekaran, & Belhadi. (2020). Agriculture supply chain risks and COVID-19: mitigation strategies and implications for the practitioners. *International Journal of Logistics Research and Applications*. doi :10.1080/13675567.2020.1830049

Sharma, M., Joshi, S., Luthra, S., & Kumar, A. (2021). *Managing disruptions and risks amidst COVID-19 outbreaks: role of blockchain technology in developing resilient food supply chains*. Operations Management Research., doi:10.100712063-021-00198-9

Sharp, J., & Lang, G. (2018). Agile in teaching and learning: Conceptual framework and research agenda. *Journal of Information Systems Education*, *29*, 45–52.

Shavitt, S., & Barnes, A. J. (2020). Culture and the Consumer Journey. *Journal of Retailing*, *96*(1), 40–54. doi:10.1016/j.jretai.2019.11.009

Sheffi, Y. (2001). Supply Chain Management under the Threat of International Terrorism. *International Journal of Logistics Management*, *12*(2), 1–11. doi:10.1108/09574090110806262

Shehzad, K., Xiaoxing, L., & Kazouz, H. (2020). COVID-19's disasters are perilous than Global Financial Crisis: A rumor or fact? *Finance Research Letters*, *36*, 1–6. doi:10.1016/j.frl.2020.101669 PMID:32837374

Shengelia, B., Tandon, A., Adams, O. B., & Murray, C. J. (2005). Access, utilization, quality, and effective coverage: An integrated conceptual framework and measurement strategy. *Social Science & Medicine*, *61*(1), 97–109.

Sherif, M., & Sherif, C. W. (1956). An outline of social psychology. Academic Press.

Sheth, J., (2020). Impact of Covid-19 on consumer behaviour: will the old habits return or die? *Journal of Business Research. 117*, 280–283.. doi:10.1016/j.jbusres.2020.05.059

Shevchuk, A., & Kalyazina, S. (2019, September). Traceability technology: fruits and vegetables trader case study. In *International Conference on Digital Technologies in Logistics and Infrastructure (ICDTLI 2019)*. Atlantis Press. 10.2991/icdtli-19.2019.70

Shi, H., & Iqbal, Q. (2020). *Chinese SMEs in Industry 4.0: Analysis and Future Trends*. IGI Global., doi:10.4018/978-1-7998-2577-7.ch001

Shin, H., Collier, D. A., & Wilson, D. D. (2000). Supply Management orientation and supplier/buyer performance. *Journal of Operations Management*, *18*(3), 317–333. doi:10.1016/S0272-6963(99)00031-5

Shleifer, A. (2004). Does competition destroy ethical behavior? *The American Economic Review*, *94*(2), 414–418. doi:10.1257/0002828041301498

Siahaan, M., Umar, H., & Purba, R. B. (2019). Fraud Star Drives to Asset Misappropriation Moderated by Internal Controls. *Journal of Southwest Jiaotong University*, *54*(4), 1–10. doi:10.35741/issn.0258-2724.54.4.24

Sidorenko, E. A. (2021). *Transformational processes of event practices: challenges of the COVID-19 pandemic* [Master's Dissertation]. National Academy of Management of Culture and Arts.

Siegel, G., & Sorensen, J. E. (1999). *Counting more, counting less. Transformation in the management accounting profession*. Institute of Managing Accountants.

Sigahi, T. F. A. C., Kawasaki, B. C., Bolis, I., & Morioka, S. N. (2021). A systematic review on the impacts of Covid-19 on work: Contributions and a path forward from the perspectives of ergonomics and psychodynamics of work. *Human Factors and Ergonomics in Manufacturing & Service Industries*, *31*(4), 375–388. https://doi.org/10.1002/hfm.20889

Silva, A. L. E., Moraes, J. A. R., Benitez, L. B., & Kaufmann, E. A. (2021). Impressão 3D: Análise da evolução e seus impactos no mundo científico. *Revista FSA*, *18*(11), 124–144. Advance online publication. doi:10.12819/2021.18.11.6

Silva, F. M. J., Zanet, G. C., Trezza, R., Lamour, L., & Beraldo, L. A. (2020). The Importance of Dental Office Management in Times of Covid-19 And How to Resume Activities in Post-Pandemic. *Brazilian Dental Science*, *23*(2).

Silva, S. C., Martins, C. C., & Sousa, J. M. (2018). Omnichannel approach: Factors affecting consumer acceptance. *Journal of Marketing Channels*, *25*(1–2), 73–84. doi:10.1080/1046669X.2019.1647910

Simatupany, T. M., & Sridharan, R. (2002). The Collaborative Supply Chain. *International Journal of Logistics Management*, *13*(1), 15–30. doi:10.1108/09574090210806333

Simchi-Levi, D. (2020). *Three scenarios to guide your global supply chain recovery*. Sloan Management Review Digital Article. Available at: https://sloanreview-mit-edu.cdn.ampproject.org/c/s/sloanreview.mit.edu/article/three-scenarios-to-guide-your-global-supply-chain-recovery/amp

Singh, G. (2020). Changes in work culture and workplace due to COVID19 crisis. PsyArXiv. doi:10.31234/osf.io/htjx5osf.io/htjx5

Singh, N. (2019). Big data technology: Developments in current research and emerging landscape. *Enterprise Information Systems*, *13*(6), 801–831. doi:10.1080/17517575.2019.1612098

Singh, S., Kumar, R., Panchal, R., & Tiwari, M. K. (2021). Impact of COVID-19 on logistics systems and disruptions in food supply chain. *International Journal of Production Research*, *59*(7), 1993–2008. doi:10.1080/00207543.2020.1792000

Singh, U. S., Singh, N., Gulati, K., Bhasin, N. K., & Sreejith, P. M. (2021). A study on the revolution of consumer relationships as a combination of human interactions and digital transformations. *Materials Today: Proceedings*. Advance online publication. doi:10.1016/j.matpr.2021.05.578

Sinkovics, N. (2016). Enhancing the foundations for theorising through bibliometric mapping. *International Marketing Review*, *33*(3), 327–350. doi:10.1108/IMR-10-2014-0341

Skojett-Larsen, T. (1999). Supply chain Management: A New Challenge for Researchers and Managers in Logistics. *International Journal of Logistics Management*, *10*(2), 41–53. doi:10.1108/09574099910805987

Slovin, M. J. (1960). *Sampling*. Simon and.

Smith, S. S. S. & R. W. (2002). Forensic psycholinguistics: Using language analysis for identifying and assessing offenders. *FBI Law Enforcement Bulletin*.

Sneader, K., & Sternfels, R. A. (2020). *From surviving to thriving: Reimagining the post-COVID-19 return*. McKinsey.

Sodhi, M. S., Tang, C. S., & Willenson, E. T. (2021). Research opportunities in preparing supply chains of essential goods for future pandemics. *International Journal of Production Research*, 1–16. doi:10.1080/00207543.2021.1884310

Soman, P., & Shroff, V. (2021). *Mental health and wellbeing of employees in a post-pandemic world: considerations for employers*. International Bar Association. https://www.ibanet.org/mental-wellbeing-of-employees-post-pandemic-considerations-for-employers

Sostero, M., Milasi, S., Hurley, J., Fernandez-Macias, E., & Bisello, M. (2020). *Teleworkability and the COVID-19 crisis: A new digital divide?* (No. 2020/05). JRC working papers series on labour, education and technology.

Sousa, M. J., & Rocha, Á. (2019). Skills for disruptive digital business. *Journal of Business Research*, *94*, 257–263. doi:10.1016/j.jbusres.2017.12.051

Şova, R. A., & Popa, A. F. (2020a). The Accounting Education, Between Digitalisation and the COVID-19 Crisis. *CECCAR Business Review, 1*(10), 3–8. doi:10.37945/cbr.2020.10.01

Spears, R. (2011). Group identities: The social identity perspective. In Handbook of identity theory and research (pp. 201-224). New York, NY: Springer.

Spielberger, C. (2004). Encyclopedia of applied psychology. Academic Press.

Spieske, A., & Birkel, H. (2021). Improving supply chain resilience through industry 4.0: A systematic literature review under the impressions of the COVID-19 pandemic. *Computers & Industrial Engineering*, *158*, 107452. doi:10.1016/j.cie.2021.107452 PMID:35313661

Spradley, R. T., & Spradley, E. (2021). The Building Blocks of Pandemic Communication Strategy: Models to Enable Resilient Risk and Crisis Communication. In Pandemic Communication and Resilience (pp. 51-73). Cham: Springer.

Spreer, P., & Rauschnabel, P. A. (2016). Selling with technology: Understanding the resistance to mobile sales assistant use in retailing. *Journal of Personal Selling & Sales Management*, *36*(3), 240–263. doi:10.1080/08853134.2016.1208100

Sreejesh, S., Sarkar, J. G., & Sarkar, A. (2019). CSR through social media: Examining the intervening factors. *Marketing Intelligence & Planning*.

Stajkovic, A. D., & Luthans, F. (1998). Social cognitive theory and self-efficacy: Goin beyond traditional motivational and behavioral approaches. *Organizational Dynamics*, *26*(4), 62–74. doi:10.1016/S0090-2616(98)90006-7

Stake, R. (2011). *Qualitative Research - Studying how things work*. ARTMED Editora, SA.

Stank, T., Esper, T., Goldsby, T. J., Zinn, W., & Autry, C. (2019). Toward a digitally dominant paradigm for twenty-first century supply chain scholarship. *International Journal of Physical Distribution & Logistics Management*, *49*(10), 956–971. doi:10.1108/IJPDLM-03-2019-0076

Stanley, A. (2018, October 8). Ready to rumble: IBM launches food trust blockchain for commercial use. *Forbes*. Available at: https://www.forbes.com/sites/astanley/2018/10/08/ready-to-rumble-ibm-launches-food-trust-blockchain-forcommercial-use/#173fb79f7439

State Program. (2020). *State program promotion to overcome the negative effects caused by restrictive measures to prevent the occurrence and spread of acute respiratory disease COVID-19 CoV-2, for 2020 – 2022*. https://ips.ligazakon.net/document/KP200534?an=19

Stephenson, N. (1992). *Snow crash*. Bantan Books Publisher.

Stevenson, C., Wakefield, J. R. H., Felsner, I., Drury, J., & Costa, S. (2021). Collectively coping with coronavirus: Local community identification predicts giving support and lockdown adherence during the COVID-19 pandemic. *British Journal of Social Psychology*, *60*(4), 1403–1418. doi:10.1111/bjso.12457 PMID:33969899

Stewart, A., & Stanford, J. (2017). Regulating work in the gig economy: What are the options? *Economic and Labour Relations Review*, *28*(3), 420–437. doi:10.1177/1035304617722461

Stieger, D., Matzler, K., Chatterjee, S., & Ladstaetter-Fussenegger, F. (2012). Democratizing Strategy: How Crowdsourcing Can be Used for Strategy Dialogues. *Calif Management Review, 54*(4).

Strachan, R. (2022). *Who will be the supply chain winners and losers in 2022?* Investment Monitor. https://www.investmentmonitor.ai/analysis/supply-chain-winners-and-losers-2022

Strange, R. (2020). Whither Globalisation? *Journal of International Management*, *26*(1), 100728. doi:10.1016/j.intman.2019.100728

Strange, R., & Magnani, G. (2018). Outsourcing, offshoring and the global factory. In G. Cook & F. McDonald (Eds.), *The Routledge companion to the geography of international business* (pp. 60–67). Routledge. doi:10.4324/9781315667379-4

Štreimikienė, D., Baležentis, T., Volkov, A., Ribašauskienė, E., Morkūnas, M., & Žičkienė, A. (2021). *Negative effects of covid-19 pandemic on agriculture: systematic literature review in the frameworks of vulnerability, resilience and risks involved.* Economic Research-Ekonomska Istraživanja. doi:10.1080/1331677X.2021.1919542

Stuart, F. I. (1997). Supply Chain Strategy: Organisational Influence through supplier alliances. *British Journal of Management, 8*(3), 223–236. doi:10.1111/1467-8551.00062

Studdert, D. M., & Hall, M. A. (2020). Disease control, civil liberties, and mass testing—Calibrating restrictions during the COVID-19 pandemic. *The New England Journal of Medicine, 383*(2), 102–104. doi:10.1056/NEJMp2007637 PMID:32272003

Su, C. W., Dai, K., Ullah, S., & Andlib, Z. (2021). COVID-19 pandemic and unemployment dynamics in European economies. *Economic Research-EkonomskaIstraživanja*, 1-13.

Subramaniam, S., & Chakraborty. (2021). COVID-19 fear index: Does it matter for stock market returns? *Review of Behavioral Finance, 13*(1), 40–50.

Subreddit Stats. (n.d.). https://subredditstats.com

Suez Group. (n.d.). *CircularChain, the circular economy blockchain.* https://www.suez.com/en/who-we-are/innovating-for-the-future/circularchain-the-circular-economy-blockchain

Sun, F. (2020). Sino-UK Science and Technology Cooperation in the Field of People's Livelihood. *Journal of Chinese Economic and Business Studies, 18*(4), 349–354. doi:10.1080/14765284.2020.1855857

SuperHot. (2022). *SuperHot Game – Time only moves when you do.* Available at https://superhotgame.com/

Superintendencia Financiera de Colombia - SFC. (n.d.). *Programa de Acompañamiento a Deudores.* https://www.superfinanciera.gov.co/inicio/consumidor-financiero/informacion-general/informacion-al-consumidor-financiero/programa-de-acompanamiento-a-deudores-pad-10104439

Supply Chain Digital. (2020). Accessed on https://supplychaindigital.com/magazine/december-2020

Surai, I. G. (2005). *Public administration of the agricultural sector of the economy of Ukraine: functional and structural aspect* [PhD Dissertation]. Dissertations and Theses database.

Surucu-Balci, E., Balci, G., & Yuen, K. F. (2020). Social media engagement of stakeholders: A decision tree approach in container shipping. *Computers in Industry, 115*, 103152. doi:10.1016/j.compind.2019.103152

Suwandee, S., Surachartkumtonkun, J., & Lertwannawit, A. (2020). EWOM firestorm: Young consumers and online community. *Young Consumers, 21*(1), 1–15. doi:10.1108/YC-03-2019-0982

Suyadal, M. (2021). Covıd-19 pandemisinde piyasa etkinliği ve davranışsal finans teorilerinin geçerliliği: uluslararası piyasalarda bir uygulama. *Erciyes Üniversitesi İktisadi ve İdari Bilimler Fakültesi Dergisi,* (60), 519-546.

Su, Z., Liu, P., & Fang, T. (2021). Pandemic-induced fear and stock market returns: Evidence from China. *Global Finance Journal.*

Svabova, L., Kramarova, K., Chutka, J., & Strakova, L. (2020). Detecting earnings manipulation and fraudulent financial reporting in Slovakia. *Oeconomia Copernicana, 11*(3), 485–508. doi:10.24136/oc.2020.020

Svajdova, L. (2021). Consumer behaviour during pandemic of COVID-19. *Journal of International Business Research and Marketing*, *6*(3), 34–37. doi:10.18775/jibrm.1849-8558.2015.63.3005

Swatch Group. (2021). *Sustainability report & social policy*. Retrieved from https://www.swatchgroup.com/en/brands-companies

Syaifullah, J., Syaifudin, M., Sukendar, M. U., & Junaedi, J. (2021). Social media marketing and business performance of MSMEs during the COVID-19 pandemic. *The Journal of Asian Finance, Economics, and Business*, *8*(2), 523–531.

Tabrizi, B., Lam, E., Girard, K., & Irvin, V. (2019). Digital transformation is not about technology. *Harvard Business Review*, 13.

Takac, P. (1994). Outsourcing: A Key to Controlling Escalating IT Cost? *International Journal of Technology Management*, *9*(2), 139–155.

Taliento, M., Favino, C., & Netti, A. (2019). Impact of environmental, social, and governance information on economic performance: Evidence of a corporate "sustainability advantage" from Europe. *Sustainability*, *11*(6), 1738. doi:10.3390u11061738

Tanahashi, T. (1978). Health service coverage and its evaluation. *Bull World Health Organ, 56*, 295–303.

Tan, K. C., Kannan, V. R., & Handfield, R. B. (1998). Supply chain management: Supplier performance and firm performance. *International Journal of Purchasing and Materials Management, 34*(3), 2–9.

Tan, K. C., Kannan, V. R., & Handfield, R. B. (1998). Supply Chain Management: Supplier Performance and firm performance. *International Journal of Purchasing and Materials Management, 34*(3), 2–9.

Tan, K. C., Lyman, S. B., & Wisner, J. D. (2002). Supply Chain Management: A strategic perspective. *International Journal of Operations & Production Management, 22*(6), 614–631. doi:10.1108/01443570210427659

Taşar, İ. (2015). *İçsel büyüme modelleri çerçevesinde Türkiye'de ekonomik büyümenin yapısal dönüşümü* (Unpublished doctoral dissertation). İnönü University, Institute of Social Sciences, Department of Economics, Malatya.

Tasavori, M., Zaefarian, R., & Eng, T. Y. (2018). Internal social capital and international firm performance in emerging market family firms: The mediating role of participative governance. *International Small Business Journal, 36*(8), 887–910. doi:10.1177/0266242618773145

Tate, S., Reinstein, A., & Churyk, N. (2017). The Impact of Online Education on Accounting Recruiting. *The CPA Journal, New York*, *87*(9), 13–15.

Taylor, P. (2021). *The good news about labor shortages*. Politico. https://www.politico.eu/article/good-news-labor-shortages-coronavirus-economic-recovery/

Taylor, S., Landry, C. A., Paluszek, M. M., Fergus, T. A., McKay, D., & Asmundson, G. J. G. (2020). Development and initial validation of the COVID stress scales. *Journal of Anxiety Disorders*, *72*, 1–7.

Teba, S. M. E., Mestanza, G. J., & Fernandez, R. M. (2020). The Application of the Inbound Marketing Strategy on Costa del Sol Planning & Tourism Board. Lessons for Post-Covid-19 Revival. *Sustainability*, *12*(23), 9926. Advance online publication. doi:10.3390u12239926

Teller, C., Brusset, X., & Kotzab, H. (2019). Physical and digital market places – where marketing meets operations. *International Journal of Retail & Distribution Management*, *47*(12), 1225–1231. doi:10.1108/IJRDM-12-2019-299

Telzer, E. H., Van Hoorn, J., Rogers, C. R., & Do, K. T. (2018). Social influence on positive youth development: A developmental neuroscience perspective. *Advances in Child Development and Behavior, 54*, 215–258. doi:10.1016/bs.acdb.2017.10.003 PMID:29455864

Temur, A. S. (2021). COVID-19 financial crisis? comparison of its impacts on borsa istanbul (bist) with history financial crises. In *International Conference on Economics*. Turkish Economic Association.

Tene, O., & Polonetsky, J. (2014). A Theory of Creepy: Technology, Privacy andv Shifting Social Norms. *Yale Journal of Law and Technology, 16*(1), 59–102.

Tey, Y. S., Brindal, M., & Dibba, H. (2018). Factors influencing willingness to pay for sustainable apparel: A literature review. *Journal of Global Fashion Marketing, 9*(2), 129–147. doi:10.1080/20932685.2018.1432407

Thakker, J. (2013). International perspectives on addiction. In *Principles of Addiction* (pp. 51–59). Academic Press. doi:10.1016/B978-0-12-398336-7.00005-X

The Economist. (2021, July 21). The Power of Proximity: Localizing Supply Chains in the Middle East. *The Economist.*

The Economist. (2022). *The Big Mac index.* https://www.economist.com/big-mac-index?utm_content=article-link-3&etear=nl_today_3&utm_campaign=a.the-economist-today&utm_medium=email.internal-newsletter.np&utm_source=salesforce-marketing-cloud&utm_term=2/3/2022&utm_id=1039508

The Economist. (2022). *Will remote work stick after the pandemic?* https://www.economist.com/finance-and-economics/2022/01/15/will-remote-work-stick-after-the-pandemic

The Open Group. (2015). *The Open Group Architecture Framework TOGAF Version 9.* Van Haren Publishing.

The Primary Health Care Performance Initiative. (n.d.). https://improvingphc.org/about-phcpi

The role of online platforms in weathering the COVID-19 shock. (2020). *OECD.* https://www.oecd.org/coronavirus/policy-responses/the-role-of-online-platforms-in-weathering-the-covid-19-shock-2a3b8434/

The Star. (2022). *Brunei gives the nod to re-open childcare centres from Jan 17.* Available at: https://www.thestar.com.my/aseanplus/aseanplus-news/2022/01/06/brunei-gives-the-nod-to-re-open-childcare-centres-from-jan-17

The White House. (2020). *Coronavirus guidelines for America.* Available online: https://www.whitehouse.gov/briefings-statements/coronavirus-guidelinesamerica/

The White House. (2020). *Proclamation on suspension of entry as immigrants and nonimmigrants of persons who pose a risk of transmitting 2019 Novel Coronavirus.* Available online: https://www.whitehouse.gov/presidentialactions/proclamation-suspension-entry-immigrants-nonimmigrants-personspose-risk-transmitting-2019-novel-coronavirus/

The World Bank In Pakistan. (2021). *World Bank.* https://www.worldbank.org/en/country/pakistan/overview#1

The World Bank. (2021). https://www.worldbank.org/en/topic/universalhealthcoverage#1

Theis, L., & Bipp, T. (2019). Workplace Goal Orientation. *European Journal of Psychological Assessment.*

Thiede, M., Akweongo, P., & McIntyre, D. (2007). Exploring the dimensions of access. In The economics of health equity. Cambridge University Press.

Thomas, S. (2018). Peace of mind: The quintessential luxury. Journal of Design. *Business & Society, 4*(2), 151–169.

Thorum, C., Ketter, S., & Merck, J. (2018). Ethik in Der Digitalisierung. Der Bedarf für eine Corporate Digital Responsibility. *Wirtschafts-und Sozialpolitik, 17.* Available at: https://library.fes.de/pdf-files/wiso/14691.pdf

Thygesen, L. C., Møller, S. P., Ersbøll, A. K., Santini, Z. I., Nielsen, M. B. D., Grønbæk, M. K., & Ekholm, O. (2021). Decreasing Mental Well-Being During the COVID-19 Pandemic: A Longitudinal Study Among Danes Before and During the Pandemic. *SSRN Electronic Journal*. doi:10.2139/ssrn.3845383

Tiwari, A., So, M. K. P., Chong, A. C. Y., Chan, J. N. L., & Chu, A. M. Y. (2021). Pandemic risk of Covid-19 outbreak in the United States: An Analysis of network connectedness with air travel data. *International Journal of Infectious Diseases*, *103*, 97–101. doi:10.1016/j.ijid.2020.11.143 PMID:33212255

Topal, ˙. I., Nart, S., Akar, C., & Erkollar, A. (2020). The effect of greenwashing on online consumer engagement: A comparative study in France, Germany, Turkey, and the United Kingdom. *Business Strategy and the Environment*, *29*(2), 465–480. doi:10.1002/bse.2380

Torgler, B. (2008). What Do We Know about Tax Fraud? An Overview of Recent Developments. *Social Research*, *75*(4), 1239–1270. doi:10.1353or.2008.0032

Torkunov, A. V., Ryazantsev, S. V., & Levashov, V. K. (Eds.). (2021). *Pandemic COVID-19: Challenges, consequences, counteraction*. Aspect Press Publishing House.

Tosun, N. (2021). *Finansal yatırım kararlarına yatırımcı duyarlılığının etkisi: Türkiye üzerine bir araştırma* (Unpublished doctoral dissertation). İnönü University, Institute of Social Sciences, Department of Economics, Malatya.

Tranfield, D., Denyer, D., & Smart, P. (2003). Towards a methodology for developing evidence-informed management knowledge by means of systematic review. *British Journal of Management*, *14*(3), 207–222. doi:10.1111/1467-8551.00375

Tran, L. T. T. (2021). Managing the effectiveness of e-commerce platforms in a pandemic. *Journal of Retailing and Consumer Services*, *58*, 102287. doi:10.1016/j.jretconser.2020.102287

Triandis, H. C. (1989). The self and social behavior in differing cultural contexts. *Psychological Review*, *96*(3), 506–520. doi:10.1037/0033-295X.96.3.506

Tricco, A.C., Langlois, E., Straus, S.E., & World Health Organization. (2017). *Rapid reviews to strengthen health policy and systems: a practical guide*. World Health Organization.

Trivellas, P., Akrivouli, Z., Tsifora, E., & Tsoutsa, P. (2015). The Impact of Knowledge Sharing Culture on Job Satisfaction in Accounting Firms. The Mediating Effect of General Competencies. *Procedia Economics and Finance*, *19*, 238–247. doi:10.1016/S2212-5671(15)00025-8

Trkman, P. (2013). Increasing process orientation with business process management: Critical practices'. *International Journal of Information Management*, *33*(1), 48–60. doi:10.1016/j.ijinfomgt.2012.05.011

Troth, A. C., Jordan, P. J., & Lawrence, S. A. (2012). Emotional intelligence, communication competence, and student perceptions of team social cohesion. *Journal of Psychoeducational Assessment*, *30*(4), 414–424. doi:10.1177/0734282912449447

Trougakos, J. P., Chawla, N., & McCarthy, J. M. (2020). Working in a pandemic: Exploring the impact of COVID-19 health anxiety on work, family, and health outcomes. *The Journal of Applied Psychology*, *105*(11), 1234–1245. doi:10.1037/apl0000739 PMID:32969707

Tsilika, T., Kakouris, A., Apostolopoulos, N., & Dermatis, Z. (2020). Entrepreneurial bricolage in the aftermath of a shock. Insights from Greek SMEs. *Journal of Small Business and Entrepreneurship*, *32*(6), 635–652. doi:10.1080/08276331.2020.1764733

Tsoutsa, P., Fitsilis, P., & Ragos, O. (2018). Service Simulation in Industry 4.0: A Comparison of Simulators. *Industry 4.0, 3*(2), 101-104.

Tsoutsa, P., & Lampropoulos, I. (2022). *Preparing for Smart Cities Future Competences: trends arising through keyword and review analysis. In Building on Smart Cities Skills and Competences*. Springer.

Tuanakotta, T. M. (2010). Akuntansi Forensik dan AuditorInvestigatif. Lembaga Penerbit Fakultas Ekonomi Universitas Indonesia (LPFE UI).

Tuikka, S. (2019). Negative relationships in the workplace. In *Workplace Communication* (pp. 136–148). Routledge. doi:10.4324/9780429196881-11

Turner, J. C. (1991). *Social influence*. Thomson Brooks/Cole Publishing Co.

Uçar, M., & Kıdemli. M. (2021). Türkiye'de Covıd-19 hasta vaka sayısı, vıx endeksi, dolar endeksi ile seçilmiş bıst sektör endeksleri arasındaki ilişki: ARDL model. *Uluslararası Kapadokya Salgın Dönemleri Kongresi. ICCET'21.*

UHC2030's mission is to create a movement for accelerating equitable and sustainable progress towards universal health coverage (UHC). (n.d.). https://www.uhc2030.org/our-mission/

UK Statutory Instruments on The Working Time (Amendment) Regulations 2020. (2020). No. 365. Academic Press.

UNCTAD. (2020a). *Impact of the Pandemic on Trade and Development: Transitioning to a new normal*. Geneva: United Nations Conference on Trade and Development. https://unctad.org/system/files/official-document/osg2020d1_en.pdf

UNDP. (2014). *Human Development Report 2014. Sustaining Human Progress: Reducing Vulnerabilities and Building Resilience*. United Nations Office for Outer Space Affairs. https://www.unoosa.org/oosa/en/ourwork/space4sdgs/sdg3.html

Unidad de Gestión de Pensiones y Parafiscales - UGPP. (n.d.). *Programa de Apoyo al Empleo Formal - PAEF*. https://paef.ugpp.gov.co/ver20/dfV3Paef

United Nations - UN. (2020). *Plan de respuesta socio-económica frente a la pandemia de la COVID-19 en Colombia*. https://colombia.un.org/es/160844-plan-de-respuesta-socio-economica-frente-la-pandemia-de-la-covid-19-en-colombia

United Nations for Development Programme. (2021). *Un año de pandemia: impacto socioeconómico de la COVID-19 en Colombia*. https://www.co.undp.org/content/colombia/es/home/-sabias-que-/un-ano-de-pandemia--impacto-socio-economico-de-la-covid-19-en-col.html#:~:text=Mas%20de%201%2C5%20millones,en%20los%20%C3%BAltimos%205%20a%C3%B1os

Universal Health Coverage Partnership. (n.d.). https://www.uhcpartnership.net/about/

Urciuoli, B. (2008). Skills and selves in the new workplace. *American Ethnologist*, *35*(2), 211–228. doi:10.1111/j.1548-1425.2008.00031.x

Uzunoğlu, E., Türkel, S., & Akyar, B. Y. (2017). Engaging consumers through corporate social responsibility messages on social media: An experimental study. *Public Relations Review*, *43*(5), 989–997. doi:10.1016/j.pubrev.2017.03.013

Van Dam, A. (2020). The unluckiest generation in US history. *Washington Post, 5*.

Van Dijk, T. A. (1990). Social cognition and discourse. In H. Giles & W. P. Robinson (Eds.), *Handbook of language and social psychology* (pp. 163–183). John Wiley & Sons Ltd.

Van Hoek, R., & Lacity, M. (2020). *How the pandemic is pushing blockchain forward*. Harvard Business Review Digital Article. Available at: https://hbr.org/2020/04/how-the-pandemic-is-pushing-blockchain-forw

Van Hoek, R. (2020). Impact Pathway Research opportunities for a more resilient post-Covid-19 Supply Chain- closing the gap between research findings and industry practice. *International Journal of Operations & Production Management*, *40*(4), 341–355. doi:10.1108/IJOPM-03-2020-0165

Van Hoorn, J., Crone, E. A., & Van Leijenhorst, L. (2017). Hanging out with the right crowd: Peer influence on risk-taking behavior in adolescence. *Journal of Research on Adolescence*, *27*(1), 189–200. doi:10.1111/jora.12265 PMID:28498538

Van Kerrebroeck, H., Willems, K., & Brengman, M. (2017). Touching the void. *International Journal of Retail & Distribution Management*, *45*(7/8), 892–909. doi:10.1108/IJRDM-09-2016-0156

Van Mieghem, J. A. (1999). Coordinating Investment, Production and Subcontracting. *Management Science*, *45*(7), 954–971. doi:10.1287/mnsc.45.7.954

Vanina, E. (2021, September 7). *Previously, peasants sold their watermelons to neighboring countries. But due to lockdown and political crises, all the usual supply channels have broken.* https://tsn.ua/ru/exclusive/nikomu-ne-nuzhen-urozhay-pochemu-fermery-za-bescenok-vynuzhdeny-prodavat-arbuzy-1862242.html

Varela, F. J. (1999). *Ethical know-how: Action, wisdom, and cognition.* Stanford University Press.

Vasileiou, E. (2021). Behavioral finance and market efficiency in the time of the COVID-19 pandemic: Does fear drive the market? *International Review of Applied Economics*, *35*(2), 224–241. doi:10.1080/02692171.2020.1864301

Vaziri, H., Casper, W. J., Wayne, J. H., & Matthews, R. A. (2020). Changes to the work–family interface during the COVID-19 pandemic: Examining predictors and implications using latent transition analysis. *The Journal of Applied Psychology*, *105*(10), 1073–1087. doi:10.1037/apl0000819 PMID:32866024

Venkatesh, V., & Davis, F. (2000). A theoretical extension of the technology acceptance model: Four longitudinal field studies. *Management Science*, *46*(2), 186–204. doi:10.1287/mnsc.46.2.186.11926

Venter, E. (2017). Bridging the communication gap between Generation Y and the Baby Boomer generation. *International Journal of Adolescence and Youth*, *22*(4), 497–507. doi:10.1080/02673843.2016.1267022

Vera, A. (2017). *Humanizing the retail experience: Experiential shopping lives offline.* https://www.retailcustomerexperience.com/blogs/humanizing-the-retail-experience-experiential-shopping-lives-offline/

Verbeke, A., & Wenlong, Y. (2020). A few Implications of The Covid-19 Pandemic for International Business Strategy Research. *Journal of Management Studies*. Advance online publication. doi:10.1111/joms.12

Verburg, R. M., Den Hartog, D. N., & Koopman, P. L. (2007). Configurations of human resource management practices: A model and test of internal fit. *International Journal of Human Resource Management*, *18*(2), 184–208. doi:10.1080/09585190601102349

Verhoef, P. C., Kannan, P. K., & Inman, J. J. (2015). From Multi-Channel Retailing to Omni-Channel Retailing: Introduction to the Special Issue on Multi-Channel Retailing. *Journal of Retailing*, *91*(2), 174–181. doi:10.1016/j.jretai.2015.02.005

Verhoef, P. C., Stephen, A. T., Kannan, P. K. K., Luo, X., Abhishek, V., Andrews, M., Bart, Y., Datta, H., Fong, N., Hoffman, D. L., Hu, M. M., Novak, T., Rand, W., & Zhang, Y. (2017). Consumer Connectivity in a Complex, Technology-enabled, and Mobile-oriented World with Smart Products. *Journal of Interactive Marketing*, *40*(1), 1–8. doi:10.1016/j.intmar.2017.06.001

Verma, A. K., & Prakash, S. (2020). Impact of covid-19 on environment and society. *Journal of Global Biosciences*, *9*(5), 7352–7363.

Verma, S. (2013). Effectiveness of social network sites for influencing consumer purchase decisions. *International Journal of Business Excellence*, *6*(5), 624–634. doi:10.1504/IJBEX.2013.056112

Vial, G. (2019). Understanding digital transformation: A review and a research agenda. *The Journal of Strategic Information Systems*, *28*(2), 118–144. doi:10.1016/j.jsis.2019.01.003

Vicari, B., Zoch, G., & Bächmann, A. (2022). Childcare, work or worries? What explains the decline in parents' well-being at the beginning of the COVID-19 pandemic in Germany? *ZtF. Zeitschrift für Familienforschung.*

Villanova, D., Bodapati, A. V., Puccinelli, N. M., Tsiros, M., Goodstein, R. C., Kushwaha, T., Suri, R., Ho, H., Brandon, R., & Hatfield, C. (2021). Retailer Marketing Communications in the Digital Age: Getting the Right Message to the Right Shopper at the Right Time. *Journal of Retailing*, *97*(1), 116–132. doi:10.1016/j.jretai.2021.02.001

Vrechopoulos, A., Lazaris, C., & Doukidis, G. (2019). From omnichannel retailing to "diachronic retailing": blending digital technologies with traditional marketing strategies and practices. *Proceedings of the 48th Annual European Marketing Academy Conference (EMAC).*

Vrijihoef, R., & Koskela, L. (1999). *Roles of Supply Chain Management in Construction.* University of California.

Wagner, A. F. (2020). What the stick market tells us about the Post-COVID-19. *Nature Human Behaviour*, *4*(5), 440. Advance online publication. doi:10.103841562-020-0869-y

Wagstaff, A., Cotlear, D., Eozenou, P. H. V., & Buisman, L. R. (2016). Measuring progress towards universal health coverage: With an application to 24 developing countries. *Oxford Review of Economic Policy*, *32*(1), 147–189.

Walker, G. (1995). Renewable Energy and the Public. *Land Use Policy*, *12*(1), 49–59. doi:10.1016/0264-8377(95)90074-C

WallstreetBets News. (2020, August 30). *Dissecting the Unique Lingo and Terminology used in the Subreddit r/Wallstreetbets.* https://www.wallstreetbets.shop/blogs/news/dissecting-the-unique-lingo-and-terminology-used-in-the-subreddit-r-wallstreetbets

Walters, L., Wade, T., & Suttles, S. (2020). Food and Agricultural Transportation Challenges Amid the COVID-19 Pandemic. *Choices.* https://www.choicesmagazine.org/choices-magazine/theme-articles/covid-19-and-the-agriculture-industry-labor-supply-chains-and-consumer-behavior/food-and-agricultural-transportation-challenges-amid-the-covid-19-pandemic

Wang, J., Yang, J., Iverson, B. C., & Kluender, R. (2020). Bankruptcy and the COVID-19 Crisis. *SSRN Electronic Journal.* doi:10.2139/ssrn.3690398

Wang, B., Luo, W., Zhang, A., Tian, Z., & Li, Z. (2020). Blockchain-enabled circular supply chain management: A system architecture for fast fashion.). https://www.sciencedirect.com/science/article/abs/pii/S0166361520305583. *Computers in Industry*, *123*, •••.

Wang, H., Tong, L., Takeuchi, R., & George, G. (2016). Corporate social responsibility: An overview and new research directions: Thematic issue on corporate social responsibility. *Academy of Management Journal*, *59*(2), 534–544. doi:10.5465/amj.2016.5001

Wang, K., Dong, J. Q., Wang, Y., & Yin, H. (2019). Securing Data with Blockchain and AI. *IEEE Access: Practical Innovations, Open Solutions*, *7*, 77981–77989. doi:10.1109/ACCESS.2019.2921555

Wang, R., & Chan-Olmsted, S. (2020). Content marketing strategy of branded YouTube channels. *Journal of Media Business Studies*, *17*(3-4), 294–316. doi:10.1080/16522354.2020.1783130

Wang, R., & Huang, Y. (2018). Communicating corporate social responsibility (CSR) on social media: How do message source and types of CSR messages influence stakeholders' perceptions? *Corporate Communications*, *23*(3), 326–341. doi:10.1108/CCIJ-07-2017-0067

Wang, S., & Chen, S. (2012). The Motivation for Tax Avoidance in Earnings Management. *International Conference on Engineering and Business Management*, 447–450.

Wang, X., Yiik Diew Wong, Y. D., & Yuen, K. F. (2021). Rise of 'Lonely' Consumers in the Post-COVID-19 Era: A Synthesised Review on Psychological, Commercial and Social Implications. *International Journal of Environmental Research and Public Health, 18*(2), 404. doi:10.3390/ijerph18020404

Ward, M. (2017). *Physical store online shopping control.* https://patents.google.com/patent/US9665881B1/en

Watson, C. (2021). *20+ Business Ideas Coming Out of COVID-19 Pandemic [Small Business Edition].* The European Business Review. https://www.europeanbusinessreview.com/20-business-ideas-coming-out-of-covid-19-pandemic-small-business-edition/

Watts, R., & Zimmerman, J. (2006). Positive Accounting Theory: A Ten Year Perspective. *Accounting Review, 65*(May), 131–156.

Wautelet, T. (2018). *Exploring the role of independent retailers in the circular economy: a case study approach.* https://www.researchgate.net/figure/The-linear-economy-The-take-make-and-waste-approach-of-production_fig2_323809440

Wechsler, H., Nelson, T. E., Lee, J. E., Seibring, M., Lewis, C., & Keeling, R. P. (2003). Perception and reality: A national evaluation of social norms marketing interventions to reduce college students' heavy alcohol use. *Journal of Studies on Alcohol, 64*(4), 484–494. doi:10.15288/jsa.2003.64.484 PMID:12921190

Wegerif, M. (2021). The impact of Covid-19 on black farmers in South Africa. *Agrekon.* Advance online publication. doi:10.1080/03031853.2021.1971097

Weißer, T., Saßmannshausen, T., Ohrndorf, D., Burggräf, P., & Wagner, J. (2020). A clustering approach for topic filtering within systematic literature reviews. *MethodsX, 7,* 100831. doi:10.1016/j.mex.2020.100831 PMID:32195145

Wells Fargo Asset Management. (2017, September 20). *Majority of Millennials Are Happy Despite Financial Anxiety, Wells Fargo Study Finds.* Wells Fargo Asset Management. https://www.wellsfargoassetmanagement.com/assets/public/pdf/press-releases/20170920-pressrelease.pdf

Wells, J. T. (2010). *Forensic Accounting and Fraud Examination.* John Wiley & Sons, Inc.

WheelockD. C. (2020). Comparing the COVID-19 recession with the Great Depression. *Available at* SSRN 3745250. doi:10.20955/es.2020.39

White, N. E. (2021). Farming in the time of pandemic: Small farms demonstrate flexibility, innovation, and hope. *Journal of Agriculture, Food Systems, and Community Development, 10*(2), 247–249. doi:10.5304/jafscd.2021.102.008

WHO & UNICEF. (2018). *A Vision for Primary Health Care in the 21st Century: Towards Universal Health Coverage and the Sustainable Development Goals.* World Health Organization. https:// apps.who.int/iris/handle/10665/328065

WHO. (2019). *Health expenditure report.* Available online at https://www.who.int/health_financing/documents/health-expenditure-report-2019.pdf

WHO. (2020). *Covid-19 disrupting mental health services in most countries.* WHO Survey. https://www.who.int/news/item/05-10-2020-covid-19-disrupting-mental-health-services-in-most-countries-who-survey#:~:text=Bereavement%2C%20isolation%2C%20loss,outcomes%20and%20even%20death

WHO. (2020). *Global surveillance for COVID-19 caused by human infection with COVID-19 virus: Interim guidance.* Available online: https://www.who.int/docs/default-source/coronaviruse/2020 03 20 surveillance.pdf

WHO. (2020). *WHO Director-General's opening remarks at the media briefing on COVID-19 - 11 March 2020.* https://www.who.int/director-general/speeches/detail/who-director-general-s-opening-remarks-at-the-media-briefing-on-covid-19---11-march-2020

WHO. (2020a). *Coronavirus disease (COVID-2019) situation reports*. Available online: https://www.who.int/emergencies/diseases/novel-coronavirus-2019/situation-reports.

WHO. (2020b). *Responding to community spread of COVID-19: interim guidance*. Available online: https://www.who.int/publications/i/item/responding-tocommunity-spread-of-covid-19.

Wikipedia Contributors. (2022). Consumer. In *Wikipedia*. https://en.wikipedia.org/wiki/Consumer

Wikström, P.-O. H., Oberwittler, D., Treiber, K., & Hardie, B. (2012). *Breaking rules: The social and situational dynamics of young people's urban crime*. OUP Oxford.

Wildman, J. L., Nguyen, D. M., Duong, N. S., & Warren, C. (2021). Student teamwork during COVID-19: Challenges, changes, and consequences. *Small Group Research, 52*(2), 119–134. doi:10.1177/1046496420985185

Willey, K. M. (2019). *Stock market short-termism: law, regulation, and reform*. Springer Berlin Heidelberg. doi:10.1007/978-3-030-22903-0

Wilson, B., & Nochajski, T. H. (2018). On the continuum of exit: Understanding the stages of change among women in commercial sexual exploitation. *Gender Issues, 35*(2), 98–112. doi:10.100712147-017-9201-1

Wilson, J., & Daugherty, P. (2018). Collaborative intelligence: Humans and AI are joining forces. *Harvard Business Review, 2018*(July-August), 1–11.

Winarsih, I. M. & Fuad, K. (2021). Impact of covid-19 on digital transformation and sustainability in small and medium enterprises (SMEs): A conceptual framework. In Advances in Intelligent Systems and Computing. Springer International Publishing.

Wing, C. S., Madub, C. N., Kueib, C.-H., Luc, M. H., Lind, C., & Tseng, H. (2008). Supply chain management in the US and Taiwan: The international journals of management science. *Omega*, 36665–36679.

Wise, J. (2020). *Covid-19: New coronavirus variant is identified in UK*. Academic Press.

WMO. (2021). *WMO Air Quality and Climate Bulletin*. https://library.wmo.int/doc_num.php?explnum_id=10887

Wong, B. (2020). *How digital entrepreneurs will help shape the world after the COVID-19 pandemic*. World Economic Forum. https://www.weforum.org/agenda/2020/06/entrepreneurs-must-embrace-digital-during-pandemic-for-society/

Workman, M. (2010). Technology Innovation Adoption and Diffusion: Contrast of Perspectives. In Cases on Technology Innovation: Entrepreneurial Successes and Pitfalls (pp. 91-106). IGI Global.

World Bank. (2020). *Confronting the socio-economic consequences of COVID-19 in Angola*. World Bank.

World Bank. (2020). *Global Economic Prospects, June 2020*. World Bank.

World Bank. (2021). Global Economy to Expand by 4% in 2021. In *Vaccine Deployment and Investment Key to Sustaining the Recovery*. Author.

World Economic Forum. (2020). *COVID-19 Has Intensified the Digital Divide*. https://www.weforum.org/agenda/2020/09/covid-19-has-intensified-the-digital-divide/

World Economic Forum. (2020). *The Future of Jobs Report 2020*. https://www3.weforum.org/docs/WEF_Future_of_Jobs_2020.pdf

World Health Organization - WHO. (2020). *Alocución de apertura del Director General de la OMS en la rueda de prensa sobre la COVID-19*. https://www.who.int/es/director-general/speeches/detail/who-director-general-s-opening-remarks-at-the-media-briefing-on-covid-19---11-march-2020

World Health Organization (WHO). (2020). *WHO Director-General's opening remarks at the media briefing on COVID-19*. https://www.who.int/dg/speeches/detail/who-director-general-s-opening-remarks-at-the-media-briefing-on-covid19

World Health Organization. (2021). *WHO Corona virus Disease (COVID-19) Dashboard*. Available online at: https://covid19.who.int/

World Tourism Organization UNWTO. (2020a). UNWTO world tourism barometer May 2020 Special focus on the impact of COVID-19. In UNWTO World Tourism Barometer. World Tourism Organization (UNWTO). doi:10.18111/9789284421817

World Tourism Organization UNWTO. (2020b). *UNWTO Global Tourism Dashboard*. https://www.unwto.org/international-tourism-and-covid-19

Wright, L. B., Haug, J. C., & Huckabee, A. (2019). Blueprint for Retail Website Design: Attracting and Retaining Millennial Online Shoppers. *Journal of Internet Commerce*, *18*(2), 170–196. doi:10.1080/15332861.2019.1584844

WTO. (2020). *COVID-19 Public Health Emergency of International Concern (PHEIC) Global research and innovation forum*. https://www.who.int/publications/m/item/covid-19-public-health-emergency-of-international-concern-(pheic)-global-research-and-innovation-forum

Wyborn, C., Louder, E., Harrison, J., Montambault, J., Montana, J., Ryan, M., ... Reed, M. (2018). Understanding the impacts of research synthesis. *Environmental Science & Policy*, *86*, 72–84. doi:10.1016/j.envsci.2018.04.013

Xinhua. (2021). *China-EU investment agreement to inject new life into global economic recovery*. Retrieved from: http://www.xinhuanet.com/english/2021-01/03/c_139638396.htm

Xu, Y., Li, J.-P., Chu, C.-C., & Dinca, G. (2021). Impact of COVID-19 on transportation and logistics: a case of China. *Economic Research-Ekonomska Istraživanja*, 1–19. doi:10.1080/1331677X.2021.1947339

Xu, Z., & Jia, H. (2022). The Influence of COVID-19 on Entrepreneur's Psychological Well-Being. *Frontiers in Psychology, 12*. doi:10.3389/fpsyg.2021.823542

Xue, B., & McMunn, A. (2021). Gender differences in unpaid care work and psychological distress in the UK Covid-19 lockdown. *PLoS One*, *16*(3), e0247959. doi:10.1371/journal.pone.0247959 PMID:33662014

Xu, Z., Elomri, A., Kerbache, L., & El Omri, A. (2020). Impacts of COVID-19 on Global Supply Chains: Facts and Perspectives. *IEEE Engineering Management Review*, *48*(3), 153–166. doi:10.1109/EMR.2020.3018420

Yang, C. C., & Chuang, H. Y. (2020). The strategy for return to work after the COVID-19 pandemic on small and medium-sized enterprises. *Journal of Occupational and Environmental Medicine*, *62*(8), e471–e472. doi:10.1097/JOM.0000000000001926 PMID:32459712

Yang, C., & Huang, J.-B. (2000). A Decision Model for IS Outsourcing. *International Journal of Information Management*, *20*(3), 225–239. doi:10.1016/S0268-4012(00)00007-4

Yao, T., Jiang, B., Young, S. T., & Talluri, S. (2010). Outsourcing Timing, Contract Selection and Negotiation. *International Journal of Production Research*, *48*(2), 305–326. doi:10.1080/00207540903174858

Yarmak, A. (2021). *How will the coronavirus affect the development of the agricultural sector in Ukraine*. https://adler.com.ua/news/yak-vpline-koronavirus-na-rozvitok-agrosektoru-v-ukrajini

Yasuda, A., & Oliveira, D. M. T. (2012). *Marketing research: Guide to the practice of market research*. Cengage Learning.

Yıldırım, E. U. (2021). Covid-19 pandemi ve 2008 ekonomik kriz dönemlerinde riskten kaçınma düzeyinin ABD ve BRIC piyasa entegrasyonu üzerindeki değişen etkisi. *Muhasebe ve Finansman Dergisi*, (90), 185-208. doi:10.25095/mufad.866684

Yıldırım, A., & Şimşek, H. (2018). *Qualitative Research Methods in Social Sciences.* Seçkin Publishing.

Yoo, B., Donthu, N., & Lee, S. (2000). An examination of selected marketing mix elements and brand equity. *Journal of the Academy of Marketing Science, 28*(2), 195–211. doi:10.1177/0092070300282002

Yoo, S. C., & Morris, P. (2015). An Exploratory Study of Successful Advertising Internships: A Survey Based on Paired Data of Interns and Employers. *Journal of Advertising Education, 19*(1), 5–16. doi:10.1177/109804821501900103

Yumurtacı Hüseyinoğlu, I. Ö., Kotzab, H., Köstepen, K. G., & Halaszovich, T. (2020). Assessing consumer logistics functions in grocery shopping: Evidence from an emerging market. *Journal of Marketing Channels, 26*(1), 72–86. doi:10.1080/1046669X.2019.1700868

Zahra, S. A. (2021). International entrepreneurship in the post Covid world. *Journal of World Business, 56*(1), 101143. doi:10.1016/j.jwb.2020.101143

Zailani, S., & Rajagopal, P. (2005). Supply Chain Integration and performance: US versus East Asian companies. *Supply Chain Management, 10*(5), 379–393. doi:10.1108/13598540510624205

Zanardo, V., Manghina, V., Giliberti, L., Vettore, M., Severino, L., & Straface, G. (2020). Psychological impact of COVID-19 quarantine measures in northeastern Italy on mothers in the immediate postpartum period. *International Journal of Gynaecology and Obstetrics: the Official Organ of the International Federation of Gynaecology and Obstetrics, 150*(2), 184–188. doi:10.1002/ijgo.13249 PMID:32474910

Zaridis, A. D., & Logotheti, A. (2020). Entrepreneurial Strategies and Practices promoting Innovations Adoption in Global Food Industry. *SSRG International Journal of Economics and Management Studies, 7*(3), 40–46.

Zatuliviter, V. (2021). Internationalization of higher education in a pandemic condition. *Scientific Notes of Young Scientists*, (8).

Zeng, A. (2000). A systematic study of sourcing strengths. *Industrial Management & Data Systems, 100*(5), 219–229. doi:10.1108/02635570010304798

Zenic, N., Taiar, R., Gilic, B., Blazevic, M., Maric, D., Pojskic, H., & Sekulic, D. (2020). Levels and changes of physical activity in adolescents during the COVID-19 pandemic: Contextualizing urban vs. rural living environment. *Applied Sciences (Basel, Switzerland), 10*(11), 3997. doi:10.3390/app10113997

Zhai, Y., & Du, X. (2020). Addressing collegiate mental health amid COVID-19 pandemic. *Psychiatry Research, 288*, 113003. doi:10.1016/j.psychres.2020.113003 PMID:32315885

Zhai, Y., & Du, X. (2020). Loss and grief amidst COVID-19: A path to adaptation and resilience. *Brain, Behavior, and Immunity, 87*, 80–81. doi:10.1016/j.bbi.2020.04.053 PMID:32335197

Zhang, D. Y. (2021). Fiscal policy benefits and green recovery of firms : An experimental exploration of Chinese listed firms. *Economic Change and Restructuring*. Advance online publication. doi:10.100710644-021-09344-6

Zhang, D. Y., Hao, M. G., & Morse, S. (2020). Is Environmental Sustainability Taking a Backseat in China after COVID-19? The Perspective of Business Managers. *Sustainability, 12*(24), 1–24. doi:10.3390u122410369

Zhang, D., Hu, M., & Ji, Q. (2020). Financial markets under the global pandemic of COVID-19. *Finance Research Letters, 36*, 101–528. doi:10.1016/j.frl.2020.101528 PMID:32837360

Zhang, T., Gerlowski, D., & Acs, Z. (2022). Working from home: Small business performance and the COVID-19 pandemic. *Small Business Economics, 58*(2), 611–636. doi:10.100711187-021-00493-6

Zhao, M., Liao, L., Xiao, W., Yu, X., Wang, H., & Wang, Q. (2020). Household materials selection for homemade cloth face coverings and their filtration efficiency enhancement with triboelectric charging. *Nano Letters*, *20*, 5544–5552. doi:10.1021/acs.nanolett.0c02211

Zhemoida, O. V. (2013). *Public administration in the field of agriculture* (Vol. K). NADU.

Zhu, G., Chou, M.C., & Tsai, W.C. (2020). *Lessons learnt from the Covid-19 pandemic. Exploring the shortcomings of current supply chain operations: A long-term Perspective Offering*. Academic Press.

Zides, M. (2021). *On-demand Learning: A Must-have in the Digital Era*. Training Industry. https://trainingindustry.com/articles/content-development/on-demand-learning-a-must-have-in-the-digital-era-spon-coreaxis/

Zoch, G., Bächmann, A., & Vicari, B. (2020). Who cares when care closes? Care-arrangements and parental working conditions during the COVID-19 pandemic in Germany. *European Societies*, *23*(sup1), S576-S588.

Zysman, A. (2004). Forensic accounting demystified: World Investigators Network Standard Practice for Investigative and Forensic. Accounting Engagements, Canadian Institute of Chartered Accountant.

About the Contributors

Ana Pego is a PhD in Geography and Territorial Planning, MBA, BSC in Economics. She is a researcher in clusters, smart cities and renewable energy, also interested in agriculture and farming sustainability. She is also a European Projects coordinator and consultant.

* * *

Shivani Agarwal is an Assistant Professor, KIET School of Management at KIET Group of Institutions, Ghaziabad, India. She has earned her PhD from Indian Institute of Technology (IIT, Roorkee) in Management. She is engaged in teaching, research and consultancy assignments. She has more than 12 years of experience in teaching and in handling various administrative positions. She also presented several research papers in national and international conferences. Dr. Agarwal has contributed chapters in different books published by Taylor and Francis, Springer and IGI Global. She has conducted and attended various workshops, FDPs and MDPs. She is the Book Series Editor of Information Technology, Management & Operations Research Practices, CRC Press, Taylor & Francis Group, USA. She is guest editor with IGI-Global, USA. Her research interests include Quality of Work life, Trust, Subjective well-being, knowledge management, Employer Branding innovation and human resource management. Dr. Shivani Agarwal can be contacted at: jindal.shivani24@gmail.com

Ayla Avcı completed her Bachelor of Business Administration degree at Anadolu University. She completed her master's and doctorate programs at Istanbul Sabahattin Zaim University. There are articles and book chapters in international and national journals.

Vincenzo Basile is currently a Researcher in Economics and Business Management, Disciplinary Scientific Sector: SECS-P/08 (13/B2), Federico II University of Naples Department: Economics, Management, Institutions. Dr Basile is a former Research Fellow on the PON Place Project (Conversion of offshore platforms for multiple eco-sustainable uses) starting from April 2019 at the Department of Economics, Management, Institutions of University FEDERICO II of Naples. He holds a PhD in Business Science (Doctor Europaeus Label) from University FEDERICO II of Naples, defending in May 2016 a thesis entitled: "Marketing Performance Measurement in FMCG - Share of Wallet in Italian Retail Industry".

Oscar Bernardes holds a Ph.D. in management, since 2013. He worked as management consultant for several years, in several organizations (social, profitable, and governmental). He is Invited Professor at Polytechnic Institute of Porto (P.Porto), Portugal, where he has been lecturing courses in the following areas: entrepreneurship, innovation, marketing and general management. His research interests include entrepreneurship, gamification, innovation, and marketing.

Anthony Bolton is a PhD graduate in the School of Computing at the University of South Africa. He is also Chief Information Officer (CIO) and Chief Technical Officer (CTO) Global Telecom, End User Infrastructure & Services, Immersive Technology Development and Engineering at General Motors in Ireland.

Federica Caboni, PhD, is an Assistant Professor in Business Communication at the University of Cagliari, Department of Economic and Business Science (Italy). Since 2017 she is a visiting researcher at the Centre for Retailing, School of Business, Economics and Law at the University of Gothenburg. Her research interests focus on retail, consumer behavior, digitalization and new technology. She is an author of several scientific publications and book chapters edited by Emerald, Springer, Palgrave.

Mariana Carmona is the founder of Immutable Oasis Labs, a consultancy firm aimed to foster blockchain education and adoption in developing countries. Holds a MSc in Digital Currencies (Cum Laude) from the University of Nicosia and a DeFi certificate by the Frankfurt School Blockchain Center. Mariana has 20 years of experience in consulting and research. She is an expert in blockchain applications, token economics and token analysis.

Vyron Damasiotis is Assistant Professor at the Department of Accounting and Finance of the University of Thessaly, Greece.

Georgios Doukidis is Professor of eBusiness in the Department of Management Science and Technology, at the Athens University of Economics and Business. He holds an MSc and PhD from the London School of Economics. He has acted as guest-editor for the Journal of the OR Society, European Journal of Information Systems, International Journal of Electronic Commerce, Journal of Information Technology, Supply Chain Management: An International Journal.

Dian Ekowati is a senior lecturer in the Business Management department, Faculty of Economics and Business, and Head of Planning and development board Universitas Airlangga. After persuading her master's degree from the University of Melbourne in organizational change, she earned her doctoral degree in management from the University of York, United Kingdom. She is the author of several book chapters, conference and journal papers, and many academic, social, and academic development projects.

Mochammad Fahlevi is Lecturer at Department of Management, BINUS Online Learning, Bina Nusantara University, Indonesia. Mochammad Fahlevi research has been published in several Scopus and WOS journals. Mochammad Fahlevi also serves as a Chief Editor of Journal of Research in Business, Economics, and Education, Journal of Business Management and Accounting, Journal of Economics and Business Letters, Priviet Multidisciplinary Journal, and Priviet Social Sciences Journal

Rakotoarisoa Maminirina Fenitra holds a Ph.D Management Science from the Faculty of Economics and Business, Department of Management, Universitas Airlangga, Surabaya Indonesia. His area of interest falls in Entrepreneurship, human behavior, tourism and marketing in particular, while general interests are related to human development approaches and empirical research. Also, Dr. Fenitra has published several papers in international journal and present his work in various international conferences.

Neha Goel is an Assistant Professor at the Faculty of Department of Business and Management Studies, Meerut Institute of Engineering and Technology, Meerut, Uttar Pradesh, India. She has 8 Years of teaching and research experience in Pure and Applied Statistics, Business Statistics and Analytics, Statistical Methods and Computational Techniques, Quantitative Techniques for Managers. Her area of specialization is Inferential Statistics and Reliability. She is Gold medalist in M.Phil. Statistics and has taught as a Guest Lecturer at the Ch. Charan Singh University, Campus, Meerut. She has written and published many research papers in International journals and also in National and International Conferences and is actively involved in the area of research. She is a member of research and development committee in MIET, College and reviewer of the International Journal of System Assurance Engineering and Technology, (Springer). Dr. Neha Goel is also involved in conducting the research projects for the management students.

Leila Goosen is a full professor in the Department of Science and Technology Education of the University of South Africa. Prof. Goosen was an Associate Professor in the School of Computing, and the module leader and head designer of the fully online signature module for the College for Science, Engineering and Technology, rolled out to over 92,000 registered students since the first semester of 2013. She also supervises ten Masters and Doctoral students, and has successfully completed supervision of 43 students at postgraduate level. Previously, she was a Deputy Director at the South African national Department of Education. In this capacity, she was required to develop ICT strategies for implementation. She also promoted, coordinated, managed, monitored and evaluated ICT policies and strategies, and drove the research agenda in this area. Before that, she had been a lecturer of Information Technology (IT) in the Department for Science, Mathematics and Technology Education in the Faculty of Education of the University of Pretoria. Her research interests have included cooperative work in IT, effective teaching and learning of programming and teacher professional development.

Mitsunori Hirogaki is an Associate Professor of Marketing Strategy at Kyushu University, Japan. He received his PhD from the Graduate School of Business Administration, Kobe University. He has been involved in big data analysis projects, as a member of a research group at the Center for the Study of the Creative Economy (Doshisha Univeristy), he works with big data analysis to construct systems that identify seeds of innovation. Dr. Hirogaki's current research focuses on Cross-Cultural Consumer Behavior in international marketing and marketing strategies in mature, developed societies. Dr. Hirogaki is a member of the Japan Society of Marketing and Distribution, the Japan Association for Consumer Studies, and the Japanese Economic Association.

Esengül Iplik is an Associate Professor in the Department of Business at the Adana Alparslan Türkeş Science and Technology University. She completed her Ph.D. at Çukurova University, Adana/Turkey in 2017. Her research interests lie in the area of management and organization, organizational behavior.

Imran Khan is an Assistant Professor in the Department of Finance at Niels Brock in Copenhagen (Denmark). He earned a Master's degree in Investments from the University of Birmingham (UK) with a Distinction and a Bachelor's degree from the London School of Economics and Political Science. As a professor, research supervisor, peer reviewer, author, and independent researcher, Imran has experience in accounting, finance, economics, and investments. Having spent a few years working in the corporate world, Imran transitioned into education, teaching and advising undergraduate and postgraduate students. Professionally, he has been in the field for over eight years. Among his research interests are FinTech, Global Economy, Financial Crisis, Financial Innovations, and Corporate Finance.

Elmarie Kritzinger joined the University of South Africa's College of Science, Engineering and Technology (CSET) in 2000 and currently holds the position of Professor in the School of Computing. Prof Kritzinger completed her PhD in 2006 and Post Graduate Certificate in Education in 2012. She has successfully completed her Master's in Education (Online Technology). Her research primarily focuses on Cyber Safety awareness, training and education for school learners, teachers and schools. The main aim is to establish and promote social responsibilities within communities to establish and grow a cyber-safety culture within South Africa. Prof Kritzinger has established herself as a mature researcher and has published in accredited national and international journals, contributed to a chapter in a book and presented at peer-reviewed conferences across the globe. Prof Kritzinger currently hold a NRF C3 rating within her research field.

Reenu Kumari is Assistant Professor in the Department of Business and Management Studies, Meerut Institute of Engineering and Technology, Meerut, Uttar Pradesh, (India). She has received Ph.D from Indian Institute of Technology, Roorkee. She has qualified UGC NET (JRF) in 2011. She has thirteen year experience in teaching as well as research also. Her area of specialization is Finance & Accounting. Her are of interest FDI, Education, Economic Growth, Digitalization and Trade Openness. She has written and published many research papers in the national & international Journal and Conferences. She has reviewer in various journals including Sage, Emerald, Inderscience, and Elsevier. International Journal of Emerging Markets (IJoEM), Management Research Review (MRR), International Journal of Comparative Management (IJoCM), the Third PAN-IIM World Management Conference, Human Development and Capabilities (JoHDC), the social science Journal (SSJ), Transnational Corporations Review (TCR), South Asian Journal of business studies.

Antonio Lanotte is a chartered tax adviser and senior auditor, international tax partner at DMG & Partners. Particularly keen on Digital Transformation (Blockchain, IoT, AI, machine learning) and also Circular Economy (Green Tech) with important contributions on IBFD-European Taxation; ITR - Tax Notes International - International Tax Review; IFRL - International Financial Law Review; HBR - Bloomberg - FinTech Review; Il Sole 24 ore; Wall Street Italia; Bollettino Tributario. Results driven finance, controlling and international taxation with years of experience in industries and consulting in Italy and abroad. He attends as panelist and often as moderator in national and international events particularly focusing on International taxation, Circular Economy (Green Finance - ESG) and Digital Transformation (Blockchain, AI, DeFi). He is also a lecturer on the above mentioned subjects within national and international Universities or Master programs. Since October 2019 he has been an active member/delegate of the Tax Technology Committee - CFE Bruxelles, and also a member of the Organization for Climate & Circular Economy - OCCE_EU Bruxelles, with an important contribution to the "Climate Bank Roadmap 2021-2025" financed by the European Investment Bank - EIB. He is among the 100 European Talents for Decentralized Finance (DeFi) certified by the Frankfurt School Blockchain Center headed by Prof. Philipp Sandner.

Chris Lazaris is a member of the Laboratory Teaching Faculty in the Department of Management Science and Technology, at the Athens University of Economics and Business (AUEB). He is senior researcher at the eBusiness Research Center (ELTRUN) of AUEB and the Interactive Marketing & Electronic Services (IMES) research group, having participated in numerous EU funded R&D projects. He has been awarded a PhD by the Department of Management Science & Technology of AUEB, studying the thematic areas of Omnichannel Retailing, Store Atmosphere and Consumer Behavior, following an interdisciplinary approach. His work appears at world-leading journals such as the International Journal of Electronic Commerce, the Journal of Retailing and Consumer Services, and the International Journal of Technology Marketing.

Etelvino Leandro is a master in GERH (Strategic Human Resources Management) by ESCE-IPS Setúbal, Portugal. Degree in Psychology from UAL (Universidade Autónoma de Lisboa). Professor at UAN-Universidade Agostinho Neto FCS (Faculty of Social Sciences) DEI-Psychology. And Head of the Scientific Department of the Psychology Department of the FCS of the UAN. Professor in Human Resources Management and Administration and Marketing at Unibelas - University of Belas, Luanda (Angola).

Gracieth de Sousa Leandro is a Master in Business Sciences in the field of Small and Medium Enterprises from ESCE-IPS, Setúbal, Portugal; Professor at the School of Hospitality and Tourism at Universidade Agostinho and Universidade de Belas, in Angola.

Nadezhda Anatolievna Lebedeva is a Doctor of Philosophy in the field of Cultural Studies, professor of the International Personnel Academy (Kyiv, Ukraine), works at the Kherson State Agrarian and Economic University, full member of the Eurasian Academy of Television and Radio. She is the author of more than 100 scientific articles. The focus of her research is the cultural and social aspects of regional development. She graduated from the Kherson State Pedagogical Institute in 1996. After graduating from the postgraduate course at the Kherson State University, became a lecturer at the History of World Culture and Literature Department of the Kherson State University. In June 2008 was enrolled in the doctoral program of the Interregional Academy of Personnel Management in Kyiv, specializing in Cultural Studies. She was awarded the medal "For Civil Courage" of the Afghan Veterans' Ukrainian Union for the book "My Afghan" by Nikolay Vishnyak". Participation in the creation of documentary films and scientific articles are marked by membership in the Eurasian Academy of Television and Radio (November 2012). The monograph "Cultural Aspect of Alexander Elagin'sCreativeness" was awarded by the 1-st place in scientific direction "Cultural Studies" in 2017 and became the winner of the competition for educational projects "Interclover - 2017" in the nomination – "Research Project".

Jahir Lombana earned a Ph.D. Economics at the Universität Göttingen (Germany), Master in International Studies (Univesidad de Chile). Associate Professor and Research Director at the Business School at the Universidad del Norte (Barranquila-Colombia).

Belén López has a Ph.D. in Communication and she is a full-time professor at ESIC University and associate researcher at the Permanent Research Unit at ESIC. Research areas: corporate social responsibility, corporate communication, corporate reputation and social impact of companies. She publishes articles in high-impact scientific journals and book chapters in international publishers and regularly attends international academic conferences. She is associated with the Academy of International Business (AiB) and the Academy of Management (AoM). She is a researcher in the Brand Management and Integrated Communication group at the Complutense University of Madrid.

Andreia Machado is a PhD in Engineering and Knowledge Management (UFSC), Master in Scientific and Technological Education (UFSC), specialist in Literacy and graduated in Pedagogy (UDESC) and in Management Processes. He is a reviewer of Revisa Educação e Pesquisa scielo. Ad Hoc evaluator of National and International Journals. He is part of the Editorial Committee of the Journal of Studies in Social Sciences and Humanities. He teaches courses in the Pedagogy undergraduate course at Faculdade Municipal da Palhoça and in Administration and Production Engineering at the Faculty of Vale do Itajaí Mirim / UNIASSELVI. Advisor professor at the Leonardo da Vinci University Center. Evaluator of the National Institute of Educational Studies and Research Anísio Teixeira (Ministry of Education). He has been working in the educational field for over 25 years. He has experience in the area: Education, Distance Education, management, hybrid teaching, digital technologies, active methodology, knowledge media, entrepreneurship, innovation habitat and knowledge management. She is the author of numerous articles and book chapters published in national and international journals. https://orcid.org/0000-0002-4404-0341.

Hesham Magd has more than twenty-five years of combined experience in traditional and nontraditional higher education teaching, training, consultancy, community development, academic administration, curricula design, organizational change and development, distinguished research and scholarly writing, resulting in Honors, awards and recognition for academic excellence and outstanding achievement. Hesham is currently heavily involved in International accreditation and reshaping the aviation education in Oman and offer strategic direction on the direction of the sector In his previous appointments throughout the world in British, European, and American oriented Curriculum (Middle East, USA, and UK), he has been the driving force behind strategic institutional development during the time of profound change in the Higher Education in the Middle East. Hesham has broad knowledge of the UK, USA, Middle East University Systems, and Quality and accreditation systems (AACSB, AABI, OAAA, NCAAA).

Sithokozile Mamba holds a Bachelor of Science in Marine Biology from the University of KwaZulu-Natal (UKZN), and a Postgraduate Diploma in Management (UKZN). Further to that, she is currently registered for her Master of Commerce in Management at UKZN. She has been an Ocean Steward for the KZN WildOceans.

John Mendy is currently a Senior Lecturer and Programme Leader for Full-Time MSc HRM. He is interested in Research, Teaching and Learning Methodologies, HRM and Organisational Behaviour, how to manage relationships between international graduates, home graduates and other employees and smart cities as learning cities. He is a Fellow of the Higher Education Academy, UK, an Associate Editor of Electronic Journal of Business Research Methods, Member of British Academy of Management and the European Academy of Management and a Chartered Member of the Chartered Institute of Personnel and Development, UK. He teaches on Undergraduate and Postgraduate programmes and supervises PhD candidates. He continues to publish in refereed journals and presents his work at international conferences.

Vladimir D. Milovidov was born in Moscow 13th of January 1960. He graduated from Moscow State University in 1984. He has extensive experience in researching the modern financial system, banking, international finance, and corporate governance. He was a postdoctoral fellow at the economic department of Yale University (1990-1991), and visiting professor of Russian summer school in Middlebury College (the USA, 1991-1996). He also has experience working high ranked governmental officers. He was the head of the Russian Financial Market Service, Russian financial market regulator (2007-2011). He also worked as a top manager of one of the largest Russian oil and gas public companies (2011-2017), responsible for innovation projects management. Since 2011 he has been taking the head of the international finance department of the School of International Economic Relation of MGIMO University. In 2021 he joined the Institute of the world economy and international relations of Russia Academy of science as a deputy director. He has extended a list of publications, including articles and monographs.

Alberto Muñoz-Santiago is a full-time professor at the Universidad del Norte (Barranquilla-Colombia), MBA, specialist in Financial Administration at Universidad del Norte and Master in Business Economics from INCAE (Costa Rica), Current Coordinator of the Masters in Business Administration and Finance of the Universidad del Norte.

Maria Ovalle is Administrative Assistant of the Business School at Universidad del Norte, Barranquilla - Colombia. Has a Master in Business Administration, and a Undergraduate degree in Economics. Researcher in Marketing and Consumer Behaviour.

Ferhat Özbay worked as a lecturer at Süleyman Demirel University for 6 months and 1 year at Isparta University of Applied Sciences. Dr Özbay has a bachelor's degree from İnönü University, Department of Econmics (2013). He received his master's degree from Süleyman Demirel University, Department of Economics (2015). He also has a PhD in Economics (2020) from Süleyman Demirel University. His research interests are Innovation, development and growth within the scope of the macroeconomy.

João Peixoto is a doctor in control and automation engineering from UFRGS, master in control and automation engineering from UFRGS, electrical engineer from UNISINOS, adjunct professor at the State University of Rio Grande do Sul - UERGS, in the Control and Automation Engineering course and collaborating professor at the Professional Master's Program PPGSTEM at UERGS. Researcher in Industry 4.0 systems and digital technologies for digital transformation.

Lucia Pizzichini, PhD, is Assistant Professor in Marketing at the Management Department at Polytechnic University of Marche (Italy). Since 2016 she is a visiting researcher at the School of Business, Economics, and Law at the University of Gothenburg. She is a Lecturer at Jönköping International Business School (Jönköping University) and Dalarna University. Her research interests focus on retailing, consumer behavior, service marketing and management.

Andrei Popescu is Founder & CEO at SCX Holdings and seasoned FinTech/DeFi/Blockchain Tech Start-Ups Investor/Advisor. PhD Candidate and a vision-driven entrepreneur/executive with career-long record of business growth and innovation. Andrei helped in building great companies in Singapore, Austria, Italy and Romania with extraordinary people, while seeking continuous intellectual stimulation through a broad set of experiences in dynamic, challenging, and high-intensity environments. He has been engaged on helping organizations that evolve in challenging markets to break down the barriers that prevent them from reaching their potential, which operate in Scandinavia, Eastern Europe, China and Asia-Pacific. His focus and interest are on Strategic Investments in Disruptive Technologies & Innovations, FinTech, Financial Innovations, Financial Digital Assets, Blockchain, DLT, Crypto Asset Trading Systems, Decentralized Finance (DeFi), dApps, Digital Markets & Trading Platforms, Data Science, Data Capital, Artificial Intelligence (ANI, AGI, ASI, ML, DL) Applications, AI based Automated Trading Strategies, Business Strategy Implementations via AI systems.

Andrisha Beharry Ramraj, lecturer at the University of KwaZulu-Natal, holds a PhD in Management studies majoring in management, leadership and governance. Further to this she holds a Diploma in Higher Education. In 2004 and 2005 she received NRF scholarships to complete her Honours and Masters degrees respectively. She has presented at local and international conference in the areas of Management, Leadership, Marketing, Global Business and Entrepreneurship. She has published in the fields of Leadership, Entrepreneurship, Human Resources and Business Management. She recently published book chapters on entrepreneurial suitability and employee wellness across the globe. In 2016 and 2017 she received best presentation awards for best paper delivered at conferences, she serves on the Teaching and Learning committee within the University of KwaZulu Natal (UKZN) and served as the Bachelor of Business Administrator Programme Manager (Self-Funding Teaching Programme) for a one term. She teaches across levels within the Discipline of Management and Entrepreneurship, from entry level to masters level. She is keen on developing undergraduate curriculum transformation within the discipline. Redesigning curricular to suite the dynamics of the modern world enabling sustainability is fast becoming her passion. Having realised her desire for higher education, Dr Beharry serves as an expert advisor for the Student Society of Entrepreneurship (CAVE) based at UKZN. Further to this she now shares her expertise as a research expert for the Centre of Entrepreneurship.

Celia Rangel has combined her academic career with professional experience. She has brand & communication experience in leadership roles within corporate entities, as well as in leading branding and communications agencies managing luxury brands. Research interests are advertising, communication, strategy, brands and luxury. Her last book chapter is Managing the intangibles of luxury brands.

Marc Richter graduated in Chemistry (1990) and PhD in Biochemistry (1995) from Albert-Ludwigs Universität Freiburg (Germany). He did postdoctoral research at Institut Pasteur in France (1995-1997), and a second one as CNPq visiting researcher at the Center of Biotechnology, Federal University of Rio Grande do Sul (UFRGS). From 2000 to 2003 he worked with the Integrated Cancer Center (ULBRA) and the South American Foundation for the Development of Anti-Cancer Drugs. He also served as a Master Advisor during the years 2006 to 2010 in the Graduate Program in Genetics and Applied Toxicology (PPGGTA of ULBRA). Currently, he serves as adjunct professor at the State University of Rio Grande do Sul as adjunct professor (since 2003). He served as Pro-Rector of Research and Graduate Studies (2010 to 2014). He was a Member of the Science and Technology Council of the Secretariat of Science, Innovation and Technological Development of the State of RS (SCIT-RS) (2012 to 2015). From 2016 to 2018 he held the position of President of the Science and Technology Foundation. Since March 2018 he is teaching and acting in research and extension projects in the areas of Environmental Management, Sustainability and Biotechnology. He is also a Member of the Council of the Technological Innovation Centre - NITUergs. In 2019 he started his activities as professor-supervisor in 2 professional Master's degrees: 1) Environment and Sustainability (PPGAS-Uergs); and 2) Food Science and Technology (PPGCTA-Uergs). He is editor-in-chief of Blog REPENSE, which carries out dissemination and awareness of issues related to sustainability.

Benson Ruzive is a faculty member at the transportation, logistics and Safety management at the Faculty of Business and Economics, Modern College of Business and Economics, Muscat, Oman.

Ashwani Sharma is an assistant professor at department of Business & Management studies, Meerut Institute of Engineering & Technology, India (MIET). He Holds a Ph.D (Commerce) degree from CCS University Meerut, received MBA Degree from AKTU University Lucknow and is certified in Digital marketing by Google. He has 12 years experience in teaching and research also. His area of Interest is Digitalisation, Cashless Economy, marketing, economics, new technology and strategies adoption and he is a Coordinator of Research and Development committee at department of Business & Management studies in MIET. He has published national and international research paper and also active on digital platform. He has also a copy right ownership of Design Thinking model for start-ups. He has always tried to expand his research areas according to the scenario.

Ayşe Aslı Sezgin is an Associate Professor in the Department of Communication Sciences at the Çukurova University Facult of Communication. Ayşe Aslı Sezgin completed her Ph.D. at Gazi University, Ankara/Turkey. Her research interests lie in the area of new media, communication technologies, social media, political communication, media literacy.

Hu Shi holds a PhD degree from Universiti Sains Malaysia. She is Chinese. She has published more than 10 international research papers. Her research interests are human resource management, workplace safety management, and organisational behaviour.

Fendy Suhariadi is Ph.D. Professor, in the department Industrial & Organizational Psychology, Faculty of Psychology, Universitas Airlangga, Surabaya, Indonesia. Now, He is a head of Doctoral Program in Human Resource Development Postgraduate School Universitas Airlangga. His research interests are industrial & organizational psychology, Human resource management, Change management, Organizational Development and Health Organization. He is author of several international, journal and conference publications.

Heru Susanto is currently as Associated Professor Research Center for Informatics, The Indonesia Institute of Sciences, Indonesia. He is also Assistant Professor of Technology Management at School of Business, Universiti Teknologi Brunei. Dr. Heru currently serves as Society and Entrepreneur Thrust Leader – SERT SB UTB and Honorary Professor in the department of Information Management at College of Management, Tunghai University, Taichung, Taiwan. Dr. Susanto has worked as an IT professional in several roles, including Consultant and Web Division Head of IT Strategic at Indomobil Group, Indonesia and Prince Muqrin Chair for Information Security Technologies, King Saud University – Saudi Arabia. His research interests are in the areas of Information Security, 5G Technologies, Grid Application, Big Data, Business Process Re-engineering, and e-Marketing. Dr. Susanto received a BSc in Computer Science; an MBA in Marketing Management; an MSc in Information Systems; and a PhD in Information Security. Dr. Heru Successfully authoring more than 35 books published by Francis & Taylor Group, IGI

Global, Springer, and Elsevier; including 8 full authored books and 30 book chapters, and more than 100 international publication in peer review journal and high impact journals indexed by SCOPUS and ISI.

Evdokia Tsifora is an Assistant Professor at the Department of Accounting and Finance of the University of Thessaly, Greece.

Paraskevi Tsoutsa is a Lecturer at the Department of Accounting and Finance of the University of Thessaly, Greece.

Amitabh Verma is working as Assistant Professor, Business Department, Sohar University, Oman. He received his Master of Computer Application in the year 2005, Ph.D. in Management in 2015. He has over 15 years of experience in both teaching and research. His research interest includes DSS, Database Management, Data Mining, MIS, E-Business, AI & Cloud Computing. He has published research papers in international journals and conferences. He is a member of IAENG (International Association of Engineers) and a life member of Indian Society for Technical Education.

Adam Vrechopoulos is Professor at the Athens University of Economics and Business (AUEB), School of Business, Department of Management Science and Technology and Scientific Coordinator of the Interactive Marketing and Electronic Services (IMES) Research Group of the ELTRUN E-Business Research Center at AUEB. He holds a Ph.D. from Brunel University, Department of Information Systems and Computing, an MBA from ALBA and a BSc from AUEB, Department of Informatics. He has served through various roles in several international scientific journals and academic conferences. His published work includes more than 140 publications in academic conference proceedings, edited volumes, books and scientific journals.

Index

A

B

C

N

O

P

R

S

T

U

V

W

Y

Recommended Reference Books

IGI Global's reference books are available in three unique pricing formats: Print Only, E-Book Only, or Print + E-Book.

Shipping fees may apply.

www.igi-global.com

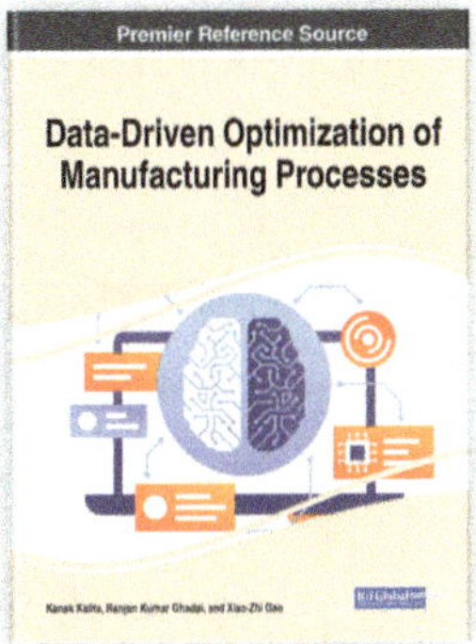

ISBN: 9781799872061
EISBN: 9781799872085
© 2021; 298 pp.
List Price: US$ **225**

ISBN: 9781799876113
EISBN: 9781799876120
© 2021; 210 pp.
List Price: US$ **225**

ISBN: 9781799847601
EISBN: 9781799847618
© 2021; 254 pp.
List Price: US$ **225**

ISBN: 9781799869924
EISBN: 9781799869948
© 2021; 522 pp.
List Price: US$ **295**

ISBN: 9781799843993
EISBN: 9781799844006
© 2021; 347 pp.
List Price: US$ **195**

ISBN: 9781799850625
EISBN: 9781799850632
© 2021; 367 pp.
List Price: US$ **215**

Do you want to stay current on the latest research trends, product announcements, news, and special offers?
Join IGI Global's mailing list to receive customized recommendations, exclusive discounts, and more.
Sign up at: **www.igi-global.com/newsletters.**

Publisher of Timely, Peer-Reviewed Inclusive Research Since 1988

IGI Global
PUBLISHER of TIMELY KNOWLEDGE

www.igi-global.com Sign up at www.igi-global.com/newsletters facebook.com/igiglobal twitter.com/igiglobal linkedin.com/igiglobal

www.ingramcontent.com/pod-product-compliance
Lightning Source LLC
LaVergne TN
LVHW060252011026
849161LV00011B/2695